TENTH EDITION

ORGANIZATIONAL BEHAVIOUR

UNDERSTANDING AND MANAGING LIFE AT WORK

GARY JOHNS
CONCORDIA UNIVERSITY

ALAN M. SAKS
UNIVERSITY OF TORONTO

PEARSON

Toronto

Editorial Director: Claudine O'Donnell
Acquisitions Editor: Carolin Sweig
Marketing Manager: Lisa Gillis
Program Manager: Karen Townsend
Project Manager: Jessica Hellen
Developmental Editor: Mary Wat
Media Developer: Kelli Cadet
Production Services: Cenveo® Publisher Services
Permissions Project Manager: Joanne Tang
Photo Permissions Research: Josh Garvin, Integra
Text Permissions Research: Renae Horstman, Integra
Interior and Cover Designer: Anthony Leung
Cover Image: © Eugene Ivanov / Shutterstock

Vice-President, Cross Media and Publishing Services: Gary Bennett

Credits and acknowledgments for material borrowed from other sources and reproduced, with permission, in this textbook appear on the appropriate page within the text.

If you purchased this book outside the United States or Canada, you should be aware that it has been imported without the approval of the publisher or the author.

7   17

Library and Archives Canada Cataloguing in Publication

Johns, Gary, 1946-, author
        Organizational behaviour : understanding and managing
life at work / Gary Johns (Concordia University), Alan M. Saks
(University of Toronto). — Tenth edition.

Includes bibliographical references and index.
ISBN 978-0-13-395162-2 (hardback)

        1. Organizational behavior—Textbooks.   2. Management—
Textbooks.   I. Saks, Alan M.   (Alan Michael), 1960-, author   II. Title.

HD58.7.J64 2016   302.3'5   C2015-908621-3

ISBN 978-0-13-395162-2

For Bill and Jean Johns and for Monika Jörg

Gary Johns

For Kelly, Justin, Brooke, and my parents
Simon and Renee Saks

Alan M. Saks

This edition is dedicated to the memory of Lyman Porter,
an inspiring academic and good friend who played
an important role in the genesis of this book.

BRIEF CONTENTS

PART ONE AN INTRODUCTION 2

Chapter 1 Organizational Behaviour and Management 2

PART TWO INDIVIDUAL BEHAVIOUR 44

Chapter 2 Personality and Learning 44
Chapter 3 Perception, Attribution, and Diversity 82
Chapter 4 Values, Attitudes, and Work Behaviour 126
Chapter 5 Theories of Work Motivation 158
Chapter 6 Motivation in Practice 200

PART THREE SOCIAL BEHAVIOUR AND ORGANIZATIONAL PROCESSES 240

Chapter 7 Groups and Teamwork 240
Chapter 8 Social Influence, Socialization, and Organizational Culture 274
Chapter 9 Leadership 318
Chapter 10 Communication 366
Chapter 11 Decision Making 398
Chapter 12 Power, Politics, and Ethics 430
Chapter 13 Conflict and Stress 462

PART FOUR THE TOTAL ORGANIZATION 500

Chapter 14 Environment, Strategy, and Structure 500
Chapter 15 Organizational Change, Development, and Innovation 542

References 580
Index 621

CONTENTS

Preface   xviii

About the Authors   xxviii

PART ONE	**AN INTRODUCTION**	2
Chapter 1	**Organizational Behaviour and Management**	2

What Are Organizations?   4

Social Inventions *4* Goal Accomplishment *5* Group Effort *5*

What Is Organizational Behaviour?   5

Why Study Organizational Behaviour?   6

Organizational Behaviour Is Interesting *6* Organizational Behaviour Is
Important *7* Organizational Behaviour Makes a Difference *7*

How Much Do You Know About Organizational Behaviour?   8

Goals of Organizational Behaviour   9

Predicting Organizational Behaviour *9* Explaining Organizational
Behaviour *9* Managing Organizational Behaviour *10*

Early Prescriptions Concerning Management   10

● YOU BE THE MANAGER

Toronto's Troubled Transit System   11

The Classical View and Bureaucracy *12* The Human Relations
Movement and a Critique of Bureaucracy *12*

Contemporary Management—The Contingency Approach   13

What Do Managers Do?   14

Managerial Roles *14* Managerial Activities *15* Managerial
Agendas *16* Managerial Minds *17* International Managers *18*

Some Contemporary Management Concerns   18

Diversity—Local and Global *19* Employee Health and Well-Being *19*

● APPLIED FOCUS

Mental Health in the County of Wellington   22

Talent Management and Employee Engagement *23* Corporate Social
Responsibility *24*

● RESEARCH FOCUS

Collective Organizational Engagement and Firm Performance   25

● THE MANAGER'S NOTEBOOK

Toronto's Troubled Transit System   27

Learning Objectives Checklist   28

Discussion Questions   28

On-the-Job Challenge Question

Pay to Work or Pay to Quit?   29

Experiential Exercise

Good Job, Bad Job   29

Experiential Exercise

OB in the News   29

Experiential Exercise
How Engaged Are You? 　30
Case Incident
My Mother's Visit 　31
Case Study
Argamassa Construction Materials 　32
Integrative Case
Ken Private Limited: Digitization Project 　36

PART TWO　　**INDIVIDUAL BEHAVIOUR**　　**44**

Chapter 2　　**Personality and Learning**　　44

What Is Personality? 　46

Personality and Organizational Behaviour 　47
The Five-Factor Model of Personality *48* Locus of Control *50*

● **RESEARCH FOCUS**
Personality and Adaptive Performance 　51
Self-Monitoring *51* Self-Esteem *52*

Advances in Personality and Organizational Behaviour 　53
Positive and Negative Affectivity *53* Proactive Personality *54* General
Self-Efficacy *54* Core Self-Evaluations *54*

What Is Learning? 　55
What Do Employees Learn? *55* Operant Learning Theory *55*

Increasing the Probability of Behaviour 　56
Positive Reinforcement *56* Negative Reinforcement *56* Organizational
Errors Involving Reinforcement *57*

Reinforcement Strategies 　58

Reducing the Probability of Behaviour 　59
Extinction *60* Punishment *60* Using Punishment Effectively *60*

Social Cognitive Theory 　62
Observational Learning *63*

● **RESEARCH FOCUS**
The Trickle-Down Effects of Abusive Management 　64
Self-Efficacy Beliefs *64* Self-Regulation *65*

Organizational Learning Practices 　66
Organizational Behaviour Modification *66* Employee Recognition
Programs *67* Training and Development Programs *69*

● **YOU BE THE MANAGER**
Calgary International Airport's YYC Miles Recognition Program 　69

● **THE MANAGER'S NOTEBOOK**
Calgary International Airport's YYC Miles Recognition Program 　70
Learning Objectives Checklist 　71
Discussion Questions 　72
Integrative Discussion Questions 　72
On-the-Job Challenge Question
18 000 Collisions 　73
Experiential Exercise
Proactive Personality Scale 　73
Experiential Exercise
General Self Efficacy 　74
Experiential Exercise
The Core Self-Evaluations Scale (CSES) 　74

Case Incident
Playing Hooky   75
Case Study
Roaring Dragon Hotel: A Second Attempt at Modernization   76

Chapter 3   Perception, Attribution, and Diversity   82

What Is Perception?   84

Components of Perception   84
The Perceiver *85* The Target *85* The Situation *86*

Social Identity Theory   86

A Model of the Perceptual Process   87

Basic Biases in Person Perception   88
Primacy and Recency Effects *88* Reliance on Central
Traits *89* Implicit Personality Theories *89* Projection *89*
Stereotyping *90*

Attribution: Perceiving Causes and Motives   91
Consistency Cues *91* Consensus Cues *92* Distinctiveness
Cues *92* Attribution in Action *92* Biases in Attribution *93*

Person Perception and Workforce Diversity   94
The Changing Workplace *95* Valuing Diversity *95* Stereotypes and
Workforce Diversity *96*

● **APPLIED FOCUS**
Police Anti-Bias Training   97

● **ETHICAL FOCUS**
What's in a Name? You're Hired ... or Not!   99
Managing Workforce Diversity *104*

Perceptions of Trust   105

● **YOU BE THE MANAGER**
American Express Canada's Skilled Immigrant Strategy   106

Perceived Organizational Support   107

Person Perception in Human Resources   108
Perceptions of Recruitment and Selection *109* Perceptions in the
Employment Interview *109* Perceptions and the Performance
Appraisal *111*

● **THE MANAGER'S NOTEBOOK**
American Express Canada's Skilled Immigrant Strategy   114
Learning Objectives Checklist   114
Discussion Questions   115
Integrative Discussion Questions   116
On-the-Job Challenge Question
Australia's Jobs Bonus Initiative   116
Experiential Exercise
Beliefs about Older Workers   117
Case Incident
The New Hiring Policy   118
Case Study
LGBTA at TD Bank Financial Group in 2012   119

Chapter 4   Values, Attitudes, and Work Behaviour   126

What Are Values?   128
Generational Differences in Values *128* Cultural Differences in
Values *129* Implications of Cultural Variation *132*

● **YOU BE THE MANAGER**
Carlsberg's *Winning Behaviours* Campaign   134

● **GLOBAL FOCUS**
Canadians Have Cultural Intelligence   135

What Are Attitudes?   136

What Is Job Satisfaction?   136

What Determines Job Satisfaction?   137
Discrepancy *137* Fairness *138* Disposition *140*

● **GLOBAL FOCUS**
Is The Importance of Fairness Universal Across Cultures?   140
Mood and Emotion *141* Some Key Contributors to Job
Satisfaction *143*

Consequences of Job Satisfaction   144
Absence from Work *144* Turnover *145* Performance *147* Organizational Citizenship Behaviour *148* Customer Satisfaction and Profit *149*

What Is Organizational Commitment?   150
Key Contributors to Organizational Commitment *150* Consequences
of Organizational Commitment *150* Changes in the Workplace and
Employee Commitment *151*

● **THE MANAGER'S NOTEBOOK**
Carlsberg's *Winning Behaviours* Campaign   152
Learning Objectives Checklist   152
Discussion Questions   153
Integrative Discussion Questions   153
On-the-Job Challenge Question
Mr. Winston   153
Experiential Exercise
Attitudes Toward Absenteeism from Work   154
Case Incident
How Much Do You Get Paid?   155
Case Study
Michael Simpson   155

Chapter 5   **Theories of Work Motivation**   158

Why Study Motivation?   160

What Is Motivation?   160
Basic Characteristics of Motivation *160* Extrinsic and Intrinsic
Motivation *161* Motivation and Performance *162* The Motivation–
Performance Relationship *164*

Need Theories of Work Motivation   164
Maslow's Hierarchy of Needs *165* Alderfer's ERG Theory *166*
McClelland's Theory of Needs *167* Research Support for Need
Theories *168* Managerial Implications of Need Theories *169*

Self-Determination Theory   169
Research Support for and Managerial Implications of Self-Determination
Theory *170*

Process Theories of Work Motivation   171
Expectancy Theory *171* Research Support for Expectancy
Theory *173* Managerial Implications of Expectancy Theory *173*
Equity Theory *174* Research Support for Equity Theory *175* Mana-
gerial Implications of Equity Theory *175* Goal Setting Theory *176*

What Kinds of Goals Are Motivational? *176* Enhancing Goal
Commitment *177* Goal Orientation *178*

- **RESEARCH FOCUS**
  Challenging Goals and Business-Unit Performance 179
  Goal Proximity *180* Research Support for Goal Setting
  Theory *180* Managerial Implications of Goal Setting Theory *181*
  Do Motivation Theories Translate Across Cultures? 181
- **ETHICAL FOCUS**
  The Dark Side of Goal Setting 182
- **YOU BE THE MANAGER**
  Your Tips or Your Job 183
  Putting It All Together: Integrating Theories of Work Motivation 185
- **THE MANAGER'S NOTEBOOK**
  Your Tips or Your Job 186
  Learning Objectives Checklist 187
  Discussion Questions 188
  Integrative Discussion Questions 189
  On-the-Job Challenge Question
  Employee Time Theft 189
  Experiential Exercise
  What Is Your Goal Orientation? 190
  Case Incident
  A Night at the Office 191
  Case Study
  Kyle Evans at Ruffian Apparel: Staffing a Retail Establishment 191

Chapter 6   **Motivation in Practice** 200
  Money as a Motivator 202
  Linking Pay to Performance on Production Jobs *202* Potential Problems
  with Wage Incentives *203* Linking Pay to Performance on White-Collar
  Jobs *205* Potential Problems with Merit Pay Plans *206*

- **RESEARCH FOCUS**
  Improving the "Line-of-Sight" in Pay-for-Performance Programs 207
- **ETHICAL FOCUS**
  Incentive Compensation and Unethical Behaviour 208
- **YOU BE THE MANAGER**
  Retention Bonuses at SNC-Lavalin Group Inc. 210
  Using Pay to Motivate Teamwork *210*
  Job Design as a Motivator 213
  Traditional Views of Job Design *214* Job Scope and
  Motivation *214* The Job Characteristics Model *215*
  Job Enrichment *219* Potential Problems with Job Enrichment *220*
  Work Design and Relational Job Design *221*
  Management by Objectives 223
  Flexible Work Arrangements as Motivators for a Diverse Workforce 224
  Flex-Time *224* Compressed Workweek *225* Job and Work
  Sharing *226* Telecommuting *227*
  Motivational Practices in Perspective 228
- **THE MANAGER'S NOTEBOOK**
  Retention Bonuses at SNC-Lavalin 229
  Learning Objectives Checklist 230

Discussion Questions   231
Integrative Discussion Questions   231
On-the-Job Challenge Question
   Your New Salary   231
Experiential Exercise
   Task Characteristics Scale   232
Case Incident
   The Junior Accountant   233
Case Study
   Dr. Jack Perry, DDS   234
Integrative Case
   Ken Private Limited: Digitization Project   238

PART THREE   SOCIAL BEHAVIOUR
AND ORGANIZATIONAL PROCESSES   240

Chapter 7   Groups and Teamwork   240

What Is a Group?   242
Group Development   242
Typical Stages of Group Development *243* Punctuated
Equilibrium *244*
Group Structure and Its Consequences   245
Group Size *245* Diversity of Group Membership *247*
Group Norms *247* Roles *248* Status *250*
Group Cohesiveness   252
Factors Influencing Cohesiveness *252* Consequences of
Cohesiveness *254*
Social Loafing   255
What Is a Team?   256
Designing Effective Work Teams   256
Self-Managed Work Teams *257*

● RESEARCH FOCUS
Supporting Teamwork on the Mission to Mars   260
Cross-Functional Teams *261* Virtual Teams *262*

● APPLIED FOCUS
Virtual Teams at Save the Children   263

● YOU BE THE MANAGER
Creating Trust in Virtual Teams at Orange   264
A Word of Caution: Teams as a Panacea   266

● THE MANAGER'S NOTEBOOK
Creating Trust in Virtual Teams at Orange   266
Learning Objectives Checklist   267
Discussion Questions   268
Integrative Discussion Questions   268
On-the-Job Challenge Question
   Self-Managed Teams at ISE Communications   268
Experiential Exercise
   NASA   269
Case Incident
   The Group Assignment   270
Case Study
   Levi Strauss & Co.'s Flirtation with Teams   271

Chapter 8   **Social Influence, Socialization, and Organizational Culture**   274

Social Influence in Organizations   276
Information Dependence and Effect Dependence *276* The Social Influence Process and Conformity *277*

Organizational Socialization   277
Stages of Socialization *279*

Unrealistic Expectations and the Psychological Contract   280
Unrealistic Expectations *280* Psychological Contract *281*

Methods of Organizational Socialization   281
Realistic Job Previews *282* Employee Orientation Programs *283* Socialization Tactics *284* Mentoring *286*

● ETHICAL FOCUS
Socialization Tactics and Ethical Conflict   287

● RESEARCH FOCUS
The Discriminatory Gap in University Mentoring   290
Proactive Socialization *291*

Organizational Culture   292
What Is Organizational Culture? *292* The "Strong Culture" Concept *294* Assets of Strong Cultures *295* Liabilities of Strong Cultures *296* Contributors to the Culture *297* Diagnosing a Culture *300*

● YOU BE THE MANAGER
Changing the Culture at Kinaxis   301

● THE MANAGER'S NOTEBOOK
Changing the Culture at Kinaxis   303
Learning Objectives Checklist   303
Discussion Questions   304
Integrative Discussion Questions   305
On-the-Job Challenge Question
Culture or Biology?   305
Experiential Exercise
Socialization Preferences and Experience   306
Case Incident
The Reality Shock   308
Case Study
The Wonderful World of Human Resources at Disney   308

Chapter 9   **Leadership**   318

What Is Leadership?   320

Are Leaders Born? The Trait Theory of Leadership   321
Research on Leadership Traits *322* Limitations of the Trait Approach *322*

● RESEARCH FOCUS
Narcissism and Leadership   323

The Behaviour of Leaders   324
Consideration and Initiating Structure *325* The Consequences of Consideration and Structure *325* Leader Reward and Punishment Behaviours *325*

Situational Theories of Leadership   326
Fiedler's Contingency Theory *326* House's Path–Goal Theory *328*

Participative Leadership: Involving Employees in Decisions   330

What Is Participative Leadership? *330* Potential Advantages of
Participative Leadership *330* Potential Problems of Participative
Leadership *331* Vroom and Jago's Situational Model of Participation *332*

Leader–Member Exchange (LMX) Theory 334

Transactional and Transformational Leadership Theory 334
Intellectual Stimulation *335* Individualized Consideration *335*
Inspirational Motivation *335* Charisma *336*

New and Emerging Theories of Leadership 337
Empowering Leadership *337*

● RESEARCH FOCUS
Empowering Leadership and Newcomer Creativity 338
Ethical Leadership *338* Authentic Leadership *339* Servant
Leadership *341*

● YOU BE THE MANAGER
Leadership at the CBC 342

Gender and Leadership 343

Culture and Leadership 345

Global Leadership 348

What Style of Leadership is Best? 349

● THE MANAGER'S NOTEBOOK
Leadership at the CBC 351
Learning Objectives Checklist 352
Discussion Questions 353
Integrative Discussion Questions 353
On-the-Job Challenge Question
  The RCMP's New Boss 354
Experiential Exercise
  Ethical Leadership Scale (ELS) 354
Experiential Exercise
  Leadership Empowerment Behaviour 355
Experiential Exercise
  Servant Leadership Scale 356
Case Incident
  Fran-Tech 357
Case Study
  Radio Station WEAA: Leading in a Challenging Situation 358

Chapter 10   **Communication** 366

What Is Communication? 368

Basics of Organizational Communication 369
Communication by Strict Chain of Command *369* Deficiencies in the
Chain of Command *369*

Voice, Silence, and the Mum Effect 370

● YOU BE THE MANAGER
Communicating Diversity and Inclusion at Ryder 371

The Grapevine 371
Characteristics of the Grapevine *372* Who Participates in the Grapevine,
and Why? *372* Pros and Cons of the Grapevine *373*

The Verbal Language of Work 373

The Non-Verbal Language of Work 374
Body Language *374* Props, Artifacts, and Costumes *375*

- **RESEARCH FOCUS**
  The Red Sneakers Effect: When Nonconformity Signals High Status   377
  Gender Differences in Communication   377
  Cross-Cultural Communication   379
  Language Differences *379* Non-Verbal Communication across
  Cultures *380*

- **GLOBAL FOCUS**
  **Self-Presentation Bias: Who's Most and Least
  Modest in Job Applications?**   381
  Etiquette and Politeness across Cultures *381* Social Conventions across
  Cultures *382* Cultural Context *383*
  Computer-Mediated Communication   384
  Personal Approaches to Improving Communication   387
  Basic Principles of Effective Communication *387* When in
  Rome... *388*
  Organizational Approaches to Improving Communication   389
  Provision of Explanations *389* 360-Degree Feedback *389* Employee
  Surveys and Survey Feedback *390* Suggestion Systems *390* Telephone
  Hotlines, Intranets, and Webcasts *390* Management Training *391*

- **THE MANAGER'S NOTEBOOK**
  Communicating Diversity and Inclusion at Ryder   392
  Learning Objectives Checklist   392
  Discussion Questions   393
  Integrative Discussion Questions   393
  On-the-Job Challenge Question
  Carol Bartz and Yahoo!   394
  Experiential Exercise
  Communication Technology and Media Dilemmas   394
  Case Incident
  Email Madness   396
  Case Study
  Facebook (A) and (B)   396

Chapter 11   Decision Making   398

  What Is Decision Making?   400
  Well-Structured Problems *400* Ill-Structured Problems *401*

  The Compleat Decision Maker—A Rational Decision-Making Model   402
  Perfect versus Bounded Rationality *402*

- **APPLIED FOCUS**
  Decision Errors Lead to Target's Failure in Canada   403
  Problem Identification and Framing *404* Information Search *405*
  Alternative Development, Evaluation, and Choice *406* Risky
  Business *407* Solution Implementation *408* Solution Evaluation *408*
  How Emotions and Mood Affect Decision Making *410*

- **YOU BE THE MANAGER**
  Preventing Surgical Decision Errors at Toronto General Hospital   412
  Rational Decision Making—A Summary *413*

  Group Decision Making   414
  Why Use Groups? *414* Do Groups Actually Make Higher-Quality
  Decisions than Individuals? *415* Disadvantages of Group Decision
  Making *416* Stimulating and Managing Controversy *417* How Do
  Groups Handle Risk? *418*

Contemporary Approaches to Improving Decision Making   419
Evidence-Based Management *419* Crowdsourcing *420*

● APPLIED FOCUS
Some Applications of Crowdsourcing   421
Analytics and Big Data *421*

● THE MANAGER'S NOTEBOOK
Preventing Surgical Decision Errors at Toronto General Hospital   422
Learning Objectives Checklist   423
Discussion Questions   424
Integrative Discussion Questions   424
On-the-Job Challenge Question
Toronto Ritz-Carlton Nixes Poppies   425
Experiential Exercise
The New Truck Dilemma   425
Case Incident
The Restaurant Review   427
Case Study
The Admissions Dilemma   427

Chapter 12   **Power, Politics, and Ethics**   430
What Is Power?   432
The Bases of Individual Power   432
Legitimate Power *432* Reward Power *433* Coercive Power *433*
Referent Power *433* Expert Power *434*

How do People Obtain Power?   434
Doing the Right Things *434* Cultivating the Right People *435*

Empowerment—Putting Power Where it is Needed   436

Influence Tactics—Putting Power to Work   438

Who Wants Power?   439

Controlling Strategic Contingencies—How Subunits Obtain Power   440
Scarcity *440* Uncertainty *441* Centrality *441* Substitutability *441*

Organizational Politics—Using and Abusing Power   442
The Basics of Organizational Politics *442*

● ETHICAL FOCUS
Knowledge Hiding in Organizations   443
The Facets of Political Skill *444* Machiavellianism—The Harder Side of
Politics *446* Defensiveness—Reactive Politics *447*

Ethics in Organizations   447
The Nature of Ethical Misconduct *448* Causes of Unethical
Behaviour *450*

● YOU BE THE MANAGER
Yahoo's Resume Scandal   451
Whistle-Blowing *453*

● RESEARCH FOCUS
Are You More Moral in the Morning?   453
Sexual Harassment—When Power and Ethics Collide *454* Employing
Ethical Guidelines *456*

● THE MANAGER'S NOTEBOOK
Yahoo's Resume Scandal   456
Learning Objectives Checklist   457
Discussion Questions   458

Integrative Discussion Questions   458
On-the-Job Challenge Question
  CBC's Steven Smart   458
Experiential Exercise
  Political Skill Inventory   459
Case Incident
  Doubling Up   460
Case Study
  To Tell the Truth   460

Chapter 13   Conflict and Stress   462

What Is Conflict?   464

Causes of Organizational Conflict   464
Group Identification and Intergroup Bias *464* Interdependence *465* Differences in Power, Status, and Culture *465* Ambiguity *466* Scarce Resources *466*

Types of Conflict   466

Conflict Dynamics   467

Modes of Managing Conflict   467
Avoiding *468* Accommodating *468* Competing *468* Compromise *468* Collaborating *469*

Managing Conflict with Negotiation   469
Distributive Negotiation Tactics *470* Integrative Negotiation Tactics *471* Third-Party Involvement *473*

Is All Conflict Bad?   474

A Model of Stress in Organizations   474
Stressors *474* Stress *474* Stress Reactions *475* Personality and Stress *475*

Stressors in Organizational Life   476
Executive and Managerial Stressors *476* Operative-Level Stressors *477* Boundary Role Stressors, Burnout, and Emotional Labour *478* The Job Demands–Resources Model and Work Engagement *479* Some General Stressors *480*

● RESEARCH FOCUS
  Get Smarty Pants   482

● YOU BE THE MANAGER
  Bullying at Veterans Affairs   483

Reactions to Organizational Stress   485
Behavioural Reactions to Stress *485* Psychological Reactions to Stress *487* Physiological Reactions to Stress *488*

Organizational Strategies for Managing Stress   488
Job Redesign *488* "Family-Friendly" Human Resource Policies *489* Stress Management Programs *489*

● APPLIED FOCUS
  Vancity Offers Family-Friendly Policies   490
  Work–Life Balance, Fitness, and Wellness Programs *491*

● THE MANAGER'S NOTEBOOK
  Bullying at Veterans Affairs   491
  Learning Objectives Checklist   492
  Discussion Questions   493

Integrative Discussion Questions   493
On-the-Job Challenge Question
Why Don't People Take Their Vacations?   493
Experiential Exercise
Strategies for Managing Conflict   494
Case Incident
Bringing Baby to Work   494
Case Study
Tough Guy   495
Integrative Case
Ken Private Limited: Digitization Project   498

PART FOUR   THE TOTAL ORGANIZATION   500

Chapter 14   Environment, Strategy, and Structure   500

The External Environment of Organizations   502
Organizations as Open Systems 503 Components of the External
Environment 503 Environmental Uncertainty 505 Resource
Dependence 507

Strategic Responses to Uncertainty and Resource Dependence   508

● RESEARCH FOCUS
CEO Narcissism and Firm Strategy   509

What Is Organizational Structure?   510
Vertical Division of Labour 510 Horizontal Division of
Labour 511 Departmentation 512 Basic Methods of Coordinating
Divided Labour 516 Other Methods of Coordination 517

Traditional Structural Characteristics   518
Span of Control 518 Flat versus Tall 519 Formalization 519
Centralization 520 Complexity 521 Size and Structure 521

● APPLIED FOCUS
Did BP's Organizational Structure Contribute to the Gulf Oil Spill? 522

Summarizing Structure—Organic versus Mechanistic   522

Contemporary Organic Structures   524
The Ambidextrous Organization 524

● YOU BE THE MANAGER
Zappos New Organizational Structure   525
Network and Virtual Organizations 526 The Modular
Organization 527 Other Forms of Strategic Response 528

● THE MANAGER'S NOTEBOOK
Zappos New Organizational Structure   531
Learning Objectives Checklist   532
Discussion Questions   533
Integrative Discussion Questions   533
On-the-Job Challenge Question
Span of Control at Google   534
Experiential Exercise
Organizational Structure Preference Scale   534
Case Incident
Conway Manufacturing   535
Case Study
Chris Peterson at DSS Consulting   535

Chapter 15   Organizational Change, Development, and Innovation   542

The Concept of Organizational Change   544
Why Organizations Must Change *544* What Organizations Can
Change *545* The Change Process *546* The Learning
Organization *548*

● RESEARCH FOCUS
Do Organizations Learn More from Success or Failure?   549

Issues in the Change Process   550
Diagnosis *550* Resistance *550* Evaluation and Institutionalization *553*

● YOU BE THE MANAGER
Transforming a Legacy Culture at 3M   554

Organizational Development: Planned Organizational Change   554

Some Specific Organizational Development Strategies   555
Team Building *555* Survey Feedback *556* Total Quality
Management *558* Reengineering *560*

Does Organizational Development Work?   562

The Innovation Process   563
What Is Innovation? *563* Generating and Implementing Innovative
Ideas *564*

● APPLIED FOCUS
Guests Help Hotels Innovate   567
Diffusing Innovative Ideas *570*

A Footnote: The Knowing–Doing Gap   571

● THE MANAGER'S NOTEBOOK
Transforming a Legacy Culture at 3M   572

Learning Objectives Checklist   572

Discussion Questions   573

Integrative Discussion Questions   574

On-the-Job Challenge Question
The Hacker Way at Facebook   574

Experiential Exercise
Measuring Tolerance for Ambiguity   574

Case Incident
Dandy Toys   575

Case Study
Ions Consulting: The MP^2 Training Program   576

Integrative Case
Ken Private Limited: Digitization Project   579

References   580

Index   621

PREFACE

Welcome to the tenth edition of *Organizational Behaviour: Understanding and Managing Life at Work*! This edition marks the 33rd anniversary of the text, which has been rigorously updated over the years to present students with the latest knowledge and research on both the science and practice of organizational behaviour. First published in 1983, *Organizational Behaviour* is the longest-running, continuously published, and regularly revised organizational behaviour textbook authored in Canada.

In writing the tenth edition of this book, we have been guided by three goals. First, we wish to convey the genuine excitement inherent in the subject of organizational behaviour by sharing our enthusiasm about the subject with students who are reading and learning about it for the first time.

Second, we want the presentation of the material to have both academic and practical integrity, acknowledging the debt of the field to both behavioural science research and organizational practice. To put it another way, we want this book to be useful and enjoyable to read without oversimplifying key subjects on the premise that this somehow makes them easier to understand. This requires striking a balance between research and theory on the one hand, and practice and application on the other hand. The tenth edition of *Organizational Behaviour* includes the most recent research and theory in the field (e.g., positive organizational behaviour, Chapter 1; cultural distance and cultural intelligence, Chapter 4; ethical, authentic, and servant leadership, Chapter 9; evidence-based management, big data, and crowdsourcing, Chapter 11; abusive supervision and cyberbullying, Chapter 13) as well as many examples of the application and practice of organizational behaviour that are throughout the text and showcased in the chapter-opening vignettes, the "Applied Focus" features, and the "You Be the Manager" features.

Third, we want students to not only learn about organizational behaviour but also to understand the connections and linkages across topics and how to integrate theory, principles, and concepts across chapters rather than see them as separate or isolated topics. Special features designed to enhance this skill include a new integrative case that runs through each section of the text and integrative discussion questions at the end of every chapter. We sincerely hope these goals have resulted in a textbook that is interesting and enjoyable to read and also conveys the importance of organizational behaviour to individuals, groups, organizations, and society.

NEW TO THE TENTH EDITION

The tenth edition of *Organizational Behaviour* involves a substantial revision to Chapters 14 (Organizational Structure) and what was Chapter 15 (Environment, Strategy, and Technology) in the previous editions. In the tenth edition, these two chapters have been merged, resulting in a new Chapter 14 (Environment, Strategy, and Structure) that covers the material on the external environment and strategic responses to uncertainty and resource dependence from the previous Chapter 15 as well as material on organizational structure and structural characteristics from the previous Chapter 14. In addition, the Appendix on Research in Organizational Behaviour that appeared in previous editions of *Organizational Behaviour* is now available online.

The tenth edition of *Organizational Behaviour* adds substantial new content, features, and pedagogy while remaining faithful to the general format and structure of the ninth edition. While the major topics of the ninth edition remain in this edition, we have added new content to reflect recent research as well as new and emerging themes in the organizational behaviour literature in every chapter of the text. Examples of new vignettes, focus boxes, topics, case studies, and definitions that can be found in the tenth edition include

- Integrative Case: Ken Private Limited: Digitization Project

Chapter 1:

- positive organizational behavior
- Chapter-Opening *Vignette*: Vega
- *Research Focus* box: Collective Organization Engagement
- *Applied Focus* box: Mental Health at Wellington County
- *Case Study:* Argamassa Construction Materials

Chapter 2:

- Chapter-Opening *Vignette*: Naheed Nenshi
- *Research Focus* box: Personality and Adaptive Performance
- *Case Study:* Roaring Dragon Hotel

Chapter 3:

- LGBT stereotypes
- Chapter-Opening *Vignette*: RBC
- *Applied Focus* box: Police Anti-Bias Training
- *Case Study:* LGBTA at TD Bank

Chapter 4:

- cultural distance and cultural intelligence
- Chapter-Opening *Vignette*: Facebook
- *You be the Manager* box: Carlsberg Group

Chapter 5:

- expanded coverage of self-determination theory (e.g., autonomy support)
- Chapter-Opening *Vignette*: DevFacto Technologies
- *Research Focus* box: Challenging Goals and Business Unit Performance
- *Ethical Focus* box: The Dark Side of Goal Setting
- *Case Study:* Kyle Evans at Ruffian Apparel: Staffing a Retail Establishment

Chapter 6:

- flexible work arrangements
- Updated Chapter-Opening *Vignette*: EllisDon
- *Research Focus* box: Improving the "Line-of-Sight" in Pay-for-Performance Programs
- *You Be the Manager:* Retention Bonuses at SNC Lavalin
- *Case Study:* Dr. Jack Perry

Chapter 7:

- *Research Focus* box: Supporting Teamwork on the Mission to Mars
- *Applied Focus* box: Virtual Teams at Save the Children
- *Case Study:* Levi Strauss & Co.'s Flirtation with Teams

Chapter 8:

- person-group (PG) fit
- Chapter-Opening *Vignette*: Kicking Horse Coffee
- *Research Focus* box: The Discriminatory Gap in University Mentoring
- *Case Study:* The Wonderful World of Human Resources at Disney

Chapter 9:

- role congruity theory
- Chapter-Opening *Vignette:* Sergio Marchionne (Fiat Chrysler Automobiles)
- *Research Focus* box*:* Narcissism and Leadership
- *Research Focus* box*:* Empowering Leadership and Newcomer Creativity
- *You Be the Manager:* Leadership at the CBC
- *Case Study:* Radio Station WEAA: Leading in a Challenging Situation

Chapter 10:

- enterprise social media
- *Chapter-Opening Vignette:* Toronto Sick Kids Hospital
- *You Be the Manager:* Communicating Diversity and Inclusion at Ryder
- *Research Focus* box: Red Sneakers Effect

Chapter 11:

- crowdsourcing
- evidence-based management
- big data
- *Applied Focus* box: Target Decision Errors
- *Applied Focus* box: Crowdsourcing
- *Case Study*: The Admissions Dilemma

Chapter 12:

- effects of extreme performance pressure on ethical lapses
- *Research Focus* box: Are you more moral in morning?
- *Case Study*: To Tell the Truth

Chapter 13:

- Chapter-opening *Vignette*: Orange France
- *Research Focus* box: Get Smarty Pants
- *Applied Focus* box*:* Vancity family-friendly

Chapter 14:

- Holacracy organizational structure
- Chapter-Opening *Vignette*: McDonald's
- *You be the Manager*: Zappos
- *Case Study*: Chris Peterson at DSS Consulting

Chapter 15:

- *Chapter-Opening Vignette:* Microsoft's Struggle
- *You Be the Manager*: Transforming 3M culture
- *Applied Focus* box*:* Guests Help Hotels Innovate
- *Case Study*: ION Consulting: The MP^2 Training Program

We have updated many other areas throughout the text with the most current and recent research from the practising management literature, academic literature, and the popular and business press. We have also replaced the content of many of the features and added new ones. In total, the tenth edition contains 11 new chapter-opening vignettes, 19 new "Focus" boxes, and 6 new "You Be the Manager" features. These features have been carefully chosen to represent current and exciting examples of organizational behaviour. Of those examples that we have retained from the ninth edition, many have been substantially updated.

In addition to new and updated content, the tenth edition includes several new exhibits. For example, Chapter 4 includes new data on what contributes to employee job satisfaction (Exhibit 4.7); Chapter 6 includes an exhibit showing the contingency factors to consider for the motivational practices discussed in the chapter (Exhibit 6.9); Chapter 9 includes a model of leadership styles, situational factors, and leader effectiveness (Exhibit 9.10); and Chapter 12 includes new data on observed ethical misconduct (Exhibit 12.6).

Finally, in the end-of-chapter material, there are thirteen new case studies, three new case incidents, and two new experiential exercises.

ABOUT THE COVER

The cover of the tenth edition of *Organizational Behaviour: Understanding and Managing Life at Work*, along with the pictures throughout the text, features musicians from a performing jazz band. What does a jazz band have to do with organizational behaviour? A great deal! Jazz has been used as a metaphor for organizations and organizational behaviour for many years.

In 1998, the journal *Organizational Science* published a special issue on jazz improvisation as a metaphor for organizations (vol. 9, no. 5), a result of a symposium called "Jazz as a Metaphor for Organizing in the Twenty-First Century" that was held at the 1995 Academy of Management Conference in Vancouver, British Columbia. The idea was to think about the twenty-first-century organization in the context of the jazz metaphor for organizing. The jazz metaphor has also been adopted by some organizations. In its 1996 annual report, the LEGO Corporation featured its top-management team as a jazz ensemble, with the CEO playing the saxophone—the CEO wanted to highlight the importance of improvisation at all levels of management.

Organizations and organizational behaviour are like jazz in many ways. Jazz involves improvisation, innovation, and flexibility, all of which are important attributes of individuals and groups in organizations as well as organizations themselves. Organizations and the people in them must be flexible and capable of innovation and improvisation to survive and adapt to change. Innovation and flexibility are especially important for contemporary organizations.

In his book *Leadership Jazz*, Max De Pree argues that leadership in organizations is like a jazz band: "Jazz-band leaders must choose the music, find the right musicians, and perform—in public. But the effect of the performance depends on so many things—the environment, the volunteers playing in the band, the need for everybody to perform as individuals and as a group, the absolute dependence of the leader on the members of the band, the need of the leader for the followers to play well. What a summary of an organization!"

Finally, as noted by Mary Jo Hatch, one of the chairs of the jazz symposium, the characteristics that are associated with the twenty-first-century organization are very similar to those of a jazz band: It is flexible, adaptable, and responsive to the environment, and it has loose boundaries and minimal hierarchy. Organizational behaviour is very much like a jazz band—individuals working together in the spirit of innovation, improvisation, and inspiration.

GENERAL CONTENT AND WRITING STYLE

Organizational Behaviour, Tenth Edition, is comprehensive—the material is authoritative and up to date and reflects current research and practical concerns. Both traditional subjects (such as expectancy theory) and newer topics (like workplace spirituality, positive organizational behaviour, cyberbullying, whistle-blowing, servant leadership, virtual teams, collective efficacy, emotional intelligence, creative deviance, and crowdsourcing) are addressed. Balanced treatment is provided to micro topics (covered in the earlier chapters) and macro topics (covered in the later chapters).

Although *Organizational Behaviour* is comprehensive, we have avoided the temptation to include too many concepts, theories, and ideas. Rather than composing a long laundry list of marginally related concepts, each chapter is organized in interlocked topics. The topics are actively interrelated and are treated in enough detail to ensure understanding. Special attention has been devoted to the flow and sequencing of the topics.

The writing style is personal and conversational. Excessive use of jargon is avoided, and important ideas are well defined and illustrated. Special attention has been paid to consistency of terminology throughout the book. We have tried to foster critical thinking about the concepts under discussion by using devices like asking the reader questions in the body of the text.

Believing that a well-tailored example can illuminate the most complex concept, we have used examples liberally throughout the text to clarify the points under consideration. The reader is not left wondering how a key idea applies to the world of organizations. The book is illustrated with exhibits, cartoons, and excerpts from the business press, such as *Report on Business*, *Canadian Business*, and *Canadian HR Reporter*, to enhance the flow of the material and reinforce the relevance of the examples for students.

We have treated the subject matter generically, recognizing that organizational behaviour occurs in all organizations. The reader will find vignettes, cases, "Focus" selections, "You Be the Manager" features, and examples drawn from a variety of settings, including large and small businesses, high-tech firms, manufacturing firms, hospitals, schools, and the military. In addition, care has been taken to demonstrate that the material covered is relevant to various levels and jobs within these organizations.

ORGANIZATION

Organizational Behaviour is organized in a simple but effective building-block manner. Part One: An Introduction defines organizational behaviour, discusses the nature of organizations, introduces the concept of management, and reviews contemporary management concerns. Part Two: Individual Behaviour covers the topics of personality, learning, perception, attribution, diversity, attitudes, job satisfaction, organizational commitment, and motivation. Part Three: Social Behaviour and Organizational Processes discusses groups, teamwork, socialization, culture, leadership, communication, decision making, power, politics, ethics, conflict, negotiation, and stress. Part Four: The Total Organization considers the environment, strategy, organizational structure, change, and innovation.

Some instructors may prefer to revise the order in which students read particular chapters, and they can accomplish this easily. However, Chapter 5, Theories of Work Motivation, should be read before Chapter 6, Motivation in Practice. The book has been designed to be used in either a quarter or semester course.

MAJOR THEMES AND CONTENT

In preparing the tenth edition of *Organizational Behaviour*, we concentrated on developing several themes that are current in contemporary organizational life. This development included adding new content, expanding previous coverage, and addressing the themes throughout the text to enhance integration.

The **global aspects of organizational life** continue to receive strong treatment in this edition to enable students to become more comfortable and competent in dealing with people from other cultures. Major sections on this theme appear in Chapters 4, 5, 9, and 10, which deal respectively with values, motivation, leadership, and communication. Pedagogical support for the global theme includes "Global Focus" features (Chapters 4 and 10), two "You Be the Manager" features (Chapters 4 and 10), a case study (Chapter 2), and the integrative case.

The changing nature of workplace demographics and a need to provide a welcoming work environment for all organizational members has led to explicit coverage of **workforce diversity**. The major treatment of this topic occurs in Chapter 3 in the context of perception and attribution. Additional treatment occurs in the context of motivation (Chapter 5), teams (Chapter 7), and communication (Chapter 10). Pedagogical support for the diversity theme can be found in the "You Be the Manager" feature in Chapters 3 and 10. We also see it in an "Applied Focus" feature (Chapter 3), a "Research Focus" feature (Chapter 8), an "Ethical Focus" feature (Chapter 3), three chapter-opening vignettes (Chapters 3, 4, and 12), a case incident (Chapter 3), two case studies (Chapters 3 and 4), and an experiential exercise (Chapter 3).

Contemporary organizations are focusing more and more on **teamwork**. This has led to expanded coverage of teams (such as virtual teams), and the most recent research findings on team characteristics and group effectiveness can be found in Chapter 7. Coverage of group decision making is included in Chapter 11. Pedagogical backup for the teamwork theme includes a chapter-opening vignette, "You Be the Manager" feature, "Research Focus" feature, "Applied Focus" feature, a case study, a case incident, and an experiential exercise (all in Chapter 7).

Many organizations continue to undergo major *change and transformation*. Interrelated topics involving organizational change such as reengineering and the use of technology continue to receive detailed coverage and are the focus of another theme highlighted in this edition. Coverage of organizational change can be found in Chapter 15. The role of technology in communication and decision making can be found in Chapters 10 and 11, where computer-mediated communication and enterprise social media are covered. Other relevant topics include telecommuting (Chapter 6) as well as sections on virtual, modular, and ambidextrous organizational structures (Chapter 14). Several passages portray the use and abuse of advanced technology, such as the discussion of cyberloafing in Chapter 10. Pedagogical backup for the change theme includes two chapter-opening vignettes (Chapters 14 and 15), three "You Be the Manager" features (Chapters 8, 14, and 15), an experiential exercise (Chapter 10), a case incident (Chapter 15), a case study (Chapter 15), and the Integrative Case.

Finally, the tenth edition of *Organizational Behaviour* reflects the continuing issue of **ethics** in organizations. The major formal coverage of ethics is included in Chapter 12 along with a discussion of power and politics. In addition, coverage of ethical leadership can be found in Chapter 9. Pedagogical support for the ethics theme can be found in a chapter-opening vignette and the "You Be the Manager" feature in Chapter 12, and several "Ethical Focus" features (Chapters 3, 5, 6, 8, and 12). Case studies are particularly good vehicles for examining the complexity surrounding ethical issues, and the case incidents in Chapters 9 and 12 and the case studies in Chapters 10 and 12 deal with explicit ethical dilemmas. One of the experiential exercises in Chapter 9 deals with ethical leadership.

PEDAGOGICAL FEATURES

The tenth edition's pedagogical features are designed to complement, supplement, and reinforce the textual material. More specifically, they are designed to promote self-awareness, critical thinking, and an appreciation of how the subject matter applies in actual organizations. The tenth edition of *Organizational Behaviour* includes all of the features found in the previous edition, including three different kinds of cases (case studies, case incidents, and a new integrative case), four types of "Focus" boxes ("Applied Focus," "Research Focus," "Ethical Focus," and "Global Focus"), "You Be the Manager" features, experiential exercises, and "On-the-Job Challenge" questions, which can be found at the end of each chapter, along with discussion questions for each chapter and integrative discussion questions.

- All chapters begin with an **Opening Vignette** chosen to stimulate interest in the chapter's subject matter. All of these vignettes concern real people in real organizations. Each vignette is carefully analyzed at several points in the chapter to illustrate the ideas under consideration. For example, Chapter 3 begins with a discussion of diversity at RBC, and Chapter 12 describes sexual harassment at the RCMP. The tenth edition of *Organizational Behaviour* includes eleven new vignettes and an updated one.

- Each chapter opens with **Learning Objectives** to help focus the student's attention on the chapter's subject matter. The Learning Objectives also appear within the chapter, in the margin, beside content relevant to each objective.

- In each chapter, students encounter a "**You Be the Manager**" feature that invites them to stop and reflect on the relevance of the material they are studying to a real problem in a real organization. Venues range from the Toronto Transit Commission (Chapter 1) and Calgary International Airport (Chapter 2) to Zappos' new holacracy organization structure (Chapter 14). Problems range from improving customer service (Chapter 1), managing diversity (Chapter 3), and changing an organization's culture (Chapter 8), to bullying at work (Chapter 13). At the end of each chapter, "**The Manager's Notebook**" offers some observations about the problem and reveals what the organization actually did or should do. The tenth edition of *Organizational Behaviour* includes six new "You Be the Manager" features.

- All chapters contain some combination of the following "Focus" features: "**Research Focus,**" "**Applied Focus,**" "**Global Focus,**" or "**Ethical Focus.**" These features illustrate or supplement the textual material with material from the practising management literature (e.g., *Canadian HR Reporter*), the research literature (e.g., *Academy of Management Journal*), and the popular press (e.g., *National Post*). They are chosen to exemplify real-world problems and practices as they relate to organizational behaviour. The "Research Focus" feature provides examples of organizational behaviour research, such as the effects of goals on business-unit performance (Chapter 5) and the red sneakers effect (Chapter 10). The "Applied Focus" features provide practical examples of the application of the text material in organizations. For example, the "Applied Focus" box in Chapter 1 describes mental health initiatives in Wellington County, and the box in Chapter 3 describes police training to address implicit biases. These two features help to reinforce the importance of both the research and practice of organizational behaviour. The "Ethical Focus" feature provides examples of ethics in organizational behaviour research, such as incentive compensation and unethical behaviour (Chapter 6) and knowledge hiding in the workplace (Chapter 12). This feature reinforces the importance of ethics in management and organizational behaviour. The "Global Focus" feature provides examples of organizational behaviour around the globe, such as illustrating who has high cultural intelligence (Chapter 4). This feature reinforces the importance of cross-cultural issues in management and organizational behaviour. The tenth edition of *Organizational Behaviour* includes 19 new Focus features.

- **Key terms** in each chapter are set in boldface type when they are discussed in the body of the text and are defined in the margin in a **running glossary**. To help students find the definitions they need, key terms are highlighted in the index, with page references for definitions, also in boldface.

- Each chapter concludes with a **Learning Objectives Checklist** (keyed to the chapter **Learning Objectives**) and **Discussion Questions**. In addition, each chapter includes at least two **Integrative Discussion Questions**. While the traditional discussion questions deal with issues within each chapter, the integrative discussion questions require students to relate and integrate the material in a current chapter with concepts and theories from previous chapters. For example, one of the questions in Chapter 12 ("Power, Politics, and Ethics") requires students to use the material on organizational learning practices (Chapter 2) and contributors to organizational culture (Chapter 8) to understand how an organization can create an ethical workplace. This feature is designed to facilitate student integration of various concepts and theories throughout the text.

- **On-the-Job Challenge Questions** appear after the Integrative Discussion Questions in each chapter. These questions differ from the other discussion questions in several respects. First, they are based on real issues and problems facing organizations. Second, they are more complex and challenging in that they require students to use their knowledge of all the material in the chapter. Third, these questions are very practical and require students to apply the text material to an actual situation or event facing an organization. For example, the question in Chapter 8 asks students to consider the role of culture in the sexual misconduct and abuse in the Canadian Forces. The answers to these questions are not simple or straightforward and require the student to apply the text material to a real issue or problem facing an organization. We hope that these questions provide students with an interesting and engaging opportunity to use their knowledge of organizational behaviour to address real problems facing organizations today. The tenth edition of *Organizational Behaviour* includes four new on-the-job challenge questions.

- Each chapter includes at least one **Experiential Exercise**. These exercises span individual self-assessment, role-playing, and group activities. In addition, to enhance student understanding and encourage discussion and interaction, most of the exercises include a group component in which groups of students work together on an exercise or discuss the results of a self-assessment and answer a series of questions. To ensure confidence in the feedback students receive, the self-assessments generally have a research base. The tenth edition of *Organizational Behaviour* includes two new experiential exercises.

- **Case Incidents** are included in every chapter. Case incidents are shorter than the case studies and are designed to focus on a particular topic within a chapter. Because they are short (one or two paragraphs) and deal with realistic scenarios of organizational life, they enable an instructor to quickly generate class discussion on a key theme within each chapter. They can be used at the beginning of a class to introduce a topic and to stimulate student thinking and interest, during the class when a particular topic is being discussed, or at the end of a class when the focus turns to applying the text material. The tenth edition of *Organizational Behaviour* includes three new case incidents.

- A **Case Study** is found in each chapter. The cases are of medium length, allowing great flexibility in tailoring their use to an instructor's personal style. We have selected cases that require active analysis and decision making, not simply passive description. Cases span important topics in contemporary organizations, such as diversity (Chapter 3), introducing teams (Chapter 7), and corporate culture (Chapter 8). The tenth edition of *Organizational Behaviour* includes thirteen new case studies.

- The **Integrative Case** is presented at the end of Part One of the text. Unlike the case studies, which focus only on the material in each chapter, the integrative case requires that students use the material throughout the text to understand the case material. Integrative case questions can be found at the end of each of the four parts of the text. The questions deal with the main issues and themes of the chapters within each part. This enables students to gain an increasing awareness and understanding of the case material upon completion of each part of the text. Answering the case questions requires the integration of material from the chapters within each part as well as preceding parts of the text. Therefore, upon completion of the text and the integrative case questions, the student will have acquired a comprehensive understanding of the case through the integration of issues pertaining to individual behaviour, social behaviour and organizational processes, and the total organization. The tenth edition of *Organizational Behaviour* includes a new integrative case: Ken Private Limited: Digitization Project.

RESOURCES FOR STUDENTS

MyManagementLab

We have created an outstanding supplements package for *Organizational Behaviour*, Tenth Canadian edition. In particular, we have provided access to MyManagementLab, which provides students with an assortment of tools to help enrich and expedite learning. MyManagementLab is an online study tool for students and an online homework and assessment tool for faculty. MyManagementLab lets students assess their understanding through auto-graded tests and assignments, develop a personalized study plan to address areas of weakness, and practise a variety of learning tools to master management principles. New and updated MyManagementLab resources include the following:

- *New Study Plan.* MyManagementLab offers students an engaging and focused self-study experience that is driven by a powerful new Study Plan. Students work through assessments in each chapter to gauge their understanding and target the topics that require additional practice. Along the way, they are recognized for their mastery of each topic and guided toward resources in areas that they might be struggling to understand.

- *Talking OB.* These self-assessment activities allow students to test their own knowledge.

- *New Personal Inventory Assessment (PIA).* Students learn better when they can connect what they are learning to their personal experience. PIA is a collection of online exercises designed to promote self-reflection and engagement in students, enhancing their ability to connect with concepts taught in principles of management, organizational behaviour, and human resource management classes. Assessments can be assigned by instructors, who can then track students' completions. Student results include a written explanation along with a graphic display that shows how their results compare to the class as a whole. Instructors will also have access to this graphic representation of results to promote classroom discussion.

- *New Dynamic Study Modules.* These new study modules allow students to work through groups of questions and check their understanding of foundational business topics. As students work through questions, the Dynamic Study Modules assess their knowledge and show only questions that still require practice. Dynamic Study Modules can be completed online using your computer, tablet, or mobile device.
- *Simulations.* Simulations walk students through key business decision-making scenarios to help them understand how business decisions are made. Students are asked to make important decisions relating to core business concepts. At each point, students receive feedback to help them understand the implications of their choices in the business environment. Both types of simulations can now be assigned by instructors and graded directly through MyManagementLab.
- *Assignable Mini-Cases.* Instructors have access to case-based assessment material for each part that can be assigned to students, with multiple-choice quizzes.
- *Pearson eText.* The Pearson eText gives students access to their textbook anytime, anywhere. In addition to note taking, highlighting, and bookmarking, the Pearson eText offers interactive and sharing features. Instructors can share their comments or highlights, and students can add their own, creating a tight community of learners within the class.
- *Glossary Flashcards.* This study aid is useful for students' review of key concepts.
- *Writing Space.* Better writers make great learners—who perform better in their courses. Providing a single location to develop and assess concept mastery and critical thinking, the Writing Space offers automatic graded, assisted graded, and create-your-own writing assignments, allowing you to exchange personalized feedback with students quickly and easily.

RESOURCES FOR INSTRUCTORS

Most of these instructor supplements are available for download from a password-protected section of Pearson Canada's online catalogue (www.pearsoncanada.ca/highered). Navigate to your book's catalogue page to view a list of those supplements that are available. See your local Pearson Canada sales representative for details and access.

- **CBC Video Library on DVD**. This DVD compilation which has been developed by the text authors includes segments from CBC programs on a range of topics relevant to issues covered in the text. Contact your local sales representative for details and access.
- **Instructor's Resource Manual with Video Guide**. Written by the text authors to ensure close coordination with the book, this extensive manual includes chapter objectives, a chapter outline, answers to all of the text questions and cases, supplemental lecture material, video case teaching notes, and teaching notes for each chapter.
- **Computerized Test Bank**. The testbank which has been developed by the text authors consists of nearly 4000 questions, including a mix of factual and application questions. Multiple-choice, true/false, fill-in-the-blank and short-answer formats are provided. For each question, we have provided the correct answer, a reference to the relevant section of the text, a difficulty rating, and a classification (recall/applied). Pearson's computerized test banks allow instructors to filter and select questions to create quizzes, tests or homework. Instructors can revise questions or add their own, and may be able to choose print or online options. These questions are also available in Microsoft Word format.
- **PowerPoint® Presentations**. Developed by the text authors, a ready-to-use PowerPoint slideshow designed for classroom presentation. Use it as is, or edit content to fit your individual classroom needs.
- **Image Library**. This package provides instructors with images to enhance their teaching.

Learning Solutions Managers

Pearson's Learning Solutions Managers work with faculty and campus course designers to ensure that Pearson technology products, assessment tools, and online course materials are tailored to meet your specific needs. This highly qualified team is dedicated to helping schools take full advantage of a wide range of educational resources, by assisting in the integration of a variety of instructional materials and media formats. Your local Pearson Education sales representative can provide you with more details on this service program.

ACKNOWLEDGMENTS

Books are not written in a vacuum. In writing *Organizational Behaviour*, Tenth Edition, we have profited from the advice and support of a number of individuals. This is our chance to say thank you.

First, we would like to thank our reviewers for this edition (including those who chose to remain anonymous), who provided us with a wealth of insights about how to improve the text:

Linda Donville, Centennial College

Kelly Dye, Acadia University

Stephen Friedman, York University

Joanne Leck, University of Ottawa

Teal McAteer, McMaster University

Don Miskiman, University of the Fraser Valley

John G. Vongas, Concordia University

Marlies Wiesel, Conestoga College

Second, we wish to thank our many colleagues who have provided us with helpful feedback, insights, and general support for the book over the years: Jennifer Berdahl, Stéphane Côté, Aaron Dresner, Jamie Gruman, Geoffrey Leonardelli, Julie McCarthy, Samantha Montes, Robert Oppenheimer, Tima Petrushka-Bordan, Phani Radhakrishnan, Simon Taggar, Soo Min Toh, John Trougakos, V.V. Baba, and David Zweig.

Third, we want to thank Samuel Tang, whose excellent research and organizational skills contributed greatly to the timeliness and relevance of the revision.

Fourth, we want to thank the team at Pearson Canada. We wish to extend our genuine appreciation to a group of extremely competent professionals who were wonderful to work with and who have greatly contributed to the quality of this text: Carolin Sweig (Senior Acquisitions Editor), Karen Townsend (Program Manager), Jessica McInnis (Marketing Manager), Mary Wat (Developmental Editor), Jessica Hellen (Project Manager), Barbara Kamienski (Copy Editor), Joanne Tang (Permissions Coordinator); and Anthony Leung (Designer). We did our best to make this book interesting, informative, and enjoyable to read; making it look as good as it does is icing on the cake. Thanks to everyone at Pearson who contributed to this book. They represent a great example of what this textbook is all about: *individuals working together to accomplish goals through group effort.*

Finally, each of us wishes to give thanks to those in our lives who have contributed to our work and the writing of this text:

I (Gary Johns) am grateful to my Concordia University Management Department colleagues for their interest, support, and ideas. Additionally, I would like to thank my students over the years. In one way or another, many of their questions, comments, challenges, and suggestions are reflected in the book. Also, thanks to all my colleagues who have taken time to suggest ideas for the book when we have met at professional conferences. Finally, thanks to Monika Jörg for her continuing enthusiasm, caring, humour, support, and advice.

I (Alan Saks) am grateful to my colleagues at the University of Toronto who have all been very supportive of this textbook. I would like to express my appreciation to my parents who have provided me with love and support throughout my career and continue to celebrate every step along the way. I also wish to thank my family, Kelly, Justin, and Brooke, who have had to endure my long hours of work for the past year. Although they did not write a single word in this book, in many ways their contribution is as significant as mine. Thanks for understanding, making me laugh, and for waiting so long for it to end!

Gary Johns Alan M. Saks

ABOUT THE AUTHORS

Gary Johns (PhD, Wayne State University) is Professor of Management in the John Molson School of Business, Concordia University, Montreal. He has research interests in absenteeism from work, presenteeism, personality, job design, research methodology, and the impact of context on organizational behaviour. He has published in *Journal of Applied Psychology, Academy of Management Journal, Academy of Management Review, Organizational Behavior and Human Decision Processes, Personnel Psychology, Journal of Management, Research in Organizational Behavior, Research in Personnel and Human Resources Management, Journal of Organizational Behavior, Journal of Vocational Behavior, Journal of Occupational and Organizational Psychology, International Review of Industrial and Organizational Psychology, Journal of Occupational Health Psychology, Canadian Psychology, Human Resource Management Review, Human Relations, Applied Psychology: An International Review, Journal of Business and Psychology, Canadian Journal of Administrative Sciences, International Journal of Cross Cultural Management, Cross Cultural Management,* and *Psychology Today.* Co-author of *Organizational Behavior: Understanding and Managing Life at Work* (10th Edition, Pearson). Recipient of Academy of Management Organizational Behavior Division's New Concept Award, Society for Industrial and Organizational Psychology's Edwin E. Ghiselli Research Design Award, the Canadian Society for Industrial and Organizational Psychology's Award for Distinguished Contributions to Industrial and Organizational Psychology, the Concordia University Research Award, the award for the Best Article published in *Human Relations* in 2007, and the award for the Outstanding Paper published in *Cross Cultural Management* in 2013. Elected Fellow of SIOP, American Psychological Association, Canadian Psychological Association, Academy of Management, and International Association of Applied Psychology. Former Chair of the Canadian Society for Industrial and Organizational Psychology. Former Associate Editor, *Journal of Organizational Behavior.* Currently on editorial boards of *Journal of Applied Psychology, Human Relations, International Journal of Selection and Assessment,* and *Applied Psychology: An International Review.* Formerly on editorial boards of *Academy of Management Journal, Journal of Management, Personnel Psychology, Organizational Behavior and Human Decision Processes, Journal of Occupational Health Psychology, Canadian Journal of Administrative Sciences,* and *Journal of Occupational and Organizational Psychology.* Held visiting positions at University of Sheffield, University of Oregon, Queensland University of Technology, Australian Graduate School of Management and Australian School of Business (University of New South Wales), Hong Kong University of Science and Technology, Singapore Management University, Australia's Griffith University, and the University of British Columbia.

Alan M. Saks (PhD, University of Toronto) is a Professor of Organizational Behaviour and Human Resources Management at the University of Toronto, where he holds a joint appointment in the Department of Management—UTSC, the Centre for Industrial Relations and Human Resources, and the Joseph L. Rotman School of Management. Prior to joining the University of Toronto, Professor Saks was a member of the Department of Management at Concordia University and the School of Administrative Studies at York University. Professor Saks earned an HBA in Psychology from the University of Western Ontario, an MASc in Industrial–Organizational Psychology from the University of Waterloo, and a PhD in Organizational Behaviour and Human Resources from the University of Toronto. His research interests include recruitment, job search, training, employee engagement, and the socialization and on-boarding of new employees. Professor Saks has published his research in refereed journals such as the *Journal of Applied Psychology, Personnel Psychology, Academy of Management Journal, Journal of Organizational Behavior, Journal of Vocational Behavior, Journal of Business and Psychology, Human Resource Management, The International Journal of Human Resource Management, International Journal of Training and Development,* and *Human Resource Management Review,* as well as in professional journals such as *HR Professional Magazine, The Learning Journal,* and *Canadian HR Reporter.* In addition to *Organizational Behaviour: Understanding and Managing Life at Work,* he is also the author of *Research, Measurement, and Evaluation of Human Resources* and co-author of *Managing Performance through Training and Development.* Professor Saks is currently on the editorial boards of the *Journal of Vocational Behavior, Human Resource Development Review, Journal of Leadership and Organizational Studies, Journal of Organizational Effectiveness: People and Performance, Journal of Management,* and *International Journal of Training and Development* and is an Associate Editor of the *Journal of Business and Psychology.*

CHAPTER 1

ORGANIZATIONAL BEHAVIOUR AND MANAGEMENT

LEARNING OBJECTIVES

After reading Chapter 1, you should be able to:

1.1 Define *organizations* and describe their basic characteristics.

1.2 Explain the concept of *organizational behaviour* and describe the goals of the field.

1.3 Define *management* and describe what managers do to accomplish goals.

1.4 Contrast the *classical viewpoint* of management with that advocated by the *human relations movement*.

1.5 Describe the *contingency approach* to management.

1.6 Explain what managers do—their roles, activities, agendas for action, and thought processes.

1.7 Describe the four contemporary management concerns facing organizations and how organizational behaviour can help organizations understand and manage these concerns.

VEGA

How would you like to work for a company that offers vegan meals prepared by an in-house chef and complimentary smoothies, soups, salads, and snacks on a daily basis? The 165 employees at Vega of Burnaby, British Columbia get this and more every day.

According to Angela Hutchinson, Vega HR Generalist, "We believe that a plant-based, whole-foods diet reduces stress so therefore it's going to be more energizing for our employees as well during the day."

Vega was founded by company President Charles Chang in his basement in 2001. The company sells plant-based natural health and performance products such as its flagship product, protein-rich powdered shake Vega One, as well as other protein smoothies and nutritional shakes. It is considered a pioneer in plant-based supplements. Vega's sales in 2004, its first year on the market, reached $1 million. By 2013, sales had reached $70 million, with projected sales of $100 million. In the United States, Vega has doubled its growth every year since it entered the market.

In addition to healthy food, Vega also offers employees an after-hours clinic with massage therapists and acupuncture, and wellness events that include foosball tournaments and team outings such as trips to a spa.

Employees also participate in events such as the Tough Mudder obstacle course challenge.

Vega fosters a culture of empowerment and entrepreneurship," says Hutchinson. "For an employee who wants to take the ball, they have the freedom to make things happen and then they're rewarded for their efforts. So whether or not you're in a management role, you are still given the opportunity to be a leader in your position."

At Vega, they refer to the company culture as Vegatopia and employees as Vegatopians. The company's culture and core values of relationships, entrepreneurship, integrity, and performance are a key source of its competitive advantage. According to Vega President Charles Chang, "We nurture a performance-driven culture with highly motivated employees who have a sense of ownership in the business. We're committed to product innovation, category creation and category leadership. And we're always fit and ready to sell. This keeps us focused on our vision, our strategy and our best practices."

Vega hires people who contribute to its spirited culture. "We look for people who have really great core values, aligned with our own," says Hutchinson, citing integrity, a passion for customer service, being performance-driven, embracing change, and thriving in

Eric Milic (ericmilic.com), by permission of Vega, Vegan Snacks

a high-paced, dynamic work environment. According to Chang, "Our primary sustainable competitive advantage lay in our ability to build a team to fulfill our vision and represent our core values."

Vega has an open-door policy, so everyone has full access to managers and the president. There are also weekly one-on-one meetings with managers and monthly staff meetings, plus a new program for coaching and career development.

Vega recently rolled out an employee survey in which it asked employees to take their lowest-scoring and highest-scoring sections and come back with action plans. "We really want to empower our employees to take charge on how they want to see their engagement level and their teams improve by doing that. We're there to support them," said Hutchinson.

Performance bonuses are based on quarterly goals, and each employee receives an annual profit-sharing bonus. Benefits include a health spending account along with life insurance, travel insurance, an education reimbursement, a green incentive, a fitness reimbursement, and free products every month.

If this sounds like a great place to work, then you are right. Vega has been named one of Canada's Best Workplaces and Best Managed Companies as well as one of British Columbia's Top Employers.[1]

What we have here is an example of work life and management—just what this book is about. The example also highlights many important aspects of organizational behaviour, such as culture, values, empowerment, health and wellness, motivation, compensation, engagement, and rewards. It raises some very interesting questions: Why does Vega offer employees vegan meals and wellness events? Why does Vega foster a culture of empowerment and entrepreneurship? Why does Vega have an open-door policy? Why do Vega employees receive a performance bonus and an annual profit-sharing bonus? This book will help you uncover the answers to these kinds of questions.

In this chapter, we will define *organizations* and *organizational behaviour* and examine their relationship to management. We will explore historical and contemporary approaches to management and consider what managers do and how they think. The chapter concludes with some issues of concern to contemporary organizations.

LO **1.1**

Define *organizations* and describe their basic characteristics.

Organizations. Social inventions for accomplishing common goals through group effort.

WHAT ARE ORGANIZATIONS?

This book is about what happens in organizations. Most of us will earn our livelihood working in organizations, and our well-being as well as that of our communities depends on organizations. We are often identified, in part, by what we do and where we do it. We live in an organizational society.[2] But what exactly is an organization?

Organizations are social inventions for accomplishing common goals through group effort. Vega is obviously an organization, but so are the Toronto Blue Jays, CTV, and college sororities or fraternities.

Social Inventions

When we say that organizations are social inventions, we mean that their essential characteristic is the coordinated presence of *people*, not necessarily things. Vega owns a lot of things, such as equipment and offices. However, you are probably aware that, through advanced information technology and contracting out work, some contemporary organizations make and sell products, such as computers or clothes, without owning much of anything. In fact, Vega outsources the manufacturing and warehousing of its products. Also, many service organizations, such as consulting firms, have little physical capital. Still, these organizations have people—people who present both opportunities and challenges. *The field of organizational behaviour is about understanding people and managing them to work effectively.*

In a variety of different organizations, individuals work together to accomplish goals through group effort. Though the motivation of a television news station might differ from that of another organization, all organizations strive for goal accomplishment and survival.

THE CANADIAN PRESS/Adrien Veczan

Goal Accomplishment

Individuals are assembled into organizations for a reason. The organizations mentioned above have the very basic goals of selling plant-based natural health and performance products, winning baseball games, delivering news, or providing social networks. Non-profit organizations have goals such as saving souls, promoting the arts, helping the needy, or educating people. Virtually all organizations have survival as a goal. Despite this, consider the list of organizations that have failed to survive: Canadian Airlines, Eaton's, the Montreal Expos, and Columbia House, to name just a few. *The field of organizational behaviour is concerned with how organizations can survive and adapt to change.* Certain behaviours are necessary for survival and adaptation. People have to

- be motivated to join and remain in the organization;
- carry out their basic work reliably, in terms of productivity, quality, and service;
- be willing to continuously learn and upgrade their knowledge and skills; and
- be flexible and innovative.[3]

The field of organizational behaviour is concerned with all these basic activities. Innovation and flexibility, which foster adaptation to change, are especially important for contemporary organizations. Management guru Tom Peters has gone so far as to advise firms to "Get Innovative or Get Dead."[4] Demonstrating the validity of his advice, layoffs and the loss of market share at Blackberry several years ago were blamed on the company's failure to innovate. Perhaps it is not surprising that 87 percent of executives believe that innovation is a strategic priority for their organizations.[5]

Group Effort

The final component of our definition of organizations is that they are based on group effort. At its most general level, this means that organizations depend on interaction and coordination among people to accomplish their goals. Much of the intellectual and physical work done in organizations is quite literally performed by groups, whether they are permanent work teams or short-term project teams. Also, informal grouping occurs in all organizations because friendships develop and individuals form informal alliances to accomplish work. The quality of this informal contact in terms of communication and morale can have a strong impact on goal achievement. For all these reasons, *the field of organizational behaviour is concerned with how to get people to practise effective teamwork.*

Now that we have reviewed the basic characteristics of organizations, let's look more directly at the meaning and scope of organizational behaviour.

WHAT IS ORGANIZATIONAL BEHAVIOUR?

Organizational behaviour refers to the attitudes and behaviours of individuals and groups in organizations. The discipline of organizational behaviour systematically studies these attitudes and behaviours and provides insight about effectively managing and changing them. It also studies how organizations can be structured more effectively and how events in their external environments affect organizations. Those who study organizational behaviour are interested in attitudes—how satisfied people are with their jobs, how committed they feel to the goals of the organization, or how supportive they are of promoting women or minorities into management positions. Behaviours such as cooperation, conflict, innovation, resignation, or ethical lapses are important areas of study in the field of organizational behaviour.

A closely related but distinct discipline is human resources management. **Human resources management** refers to programs, practices, and systems to acquire, develop, motivate, and retain employees in organizations. You are probably familiar with many

LO 1.2

Explain the concept of *organizational behaviour* and describe the goals of the field.

Organizational behaviour. The attitudes and behaviours of individuals and groups in organizations.

Human resources management. Programs, practices, and systems to acquire, develop, motivate, and retain employees in organizations.

human resource practices such as recruitment and selection, compensation, and training and development. As you will see throughout this text, knowledge of organizational behaviour will help you understand human resource management. For example, in Chapter 3 you will learn about the role that perceptions play in recruitment, the employment interview, and performance appraisals. In Chapter 4, you will learn about the factors that contribute to employee absenteeism and turnover, knowledge of which is necessary for developing effective human resource practices to lower absenteeism and retain employees. In Chapters 5 and 6 you will learn how theories of motivation help us understand the effects of different compensation strategies on employee motivation and performance. In Chapter 8 you will learn how human resource practices such as realistic job previews and employee orientation programs contribute to the on-boarding and socialization process in organizations. Thus, learning about organizational behaviour will improve your understanding of human resources management.

Using an organizational behaviour perspective, reconsider the Vega vignette that opened the chapter. The immediate question is, *What are the factors that make an organization successful and a great place to work?* Although we will not answer this question directly, we can pose some questions highlighting some of the topics that the field of organizational behaviour covers, which we will explore in later chapters.

- What can organizations do to help employees manage stress? Vega provides employees with healthy food choices and wellness programs. The topic of stress and organizational strategies for managing it are the focus of Chapter 13.
- What does it mean to empower employees, and why is this important? Vega fosters a culture of empowerment, and employees have the freedom to make things happen. Empowerment and its consequences are discussed in Chapter 12.
- How can organizations motivate employees, and how important is compensation? Vega provides performance bonuses to employees, and employees receive an annual profit-sharing bonus. Chapter 5 describes different theories of motivation, and the role of money as a motivator is discussed in Chapter 6.
- What is the purpose of an employee survey? Vega conducts an employee survey and asks employees to come up with action plans. An employee survey is an organizational approach to improve communication, which is covered in Chapter 10.
- What is an organizational culture, and what role does it play in an organization's success? The culture at Vega emphasizes relationships, entrepreneurship, integrity, and performance. How cultures are built and maintained and their role in organizational effectiveness is covered in Chapter 8.

These questions provide a good overview of some issues that those in the field of organizational behaviour study. Accurate answers to these questions would go a long way toward understanding why Vega is a successful organization and how other organizations can make changes to become more effective. Analysis followed by action is what organizational behaviour is all about.

WHY STUDY ORGANIZATIONAL BEHAVIOUR?

Why should you attempt to read and understand the material in *Organizational Behaviour*? As described below, organizational behaviour is interesting and important, and it makes a difference for employees and organizations.

Organizational Behaviour Is Interesting

At its core, organizational behaviour is interesting because it is about people and human nature. Why does Vega have a culture of empowerment and entrepreneurship, and what effect does this have on employee attitudes and behaviour? These questions are interesting because they help us understand why employees become committed to an organization and what motivates them to work hard.

Organizational behaviour includes interesting examples of success as well as failure. Later in the text, we will study a company that promotes job satisfaction among its mostly young workforce (Facebook, Chapter 4); an organization that provides all employees $2500 per year for any vocational training, $100 per month for travel expenses, an annual $1200 cell-phone and home-internet subsidy, and free beer on Fridays from the company's beer fridge (DevFacto Technologies Inc., Chapter 5); an organization that has a strong commitment to recruiting, hiring, and developing persons with disabilities (RBC, Chapter 3); a company that excels at staffing project teams (IDEO, Chapter 7); and a company where employees have flexible work hours, daily workout breaks, catered monthly meetings called "pow-wows," and fun days for outdoor activities like hiking, rafting, kayaking, mountain bike excursions, and skiing (Kicking Horse Coffee, Chapter 8). All of these companies are extremely success-ful, and organizational behaviour helps explain why.

Organizational behaviour does not have to be exotic to be interesting. Anyone who has negotiated with a recalcitrant bureaucrat or had a really excellent boss has probably wondered what made them behave the way they did. Organizational behaviour provides the tools to find out why.

Organizational Behaviour Is Important

Looking through the lens of other disciplines, it would be possible to frame Vega's success in terms of marketing and sales. Notice, however, that underlying these perspectives, it is *still* about organiza-tional behaviour. What happens in organizations often has a profound impact on people. It is clear that the impact of organizational behaviour does not stop at the walls of the organization. The con-sumers of an organization's products and services, such as the customers who purchase Vega's prod-ucts, are also affected. Thus, organizational behaviour is important to managers, employees, and consumers, and understanding it can make us more effective managers, employees, or consumers.

We sometimes fail to appreciate that there is tremendous variation in organizational behaviour. For example, skilled salespeople in insurance or real estate make many, many more sales than some of their peers. Similarly, for every Greenpeace or Sierra Club, there are dozens of failed organizations that were dedicated to saving the environment. The field of organizational behaviour is concerned with explaining these differences and using the explanations to improve organizational effectiveness and efficiency.

Organizational Behaviour Makes a Difference

In his book *Competitive Advantage Through People*, Jeffrey Pfeffer argued that organizations can no longer achieve a competitive advantage through the traditional sources of success, such as technology, regulated markets, access to financial resources, and economies of scale.[6] Today, the main factor that differentiates organizations is their workforce and human capital. The results of a study that reviewed research on human capital are unequivocal: Human capital is strongly related to and a key determinant of firm performance.[7] Thus, sustained competitive advantage and organizational effectiveness are increasingly related to the management of human capital and organizational behaviour.

Pfeffer identified 16 practices of companies that are effective through their management of people. Many of these practices, such as incentive pay, participation and empowerment, teams, job redesign, and training and skill development, are important topics in organiza-tional behaviour and are discussed in this book. Pfeffer's research helps to point out that organizational behaviour is not just interesting and important but that it also makes a big difference for the effectiveness and competitiveness of organizations.

Many of the best companies to work for and organizations like Vega that have been named best workplaces, best managed companies, and top employers are living examples of

EXHIBIT 1.1
Management practices of the best companies to work for in Canada.
Sources: Brearton, S., & Daly, J. (2003, January). The 50 best companies to work for in Canada. *Report on Business Magazine, 19*(2), 53–66; Hannon, G. (2002, January). The 50 best companies to work for. *Report on Business Magazine, 18*(7), 41–52.

- Flexible work schedules (flex-time, telecommuting, job sharing, and compressed workweek)
- Stock options, profit sharing plans, and performance bonuses
- Extensive training and development programs
- Family assistance programs
- On-site fitness facilities, daycare, and wellness programs
- Career days and formal career plans
- Flexible or cafeteria-style benefit plans
- Monthly staff socials, family Christmas parties, and picnics
- Stress reduction programs
- Monthly all-employee meetings
- Formal workplace diversity programs to encourage women and minorities
- Employee recognition and reward programs

the importance of organizational behaviour. As shown in Exhibit 1.1, the best companies to work for in Canada have implemented management practices that have their basis in organizational behaviour such as flexible work schedules, diversity programs, and employee recognition and reward programs. This raises an interesting question: Are the best companies to work for also the most profitable? Some might argue that just because an organization is a great place to work does not necessarily mean that it is a great organization when it comes to competitiveness and performance. What do you think?

As it turns out, the best companies to work for are also the most successful. Research has found that the best companies outperformed a matched group of companies that have never been on the 100 best list but are comparable in terms of industry, size and operating performance, financial performance and stock returns.[8] Thus, it makes good business sense for organizations to be great places to work, and that is what organizational behaviour is all about.

HOW MUCH DO YOU KNOW ABOUT ORGANIZATIONAL BEHAVIOUR?

Although this is probably your first formal course in organizational behaviour, you already have a number of opinions about the subject. To illustrate this, consider whether the following statements are true or false. Please jot down a one-sentence rationale for your answer. There are no tricks involved!

1. Effective organizational leaders tend to possess identical personality traits.
2. Nearly all workers prefer stimulating, challenging jobs.
3. Managers have a very accurate idea about how much their peers and superiors are paid.
4. Workers have a very accurate idea about how often they are absent from work.
5. Pay is the best way to motivate most employees and improve job performance.
6. Women are just as likely to become leaders in organizations as men.

Now that you have your answers, do one more thing. Assume that the correct answer is opposite to the one you have given; that is, if your answer is true for a statement, assume that it is actually false, and vice versa. Now, give a one-sentence rationale for why this opposite answer could also be correct.

Each of these statements concerns the behaviour of people in organizations. Furthermore, each statement has important implications for the functioning of organizations. If effective leaders possess identical personality traits, then organizations might sensibly hire leaders who have such traits. Similarly, if most employees prefer stimulating jobs, there are many jobs that could benefit from upgrading. In this book, we will investigate the extent to which statements such as these are true or false and why they are true or false.

The answers to this quiz may surprise you. Substantial research indicates that each of the statements in the quiz is essentially false. Of course, there are exceptions, but in general, researchers have found that the personalities of effective leaders vary a fair amount, many people prefer routine jobs, managers are not well informed about the pay of their peers and superiors, workers underestimate their own absenteeism, pay is not always the most effective way to motivate workers and improve job performance, and women are underrepresented in leadership roles in organizations. However, you should not jump to unwarranted conclusions based on the inaccuracy of these statements until we determine *why* they tend to be incorrect. There are good reasons for an organization to tie pay to job performance to motivate employees and to improve their performance. Also, we can predict who might prefer challenging jobs and who will be motivated by pay. We will discuss these issues in more detail in later chapters.

Experience indicates that people are amazingly good at giving sensible reasons why the same statement is either true or false. Thus, pay will always motivate workers because most people want to make more money and will work harder to get more pay. Conversely, workers will work only as hard as they have to, regardless of how much money they are paid. The ease with which people can generate such contradictory responses suggests that "common sense" develops through unsystematic and incomplete experiences with organizational behaviour.

However, because common sense and opinions about organizational behaviour do affect management practice, practice should be based on informed opinion and systematic study. Now, let's consider the goals of organizational behaviour.

GOALS OF ORGANIZATIONAL BEHAVIOUR

Like any discipline, the field of organizational behaviour has a number of commonly agreed-upon goals. Chief among these are effectively predicting, explaining, and managing behaviour that occurs in organizations. For example, in Chapter 6 we will discuss the factors that predict which pay plans are most effective in motivating individuals and groups. Then we will explain the reasons for this effectiveness and describe how managers can implement effective pay plans.

Predicting Organizational Behaviour

Predicting the behaviour of others is an essential requirement for everyday life, both inside and outside of organizations. Our lives are made considerably easier by our ability to anticipate when our friends will get angry, when our professors will respond favourably to a completed assignment, and when salespeople and politicians are telling us the truth about a new product or the state of the nation. In organizations, there is considerable interest in predicting when people will make ethical decisions, create innovative products, or engage in sexual harassment.

The very regularity of behaviour in organizations permits the prediction of its future occurrence. However, untutored predictions of organizational behaviour are not always as accurate. Through systematic study, the field of organizational behaviour provides a scientific foundation that helps improve predictions of organizational events. Of course, being able to predict organizational behaviour does not guarantee that we can explain the reason for the behaviour and develop an effective strategy to manage it. This brings us to the second goal of the field.

Explaining Organizational Behaviour

Another goal of organizational behaviour is to explain events in organizations—why do they occur? Prediction and explanation are not synonymous. Ancient societies were capable of predicting the regular setting of the sun but were unable to explain where it went or why it went there. In general, accurate prediction precedes explanation. Thus, the very regularity of the sun's disappearance gave some clues about why it was disappearing.

Organizational behaviour is especially interested in determining why people are more or less motivated, satisfied, or prone to resign. Explaining events is more complicated than predicting them. For one thing, a particular behaviour could have multiple causes. People may resign from their jobs because they are dissatisfied with their pay, because they are discriminated against, or because they have failed to respond appropriately to an organizational crisis. An organization that finds itself with a "turnover problem" is going to have to find out why this is happening before it can put an effective correction into place. This behaviour could have many different causes, each of which would require a specific solution. Furthermore, explanation is also complicated by the fact that the underlying causes of some event or behaviour can change over time. For example, the reasons people quit may vary greatly depending on the overall economy and whether there is high or low unemployment in the field in question. Throughout the book, we will consider material that should improve your grasp of organizational behaviour. The ability to understand behaviour is a necessary prerequisite for effectively managing it.

Managing Organizational Behaviour

LO 1.3

Define *management* and describe what managers do to accomplish goals.

Management. The art of getting things accomplished in organizations through others.

Management is defined as the art of getting things accomplished in organizations through others. Managers acquire, allocate, and utilize physical and human resources to accomplish goals.[9] This definition does not include a prescription about how to get things accomplished. As we proceed through the text, you will learn that a variety of management styles might be effective, depending on the situation at hand.

If behaviour can be predicted and explained, it can often be managed. That is, if we truly understand the reasons for high-quality service, ethical behaviour, or anything else, we can often take sensible action to manage it effectively. If prediction and explanation constitute analysis, then management constitutes action. Unfortunately, we see all too many cases in which managers act without analysis, looking for a quick fix to problems. The result is often disaster. The point is not to overanalyze a problem. Rather, it is to approach a problem with a systematic understanding of behavioural science and organizational behaviour and to use that understanding to make decisions; this is known as evidence-based management.

Evidence-based management. Translating principles based on the best scientific evidence into organizational practices.

Evidence-based management involves translating principles based on the best scientific evidence into organizational practices. By using evidence-based management, managers can make decisions based on the best available scientific evidence from social science and organizational research, rather than personal preference and unsystematic experience. Evidence-based management derives principles from research evidence and translates them into practices that solve organizational problems. The use of evidence-based management is more likely to result in the attainment of organizational goals, including those affecting employees, stockholders, and the public in general (see Chapter 11 for a more detailed discussion of evidence-based management and decision making).[10]

Now that you are familiar with the goals of organizational behaviour, read You Be the Manager: *Toronto's Troubled Transit System* and answer the questions. In The Manager's Notebook at the end of the chapter, find out what the TTC is doing. This is not a test but rather an exercise to improve critical thinking, analytical skills, and management skills. Pause and reflect on these application features as you encounter them in each chapter.

LO 1.4

Contrast the *classical viewpoint* of management with that advocated by the *human relations movement*.

EARLY PRESCRIPTIONS CONCERNING MANAGEMENT

For many years, experts interested in organizations were concerned with prescribing the "correct" way to manage an organization to achieve its goals. There were two basic phases to this prescription, which experts often call the classical view and the human relations view. A summary of these viewpoints will illustrate how the history of management thought and organizational behaviour has developed.

YOU BE THE MANAGER

Toronto's Troubled Transit System

The Toronto Transit Commission (TTC) is the third-largest public transit system in North America, after New York and Mexico City. With 12 500 employees, the TTC moves 1.5 million riders every weekday.

In January of 2010, on the heels of a TTC fare hike and token shortages, a TTC rider took a photo of a subway ticket collector sprawled back in his chair, his mouth agape, and apparently snoozing while on the job. The photo was posted on the web and went viral.

At first people were amused, but then reaction grew rapidly into anger, and the sleeping ticket collector who became known as "TTC Sleeper" became a lightning rod for transit riders frustrated with the TTC.

Soon more photos of sleeping TTC employees began to surface, and riders complained about everything from TTC employees sleeping, reading, or watching DVDs, to more serious allegations of dangerous driving, verbal rudeness, and even assault. And then in February the TTC was once again under fire for a video taken of an employee who left a bus idling while he took a lengthy, unscheduled break in a doughnut shop.

Reports of customer complaints indicate that they increased by nearly 20 percent, from about 26 000 in the first 11 months of 2008 to about 31 000 in the same period the following year. While many riders complained about the fare increase, the top two complaints for the year were bus and streetcar delays and "discourtesy" from TTC workers. There were 3851 complaints about discourteous employees.

Former TTC chief general manager Gary Webster issued a scolding memo to all employees, declaring, "The culture of complacency and malaise that has seeped into our organization will end," and he warned that workers would be "held accountable for their poor performance."

Then TTC chairman Adam Giambrone announced the creation of a blue-ribbon customer service advisory panel of private-sector experts to review the TTC's customer service practices and make recommendations on how the TTC could improve customer service. The Amalgamated Transit Union Local 113 announced that it would hold a series of town hall meetings to address the strained relationship between passengers and workers.

In April 2010, the TTC released hundreds of customer complaints to the *Toronto Star* through a freedom of information request. The complaints painted a picture of a transit system troubled by a culture of

Customer complaints paint a picture of a transit system troubled by a culture of indifference and disdain toward customers.

indifference and disdain toward customers. Riders said they were verbally abused and harassed by TTC staff daily. Poor people skills, not delays or fare disputes, appeared to be the main concern for transit customers.

Questions

1. What issues at the TTC are particularly relevant from an organizational behaviour perspective? What can the TTC learn about the customer service problem from organizational behaviour?

2. How can the goals of organizational behaviour help solve the problems at the TTC and improve customer service?

To find out what the TTC is doing to improve customer service, see The Manager's Notebook at the end of the chapter.

Sources: Kalinowski, T. (2010, January 20). TTC seeks outside aid to fix customer beefs. *Toronto Star*, GT5; Kalinowski, T. (2010, January 28). "We owe our riders an apology," TTC boss concedes, Giambrone's news conference was classic damage control. But will it work? *Toronto Star*, A1; Kalinowski, T. (2010, January 28). Customer service checklist. *Toronto Star*, A19; Ferenc, L. (2010, February 3). Can much-maligned TTC pass our test? After all the promises on improvements, Star reporter boards for 2 hours of scrutiny. *Toronto Star*, GT3; Kalinowski, T. (2010, February 4). TTC driver takes coffee break as fuming riders wait and wait. *Toronto Star*, A2; TTC's culture of complacency. (2010, February 9). *Toronto Star*, A18; Kennedy, B. (2010, April 1). Unhappy TTC riders get chance to sound off to employees. *Toronto Star*, 1; Doolittle, R. (2010, April 20). Crude, rude TTC staff top list of complaints; Dreadful lack of people skills, not delays or fare disputes, main concern for commuters. *Toronto Star*, 1; Yang, J. (2010, January 22). TTC catnaps ignite rider fury amid higher fares. *Toronto Star*, www.thestar.com/printarticle/754753; TTC Customer Service Advisory Panel Report. (2010, August 23).

The Classical View and Bureaucracy

Most of the major advocates of the classical viewpoint were experienced managers or consultants who took the time to write down their thoughts on organizing. For the most part, this activity occurred in the early 1900s. The classical writers acquired their experience in military settings, mining operations, and factories that produced everything from cars to candy. Prominent names include Henri Fayol, General Motors executive James D. Mooney, and consultant Lyndall Urwick.[11] Although exceptions existed, the **classical viewpoint** tended to advocate a very high degree of specialization of labour and a very high degree of coordination. Each department was to tend to its own affairs, with centralized decision making from upper management providing coordination. The classical view suggested that, to maintain control, managers have fairly few workers, except for lower-level jobs, where machine pacing might substitute for close supervision.

Frederick Taylor (1856–1915), the father of **scientific management**, was also a contributor to the classical school, although he was mainly concerned with job design and the structure of work on the shop floor.[12] Rather than informal "rules of thumb" for job design, Taylor's scientific management advocated the use of careful research to determine the optimum degree of specialization and standardization. He also supported the development of written instructions that clearly defined work procedures, and he encouraged supervisors to standardize workers' movements and breaks for maximum efficiency. Taylor even extended scientific management to the supervisor's job, advocating "functional foremanship," whereby supervisors would specialize in particular functions. For example, one might become a specialist in training workers, while another might fulfill the role of a disciplinarian.

The practising managers and consultants had an academic ally in Max Weber (1864–1920), the distinguished German social theorist. Weber made the term *bureaucracy* famous by advocating it as a means of rationally managing complex organizations. During Weber's lifetime, managers were certainly in need of advice. In this time of industrial growth and development, most management was done by intuition, and nepotism and favouritism were rampant. According to Weber, a **bureaucracy** has the following qualities:

- A strict chain of command in which each member reports to only a single superior.
- Criteria for selection and promotion based on impersonal technical skills rather than nepotism or favouritism.
- A set of detailed rules, regulations, and procedures ensuring that the job gets done regardless of who the specific worker is.
- The use of strict specialization to match duties with technical competence.
- The centralization of power at the top of the organization.[13]

Weber saw bureaucracy as an "ideal type" or theoretical model that would standardize behaviour in organizations and provide workers with security and a sense of purpose. Jobs would be performed as intended rather than following the whims of the specific role occupant. In exchange for this conformity, workers would have a fair chance of being promoted and rising in the power structure. Rules, regulations, and a clear-cut chain of command that further clarified required behaviour provided the workers with a sense of security.

Even during this period, some observers, such as the "business philosopher" Mary Parker Follett (1868–1933), noted that the classical view of management seemed to take for granted an essential conflict of interest between managers and employees.[14] This sentiment found expression in the human relations movement.

The Human Relations Movement and a Critique of Bureaucracy

The human relations movement generally began with the famous **Hawthorne studies** of the 1920s and 1930s.[15] These studies, conducted at the Hawthorne plant of Western Electric

---

Classical viewpoint. An early prescription on management that advocated a high specialization of labour, intensive coordination, and centralized decision making.

Scientific management. Frederick Taylor's system for using research to determine the optimum degree of specialization and standardization of work tasks.

Bureaucracy. Max Weber's ideal type of organization that included a strict chain of command, detailed rules, high specialization, centralized power, and selection and promotion based on technical competence.

Hawthorne studies. Research conducted in the 1920s and 1930s at the Hawthorne plant of Western Electric near Chicago that illustrated how psychological and social processes affect productivity and work adjustment.

near Chicago, began in the strict tradition of industrial engineering. They were concerned with the impact of fatigue, rest pauses, and lighting on productivity. However, during the course of the studies, the researchers (among others, Harvard University's Elton Mayo and Fritz Roethlisberger, and Hawthorne's William J. Dickson) began to notice the effects of psychological and social processes on productivity and work adjustment. This impact suggested that there could be dysfunctional aspects to how work was organized. One obvious sign was resistance to management through strong informal group mechanisms, such as norms that limited productivity to less than what management wanted.

After the Second World War, a number of theorists and researchers, who were mostly academics, took up the theme begun at Hawthorne. Prominent names included Chris Argyris, Alvin Gouldner, and Rensis Likert. The **human relations movement** called attention to certain dysfunctional aspects of classical management and bureaucracy and advocated more people-oriented styles of management that catered more to the social and psychological needs of employees. This critique of bureaucracy addressed several specific problems:

- Strict specialization is incompatible with human needs for growth and achievement.[16] This can lead to employee alienation from the organization and its clients.

- Strong centralization and reliance on formal authority often fail to take advantage of the creative ideas and knowledge of lower-level members, who are often closer to the customer.[17] As a result, the organization will fail to learn from its mistakes, which threatens innovation and adaptation. Resistance to change will occur as a matter of course.

- Strict, impersonal rules lead members to adopt the minimum acceptable level of performance that the rules specify.[18] If a rule states that employees must process at least eight claims a day, eight claims will become the norm, even though higher performance levels are possible.

- Strong specialization causes employees to lose sight of the overall goals of the organization.[19] Forms, procedures, and required signatures become ends in themselves, divorced from the true needs of customers, clients, and other departments in the organization. This is the "red-tape mentality" that we sometimes observe in bureaucracies.

Obviously, not all bureaucratic organizations have these problems. However, they were common enough that human relations advocates and others began to call for the adoption of more flexible systems of management and the design of more interesting jobs. They also advocated open communication, more employee participation in decision making, and less rigid, more decentralized forms of control.

Human relations movement. A critique of classical management and bureaucracy that advocated management styles that were more participative and oriented toward employee needs.

CONTEMPORARY MANAGEMENT— THE CONTINGENCY APPROACH

LO 1.5

Describe the *contingency approach* to management.

How has the apparent tension between the classical approach and the human relations approach been resolved? First, contemporary scholars and managers recognize the merits of both approaches. The classical advocates pointed out the critical role of control and coordination in getting organizations to achieve their goals. The human relationists pointed out the dangers of certain forms of control and coordination and addressed the need for flexibility and adaptability. Second, as we will study in later chapters, contemporary scholars have learned that management approaches need to be tailored to fit the situation. For example, we would generally manage a payroll department more bureaucratically than a research and development department. Getting out a payroll every week is a routine task with no margin for error. Research requires creativity that is fostered by a more flexible work environment.

Reconsider the five questions we posed earlier about the factors that make an organization successful and a great place to work. Answering these questions is not an easy task, partly because human nature is so complex. This complexity means that an organizational behaviour text cannot be a "cookbook." In what follows, you will not find recipes to improve job satisfaction or service quality, with one cup of leadership style and two cups of group dynamics. We have not discovered a simple set of laws of organizational behaviour that you can memorize and then retrieve when necessary to solve any organizational problem. It is this "quick fix" mentality that produces simplistic and costly management fads and fashions.[20]

There is a growing body of research and management experience to help sort out the complexities of what happens in organizations. However, the general answer to many of the questions we will pose in the following chapters is: *It depends.* Which leadership style is most effective? This depends on the characteristics of the leader, those of the people being led, and what the leader is trying to achieve. Will an increase in pay lead to an increase in performance? This depends on who is getting the increase and the exact reason for the increase.

These dependencies are called contingencies. The **contingency approach** to management recognizes that there is no one best way to manage; rather, an appropriate style depends on the demands of the situation. Thus, the effectiveness of a leadership style is contingent on the abilities of the followers, and the consequence of a pay increase is partly contingent on the need for money. Contingencies illustrate the complexity of organizational behaviour and show why we should study it systematically. Throughout the text we will discuss organizational behaviour with the contingency approach in mind.

Contingency approach. An approach to management that recognizes that there is no one best way to manage, and that an appropriate management style depends on the demands of the situation.

LO 1.6

Explain what managers do—their roles, activities, agendas for action, and thought processes.

 Simulate

WHAT IS MANAGEMENT?

PERSONAL INVENTORY ASSESSMENT
Learn About Yourself
Personal Assessment of Management Skills (PAMS)

WHAT DO MANAGERS DO?

Organizational behaviour is not just for managers or aspiring managers. As we noted earlier, a good understanding of the field can be useful for consumers or anyone else who has to interact with organizations or get things done through them. Nevertheless, many readers of this text have an interest in management as a potential career. Managers can have a strong impact on what happens in and to organizations. They both influence and are influenced by organizational behaviour, and the net result can have important consequences for organizational effectiveness.

There is no shortage of texts and popular press books oriented toward what managers *should* do. However, the field of organizational behaviour is also concerned with what really happens in organizations. Let's look at several research studies that explore what managers *do* do. This provides a context for appreciating the usefulness of understanding organizational behaviour.

Managerial Roles

Canadian management theorist Henry Mintzberg conducted an in-depth study of the behaviour of several managers.[21] The study earned him a PhD from the Massachusetts Institute of Technology (MIT) in 1968. Mintzberg discovered a rather complex set of roles played by the managers: figurehead, leader, liaison person, monitor, disseminator, spokesperson, entrepreneur, disturbance handler, resource allocator, and negotiator. These roles are summarized in Exhibit 1.2.

EXHIBIT 1.2
Mintzberg's managerial roles.
Source: Reprinted by permission of Dr. Henry Mintzberg.

Informational Roles	Interpersonal Roles	Decisional Roles
Monitor	Figurehead	Entrepreneur
Disseminator	Leader	Disturbance handler
Spokesperson	Liaison	Resource allocator
		Negotiator

INTERPERSONAL ROLES Interpersonal roles are expected behaviours that have to do with establishing and maintaining interpersonal relations. In the *figurehead role*, managers serve as symbols of their organization rather than active decision makers. Examples of the figurehead role are making a speech to a trade group, entertaining clients, or signing legal documents. In the *leadership role*, managers select, mentor, reward, and discipline employees. In the *liaison role*, managers maintain horizontal contacts inside and outside the organization. This might include discussing a project with a colleague in another department or touching base with an embassy delegate of a country where the company hopes to do future business.

INFORMATIONAL ROLES These roles are concerned with the various ways managers receive and transmit information. In the *monitor role*, managers scan the internal and external environments of the firm to follow current performance and to keep themselves informed of new ideas and trends. For example, the head of research and development might attend a professional engineering conference. In the *disseminator role*, managers send information on both facts and preferences to others. For example, the R&D head might summarize what he or she learned at the conference in an email to employees. The *spokesperson role* concerns mainly sending messages into the organization's external environment—for example, drafting an annual report to stockholders or giving an interview to the press.

DECISIONAL ROLES The final set of managerial roles Mintzberg discussed deals with decision making. In the *entrepreneur role*, managers turn problems and opportunities into plans for improved changes. This might include suggesting a new product or service that will please customers. In the *disturbance handler role*, managers deal with problems stemming from employee conflicts and address threats to resources and turf. In their *resource allocation role*, managers decide how to deploy time, money, personnel, and other critical resources. Finally, in their *negotiator role*, managers conduct major negotiations with other organizations or individuals.

Of course, the relative importance of these roles will vary with management level and organizational technology.[22] First-level supervisors do more disturbance handling and less figure heading. Still, Mintzberg's major contribution to organizational behaviour is to highlight the *complexity* of the roles managers are required to play and the variety of skills they must have to be effective, including leadership, communication, and negotiation. His work also illustrates the complex balancing act managers face when they must play different roles for different audiences. A good grasp of organizational behaviour is at the heart of acquiring these skills and performing this balancing act.

Managerial Activities

Fred Luthans, Richard Hodgetts, and Stuart Rosenkrantz studied the behaviour of a large number of managers in a variety of different kinds of organizations.[23] They determined that the managers engage in four basic types of activities:

- *Routine communication.* This includes the formal sending and receiving of information (as in meetings) and the handling of paperwork.

- *Traditional management.* Planning, decision making, and controlling are the primary types of traditional management.

- *Networking.* Networking consists of interacting with people outside of the organization and informal socializing and politicking with insiders.

- *Human resource management.* This includes motivating and reinforcing, disciplining and punishing, managing conflict, staffing, and training and developing employees.

Exhibit 1.3 summarizes these managerial activities and shows how a sample of 248 managers divided their time and effort, as determined by research observers (discipline

EXHIBIT 1.3
Summary of managerial activities.

Source: Adapted from Luthans, F., Hodgetts, R.M., & Rosenkrantz, S.A. (1988). *Real managers.* Cambridge, MA: Ballinger. Reprinted by permission of Dr. F. Luthans on behalf of the authors.

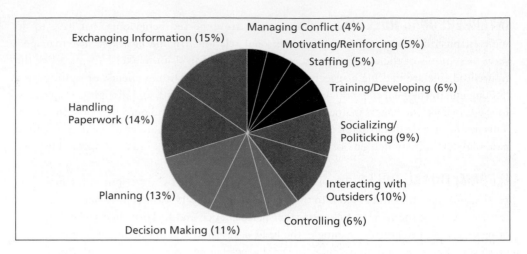

and punishment were done in private and were not open to observation). Perhaps the most striking observation about this figure is how all these managerial activities involve dealing with people.

One of Luthans and his colleagues' most fascinating findings is how emphasis on these various activities correlated with managerial success. If we define success as moving up the ranks of the organization quickly, networking proved to be critical. The people who were promoted quickly tended to do more networking (politicking, socializing, and making contacts) and less human resource management than the averages in Exhibit 1.3. If we define success in terms of unit effectiveness and employee satisfaction and commitment, the more successful managers were those who devoted more time and effort to human resource management and less to networking than the averages in the exhibit. A good understanding of organizational behaviour should help you manage this trade-off more effectively, reconciling the realities of organizational politics with the demands of accomplishing things through others.

Managerial Agendas

John Kotter studied the behaviour patterns of a number of successful general managers.[24] Although he found some differences among them, he also found a strong pattern of similarities that he grouped into the categories of agenda setting, networking, and agenda implementation.

AGENDA SETTING Kotter's managers, given their positions, all gradually developed agendas of what they wanted to accomplish for the organization. Many began these agendas even before they assumed their positions. These agendas were almost always informal and unwritten, and they were much more concerned with "people issues" and were less numerical than most formal strategic plans. The managers based their agendas on wide-ranging informal discussions with a wide variety of people.

NETWORKING Kotter's managers established a wide formal and informal network of key people both inside and outside of their organizations. Insiders included peers, employees, and bosses, but they also extended to these people's employees and bosses. Outsiders included customers, suppliers, competitors, government officials, and the press. This network provided managers with information and established cooperative relationships relevant to their agendas. Formal hiring, firing, and reassigning shaped the network, but so did informal liaisons in which managers created dependencies by doing favours for others.

AGENDA IMPLEMENTATION The managers used networks to implement the agendas. They would go *anywhere* in the network for help—up or down, in or out of the organization.

Fernando Morales/The Globe and Mail

John Kotter's research of successful business managers showed that exemplary managers practise agenda setting, networking, and agenda implementation. Heather Reisman of Indigo Books and Music, is an example of such a manager.

In addition, they employed a wide range of influence tactics, from direct orders to subtle language and stories that conveyed their message indirectly.

The theme that runs through Kotter's findings is the high degree of informal interaction and concern with people issues that were necessary for the managers to achieve their agendas. To be sure, the managers used their formal organizational power, but they often found themselves dependent on people over whom they wielded no power. An understanding of organizational behaviour helps to recognize and manage these realities.

Managerial Minds

In contrast to exploring how managers act, which is the focus of the previous section, Herbert Simon and Daniel Isenberg explored how managers think.[25] Although they offer a wealth of observations, we will concentrate here on a specific issue that each examined in independent research—managerial intuition.

Some people think that organizational behaviour and its implications for management are just common sense. However, careful observers of successful managers have often noted that intuition seems to guide many of their actions. Isenberg's research suggests that experienced managers use intuition in several ways:

- to sense that a problem exists;
- to perform well-learned mental tasks rapidly (e.g., sizing up a written contract);
- to synthesize isolated pieces of information and data; and
- to double-check more formal or mechanical analyses ("Do these projections look correct?").

Does the use of intuition mean that managerial thinking is random, irrational, or undisciplined? Both Simon and Isenberg say no. In fact, both strongly dispute the idea that intuition is the opposite of rationality or that intuitive means unanalytical. Rather, good intuition is problem identification and problem solving based on a long history of systematic and extensive education and experience that enables the manager to locate problems within a network of previously acquired information. The theories, research, and management practices that we cover in *Organizational Behaviour* will contribute to your own information network and give you better managerial intuition about decisions that involve how to make an organization a great place to work and a financial success.

International managers must adapt to cross-cultural differences to successfully interact with potential clients and overseas affiliates.

© michaeljung/Fotolia

International Managers

The research we discussed above describes how managers act and think in North America. Would managers in other global locations act and think the same way? Up to a point, the answer is probably yes. After all, we are dealing here with some very basic behaviours and thought processes. However, the style in which managers do what they do and the emphasis they give to various activities will vary greatly across cultures because of cross-cultural variations in values that affect both managers' and employees' expectations about interpersonal interaction. Thus, in Chapter 5 we study cross-cultural differences in motivation. In Chapter 9 we study cultural differences in leadership, and in Chapter 10 we explore how communication varies across cultures.

Geert Hofstede has done pioneering work on cross-cultural differences in values that we will study in Chapter 4. Hofstede provides some interesting observations about how these value differences promote contrasts in the general role that managers play across cultures.[26] He asserts that managers are cultural heroes and are even a distinct social class in North America, where individualism is treasured. In contrast, Germany tends to worship engineers and has fewer managerial types. In Japan, managers are required to pay obsessive attention to group solidarity rather than to star employees. In the Netherlands, managers are supposed to exhibit modesty and strive for consensus. In the family-run businesses of Taiwan and Singapore, "professional" management, North American style, is greatly downplayed. The contrasts that Hofstede raises are fascinating because the technical requirements for accomplishing goals are actually the same across cultures. It is only the *behavioural* requirements that differ. Thus, national culture is one of the most important contingency variables in organizational behaviour. The appropriateness of various leadership styles, motivation techniques, and communication methods depends on where one is in the world.

LO 1.7

Describe the four contemporary management concerns facing organizations and how organizational behaviour can help organizations understand and manage these concerns.

SOME CONTEMPORARY MANAGEMENT CONCERNS

To conclude the chapter, we will briefly examine four issues with which organizations and managers are currently concerned. As with previous sections, our goal is to illustrate how the field of organizational behaviour can help you understand and manage these issues.

Diversity—Local and Global

The demographics of the North American population and workforce has been changing and, as a result, both the labour force and customers are becoming increasingly culturally diverse. In Canada, visible minorities are the fastest-growing segment of the population.[27] Employment and Immigration Canada has projected that two-thirds of today's new entrants to the Canadian labour force will be women, visible minorities, Aboriginal people, and persons with disabilities.[28] By 2031, 30.6 percent of the Canadian population will be visible minorities, and 60 percent of the population in Toronto and Vancouver will belong to a visible minority group.[29]

Diversity of age is also having an impact in organizations. In less than a decade, the workforce will be dominated by people over the age of 40. With the elimination of mandatory retirement at age 65, along with the recent global recession in which many people saw their life savings diminish, a growing number of Canadians over 65 will remain in the workforce. A survey found that older Canadians are redefining the concept of retirement and that 75 percent of the participants who had not yet retired expected to continue working past the age of 65.[30] Perhaps you have observed people of various ages working in fast-food restaurants that were at one time staffed solely by young people. Both the re-entry of retired people into the workforce and the trend to remove vertical layers in organizations have contributed to much more intergenerational contact in the workplace than was common in the past. In response to this demographic shift, organizations are beginning to adopt new programs, such as flexible benefit plans, compressed workdays, and part-time jobs, to attract and retain older workers. For example, Orkin/PCO Services Corp. of Mississauga, a pest-control service, dealt with a shortage of pest control specialists by introducing a more flexible part-time schedule with benefits to attract and retain employees who would otherwise have retired or left the industry.[31]

Diversity is also coming to the fore as many organizations realize that in many aspects of employment, they have not treated certain segments of the population fairly, for instance, women; members of the lesbian, gay, bisexual, and transgender (LGBT) community; and the disabled. Organizations have to be able to get the best from *everyone* to be truly competitive. Although legal pressures (such as the *Employment Equity Act*) have contributed to this awareness, general social pressure, especially from customers and clients, has also done so.

Finally, diversity issues are having an increasing impact as organizations "go global." Foreign sales by multinational corporations have exceeded $7 trillion and are growing 20 to 30 percent faster than their sales of exports.[32] Multinational expansion, strategic alliances, and joint ventures increasingly require employees and managers to come into contact with their counterparts from other cultures. Although many of these people have an interest in North American consumer goods and entertainment, it is naïve to assume that business values are rapidly converging on a North American model. As a result, North American organizations that operate in other countries need to understand how the workforce and customers in those countries are diverse and culturally different.

What does diversity have to do with organizational behaviour? The field has long been concerned with stereotypes, conflict, cooperation, and teamwork. These are just some of the factors that managers must manage effectively for organizations to benefit from the considerable opportunities that a diverse workforce affords. We will have more to say about workforce diversity in Chapter 3 and cultural differences in values in Chapter 4.

Employee Health and Well-Being

During the past decade, employees have faced increasing concerns over job security, increasing job demands, and work-related stress, all of which have contributed to a deterioration of their physical and psychological health and well-being. At the same time, organizations are faced with employees who are disengaged, disillusioned, and suffering from physical and mental sicknesses.

EXHIBIT 1.4
**Work–life conflict in
Canadian organizations.**
Source: Based on Higgins, C.,
& Duxbury, L. (2003). *2001
national work–life conflict study*
(Ottawa: Health Canada).

These findings are based on a sample of 31 571 Canadian employees who work for 100 medium to large organizations in the public, private, and nonprofit sections of the economy. The authors of the report concluded that the majority of Canada's largest employers cannot be considered to be best-practice employers.

What Workers Experience	Percentage of Employees
Employees reporting high levels of role overload	58%
Work responsibilities interfering with the ability to fulfill responsibilities at home	28%
Negative spillover from work to family	44%
Employees reporting high levels of stress	33%
Employees reporting high levels of burnout	32%
Employees reporting highly depressed mood	36%
Employees reporting high levels of job satisfaction	46%
Employees reporting high levels of organizational commitment	53%
Employees who think of leaving their current organization once a week or more	28%
Employees indicating high levels of absenteeism	46%
Employees reporting high levels of life satisfaction	41%

Absenteeism and employee turnover in Canadian organizations are also on the rise. According to Statistics Canada, there has been an alarming and unprecedented increase in absenteeism rates since the mid-1990s. The increase in absenteeism has been found across all age groups and sectors and translates into millions of dollars in lost productivity. It has been estimated that the total cost of reported absenteeism in Canada is $16.6 billion annually. Although there is no one definitive cause, increasing stress levels and poorly designed jobs are major contributors. In fact, all types of employees are experiencing more workplace stress today than a decade ago, and the incidence of work-related illness is also on the rise. A study of professionals found that 46 percent of Canadian workers feel more stressed out today than they did five years ago. In addition, an increasing number of Canadian workers, especially women (more than half), are struggling to achieve work–life balance.[33]

Work-life conflict is also a major stressor for employees. A study of Canadian employees estimated that the direct cost of absenteeism due to high work–life conflict is approximately $3 to $5 billion per year, and when both direct and indirect costs are included in the calculation, work–life conflict costs Canadians approximately $6 to $10 billion per year.[34] Exhibit 1.4 presents some of the major findings from this study.

In addition, there has been an increasing awareness of mental health in the workplace. Mental illness in Canada is said to be costing business billions of dollars in lost productivity and absenteeism. As shown in Exhibit 1.5, it is estimated that by 2020 mental health problems will be the second cause of disability. Workplace mental health and safety have become so important that in 2013 a new national standard for workplace mental health and safety (Psychological Health and Safety in the Workplace) was introduced to help Canadian organizations create workplaces that promote a mentally healthy workplace and support employees dealing with mental illness. The standard provides guidelines to help organizations identify potential hazards to mental health and how they can improve policies and practices.[35] In response, organizations have begun to implement mental health initiatives and to make mental health a priority at work. While organization wellness programs in the

- An average of $51 billion is lost each year to the Canadian economy due to the impact of mental illness.

- Mental health problems will cost $198 billion in lost productivity over the next 30 years.

- Lost labour-force participation due to mental illness costs $20.7 billion a year.

- 44 percent of workers say they have or have had a mental health issue at work.

- On any given week, more than 500 000 Canadians will not go to work due to mental illness.

- One in five people will experience a mental illness in their lifetime

- More than 30 percent of disability claims and 70 percent of disability claim costs are due to mental health concerns.

- Mental health problems will be the number two cause of disability by 2020.

EXHIBIT 1.5   Mental health in the workplace.

Sources: Alderson, P. (2015, March 23). Do EAPs really make a difference? *Canadian HR Reporter, 28*(5), 13; Jurgens, K. (2014, February). Fostering mental health in the workplace. *Media Planet* (Sponsored Feature in the *Toronto Star*), 5; Grant, T. (2015, February 1). How Canadian employers are tackling the terrain where office culture, productivity and mental health intersect. Balancing office culture and productivity with mental health. *The Globe and Mail*, http://www.theglobeandmail.com/life/health-and-fitness/health/balancing-office-culture-and-productivity-with-mental-health/article22725410/.

past focused primarily on physical health, an increasing number of organizations are now also focusing on mental health. For a good example, see Applied Focus: *Mental Health in the County of Wellington*.

In response to these concerns, employees are searching for meaning and purpose in their work lives, and organizations like Vega have begun to focus on employees' physical and mental health by providing wellness initiatives and creating more positive work environments. What does a positive work environment and employee mental health and well-being have to do with organizational behaviour?

For one thing, organizational behaviour is concerned with creating positive work environments that contribute to employee health and wellness. Two examples of this are workplace spirituality (or a spiritual workplace) and positive organizational behaviour. Let's take a closer look at each of these.

WORKPLACE SPIRITUALITY Workplace spirituality is found in workplaces that provide employees with meaning, purpose, a sense of community, and a connection to others. It is important to realize that workplace spirituality is not about religion in the workplace, but rather providing employees with a meaningful work life that is aligned with their values. In a spiritual workplace, employees have interesting work that provides meaning and a feeling of purpose, a sense that they belong to and are part of a caring and supportive community, and a sense of connection to their work and others. Employees in a spiritual workplace have opportunities for personal growth and development, and they feel valued and supported.[36]

An increasing number of organizations are showing interest in spiritual workplaces. For example, TELUS provides quiet rooms where employees can decompress, meditate, or pray; it offers seminars on topics such as nutrition, parenting, and work–life balance, and employees have access to books and CDs on spirituality; on-site fitness classes in such disciplines as yoga and tai chi are also available. Employees at TELUS annually get three personal days off to use at their discretion and can work from home. These spirituality initiatives help to create a positive work environment that promotes health and wellness and reduces absenteeism.[37]

Workplace spirituality.
A workplace that provides employees with meaning, purpose, a sense of community, and a connection to others.

APPLIED FOCUS

MENTAL HEALTH IN THE COUNTY OF WELLINGTON

Employees at the County of Wellington are not just protected from slips, falls, and workplace accidents. The county also places a strong emphasis on psychological safety and mental wellness.

Wellington County is located in southern Ontario and encompasses the area that includes the City of Guelph. In 2014, the County of Wellington won the inaugural psychological safety gold award in Canada's Safest Employers awards. The psychological safety award is the first-ever national award that focuses exclusively on mitigating risks to employees' psychological safety.

The county's many mental health and wellness initiatives are built on a culture of respect, said Michele Richardson, health and safety coordinator at the County of Wellington. "It really [requires] a culture of respect to make a psychologically safe workplace, and we start that right from day one here, at our new hire orientation," she said.

One of the county's most popular initiatives is called "Walk the Talk," in which employees are encouraged to have face-to-face conversations instead of sending emails all day, said Richardson. Training and education are also a critical part of the county's mental health initiatives. Employees receive training to learn about a respectful workplace, verbal de-escalation techniques, and workplace violence policies, and learn to report psychologically unhealthy situations to managers. The county has also introduced mandatory mental-health tool-kit training for all employees across the organization. Managers also receive in-depth training on recognizing and responding to mental health issues. "We [train] our managers to recognize if there's been a change in their staff, so they've got formal training on how to approach the difficult subjects," said Andrea Lawson, Human Resources Director.

"We have two gyms which are extremely well utilized, we do yoga in the park, social services has meditation sessions...so there's something for everybody," said Lawson, adding that by participating, staff feel like they are part of a family. "That contributes to the psychological wellness of an employee. If you like coming to work, you feel valued, you feel that there are outlets and resources for you when you get here, you're preventing issues before they even occur."

The initiatives are not just about recognizing and responding to crises—they're about building and maintaining mental wellness and taking preventative measures before mental health problems arise. According to Lawson, the costs of the programs are minimal but the benefits are huge, and the support from all levels of the organization has made the initiatives easy to implement.

Source: Reprinted by permission of Canadian HR Reporter. © Copyright Thomson Reuters Canada Ltd., (2014, December 1), 27(21), 11, Toronto, Ontario, 1-800-387-5164. Web: www. hrreporter.com

---

Positive organizational behaviour (POB). The study and application of positively oriented human resource strengths and psychological capacities that can be measured, developed, and effectively managed for performance improvement.

Psychological capital (PsyCap). An individual's positive psychological state of development that is characterized by self-efficacy, optimism, hope, and resilience.

POSITIVE ORGANIZATIONAL BEHAVIOUR Organizational behaviour is concerned with developing employees and providing them with the resources they need to achieve their goals and for their well-being. This is best reflected in what is known as positive organizational behaviour. **Positive organizational behaviour (POB)** is "the study and application of positively oriented human resource strengths and psychological capacities that can be measured, developed, and effectively managed for performance improvement in today's workplace."[38] The psychological capacities that can be developed in employees are known as psychological capital (PsyCap). **Psychological capital** refers to an individual's positive psychological state of development that is characterized by self-efficacy, optimism, hope, and resilience. *Self-efficacy* refers to one's confidence to take on and put in the necessary effort to succeed at challenging tasks (see Chapter 2 for a more detailed discussion of self-efficacy); *optimism* involves making internal attributions about positive events in the present and future and external attributions about negative events (see Chapter 3 for a more detailed discussion on attributions); *hope* refers to persevering toward one's goals and, when necessary, making changes and using multiple pathways to achieve one's goals (see Chapter 5 for a more detailed discussion of goals and goal setting); and *resilience* refers to one's ability to bounce back or rebound from adversity and setbacks to attain success.[39]

It is important to note that each of the components of PsyCap are considered to be states or positive work-related psychological resources that can be changed, modified, and developed. In other words, they are not fixed, stable, or static personality traits.[40]

Research on POB has found that PsyCap is positively related to employee psychological well-being as well as more positive job attitudes, behaviours, and job performance, and negatively related to undesirable attitudes and behaviours such as employee anxiety, stress, and turnover intentions.[41] There is also evidence that PsyCap interventions (PCI) that focus on enhancing each of the components of PsyCap are effective for developing employees' PsyCap. Thus, POB is an effective approach for organizations to improve employee health and well-being by developing employees' PsyCap.[42]

Talent Management and Employee Engagement

During the past decade, organizations have become increasingly concerned about talent management and employee engagement. Consider this: a survey of senior executives from all over the world found that talent was ranked as the second most critical challenge just behind business growth.[43] Let's take a closer look at talent management and employee engagement.

TALENT MANAGEMENT **Talent management** refers to an organization's processes for attracting, developing, retaining, and utilizing people with the required skills to meet current and future business needs.[44]

The ability of organizations to attract and retain talent has always been important; however, today it has become especially critical for many organizations that are struggling to find the employees they need to compete and survive. As a result, the management of talent has become a major organizational concern that involves a concerted effort and the involvement of all levels of management.

An increasing number of organizations are having trouble finding qualified talent, a problem stemming in part from changing demographics that will result in a dramatic shortage of skilled workers over the next 10 years, as the baby boomers begin to retire, leaving a large skills gap. It is predicted that there will be a 30 percent shortfall of workers between the ages of 25 and 44. This, combined with the increasing willingness of knowledge workers to relocate anywhere in the world and fewer Canadians entering the skilled trades, means that Canadian organizations will increasingly face severe labour shortages. There are already shortages in scientific, technical, and high-tech industries and in senior management, communications, and marketing positions. A recent poll found that more than 60 percent of Canadian employers say that labour shortages are limiting their productivity and efficiency. Most of Canada's top CEOs believe that retaining talent has become their number-one priority, and attracting new talent is their fourth priority, just behind financial performance and profitability. Three-quarters of CEOs say they cannot find enough competent employees.[45]

EMPLOYEE ENGAGEMENT Organizations have also become increasingly concerned about employee engagement. As you will learn in Chapter 13, **work engagement** is a positive work-related state of mind that is characterized by vigour, dedication, and absorption.[46] It has been reported that only one-third of workers are engaged, and yet engaged workers have more positive work attitudes and higher job performance. Employee engagement is considered to be key to an organization's success and competitiveness, and it can have a significant impact on productivity, customer satisfaction, profitability, innovation, and quality. One study found that in a sample of 65 firms from different industries, the top 25 percent on an engagement index had greater return on assets (ROA), greater profitability, and more than double the shareholder value compared to the bottom 25 percent. What's more, it has been estimated that disengaged employees are costing organizations billions of dollars a

Talent management. An organization's processes for attracting, developing, retaining, and utilizing people with the required skills to meet current and future business needs.

Work engagement. A positive work-related state of mind that is characterized by vigour, dedication, and absorption.

year.[47] While this research has focused on the engagement of individual employees, there is also evidence that engagement levels also differ from one organization to another; this is known as collective organizational engagement and has implications for firm performance. To learn more, see Research Focus: *Collective Organizational Engagement and Firm Performance.*

What does organizational behaviour have to do with talent management and employee engagement? Organizational behaviour provides the means for organizations to be designed and managed in ways that optimize the attraction, development, retention, engagement, and performance of talent.[48] For example, providing opportunities for learning and designing jobs that are challenging, meaningful, and rewarding; providing recognition and monetary rewards for performance; managing a diverse workforce; offering flexible work arrangements; and providing effective leadership are just some of the factors that are important for the effective management of talent and employee engagement. These are, of course, some of the practices of the best companies to work for in Canada (see Exhibit 1.1), and their annual rate of turnover is lower than the national average and half that of some other companies.[49] As described in the chapter-opening vignette, Vega is a great example of an organization that excels at talent management and employee engagement.

Corporate Social Responsibility

Corporate social responsibility (CSR).
An organization taking responsibility for the impact of its decisions and actions on its stakeholders.

Organizations have become increasingly concerned about corporate social responsibility (CSR) and the need to be good corporate citizens. **Corporate social responsibility** refers to an organization's taking responsibility for the impact of its decisions and actions on its stakeholders (e.g., employees, customers, suppliers, environmentalists, the community, owners/shareholders). It has to do with an organization's overall impact on society at large and extends beyond the interests of shareholders to the interests and needs of employees and the community in which it operates. CSR involves a variety of issues that range from community involvement, environmental protection, product safety, ethical marketing, employee diversity, and local and global labour practices. Ultimately, CSR has to do with how an organization performs its core functions of producing goods and providing services while doing so in a socially responsible way.[50]

What does a focus on social responsibility have to do with organizational behaviour? For starters, many CSR issues have to do with organizational behaviour, such as an organization's treatment of employees, management practices such as promoting diversity, work–family balance, and employment equity. Organizations that rank high on CSR are good employers because of the way they treat their employees and because of management practices that promote employee well-being. As indicated earlier, these are the kinds of practices employed by the best companies to work for in Canada.

CSR also involves environmental, social, and governance (ESG) issues. Organizations' social and environmental actions are increasingly being scrutinized, and shareholders and consumers are holding firms to higher CSR standards on the environment, employment, and other social issues. Governance issues such as executive compensation have also begun to receive greater attention. CSR is so important that a number of research firms now rank and rate organizations on CSR.[51]

In 2009, *Maclean's* published its inaugural list of the 50 Most Socially Responsible Corporations in Canada, corporations that are raising the standard of what it means to be a good corporate citizen.[52] These rankings, along with the belief that CSR has implications for an organization's reputation and financial performance, have led to an increasing number of organizations placing greater emphasis on CSR initiatives.

For example, many organizations make donations to charitable organizations and have implemented programs to help their communities. Cameo Corp. of Saskatoon, one of the world's largest producers of uranium, has a community investment program that focuses on improving the quality of life for people in the communities in which it operates. The

RESEARCH FOCUS

COLLECTIVE ORGANIZATIONAL ENGAGEMENT AND FIRM PERFORMANCE

In the past decade, an increasing number of studies have found that employees who are more engaged have more positive job attitudes and higher job performance. Although it has often been assumed that employee engagement will have positive effects for organizational-level outcomes such as organizational performance, there has been little research linking engagement at the organizational level to organizational outcomes.

To learn more about the link between engagement at the organizational level and organizational outcomes, Murray R. Barrick, Gary R. Thurgood, Troy A. Smith, and Stephen H. Courtright conducted a study on what they called collective organizational engagement. Collective organizational engagement is defined as the shared perceptions of organizational members that members of the organization are, as a whole, physically, cognitively, and emotionally invested in their work. Thus, it exists at the organizational level, which means that organizations differ in terms of their level of collective organizational engagement.

The authors tested a model in which several factors predicted collective organizational engagement, which in turn predicts firm performance. First, they suggested that three organizational-level resources would lead to collective organizational engagement: motivating work design, human resource management (HRM) practices, and CEO transformational leadership behaviours.

Motivating work design has to do with the extent to which the work of entry-level employees is enriched through the use of five job characteristics from the job characteristics model (autonomy, skills variety, task significance, task identity, and feedback; see Chapter 6 for a complete description of the job characteristics model). Human resource practices are expected to lead to collective organizational engagement when they focus on a firm's expectations of employees and enhance employees' expected rewards and outcomes (pay equity, job security, developmental feedback, and pay for performance). The third organizational resource they predicted to influence collective organizational engagement is CEO transformational leadership, which has to do with the extent to which the CEO shares a compelling vision, intellectually stimulates followers, and sets challenging goals and expectations (see Chapter 9 for a complete description of transformational leadership). Transformational leaders encourage followers to rise above their own self-interests in pursuit of organization objectives.

Second, the authors suggested that the relationship between the organizational resources and collective organizational engagement would be strongest when strategic implementation is high. Strategic implementation has to do with the extent to which top management in an organization specify, pursue, and monitor the organization's strategic objectives. Thus, the effect of the organizational resources on collective organizational engagement will be augmented when senior management effectively implements the organization's strategic objectives. Third, the authors predicted that collective organizational engagement would create value for an organization and would be positively related to firm performance.

To test their model, the authors conducted a study of 83 small- to medium-sized credit unions located throughout the United States. The study participants included employees from various levels in each organization (top management, mid-level managers, and entry-level employees). The results indicated that all three of the organizational-level resources (motivating work design, HRM practices, and CEO transformational leadership) were positively related to collective organizational engagement, and these relationships were strongest when top management was high on implementing the organization's objectives and strategies. In addition, collective organizational engagement was positively related to firm performance.

The results of this study indicate that an organization can enhance its performance and gain a competitive advantage by creating high levels of collective organizational engagement, and this can be achieved by enriching the jobs of entry-level employees and using HRM practices that are expectation-enhancing and provide employees with rewards and outcomes, and when the CEO is a transformational leader and top management actively strives to implement the organization's objectives and strategy. The study also shows that collective organizational engagement is a key mechanism for explaining the effects of organizational resources on firm performance.

Source: Based on Barrick, M.R., Thurgood, G.R, Smith, T.A., & Courtright, S.H. (2015). Collective organizational engagement: Linking motivational antecedents, strategic implementation, and firm performance. *Academy of Management Journal, 58,* 111–135.

company has contributed $3 million to the University of Saskatchewan to promote greater access for Aboriginal peoples, women, and northerners to studies in engineering and science. Unilever Canada has a community vitality fund and donates 1 percent of pre-tax profits to initiatives in children's health and water resources, which are both linked to its products. The company also encourages volunteerism and gives employees four afternoons off each year for community activities.[53]

A concern for the environment and green initiatives is also an example of CSR. What does going green have to do with organizational behaviour? Green programs require changes in employees' attitudes and behaviours. For example, at Fairmont Hotels and Resorts, employees volunteer to be on green teams that meet monthly to brainstorm environmental initiatives. The company also recognizes and rewards employees for their efforts. The program has had a positive effect on employee engagement and motivation, and employees are proud to be working for an environmentally responsible organization.[54]

In summary, CSR is becoming a major concern for organizations today, and some organizations even issue CSR reports along with their annual reports. Hudson's Bay Company (HBC) publishes an annual Corporate Social Responsibility Report that is available on its website. An organization's CSR activities and policies are associated with a firm's financial performance as well as positive employee attitudes, engagement, and performance.[55] CSR also has implications for the recruitment and retention of employees, as an increasing number of workers want to work for organizations that are environmentally friendly and rank high on CSR. For example, job candidates are attracted to HBC because of its corporate social responsibility program. At Husky Injection Molding Systems Ltd. in Bolton, Ontario, job candidates and employees choose to work at the company because of its environmental responsibility program.[56] Organizations that communicate their CSR values during recruitment will be more attractive to job seekers, especially those who want to have a significant impact through work.[57] Thus, organizational behaviour has much to offer organizations in their quest to become more socially responsible.

We hope this brief discussion of some of the issues that are of concern to organizations and managers has reinforced your awareness of using organizational behaviour to better understand and manage life at work. These concerns permeate today's workplace, and we will cover them in more detail throughout the text.

Fairmont Hotels and Resorts recognizes and rewards employees for their involvement in enviornmental initiatives.

© jiawangkun/Fotolia

THE MANAGER'S NOTEBOOK

Toronto's Troubled Transit System

1. Organizational behaviour refers to the attitudes and behaviours of individuals and groups in organizations, and the discipline of organizational behaviour provides insight about effectively managing and changing attitudes and behaviours. The complaints made by TTC riders indicate employee indifference and disdain toward customers and discourteous and rude behaviour. Organizational behaviour can help to address the TTC's customer service problems by creating positive attitudes toward customer service and changing employee behaviours when interacting with customers. This might involve motivating employees to be more courteous, and it will probably involve a change in the culture of the TTC toward a greater emphasis on customer service. Organizational behaviour topics that are particularly relevant include learning (Chapter 2), attitudes (Chapter 4), motivation (Chapters 5 and 6), socialization and organizational culture (Chapter 8), leadership (Chapter 9), communication (Chapter 10), and organizational change (Chapter 15).

2. The goals of organizational behaviour are predicting, explaining, and managing organizational behaviour. Based on customer complaints, it is possible to predict the things that customers will complain about; many of the complaints will be about poor customer service and discourteous employee behaviour. However, less clear are the reasons for discourteous and rude behaviour. Yet explaining such behaviours is an important prerequisite to managing them, and there are many possible reasons for discourteous behaviour and poor customer service. Lack of learning is one: perhaps employees have not be trained to provide good customer service or maybe they are not rewarded for it. Or perhaps the importance of customer service has not been clearly communicated to employees and they are not given feedback about their customer service performance. Each of these explanations will require a different and specific solution. So if we understand the reasons for poor customer service, we can take action to manage and improve it. Along these lines, the TTC announced a series of customer service improvements that they promise will make the TTC "the better way" in Toronto. The TTC promised better communication and courtesy and announced it would be screening new hires for "customer service aptitude" and evaluating all 12 000 employees on their customer service performance. A comprehensive review of customer service training for new employees and recertification for older staff is also planned. The report by the Customer Service Advisory Panel made a number of recommendations that involve a renewed focus on customer service. Many of the recommendations involve organizational behaviour such as the creation of a culture of customer service, improving internal communications, customer service training courses, and a review of recognition programs.

MyManagementLab Study, practise, and explore real management situations with these helpful resources:

- **Interactive Lesson Presentations:** Work through interactive presentations and assessments to test your knowledge of management concepts.
- **PIA (Personal Inventory Assessments):** Enhance your ability to connect with key concepts through these engaging, self-reflection assessments.
- **Study Plan:** Check your understanding of chapter concepts with self-study quizzes.
- **Videos:** Learn more about the management practices and strategies of real companies.
- **Simulations:** Practise decision-making in simulated management environments.

LEARNING OBJECTIVES CHECKLIST

1.1 *Organizations* are social inventions for accomplishing common goals through group effort. The basic characteristic of organizations is that they involve the coordinated efforts of people working together to accomplish common goals.

1.2 *Organizational behaviour* refers to the attitudes and behaviours of individuals and groups in an organizational context. The field of organizational behaviour systematically studies these attitudes and behaviours and provides advice about how organizations can manage them effectively. The goals of the field include the prediction, explanation, and management of organizational behaviour.

1.3 *Management* is the art of getting things accomplished in organizations through others. It consists of acquiring, allocating, and utilizing physical and human resources to accomplish goals.

1.4 The *classical view* of management advocated a high degree of employee specialization and a high degree of coordination of labour from the top of the organization. Taylor's scientific management and Weber's views on bureaucracy are in line with the classical position. The *human relations movement* pointed out the "people problems" that the classical management style sometimes provoked, advocating instead for more interesting job design, more employee participation in decisions, and less centralized control.

1.5 The *contingency approach* to management suggests that the most effective management styles and organizational designs are dependent on the demands of the situation.

1.6 Research on what managers do shows that they fulfill interpersonal, informational, and decisional roles. Important activities include routine communication, traditional management, networking, and human resource management. Managers pursue agendas through networking and use intuition to guide decision making. The demands on managers vary across cultures. A good grasp of organizational behaviour is essential for effective management.

1.7 A number of societal and global trends are shaping contemporary management concerns, including local and global diversity; employee health and well-being; talent management and employee engagement; and a focus on corporate social responsibility. The field of organizational behaviour can help organizations understand and manage these concerns.

DISCUSSION QUESTIONS

1. Consider absence from work as an example of organizational behaviour. What are some of the factors that might predict who is likely to be absent from work? How might you explain absence from work? What are some techniques that organizations use to manage absence? Now do the same for turnover as an example of organizational behaviour.

2. To demonstrate that you grasp the idea of contingencies in organizational behaviour, consider how closely managers should supervise the work of their employees. What are some factors on which closeness of supervision might be contingent?

3. Use the contingency approach to describe a task or an organizational department where a more classical management style might be effective. Then do the same for a task or department where the human relations style would be effective.

4. Describe how management practices and organizational behaviour can help organizations deal with the contemporary management concerns discussed in the chapter. In other words, what are some of the things that organizations can do to (a) manage local and global diversity, (b) improve employee health and well-being, (c) facilitate the management of talent and employee engagement, and (e) promote corporate social responsibility?

5. What is the meaning of psychological capital and what does it have to do with positive organizational behaviour? Describe each of the components of psychological capital and how it can help you in your studies and employees in organizations.

ON-THE-JOB CHALLENGE QUESTION

Pay to Work or Pay to Quit?

What would you do if your employer offered you $2000 to quit? Would you stay or would you take the money and run? That is a decision that employees at Amazon and Zappos must make. Zappos offers new hires $2000 to quit. However, less than 2 percent of its employees have accepted the offer. Amazon, which acquired Zappos in 2009, also has a pay-to-quit program. Amazon offers its fulfillment centre employees $2000 to quit to start and up to $1000 more per year up to $5000. However, only a small percentage of employees accept the offer. According to Amazon, "The goal is to encourage folks to take a moment and think about what they really want. In the long run, an employee staying somewhere they don't want to be isn't healthy for the employee or the company."

What do you think about Zappos and Amazon's pay-to-quit programs? Using an organizational behaviour perspective, what effect do you think it would have on employees' attitudes and behaviour? Discuss the program in terms of the goals of organizational behaviour. In other words, what can be predicted, how can you explain it, and what is being managed? Does a pay-to-quit program make sense in terms of any of the contemporary management concerns discussed in the chapter? Do you think it is a good idea for organizations to have pay-to-quit programs? Explain your answer.

Source: Based on Dobson, S. (2014, May 19). Quitting for money. *Canadian HR Reporter, 27*(10), 1, 16.

EXPERIENTIAL EXERCISE

Good Job, Bad Job

The purpose of this exercise is to help you get acquainted with some of your classmates by learning something about their experiences with work and organizations. To do this, we will focus on an important and traditional topic in organizational behaviour—what makes people satisfied or dissatisfied with their jobs (a topic that we will cover in detail in Chapter 4).

1. Students should break into groups of four to six people. Each group should choose a recording secretary.

2. In each group, members should take turns introducing themselves and then describing to the others either the best job or the worst job that they have ever had. Take particular care to explain why this particular job was either satisfying or dissatisfying. For example, did factors such as pay, co-workers, your boss, or the work itself affect your level of satisfaction? The recording secretary should make a list of the jobs group members held, noting which were "good" and which were "bad." (15 minutes)

3. Using the information from Step 2, each group should develop a profile of four or five characteristics that seem to contribute to dissatisfaction in a job and four or five characteristics that contribute to satisfaction. In other words, are there some common experiences among the group members? (10 minutes)

4. Each group should write its "good job" and "bad job" characteristics on the board. (3 minutes)

5. The class should reconvene, and each group's recording secretary should report on the specific jobs the group considered good or bad. The instructor will discuss the profiles on the board, noting similarities and differences. Other issues worth probing are behavioural consequences of job attitudes (e.g., quitting) and differences of opinion within the groups (e.g., one person's bad job may have seemed attractive to someone else). (15 minutes)

6. Why do you think that a good job for one person might be a bad job for another and vice versa? What are the implications of this for management and organizational behaviour?

EXPERIENTIAL EXERCISE

OB in the News

Every day there are stories in the news about organizations, the workplace, careers, and jobs. Now that you are learning about organizational behaviour, you can begin to interpret and understand these stories in a more informed manner. So let's get started. Look for a recent news story that has something to do with work or organizations. Pay particular attention to articles in the business or careers section of newspapers. Read the article as you normally would, and then write a short summary of the article and what you have learned from it. Then read the article again, but this time answer the following questions:

1. What does the article tell you about organizational behaviour? Refer to the sections *What Are Organizations?* and *What Is Organizational Behaviour?* in this chapter to answer this question.

2. Use the events described in the article to explain why organizational behaviour is important and makes a difference.

3. How can the goals of organizational behaviour be used to better understand the events in the article or solve a problem or concern that is noted in the article? Be sure to relate each of the goals of organizational behaviour to the article (i.e., predicting, explaining, and managing behaviour).

4. Does the article address any of the contemporary management concerns described in the chapter? Try to interpret the article in terms of one or more of the contemporary management concerns.

5. Compare your first reading and interpretation of the article to your second reading and interpretation. What did you learn about the events in the article when interpreting it through your new organizational behaviour "lens"?

6. How can learning about organizational behaviour improve your understanding and interpretation of stories and events like the one described in your article?

EXPERIENTIAL EXERCISE

How Engaged Are You?

To find out about your work or student engagement, answer the 17 questions below as frankly and honestly as possible. Note that to answer the questions for work engagement you should refer to your current or most recent job. Refer to the wording in parentheses if you are answering the questions as a student rather than an employee. Use the following response scale:

0–Never

1–Almost never

2–Rarely

3–Sometimes

4–Often

5–Very often

6–Always

____ 1. When I get up in the morning, I feel like going to work (class).

____ 2. To me, my job (studies) is (are) challenging.

____ 3. When I am working (studying), I forget everything else around me.

____ 4. At my work (When I'm doing my work as a student), I feel bursting with energy.

____ 5. My job (study) inspires me.

____ 6. Time flies when I am working (studying).

____ 7. At my work (As far as my studies are concerned), I always persevere, even when things do not go well.

____ 8. I am enthusiastic about my job (studies).

____ 9. I get carried away when I am working (studying).

____ 10. I can continue working (studying) for very long periods at a time.

____ 11. I am proud of the work (my studies) that I do.

____ 12. It is difficult to detach myself from my job (studies).

____ 13. At my job (As far as my studies are concerned), I am very resilient, mentally.

____ 14. I find the work (my studies) that I do full of meaning and purpose.

____ 15. I am immersed in my work (studies).

____ 16. At my job (When I'm studying or going to class), I feel strong and vigorous.

____ 17. I feel happy when I am working (studying) intensely.

Source: Republished with permission of Kluwer Academic Publishers (Dordrecht), from Schaufeli, W.B., Salanova, M., González-Romá, V., & Bakker, A.B. (2002). The measurement of engagement and burnout: A two sample confirmatory factor analystic approach. *Journal of Happiness Studies, 3,* 71–92; permission conveyed through Copyright Clearance Center, Inc.

Scoring and Interpretation

You have just completed the UWES work engagement scale developed by Wilmar B. Schaufeli, Marisa Salanova, Vicente González-Romá, and Arnold B. Bakker. Work engagement is a positive work-related state of mind that is characterized by vigour, dedication, and absorption. Vigour is characterized by high levels of energy and mental resilience while working, the willingness to invest effort into one's work, and persistence even in the face of difficulties. Dedication is characterized by a sense of significance, enthusiasm, inspiration, pride, and challenge. Absorption is characterized by being fully concentrated and deeply engrossed in one's work to such a degree that time passes quickly and one has difficulties detaching oneself from work. The average score of a sample of undergraduate students on each dimension was as follows: Vigour, 3.30; Dedication 4.41; and Absorption, 3.37. The average score of a sample of employees was as follows: Vigour, 3.82; Dedication 3.74; and Absorption, 3.53.

To obtain your score on each dimension of work engagement (vigour, dedication, and absorption), calculate the average of the items for each dimension as indicated below. To obtain your overall engagement score, calculate the average of your responses to all 17 questions.

Vigour: Add 1, 4, 7, 10, 13, and 16 and divide by 6.

Dedication: Add 2, 5, 8, 11, and 14 and divide by 5.

Absorption: Add 3, 6, 9, 12, 15, and 17 and divide by 6.

Overall engagement score: Add all 17 items and divide by 17.

Questions

To facilitate class discussion and your understanding of work engagement, form a small group with several other members of the class and consider the following questions:

1. Compare your own scores on each work engagement dimension. Which dimension is highest and which is lowest? What does this say about your own work or student engagement?

2. Each group member should present their scores on each dimension of work or student engagement as well as their overall work engagement score. What is the range of group members' scores on each dimension and overall work or student engagement? What dimensions do group members have high and low scores on? What is the average overall work or student engagement score in your group?

3. Try to understand why some group members have a low or high work or student engagement score. Each group member should try to explain what factors they think account for their low or high engagement score. If the group completed the scale for student engagement, you might discuss the courses you are taking, how many courses you are taking, course assignments, and your course instructors. If you completed the scale for work engagement, you might discuss the type of job each group member has, the type of tasks they perform, and the amount of autonomy and control they have in how they perform their job. Can you explain and understand why some group members have higher engagement scores than others?

4. What effect do you think your level of engagement has on your attitudes, behaviour, and performance? If you completed the scale for student engagement, consider your attitudes toward your program and your grades. If you completed the scale for work engagement, consider your job attitudes and job performance. Do students with higher engagement scores have more positive attitudes and higher grades or job performance?

5. Based on your work or student engagement score, what have you learned about yourself as a student or an employee? What are the implications of this for your attitudes and grades or performance?

6. How can knowledge of your work or student engagement help you as a student and as an employee? What can you do to become a more engaged student and employee? What are the potential consequences of being a more engaged student and employee?

CASE INCIDENT

My Mother's Visit

Last year, George was preparing for his mother's first visit to Canada. George had immigrated to Canada from Haiti six years earlier. His dream was for his mother to come to Canada to meet his new family and live with them. He had been working hard and saving money for many years to pay for his mother's airfare. Finally, everything was coming together. His mother's flight was booked, and a big celebration was planned to mark her arrival. George had arranged to leave work at lunchtime to pick his mother up at the airport and take her to his house, where the guests would be waiting. He had spent months planning the celebration and making the arrangements.

However, when the big day arrived, George's boss handed him an assignment and told him he was not to leave until it was completed. When George described his plans, his boss cut him off and reminded him that the organization depended on employees to do whatever it took to get the job done: "No excuses, George. You are not to leave until the job is done!" George had to arrange for a taxi to pick up his mother, and her welcome celebration took place without him. George did not get home until late in the evening. The guests had left, and his mother had gone to bed. George wondered why the assignment could not have waited until the next day, or why one of his co-workers couldn't have done it.

1. What does this incident tell you about management and organizational behaviour at George's organization?

2. How can organizational behaviour help to predict and explain the behaviour of George and his boss? What advice would you give to George and his boss in terms of managing organizational behaviour in the future?

3. What does this incident tell you about management and organizational behaviour in general?

CASE STUDY

Argamassa Construction Materials

At what point had Eduardo Santiago, plant manager at Argamassa, a construction materials company in Rio de Janeiro, Brazil, moved from admiring his boss to feeling like walking out? After all, if it weren't for Leandro Giuntini, the director of Argamassa, Santiago may not have had the opportunity to move into management—something he deeply wanted. Yet by the end of 2010, Santiago was feeling something less than gratitude toward Giuntini, who also happened to be a longtime friend. Santiago disagreed with the cost-cutting strategy Giuntini had implemented the previous year. And he believed that other more recent changes Giuntini had made had created an adversarial environment between management and labour.

Struggling with the situation while trying to remain professional, Santiago decided to arrange a dinner meeting with Giuntini. Now he wondered whether he should go ahead with his plan to give feedback to his boss or keep his thoughts to himself and view the outing as a personal dinner between friends.

Brazil and the Labour Market

With a population of slightly less than 200 million in 2010, Brazil was by far the most populated country in South America; its work force was also among the largest, at roughly 102 million.[1] Considered a developing economy, Brazil's industrial sectors, such as aircraft, cars and car parts, cement, chemicals, iron ore, lumber, steel, textiles, and tin made up 26% of its GDP. Unskilled labourers to fill positions in these sectors were in demand. Despite the need, workers' salaries were low. More than 60% of the population lived on BRL230 (USD70) per month.[2]

The Brazilian work force was correlated with the country's social class categories—a calculated system using the letters A, B, C, D, and E to indicate decreasing levels of income (see Table 1)—which determined one's position in life. Those capable of earning higher levels of income were considered Class A and B and tended to be mostly white. Most who had finished high school, a technical school, or some college tended to fit in Class C (50.4% of Brazilians fell in this category).[3] Those who had no high school diploma made

1 The World Bank, "Labor Force, Total," http://data.world-bank.org/indicator/SL.TLF.TOTL.IN (accessed Feb. 27, 2015).

2 BRL = Brazilian real. USD = U.S. dollar. Causa Operaria Online, "60% do brasilerios vivem com menos de um salario minimo," http://www.pco.org.br/nacional/60-dos-brasileiros-vivem-com-menos-de-um-salario-minimo/asia,e.html, and historical currency conversion: http://www.x-rates.com/historical/?from=USD&amount=70&date=2015-03-19 (both accessed Mar. 19, 2015).

3 "Meet the 'C' Class—Brazil's Rising Middle Class, The Hope of a Nation," *Worldcrunch,* July 19, 2012, http://www.worldcrunch.com/culture-society/meet-the-c-class-brazil-s-rising-middle-class-the-hope-of-a-nation/c3s5888/#.VPDz4zYo6Uk; and https://www.jpmorgan.com/cm/Blob-Server/Brazil_101_the_2011_country_handbook.pdf?blobkey=id&blobnocache=true&blobwhere=1158631510475&blobheader=application/pdf&blobcol=urldata&blobtable=MungoBlobs, 11 (both accessed Jul. 17, 2015).

TABLE 1   Distribution of social class system in 2009 and gross monthly earnings per household.

Class	Income (BRL)[4]	% Total Population
A	Above 10,200	5.1
B	Above 5,100	5.5
C	Above 2,040	50.4
D	Above 1,020	23.6
E	Below 1,020	15.3

Data sources: Andréa Novais, "Social Classes in Brazil," The Brazil Business, October 7, 2011, http://thebrazilbusiness.com/article/social-classes-in-brazil; and Emy Shayo Cherman and Fabio Akira, "Brazil 101: The 2011 Country Handbook," J.P.Morgan Latin America Equity Research, April 18, 2011, https://www.jpmorgan.com/cm/BlobServer/Brazil_101_the_2011_country_handbook.pdf?blobkey=id&blobnocache=true&blobwhere=1158631510475&blobheader=application/pdf&blobcol=urldata&blobtable=MungoBlobs (both accessed Jul. 17, 2015).

up Class D, and those who did not finish elementary school or who were illiterate usually had income levels more aligned with Class E. Both D and E classes tended to be mostly nonwhite.

Although wages were low, employee benefits were generous. Under Brazilian law, employers in the manufacturing industry were obligated to provide transportation costs to and from work, provide a meal inside the workplace (or give employees the price of a standard meal or provide a *cesta básica* (a boxed meal with rice, beans, sugar, coffee, pasta, etc.), give 30 days' paid vacation a year, and pay a 13th month's salary, which was equal to one month's pay. And although not the law, employers commonly provided daycare assistance for employees' families (spouses and children) too.

Argamassa and Leandro Giuntini

After learning the cement mortar business by working for his father's company, Leandro Giuntini and his brother Flavio founded Argamassa in 2003. Their father provided financial backing as well as connections in the industry. The company grew to become a medium-sized Brazilian construction materials firm focused on the production and distribution of cement mortar and colored grout. The firm competed on cost and relied on economies of scale for generating profits. Given the heavy weight of its products and significant transportation costs, Argamassa served only clients within a 300-kilometer radius of Rio de Janeiro. Argamassa had two types of clients—small-to-medium retailers and medium-to-large construction firms. And customers were loyal to Argamassa because it guaranteed a two- to three-day lead time delivery—significantly quicker than competitors—and very effective customer service.

By 2010, Argamassa owned three manufacturing plants and employed over 90 people. Most employees were from Class D and Class E. All lived paycheck to paycheck and worked in an industry where labourers were not generally well treated. They were usually pejoratively mistreated as *peões* (drudges) and when executives and labourers encountered each other, workers tended to neither be acknowledged nor greeted—indeed, they were usually perceived as potential thieves. More often than not, companies had some type of inspector who checked on employees to ensure they weren't stealing products or company assets.

While employees may have been mistreated in the greater area, at Argamassa, they were treated respectfully—Giuntini knew most by name. And it was common knowledge that he helped employees build homes and that he lent money for motorcycle purchases. From motivating employees to get their driver's licences to providing capital to purchase items to improve their lives, Argamassa employees appreciated Giuntini. Argamassa employees were also paid a higher wage than others in the industry. Giuntini celebrated the company's anniversaries and Christmases with gifts and prizes (televisions, fridges, and microwave ovens)—gestures that went a long way with employees. And benefits such as lunch and groceries went beyond what most firms provided employees. For those reasons, retention was high.

While Flavio focused on sales, Leandro Giuntini worked on manufacturing operations and product formulas. It was clear to everyone that the real engine of Argamassa's phenomenal growth was Leandro Giuntini's dogged determination and capacity to handle many tasks at the same time. Regardless of his generous nature, Leandro Giuntini's managerial style was demanding, and almost every decision passed through him. He calculated raw material purchases, defined optimum delivery routes, set production schedules, and organized marketing efforts. He managed all these technical tasks while at the same time serving as the general director of the company.

Despite the great time commitment of these varied responsibilities, Leandro Giuntini managed to deliver a high-quality product with greater speed than his competitors. The company thrived under his micromanagement. Sales increased by 86% in 2005 and another 48% in 2006. The company attracted the attention of many in the business community. Several

4 BRL1 = USD0.35.

potential buyers made lucrative offers for the company—Leandro Giuntini confidently rejected each one. The sky seemed to be the limit. In 2007, however, the company's rapid growth ground to a halt. Seeking some advice about the abrupt turn of events, one of the people Leandro Giuntini spoke with was his old friend, Eduardo Santiago.

Eduardo Santiago

Born in rural northeastern Brazil, Eduardo Santiago studied electrical engineering and later finance at the University of Pernambuco. He spent five years in the IT industry working on enterprise resource planning and improving and streamlining company processes. Although it seemed clear he could rise to the top in that field, Santiago's real desire was to work in business administration—a notion that seemed like a pipe dream. Then his childhood friend and owner of Argamassa presented him with an opportunity.

Leandro Giuntini shared some of his company's issues with Santiago, asked for his advice, and offered Santiago the opportunity to work as an independent consultant on a seven-month project to align processes. Deciding to drop his more immediate plans to apply to an MBA program, Santiago accepted the position at Argamassa. At the end of his tenure, Santiago had produced an impressive list of recommendations that would help Argamassa break out of its rut. Convinced that Santiago's proposed changes were on the right track, Leandro Giuntini asked him to join the company to spearhead the project himself. Santiago was thrilled about the opportunity. He could implement his recommendations to address Argamassa's issues, help out a long-time friend, and at the same time make the jump into his aspired career track. Santiago began the position as plant manager in March 2008.

Argamassa, Leandro Giuntini, and Eduardo Santiago

When Santiago joined Argamassa, Leandro Giuntini told him that he had free rein to manage and execute the restructuring. He was to solve the rampant disorganization and inefficiency. Production was using 55% of its capacity, yet employees were consistently working overtime. Variable costs had increased by 15% and fixed costs by 10% in 2007, resulting in an 81% drop in profits. Santiago reorganized divisions to create economies of scale, and he appointed a new crop of competent managers. Key performance indicators were chosen to generate continuous improvement throughout the company. In addition, Santiago reduced material wastage and, by the end of 2008, there was no overtime pay.

Things were humming along smoothly until Leandro Giuntini made a decision to increase prices just as two new entrants joined the market with reduced prices. Sales dropped by 10%. When the company looked as though it was headed toward serious financial trouble in 2009, harsh cutbacks were instituted. Leandro Giuntini stopped consulting Santiago and reduced employee benefits to just above the minimum required by law: he stopped paying for lunches or groceries, a large part of the reason why some employees came to work with Argamassa; ended a policy of salary advances; and greatly reduced Christmas bonuses and gifts. The workers, to their credit, accepted the cuts because Santiago promised them that benefits would return when profits did, and they trusted Leandro Giuntini.

Eventually the cost reductions seemed to be paying off as Argamassa's profitability started to recover by the first quarter of 2010. Instead of reinstating the firm's previously generous benefits, money was instead spent on new trucks and on a new product line. Employees became disgruntled.

By the end of 2010, it seemed as though the company was headed toward another loss. Santiago could feel the toxic relationship between labour and management. Employees were taking longer to do their jobs, and they were less productive. Some were doing poor work so that they could stay later and receive overtime pay as compensation for their slashed benefits. Others were simply quitting and, although they were easily replaced, new hires immediately adopted their bad habits.

Leandro Giuntini went directly to Santiago's managers and ordered them to fix employee production issues. That directive resulted in two bitter public firings by one manager. Santiago was frustrated. He believed that at the first sign of trouble, Leandro Giuntini had begun his obsessive micromanaging again.

Production wasn't the only area suffering from low morale; sales reps who normally pushed Argamassa products started dedicating more time to other companies' products, and sales growth dropped. Discouraged over the situation, Santiago sought the counsel of another friend and co-worker at Argamassa, Bruno Fonseca. As he listened to Santiago vent about his boss, Fonseca reminded him that it was Leandro Giuntini who was the driver who had built a successful company. And it was Leandro Giuntini who took a chance by hiring Santiago to fix some issues in the first place. Fonseca continued:

> You're not the only one who owes something to Leandro. We all do. He helped me when I had a severe financial problem. He helped Ediliea in financial management to buy a nice home to raise her family in. You can ask nearly every worker in the shop—they are all thankful to Leandro for something, whether a motorcycle, car, or grocery payments. Behind the temper and hunger for results, he really is a good man. At the moment, the intense pressure for numbers has obscured that in the eyes of the workers.

Their conversation had Santiago deeply worried. Fonseca's insights regarding how much employees depended upon the company to take care of them reminded him of something else. Leandro Giuntini had just decided to cut the snack budget for the transportation team—again. He had reinstated it when things improved after the first round of cost cutting.

Fix it—Again?

In his mind, Santiago had two choices to change the firm's situation, which he figured would otherwise end with bankruptcy or a takeover. He could apply to MBA programs and quit his job before he was fired, or he could stay and try to tackle the problems. He wondered how he would explain working at the company for only three years and being part of its second major loss in profits—not a successful track record that he would be proud to show potential employers or write on MBA program applications.

For Santiago, staying at Argamassa implied approaching Leandro Giuntini about a plan to turn things around. In Santiago's view, the problems had little to do with the high costs Giuntini was determined to continue fixing. Instead he felt the root cause of Argamassa's issues was that both he and Leandro Giuntini were doing practically the same job. This confused and upset employees and prevented the company from having clear leadership.

Santiago's plan to turn things around was two-fold. First, he would propose to increase Argamassa's sales. Cost-cutting measures had been tried and had not worked. It was clear to him that if management wanted to fix Argamassa's bottom line and growth in sales, cost-cutting measures would not be the proper means. Santiago would achieve sales growth by focusing on the marketing and commercial division and by finding ways to acquire new customers.

This, Santiago thought, was the right way to stop the company's losses. Second, he would revive employee morale by rebuilding the company's earlier positive culture. He would do more to engage employees and clients in the company and show that management really did care. Santiago believed his plan would work *only* if Leandro Giuntini took a big step back from the plant and gave him complete freedom to implement it.

Santiago's head hurt from the lack of sleep over the way things could play out at Argamassa. His mind turned to his complicated working relationship with Leandro Giuntini and the unknown if he decided to leave the firm. How would he approach his conversation with Giuntini? Was dinner with him going to be one between a boss and his manager or between two old friends?

QUESTIONS

1. Explain the relevance and importance of organizational behaviour for the issues described in the case and the problems at Argamassa. What are the main issues, and what do they have to do with organizational behaviour?

2. Describe employee attitudes, behaviour, and performance at the following time periods: (a) 2003 to 2008; (b) after Giuntini's cutbacks in 2009; and (c) by the end of 2010. How, when, and why did employees' attitudes, behaviour, and performance change?

3. Using the goals of organizational behaviour, discuss the impact of Giuntini's cutbacks on employees and the relationship between labour and management. In other words, predict and explain the effects of the cutbacks and describe what you would do to manage them.

4. Consider Leandro Giuntini's performance in terms of managerial roles and activities. What roles and activities does he engage in, and how effective is he in performing them? What roles and activities does he need to do more or less of and why?

5. Do you think Santiago's plan to turn things around will be successful? What changes would you recommend for returning the company to profitability and why?

INTEGRATIVE CASE

IVEY | Publishing

Ken Private Limited: Digitization Project

Late one evening in August 2004, Saiyumn Savarker, chief operating officer (COO) of Ken Private Limited (Ken), was sitting alone in his corporate office. While he gazed at the panoramic view from his workplace in the Philippines, his thoughts raced to the vexing problems encountered in the first phase of the Genesis Digitization Project.

The Genesis Digitization Project required Ken to create digital archives of an American daily newspaper, *The Genesis Times*,[1] for its client, Dogma International. The coverage of this newspaper spanned 150 years. Ken had begun the project in April 2004 and had promised 10 years of digitized newspaper to the client by the end of July 2004. Unfortunately, Ken could not meet this deadline, and the delay did not sit well with Dogma International, since it had, in turn, already made a commitment to its customers. Infuriated by the delay, Dogma International sent out a dire warning: If Ken was unable to honour the commitment, Dogma International would not hesitate to cancel the project.

The project was in a state of flux. Ken had to deliver 35 years of digitized newspapers with enhanced image quality to Dogma International in a time frame of just two months. Moreover, the cross-cultural context exacerbated Ken's problems and presented Savarker with a tough business issue. The gravity of the situation forced him to call an emergency meeting with the various managers of the Genesis Digitization Project to discuss and develop an action plan for successful execution and on-time delivery of the project to the client.

COMPANY BACKGROUND

Ken Private Limited

Ken Private Limited was established in March 1991 in Texas, United States, and was in the business of providing knowledge outsourcing and technology services. The firm helped its clients to use information efficiently as well as cost-effectively. The outsourcing content services of the company focused on fabrication services and knowledge services. Included in Ken's fabrication services were processes such as digitization, XML and mark-up services, imaging, data conversion, content creation services, and language translation services. Knowledge services, on the other hand, included content enhancement, vocabulary development, taxonomy, hyperlinking mark-up, indexing and abstracting, and other general editorial services. The technology services focused on the design, implementation, integration and deployment of systems to author, manage and distribute content. By 2004, Ken had earned a great reputation in the market for its excellent performance. It had established offices in America, Europe, and Asia, employing more than 5000 employees, and its net profit in 2004 amounted to $90 million. Ken was one of the best market players in the industry, having earned many accolades for its superior performance, and its client base included many of the world's pre-eminent information, media and publishing companies, as well as leading enterprises in information-intensive industries.

Dogma International

Dogma International was a leading global content-publishing company, located in Michigan, United States. The company's history spanned 55 years, and its

---

1 *The name of the newspaper has been disguised to protect confidentiality.*

reputation in the market was based on the high quality and excellence of its services. The company developed information databases through multiple sources like newspapers, magazines, journals and from the works of thousands of publishers, in turn making the information available to customers through a web-based online information system. Large organizations and individuals alike depended on Dogma International to provide reliable and trustworthy information.

Dogma International acquired the rights to the microfilm archives of *The Genesis Times,* one of the most prestigious newspapers in America. The company considered it advantageous to shift from microfilm to a web-based product and decided to digitize the newspaper. For Dogma International, this decision represented a key strategic move as well as a prestigious project—to make available over the web millions of pages currently on microfilm, dating as far back as the 18th century.

As a part of this project, Dogma International aimed to convert the microfilm archives of the newspaper into a comprehensive digital archive. The main goal of the project was to make the content available and accessible, from anywhere in the world, to scholars, researchers, students, teachers, libraries, and others needing the information. Every issue was to be digitized from cover to cover in an easily searchable, user-friendly format. Thus, the company sought to provide the information in both text-only format and full-page format so that users could view the information as originally published. The company also planned to index every issue thoroughly in order to enhance the browsing experience of the user, an effort that would require additional features, such as the ability to narrow searches (by date, author's name, keyword, etc.), view brief abstracts, and access each page with a user-friendly URL. Dogma International approached Ken to take on this task.

STRATEGIC AGREEMENT: DIGITIZING 150 YEARS OF HISTORY

On March 21, 2004, Ken entered into an agreement with Dogma International to provide its services for the Digitization Project, creating a digital historical archive of full runs of *The Genesis Times.* Under the agreement, Ken was expected to provide the client with a range of services that included product manufacturing services, such as digitization and imaging services; XML conversion and transformation services, professional services; and editorial services, such as abstracting and indexing. (See Exhibit 1 for project summary.)

The history of the newspaper spanned almost 150 years, from its first issue in 1851 until 1999, which included more than 3.4 million pages and represented a 15-month project for Ken. As per the agreement, Ken had to deliver the first batch (i.e., 10 years of digitized newspaper) within four months of the project's commencement. Thereafter, Ken was to deliver a bulk order of 25 years' worth of digitized newspaper content every two months.

THE PREPARATION: TECHNOLOGY AND CONTENT STRATEGY

Shekhar Sharma, who had recently joined Ken's Hyderabad office, was appointed as project manager for the Genesis Digitization Project. Sharma, an Indian, had six years of experience working for an Indian information technology (IT) company and four years of formal education in technology.

The digitization of *The Genesis Times* represented the first time that Ken had handled a project of this kind. So far, the company had been using the traditional method of web-page delivery, wherein PCs were used to access HTML web pages that were displayed page by page. However, owing to the large volume of data in the newspapers and the requirements of the client, the Genesis Digitization Project could not be carried out using this method. Further, XML was rapidly replacing HTML as a standard format within the industry, and the project required the newspaper data to be converted to the XML format, which demanded an XML-based repository structure. However, compared to HTML and other conventional data sets, the use of XML posed a unique set of challenges. The XML format required creation of rich metadata with a high degree of precision and consistency, as well as a technology-intensive manufacturing environment.

Ken's recently established XML content factory in Tacloban City, Philippines, was thought to be the appropriate location to carry out a large-scale project like this. The factory was equipped with all the tools required to meet the challenges posed by the newspaper digitization process.

A new process and methodology were created for the project. The process involved gathering data from the microfilms, normalizing disparate data formats, digitizing non-digital assets and creating XML files, which were uploaded to the client's digital warehouse. However, to implement the conversion process, it was essential for Ken to operate on advanced technological platforms, which had to be built to facilitate the needs

EXHIBIT 1   Project Summary

Project Description	A newspaper digitization project required to create digital archives of 150 years of the newspaper, *The Genesis Times*.
Input Materials	Newspapers in 35 mm roll microfilm. Each shipment will contain multiple reels. <ul><li>Each reel may contain several complete issues; an issue will not span more than one reel.</li><li>Each issue may contain several pages.</li><li>Each page contains a number of articles.</li></ul>
Output Requirements	Both full page and clipped images (of individual article zones) are required. Text will be delivered in XML. For each article (which may include ads and other non-article kinds of individual content): <ul><li>One XML file, containing all the metadata and zone content for the article.</li><li>One tagged image file (TIFF) containing article images.</li><li>Exception: photographic zones and charts are to be provided as jpeg images instead of TIFF.</li></ul>
Accuracy Requirement	<ul><li>99.95 percent character accuracy for header information (headlines, sub-headlines, bylines, photo captions, and first full paragraph of the article)</li><li>100 percent accuracy for quality pre-audit of the product submitted.</li><li>100 percent tag accuracy.</li></ul>
Mode of Transmission	Processed files shall be burn-in DLT tapes
Special Project Requirements	Processed file should be delivered issue by issue directory as follows: newspaper_issuedate (directory) → each article XML file and all article TIFF or JPEG files from that issue → page (directory) → all full-page TIFF files from that issue Each file (whether XML, TIFF or JPEG) will be uniquely named. In addition to the required deliverable are <ul><li>exact count of pages in each reel delivered to IDI;</li><li>exact count of pages in each batch delivered to client;</li><li>exact count of articles (by headline) of each batch delivered to the client (transmitted);</li><li>exact count of articles (per batch delivered) not processed.</li></ul>

Source: Company files.

of the project. Such technology development functions were, by and large, performed at the company's office in Hyderabad, India.

Both tasks—content processing and technology development—were indispensable for the project. Keeping this fact in mind, Sharma decided to split the activities of the production and technology development between the Philippines office and the Indian office. It was the first time that the company had adopted this kind of an arrangement to execute a project. The Indian team was given the responsibility of developing a technological platform and transferring it to the Filipino team, whereas the latter was given the task of content processing and production, using the newly developed technical platform.

DISTANT TEAMS, DIFFERENT BACKGROUNDS

Sharma, the project manager, took charge of the Genesis Digitization Project, relocated to the Philippines, and decided to start work simultaneously at both locations to save time. The project started on April 1, 2004.

To carry out the project, Ken created a team of 1600 employees, with 1400 members in the Philippines and 200 in India. The Filipino team was segregated into five departments: Production Planning and Control (PPC), Initial Process Imaging (IPI), Document Control and Distribution (DCD), Non-Production Staff (NPS) and Quality Assurance (QA) (see Exhibit 2). The employees in each department were assigned clear tasks. A department manager was associated with each department and was accountable for the department he or she managed. The Indian team had three assistant managers supervising the project in India in three shifts. Each of the three managers was responsible for delivery from their respective teams.

The Indian team initiated the project through the planning and design of the technological platform,

EXHIBIT 2
Process Flow

Source: Company files.

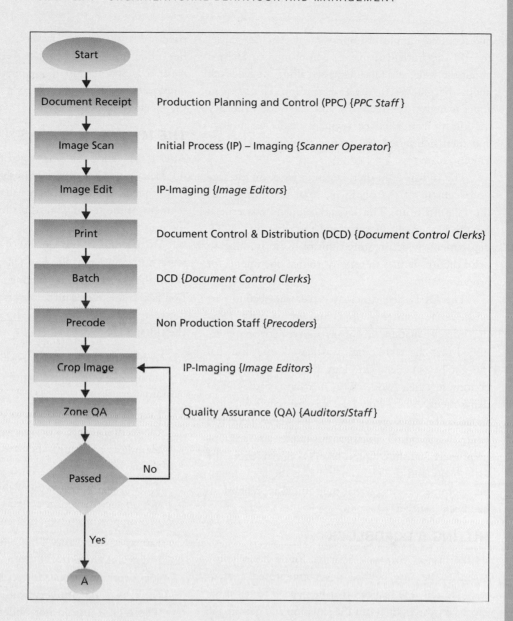

transferring each technology segment to the Filipino team throughout each stage of the development process. While the Indian team was working on the first segment of the technology, the Production Planning and Control department of the Filipino team had the task of receiving the input from the client in the form of microfilms.

The Filipino team members were very comfortable working with the current form of *pragmatic workflow* (a term used for work that required minimal use of high-end technology) since it offered enough flexibility to carry out operations. The members of the Filipino team, however, did not see the benefits of switching over to the new workflow. They were quite skeptical about the new technology that was being developed by

the Indian team, and they had reservations about the value of the technology, both to their own team and to the project. Although the team members discussed this issue among themselves, they did not share their concerns with their project manager.

THE WIDENING GAP

While the Filipino team continued to express concerns among themselves about the new workflow, the Indian team was ready with the first segment of the technological platform. The Filipino team received the technology, and its IPI department initiated the scanning of microfilms to create electronic images. The members of the IPI department found the technology frustrating because, in their opinion, it was not very user friendly and required significant improvement. Michael Tajale, the IPI department manager, complained to Sharma about the issue, and Sharma passed along the feedback about the glitches to the Indian team. The team in India reviewed the feedback and made the necessary modifications in the first segment of the technology and then transferred the revised version back to the Filipino team.

The Indian team then began to work on the second segment of the platform, soon delivering it to the Filipino team. The second segment was crucial for the Document Control and Distribution (DCD) department, which required this platform in order to print the image files to serve as source documents for production.

The DCD department received the second part of the technological platform and got to work. During implementation, however, the employees determined that the technology was flawed, asserting that the glitches in the technology prevented them from continuing their work. The manager of the DCD department, Albert Lumapas, was frustrated with the situation because production in his department had come to a standstill. Further, this unpleasant development increased the Filipino team's concerns about the technology and the team in India, as the team members became convinced that their initial apprehensions had been justified.

HITTING A ROADBLOCK

As the project manager, Sharma, found himself in a quandary because he had never anticipated a situation like this. He realized that he needed to get more involved to straighten out the situation and get the job back on track. With this goal in mind, he convened a meeting with all five department managers and a few employees from each department.

He started off with a general discussion and then gradually began to make inquiries about the delay in the project. He addressed the managers but was met with a stony silence; none of them expressed their concerns. This did not deter Sharma. He insisted that each employee share their views regarding the problems. An employee from the DCC department murmured something about there being a lot of errors in the technology delivered to them and that the team in India was not sensitive to the production department's needs. Sharma took note of the response, tried to find out more about the problem, and asked the employee to explain what the glitches were; however, the employee refused to share anything more. Sharma

tried yet again to get answers from the employees, but none were forthcoming. Feeling irritated and frustrated, Sharma lost his temper and yelled at the employees but still could not get a response. He called the meeting to a close.

THE MYSTERY DEEPENS

After the meeting, Sharma urged the Indian team to do their job more conscientiously and also directed them to resolve the errors they had made in the second segment of the technological platform before resending it to the Filipino team.

By this time, it was already May 2004, and things were not improving. Sharma felt genuinely worried about the project. While walking around the production facility, he overheard a conversation in the hallway between Tajale and Lumapas, who respectively headed the IPI and DCC departments.

Tajale: Hey, Lumapas. How's the production going in your department? Are things getting any better?

Lumapas: Not really. There are a lot of issues in the technical part. I don't know what the Indian team is up to. I think they are just not concerned about our problems.

Tajale: I agree with you. While we were working on the microfilm conversion, we had minimal support from the engineering department.

Lumapas: Very true. The other day I sent a very important email to the team in India for resolving a technical issue. It was an urgent one, but there was no answer from the Indian team. Those guys just do not understand the urgency and take their own sweet time to get back to us. My department had to sit idle for the whole day because of the unresolved problem. My team felt frustrated. This was, of course, not the first time that such an incident happened. It's an everyday scenario now with the engineering team.

Tajale: Yeah. That's sad. We didn't have a great experience working with them either. The technology that was transferred to us was not at all user friendly, and moreover, I feel those guys aren't even looking out for inputs from the production department.

Lumapas: That's right, and this is a big barrier. Our team members are not well versed in the use of technology. Of course, the engineering team didn't organize any knowledge-sharing sessions or training. The lack of awareness on the use of technology has made it even more difficult for us to reduce the problems.

Tajale: The Indian team did resolve some issues by making some modifications in the technology and transferred that to us a second time. It became all the more complicated to work on those platforms as the rework processes were not clearly defined.

Lumapas: Oh, I see. I wasn't aware of these intricacies. Thanks, Tajale, for sharing this piece of information.

Tajale: Lumapas, there's one thing that I fail to understand. The problem lies with the Indian team, and the project manager keeps asking us, "What's the problem?"

Lumapas: I know, and finally, if something goes wrong, it is always our team that is blamed. Nobody blames them.

Tajale: Yeah … alright then, Lumapas. I have someone waiting for me at reception. I'll catch you later.

Lumapas: Sure, Tajale. Thanks.

After Sharma overheard the conversation, he felt even more perplexed and overwhelmed by the whole situation, which seemed to be rapidly spinning out of control.

THE OTHER SIDE

Sharma believed it was essential to talk to the Indian managers before taking any further steps. Consequently, he connected with Rajeev Anand, one of the three assistant managers in India. Sharma expressed his disappointment over the results delivered by the Indian team. He also asked Anand to clarify why things were not proceeding according to the original plan, to which Anand replied:

The team here in India has its expertise in developing technology, but at the moment, we are dealing with a new project. This project is not like any of the usual projects and requires a different kind of treatment. Technology of this kind has not been established in the company and thus has required extra time, effort and even refinement. There are a few inevitable bottlenecks in technology at the moment. Despite this, the team is trying to fix all the issues and enhance the applications as and when reported.

As far as the Filipino team is concerned, sir, I try to ensure that all their concerns are immediately *addressed, and they get a timely response. They are not at all patient, and they create an uproar over every petty issue. I believe there aren't as many errors in the technology as they have made out, and I feel they lack the inclination to learn the processes involved. I wonder if they even understand the project they are working on. We will, of course, take your suggestions into consideration and ensure successful delivery of the technology.*

THE DEADLINE APPROACHES

The project manager's attempts at mediation brought some success. After fixing the errors, the Indian team passed on the technology to the Filipino team, and production in the Philippines finally resumed. The DCC department printed the image files to serve as documents for production and, thereafter, batched source documents per page for easier data tracking and processing.

Meanwhile, the Indian team was preparing its third segment of the technical platform. As a part of the third segment of technical work, the Indian team engineered links that would enable the Filipino team to provide the abstracting, indexing, and other editorial services to the client. This time, they were certain that there were minimal errors.

With the help of the third segment of technology, the NPS department of the Filipino team inserted tags within the content to provide markers that the computer could process. They were also expected to provide the client with certain other services, such as content enhancement, hyper-linking, indexing, abstracting, and general editorial services, which once again proved to be taxing for the Filipinos.

The NPS department faced major difficulties in delivering these services. The team members were not able to comprehend the style of language used in the newspaper as they had never been exposed to such writing before. It was with great difficulty that the project moved to the next step.

The IPI department edited the images in this stage. They cropped the corresponding image file according to the pre-coded source document. The project was subsequently passed on to the Quality Assurance (QA) department to perform the procedures required in order to certify that the processed zones met the zoning quality requirement. The department ascertained that the product being extended to the client was of suitable quality and that it met all the required standards. According to the QA department, there were no errors in the digitization of the newspapers.

Despite the team's best efforts, Ken was prepared to deliver only two years' worth of digitized newspapers on July 31, 2004.

THE ANGRY CLIENT

After four months, it was time for the first delivery to be made, as per the agreement. But to the shock of the client, Ken could deliver just two years of digitized newspapers, not even one-quarter of what it had promised.

Not surprisingly, the client was appalled. Dogma International was extremely unhappy, not just with the delay, but also the quality of the delivery. The company issued an ultimatum to Ken: either Ken would deliver high-quality digitized archives of the newspaper, as per the agreement, within a period of two months, or it would lose the project.

The client's warning was a major wake-up call for Ken. The company managers realized that if they wanted to retain the project, they had no other choice but to deliver the product as per the client's requirement. The loss of an important client and potential damage to Ken's own reputation was at stake. The board of the company got together to find a way out. They zeroed in on COO Saiyumn Savarker as their point man to handle the project at this critical juncture.

Prior to attaining this COO position, Savarker had served as assistant vice-president of project delivery at Ken. He had a long and successful record of managing many national and international project deliveries for the company, and the board appreciated his work and the corporate contributions he had made. Savarker flew from India to the Philippines to assess the issue.

THE MISSING LINK

Savarker's primary focus was to get acquainted with the situation. He met with Sharma, who briefed him about the state of affairs and shared everything that had happened during the four-month period. With the information he gleaned, Savarker gained some insight into the client's disappointment with the deadlines, but he still could not identify the source of the problem.

Savarker's next step was to go to the QA department in search of further insights. To his surprise, he was told that the product that had been offered to the client was of good quality. The department manager said, "The team captured the client's relevant content and converted it into XML as per the standards. The 99.95 percent character accuracy requirement for header information for headlines, sub-headlines, bylines, photo captions, and first full paragraph of the article was ensured. The team also ensured 100 percent tag accuracy and 100 percent accuracy for quality pre-audit of the product submitted."

Upon discovering this information, Savarker wondered about the all-important missing link. He decided it would be helpful to find out more from the client, so he promptly arranged for a meeting in order to gain a clear understanding as to why Dogma International considered the product to be inadequate. The client replied by saying, "Though the text part was digitized in a correct manner, the quality of the images was really poor." The client told Savarker that they considered the image part important because it had tremendous power to attract users to the product. With the growth of the Internet, they expected the demand for images to be huge. As the meeting was about to come to an end, the client exclaimed, "At least you talked to us! This is the first time that somebody from your company has asked for input or feedback from us, so we thought our specifications and expectations must be clear to your company."

Savarker returned to his office and met with Sharma. He explained his conversation with the staff at Dogma International and asked Sharma for an explanation. Sharma said, "We weren't aware that the client was concerned about the aesthetics as well. We had no clue about this requirement. If we replace our current scanners with high-resolution scanners, we will be able to deliver high-quality images to the client as per their requirement."

After winding up his meeting with Sharma, Savarker walked directly into his office on the fourth floor. He called his assistant and asked her not to let anybody disturb him for next two hours. He then sat on his chair and said to himself, "There is no time for crying over spilt milk and blaming anybody, but it is sad that this lack of competency or comprehension of the client's need was attributed to poor knowledge on the company's part."

He pondered the situation and realized that Ken needed to digitize approximately 35 years' worth of newspaper afresh, and it also needed to improve the image quality throughout the process. The task seemed enormous since it had to be done within a period of just two months. As he grappled with the situation, Savarker worked toward finding a solution that would steer the project out of dangerous waters.

QUESTIONS

1. Discuss the relevance of organizational behaviour for the issues and problems facing Ken Private Limited with respect to the Genesis Digitization Project. What topics in organizational behaviour help to explain the problems with the Genesis Digitization Project, and what topics are important for the success of the Genesis Digitization Project?

2. Explain how the goals of organizational behaviour would have been helpful for the Genesis Digitization Project. Describe some of the things that Shekhar Sharma might have predicted, explained, and managed.

3. Consider Shekhar Sharma's role as project manager for the Genesis Digitization Project in terms of Mintzberg's managerial roles and Luthans, Hodgetts, and Rosenkrantz's managerial activities. What managerial roles and activities does he exhibit, and how effective is he in performing them? What roles and activities are most important for him to perform and why?

4. To what extent are the contemporary management concerns described in Chapter 1 relevant for Ken Private and the Genesis Digitization Project? What should Ken Private be most concerned about, and what should they do to effectively manage the contemporary management concerns?

5. How can organizational behaviour help Saiyumn Savarker find a solution to steer the Genesis Digitization Project out of dangerous waters and to successfully complete the project? What should Savarker do to ensure Ken's successful delivery of the project?

CHAPTER 2 PERSONALITY AND LEARNING

LEARNING OBJECTIVES

After reading Chapter 2, you should be able to:

2.1 Define *personality* and describe the *dispositional*, *situational*, and *interactionist* approaches to organizational behaviour.

2.2 Discuss the Five-Factor Model of personality, *locus of control*, *self-monitoring*, and *self-esteem*.

2.3 Discuss *positive* and *negative affectivity*, *proactive personality*, *general self-efficacy*, and *core self-evaluations* and their consequences.

2.4 Define *learning,* and describe what is learned in organizations.

2.5 Explain *operant learning theory,* differentiate between *positive* and *negative reinforcements, and extinction and punishment,* and explain how to use punishment effectively.

2.6 Explain when to use immediate versus delayed reinforcement and when to use continuous versus partial reinforcement.

2.7 Explain social cognitive theory and discuss *observational learning, self-efficacy beliefs*, and *self-regulation*.

2.8 Describe the following organizational learning practices: *organizational behaviour modification, employee recognition programs*, and *training and development programs*.

NAHEED NENSHI

What does it take to be the best mayor in the world? Some say politics, some say personality, while others say both. Whatever it takes, Calgary mayor Naheed Nenshi has it. In 2014, the City Mayors Foundation awarded Nenshi the World Mayor Prize which recognizes mayors who have made outstanding contributions to their communities. A year earlier, *Maclean's* magazine named him the second most powerful person in Canada, second only to the prime minister.

Naheed Nenshi was born in Toronto shortly after his family immigrated from Tanzania in the 1970s. They then moved to Calgary, where Nenshi was raised. After graduating from the University of Calgary with a bachelor of commerce degree and then Harvard University with a master's degree in public policy, he worked for the consulting firm McKinsey & Company before returning to Calgary, where he started his own business and worked as a professor at Mount Royal University.

His interest in civic affairs led him to consider a run for mayor of Calgary in 2010. Few people knew who he was when he entered the race, and he was considered an outside candidate. However, during the final weeks of the campaign, his support and momentum surged. To everyone's surprise, he was elected with 39 percent of the vote, making him the 36th mayor of Calgary and the first Muslim mayor of a major North American city.

Nenshi ran a grassroots campaign that was made up of volunteers. His campaign and surprise victory was called the "Purple Revolution" because of the campaign colour and broad demographic and strong youth support. Supporters were seen in purple clothes, social media accounts had purple backgrounds, and Nenshi's campaign headquarters was painted purple.

His campaign emphasized community activism with the campaign slogan "Better Ideas" and focused on things such as safe neighbourhoods, poverty reduction, improved transportation, transparent city hall, complete communities, and quick access to the airport. His campaign was also noted for its use of social media, including Twitter, Facebook, and YouTube. He wore a

Courtesy of the City of Calgary, Office of the Mayor

button with the number 3 to urge Calgarians to do three things to better their community. In his acceptance speech to his supporters he said, "Today Calgary is a different place than it was yesterday. A better place."

During the Calgary floods of June of 2013, Nenshi obtained superhero and rock-star status as he worked tirelessly around the clock. Photos of the mayor were superimposed on Superman movie posters. People sported T-shirts of a smiling Nenshi with goggles and snorkel while others featured a cowboy hat and read "Keep Calm and Nenshi On." Nenshi worked for 43 hours straight and urged residents to help their neighbours and hug emergency providers. Many people lined up to hug him.

He was in helicopters, in front of news cameras, providing updates several times a day, visiting flood-struck zones, and he went door-to-door to people's homes to see how they were doing. He used traditional and social media to provide Calgarians with up-to-date information. His constant presence led to a social media movement to get him to go home and get some sleep.

During one of many interviews, Nenshi spotted a five-year-old girl. Once he was free, he approached the girl and kneeled down to her height. She then handed him a hand-drawn card with a picture of Pete the Cat, a main character in a book he had read to her class. Inside the card it read, "Dear Mayor Nenshi, thank you for keeping Calgary strong!"

In an editorial that appeared in the *Calgary Sun*, Nenshi was commended "for his amazing leadership under the most trying of circumstances … He has been a beacon of strength, support and optimism as Calgary battles the effects of the single-biggest disaster to hit our city … But most importantly, he has been positive in the face of unprecedented chaos."

The flood crisis confirmed Nenshi's leadership ability, and in October 2013 he was re-elected as mayor of Calgary in a landslide victory. Now in his second term, Naheed Nenshi is the most admired and popular mayor in Canada. He is considered a role model for decisive management, inclusivity, and forward planning.

Many have described Naheed Nenshi as a people person who is whip-smart and jolly. He has a track record of success and a reputation for innovative thinking and is a great communicator. Nenshi's popularity and success have led some to suggest that he would be the ideal candidate for premier of Alberta. For now, however, he is just the best mayor in the world.[1]

Naheed Nenshi seems to have what it takes to be a successful leader and politician. But what is it about him that has contributed to his success? Does it have something to do with his personality? What kind of personality does he have? And what kind of personality is important for leadership and career success? In this chapter, we will try to answer these questions. While research in organizational behaviour has shown that behaviour is partly a function of people's personalities, learning is also a critical requirement for effective organizational behaviour. Therefore, we will also consider the role of learning in this chapter. But first, we begin with the important role of personality in organizational behaviour.

WHAT IS PERSONALITY?

LO 2.1

Define *personality* and describe the *dispositional, situational,* and *interactionist* approaches to organizational behaviour.

PERSONAL INVENTORY ASSESSMENT

Learn About Yourself
Psychological Personality Types/Preferences

Personality. The relatively stable set of psychological characteristics that influences the way an individual interacts with his or her environment.

The notion of personality permeates thought and discussion in our culture. We are bombarded with information about "personalities" in the print and broadcast media. We are sometimes promised exciting introductions to people with "nice" personalities. We occasionally meet people who seem to have "no personality."

Personality is so important that some companies focus on personality when hiring employees. For example, Kirmac Collision Services, an automotive collision repair company based in Coquitlam, British Columbia, focuses more on personality and less on industry-specific experience and skills when recruiting and hiring employees. And if you are interested in participating in the Mars One mission, which will send a crew of four to Mars in 2024, it is your personality, not your knowledge or technical skills, that is the focus of the selection process. A recent survey of Canadian organizations found that when it comes to hiring recent graduates, many employers rank personality as more important than work experience and education.[2] But what exactly *is* personality?

Personality is the relatively stable set of psychological characteristics that influences the way an individual interacts with his or her environment and how he or she feels, thinks, and behaves. An individual's personality summarizes his or her personal style of dealing with the world. You have certainly noticed differences in personal style among your parents, friends, professors, bosses, and employees. They are reflected in the distinctive ways that they react to people, situations, and problems.

Where does personality come from? Personality consists of a number of dimensions and traits that are determined in a complex way by genetic predisposition and by one's long-term learning history. Although personality is relatively stable, it is certainly susceptible to change through adult learning experiences. And while we often use labels such as "high self-esteem" to describe people, we should always remember that people have a *variety* of personality characteristics. Excessive typing of people does not help us to appreciate their unique potential to contribute to an organization.

Personality is the focus of the selection process for the Mars One Mission which will send a crew of four to Mars in 2024.

NASA/Goddard Space Flight Center

PERSONALITY AND ORGANIZATIONAL BEHAVIOUR

◄⊙─Simulate

**INDIVIDUAL
BEHAVIOUR**

Personality has a rather long history in organizational behaviour. Initially, it was believed that personality was an important factor in many areas of organizational behaviour, including motivation, attitudes, performance, and leadership. In fact, after the Second World War, the use of personality tests for the selection of military personnel became widespread, and in the 1950s and 1960s it became popular in business organizations.

This approach to organizational behaviour is known as the **dispositional approach** because it focuses on individual dispositions and personality. According to the dispositional approach, individuals possess stable traits or characteristics that influence their attitudes and behaviours. In other words, individuals are predisposed to behave in certain ways. However, decades of research produced mixed and inconsistent findings that failed to support the usefulness of personality as a predictor of organizational behaviour and job performance. As a result, there was a dramatic decrease in personality research and a decline in the use of personality tests for selection.

Researchers began to shift their attention to factors in the work environment that might predict and explain organizational behaviour. This approach became known as the **situational approach**. According to the situational approach, characteristics of the organizational setting, such as rewards and punishment, influence people's feelings, attitudes, and behaviour. For example, many studies have shown that job satisfaction and other work-related attitudes are largely determined by situational factors, such as the characteristics of work tasks.[3]

Over the years, proponents of both approaches have argued about the importance of dispositions versus the situation in what is known as the "person–situation debate." Although researchers argued over which approach was the right one, it is now believed that both approaches are important for predicting and understanding organizational behaviour. This led to a third approach to organizational behaviour, known as the "interactionist approach," or "interactionism." According to the **interactionist approach**, organizational behaviour is a function of both dispositions and the situation. In other words, to predict and understand organizational behaviour, one must know something about an individual's personality and the setting in which he or she works. This approach is now the most widely accepted perspective within organizational behaviour.[4]

To give you an example of the interactionist perspective, consider the role of personality in different situations. To keep it simple, we will describe situations as being either "weak" or "strong." In weak situations it is not always clear how a person should behave, while in strong situations there are clear expectations for appropriate behaviour. As a result, personality has the most impact in weak situations. This is because in these situations (e.g., a newly formed volunteer community organization) there are loosely defined roles, few rules,

Dispositional approach.
Individuals possess stable traits or characteristics that influence their attitudes and behaviours.

Situational approach.
Characteristics of the organizational setting influence people's attitudes and behaviour.

Interactionist approach.
Individuals' attitudes and behaviour are a function of both dispositions and the situation.

"You clearly know about his toxic personality."

and weak reward and punishment contingencies. However, in strong situations, which have more defined roles, rules, and contingencies (e.g., routine military operations), personality tends to have less impact.[5] Thus, as you can see, the extent to which personality influences people's attitudes and behaviour depends on the situation. Later in the text, you will learn that the extent to which people perceive stressors as stressful and the way they react to stress is also influenced by their personality. This is another example of the interactionist approach to organizational behaviour.

One of the most important implications of the interactionist perspective is that some personality characteristics are most useful in certain organizational situations. According to **trait activation theory**, personality traits lead to certain behaviours only when the situation makes the need for that trait salient. In other words, personality characteristics influence people's behaviour when the situation calls for a particular personality characteristic.[6] Thus, there is no one best personality, and managers need to appreciate the advantages of employee diversity. A key concept here is *fit*: putting the right person in the right job, group, or organization and exposing different employees to different management styles.

In recent years, there has been a resurgence of interest in personality research in organizational behaviour. One of the main problems with the early research on personality was the use of inadequate measures of personality characteristics. However, advances in measurement and trends in organizations have prompted renewed interest. For example, increased emphasis on service jobs with customer contact, concern about ethics and integrity, and contemporary interest in teamwork and cooperation all point to the potential contribution of personality.[7]

Another reason for the renewed interest in personality has been the development of a framework of personality characteristics known as the Five-Factor Model, or the "Big Five," which provides a framework for classifying personality characteristics into five general dimensions. This framework makes it much easier to understand and study the role of personality in organizational behaviour.[8]

In what follows, we discuss the five general personality dimensions of the Five-Factor Model. Then we cover three well-known personality characteristics with special relevance to organizational behaviour. We then discuss recent developments and advances in personality research. Later in the text, we will explore the impact of personality characteristics on job satisfaction, motivation, leadership, ethics, organizational politics, and stress.

The Five-Factor Model of Personality

People are unique, people are complex, and there are literally hundreds of adjectives that we can use to reflect this unique complexity. Yet, over the years, psychologists have discovered that there are about five basic but general dimensions that describe personality. These Big Five dimensions are known as the Five-Factor Model (FFM) of personality and are summarized in Exhibit 2.1 along with some illustrative traits.[9] The dimensions are:

- **Extraversion.** This is the extent to which a person is outgoing versus shy. Persons who score high on extraversion tend to be sociable, outgoing, energetic, joyful, and assertive. High extraverts enjoy social situations, while those low on this dimension (introverts) avoid them. Extraversion is especially important for jobs that require a

Trait activation theory.
Traits lead to certain behaviours only when the situation makes the need for the trait salient.

LO 2.2

Discuss the Five-Factor Model of personality, *locus of control*, *self-monitoring*, and *self-esteem*.

PERSONAL INVENTORY ASSESSMENT

Learn About Yourself
Core Five Personality Dimensions

EXHIBIT 2.1
The Five-Factor Model of personality.

Extraversion	Emotional Stability	Agreeableness	Conscientiousness	Openness to Experience
Sociable, Talkative vs. Withdrawn, Shy	Stable, Confident vs. Depressed, Anxious	Tolerant, Cooperative vs. Cold, Rude	Dependable, Responsible vs. Careless, Impulsive	Curious, Original vs. Dull, Unimaginative

lot of interpersonal interaction, such as sales and management, where being sociable, assertive, energetic, and ambitious is important for success.

- **Emotional stability/Neuroticism.** This is degree to which a person has appropriate emotional control. People with high emotional stability (low neuroticism) are self-confident and have high self-esteem. Those with lower emotional stability (high neuroticism) tend toward self-doubt and depression. They tend to be anxious, hostile, impulsive, depressed, insecure, and more prone to stress. As a result, for almost any job the performance of persons with low emotional stability is likely to suffer. Persons who score high on emotional stability are likely to have more effective interactions with co-workers and customers because they tend to be more calm and secure.

- **Agreeableness.** This is the extent to which a person is friendly and approachable. More agreeable people are warm, considerate, altruistic, friendly, sympathetic, cooperative, and eager to help others. Less agreeable people tend to be cold and aloof. They tend to be more argumentative, inflexible, uncooperative, uncaring, intolerant, and disagreeable. Agreeableness is most likely to contribute to job performance in jobs that require interaction and involve helping, cooperating, and nurturing others, as well as in jobs that involve teamwork and cooperation.

- **Conscientiousness.** This is the degree to which a person is responsible and achievement oriented. More conscientious people are dependable and positively motivated. They are orderly, self-disciplined, hard working, and achievement striving, while less conscientious people are irresponsible, lazy, and impulsive. Persons who are high on conscientiousness are likely to perform well on most jobs, given their tendency toward hard work and achievement.

- **Openness to experience.** This is the extent to which a person thinks flexibly and is receptive to new ideas. More open people tend toward creativity and innovation. Less open people favour the status quo. People who are high on openness to experience are likely to do well in jobs that involve learning and creativity, given that they tend to be intellectual, curious, and imaginative, and to have broad interests.

The Big Five dimensions are relatively independent. That is, you could be higher or lower in any combination of dimensions. Also, they tend to hold up well cross-culturally. Thus, people in different cultures use these same dimensions when describing the personalities of friends and acquaintances. There is also evidence that the Big Five traits have a genetic basis.[10]

RESEARCH EVIDENCE Research has linked the Big Five personality dimensions to organizational behaviour. First, there is evidence that each of the Big Five dimensions is related to job performance and organizational citizenship behaviours (voluntary behaviour that contributes to organizational effectiveness, such as helping co-workers; see Chapter 4 for a detailed discussion of organizational citizenship behaviour).[11] Generally, traits like those in the top half of Exhibit 2.1 lead to better job performance and more citizenship behaviours. Further, the Big Five dimensions that best predict job performance depend on the occupation. For example, high extraversion is important for managers and salespeople. Nonetheless, high conscientiousness predicts performance in all jobs across occupations and is the strongest predictor of all the Big Five dimensions of overall job performance.[12] However, an exception to this is the prediction of a particular kind of performance known as adaptive performance. To find out more, see the Research Focus: *Personality and Adaptive Performance.*

Second, research has also found that the Big Five are related to other work behaviours. For example, one study found that conscientiousness is related to retention and attendance at work and is also an important antidote for counterproductive behaviours such as theft, absenteeism, and disciplinary problems.[13] Extraversion has also been found to be related to absenteeism; extraverts tend to be absent more often than introverts. There is also evidence of relationships between personality and unsafe work behaviour and workplace deviance. For example, while high levels of conscientiousness and agreeableness are associated with fewer unsafe behaviours, high levels of extraversion and low emotional stability (neuroticism) are associated with more unsafe behaviours. In addition, higher levels of conscientiousness, agreeableness, and emotional stability are associated with lower levels of workplace deviance.[14]

The Big Five are also related to work motivation and job satisfaction. In a study that investigated the relationship between the Big Five and different indicators of work motivation, the Big Five were found to be significantly related to motivation. Among the five dimensions, neuroticism and conscientiousness were the strongest predictors of motivation, with the former being negatively related and the latter being positively related.[15] In another study, the Big Five were shown to be significantly related to job satisfaction. The strongest predictor was emotional stability, followed by conscientiousness, extraversion, and, to a lesser extent, agreeableness. Openness to experience was not related to job satisfaction. Similar results have been found for life satisfaction. In addition, individuals with higher conscientiousness, extraversion, agreeableness, and emotional stability perform better on a team in terms of their performance of important team-relevant behaviours such as cooperation, concern, and courtesy to team members.[16]

The Big Five are also related to career success. High conscientiousness, extraversion, and emotional stability have been found to be associated with a higher income and occupational status. These personality traits were related to career success even when the influence of general mental ability was taken into account. Furthermore, both childhood and adult measures of personality predicted career success during adulthood over a period of 50 years. Thus, the effects of personality on career success are relatively enduring.[17]

Now that you are familiar with the big five personality dimensions, read the chapter-opening vignette again about Naheed Nenshi and try to answer some of the questions we posed at the beginning of the chapter. For example, what kind of personality does Naheed Nenshi have with regard to the Five-Factor Model? Which of the five factors do you think best explains Naheed Nenshi's success as a political leader?

EXHIBIT 2.2
The internal/external locus of control continuum.

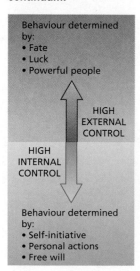

Behaviour determined by:
• Fate
• Luck
• Powerful people

HIGH EXTERNAL CONTROL

HIGH INTERNAL CONTROL

Behaviour determined by:
• Self-initiative
• Personal actions
• Free will

Locus of control. A set of beliefs about whether one's behaviour is controlled mainly by internal or external forces.

Locus of Control

Consider the following comparison. Laurie and Stan are both management trainees in large banks. However, they have rather different expectations regarding their futures. Laurie has just enrolled in an evening master of business administration (MBA) program in a nearby university. Although some of her MBA courses are not immediately applicable to her job, Laurie feels that she must be prepared for greater responsibility as she moves up in the bank hierarchy. Laurie is convinced that she will achieve promotions because she studies hard, works hard, and does her job properly. She feels that an individual makes her own way in the world and that she can control her own destiny. She is certain that she can someday be the president of the bank if she really wants to be. Her personal motto is "I can do it."

Stan, on the other hand, sees no use in pursuing additional education beyond his bachelor's degree. According to him, such activities just do not pay off. People who get promoted are just plain lucky or have special connections, and further academic preparation or hard work has nothing to do with it. Stan feels that it is impossible to predict his own future, but he knows that the world is pretty unfair.

Laurie and Stan differ on a personality dimension called **locus of control**. This variable refers to individuals' beliefs about the *location* of the factors that control their behaviour. At one end of the continuum are high internals (like Laurie), who believe that the opportunity to control their own behaviour resides within themselves. At the other end of the continuum are high externals (like Stan), who believe that external forces determine their behaviour. Not surprisingly, compared with internals, externals see the world as an unpredictable, chancy place in which luck, fate, or powerful people control their destinies (see Exhibit 2.2).[18]

Internals tend to see stronger links between the effort they put into their jobs and the performance level that they achieve. In addition, they perceive to a greater degree than externals

■ RESEARCH FOCUS ■

PERSONALITY AND ADAPTIVE PERFORMANCE

Changes in technology and the design of work have made it increasingly important and necessary for employees to be able to adapt quickly to changes and novel situations in the workplace. The increasing uncertainty in organizational environments means that employees and managers must be attuned to workplace changes and adjust and modify their behaviour accordingly. Being able to adjust and adapt to changes is key to the success of employees and their organizations.

The ability to adapt to changes is a particular kind of job performance known as adaptive performance. Adaptive performance has been defined as the proficiency with which an individual alters his or her behaviour in response to the demands of a new task, event, situation, or environmental constraints. Thus, adaptive performance involves responding to environmental changes by modifying one's behaviour.

Personality is believed to be an important predictor of adaptive performance. Among the Big Five dimensions, emotional stability, extraversion, and openness to experience are believed to be especially important. Emotional stability should be related to adaptive performance because of the propensity to stay calm and level-headed in the face of challenge and difficulty and a greater willingness to face and deal with change. Extraversion is also expected to predict adaptive performance because extraverts are more likely to welcome challenge when confronted with a novel task or work environment and to initiate changes (e.g., enterprising activities). This is especially likely for ambition, which is a specific aspect of extraversion. Openness to experience should also be related to adaptive performance because there is evidence that it relates to the pursuit of and adjustment to new environments. On the other hand, because conscientiousness is associated with a preference for routine and structure, consciencious individuals might be too inflexible to cope with and adjust to changes in the work environment. Finally, agreeableness is not likely to be related to adaptive performance, given that it is of most importance for interpersonal interactions.

The relationship between personality and adaptive performance was investigated in a study that analyzed the results of 71 independent samples of employees and managers from a variety of industries. The results indicated that only emotional stability and ambition were positively related to adaptive performance for both employees and managers. These relationships were stronger for managers than for employees because managers have more opportunities to engage in adaptive performance.

Given the increasing importance of adaptive performance in the workplace today, organizations will increasingly want to identify individuals who can adapt to changing tasks and dynamic situations, because they can help a business gain a competitive advantage. The results of this study indicate that emotional stability and extraversion are two personality variables that predict adaptive performance in the workplace.

Source: Based on Huang, J.L., Ryan, A.M., Zabel, K.L., & Palmer, A. (2014). Personality and adaptive performance at work: A meta-analytic investigation. *Journal of Applied Psychology, 99*, 162–179.

---

that the organization will notice high performance and reward it.[19] Since internals believe that their work behaviour will influence the rewards they achieve, they are more likely to be aware of and to take advantage of information that will enable them to perform effectively.[20]

Research shows that locus of control influences organizational behaviour in a variety of occupational settings. Evidently, because they perceive themselves as being able to control what happens to them, people who are high on internal control are more satisfied with their jobs and more committed to their organizations, and they earn more money and achieve higher organizational positions.[21] In addition, they seem to perceive less stress, cope with stress better, experience less burnout, and engage in more careful career planning. They are also less likely to be absent from work and more likely to be satisfied with their lives.[22]

Self-Monitoring

We are sure that you have known people who tend to "wear their heart on their sleeve." These are people who act the way they feel and say what they think in spite of their social surroundings. We are also sure that you have known people who are a lot more sensitive to

Self-monitoring. The extent to which people observe and regulate how they appear and behave in social settings and relationships.

their social surroundings, a lot more likely to fit what they say and do to the nature of those surroundings, regardless of how they think or feel. What we have here is a contrast in **self-monitoring**, which is the extent to which people observe and regulate how they appear and behave in social settings and relationships.[23] The people who "wear their heart on their sleeve" are low self-monitors. They are not so concerned with scoping out and fitting in with those around them. Their opposites are high self-monitors, who take great care to observe the thoughts, actions, and feelings of those around them and control the images that they project. In this sense, high self-monitors behave somewhat like actors. In particular, high self-monitors tend to show concern for socially appropriate emotions and behaviours, to tune in to social and interpersonal cues, and to regulate their behaviour and self-presentation according to these cues.

How does self-monitoring affect organizational behaviour?[24] For one thing, high self-monitors tend to gravitate toward jobs that require, by their nature, a degree of role-playing and the exercise of their self-presentation skills. Sales, law, public relations, and politics are examples. In such jobs, the ability to adapt to one's clients and contacts is critical; so are communication skills and persuasive abilities, characteristics that high self-monitors frequently exhibit. High self-monitors perform particularly well in occupations that call for flexibility and adaptiveness in dealings with diverse constituencies. As well, a number of studies show that managers are inclined to be higher self-monitors than non-managers in the same organization. High self-monitors tend to be more involved in their jobs, to perform at a higher level, and to be more likely to emerge as leaders. However, high self-monitors are also likely to experience more role stress and show less commitment to their organization.[25]

Are high self-monitors always at an organizational advantage? Not likely. They are unlikely to feel comfortable in ambiguous social settings in which it is hard to determine exactly what behaviours are socially appropriate. Dealing with unfamiliar cultures (national or corporate) might provoke stress. Also, some roles require people to go against the grain or really stand up for what they truly believe in. Thus, high self-monitoring types would seem to be weak innovators and would have difficulty resisting social pressure.

Self-Esteem

Self-esteem. The degree to which a person has a positive self-evaluation.

How well do you like yourself? This is the essence of the personality characteristic called self-esteem. More formally, **self-esteem** is the degree to which a person has a positive self-evaluation. People with high self-esteem have favourable self-images. People with low self-esteem have unfavourable self-images. They also tend to be uncertain about the correctness of their opinions, attitudes, and behaviours. In general, people tend to be highly motivated to protect themselves from threats to their self-esteem.

Behavioural plasticity theory. People with low self-esteem tend to be more susceptible to external and social influences than those who have high self-esteem.

One of the most interesting differences between people with high and low self-esteem has to do with the *plasticity* of their thoughts, attitudes, and behaviour, or what is known as "behavioural plasticity." According to **behavioural plasticity theory**, people with low self-esteem tend to be more susceptible to external and social influences than those who have high self-esteem—that is, they are more pliable. Thus, events and people in the organizational environment have more impact on the beliefs and actions of employees with low self-esteem. This occurs because, being unsure of their own views and behaviour, they are more likely to look to others for information and confirmation. In addition, people who have low self-esteem seek social approval from others, approval that they might gain from adopting others' views, and they do not react well to ambiguous and stressful situations. This is another example of the interactionist approach, in that the effect of the work environment on people's beliefs and actions is partly a function of their self-esteem.[26]

Employees with low self-esteem also tend to react badly to negative feedback—it lowers their subsequent performance.[27] This means that managers should be especially cautious when using punishment, as discussed later in this chapter, with employees with low self-esteem. If external causes are thought to be responsible for a performance problem, this should be made very clear. Also, managers should direct criticism at the performance difficulty and not at the person. As we will explain shortly, modelling the correct behaviour should be especially effective with employees with low self-esteem, who are quite willing to imitate credible models and who also respond well to mentoring. Finally, organizations should try to avoid assigning those with low self-esteem to jobs (such as life insurance sales) that inherently provide a lot of negative feedback.

Organizations will generally benefit from a workforce with high self-esteem. Such people tend to make more fulfilling career decisions, they exhibit higher job satisfaction and job performance, and they are generally more resilient to the strains of everyday worklife.[28] What can organizations do to bolster self-esteem? Opportunity for participation in decision making, autonomy, and interesting work have been fairly consistently found to be positively related to self-esteem.[29] Also, organizations should avoid creating a culture with excessive and petty work rules that signal to employees that they are incompetent or untrustworthy.[30]

ADVANCES IN PERSONALITY AND ORGANIZATIONAL BEHAVIOUR

LO 2.3

In recent years, there has been increased attention to the role of personality and organizational behavior, and this has led to a number of advances in personality research. In this section, we describe five more personality variables that are important for organizational behaviour: positive and negative affectivity, proactive personality, general self-efficacy, and core self-evaluations.

Discuss *positive* and *negative affectivity*, *proactive personality*, *general self-efficacy*, and *core self-evaluations* and their consequences.

Positive and Negative Affectivity

Have you ever known somebody who is always happy, cheerful, and in a good mood? Or perhaps you know someone who is always unhappy and in a bad mood. Chances are you have noticed these differences in people. These differences reflect two affective dispositions known as positive affectivity (PA) and negative affectivity (NA). Research has found that they are enduring personality characteristics and that there may be a genetic and biological basis to them.

People who are high on **positive affectivity** experience positive emotions and moods like joy and excitement and view the world, including themselves and other people, in a positive light. They tend to be cheerful, enthusiastic, lively, sociable, and energetic. People who are high on **negative affectivity** experience negative emotions and moods like fear and anxiety and view the world in a negative light. They have an overall negative view of themselves and the world around them, and they tend to be distressed, depressed, and unhappy.[31] It is important to understand that PA and NA are not opposite ends of a continuum but are relatively independent dimensions.[32]

Unlike the other personality traits discussed in this chapter, positive and negative affectivity are emotional dispositions that predict people's general emotional tendencies. Thus, they can influence people's emotions and mood states at work and influence job attitudes and work behaviours. Research has found that people who are high on PA have higher job satisfaction and job performance and engage in more organizational citizenship behaviours. High PA employees are also more creative at work, and there is some evidence that PA is a key factor that links happiness to success at work and in life. Individuals who are high on NA report lower job satisfaction and have poorer job performance. High NA employees experience more stressful work conditions and report higher levels of workplace stress and strain. NA has also been found to be associated with counterproductive work behaviours (e.g., harassment and physical aggression), withdrawal behaviours (e.g., absenteeism and turnover), and occupational injury.[33]

Positive affectivity.
Propensity to view the world, including oneself and other people, in a positive light.

Negative affectivity.
Propensity to view the world, including oneself and other people, in a negative light.

Proactive Personality

Proactive behaviour.
Taking initiative to improve
current circumstances or
creating new ones.

Proactive personality. A
stable personal disposition
that reflects a tendency
to take personal initiative
across a range of activities
and situations and to effect
positive change in one's
environment.

How effective are you at taking initiative and changing your circumstances? Taking initiative to improve one's current circumstances or creating new ones is known as **proactive behaviour**. It involves challenging the status quo rather than passively adapting to present conditions. Some people are very good at this because they have a stable disposition toward proactive behaviour, known as a "proactive personality." Individuals who have a **proactive personality** are relatively unconstrained by situational forces and act to change and influence their environment. Proactive personality is a stable personal disposition that reflects a tendency to take personal initiative across a range of activities and situations and to effect positive change in one's environment.[34]

Proactive individuals search for and identify opportunities, show initiative, take action, and persevere until they bring about meaningful change. People who do not have a proactive personality are more likely to be passive and to react and adapt to their environment. As a result, they tend to endure and to be shaped by the environment instead of trying to change it.[35]

Proactive personality has been found to be related to a number of work outcomes, including job satisfaction, job performance, organizational citizenship behaviours, tolerance for stress in demanding jobs, leadership effectiveness, participation in organizational initiatives, work-team performance, and entrepreneurship. One study found that proactive personality is associated with higher performance evaluations because individuals with a proactive personality develop strong supportive networks and perform initiative-taking behaviours, such as implementing solutions to organizational or departmental problems or spearheading new programs. Individuals with a proactive personality have also been found to have high-quality relationships with their supervisors. There is also evidence that persons with a proactive personality are more successful in searching for employment and career success. They are more likely to find jobs, receive higher salaries and more frequent promotions, and have more satisfying careers.[36]

General Self-Efficacy

General self-efficacy (GSE). A general trait that refers to an individual's belief in his or her ability to perform successfully in a variety of challenging situations.

General self-efficacy (GSE) is a general trait that refers to an individual's belief in his or her ability to perform successfully in a variety of challenging situations.[37] GSE is considered to be a *motivational* trait rather than an *affective* trait, because it reflects an individual's belief that he or she can succeed at a variety of tasks rather than how an individual feels about him- or herself. An individual's GSE is believed to develop over the lifespan as repeated successes and failures are experienced across a variety of tasks and situations. Thus, if you have experienced many successes in your life, you probably have high GSE, whereas somebody who has experienced many failures probably has low GSE. Individuals who are high on GSE are better able to adapt to novel, uncertain, and adverse situations. In addition, employees with higher GSE have higher job satisfaction and job performance.[38]

Core Self-Evaluations

Core self-evaluations. A
broad personality concept
that consists of more
specific traits that reflect
the evaluations people hold
about themselves and their
self-worth.

Unlike the other personality characteristics described in this chapter, **core self-evaluations** refers to a broad personality concept that consists of more specific traits. The idea behind the theory of core self-evaluations is that individuals hold evaluations about themselves and their self-worth or worthiness, competence, and capability.[39] In a review of the personality literature, Timothy Judge, Edwin Locke, and Cathy Durham identified four traits that make up a person's core self-evaluation. The four traits have already been described in this chapter; they include self-esteem, general self-efficacy, locus of control, and neuroticism (emotional stability).

Research on core self-evaluations has found that these traits are among the best dispositional predictors of job satisfaction and job performance. People with more positive core self-evaluations have higher job satisfaction, organizational commitment, and job performance. Furthermore, research has shown that core self-evaluations measured in childhood

PERSONAL INVENTORY ASSESSMENT

Learn About Yourself
Core Self Evaluation Scale

and in early adulthood are related to job satisfaction in middle adulthood. This suggests that core self-evaluations are related to job satisfaction over time. Core self-evaluations have also been found to be positively related to life and career satisfaction, and individuals with higher CSE perceive fewer stressors and experience less stress and conflict at work. One of the reasons for the relationship between core self-evaluations and work outcomes is that individuals with a positive self-regard are more likely to perceive and pay attention to the positive aspects of their environments. They experience their job as more intrinsically satisfying and have higher perceptions of fairness and support.[40]

WHAT IS LEARNING?

So far in this chapter we have described how people's personalities can influence their work attitudes and behaviours. However, recall our earlier discussion that the organizational setting can also have a strong effect on an individual's attitudes and behaviour. As you will learn in this section, the environment can change people's behaviour and even shape personalities. But how does this happen? How and why do people change their behaviour? To try and answer this question, let's examine the concept of learning.

Learning occurs when practice or experience leads to a relatively permanent change in behaviour potential. The words *practice* or *experience* rule out viewing behavioural changes caused by factors like drug intake or biological maturation as learning. One does not learn to be relaxed after taking a tranquilizer, and a child does not suddenly learn to be a bass singer at the age of 14. The practice or experience that prompts learning stems from an environment that gives feedback concerning the consequences of behaviour. But what do employees learn in organizations?

What Do Employees Learn?

Learning in organizations can be understood in terms of taxonomies that indicate what employees learn, how they learn, and different types of learning experiences. The "what" aspect of learning can be described as learning content, of which there are four primary categories: practical skills, intrapersonal skills, interpersonal skills, and cultural awareness.[41]

Practical skills include job-specific skills, knowledge, and technical competence. Employees frequently learn new skills and technologies to continually improve performance and to keep organizations competitive. Constant improvement has become a major goal in many organizations today, and learning can give an organization a competitive advantage.[42] *Intrapersonal skills* are skills such as problem solving, critical thinking, learning about alternative work processes, and risk taking. *Interpersonal skills* include interactive skills such as communicating, teamwork, and conflict resolution. Later in this book, we will discuss the ways in which teams are becoming the major building blocks of organizations, as well as the importance of effective communication for organizational success.

Finally, *cultural awareness* involves learning the social norms of organizations and understanding company goals, business operations, and company expectations and priorities. All employees need to learn the cultural norms and expectations of their organizations to function as effective organizational members. We discuss the learning of social norms and organizational culture in more detail in Chapter 8.

Now that we have considered what people learn in organizations, let's turn to two theories that describe how people learn.

Operant Learning Theory

In the 1930s, psychologist B.F. Skinner investigated the behaviour of rats confined in a box containing a lever that delivered food pellets when pulled. Initially, the rats ignored the lever, but at some point they would accidentally pull it and a pellet would appear. Over time, the rats gradually acquired the lever-pulling response as a means of obtaining food. In other words,

LO 2.4

Define *learning*, and describe what is learned in organizations.

Learning. A relatively permanent change in behaviour potential that occurs due to practice or experience.

PERSONAL INVENTORY ASSESSMENT

Learn About Yourself
Learning Styles

LO 2.5

Explain *operant learning theory*, differentiate between *positive* and *negative reinforcements*, and *extinction* and *punishment*, and explain how to use punishment effectively.

Operant learning. Learning by which the subject learns to operate on the environment to achieve certain consequences.

they *learned* to pull the lever. The kind of learning Skinner studied is called **operant learning** because the subject learns to operate on the environment to achieve certain consequences. The rats learned to operate the lever to achieve food. Notice that operantly learned behaviour is controlled by the consequences that follow it. These consequences usually depend on the behaviour, and this connection is what is learned. For example, salespeople learn effective sales techniques to achieve commissions and avoid criticism from their managers. The consequences of commissions and criticism depend on which sales behaviours salespeople exhibit.

Operant learning can be used to increase the probability of desired behaviours and to reduce or eliminate the probability of undesirable behaviours. Let's now consider how this is done.

INCREASING THE PROBABILITY OF BEHAVIOUR

Reinforcement. The process by which stimuli strengthen behaviours.

One of the most important consequences that influences behaviour is reinforcement. **Reinforcement** is the process by which stimuli strengthen behaviours. Thus, a *reinforcer* is a stimulus that follows some behaviour and increases or maintains the probability of that behaviour. The sales commissions and criticism mentioned earlier are reinforcers for salespeople. In each case, reinforcement serves to strengthen behaviours, such as proper sales techniques, that fulfill organizational goals. In general, organizations are interested in maintaining or increasing the probability of behaviours such as correct performance, prompt attendance, and accurate decision making. As we shall see, positive reinforcers work by their application to a situation, while negative reinforcers work by their removal from a situation.

Positive Reinforcement

Positive reinforcement. The application or addition of a stimulus that increases or maintains the probability of some behaviour.

Positive reinforcement increases or maintains the probability of some behaviour by the *application* or *addition* of a stimulus to the situation in question. Such a stimulus is a positive reinforcer. In the basic Skinnerian learning situation described earlier, we can assume that reinforcement occurred because the probability of the lever operation increased over time. We can further assume that the food pellets were positive reinforcers because they were introduced after the lever was pulled.

Consider the experienced securities analyst who tends to read a particular set of financial newspapers regularly. If we had been able to observe the development of this reading habit, we might have found that it occurred as the result of a series of successful business decisions. That is, the analyst has learned to scan those papers because his or her reading is positively reinforced by subsequent successful decisions. In this example, something is added to the situation (favourable decisions) that increases the probability of certain behaviour (selective reading). Also, the appearance of the reinforcer is dependent or contingent on the occurrence of that behaviour.

In general, positive reinforcers tend to be pleasant things, such as food, praise, money, or business success. However, the intrinsic character of stimuli does not determine whether they are positive reinforcers, and pleasant stimuli are not positive reinforcers when considered in the abstract. Whether or not something is a positive reinforcer depends only on whether it increases or maintains the occurrence of some behaviour by its application. Thus, it is improbable that the holiday turkey that employers give to all the employees of a manufacturing plant positively reinforces anything. The only behaviour that the receipt of the turkey is contingent on is being employed by the company during the third week of December. It is unlikely that the turkey increases the probability that employees will remain for another year or work harder.

Negative Reinforcement

Negative reinforcement. The removal of a stimulus that in turn increases or maintains the probability of some behaviour.

Negative reinforcement increases or maintains the probability of some behaviour by the *removal* of a stimulus from the situation in question. Also, negative reinforcement occurs when a response *prevents* some event or stimulus from occurring. In each case, the removed or prevented stimulus is a *negative reinforcer.* Negative reinforcers are usually aversive or unpleasant stimuli, and it stands to reason that we will learn to repeat behaviours that remove or prevent these stimuli.

Let's repeat this point, because it frequently confuses students of organizational behaviour: Negative reinforcers *increase* the probability of behaviour.

Managers who continually nag their employees unless the employees work hard are attempting to use negative reinforcement. The only way employees can stop the aversive nagging is to work hard and be diligent. The nagging maintains the probability of productive responses by its removal. In this situation, employees often get pretty good at anticipating the onset of nagging by the look on their boss's face. This look serves as a signal that they can avoid the nagging altogether if they work harder.

Negative reinforcers generally tend to be unpleasant things, such as nagging or the threat of fines. Again, however, negative reinforcers are defined only by what they do and how they work, not by their unpleasantness. Above, we indicated that nagging could serve as a negative reinforcer to increase the probability of productive responses. However, nagging could also serve as a positive reinforcer to increase the probability of unproductive responses if an employee has a need for attention and nagging is the only attention the manager provides. In the first case, nagging is a negative reinforcer—it is terminated following productive responses. In the second case, nagging is a positive reinforcer—it is applied following unproductive responses. In both cases, the responses increase in probability.

Organizational Errors Involving Reinforcement

Experience indicates that managers sometimes make errors in trying to use reinforcement. The most common errors are confusing rewards with reinforcers, neglecting diversity in preferences for reinforcers, and neglecting important sources of reinforcement.

CONFUSING REWARDS WITH REINFORCERS Organizations and individual managers frequently "reward" workers with things such as pay, promotions, fringe benefits, paid vacations, overtime work, and the opportunity to perform challenging tasks. Such rewards can fail to serve as reinforcers, however, because organizations do not make them contingent on specific behaviours that are of interest to the organization, such as attendance, innovation, or productivity. For example, many organizations assign overtime work on the basis of seniority, rather than performance or good attendance, even when the union contract does not require it. Although the opportunity to earn extra money might have strong potential as a reinforcer, it is seldom made contingent on some desired behaviour.

NEGLECTING DIVERSITY IN PREFERENCES FOR REINFORCERS Organizations often fail to appreciate individual differences in preferences for reinforcers. In this case, even if managers administer rewards after a desired behaviour, they may fail to have a reinforcing effect. Intuitively, it seems questionable to reinforce a workaholic's extra effort with time off from work, yet such a strategy is fairly common. A more appropriate reinforcer might be the assignment of some challenging task, such as work on a very demanding key project. Some labour contracts include clauses that dictate that supervisors assign overtime to the workers who have the greatest seniority. Not surprisingly, high-seniority workers are often the best paid and the least in need of the extra pay available through overtime. Even if it is administered so that the best-performing high-seniority workers get the overtime, such a strategy might not prove reinforcing—the usual time off might be preferred over extra money.

Managers should carefully explore the possible range of stimuli under their control (such as task assignment and time off from work) for their applicability as reinforcers for particular employees. For example, there is some evidence that employee reward preferences vary as a function of generational differences. One survey of workers found that generation Y prefers non-monetary rewards to a greater extent than generation X and baby boomers.[43] Furthermore, organizations should attempt to administer their formal rewards (such as pay and promotions) to capitalize on their reinforcing effects for various individuals.

NEGLECTING IMPORTANT SOURCES OF REINFORCEMENT There are many reinforcers of organizational behaviour that are not especially obvious. While concentrating on potential reinforcers of a formal nature, such as pay or promotions, organizations and their managers often neglect those that are administered by co-workers or are intrinsic to the jobs being performed. Many managers cannot understand why a worker would persist in potentially dangerous horseplay despite threats of a pay penalty or dismissal. Frequently, such activity is positively reinforced by the attention provided by the joker's co-workers. In fact, on a particularly boring job, such threats might act as positive reinforcers for horseplay by relieving the boredom, especially if the threats are never carried out. Two important sources of reinforcement that managers often ignore are performance feedback and social recognition.

> **Performance feedback.**
> Providing quantitative or qualitative information on past performance for the purpose of changing or maintaining performance in specific ways.

Performance feedback involves providing quantitative or qualitative information on past performance for the purpose of changing or maintaining performance in specific ways. This reinforcement is available for jobs that provide feedback concerning the adequacy of performance. For example, in some jobs, feedback contingent on performance is readily available. Doctors can observe the success of their treatment by observing the progress of their patients' health, and mechanics can take the cars they repair for a test drive. In other jobs, organizations must build some special feedback mechanism into the job. Performance feedback is most effective when it is (a) conveyed in a positive manner, (b) delivered immediately after the performance is observed, (c) represented visually, such as in graph or chart form, and (d) specific to the behaviour that is being targeted for feedback.[44]

> **Social recognition.**
> Informal acknowledgement, attention, praise, approval, or genuine appreciation for work well done from one individual or group to another.

Social recognition involves informal acknowledgement, attention, praise, approval, or genuine appreciation for work well done from one individual or group to another. Research has shown that when social recognition is made contingent on employee behaviour it can be an effective means for performance improvement.[45]

In summary, managers should understand that positive feedback and a "pat on the back" for a job well done are positive reinforcers that are easy to administer and likely to reinforce desirable behaviours.

LO 2.6

Explain when to use immediate versus delayed reinforcement and when to use continuous versus partial reinforcement.

REINFORCEMENT STRATEGIES

What is the best way to administer reinforcers? Should we apply a reinforcer immediately after the behaviour of interest occurs, or should we wait for some period of time? Should we reinforce every correct behaviour, or should we reinforce only a portion of correct responses?

To obtain the *fast acquisition* of some response, continuous and immediate reinforcement should be used—that is, the reinforcer should be applied every time the behaviour of interest occurs, and it should be applied without delay after each occurrence. Many conditions exist in which the fast acquisition of responses is desirable. These include correcting the behaviour

© David Anderson

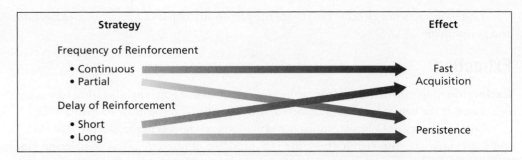

EXHIBIT 2.3
Summary of reinforcement strategies and their effects.

of "problem" employees, training employees for emergency operations, and dealing with unsafe work behaviours. Consider the otherwise excellent performer who tends to be late for work. Under pressure to demote or fire this good worker, the boss might sensibly attempt to positively reinforce instances of prompt attendance with compliments and encouragement. To modify the employee's behaviour as quickly as possible, the supervisor might station herself near the office door each morning to supply these reinforcers regularly and immediately.

You might wonder when one would not want to use a continuous, immediate reinforcement strategy to change organizational behaviour. Put simply, behaviour that individuals learn under such conditions tends not to persist when reinforced less frequently or stopped. Intuitively, this should not be surprising. For example, under normal conditions, operating the power switch on your iPod is continuously and immediately reinforced by music. If the system develops a short circuit and fails to produce music, your switch-operating behaviour will cease very quickly. In the example in the preceding paragraph, the need for fast learning justified the use of continuous, immediate reinforcement. Under more typical circumstances, we would hope that prompt attendance could occur without such close attention.

Behaviour tends to be *persistent* when it is learned under conditions of partial and delayed reinforcement. That is, it will tend to persist under reduced or terminated reinforcement when not every instance of the behaviour is reinforced during learning or when some time period elapses between its enactment and reinforcement. In most cases, the supervisor who wishes to reinforce prompt attendance knows that he or she will not be able to stand by the shop door every morning to compliment the crew's timely entry. Given this constraint, the supervisor should compliment prompt attendance occasionally, perhaps later in the day. This should increase the persistence of promptness and reduce the employees' reliance on the boss's monitoring.

Let's recap. Continuous, immediate reinforcement facilitates fast learning, and delayed, partial reinforcement facilitates persistent learning (see Exhibit 2.3). Notice that it is impossible to maximize both speed and persistence with a single reinforcement strategy. Also, many responses in our everyday lives cannot be continuously and immediately reinforced, so in many cases it pays to sacrifice some speed in learning to prepare the learner for this fact of life. All this suggests that managers have to tailor reinforcement strategies to the needs of the situation. Often, managers must alter the strategies over time to achieve effective learning and maintenance of behaviour. For example, the manager training a new employee should probably use a reinforcement strategy that is fairly continuous and immediate (whatever the reinforcer). Looking over the employee's shoulder to obtain the fast acquisition of behaviour is appropriate. Gradually, however, the supervisor should probably reduce the frequency of reinforcement and perhaps build some delay into its presentation to reduce the employee's dependency on his or her attention.

REDUCING THE PROBABILITY OF BEHAVIOUR

Thus far in our discussion of learning, we have been interested in *increasing* the probability of various work behaviours, such as attendance or good performance. Both positive and negative reinforcement can accomplish this goal. However, in many cases, we encounter learned behaviours that we wish to *stop* from occurring. Such behaviours are detrimental to the operation of the organization and could be detrimental to the health or safety of an individual employee.

There are two strategies that can reduce the probability of learned behaviour: extinction and punishment.

Extinction

Extinction simply involves terminating the reinforcement that is maintaining some unwanted behaviour. If the behaviour is not reinforced, it will gradually dissipate or be extinguished.

Consider the case of a bright, young marketing expert who was headed for the "fast track" in his organization. Although his boss, the vice-president of marketing, was considering him for promotion, the young expert had developed a very disruptive habit—the tendency to play comedian during department meetings. The vice-president observed that this wisecracking was reinforced by the appreciative laughs of two other department members. He proceeded to enlist their aid to extinguish the joking. After the vice-president explained the problem to them, they agreed to ignore the disruptive one-liners and puns. At the same time, the vice-president took special pains to positively reinforce constructive comments by the young marketer. Very quickly, joking was extinguished, and the young man's future with the company improved.[46]

This example illustrates that extinction works best when coupled with the reinforcement of some desired substitute behaviour. Remember that behaviours that have been learned under delayed or partial reinforcement schedules are more difficult to extinguish than those learned under continuous, immediate reinforcement. Ironically, it would be harder to extinguish the joke-telling behaviour of a committee member who was only partially successful at getting a laugh than of one who was always successful at getting a laugh.

Punishment

Punishment involves following an unwanted behaviour with some unpleasant, aversive stimulus. In theory, when the actor learns that the behaviour leads to unwanted consequences, this should reduce the probability of the response. Notice the difference between punishment and negative reinforcement. In negative reinforcement a nasty stimulus is *removed* following some behaviour, increasing the probability of that behaviour. With punishment, a nasty stimulus is *applied* after some behaviour, *decreasing* the probability of that behaviour. If a boss criticizes her assistant after seeing her use the office phone for personal calls, we expect to see less of this activity in the future. Exhibit 2.4 compares punishment with reinforcement and extinction.

Using Punishment Effectively

In theory, punishment should be useful in eliminating unwanted behaviour. After all, it seems unreasonable to repeat actions that cause us trouble. Unfortunately, punishment has some unique characteristics that often limit its effectiveness in stopping unwanted activity.

© wavebreakmedia/Shutterstock.com

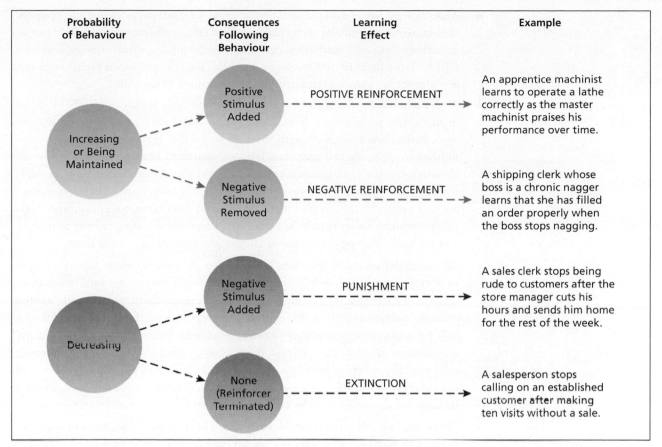

Probability of Behaviour	Consequences Following Behaviour	Learning Effect	Example
Increasing or Being Maintained	Positive Stimulus Added	POSITIVE REINFORCEMENT	An apprentice machinist learns to operate a lathe correctly as the master machinist praises his performance over time.
	Negative Stimulus Removed	NEGATIVE REINFORCEMENT	A shipping clerk whose boss is a chronic nagger learns that she has filled an order properly when the boss stops nagging.
Decreasing	Negative Stimulus Added	PUNISHMENT	A sales clerk stops being rude to customers after the store manager cuts his hours and sends him home for the rest of the week.
	None (Reinforcer Terminated)	EXTINCTION	A salesperson stops calling on an established customer after making ten visits without a sale.

EXHIBIT 2.4
Summary of learning effects.

First, while punishment provides a clear signal as to which activities are inappropriate, it does not by itself demonstrate which activities should *replace* the punished response. Reconsider the executive who chastises her assistant for making personal calls at the office. If the assistant makes personal calls only when she has caught up on her work, she might legitimately wonder what she is supposed to be doing during her occasional free time. If the boss fails to provide substitute activities, the message contained in the punishment may be lost.

Both positive and negative reinforcers specify which behaviours are appropriate. Punishment indicates only what is not appropriate. Since no reinforced substitute behaviour is provided, punishment only temporarily suppresses the unwanted response. When surveillance is removed, the response will tend to recur. Constant monitoring is very time consuming, and individuals become amazingly adept at learning when they can get away with the forbidden activity. The assistant will soon learn when she can make personal calls without detection. The moral here is clear: *Provide an acceptable alternative for the punished response.*

A second difficulty with punishment is that it has a tendency to provoke a strong emotional reaction on the part of the punished individual.[47] This is especially likely when the punishment is delivered in anger or perceived to be unfair. Managers who try overly hard to be patient with employees and then finally blow up risk over-emotional reactions. So do those who tolerate unwanted behaviour on the part of their employees and then impulsively decide to make an example of one individual by punishing him or her. Managers should be sure that their own emotions are under control before punishing, and they should generally avoid punishment in front of observers.[48] Because of the emotional problems involved in the use of punishment, some organizations downplay its use in discipline systems. They give employees who have committed infractions *paid* time off to think about their problems.

In addition to providing correct alternative responses and limiting the emotions involved in punishment, there are several other principles that can increase the effectiveness of punishment.

- *Make sure the chosen punishment is truly aversive.* Organizations frequently "punish" chronically absent employees by making them take several days off work. Managers sometimes "punish" ineffective performers by requiring them to work overtime, which allows them to earn extra pay. In both cases, the presumed punishment may actually act as a positive reinforcer for the unwanted behaviour.

- *Punish immediately.* Managers frequently overlook early instances of rule violations or ineffective performance, hoping that things will "work out."[49] This only allows these behaviours to gain strength through repetition. If immediate punishment is difficult to apply, the manager should delay action until a more appropriate time and then reinstate the circumstances surrounding the problem behaviour. For example, the bank manager who observes her teller exhibiting inappropriate behaviour might ask this person to remain after work. She should then carry out punishment at the teller's window rather than in her office, perhaps demonstrating correct procedures and then role-playing a customer to allow the employee to practise them.

- *Do not reward unwanted behaviours before or after punishment.* Many supervisors join in horseplay with their employees until they feel it is time to get some work done. Then, unexpectedly, they do an about-face and punish those who are still "goofing around." Sometimes, managers feel guilty about punishing their employees for some rule infraction and then quickly attempt to make up with displays of good-natured sympathy or affection. For example, the boss who criticizes her assistant for personal calls might show up an hour later with a gift. Such actions present employees with extremely confusing signals about how they should behave, since the manager could be unwittingly reinforcing the very response that he or she wants to terminate.

- *Do not inadvertently punish desirable behaviour.* This happens commonly in organizations. The manager who does not use all his capital budget for a given fiscal year might have the department's budget for the next year reduced, punishing the prudence of his employees. Government employees who "blow the whistle" on wasteful or inefficient practices might find themselves demoted.[50] University professors who are considered excellent teachers might be assigned to onerous, time-consuming duty on a curriculum committee, cutting into their class preparation time.

In summary, punishment can be an effective means of stopping undesirable behaviour. However, managers must apply it very carefully and deliberately to achieve this effectiveness. In general, reinforcing correct behaviours and extinguishing unwanted responses are safer strategies for managers than the frequent use of punishment.

LO 2.7

Explain social cognitive theory and discuss *observational learning, self-efficacy beliefs,* and *self-regulation.*

Social cognitive theory (SCT). Emphasizes the role of cognitive processes in learning and in the regulation of people's behaviour.

SOCIAL COGNITIVE THEORY

It has perhaps occurred to you that learning and behaviour sometimes take place without the conscious control of positive and negative reinforcers by managers. People often learn and behave through their own volition and self-influence. Thus, human behaviour is not simply due to environmental influences. Rather, people have the cognitive capacity to regulate and control their own thoughts, feelings, motivation, and actions. Unlike operant learning theory, **social cognitive theory (SCT)** emphasizes the role of *cognitive processes* in regulating people's behaviour.

According to SCT, people learn by observing the behaviour of others. Individuals also manage their own behaviour by thinking about the consequences of their actions (forethought), setting performance goals, monitoring their performance and comparing it to their goals, and rewarding themselves for goal accomplishment. People also develop beliefs about their abilities through their interaction with the environment, and these beliefs influence their thoughts and behaviour.[51]

Social cognitive theory suggests that human behaviour can best be explained through a system of *triadic reciprocal causation,* in which personal factors and environmental factors work together and interact to influence people's behaviour. In addition, people's behaviour can also influence personal factors and the environment. Thus, SCT complements operant learning in explaining how people learn and organizational behaviour.[52]

According to Albert Bandura, who is responsible for the development of social cognitive theory, SCT involves three key components: observational learning, self-efficacy beliefs, and self-regulation.[53]

Observational Learning

Besides directly experiencing consequences, people also learn by observing the behaviour of others. For instance, after experiencing just a couple of executive committee meetings, a newly promoted vice-president might look like an "old pro," bringing appropriate materials to the meeting, asking questions in an approved style, and so on. How can we account for such learning?

Observational learning is the process of observing and imitating the behaviour of others. With observational learning, learning occurs by observing or imagining the behaviour of others (models), rather than through direct personal experience.[54] Generally, observational learning involves examining the behaviour of others, seeing what consequences they experience, and thinking about what might happen if we were to act the same way. If we expect favourable consequences, we might imitate the behaviour. Thus, the new vice-president doubtless modelled his behaviour on that of the more experienced peers on the executive committee. But has reinforcement occurred here? It is *self-reinforcement* that occurs in the observational learning process. For one thing, it is reinforcing to acquire an understanding of others who are viewed positively. In addition, we are able to imagine that the reinforcers that the model experiences will come our way when we imitate his or her behaviour. Surely, this is why we imitate the behaviour of sports heroes and entertainers, a fact that advertisers capitalize on when they choose them to endorse products.

What kinds of models are likely to provoke the greatest degree of imitation? In general, attractive, credible, competent, high-status people stand a good chance of being imitated. In addition, it is important that the model's behaviour provoke consequences that are seen as positive and successful by the observer.

Finally, it helps if the model's behaviour is vivid and memorable—bores do not make good models.[55] In business schools, it is not unusual to find students who have developed philosophies or approaches that are modelled on credible, successful, high-profile business leaders. Popular examples include Microsoft's Bill Gates and former General Electric CEO Jack Welch, both of whom have been the object of extensive coverage in the business and popular press.

The extent of observational learning as a means of learning in organizations suggests that managers should pay more attention to the process. For one thing, managers who operate on a principle of "Do as I say, not as I do" will find that what they do is more likely to be imitated, including undesirable behaviours such as expense account abuse. Also, in the

Observational learning.
The process of observing and imitating the behaviour of others.

© E.D. Torial / Alamy Stock Photo

Observational learning involves observing and imitating the behaviour of others.

■ RESEARCH FOCUS

THE TRICKLE-DOWN EFFECTS OF ABUSIVE MANAGEMENT

There is strong evidence that abusive behaviour by supervisors (e.g., telling a subordinate that his or her thoughts or feelings are stupid or putting the subordinate down in front of others) results in negative employee attitudes, behaviours, and psychological health. But why are supervisors abusive, and why does their abusive behaviour make their employees more likely to be abusive?

To find out, Mary Bardes Mawritz and colleagues tested a model of the trickle-down effects of abusive manager behaviour that suggests that abusive behaviour in organizations can flow downward from higher levels of management to lower-level employees. The model predicts that employees will be negatively impacted by abusive manager behaviour through their direct supervisor's abusive behaviour.

The model and predictions are based on social cognitive theory and observational learning, positing that abusive behaviour at higher levels in an organization is role modelled by those at lower levels (i.e., supervisors and employees). In other words, supervisors role model the abusive behaviour of their managers and engage in similar abusive behaviour with their own employees. Employees then model their supervisor's abusive behaviour which leads to work-group interpersonal deviance (i.e., employees' abusive behaviours directed at other organizational members).

The researchers also predicted that the effect of abusive supervisor behaviour on work-group interpersonal deviance would be especially strong when the work-group climate was hostile (i.e., characterized by consistent acrimonious, antagonistic, and suspicious feelings within the work group). In a hostile climate, work-group members feel envious, less trusting, and aggressive toward others.

Employees in different organizations completed a survey and asked four of their co-workers and their immediate supervisor to also complete the survey. As expected, abusive manager behaviour was positively related to abusive supervisor behaviour, and abusive supervisor behaviour was positively related to work-group interpersonal deviance. In other words, supervisors who have managers who are abusive toward them are abusive toward their employees, who in turn treat each other in an abusive manner.

The results also indicated that employees were more likely to model their supervisor's abusive behaviour when the climate of their work group was hostile. When the work-group climate was non-hostile it actually reversed the negative effects of abusive supervisor behaviour on work-group interpersonal deviance. Thus, employees in a non-hostile work climate did not model their supervisor's abusive behaviour.

These results indicate that employees observe and imitate their supervisor's negative and abusive behaviours. Thus, managers and supervisors should act as positive role models because their behaviours, both positive and negative, will trickle down and be observed and imitated by their employees.

Source: Based on Bardes Mawritz, M., Mayer, D.M., Hoobler, J.M., Wayne, S.J., & Marinova, S.V. (2012). A trickle-down model of abusive supervision. *Personnel Psychology, 65,* 325–357.

absence of credible management models, workers might imitate dysfunctional peer behaviour if peers meet the criteria for strong models. For example, one study found that the antisocial behaviour of a work group was a significant predictor of an individual's antisocial workplace behaviour. Thus, an individual's antisocial workplace behaviour can be shaped, in part, through the process of observation.[56] Furthermore, as described in the Research Focus: *The Trickle-Down Effects of Abusive Management,* abusive behaviour on the part of managers and supervisors can lead to abusive behaviour among employees. On a more positive note, well-designed performance appraisal and reward systems permit organizations to publicize the kind of organizational behaviour that should be learned and imitated.

Self-Efficacy Beliefs

Self-efficacy beliefs.
Beliefs people have about their ability to successfully perform a specific task.

While observational learning may have helped the vice-president learn how to behave in an executive committee meeting, you may have wondered what made him so confident. Was he not full of self-doubt and worried that he would fail? This belief is known as self-efficacy. **Self-efficacy beliefs** refer to beliefs people have about their ability to successfully perform a specific task. At this point, it is important to note the difference between task-specific

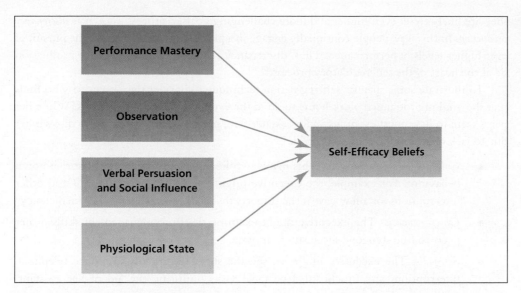

EXHIBIT 2.5
Determinants of self-efficacy beliefs.

self-efficacy and some of the general personality traits discussed earlier in the chapter. In particular, unlike self-esteem and general self-efficacy, which are general personality traits, self-efficacy is a task-specific cognitive appraisal of one's ability to perform a specific task. Furthermore, people can have different self-efficacy beliefs for different tasks. For example, the vice-president might have strong self-efficacy for conducting an executive committee meeting, but low self-efficacy for doing well in a course on organizational behaviour![57]

Because self-efficacy is a cognitive belief rather than a stable personality trait, it can be changed and modified in response to different sources of information. As shown in Exhibit 2.5, self-efficacy beliefs are influenced by one's experiences and success performing the task in question (performance mastery), observation of others performing the task, verbal persuasion and social influence, and one's physiological or emotional state. Thus, the self-efficacy of the vice-president could have been strengthened by observing the behaviour of others during meetings, by encouragement from peers that he would do a great job, and perhaps by his own sense of comfort and relaxation rather than feelings of anxiety and stress while attending meetings. Finally, his mastery displayed during the meeting is also likely to have further strengthened his self-efficacy beliefs.

Self-efficacy beliefs are important because they influence the activities people choose to perform, the amount of effort and persistence they devote to a task, affective and stress reactions, and job performance.[58] In the case of the vice-president, his strong sense of self-efficacy beliefs obviously contributed to his ability to perform like an "old pro" at the meeting.

Self-Regulation

In much of this chapter we have been concerned with how organizations and individual managers can use learning principles to manage the behaviour of organizational members. However, according to social cognitive theory, employees can use learning principles to manage their *own* behaviour, making external control less necessary. This process is called **self-regulation**.[59]

How does self-regulation occur? You will recall that observational learning involved factors such as observation of models, imagination, imitation, and self-reinforcement. Individuals can use these and similar techniques in an intentional way to control their own behaviour. The basic process involves observing one's own behaviour (i.e., self-observation), comparing the behaviour with a standard (i.e., self-evaluation), and rewarding oneself if the behaviour meets the standard (i.e., self-reinforcement). A key part of the process is people's pursuit of self-set goals that guide their behaviour. When a discrepancy exists between one's goals and performance, individuals are motivated to modify their behaviour in the pursuit of goal attainment, a process known as *discrepancy reduction*. When individuals attain their goals,

Self-regulation. The use of learning principles to regulate one's own behaviour.

they are likely to set even higher and more challenging goals, a process known as *discrepancy production*. In this way, people continually engage in a process of setting goals in the pursuit of ever higher levels of performance. Thus, discrepancy reduction and discrepancy production lie at the heart of the self-regulatory process.[60]

To illustrate some specific self-regulation techniques, consider the executive who finds that she is taking too much work home to do in the evenings and over weekends. While her peers seem to have most evenings and weekends free, her own family is ready to disown her due to lack of attention! What can she do?[61]

- *Collect self-observation data.* This involves collecting objective data about one's own behaviour. For example, the executive might keep a log of phone calls and other interruptions for a few days if she suspects that these contribute to her inefficiency.

- *Observe models.* The executive might examine the time-management skills of her peers to find someone successful to imitate.

- *Set goals.* The executive might set specific short-term goals to reduce telephone interruptions and unscheduled personal visits, enlisting the aid of her assistant, and using self-observation data to monitor her progress. Longer-term goals might involve four free nights a week and no more than four hours of work on weekends.

- *Rehearse.* The executive might anticipate that she will have to educate her co-workers about her reduced availability. So as not to offend them, she might practise explaining the reason for her revised accessibility.

- *Reinforce oneself.* The executive might promise herself a weekend at the beach with her family the first time she gets her take-home workload down to her target level.

Research has found that self-regulation can improve learning and result in a change in behaviour. For example, one study showed how a self-regulation program was used to improve work attendance among unionized maintenance employees. Those who had used over half their sick leave were invited by the human resources department to participate in an eight-week self-regulation program. Compared with a group of employees who did not attend the program, the employees who were exposed to the program achieved a significant improvement in attendance, and they also felt more confident (i.e., higher self-efficacy) that they would be able to come to work when confronted with various obstacles to attendance.[62] In another study, training in self-regulation was found to significantly improve the sales performance of a sample of insurance salespeople.[63] Self-regulation programs have been successful in changing a variety of work behaviours and are an effective method of training and learning.[64]

ORGANIZATIONAL LEARNING PRACTICES

LO 2.8

Describe the following organizational learning practices: *organizational behaviour modification, employee recognition programs*, and *training and development programs*.

Organizational behaviour modification (O.B. Mod).
The systematic use of learning principles to influence organizational behaviour.

We began our discussion of learning by defining learning and describing learning content, and then we focused on theories of how people learn. In this final section, we review a number of organizational learning practices including organizational behaviour modification, employee recognition programs, and training and development programs.

Organizational Behaviour Modification

Organizational behaviour modification (O.B. Mod) involves the systematic use of learning principles to influence organizational behaviour. For example, consider how one company used organizational behaviour modification through the reinforcement of safe working behaviour in a food-manufacturing plant. At first glance, accidents appeared to be chance events or wholly under the control of factors such as equipment failures. However, the researchers felt that accidents could be reduced if specific safe working practices could be identified and reinforced. These practices were identified with the help of past accident reports and advice from

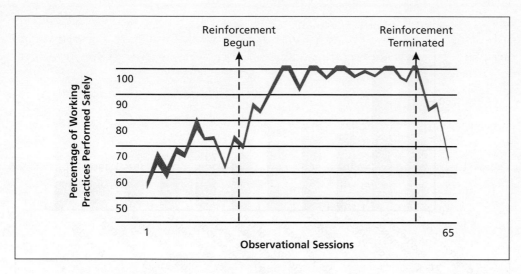

EXHIBIT 2.6
Percentage of safe working practices achieved with and without reinforcement.
Source: Adapted from Komaki, J., et al. (1978, August). A behavioral approach to occupational safety: Pinpointing and reinforcing safe performance in a food manufacturing plant. *Journal of Applied Psychology, 63* (4), 439. Copyright © 1978 by American Psychological Association.

supervisors. Systematic observation of working behaviour indicated that employees followed safe practices only about 74 percent of the time. A brief slide show was prepared to illustrate safe versus unsafe job behaviours. Then, two reinforcers of safe practices were introduced into the workplace. The first consisted of a feedback chart that was conspicuously posted in the workplace to indicate the percentage of safe behaviours observers noted. This chart included the percentages achieved in observational sessions before the slide show, as well as those achieved every three days after the slide show. A second source of reinforcement was supervisors, who were encouraged to praise instances of safe performance that they observed. These interventions were successful in raising the percentage of safe working practices to around 97 percent almost immediately. The plant moved from last to first place in the company standings and received a safety plaque from the company "in recognition of successfully working 280 000 hours without a disabling injury" over a period of 10 months. (See Exhibit 2.6.)[65]

In addition to improvements in safety, O.B. Mod has also been found to have a positive effect on improving work attendance and task performance. The effects on task performance, however, tend to be stronger in manufacturing than in service organizations. As well, money, feedback, and social recognition have all been found to be effective forms of positive reinforcement. Although money has been found to have stronger effects on performance than social recognition and performance feedback, the use of all three together has the strongest effect on task performance. Research has also found that the effect of money on performance is greater when it is provided systematically through O.B. Mod compared to a routine pay-for-performance program.[66]

Employee Recognition Programs

A popular example of an organizational learning practice that uses positive reinforcement is employee recognition programs. **Employee recognition programs** are formal organizational programs that publicly recognize and reward employees for specific behaviours. Exhibit 2.7 shows some of the most popular types of employee recognition programs.

Many companies in Canada have some form of employee recognition program, and employees in the best companies to work for in Canada believe that they receive adequate recognition beyond compensation for their contributions and accomplishments. To be effective, however, a formal employee recognition program must specify (a) how a person will be recognized, (b) the type of behaviour being encouraged, (c) the manner of the public acknowledgement, and (d) a token or icon of the event for the recipient. A key part of an employee recognition program is public acknowledgement. Thus, a financial reward for good performance would not qualify as an employee recognition program if it was not accompanied by some form of public praise and recognition.[67]

Employee recognition programs. Formal organizational programs that publicly recognize and reward employees for specific behaviours.

EXHIBIT 2.7
Types of recognition programs.

Source: Based on Trends in Employee Recognition/WorldatWork. (2008, August 11). Service awards most popular. *Canadian HR Reporter, 21* (14), 4.

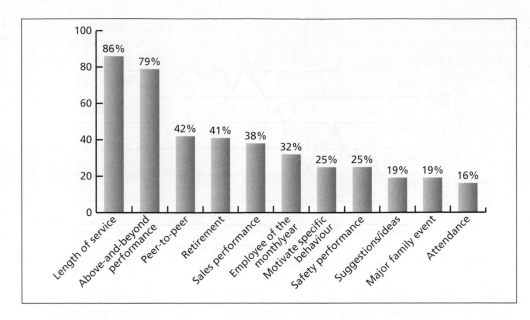

Peer recognition programs. Formal programs in which employees can publicly acknowledge, recognize, and reward their co-workers for exceptional work and performance.

An increasing number of organizations have begun to implement a new kind of recognition program called peer recognition. **Peer recognition programs** are formal programs in which employees can publicly acknowledge, recognize, and reward their co-workers for exceptional work and performance. For example, IT/NET Ottawa Inc. has a peer-to-peer recognition program called "My Thanks," in which employees are encouraged to acknowledge co-workers' exceptional work by sending them a cash-valued gift certificate. The value of the certificate is determined by the person who is awarding it and it can be done any time and as often as employees choose to recognize a co-worker.

With the increasing use of technology, many organizations have begun to use social recognition platforms for peer recognition. For example, RBC launched a social recognition platform that allows all of its employees to send a thank you message to another employee. The program has had a positive effect on employee engagement and loyalty. Pharmaceutical company Eli Lilly Canada implemented an online recognition program in which employees choose a value from the company's value statement that represents an action being rewarded, and then allocate points to the person being rewarded. Employees can use their points for items such as electronics and gift cards.[68] Before continuing, consider You Be the Manager: *Calgary International Airport's YYC Miles Recognition Program* on the following page.

Employee recognition programs have been found to result in individual and organizational outcomes, including job satisfaction, performance and productivity, and lower turnover.[69] One study compared a public recognition program for improving work attendance

with several other interventions. Employees with perfect attendance for an entire month had their names posted with a gold star for that month. At the end of each quarter, employees with no more than two absences received a personal card notifying and congratulating them. In addition, at the end of the year there was a plant-wide meeting to recognize good attendance, and small engraved mementos were awarded to employees who had perfect attendance during the entire year. The results indicated that employees had favourable perceptions of the program and that the program resulted in a decrease in absenteeism.[70] A survey of 26 000 employees in 31 organizations in the United States found that companies that invest the most in recognition programs have more than triple the profits of those that invest the least.[71]

Training and Development Programs

Training and development are among the most common types of formal learning in organizations. Training refers to planned organizational activities that are designed to facilitate knowledge and skill acquisition to change behaviour and improve performance on one's current job; development focuses on future job responsibilities.[72] Employees learn a variety of skills by attending formal training and development programs. In addition to teaching

Training and development. Training is planned organizational activities that are designed to facilitate knowledge and skill acquisition to change behaviour and improve performance on one's current job; development focuses on future job responsibilities.

◼ YOU BE THE MANAGER

Calgary International Airport's YYC Miles Recognition Program

The Calgary Airport Authority is a not-for-profit corporation that is responsible for the management, maintenance, operation, and development of Calgary International Airport and Springbank Airport.

Several years ago, a volunteer employee committee developed a recognition program in response to a low score to a question on an employee engagement survey. The low score was for the statement "I feel my contributions are recognized and valued."

According to Cynthia Tremblay, Vice President of Human Resources at the Calgary Airport Authority, "We did some employee focus groups [asking], 'What can we do to help address this issue?' and a recognition program was the idea that came out of that. It is very much employee-driven," she says.

The program, called the YYC Miles recognition program—based on the Calgary airport locator code—allows employees to recognize their co-workers for going above and beyond their role, such as helping a confused passenger find his/her way around the airport.

When the program was launched, the employee committee made a promotional video based on the TV show *The Office* and showed it to all employees at a company retreat. To make sure they are continually promoting the program, the committee writes regular articles about it for the company newsletter and mentions it in meetings.

What do you think of the Calgary Airport's YYC Miles recognition program? You be the manager.

Employees at the Calgary International Airport can recognize their co-workers for going above and beyond their role.

Questions

1. How would you design the YYC Miles peer recognition program if you were using the principles of operant learning theory?

2. How should peer recognition programs be designed to be most effective?

To learn more about the YYC miles recognition program, see The Manager's Notebook.

Sources: Based on Silliker, A. (2011, October 10). Calgary airport's recognition program—YYC Miles—takes flight. *Canadian HR Reporter, 24* (17), 19; information on Calgary International Airport (www.calgaryairport.com).

employees technical skills required to perform their jobs, training and development programs also teach employees non-technical skills such as how to work in teams, how to provide excellent customer service, and how to understand and appreciate cultural diversity.

Effective training and development programs include many of the principles of learning described earlier in the chapter, such as positive reinforcement, feedback, observational learning, strengthening employees' self-efficacy beliefs, and self-regulation. One of the most widely used and effective methods of training is **behaviour modelling training** (BMT), which is based on the observational learning component of social cognitive theory and involves the following steps:[73]

Behaviour modelling training (BMT). One of the most widely used and effective methods of training, involving five steps based on the observational learning component of social cognitive theory.

- Describe to trainees a set of well-defined behaviours (skills) to be learned.
- Provide a model or models displaying the effective use of those behaviours.
- Provide opportunities for trainees to practise using those behaviours.
- Provide feedback and social reinforcement to trainees following practice.
- Take steps to maximize the transfer of those behaviours to the job.

Many organizations have used behavioural modelling training to develop supervisory, communications, sales, and customer service skills. A review of BMT research concluded that it has a positive effect on learning, skills, and job behaviour. The effects on behaviour were greatest when trainees were instructed to set goals and when rewards and sanctions were used in the trainees' work environment.[74]

THE MANAGER'S NOTEBOOK

Calgary International Airport's YYC Miles Recognition Program

1. According to operant learning theory, rewards should be contingent on specific behaviours that are of interest to the organization, such as attendance, innovation, or productivity. Thus, the program must be designed so that there is a clear connection between recognition and rewards, and specific employee behaviours that are important for the organization. This is especially a concern in peer recognition programs, because employees are responsible for choosing co-workers for recognition, and such choices should not simply be based on who is most liked or who has the most friends in the company. The program also has to consider individual preferences for reinforcers. Rewards will not have a reinforcing effect if they are not desired by employees. Therefore, it is important that a variety of rewards be available to suit individual preferences. With respect to the YYC Miles program, each employee is given 1000 points per month to recognize co-workers. When an employee sees a co-worker go above and beyond his role, he or she fills out a form online stating the reason for the recognition and how many points the co-worker is receiving—which is completely at the discretion of the employee. One point is equivalent to one cent and points can be accumulated for a wide range of gifts from the YYC Miles online catalogue, starting at 1250 points for a movie ticket all the way up to 450 000 points for an LCD TV.

2. Peer recognition programs should be designed in the same manner as formal employee recognition programs. To be effective, they should specify (a) how a person will be recognized, (b) the type of behaviour being encouraged, (c) the manner of the public acknowledgement, and (d) a token or icon of the event for the recipient. Because the employee's peers are responsible for deciding who will be recognized, careful attention should be given to how this is done to ensure that the process is fair and that the expected behaviour has been demonstrated. With respect to the YYC Miles program, the committee monitors the program to make sure people are nominating each other for appropriate things. When filling out a recognition form, employees need to specify which of five pillars of excellence the co-worker displayed—dedication, responsible investing, great partnerships, operational efficiency, or Western hospitality.

LEARNING OBJECTIVES CHECKLIST

2.1 *Personality* is the relatively stable set of psychological characteristics that influences the way we interact with our environment. It has more impact on behaviour in weak situations than in strong situations. According to the *dispositional approach*, stable individual characteristics influence people's attitudes and behaviours. The *situational approach* argues that characteristics in the work environment influence people's attitudes and behaviour. The *interactionist approach* posits that organizational behaviour is a function of both dispositions and the situation.

2.2 The Five-Factor Model consists of five basic dimensions of personality: *extraversion*, *emotional stability/neuroticism*, *agreeableness*, *conscientiousness*, and *openness to experience*. Research has found that the Big Five are related to job performance, motivation, job satisfaction, and career outcomes. *Locus of control* refers to individuals' beliefs about the location of the factors that control their behaviour. High internals believe that the opportunity to control their own behaviour resides within themselves, while high externals believe that external forces determine their behaviour. *Self-monitoring* is the extent to which people observe and regulate how they appear and behave in social settings and relationships. *Self-esteem* is the degree to which a person has a positive self-evaluation.

2.3 People who are high on *positive affectivity* experience positive emotions and moods and tend to view the world in a positive light, including themselves and other people. People who are high on *negative affectivity* experience negative emotions and moods and tend to view the world in a negative light. *Proactive personality* is a stable

personal disposition that reflects a tendency to take personal initiative across a range of activities and situations and to effect positive change in one's environment. *General self-efficacy* (GSE) is a general trait that refers to an individual's belief in his or her ability to perform successfully in a variety of challenging situations. *Core self-evaluations* refer to a broad personality concept that consists of more specific traits.

2.4 *Learning* occurs when practice or experience leads to a relatively permanent change in behaviour potential. The content of learning in organizations consists of practical, intrapersonal and interpersonal skills, and cultural awareness.

2.5 *Operant learning* occurs as a function of the consequences of behaviour. If some behaviour is occurring regularly or increasing in probability, you can assume that it is being reinforced. If the reinforcer is added to the situation following the behaviour, it is a *positive reinforcer*. If the reinforcer is removed from the situation following the behaviour, it is a *negative reinforcer*. If some behaviour decreases in probability, you can assume that it is being either extinguished or punished. If the behaviour is followed by no observable consequence, it is being extinguished; that is, some reinforcer that was maintaining the behaviour has been terminated. If the behaviour is followed by the application of some unpleasant consequence, it is being punished. For punishment to be effective, it is important that the emotions involved be limited and that correct alternative responses be provided.

2.6 Behaviour is learned quickly when it is reinforced immediately and continuously. Behaviour tends to be persistent under reduced or terminated reinforcement when it is learned under conditions of delayed or partial reinforcement.

2.7 According to social cognitive theory, people have the cognitive capacity to regulate and control their own thoughts, feelings, motivation, and actions. The main components of social cognitive theory are observational learning, self-efficacy beliefs, and self-regulation. *Observational learning* is the process of imitating others. *Self-efficacy beliefs* refer to beliefs that one can successfully perform specific tasks and are influenced by performance mastery, observation of others performing the same tasks, verbal persuasion and social influence, and physiological arousal. *Self-regulation* occurs when people use learning principles to manage their own behaviour, thus reducing the need for external control. Aspects of self-regulation include collecting self-observation data, observing models, goal setting, rehearsing, and using self-reinforcement.

2.8 Organizational learning practices include organizational behaviour modification, employee recognition programs, and training and development programs. *Organizational behaviour modification* is the systematic use of learning principles to influence organizational behaviour. Companies have successfully used it to improve employees' attendance, task performance, and workplace safety. *Employee recognition programs* are formal organizational programs that publicly recognize and reward employees for specific behaviours. *Training programs* involve planned organizational activities that are designed to facilitate knowledge and skill acquisition and to change behaviour and improve performance on one's current job, while *development* focuses on future job responsibilities.

DISCUSSION QUESTIONS

1. Describe a situation in which you think an employer could use organizational behaviour modification and an employee recognition program to improve or correct employee behaviour. Can you anticipate any dangers in using these approaches?

2. A supervisor in a textile factory observes that one of her employees is violating a safety rule that could result in severe injury. What combination of reinforcement, punishment, and extinction could she use to correct this behaviour? What does social cognitive theory suggest that she do to correct the behaviour?

3. Describe a job in which you think an employee recognition program might be an effective means for changing and improving employee behaviour. Explain how you would design the program and how you would use principles from operant learning theory and social cognitive theory.

4. Do you think that organizations should base their hiring decisions on applicants' personalities? What are the advantages and disadvantages of doing this? If an organization were to do this, what personality characteristics do you think they should focus on when assessing and choosing applicants?

5. Employee of the month (EOM) programs are one of the most popular forms of recognition in organizations. However, there is some evidence that such programs are not effective and can even have detrimental effects, such as sabotage and unhealthy competition. Based on the material presented in this chapter, why do you think that the typical EOM program is not effective, and how should EOM programs be designed to make them more effective?

INTEGRATIVE DISCUSSION QUESTIONS

1. Refer to the material in Chapter 1 on Mintzberg's managerial roles and consider how personality might be a factor in how effectively a manager performs each role. Discuss the relationships among the Big Five personality dimensions, locus of control, self-monitoring, self-esteem, proactive personality, and general self-efficacy with each of the managerial roles.

2. Discuss how each of the organizational learning practices described in the chapter can be used by organizations to deal effectively with the contemporary management concerns discussed in Chapter 1.

ON-THE-JOB CHALLENGE QUESTION

18 000 Collisions

It has been reported that since 2009, 5300 Toronto Transit Commission (TTC) drivers have been involved in almost 18 000 collisions, with nearly 5000 deemed preventable by the transit commission's own investigators. This works out to an average of 3564 collisions a year. One bus driver was involved in 30 crashes in the past five years, and 181 drivers have been in 10 collisions or more. While some accidents are bound to happen, city councillors and the head of the TTC union expressed alarm at the number of drivers with double-digit collision figures.

According to Councillor Denzil Minnan-Wong, "That's really troubling. When they're having this many accidents, we have to understand the nature of those accidents, why they're having those accidents, and whether some of those drivers should still be behind the wheel of a TTC vehicle."

When a bus or streetcar gets into an accident, a TTC manager goes to the scene and determines whether the collision was "preventable" or "not preventable." On average, a little more than a quarter of accidents received the "preventable" designation.

What do you think is the reason for so many TTC accidents? Is it due to driver personality or characteristics of the work environment? Use learning theory to explain what the TTC can do to reduce the number of accidents. What organizational learning practices might help to lower the number of accidents? Explain your answers.

Source: Based on Andrew-Gee, E. (2014, July 4). TTC in 18 000 crashes since 2009. *Toronto Star*, A1, A4

EXPERIENTIAL EXERCISE

Proactive Personality Scale

Do you have a proactive personality? To find out, answer the 17 questions below as frankly and honestly as possible, using the following response scale:

1–Disagree very much

2–Disagree moderately

3–Disagree slightly

4–Neither agree or disagree

5–Agree slightly

6–Agree moderately

7–Agree very much

____ 1. I am constantly on the lookout for new ways to improve my life.

____ 2. I feel driven to make a difference in my community, and maybe the world.

____ 3. I tend to let others take the initiative to start new projects.

____ 4. Wherever I have been, I have been a powerful force for constructive change.

____ 5. I enjoy facing and overcoming obstacles to my ideas.

____ 6. Nothing is more exciting than seeing my ideas turn into reality.

____ 7. If I see something I don't like, I fix it.

____ 8. No matter what the odds, if I believe in something I will make it happen.

____ 9. I love being a champion for my ideas, even against others' opposition.

____ 10. I excel at identifying opportunities.

____ 11. I am always looking for better ways to do things.

____ 12. If I believe in an idea, no obstacle will prevent me from making it happen.

____ 13. I love to challenge the status quo.

____ 14. When I have a problem, I tackle it head-on.

____ 15. I am great at turning problems into opportunities.

____ 16. I can spot a good opportunity long before others can.

____ 17. If I see someone in trouble, I help out in any way I can.

Source: Republished with permission of John Wiley & Sons, Inc., from Bateman, T.S., & Crant, J.M. (1993). The proactive component of organizational behavior: A measure and correlates. *Journal of Organizational Behavior, 14,* 103–118; permission conveyed through Copyright Clearance Center, Inc.

Scoring and Interpretation

You have just completed the Proactive Personality Scale developed by Thomas Bateman and J. Michael Crant. To obtain your score, first subtract your response to question 3 from 8. For example, if you gave a response of 7 to question 3, give yourself a 1 (8 minus 7). Then add up your scores to all 17 items. Your total should be somewhere between 17 and 119. The higher you scored, the more proactive your personality is—you feel that you can change things in your environment.

The average score of 134 first-year MBA students with full-time work experience was 90.7. Thus, these people tended to see themselves as very proactive. In this research, people with a proactive personality tended to report more extracurricular and service activities and major personal achievements that involve making constructive changes to the world around them.

General Self-Efficacy

Want to learn about your general self-efficacy? Answer the eight questions below as frankly and honestly as possible, using the following response scale:

1–Strongly disagree

2–Disagree

3–Neither agree nor disagree

4–Agree

5–Strongly agree

____ 1. I will be able to achieve most of the goals that I have set for myself.

____ 2. When facing difficult tasks, I am certain that I will accomplish them.

____ 3. In general, I think that I can obtain outcomes that are important to me.

____ 4. I believe I can succeed at most any endeavour to which I set my mind.

____ 5. I will be able to successfully overcome many challenges.

____ 6. I am confident that I can perform effectively on many different tasks.

____ 7. Compared to other people, I can do most tasks very well.

____ 8. Even when things are tough, I can perform quite well.

Source: Chen, G., Gully, S.M., & Eden, D. (2001). Validation of a new general self-efficacy scale. *Organizational Research Methods, 4,* 62–83. Copyright © 2001 by SAGE Publications, Inc. Reprinted by permission of SAGE Publications, Inc.

Scoring and Interpretation

You have just completed the New General Self-Efficacy Scale developed by Gilad Chen, Stanley M. Gully, and Dov Eden. To obtain your general self-efficacy (GSE) score, add up your scores to all 8 items and divide by 8. Your score should be somewhere between 1 and 5. The higher your score, the greater your general self-efficacy.

GSE enables individuals to effectively adapt to novel and adverse environments and can help to explain motivation and performance in a variety of work contexts. The average score of 323 undergraduate students enrolled in several upper-level psychology courses was 3.87.

The Core Self-Evaluations Scale (CSES)

To find out about your core self-evaluations, answer the 12 questions below as frankly and honestly as possible, using the following response scale:

1–Strongly disagree

2–Disagree

3–Neither agree nor disagree

4–Agree

5–Strongly agree

____ 1. I am confident I get the success I deserve in life.

____ 2. Sometimes I feel depressed.

____ 3. When I try, I generally succeed.

____ 4. Sometimes when I fail I feel worthless.

____ 5. I complete tasks successfully.

____ 6. Sometimes I do not feel in control of my work.

____ 7. Overall, I am satisfied with myself.

____ 8. I am filled with doubts about my competence.

____ 9. I determine what will happen in my life.

____ 10. I do not feel in control of my success in my career.

_____ 11. I am capable of coping with most of my problems.

_____ 12. There are times when things look pretty bleak and hopeless to me.

Source: Republished with permission of John Wiley & Sons, Inc., from Judge, T.A., Erez, A., Bono, J.E., & Thoresen, C.J. (2003). The core self-evaluations scale: Development of a measure. *Personnel Psychology, 56*, 303–313; permission conveyed through Copyright Clearance Center, Inc.

Scoring and Interpretation

You have just completed the Core Self-Evaluations Scale (CSES) developed by Timothy Judge, Amir Erez, Joyce Bono, and Carl Thoresen. To obtain your score, first subtract your response to questions 2, 4, 6, 8, 10, and 12 from 6. For example, if you gave a response of 1 to question 2, give yourself a 5 (6 minus 1). Then add up your scores to all 12 items and divide by 12. Your score should be somewhere between 1 and 5. The higher your score, the higher your core self-evaluations.

Core self-evaluations (CSE) are a broad personality concept that reflect evaluations people hold about themselves and their self-worth. Core self-evaluations consist of self-esteem, general self-efficacy, locus of control, and neuroticism. The average score of undergraduate students in two studies was 3.83 and 3.78. Scores on the CSES have been found to be positively related to job satisfaction, job performance, and life satisfaction.

To facilitate class discussion and your understanding of proactive personality, GSE, and CSE, form a small group with several other members of the class and consider the following questions:

1. Each group member should present their proactive personality, GSE, and CSE scores. Next, consider the extent to which each member has been involved in extracurricular and service activities and in personal accomplishments that involved making changes to their circumstances and how they have adapted to novel and difficult situations. Each member should also consider how satisfied they are with a current or previous job and how satisfied they are with their life (1 = not satisfied at all to 5 = very satisfied). Have students with higher proactive personality scores been more involved in extracurricular and service activities? What about personal accomplishments and constructive change? Have students with higher GSE scores been more effective in adapting to novel and difficult situations? And are students with higher CSE scores more satisfied with their current or a previous job, and are they more satisfied with their life? (Alternatively, members of the class may write their proactive personality, GSE, and CSE scores, extracurricular and service activities, personal accomplishments, experiences adapting to novel and difficult situations, and job and life satisfaction on a piece of paper and hand it in to the instructor. The instructor can then write the responses on the board for class discussion.)

2. When are a proactive personality, GSE, and CSE most likely to be beneficial? When are they least likely to be beneficial?

3. Do you think organizations should hire people based on whether they have a proactive personality and on their GSE and CSE scores? What are the implications of this?

4. Based on your proactive personality, GSE, and CSE scores, what have you learned about yourself and your behaviour in different situations?

5. How can your knowledge of your proactive personality, GSE, and CSE scores help you at school and at work? What can you do to become more proactive? What can you do to strengthen your GSE and CSE?

CASE INCIDENT

Playing Hooky

Several years ago, a *Toronto Star* investigation reported that construction and maintenance workers who were supposed to be working at Toronto public schools were spending their mornings at Tim Hortons, drinking in bars, and even kissing in cars. One worker was spotted delivering pamphlets to houses and offering to perform odd jobs for pay on school board time. Some workers did not show up at jobs even though time cards indicated they did. The workers submitted time sheets and were paid their wages as if they had put in a full day's work.

In some cases, workers signed in to work at a school, then announced that they had to go get "parts," and were later discovered by Toronto District School Board officials drinking in a bar. In another case, a male worker was found in a board vehicle with a female "fooling around," according to a board source. In the case of the pamphlets, board sources say a worker was using board time to distribute flyers advertising his services for odd jobs, apparently using board equipment.

Following the *Toronto Star* investigation, the school board cracked down on wasteful activities and fired or disciplined 150 construction and maintenance workers over allegations of fraud and time theft. The school board also installed GPS tracking devices on all board vehicles and began to bundle jobs, so that a worker would spend the full day at one school rather than doing a series of small jobs at different schools.

Sources: Donovan, K., & Welsh, M. (2012, June 22). School workers playing hooky. *Toronto Star,* A1, A4; Donovan, K. (2014, June 18). TDSB cracking down on fraud and waste in maintenance. *Toronto Star,* http://www.thestar.com/news/investigations/2014/06/18/tdsb_cracking_down_on_fraud_and_waste_in_maintenance.html.

1. Based on what you know about learning theory, explain why the workers engaged in inappropriate behaviours during work hours and why they were not doing what they were supposed to be doing.

2. Use operant learning theory and social cognitive theory to explain what can be done to eliminate undesirable behaviours and increase desirable behaviours. What approach do you recommend?

3. What do you think of the way the school board responded to the *Toronto Star* investigation? Do you think it will eliminate the problems? Explain your answer.

4. Do you think that organizational learning practices can be used to change employee behaviours? Consider the potential of organizational behaviour modification, employee recognition programs, and training and development. What practices would you recommend and why?

CASE STUDY

IVEY | Publishing

Roaring Dragon Hotel: A Second Attempt at Modernization

Source: Stephan Grainger wrote this case solely to provide material for class discussion. The author does not intend to illustrate either effective or ineffective handling of a managerial situation. The author may have disguised certain names and other identifying information to protect confidentiality. Richard Ivey School of Business Foundation prohibits any form of reproduction, storage or transmission without its written permission. Reproduction of this material is not covered under authorization by any reproduction rights organization. To order copies or request permission to reproduce materials, contact Ivey Publishing,

Richard Ivey School of Business Foundation, The University of Western Ontario, London, Ontario, Canada, N6A 3K7; phone (519) 661-3208; fax (519) 661-3882; e-mail cases@ivey.uwo.ca. Copyright © 2012, Richard Ivey School of Business Foundation. Version: 2012-12-17.

One time permission to reproduce granted by Richard Ivey School of Business Foundation on October 14, 2015.

The Roaring Dragon Hotel (RDH) was constructed in south-west China in the 1950s as a state owned enterprise (SOE) and was viewed primarily as a premier guest house for visiting dignitaries and officials, Communist party members, and guests. As for many SOE hotels at that time, historically the RDH had the characteristics of overstaffing, archaic work practices and technology, unsystematic production systems and a dysfunctional motivation system unrelated to performance. In 2000, the RDH board and provincial government made their first attempt at modernizing the hotel,[1] but the internationalization process failed due to a number of problems including the collision[2]

1 S. Grainger, *Organisational Guanxi in a State Owned Enterprises in South-west China,* VDM Verlag, Saarbrücken, Germany, 2005.

2 D.E. Warren, T.W. Dunfee and N. Li, "Social Exchange in China: The Double-Edged Sword of Guanxi," *Journal of Business Ethics,* 55, 2004, pp. 355–372.

between cultural characteristics like *guanxi* and *mianzi*.[3] A disastrous outcome caused the provincial government and RDH stakeholders to lose heart, momentum and the motivation to modernize. After 2000, as the Chinese market economy continued to develop, a number of human resource problems emerged at the RDH. Solving these problems became a priority. Six years later, the RDH board and new joint venture owner had recovered enough confidence to attempt the service standard upgrade for a second time. In 2005, the global company, Premium Hotel Services (PHS), was contracted to complete the task and found that the quality and retention of older employees, increased turnover of younger staff, and Chinese economic policies were impeding progress. How can the Premium Hotel Services and RDH solve these problems so the hotel can emerge as a five-star operation?

BACKGROUND

Up until the late 1990s, the RDH management had little concern for profit and primarily focused its efforts on serving and meeting the needs of officials and party members. The majority of managers were untrained, and internal family cliques within the hotel departments were prominent. These were built upon trust and they were known to use the hotel's resources to ameliorate the wants of clique members. Clique insiders were able to conduct their own private external business during working hours and use the hotel's facilities free of charge. Government officials provided protection for well connected employees, and nepotism was common. Again, powerful *guanxi* was an important tool in facilitating these outcomes.

In 1999, after a long history of government-funded losses, the local provincial government and RDH board decided they had to make the hotel profitable, meet the demands of the encroaching Chinese market economy, and modernize the

management practices for the expected growth in tourism in China's south-west. In its first attempt, the local government invited the Hotel International (HI) group to take over the management and upgrade of the RDH in April 1999. The experiment failed to convert the RDH from a state-owned hotel into a competitive, market-driven hotel. The bad experience greatly discouraged the RDH board and local government from developing a modern, market-driven hotel. After HI's departure, the pre-HI Chinese management team came back in to resume its management. The patient Chinese managers had been waiting in the wings, watching every mistake HI had made, and now felt they were resuming their rightful place managing the RDH.

The local government's experience with HI had not been completely in vain, though. During this nine-month period, the Chinese deputy departmental managers had documented all HI's international operations and practices. With this documentation secured, could the Chinese employees and managers reach the same level of service quality as HI was renowned for in its global operations?

The Second Attempt in 2005

After a five-year wait and a new co-ownership arrangement with a private, state-controlled tobacco company, the RDH board had renewed confidence to modernizing the hotel a second time. The goal was to contract a proven international company able to successfully raise the skills of existing staff to a five-star standard of quality. With the scars of the HI experience still present in its mind, the RDH board took care to choose an international service training company based on its track record rather than its brand. The board understood that the quality of expertise and training had to be at the cutting edge to produce the desired outcome.

In 2004, two other new five-star hotels were completed in the region, with two more under construction and one under planning and development. With competition growing, developing the human resources to deliver a five-star service experience for RDH clientele was paramount. With the number of domestic and international business and holiday clients visiting the region continuing to grow, the board realized an old section of the hotel required demolition and replacement by a new five-star facility.

An agreement was finalized in January 2005 to demolish the old section and replace it with a modern,

---

3 *Guanxi*-a personal relationship between two people facilitating the exchange of favours. L.W. Pye, *Chinese Negotiating Style,* Quorum Books, Westport, Connecticut, 1992; Mianzi - the respectability a person can claim for themselves from others by virtue of the relative position and status they have in their social network. S. Grainger, "The Privatisation of China's SOE: How Is It Affecting the Production of Guanxi?" *International Journal of Management and Enterprise Development,* Vol. 10 No. 2/3, 2011, pp. 156–172.

five-storey, state-of-the-art facility. The opening of the newly constructed wing was planned for November 2006. This new facility would feature a large open entry hall complemented by two five-star restaurants and a business centre, two large modern banquet halls on the first floor, an executive club and tea house on the second floor, and a heated indoor swimming pool on the third floor, adjacent to the spa and beauty centre. This new facility would complement the adjacent 16-storey accommodation wing built in 1992, which contained 392 quality guest rooms.

After extensive research, the RDH committee chose to commence discussions with Premium Hotel Services (PHS), a mid-sized global hotel training company. After negotiations were complete, the committee contracted PHS to come to the hotel and upgrade all the employees' skills between October 2005 and October 2006 to prepare for the re-opening of the new premises in November 2006. During the period of the PHS contract, the hotel would be closed for reconstruction, providing the opportunity for the employees to partake in full-time training.

The first representatives of the PHS team arrived in September 2005, and their initial goal was to assess the hotel's existing standards of service and design a training program targeted to produce a five-star outcome. The PHS would not be able to hire any new employees. Many department managers remaining at the RDH had endured the experience with HI in 1999/2000 and had since been promoted to head their respective departments. Many of the employees made redundant by HI in 1999/2000, especially those with strong *guanxi* with powerful officials, had managed to get their jobs back six months later. Consequently, some of the former SOE work practices had also crept back into the hotel operations after 2000.

The RDH board had implemented a new rule in late 2004 to replace all departmental managers older than 45 years of age. This appeared to be an injection of youth into the RDH management and culture, as only one of the existing department managers or their deputies retained a position of seniority. In reality, however, the former departmental heads had merely been moved sideways and still had some influence on the younger managers. None of the incumbent departmental managers from before 2004 had been made redundant or asked to retire, partially due to the loss of face, or *mianzi,* it would have generated.

After a month on site, the PHS leadership team completed the design of an intense training program it thought would effectively develop a human resource team able to produce the five-star standard of hotel service. Soon after, the PHS's training team began to arrive from a variety of locations around the world and the intense training sessions commenced.

After a short time, the PHS staff noticed two interesting conditions in the workplace that had the potential to create new problems not previously experienced at the RDH. In the developing Chinese market economy, changing government labour policies were enabling employees to change jobs more easily as well as their location from one city to another. Under the former planned-economy conditions, this had been forbidden or very difficult to do. The increasing demand for quality hotel employees to staff the growing number of new hotels in the region heralded the emergence of Chinese-style head hunting for quality hotel staff. Rival hotels' HR departments targeted talented employees from private, state-owned and semi-private accommodation providers for recruitment. Smart recruiters enjoyed great success in attracting skilled and trained hotel employees by offering them significantly higher salaries and benefits.

Another new phenomenon concerned the emerging one-child generation. This generation had not experienced previously difficult living and working conditions under SOE or China's planned economy. They wanted opportunities and a clear career path (see Exhibit 1). They were confident enough to change jobs if their existing conditions were not suitable or if they were made an attractive offer. The previous generations had survived much tougher working conditions and fewer education opportunities and had cherished their SOE job-for-life status.

The one-child generation's attitude was significantly different, best summed up during an interview with the RDH housekeeping departmental manager in 2011. She wanted to encourage her son to take a position at the RDH but commented that her son "did not want to work in a hotel." He wanted to work in a place "where he could be served." This comment perhaps reflects the profile of a son coming from a semi-wealthy background and the choices he enjoyed in having two parents, four grandparents, and no competition for attention from any fellow siblings. This generation's expectations reflected the attitudes of the growing Chinese middle class.

EXHIBIT 1
Nation's workers unhappy with jobs
Source: Wang Huazhong, China Daily, July 10, 2012, p. 9.

"China's workers are among the least likely in Asia to say their jobs are ideal, despite China having one of the regions lowest unemployment rates . . . . Providing an adequate number of jobs in China alone is not enough to fulfill the career expectations of its workforce or to sustain and grow a productive labour pool .... This likely means that many Chinese workers will not be looking for just any job but a great job – one that offers a good workplace where they can use their unique talents. . . .

Concerns have been raised about the high expectations of Chinese job seekers, with several incidents highlighting the extreme pressures placed on well-educated students with master's degrees or doctorates unable to find work.

In October 2009, a graduate student who had been unemployed for over a year jumped off a building of China West Normal University with his degree certificate in his arms and died at the scene.

Du Hanqi, a psychologist with Mind Care Counseling said job seekers' views of value have changed as the market has become increasingly competitive in the fast-growing economy. "Years ago people were willing to build their career gradually from a low stating point. . . . Peer pressure meant graduates were looking for high-powered jobs without working their way up the career ladder."

Incomes: Urban, rural residents see their wallets bulge

"The growth of urban and rural incomes has maintained good momentum, with rural incomes growing quicker than the urban equivalents. In the first half of the year, the per capita disposable income of urban residents was 12,509 yuan (~$2000 US), a year-on-year growth of 13.3percent, which was 2.1 percentage points higher than that in the same period of 2011.

The per capita cash income of rural residents was 4,303 yuan (~$825), up by 16.1 percent year-on-year. Wang Jun, a senior economist ... said the government's increasing investment in agricultural production and rural infrastructure has played a role in lifting up the rural incomes [and increases in income could be seen across the board in rural and urban income]. The average monthly income of migrant workers also rose to 2,200 yuan, up by 14.9 percent year-on-year."

Source: Wang Zhouqlong, *China Daily* – Business, July 14 15, 2012, p. 10.

The social environment in the vicinity of the RDH was also changing. Nearby, one could now find clubs presenting live modern music every night to young customers from one-child backgrounds that proudly exhibited their dyed hair, modern clothing, and fashion trends. In contrast, during the day, hundreds of older Chinese people from large families, some clad in former blue Communist Party clothing, would gather in the vicinity of the nearby park to play traditional acoustic music on a variety of instruments, play chess-like games, and enjoy old style dances and customs together. At the turn of the century, these contrasting characteristics could not have been imagined.

Collectively, these conditions meant the RDH human resources department had to work harder to retain their good employees and to attract young recruits. Younger employees now had less concern about having a secure position with a famous five-star hotel like the RDH. They were more interested in making money, and short-term outcomes were their priority.

The PHS trainers noticed these conditions and, in discussions with the GM, suggested the RDH human resources department must take care to place reliable dedicated employees with proven ability, the right attitude, and problem solving skills in key decision-making positions. They noted the increased demands on the RDH HR team and were concerned the older managers might not have the capability to produce five-star outcomes. The long-serving RDH general manager said he would take care of this concern. However, he failed to raise the issue as a priority among his fellow directors and departmental managers.

With most of the PHS training contract complete, only two PHS trainers remained when the RDH re-opened with new facilities in November 2006. Not long after, a number of problems began to surface and two critical errors affected the RDH's status and placed the spotlight firmly on the quality of the hotel's human resources.

A Japanese couple were given the keys to their "Superior Room" on the eighth level and, rather than being guided and accompanied to their room by a bell boy, were allowed to check in unaccompanied. They found the room had not been made up after the previous guests had checked out late earlier in the day. The housekeeping department head was notified and had to take urgent action to find the guests another room. The guests had to wait for a further 45 minutes in the hotel lobby for the problem to be solved. As they had just arrived from a long flight and had paid for a superior suite at 1950rmb (US$330) per night, the couple was not happy and wrote a letter of complaint to the RDH general manager. An older employee had failed to complete the relevant paper work correctly earlier in the day. Since it occurred at a demanding period with a significant number of new guests arriving, the supervisor had been called away and had not been present to double check the documentation.

A week later, three meals were delivered to the wrong room on the executive level. As the room was empty, no guests answered the door. The food and beverage staff member returned to the ground floor with the meals to the kitchen and no one was sure of what to do. A female employee, a recent transfer from the supply department, had written the wrong room number on the delivery sheet. The supervisor was again taking care of another urgent duty and by the time she returned, nearly 40 minutes had passed and the food was cold. The guests in the room had rung the front desk to ask why it was taking so long. The food

had to be prepared again, resulting in a 90-minute wait for the guests from the time they placed their order. These guests included a senior executive from petroleum giant Sinopec. The GM received another formal complaint about this matter. Even though the RDH general manager went to the room to personally apologize and give the guests a complimentary bottle of French wine, the damage to the hotel's reputation was complete. A week later, Sinopec cancelled the bookings for its annual conference at the RDH and rebooked with a competitor.

Long-term customers began to notice some small idiosyncrasies in the housekeeping and bellboy services. After the daily servicing of their rooms, customers noticed that some days two sachets of coffee, two of sugar and two of powdered milk would be left in their side table drawer. The next day, there would be four of each and then a week later, the whole set of sachets may have been forgotten. In a two- or three-star hotel, this detail may have been forgiven, but not at the now five-star RDH. This kind of variability was not tolerated in a five-star hotel, and the problem seemed to be the complacent attitude of the small number of younger staff, coupled with greater demands on the supervisory staff.

In the first three months of 2007, the attraction of higher salaries and a promotion had caused three senior managers and 14 junior and middle-level staff to leave and take up new positions locally, in Beijing, Nanjing, and Shanghai. The employee turnover was expected to intensify in late 2007, when two more five-star hotels would open in the city and continue placing pressure on human resources.

These worsening conditions and problems were increasingly significant. Several senior government officials and RDH board members decided to call an urgent meeting to decide on how to proceed. The board and officials had to decide whether they should contact the PHS senior management to gain its input and also whether the PHS team would be contracted to stay on the site until these problems were resolved.

QUESTIONS

1. What are the main problems at the Roaring Dragon Hotel? Use operant learning theory and social cognitive theory to explain why the hotel is having these problems.

2. Do you think it was a good idea to train all of the hotels employees? How effective was the

training? Did the training result in a five-star standard of hotel service? Explain your answer.

3. What behaviours need to be maintained or increased, and what behaviours should be reduced or eliminated? Be specific about the

behaviours that need to be improved and those that need to be eliminated.

4. Use the concepts and principles from operant learning theory and social cognitive theory to explain how the hotel can address its problems. What are some of the most important things it should do?

5. What organizational learning practices might be effective for changing employee behaviours and improving the quality of the hotel's service? Con-sider the potential of organizational behaviour modification, employee recognition programs, and additional training and development. Explain how you would implement each of these practices and predict their potential effectiveness.

6. What advice would you give the Roaring Dragon Hotel on how to address the problems they are having? What do they need to do to achieve a five-star standard of quality? Explain your answer.

3 PERCEPTION, ATTRIBUTION, AND DIVERSITY

LEARNING OBJECTIVES

After reading Chapter 3, you should be able to:

3.1 Define *perception*, and discuss some of the general factors that influence perception.

3.2 Explain *social identity theory* and *Bruner's model* of the perceptual process.

3.3 Describe the main biases in person perception.

3.4 Describe how people form *attributions* about the causes of behaviour and various biases in attribution.

3.5 Discuss the concepts of *workforce diversity* and valuing diversity and how racial, ethnic, religious, gender, age, and LGBT *stereotypes* affect organizational behaviour, and what organizations can do to manage diversity.

3.6 Define *trust* perceptions and *perceived organizational support*, and describe *organizational support theory*.

3.7 Discuss person perception and perceptual biases in human resources.

RBC

Douglas Dow has been legally blind since birth; Lawrence Young was born with a severe vision impairment; Courtney Sheldon lost her eyesight shortly after her 22nd birthday. All three are successfully employed in good careers. And while they have all faced challenges in their day-to-day work, their challenges have been greatly lessened by their employer, RBC.

RBC is one of the largest banks in Canada and the world. In addition to Canada and the United States, RBC has offices in 40 other countries and employs more than 79 000 full- and part-time employees. The organization has a strong commitment to recruiting, hiring, and developing persons with disabilities as part of its overall diversity strategy. In 2014, persons with disabilities made up 4.6 percent of RBC's workforce.

The commitment to persons with disabilities begins during the recruitment process when a person applies for a job at RBC. According to Norma Tombari, director of global diversity, human resources at RBC, "We always ensure that a person with a disability who has particular needs can be accommodated during the interview process, so our recruiters always will ask that question as a normal

course of business." The company also has a "Pursue Your Potential" recruitment program that links job candidates with RBC's diversity coordinators, who work to understand their interests and capabilities and how they can better apply and market themselves within RBC.

Once someone is hired, RBC has a number of programs and initiatives to provide mentoring, coaching, networking, and professional development. For example, a new initiative is Persons with Disabilities @ RBC community on RBC Connect, a social site and discussion forum. It's a community that goes beyond just connecting people in a conversation because it does provide resources, tools, and tips and information ... it's a great way to learn and connect in a very, very comfortable setting," said Tombari. The site also has information on myths and misconceptions around disabilities, mental health, and visible and invisible disabilities.

There is also a REACH employee resource group that enables employees to connect with each other and provide peer support, coaching, and mentoring; a Diversity Dialogue Reciprocal Mentoring Program, which links diverse employees and senior leaders to facilitate

RBC has been named one of Canada's Best Diversity Employers and one of the Best Workplaces in Canada.

mutual learning opportunities; and web-based training for managers and colleagues. And in partnership with REACH, RBC organized a communication campaign called "Let's Talk About It" to increase all employees' awareness of disability issues.

"That's the other side of the equation," says Tombari, "If you want to be inclusive and be supportive and help develop (talent), we do all have some learning to do ourselves to better understand what the right approaches are."

But perhaps the most important element that RBC offers is a supportive, inclusive culture, says Douglas Dow. "People with disabilities, we have unique needs, and RBC meets those needs by providing a supportive environment and one that addresses the needs of visible and invisible disabilities. It's such a wonderful feeling to work for a company that's always striving to find innovative ways to help people with disabilities beyond the technology."

In addition to its programs for persons with disabilities, RBC also has diversity programs for women, visible minorities, Aboriginal and Indigenous peoples, and LGBT people. RBC has been named as one of Canada's Best Diversity Employers in recognition of its initiatives to attract, develop, and retain a diversity of employees and has also been named one of the Best Workplaces in Canada. At RBC, they like to say, "Diversity Works Here" because it is the right thing to do and the smart thing to do.[1]

Why does RBC have a strong commitment to recruiting, hiring, and developing persons with disabilities as well as diversity programs for women, visible minorities, Aboriginal and Indigenous peoples, and LGBT people? What effect do diversity programs have on employee attitudes and behaviour? And why do organizations often harbour false assumptions and myths about women, visible minority employees, older workers, and persons with disabilities? These are the kinds of questions that we will attempt to answer in this chapter. First, we will define *perception* and examine how various aspects of the perceiver, the object or person being perceived, and the situation influence perception. Following this, we will present a theory and model of the perceptual process and we will consider some of the perceptual tendencies that we employ in forming impressions of people and attributing causes to their behaviour. We will then examine the role of perception in achieving a diverse workforce and how to manage diversity, perceptions of trust, perceived organizational support, and person perception in human resources. In general, you will learn that perception and attribution influence who gets into organizations, how they are treated as members, and how they interpret this treatment.

WHAT IS PERCEPTION?

LO 3.1

Define *perception*, and discuss some of the general factors that influence perception.

Perception. The process of interpreting the messages of our senses to provide order and meaning to the environment.

Perception is the process of interpreting the messages of our senses to provide order and meaning to the environment. Perception helps us sort out and organize the complex and varied input received by our senses of sight, smell, touch, taste, and hearing. The key word in this definition is *interpreting*. People frequently base their actions on the interpretation of reality that their perceptual system provides, rather than on reality itself. If you perceive your pay to be very low, you might seek employment in another firm. The reality—that you are the best-paid person in your department—will not matter if you are unaware of the fact. However, to go a step further, you might be aware that you are the best-paid person and *still* perceive your pay as low in comparison with that of the CEO of your organization or your ostentatious next-door neighbour.

Some of the most important perceptions that influence organizational behaviour are the perceptions that organizational members have of each other. Because of this, we will concentrate on person perception in this chapter.

COMPONENTS OF PERCEPTION

Perception has three components—a perceiver, a target that is being perceived, and some situational context in which the perception is occurring. Each of these components influences the perceiver's impression or interpretation of the target (Exhibit 3.1).

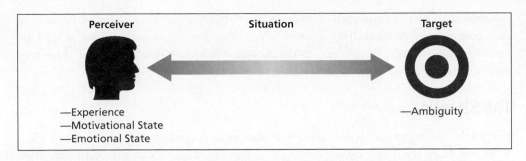

EXHIBIT 3.1
Factors that influence perception.

The Perceiver

The perceiver's experience, needs, and emotions can affect his or her perceptions of a target.

One of the most important characteristics of the perceiver that influences his or her impressions of a target is experience. Past experiences lead the perceiver to develop expectations, and these expectations affect current perceptions. An interesting example of the influence of experience on perception is shown in Exhibit 3.2. It illustrates the perceptions of 268 managerial personnel in a Fortune 500 company concerning the influence of race and gender on promotion opportunities. As you can see, Caucasian men were much less likely to perceive race or gender barriers to promotion than were Caucasian women, non-Caucasian men, and non-Caucasian women.⁷ Remember, these people were ostensibly viewing the same "objective" promotion system.

Frequently, our needs unconsciously influence our perceptions by causing us to perceive what we wish to perceive. Research has demonstrated that perceivers who have been deprived of food will tend to "see" more edible things in ambiguous pictures than will well-fed observers. Similarly, lonely university students might misperceive the most innocent actions of members of the opposite sex as indicating interest in them.

Emotions, such as anger, happiness, or fear, can influence our perceptions. We have all had the experience of misperceiving the innocent comment of a friend or acquaintance when we were angry. For example, a worker who is upset about not getting a promotion might perceive the consolation provided by a co-worker as gloating condescension. On the other hand, consider the worker who does get a promotion. She is so happy that she fails to notice how upset her co-worker is that he was not the one promoted.

In some cases, our perceptual system serves to defend us against unpleasant emotions. This phenomenon is known as **perceptual defence**. We have all experienced cases in which we "see what we want to see" or "hear what we want to hear." In many of these instances, our perceptual system is working to ensure that we do not see or hear things that are threatening.

Perceptual defence.
The tendency for the perceptual system to defend the perceiver against unpleasant emotions.

EXHIBIT 3.2
Ratings of the perceived importance of race and gender for promotion opportunity in executive jobs.
Note: Table values are the percentages saying that race or gender was important or very important. N = number of cases.
Source: Reprinted with permission of the publisher from *Cultural diversity in organizations: Theory, research, & practice.* © 1993 by T. Cox Jr. Berrett-Koehler Publishers, Inc., San Francisco, CA. All rights reserved. www.bkconnection. com.

The Target

Perception involves interpretation and the addition of meaning to the target, and ambiguous targets are especially susceptible to interpretation and addition. Perceivers have a need to resolve such ambiguities. You might be tempted to believe that providing more information about the target will improve perceptual accuracy. Unfortunately, this is not always the case. Writing clearer memos might not always get the message across. Similarly, assigning

	Caucasian Men (N = 123)	Caucasian Women (N = 76)	Non-Caucasian Men (N = 52)	Non-Caucasian Women (N = 17)
Race	26	62	75	76
Gender	31	87	71	82

minority workers to a prejudiced manager will not always improve his or her perceptions of their true abilities. As we shall see shortly, the perceiver does not or cannot always use all the information provided by the target. In these cases, a reduction in ambiguity might not be accompanied by greater accuracy.

The Situation

Every instance of perception occurs in some situational context, and this context can affect what one perceives. The most important effect that the situation can have is to add information about the target. Imagine a casual critical comment about your performance from your boss the week before she is to decide whether or not you will be promoted. You will likely perceive this comment very differently from the way you would if you were not up for promotion. Also, a worker might perceive a racial joke overheard on the job very differently before and after racial strife has occurred in the plant. In both of these examples, the perceiver and the target are the same, but the perception of the target changes with the situation.

LO **3.2**

Explain *social identity theory* and *Bruner's model* of the perceptual process.

Social identity theory. A theory that states that people form perceptions of themselves based on their personal characteristics and memberships in social categories.

PERSONAL INVENTORY ASSESSMENT

Learn About Yourself
Self-Awareness Assessment

SOCIAL IDENTITY THEORY

In the previous section, we described how characteristics of the perceiver, the target, and the situation influence the perceiver's interpretation of the target. In this section, we discuss social identity theory to help us understand how this happens. Let's begin with a simple question: "Who are you?" Chances are that when you answer this question you say things like "student," "Canadian," "accountant," and so on. In other words, you respond in terms of various social categories to which you believe you belong. This is what social identity theory is all about.

According to **social identity theory**, people form perceptions of themselves based on their personal characteristics and memberships in social categories. As a result, our sense of self is composed of a personal identity and a social identity. Our *personal identity* is based on our unique personal characteristics, such as our interests, abilities, and traits. *Social identity* is based on our perception that we belong to various social groups, such as our gender, nationality, religion, occupation, and so on. Personal and social identities help us answer the question "Who am I?"

But why and how do we do this? As individuals, we categorize ourselves and others to make sense of and understand the social environment. The choice of specific categories depends on what is most salient and appropriate to the situation. For example, we might define people in a meeting according to their job titles. Once a category is chosen, we tend to see members of that category as embodying the most typical attributes of that category, or what are called "prototypes." Similarly, once we locate ourselves in a social category we tend to perceive ourselves as embodying the prototypical characteristics of the category. In this way, we develop a sense of who and what we are, as well as our values, beliefs, and ways of thinking, acting, and feeling.[3]

In addition to forming self-perceptions based on our social memberships, we also form perceptions of others based on their memberships in social categories. This is because social identities are relational and comparative. In other words, we define members of a category relative to members of other categories. For example, the category of professor is meaningful in relation to the category of student. As the comparison category changes, so will certain aspects of the focal social identity. So when the authors of this text are in the classroom, they are perceived as professors by their students and as having whatever attributes the students attribute to professors. However, one of the authors of this text lives next door to a university student who perceives him not as a professor but as a "baby boomer." Notice how her social categorization differs from those of the students in the classroom. As a result, her perception of the author will also differ, because the attributes and characteristics associated with the generation category of a "baby boomer" differ from those of the occupational category of "professor."

Social identity theory helps us understand how the components of the perceptual system operate in the formation of perceptions. We perceive people in terms of the attributes and characteristics that we associate with their social category relative to other categories. Thus, your perception of others is a function of how you categorize yourself (e.g., student) and your target (e.g., professor). If the situation changes, so might the categorization and the relation between the perceiver and the target. For example, in a hospital, medical students might be perceived as doctors by nurses and patients, but in the classroom they are perceived as medical students by their professors.[4]

Because people tend to perceive members of their own social categories in more positive and favourable ways than those who are different and belong to other categories, social identity theory is useful for understanding stereotyping and discrimination, topics we discuss later in this chapter. Now let's turn to a more detailed understanding and model of the perceptual process.

A MODEL OF THE PERCEPTUAL PROCESS

In the previous section, we described how we form perceptions of ourselves and others based on social categories. But exactly how does the perceiver go about putting together the information contained in the target and the situation to form a picture of the target? Respected psychologist Jerome Bruner has developed a model of the perceptual process that can provide a useful framework for this discussion.[5] According to Bruner, when the perceiver encounters an unfamiliar target, the perceiver is very open to the informational cues contained in the target and the situation surrounding it. In this unfamiliar state, the perceiver needs information on which to base perceptions of the target and will actively seek out cues to resolve this ambiguity. Gradually, the perceiver encounters some familiar cues (note the role of the perceiver's experience here) that enable her or him to make a crude categorization of the target, which follows from social identity theory. At this point, the cue search becomes less open and more selective. The perceiver begins to search out cues that confirm the categorization of the target. As this categorization becomes stronger, the perceiver actively ignores or even distorts cues that violate initial perceptions (see the left side of Exhibit 3.3). This does not mean that an early categorization cannot be changed. It does mean, however, that it will take a good many contradictory cues before one recategorizes the target, and that these cues will have to overcome the expectations that have been developed.

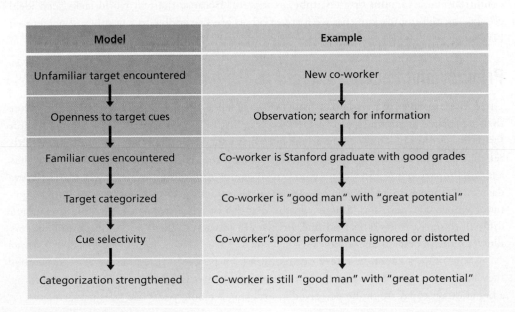

Model	Example
Unfamiliar target encountered	New co-worker
Openness to target cues	Observation; search for information
Familiar cues encountered	Co-worker is Stanford graduate with good grades
Target categorized	Co-worker is "good man" with "great potential"
Cue selectivity	Co-worker's poor performance ignored or distorted
Categorization strengthened	Co-worker is still "good man" with "great potential"

EXHIBIT 3.3
Bruner's model of the perceptual process and an example.

Let's clarify your understanding of Bruner's perceptual model with an example, shown on the right side of Exhibit 3.3. Imagine that a woman who works as an engineer for a large aircraft company is trying to size up a newly hired co-worker. Since he is an unfamiliar target, she will be especially open to any cues that might provide information about him. In the course of her cue search, she discovers that he has a master's degree in aeronautical engineering from Stanford University and that he graduated with top grades. These are familiar cues because she knows that Stanford is a top school in the field, and she has worked with many excellent Stanford graduates. She then proceeds to categorize her new co-worker as a "good man" with "great potential." With these perceptions, she takes a special interest in observing his performance, which is good for several months. This increases the strength of her initial categorization. Gradually, however, the engineer's performance deteriorates for some reason, and his work becomes less and less satisfactory. This is clear to everyone except the other engineer, who continues to see him as adequate and excuses his most obvious errors as stemming from external factors beyond his control.

Bruner's model demonstrates three important characteristics of the perceptual process. First, perception is *selective*. Perceivers do not use all the available cues, and those they do use are thus given special emphasis. This means that our perception is efficient, and this efficiency can both aid and hinder our perceptual accuracy. Second, Bruner's model illustrates that our perceptual system works to paint a constant picture of the target. Perceptual *constancy* refers to the tendency for the target to be perceived in the same way over time or across situations. We have all had the experience of "getting off on the wrong foot" with a teacher or a boss and finding it difficult to change his or her constant perception of us. Third, the perceptual system also creates a consistent picture of the target. Perceptual *consistency* refers to the tendency to select, ignore, and distort cues in such a manner that they fit together to form a homogeneous picture of the target. We strive for consistency in our perception of people. We do not tend to see the same person as both good and bad or dependable and untrustworthy. Often, we distort cues that are discrepant with our general image of a person to make the cues consistent with this image. In the next section, we consider some specific perceptual biases that contribute to selectivity, constancy, and consistency in our perception of people.

LO 3.3

Describe the main biases in person perception.

BASIC BIASES IN PERSON PERCEPTION

For accuracy's sake, it would be convenient if we could encounter others under laboratory conditions, in a vacuum or a test tube, as it were. Because the real world lacks such ideal conditions, the impressions that we form of others are susceptible to a number of perceptual biases.

Primacy and Recency Effects

Given the examples of person perception that we have discussed thus far, you might gather that we form our impressions of others fairly quickly. One reason for this fast impression formation is our tendency to rely on the cues that we encounter early in a relationship. This reliance on early cues or first impressions is known as the **primacy effect**. Primacy often has a lasting impact. Thus, the worker who can favourably impress his or her boss in the first few days on the job is in an advantageous position due to primacy. Similarly, the labour negotiator who comes across as "tough" on the first day of contract talks might find this image difficult to shake as the talks continue. Primacy is a form of selectivity, and its lasting effects illustrate the operation of constancy.

Sometimes, a **recency effect** occurs, in which people give undue weight to the cues they have encountered most recently. In other words, last impressions count most. Landing a big contract today might be perceived as excusing a whole year's bad sales performance.

Primacy effect. The tendency for a perceiver to rely on early cues or first impressions.

Recency effect. The tendency for a perceiver to rely on recent cues or last impressions.

Reliance on Central Traits

Even though perceivers tend to rely on early information when developing their perceptions, these early cues do not receive equal weight. People tend to organize their perceptions around **central traits**, personal characteristics of the target that are of special interest to them. In developing her perceptions of her new co-worker, the experienced engineer seemed to organize her impressions around the trait of intellectual capacity. The centrality of traits depends on the perceiver's interests and the situation. Thus, not all engineers would organize their perceptions of the new worker around his intellectual abilities, and the established engineer might not use this trait as a central factor in forming impressions of the people she meets at a party.

Central traits often have a very powerful influence on our perceptions of others. In work settings, physical appearance is a common central trait that is related to a variety of job-related outcomes. Research shows an overwhelming tendency for those who are "attractive" to also be perceived as "good," especially when it comes to judgments about their social competence, qualifications, and potential job success.[6]

In general, research shows that conventionally attractive people are more likely to fare better than unattractive people in terms of a variety of job-related outcomes, including employment potential, getting hired, being chosen as a business partner, receiving good performance evaluations, or being promoted.[7] Physical height, which is one of the most obvious aspects of appearance, has also been found to be related to job performance, promotions, and career success. Taller and more attractive people are also more likely to be paid more.[8] And when it comes to weight, research has found that individuals who are overweight tend to be evaluated negatively on a number of workplace outcomes, including hiring, promotion decisions, and performance evaluations.[9] This bias is particularly troublesome, given that the rate of obesity among adults in North America is increasing.

> **Central traits.** Personal characteristics of a target person that are of particular interest to a perceiver.

Implicit Personality Theories

Each of us has a "theory" about which personality characteristics go together. These are called **implicit personality theories**. Perhaps you expect hardworking people to also be honest. Perhaps you feel that people of average intelligence tend to be most friendly. To the extent that such implicit theories are inaccurate, they provide a basis for misunderstanding.[10] The employee who assumes that her very formal boss is also insensitive might be reluctant to discuss with him a work-related problem that could be solved fairly easily.

> **Implicit personality theories.** Personal theories that people have about which personality characteristics go together.

Projection

In the absence of information to the contrary, and sometimes in spite of it, people often assume that others are like themselves. This tendency to attribute one's own thoughts and feelings to others is called **projection**. In some cases, projection is an efficient and sensible perceptual strategy. After all, people with similar backgrounds or interests often *do* think and feel similarly. Thus, it is not unreasonable for a capitalistic business person to assume that other business people favour the free enterprise system and disapprove of government intervention in this system. However, projection can also lead to perceptual difficulties. The chairperson who feels that an issue has been resolved and perceives committee members to feel the same way might be very surprised when a vote is taken. The honest warehouse manager who perceives others as honest might find inventory disappearing. In the case of threatening or undesirable characteristics, projection can serve as a form of perceptual defence. The dishonest worker might say, "Sure I steal from the company, but so does everyone else." Such perceptions can be used to justify the perceiver's thievery.

> **Projection.** The tendency for perceivers to attribute their own thoughts and feelings to others.

Stereotyping

Stereotyping. The tendency to generalize about people in a certain social category and ignore variations among them.

One way to form a consistent impression of other people is simply to assume that they have certain characteristics by virtue of some category that they fall into as suggested by social identity theory. This perceptual tendency is known as **stereotyping**, or the tendency to generalize about people in a social category and ignore variations among them. Categories on which people might base a stereotype include race, age, gender, ethnic background, religion, social class, and occupation.[11] There are three specific aspects to stereotyping.[12]

- We distinguish some category of people (university professors).
- We assume that the individuals in this category have certain traits (absent-minded, disorganized, ivory-tower mentality).
- We perceive that everyone in this category possesses these traits ("All my professors this year will be absent-minded, disorganized, and have an ivory-tower mentality").

People can evoke stereotypes with incredibly little information. In a "first impressions" study, the mere fact that a woman preferred to be addressed as "Ms." led to her being perceived as more masculine, more achievement-oriented, and less likeable than those who preferred the traditional titles "Miss" or "Mrs."[13]

Not all stereotypes are unfavourable. You probably hold favourable stereotypes of the social categories of which you are a member, such as student. However, these stereotypes are often less well developed and less rigid than others you hold. Stereotypes help us develop impressions of ambiguous targets, and we are usually pretty familiar with the people in our own groups. In addition, this contact helps us appreciate individual differences among group members, and such differences work against the development of stereotypes.

Language can be easily twisted to turn neutral or even favourable information into a basis for unfavourable stereotypes. For example, if British people do tend to be reserved, it is fairly easy to interpret this reserve as snobbishness. Similarly, if women who achieve executive positions have had to be assertive, it is easy to interpret this assertiveness as pushiness.

Knowing a person's occupation or field of study, we often make assumptions about his or her behaviour and personality. Accountants might be stereotyped as compulsive, precise, and one-dimensional, while engineers might be perceived as cold and calculating. Reflect on your own stereotypes of music or business students.

Not all stereotypes are inaccurate. You probably hold fairly correct stereotypes about the educational level of the typical university professor and the on-the-job demeanour of the typical telephone operator. These accurate stereotypes ease the task of developing perceptions of others.

The tendency to assume that all professors have certain characteristics and to ignore variations among them is an example of stereotyping.

Rawpixel.com/Shutterstock.com

However, it is probably safe to say that most stereotypes are inaccurate, especially when we use them to develop perceptions of specific individuals. This follows from the fact that stereotypes are most likely to develop when we do not have good information about a particular group.

This raises an interesting question: If many stereotypes are inaccurate, why do they persist?[14] After all, reliance on inaccurate information to develop our perceptions would seem to be punishing in the long run. In reality, a couple of factors work to *reinforce* inaccurate stereotypes. For one thing, even incorrect stereotypes help us process information about others quickly and efficiently. Sometimes, it is easier for the perceiver to rely on an inaccurate stereotype than it is to discover the true nature of the target. The male manager who is required to recommend one of his 20 employees for a promotion might find it easier to automatically rule out promoting a woman than to carefully evaluate all his employees, regardless of gender. Second, inaccurate stereotypes are often reinforced by selective perception and the selective application of language that was discussed above. The Hispanic worker who stereotypes all non-Hispanic managers as unfair might be on the lookout for behaviours to confirm these stereotypes and fail to notice examples of fair and friendly treatment. If such treatment *is* noticed, it might be perceived as patronizing rather than helpful.

ATTRIBUTION: PERCEIVING CAUSES AND MOTIVES

LO

Describe how people form *attributions* about the causes of behaviour and various biases in attribution.

Thus far, we have considered the components of perception, social identity theory, and Bruner's model of the perceptual process, and we have discussed some specific perceptual tendencies that operate as we form impressions of others. We will now consider a further aspect of impression formation—how we perceive people's motives. **Attribution** is the process by which we assign causes or motives to explain people's behaviour. The attribution process is important because many rewards and punishments in organizations are based on judgments about what caused a target person to behave in a certain way.

In making attributions about behaviour, an important goal is to determine whether the behaviour is caused by dispositional or situational factors. **Dispositional attributions** suggest that some personality or intellectual characteristic unique to the person is responsible for the behaviour and that the behaviour thus reflects the "true person." If we explain a behaviour as a function of intelligence, greed, friendliness, or laziness, we are making dispositional attributions.

Situational attributions suggest that the external situation or environment in which the target person exists was responsible for the behaviour and that the person might have had little control over the behaviour. If we explain behaviour as a function of bad weather, good luck, proper tools, or poor advice, we are making situational attributions.

Obviously, it would be nice to be able to read minds to understand people's motives. Since we cannot do this, we are forced to rely on external cues and make inferences from these cues. Research indicates that as we gain experience with the behaviour of a target person, three implicit questions guide our decisions as to whether we should attribute the behaviour to dispositional or situational causes.[15]

Attribution. The process by which causes or motives are assigned to explain people's behaviour.

Dispositional attributions. Explanations for behaviour based on an actor's personality or intellect.

Situational attributions. Explanations for behaviour based on an actor's external situation or environment.

- Does the person engage in the behaviour regularly and consistently? (Consistency cues)
- Do most people engage in the behaviour, or is it unique to this person? (Consensus cues)
- Does the person engage in the behaviour in many situations, or is it distinctive to one situation? (Distinctiveness cues)

Let's examine consistency, consensus, and distinctiveness cues in more detail.

Consistency Cues

Consistency cues reflect how consistently a person engages in a behaviour over time. For example, unless we see clear evidence of external constraints that force a behaviour to occur, we tend to perceive behaviour that a person performs regularly as indicative of his or her true

Consistency cues. Attribution cues that reflect how consistently a person engages in a behaviour over time.

motives. In other words, high consistency leads to dispositional attributions. Thus, one might assume that the professor who has generous office hours and is always there for consultation really cares about his or her students. Similarly, we are likely to make dispositional attributions about workers who are consistently good or poor performers, perhaps perceiving the former as "dedicated" and the latter as "lazy." When behaviour occurs inconsistently, we begin to consider situational attributions. For example, if a person's performance cycles between mediocre and excellent, we might look to variations in workload to explain the cycles.

Consensus Cues

Consensus cues.
Attribution cues that reflect how a person's behaviour compares with that of others.

Consensus cues reflect how a person's behaviour compares with that of others. In general, acts that deviate from social expectations provide us with more information about the actor's motives than conforming behaviours do. Thus, unusual, low-consensus behaviour leads to more dispositional attributions than typical, high-consensus behaviour. The person who acts differently from the majority is seen as revealing more of his or her true motives. The informational effects of low-consensus behaviour are magnified when the actor is expected to suffer negative consequences because of the deviance. Consider the job applicant who makes favourable statements about the role of big business in society while being interviewed for a job at General Electric. Such statements are so predictable in this situation that the interviewer can place little confidence in what they really indicate about the candidate's true feelings and motives. On the other hand, imagine an applicant who makes critical comments about big business in the same situation. Such comments are hardly expected and could clearly lead to rejection. In this case, the interviewer would be more confident about the applicant's true disposition regarding big business.

Distinctiveness Cues

Distinctiveness cues.
Attribution cues that reflect the extent to which a person engages in some behaviour across a variety of situations.

Distinctiveness cues reflect the extent to which a person engages in some behaviour across a variety of situations. When a behaviour occurs across a variety of situations, it lacks distinctiveness, and the observer is prone to provide a dispositional attribution about its cause. We reason that the behaviour reflects a person's true motives if it "stands up" in a variety of environments. Thus, the professor who has generous office hours, stays after class to talk to students, and attends student functions is seen as truly student oriented. The worker whose performance was good in his first job as well as several subsequent jobs is perceived as having real ability. When a behaviour is highly distinctive, in that it occurs in only one situation, we are likely to assume that some aspect of the situation has caused the behaviour. If the only student-oriented behaviour that we observe is generous office hours, we assume that they are dictated by department policy. If a worker performed well on only one job, back in 2010, we suspect that his uncle owned the company!

Attribution in Action

Frequently, observers of real-life behaviour have information at hand about consistency, consensus, and distinctiveness. Let's take an example that shows how the observer puts such information together in forming attributions. At the same time, the example will serve to review the previous discussion. Imagine that Roshani, Mika, and Sam are employees who work in separate firms. Each is absent from work today, and a manager must develop an attribution about the cause to decide which action is warranted.

- *Roshani.* Roshani is absent a lot, her co-workers are seldom absent, and she was absent a lot in her previous job.
- *Mika.* Mika is absent a lot, her co-workers are also absent a lot, but she was almost never absent in her previous job.

	Consistency	Consensus	Distinctiveness	Likely Attribution
Roshani	High	Low	Low	Disposition
Mika	High	High	High	Situation
Sam	Low	High	Low	Temporary Situation

EXHIBIT 3.4
Cue combinations and resulting attributions.

- *Sam.* Sam is seldom absent, her co-workers are seldom absent, and she was seldom absent in her previous job.

Just what kind of attributions are managers likely to make regarding the absences of Roshani, Mika, and Sam? Roshani's absence is highly consistent, it is a low-consensus behaviour, and it is not distinctive, since she was absent in her previous job. As shown in Exhibit 3.4, this combination of cues is very likely to prompt a dispositional attribution, perhaps that Roshani is lazy or irresponsible. Mika is also absent consistently, but it is high-consensus behaviour in that her peers also exhibit absence. In addition, the behaviour is highly distinctive—she is absent only on this job. As indicated, this combination of cues will usually result in a situational attribution, perhaps that working conditions are terrible, or that the boss is nasty. Finally, Sam's absence is inconsistent. In addition, it is similar to that of co-workers and not distinctive, in that she was inconsistently absent on her previous job as well. As shown, this combination of cues suggests that some temporary, short-term situational factor is causing her absence. It is possible that a sick child occasionally requires her to stay home.

Biases in Attribution

As the preceding section indicates, observers often operate in a rational, logical manner in forming attributions about behaviour. The various cue combinations and the resulting attributions have a sensible appearance. This does not mean that such attributions are always correct, but they do represent good bets about why some behaviour has occurred. Having made this observation, it would be naïve to assume that attributions are always free from bias or error. Earlier, we discussed a number of very basic perceptual biases, and it stands to reason that the complex task of attribution would also be open to bias. Let's consider three biases in attribution: the fundamental attribution error, actor–observer effect, and self-serving bias.[16]

FUNDAMENTAL ATTRIBUTION ERROR
Suppose you make a mistake in attributing a cause to someone else's behaviour. Would you be likely to err on the side of a dispositional cause or a situational cause? Substantial evidence indicates that when we make judgments about the behaviour of people other than ourselves, we tend to overemphasize dispositional explanations at the expense of situational explanations. This is called the **fundamental attribution error**.[17]

Why does the fundamental attribution error occur? For one thing, we often discount the strong effects that social roles can have on behaviour. We might see bankers as truly conservative people because we ignore the fact that their occupational role and their employer dictate that they act conservatively. Second, many people whom we observe are seen in rather constrained, constant situations (at work or at school) that reduce our appreciation of how their behaviour may vary in other situations. Thus, we fail to realize that the observed behaviour is distinctive to a particular situation. That conservative banker might actually be a weekend skydiver!

The fundamental attribution error can lead to problems for managers of poorly performing employees. It suggests that dispositional explanations for the poor performance will sometimes be made even when situational factors are the true cause. Laziness or low aptitude might be cited, while poor training or a bad sales territory is ignored. However, this is less likely when the manager has had actual experience in performing the employee's job and is thus aware of situational roadblocks to good performance.[18]

Fundamental attribution error. The tendency to overemphasize dispositional explanations for behaviour at the expense of situational explanations.

Actor–observer effect.
The propensity for actors and observers to view the causes of the actor's behaviour differently.

ACTOR–OBSERVER EFFECT It is not surprising that actors and observers often view the causes for the actor's behaviour very differently. This difference in attributional perspectives is called the **actor–observer effect**.[19] Specifically, while the observer might be busy committing the fundamental attribution error, the actor might be emphasizing the role of the situation in explaining his or her own behaviour. Thus, as actors, we are often particularly sensitive to those environmental events that led us to be late or absent. As observers of the same behaviour in others, we are more likely to invoke dispositional causes.

We see some of the most striking examples of this effect in cases of illegal behaviour, such as price fixing and the bribery of government officials. The perpetrators and those close to them often cite stiff competition or management pressure as causes for their ethical lapses. Observers see the perpetrators as immoral or unintelligent.[20]

Why are actors prone to attribute much of their own behaviour to situational causes? First, they might be more aware than observers of the constraints and advantages that the environment offered. At the same time, they are aware of their private thoughts, feelings, and intentions regarding the behaviour, all of which might be unknown to the observer. Thus, I might know that I sincerely wanted to get to the meeting on time, that I left home extra early, and that the accident that delayed me was truly unusual. My boss might be unaware of all of this information and figure that I am just unreliable.

Research on the actor–observer effect has found that the effect is not as pervasive as once believed. For example, it appears to be more likely under particular conditions, such as when explaining negative events. The opposite effect seems to occur for positive events (i.e., the actor makes a dispositional attribution while the observer makes a situational attribution).[21]

Self-serving bias. The tendency to take credit for successful outcomes and to deny responsibility for failures.

SELF-SERVING BIAS It has probably already occurred to you that certain forms of attributions have the capacity to make us feel good or bad about ourselves. In fact, people have a tendency to take credit and responsibility for successful outcomes of their behaviour and to deny credit and responsibility for failures.[22] This tendency is called **self-serving bias**, and it is interesting because it suggests that people will explain the very same behaviour differently on the basis of events that happened *after* the behaviour occurred. If the vice-president of marketing champions a product that turns out to be a sales success, she might attribute this to her retailing savvy. If the very same marketing process leads to failure, she might attribute this to the poor performance of the marketing research firm that she used. Notice that the self-serving bias can overcome the tendency for actors to attribute their behaviour to situational factors. In this example, the vice-president invokes a dispositional explanation ("I'm an intelligent, competent person") when the behaviour is successful.

Self-serving bias can reflect intentional self-promotion or excuse making. However, again, it is possible that it reflects unique information on the part of the actor. Especially when behaviour has negative consequences, the actor might scan the environment and find situational causes for the failure.[23] To be sure, when a student does very well on an exam, she is very likely to make a dispositional attribution. However, upon receiving a failing grade, the same student is much more likely to find situational causes to explain her grade!

Workforce diversity.
Differences among recruits and employees in characteristics such as gender, race, age, religion, cultural background, physical ability, or sexual orientation.

LO 3.5

Discuss the concepts of *workforce diversity* and valuing diversity and how racial, ethnic, religious, gender, age, and LGBT *stereotypes* affect organizational behaviour, and what organizations can do to manage diversity.

PERSON PERCEPTION AND WORKFORCE DIVERSITY

The realities of workforce diversity have become an important factor for many organizations in recent years. **Workforce diversity** refers to differences among employees or potential recruits in characteristics such as gender, race, age, religion, cultural background, physical ability, or sexual orientation. The interest in diversity stems from at least two broad facts. First, the workforce is becoming more diverse. Second, there is growing recognition that many organizations have not successfully managed workforce diversity.

The Changing Workplace

As we mentioned in Chapter 1, the composition of the Canadian labour force is changing.[24] Fifty years ago, it was mainly Caucasian and male. Now, changing immigration patterns, the aging of baby boomers, and the increasing movement of women into paid employment result in a lot more variety. Immigrants to Canada from all parts of the world are making the Canadian population and labour force increasingly multicultural and multiethnic. The diversity of Canada's population is expected to continue to grow during the next 20 years. By 2031, 30.6 percent of the population will be visible minorities, and 60 percent of the population in Toronto and Vancouver will belong to a visible minority group making them "majority-minority" cities. If current trends continue, one in every five persons in Canada will be non-white when Canada celebrates its 150th birthday in 2017.[25] According to projections, between 25 and 28 percent of the Canadian population will be foreign born by 2031, and in less than a decade 48 percent of Canada's working-age population will be between the ages of 45 and 64.[26]

The labour pool is changing, and at the same time many organizations are seeking to recruit more representatively from this pool so that they employ people who reflect their customer base—an effort to better mirror their markets. This is especially true in the growing service sector, where contact between organizational members and customers is very direct. As discussed in the chapter-opening vignette, RBC has been very active in developing programs to recruit, hire, and develop persons with disabilities. Many other organizations, including the YMCA in Toronto, Shell Canada Ltd., Federal Express Canada Ltd., the City of Ottawa, the City of Vancouver, and Manitoba Hydro have been recognized for their diversity programs.[27]

The changing employment pool is not the only factor that has prompted interest in diversity issues. Globalization, mergers, and strategic alliances mean that many employees are required to interact with people from substantially different national or corporate cultures. Compounding all this is an increased emphasis on teamwork as a means of job design and quality enhancement.

Valuing Diversity

In the past, organizations were thought to be doing the right thing if they merely tolerated diversity—that is, if they engaged in fair hiring and employment practices with respect to women and minorities. Firms were considered to be doing especially well if they assisted these people to "fit in" with the mainstream corporate culture by "fixing" what was different about them.[28] For example, women managers were sometimes given assertiveness training to enable them to be as hard-nosed and aggressive as their male counterparts!

Recently, some have argued that organizations should *value* diversity, not just tolerate it or try to blend everyone into a narrow mainstream. To be sure, a critical motive is the basic fairness of valuing diversity. However, there is also increasing awareness that diversity and its proper management can yield strategic and competitive advantages. These advantages include the potential for improved problem solving and creativity when diverse perspectives are brought to bear on an organizational problem, such as product or service quality. Advantages also include improved recruiting and marketing when the firm's human resources profile matches that of the labour pool and customer base (see Exhibit 3.5). As a result, more organizations are adopting diversity as part of their corporate strategy to improve their competitiveness in global markets. Furthermore, a diversity climate (the extent to which an organization promotes equal employment opportunity and inclusion) has been found to be associated with business-unit performance. There is also evidence that retail stores have higher customer satisfaction and productivity when their employees represent the ethnicity of their customers. In addition, organizations with more gender-diverse management teams have superior financial performance.[29]

However, if there is a single concept that serves as a barrier to valuing diversity, it is the stereotype. Let's now examine several workplace stereotypes and their consequences.

◄⊙ Simulate

HUMAN RESOURCES AND DIVERSITY

EXHIBIT 3.5
Competitive advantages to valuing and managing a diverse workforce.
Source: Cox, T.H., & Blake, S. (1991, August). Managing cultural diversity: Implications for organizational competitiveness. *Academy of Management Executive, 47,* 45–56.

1. Cost Argument	As organizations become more diverse, the cost of a poor job in integrating workers will increase. Those who handle this well will thus create cost advantages over those who don't.
2. Resource-Acquisition Argument	Companies develop reputations on favourability as prospective employers for women and ethnic minorities. Those with the best reputations for managing diversity will win the competition for the best personnel. As the labour pool shrinks and changes composition, this edge will become increasingly important.
3. Marketing Argument	For multinational organizations, the insight and cultural sensitivity that members with roots in other countries bring to the marketing effort should improve these efforts in important ways. The same rationale applies to marketing to subpopulations within domestic operations.
4. Creativity Argument	Diversity of perspectives and less emphasis on conformity to norms of the past (which characterize the modern approach to management of diversity) should improve the level of creativity.
5. Problem-Solving Argument	Heterogeneity in decision and problem solving groups potentially produces better decisions through a wider range of perspectives and more thorough critical analysis of issues.
6. System Flexibility Argument	An implication of the multicultural model for managing diversity is that the system will become less determinant, less standardized, and therefore more fluid. The increased fluidity should create greater flexibility to react to environmental changes (i.e., reactions should be faster and at less cost).

Stereotypes and Workforce Diversity

As described earlier, a stereotype is the tendency to generalize about people in a certain social category and ignore variations among them. Common workplace stereotypes are based on gender, age, race, religion, ethnicity, and sexual orientation. In the following section, we describe how stereotypes can have negative effects on how individuals are treated in organizations. It is also worth noting that in some situations in which a negative stereotype is salient, just the perception that one might be judged on the basis of a stereotype can have a negative effect on a person's behaviour and performance, a phenomenon known as stereotype threat.

Stereotype threat occurs when members of a social group (e.g., visible minorities or women) feel they might be judged or treated according to a stereotype and that their behaviour

Stereotype threat.
Members of a social group feel they might be judged or treated according to a stereotype and that their behaviour and/or performance will confirm the stereotype.

Many organizations today are adopting diversity as part of their corporate strategy to improve their competitiveness.

Rawpixel.com/Fotolia

APPLIED FOCUS

POLICE ANTI-BIAS TRAINING

Stereotypes and bias can have negative effects on hiring and promotion decisions in all organizations. But when it comes to policing, stereotypes and bias can result in tragic events that receive massive media attention and lead to public anger, protests, and even violence. Biased policing, however, is not due to widespread racism. Rather, it has more to do with implicit biases.

Fair and Impartial Policing (FIP) is an organization that has developed a training program to train police officers on bias, especially implicit bias. According to FIP's Dr. Lorie Fridell, who developed the program, "We are educating them on implicit biases, talking about how implicit biases might manifest in policing, what it might look like, and then we give them skills for reducing and managing their implicit biases."

Unlike an explicit bias, in which a person is aware of the stereotype and negative perception he or she has of a particular group, an implicit bias is outside of one's conscious awareness. Thus, a person might be unaware of associating a particular group with a stereotype. "This means even well-intentioned individuals, even well-intentioned law enforcement, can have implicit biases that impact on their perceptions and impact on their behaviours," says Fridell.

One implicit bias that is particularly relevant for policing is the implicit association between minorities and crime. Decades of research has shown that even people who are non-prejudiced and consciously tolerant have an implicit bias that links minorities to crime, and this impacts their perceptions and behaviour. However, when people are made aware of their implicit biases, the impact can be reduced or eliminated.

FIP has provided training on implicit bias to many police forces in North America, including the Toronto Police Service and the Metro Vancouver Transit Police. The training focuses on various biases that can influence police, such as stereotypes associated with who commits crime as well as stereotypes about who the police are most likely to believe (e.g., a rich person versus a low-income person). In addition to race and ethnicity, the training also considers socio-economic status, sexual orientation, gender, and religious biases because police officers might be less vigilant with certain groups, such as women or those who are professionally dressed.

FIP training informs police officers of their implicit biases and the effect it has on their perceptions and behaviour, and provides them with skills to reduce and manage their biases. Police officers are provided with two tactics to help them combat implicit biases. The first is to recognize one's own biases and actively choose to implement unbiased behaviour. The second tactic is to interact in a positive way with people who are different from oneself, because that interaction will reduce one's conscious and implicit biases.

FIP training provides police officers with information and motivation that enables them to engage in controlled and unbiased behaviour that will override implicit biases and result in fair, impartial, and effective policing.

Sources: Bernier, L. (2015, April 20). Policing implicit bias. *Canadian HR Reporter, 28*(7), 2, 12; Laszlo, A. T., & Fridell, I. A. (2012). Fair and impartial policing: Social psychology transforms law enforcement training. *Royal Canadian Mounted Police Gazette, 74*(3), 22–23; Tucker, E. (2014, August 21). What Canadian police are doing so Ferguson doesn't happen here. *Global News*, www.globalnews.ca/news/1520068/; Fair and impartial policing, www.fairimpartialpolicing.com/.

and/or performance will confirm the stereotype. The activation of a salient negative stereotype threat in a testing situation (e.g., asking test takers to report demographics prior to taking a test) has been found to result in lower cognitive ability and math test performance scores of minorities and women compared to their performance in non-threatening situations.[30]

There is also some evidence that workers are often pressured to cover up or downplay their membership in a particular group (e.g., racial, ethnic, religious, LGBT), and they comply by changing their appearance or minimizing their affiliation and association with their group and other members of it. This can have a negative effect on a person's work attitudes and behaviour.[31] In the remainder of this section, we will consider the nature of several common stereotypes and their consequences in the workplace. But first, see the Applied Focus: *Police Anti-Bias Training* to find out what some police forces are doing to combat stereotypes and bias.

Learn About Yourself
Multicultural Awareness Scale

RACIAL, ETHNIC, AND RELIGIOUS STEREOTYPES   Racial, ethnic, and religious stereotypes are pervasive, persistent, frequently negative, and often self-contradictory. Most of us hold at least some stereotypical views of other races, religions, or cultures. Over the years, such stereotypes exhibit remarkable stability unless some major event, such as a war, intervenes to change them. Then, former allies can acquire negative attributes in short order.

Personal experience is unnecessary for such stereotype formation. In one study, people were asked to describe the traits of a number of ethnic groups, including several fictional ones. Although they had never met a Danerian, a Pirenian, or a Wallonian, this did not inhibit them from assigning traits—and those they assigned were usually unfavourable![32] Such stereotypes often contain contradictory elements. A common reaction is to describe a particular group as being too lazy, while at the same time criticizing it for taking one's own job opportunities away.

Research evidence suggests that just getting in the door can be a problem. For example, whites have been found to advance further in the hiring process than blacks, even when the applicants are the same age and physical size, have identical education and work experience, and share similar personalities.[33] A study on religious discrimination found that female job applicants who appeared to be Muslim experienced more negative interpersonal behaviour and discrimination (e.g., rudeness or hostility) than non-Muslim female applicants.[34] Discrimination in hiring has also been found to occur when job applicants have an ethnic-sounding name. To learn more, see the Ethical Focus: *What's in a Name? You're Hired . . . or Not!*

Even after visible minorities get in the door, career advancement based on racial or ethnic stereotypes are common. A study on the career satisfaction and advancement of visible minorities in Canada found that visible minorities perceive more barriers in their career advancement, including a lack of fairness in the process, and report less career satisfaction than white colleagues. In addition, 47 percent of visible minority managers and professionals reported feeling they were held to a higher standard of performance, and 69 percent of visible minority respondents reported that in their career, "who you know" was more important than "what you know."[35] In the United States, almost one-quarter of workers from diverse backgrounds reported being discriminated against or treated unfairly at work. The most common example was not receiving credit for their work.[36]

Attributions can play an important role in determining how job performance is interpreted. For example, one study found that good performance on the part of African-American managers was seen to be due to help from others (a situational attribution), while good performance by Caucasian managers was seen to be due to their effort and abilities (a dispositional attribution).[37]

Racial and ethnic stereotypes are also important in the context of the increasing globalization of business. In one study, researchers asked American business students to describe Japanese and American managers along a number of dimensions. The students viewed Japanese managers as having more productive employees and being better overall managers. However, the students preferred to work for an American manager.[38] One can wonder how such students would respond to international assignments. Of course, all groups have stereotypes of each other. Japanese stereotypes of Americans probably contribute to Americans not being promoted above a certain level in Japanese firms.

GENDER STEREOTYPES   One of the most problematic stereotypes for organizations is the gender stereotype. Considering their numbers in the workforce, women are severely under-represented in managerial and administrative jobs. Although women now occupy a significant and growing proportion of entry- and mid-level management positions, this is not the case for top-level positions, where they remain significantly under-represented. According to a study of 500 of Canada's top companies by Catalyst Canada, women hold only

ETHICAL FOCUS

WHAT'S IN A NAME? YOU'RE HIRED ... OR NOT!

Have you ever thought about how your name might influence your chances of being invited for a job interview or receiving a job offer? Chances are you probably have not thought about this.

However, there is evidence that name discrimination is a problem when it comes to screening resumés and that having an ethnic-sounding name might put a job applicant at a disadvantage. Furthermore, this might explain in part why the unemployment rate of recent immigrants to Canada is almost twice as high as similarly aged non-immigrants even though Canada's immigration policy focuses on skilled immigrants with high levels of education and experience.

To find out if the name of a job applicant influences recruiter decisions, a study was conducted by Metropolis British Columbia and authors Philip Oreopoulos and Diane Dechief of the University of Toronto. The study involved sending over 7000 resumés by email in response to job postings across multiple occupations in Toronto, Montreal, and Vancouver. The jobs required at least a bachelor's degree, fluency in English, and four to six years of work experience. All of the resumés indicated that the applicant had Canadian work experience, Canadian education, and solid credentials. However, they differed in terms of the name of the applicant. Some of the resumés had common Anglophone-sounding names such as John Smith, while others had popular Greek, Indian, or Chinese names.

The main outcome variable of the study was whether or not a resumé generated a callback from an employer indicating interest in meeting or further discussing the applicant's credentials. A callback is the most important step for obtaining a job offer.

The results indicated that resumés with English-sounding names were 35 percent more likely to receive a callback for a job interview than resumés with Indian or Chinese names across the three cities. Resumés with English-sounding names also received more callbacks than resumés with Greek-sounding names. These results remained even when taking into account many other factors on the resumés, such as a degree from a top-ranking university, active social extracurricular activities, or job experience from a large, multinational firm.

These results indicate the existence of employer discrimination against job applicants with ethnic-sounding names. According to the authors of the study, subconscious or implicit discrimination may be one reason why recruiters are less likely to call back applicants with ethnic-sounding names. An applicant's name or country of origin may trigger stereotypes that cause employers to focus on the stereotype and overemphasize potential concerns, such as social and language skills, and to ignore other important factors on the resumé, such as education and experience.

These results provide one explanation for a common complaint from immigrants to Canada that they never hear back from prospective employers, even when they apply for jobs that precisely match their expertise. What's more, the results also indicate that even Canadian raised and educated job applicants might be discriminated against if they have ethnic-sounding names.

Sources: Oreopoulos, P., & Dechief, D. (2011). *Why do some employers prefer to interview Matthew, but not Samir? New evidence from Toronto, Montreal, and Vancouver.* Metropolis British Columbia Centre of Excellence for Research on Immigration and Diversity, Working Paper Series, No.11–13; Silliker, A. (2011, November 21). "Matthew, you're hired. Good luck next time, Samir." *Canadian HR Reporter,* 24(20), 1, 20; Immen, W. (2011, November 18). How an ethnic-sounding name may affect the job hunt: Hiring managers tend to bypass resumés with foreign-sounding names even if education, experience meet the grade, study finds. *The Globe and Mail,* B21.

14.4 percent of corporate officer positions, including that of president, executive vice–president, and chief operating officer. As a result, it's predicted that women's overall representation in corporate Canada will not reach 25 percent until 2025.[39]

There is evidence that gender stereotypes are partially responsible for discouraging women from business careers and blocking their ascent to managerial positions. This under-representation of women managers and administrators happens because stereotypes of women do not correspond especially well with stereotypes of business people or managers.

What is the nature of gender stereotypes? A series of studies have had managers describe men in general, women in general, and typical "successful middle managers." These studies have determined that successful middle managers are perceived as having traits and attitudes that are similar to those generally ascribed to men. That is, successful managers are seen as more similar to men in qualities such as leadership ability, competitiveness, self-confidence, ambitiousness, and objectivity.[40] Thus, stereotypes of successful middle managers do not correspond to stereotypes of women. The trend over time in the results of these studies contains some bad news and some good news. The bad news is that *male* managers today hold the same dysfunctional stereotypes about women and management that they held in the early 1970s, when researchers conducted the first of these studies. At that time, women managers held the same stereotypes as the men. The good news is that the recent research shows a shift by the women—they now see successful middle managers as possessing attitudes and characteristics that describe *both* men and women in general. However, although good managers are described today as possessing fewer masculine characteristics than in past decades, the recent research indicates that both men and women of varying age, education, and work experience still describe a good manager as possessing predominantly masculine characteristics. In other words, the stereotype of a leader is culturally masculine. People perceive leaders as similar to men but not very similar to women. In addition, men continue to be rated more favourably than women for male-dominated jobs, especially by male raters.[41]

Granting that gender stereotypes exist, do they lead to biased human resources decisions? The answer would appear to be yes. In a typical study, researchers asked male bank supervisors to make hypothetical decisions about workers who were described equivalently except for gender.[42] Women were discriminated against for promotion to a branch manager's position. They were also discriminated against when they requested to attend a professional development conference. In addition, female supervisors were less likely than their male counterparts to receive support for their request that a problem employee be fired. In one case, bias worked to *favour* women. The bank supervisors were more likely to approve a request for a leave of absence to care for one's children when it came from a female. This finding is similar to others that show that gender stereotypes tend to favour women when they are being considered for "women's" jobs (such as secretary) or for "women's" tasks (such as supervising other women), but not for traditional male jobs.[43] One study found that when women are successful in traditional male jobs, they are less liked, and being disliked had a negative effect on their evaluations and recommendations for rewards, including salary and special job opportunities.[44]

In general, research suggests that the above findings are fairly typical. Women suffer from a stereotype that is detrimental to their hiring, development, promotion, and salaries. Even women with MBAs earn less than men in their first year of work, start in more junior positions, and are offered fewer career-accelerating work experiences and international assignments. Women have fewer opportunities to be mentored or coached, and are less likely to receive job rotation assignments, line management experience, and access to professional development training. Female managers are also more likely than male managers to have to make off-the-job sacrifices and compromises in family life to maintain their careers.[45]

However, there is growing evidence that the detrimental effects of gender stereotypes are reduced or removed when decision makers have increased experience and training, are held accountable for their decisions, and have good job-related information about the qualifications, competence, and performance of particular women and an accurate picture of the job that they are applying for or seeking promotion into.[46] In particular, several studies reveal convincingly that women do not generally suffer from gender stereotypes in *performance evaluations* that their supervisors provide.[47] This is not altogether surprising. As we noted earlier, stereotypes help us process information in ambiguous situations. To the extent that we have good information on which to base our perceptions of people, reliance on stereotypes is less necessary. Day-to-day performance is often fairly easy to observe, and gender stereotypes do not intrude on evaluations. Along these lines, a review of research on gender

1. L.V. Lomas Limited
2. Admiral Insurance
3. DEL Property Management Inc.
4. Nycomed, a Takeda Company
5. Royal Lepage Performance Realty
6. SaskCentral (Credit Union Central of Saskatchewan)
7. Ariad Communications
8. T4G Limited
9. Lutherwood
10. Achievers (Formerly I Love Rewards)

EXHIBIT 3.6
2015 Best workplaces for women in Canada.
Note: Listed are the top 10 of the 50 workplaces recognized as best workplaces in Canada for women.
Source: © 2015 Great Place to Work® Institute, Inc. All Rights Reserved.

differences in job performance ratings found that females scored slightly higher than males, while males received higher ratings of promotion potential.[48] However, a recent review of male and female performance reviews found that women are more likely to receive negative comments about their personality (e.g., abrasive, emotional) than men.[49]

Fortunately, as shown in Exhibit 3.6, many Canadian organizations have made efforts to ensure that women are represented in senior positions and have been recognized for their endeavours. For example, at Shell Canada Ltd. of Calgary, there are more women than men on the list of potential senior managers.[50] Women have made the most significant progress moving into senior management and executive positions in the financial services industry. In fact, Canada's financial services sector ranks third in the world in terms of the percentage of women in executive positions: 23 percent. Canada's five largest banks have women in senior executive positions. On the other hand, industries that tend to be stereotypically male, such as paper and forest products, steel production, motor vehicles and parts, oil and gas, and general manufacturing and construction, continue to have the lowest representation of women in senior positions.[51]

AGE STEREOTYPES Another kind of stereotype that presents problems for organizations is the age stereotype. Knowing that a person falls into a certain age range or belongs to a particular age generation, we have a tendency to make certain assumptions about the person's physical, psychological, and intellectual capabilities. We will have more to say about generation differences and values in Chapter 4.

What is the nature of work-related age stereotypes? Older workers are seen as having less *capacity for performance.* They tend to be viewed as less productive, creative, logical, and capable of performing under pressure than younger workers. In addition, older workers are seen as having less *potential for development.* Compared with younger workers, they are considered more rigid and dogmatic and less adaptable to new corporate cultures. Not all stereotypes of older workers are negative, however. They tend to be perceived as more honest, dependable, and trustworthy (in short, more *stable*). In general, these stereotypes are held by both younger and older individuals.[52]

It is worth noting that these stereotypes are essentially inaccurate. For example, age seldom limits the capacity for development until post-employment years.[53] Furthermore, the most comprehensive study on age and job performance found that age is not related to task performance or creativity, but it is related to other forms of job performance. For example, older workers were found to exhibit more citizenship behaviours and greater safety-related behaviour, and fewer counterproductive work behaviours. Older workers were also found to exhibit less workplace aggression, on-the-job substance use, tardiness, and absenteeism. Thus, by all accounts older workers perform as well or better than younger workers across numerous dimensions of job performance.[54]

Walmart Canada is a repeat winner of the Best Employer Awards for 50-plus Canadians for its efforts in attracting and hiring older workers.

Dick Loek/Newscom

However, the relevant question remains: Do age stereotypes affect human resources decisions? It would appear that such stereotypes can affect decisions regarding hiring, promotion, and skills development. In one study, researchers had university students make hypothetical recommendations regarding younger and older male workers. An older man was less likely to be hired for a finance job that required rapid, high-risk decisions. An older man was considered less promotable for a marketing position that required creative solutions to difficult problems. Finally, an older worker was less likely to be permitted to attend a conference on advanced production systems.[55] These decisions reflect the stereotypes of the older worker depicted above, and they are doubtless borne out by the tendency for older employees to be laid off during corporate restructuring.

Unfortunately, the reality for older workers is consistent with the research. According to the Ontario Human Rights Commission, discrimination on the basis of age is experienced by people as young as 40 to 45, who are often passed over for merit pay and promotions or pressured to take early retirement. In a blatant example of such discrimination, a job fair held in Toronto several years ago stated that the target audience was 18- to 54-year-olds. Many older workers were offended, and a complaint was made to the Ontario Human Rights Commission.[56] Again, however, we should recognize that age stereotypes may have less impact on human resources decisions when managers have good information about the capacities of the particular employee in question.

Some organizations have implemented programs and practices to promote the hiring and retention of older workers. A good example is Walmart Canada, which has been recognized for its efforts in attracting and hiring older workers. The company is a repeat winner of the Best Employer Awards for 50-plus Canadians. Home Depot also actively recruits older workers; nearly one-third of its employees are over 50, and 6 percent are 65 or older. At HP Advanced Solutions, an IT provider in Victoria that has been recognized as a top employer for Canadians over 40, mature workers train younger generations of workers in key skills that they have developed.

Unfortunately, many organizations do not actively recruit and hire older workers. A recent survey found that 71.5 percent of small- and medium-sized organizations across Canada said that they were not likely to fill a job opening with someone older than 65 now or in the future. This is unfortunate, as an increasing number of older workers are returning to work and want to continue working past the age of 65. Thus, inaccurate perceptions and stereotypes continue to have a negative effect on the hiring of older workers.[57]

LGBT STEREOTYPES In 2014, Apple CEO Tim Cook became the first CEO of a Fortune 500 company to publicly announce that he was gay. This is no small feat, especially since employees who are members of the lesbian, gay, bisexual, and transgender (LGBT) community fear that coming out will result in bias and discrimination toward them. Although there are laws in Canada that protect the rights of LGBT workers, LGBT employees nonetheless face barriers and discrimination in the workplace that can limit their career advancement.

The results of several surveys found that LGBT employees face discrimination at work. While 67 percent of heterosexual respondents indicated there was no discrimination against LGBT employees, 29 percent of LGBT employees said they had experienced it, and 33.2 percent reported having witnessed discrimination against LGBT colleagues. Another survey reported that 35 percent of gay men and 40 percent of lesbian respondents said they had experienced discrimination during their professional lives. Further, LGBT men and women report exclusion from the "old boys' club" and LGBT women report a less friendly workplace and more hurdles than LGBT men. As a result, many LGBT employees do not come out at work for fear of the potential repercussions and negative consequences.

Why do LGBT employees face these barriers and fear coming out at work? One report found that a lack of education and awareness and a reliance on stereotypes is the root of the problem. These misperceptions and stereotypes lead to discriminatory behaviours towards LGBT employees, such as homophobia, inappropriate humour, exclusion from networks inside and outside of the organization, social exclusion, ridicule, and a lack of role models. Further, LGBT employees who do not feel safe to come out at work are up to 30 percent less productive, more likely to suffer from depression and stress, and more likely to quit. And LGBT employees who are not out at work report greater feelings of being stalled in their careers, and dissatisfaction with their rate of promotion and advancement. LGBT employees who are not out at work are 40 percent less likely to trust their employers, and 73 percent more likely to leave within three years compared to those who have come out at work.

In recent years, an increasing number of organizations have begun to make their workplaces more inclusive for LGBT employees. For example, IBM has LGBT resource groups and Scotiabank created an employee group for LGBT employees called Scotia Pride. LGBT-inclusive workplaces can increase employee engagement because they allow employees to be authentic and spend less time self-editing, which can also increase loyalty and reduce turnover. When organizations implement programs to create LGBT-inclusive workplaces, they improve LGBT employee relationships with co-workers, increase perceptions of fairness, and increase organizational commitment and career satisfaction, which can lead to increased productivity.[58] To learn more on how to make a workplace more LGBT-inclusive, see Exhibit 3.7.

• Increase awareness by identifying and tackling organizational issues related to LGBT employees company-wide.
• Create and enforce anti-discriminatory policies and practices and communicate these externally as well as internally to all employees.
• Implement diversity training to help dispel LGBT myths and stereotypes.
• Help LGBT employees find mentors and form employee groups.
• Make consistent and inclusive communications a core goal. For example, organizations should make it clear partners of employees, regardless of sex, are invited to corporate events and discrimination, in any form, will not be tolerated.
• Include LGBT identity in diversity metrics to help ensure these employees, and candidates, aren't overlooked in recruiting and promotion.
• Leverage general talent management practices to support all employees. Broad talent management practices without a specific focus on diversity and inclusion will help develop all employees and improve workplace experiences.

EXHIBIT 3.7
Making workplaces LGBT-inclusive.

Source: Reprinted by permission of Canadian HR Reporter. © Copyright Thomson Reuters Canada Ltd., (2009, July 13), 22(13), 8, Toronto, Ontario, 1-800-387-5164. Web: www.hrreporter.com.

Managing Workforce Diversity

Given the prevalence of the stereotypes noted above, valuing diversity is not something that occurs automatically. Rather, diversity needs to be *managed* to have a positive impact on work behaviour and an organization. What can organizations do to achieve and manage a diverse workforce? Before continuing, try to answer this question by taking a closer look at the chapter-opening vignette on RBC, paying particular attention to how they recruit, hire, and develop persons with disabilities.

Exhibit 3.8 lists some of the common activities that are often included in diversity programs. Some additional examples are listed below.[59]

- Select enough minority members to get them beyond token status. When this happens, the majority starts to look at individual accomplishments rather than group membership, because they can see variation in the behaviours of the minority. In recent years, an increasing number of Canadian organizations have become more interested in diversity recruiting and, as indicted in the chapter-opening vignette, RBC actively recruits and hires persons with disabilities.[60]

- Encourage teamwork that brings minority and majority members together.

- Ensure that those making career decisions about employees have accurate information about them rather than having to rely on hearsay and second-hand opinion.

EXHIBIT 3.8
Common activities included in diversity programs.
Source: Republished with permission of John Wiley & Sons, Inc., from Jayne, M.E.A., & Dipboye, R.L. (2004, Winter). Leveraging diversity to improve business performance: Research findings and recommendations for organizations. *Human Resource Management*, *43*(4), 409–424; permission conveyed through Copyright Clearance Center, Inc.

Strategic Initiative	Sample Interventions
Recruiting	• Employee referral programs • Diverse recruiting teams • Internship programs and sponsored scholarships • Job posting and advertising initiatives targeting specific groups • Minority conference and job fair attendance • Recruiting efforts targeting universities and community colleges with diverse student bodies
Retention	• Corporate-sponsored employee resource or affinity groups • Employee benefits (e.g., adoption, domestic partner, elder care, flexible health, and dependent spending accounts) • Work–life programs and incentives (e.g., on-site child care, flexible work schedules, and on-site lactation facilities)
Development	• Leadership development training programs • Mentoring programs
External Partnership	• Minority supplier programs • Community service outreach
Communication	• Award programs providing public recognition of managers and employees for diversity achievement • Newsletters, internal websites on diversity • Senior leadership addresses, town hall meetings, business updates
Training	• Awareness training on the organization's diversity initiative • Issue-based/prevention training (e.g., sexual harassment and men and women as colleagues) • Team-building and group-process training
Staffing and Infrastructure	• Dedicated diversity staff • Executive and local diversity councils

- Train people to be aware of stereotypes and to value diversity. As indicated in the chapter-opening vignette, RBC provides web-based training for its managers. At TD Bank, all managers are required to take cross-cultural training as well as workshops on diversity and on interviewing and hiring, to prevent hiring bias.[61]

Although diversity training programs are one of the most common approaches for managing diversity, there is little hard research on the success of these programs. However, there is some anecdotal evidence that these programs can actually cause disruption and bad feelings when all they do is get people to open up and voice their stereotypes and then send them back to work.[62] Awareness training should be accompanied by skills training that is relevant to the particular needs of the organization. This might include training in resolving intercultural conflict, team building, handling a charge of sexual harassment, or learning a second language. Basic awareness and skills training are not the only components of managing diversity. Organizations must use a number of other tactics. What is perhaps most important is that organizations integrate diversity into all their policies and practices rather than treat diversity as a stand-alone practice. Organizations that have been successful in managing diversity have an inclusive culture that values individual differences. And in those organizations that have been recognized as Canada's Best Diversity Employers, diversity is an integral part of the culture.[63]

In future chapters, we will consider the following diversity practices:

- Generational differences in values and work attitudes (Chapter 4).
- Recognizing diversity in employee needs and motives (Chapter 5).
- Using flexible work arrangements to offer employees flexibility (Chapter 6).
- Using employee surveys to foster better communication (Chapters 10 and 15).

Finally, one area of diversity that is of particular concern to governments and organizations is the hiring and integration of skilled immigrants. To find out how one organization does this, see You Be the Manager: *American Express Canada's Skilled Immigrant Strategy*.

PERCEPTIONS OF TRUST

Do you trust your boss and organization? What about your co-workers? These are questions that more and more people are asking themselves. Research has found that employee trust toward management is on the decline.[64] One survey found that 47 percent of respondents agreed that a lack of trust is a problem in their organization. In another survey, 40 percent indicated that they do not believe what management says.[65] In the United States, one in four workers do not trust their employer, while 61 percent of Canadian workers do not trust what their senior leaders say.[66] A lack of trust can be a serious problem, because trust perceptions influence organizational processes and outcomes, such as sales levels, net profits, and employee turnover.[67]

Trust has been defined as a willingness to be vulnerable and to take risks with respect to the actions of another party.[68] More specifically, "Trust is a psychological state comprising the intention to accept vulnerability based upon positive expectations of the intentions or behaviour of another."[69] Trust perceptions toward management are based on three distinct perceptions: ability, benevolence, and integrity.[70] *Ability* refers to employee perceptions regarding management's competence and skills. *Benevolence* refers to the extent that employees perceive management as caring and concerned for their interests and willing to do good for them. *Integrity* refers to employee perceptions that management adheres to and behaves according to a set of values and principles that the employee finds acceptable. The combination of these three factors influences trust perceptions.

LO **3.6**

Define *trust* perceptions and *perceived organizational support*, and describe *organizational support theory*.

Trust. A psychological state in which one has a willingness to be vulnerable and to take risks with respect to the actions of another party.

◼ YOU BE THE MANAGER ◼

American Express Canada's Skilled Immigrant Strategy

American Express in Canada operates as AMEX Canada Inc. and AMEX Bank of Canada. AMEX Canada Inc. and AMEX Band of Canada employ over 3000 Canadians in 13 cities coast to coast.

AMEX Canada has had a diverse workforce for many years. However, with the expected company growth in the coming years, AMEX realized that it needed to do more to attract, retain, and develop skilled immigrants.

Nancy Steele, Director of AMEX technologies (AET), was puzzled that the company's policy of hiring skilled immigrant workers seemed to be failing. "Quite often, you would on-board them, then find they weren't successful and have to remove them and have them leave the organization," she said.

As a solution, Steele initiated a skilled immigrant strategy. "The broader strategy was to look at talent in general across the organization," she said. "As we're going to grow, take on new people and invest a lot in Canada, we looked at what we're going to do to keep up the pace of growth and diversity a little bit."

In looking at ways to hire new employees, she realized there needed to be more work done to hire immigrants. "There were a lot of gaps in the process of how we hire and recruit, where we hire and recruit, and the type of talent we're getting," she said. "There were many opportunities we didn't see."

Furthermore, managers sometimes struggled to understand other cultures and help staff to succeed.

To retain skilled immigrants, Steele implemented initiatives to encourage these employees to grow within the company. "We looked at strategies to improve the process to help individuals not only get better jobs or jobs that are more suited to their skills, but develop them when they're on-site and help them progress in their career," she said.

What should AMEX Canada do to improve the hiring and retention of skilled immigrants? You be the manager.

Fernanda Silva (left) is a Brazilian immigrant who was hired by AMEX technologies as a quality assurance analyst through a skilled immigrant hiring program that was initiated by company director, Nancy Steele.

Questions

1. What should AMEX Canada do to attract and hire skilled immigrants?

2. What strategies are needed to develop and retain skilled immigrants?

To find out what AMEX Canada did, consult The Manager's Notebook at the end of the chapter.

Sources: Based on Silliker, A. (2011, March 28). Firms honoured for work with skilled immigrants. *Canadian HR Reporter, 24*(6), 1, 20; Dalby, P. (2011, March 9). New hiring approach improves success rate for immigrants. *Toronto Star,* www.thestar.com/printarticle/950769; Nancy Steele spearheads skilled immigrant strategy at American Express Canada. (2011, October 6). *TRIEC,* www.triec.ca/2011/nancy-steele-spearheads-skilled-immigrant-strategy; www.americanexpress.com/ca.

Not surprisingly, higher perceptions of management ability, benevolence, and integrity are associated with greater perceptions of trust. There is also some evidence that perceptions of fairness (see Chapter 4 for a discussion of fairness) are associated with trust perceptions. Employees who perceived their supervisor as more fair report higher levels of trust.[71] Furthermore, perceptions of trust in management are positively related to job satisfaction, organizational commitment, job performance, and organizational citizenship behaviour, and negatively related to turnover intentions.[72] Trust among co-workers is also important. A study of firefighters found that higher levels of trust toward one's co-workers was related to fewer physical symptoms (e.g., trouble sleeping) and less withdrawal (e.g., thoughts of being absent).[73]

EXHIBIT 3.9
Trust model.
Source: © 2005 Great Place to Work® Institute, Inc. All Rights Reserved.

CREDIBILITY
- Being approachable and easy to talk with, answering hard questions, and making expectations clear
- Trusting people without looking over their shoulders
- Being reliable, delivering on promises, and "walking the talk"
- Articulating a clear vision for the company or department

RESPECT
- Showing appreciation for employees' efforts and contributions
- Ensuring that people have the equipment they need to do their jobs
- Seeking employees' opinions and involving them in important decisions
- Caring for employees as people with lives outside of work

FAIRNESS
- Ensuring all employees have opportunities for rewards and recognition
- Avoiding playing favourites, especially when promoting people
- Treating all employees fairly, regardless of age, race, or sex
- Ensuring employees are paid fairly

PRIDE
- Helping employees feel they personally make a difference in their work
- Inspiring employees to feel pride in team accomplishments
- Helping employees feel proud of the whole company and its contributions to the community

CAMARADERIE
- Creating a workplace atmosphere where employees can be themselves and care about each other
- Welcoming new employees to a friendly environment and celebrating special events
- Creating a cooperative work environment and demonstrating that people are "all in this together"

Trust is also considered to be the most critical factor when judging best workplaces in Canada. According to the Great Place to Work Institute Canada, trust is the foundation for quality jobs and performance excellence. When the institute evaluates organizations for the best workplaces, they use a "Trust Index" to assess employees' perspective on what it is like to work in their organization. As shown in Exhibit 3.9, the trust model consists of five dimensions. To create a great workplace, managers need to build trust, which is achieved by practising credibility, respect, and fairness, and by encouraging pride and camaraderie among employees.[74]

PERCEIVED ORGANIZATIONAL SUPPORT

Whether or not you trust your boss and organization probably has a lot to do with how much they support you or, rather, your perceptions of support. **Perceived organizational support** (POS) refers to employees' general belief that their organization values their contribution and cares about their well-being. When employees have positive perceptions of organizational support, they believe their organization will provide assistance when they need it to perform their job effectively and to deal with stressful situations.[75]

According to **organizational support theory**, employees who have strong perceptions of organizational support feel an obligation to care about the organization's welfare and to help the organization achieve its objectives. They feel a greater sense of purpose

Perceived organizational support (POS). Employees' general belief that their organization values their contribution and cares about their well-being.

Organizational support theory. A theory that states that employees who have strong perceptions of organizational support feel an obligation to care about the organization's welfare and to help the organization achieve its objectives.

EXHIBIT 3.10
**Predictors and
consequences of
perceived organizational
support.**
Source: Based on Rhoades,
L., & Eisenberger, R. (2002).
Perceived organizational support: A review of the literature.
Journal of Applied Psychology,
87, 698–714.

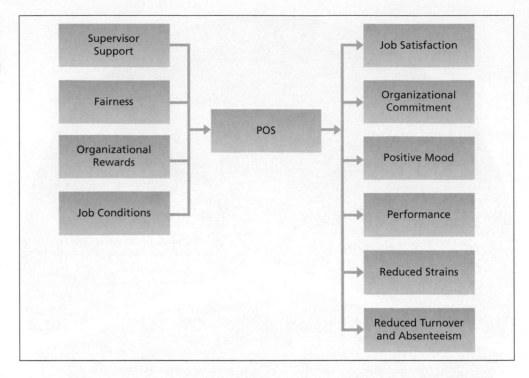

and meaning, and a strong sense of belonging to the organization. As a result, employees incorporate their membership and role within the organization into their social identity. In addition, when POS is strong, employees feel obligated to reciprocate the organization's care and support.

Research has found that employees who have greater POS have higher job performance and are more satisfied with their jobs, more committed to the organization, and less likely to be absent from work and to quit. They are also more likely to have a positive mood at work and to be more involved in their job, and they are less likely to experience strain symptoms such as fatigue, burnout, anxiety, and headaches.[76]

As shown in Exhibit 3.10, there are a number of factors that contribute to employees' POS. First, because supervisors function as representatives of the organization through their actions and decisions, they represent the organization to employees. As a result, favourable treatment, support, and concern for one's well-being from supervisors, or **perceived super-visor support**, contributes strongly to POS. Interestingly, supervisors with more positive perceptions of POS are themselves perceived by employees as being more supportive. In addition, fair organizational procedures as well as favourable rewards and job conditions are also strongly related to POS.[77]

What can organizations do to improve employee perceptions of organizational support? One study found that supportive human resources practices that demonstrate an investment in employees and recognition of employee contributions are most likely to lead to the development of greater POS. Such practices signal to employees that the organization values and cares about them. Some examples of supportive human resources practices include participation in decision making, opportunities for growth and development, and a fair reward and recognition system.[78]

**Perceived supervisor
support (PSS).** Employees'
general belief that their
supervisor values their
contribution and cares
about their well-being.

LO **3.7**

Discuss person
perception and
perceptual biases in
human resources.

PERSON PERCEPTION IN HUMAN RESOURCES

Perceptions play an important role in human resources and can influence who gets hired and how employees are evaluated once they are hired. Job applicants also form perceptions during the recruitment and selection process, and their perceptions influence their attraction to an organization and whether or not they decide to accept a job offer.

In this section, we consider the role of perceptions in three areas of human resources: recruitment and selection, the employment interview, and the performance appraisal.

Perceptions of Recruitment and Selection

When you meet recruiters and complete employment tests, chances are you form perceptions of the organization. In fact, research indicates that the way job applicants are treated during the recruitment and selection process influences their perceptions toward the organization and their likelihood of accepting a job offer. According to **signalling theory**, job applicants have incomplete information about jobs and organizations, so they interpret their recruitment experiences as cues or signals about unknown characteristics of a job and organization and what it would be like to work there. For example, questions that are invasive and discriminatory might send a signal that the organization discriminates and does not value diversity; poor treatment during the hiring process might signal a lack of professionalism and respect of employees. These perceptions are important, because they influence a job applicant's likelihood of remaining in the selection process and accepting a job offer.[79]

Applicants also form perceptions toward organizations based on the selection tests used for hiring. This research has its basis in *organizational justice theory and fairness*, which is described in more detail in Chapter 4. Essentially, job applicants form more positive perceptions of the selection process when selection procedures are perceived to be fair. Furthermore, applicants who have more positive perceptions of selection fairness are more likely to view the organization favourably and to have stronger intentions to accept a job offer and recommend the organization to others. Among various selection procedures, employment interviews and work samples are perceived more favourably than cognitive ability tests, which are perceived more favourably than personality tests and honesty tests.[80]

The interview is a difficult setting in which to form accurate impressions about a candidate. Interview validity increases when interviews are more structured.

Signalling theory. Job applicants interpret their recruitment experiences as cues or signals about unknown characteristics of a job and an organization and what it will be like to work in an organization.

Perceptions in the Employment Interview

You have probably had the pleasure (or displeasure!) of sitting through one or more job interviews in your life. After all, the interview is one of the most common organizational selection devices, applied with equal opportunity to applicants for everything from the janitorial staff to the executive suite. With our futures on the line, we would like to think that the interview is a fair and accurate selection device, but is it? Research shows that the interview is a valid selection device, although it is far from perfectly accurate, especially when the interviewer conducts it in an unstructured, free-form format. The validity of the interview improves when interviewers conduct a more structured interview.[81]

What factors threaten the validity of the interview? To consider the most obvious problem first, applicants are usually motivated to present an especially favourable impression of themselves. As our discussion of the perception of people implies, it is difficult enough to gain a clear picture of another individual without having to cope with active deception! A couple of the perceptual tendencies that we already discussed in this chapter can also operate in the interview. For one thing, there is evidence that interviewers compare applicants to a stereotype of the ideal applicant.[82] In and of itself, this is not a bad thing. However, this ideal stereotype must be accurate, and this requires a clear understanding of the nature of the job in question and the kind of person who can do well in this job. This is a tall order, especially

EXHIBIT 3.11
Two examples of contrast effects.

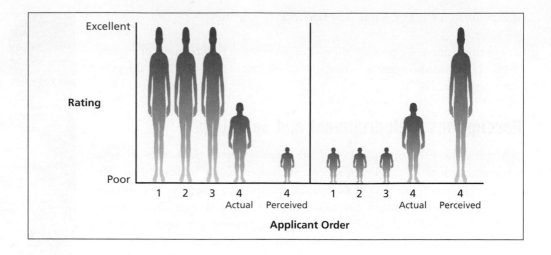

for the interviewer who is hiring applicants for a wide variety of jobs. Second, interviewers have a tendency to exhibit primacy reactions.[83] Minimally, this means that information the interviewer acquires early in the interview will have an undue impact on the final decision. However, it also means that information the interviewer obtains *before* the interview (for instance, by scanning the application form or resumé) can have an exaggerated influence on the interview outcome.

A couple of perceptual tendencies that we have not discussed are also at work in interviews. First, interviewers have a tendency to give less importance to positive information about the applicant.[84] This tendency means that negative information has undue impact on the decision.[85] It might occur because interviewers get more feedback about unsuccessful hiring than successful hiring ("Why did you send me that idiot?"). It might also happen because positive information is not perceived as telling the interviewer much, since the candidate is motivated to put up a good front. In addition, **contrast effects** sometimes occur in the interview.[86] This means that the applicants who have been interviewed earlier affect the interviewer's perception of a current applicant, leading to an exaggeration of differences between applicants. For example, an interviewer who has seen two excellent candidates and then encounters an average candidate, might rate this person lower than an applicant preceded by two average ones (see Exhibit 3.11). This is an example of the impact of the situation on perception.

It is clear that the interview constitutes a fairly difficult setting in which to form accurate impressions about others. It is of short duration, a lot of information is generated, and the applicant is motivated to present a favourable image. Thus, interviewers often adopt "perceptual crutches" that hinder accurate perception.

Earlier, we noted that the validity of the interview improves when it is structured. But what exactly is a structured interview? According to a study by Derek Chapman of the University of Calgary and David Zweig of the University of Toronto, interview structure involves four dimensions: *evaluation standardization* (the extent to which the interviewer uses standardized and numeric scoring procedures); *question sophistication* (the extent to which the interviewer uses job-related behavioural questions and situational questions); *question consistency* (the extent to which the interviewer asks the same questions in the same order of every candidate); and *rapport building* (the extent to which the interviewer does *not* ask personal questions that are unrelated to the job). They also found that interviews were more likely to be structured when the interviewer had formal interview training and focused on selection rather than recruitment during the interview.[87] Structured interviews probably reduce information overload and ensure that applicants can be more easily compared, since they have all responded to an identical sequence of questions.[88]

Contrast effects.
Previously interviewed job applicants affect an interviewer's perception of a current applicant, leading to an exaggeration of differences between applicants.

Perceptions and the Performance Appraisal

Once a person is hired, however imperfectly, further perceptual tasks confront organization members. Specifically, the organization will want some index of the person's job performance for decisions regarding pay raises, promotions, transfers, and training needs. The question is what role do perceptions play in the performance appraisal process? Well, consider this. A recent study found that employees with late start times received lower job performance ratings from their supervisors than employees with early start times. The authors refer to this as a *morning bias* that is due to the negative stereotype of employees with late start times being perceived as less conscientious.[89] Let's now consider some other perceptual biases in the performance appraisal.

OBJECTIVE AND SUBJECTIVE MEASURES It is possible to find objective measures of performance for certain aspects of some jobs. These are measures that do not involve a substantial degree of human judgment. The number of publications that a professor has in top journals is a good example. In general, though, as we move up the organizational hierarchy, it becomes more difficult to find objective indicators of performance. Thus, it is often hard to find quantifiable evidence of a manager's success or failure. When objective indicators of performance do exist, they are often contaminated by situational factors. For example, it might be very difficult to compare the dollar sales of a snowmobile salesperson whose territory covers British Columbia with one whose territory is Nova Scotia. Also, while dollar sales might be a good indicator of current sales performance, it says little about a person's capacity for promotion to district sales manager.

Because of the difficulties that objective performance indicators present, organizations must often rely on subjective measures of effectiveness, usually provided by managers. However, the manager is confronted by a number of perceptual roadblocks. He or she might not be in a position to observe many instances of effective and ineffective performance. This is especially likely when the employee's job activities cannot be monitored directly. For example, a police sergeant cannot ride around in six squad cars at the same time, and a telephone company supervisor cannot visit customers' homes or climb telephone poles with all of his or her installers. Such situations mean that the target (the employee's performance) is frequently ambiguous, and we have seen that the perceptual system resolves ambiguities in an efficient but often inaccurate manner. Even when performance is observable, employees often alter their behaviour so that they look good when their manager is around.

RATER ERRORS Subjective performance appraisal is susceptible to some of the perceptual biases we discussed earlier—primacy, recency, and stereotypes. In addition, a number of other perceptual tendencies occur in performance evaluation. They are often called rater errors. One interrelated set of these tendencies includes leniency, harshness, and central tendency (Exhibit 3.12). **Leniency** refers to the tendency to perceive the performance of one's ratees as especially good, while **harshness** is the tendency to see their performance as especially ineffective. Lenient raters tend to give "good" ratings, and harsh raters tend to give "bad" ratings. Professors with reputations as easy graders or tough graders exemplify these types of raters. **Central tendency** involves assigning most ratees to a middle-range performance category—the extremes of the rating categories are not used. The professor who assigns 80 percent of her students Cs is committing this error.

Each of these three rating tendencies is probably partially a function of the rater's personal experiences. For example, the manager who has had an especially good group of employees might respond with special harshness when management transfers him to supervise a group of slightly less able workers. It is worth noting that not all instances

Leniency. The tendency to perceive the job performance of ratees as especially good.

Harshness. The tendency to perceive the job performance of ratees as especially ineffective.

Central tendency. The tendency to assign most ratees to middle-range job performance categories.

EXHIBIT 3.12
Leniency, harshness, and central tendency rater errors.

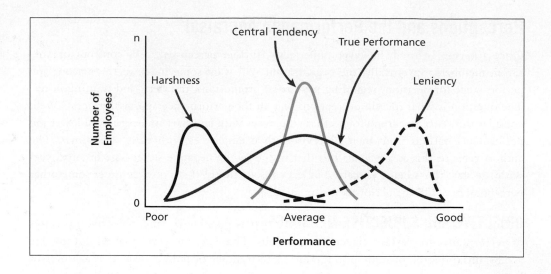

of leniency, harshness, and central tendency necessarily represent perceptual errors. In some cases, raters intentionally commit these errors, even though they have accurate perceptions of workers' performance. For example, a manager might use leniency or central tendency in performance reviews so that his employees do not react negatively to his evaluation.

Another perceptual error that is frequently committed by performance raters is called the **halo effect**.[90] The halo effect occurs when the observer allows the rating of an individual on one trait or characteristic to colour the ratings on other traits or characteristics. For example, in a teacher evaluation system, a student might perceive his instructor as a nice person, and this might favourably influence his perception of the instructor's knowledge of the material and speed in returning exams and papers. Similarly, a manager might rate an employee as frequently late for work, and this might in turn lead her to devalue the employee's productivity and quality of work. As these examples illustrate, halo can work either for or against the ratee. In both cases, the rater fails to perceive differences *within* ratees. The halo effect tends to be organized around central traits that the rater considers important. The student feels that being nice is an especially important quality, while the manager places special emphasis on promptness. Ratings on these characteristics then affect the rater's perceptions of other characteristics.

The **similar-to-me effect** is an additional rater error that may, in part, reflect perceptual bias. The rater tends to give more favourable evaluations to people who are similar to the rater in terms of background or attitudes. For example, the manager with an MBA degree who comes from an upper-middle-class family might perceive a similar employee as a good performer, even though the person is only average. Similarly, a rater might overestimate the performance of an individual who holds similar religious and political views. Such reactions probably stem from a tendency to view our own performance, attitudes, and background as "good." We then tend to generalize this evaluation to others who are, to some degree, similar to us. Raters with diverse employees should be especially wary of this error.

Given all these problems, it should be clear that it is difficult to obtain good subjective evaluations of employee performance. Because of this, human resources specialists have explored various techniques for reducing perceptual errors and biases. There has been a tendency to attempt to reduce rater errors by using rating scales with more specific behavioural labels. The assumption here is that giving specific examples of effective and ineffective performance will facilitate the rater's perceptual processes and recall.

Halo effect. The rating of an individual on one trait or characteristic tends to colour ratings on other traits or characteristics.

Similar-to-me effect. A rater gives more favourable evaluations to people who are similar to the rater in terms of background or attitudes.

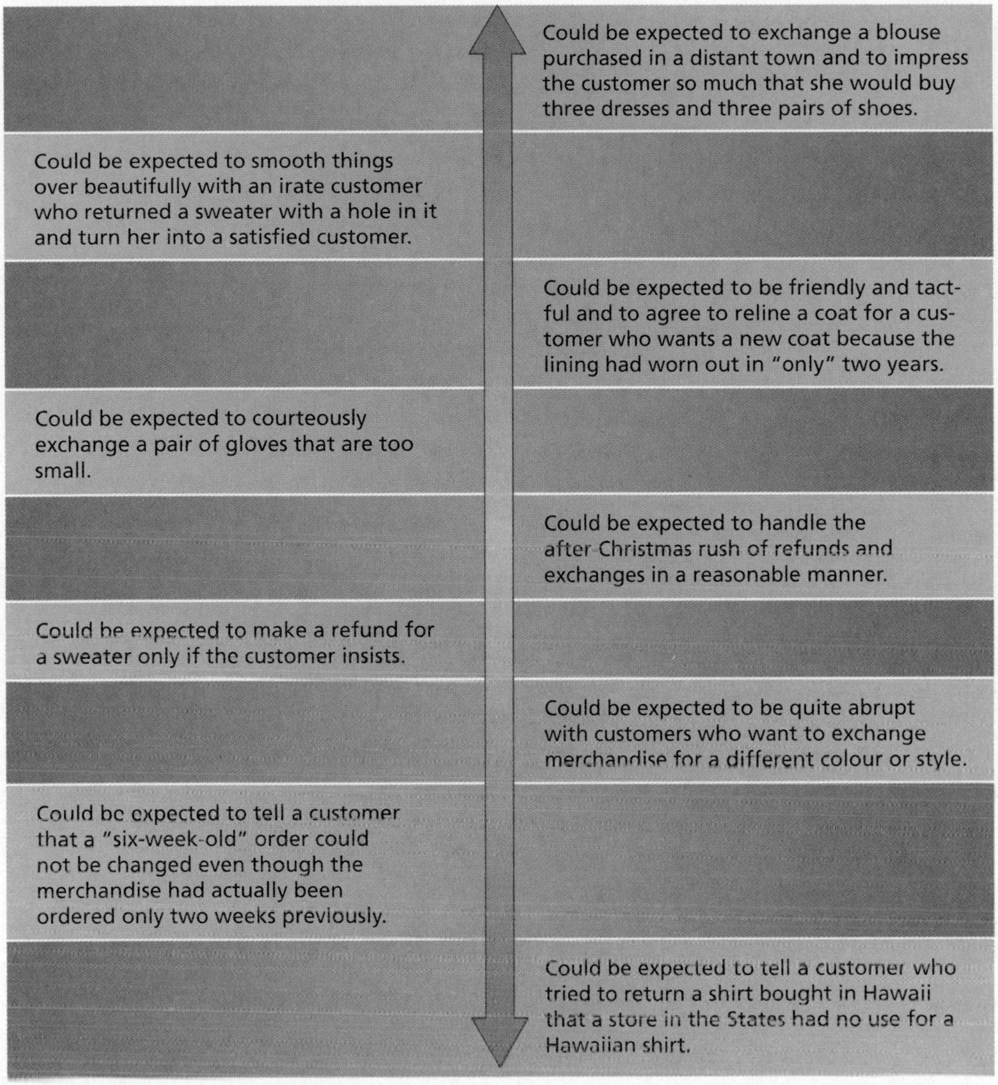

Could be expected to exchange a blouse purchased in a distant town and to impress the customer so much that she would buy three dresses and three pairs of shoes.

Could be expected to smooth things over beautifully with an irate customer who returned a sweater with a hole in it and turn her into a satisfied customer.

Could be expected to be friendly and tactful and to agree to reline a coat for a customer who wants a new coat because the lining had worn out in "only" two years.

Could be expected to courteously exchange a pair of gloves that are too small.

Could be expected to handle the after-Christmas rush of refunds and exchanges in a reasonable manner.

Could be expected to make a refund for a sweater only if the customer insists.

Could be expected to be quite abrupt with customers who want to exchange merchandise for a different colour or style.

Could be expected to tell a customer that a "six-week-old" order could not be changed even though the merchandise had actually been ordered only two weeks previously.

Could be expected to tell a customer who tried to return a shirt bought in Hawaii that a store in the States had no use for a Hawaiian shirt.

EXHIBIT 3.13
Behaviourally anchored rating scale (BARS) for rating customer service.
Source: Campbell, J.P., Dunnette, M.D., Lawler, E.E., III, & Weick, K.E., Jr. (1970). *Managerial behavior, performance, and effectiveness.* New York: McGraw-Hill. © The McGraw-Hill Companies, Inc. Used by permission.

Exhibit 3.13 shows a **behaviourally anchored rating scale (BARS)** that gives very specific behavioural examples (from top to bottom) of good, average, and poor customer service. With such an aid, the rater may be less susceptible to perceptual errors when completing the rating task, although the evidence for this is mixed.[91]

Another approach for reducing perceptual errors and biases and improving the accuracy of performance appraisals is rater training. One of the best known approaches is called **frame-of-reference (FOR) training**. FOR training involves providing raters with a common frame of reference to use when rating individuals. Raters learn about each performance dimension and are provided with examples of good, average, and poor performance. They then practise making performance ratings and receive feedback on their accuracy. As a result, raters learn what behaviours reflect different levels of performance on each performance dimension and to use the same frame of reference when rating all individuals. Research on FOR training has shown that it is an effective method for improving rating accuracy.[92]

Behaviourally anchored rating scale (BARS). A rating scale with specific behavioural examples of good, average, and poor performance.

Frame-of-reference (FOR) training. A training method to improve rating accuracy that involves providing raters with a common frame of reference to use when rating individuals.

THE MANAGER'S NOTEBOOK

American Express Canada's Skilled Immigrant Strategy

AMEX Canada's skilled immigrant strategy was implemented in 2009 and earned Nancy Steele the *Canadian HR Reporter* Individual Achievement Award in 2011 at the Immigrant Success Awards presented by the Toronto Region Immigrant Employment Council (TRIEC). AMEX Canada has also been recognized as one of Canada's Best Diversity Employers.

1. To recruit skilled immigrants, Nancy Steele worked with TRIEC and organized a mass recruitment day. TRIEC, which pre-screens applicants, brought in 200 immigrants and 10 managers and went through the interview process with the recruits. There have been two sessions like this to date, with more scheduled. So far, 11 skilled immigrants have been hired through the program, or 10 percent of hires in the AET division. They have filled key positions including quality assurance analysts, business analysts, project managers, and programmers.

2. To develop and retain skilled immigrants, a number of initiatives were implemented. Language training is available for those skilled immigrants whose language skills many not be "quite as robust" as what is needed, said Steele. English language training enhances integration and promotion. Managers undergo cross-cultural training to learn how to understand the challenges immigrants might be facing and evaluate any potential gaps in their training or performance, so they can coach them appropriately. The success of the program is demonstrated in improved retention rates. "What makes me most proud is the feedback I get directly from our new skilled immigrant hires. They thank me for the opportunity to work here and grow their career with the company," says Steele.

Sources: Based on Silliker, A. (2011, March 28). Firms honoured for work with skilled immigrants. *Canadian HR Reporter*, 24(6), 1, 20; Dalby, P. (2011, March 9). New hiring approach improves success rate for immigrants. *Toronto Star*, www.thestar.com/printarticle/950769; Anonymous (2011, October 6). Nancy Steele spearheads skilled immigrant strategy at American Express Canada. *TRIEC*, www.triec.ca/2011/nancy-steele-spearheads-skilled-immigrant-strategy; www.americanexpress.com/ca.

MyManagementLab   Study, practise, and explore real management situations with these helpful resources:

- **Interactive Lesson Presentations:** Work through interactive presentations and assessments to test your knowledge of management concepts.
- **PIA (Personal Inventory Assessments):** Enhance your ability to connect with key concepts through these engaging, self-reflection assessments.   **P I A** PERSONAL INVENTORY ASSESSMENT
- **Study Plan:** Check your understanding of chapter concepts with self-study quizzes.
- **Videos:** Learn more about the management practices and strategies of real companies.
- **Simulations:** Practise decision-making in simulated management environments.

LEARNING OBJECTIVES CHECKLIST

3.1 *Perception* involves interpreting the input from our senses to provide meaning to our environment. Any instance of perception involves a perceiver, a target, and a situational context. The experience, needs, and emotions of the perceiver affect perception, as does the ambiguity of the target.

3.2 According to *social identity theory*, people form perceptions of themselves and others based on their characteristics and memberships in social categories. Bruner's model of the perceptual process suggests that we are very receptive to cues provided by the target and the situation when we encounter an unfamiliar target.

However, as we discover familiar cues, we quickly categorize the target and process other cues in a selective manner to maintain a consistent and constant picture of the target.

3.3 The main biases in person perception include primacy, recency, implicit personality theory, reliance on central traits, projection, *and* stereotyping. *Primacy* is the tendency for a perceiver to rely on early cues or first impressions, while *recency* is the tendency for a perceiver to rely on recent cues or last impressions. *Central traits* involves personal characteristics of a target person that are of particular interest to a perceiver. *Implicit personality theory* involves personal theories that people have about which personality characteristics go together. *Projection* is the tendency for perceivers to attribute their own thoughts and feelings to others. *Stereotyping* is the tendency to generalize about people in a certain social category and ignore variations among them.

3.4 *Attribution* is the process of assigning causes or motives to people's behaviour. The observer is often interested in determining whether the behaviour is due to *dispositional* (internal) or *situational* (external) causes. Behaviour is likely to be attributed to the disposition of the actor when the behaviour (1) is performed consistently, (2) differs from that exhibited by other people, and (3) occurs in a variety of situations or environments. An opposite set of cues will prompt a situational attribution. The tendency of observers to overemphasize dispositional attributions is known as the *fundamental attribution error,* and the tendency for actors to be more likely to explain their own behaviour in situational terms is the *actor–observer effect.* Our tendency to take credit for success and to deny responsibility for failure is known as the *self-serving bias.*

3.5 The changing nature of the workplace and increasing diversity have highlighted the importance of valuing and managing employee diversity, which can yield strategic, competitive, and performance advantages for the organization. Racial, ethnic, religious, gender, age, and LGBT stereotypes can result in discriminatory human resources decisions and are a major barrier to valuing diversity. Organizations can use a number of tactics, including training, to manage diversity. However, to be most effective, diversity should be integrated into all organization policies and practices and be part of an inclusive culture that values individual differences.

3.6 Perceptions of *trust* involve a willingness to be vulnerable and to take risks with respect to the actions of another party. Trust perceptions toward management are based on perceptions of ability, benevolence, and integrity. *Perceived organizational support* (POS) refers to perceptions about how much an organization values an individual's contribution and cares about one's well-being. According to *organizational support theory,* employees who have strong perceptions of organizational support feel an obligation to care about the organization's welfare and to help the organization achieve its objectives.

3.7 According to *signalling theory,* job applicants have incomplete information about jobs and organizations, so they interpret their recruitment and selection experiences as cues or signals about unknown characteristics of a job and an organization. Job applicants form more positive perceptions of the selection process when the selection procedures are perceived to be fair. Interviewers and performance raters exhibit a number of perceptual tendencies that are reflected in inaccurate judgments, including *leniency, harshness, central tendency,* and *contrast, halo,* and *similar-to-me effects.* Structured interviews can improve the accuracy of perceptions in the employment interview, and *behaviourally anchored rating scales (BARS)* and *frame-of-reference (FOR)* training can improve the accuracy of performance appraisals.

DISCUSSION QUESTIONS

1. Suppose an employee does a particularly poor job on an assigned project. Discuss the attribution process that this person's manager will use to form judgments about this poor performance. Be sure to discuss how the manager will use consistency, consensus, and distinctiveness cues.

2. Discuss the factors that make it difficult for employment interviewers to form accurate perceptions of interviewees. Explain why a gender or racial stereotype might be more likely to affect a hiring decision than a performance appraisal decision. How can interviews and

performance appraisals be designed to improve the accuracy of perceptions?

3. What are the implications of social identity theory for diversity in organizations? Describe some of the things that an organization can do to remove the barriers to workplace diversity. List some of the advantages gained by organizations that effectively manage a diverse workforce.

4. Explain stereotype threat effects and provide some examples of how they might occur in organizations and the consequences. What can organizations do to prevent stereotype threat effects?

5. Review the Ethical Focus feature, *What's in a Name? You're Hired ... or Not!*, and use Bruner's model of the perceptual process to explain why job applicants with ethnic-sounding names are less likely to receive callbacks. What perceptual biases might explain the lower callbacks received for resumés with ethnic-sounding names? What should organizations do to avoid name discrimination? What should job applicants do?

INTEGRATIVE DISCUSSION QUESTIONS

1. Describe how the principles of operant learning theory and social cognitive theory can be used to manage workplace diversity and reduce the effects of workplace stereotypes. How can the organizational learning practices described in Chapter 2 be used for managing diversity?

2. Consider how the four basic types of managerial activities described in Chapter 1 (i.e., routine communication, traditional management, networking, and human resource management) can influence employees' perceptions of trust and perceived organizational support (POS). How should managers perform each of these activities to improve employees' perceptions of trust and POS?

ON-THE-JOB CHALLENGE QUESTION

Australia's Jobs Bonus Initiative

In 2012, the Australian government launched a new initiative that will pay employers to hire older workers. Employers will receive $1000 for every worker aged 50 or older that they hire and retain for at least three months. The government has committed $10 million over four years to the Jobs Bonus initiative in response to a report that highlights the value of older workers.

According to Mark Butler, the former Minister for Mental Health and Ageing, "We still need to deal with a cultural issue in the Australian business community that sometimes looks past the value of older workers. We know that older workers have lower absenteeism; they have higher retention rates; and they bring with them extraordinary wisdom and experience. We just need to push through this barrier that some Australian employers still have."

However, according to Susan Eng, vice-president for advocacy at CARP, a Toronto-based advocacy group for people over 50, this may not be the right course of action. "I understand the motivation, but I'm not particularly thrilled with the method. It suggests that an older worker is somehow flawed and you, therefore, have to pay somebody to hire them," she said. "If you're trying to resolve and overcome age discrimination in hiring, why reinforce this stereotype by offering a sweetener?"

What do you think about the Australian government's Jobs Bonus initiative? Do perceptions have anything to do with this initiative? Do you think this will help or hurt older workers and the perception and stereotype of them? Is this something that Canadian governments should consider doing? What are the implications for employees and organizations?

Source: Reprinted by permission of Silliker, A. (2012, May 21). Australia offers $1000 for hiring of older workers. *Canadian HR Reporter, 25*(10), 1, 10.

EXPERIENTIAL EXERCISE

Beliefs about Older Workers

Answer the 27 questions listed here. The questions are an attempt to assess the attitudes people have about older workers. The statements cover many different points of view; you may find yourself agreeing strongly with some of the statements, disagreeing just as strongly with others, and perhaps feeling uncertain about others. After you have answered all 27 questions, follow the instructions below to obtain your score.

Read each statement carefully. Using the numbers from 1 to 5 on the rating scale, mark your personal opinion about each statement in the blank space next to each statement. Remember, give your personal opinion according to how much you agree or disagree with each item. In all cases, *older* refers to people who are 50 years of age or older.

1–Strongly disagree

2–Disagree

3–Neither agree or disagree

4–Agree

5–Strongly agree

_____ 1. Older employees have fewer accidents on the job.

_____ 2. Most companies are unfair to older employees.

_____ 3. Older employees are harder to train for jobs.

_____ 4. Older employees are absent more often than younger employees.

_____ 5. Younger employees have more serious accidents than older workers.

_____ 6. If two workers had similar skills, I'd pick the older worker to work with me.

_____ 7. Occupational diseases are more likely to occur among younger employees.

_____ 8. Older employees usually turn out work of higher quality.

_____ 9. Older employees are grouchier on the job.

_____ 10. Younger workers are more cooperative on the job.

_____ 11. Older workers are more dependable.

_____ 12. Most older workers cannot keep up with the speed of modern industry.

_____ 13. Older employees are most loyal to the company.

_____ 14. Older workers resist change and are too set in their ways.

_____ 15. Younger workers are more interested than older workers in challenging jobs.

_____ 16. Older workers can learn new skills as easily as other employees.

_____ 17. Older employees are better employees.

_____ 18. Older employees do not want jobs with increased responsibilities.

_____ 19. Older workers are not interested in learning new skills.

_____ 20. Older employees should "step aside" (take a less demanding job) to give younger employees advancement opportunities.

_____ 21. The majority of older employees would quit work if they could afford it.

_____ 22. Older workers are usually outgoing and friendly at work.

_____ 23. Older workers prefer less challenging jobs than those they held when they were younger.

_____ 24. It is a better investment to train younger workers rather than older workers.

_____ 25. Older employees in our department work just as hard as anyone else.

_____ 26. Given a choice, I would not work with an older worker on a daily basis.

_____ 27. A person's performance declines significantly with age.

Scoring and Interpretation

The scale you have just completed measures your attitudes toward older workers. To score your beliefs about older workers, subtract your responses to each of the following items from 6: 3, 4, 9, 10, 12, 14, 15, 18, 19, 20, 21, 23, 24, 26, and 27. For example, if you put 2 for item 3, give yourself a 4 (6 minus 2). Then simply add up your resulting responses to all 27 items. Your score should fall somewhere between 27 and 135. Low scores indicate an overall negative belief about older workers, while high scores indicate positive beliefs. The higher your score, the more favourable your attitudes are toward older workers.

Research on older workers has generally found that a negative stereotype of older workers exists in organizations. The danger of this is that it can lead to negative attitudes and discriminatory behaviour toward older workers.

A study of 179 employees from three organizations obtained scores that ranged from 54 to 118. The average score was 90, which indicated somewhat positive beliefs about older workers. As reported in other studies, older workers had more positive beliefs about older workers than did younger workers. However, younger workers who had more interactions with older workers were found to have more positive beliefs about older workers.

To facilitate class discussion and your understanding of age stereotypes, form a small group with several other members of the class and consider the following questions. (Note that the instructor can also do this as a class exercise. Students should write their score, age, and interactions with older workers on a piece of paper and hand it in to the instructor, who can then determine the relationship between age, interactions with older workers, and beliefs about older workers.)

1. Students should first compare their scores to each other's and to the average score indicated above (90). Do group members have positive or negative beliefs about older workers? Do some group members have more positive or negative beliefs than others in the group?

2. Each member of the group should indicate his or her age. Determine the average age of the group and categorize those members above the average as being "older" and those below the average as being "younger." Then calculate the average score of the two age groups. Is there a difference in beliefs about older workers between older and younger group members?

3. Each group member should indicate how often they interact with older workers (daily, several times a week, once a week, or monthly). Based on group members' responses, create two categories that correspond to high and low interactions with older workers. Calculate the average score of these two groups. Is there a difference in beliefs about older workers between those who have more and those you have less interaction with older workers?

4. Why do some students have positive or negative beliefs about older workers? What are the implications of these beliefs at work and outside of work?

5. What can you do to develop more positive beliefs about older workers? What are the implications of doing so?

Source: Republished with permission of John Wiley & Sons, Inc., from Hassell, B.L., & Perrewe, P.L. (1995). An examination of beliefs about older workers: Do stereotypes still exist? *Journal of Organizational Behavior*, 16, 457–468; permission conveyed through Copyright Clearance Center, Inc.

CASE INCIDENT

The New Hiring Policy

Citizens Medical Centre, a hospital in Victoria, Texas, recently instituted a new hiring policy that bans job applicants from employment for being overweight. The new policy states that the hospital will not hire anyone with a body mass index (BMI which is a formula used to determine fat) of 35 or higher. This is the equivalent of someone who is 5 feet 5 inches tall and weighs 210 pounds or someone who is 5 feet 10 inches tall and weighs 245 pounds.

According to the policy, an employee's physique "should fit with a representational image or specific mental projection of the job of a health-care professional." David Brown, the hospital's former CEO, stated, "The majority of our patients are over 65 and they have expectations that cannot be ignored in terms of personal appearance." He further stated, "We have the ability as an employer to characterize our process and to have a policy that says what's best for our business and our patients."

As part of the hiring process, job applicants are screened by a physician who assesses their fitness for work, which includes their body mass index. Existing workers who become obese during employment are not terminated; however, job applicants have been turned away as a result of the policy.

Although the laws in Texas do not prohibit weight discrimination in hiring, they do prohibit discrimination based on race, age, or religion.

However, according to Peggy Howell, public relations director for the National Association to Advance Fat Acceptance, "This is discrimination plain and simple. So the field of medicine is no longer an option for people of larger body size? What a waste of talent." She said that a hospital should know that lots of medical conditions lead to obesity or weight gain.

According to former CEO David Brown, excessive weight has "all kinds of encumbrances" for the hospital and its health plan, and there's evidence that extremely obese employees are absent from work more often.

1. Discuss the role of perceptions and attributions in the new hiring policy. Do perceptions and attributions have anything to do with the hiring policy?

2. Discuss the role of stereotypes and bias in the new hiring policy. Do stereotypes and bias have anything to do with the hiring policy? Is it discrimination?

3. Do you agree with the hospital's new hiring policy? What are the implications of the policy for the hospital, its employees, and patients?

Sources: Silliker, A. (2012, May 21). U.S. hospital balks at hiring obese workers. *Canadian HR Reporter, 25*(10), 1, 3; Ramshaw, E. (March 26, 2012). Victoria hospital won't hire very obese workers. *The Texas Tribune*, www.texastribune.org; (2012, April 5). Hospital in weight row after hiring policy BANS obese job applicants. *Daily Mail Reporter*, www.dailymail.co.uk/news/article-2125385.

CASE STUDY

IVEY | Publishing

LGBTA at TD Bank Financial Group in 2012

Ron Puccini, senior manager of corporate diversity at TD Bank Financial Group (TD), was rubbing his temples as he sat in his office at the end of a long day in January 2012.[1] He opened the report in front of him, part of a review by the corporate diversity department of the strategic direction of TD's LGBTA[2] initiatives. Ever since the Diversity Leadership Council (DLC) was created in 2006, engagement from the LGBTA employees at TD had risen exponentially. The corporate diversity group had been providing a growing number of resources, events, and LGBTA-related sponsorship over the past six years to promote a comfortable, barrier-free and inclusive work environment for all employees.

However, the report also revealed that, as of late, TD's competitors and other large companies were catching up to TD. Puccini had also been notified that there was a large variance in the quality of experience between the different subgroups of TD's LGBTA community. He wondered how TD should continue to grow these initiatives to ensure the bank would maintain its position as the "Employer of Choice" for the LGBTA community and be among the "Top 100 Diversity Employers for 2012." The DLC was expecting a report by the end of the week.

TD Bank Financial Group[3]

At the time, the Toronto-Dominion Bank (TSX:TD) was the sixth largest bank in North America,[4] with more than 2300 retail locations in Canada and the United States, serving more than 19 million customers around the world. With headquarters in Toronto, the bank was divided into four main sectors: Canadian personal and commercial banking, U.S. personal and commercial banking, wholesale banking, and wealth management.

TD primarily competed with the other major Canadian banks: Royal Bank of Canada (RBC), Canadian Imperial Bank of Commerce (CIBC), Bank of Nova Scotia (Scotia), and Bank of Montreal (BMO). As of 2011, TD placed second behind RBC in total asset value and market capitalization, with Scotia Bank in third place.[5]

In 2011, TD had earned $5.89 billion in net income on $21.59 billion of revenue. Despite the bank's conservative values and strong risk-management

1 The case writer gathered all direct quotes in this case from the company during multiple interviews and phone calls with the decision maker between February and April of 2012.
2 LGBTA stands for lesbian, gay, bisexual, transgendered, and allies.

3 http://www.w3.td.com/intranet/tdweb, accessed on March 15, 2012.
4 Measured by number of branches.
5 http://www.bankingcanada.net/big+five+banks+in+canada/, accessed on April 3, 2012.

EXHIBIT 1   2011 Sustainalytics Scores for the Big Five Canadian Banks

The Toronto-Dominion Bank	73
Royal Bank of Canada	72
Canadian Imperial Bank of Commerce	68
Bank of Nova Scotia	67
Bank of Montreal	66

Source: http://www.sustainalytics.com; assessed April 3, 2012.

principles, it had experienced strong revenue growth over the past five years, at an average of 10 per cent per annum.[6]

TD was committed to being the "better bank" and had built its reputation on being growth-orientated and customer-focused. The company dedicated itself to transparency and follow-through on its promises. It had won numerous awards, including one of *Financial Post's* "Ten Best Companies to Work For." In 2011, there were 75 631 full-time employees at TD. The bank had reported an employee turnover rate of 7.8 per cent in Canada and 8.7 per cent in the United States.

Corporate Responsbility and Diversity at TD[7]

Executives at TD considered corporate social responsibility a key driver of TD's bottom line. The bank's multifaceted strategy of better serving the community comprised three main areas: education and financial literacy, creating opportunities for young people, and the environment. Every year, the bank made donations of millions of dollars to not-for-profit organizations and provided employees with paid time off for volunteer work.

Compared to its competitors, TD currently ranked the highest in its sustainability performance with an overall score of 73 out of 100, as assessed in an annual report by Sustainalytics.[8] Sustainalytics is a global investment research company, formerly known as Jantzi Research, that researches, analyzes and reports on ESG and SRI performance of a large number of firms. ESG refers to economic, social and corporate governance issues. SRI, or social responsibility index, is Canadian stock market index that measures a firm's environmental and social performance. Anyone interested in ESG and SRI scores could access them, typically for a small fee including investors, customers and employees.

Exhibits 1 and 2 offer a comparison of competitors' scores and a breakdown of TD's social score. Regarding TD's overall sustainability performance, the Sustainalytics report stated that "Toronto-Dominion Bank (TD)'s reporting on ESG issues is considered strong and the company is highly transparent. The company publishes a CSR report annually accord-

EXHIBIT 2
TD's Sustainalytics Social Score
Source: Adapted by case writers from data available on http://www.sustainalytics.com; assessed April 3, 2012.

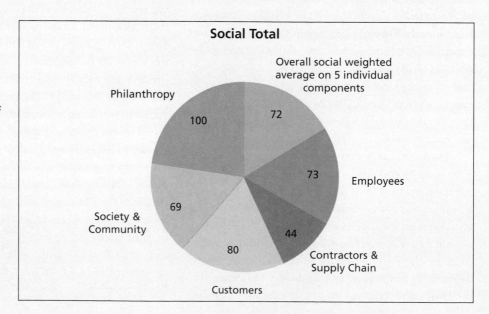

6 Mergent online, assessed on October 12, 2012.

7 http://www.td.com/corporate-responsibility/index.jsp, accessed on March 15, 2012.

8 Sustainalytics measures companies against each other based on corporate social responsibility practices. The maximum score is 100. http://www.sustainalytics.com.

EXHIBIT 3 Excerpt from TD's Corporate Policy on Diversity

Fostering Diversity

- Fostering diversity has been important to TD for many years, but as we weren't making the progress we wanted we made it a strategic business priority—to make sure it is part of everything we do and won't be set aside in tough times.
- At TD diversity means being an inclusive work environment, a place where
  - No one is overlooked on the basis of their unique background, be that gender, ethnic origin, physical ability, sexual orientation, or anything else.
  - People's differences are respected, valued, and supported.
  - Barriers are taken down to create a place where all employees have the opportunity to reach their full potential based on their merits.
  - Customers feel comfortable.
  - The communities we serve are reflected in our workforce and supported in our actions.
- TD's Diversity Leadership Council (DLC) champions diversity programs across TD. The DLC is made up of senior leaders with established committees that support and focus on key areas:
  - Aboriginal peoples.
  - Serving diverse communities.
  - Promoting and enhancing an inclusive environment for lesbian, gay, bisexual, transgender, and allies (LGBTA) employees and customers.
  - Building an agenda for people with disabilities.
  - Expanding leadership opportunities for members of visible minority groups.
  - Expanding leadership opportunities for women.
- Our diversity initiatives start with talking to employees and customers. In this way we are building inclusiveness one conversation at a time.
- According to the 2006 Canadian census, about 13 million people, or just over 40 percent of Canadians, fall into one of our diversity areas of focus (excluding women who aren't also part of another area of focus). Even taking into account some people who fall into more than one category, we're still talking about a third of our population.
- Diversity is not in itself a numbers game—numbers are only a measure of our progress. Our focus is on engaging in initiatives that make an impact and that lead to a long-lasting cultural change. This is what will continue to make TD the better bank in the challenging times ahead.

Source: Company documents.

ing to GRI guidelines to application level B+ and its GRI table is externally verified.[9]" On the social subcategory, the report noted that "TD reports on programs to increase workforce diversity, although it has not disclosed a formal policy on the freedom of association."[10]

As part of its overall emphasis on sustainability, TD had made the promotion of diversity and inclusivity a priority for many years, and in 2005 diversity was integrated into the business strategy. Soon after, the bank created the DLC in response to a seemingly slow adoption of the concept of diversity throughout the bank. The DLC allowed senior executives to take owner-

ship of diversity and inclusivity by figuring out how to implement these priorities across the bank. The DLC oversaw a multitude of diversity initiatives and ensured that no one in the organization was mistreated on any dimension, including gender, ethnic origin, physical ability, or sexual orientation. The committee focused on creating programs that led to long-term organizational change and impacted a wide range of subcultures within TD. (See Exhibit 3 for an excerpt of TD's corporate policy on diversity.)

The bank had a formal policy on the elimination of discrimination and formal programs to increase workforce diversity:

TD's code of ethics prohibits any behaviour that could be construed as harassment or discrimination on the grounds of sex, race, national or

---

9 GRI stands for global reporting initiative. It is a non-profit organization that promotes economic sustainability.

10 Sustainalytics, Company Sustainability Summary, April 3, 2012.

ethnic origin, colour, religion, age, disability, marital status, family status, sexual orientation or criminal convictions from which a pardon has been granted. The company also upholds the Universal Declaration of Human Rights, which prohibits discrimination; however, it does not explicitly refer to the ILO [International Labour Organization] conventions.

TD has initiatives to increase diversity, including recruitment, engagement with employees, mentoring and networking, as well as training and development. The company reported that as of FY2009, women accounted for 65.60% of its Canadian workforce, 33.13% of senior management, and 46.63% of middle management and equivalent positions. Diversity figures for minorities, Aboriginal peoples and persons with disabilities have also been disclosed. The company has not reported global figures and has not disclosed quantitative targets and deadlines to workforce diversity.[11]

LGBTA Initiatives at TD

A survey in 2006 revealed that TD was below the banking industry norm of providing benefits to same-sex couples, particularly at the executive level. This insight created urgency for change at the bank. The LGBTA committee was formed within the DLC. Paul Douglas, an executive vice-president at TD, was appointed as its chair. At the time, there were no "out" executives at the bank, which seemed not to capture the underlying reality. TD wanted to implement policies to provide better experience to LGBTA employees and raise awareness about same-sex benefits. Douglas stated:

> While we had same-sex benefits available for many years, only 94 employees were signed up for them. With 47 000 employees in Canada, this didn't make sense. We also knew that some people, including executives, didn't feel at ease being upfront about their sexuality as they thought it would limit their careers.[12]

The response from TD's stakeholders was mixed. There were many employees, customers, and share-

holders who were either indifferent or in support of TD's decision to actively support the LGBTA community through its strategic plan. However, some stakeholders were anti-LGBTA for personal, traditional, or religious reasons. A number of complaints were received, and some clients and investors threatened to leave the bank. TD kept track of all negative feedback, but its stance remained firm—no employee would be discriminated against based on his or her sexual orientation. Puccini remembered that he had once said, that "banks and big businesses need to be change-makers, so there was no threshold to pull the switch."

The DLC's efforts began to pay off soon after its first year. Between March 2006 and March 2008, the number of employees with same-sex benefits had increased by 36 per cent.

Core Employee Programs and Sponsorships

TD provides many LGBTA-related programs and services to its employees. Some examples include mentors, networking events, internal social networks, and HIV/AIDS programs.

After forming the DLC in 2005, TD started rolling out its strategy in 2006. In the beginning, the focus was on grassroots initiatives such as HIV/AIDS awareness programs. Over time, these initiatives transformed from a business strategy into "the right thing to do." This philosophy drove the bank to move beyond common programming by expanding to underserved areas of the LGBTA community. One such program was Youthline, TD's helpline for LGBTA youth.

TD offers mentoring opportunities in its regional offices to teach newer employees how to use their identification as LGBTA as an advantage and how to build a successful career at the bank. TD also organizes networking events for LGBTA employees as well as allies twice a year across North America. Members of senior management, including Ed Clark, the CEO, attend all of these events. He had been deeply committed to LGBTA initiatives:

> I care that our customers and employees who are gay, lesbian, bisexual or transgender have a comfortable experience at TD. I don't want people to feel they have to hide who they are because they're afraid we'll discriminate against them. In fact, I look forward to the day when all employees feel that their sexual orientation is a non-issue.[13]

11 Company documents.

12 Paul Douglas, 2007, "Diversity and the Gay and Lesbian Community: More Than Chasing the Pink Dollar," Ivey Business Journal online; http://www.iveybusinessjournal.com/topics/the-organization/diversity-and-the-gay-and-lesbian-community-more-than-chasing-the-pink-dollar#.UHg7MEJgPlI, accessed April 3, 2012.

13 Ibid.

Three years after initiating the LGBTA strategy, the Employee Pride Network (EPN) was created. The EPN acted as a communication tool for LGBTA events, sponsorships, and other initiatives. In 2011, the EPN had grown to 2100 members across North America. LGBTA awareness training was optional for new employees, and the responsibility for promoting resource groups such as EPN fell on managers.

In 2011, TD unveiled an internal social media application called Connections, which was the bank's adaptation of Facebook for the office. Users were able to join different communities depending on their interests and thus to interact with TD employees with similar interests. Near the end of 2011, TD launched a LGBTA Community within Connections, which at the time had 426 members. Employees could benefit from the community based on their comfort level: those not wishing to identify could "follow" the page, while those wishing to identify could "join." Regardless of which they chose, all employees who "followed" or "joined" the LGBTA Community were sent frequent updates on events and initiatives in their region.

Each year, TD contributed more than $1 million towards LGBTA organizations such as Pride Toronto, PFLAG Canada, Ontario Gay & Lesbian Chamber of Commerce, Inside Out Film Festival, and Out on Bay Street. This was a fixed amount of approximately $56 million of total sponsorship per year, and poor economic times did not impact TD's corporate giving.

Customer Strategies

TD aimed to provide its LGBTA customers with a comfortable banking experience, although no customized products and services were designed specifically for them. The value lay in precise target marketing to promote a broad range of products and services as an overall extension of the TD brand. Paul Douglas had noted,

> In Canada, LGBTA consumers have an estimated buying power of more than $75 billion. . . . It would be foolish not to pursue such a potentially profitable client group.[14]

TD's LGBTA marketing strategy included targeted advertising to LGBTA publications in major centers as well as overt mainstream advertisements. There was also some local advertising in branches.

Competition on Being a Top Diversity Employer

TD was the first bank to make specific inroads into the LGBTA community. Their support was consistent and multi-pronged, as they contributed to numerous LGBTA organizations and implemented large-scale programming from the beginning. In contrast, other banks would sponsor a LGBTA event but would exit the community soon after.

Although their competitors were certainly aiming to implement similar strategies, TD did not specifically research what the other banks were doing for LGBTA. Since TD was focused on doing the right thing, getting an edge over its competitors was secondary.

However, other banks have learned quickly from TD's success and have adopted many similar initiatives and contributions to LGBTA organizations. While TD was once the dominant organization supporting the LGBTA community, other banks were slowly marginalizing their position as "employer of choice."

Initial Challenges

Although their change efforts have made significant progress in the organization, Puccini thought that he and the DLC had struggled with prioritization of issues when first rolling out the strategy in 2006. He believed that they had tried to tackle too many issues at once instead of implementing programs gradually and in stages. In 2006, there had also been no plan to create opportunities across Canada.

Many employees were hesitant to identify as LGBTA because they perceived a possible trade-off between feeling comfortable at work and successful career progression. Often there were communication barriers within the bank. Managers were the main communication mechanism for reaching all employees in North America. During 2007–08, managers and executives participated in "Embracing Diversity" training. This was general training that included multiple areas of diversity. In 2010, "The Value of Allies" presentation was added. Despite this training, numerous managers were showing resistance toward this responsibility. This was particularly an issue in smaller cities. There was also no incentive system in place to motivate managers to champion diversity or LGBTA-specific initiatives.

Another early mistake had been to not recognize differences between the subgroups of the LGBTA community. As Amin Sunderji, associate vice president at TD, had noted: "One mistake made by TD early

---

14 Ibid.

in the process was painting the LGBTA community with one brush. We didn't realize that there was actual diversity within the community."

This was an issue at the employee and customer level. Since a large number of gay men had identified themselves as LGBTA at the beginning, TD began to roll out programs that were specifically targeted toward them. As a result, its advertising strategy was negatively impacted. Without the lesbian and transgender employees voluntarily identifying as part of the program, TD did not fully understand how to market to these communities, and it centred advertisements only around gay men. The DLC realized that all subgroups needed to be considered equally if their initiatives were truly going to succeed.

Expanding the Strategy

By 2009, many LGBTA employees within the bank were benefiting from its programs. TD turned its attention to talent acquisition to become the "employer of choice" for the LGBTA community in the financial sector. To accomplish this, the bank reached out to certain universities in Canada to build stronger relationships with their pride networks and MBA student associations. The bank also heavily sponsored career-related LGBTA organizations such as Pride at Work and Out on Bay Street.

All change initiatives at TD were targeted toward its goal of being the "better bank" through customer-focused and growth-orientated thinking. Like the other components of the DLC, the purpose of the LGBTA Committee was to ultimately increase shareholder value while providing the best experience possible for customers and employees.

Hiring certain minorities (e.g., visible minorities, Aboriginal peoples, and women) is bound by employment equity law in Canada, and corporations that don't meet certain quotas can be perceived as biased against these minorities. LGBTA was excluded from equity employment law, so there were no quotas for hiring LGBTA employees. Therefore, LGBTA initiatives were treated as a business strategy instead of a compliance tactic.

The current LGBTA strategy at TD was comprised of four elements:

1. Acknowledging and valuing differences in customers, employees and shareholders.

2. Attracting and retaining the best talent available and having access to the most diverse and creative work force.

3. Improving the value of TD's franchise for future generations.

4. Achieving long-term sustainability as an organization that resonates with customers, employees and the communities it serves.

Advancing LGBTA Initiatives

Puccini put down the report, looking at his map of the current issues facing his team. Although he was fully supportive of TD's LGBTA initiatives, it was clear that some of the bank's managers did not see LGBTA as a priority. Puccini wondered how he could motivate these managers to take LGBTA initiatives more seriously and if there were more effective ways to promote these initiatives to employees.

Although TD had worked hard to close the gap between the subcultures of their LGBTA employees over the last few years, the lesbian, bisexual, and transgendered community still seemed to have a lower quality of experience with the bank's initiatives. Puccini questioned if TD was overlooking something and how current programs could be altered to be more inclusive of this area of the community.

He glanced at the long list of emails in his inbox regarding LGBTA initiatives and realized that he needed to form an action plan by the end of the week to present to the DLC.

QUESTIONS

1. Discuss what it means to value diversity. Does TD Bank value diversity? Provide some examples to support your answer.

2. What are some of the initiatives that TD Bank has implemented to increase diversity? What effect has this had on the bank and its employees?

3. When TD bank formed the LGBTA committee, only 94 employees were signed up for same-sex benefits and there were no "out" executives at the bank. Why do you think so few employees were signed up for same-sex benefits and there were no "out" executives? Use the material in the chapter to explain your answer.

4. The response from stakeholders to TD's LGBTA initiatives was mixed. Some stakeholders were indifferent, others were supportive, and some were anti-LGBTA. In addition, some clients and investors threatened to leave the bank. What role

do perceptions and perceptual biases in person perception play in the different stakeholder reactions? Explain your answer.

5. What are some of the LGBTA programs that TD bank implemented, and what effect did this have on the organization, employees, customers, and other banks?

6. Why were some employees hesitant to identify as LGBTA? Why were some managers resistant to the LGBTA initiatives and their responsibility, even after they received diversity training?

7. What are some of the mistakes that the bank made with its LGBTA initiatives? Do you think this had anything to do with perceptions and stereotypes? Explain your answer and consider the relevance of social identity theory.

8. Why don't all of the bank's managers see LGBTA as a priority, and what can be done to change this? What can be done to better promote the LGBTA initiatives to employees?

CHAPTER 4

VALUES, ATTITUDES, AND WORK BEHAVIOUR

LEARNING OBJECTIVES

After reading Chapter 4, you should be able to:

4.1 Define *values*, and discuss the implications of cross-cultural variation in values for organizational behaviour.

4.2 Define *attitudes*, and explain how people develop attitudes.

4.3 Explain the concept of *job satisfaction*, and discuss some of its key contributors, including discrepancy, fairness, disposition, mood, and emotion.

4.4 Explain the relationship between job satisfaction and absenteeism, turnover, performance, organizational citizenship behaviour, and customer satisfaction.

4.5 Differentiate *affective*, *continuance*, and *normative commitment*, and explain how organizations can foster *organizational commitment*.

FACEBOOK

For much of corporate America, the millennial generation is a puzzle. At Facebook Inc., it became the answer. Born after 1980, millennials are often thought of as feeling entitled and clinging to a fantasy that work should be fun. They are also a majority of Facebook's 8000 employees. A Payscale study in December 2014 found the median age at Facebook was 28, compared with 30 at Google Inc. and 31 at Apple Inc. Rather than shrink from the stereotypes, Facebook embraced them and crafted management techniques around them. Managers are told performance reviews should be 80 percent "focused on strengths." Employees aren't "entitled"—they have "an intense sense of ownership." Employees are given unusual freedom to choose, and change, assignments, even outside their areas of expertise.

Even low-level employees are encouraged to question and criticize managers. Shortly after Don Faul joined Facebook's online-operations team from Google, he scheduled an 8 a.m. meeting for staffers. Employees resisted, which rattled the former Marines special-forces commander. "I was walking on eggshells from minute one," Mr. Faul says. Staffers ultimately went along when Mr. Faul said the early start was necessary to accommodate employees in a soon-to-be-opened office in Ireland. Mr. Faul says Google is more structured, and being a manager meant more. At Facebook, "You get zero credit for your title," he said. "It's all about the quality of the work, the power of your conviction, and the ability to influence people."

Facebook can be disorienting for some older employees, who feel their past experience and accomplishments aren't valued. Peter Yewell, who was in his mid-to-late 30s when he worked on Facebook's sales team from 2006 to 2012, said the company chose not to hire some job candidates his age or older—for good reason. "A lot of people who were really talented just wouldn't work in that environment," he said. At other places he worked, including Yahoo Inc. and CBS Radio, Mr. Yewell said managers told employees what to do. At Facebook, "sometimes their role is to help you get the resources you need and to move things out of your way," he says.

To be sure, Facebook doesn't give employees free rein. Executives describe a balance between keeping young workers productive and doing what's practical. Facebook staffers are rated on a bell curve relative to peers. That can jolt young employees accustomed to being told they are high achievers. For some, an average performance review compared with others was "the worst thing that ever happened in their career," Mr. Faul said.

It is unclear how Facebook's management system will evolve as Facebook's young employees age and work alongside even younger colleagues. "I don't think many people could make it at Facebook for more than 10 years," says Karel Baloun, who was among the oldest employees when, in his early 30s, he worked at Facebook in 2005 and 2006. Mr. Baloun, who wrote a book about the experience, says working at Facebook is hectic and

Facebook manages generational differences in values.

© Monkey Business Images/Fotolia

intense. "After seven or eight years or ten years, you're done, you're burned out, you get replaced," he says.

Gretchen Spreitzer, a management professor at the University of Michigan's Steven M. Ross School of Business, says Facebook's approach reflects the changing demographics of the workplace. "Employees want more power," she says. "They want jobs that are more interesting." At Facebook, that can mean frequent job changes. Paddy Underwood, 28, joined Facebook in 2011 as a lawyer on the privacy team. Two years later, Mr. Underwood decided he wanted to build products instead of practise law. He called his supervisor into a conference room and floated the idea. Two weeks later, Mr. Underwood was named a product manager in the Privacy and Trust group. Because he loves the new assignment, Mr. Underwood says, "I'm totally happy working as many hours as I need to."

Peter Cappelli, a professor of management at the University of Pennsylvania's Wharton School, says Facebook's approach helps retain employees at a time when tech talent is scarce. "Employers haven't really been paying attention to being nice to employees over the past few years—except maybe in Silicon Valley," he says. But current and former employees say Facebook's culture is unique, even in Silicon Valley. "It's the first Fortune 500 company built by millennials," says Molly Graham, a former human resources and product manager at Facebook.[1]

The Facebook story illustrates how generational differences in values and work attitudes affect workplace behaviour. In this chapter we will discuss such values and attitudes. Our discussion of values will be particularly oriented toward cross-cultural variations in values and their implications for organizational behaviour. Our discussion of attitudes will explain attitude formation. Two critical attitudes are job satisfaction and organizational commitment. We will consider the causes and consequences of both.

WHAT ARE VALUES?

LO 4.1

Define *values*, and discuss the implications of cross-cultural variation in values for organizational behaviour.

Values. A broad tendency to prefer certain states of affairs over others.

We can define **values** as "a broad tendency to prefer certain states of affairs over others."[2] The *preference* aspect of this definition means that values have to do with what we consider good and bad. Values are motivational, since they signal the attractive aspects of our environment that we seek and the unattractive aspects that we try to avoid or change. They also signal how we believe we *should* and *should not* behave.[3] The words *broad tendency* mean that values are very general and that they do not predict behaviour in specific situations very well. Knowing that a person generally embraces the values that support capitalism does not tell us much about how he or she will respond to a homeless person on the street this afternoon.

People tend to hold values structured around such factors as achievement, power, autonomy, conformity, tradition, and social welfare.[4] Not everyone holds the same values. Managers might value high productivity (an achievement value), while union officials might be more concerned with enlightened supervision and full employment (social values). We learn values through the reinforcement processes we discussed in Chapter 2. Most are socially reinforced by parents, teachers, and representatives of religions.

To solidify your understanding of values and their impact on organizational behaviour, let's examine some generational differences in values and see how work values differ across cultures.

Generational Differences in Values

Like Facebook, many contemporary organizations are attempting to understand the implications of having different generations in the workplace who are required to work with one another. As shown in Exhibit 4.1, these generations comprise what are often called the Traditionalists, the Baby Boomers, Generation X, and the Millennials (or Generation Y). These generations are of course demarcated by being of different ages, but they are also distinguished by having grown up under rather different socialization experiences. For example, many Traditionalists grew up in the shadow of two wars; Baby Boomers faced a vibrant

EXHIBIT 4.1
Four generations in today's workplace.
Source: Society for Human Resource Management (2009). The multigenerational workforce: Opportunity for competitive success. *SHRM Research Quarterly*, First Quarter, 1–9. Compiled from AARP (2007). *Leading a multigenerational workforce*. Washington, DC: AARP; Sabatini Fraone, J., Hartmann, D., & McNally, K. (2008). *The multigenerational workforce: Management implications and strategies for collaboration*. Boston: Boston College Center for Work & Family; Zemke, R., Raines, C., & Filipezak, B. (2000). *Generations at work*. New York: American Management Association.

Generation	Percentage of Workforce	Assets in the Workplace	Leadership Style Preferences
Traditionalists Born 1922–1945	8%	Hard working, stable, loyal, thorough, detail-oriented, focused, emotional maturity	Fair, consistent, clear, direct, respectful
Baby Boomers Born 1946–1964	44%	Team perspective, delicated, experienced, knowledgeable, service-oriented	Treat as equals, warm and caring, mission-defined, democratic approach
Generation X Born 1965–1980	34%	Independent, adaptable, creative, techno-literate, willing to challenge the status quo	Direct, competent, genuine, informal, flexible, results-oriented, supportive of learning opportunities
Millennials Born 1981–2000	14% and increasing rapidly	Optimistic, able to multitask, tenacious, technologically savvy, driven to learn and grow, team-oriented, socially responsible	Motivational, collaborative, positive, educational, organized, achievement-oriented, able to coach

economy (not to mention the sexual revolution and the advent of rock 'n' roll!); and Gen X and Y experienced more dual-career families and more divorce when growing up. It has been argued that these contrasting experiences, in turn, have led to notable value differences between the generations. For example, "latchkey kids" and those who know divorce might come to value the advice of authority figures less and the advice of friends more, compared to earlier generations. Such value differences might then underlie the differential workplace assets and preferences for leadership style highlighted in Exhibit 4.1.

The popular press contains many stereotypes (Chapter 3) concerning the generations, some of which are apparent in the exhibit.[5] Thus, the Traditionalists are portrayed as being respectful of authority and having a high work ethic; Boomers are viewed as optimistic workaholics; Gen X is seen as cynical, confident, and pragmatic; and Gen Y is said to be confident, social, demanding of feedback, and somewhat unfocused. In general, the latter two generations are seen as more accepting of diversity and striving for good work–life balance, and their comfort with technology is notable.

Are these stereotypes accurate? It has to be said that the study of intergenerational values and of related attitudes and behaviour is in its early stages. And it is inherently hard to tease out generational effects from those that simply reflect age or work experience.[6] Most recent research points to more similarities than differences in values across generations.[7] However, there is some indication that Gen X and Y are more inclined to value money, status, and rapid career growth than are Boomers.[8] This may reflect valuing what one does not yet have, but it could also reflect the positive self-esteem movement to which later generations have been exposed. Indeed, there is evidence that the self-esteem of university students has increased over the years, along with narcissism.[9] There is also evidence that Gen Ys and Xs, compared to Boomers, see work as less central, value leisure more, and are more inclined toward work–life balance.[10] Research conducted by the Center for Creative Leadership concluded that all work generations share the same values but express them differently. For instance, most people value respect, but for older employees this means being deferred to, while for Gen X and Y it means being listened to.[11]

Any generational differences in work values or in the way values are expressed is important, because there is much evidence that a good "fit" between a person's values and those of the organization (person–organization fit) leads to positive work attitudes and behaviours, including reduced chances of quitting.[12] This means that organizations may have to tailor job designs, leadership styles, and benefits to the generational mix of their workforces.

Cultural Differences in Values

It is by now a cliché to observe that business has become global in its scope—Korean cars dot North American roads, your Dell helpdesk service provider resides in India, and entire lines of "Italian" cookware are made in China. All this activity obscures just how difficult it can be to forge business links across cultures. For example, research shows that anywhere from 16 to 40 percent of managers who receive foreign assignments terminate them early because they perform poorly or do not adjust to the culture.[13] Similarly, a lengthy history of failed business negotiations is attributable to a lack of understanding of cross-cultural differences. At the root of many of these problems is a lack of appreciation of basic differences in work-related values across cultures.

WORK CENTRALITY Work itself is valued differently across cultures. One large-scale survey of over 8000 individuals in several nations found marked cross-national differences in the extent to which people perceived work as a central life interest.[14] Japan topped the list, with very high work centrality. Belgians and Americans exhibited average work centrality, and the British scored low. One question in the survey asked respondents whether they would continue working if they won a large amount of money in a lottery. Those with more central interest in work were more likely to report that they would continue working despite the new-found wealth.

The centrality of work in life varies across cultures.

© oneinpunch/Fotolia

The survey also found that people for whom work was a central life interest tended to work more hours. A reflection of this can be seen in Exhibit 4.2, which shows great variation in vacation time across cultures. This illustrates how cross-cultural differences in work centrality can lead to adjustment problems for foreign employees and managers. Imagine the unprepared British executive who is posted to Japan only to find that Japanese managers commonly work late and then socialize with co-workers or customers long into the night. In Japan, this is all part of the job, often to the chagrin of the lonely spouse. On the other hand, consider the Japanese executive posted to Britain who finds out that an evening at the pub is *not* viewed as an extension of the day at the office and is therefore not a time to continue talking business.

HOFSTEDE'S STUDY Dutch social scientist Geert Hofstede questioned over 116 000 IBM employees located in 40 countries about their work-related values. In subsequent work he added another 36 countries and regions to his database.[15] When Hofstede analyzed the

EXHIBIT 4.2
Vacation time across cultures.

Source: Based on World Tourism Organization (1999). Changes in Leisure Time: The Impact on Tourism, UNWTO, Madrid, p. 122. © UNWTO, 92844/02/16.

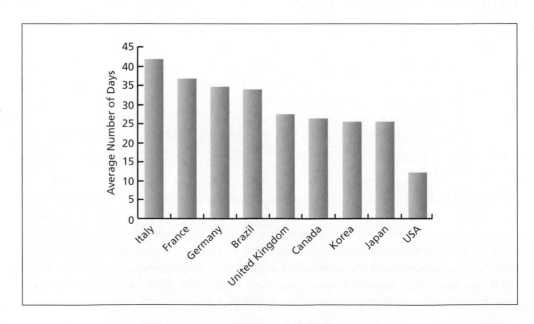

results, he discovered four basic dimensions along which work-related values differed across cultures: power distance, uncertainty avoidance, masculinity/femininity, and individualism/collectivism. Subsequent work with Canadian Michael Bond that catered more to Eastern cultures resulted in a fifth dimension, the long-term/short-term orientation.[16] More recently, the dimensions were verified and supplemented by the GLOBE project, headed by Professor Robert House.[17] You will learn more about this research, which involved more than 17 000 managers in 62 societies, when we cover leadership in Chapter 9.

- *Power distance.* **Power distance** refers to the extent to which society members accept an unequal distribution of power, including those who hold more power and those who hold less.[18] In small power distance cultures, inequality is minimized, superiors are accessible, and power differences are downplayed. In large power distance societies, inequality is accepted as natural, superiors are inaccessible, and power differences are highlighted. Small power distance societies include Denmark, New Zealand, Israel, and Austria. Large power distance societies include the Philippines, Russia, and Mexico. Out of 76 countries and regions, Canada and the United States rank 15 and 16, respectively, falling on the low power distance side of the average, which would be 38.

- *Uncertainty avoidance.* **Uncertainty avoidance** refers to the extent to which people are uncomfortable with uncertain and ambiguous situations. Strong uncertainty avoidance cultures stress rules and regulations, hard work, conformity, and security. Cultures with weak uncertainty avoidance are less concerned with rules, conformity, and security, and hard work is not seen as a virtue. However, risk taking is valued. Strong uncertainty avoidance cultures include Japan, Greece, and Portugal. Weak uncertainty avoidance cultures include Singapore, Denmark, and Sweden. On uncertainty avoidance, the United States and Canada are well below average (i.e., exhibiting weak uncertainty avoidance), ranking 13 and 15, respectively, out of 76.

- *Masculinity/femininity.* More masculine cultures clearly differentiate gender roles, support the dominance of men, and stress economic performance. More feminine cultures accept fluid gender roles, stress sexual equality, and stress quality of life. In Hofstede's research, Slovakia and Japan are the most masculine societies, followed by Austria, Venezuela, and Mexico. The Scandinavian countries are the most feminine. Canada ranks about mid-pack, and the United States is fairly masculine, falling about halfway between Canada and Japan. The GLOBE research identified two aspects to this dimension—how assertive people are and how much they value gender equality.

- *Individualism/collectivism.* More **individualistic** societies tend to stress independence, individual initiative, and privacy. More **collective** cultures favour interdependence and loyalty to one's family or clan. The United States, Australia, Great Britain, and Canada are among the most individualistic societies. Venezuela, Columbia, and Pakistan are among the most collective, with Japan falling about mid-pack. The GLOBE research uncovered two aspects to this dimension—how much the collective distribution of resources is stressed and how much one's group or organization elicits loyalty.

- *Long-term/short-term orientation.* Cultures with a long-term orientation tend to stress persistence, perseverance, thrift, and close attention to status differences. Cultures with a short-term orientation stress personal steadiness and stability, face-saving, and social niceties. China, Hong Kong, Taiwan, Japan, and South Korea tend to be characterized by a long-term orientation. The United States, Canada, Great Britain, Zimbabwe, and Nigeria are characterized by a more short-term orientation. Hofstede and Bond argue that the long-term orientation, in part, explains prolific East Asian entrepreneurship.

Power distance. The extent to which an unequal distribution of power is accepted by society members.

Uncertainty avoidance. The extent to which people are uncomfortable with uncertain and ambiguous situations.

Individualism versus collectivism. Individualistic societies stress independence, individual initiative, and privacy. Collective cultures favour interdependence and loyalty to family or clan.

EXHIBIT 4.3
Cross-cultural value comparisons.

Note: Time orientation data for Mexico unavailable.

Source: Based on data from Hofstede, G. (2005). *Cultures and organizations: Software of the mind.*

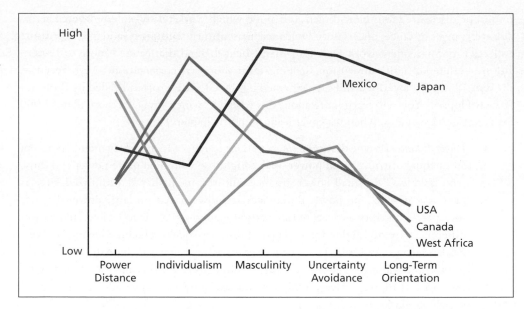

Exhibit 4.3 compares the United States, Canada, Mexico, Japan, and West Africa on Hofstede's value dimensions. Note that the profiles for Canada and the United States are very similar, but they differ considerably from that of Mexico.

Hofstede has produced a number of interesting "cultural maps" that show how countries and regions cluster together on pairs of cultural dimensions. The map in Exhibit 4.4 shows the relationship between power distance and degree of individualism. As you can see, these two values tend to be related. Cultures that are more individualistic tend to downplay power differences, while those that are more collectivistic tend to accentuate power differences.[19]

Cultural distance. The extent to which cultures differ in values.

Cultural distance refers to the extent to which cultures differ in values. As shown in Exhibit 4.3, Canada and the United States have very similar value profiles, and they both differ markedly from Japan. Hence, Canada is considerably more culturally distant from Japan than from the U.S. In general, greater cultural distance impedes communication (Chapter 10) and makes negotiations, mergers, acquisitions, and joint ventures more difficult. In addition, expatriates working abroad will generally find it more difficult to adjust to more distant cultures.[20] However, exposure to distant cultures can have its benefits. A study determined that leaders with more global work experience had more strategic competence, especially when they had been posted to more distant cultures.[21]

Implications of Cultural Variation

EXPORTING OB THEORIES
An important message from the cross-cultural study of values is that organizational behaviour theories, research, and practices from North America might not translate well to other societies, even the one located just south of Texas.[22] The basic questions (How should I lead? How should we make this decision?) remain the same. It is just the *answers* that differ. For example, North American managers tend to encourage participation in work decisions by employees. This corresponds to the fairly low degree of power distance valued here. Trying to translate this leadership style to cultures that value high power distance might prove unwise. In these cultures, people might be more comfortable deferring to the boss's decision. Similarly, in individualistic North America, calling attention to one's accomplishments is expected and often rewarded in organizations. In more collective Asian or South American cultures, individual success might be devalued, and it might make sense to reward groups rather than individuals. Finally, in extremely masculine cultures, integrating women into management positions might require special sensitivity.

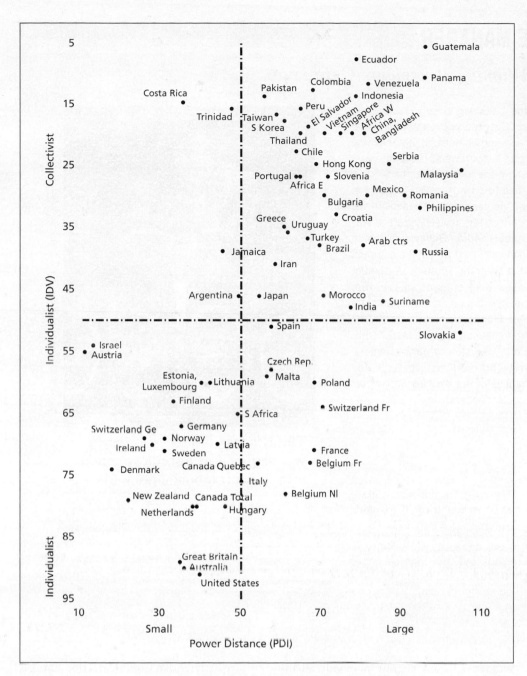

EXHIBIT 4.4
Power distance and individualism values for various countries and regions.

Source: Adapted from Hofstede, G., Hofstede, G.J., & Minkov, M. (2010). *Cultures and organizations: Software of the mind* (3rd ed.). New York: McGraw-Hill, p. 103. Used by permission from Geert Hofstede.

IMPORTING OB THEORIES Not all theories and practices that concern organizational behaviour are designed in North America or even in the West. The most obvious examples are "Japanese management" techniques, such as quality circles, total quality management, and just-in-time production. Although there are success stories of importing these techniques from Japan to North America, there are also examples of difficulties and failure. Many of the problems stem from basic value differences between Japan and North America. For example, the quest for continuous improvement and the heavy reliance on employee suggestions for improvement has had a mixed reaction.[23] In Japan, cultural values have traditionally dictated a fairly high degree of employment security. Thus, working at a fast pace and providing suggestions for improvement will not put one out of a job. North American workers are uncertain about this.

Many of the Japanese-inspired means of organizing work are team oriented. Since Japan has fairly collective cultural values, submerging one's own interests in those of the team is natural. Although employers have successfully used teams in North America, as you

YOU BE THE MANAGER

Carlsberg's *Winning Behaviours* Campaign

Founded in 1847, the Carlsberg Group is based in Copenhagen, Denmark. Over the years, through global expansion, mergers, and acquisitions, it has become the world's fourth-largest beer brewery. In recent years the executive group saw the need to embark on a revised strategy designed to provide better integration of its global efforts and greater competitiveness in the global marketplace. Part of this revised strategy was a strategic concept called *Winning Behaviours*, which was designed (among other things) to instill a common organizational culture, a "winning" culture. A number of values and behaviours were stressed in the *Winning Behaviours* campaign, including: we appreciate diversity but share best practices across borders; we are proactive and entrepreneurial; we take responsibility and don't fear failure; we listen to our customers. Malaysia and China are important markets for Carlsberg, so the reception there for the *Winning Behaviours* campaign was of particular concern.

The *Winning Behaviours* campaign was designed to instill a common organizational culture.

To find out what happened at Carlsberg, see The Manager's Notebook at the end of the chapter.

Questions

1. The goal of top management is to instill a common organizational culture. Is this possible, given the considerable differences in national culture between Denmark and Asian countries? If so, how?

2. Exhibit 4.4 shows that Denmark is fairly individualistic and low on power distance, while Malaysia and China are more collective and high on power distance. How might this affect the reception of the *Winning Behaviours* campaign in Asia?

Source: Adapted from Søderberg, A.M. (2015). Recontextualising a strategic concept within a globalising company: A case study on Carlsberg's "Winning Behaviours" strategy. *International Journal of Human Resource Management, 26*, 231-257.

will see in Chapter 7, our more individualistic culture dictates that careful selection of team members is necessary.

Understanding cultural value differences can enable organizations to successfully import management practices by tailoring the practice to the home culture's concerns. In this regard, see You Be the Manager: *Carlsberg's Winning Behaviours Campaign.*

APPRECIATING GLOBAL CUSTOMERS An appreciation of cross-cultural differences in values is essential to understanding the needs and tastes of customers or clients around the world. Once relegated to the status of a marketing problem, it is now clear that such understanding fundamentally has to do with organizational behaviour. Errors occur with regularity. For instance, the initial French response to the Disneyland Paris theme park was less enthusiastic than Disney management had expected, probably due in part to Disney's failure to truly appreciate French tastes in food, lifestyle, and entertainment. South Korea's Samsung recalled a calendar, featuring female models displaying its products, that was destined for overseas customers. Some North Americans were offended by Miss July's see-through blouse.

Appreciating the values of global customers is also important when the customers enter your own culture. Many firms have profited from an understanding of the increasing ethnic diversity in the United States, Canada, and Australia.

DEVELOPING GLOBAL EMPLOYEES Success in translating management practices to other cultures, importing practices developed elsewhere, and appreciating global customers are not things that happen by accident. Rather, companies need to select, train, and develop employees to have a much better appreciation of differences in cultural values and the implications of these differences for behaviour in organizations.

To get their designers to better appreciate the values of the North American market, Japanese and Korean carmakers, including Nissan, Toyota, Hyundai, and Kia, have design studios in California. The top ranks of Detroit's automakers, once the protected realm of Midwesterners, are now liberally filled with Europeans or those with European or Asian experience.

The goal here is to foster **cultural intelligence**, the capability to function and manage well in culturally diverse environments.[24] It encompasses knowledge, motivation, and behaviour that contribute to good cross-cultural functioning, and people with high cultural intelligence tend to score high on intercultural adjustment, global leadership, and performance in intercultural settings. Before continuing, please see Global Focus: *Canadians Have Cultural Intelligence*.

As you proceed through the text, you will encounter further discussion about the impact of cultural values on organizational behaviour and further opportunities to sharpen

Cultural intelligence. The capability to function and manage well in culturally diverse environments.

PERSONAL INVENTORY ASSESSMENT

Learn About Yourself
Intercultural Sensitivity Scale

GLOBAL FOCUS

CANADIANS HAVE CULTURAL INTELLIGENCE

First there was IQ—intelligence quotient. Then there was EQ—emotional intelligence. Now there's a new kind of intelligence that is increasingly indispensable in today's global village. CQ—cultural intelligence—is a must-have skill, not just for foreign diplomats but also for business people, public sector workers, military personnel, and just about everyone in multicultural societies. And Canadians score more highly in it than people in the United States, United Kingdom, and France, according to a recent study.

CQ is a heightened awareness of cultures—including one's own—that makes a person more sensitive to people from diverse origins. It implies having a broad knowledge of customs and beliefs among different nationalities, ethnic groups, and faiths. It also reflects a person's motivation to overcome cultural barriers, and confidence in one's ability to communicate with people from different cultures.

Four out of ten Canadians strongly agreed with the statement "I enjoy interacting with people from different cultures," compared with 37 percent of Americans, 24 percent of Britons, and 30 percent of French

respondents. Sixteen percent of Canadians strongly agreed that "I have a good knowledge of the cultural values and religious beliefs of some other cultures," compared with 13 percent of Americans, 9 percent of Britons, and 5 percent of French respondents. Fifteen percent of Canadians strongly agreed that "I adjust my behaviour when I meet people from a culture that is unfamiliar to me," compared with 13 percent of Americans, 10 percent of British residents, and 12 percent of people in France.

Canadians' relatively high CQ reflects the fact that multicultural cities like Toronto, Vancouver, and Montreal give citizens plenty of opportunities to interact with people from diverse origins, said Jack Jedwab, executive director of the Association for Canadian Studies. The internet survey was carried out among 3000 international respondents and 2345 Canadians by Léger Marketing.

Source: Material reprinted with the express permission of: Montreal Gazette, a division of Postmedia Network Inc.

your cultural intelligence. For now, let's examine attitudes and see how they are related to values.

WHAT ARE ATTITUDES?

LO **4.2**

Define *attitudes*, and explain how people develop attitudes.

Attitude. A fairly stable evaluative tendency to respond consistently to some specific object, situation, person, or category of people.

An **attitude** is a fairly stable evaluative tendency to respond consistently to some specific object, situation, person, or category of people. First, notice that attitudes involve *evaluations* directed toward *specific* targets. If I inquire about your attitude toward your boss, you will probably tell me something about how well you *like* him or her. This illustrates the evaluative aspect of attitudes. Attitudes are also much more specific than values, which dictate only broad preferences. For example, you could value working quite highly but still dislike your specific job.

Our definition indicates that attitudes are *tendencies to respond* to the target of the attitude. Thus, attitudes often influence our behaviour toward some object, situation, person, or group.

Attitude ⟶ Behaviour

Of course, not everyone who likes the boss goes around praising him or her in public for fear of being seen as too political. Similarly, people who dislike the boss do not always engage in public criticism for fear of retaliation. These examples indicate that attitudes are not always consistent with behaviour and that attitudes provide useful information over and above the actions that we can observe. Behaviour is most likely to correspond to attitudes when people have direct experience with the target of the attitude and when the attitude is held confidently.[25]

Where do attitudes come from? Put simply, attitudes are a function of what we think and what we feel. That is, attitudes are the product of a related belief and value.[26] Given this point of view, we can now expand the attitude model presented above to include the thinking and feeling aspects of attitudes represented by beliefs and values.

BELIEF + VALUE ⟹ Attitude ⟶ Behaviour

Thus, we can imagine the following sequence of ideas in the case of a person experiencing work–family conflict:

"My job is interfering with my family life." (Belief)
"I dislike anything that hurts my family." (Value)
"I dislike my job." (Attitude)
"I'll search for another job." (Behaviour)

This simple example shows how attitudes (in this case, job satisfaction) develop from basic beliefs and values, and how they affect organizational behaviour (in this case, turnover from the organization). The specific attitudes we are now going to cover, job satisfaction and organizational commitment, have a strong impact on people's positive contributions to their work.[27]

WHAT IS JOB SATISFACTION?

LO **4.3**

Explain the concept of *job satisfaction*, and discuss some of its key contributors, including discrepancy, fairness, disposition, mood, and emotion.

Job satisfaction. A collection of attitudes that workers have about their jobs.

Job satisfaction refers to a collection of attitudes that people have about their jobs. We can differentiate two aspects of satisfaction. The first of these is facet satisfaction, the tendency for an employee to be more or less satisfied with various facets of the job. The notion of facet satisfaction is obvious when we hear someone say "I love my work but hate my boss" or "This place pays lousy, but the people I work with are great." Both these statements represent different attitudes toward separate facets of the speaker's job. The most relevant attitudes toward jobs are contained in a rather small group of facets: the work itself, compensation, career opportunities, recognition, benefits, working conditions, supervision, co-workers, and organizational policy.[28]

In addition to facet satisfaction, we can also conceive of overall satisfaction, an overall or summary indicator of a person's attitude toward his or her job that cuts across the various facets.[29] The statement "On the whole, I really like my job, although a couple of aspects could stand some improvement" is indicative of the nature of overall satisfaction. Overall satisfaction is an average or total of the attitudes individuals hold toward various facets of the job. Thus, two employees might express the same level of overall satisfaction for different reasons.

A popular measure of job satisfaction is the *Job Descriptive Index* (JDI).[30] This questionnaire is designed to evaluate five facets of satisfaction: people, pay, supervision, promotions, and the work itself. Employees are asked to respond "yes," "no," or "?" (cannot decide) in describing whether a particular word or phrase is descriptive of these facets. For example, for the pay facet, they are asked whether they are "well paid." A scoring system is available to provide an index of satisfaction for each facet. In addition, there is a scale that provides an overall measure of satisfaction.

Another carefully constructed measure of satisfaction, using a somewhat different set of facets, is the *Minnesota Satisfaction Questionnaire* (MSQ).[31] On this measure, respondents indicate how happy they are with various aspects of their job on a scale ranging from "very satisfied" to "very dissatisfied." Sample items from the short form of the MSQ include

- the competence of my supervisor in making decisions;
- the way my job provides for steady employment; and
- my pay and the amount of work I do.

Scoring the responses to these items provides an index of overall satisfaction as well as satisfaction on the facets on which the MSQ is based.

Firms such as Best Buy, Marriott, Scotiabank, The Keg, and Microsoft make extensive use of employee attitude surveys. We will cover the details of such surveys in Chapter 10 when we explore communication and in Chapter 15 when we cover organizational change and development.

WHAT DETERMINES JOB SATISFACTION?

When employees on a variety of jobs complete the JDI or the MSQ, we often find differences in the average scores across jobs. Of course, we could almost expect such differences. The various jobs might differ objectively in the facets that contribute to satisfaction. Thus, you would not be astonished to learn that a corporate vice-president was more satisfied with his or her job than a janitor in the same company. Of greater interest is the fact that we frequently find decided differences in job satisfaction expressed by individuals performing the same job in a given organization. For example, two nurses who work side by side might indicate radically different satisfaction in response to the MSQ item "The chance to do things for other people." How does this happen?

Discrepancy

You will recall that attitudes, such as job satisfaction, are the product of associated beliefs and values. These two factors cause differences in job satisfaction even when jobs are identical. First, people might differ in their beliefs about the job in question. That is, they might differ in their *perceptions* concerning the actual nature of the job. For example, one of the nurses might perceive that most of her working time is devoted to direct patient care, while the other might perceive that most of her time is spent on administrative functions. To the extent that they both value patient care, the former nurse should be more satisfied with this aspect of the job than the latter. Second, even if individuals perceive their jobs as equivalent, they might differ in what they *want* from the jobs. Such desires are preferences that are dictated, in part, by the workers' value systems. Thus, if the two nurses perceive their opportunities to engage in direct patient care as high, the one who values this activity more will be more satisfied with the patient care aspect of work. The **discrepancy theory** of job satisfaction asserts that satisfaction is a function of the discrepancy between the job outcomes people want and the outcomes that they perceive they obtain.[32] For instance, there is strong evidence that satisfaction with one's pay is high when the gap between the pay received and the perception of how much pay *should* be received is small.[33] For example, at Facebook generational differences in values could have an impact on job satisfaction levels.

Discrepancy theory. A theory that job satisfaction stems from the discrepancy between the job outcomes wanted and the outcomes that are perceived to be obtained.

Fairness

In addition to the discrepancy between the outcomes people receive and those they desire, another factor that determines job satisfaction is fairness. Issues of fairness affect both what people want from their jobs and how they react to the inevitable discrepancies of organizational life. As you will see, there are three basic kinds of fairness. Distributive fairness has to do with the outcomes we receive; procedural fairness concerns the process that led to those outcomes; and interactional fairness concerns how these matters were communicated to us.[34]

DISTRIBUTIVE FAIRNESS **Distributive fairness** (often called *distributive justice*) occurs when people receive the outcomes they think they deserve from their jobs; that is, it involves the ultimate *distribution* of work rewards and resources. Above, we indicated that what people want from their jobs is a partial function of their value systems. In fact, however, there are practical limitations to this notion. You might value money and the luxurious lifestyle that it can buy very highly, but this does not suggest that you expect to receive a salary of $200 000 a year. In the case of many job facets, individuals want "what's fair." And how do we develop our conception of what is fair? **Equity theory** states that the inputs that people perceive themselves as investing in a job and the outcomes that the job provides are compared against the inputs and outcomes of some other relevant person or group.[35] Equity will be perceived when the following distribution ratios exist:

Distributive fairness. Fairness that occurs when people receive the outcomes they think they deserve from their jobs

Equity theory. A theory that job satisfaction stems from a comparison of the inputs one invests in a job and the outcomes one receives in comparison with the inputs and outcomes of another person or group.

$$\frac{\text{My outcomes}}{\text{My inputs}} = \frac{\text{Others' outcomes}}{\text{Others' inputs}}$$

In these ratios, **inputs** consist of anything that individuals consider relevant to their exchange with the organization, anything that they give up, offer, or trade to their organization. These might include factors such as education, training, seniority, hard work, and high-quality work. **Outcomes** are those factors that the organization distributes to employees in return for their inputs. The most relevant outcomes are represented by the job facets we discussed earlier—pay, career opportunities, supervision, the nature of the work, and so on. The "other" in the ratio above might be a co-worker performing the same job, a number of co-workers, or even one's conception of all the individuals in one's occupation.[36] For example, the CEO of Microsoft probably compares his outcome/input ratio with those that he assumes exist for the CEOs of Google and Intel. You probably compare your outcome/input ratio in your organizational behaviour class with that of one or more fellow students.

Inputs. Anything that people give up, offer, or trade to their organization in exchange for outcomes.

Outcomes. Factors that an organization distributes to employees in exchange for their inputs.

Equity theory has important implications for job satisfaction. First, inequity itself is a dissatisfying state, especially for those on the "short end of the stick." For example, suppose you see the hours spent studying as your main input to your organizational behaviour class and the final grade as an important outcome. Imagine that a friend in the class is your comparison person. Under these conditions, the following situations appear equitable and should not provoke dissatisfaction on your part:

You	**Friend**		**You**	**Friend**
C grade	A grade	Or	A grade	C grade
50 hours	100 hours		60 hours	30 hours

In each of these cases, a fair relationship seems to exist between study time and grades distributed. Now consider the following relationships:

You	**Friend**		**You**	**Friend**
C grade	A grade	Or	A grade	C grade
100 hours	50 hours		30 hours	60 hours

In each of these situations, an unfair connection appears to exist between study time and grades received, and you should perceive inequity. However, the situation on the left, in which you put in more work for a lower grade, should be most likely to prompt dissatisfaction. This is a "short end of the stick" situation. For example, the employee who frequently remains on the job after regular hours (input) and receives no special praise or extra pay (outcome) might perceive inequity and feel dissatisfied. Equity considerations also have an indirect effect on job satisfaction by influencing what people want from their jobs. If you study for 100 hours while the rest of the class averages 50 hours, you will expect a higher grade than the class average.

Consider a practical example of equity in action. During a business recession, the Canadian-based luxury hotel company Four Seasons did not lay off employees and thus threaten customer service like many of its competitors. Rather, executives accepted a pay freeze and workers were asked to vote on a temporary move to a four-day work week rather than five. The offer was accepted enthusiastically because it was seen as fair, given extensive industry layoffs and the sacrifices made by company executives.[37]

The equity concept suggests that outcomes should be tied to individual contributions or inputs. This corresponds well with the individualistic North American culture. In more collective cultures, *equality* of outcomes might produce more feelings of distributive fairness. In more feminine cultures, allocating outcomes according to *need* (rather than performance) might provide for distributive fairness.

PROCEDURAL FAIRNESS

Procedural fairness (often called *procedural justice*) occurs when individuals see the process used to determine outcomes as reasonable; that is, rather than involving the actual distribution of resources or rewards, it is concerned with how these outcomes are decided and allocated. An example will illustrate the difference between distributive and procedural fairness. Out of the blue, Greg's boss tells him that she has completed his performance evaluation and that he will receive a healthy pay raise starting next month. Greg has been working very hard, and he is pleased with the pay raise (distributive fairness). However, he is vaguely unhappy about the fact that all this occurred without his participation. Where he used to work, the employee and the boss would complete independent performance evaluation forms and then sit down and discuss any differences. This provided good feedback for the employee. Greg wonders how his peers who got less generous raises are reacting to the boss's style.

Procedural fairness is particularly relevant to outcomes such as performance evaluations, pay raises, promotions, layoffs, and work assignments. In allocating such outcomes, the following factors contribute to perceptions of procedural fairness.[38] The allocator

- follows consistent procedures over time and across people;
- uses accurate information and appears unbiased;
- allows two-way communication during the allocation process; and
- welcomes appeals of the procedure or allocation.

Procedural fairness.
Fairness that occurs when the process used to determine work outcomes is seen as reasonable.

Procedural fairness is especially likely to provoke dissatisfaction when people also see distributive fairness as being low.[39] One view notes that dissatisfaction will be "maximized when people believe that they *would* have obtained better outcomes if the decision maker had used other procedures that *should* have been implemented."[40] (Students who receive lower grades than their friends will recognize the wisdom of this observation!) Thus, Greg, mentioned above, will probably not react too badly to the lack of consultation, while his peers who did not receive large raises might strongly resent the process that the boss used.

Interactional fairness.
Fairness that occurs when people feel they have received respectful and informative communication about an outcome.

INTERACTIONAL FAIRNESS Interactional **fairness** (often called *interactional justice*) occurs when people feel that they have received respectful and informative communication about some outcome.[41] In other words, it extends beyond the actual procedures used to the interpersonal treatment received when learning about the outcome. Respectful communication is sincere and polite and treats the individual with dignity; informative communication is candid, timely, and thorough. Interactional fairness is important because it is possible for absolutely fair outcomes or procedures to be perceived as unfair when they are inadequately or uncaringly explained.

Sometimes, lower-level managers have little control over procedures that are used to allocate resources. However, they almost always have the opportunity to explain these procedures in a thorough, truthful, and caring manner. Frequently, people who experience procedural unfairness are dissatisfied with the "system." On the other hand, people who experience interactional unfairness are more likely to be dissatisfied with the boss. Both procedural and interactional fairness can to some extent offset the negative effects of distributive unfairness.

Before continuing, see the Global Focus: *Is the Importance of Fairness Universal across Cultures?*

Disposition

Could your personality contribute to your feelings of job satisfaction? This is the essential question guiding research on the relationship between disposition and job satisfaction.

GLOBAL FOCUS

IS THE IMPORTANCE OF FAIRNESS UNIVERSAL ACROSS CULTURES?

Most research concerning fairness at work has been done in North America. In general, this research shows that fairness is an important determinant of job satisfaction, commitment to the organization, and trust in the organization and managers. But are these findings universal across cultures, or is fairness a particular preoccupation of North Americans?

Andrew Li and Russell Cropanzano compared the research on fairness at work that has been done in North America with that conducted in East Asia (mainland China, Japan, Hong Kong, South Korea, Taiwan, and Singapore). On one hand, we might guess that individualistic, low power distance North Americans would be more sensitive to incidents of unfairness. On the other hand, most such incidents are interpersonal (e.g., a boss gives a biased performance evaluation), and the more collective, social features of East Asian cultures might point to greater fairness sensitivity.

Li and Cropanzano found that distributive and procedural fairness predicted satisfaction, commitment, and trust in both regions. However, the associations were somewhat weaker in East Asia, suggesting a greater tolerance for unfairness there. The authors suggested that a need for interpersonal harmony, prevalent in the more collective East Asian cultures, might have led to this result.

The authors concluded that fairness seems important for people with a range of cultural backgrounds. However, they also noted that managers should be extra alert for feelings of unfairness among East Asians, because in hoping to maintain social harmony they might not signal it in their attitudes and behaviour.

Source: Li, A., & Cropanzano, R. (2009). Do East Asians respond more/less strongly to organizational justice than North Americans? *Journal of Management Studies, 46,* 787–805. See also Shao, R., Rupp, D.E., Skarlicki, D.P., & Jones, K.S. (2013). Employee justice across cultures: A meta-analytic review. *Journal of Management, 39,* 263–301.

Underlying the dispositional view is the idea that some people are *predisposed* by virtue of their personalities to be more or less satisfied despite changes in discrepancy or fairness. Some of the research that suggests that disposition contributes to job satisfaction is fascinating:[42]

- Identical twins raised apart from early childhood tend to have similar levels of job satisfaction.

- Job satisfaction tends to be fairly stable over time, even when changes in employer occur.

- Disposition measured early in adolescence is correlated with one's job satisfaction as a mature adult.

Taken together, these findings suggest that some personality characteristics originating in genetics or early learning contribute to adult job satisfaction. In fact, recent research has linked dopamine and serotonin genes to satisfaction.[43]

Research on disposition and job satisfaction has centred around the Big Five personality traits (Chapter 2). People who are extraverted and conscientious tend to be more satisfied with their jobs, while those high in neuroticism are less satisfied.[44] Also, people who are high in self-esteem and internal locus of control are more satisfied.[45] Thus, in general, people who are more optimistic and proactive report higher job satisfaction. Mood and emotion may contribute to this connection, so we will now examine these topics.

Mood and Emotion

The picture we have painted so far of the determinants of job satisfaction has been mostly one of calculation and rationality: people calculate discrepancies, compare job inputs to outcomes, and so on. But what about the intense feelings that are sometimes seen in work settings—the joy of a closed business deal or the despair that leads to workplace homicides? Or what about that vague feeling of a lack of accomplishment that blunts the pleasure of a dream job? We are speaking here about the role of affect as a determinant of job satisfaction. *Affect* is simply a broad label for feelings. These feelings include **emotions**, which are intense, often short-lived, and caused by a particular event such as a bad performance appraisal. Common emotions include joy, pride, anger, fear, and sadness. Affect also refers to **moods**, which are less intense, longer-lived, and more diffuse feelings.

How do emotions and moods affect job satisfaction? Affective events theory, proposed by Howard Weiss and Russell Cropanzano, addresses this question.[46] Basically, the theory reminds us that jobs actually consist of a series of events and happenings that have the potential to provoke emotions or to influence moods, depending on how we appraise these events and happenings. Thus, seeing a co-worker being berated by a manager might provoke emotional disgust and lower one's job satisfaction, especially if it is a frequent occurrence. This illustrates that perceived unfairness, as discussed earlier, can affect job satisfaction via emotion.[47] Also, a person's disposition can interact with job events to influence satisfaction. For instance, those who are neurotic and pessimistic may react to a minor series of job setbacks with a negative mood that depresses their job satisfaction.

An interesting way in which mood and emotion can influence job satisfaction is through **emotional contagion**. This is the tendency for moods and emotions to spread between people or throughout a group.[48] Thus, people's moods and emotions tend to converge with interaction. Generally, teams experiencing more positive affect tend to be more cooperative, helpful, and successful, all of which are conditions that contribute to job satisfaction.[49] Emotional contagion can also occur in dealing with customers such that pleasant service encounters contribute to the service provider's satisfaction as well as to that of the customer.

Another interesting way in which mood and emotion can influence job satisfaction is through the need for **emotional regulation**. This is the requirement for people to conform

Emotions. Intense, often short-lived feelings caused by a particular event.

Moods. Less intense, longer-lived, and more diffuse feelings.

Emotional contagion. Tendency for moods and emotions to spread between people or throughout a group.

Emotional regulation. Requirement for people to conform to certain "display rules" in their job behaviour in spite of their true mood or emotions.

to certain "display rules" in their job behaviour, in spite of their true mood or emotions. Often, this is referred to informally as "emotional labour." In one version, employees are expected to be perky and upbeat whether they feel that way or not, thus exaggerating positive emotions. In the other version, employees are supposed to remain calm and civil even when hassled or insulted, thus suppressing negative emotions. One study found that call centre employees averaged 10 incidents of customer aggression a day.[50] All jobs have their implicit display rules, such as not acting angry in front of the boss. However, service roles such as those of waiters, bank tellers, and flight attendants are especially laden with display rules, some of which may be made explicit in training and via cues from managers.

What are the consequences of the requirement for emotional regulation? There is solid evidence that the frequent need to suppress negative emotions and fake emotions that you do not really feel takes a toll on job satisfaction and increase stress. Flight attendants can humour only so many drunk or angry air passengers before the experience wears thin! On the other hand, the requirement to express positive emotions, especially when you really are feeling positive, boosts job satisfaction and reduces stress.[51] Positive contagion from happy customers may be responsible.[52] Of course, disposition may again enter the picture, as extraverts may be energized by requirements for positive display.

Do organizations pay a premium for emotional labour? The answer is "sometimes." Theresa Glomb, John Kammeyer-Mueller, and Maria Rotundo studied the emotional labour and cognitive demands (thinking, decision making) required in various occupations (see Exhibit 4.5).[53] They found that those in occupations with high cognitive demands (the upper portion of the exhibit) tend to be paid more when the jobs are also high in emotional

EXHIBIT 4.5
Occupations plotted by emotional labour and cognitive demands.

Source: Adapted from Glomb, T.M., Kammeyer-Mueller, J.D., & Rotundo, M. (2004). Emotional labor demands and compensating wage differentials. *Journal of Applied Psychology, 89*, 700–714.

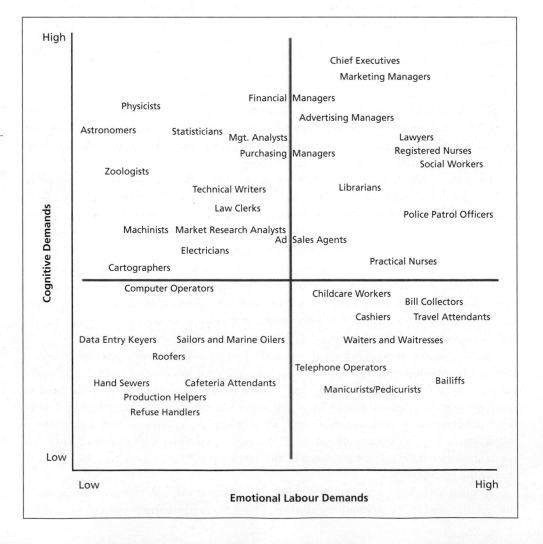

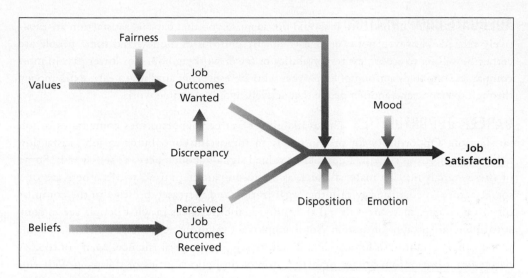

EXHIBIT 4.6
How discrepancy, fairness, disposition, mood, and emotion affect job satisfaction.

labour. Thus, lawyers tend to earn more than zoologists. On the other hand, occupations with low cognitive demands entail a wage penalty when emotional labour is higher. Thus, the "people jobs" in the lower right quadrant of the exhibit tend to be less well paid than the jobs in the lower left quadrant. As we will see shortly, pay is an important determinant of job satisfaction.

Consideration of mood and emotion helps explain a curious but commonplace phenomenon: how people with similar beliefs and values doing the same job for the same compensation can still exhibit very different satisfaction levels. This difference is probably a result of emotional events and subtle differences in mood that add up over time. We will revisit emotion when we study emotional intelligence (Chapter 5), decision making (Chapter 11) stress (Chapter 13), and organizational change (Chapter 15).

Exhibit 4.6 summarizes what research has to say about the determinants of job satisfaction. To recapitulate, satisfaction is a function of certain dispositional factors, the discrepancy between the job outcomes a person wants and the outcomes received, and mood and emotion. More specifically, people experience greater satisfaction when they meet or exceed the job outcomes they want, perceive the job outcomes they receive as equitable compared with those others receive, and believe that fair procedures determine job outcomes. The outcomes that people want from a job are a function of their personal value systems, moderated by equity considerations. The outcomes that people perceive themselves as receiving from the job represent their beliefs about the nature of that job.

Some Key Contributors to Job Satisfaction

From what we have said thus far, you might expect that job satisfaction is a highly personal experience. While this is essentially true, we can make some general statements about the facets that seem to contribute the most to feelings of job satisfaction for most North American workers. These include mentally challenging work, adequate compensation, career opportunities, and friendly or helpful colleagues.[54]

MENTALLY CHALLENGING WORK This is work that tests employees' skills and abilities and allows them to set their own working pace. Employees usually perceive such work as personally involving and important. It also provides the worker with clear feedback regarding performance. Of course, some types of work can be too challenging, and this can result in feelings of failure and reduced satisfaction. In addition, some employees seem to prefer repetitive, unchallenging work that makes few demands on them. At Facebook, frequent job changes contribute to mentally challenging work.

ADEQUATE COMPENSATION It should not surprise you that pay and satisfaction are positively related. However, not everyone is equally desirous of money, and some people are certainly willing to accept less responsibility or fewer working hours for lower pay. In most companies, one finds a group of employees who are especially anxious to earn extra money through overtime and another group that actively avoids overtime work.

CAREER OPPORTUNITIES The availability of career opportunities contributes to job satisfaction. Opportunity for promotion is an important contributor to job satisfaction because promotions contain a number of valued signals about a person's self-worth. Some of these signals may be material (such as an accompanying raise), while others are of a social nature (recognition within the organization and increased prestige in the community). Of course, there are cultural and individual differences in what people see as constituting a fair promotion system. Some employees might prefer a strict seniority system, while others might wish for a system based strictly on job performance. Many of today's flatter organizations no longer offer the promotion opportunities of the past. Well-run firms have offset this by designing lateral moves that provide for challenging work. Also, as discussed in Chapter 2, career development helps prepare employees to assume challenging assignments.

PEOPLE It should not surprise you that friendly, considerate, good-natured superiors and co-workers contribute to job satisfaction, especially via positive moods and emotions. There is, however, another aspect to interpersonal relationships on the job that contributes to job satisfaction. Specifically, we tend to be satisfied in the presence of people who help us attain job outcomes that we value. Such outcomes might include doing our work better or more easily, obtaining a raise or promotion, or even staying alive. For example, a company of soldiers in battle might be less concerned with how friendly their commanding officer is than with how competently he is able to act to keep them from being overrun by the enemy. Similarly, an aggressive young executive might like a considerate boss but prefer even more a boss who can clearly define work objectives and reward their attainment. The friendliness aspect of interpersonal relationships seems most important in lower-level jobs with clear duties and in various dead-end jobs. If pay is tied to performance or as jobs become more complex or promotion opportunities increase, the ability of others to help us do our work well contributes more to job satisfaction.

Context can certainly affect what contributes most to job satisfaction. Exhibit 4.7 shows the results of a recent survey conducted by the Society for Human Resource Management. As you can see, compensation and job security were high on the list.

In the high-tech and creative domains, organizational success depends on attracting and retaining the very best talent and creating an atmosphere free from distractions and inconveniences so that the creative juices can flow. The stress of project deadlines is commonplace. Because of these factors, firms such as Google, Microsoft, Pixar, and BlackBerry go to extraordinary lengths to foster employee job satisfaction. Perks range from the provision of "fun" campus-like environments to free meals and the availability of services such as transportation, dry cleaning, and car washes.

CONSEQUENCES OF JOB SATISFACTION

LO 4.4

Explain the relationship between job satisfaction and absenteeism, turnover, performance, organizational citizenship behaviour, and customer satisfaction.

Many prominent firms have maintained a competitive advantage by paying particular attention to employee satisfaction. Why is this so? Let's look at some consequences of job satisfaction.

Absence from Work

Absenteeism is an expensive behaviour in North America, costing billions of dollars each year. Such costs are attributable to "sick pay," lost productivity, and chronic overstaffing to

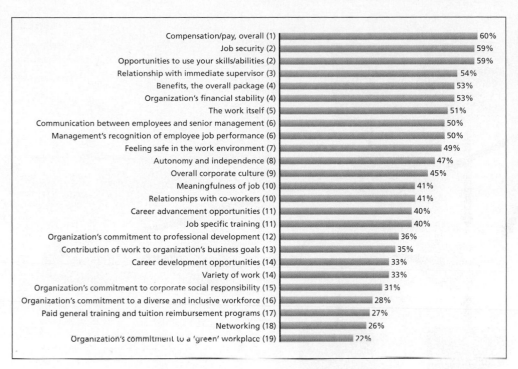

EXHIBIT 4.7
"Very important"
aspects of employee job satisfaction.
Note: Percentages reflect respondents who answered "very important" on a scale where 1 = "very unimportant" and 4 = "very important."
Source: Data from Society for Human Resource Management. (2014). *Employee job satisfaction and engagement.* Alexandria, VA: SHRM, p.4.

compensate for absentees. Many more days are lost to absenteeism than to strikes and other industrial disputes. Research shows that less-satisfied employees are more likely to be absent and that satisfaction with the content of the work is the best predictor of absenteeism.[55] However, the absence–satisfaction connection is not very strong. Several factors constrain the ability of many people to convert their like or dislike of work into corresponding attendance patterns:

- Some absence is simply unavoidable because of illness, weather conditions, or child-care problems. Thus, some very happy employees will occasionally be absent owing to circumstances beyond their control.

- Some organizations have attendance control policies that influence absence more than satisfaction does. In a company that does not pay workers for missed days (typical of many workplaces with hourly pay), absence may be more related to economic needs than to dissatisfaction. The unhappy worker who absolutely needs money will probably show up for work. By the same token, dissatisfied and satisfied workers might be equally responsive to threats of dismissal for absenteeism.

- In many jobs, it may be unclear to employees how much absenteeism is reasonable or sensible. With a lack of company guidelines, workers may look to the behaviour of their peers for a norm to guide their behaviour. This norm and its corresponding "absence culture" might have a stronger effect than individual employees' satisfaction with their jobs.[56]

Turnover

Turnover refers to resignation from an organization, and it can be incredibly expensive. For example, it costs several thousand dollars to replace a nurse or a bank teller who resigns.[57] As employees move up the organizational hierarchy, or into technologically complex jobs, such costs escalate dramatically. For example, it costs millions of dollars to hire and train a single military fighter pilot. Estimates of turnover costs usually include the price of hiring, training, and developing to proficiency a replacement employee. Such figures probably

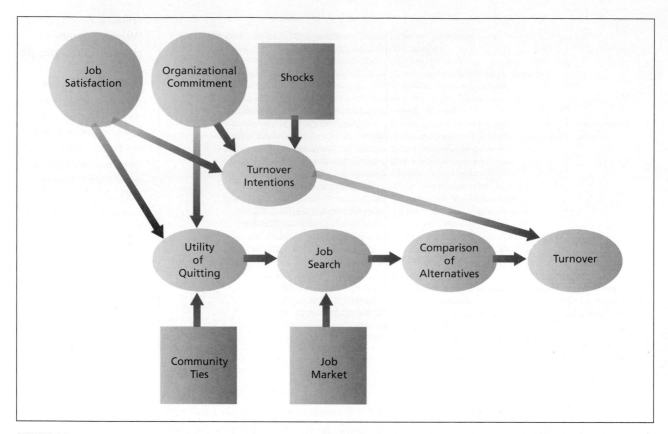

EXHIBIT 4.8
A model of employee turnover.

underestimate the true costs of turnover, however, because they do not include intangible costs, such as work-group disruption or the loss of employees who have informally acquired special skills and knowledge over time on a job. All this would not be so bad if turnover were concentrated among poorer performers. Unfortunately, this is not always the case. In one study, 23 percent of scientists and engineers who left an organization were among the top 10 percent of performers.[58] Given this, it is not surprising that high turnover rates damage organizational financial performance.[59]

What is the relationship between job satisfaction and turnover? Research indicates a moderately strong connection, with less-satisfied workers being more likely to quit.[60] However, the relationship between the attitude (job satisfaction) and the behaviour in question (turnover) is far from perfect. Exhibit 4.8 presents a model of turnover that can help explain this.[61] In the model, circles represent attitudes, ovals represent elements of the turnover process, and squares denote situational factors. The model shows that job satisfaction as well as commitment to the organization and various "shocks" (both discussed below) can contribute to intentions to leave. Research shows that such intentions are very good predictors of turnover.[62] As shown, such intentions sometimes prompt turnover directly, even impulsively. On the other hand, reduced satisfaction or commitment can also stimulate a more deliberate evaluation of the utility of quitting and a careful job search and evaluation of job alternatives. The following are some reasons why satisfied people sometimes quit their jobs or dissatisfied people stay:[63]

- Certain "shocks," such as a marital breakup, the birth of a child, or an unsolicited job offer in an attractive location, might stimulate turnover despite an employee's satisfaction with the current job.

- An employee's dissatisfaction with his or her specific job might be offset by a strong commitment to the overall values and mission of the organization.

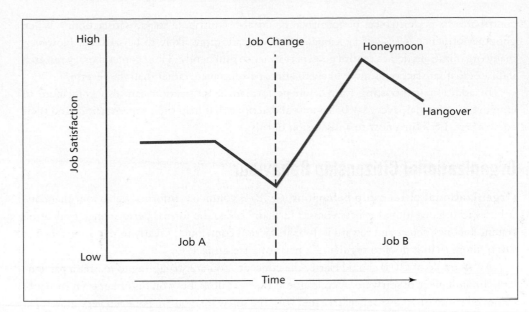

EXHIBIT 4.9
The honeymoon–hangover effect.
Source: Drawing by the authors, based on Boswell, W.R., Boudreau, J.W., & Tichy, J. (2005). The relationship between employee job change and job satisfaction: The honeymoon–hangover effect. *Journal of Applied Psychology, 90,* 882–892.

- An employee might be so embedded in the community (due to involvement with churches, schools, or sports) that he or she is willing to endure a dissatisfying job rather than move.
- A weak job market might result in limited employment alternatives. Dissatisfaction is most likely to result in turnover when jobs are plentiful.[64]

Despite these exceptions, a decrease in job satisfaction often precedes turnover, and an employee who quits experiences a boost in satisfaction in the new job. However, some of this boost might be due to a "honeymoon effect," in which the bad facets of the old job are gone, the good facets of the new job are apparent, and the bad facets of the new job are not yet known. Over time, as these bad facets are recognized, a "hangover effect" can occur, in which overall satisfaction with the new job decreases.[65] This pattern is shown in Exhibit 4.9, which traces job satisfaction at five points in time as a person moves between jobs A and B.

Performance

It seems to make sense that job satisfaction contributes to less absenteeism and turnover, but does it also lead to improved job performance? After all, employees might be so "satisfied" that no work is accomplished! In fact, research has confirmed what folk wisdom and business magazines have advocated for many years—job satisfaction is associated with enhanced performance.[66] However, the connection between satisfaction and performance is complicated, because many factors besides job satisfaction influence motivation and performance (as we'll see in Chapter 5). Thus, research has led to some qualifications to the idea that "a happy worker is a productive worker."

All satisfaction facets are not equal in terms of stimulating performance. The most important facet has to do with the content of the work itself.[67] Thus, interesting, challenging jobs are most likely to stimulate high performance (we will see how to design such jobs in Chapter 6). One consequence of this is the fact that the connection between job satisfaction and performance is stronger for complex, high-tech jobs in science, engineering, and computers and less strong for more routine labour jobs. In part, this is because people doing complex jobs have more control over their level of performance.

Another issue in the connection between job satisfaction and performance has to do with the question of which of these is the cause and which the effect. Although job satisfaction contributes to performance, performance could also contribute to job satisfaction.[68] When good performance is *followed by rewards*, employees are more likely to be satisfied. However, many organizations do not reward good performance sufficiently. Thus, contemporary research indicates that satisfaction is more likely to affect performance, rather than the reverse.[69]

In addition to boosting formal job performance, satisfaction can also contribute to employees' informal, everyday behaviour and actions that help their organizations and their co-workers. Let's turn now to a discussion of this.

Organizational Citizenship Behaviour

Organizational citizenship behaviour (OCB) is voluntary, informal behaviour that contributes to organizational effectiveness.[70] In many cases, the formal performance evaluation system does not detect and reward it. Job satisfaction contributes greatly to the occurrence of OCB, more than it does to regular task performance, in fact.[71]

An example of OCB should clarify the concept. You are struggling to master a particularly difficult piece of software. A colleague at the next desk, busy on his or her own rush job, comes over and offers assistance. Irritated with the software, you are not even very grateful at first, but within 10 minutes you have solved the problem with your colleague's help. Notice the defining characteristics of this example of OCB:

- The behaviour is voluntary. It is not included in the person's job description.

- The behaviour is spontaneous. No one ordered or suggested it.

- The behaviour contributes to organizational effectiveness. It extends beyond simply doing you a personal favour.

- The behaviour is unlikely to be explicitly picked up and rewarded by the performance evaluation system, especially since it is not part of the job description.

What forms might OCB take? As the software example indicates, one prominent form is *helping* behaviour, offering assistance to others. Another might be *conscientiousness* to the details of work, including getting in on the snowiest day of the year and not wasting organizational resources. A third involves being a *good sport* when the inevitable frustrations of organizational life crop up—not everyone can have the best office or the best parking spot. A final form of OCB is *courtesy and cooperation*.[72] Examples might include warning the photocopy unit about a big job that is on the way or delaying one's own work to assist a colleague on a rush job.

Just how does job satisfaction contribute to OCB? Fairness is the key. Although distributive fairness (especially in terms of pay) is important, procedural and interactional fairness from a supportive manager seem especially critical.[73] If the manager strays from the prescriptions for procedural fairness we gave earlier, OCB can suffer. If one feels unfairly treated, it might be difficult to lower formal performance for fear of dire consequences. It might be much easier to withdraw the less visible, informal activities that make up OCB. On the other hand, fair treatment and its resulting satisfaction might be reciprocated with OCB, a truly personalized input. OCB is also influenced by employees' mood at work. People in a pleasant, relaxed, optimistic mood are more likely to provide special assistance to others.[74] OCB contributes to organizational productivity and efficiency and to reduced turnover.[75]

Research shows that there is sometimes a progression of withdrawal in response to job dissatisfaction (and to reduced commitment, discussed below).[76] That is, people withdraw their attention or work effort in an attempt to compensate for dissatisfaction, beginning with more subtle behaviours and progressing to more extreme, until some equilibrium is struck. As shown in Exhibit 4.10, reduction of OCB is often the first withdrawal response, as these are voluntary behaviours. This may be followed, in turn, by coming to work late, then absenteeism, and ultimately turnover. Managers should be alert to increases in the lower forms of withdrawal, because they may signal bigger problems in the future.

Organizational citizenship behaviour (OCB). Voluntary, informal behaviour that contributes to organizational effectiveness.

EXHIBIT 4.10
Progression of
withdrawal

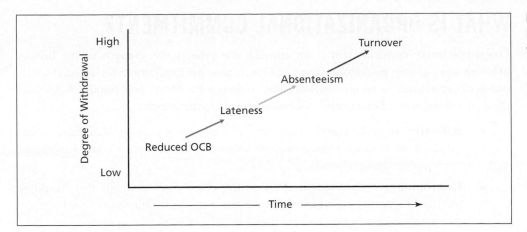

Customer Satisfaction and Profit

Is it possible that employee satisfaction could actually affect *customer* satisfaction? That is, do happy employees translate into happy customers? And do happy employees actually contribute to the bottom line of the organization by increasing organizational profits?

A growing body of evidence has established that employee job satisfaction is indeed translated into customer or client satisfaction and organizational profitability.[77] Thus, organizations with higher average levels of employee satisfaction are more effective. For instance, firms in the 100 Best Companies to Work for in America have consistently generated higher stock returns than their corporate peers.[78] The same applies to units within larger organizations. Hence, local bank branches or insurance claims offices with more satisfied employees should tend to have more satisfied clients and generate more profits for the larger firm. Thus, it makes good sense to use employee satisfaction as one criterion in judging the effectiveness of local unit managers.

How does employee satisfaction translate into customer satisfaction? Reduced absenteeism and turnover contribute to the seamless delivery of service, as do the OCBs that stimulate good teamwork. Also, the mood mechanism, mentioned earlier, should not be discounted, as good mood among employees can be contagious for customers.

Let's turn now to another important work attitude—organizational commitment.

One worker voluntarily helping out another is an example of organizational citizenship, which positively affects organizational effectiveness.

© Monkey Business Images/Shutterstock.com

LO 4.5

Differentiate *affective*, *continuance*, and *normative commitment*, and explain how organizations can foster *organizational commitment*.

Organizational commitment. An attitude that reflects the strength of the linkage between an employee and an organization.

Affective commitment. Commitment based on identification and involvement with an organization.

Continuance commitment. Commitment based on the costs that would be incurred in leaving an organization.

Normative commitment. Commitment based on ideology or a feeling of obligation to an organization.

WHAT IS ORGANIZATIONAL COMMITMENT?

Organizational commitment is an attitude that reflects the strength of the linkage between an employee and an organization. This linkage has implications for whether someone tends to remain in an organization. Researchers John Meyer and Natalie Allen have identified three very different types of organizational commitment:[79]

- **Affective commitment** is commitment based on a person's identification and involvement with an organization. People with high affective commitment stay with an organization because they *want* to.

- **Continuance commitment** is commitment based on the costs that would be incurred in leaving an organization. People with high continuance commitment stay with an organization because they *have* to.

- **Normative commitment** is commitment based on ideology or a feeling of obligation to an organization. People with high normative commitment stay with an organization because they think that they *should* do so.

Employees can be committed not only to their organization but also to various constituencies within and outside the organization. Thus, each type of commitment could also apply to one's work team, union, or profession.[80]

Key Contributors to Organizational Commitment

The best predictor of affective commitment is interesting, satisfying work of the type found in enriched jobs (see Chapter 6).[81] One mistake that organizations sometimes make is starting employees out in unchallenging jobs so they do not make any serious errors. This can have a negative impact on affective commitment. Role clarity and having one's expectations met after being hired also contribute to affective commitment.[82]

Continuance commitment occurs when people feel that leaving the organization will result in personal sacrifice, or they perceive that good alternative employment is lacking. Building up "side bets" in pension funds, obtaining rapid promotion, or being well integrated into the community where the firm is located can lock employees into organizations even though they would rather go elsewhere. Not surprisingly, continuance commitment increases with the length of time a person is employed by an organization.

Normative commitment ("I *should* stay here") can be fostered by benefits that build a sense of obligation to the organization. These might include tuition reimbursements or special training that enhances one's skills. Strong identification with an organization's product or service ("I should stay here because the Sierra Club is doing important work") can also foster normative commitment. Finally, certain socialization practices (see Chapter 8) that emphasize loyalty to the organization can stimulate normative commitment. For example, sports coaches often haze players who miss practice to stress the importance of loyalty to the team.

Consequences of Organizational Commitment

All forms of commitment reduce turnover intentions and actual turnover.[83] Organizations plagued with turnover problems among key employees should look carefully at tactics that foster commitment. This is especially called for when turnover gets so bad that it threatens customer service. Many service organizations (e.g., restaurants and hotels), however, have traditionally accepted high turnover rates.

Organizations should take care, though, in their targeting of the kind of commitment to boost. Affective commitment is positively related to performance because it focuses attention on goals and thus enhances motivation (see Chapter 5).[84] However, continuance commitment is *negatively* related to performance, something you might have observed in dealing with burned-out bureaucrats.[85] An especially bad combination for both the employee and the organization is high continuance commitment coupled with low affective commitment—people locked into organizations that they detest. This happens very frequently during recessions.

Is there a downside to organizational commitment? Very high levels of commitment can cause conflicts between family life and work life. Also, very high levels of commitment have often been implicated in unethical and illegal behaviour, including a General Electric price-fixing conspiracy. Finally, high levels of commitment to a particular *form* or *style* of organization can cause a lack of innovation and lead to resistance when a change in the culture is necessary.[86]

Changes in the Workplace and Employee Commitment

Organizations are experiencing unprecedented change as a result of shifts in workforce demographics, technological innovations, and global competition. John Meyer, Natalie Allen, and Laryssa Topolnytsky explain that the impact of these changes in the workplace on employee commitment can be seen in three main areas:[87]

- *Changes in the nature of employees' commitment to the organization.* Depending on the nature of workplace changes and how they are managed, employees' levels of affective, continuance, and normative commitment can increase or decrease. Thus, the commitment profiles of employees following a change will be different from what they were prior to the change, and maintaining high levels of affective commitment will be particularly challenging. Changes that are made in the organization's best interest but that are detrimental to employees' well-being are most likely to damage affective commitment.

- *Changes in the focus of employees' commitment.* Employees generally have multiple commitments. In particular, employee commitment can be directed to others within the organization, such as subunits or divisions, teams, the "new" organization, as well as entities outside the organization, such as one's occupation, career, or union. Therefore, changes in the workplace might alter the focus of employees' commitments both within and outside of the organization. As organizations increase in size following mergers and acquisitions, for example, employees are likely to shift their commitment to smaller organizational units, such as their particular division, branch, or team. As well, changes that threaten employees' future in the organization might result in a shift in commitment to entities outside the organization, such as one's profession, occupation, or personal career.

- *The multiplicity of employer–employee relationships within organizations.* As organizations attempt to cope and adapt to rapid change, they need to be flexible enough to shrink or expand their workforce. At the same time, they need a workforce that is flexible enough to get any job done. This creates a potential conflict, as employees who do not have guaranteed job security may be unwilling to be as flexible as the organization would like or to have a strong affective commitment toward the organization. A potential solution to this problem is for organizations to have different relationships with employee groups. For example, an organization might have a group of core employees who perform the key operations required for organizational success. It would be important for this group of employees to have a high level of affective organizational commitment. Other employee groups would consist of those with contractual arrangements or individuals hired on a temporary basis who do not perform the core tasks and whose commitment to the organization is not as important.

In summary, changes in the workplace are having an impact on the nature of employee commitment and employee–employer relationships. It is therefore important that organizations understand the way in which changes in the workplace can change the profile and focus of employees' commitment and the impact this can have on employee behaviour and organizational success.

THE MANAGER'S NOTEBOOK

Carlsberg's *Winning Behaviours* Campaign

1. It is possible to instill a common organizational culture globally as long as some adjustments are made to respect variations in national culture. With the help of headquarters HR and communications specialists, local managers employed a "glocal" approach, tailoring Carlsberg's global strategy to local values and preferences. Thus, diversity is accepted even as people are encouraged to pull in the same strategic direction. As examples of "glocalization," the Malaysian operation created a unique logo to highlight the winning behaviours that employed preferred regional esthetic cues and also created an indigenous video illustrating the behaviours. Awards were instituted for individuals and teams who exemplified the winning behaviours.

2. In particular, the fairly high power distance (and uncertainty avoidance) prevalent in both Malaysia and China posed some challenges, since the winning behaviours had to do with being proactive, being entrepreneurial, taking responsibility, and risking failure. Taking initiative without close supervision and direction was challenging for some employees, and a strong tendency for face saving meant that it was hard to risk failure. Managers found that these particular aspects of the *Winning Behaviours* campaign required more training and patience in implementation. Nonetheless, the campaign was generally considered successful.

MyManagementLab   Study, practise, and explore real management situations with these helpful resources:

- **Interactive Lesson Presentations:** Work through interactive presentations and assessments to test your knowledge of management concepts.
- **PIA (Personal Inventory Assessments):** Enhance your ability to connect with key concepts through these engaging, self-reflection assessments.
- **Study Plan:** Check your understanding of chapter concepts with self-study quizzes.
- **Videos:** Learn more about the management practices and strategies of real companies.
- **Simulations:** Practise decision-making in simulated management environments.

LEARNING OBJECTIVES CHECKLIST

4.1 *Values* are broad preferences for particular states of affairs. Values tend to differ across generations and across cultures. Critical cross–cultural dimensions of values include power distance, uncertainty avoidance, masculinity/femininity, individualism/collectivism, and time orientation. Differences in values across cultures set constraints on the export and import of organizational behaviour theories and management practices. They also have implications for satisfying global customers and developing globally aware employees.

4.2 *Attitudes* are a function of what we think about the world (our beliefs) and how we feel about the world (our values). Attitudes are important because they influence how we behave, although we have

discussed several factors that reduce the correspondence between our attitudes and behaviours.

4.3 *Job satisfaction* is an especially important attitude for organizations. Satisfaction is a function of the discrepancy between what individuals want from their jobs and what they perceive that they obtain, taking into account fairness. Dispositional factors, moods, and emotions also influence job satisfaction. Factors such as challenging work, adequate compensation, career opportunities, and friendly, helpful co-workers contribute to job satisfaction.

4.4 Job satisfaction is important because it promotes several positive outcomes for organizations. Satisfied employees tend to be less likely to be absent or leave their jobs. While links between satisfaction and performance are not always strong, satisfaction with the work itself has been linked to better performance. Satisfaction linked to perceptions of fairness can also lead to citizenship behaviours on the part of employees. Satisfied workers may also enhance customer satisfaction.

4.5 *Organizational commitment* is an attitude that reflects the strength of the linkage between an employee and an organization. *Affective commitment* is based on a person's identification with an organization. *Continuance commitment* is based on the costs of leaving an organization. *Normative commitment* is based on ideology or feelings of obligation. Changes in the workplace can change the nature and focus of employee commitment as well as employer–employee relationships. To foster commitment, organizations need to be sensitive to the expectations of employees and consider the impact of policy decisions beyond economic issues.

DISCUSSION QUESTIONS

1. Explain how these people might have to regulate their emotions when doing their jobs: hair salon owner, bill collector, police officer, teacher. How will this regulation of emotion affect job satisfaction?

2. Using the model of the turnover process in Exhibit 4.8, explain why a very dissatisfied employee might not quit his or her job.

3. Use equity theory to explain why a dentist who earns $100 000 a year might experience more job dissatisfaction than a factory worker who earns $40 000.

4. Mexico has a fairly high power distance culture, while the United States and Canada have lower power distance cultures. Discuss how effective management techniques might vary between Mexico and its neighbours to the north.

5. Give an example of an employee who is experiencing distributive fairness but not procedural fairness. Give an example of an employee who is experiencing procedural fairness but not distributive fairness.

INTEGRATIVE DISCUSSION QUESTIONS

1. What role do perceptions play in the determination of job satisfaction? Refer to the components of perception in Chapter 3 and describe how perception plays a role in the determination of job satisfaction according to discrepancy theory, equity theory, and dispositions. How can perceptions be changed to increase job satisfaction?

2. Does personality influence values and job attitudes? Discuss how the Big Five personality dimensions, locus of control, self-monitoring, self-esteem, and positive and negative affectivity might influence occupational choice, job satisfaction, and organizational commitment (affective, continuance, and normative). If personality influences job satisfaction and organizational commitment, how can organizations foster high levels of these attitudes?

ON-THE-JOB CHALLENGE QUESTION

Mr. Winston

In 2006, Arthur Winston died at age 100. He had worked for 76 years for the Los Angeles Metropolitan Transportation Authority cleaning trains and buses. Although this is remarkable enough, it is even more remarkable that he missed only one day of work in his last 72 years, the day of his wife's funeral in 1988. At the time of his retirement on the eve of becoming 100, he headed a crew of 11 workers. Although

he had aspired to become a mechanic when younger, the racial biases of the 1930s and 1940s prevented this career advancement. In 1996, Mr. Winston received a congressional citation from the U.S. president as "Employee of the Century." Mr. Winston's incredible record was the object of extensive media coverage, both at home and abroad.

Use the material in the chapter to speculate on various reasons for Mr. Winston's awesome attendance record. What accounts for the great media interest in Mr. Winston?

Sources: (2006, April 14). MTA employee who retired at 100 has died in his sleep. http://cbs2.com/local/Arthur.Winston. MTA.2.515610.html; Marquez, M. (2006, March 22). Los Angeles man retires at 100. abcnews.go.com/US/WNT/story?id=1756219.

EXPERIENTIAL EXERCISE

Attitudes Toward Absenteeism from Work

In this exercise we will examine your attitudes toward absenteeism from work. Although you learned in the chapter that absence can stem from job dissatisfaction, the scenarios below show that a number of other factors can also come into play.

1. Working alone, please indicate the extent to which you think that the employee's absence in each of the following scenarios is legitimate or illegitimate by using one of the six answer categories that appear below. A legitimate absence might be considered acceptable, while an illegitimate absence might be considered unacceptable. This is a measure of your personal attitudes; there are no right or wrong answers. Add up your scores and divide by 7 to obtain an average. Lower scores represent less favourable attitudes toward absenteeism.

2. Working in groups of 3 to 5 people, discuss the ratings that each of you gave to each scenario. What are the major reasons that contributed to each of your ratings? Compare your average scores.

3. As a group, decide which scenario is *most* legitimate, and explain why. Then decide which scenario is *least* legitimate, and explain why. Compare with the norms provided below.

4. As managers, how would you react to the least legitimate situation? What would you do?

6	5	4	3	2	1
Extremely legitimate	Moderately legitimate	Slightly legitimate	Slightly illegitimate	Moderately illegitimate	Extremely illegitimate

1. Susan is a highly productive employee, but she is absent more often than her co-workers. She has decided to be absent from work to engage in some recreational activities because she believes that her absence would not affect her overall productivity. _____

2. John is an active member of his community social club. Occasionally, the club organizes community activities with the aim of improving the quality of community life. A few days before a planned community activity, much of the work has not been done, and the club members are concerned that the activities will be unsuccessful. John has therefore decided to be absent from work to help the club organize its forthcoming activities. _____

3. Peter is a member of a project team that was charged with the responsibility of converting the company's information systems. The work entailed long hours, but the team was able to finish the project on time. Now that the project is completed, the long working hours have taken a toll and Peter feels quite stressed, so he has decided to stay away from work to recuperate. _____

4. Jane works in a low-paying job for which she is overqualified. She has been searching for a more suitable job through advertisements in the newspapers. She has been called for a job interview and has decided to call in sick to attend the interview. _____

5. Frank has a few months before his retirement and has lost the enthusiasm he used to have for his work. He believes he has contributed to making the company the success it is today. He recently joined a retired persons association where he feels his services are needed more. The association is organizing a safety awareness program for senior citizens, so he has decided to stay away from work to help. _____

6. Joan's co-workers normally use up all their sick leave. She is moving into a new house, and since she has not used up all her permitted sick leave, she has decided to call in sick so that she can finish packing for the move. _____

7. Anne does not feel challenged by her job and believes that she is not making any meaningful contribution to her organization. Her mother is going to the doctor for a routine medical

checkup and because Anne believes the company will not miss her, she decided to stay away from work to accompany her mother. _____

the scenarios, administered them to over 1500 employees in nine countries. The average rating across the 7 scenarios was 3.09. Respectively, the average ratings for each scenario were: S1 = 2.39; S2 = 2.88; S3 = 3.96; S4 = 3.52; S5 = 3.12; S6 = 3.03; S7 = 2.70. Higher numbers indicate more legitimacy.

Source: Scenarios developed by Helena M. Addae. Used with permission.

Scoring and Interpretation

As noted, lower scores represent less favourable attitudes toward absenteeism. Helena Addae, who developed

CASE INCIDENT

How Much Do You Get Paid?

Joan had been working as a reporter for a large television network for seven years. She was an experienced and hardworking reporter who had won many awards over the years for her outstanding work. The work was exciting and challenging, and at $75 000 a year plus benefits she felt well paid and satisfied. Then she found out that two recent graduates from one of the best schools of journalism in the United States had just been hired by her network at a starting salary of $80 000. Further,

two other reporters who worked with Joan and had similar track records had just received job offers from American networks and were being offered $150 000 plus $10 000 for every award won for their reporting.

1. According to equity theory, how will these incidents influence Joan's job satisfaction and behaviour?

2. What should Joan do in response to her situation? What should her organization do?

CASE STUDY

Michael Simpson

Michael Simpson is one of the most outstanding managers in the management consulting division of Avery McNeil and Co. (Avery McNeil is primarily an accounting firm, but it also has two divisions besides accounting: tax and management consulting.) A highly qualified individual with a deep sense of responsibility, Simpson obtained his M.B.A. two years ago from one of the leading northeastern schools. Before graduating from business school, Simpson interviewed a number of consulting firms and decided that the consulting division of Avery McNeil offered the greatest potential for rapid advancement.

At the time of the events in this story, Simpson had recently been promoted to manager, making him the youngest individual at this level in the consulting group. Two years with the firm was an exceptionally short period of time in which to

achieve this promotion. Although the promotions had been announced, Simpson had not yet been informed of his new salary. Despite the fact that his career had progressed well, he was concerned that his salary would be somewhat lower than the current market value that a headhunter had recently quoted him.

Simpson's wife, Diane, soon would be receiving her M.B.A. One night over dinner, Simpson was amazed to hear the level of the salaries being offered to new M.B.A.s. Simpson commented to Diane, "I certainly hope I get a substantial raise this time. I mean, it just wouldn't be fair to be making the same amount as recent graduates when I've been at the company now for over two years! I'd like to buy a house soon, but with housing costs rising and inflation following, that will depend on my pay raise."

Several days later, Simpson was working at his desk when Dave Barton, a friend and colleague, came across to Simpson's office. Barton had been hired at the same time as Simpson and had also been promoted recently. Barton said, "Hey, Mike, look at this! I was walking past Jane's desk and saw this memo from the personnel manager lying there. She obviously forgot to put it away. Her boss would kill her if he found out!"

The memo showed the proposed salaries for all the individuals in the consulting group that year. Simpson looked at the list and was amazed by what he saw. He said, "I can't believe this, Dave! Walt and Rich will be getting $12,000 more than I am." Walt Gresham and Rich Watson had been hired within the past year. Before coming to Avery McNeil they had both worked one year at another consulting firm. Barton spoke angrily: "Mike, I knew the firm had to pay them an awful lot to attract them, but to pay them more than people above them is ridiculous!" Simpson responded, "You know, if I hadn't seen Walt and Rich's salaries, I would think I was getting a reasonable raise. Hey listen, Dave, let's get out of here. I've had enough of this place for one day." Barton replied, "Okay, Mike, just let me return this memo. Look, it's not that bad; after all, you are getting the largest raise."

On his way home, Simpson tried to think about the situation more objectively. He knew that there were a number of pressures on the compensation structure in the consulting division. If the division wished to continue attracting M.B.A.s from top schools, it would have to offer competitive salaries. Starting salaries had increased about $23,000 during the last two years. As a result, some of the less experienced M.B.A.s were earning nearly the same amounts as others who had been with the firm several years but had come in at lower starting salaries, even though their pay had been gradually increasing over time. Furthermore, because of expanding business, the division had found it necessary to hire consultants from other firms. In order to do so effectively, Avery McNeil had found it necessary to upgrade the salaries they offered. The firm as a whole was having problems meeting the federally regulated Equal Opportunity Employment goals and was trying especially hard to recruit women and minorities.

One of Simpson's colleagues, Martha Lohman, had been working in the consulting division of Avery McNeil and Company until three months ago, when she was offered a job at another consulting firm. She had become disappointed with her new job and on returning to her previous position at Avery McNeil was rehired at a salary considerably higher than her former level. Simpson had noticed on the memo that she was earning more than he was, even though she was not given nearly the same level of responsibility as he was. Simpson also realized that the firm attempted to maintain some parity between salaries in the auditing and consulting divisions.

When Simpson arrived home, he discussed the situation with his wife:

Simpson: Diane, I know I'm getting a good raise, but I am still earning below my market value—$20,000 less than that headhunter told me last week. And the fact that those two guys from the other consulting firm are getting more than I shows the firm is prepared to pay competitive rates.

Diane: I know it's unfair, Mike, but what can you do? You know your boss won't negotiate salaries after they have been approved by the compensation committee, but it wouldn't hurt to at least talk to him about your dissatisfaction. I don't think you should let a few thousand dollars a year bother you. You will catch up eventually, and the main thing is that you really enjoy what you are doing.

Simpson: Yes I do enjoy what I'm doing, but that is not to say that I wouldn't enjoy it elsewhere. I really just have to sit down and think about all the pros and cons in my working for Avery McNeil. First of all, I took this job because I felt that I could work my way up quickly. I think that I have demonstrated this, and the firm has also shown that they are willing to help me achieve this goal. If I left this job for a better-paying one, I might not get the opportunity to work on the exciting jobs that I am currently working on. Furthermore, this company has time and money invested in me. I'm the only one at Avery that can work on certain jobs, and the company has several lined up. If I left the company now, they would not only lose me, but they would probably lose some of their billings as well. I really don't know what to do at this point, Diane. I can either stay with Avery McNeil or look for a higher-paying job elsewhere; however, there is no guarantee that my new job would be a "fast track" one like my job at Avery. One big plus at Avery is that the people there already know me and the kind of work I produce. If I went elsewhere, I'd essentially have to start all over again. What do you think I should do, Diane?

Source: From Nadler, D. A., Tushman, M. L., & Hatvany, N. G. (1982). *Managing organizations: Readings and cases*. Used with permission.

QUESTIONS

1. Use discrepancy theory concepts to explain Michael Simpson's feelings.
2. Use equity theory to explain Michael's feelings. Provide details about inputs, outcomes, and likely comparison people.
3. Comment on Mike's likely perceptions about procedural fairness at Avery McNeil and Co.
4. Apply affective events theory to the case. How did the memo affect the mood in the office? What emotions are at play?
5. Use Exhibit 4.8 to analyze the factors that might determine if Mike quits his job at Avery McNeil.
6. Speculate on the likely consequences of Mike's dissatisfaction if he does not quit the firm.
7. Comment on how Mike's organizational commitment may be changing.
8. What should Mike do now?

CHAPTER 5
THEORIES OF WORK MOTIVATION

LEARNING OBJECTIVES

After reading Chapter 5, you should be able to:

5.1 Define *motivation*, discuss its basic properties, and distinguish it from *performance*.

5.2 Compare and contrast *intrinsic* and *extrinsic motivation*.

5.3 Explain and discuss the different factors that predict *performance*, and define *general cognitive ability* and *emotional intelligence*.

5.4 Explain and discuss *need theories* of motivation and *self-determination theory*.

5.5 Explain and discuss the *process theories of motivation*.

5.6 Discuss the cross-cultural limitations of theories of motivation.

5.7 Summarize the relationships among the various theories of motivation, performance, and job satisfaction.

DEVFACTO TECHNOLOGIES INC.

Mike McKinnon had a lot going on. In fact, that's an understatement. With a newborn at home, the developer was still spending long hours at Edmonton IT consultancy DevFacto Technologies Inc. He was working on a big project that had run into some snags, and the pressure was on. If the job was successful, the company would bankroll a trip for all its employees to Las Vegas. Instead of grumbling, the sleep-deprived McKinnon doubled his efforts to make sure the job was done right. And when he and his wife finally did board the plane to Las Vegas, his company gave them a pair of tickets to catch a show as a further thank you.

DevFacto Technologies in Edmonton was founded by Chris Izquierdo and David Cronin in 2007. Both had previously worked as software developers in rigidly bureaucratic firms and decided to start their own IT consulting practice. Their dream was to create a different kind of organization with a healthy workplace that allowed talent to flourish, while building superior software that had a brilliant customer-service edge.

In starting their own company, the thinking was that a self-motivated workforce would make for a less hierarchical, more efficient, and more productive business. "If you get a bunch of driven people who are intrinsically motivated to do good work, you shouldn't have to monitor them using managers," says Cronin. "If you give them a purpose that's larger than themselves, you can lead them to results."

DevFacto has more than doubled in size since 2010 and now has offices in Regina and Calgary. Job applicants go through a lengthy culture-fit interview with Cronin or a regional director. "I'm looking for evidence of intrinsic motivation, that thing that's driving them to be better," says Cronin. Employees also participate in group interviews to assess candidates and have the power to veto a hire who won't fit in.

DevFacto employees are responsible for keeping one another accountable to deadlines, budgets, and other concerns. "People do need some pressure and attention put on them," Cronin says. "That can come from a boss

DevFacto Technologies

Motivated employees are the key to the success of DevFacto Technologies Inc., which has been named one of the Best Workplaces in Canada and the best place for millennials to work in Alberta.

walking around, or it can come from peers giving you feedback and challenging you," says Cronin. He feels the latter approach is a more potent way to make people understand their own role in the overall health of the organization.

Motivation at DevFacto is more than just intrinsic. For example, new hires receive three weeks of vacation per year to start. The company offers all employees $2500 per year for any vocational training (including photography classes, cooking classes, public speaking classes, and self-help books), $100 per month for travel expenses (including a bus pass), and free beer on Fridays from the company's beer fridge. Employees also receive an annual $1200 cell-phone and home-internet subsidy. The company also has a profit sharing program that they use every year to implement two new benefit programs for its employees. For example, in 2011 the company introduced a $500-per-year wellness fund that can be used for anything from a gym membership to a tablet computer, and a 52-cent-per-kilometre subsidy when-ever an employee has to travel for work. In 2012, the company introduced a $1000-per-year vacation subsidy to encourage employees to use their minimum three weeks of vacation per year. The second program in 2012 was a plan to match a percentage of each employee's RRSP contributions.

The company also hosts DevFacto Development Days four times a year. Employees are split into teams and have free rein to create whatever they want, be it a technical process or a mobile application. At the end of the day, their creations are showcased to the rest of the DevFacto team.

DevFacto has been named one of the Best Workplaces in Canada and the best place for millennials to work in Alberta. Its average annual employee retention rate is 98 percent. Cronin believes that by investing in their young employees "they will return the favour by working hard and being loyal."[1]

Would you be motivated if you worked for DevFacto Technologies? What kind of person would respond well to the company's motivational techniques? What underlying philosophy of motivation is being used, and what effect does it have on employees' motivation and performance? These are some of the questions that this chapter will explore.

First we will define *motivation* and distinguish it from *performance*. After that, we will describe several popular theories of work motivation and contrast them. Then, we will explore whether these theories translate across cultures. Finally, we will present a model that links motivation, performance, and job satisfaction.

WHY STUDY MOTIVATION?

Motivation is one of the most traditional topics in organizational behaviour, and it has interested managers, researchers, teachers, and sports coaches for years. However, a good case can be made that motivation has become even more important in contemporary organizations. Much of this is a result of the need for increased productivity for organizations to be globally competitive. It is also a result of the rapid changes that contemporary organizations are undergoing. Stable systems of rules, regulations, and procedures that once guided behaviour are being replaced by requirements for flexibility and attention to customers that necessitate higher levels of initiative. This initiative depends on motivation.

What would a good motivation theory look like? In fact, as we shall see, there is no single, all-purpose motivation theory. Rather, we will consider several theories that serve somewhat different purposes. In combination, though, a good set of theories should recognize human diversity and consider that the same conditions will not motivate everyone. Also, a good set of theories should be able to explain how it is that some people like those who work at DevFacto Technologies seem to be self-motivated, while others seem to require external motivation. Finally, a good set of theories should recognize the social aspect of human beings—people's motivation is often affected by how they see others being treated. Before getting to our theories, let's first define motivation more precisely.

Define *motivation*, discuss its basic properties, and distinguish it from *performance*.

Motivation. The extent to which persistent effort is directed toward a goal.

WHAT IS MOTIVATION?

The term *motivation* is not easy to define. However, from an organization's perspective, when we speak of a person as being motivated, we usually mean that the person works "hard," "keeps at" his or her work, and directs his or her behaviour toward appropriate outcomes.

Basic Characteristics of Motivation

We can formally define **motivation** as the extent to which persistent effort is directed toward a goal.[2]

EFFORT The first aspect of motivation is the strength of the person's work-related behaviour, or the amount of *effort* the person exhibits on the job. Clearly, this involves different kinds of activities on different kinds of jobs. A loading-dock worker might exhibit greater effort by carrying heavier crates, while a researcher might reveal greater effort by searching out an article in some obscure foreign technical journal. Both are exerting effort in a manner appropriate to their jobs.

PERSISTENCE The second characteristic of motivation is the *persistence* that individuals exhibit in applying effort to their work tasks. The organization would not be likely to think of the loading-dock worker who stacks the heaviest crates for two hours and then goofs off for six hours as especially highly motivated. Similarly, the researcher who makes an important discovery early in her career and then rests on her laurels for five years would not be considered especially highly motivated. In each case, workers have not been persistent in the application of their effort.

DIRECTION Effort and persistence refer mainly to the quantity of work an individual produces. Of equal importance is the quality of a person's work. Thus, the third characteristic of motivation is the *direction* of the person's work-related behaviour. In other words, do workers channel persistent effort in a direction that benefits the organization? Employers expect motivated stockbrokers to advise their clients of good investment opportunities and motivated software designers to design software, not play computer games. These correct decisions increase the probability that persistent effort is actually translated into accepted organizational outcomes. Thus, motivation means working smart as well as working hard.

GOALS Ultimately, all motivated behaviour has some goal or objective toward which it is directed. We have presented the preceding discussion from an organizational perspective— that is, we assume that motivated people act to enhance organizational objectives. In this case, employee goals might include high productivity, good attendance, or creative decisions. Of course, employees can also be motivated by goals that are contrary to the objectives of the organization, including absenteeism, sabotage, and embezzlement. In these cases, they are channelling their persistent efforts in directions that are dysfunctional for the organization.

Extrinsic and Intrinsic Motivation

LO 5.2

Some hold the view that people are motivated by factors in the external environment (such as supervision or pay), while others believe that people can, in some sense, be self-motivated without the application of these external factors. You might have experienced this distinction. As a worker, you might recall tasks that you enthusiastically performed simply for the sake of doing them and others that you performed only to keep your job or placate your boss.

Experts in organizational behaviour distinguish between intrinsic and extrinsic motivation. At the outset, we should emphasize that there is only weak consensus concerning the exact definitions of these concepts and even weaker agreement about whether we should label specific motivators as intrinsic or extrinsic.[3] However, the following definitions and examples seem to capture the distinction fairly well.

Intrinsic motivation stems from the direct relationship between the worker and the task and is usually self-applied. Feelings of achievement, accomplishment, challenge, and competence derived from performing one's job are examples of intrinsic motivators, as is sheer interest in the job itself. Off the job, avid participation in sports and hobbies is often intrinsically motivated. As described in the chapter-opening vignette, DevFacto Technologies emphasizes intrinsic motivation even when hiring employees.

Extrinsic motivation stems from the work environment external to the task and is usually applied by someone other than the person being motivated. Pay, fringe benefits, company policies, and various forms of supervision are examples of extrinsic motivators. At DevFacto Technologies, the trip to Las Vegas and the vacation subsidy are examples of extrinsic motivators.

Obviously, employers cannot package all conceivable motivators as neatly as these definitions suggest. For example, a promotion or a compliment might be applied by the boss but might also be a clear signal of achievement and competence. Thus, some motivators have both extrinsic and intrinsic qualities.

The relationship between intrinsic and extrinsic motivators has been the subject of a great deal of debate.[4] Some research studies have reached the conclusion that the availability of extrinsic motivators can reduce the intrinsic motivation stemming from the task itself.[5] The notion is that when extrinsic rewards depend on performance, then the motivating potential of intrinsic rewards decreases. Proponents of this view have suggested that making extrinsic rewards contingent on performance makes individuals feel less competent and less

Compare and contrast *intrinsic* and *extrinsic motivation.*

Intrinsic motivation. Motivation that stems from the direct relationship between the worker and the task; it is usually self-applied.

Extrinsic motivation. Motivation that stems from the work environment external to the task; it is usually applied by others.

EXHIBIT 5.1
Factors contributing to individual job performance.

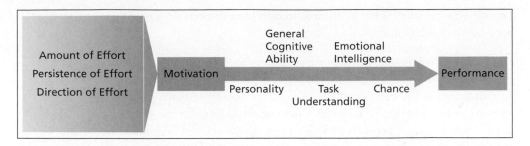

in control of their own behaviour. That is, they come to believe that their performance is controlled by the environment and that they perform well only because of the money.[6] As a result, their intrinsic motivation suffers.

However, a review of research in this area reached the conclusion that the negative effect of extrinsic rewards on intrinsic motivation occurs only under very limited conditions, and they are easily avoidable.[7] As well, in organizational settings in which individuals see extrinsic rewards as symbols of success and as signals of what to do to achieve future rewards, they increase their task performance.[8] Thus, it is safe to assume that both kinds of rewards are important and compatible in enhancing work motivation. Further, as you will see later in the chapter, many theories of work motivation make the distinction between intrinsic and extrinsic motivation.

Motivation and Performance

LO **5.3**

Explain and discuss the different factors that predict *performance*, and define *general cognitive ability* and *emotional intelligence*.

Performance. The extent to which an organizational member contributes to achieving the objectives of the organization.

At this point, you may well be saying, "Wait a minute, I know many people who are 'highly motivated' but just don't seem to perform well. They work long and hard, but they just don't measure up." This is certainly a sensible observation, and it points to the important distinction between motivation and performance. **Performance** can be defined as the extent to which an organizational member contributes to achieving the objectives of the organization.

Some of the factors that contribute to individual performance in organizations are shown in Exhibit 5.1.[9] While motivation clearly contributes to performance, the relationship is not one to one, because a number of other factors also influence performance. For example, recall from Chapter 2 that personality traits such as the Big Five and core self-evaluations also predict job performance. You might also be wondering about the role of intelligence: Doesn't it influence performance? The answer, of course, is yes—intelligence, or what is also known as mental ability, does predict performance. Two forms of intelligence that are particularly important for performance are general cognitive ability and emotional intelligence. Let's consider each before we discuss motivation.

Motivation is just one of several factors that contributes to performance.

© Cathy Yeulet/123rf

GENERAL COGNITIVE ABILITY The term *cognitive ability* is often used to refer to what most people call intelligence or mental ability. Although there are many different types of specific cognitive abilities, in organizational behaviour we are often concerned with what is known as *general cognitive ability*. **General cognitive ability** is a term used to refer to a person's basic information-processing capacities and cognitive resources. It reflects an individual's overall capacity and efficiency for processing information, and it includes a number of cognitive abilities, such as verbal, numerical, spatial, and reasoning abilities, that are required to perform mental tasks. Cognitive ability is usually measured by a number of specific aptitude tests that measure these abilities.[10]

Research has found that general cognitive ability predicts learning, training, career success, and job performance in all kinds of jobs and occupations, including those that involve both manual and mental tasks. This should not be surprising, because many cognitive skills are required to perform most jobs. General cognitive ability is an even better predictor of performance for more complex and higher-level jobs that require the use of more cognitive skills and involve more information processing.[11] Thus, both general cognitive ability and motivation are necessary for performance.

EMOTIONAL INTELLIGENCE Although the importance of general cognitive ability for job performance has been known for many years, researchers have only recently begun to study emotional intelligence. **Emotional intelligence** (EI) has to do with an individual's ability to understand and manage his or her own and others' feelings and emotions. It involves the ability to perceive and express emotion, assimilate emotion in thought, understand and reason about emotions, and manage emotions in oneself and others. Individuals high in EI are able to identify and understand the meanings of emotions and to manage and regulate their emotions as a basis for problem solving, reasoning, thinking, and action.[12]

Peter Salovey and John Mayer, who are credited with first coining the term *emotional intelligence*, have developed an EI model that consists of four interrelated sets of skills, or branches. The four skills represent sequential steps that form a hierarchy. The perception of emotion is at the bottom of the hierarchy, followed by (in ascending order) using emotions to facilitate thinking, understanding emotions, and managing and regulating emotions. The four-branch model of EI is shown in Exhibit 5.2 and described below.[13]

1. *Perceiving emotions accurately in oneself and others:* This involves the ability to perceive emotions and to accurately identify one's own emotions and the emotions of others. An example of this is the ability to accurately identify emotions in people's faces and in non-verbal behaviour. People differ in the extent to which they can accurately identify emotions in others, particularly from facial expressions.[14] This step is the most basic level of EI and is necessary to be able to perform the other steps in the model.

2. *Using emotions to facilitate thinking:* This refers to the ability to use and assimilate emotions and emotional experiences to guide and facilitate one's thinking and reasoning. This means that one is able to use emotions in functional ways, such as making decisions and other cognitive processes (e.g., creativity, integrative thinking, and inductive reasoning). This stage also involves being able to shift one's emotions and generate new emotions that can help one to see things in different ways and from different perspectives. This is an important skill because, as will be described in Chapter 11, emotions and moods affect what and how people think when making decisions.[15]

3. *Understanding emotions, emotional language, and the signals conveyed by emotions:* This stage involves being able to understand emotional information, the determinants and consequences of emotions, and how emotions evolve and change over time. At this stage, people understand how different situations and events generate emotions as well as how they and others are influenced by various emotions.[16] Individuals who are good at this know not to ask somebody who is in a bad mood for a favour, but rather to wait until the person is in a better mood or to just ask somebody else!

Emotional intelligence. The ability to understand and manage one's own and other's feelings and emotions.

Managing emotions so as to attain specific goals

Understanding emotions, emotional language, and the signals conveyed by emotions

Using emotions to facilitate thinking

Perceiving emotions accurately in oneself and others

EXHIBIT 5.2
Four-branch model of emotional intelligence.
Source: Based on Mayer, J.D., Caruso, D.R., & Salovey, P. (2000). Emotional Intelligence meets traditional standards for an intelligence. *Intelligence, 27,* 267–298; Salovey, P., & Mayer, J.D. (1990). Emotional Intelligence. *Imagination, Cognition & Personality, 9,* 185–211.

4. *Managing emotions so as to attain specific goals:* This involves the ability to manage one's own and others' feelings and emotions as well as emotional relationships. This is the highest level of EI because it requires one to have mastered the previous stages. At this stage, an individual is able to regulate, adjust, and change his or her own emotions as well as others' emotions to suit the situation. Examples of this include being able to stay calm when feeling angry or upset; being able to excite and enthuse others; or being able to lower another person's anger. To be effective at managing emotions, one must be able to perceive emotions, integrate and assimilate emotions, and be knowledgeable of and understand emotions.

Research on EI has found that it predicts job performance and academic performance.[17] One study found that college students' EI measured at the start of the academic year predicted their grade point averages at the end of the year. A review of research on emotional intelligence and job performance found that not only is EI positively related to job performance, it also predicts job performance above and beyond cognitive ability and the Big Five personality variables.[18] There is also some evidence that EI is most strongly related to job performance in jobs that require high levels of emotional labour, such as police officers and customer service representatives.[19] According to the results of one study, emotional intelligence is most important for the job performance of employees with lower levels of cognitive ability and of less importance for the job performance of employees with high levels of cognitive ability.[20]

The Motivation–Performance Relationship

As shown in Exhibit 5.1, it is certainly possible for performance to be low even when a person is highly motivated. In addition to personality, general cognitive ability, and emotional intelligence, poor performance could also be due to a poor understanding of the task or luck and chance factors that can damage the performance of the most highly motivated individuals. Of course, an opposite effect is also possible. An individual with rather marginal motivation might have high general cognitive ability or emotional intelligence or might understand the task so well that some compensation occurs—what little effort the individual makes is expended very efficiently in terms of goal accomplishment. Also, a person with weak motivation might perform well because of some luck or chance factor that boosts performance. Thus, it is no wonder that workers sometimes complain that they receive lower performance ratings than colleagues who "don't work as hard."

In this chapter, we will concentrate on the motivational components of performance rather than on the other determinants in Exhibit 5.1. However, the message here should be clear: we cannot consider motivation in isolation. High motivation will not result in high performance if employees have low general cognitive ability and emotional intelligence, do not understand their jobs, or encounter unavoidable obstacles over which they have no control. Motivational interventions, such as linking pay to performance, simply *will not work* if employees are deficient in important skills and abilities.[21] Let's now turn to theories of work motivation to better understand what motivates people, and the process of motivation.

NEED THEORIES OF WORK MOTIVATION

The first three theories of motivation that we will consider are **need theories**. These theories attempt to specify the kinds of needs people have and the conditions under which they will be motivated to satisfy these needs in a way that contributes to performance. Needs are physiological and psychological wants or desires that individuals can satisfy by acquiring certain incentives or achieving particular goals. It is the behaviour stimulated by this acquisition process that reveals the motivational character of needs:

NEEDS → BEHAVIOUR → INCENTIVES AND GOALS

LO 5.4

Explain and discuss *need theories* of motivation and *self-determination theory.*

Need theories. Motivation theories that specify the kinds of needs people have and the conditions under which they will be motivated to satisfy these needs in a way that contributes to performance.

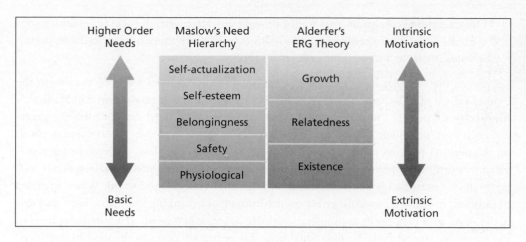

EXHIBIT 5.3
Relationship between Maslow's and Alderfer's need theories.

Notice that need theories are concerned with *what* motivates workers (needs and their associated incentives or goals). They can be contrasted with *process theories*, which are concerned with exactly *how* various factors motivate people. Need and process theories are complementary rather than contradictory. Thus, a need theory might contend that money can be an important motivator (what), and a process theory might explain the actual mechanics by which money motivates (how).[22] In this section, we will examine three prominent need theories of motivation.

Maslow's Hierarchy of Needs

Abraham Maslow was a psychologist who developed and refined a general theory of human motivation.[23] According to Maslow, humans have five sets of needs that are arranged in a hierarchy, beginning with the most basic and compelling needs (see the left side of Exhibit 5.3). These needs include

1. *Physiological needs.* These include the needs that must be satisfied for the person to survive, such as food, water, oxygen, and shelter. Organizational factors that might satisfy these needs include the minimum pay necessary for survival and working conditions that promote existence.

2. *Safety needs.* These include needs for security, stability, freedom from anxiety, and a structured and ordered environment. Organizational conditions that might meet these needs include safe working conditions, fair and sensible rules and regulations, job security, a comfortable work environment, pension and insurance plans, and pay above the minimum needed for survival.

3. *Belongingness needs.* These include needs for social interaction, affection, love, companionship, and friendship. Organizational factors that might meet these needs include the opportunity to interact with others on the job, friendly and supportive supervision, opportunity for teamwork, and opportunity to develop new social relationships.

4. *Esteem needs.* These include needs for feelings of adequacy, competence, independence, strength, and confidence, and the appreciation and recognition of these characteristics by others. Organizational factors that might satisfy these needs include the opportunity to master tasks leading to feelings of achievement and responsibility. Also, awards, promotions, prestigious job titles, professional recognition, and the like might satisfy these needs when they are felt to be truly deserved.

5. *Self-actualization needs.* These needs are the most difficult to define. They involve the desire to develop one's true potential as an individual to the fullest extent and to express one's skills, talents, and emotions in a manner that is most personally fulfilling. Maslow suggests that self-actualizing people have clear perceptions of reality, accept themselves and others, and are independent, creative, and appreciative of the world around them.

Organizational conditions that might provide self-actualization include absorbing jobs with the potential for creativity and growth as well as a relaxation of structure to permit self-development and personal progression.

Given the fact that individuals may have these needs, in what sense do they form the basis of a theory of motivation? That is, what exactly is the motivational premise of **Maslow's hierarchy of needs**? Put simply, the lowest-level unsatisfied need category has the greatest motivating potential. Thus, none of the needs is a "best" motivator; motivation depends on the person's position in the need hierarchy. According to Maslow, individuals are motivated to satisfy their physiological needs before they reveal an interest in safety needs, and safety must be satisfied before social needs become motivational, and so on. When a need is unsatisfied, it exerts a powerful effect on the individual's thinking and behaviour, and this is the sense in which needs are motivational. However, when needs at a particular level of the hierarchy are satisfied, the individual turns his or her attention to the next higher level. Notice the clear implication here that a *satisfied need is no longer an effective motivator.* Once one has adequate physiological resources and feels safe and secure, one does not seek more of the factors that met these needs but looks elsewhere for gratification. According to Maslow, the single exception to this rule involves self-actualization needs. He felt that these were "growth" needs that become stronger as they are gratified.

Alderfer's ERG Theory

Clayton Alderfer developed another need-based theory, called **ERG theory**.[24] It streamlines Maslow's need classifications and makes some different assumptions about the relationship between needs and motivation. The name ERG stems from Alderfer's compression of Maslow's five-category need system into three categories: existence, relatedness, and growth needs.

1. *Existence needs.* These are needs that are satisfied by some material substance or condition. As such, they correspond closely to Maslow's physiological needs and to those safety needs that are satisfied by material conditions rather than interpersonal relations. These include the need for food, shelter, pay, and safe working conditions.

2. *Relatedness needs.* These are needs that are satisfied by open communication and the exchange of thoughts and feelings with other organizational members. They correspond fairly closely to Maslow's belongingness needs and to those esteem needs that involve feedback from others. However, Alderfer stresses that relatedness needs are satisfied by open, accurate, honest interaction rather than by uncritical pleasantness.

3. *Growth needs.* These are needs that are fulfilled by strong personal involvement in the work setting. They involve the full utilization of one's skills and abilities and the creative development of new skills and abilities. Growth needs correspond to Maslow's need for self-actualization and the aspects of his esteem needs that concern achievement and responsibility.

As you can see in Exhibit 5.3, Alderfer's need classification system does not represent a radical departure from that of Maslow. In addition, Alderfer agrees with Maslow that as lower-level needs are satisfied, the desire to have higher-level needs satisfied will increase. Thus, as existence needs are fulfilled, relatedness needs gain motivational power. Alderfer explains this by arguing that as more "concrete" needs are satisfied, energy can be directed toward satisfying less concrete needs. Finally, Alderfer agrees with Maslow that the least concrete needs—growth needs—become *more* compelling and *more* desired as they are fulfilled.

It is, of course, the differences between ERG theory and the need hierarchy that represent Alderfer's contribution to the understanding of motivation. First, unlike the need hierarchy, ERG theory does not assume that a lower-level need *must* be gratified before a less concrete need becomes operative. Thus, ERG theory does not propose a rigid hierarchy

Maslow's hierarchy of needs. A five-level hierarchical need theory of motivation that specifies that the lowest-level unsatisfied need has the greatest motivating potential.

ERG theory. A three-level hierarchical need theory of motivation (existence, relatedness, growth) that allows for movement up and down the hierarchy.

of needs. Some individuals, owing to background and experience, might seek relatedness or growth even though their existence needs are ungratified. Hence, ERG theory seems to account for a wide variety of individual differences in motive structure. Second, ERG theory assumes that if the higher-level needs are ungratified, individuals will increase their desire for the gratification of lower-level needs. Notice that this represents a *radical* departure from Maslow. According to Maslow, if esteem needs are strong but ungratified, a person will not revert to an interest in belongingness needs, because these have necessarily already been gratified. (Remember, he argues that satisfied needs are not motivational.) According to Alderfer, however, the frustration of higher-order needs will lead workers to regress to a more concrete need category. For example, the software designer who is unable to establish rewarding social relationships with superiors or co-workers might increase his or her interest in fulfilling existence needs, perhaps by seeking a pay increase. Thus, according to Alderfer, an apparently satisfied need can act as a motivator by substituting for an unsatisfied need.

Given the preceding description of ERG theory, we can identify its two major motivational premises as follows:

1. The more lower-level needs are gratified, the more higher-level need satisfaction is desired.

2. The less higher-level needs are gratified, the more lower-level need satisfaction is desired.

McClelland's Theory of Needs

Psychologist David McClelland spent several decades studying the human need structure and its implications for motivation. According to **McClelland's theory of needs**, needs reflect relatively stable personality characteristics that one acquires through early life experiences and exposure to selected aspects of one's society. Unlike Maslow and Alderfer, McClelland has not been interested in specifying a hierarchical relationship among needs. Rather, he has been more concerned with the specific behavioural consequences of needs. In other words, under what conditions are certain needs likely to result in particular patterns of motivation? The three needs that McClelland studied most have special relevance for organizational behaviour: needs for achievement, affiliation, and power.[25]

Individuals who are high in **need for achievement** (*n* Ach) have a strong desire to perform challenging tasks well. More specifically, they exhibit the following characteristics:

- *A preference for situations in which personal responsibility can be taken for outcomes.* Those high in *n* Ach do not prefer situations in which outcomes are determined by chance, because success in such situations does not provide an experience of achievement.

McClelland's theory of needs. A nonhierarchical need theory of motivation that outlines the conditions under which certain needs result in particular patterns of motivation.

Need for achievement. A strong desire to perform challenging tasks well.

People with a high need for power have a desire to influence others.

© alotofpeople/Fotolia

- *A tendency to set moderately difficult goals that provide for calculated risks.* Success with easy goals will provide little sense of achievement, while extremely difficult goals might never be reached. The calculation of successful risks is stimulating to the high–*n* Ach person.

- *A desire for performance feedback.* Such feedback permits individuals with high *n* Ach to modify their goal attainment strategies to ensure success and signals them when success has been reached.[26]

People who are high in *n* Ach are concerned with bettering their own performance or that of others. They are often concerned with innovation and long-term goal involvement. However, these things are not done to please others or to damage the interests of others. Rather, they are done because they are *intrinsically* satisfying. Thus, *n* Ach would appear to be an example of a growth or self-actualization need.

Need for affiliation. A strong desire to establish and maintain friendly, compatible interpersonal relationships.

People who are high in **need for affiliation** (*n* Aff) have a strong desire to establish and maintain friendly, compatible interpersonal relationships. In other words, they like to like others, and they want others to like them! More specifically, they have an ability to learn social networking quickly and a tendency to communicate frequently with others, either face to face, by telephone, or in writing. Also, they prefer to avoid conflict and competition with others, and they sometimes exhibit strong conformity to the wishes of their friends. The *n* Aff motive is obviously an example of a belongingness or relatedness need.

Need for power. A strong desire to influence others, making a significant impact or impression.

People who are high in **need for power** (*n* Pow) strongly desire to have influence over others. In other words, they wish to make a significant impact or impression on them. People who are high in *n* Pow seek out social settings in which they can be influential. When in small groups, they act in a "high-profile," attention-getting manner. There is some tendency for those who are high in *n* Pow to advocate risky positions. Also, some people who are high in *n* Pow show a strong concern for personal prestige. The need for power is a complex need because power can be used in a variety of ways, some of which serve the power seeker and some of which serve other people or the organization. However, *n* Pow seems to correspond most closely to Maslow's self-esteem need.

McClelland predicts that people will be motivated to seek out and perform well in jobs that match their needs. Thus, people with high *n* Ach should be strongly motivated by sales jobs or entrepreneurial positions, such as running a small business. Such jobs offer the feedback, personal responsibility, and opportunity to set goals, as noted above. People who are high in *n* Aff will be motivated by jobs such as social work or customer relations because these jobs have as a primary task establishing good relations with others.

Finally, high *n* Pow will result in high motivation in jobs that enable one to have a strong impact on others—jobs such as journalism and management. In fact, McClelland has found that the most effective managers have a low need for affiliation, a high need for power, and the ability to direct power toward organizational goals.[27] (We will study this further in Chapter 12.)

Research Support for Need Theories

Maslow's need hierarchy suggests two main hypotheses. First, specific needs should cluster into the five main need categories that Maslow proposes. Second, as the needs in a given category are satisfied, they should become less important, while the needs in the adjacent higher-need category should become more important. This second hypothesis captures the progressive, hierarchical aspect of the theory. In general, research support for both these hypotheses is weak or negative. This is probably a function of the rigidity of the theory, which suggests that most people experience the same needs in the same hierarchical order. However, there is fair support for a simpler, two-level need hierarchy comprising the needs toward the top and the bottom of Maslow's hierarchy.[28]

This latter finding provides some indirect encouragement for the compressed need hierarchy found in Alderfer's ERG theory. Several tests indicate fairly good support for many of the predictions generated by the theory, including expected changes in need strength. Particularly interesting is the confirmation that the frustration of relatedness needs increases the strength of existence needs.[29] The simplicity and flexibility of ERG theory seem to capture the human need structure better than the greater complexity and rigidity of Maslow's theory.

McClelland's need theory has generated a wealth of predictions about many aspects of human motivation. Researchers have tested more and more of these predictions in organizational settings, and the results are generally supportive of the idea that particular needs are motivational when the work setting permits the satisfaction of these needs.[30]

Managerial Implications of Need Theories

The need theories have some important things to say about managerial attempts to motivate employees.

APPRECIATE DIVERSITY The lack of support for the fairly rigid need hierarchy suggests that managers must be adept at evaluating the needs of individual employees and offering incentives or goals that correspond to their needs. Unfounded stereotypes about the needs of the "typical" employee and naïve assumptions about the universality of need satisfaction are bound to reduce the effectiveness of chosen motivational strategies. The best salesperson might not make the best sales manager! The needs of a young recent college graduate probably differ from those of an older employee preparing for retirement. Thus, it is important to survey employees to find out what their needs are and then offer programs that meet their needs.

APPRECIATE INTRINSIC MOTIVATION The need theories also serve the valuable function of alerting managers to the existence of higher-order needs (whatever specific label we apply to them). The recognition of these needs in many employees is important for two key reasons. One of the basic conditions for organizational survival is the expression of some creative and innovative behaviour on the part of members. Such behaviour seems most likely to occur during the pursuit of higher-order need fulfillment, and ignorance of this factor can cause the demotivation of the people who have the most to offer the organization. Second, observation and research evidence support Alderfer's idea that the frustration of higher-order needs prompts demands for greater satisfaction of lower-order needs. This can lead to a vicious motivational cycle—that is, because the factors that gratify lower level needs are fairly easy to administer (e.g., pay and fringe benefits), management has grown to rely on them to motivate employees. In turn, some employees, deprived of higher-order need gratification, come to expect more and more of these extrinsic factors in exchange for their services. Thus, a cycle of deprivation, regression, and temporary gratification continues, at great cost to the organization.[31]

How can organizations benefit from the intrinsic motivation that is inherent in strong higher-order needs? First, such needs will fail to develop for most employees unless lower-level needs are reasonably well gratified.[32] Thus, very poor pay, job insecurity, and unsafe working conditions will preoccupy most workers at the expense of higher-order outcomes. Second, if basic needs are met, jobs can be "enriched" to be more stimulating and challenging and to provide feelings of responsibility and achievement (we will have more to say about this in Chapter 6). Finally, organizations could pay more attention to designing career paths that enable interested workers to progress through a series of jobs that continue to challenge their higher-order needs. Individual managers could also assign tasks to employees with this goal in mind.

SELF-DETERMINATION THEORY

A more recent theory of motivation that involves needs is self-determination theory. However, unlike the need theories described in the previous section, self-determination theory makes a distinction between two types of motivation: autonomous (or self-determined)

EXHIBIT 5.4
Self-Determination
Theory.

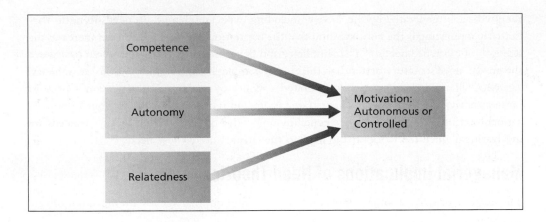

Self-determination theory. A theory of motivation that considers whether people's motivation is autonomous or controlled.

motivation and controlled (or not self-determined) motivation. Thus, **self-determination theory** (SDT) explains what motivates people and whether motivation is autonomous or controlled.[33]

If you refer to the chapter-opening vignette, you will see that when it comes to motivation at DevFacto Technologies, the emphasis is self-motivation, or what SDT calls autonomous motivation. **Autonomous motivation** is self-motivation or intrinsic motivation and occurs when people feel they are in control of their motivation, and they are performing a task because it is interesting, and they have chosen to do it. Thus, when motivation is autonomous, individuals are engaged in a task because they have made a choice to do the task and their actions are internally rather than externally regulated.

Autonomous motivation. Self-motivation or intrinsic motivation that occurs when people feel they are in control of their motivation.

Controlled motivation. Motivation that is externally controlled, such as when one is motivated to obtain a desired consequence or extrinsic reward.

Controlled motivation occurs when people are motivated to obtain a desired consequence or extrinsic reward. When motivation is controlled, individuals feel they are pressured and have no choice but to engage in a task. Thus, their motivation is externally rather than internally regulated. This is the case when people do something to obtain a desired consequence, avoid punishment, or because their boss is watching them. Controlled motivation is similar to extrinsic motivation.

The extent to which a person's motivation is autonomous or controlled depends on the satisfaction of basic psychological needs. According to self-determination theory, needs are universal necessities for psychological health. Thus, unlike the need theories described in the previous section, self-determination theory posits that needs are not hierarchical and people do not differ in the strength of particular needs. Rather, according to SDT, there are three basic psychological needs that are important for all individuals: competence, autonomy, and relatedness. As shown in Exhibit 5.4, these three needs influence people's motivation. When people have their basic psychological needs for competence, autonomy, and relatedness satisfied, their motivation will be autonomous. When these needs are not satisfied, motivation will be controlled. Thus, the basic premise of SDT is that work environments that lead to the satisfaction of the three psychological needs will promote autonomous motivation, which will then lead to more effective performance and positive work outcomes.[34]

Research Support for and Managerial Implications of Self-Determination Theory

Research on self-determination theory has investigated the predictors of autonomous and controlled motivation as well as the three psychological needs. A key predictor variable is autonomy support from one's direct supervisor. **Autonomy support** involves providing employees with choice and encouragement for personal initiative. Managers provide employees with autonomy support when they give a meaningful rationale for performing an activity or task, they emphasize and enable some choice rather than control, and they understand and

Autonomy support. Providing employees with choice and encouragement for personal initiative.

acknowledge employees' feelings and perspectives. They also encourage employees to take initiative and convey confidence in employees' abilities. Research has found that autonomy support is positively related to the satisfaction of the needs for competence, relatedness, and autonomy as well as autonomous motivation. In addition, autonomous motivation is related more effective job performance, especially on complex tasks. It is also associated with re positive job attitudes, such as organizational commitment, job satisfaction, and psycho- al well-being, while controlled motivation is associated with negative outcomes, such as psychological distress and turnover intentions.[35]

The most important managerial implication of SDT is that organizations need to create work environments that will satisfy employees' needs for competence, autonomy, and relatedness and facilitate autonomous motivation. Thus, managers should provide employees with autonomy support as well as jobs that are interesting and challenging and that allow employees some choice. Structuring work to allow interdependence among employees can also facilitate autonomous motivation by satisfying the need for relatedness.[36]

PROCESS THEORIES OF WORK MOTIVATION

In contrast to need theories of motivation and self-determination theory, which concentrate on *what* motivates people, **process theories** concentrate on *how* motivation occurs. In this section, we will examine three important process theories: expectancy theory, equity theory, and goal setting theory.

Expectancy Theory

The basic idea underlying **expectancy theory** is the belief that motivation is determined by the outcomes that people expect to occur as a result of their actions on the job. Psychologist Victor Vroom is usually credited with developing the first complete version of expectancy theory and applying it to the work setting.[37] The basic components of Vroom's theory are shown in Exhibit 5.5 and are described in more detail below.

- **Outcomes** are the consequences that may follow certain work behaviours. Of particular interest to the organization are first-level outcomes, such as high productivity versus average productivity, illustrated in Exhibit 5.5, or good attendance versus poor attendance. Expectancy theory is concerned with specifying how an employee might attempt to choose one first-level outcome instead of another. Second-level outcomes are consequences that follow the attainment of a particular first-level outcome. Contrasted with first-level outcomes, second-level outcomes are most personally relevant to the individual worker and might involve amount of pay, sense of accomplishment, acceptance by peers, fatigue, and so on.

- **Instrumentality** is the probability that a particular first-level outcome (such as high productivity) will be followed by a particular second-level outcome (such as pay) (this is also known as the *performance → outcome* link). For example, a bank teller might figure that the odds are 50/50 (instrumentality = .5) that a good performance rating will result in a pay raise.

- **Valence** is the expected value of outcomes, the extent to which they are attractive or unattractive to the individual. Thus, good pay, peer acceptance, the possibility of being fired, or any other second-level outcome might be more or less attractive to particular workers. According to Vroom, the valence of first-level outcomes is the sum of products of the associated second-level outcomes and their instrumentalities—that is,

$$\text{the valence of particular first-level outcome} = \sum \text{instrumentalities} \times \text{second-level valences}$$

Simulate

MOTIVATION

LO 5.5

Explain and discuss the *process theories of motivation*.

Process theories. Motivation theories that specify the details of how motivation occurs.

Expectancy theory. A process theory that states that motivation is determined by the outcomes that people expect to occur as a result of their actions on the job.

Outcomes. Consequences that follow work behaviour.

Instrumentality. The probability that a particular first-level outcome will be followed by a particular second-level outcome.

Valence. The expected value of work outcomes; the extent to which they are attractive or unattractive.

EXHIBIT 5.5
**A hypothetical
expectancy model
(E = Expectancy,
I = Instrumentality,
V = Valence).**

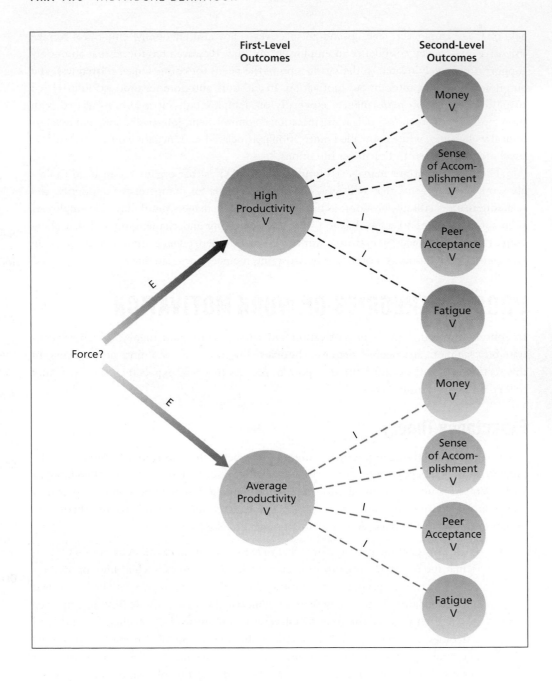

In other words, the valence of a first-level outcome depends on the extent to which
it leads to favourable second-level outcomes.

Expectancy. The
probability that a particular
first-level outcome can be
achieved.

- **Expectancy** is the probability that the worker can actually achieve a particular
first-level outcome (this is also known as the *effort → performance* link). For example,
a machinist might be absolutely certain (expectancy = 1.0) that she can perform at
an average level (producing 15 units a day) but less certain (expectancy = .6) that
she can perform at a high level (producing 20 units a day).

Force. The effort directed
toward a first-level outcome.

- **Force** is the end product of the other components of the theory. It represents
the relative degree of effort that will be directed toward various first-level
outcomes.

According to Vroom, the force directed toward a first-level outcome is a product of the
valence of that outcome and the expectancy that it can be achieved. Thus,

$$\text{Force} = \text{First-level valence} \times \text{Expectancy}$$

We can expect an individual's effort to be directed toward the first-level outcome that has the largest force product. Notice that no matter the valence of a particular first-level outcome, a person will not be motivated to achieve it if the expectancy of accomplishment approaches zero.

Believe it or not, the mechanics of expectancy theory can be distilled into a couple of simple sentences! In fact, these sentences nicely capture the premises of the theory:

- People will be motivated to perform in those work activities that they find attractive and that they feel they can accomplish.

- The attractiveness of various work activities depends on the extent to which they lead to favourable personal consequences.

It is extremely important to understand that expectancy theory is based on the perceptions of the individual worker. Thus, expectancies, valences, instrumentalities, and relevant second-level outcomes depend on the perceptual system of the person whose motivation we are analyzing. For example, two employees performing the same job might attach different valences to money, differ in their perceptions of the instrumentality of performance for obtaining high pay, and differ in their expectations of being able to perform at a high level. Therefore, they would likely exhibit different patterns of motivation.

Although expectancy theory does not concern itself directly with the distinction between extrinsic and intrinsic motivators, it can handle any form of second-level outcome that has relevance for the person in question. Thus, some people might find second-level outcomes of an intrinsic nature, such as feeling good about performing a task well, positively valent. Others might find extrinsic outcomes, such as high pay, positively valent.

Research Support for Expectancy Theory

Tests have provided moderately favourable support for expectancy theory.[38] In particular, there is especially good evidence that the valence of first-level outcomes depends on the extent to which they lead to favourable second-level consequences. We must recognize, however, that the sheer complexity of expectancy theory makes it difficult to test. Some research studies show that individuals have a difficult time discriminating between instrumentalities and second-level valences. Despite this and other technical problems, experts in motivation generally accept expectancy theory.

Managerial Implications of Expectancy Theory

The motivational practices suggested by expectancy theory involve "juggling the numbers" that individuals attach to expectancies, instrumentalities, and valences.

BOOST EXPECTANCIES One of the most basic things managers can do is ensure that their employees *expect* to be able to achieve first-level outcomes that are of interest to the organization. No matter how positively valent high productivity or good attendance might be, the force equation suggests that workers will not pursue these goals if expectancy is low. Low expectancies can take many forms, but a few examples will suffice to make the point.

- Employees might feel that poor equipment, poor tools, or lazy co-workers impede their work progress.

- Employees might not understand what the organization considers to be good performance or see how they can achieve it.

- If performance is evaluated by a subjective supervisory rating, employees might see the process as capricious and arbitrary, not understanding how to obtain a good rating.

Although the specific solutions to these problems vary, expectancies can usually be enhanced by providing proper equipment and training, demonstrating correct work procedures, carefully explaining how performance is evaluated, and listening to employee performance problems. The point of all this is to clarify the path to beneficial first-level outcomes.

CLARIFY REWARD CONTINGENCIES Managers should also attempt to ensure that the paths between first- and second-level outcomes are clear. Employees should be convinced that first-level outcomes desired by the organization are clearly *instrumental* in obtaining positive second-level outcomes and avoiding negative outcomes. If managers have a policy of recommending good performers for promotion, they should spell out this policy. Similarly, if managers desire regular attendance, they should clarify the consequences of good and poor attendance. To ensure that instrumentalities are strongly established, they should be clearly stated and then acted on by the manager. Managers should also attempt to provide stimulating, challenging tasks for workers who appear to be interested in such work. On such tasks, the instrumentality of good performance for feelings of achievement, accomplishment, and competence is almost necessarily high. The ready availability of intrinsic motivation reduces the need for the manager to constantly monitor and clarify instrumentalities.[39]

APPRECIATE DIVERSE NEEDS Obviously, it might be difficult for managers to change the valences that employees attach to second-level outcomes. Individual preferences for high pay, promotion, interesting work, and so on are the product of a long history of development and are unlikely to change rapidly. However, managers would do well to analyze the diverse preferences of particular employees and attempt to design individualized "motivational packages" to meet their needs. Of course, all concerned must perceive such rewards to be fair. Let's examine another process theory that is concerned specifically with the motivational consequences of fairness.

Equity Theory

Equity theory. A process theory that states that motivation stems from a comparison of the inputs one invests in a job and the outcomes one receives in comparison with the inputs and outcomes of another person or group.

In Chapter 4, we discussed the role of **equity theory** in explaining job satisfaction. To review, the theory asserts that workers compare the inputs that they invest in their jobs and the outcomes that they receive against the inputs and outcomes of some other relevant person or group. When these ratios are equal, the worker should feel that a fair and equitable exchange exists with the employing organization. Such fair exchange contributes to job satisfaction. When the ratios are unequal, workers perceive inequity, and they should experience job dissatisfaction, at least if the exchange puts the worker at a disadvantage vis-à-vis others.

But in what sense is equity theory a theory of motivation? Put simply, *individuals are motivated to maintain an equitable exchange relationship.* Inequity is unpleasant and tension producing, and people will devote considerable energy to reducing inequity and achieving equity. What tactics can do this? Psychologist J. Stacey Adams has suggested the following possibilities:[40]

- Perceptually distort one's own inputs or outcomes.
- Perceptually distort the inputs or outcomes of the comparison person or group.
- Choose another comparison person or group.
- Alter one's inputs or alter one's outcomes.
- Leave the exchange relationship.

Notice that the first three tactics for reducing inequity are essentially psychological, while the last two involve overt behaviour.

To clarify the motivational implications of equity theory, consider Terry, a middle manager in a consumer products company. He has five years' work experience and an MBA degree and considers himself a good performer. His salary is $75 000 a year. Terry finds out that Maxine, a co-worker with whom he identifies closely, makes the same salary he does.

However, she has only a bachelor's degree and one year of experience, and he sees her performance as average rather than good. Thus, from Terry's perspective, the following outcome/input ratios exist:

$$\frac{\text{TERRY \$75 000}}{\text{Good performance, MBA, 5 years}} \neq \frac{\text{MAXINE \$75 000}}{\text{Average performance, bachelor's, 1 year}}$$

In Terry's view, he is underpaid and should be experiencing inequity. What might he do to resolve this inequity? Psychologically, he might distort the outcomes that he is receiving, rationalizing that he is due for a certain promotion that will bring his pay into line with his inputs. Behaviourally, he might try to increase his outcomes (by seeking an immediate raise) or reduce his inputs. Input reduction could include a decrease in work effort or perhaps excessive absenteeism. Finally, Terry might resign from the organization to take what he perceives to be a more equitable job somewhere else.

Let's reverse the coin and assume that Maxine views the exchange relationship identically to Terry—same inputs, same outcomes. Notice that she too should be experiencing inequity, this time from relative overpayment. It does not take a genius to understand that Maxine would be unlikely to seek equity by marching into the boss's office and demanding a pay cut. However, she might well attempt to increase her inputs by working harder or enrolling in an MBA program. Alternatively, she might distort her view of Terry's performance to make it seem closer to her own. As this example implies, equity theory is somewhat vague about just when individuals will employ various inequity reduction strategies.

GENDER AND EQUITY As an addendum to the previous example, it is extremely interesting to learn that both women and men have some tendency to choose same-sex comparison persons—that is, when judging the fairness of the outcomes that they receive, men tend to compare themselves with other men, and women tend to compare themselves with other women. This might provide a partial explanation for why women are paid less than men, even for the same job. If women restrict their equity comparisons to (lesser-paid) women, they are less likely to be motivated to correct what we observers see as wage inequities.[41]

Research Support for Equity Theory

Most research on equity theory has been restricted to economic outcomes and has concentrated on the alteration of inputs and outcomes as a means of reducing inequity. In general, this research is very supportive of the theory when inequity occurs because of *underpayment*.[42] For example, when workers are underpaid on an hourly basis, they tend to lower their inputs by producing less work. This brings inputs in line with (low) outcomes. Also, when workers are underpaid on a piece-rate basis (e.g., paid $1 for each market research interview conducted), they tend to produce a high volume of low-quality work. This enables them to raise their outcomes to achieve equity. Finally, there is also evidence that underpayment inequity leads to resignation. Presumably, some underpaid workers seek equity in another organizational setting.

The theory's predictions regarding *overpayment* inequity have received less support.[43] The theory suggests that such inequity can be reduced behaviourally by increasing inputs or by reducing one's outcomes. The weak support for these strategies suggests either that people tolerate overpayment more than underpayment or that they use perceptual distortion to reduce overpayment inequity.

Managerial Implications of Equity Theory

The most straightforward implication of equity theory is that perceived underpayment will have a variety of negative motivational consequences for the organization, including low productivity, low quality, theft, or turnover. On the other hand, attempting to solve organizational problems through overpayment (disguised bribery) might not have the intended motivational effect. The trick here is to strike an equitable balance.

But how can such a balance be struck? Managers must understand that feelings about equity stem from a *perceptual* social comparison process in which the worker "controls the equation"—that is, employees decide what are considered relevant inputs, outcomes, and comparison persons, and management must be sensitive to these decisions. For example, offering the outcome of more interesting work might not redress inequity if better pay is considered a more relevant outcome. Similarly, basing pay only on performance might not be perceived as equitable if employees consider seniority an important job input.

Understanding the role of comparison people is especially crucial.[44] Even if the best engineer in the design department earns $2000 more than anyone else in the department, she might still have feelings of inequity if she compares her salary with that of more prosperous colleagues in *other* companies. Awareness of the comparison people chosen by workers might suggest strategies for reducing perceived inequity. Perhaps the company will have to pay even more to retain its star engineer.

Goal Setting Theory

Goal. The object or aim of an action.

At the beginning of the chapter, motivation was defined as persistent effort directed toward a goal. But what is a goal? A **goal** is the object or aim of an action.[45] One of the basic characteristics of all organizations is that they have goals. Thus, if employees are to achieve acceptable performance, some method of translating organizational goals into individual goals must be implemented.

Unfortunately, there is ample reason to believe that personal performance goals are vague or nonexistent for many organizational members. Employees frequently report that their role in the organization is unclear, or that they do not really know what their boss expects of them. Even in cases in which performance goals would seem to be obvious because of the nature of the task (e.g., filling packing crates to the maximum to avoid excessive freight charges), employees might be ignorant of their current performance. This suggests that the implicit performance goals simply are not making an impression.

The notion of goal setting as a motivator has been around for a long time. However, theoretical developments and some very practical research have demonstrated when and how goal setting can be effective.[46]

What Kinds of Goals Are Motivational?

Goal setting theory. A process theory that states that goals are motivational when they are specific and challenging, when organizational members are committed to them, and when feedback about progress toward goal attainment is provided.

According to **goal setting theory**, goals are most motivational when they are *specific* and *challenging* and when organizational members are *committed* to them. In addition, *feedback* about progress toward goal attainment should be provided.[47] The positive effects of goals are due to four mechanisms:[48]

- They *direct* attention toward goal-relevant activities.
- They lead to greater *effort*.
- They increase and prolong *persistence*.
- They lead to the discovery and use of task-relevant *strategies* for goal attainment.

Exhibit 5.6 shows the characteristics of goals that are motivational and the mechanisms that explain the effects of goals on performance. Let's now consider the motivational characteristics of goal setting theory in more detail.

GOAL SPECIFICITY   Specific goals are goals that specify an exact level of achievement for people to accomplish in a particular time frame. For example, "I will enrol in five courses next semester and achieve a B or better in each course" is a specific goal. Similarly, "I will

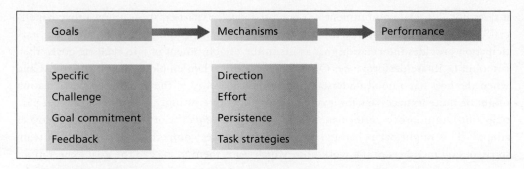

EXHIBIT 5.6
The mechanisms of goal setting.
Source: Locke, E.A., & Latham, G.P. (2002). Building a practically useful theory of goal setting and task motivation. *American Psychologist, 57,* 705–717.

increase my net sales by 20 percent in the coming business quarter" is a specific goal. On the other hand, "I will do my best" is not a specific goal, since level of achievement and time frame are both vague.

GOAL CHALLENGE Obviously, specific goals that are especially easy to achieve will not motivate effective performance. But goal challenge is a much more personal matter than goal specificity, since it depends on the experience and basic skills of the organizational member. One thing is certain, however: when goals become so difficult that they are perceived as *impossible* to achieve, they will lose their potential to motivate. Thus, goal challenge is best when it is pegged to the competence of individual workers and increased as the particular task is mastered. One practical way to do this is to base initial goals on past performance. For example, an academic counsellor might encourage a D student to set a goal of achieving Cs in the coming semester and encourage a C student to set a goal of achieving Bs. Similarly, a sales manager might ask a new salesperson to try to increase their sales by 5 percent in the next quarter and ask an experienced salesperson to try to increase their sales by 10 percent.

GOAL COMMITMENT Individuals must be committed to specific, challenging goals if the goals are to have effective motivational properties. The effect of goals on performance is strongest when individuals have high goal commitment. In a sense, goals really are not goals and cannot improve performance unless an individual accepts them and is committed to working toward them. This is especially important when goals are challenging and difficult to achieve. In a following section, we will discuss some factors that affect goal commitment.

GOAL FEEDBACK Specific and challenging goals have the most beneficial effect when they are accompanied by ongoing feedback that enables the person to compare current performance with the goal. This is why a schedule of tasks to be completed often motivates goal accomplishment. Progress against the schedule provides feedback. To be most effective, feedback should be accurate, specific, credible, and timely. Performance feedback is also obtained from co-workers and managers who are familiar with each employee's work, and informal progress reviews are also held throughout the year.

Enhancing Goal Commitment

It has probably not escaped you that the requirements for goal challenge and goal commitment seem potentially incompatible. After all, you might be quite amenable to accepting an easy goal but balk at accepting a tough one. Therefore, it is important to consider some of the factors that might affect commitment to challenging, specific goals, including participation, rewards, and management support.

PARTICIPATION It seems reasonable that organizational members should be more committed to goals that are set with their participation than to those simply handed down by their superior. Sensible as this sounds, the research evidence on the effects of participation is very mixed—sometimes participation in goal setting increases performance, and sometimes it does not.[49] If goal commitment is a potential *problem*, participation might prove beneficial.[50] When a climate of distrust between superiors and employees exists, or when participation provides information that assists in the establishment of fair, realistic goals, then it should facilitate performance. On the other hand, when employees trust their boss and when the boss has a good understanding of the capability of the employees, participation might be quite unnecessary for goal commitment.[51] Interestingly, research shows that participation can improve performance by increasing the *difficulty* of the goals that employees adopt.[52] This might occur because participation induces competition or a feeling of team spirit among members of the work unit, which leads them to exceed the goal expectations of the supervisor.

REWARDS   Will the promise of extrinsic rewards (such as money) for goal accomplishment increase goal commitment? Probably, but there is plenty of evidence that goal setting has led to performance increases *without* the introduction of monetary incentives for goal accomplishment. One reason for this might be that many ambitious goals involve no more than doing the job as it was designed to be done in the first place. For example, encouraging employees to pack crates or load trucks to within 5 percent of their maximum capacity does not really involve a greater expenditure of effort or more work. It simply requires more attention to detail. Goal setting should, however, be compatible with any system to tie pay to performance that already exists for the job in question.

MANAGEMENT SUPPORT   There is considerable agreement about one factor that will *reduce* commitment to specific, challenging performance goals. When supervisors behave in a coercive manner to encourage goal accomplishment, they can badly damage employee goal commitment. For goal setting to work properly, supervisors must demonstrate a desire to assist employees in goal accomplishment and behave supportively if failure occurs, even adjusting the goal downward if it proves to be unrealistically high. Threat and punishment in response to failure will be extremely counterproductive.[53] In addition, trust in the manager who assigns challenging goals is also important for goals to lead to improved performance. To learn more, see Research Focus: *Challenging Goals and Business-Unit Performance*.

Goal Orientation

Goal orientation. An individual's goal preferences in achievement situations.

Learning goal orientation. A preference to learn new things and develop competence in an activity by acquiring new skills and mastering new situations.

Performance-prove goal orientation. A preference to obtain favourable judgments about the outcome of one's performance.

Performance-avoid goal orientation. A preference to avoid negative judgments about the outcome of one's performance.

A recent development in goal setting is research on people's preferences for different kinds of goals, or what is known as *goal orientation*. **Goal orientation** refers to an individual's goal preferences in achievement situations. It is a stable individual difference that affects performance. Some individuals have a preference for learning goals while others have a preference for performance goals (performance-prove or performance-avoid goals). Individuals with a **learning goal orientation** are most concerned about learning something new and developing their competence in an activity by acquiring new skills and mastering new situations; they focus on acquiring new knowledge and skills and developing their competence. Individuals with a **performance-prove goal orientation** are concerned about demonstrating their competence in performing a task by seeking favourable judgments about the outcome of their performance. Individuals with a **performance-avoid goal orientation** are concerned about avoiding negative judgments about the outcome of their performance.[54]

Research on goal orientation has found that learning goal orientation is positively related to learning as well as academic, task, and job performance, while a performance-avoid orientation is negatively related to learning and lower task and job performance. A performance-prove orientation is not related to learning or performance outcomes. Thus, a learning goal orientation is most effective for learning and performance outcomes, while a performance-avoid goal orientation is detrimental for learning and performance.[55]

RESEARCH FOCUS

CHALLENGING GOALS AND BUSINESS-UNIT PERFORMANCE

Although challenging goals can improve performance, much less is known about what kind of manager will set challenging goals and when challenging goals are most likely to improve performance. To learn more about this, Craig Crossley, Cecily Cooper, and Tara Wernsing conducted a study in which they investigated the effects of challenging business-unit goals on business-unit sales performance in one of the largest sales organizations in the United States.

First, they considered the proactivity of senior managers as an important factor in the setting of challenging business-unit goals and sales performance (see Chapter 2 on proactive behaviour). Second, they suggested that trust in senior managers who assign challenging goals will be important for goal acceptance and commitment and, ultimately, business-unit performance.

As indicated in Chapter 2, proactive behaviour involves taking initiative to improve current circumstances or creating new ones. The authors suggested that proactive senior managers will set higher and more challenging goals for their units and that these higher goals will lead to greater unit sales performance. They also suggested that in order for challenging goals to lead to unit sales performance, there must be trust in the manager who assigns the goals. As indicated in Chapter 3, trust involves a willingness to be vulnerable and to take risks with respect to the actions of another party. Supervisors are expected to be more accepting of and committed to goals that are set by a senior manager they trust. As a result, they will be more likely to encourage employees to support the goals. Thus, challenging unit goals are expected to lead to higher unit sales performance when trust in the senior leader who assigns the goal is high rather than low.

To test these relationships, a study was conducted with senior (i.e., district) managers and their business units in a large consumer packaged goods company in the United States. Supervisors rated their trust in the district manager as well as his/her proactivity. District managers set their unit goals for monthly dollar sales with higher values representing more challenging goals. Unit sales performance was measured in terms of the monthly amount of sales attained in dollars by each district.

The results indicated that district manager proactivity was positively related to unit sales performance. In addition, district managers who were more proactive set more challenging unit goals, and more challenging unit goals were positively related to unit sales performance. Thus, proactive managers achieve higher unit sales performance because they set more challenging unit goals. Finally, challenging unit goals was more likely to lead to greater unit sales performance when trust in the manager was high. In other words, there needs to be a high level of trust in managers who assign challenging goals in order for the goals to result in higher unit performance.

The results of this research indicate that challenging goals are more likely to be set by proactive managers and that challenging goals are more likely to result in greater business unit sales performance when there is a high level of trust in the manager who assigns the goals.

Source: Based on Crossley, C.D., Cooper, C.D., & Wernsing, I.S. (2013). Making things happen through challenging goals: Leader proactivity, trust, and business-unit performance. *Journal of Applied Psychology, 98,* 540–549.

"Nobody came back from the Goal Setting Workshop. They all left to find better jobs."

Glasbergen Cartoons

Goal Proximity

Distal goal. Long-term or end goal.

Proximal goal. Short-term goal or sub-goal.

Goals can also be distinguished in terms of whether they are distal or proximal goals. A **distal goal** is a long-term or end goal, such as achieving a certain level of sales performance. A **proximal goal** is a short-term goal or sub-goal that is instrumental for achieving a distal goal. Proximal goals involve breaking down a distal goal into smaller, more attainable sub-goals. Proximal goals provide clear markers of progress toward a distal goal because they result in more frequent feedback. As a result, individuals can evaluate their ongoing performance and identify appropriate strategies for the attainment of a distal goal. Distal goals are too far removed to provide markers of one's progress, making it difficult for individuals to know how they are doing and to adjust their strategies.[56]

Proximal goals have been found to be especially important for novel and complex tasks, and distal goals can have a negative effect. However, when distal goals are accompanied with proximal goals, they have a significant positive effect on the discovery and use of task-relevant strategies, self-efficacy, and performance.[57]

Research Support for Goal Setting Theory

Goal setting theory is considered to be one of the most valid and practical theories of employee motivation. Several decades of research have demonstrated that specific, difficult goals lead to improved performance and productivity on a wide variety of tasks and occupations, including servicing drink machines, entering data, selling, teaching, and typing text. Further, the effect of group goal setting on group performance is similar to the effect of individual goal setting. Group goals result in superior group performance, especially when groups set specific goals and when the group members participate in setting the goals.[58] Studies also reveal that the positive effects of goal setting are not short lived—they persist over a long enough time to have practical value.[59]

For example, in a now classic study conducted at Weyerhaeuser Company, a large forest products firm headquartered in Tacoma, Washington, truck drivers were assigned the specific, challenging performance goal of loading their trucks to 94 percent of legal weight capacity. Before setting this goal, management had simply asked the drivers to do their best to maximize their weight. Over the first several weeks, load capacity gradually increased to more than

Drivers at Weyerhaeuser Company were assigned the specific, challenging performance goal of loading their trucks to 94 percent of legal weight capacity.

90 percent and remained at this high level for seven years! In the first nine months alone, the company accountants conservatively estimated the savings at $250 000. These results were achieved without driver participation in setting the goal and without monetary incentives for goal accomplishment. Drivers evidently found the 94 percent goal motivating in and of itself; they frequently recorded their weights in informal competition with other drivers.[60]

In recent years, research has found that the effects of goal setting on performance depend on a number of factors. For example, when individuals lack the knowledge or skill to perform a novel or complex task, a specific and challenging performance goal can decrease rather than increase performance relative to a do-your-best goal. On the other hand, when a task is straightforward, a specific, high-performance goal results in higher performance than a do-your-best goal. Thus, a high-performance goal is most effective when individuals already have the ability to perform a task. However, when individuals are learning to perform a novel or complex task, setting a specific, high-learning goal that focuses on knowledge and skill acquisition will be more effective than a specific, high-performance goal or a do-your-best goal. This is because effective performance of complex tasks requires the acquisition of knowledge and skills, and a specific learning goal focuses one's attention on learning.[61]

In addition, a new stream of goal setting research has found that subconscious goals can be activated by exposing participants to achievement-related stimuli such as a word or photograph and that these primed goals also have a positive effect on performance.[62] Finally, it is worth noting some research has suggested that there might be a dark side to goal setting. To learn more, see Ethical Focus: *The Dark Side of Goal Setting*.

Managerial Implications of Goal Setting Theory

The managerial implications of goal setting theory seem straightforward: set specific and challenging goals and provide ongoing feedback so that individuals can compare their performance with the goal. While goals can be motivational in certain circumstances, they obviously have some limitations. For example, as indicated earlier, the performance impact of specific, challenging goals is stronger for simpler jobs than for more complex jobs, such as scientific and engineering work. Thus, when a task is novel or complex and individuals need to acquire new knowledge and skills for good performance, setting a specific learning goal will be more effective than setting a high-performance goal. Setting a high-performance goal will be most effective when individuals already have the ability to perform a task effectively. In addition, proximal goals should be set in conjunction with distal goals when employees are learning a new task or performing a complex one.[63] In the next chapter, we will discuss a more elaborate application of goal setting theory, called *Management by Objectives*.

Now that you are familiar with the motivation theories, please consult You Be the Manager: *Your Tips or Your Job*.

DO MOTIVATION THEORIES TRANSLATE ACROSS CULTURES?

LO 5.6

Discuss the cross-cultural limitations of theories of motivation.

Are the motivation theories that we have described in this chapter culture-bound? That is, do they apply only to North America, where they were developed? The answer to this question is important for North American organizations that must understand motivational patterns in their international operations. It is also important to foreign managers, who are often exposed to North American theory and practice as part of their training and development.

It is safe to assume that most theories that revolve around human needs will come up against cultural limitations to their generality. For example, both Maslow and Alderfer suggest that people pass through a social stage (belongingness, relatedness) on their way

ETHICAL FOCUS

THE DARK SIDE OF GOAL SETTING

A number of studies have found that there is a dark side to goal setting in organizations. These studies have shown that in some situations high performance goals can lead to undesirable outcomes, such as stress and unethical behaviour. In some cases, failure to meet a high performance goal has led to poorer performance than having no goal at all.

To find out why and when high performance goals might have negative effects, David Welsh and Lisa Ordonez conducted a laboratory experiment that tested the effects of different goal structures across multiple rounds. In particular, they considered the effects of high and low goals as well as consecutive goals in which the assignment of a new goal immediately follows the completion of an existing goal. They suggested that a series of consecutive high performance goals can result in unethical behaviour because they diminish an individual's capacity for self-regulation.

Recall from Chapter 2 that self-regulation involves the use of learning principles to regulate one's own behaviour. Individuals, however, have a limited capacity for self-regulation, which means that certain tasks can drain or deplete self-regulatory resources. The authors suggested that consecutive high performance goals will have a depleting effect on self-regulatory resources compared to do-your-best (DYB) and low performance goals. This is because high performance goals require motivation, focus, and persistence, which will consume and diminish self-regulatory resources. In addition, the authors also predicted that goals that start high and then decrease over time will consume more self-regulatory resources because, compared to goals that start low and increase over time, there is little opportunity for recovery. Finally, based on research that has found a relationship between diminished self-regulatory resources and unethical behaviour, the authors predicted that consecutive high performance goals will lead to increased unethical behaviour. This is because there is a greater temptation to cheat to reach one's goal when one's capacity for self-regulation is depleted.

To test the effects of goals and depletion on unethical behaviour, the authors conducted a laboratory experiment with a sample of undergraduate students. The participants were randomly assigned to goal setting conditions (high, low, increasing, decreasing, and DYB). They then completed five rounds of a problem-solving task in which they had to solve a series of 20 numbered matrices per round. They also completed a depletion survey before each round. Participants were told that they would receive $1 for each round in which they achieved the performance goal except for the DYB condition, for which they were told they would be paid a flat fee of $5, since no goals were assigned. The participants were told that they could throw away their worksheets for each round at the end of the experiment and would hand in only the task packet that contained their self-reported performance and the depletion survey. Thus, their work was not checked, and they could cheat by overstating their performance. However, unbeknown to the participants, the worksheets and task packets were coded so that the two could be linked after participants disposed of their materials. Over-reporting of correctly solved matrices was used to measure unethical behaviour.

The results indicated that goals improved performance on the task, and the average performance was best in the high goal condition. However, consecutive high goals increased depletion more than low and DYB goals. In addition, goals that started high and then decreased over time (decreasing goals) increased depletion more than consecutive low and DYB goals and more than goals that started low and increased over time (increasing goals). Finally, high performance goals were associated with increased unethical behaviour. Participants in the high goal condition had the highest level of unethical behaviour.

The results of this study indicate a dark side of goal setting in that high performance goals can increase unethical behaviour by depleting self-regulatory resources. The overuse of high performance goals over time can lead to diminished self-regulatory resources and unethical behaviour. Thus, managers should think very carefully about the frequency and difficulty of the goals they assign to employees, as there are both performance and ethical consequences of high performance goals.

Source: Based on Welsh, D.T., & Ordonez, L.D. (2014). The dark side of consecutive high performance goals: Linking goal setting, depletion, and unethical behavior. *Organizational Behavior and Human Decision Processes, 123,* 79-89.

YOU BE THE MANAGER

Your Tips or Your Job

During the summer of 2012, a Marriott beach resort hotel in Ontario, The Rousseau Muskoka, issued an ultimatum to its spa employees. The ultimatum came in the form of a three-page letter to employees that made the front page of the *Toronto Star*.

In the letter, the employees were informed that spa customers would be charged a new higher gratuity fee (20 percent) on manicures, body wraps, massages, and other treatments, and that spa employees would receive 50 percent of the gratuity.

The gratuity had previously been 18 percent, with 2 percent going to the spa's administrative staff and the rest to the spa employee who had performed the service. Under the new gratuity policy, the spa staff would receive 10 percent, 8.75 percent would go to the hotel, and 1.25 would go to administrative staff. If customers wished to tip more than the 20 percent gratuity, the extra portion would go to the employee.

The letter indicated that the new policy was necessary to efficiently manage costs and to remain competitive within the industry. Employees were told that if the new policy was not acceptable to them, their employment would be terminated.

Under the *Employment Standards Act*, there is nothing to stop organizations and managers from taking tips from their employees. However, at the time of the letter, New Democrat MPP Michael Prue introduced a private member's bill at Queen's Park that would outlaw owners and managers from taking a cut of worker's tips. Prue's proposal would amend the law to specify "an employer shall not take any portion of an employee's tips or other gratuities."

In the *Toronto Star* article, it was reported that sources at the hotel said most spa employees had reluctantly consented to the new policy because they

Employees at the Rousseau Muskoka were told to accept a reduction in gratuities or have their employment terminated.

need their jobs. But what about their motivation and job performance? You be the manager.

Questions

1. What do you think of the resort's new policy? Use the theories of motivation to explain the effects it might have on employees' motivation and performance.

2. Do you think the resort should proceed with its new policy? Explain your answer.

To find out what happened, see The Manager's Notebook at the end of the chapter.

Sources: Based on Ferguson, R. (June 27, 2012). Your tips or your jobs, posh hotel warns staff. *Toronto Star*, A1, A6; Ferguson, R. (June 29, 2012). Staff can keep tips and their jobs. *Toronto Star*, A1, A14; Silliker, A. (2012). Hotel nixes plan to skim employee tips. *Canadian HR Reporter*, 25(14), 3, 6.

to a higher-level personal growth or self-actualization stage. However, as we discussed in Chapter 4, it is well established that there are differences in the extent to which societies value a more collective or a more individualistic approach to life.[64] In individualistic societies (e.g., Canada, the United States, Great Britain, and Australia), people tend to value individual initiative, privacy, and taking care of oneself. In more collective societies (e.g., Mexico, Singapore, and Pakistan), more closely knit social bonds are observed, in which members of one's in-group (family, clan, or organization) are expected to take care of each other in exchange for strong loyalty to the in-group.[65] This suggests that there might be no superiority to self-actualization as a motive in more collective cultures. In some cases, for example, appealing to employee loyalty might prove more motivational than the opportunity for self-expression, because it relates to strong belongingness needs that stem from cultural values. Also, cultures differ in the extent to which they value achievement as it is

Cultures differ in how they define achievement. In collective societies where group solidarity is dominant, achievement may be more group oriented than in individualistic societies.

AP/Bebeto Matthews

defined in North America, and conceptions of achievement might be more group-oriented in collective cultures than in individualistic North America. Similarly, the whole concept of intrinsic motivation might be more relevant to wealthy societies than to developing societies.

Research on self-determination theory across various cultures, however, has been largely supportive. For example, a study of SDT in nine different countries found that the three psychological needs are positively related to autonomous motivation, although the size of the relationships varied across countries for competence and autonomy, which suggests that the importance of the three needs might vary across cultures. In addition, positive relationships between autonomous motivation and work outcomes were found across the countries studied. The authors concluded that motivation type matters in all cultures and organizational contexts and that SDT is cross-culturally valid.[66]

With respect to equity theory, we noted earlier that people should be appropriately motivated when outcomes received "match" job inputs. Thus, higher producers are likely to expect superior outcomes compared with lower producers. This is only one way to allocate rewards, however, and it is one that is most likely to be endorsed in individualistic cultures. In collective cultures, there is a tendency to favour reward allocation based on equality rather than equity.[67] In other words, everyone should receive the same outcomes despite individual differences in productivity, and group solidarity is a dominant motive. Trying to motivate employees with a "fair" reward system might backfire if your definition of fairness is equity and theirs is equality.

Because of its flexibility, expectancy theory is very effective when applied cross-culturally. The theory allows for the possibility that there may be cross-cultural differences in the expectancy that effort will result in high performance. It also allows for the fact that work outcomes (such as social acceptance versus individual recognition) may have different valences across cultures.[68]

Finally, setting specific and challenging goals should also be motivational when applied cross-culturally, and, in fact, goal setting has been found to predict, influence, and explain behaviour in numerous countries around the world.[69] However, for goal setting to be effective, careful attention will be required to adjust the goal setting process in different cultures. For example, individual goals are not likely to be accepted or motivational in collectivist cultures, where group rather than individual goals should be used. Power distance is also likely to be important in the goal setting process. In cultures where power distance is large, it would be expected that goals be assigned by superiors. However, in some small power distance cultures in which power differences are downplayed, participative goal setting would be more appropriate. One limitation to the positive effect of goal setting might occur in cultures (mainly Far Eastern) in which saving face is important. That is, a specific and challenging goal may not be very motivating if it suggests that failure could occur and if it results in a negative reaction. This would seem to be especially bad if it were in the context of the less-than-preferred individual goal setting. Failure in the achievement of a very specific goal could lead to loss of face. As well, in the so-called being-oriented cultures, where people work only as much as needed to live and avoid continuous work, there tends to be some resistance to goal setting.[70]

International management expert Nancy Adler has shown how cultural blinders often lead to motivational errors.[71] A primary theme running through this discussion is that appreciating cultural diversity is critical in maximizing motivation.

PUTTING IT ALL TOGETHER: INTEGRATING THEORIES OF WORK MOTIVATION

In this chapter, we have presented several theories of work motivation and attempted to distinguish between motivation and performance. In Chapter 4, we discussed the relationship between job performance and job satisfaction. At this point, it seems appropriate to review how all these concepts fit together. Exhibit 5.7 presents a model that integrates these relationships.

Each of the theories helps us to understand the motivational process. First, for individuals to obtain rewards they must achieve designated levels of performance. We know from earlier in this chapter that performance is a function of motivation as well as other factors, such as personality, general cognitive ability, emotional intelligence, understanding of the task, and chance. In terms of motivation, we are concerned with the amount, persistence, and direction of effort as well as whether it is autonomous or controlled motivation. Therefore, Boxes 1 through 5 in Exhibit 5.7 explain these relationships.

Perceptions of expectancy and instrumentality (expectancy theory) relate to all three components of motivation (Box 1). In other words, individuals direct their effort toward a particular first-level outcome (expectancy) and increase the amount and persistence of effort to the extent that they believe it will result in second-level outcomes (instrumentality). Goal setting theory (Box 2) indicates that specific and challenging goals that people are committed to, as well as feedback about progress toward goal attainment, will have a positive effect on amount, persistence, and direction of effort. Goal specificity should also strengthen both expectancy and instrumentality connections. The individual will have a clear picture of a first-level outcome to which his or her effort should be directed and greater certainty about the consequences of achieving this outcome.

LO 5.7

Summarize the relationships among the various theories of motivation, performance, and job satisfaction.

PERSONAL INVENTORY ASSESSMENT
Learn About Yourself
Diagnosing Poor Performance and Enhancing Motivation

EXHIBIT 5.7
Integrative model of motivation theories.

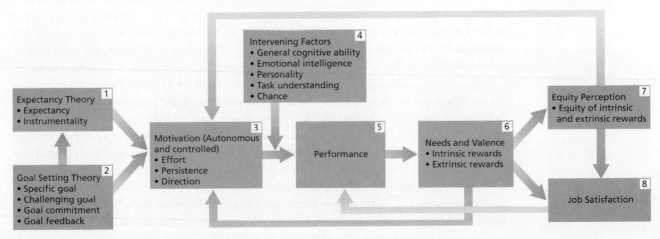

THE MANAGER'S NOTEBOOK

Your Tips or Your Job

1. According to one employee at the spa, "Everyone feels disgusted. Morale is low." The theories of motivation suggest that the new policy is going to hurt employee motivation. The employees are probably motivated to fulfill their physiological or existence needs and are thus motivated to earn the extra money they receive from tips. The reduction in tips will lower their motivation, given that they will be receiving lower tips for the same work. Their lower motivation is most clearly evident from an equity theory perspective. According to equity theory, workers compare the inputs that they invest in their jobs and the outcomes that they receive against the inputs and outcomes of some other relevant person or group. When these ratios are equal, the worker should feel that a fair and equitable exchange exists with the employing organization. When the ratios are unequal, workers perceive inequity. The employees at the resort will perceive their situation as inequitable because they will be obtaining lower outcomes (i.e., tips) for the same amount of work (i.e., inputs). Given that individuals are motivated to maintain an equitable exchange relationship, we would expect the employees to lower their inputs to bring them in line with the lower tips they will be receiving. This could include a decrease in work effort or quality, or perhaps excessive absenteeism. Employees might also try to increase their outcomes through theft. Expectancy theory also suggests that employees will lower their motivation, because performing at the same level will no longer result in the same outcome. As a result, employees might be motivated to work at a lower level given that a high level of performance is not going to result in the same outcome as previously. In expectancy theory terms, the valence of the tip (second-level outcome) might be reduced, thereby lowering the valence of the first-level outcome (e.g., high performance). Ultimately, what might happen is that the employees will work faster so that they can service more clients, which will result in more tips. This will probably result in poorer customer service (e.g., less time to chat with customers), lower quality work, and a greater potential for mistakes.

2. It didn't take long for the resort to change its mind about the new policy. An angry public and media backlash forced them to scrap the new policy just two days after the story appeared on the front page of the *Toronto Star*. In a statement to the *Star*, the general manager said, "In response to feedback from staff and clientele about our company's recent decision to change our current gratuity structure at Spa Rousseau, we believe it prudent to reverse this decision and to maintain the gratuity structure as it is." He also told the *Star* that other steps would be taken to ensure the financial viability of the spa.

Sources: Based on Ferguson, R. (June 27, 2012). Your tips or your jobs, posh hotel warns staff. *Toronto Star*, A1, A6; Ferguson, R. (June 29, 2012). Staff can keep tips—and their jobs. *Toronto Star*, A1, A14.

Boxes 3 through 5 illustrate that motivation (Box 3) will be translated into good performance (especially if it is autonomous motivation—Box 5) if the worker has the levels of general cognitive ability and emotional intelligence relevant to the job, and if the worker understands the task (Box 4). Chance can also help to translate motivation into good performance. If these conditions are not met, high motivation will not result in good performance.

Second, a particular level of performance (Box 5) will be followed by certain outcomes. To the extent that performance is followed by outcomes that fulfill individual needs (need theory) and are positively valent second-level outcomes (expectancy theory), they can be considered rewards for good performance (Box 6). In general, the connection between performance and the occurrence of intrinsic rewards should be strong and reliable because such rewards are self-administered. For example, the nurse who assists several very sick patients back to health is almost certain to feel a sense of competence and achievement because such feelings stem directly from the job. On the other hand, the connection between performance and extrinsic rewards might be much less reliable because the occurrence of such rewards depends on the actions of management. Thus, the head nurse may or may not recommend attendance at a nursing conference (an extrinsic fringe benefit) for the nurse's good performance.

Third, to the extent that the rewards fulfill individual needs (need theory), then they will be motivational, as depicted by the path from rewards (Box 6) to motivation (Box 3). However, in accordance with self-determination theory, intrinsic rewards will influence autonomous motivation, while extrinsic rewards will influence controlled motivation. In addition, the rewards that individuals receive are also the outcomes of the equity theory equation and will be used by individuals to form perceptions of equity (Box 7). Perceptions of equity also influence motivation (Box 3) and job satisfaction (Box 8). You will recall that this relationship between job outcomes, equity, and job satisfaction was discussed in Chapter 4. According to equity theory, individuals in a state of equity have high job satisfaction. Individuals who are in a state of inequity experience job dissatisfaction. Also, recall from Chapter 4 that good performance leads to job satisfaction if that performance is rewarded, and job satisfaction in turn leads to good performance.

In summary, each theory of motivation helps us to understand a different part of the motivational process. Understanding how the different theories of motivation can be integrated brings us to the topic of the next chapter—practical methods of motivation that apply the theories we have been studying in this chapter.

MyManagementLab Study, practise, and explore real management situations with these helpful resources:

- **Interactive Lesson Presentations:** Work through interactive presentations and assessments to test your knowledge of management concepts.
- **PIA (Personal Inventory Assessments):** Enhance your ability to connect with key concepts through these engaging, self-reflection assessments.   PERSONAL INVENTORY ASSESSMENT
- **Study Plan:** Check your understanding of chapter concepts with self-study quizzes.
- **Videos:** Learn more about the management practices and strategies of real companies.
- **Simulations:** Practise decision-making in simulated management environments.

LEARNING OBJECTIVES CHECKLIST

5.1 *Motivation* is the extent to which persistent effort is directed toward a goal. *Performance* is the extent to which an organizational member contributes to achieving the objectives of the organization.

5.2 *Intrinsic motivation* stems from the direct relationship between the worker and the task and is usually self-applied. *Extrinsic motivation* stems from the environment surrounding the task and is applied by others.

5.3 *Performance* is influenced by motivation as well as personality, general cognitive ability, emotional intelligence, task understanding, and chance factors. *General cognitive ability* refers to a person's basic information-processing capacities and cognitive resources. *Emotional intelligence* refers to the ability to manage one's own and other's feelings and emotions. Motivation will be translated into good performance if an individual has the general cognitive ability and emotional intelligence relevant to the job, and if he or she understands the task.

5.4 *Need theories* propose that motivation will occur when employee behaviour can be directed toward goals or incentives that satisfy personal wants or desires. The three need theories discussed are *Maslow's need hierarchy*, *Alderfer's ERG theory*, and *McClelland's theory of needs* for achievement, affiliation, and power. Maslow and Alderfer have concentrated on the hierarchical arrangement of needs and the distinction between intrinsic and extrinsic motivation. McClelland has focused on the conditions under which particular need patterns stimulate high motivation. *Self-determination theory* focuses on whether motivation is autonomous or controlled. Motivation is *autonomous* when people are motivated by intrinsic factors and they are in control of their motivation. Motivation is *controlled* when people are motivated to obtain a desired consequence or extrinsic reward. According to SDT, three basic psychological needs are important for all individuals (competence, autonomy, and relatedness).

5.5 *Process theories* attempt to explain how motivation occurs rather than what specific factors are motivational. *Expectancy theory* argues that people will be motivated to engage in work activities that they find attractive and that they feel they can accomplish. The attractiveness of these activities depends on the extent to which they lead to favourable personal consequences. *Equity theory* states that workers compare the inputs that they apply to their jobs and the outcomes that they get from their jobs with the inputs and outcomes of others. When these outcome/input ratios are unequal, inequity exists, and workers will be motivated to restore equity. *Goal setting theory* states that goals are motivational when they are specific and challenging and when workers are committed to them and receive feedback about progress toward goal attainment. In some cases, companies can facilitate goal commitment through employee participation in goal setting and by financial incentives for goal attainment, but freedom from coercion and punishment seems to be the key factor in achieving goal commitment.

5.6 There are some cross-cultural limitations of the theories of motivation. For example, most theories that revolve around human needs will come up against cultural limitations to their generality as a result of differences in values across cultures. However, research across various countries has provided support for self-determination theory. As for equity theory, trying to motivate employees with a "fair" reward system might backfire if the definition of fairness is other than equity (e.g., equality). Because of its flexibility, expectancy theory is very effective when applied cross-culturally and allows for the possibility that there may be cross-cultural differences in the expectancy that effort will result in high performance. It also allows for the fact that work outcomes (such as social acceptance versus individual recognition) may have different valences across cultures. Setting specific and challenging goals should also be motivational when applied cross-culturally. However, for goal setting to be effective, careful attention is required to adjust the goal setting process in different cultures.

5.7 Performance is a function of motivation as well as other factors, such as personality, general cognitive ability, emotional intelligence, understanding of the task, and chance. Perceptions of expectancy and instrumentality influence motivation, as do specific and challenging goals that people are committed to and that are accompanied with feedback. Motivation will be translated into good performance if the worker has the levels of general cognitive ability and emotional intelligence relevant to the job and if the worker understands the task. Chance can also help to translate motivation into good performance. To the extent that performance leads to rewards that fulfill individual needs and are positively valent, they will be motivational. When the rewards are perceived as equitable, they will have a positive effect on motivation and job satisfaction. Furthermore, good performance leads to job satisfaction if that performance is rewarded, and job satisfaction in turn leads to good performance.

DISCUSSION QUESTIONS

1. Many millionaires continue to work long, hard hours, sometimes even beyond the usual age of retirement. Use the ideas developed in the chapter to speculate about the reasons for this motivational pattern. Is the acquisition of wealth still a motivator for these individuals?

2. Discuss a time when you were highly motivated to perform well (at work, at school, in a sports contest) but performed poorly in spite of your high motivation. How do you know that your motivation was really high? What factors interfered with good performance? What did you learn from this experience?

3. What are the implications of goal orientation for motivating a group of employees? When would it be best to set a learning goal versus a

performance goal? When would it be best to set a proximal versus a distal goal? Describe a situation in which it would be best to set a learning goal and a situation in which it would be best to set a performance goal. Describe a situation in which it would be best to set a proximal goal and a situation in which it would be best to set a distal goal.

4. Describe self-determination theory, and provide an example of when your motivation was controlled and when it was autonomous. What factors contributed to your autonomous and controlled motivation, and what effect did your motivation have on your performance? What effect did it have on your job attitudes and well-being?

5. What is the relationship between cognitive ability and emotional intelligence with job performance? When would emotional intelligence be most important for a person's job performance? When is cognitive ability especially important for job performance?

INTEGRATIVE DISCUSSION QUESTIONS

1. Refer to the cross-cultural dimensions of values described in Chapter 4 (i.e., work centrality, power distance, uncertainty avoidance, masculinity/femininity, individualism/collectivism, and long-term/short-term orientation) and discuss the implications of each value for exporting the work motivation theories discussed in this chapter across cultures. Based on your analysis, how useful are the theories described in this chapter for understanding and managing motivation across cultures? What are the implications?

2. Consider the basic characteristics of motivation in relation to operant learning theory and social cognitive theory. What are the implications of operant learning theory and social cognitive theory for motivation, and how do they compare to the theories of work motivation described in this chapter?

ON-THE-JOB CHALLENGE QUESTION

Employee Time Theft

Employee theft is a major problem for organizations in Canada and the United States. According to one study, employee theft costs Canadian organizations more than $120 billion a year and is the cause of 30 percent of business failures. The study also found that 79 percent of employees admit to stealing or considering it. Another study found that as many as one out of every 28 employees was apprehended for theft in 2007 in the United States. Although employee theft has usually involved things like inflated expense accounts, cooking the books, stealing merchandise, or pocketing money from cash sales, organizations are increasingly finding themselves the victims of time theft.

Time theft occurs when employees steal their employer's time by engaging in unauthorized personal activities during working hours, such as visiting social networking sites and chat lines or spending time out of the office fulfilling their personal agendas (e.g., playing golf) rather than meeting with clients or making sales calls. Time theft also occurs when employees take longer breaks for coffee or meals, make personal phone calls at work, send or receive email not related to work, and surf the web for personal reasons.

Why are employees motivated to steal from their organization? Use the theories of motivation discussed in the chapter to answer this question. What can organizations do to prevent employee time theft? Consider the implications of each theory of motivation for preventing all forms of employee theft.

Sources: Sherr, I. (2009, July 11). U.S. retailers struggle with theft by employees; Outpaces shoplifting, fraud. Tech solutions yield surprises. *Gazette* (Montreal), C6; Levitt, H. (2009, May 20). Employers must beware of the time wasters: Ways to make staff accountable for time away from the office. *Edmonton Journal*, F4; Levitt, H. (2008, August 20). Hands off the cookie jar or pay the price. *Ottawa Citizen*, F3; Buckingham, R. (2008, April 1). Time theft growing in the workplace. *Telegraph-Journal* (Saint John), B1.

EXPERIENTIAL EXERCISE

What Is Your Goal Orientation?

The following scale is a measure of goal orientation. Answer each of the statements as accurately and honestly as possible using the following response scale:

1–Strongly disagree

2–Moderately disagree

3–Slightly disagree

4–Neither disagree nor agree

5–Slightly agree

6–Moderately agree

7–Strongly agree

____ 1. It's important for me to impress others by doing a good job.

____ 2. If I don't succeed at a difficult task, I plan to try harder the next time.

____ 3. I worry that I won't always be able to meet the standards set by others.

____ 4. I avoid tasks that I may not be able to complete.

____ 5. It's better to stick with what works than risk failing at a task.

____ 6. The opportunity to extend my range of abilities is important to me.

____ 7. I avoid circumstances where my performance will be compared to that of others.

____ 8. I like to meet others' expectations of me.

____ 9. The opportunity to learn new things is important to me.

____ 10. I'm not interested in impressing others with my performance.

____ 11. I am always challenging myself to learn new concepts.

____ 12. I get upset when other people do better than I do.

____ 13. Most of the time, I stay away from tasks that I know I won't be able to complete.

____ 14. I don't care what others think of my performance.

____ 15. I don't enjoy taking on tasks if I am unsure whether I will complete them successfully.

____ 16. The opportunity to do challenging work is important to me.

____ 17. Typically, I like to be sure that I can successfully perform a task before I attempt it.

____ 18. I value what others think of my performance.

____ 19. I prefer to work on tasks that force me to learn new things.

____ 20. In learning situations, I tend to set fairly challenging goals for myself.

____ 21. I don't like having my performance compared negatively to that of others.

Scoring and Interpretation

To obtain your score, first subtract your response to questions 10 and 14 from 8. For example, if you gave a response of 1 to question 10, give yourself a 7 (8 minus 1). To obtain your score on each type of goal orientation, add your scores as follows:

Learning goal orientation: Add items 2, 6, 9, 11, 16, 19, and 20.

Performance-prove goal orientation: Add items 1, 5, 8, 10, 12, 14, and 18.

Performance-avoid goal orientation: Add items 3, 4, 7, 13, 15, 17, and 21.

Your total for each of the three goal orientations should be somewhere between 7 and 49. The higher your score, the higher your goal orientation. Rank your scores from highest to lowest to identify your primary goal orientation. To facilitate class discussion and your understanding of goal orientation, form a small group with several other members of the class and consider the following questions:

1. Each group member should present their goal orientation scores. Rank your three scores from highest to lowest. What is your primary goal orientation? What is the primary goal orientation of most members of your group?

2. Given your primary goal orientation, how might it affect your academic performance? How might it affect your performance at work?

3. Given your primary goal orientation, what type of goal should you set for yourself in the future? When should you set a learning goal versus a performance goal?

4. How can knowledge of your primary goal orientation help you in your future studies and grades? How can it help you at work and in your career?

5. Based on the results of this exercise, what have you learned about yourself? What kind of goals should you focus on at school and at work? Explain your answers.

Source: Validation of a multidimensional measure of goal orientation. *Canadian Journal of Behavioural Science*, 36(3), 232–243. Used by permission from the Canadian Psychological Association.

CASE INCIDENT

A Night at the Office

Professor Hackenbush was one of the most popular professors at his university. Students couldn't wait to take his courses. One year there were so many students on the waiting list to get into his course that the department decided to double the class size. Professor Hackenbush didn't mind, but he knew that he would need more teaching assistants (TAs) to help with the grading of assignments and exams.

Although he was given two TAs, the larger class size meant that much more time was needed to get exams and assignments graded. Unfortunately, final grades had to be submitted one week after the final exam. The two TAs had taken too long to mark tests and exams during the term, and Professor Hackenbush was concerned that he would not be able to submit the final grades by the deadline. In an attempt to speed things up, he decided to set a challenging goal for the TAs. He asked them to mark 50 exams each day. The TAs told Professor Hackenbush that this might not be possible because they had several exams themselves. Regardless, Professor Hackenbush told them to each mark 50 exams a day and to return the graded exams to him the day before final grades were due.

Professor Hackenbush was pleased when the TAs arrived at his office with the graded exams right on time. "You finished them all?" he asked. "We sure did,"

said one of the TAs, "It was no problem." "Wonderful" said Professor Hackenbush, "How did they do?" "Very good" said one of the TAs, "They must have really enjoyed your class."

After the students left his office, Professor Hackenbush began to review the exams before calculating final grades. To his dismay, he realized that many of the grades on each exam were the same for every question, and some of the questions had not even been graded. The professor was furious and realized that his two TAs had done a poor job and that he would now have to stay at his office all night to re-mark the exams himself. "Ah, students today" he said to himself. "What am I going to do?"

1. Do you think it was a good idea for Professor Hackenbush to use goal setting to motivate the TAs? How effective was this motivational strategy?

2. Use goal setting theory to explain why setting goals for the TAs was not very effective and how it could have been more effective.

3. What advice would you give Professor Hackenbush next time he needs to motivate his TAs to mark exams? Refer to the different theories of motivation to answer this question.

CASE STUDY

Ivey | Publishing

Kyle Evans at Ruffian Apparel: Staffing a Retail Establishment

Source: Kevin Hewins wrote this case under the supervision of Professor Ann Frost solely to provide material for class discussion. The authors do not intend to illustrate either effective or ineffective handling of a managerial situation. The authors may have disguised certain names and other identifying information to protect confidentiality.

Ivey Management Services prohibits any form of reproduction, storage or transmittal without its written permission. Reproduction of this material is not covered under authorization by any

reproduction rights organization. To order copies or request permission to reproduce materials, contact Ivey Publishing, Ivey Management Services, c/o Richard Ivey School of Business, The University of Western Ontario, London, Ontario, Canada, N6A 3K7; phone (519) 661-3208; fax (519) 661-3882; e-mail cases@ivey.uwo.ca. Copyright © 2009, Ivey Management Services. Version: (A) 2010-01-27.

One time permission to reproduce granted by Richard Ivey School of Business Foundation on October 14, 2015.

INTRODUCTION

It was July 1, 2007, and the newly hired regional manager of Ruffian Apparel, Kyle Evans, sat in the Juniper Mall food court in Kelowna, British Columbia, sipping on his coffee. With the back-to-school rush fast approaching, it was critical to get the Kelowna store back on track. The store had been without a capable store manager for several months, and sales figures were

far from optimal. In the interim, Ruffian Kelowna was being run by an inexperienced full-time employee who had been granted store manager status and who was dealing with a significant staffing shortage. It was clear to Evans that this store needed help.

With his own performance evaluation and compensation tied to the success of the stores in his region, Evans needed those Kelowna sales figures to go up, and soon.

Was it as simple as finding a new store manager? What other changes might be required to turn things around? It was up to Evans to figure things out prior to returning to Vancouver in two days. There, he was to report to his new boss, operations manager Jason Wilcox.

KYLE EVANS

Born in Victoria, British Columbia, in 1977, Evans had spent the majority of his youth in Vancouver and surrounding area. At the age of 18, he ventured east to obtain his undergraduate degree in commerce from the University of Alberta. During his four years at the University of Alberta, Evans had worked at numerous locations in the famous West Edmonton Mall, including Orange Julius and BootLegger, in order to pay his tuition. His last position prior to graduation took him outside of the mall to an independent unisex apparel store called E-Zone Clothing, where he excelled in sales and, upon graduation, moved into management. Evans worked for E-Zone Clothing until 2000, when SportChek, a franchised sporting goods store, offered him a regional sales management position supervising several stores within Alberta. He loved the SportChek job and enjoyed the travelling, but after a few years, Evans felt there was little challenge and limited opportunity to advance beyond his current position. At this time, he came across an advertisement for employment in British Columbia, where Ruffian Apparel was looking for a regional manager who would be in charge of overseeing all B.C. stores as well as supervising and assisting the regional sales manager. (Refer to the following sections for a more detailed breakdown of Ruffian Apparel.) Although the compensation was similar to what Evans was currently making, the opportunity to move back to British Columbia and challenge himself was enough to convince him to apply for the job. After several interviews, in June 2007, Evans was hired as the new B.C. regional manager for Ruffian Apparel.

COMPANY/STORE DESCRIPTION

Established in Vancouver by three University of British Columbia graduates, Ruffian Apparel primarily sold both brand name and exclusive men's apparel. The name, Ruffian Apparel, was based on a nickname of one of the three founders (Jamie "The Ruffian" Clark) and was agreed upon for its simplicity and the fact that nothing better could be thought of at the time a business licence was obtained. Since the company's inception in 1974, Ruffian Apparel had slowly expanded throughout Western Canada to a point where it had 68 locations and employed over 1200 people. In British Columbia alone, Ruffian Apparel had 19 locations, the majority of which were in Vancouver and the surrounding area. Commonly found in local shopping centres and strip malls, with the exception of an outlet store located in Abbotsford, British Columbia, Ruffian Apparel competed with such stores as Below the Belt, Bootlegger, Thriftys, Extreme, and West 49. Brands commonly sold in the store included Volcom, Quiksilver, Hurley, Billabong, DC, and Element.

REGIONAL MANAGER POSITION

Evans's new job duties were almost identical to those of his previous job. He was responsible for overseeing the operations of all 19 B.C. stores, and his duties consisted of making key staffing decisions, conducting store shrinkage checks, monitoring the newly installed intranet system, taking care of cross-regional product transfers, and attending to workplace emergencies and issues as they arose. Although Evans was not technically in charge of the regional sales manager, he would supervise this position and work in tandem with the regional sales manager in an effort to monitor all 19 locations in a more efficient manner. The difference between the two positions related to sales (hence the title) as the regional sales manager was in charge of in-store promotions and product displays. Compensation for both the regional manager and the regional sales manager was directly linked to the success of the stores. Both positions received a negotiated salary in the range of $40 000 to $50 000 a year, with the potential to make upwards of an additional $25,000 based on store performance. In determining this additional compensation, semi-annual performance reviews would take into account sales goals versus results, shrinkage percentage (the percentage of goods in a store gone missing from inventory), and performance goals versus results (high profit items for which employees were given targets) for all stores. When compared to exceeding goals, failing to meet goals had a far greater impact on compensation. As a result of this compensation system, both the regional sales manager and the regional manager required constant updates as to how each store was performing, and both managers were highly invested in ensuring that all goals were met.

COMMON STORE OPERATIONS AND STANDARDS

Employee Expectations/Duties

Depending on both the size and traffic expected at a particular store, staff numbers ranged from 10 to 20, with an average store employing around 12 people. Each store consisted of one store manager, plus a minimum of one assistant manager and one full-time associate and numerous part-time associates who were scheduled according to expected sales figures, store traffic, and other tasks. Typical duties of a Ruffian part-time employee involved assisting customers, answering the phone, using the cash register, cleaning and straightening, checking off incoming stock, putting out stock, "merchandizing" the store, and assisting those in charge as needed (e.g. taking out garbage, making bank runs, etc.). Paramount to their job, however, was the expectation of making sales through what Ruffian called "Extreme Customer Service." The idea was that employees were expected to go above and beyond when it came to understanding customer needs, providing advice and opinions when necessary, and generally making the shopping experience an exceptionally pleasant one. Realizing that customer service was one of few ways to separate itself from other apparel providers, Ruffian deemed it critical for all employees, not just part-timers, to be trained in such a manner.

Aside from the duties common to all employees, full-time associates had additional responsibilities such as opening and closing the store, managing part-time employees when the manager and assistant manager were not working, and conducting returns and stock transfers. The assistant managers' duties would include these same responsibilities along with shrinkage checks (counting items and comparing counts to computer figures to check whether items were missing) and payroll duties. Finally, the store manager would be required to do all store tasks including the majority of paperwork relevant to inventory control, along with all of the human resource duties (e.g. hiring, scheduling, training, termination, performance evaluations, etc.).

Goals and Compensation

Given the diverse responsibilities at each level (part-time, full-time, assistant manager, and store manager), goal structure and compensation systems were set up differently. Part-time employees started out at minimum wage ($8.15 per hour) but could make a commission of four per cent during any individual shift if this figure were to exceed their hourly rate. This goal translated into sales of just over $200 per hour during a part-time employee's shift. Although the majority of items sold at Ruffian Apparel had an average sales price of $60 (balancing tops and bottoms), achieving this commission figure appeared to depend just as much on store location and the day and time of the shift worked as it did on the sales ability of the employee. Sales goals for part-time employees were typically assigned by the store

manager; however, it had become a standard within the company for an employee to sell $100 per hour. It had also become quite common for the regional sales manager or regional manager to question store managers about employees who did not meet this goal.

Unlike part-time employees, full-time employees and assistant managers were guaranteed a commission, supplementing their slightly higher hourly rate of approximately $9 and $12 respectively. The commission rate for these positions was two per cent of all sales, typically adding anywhere from $60 to $200 a week to their paycheques. Sales goals for both full-time employees and assistant managers were similar to (and sometimes slightly higher than) the $100 per hour required of part-time employees, due to the fact that having attained such a position within the company reflected superior sales abilities.

Finally, store managers were placed on salary and had no opportunity to make commissions on their sales. This salary figure was somewhat negotiable and depended heavily on seniority (experience), along with store size and sales volume. Recent figures showed managers making between $650 and $1150 a week. Supply and demand played a significant role in determining these figures. To supplement their pay, some store managers took on additional duties, such as the training of new store managers, which also looked good in the eyes of management. Further, sales goals for store managers were typically lower than those for full-time employees and assistant managers (generally set at $80 to $100 per hour), as store managers had a number of non-sales-related duties that kept them off the sales floor.

Along with the sales goals common to all positions within the store, there were other goals that employees were challenged to achieve. Ruffian Apparel had analyzed the profitability of certain products along with sales strategy and had decided (more than five years ago) to institute performance goals for low price point accessories (e.g. belts, caps, wallets), high price point accessories (e.g. watches, sunglasses), and "multiples" (i.e. selling more than one item per transaction). Not only would the sales of such products benefit the company's bottom line, but their use as a performance goal served as a way to ensure that employees were up-selling (trying to add additional items to a sale) and providing sufficient customer service to all customers. These goals were commonly based on the previous year's results; however, a typical four-hour shift would have the goal of two low price point accessories, one high price point accessory, and 60 per cent multiples (i.e. 60 per cent of all transactions would include more than one item). Stores in general and employees in particular were commonly judged by their ability to hit these targets, with verbal and written warnings issued if goals were not met. The cascading effect of this negative reinforcement encouraged managers to push employees to hit their goals.

Typical Employees

Typical of the majority of service sector positions of this sort, employees tended to reflect a store's target market, consisting of relatively young individuals who met minimal hiring standards and were willing to work for relatively low wages. With this in mind, Ruffian Apparel tended to employ male and female part-time sales associates ranging from 15 to 25 years old. These employees were more apt to work for minimum wage, given that the majority of them had little advanced education or experience and therefore felt unable to successfully acquire a more prestigious position in the workforce. Also, school and other obligations made these employees ideal, as jobs of this nature required flexibility in scheduling and could not provide full-time hours to everyone. Job requirements tended to focus on soft skills (such as attitude, co-operation, and problem-solving) more than on hard skills (such as computer skills or cash training), which made for a more informal and subjective hiring process. As an example, competent employees were often asked whether they had any friends who might need work if a spot opened up.

The majority of full-time employees, assistant managers and store managers were promoted from within or were found in similar stores doing similar work. For example, it was not uncommon for a full-time sales associate at another store in a local mall to be hired by Ruffian Apparel to fill a position at the same or higher level of the hierarchy. As a result of this process, the majority of managers had little post-secondary education as they tended to work their way up the ranks. Also, this method of hiring kept the average age of full-time employees and management relatively close to that of the part-time employees, usually between 22 and 30. Although turnover for management was lower than that of part-time employees, it still remained fairly high for both, tied to the nature of the work, along with the fact that Ruffian Apparel's pay level was relatively low compared to similar positions at other companies.

SINK OR SWIM: RUFFIAN KELOWNA
Evans's First Meeting

Just prior to Evans's start date, it was evident that the new regional manager of Ruffian Apparel was going to be baptized by fire. Several Ruffian Apparel stores were in similar states of turmoil that would also require some time and attention. Jason Wilcox, Ruffian Apparel's operations manager and Evans's new boss, scheduled a meeting for Evans's first day to bring him up to date regarding the region and Wilcox's own expectations. First off was Ruffian Vernon, which had just recently been given a complete overhaul as the store's last shrinkage check reported a loss of $30 000, the majority of which was thought to be due to internal theft. Although this situation was quite alarming, the store was beginning to turn around with an entirely new staff and would require little in the way of increased supervision as long as shrinkage checks maintained an acceptable level. Second was the Prince George store and the pending hike in mall leasing fees. Ruffian Apparel's contract with the Nechako River Mall was up, and it appeared that the store might not be profitable under the new leasing agreement. Third was the Cranbrook store, which had recently trained an assistant manager to become a store manager. This employee had agreed to relocate to any store within British Columbia but had refused to move to Kelowna when a store manager's job became open at that location. It was evident that this employee had breached the agreement, and some form of discipline would be necessary. Finally there was the Kelowna store itself. The recent turnover of store managers in Kelowna had left the store with huge staffing issues, along with falling sales and disappointing performance numbers. Wilcox stated his expectations when he met with Evans.

I expect that Kelowna will require your immediate attention. I know you've barely had time to read up on some of our policies and procedures, but I'm confident that you'll be able to sort things out. It's in all our best interests that Kelowna gets back on track as you and I both know that your compensation is tied to the store's success. It may be as simple as hiring another store manager, but you'll have to be the judge. Let's schedule a meeting in July, and you can let me know how you plan to address the Kelowna issue and fill the vacancy. Also, given that you're new, I'd appreciate any other suggestions you might have. Once again, I'm sorry that we won't have time to ease you into things, but your experience should make up for that.

With those final comments, Wilcox dismissed Evans, leaving him to ponder whether he made the right decision in leaving SportChek.

The Kelowna Store

When Ruffian Apparel had decided to expand, the Kelowna location was one of the first stores to be situated outside the Vancouver area. The decision to move to Kelowna in 1986 was largely based on the low leasing costs associated with the brand new Juniper Mall, coupled with the fact that Kelowna was known for hosting numerous sporting and cultural events due to its climate and central location in British Columbia. In June 2007, outside the Vancouver area, Kelowna was the second largest city in British Columbia, with a population close to 110 000. Moreover, the local post-secondary institution had recently gained university status as part of the University of British Columbia and had been rapidly expanding. This development, coupled with the city's new "destination" marketing initiative, made Kelowna an attractive location.

Since its opening in the fall of 1986, Ruffian Kelowna had fared well, consistently making average to above-average returns for the company and requiring very little maintenance. Many people within the company had attributed the past success of the Kelowna store to its solid, stable management, as the store was under the control of Samantha Abbott from 1995 to 2005. Abbott had started working at Ruffian in 1993 and had subsequently moved to a store manager's position in 1995. She had an enthusiasm for her work and, as a result, kept her job well beyond the average three-year turnover rate of a store manager. For the majority of Abbott's tenure, both the regional sales manager and the regional manager would rarely visit, assuming that she would let them know if there was a problem. Abbott was likely to know more about the store and the company than either of her two supervisors anyway. Her enthusiasm was contagious, and her store and its employees consistently met or exceeded goals and expectations, winning Abbott managerial awards along the way.

However, things changed in November of 2005. Tired of being underappreciated, Abbott decided she wanted to explore other options at a time when she was financially secure. She handed in her resignation effective December 31, 2005, which began a period of managerial turnover at the Kelowna store, with three different managers running the operation from January 2006 to May 2007. The first manager, Grace Williams, was a previous employee who had quit due to the lack of upward mobility. Once the store manager job became available, she eagerly returned. However, when she became pregnant, she decided it was in her best interest to resign in July 2006. The second manager, Sara Teegs, was hired away from a ladies retail store in the mall. Although Teegs had excellent references, her laid-back style and a souring of the relationship with the company led to her resignation in October 2006, just three months after she started. Finally, a third manager, Wayne Price, was quickly hired away from a local video games store. His management experience and his friends within Ruffian Apparel had helped him secure the job. Price left Ruffian Apparel in order to further his educational and career aspirations. His departure came as somewhat of a surprise to the regional sales manager, who had grown fond of Price and felt that he was just what Ruffian Kelowna needed to straighten things out.

Since the beginning of May 2007, Ruffian Kelowna had been looking for a store manager. In the meantime, Mark Asselhoff, the assistant manager (who had been hired by Price and was a former colleague of Price's at the video games store) initially took over. Asselhoff had been offered the store manager's position but he had refused it, citing that he had taken the job at Ruffian Apparel only as a favour to Price and that he soon planned to change jobs to make more money. He gave his two weeks' notice almost immediately, forcing the regional sales manager, Darnell Wolford, to replace him as soon as possible. Since he had to attend to business elsewhere in the province, Wolford conducted interviews over the phone and came to Kelowna only for the final interview to confirm his choice. With only three days left before Asselhoff was to leave, Jennifer Sands, an assistant manager at a jeans store in the mall, was hired and began training with Asselhoff prior to his departure. Wolford made the choice to hire Sands, a 25-year-old retail veteran, and he flew in additional people to train her in all aspects of the job. Unfortunately for Ruffian Apparel, Sands soon found a job at a local art museum that paid her significantly more money, with better hours and less responsibility. She submitted her two weeks' notice just after finishing her training. Again, it was up to Wolford to find a replacement, but personal issues led him to take a leave of absence, leaving the problem in the hands of the soon-to-be-hired regional manager, Kyle Evans. Realizing the predicament in which she was leaving Ruffian Kelowna, Sands spent her last two weeks training a newly appointed full-time employee (as there was no assistant manager as of yet) in how to manage the store. This full-time employee, Nathan Edwards, had been running the store since June, but all signs indicated that he was likely to leave as well.

Looking into the Problem

As a new hire at Ruffian Apparel, Kyle Evans was still in the midst of getting to know the company. The personal issues that led to Wolford's leave of absence were quite unexpected and, as a result, Evans had little help with staffing the management position in Kelowna. He had done some recruitment and hiring for SportChek, but usually he had more time and more options. SportChek was fairly proactive in that succession plans were often in place, and the hiring process required little more than verification of qualifications and references. Ruffian Apparel had only recently begun to train people to take over management positions, but the Cranbrook issue had provided evidence that there were several weak points in the company's hiring processes. Evans would need to move quickly to address the vacancy. With this in mind, he began looking over the reported sales figures and speaking to the experienced members of Ruffian Apparel's management team in order to get an idea of what was going on in Kelowna.

Current Staff A store of Ruffian Kelowna's size and sales figures would typically employ between 10 and 12 people: one store manager, one assistant manager, one full-time sales associate, and seven to nine part-time sales associates. The three employees who worked full-time hours could rotate so that one of them was always present in the store, able to open and close the store and handle returns, thereby keeping security issues to a minimum. At the end of June 2007, Ruffian Kelowna was being managed by Nathan Edwards with no assistant manager and no full-time employees. There were six part-time employees, one of whom was working full-time hours as a favour to Edwards, four working between 15 and 30 hours a week, and one who was on the schedule but was never available and had not worked in over three months. Ironically, the only part-time employee with any seniority was the one who never worked. The remaining five had been hired only within the last several months and, due to the high level of management turnover, were undertrained and inexperienced

at dealing with customers and speaking about the product (see Exhibit 1).

Edwards, who had been hired by Samantha Abbott in 2004, had only recently moved to full-time status due to fact that he had been in school. He had seen significant turnover during the Past three years, but had remained with Ruffian Apparel due to its flexibility in scheduling. Edwards's appointment to store manager appeared to be a short-term solution until Evans could fill the position. Evans had initially thought about possibly offering the store manager's job to Edwards, but the manager of the Prince George store had been quick to point out that she had talked to Edwards about the job, and it was apparent to her that Edwards was planning to move on in the near future. With this in mind, Evans decided to give Edwards a call in mid-June to see how things were going at the Kelowna store and to provide an update on the search for a new manager. Evans expected this call to go fairly smooth, but it was evident that Edwards had some viable concerns.

Phone Conversation With Nathan Edwards

Apparently Edwards was upset with the company's lack of progress in finding a replacement. It was evident that he felt used and that the company was making no effort to replace him, given that he was capable of doing most of the work for far less money than a store manager would demand. "As long as I keep the store afloat, nobody wants to hear from me or talk to me. I feel totally left out of the loop. I'm short-staffed and underappreciated. Why should I care about Ruffian?" Edwards mentioned that he was looking to hire more part-timers, but it was hard, given that everyone in the mall was hiring. Apparently it was not uncommon to see help-wanted signs at the front of almost every store. Edwards even spoke of an instance where he was looking over someone's resume when a customer saw what was going on and offered the person a job in construction on the spot (see Exhibit 2). "We don't pay enough, and the commission is a joke. Part-timers rarely ever sell $200 per hour worth of product in Kelowna. Maybe they make commission all the time in Vancouver, but not here. And management doesn't get paid much better. Any comparable job in the mall makes at least a couple hundred more a month than this place. You might want to look into that if you want to fill this spot quickly."

More importantly, sales figures had begun to reflect the staffing issues at Ruffian Kelowna. Not only had total sales figures plummeted, but both accessories

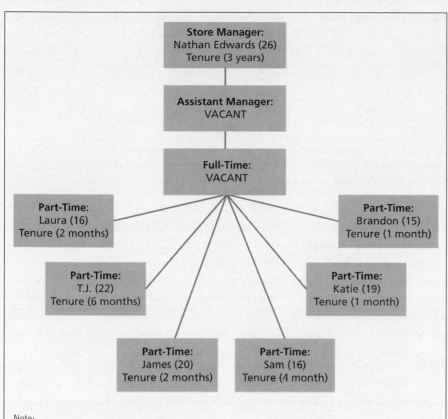

EXHIBIT 1
Kelowna Staff (as of July 1, 2007)

Note:

- James held the second key to the store and was therefore responsible for opening and closing the store along with conducting returns when Nathan was not available.

- T.J. had not worked in the past three months.

- Brandon worked close to full-time hours while the remaining staff (with the exception of T.J.) worked anywhere from 15 to 30 hours a week.

EXHIBIT 2 British Columbia Unemployment Rate (2000–2007)—BC Stats 2008

Year	2000	2001	2002	2003	2004	2005	2006	2007
UI %	7.1	7.7	8.5	8.0	7.2	5.9	4.8	4.2

EXHIBIT 3 Kelowna Total Sales Figures by Week (Goals vs. Results for May/June)

Week	1	2	3	4*	5	6	7	8	9
Goal ($)	10 500	11 100	11 500	13 500	11 200	12 400	11 900	12 600	12 800
Result ($)	10 442	11 589	11 222	10 490	10 295	10 110	10 702	9976	10 938
Diff. ($)	−58	489	−278	−3010	−905	−2290	−1198	−2624	−1862

Note: Goals were based on a $200 increase in the sales result of the same week last year.

* Week 4 Goal was relatively high due to the fact that, in 2006, Kelowna was host to a provincial cultural event during that week.

figures as well as multiple figures were horrendous (see Exhibits 3 and 4). Edwards was quick to point out that these goals seemed irrelevant as there were no repercussions for not meeting them. "I've hit my goals and I've missed my goals, and I don't receive any praise or criticism. I see no reason in forcing the part-timers to hit these goals if I don't care about them and they don't mean anything."

It was quite evident that Edwards was in need of some help. He was basically holding the store together single-handedly, and if he decided to play hardball, he could easily use his leverage to demand more money. With this in mind, Evans informed Edwards via the company's intranet system that he was raising his wage from $450 per week to $600 per week, and he also told Edwards that he was sending additional support. Evans

EXHIBIT 4   Kelowna Low Price Accessories/High Price Accessories/Multiples - Figures by Week (Goals vs. Results for May/June)

Week	1	2	3	4*	5	6	7	8	9
Low Price Accessories (G/A)	25/26	25/21	22/24	35/22	20/18	30/18	28/21	28/22	25/17
High Price Accessories (G/A)	8/8	9/6	9/4	15/4	12/6	13/2	10/5	12/7	12/2
Multiples (60% Goal)	62%	55%	68%	44%	55%	48%	38%	53%	45%
Total Goals Met	3	0	2	0	0	0	0	0	0

Note: Goals were based on adding 1 to each of the previous year's results for accessories. Unlike total sales figures, it was more common to compare accessory results between stores of similar size.

*Week 4 Goals were relatively high due to the fact that, in 2006, Kelowna was host to a provincial cultural event during that week.

contacted Chris Matthews, an experienced store manager from one of the Victoria locations, and sent him to Kelowna to give Edwards some training and a few days off. Evans also booked a trip to Kelowna for the end of the month so that he could see first-hand what was going on. In the meantime, he planned on talking to other employees and managers about some of the issues that Edwards had brought up regarding goals and commission.

Kyle Evans Visits the Store

Upon arriving in Kelowna, Evans checked into his hotel, dropped off his luggage and made his way over to Juniper Mall. Having never met Edwards in person, Evans decided to play the role of "secret shopper" and observe how things were going. It quickly became evident that only Edwards had any real experience and knowledge regarding the sales process and the products sold. The two part-time staff members appeared confused and constantly in need of advice or assistance. Whether it involved correcting a problem at the cash register or figuring out what size or cut in one brand would compare with another, Edwards was the only employee with the answers, and he was on the run constantly. And along with the lack of experience exhibited by the part-timers, the Kelowna employees were clearly not at all concerned with up-selling or attempting to move accessories. Ruffian Apparel employees were told to at least mention these additional items and accessories while in the midst of a sale or at the cash register, but at no time did this occur while Evans was looking on. No wonder the sales and performance goals were not being met.

After he felt satisfied that he had seen what he needed to see, Evans finally introduced himself, and when the store traffic had died down, he took Edwards aside to discuss the current state of affairs. Evans immediately raised his concerns regarding what he had seen with respect to sales and performance goals. Edwards was quick to respond.

You can't blame the part-timers. I'll admit I'm not the best role model. I don't see a need to push stuff on people that I wouldn't want pushed on me. Sure, everyone might need a watch, but trying to sell one to somebody who's wearing one isn't exactly easy. If customers want a watch or sunglasses, they'll ask about them. Otherwise, I don't want to be the guy pushing it on them, and I think they appreciate that. Besides, we don't have the selection that stores in Vancouver have. If they don't like one of three wallets, it's a no go. And as far as sales are concerned, we've got enough problems around here. Nobody is experienced enough to train anyone else, and we just don't have the time. They know about commission but they're not stupid. I think we've hit commission maybe once or twice in the last month, and that had nothing to do with being good at sales. And, just to let you know, the whole "multiples" thing can easily be manipulated. With our new cash registers, I can easily split a four-item sale between two people so each gets two items and increases their – and the store's – multiples. I usually don't bother because everyone needs all the sales they can get, and splitting sales to get multiples isn't necessarily a good trade, but I thought you should know because other stores are doing it. Anyway, let's face it, in the end, as long as the customers leave here happy with what they bought, that's about all you can ask of us right now.

Based on the discussions Evans had with other managers, and by taking a look at the numbers, it was clear that Edwards had some legitimate complaints. It was quite common for store location to be an accurate predictor of sales levels, even above the salesmanship skills of the staff at a given store. It was true that some people hit commission more than others, but in general, it was rare for stores outside the Vancouver area to hit their commission mark. With respect to the performance goals regarding accessories and multiples, most stores appeared to have this under control. Until recently, the Kelowna store had been able to meet its own goals;

however, the across-the-board policy for up-selling products was a sore spot with many of the employees. After all, trying to sell a pair of sunglasses in the winter or a belt to someone who wasn't buying jeans was a difficult task for the best of salespeople.

Store Manager: What to Do

It was clear to Evans that hiring a store manager for Ruffian Kelowna was a priority. Where and how he would find someone, however, was a problem. It had been common for Ruffian Apparel to simply promote an assistant manager, but in this case, that would not work: even the Cranbrook employee who was trained to take over had refused the job. Looking at the current staff, it was evident that few options existed. Until now, it had been assumed that Edwards was not interested in the position, and the experience of the remaining employees was limited. Besides, with only one exception, no part-time employee was over 20 years old. Outside Ruffian Apparel, the market was not much better. Although people could be found, the low unemployment rate combined with Ruffian Apparel's below-average salaries and lack of competent and experienced staff made the job of store manager extremely undesirable to an outsider. Jennifer Sands had been lured away from the jeans store only after extensive negotiations had provided her with compensation that was above Ruffian Apparel's average

salary for store managers. Surely there were people willing to take the job, but would they be the right people? Would it make sense to postpone hiring someone and instead address the training and other staffing issues that currently plagued the store? And Edwards was right: his $600 a week salary offer was going to be far less than a competent new store manager would require. Waiting might allow for a more comprehensive search; however, time was still an issue, and Edwards might choose to leave suddenly, causing much bigger problems.

Conclusion

Evans purchased a large cup of coffee and took a seat in the food court in Juniper Mall. It was now more apparent than ever that Ruffian Kelowna was in need of a great deal of help. Inexperienced staff, part-time vacancies, no assistant manager, no store manager, and an overworked full-time/interim store manager represented a host of issues that all appeared to be tied to the store's low sales and performance numbers. Evans knew he had only two days before his meeting with Jason Wilcox. How could he turn Ruffian Kelowna around? Were there other problems that plagued Ruffian Apparel? Was Kelowna simply in need of a good store manager, and if so, how should he go about hiring one? The smell of pizza wafted over the food court as Evans finished his coffee and made his way back to the hotel.

QUESTIONS

1. Discuss the motivation and the motivational strategies being used at Ruffian Apparel for each group of employees (store manager, assistant manager, part-time and full-time associates). How motivated are employees, and what are they motivated to do? How do the theories of motivation help us understand employees' motivation and performance and the effectiveness of the motivational strategies?

2. Discuss the use of goals at Ruffian Apparel. How effective are the sales goals and performance goals for employee motivation and performance? Use goal setting theory to explain your answer. Based on goal setting theory, how would you improve the goal setting process and the motivational potential of goals?

3. Consider the needs of employees at Ruffian Apparel. What are their primary needs and what is most likely to motivate them? How important are intrinsic and extrinsic motivators? Based on your answers, what do you recommend for improving employees' motivation?

4. Use expectancy theory and equity theory to explain the motivation of employees at Ruffian Apparel. What do these theories say about the effectiveness of the current motivational system and how to improve it?

5. What factors do you think contribute to the performance of the employees at Ruffian Kelowna? Refer to Exhibit 5.1 to explain your answer. Based on your analysis, what needs to be done to improve employee and store performance?

6. Using the theories of motivation, what advice would you give Kyle Evans on how to motivate employees at Ruffian Kelowna? Be sure to refer to the need theories and the process theories of motivation.

7. What should Kyle do to get Ruffian Kelowna back on track and improve sales? Do you think it is as simple as hiring a new store manager? Explain your answer. If not, what other changes should he make? Be specific in terms of what he should do to meet the store's sales and performance goals.

CHAPTER

6 MOTIVATION IN PRACTICE

LEARNING OBJECTIVES

After reading Chapter 6, you should be able to:

6.1 Discuss how to tie pay to performance on production jobs and the difficulties of *wage incentive plans*.

6.2 Explain how to tie pay to performance on white-collar jobs and the difficulties of *merit pay plans*.

6.3 Explain the various approaches to use pay to motivate teamwork.

6.4 Compare and contrast the different approaches to job design, including the traditional approach, the *Job Characteristics Model*, *job enrichment*, *work design*, and *relational job design*.

6.5 Understand the connection between goal setting and *Management by Objectives*.

6.6 Explain how flexible work arrangements respect employee diversity.

6.7 Describe the factors that organizations should consider when choosing motivational practices.

ELLISDON CORPORATION

EllisDon Corporation is a privately and employee-held company and one of the largest general contracting, construction, and project management organizations in Canada. The company has been involved in construction projects across the country and around the world. Some of its best known projects in Canada include the Rogers Centre in Toronto, the Centre for the Built Environment at the Nova Scotia Community College, Edmonton International Airport's LEED-certified control tower, and the Sioux Lookout Meno Ya Win Health Centre. In 2014, EllisDon received a Vancouver Regional Construction Association Silver Award of Excellence in the General Contractor category for the construction of the $23-million TRIUMF ARIEL (Advanced Rate IsotopE Laboratory) at the University of British Columbia.

Geoff Smith, president and CEO of EllisDon Corporation, took over the family business in 1996 when it was struggling, and implemented his employee-first mantra: "We are here for our employees to have great careers." Smith's thinking was that when your employees are well led, properly compensated, and challenged to do their best, they'll look after your customers—and then shareholder value will look after itself. EllisDon is now a different company. Smith says it was entrepreneurial thinking that took the company from a $500-million construction

company in 1998 to a $3.5-billion multi-disciplinary global enterprise. In the past decade the company's revenues have soared three and a half times. In 2013, Smith was named Canada's EY, Entrepreneur of the Year.

According to Neil Crawford, leader of Aon Hewitt's Best Employer surveys, EllisDon fosters "an entrepreneurial culture where people have a lot of freedom in how they're going to get things done. . . . They give people new challenges and support them. They create opportunities for individuals to make what they want of their employment." Geoff Smith says that the entrepreneurial culture allows individuals freedom to do their jobs. "That allows people to be self-confident and free-thinking. If you like structure, you won't like working here."

When working on the George Brown College Centre for Health Sciences building in Toronto, assistant project manager Lee Parsons and his team made decisions every day about scheduling, making the tower crane available as needed, working overtime when necessary, all to reach the goal of a closed-in building by Christmas. "We have the freedom to govern ourselves on site as required," said Parsons. "It's almost like it's our own little mini-business."

According to Janine Szczepanowski, EllisDon Vice-President of Leadership and Development, "We put the

Kevin Van Paassen/The Globe and Mail/Canadian Press Images

accountability and decision making with the people who are closest to the opportunity, the problem, the client, the issue." The result is a company full of people "who are running their own thing."

In addition to fostering an entrepreneurial culture, EllisDon has also created a feeling of employee ownership as the company shares its success with all of its employees. It provides employees with generous compensation, a profit-sharing plan, and a share-purchase plan. Employees are allowed to buy an equity stake in the company on an annual basis. It introduced employee shareholding in 2000, and the company is now half owned by employees.

Every 12 months, the company participates in salary surveys to keep salaries competitive, and it reviews individual salaries. Other perks include early closing time on Friday afternoons in the summer, sports ticket giveaways, and use of box seats at the Rogers Centre. In addition, the company owns and operates the Windjammer Landing Resort in St. Lucia and offers discounted accommodation packages to employees and their families.

The company's financial benefits and compensation are rated as exceptional. Benefits include a defined contribution pension plan with employer contributions (up to 5 percent of salary), subsidies for tuition and professional accreditation, retirement planning assistance, and subsidized home and auto insurance. The company also encourages employees to balance work and their personal life with alternative work arrangements such as flexible work hours, telecommuting, a shortened workweek, and a reduced summer hours program. Employees receive paid time off to volunteer with local charitable organizations, and the company donates up to $1000 for every 25 volunteer hours contributed.

In 2015, EllisDon was ranked as one of Canada's 50 Best Managed Companies, one of the Ten Best Companies to Work For, one of Canada's Top 100 Employers, and a Top Employer for Canadians over 40.[1]

Notice the motivational strategies that EllisDon employs: generous compensation, a profit-sharing plan, employee stock ownership, flexible work arrangements, and considerable freedom and autonomy in how to perform one's job. In this chapter, we will discuss four motivational techniques: money, job design, Management by Objectives, and flexible work arrangements. In each case, we will consider the practical problems that are involved in implementing these techniques. The chapter will conclude with a discussion of the factors that an organization needs to consider when choosing a motivational strategy.

MONEY AS A MOTIVATOR

PERSONAL INVENTORY ASSESSMENT

Learn About Yourself
Work Motivation Indicator

The money that employees receive in exchange for organizational membership is in reality a package made up of pay and various fringe benefits that have dollar values, such as insurance plans, sick leave, and vacation time—or what is sometimes referred to as "total rewards." Here, we will be concerned with the motivational characteristics of pay itself.

So just how effective is pay as a motivator? How important is pay for you? Chances are you do not think pay is as important as it really is for you. In fact, employees and managers seriously underestimate the importance of pay as a motivator.[2] Yet the motivation theories described in Chapter 5 suggest that pay is, in fact, a very important motivator.

According to Maslow and Alderfer, pay should prove especially motivational to people who have strong lower-level needs. For these people, pay can be exchanged for food, shelter, and other necessities of life. However, suppose you receive a healthy pay raise. Doubtless, this raise will enable you to purchase food and shelter, but it might also give you prestige among friends and family, signal your competence as a worker, and demonstrate that your boss cares about you. Thus, using need hierarchy terminology, pay can also function to satisfy social, self-esteem, and self-actualization needs. If pay has this capacity to fulfill a variety of needs, then it should have especially good potential as a motivator. How can this potential be realized? Expectancy theory provides the clearest answer to this question. According to expectancy theory, if pay can satisfy a variety of needs, it should be highly valent, and it should be a good motivator to the extent that *it is clearly tied to performance.*

Research on pay and financial incentives is consistent with the predictions of need theory and expectancy theory. Financial incentives and pay-for-performance plans have been found to increase performance and lower turnover. Research not only supports the motivational effects of pay but also suggests that pay may well be the most important and effective motivator of performance. In general, the ability to earn money for outstanding performance is a competitive advantage for attracting, motivating, and retaining employees, and recent reports indicate that an increasing number of Canadian organizations are using financial incentives.[3] Let's now consider how to link pay to performance on production jobs.

LO 6.1

Discuss how to tie pay to performance on production jobs and the difficulties of *wage incentive plans.*

Piece-rate. A pay system in which individual workers are paid a certain sum of money for each unit of production completed.

Wage incentive plans. Various systems that link pay to performance on production jobs.

Linking Pay to Performance on Production Jobs

The prototype of all schemes to link pay to performance on production jobs is piece-rate. In its pure form, **piece-rate** is set up so that individual workers are paid a certain sum of money for each unit of production they complete. For example, sewing machine operators might be paid $2 for each dress stitched, or punch press operators might be paid a few cents for each piece of metal fabricated. More common than pure piece-rate is a system whereby workers are paid a basic hourly wage and paid a piece-rate differential on top of this hourly wage. For example, a forge operator might be paid $15 an hour plus 50 cents for each unit he produces. In some cases, of course, it is very difficult to measure the productivity of an individual worker because of the nature of the production process. Under these circumstances, group incentives are sometimes employed. For example, workers in a steel mill might be paid an hourly wage and a monthly bonus for each tonne of steel produced over some minimum quota. These various schemes to link pay to performance on production jobs are called **wage incentive plans**.

© David Anderson

Compared with straight hourly pay, the introduction of wage incentives usually leads to substantial increases in productivity.[4] One review reports a median productivity improvement of 30 percent following the installation of piece-rate pay, an increase not matched by goal setting or job enrichment.[5] Also, a study of 400 manufacturing companies found that those with wage incentive plans achieved 43 to 64 percent greater productivity than those without such plans.[6]

One of the best examples of the successful use of a wage incentive plan is the Lincoln Electric Company. Lincoln Electric is the world's largest producer of arc welding equipment, and it also makes electric motors. The company offers what some say are the best-paid factory jobs in the world. They use an intricate piece-rate pay plan that rewards workers for what they produce. The firm has turned a handsome profit every quarter for more than 50 years and has not laid off anyone for more than 40 years. Employee turnover is extremely low, and Lincoln workers are estimated to be roughly twice as productive as other manufacturing workers.[7] Other companies that use wage incentive plans include Steelcase, the Michigan manufacturer of office furniture, and Nucor, a steel producer. However, not as many organizations use wage incentives as we might expect. What accounts for this relatively low utilization of a motivational system that has proven results?[8]

Potential Problems with Wage Incentives

Despite their theoretical and practical attractiveness, wage incentives have some potential problems when they are not managed with care.

LOWERED QUALITY   It is sometimes argued that wage incentives can increase productivity at the expense of quality. While this may be true in some cases, it does not require particular ingenuity to devise a system to monitor and maintain quality in manufacturing. However, the quality issue can be a problem when employers use incentives to motivate faster "people processing," such as conducting consumer interviews on the street or in stores. Here, quality control is more difficult.

DIFFERENTIAL OPPORTUNITY   A threat to the establishment of wage incentives exists when workers have different opportunities to produce at a high level. If the supply of raw materials or the quality of production equipment varies from workplace to workplace, some workers will be at an unfair disadvantage under an incentive system. In expectancy theory terminology, workers will differ in the expectancy that they can produce at a high level.

Wage incentive programs that link pay to performance on production jobs have been shown to improve employee productivity.

© Monkey Business/Fotolia

REDUCED COOPERATION Wage incentives that reward individual productivity might decrease cooperation among workers. For example, to maintain a high wage rate, machinists might hoard raw materials or refuse to engage in peripheral tasks, such as keeping the shop clean or unloading supplies.

Consider what happened when Solar Press, an Illinois printing and packaging company, installed a team wage incentive. It was not long before both managers and employees began to spot problems. Because of the pressure to produce, teams did not perform regular maintenance on the equipment, so machines broke down more often than before. When people found better or faster ways to do things, some hoarded them from fellow employees for fear of reducing the amount of their own payments. Others grumbled that work assignments were not fairly distributed, that some jobs demanded more work than others. They did, but the system did not take this into account.[9]

INCOMPATIBLE JOB DESIGN In some cases, the way jobs are designed can make it very difficult to implement wage incentives. On an assembly line it is almost impossible to identify and reward individual contributions to productivity. As pointed out above, wage incentive systems can be designed to reward team productivity in such a circumstance. However, as the size of the team *increases*, the relationship between any individual's productivity and his or her pay *decreases*. For example, the impact of your productivity in a team of two is much greater than the impact of your productivity in a team of ten. As team size increases, the linkage between your performance and your pay is erased, removing the intended incentive effect.

RESTRICTION OF PRODUCTIVITY A chief psychological impediment to the use of wage incentives is the tendency for workers to restrict productivity. This restriction is illustrated graphically in Exhibit 6.1. Under normal circumstances, without wage incentives, we can often expect productivity to be distributed in a "bell-shaped" manner—a few workers are especially low producers, a few are especially high producers, and most produce in the middle range. When wage incentives are introduced, however, workers sometimes come to an informal agreement about what constitutes a fair day's work and artificially limit their output accordingly. In many cases, this **restriction of productivity** can decrease the expected benefits of the incentive system, as in Exhibit 6.1.

Why does restriction often occur under wage incentive systems? Sometimes it happens because workers feel that increased productivity due to the incentive will lead to reductions in the workforce. More frequently, however, employees fear that if they produce at

Restriction of productivity. The artificial limitation of work output that can occur under wage incentive plans.

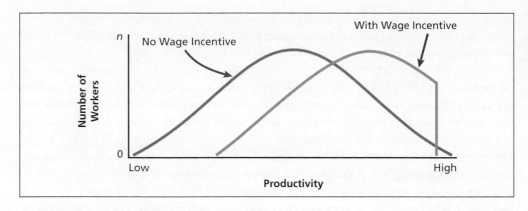

EXHIBIT 6.1
Hypothetical productivity distributions, with and without wage incentives, when incentives promote restriction.

an especially high level, an employer will reduce the rate of payment to cut labour costs. In the early days of industrialization, when unions were non-existent or weak, this often happened. Engineers studied workers under normal circumstances, and management would set a payment rate for each unit of productivity. When management introduced the incentive system, workers employed legitimate shortcuts that they had learned on the job to produce at a higher rate than expected. In response to this, management simply changed the rate to require more output for a given amount of pay! Stories of such rate-cutting are often passed down from one generation of workers to another in support of restricting output under incentive systems. As you might expect, restriction seems less likely when a climate of trust and a history of good relations exist between employees and management.

Linking Pay to Performance on White-Collar Jobs

Compared to production jobs, white-collar jobs (including clerical, professional, and managerial) frequently offer fewer objective performance criteria to which pay can be tied. To be sure, company presidents are often paid annual bonuses that are tied to the profitability of the firm, and salespeople are frequently paid commissions on sales. However, trustworthy objective indicators of individual performance for the majority of white-collar jobs are often difficult to find. Thus, performance in many such jobs is evaluated by the subjective judgment of the performer's manager (see Chapter 3 on objective and subjective measures of performance).

Attempts to link pay to performance on white-collar jobs are often called **merit pay plans**. Just as straight piece-rate is the prototype for most wage incentive plans, there is also a prototype for most merit pay plans: periodically (usually yearly), managers are required to evaluate the performance of employees on some form of rating scale or by means of a written description of performance. Using these evaluations, the managers then recommend that some amount of merit pay be awarded to individuals over and above their basic salaries. This pay is usually incorporated into the subsequent year's salary. Since the indicators of good performance on some white-collar jobs (especially managerial jobs) can be unclear or highly subjective, merit pay can provide an especially tangible signal that the organization considers an employee's performance "on track." Individuals who see a strong link between rewards and performance tend to perform better.[10] In addition, white-collar workers (especially managers) particularly support the notion that performance should be an important determinant of pay.[11]

Merit pay plans are employed with a much greater frequency than wage incentive plans and have become one of the most common forms of motivation in Canadian organizations.[12] In a tight labour market, merit pay is often used by organizations to attract and retain employees and as an alternative to wage increases.[13] Furthermore, there is some evidence that pay-for-performance merit pay plans can be effective for improving the performance of professionals.[14]

However, despite the fact that merit pay can stimulate effective performance, that substantial support exists for the idea of merit pay, and that most organizations claim to provide

LO 6.2

Explain how to tie pay to performance on white-collar jobs and the difficulties of *merit pay plans*.

Merit pay plans. Systems that attempt to link pay to performance on white-collar jobs.

merit pay, it appears that many of these systems now in use are *ineffective*. In reality, a survey found that 83 percent of organizations with a pay-for-performance system said it was only somewhat successful or not working at all.[15]

Many individuals who work under such plans do not perceive a link between their job performance and their pay. There is also evidence that pay is, in fact, *not* related to performance under some merit plans.[16] Adding more evidence of ineffectiveness are studies that track pay increases over time. For example, one study of managers showed that pay increases in a given year were often uncorrelated with pay increases in adjacent years.[17] From what we know about the consistency of human performance, such a result seems unlikely if organizations are truly tying pay to performance. In most organizations, seniority, the number of employees, and job level account for more variation in pay than performance does. However, there are ways to make merit pay plans more effective. To learn more, see Research Focus: *Improving the "Line-of-Sight" in Pay-for-Performance Programs.*

Potential Problems with Merit Pay Plans

As with wage incentive plans, merit pay plans have several potential problems if employers do not manage them carefully.

LOW DISCRIMINATION   One reason that many merit pay plans fail to achieve their intended effect is that managers might be unable or unwilling to discriminate between good performers and poor performers. In Chapter 3, we pointed out that subjective evaluations of performance can be difficult to make and are often distorted by a number of perceptual errors. In the absence of performance rating systems designed to control these problems, managers might feel that the only fair response is to rate most employees as equal performers. Effective rating systems are rarely employed. Surveys show consistent dissatisfaction with both giving and receiving performance evaluations.[18] Even when managers feel capable of clearly discriminating between good and poor performers, they might be reluctant to do so. If the performance evaluation system does not assist the manager in giving feedback about his or her decisions to employees, the equalization strategy might be employed to prevent conflicts with them or among them. If there are true performance differences among employees, equalization over-rewards poorer performers and under-rewards better performers.[19]

SMALL INCREASES   A second threat to the effectiveness of merit pay plans exists when merit increases are simply too small to be effective motivators. In this case, even if rewards are carefully tied to performance and managers do a good job of discriminating between more and less effective performers, the intended motivational effects of pay increases may not be realized. Ironically, some firms all but abandon merit pay when inflation soars or when they encounter economic difficulties. Just when high motivation is needed, the motivational impact of merit pay is removed. Sometimes a reasonable amount of merit pay is provided, but its motivational impact is reduced because it is spread out over a year or because the organization fails to communicate how much of a raise is for merit and how much is for cost of living.

Lump sum bonus. Merit pay that is awarded in a single payment and not built into base pay.

To overcome this visibility problem, some firms have replaced conventional merit pay with a **lump sum bonus** that is paid out all at one time and not built into base pay. Such bonuses have become a common method to motivate and retain employees at all levels of an organization. They get people's attention! In 2011, the Ontario Lottery and Gaming Corporation (OLG) paid out $11.6 million in one-time pay-for-performance bonuses to about 6000 employees.[20]

Although bonuses can overcome the problem of small increases, if they are not carefully designed they might encourage unethical behaviour. To learn more about how this can happen, see the Ethical Focus: *Incentive Compensation and Unethical Behaviour.*

PAY SECRECY   A final threat to the effectiveness of merit pay plans is the extreme secrecy that surrounds salaries in most organizations. It has long been a principle of human resource management that salaries are confidential information, and management frequently implores

RESEARCH FOCUS

IMPROVING THE "LINE-OF-SIGHT" IN PAY-FOR-PERFORMANCE PROGRAMS

Many organizations today use some form of individual pay-for-performance program in which they link employees' pay to their job performance. Individual pay-for-performance programs such as merit pay plans are fairly straightforward. The basic idea is to provide monetary rewards to employees based on their individual job performance.

However, many employees do not perceive a link between their job performance and pay, or what is known as a line-of-sight and performance-reward expectancy (instrumentality in expectancy theory terms). This is even the case in organizations that say that they have individual pay-for-performance programs. *Line-of-sight* is the degree to which a pay-for-performance program enables employees to recognize a clear connection or line-of-sight between work behaviours that they might enact and those measured and rewarded. Performance-reward expectancy is the degree to which employees believe that their performance will be rewarded by their organization. Thus, employees' lack of a line-of-sight and belief in a performance-pay contingency may represent an important problem that undermines the effectiveness of individual pay-for-performance programs.

It is therefore critical to understand the conditions under which employees will perceive a strong link between their performance and pay in pay-for-performance programs. Two conditions that might be especially important for increasing employees' "line-of-sight" and performance-reward expectancy of pay-for-performance programs are their immediate manager's behaviour and other pay-for-performance programs.

Although pay-for-performance programs are designed by human resource (HR) departments, it is employees' immediate managers who actually deliver pay-for-performance to employees. Therefore, managers' behaviour is key to the success of pay-for-performance programs. One particular type of behaviour that is especially important is called contingent reward leadership in which managers' reward employees for accomplishing agreed-upon objectives. With contingent reward leadership, managers clearly define employee goals and expectations and more reliably evaluate and differentiate employee performance.

An organization's use of profit sharing might also improve the effectiveness of pay-for-performance programs. This is because profit-sharing programs demonstrate to employees that the organization is concerned about performance and intends to reward employees for their performance in several ways. Furthermore, the existence of a profit sharing program reinforces and supports individual pay-for-performance programs and an organization's commitment to reward employee performance.

To investigate the role of contingent reward leadership and profit sharing for the effectiveness of individual pay-for-performance programs, Joo Hun Han, Kathryn Bartol, and Seongsu Kim conducted a study in 45 Korean companies from eight different industries. Surveys in each company were completed by HR managers, non-managerial employees, and their immediate managers.

As expected, the results indicated that the relationship between an organization's pay-for-performance program and employee perceptions of performance-reward expectancy were stronger when the manager was high on contingent reward leadership behaviour and the organization had a profit-sharing plan. Furthermore, there was a positive relationship between employees' performance-reward expectancy and their job performance. In other words, pay-for-performance was more likely to lead to higher perceptions of performance-reward expectancy and job performance when an employee's manager exhibited high contingent reward leadership and the organization had a profit-sharing plan.

The results of this study indicate that pay-for-performance programs will be more effective in terms of employees' performance-reward expectancy and job performance when accompanied by immediate managers' contingent reward leadership and organizational profit sharing. Thus, organizations can improve employees' motivation and job performance with pay-for-performance programs as long as they are accompanied with contingent reward leadership and profit sharing.

Source: Based on Han, J.H., Bartol, K. M, & Kim, S. (2015). Tightening up the performance-pay linkage: Roles of contingent reward leadership and profit-sharing in the cross-level influence of individual pay-for-performance. *Journal of Applied Psychology*, 100, 417–430.

employees who receive merit increases not to discuss these increases with their co-workers. Notice the implication of such secrecy for merit pay plans: even if merit pay is administered fairly, it is contingent on performance, and is generous, employees might remain ignorant of these facts because they have no way of comparing their own merit treatment with that of others. As a consequence, such secrecy might severely damage the motivational impact of a well-designed merit plan. Rather incredibly, many organizations fail to inform employees about the average raise received by those doing similar work.

ETHICAL FOCUS

INCENTIVE COMPENSATION AND UNETHICAL BEHAVIOUR

In the United States, executive compensation is believed to be one of the reasons why many companies engaged in the kind of risky and unethical behaviour that helped trigger the financial crisis and a global recession. It is believed that the lure of financial incentives contributed to an increase in accounting fraud and risky and unethical behaviours. But how and why does this happen?

One explanation is the use of target-based incentive systems. With a target-based incentive, an employee has to achieve a certain level of performance to obtain a bonus. As a result, employees might be tempted to lie about their performance (e.g., billable hours), take short cuts, and engage in risky and unethical behaviours to reach the target and receive the bonus.

To find out if target-based bonuses encourage unethical behaviour, C. Bram Cadsby, Fei Song, and Francis Tapon conducted an experiment in which university students performed an anagram task that required them to make as many words as possible out of seven letters.

The experiment involved seven 1-minute rounds and consisted of three different compensation schemes: 1. *Linear piece-rate:* participants were paid 40 or 10 cents for each word they created; 2. *Target-based bonus:* participants were paid $3.60 for each of the seven rounds in which they created nine words or more; and 3. *Tournament-based bonus:* participants were paid $3.60 for each of the seven rounds in which their performance was at or above the 85th percentile relative to other participants in the same session.

At the end of the seven sessions, the participants had to check the words of another participant while one of the participants checked their words. Participants then had their work returned to them and were told to check their work to make sure that all the correct words had been marked "correct" and the incorrect words had been marked "incorrect." They were given permission to correct any mistakes that had been made and were told to accurately report the number of correct words they had created. Participants were then asked to record the number of correct words they had created on a performance record sheet and to hand it in to get paid.

The results indicated that the number of correct words that a participant created during the seven rounds did not differ across the three compensation schemes. In other words, all three compensation schemes resulted in the same performance.

However, the results for over-reporting of performance (i.e., cheating) indicated that the number of words reported by participants in the target-based bonus condition that were incorrect was two and a half times higher than the other conditions. In other words, participants in the target-based bonus condition lied about the number of correct words they had created.

The results of this study indicate that incentive compensation programs that link pay to numerical targets result in more cheating than other compensation systems. Thus, incentive compensation systems need to be carefully designed to encourage appropriate behaviours and to discourage inappropriate and unethical behaviours.

Source: Based on Cadsby, C.B., Song, F., & Tapon, F. (2010). Are you paying your employees to cheat? An experimental investigation. *The B.E. Journal of Economic Analysis and Policy*, 10(1), 1–30.

Given this extreme secrecy, you might expect that employees would profess profound ignorance about the salaries of other organizational members. In fact, this is not true—in the absence of better information, employees are inclined to "invent" salaries for other members. Unfortunately, this invention seems to reduce both satisfaction and motivation. Specifically, several studies have shown that managers have a tendency to overestimate the pay of their employees and their peers and to underestimate the pay of their superiors (see Exhibit 6.2).[21] In general, these tendencies will reduce satisfaction with pay, damage perceptions of the linkage between performance and rewards, and reduce the valence of promotion to a higher level of management.

An interesting experiment examined the effects of pay disclosure on the performance and satisfaction of pharmaceutical salespeople who operated under a merit pay system. At the time of a regularly scheduled district sales meeting, each of the 14 managers in the experimental group presented to his or her employees the new open salary administration program. The sales staff were given the individual low, overall average, and individual high merit raise amounts for the previous year. The raises ranged from no raise to $75 a month, with a

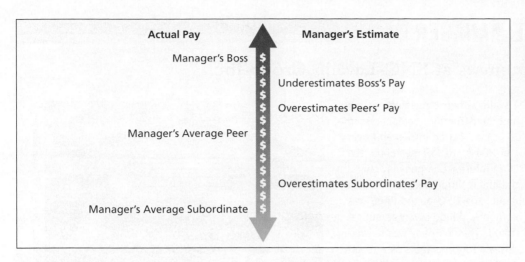

company average of $43. Raises were classified according to district, region, and company increases in pay. Likewise, salary levels (low, average, and high) were given for sales staff on the basis of their years with the company (1 to 5; 5 to 10; 10 to 20; and more than 20 years). Specific individual names and base salaries were not disclosed to the sales staff. However, this information could be obtained from the supervisor. Each person's performance evaluation was also made available by the district manager for review by his or her other sales staff.[22]

After the pay disclosure was implemented, the sales staff in the experimental group revealed significant increases in performance and satisfaction with pay. However, since performance consisted of supervisory ratings, it is possible that supervisors felt pressured to give better ratings under the open pay system, in which their actions were open to scrutiny. This, of course, raises an important point. If performance evaluation systems are inadequate and poorly implemented, a more open pay policy will simply expose the inadequacy of the merit system and lead managers to evaluate performance in a manner that reduces conflict. Unfortunately, this might be why most organizations maintain relative secrecy concerning pay. An exception is Whole Foods, a grocery chain with 80 000 employees. Whole Foods has an open-book policy that allows employees to see the compensation of others. Employees can request the company's wage disclosure report from an in-store HR representative and are allowed to take notes but can't copy or take the report home. MASS, a public consultation firm in Toronto also has an open compensation policy, although such policies in Canada are more the exception than the rule.[23]

In the next section, we will consider how to use pay to motivate teamwork. But first, read You Be the Manager: *Retention Bonuses at SNC-Lavalin.*

Whole Foods has an open-book pay policy that allows employees to see the compensation of others.

YOU BE THE MANAGER

Retention Bonuses at SNC-Lavalin Group Inc.

Montreal-based SNC-Lavalin Group Inc. is one of the largest engineering and construction companies in the world, with offices in over 50 countries and over 40 000 employees. In 2012, RCMP searched the company's offices after an internal company investigation uncovered $56 million in improperly authorized payments. Pierre Duhaime, the CEO at the time, was let go for breaching company policy and was subsequently charged with fraud. The company was so worried about losing employees and managers as a result of the scandal that they decided to pay out millions of dollars in special retention bonuses to a select group of managers and employees.

In March of 2013, a proxy management circular indicated that "in light of all the changes that took place in 2012," it had handed out awards as retention measures to certain members of management and key employees. The special retention awards were for employees below the executive vice-president level who were judged to be "high potential" or "key project" employees.*

SNC-Lavalin guaranteed that if budgeted financial targets were not met, employees participating in the management incentive program (MIP) would receive one-third of the target bonus (representing 50 percent of the financial component), and if they met expectations on their individual performance, they would also receive one-third of their target bonus. So they received a minimum of two-thirds of their target bonus for 2012.

They were also given a special cash bonus equivalent to one-half of their 2012 MIP target, representing $15.3 million. In addition, 47 key employees received restricted stock-unit (RSU) grants at a value of 50 percent of their annual base salary, while eight key employees received a cash award equal to one-half of their base salary.

SNC spokesperson Leslie Quinton said it is considered "best-practice and quite customary" among large companies in times of turmoil to offer short-term compensatory measures to retain staff. "Particularly in companies like ours, which is dependent on our people (versus technology or assets) and which has been going through a vulnerable period, it is important to provide

THE CANADIAN PRESS/Ryan Remiorz

SNC-Lavalin handed out retention bonuses to some managers and key employees.

incentives to employees to provide some stability," she said. SNC considers the bonuses a one-time cost that will not be repeated.

What do you think of SNC-Lavalin's retention bonuses? You be the manager.

Questions

1. Do you think SNC's bonuses were a good idea? Comment on the pros and cons of the retention bonuses.

2. What are some other ways that the bonuses might have been provided?

To find out more about the SNC's retention bonuses, see The Manager's Notebook at the end of the chapter.

Sources: Dobson, S. (2013, May 6). Retention bonuses help during time of crisis: Experts. *Canadian HR Reporter*, 26(9), 2, 3; Van Praet, N. (2013, April 8). SNC-Lavalin paid out millions in retention bonuses in midst of ethics scandal. *Financial Post*, http://business.financialpost.com/news/snc-lavalin-paid-out-millions-in-retention-bonuses-in-midst-of-ethics-scandal.

*Reprinted by permission of *Canadian HR Reporter*. © Copyright Thomson Reuters Canada Ltd., (2013, May 6), 26(9), 2, 3, Toronto, Ontario, 1-800-387-5164. Web: www.hrreporter.com.

LO **6.3**

Explain the various approaches to use pay to motivate teamwork.

Using Pay to Motivate Teamwork

Some of the dysfunctional aspects of wage incentives and merit pay stem from their highly individual orientations. People sometimes end up pursuing their own agendas (and pay) at the expense of the goals of their work group, department, or organization. As a result, some firms have either replaced or supplemented individual incentive pay with plans designed to foster more cooperation and teamwork.[24] Notice that each of the plans we discuss below has a somewhat different motivational focus. Organizations have to choose pay plans that support their strategic needs.

PROFIT SHARING **Profit sharing** is one of the most commonly used group-oriented incentive systems and, as described at the beginning of the chapter, it is a key component of Ellis-Don's motivational system. In years in which the firm makes a profit, some of this is returned to employees in the form of a bonus, sometimes in cash and sometimes in a deferred retirement fund. Such money is surely welcome, and it may reinforce some identification with the organization. For example, at Apex Public Relations in Toronto, the company allocates 15 percent of its profit to all of its employees every year. Larsen & Shaw Ltd., a hinge-making company in Walkerton, Ontario, has a profit-sharing plan for its 100 employees. The company shares 11 percent of its pre-tax profits every December and June. The amount an employee receives is based on his or her years of service, base pay, and performance, which is evaluated twice a year.[25]

However, it is unlikely that profit sharing, as normally practised, is highly motivational. Its greatest problem is that too many factors beyond the control of the workforce (such as the general economy) can affect profits, no matter how well people perform their jobs. Also, in a large firm, it is difficult to see the impact of one's own actions on profits. Profit sharing seems to work best in smaller firms that regularly turn a handsome profit, like WestJet Airlines. The company is small and has consistently been profitable.

EMPLOYEE STOCK OWNERSHIP PLANS (ESOPS) In recent years, **employee stock ownership plans (ESOPs)** have become a popular group-oriented incentive. These plans allow employees to own a set amount of the company's shares that they are allowed to purchase at a fixed price. For example, employees at EllisDon are allowed to buy an equity stake in the company on an annual basis. Some organizations like WestJet match employee contributions.

ESOPs provide employees with a stake in a company's future earnings and success and help to create a sense of ownership. They also serve a number of other purposes, including attracting and retaining talent, motivating employee performance, focusing employee attention on organizational performance, creating a culture of ownership, educating employees about the business, and conserving cash by substituting options for cash.[26]

In Canada, many of the best companies to work for, including EllisDon, offer stock options to a majority of their employees. For example, at the Royal Bank of Canada, 85 percent of employees are enrolled in a share ownership plan that matches 50 cents for every dollar an employee invests, up to 6 percent of his or her salary. At PCL Constructors in Edmonton, only employees are permitted to own company stock. The company has realized a profit every year since 1977, when it became 100 percent employee owned.[27] Husky Injection Molding Systems Ltd. has a share-purchasing plan in which approximately 25 percent of the company's shares are held by employees. Employees at Husky can earn company shares by doing things that help the environment and community. At Hudson's Bay Company, employees receive $1 worth of company shares for every $6 they invest, an immediate return of 17 percent.[28]

Employee stock options are believed to increase employees' loyalty and motivation, because they align employees' goals and interests with those of the organization and create a sense of legal and psychological ownership. There is some evidence that ESOPs can improve employee retention and profitability.[29] A study conducted by the Toronto Stock Exchange found that companies with employee stock ownership plans outperformed those that do not on a number of performance indicators, including profit growth, net profit margin, productivity, return on average total equity, and return on capital.[30]

However, like profit sharing, ESOPs work best in small organizations that regularly turn a profit. In larger organizations it is more difficult for employees to see the connection between their efforts and company profits, because many factors can influence the value of a company's stock besides employee effort and performance. In addition, ESOPs lose their motivational potential in a weak economy when a company's share price goes down.

Profit sharing. The return of some company profit to employees in the form of a cash bonus or a retirement supplement.

Employee stock ownership plans (ESOPs). Incentive plans that allow employees to own a set amount of a company's shares and provide employees with a stake in the company's future earnings and success.

Gainsharing. A group pay incentive plan based on productivity or performance improvements over which the workforce has some control.

GAINSHARING **Gainsharing** plans are group incentive plans that are based on improved productivity or performance over which the workforce has some control.[31] Such plans often include reductions in the cost of labour, material, or supplies. When measured costs decrease, the company pays a monthly bonus according to a predetermined formula that shares this "gain" between employees and the firm. For example, a plan installed by Canadian pulp and paper producer Fraser Papers rewards employees for low scrap and low steam usage during production. The plan sidesteps the cost of steam generation and the international price for paper, things over which the workforce lacks control.[32]

Gainsharing plans have usually been installed using committees that include extensive workforce participation. This builds trust and commitment to the formulas that are used to convert gains into bonuses. Also, most plans include all members of the work unit, including production people, managers, and support staff.

The most common gainsharing plan is the Scanlon Plan, developed by union leader Joe Scanlon in the 1930s.[33] The plan stresses participatory management and joint problem solving between employees and managers, but it also stresses using the pay system to reward employees for this cooperative behaviour. Thus, pay is used to align company and employee goals. The Scanlon Plan has been used successfully by many small, family-owned manufacturing firms. Also, in recent years, many large corporations (such as General Electric, Motorola, Carrier, and Dana) have installed Scanlon-like plans in some manufacturing plants.[34] The turnaround of the motorcycle producer Harley-Davidson is, in part, attributed to the institution of gainsharing.

In a study in a unionized auto parts manufacturing plant, a Scanlon gainsharing program was negotiated as part of a joint union–management effort to respond to economic downturns and competitive challenges in the auto industry. Management and the union were extensively involved in the development and implementation of the plan, which consisted of a formal employee suggestion program and a formula for determining the amount of total cost savings that was to be divided equally among plant employees. The plan had a positive effect on the number of suggestions provided by employees, and the cumulative number of suggestions implemented was associated with lower production costs.[35] In general, productivity improvements following the introduction of Scanlon-type plans support the motivational impact of this group wage incentive.[36] However, perception that the plan is fair is critical.[37]

Skill-based pay. A system in which people are paid according to the number of job skills they have acquired.

SKILL-BASED PAY The idea behind **skill-based pay** (also called *pay for knowledge*) is to motivate employees to learn a wide variety of work tasks, irrespective of the job that they might be doing at any given time. The more skills that are acquired, the higher the person's pay.[38] Companies use skill-based pay to encourage employee flexibility in task assignments and to give them a broader picture of the work process. It is especially useful on self-managed teams (Chapter 7), in which employees divide up the work as they see fit.

At Quebec's Bell Helicopter Textron plant, skill-based pay encourages flexibility in the aircraft assemblers' work assignments and provides them with an overall picture of the work process.

© Jean B. Heguy/First Light

PAY PLAN	DESCRIPTION	ADVANTAGES	DISADVANTAGES
Profit sharing	Employees receive a cash bonus based on organization profits	• Employees have a sense of ownership. • Aligns employee goals with organization goals. • Only pays when the organization makes a profit.	• Many factors beyond the control of employees can affect profits. • It is difficult for employees to see the impact of their actions on organization profits.
Employee stock ownership	Employees can own a set amount of the organization's shares.	• Creates a sense of legal and psychological ownership for employees. • Aligns employees' goals and interests with those of the organization.	• Many factors can influence the value of an organization's shares, regardless of employees' effort and performance. • It is difficult for employees to see the connection between their efforts and the value of their organization's stocks. • They lose their motivational potential in a weak economy when the value of an organization's stocks decline.
Gainsharing	When measured costs decrease, employees receive a bonus based on a predetermined formula.	• Aligns organization and employee goals. • Encourages teamwork and cooperative behaviour.	• Bonuses might be paid even when the organization does not make a profit. • Employees might neglect objectives that are not included in the formula.
Skill-based pay	Employees are paid according to the number of job skills they acquire.	• Encourages employees to learn new skills. • Greater flexibility in task assignments. • Provides employees with a broader picture of the work process.	• Increases the cost of training. • Labour costs can increase as employees acquire more skills.

EXHIBIT 6.3
Teamwork pay plans.

It is also useful in flexible manufacturing in which rapid changes in job demands can occur. Quebec's Bell Helicopter Textron plant uses skill-based pay for its aircraft assemblers to enhance their flexibility.

Training costs can be high with a skill-based pay system. Also, when the system is in place, it has to be used. Sometimes managers want to keep employees on a task they are good at rather than letting them acquire new skills. However, skill-based programs can have positive consequences. A study on the effects of a skill-based pay system in a large organization that manufactures vehicle safety systems reported an increase in productivity, lower labour costs per part, and a reduction in scrap following implementation of a skill-based pay program.[39]

Exhibit 6.3 compares the various pay plans that organizations use to motivate teamwork. Research has found that group-based financial incentives can have a positive effect on the collective efforts of employees and business-unit outcomes.[40]

JOB DESIGN AS A MOTIVATOR

If the use of money as a motivator is primarily an attempt to capitalize on extrinsic motivation, current approaches to using job design as a motivator represent an attempt to capitalize on intrinsic motivation. **Job design** refers to the structure, content, and configuration of a person's work tasks and roles.[41] In essence, the goal of job design is to identify the characteristics that make some tasks more motivating than others and to capture these characteristics in the design of jobs. Although it is often believed that money is the primary work motivator, many workers are actually motivated more by stimulating, challenging, and meaningful work.[42] But how do you design jobs to make them more motivating? Let's begin with a review of traditional views of job design.

LO 6.4

Compare and contrast the different approaches to job design, including the traditional approach, the *Job Characteristics Model*, *job enrichment*, *work design*, and *relational job design*.

Job design. The structure, content, and configuration of a person's work tasks and roles.

Traditional Views of Job Design

From the beginning of the Industrial Revolution until the 1960s, the prevailing philosophy regarding the design of most non-managerial jobs was job simplification. The historical roots of job simplification are found in social, economic, and technological forces that existed even before the Industrial Revolution. This pre-industrial period was characterized by increasing urbanization and the growth of a free market economy, which prompted a demand for manufactured goods. Thus, a division of labour within society occurred, and specialized industrial concerns using newly developed machinery emerged to meet this demand. With complex machinery and an uneducated, untrained workforce, these organizations recognized that *specialization* was the key to efficient productivity. If the production of an object could be broken down into very basic, simple steps, even an uneducated and minimally trained worker could contribute his or her share by mastering one of these steps.

The zenith of job simplification occurred in the early 1900s, when industrial engineer Frederick Winslow Taylor presented the industrial community with his principles of scientific management.[43] From Chapter 1, you will recall that Taylor advocated extreme division of labour and specialization, even extending to the specialization of supervisors in roles such as trainer, disciplinarian, and so on. Also, he advocated careful standardization and regulation of work activities and rest pauses. Intuitively, jobs designed according to the principles of scientific management do not seem intrinsically motivating. The motivational strategies that management used during this period consisted of close supervision and the use of piece-rate pay. But it would do a disservice to history to conclude that job simplification was unwelcomed by workers, who were mostly non-unionized, uneducated, and fighting to fulfill their basic needs. Such simplification helped them to achieve a reasonable standard of living. However, with a better-educated workforce whose basic needs are fairly well met, behavioural scientists have begun to question the impact of job simplification on performance, customer satisfaction, and the quality of working life.

Job Scope and Motivation

Job scope. The breadth and depth of a job.

Breadth. The number of different activities performed on a job.

Depth. The degree of discretion or control a worker has over how work tasks are performed.

Job scope can be defined as the breadth and depth of a job.[44] **Breadth** refers to the number of different activities performed on the job, while **depth** refers to the degree of discretion or control the worker has over how these tasks are performed. "Broad" jobs require workers to *do* a number of different tasks, while "deep" jobs emphasize freedom in *planning* how to do the work.

As shown in Exhibit 6.4, jobs that have great breadth and depth are called high-scope jobs. A professor's job is a good example of a high-scope job. It is broad because it involves the performance of a number of different tasks, such as teaching, grading, doing research, writing, and participating in committees. It is also deep because there is considerable discretion in how academics perform these tasks. In general, professors have a fair amount of freedom to choose a particular teaching style, grading format, and research area. Similarly, management jobs are high-scope jobs. Managers perform a wide variety of activities (supervision, training, performance evaluation, report writing) and have some discretion over how they accomplish these activities.

The classic example of a low-scope job is the traditional assembly line job. This job is both "shallow" and "narrow" in the sense that a single task (such as bolting on car wheels) is performed repetitively and ritually, with no discretion as to method. Traditional views of job design were attempts to construct low-scope jobs in which workers specialized in a single task.

Occasionally, we encounter jobs that have high breadth but little depth, or vice versa. For motivational purposes, we can also consider these jobs to be relatively low in scope. For example, a utility worker on an assembly line fills in for absent workers on various parts

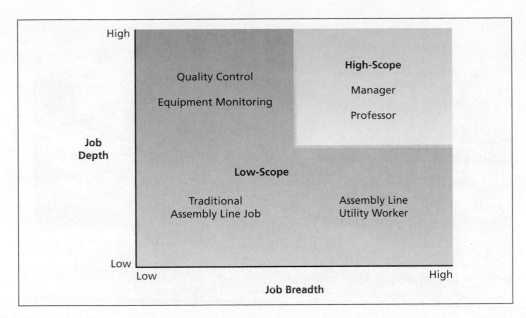

EXHIBIT 6.4
Job scope as a function of job depth and job breadth.

of the line. While this job involves the performance of a number of tasks, it involves little discretion as to when or how the worker performs the tasks. On the other hand, some jobs involve a fair amount of discretion over a single, narrowly defined task. For example, quality control inspectors perform a single, repetitive task, but they might be required to exercise a fair degree of judgment in performing this task. Similarly, workers who monitor the performance of equipment (such as in a nuclear power plant) might perform a single task but again be required to exercise considerable discretion when a problem arises.

The motivational theories we discussed in the previous chapter suggest that high-scope jobs (both broad *and* deep) should provide more intrinsic motivation than low-scope jobs. Maslow's need hierarchy and ERG theory both seem to indicate that people can fulfill higher-order needs by the opportunity to perform high-scope jobs. Expectancy theory suggests that high-scope jobs can provide intrinsic motivation if the outcomes derived from such jobs are attractive.

One way to increase the scope of a job is to assign employees *stretch assignments*, something that many organizations have begun to do. Stretch assignments offer employees challenging opportunities to broaden their skills by working on a variety of tasks with new responsibilities. Oakville, Ontario–based Javelin Technologies Inc., which develops design and engineering software for the manufacturing industry, uses stretch assignments as a way to keep employees interested and challenged in their positions.[45]

Another approach for increasing the scope of an individual's job is **job rotation**, which involves rotating employees to different tasks and jobs in an organization. This often involves working in different functional areas and departments. Job rotation is used by many companies, such as Bell Canada, Telus Corp., and Pitney Bowes, and it has been increasing in popularity. In addition to providing employees with a variety of challenging assignments, job rotation is also effective for developing new skills and expertise that can prepare employees for future roles.[46] In the next section, we discuss a model of how to design high-scope jobs.

Job rotation. Rotating employees to different tasks and jobs in an organization.

The Job Characteristics Model

The concept of job scope provides an easy-to-understand introduction to why some jobs seem more intrinsically motivating than others. However, we can find a more rigorous delineation of the motivational properties of jobs in the Job Characteristics Model that J. Richard Hackman and Greg Oldham developed (Exhibit 6.5).[47] As you can observe, the

In his classic film *Modern Times*, Charlie Chaplin performed a typical low-scope job working on an assembly line.

Photofest

EXHIBIT 6.5
The Job Characteristics Model.

Source: J. Richard Hackman & Greg R. Oldham, *Work Redesign*, 1st Ed., ©1980, p. 90. Reprinted and Electronically reproduced by permission of Pearson Education, Inc., New York, NY.

Job Characteristics Model proposes that there are several "core" job characteristics that have a certain psychological impact on workers. In turn, the psychological states induced by the nature of the job lead to certain outcomes that are relevant to the worker and the organization. Finally, several other factors (moderators) influence the extent to which these relationships hold true.

CORE JOB CHARACTERISTICS The Job Characteristics Model shows that there are five core job characteristics that have particularly strong potential to affect worker motivation: skill variety, task identity, task significance, autonomy, and job feedback. In general, higher levels of these characteristics should lead to the favourable outcomes shown in Exhibit 6.5.

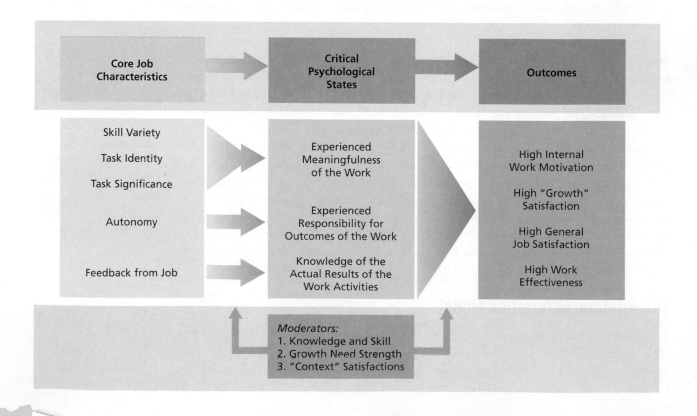

EXHIBIT 6.6
Core job characteristics
examples.

1. Skill variety
High variety: The owner-operator of a garage who does electrical repair, rebuilds engines, does body work, and interacts with customers.
Low variety: A body shop worker who sprays paint eight hours a day.

2. Task identity
High identity: A cabinet maker who designs a piece of furniture, selects the wood, builds the object, and finishes it to perfection.
Low identity: A worker in a furniture factory who operates a lathe solely to make table legs.

3. Task significance
High significance: Nursing the sick in a hospital intensive care unit.
Low significance: Sweeping hospital floors.

4. Autonomy
High autonomy: A telephone installer who schedules his or her own work for the day, makes visits without supervision, and decides on the most effective techniques for a particular installation.
Low autonomy: A telephone operator who must handle calls as they come according to a routine, highly specified procedure.

5. Job feedback
High feedback: An electronics factory worker who assembles a radio and then tests it to determine if it operates properly
Low feedback: An electronics factory worker who assembles a radio and then routes it to a quality control inspector who tests it for proper operation and makes needed adjustments.

Notice that **skill variety**, the opportunity to do a variety of job activities using various skills and talents, corresponds fairly closely to the notion of job breadth we discussed earlier. **Autonomy**, the freedom to schedule one's own work activities and decide work procedures, corresponds to job depth. However, Hackman and Oldham recognized that one could have a high degree of control over a variety of skills that were perceived as meaningless or fragmented. Thus, the concepts of task significance and task identity were introduced. **Task significance** is the impact that a job has on others. **Task identity** is the extent to which a job involves doing a complete piece of work, from beginning to end. In addition, they recognized that **feedback**, information about one's performance effectiveness, is also essential for high intrinsic motivation. People are not motivated for long if they do not know how well they are doing. High and low levels of each of the core job characteristics are described in Exhibit 6.6.

Hackman and Oldham developed a questionnaire called the Job Diagnostic Survey (JDS) to measure the core characteristics of jobs. The JDS requires job holders to report the amount of the various core characteristics contained in their jobs. From these reports, we can construct profiles to compare the motivational properties of various jobs. For example, consider the JDS profiles for lower-level managers in a utility company (collected by one of the authors of this text) and those for keypunchers in another firm (reported by Hackman and Oldham). While the managers perform a full range of managerial duties, the keypunchers perform a highly regulated job—anonymous work from various departments is assigned to them by a supervisor, and their output is verified for accuracy by others. Not surprisingly, the JDS profiles reveal that the managerial jobs are consistently higher on the core characteristics than are the keypunching jobs.

According to Hackman and Oldham, an overall measure of the motivating potential of a job can be calculated by the following formula:

$$\text{Motivating potential score} = \frac{\text{Skill variety} + \text{Task identity} + \text{Task significance}}{3} \times \text{Autonomy} \times \text{Job feedback}$$

Skill variety. The opportunity to do a variety of job activities using various skills and talents.

Autonomy. The freedom to schedule one's own work activities and decide work procedures.

Task significance. The impact that a job has on other people.

Task identity. The extent to which a job involves doing a complete piece of work, from beginning to end.

Feedback. Information about the effectiveness of one's work performance.

Since the JDS measures the job characteristics on seven-point scales, a motivating potential score could theoretically range from 1 to 343. For example, the motivating potential score for the keypunchers' jobs is 20, while that for the managers' jobs is 159. Thus, the managers are more likely than the keypunchers to be motivated by the job itself. The average motivating potential score for 6930 employees on 876 jobs has been calculated at 128.[48]

CRITICAL PSYCHOLOGICAL STATES Why are jobs that are higher on the core characteristics more intrinsically motivating? What is their psychological impact? Hackman and Oldham argue that work will be intrinsically motivating when it is perceived as meaningful, when the worker feels responsible for the outcomes of the work, and when the worker has knowledge about his or her work progress. As shown in Exhibit 6.5, the Job Characteristics Model proposes that the core job characteristics affect meaningfulness, responsibility, and knowledge of results in a systematic manner. When an individual uses a variety of skills to do a "whole" job that is perceived as significant to others, he or she perceives the work as meaningful. When a person has autonomy to organize and perform the job as he or she sees fit, the person feels personally responsible for the outcome of the work. Finally, when the job provides feedback about performance, the worker will have knowledge of the results of this opportunity to exercise responsibility.

OUTCOMES The presence of the critical psychological states leads to a number of outcomes that are relevant to both the individual and the organization. Chief among these is high intrinsic motivation. When the worker is truly in control of a challenging job that provides good feedback about performance, the key prerequisites for intrinsic motivation are present. The relationship between the work and the worker is emphasized, and the worker is able to draw motivation from the job itself. This will result in high-quality productivity. By the same token, workers will report satisfaction with higher-order needs (growth needs) and general satisfaction with the job itself. This should lead to reduced absenteeism and turnover.

MODERATORS Hackman and Oldham recognize that jobs that are high in motivating potential do not always lead to favourable outcomes. Thus, as shown in Exhibit 6.5, they propose certain moderator or contingency variables (see Chapter 1) that intervene between job characteristics and outcomes. One of these is the job-relevant knowledge and skill of the worker. Put simply, workers with weak knowledge and skills should not respond favourably to jobs that are high in motivating potential, since such jobs will prove too demanding. Another proposed moderator is **growth need strength**, which refers to the extent to which people desire to achieve higher-order need satisfaction by performing their jobs. Hackman and Oldham argue that those with high growth needs should be most responsive to challenging work. Finally, they argue that workers who are dissatisfied with the context factors surrounding the job (such as pay, supervision, and company policy) will be less responsive to challenging work than those who are reasonably satisfied with context factors.

RESEARCH EVIDENCE In tests of the Job Characteristics Model, researchers usually require workers to describe their jobs by means of the JDS and then measure their reactions to these jobs. Although there is some discrepancy regarding the relative importance of the various core characteristics, these tests have generally been very supportive of the basic prediction of the model—workers tend to respond more favourably to jobs that are higher in motivating potential.[49]

A review of research on the Job Characteristics Model found that all five core job characteristics were positively related to the outcomes in the model (i.e., job satisfaction, growth satisfaction, and internal work motivation) as well as other outcomes, including supervisor satisfaction, co-worker satisfaction, compensation satisfaction, promotion satisfaction, organizational commitment, and job involvement. In addition, some of the core job characteristics (e.g., autonomy and feedback from the job) were also related to behavioural (e.g., absenteeism

Growth need strength.
The extent to which people desire to achieve higher-order need satisfaction by performing their jobs.

and performance) and well-being (e.g., anxiety and stress) outcomes. With respect to the critical psychological states, there was strong support for the role of experienced meaningfulness of the work but less support for experienced responsibility and no support for the role of knowledge of results. These results suggest that experienced meaningfulness is the most critical psychological state.[50] Where the model seems to falter is in its predictions about growth needs and context satisfaction. Evidence that these factors influence reactions to job design is weak or contradictory.[51]

Job Enrichment

Job enrichment is the design of jobs to enhance intrinsic motivation, the quality of working life, and job involvement. **Job involvement** refers to a cognitive state of psychological identification with one's job and the importance of work to one's total self-image. Employees who have challenging and enriched jobs tend to have higher levels of job involvement. In fact, all of the core job characteristics have been found to be positively related to job involvement. Employees who are more involved in their job have higher job satisfaction and organizational commitment and are less likely to consider leaving their organization.[52]

EllisDon is a good example of an organization that has designed jobs according to the principles of job enrichment. As indicated in the chapter-opening vignette, employees at EllisDon have a great deal of autonomy in how they perform their jobs and the freedom to make important decisions. In general, job enrichment involves increasing the motivating potential of jobs via the arrangement of their core characteristics. There are no hard and fast rules for the enrichment of jobs. Specific enrichment procedures depend on a careful diagnosis of the work to be accomplished, the available technology, and the organizational context in which enrichment is to take place. However, many job enrichment schemes combine tasks, establish client relationships, reduce supervision, form teams, or make feedback more direct.[53]

- *Combining tasks.* This involves assigning tasks that might be performed by different workers to a single individual. For example, in a furniture factory a lathe operator, an assembler, a sander, and a stainer might become four "chair makers"; each worker would then do all four tasks. Such a strategy should increase the variety of skills employed and might contribute to task identity as each worker approaches doing a unified job from start to finish.

- *Establishing external client relationships.* This involves putting employees in touch with people outside the organization who depend on their products or services. An example of this might be to give line workers letters from customers who have problems with service or a product.[54] Such a strategy might involve the use of new (interpersonal) skills, increase the identity and significance of the job, and increase feedback about one's performance.

- *Establishing internal client relationships.* This involves putting employees in touch with people who depend on their products or services within the organization. For example, billers and expediters in a manufacturing firm might be assigned permanently to certain salespeople, rather than working on any salesperson's order as it comes in. The advantages are similar to those mentioned for establishing external client relationships.

- *Reducing supervision or reliance on others.* The goal here is to increase autonomy and control over one's own work. For example, management might permit clerical employees to check their own work for errors instead of having someone else do it. Similarly, firms might allow workers to order needed supplies or contract for outside services up to some dollar amount without obtaining permission.

- *Forming work teams.* Management can use this format as an alternative to a sequence of "small" jobs that individual workers perform when a product or service is too

Job enrichment. The design of jobs to enhance intrinsic motivation, quality of working life, and job involvement.

Job involvement. A cognitive state of psychological identification with one's job and the importance of work to one's total self-image.

large or complex for one person to complete alone. For example, social workers who have particular skills might operate as a true team to assist a particular client, rather than passing the client from person to person. Similarly, stable teams can form to construct an entire product, such as a car or boat, in lieu of an assembly-line approach. Such approaches should lead to the formal and informal development of a variety of skills and increase the identity of the job.

- *Making feedback more direct.* This technique is usually used in conjunction with other job design aspects that permit workers to be identified with their "own" product or service. For example, an electronics firm might have assemblers "sign" their output on a tag that includes an address and toll-free phone number. If a customer encounters problems, he or she contacts the assembler directly. In Sweden, workers who build trucks by team assembly are responsible for service and warranty work on "their" trucks that are sold locally.

Potential Problems with Job Enrichment

Despite the theoretical attractiveness of job enrichment as a motivational strategy, and despite the fact that many organizations have experimented with such programs, enrichment can encounter a number of challenging problems.

POOR DIAGNOSIS Problems with job enrichment can occur when it is instituted without a careful diagnosis of the needs of the organization and the particular jobs in question. Some enrichment attempts might be half-hearted tactical exercises that really do not increase the motivating potential of the job adequately. An especially likely error here is increasing job breadth by giving employees more tasks to perform at the same level while leaving the other crucial core characteristics unchanged—a practice known as **job enlargement**. Thus, workers are simply given *more* boring, fragmented, routine tasks to do, such as bolting intake manifolds and water pumps onto engines. On the other side of the coin, in their zeal to use enrichment as a cure-all, organizations might attempt to enrich jobs that are already perceived as too rich by their incumbents (some refer to this as *job engorgement*!).[55] This has happened in some "downsized" firms in which the remaining employees have been assigned too many extra responsibilities. Rather than increasing motivation, this can lead to role overload and work stress.

LACK OF DESIRE OR SKILL Put simply, some workers do not *desire* enriched jobs. Almost by definition, enrichment places greater demands on workers, and some might not relish this extra responsibility. Even when people have no basic objections to enrichment in theory, they might lack the skills and competence necessary to perform enriched jobs effectively. Thus, for some poorly educated or trained workforces, enrichment might entail substantial training costs. In addition, it might be difficult to train some workers in certain skills required by enriched jobs, such as social skills.

DEMAND FOR REWARDS Occasionally, workers who experience job enrichment ask that greater extrinsic rewards, such as pay, accompany their redesigned jobs. Most frequently, this desire is probably prompted by the fact that such jobs require the development of new skills and entail greater responsibility. Sometimes such requests are motivated by the wish to share in the financial benefits of a successful enrichment exercise. In one documented case, workers with radically enriched jobs in a General Foods dog food plant in Topeka, Kansas, sought a financial bonus based on the system's success.[56] Equity in action!

UNION RESISTANCE Traditionally, North American unions have not been enthusiastic about job enrichment. In part, this is due to a historical focus on negotiating with management about easily quantified extrinsic motivators, such as money, rather than the soft stuff of

Job enlargement.
Increasing job breadth by giving employees more tasks at the same level to perform but leaving other core characteristics unchanged.

job design. Also, unions have tended to equate the narrow division of labour with preserving jobs for their members. Faced with global competition, the need for flexibility, and the need for employee initiative to foster quality, companies and unions have begun to dismantle restrictive contract provisions regarding job design. Fewer job classifications mean more opportunities for flexibility by combining tasks and using team approaches.

SUPERVISORY RESISTANCE Even when enrichment schemes are carefully implemented to truly enhance the motivating potential of deserving jobs, they might fail because of their unanticipated impact on other jobs or other parts of the organizational system. A key problem here concerns the supervisors of the workers whose jobs have been enriched. By definition, enrichment increases the autonomy of employees. Unfortunately, such a change might "dis-enrich" the boss's job, a consequence that will hardly facilitate the smooth implementation of the job redesign. Some organizations have responded to this problem by effectively doing away with direct supervision of workers performing enriched jobs. Others use the supervisor as a trainer and developer of individuals in enriched jobs. Enrichment can increase the need for this supervisory function.

Work Design and Relational Job Design

In recent years, new models of job design have been developed that go beyond the core job characteristics and job enrichment and include other important aspects of job design, such as social and contextual characteristics. Two models of particular note are work design and relational job design.

Frederick Morgeson and Stephen Humphrey developed a work design model (they use the term *work design* as opposed to *job design* because it acknowledges both the job and the broader work environment) that consists of a wider variety of work design characteristics.

Work design characteristics refer to the attributes of the task, job, and social and organizational environment and consist of three categories: motivational characteristics, social characteristics, and work context characteristics. The motivational characteristics category includes *task characteristics*, which are similar to the core job characteristics of the Job Characteristics Model (autonomy, task variety, task significance, task identity, and feedback from the job), as well as *knowledge characteristics* that refer to the kinds of knowledge, skill, and ability demands required to perform a job. They also make a distinction between task variety and skill variety in that task variety involves the degree to which a job requires employees to perform a wide range of tasks on the job, while skill variety reflects the extent to which a job requires an individual to use a variety of different skills to perform a job.

Social characteristics have to do with the interpersonal and social aspects of work and include social support, interdependence, interaction outside of the organization, and feedback from others. *Work context characteristics* refer to the context within which work is performed and consist of ergonomics, physical demands, work conditions, and equipment use. See Exhibit 6.7 for more detail on the work design characteristics.

Morgeson and Humphrey developed a scale called the Work Design Questionnaire (WDQ) to measure the work design characteristics, and it is currently the most comprehensive measure of work design available. The scale can be used for research purposes and as a diagnostic tool to assess the motivational properties of jobs prior to work redesign.

Although much less research has been conducted on the knowledge, social, and work context characteristics than the task characteristics, research has found that they are also related to job attitudes and behaviours. In fact, the social characteristics are even more strongly related to some outcomes (i.e., turnover intentions and organizational commitment) than the motivational characteristics (i.e., task characteristics and knowledge characteristics). Overall, the work design characteristics have a large and significant effect on employee attitudes and behaviours.[57]

Work design characteristics. Attributes of the task, job, and social and organizational environment.

EXHIBIT 6.7
Work design characteristics.

Source: Morgeson, F.P., & Humphrey, S.E. (2006). The work design questionnaire (WDQ): Developing and validating a comprehensive measure for assessing job design and the nature of work, Journal of Applied Psychology, 91, 1321–1339; Humphrey, S.E. Nahrgang, J.D., & Morgeson, F.P. (2007). Integrating motivational, social, and contextual work design features: A meta-analytic summary and theoretical extension of the work design literature. *Journal of Applied Psychology*, 92, 1332–1356.

Task Characteristics. How the work itself is accomplished and the range and nature of tasks associated with a particular job.
  a. *Autonomy.* The extent to which a job allows freedom, independence, and discretion to schedule work, make decisions, and choose the methods used to perform tasks.
  b. *Task variety.* The degree to which a job requires employees to perform a wide range of tasks on the job.
  c. *Task significance.* The degree to which a job influences the lives of others, whether inside or outside the organization.
  d. *Task identity.* The degree to which a job involves a whole piece of work, the results of which can be easily identified.
  e. *Feedback from job.* The degree to which the job provides direct and clear information about the effectiveness of task performance.

Knowledge Characteristics. The kinds of knowledge, skill, and ability demands that are placed on an individual as a function of what is done on the job.
  a. *Job complexity.* The extent to which the tasks on a job are complex and difficult to perform.
  b. *Information processing.* The degree to which a job requires attending to and processing data or other information.
  c. *Problem solving.* The degree to which a job requires unique ideas or solutions and reflects the more active cognitive processing requirements of a job.
  d. *Skill variety.* The extent to which a job requires an individual to use a variety of different skills to complete the work.
  e. *Specialization.* The extent to which a job involves performing specialized tasks or possessing specialized knowledge and skill.

Social Characteristics. The interpersonal and social aspects of work.
  a. *Social support.* The degree to which a job provides opportunities for advice and assistance from others.
  b. *Interdependence.* The degree to which the job depends on others and others depend on it to complete the work.
  c. *Interaction outside the organization.* The extent to which the job requires employees to interact and communicate with individuals external to the organization.
  d. *Feedback from others.* The extent to which others (e.g., co-workers and supervisors) in the organization provide information about performance.

Contextual Characteristics. The context within which work is performed, including the physical and environmental contexts.
  a. *Ergonomics.* The degree to which a job allows correct or appropriate posture and movement.
  b. *Physical demands.* The amount of physical activity or effort required on the job.
  c. *Work conditions.* The environment within which a job is performed (e.g., the presence of health hazards, noise, temperature, and cleanliness of the working environment).
  d. *Equipment use.* The variety and complexity of the technology and equipment used in a job.

Relational architecture of jobs. The structural properties of work that shape employees' opportunities to connect and interact with other people.

Prosocial motivation. The desire to expend effort to benefit other people.

Another recent model of job design was developed by Adam Grant. It is a relational approach to job design that Grant calls the **relational architecture of jobs**—referring to the structural properties of work that shape employees' opportunities to connect and interact with other people. The idea behind this approach to job design is to motivate employees to make a difference in other people's lives; this is known as prosocial motivation. **Prosocial motivation** refers to the desire to expend effort to benefit other people.[58]

Jobs vary in terms of their potential to have an impact on the lives of others. For example, firefighters and surgeons have frequent opportunities to make a lasting difference in the lives of others, while janitorial jobs and cashiers have few such opportunities. However, jobs can be relationally designed to provide employees with opportunities to interact and communicate with the people affected by their work, thereby allowing them to see the benefits and significance of their work for others.[59]

For example, call centre employees raising funds for a university showed a significant increase in persistence (i.e., time spent on the phone) and performance (i.e., money raised) when they were provided with a brief exposure to a scholarship recipient who had benefited from their work. In another study, callers more than doubled the number of weekly pledges they earned and the amount of weekly donations they raised when they read stories about how former callers had helped to finance student scholarships. These studies demonstrate that it is possible to improve employee motivation and performance by redesigning jobs to emphasize their social impact. Thus, jobs should be designed so that employees have contact with or are aware of those who benefit from their work.[60]

MANAGEMENT BY OBJECTIVES

LO 6.5

Understand the connection between goal setting and *Management by Objectives*.

In Chapter 5, we discussed goal setting theory, which states that goals are most motivational when they are specific and challenging, when organizational members are committed to them, and when feedback about progress toward goal attainment is provided. **Management by Objectives (MBO)** is an elaborate, systematic, ongoing management program designed to facilitate goal establishment, goal accomplishment, and employee development.[61]

The concept was developed by management theorist Peter Drucker. The objectives in MBO are simply another label for goals. In a well-designed MBO program, objectives for the organization as a whole are developed by top management and diffused down through the organization through the MBO process. In this manner, organizational objectives are translated into specific behavioural objectives for individual members. Our primary focus here is with the nature of the interaction between managers and individual workers in an MBO program.

Although there are many variations on the MBO theme, most manager–employee interactions share the following similarities:

1. The manager meets with individual workers to develop and agree on employee objectives for the coming months. These objectives usually involve both current job performance and personal development that may prepare the worker to perform other tasks or seek promotion. The objectives are made as specific as possible and quantified, if feasible, to assist in subsequent evaluation of accomplishment. Time frames for accomplishment are specified, and the objectives may be given priority according to their agreed-upon importance. The methods to achieve the objectives may or may not be topics of discussion. Objectives, time frames, and priorities are put in writing.

2. There are periodic meetings to monitor employee progress in achieving objectives. During these meetings, people can modify objectives if new needs or problems are encountered.

3. An appraisal meeting is held to evaluate the extent to which the agreed-upon objectives have been achieved. Special emphasis is placed on diagnosing the reasons for success or failure so that the meeting serves as a learning experience for both parties.

4. The MBO cycle is repeated.

Over the years, a wide variety of organizations have implemented MBO programs. At Hewlett-Packard, MBO and metrics to measure progress were the cornerstone of the company's management philosophy for nearly six decades.[62] At Toronto-based pharmaceutical firm Janssen-Ortho Inc., each employee's goals are tied to a list of corporate objectives. Employees can earn a yearly bonus of up to 20 percent if they and the company meet their goals.[63]

RESEARCH EVIDENCE The research evidence shows that MBO programs result in clear productivity gains.[64] However, a number of factors are associated with the failure of MBO programs. For one thing, MBO is an elaborate, difficult, time-consuming process, and its implementation must have the full commitment of top management. One careful review showed a 56 percent average gain in productivity for programs with high top management commitment, and a 6 percent gain for those with low commitment.[65] If such commitment is absent, managers at lower levels simply go through the motions of practising MBO. At the very least, this reaction will lead to the haphazard specification of objectives and thus

Management by Objectives (MBO). An elaborate, systematic, ongoing program designed to facilitate goal establishment, goal accomplishment, and employee development.

subvert the very core of MBO: goal setting. A frequent symptom of this degeneration is the complaint that MBO is "just a bunch of paperwork."[66] Indeed, at this stage, it is!

Even with the best of intentions, setting specific, quantifiable objectives can be a difficult process. This might lead to an overemphasis on measurable objectives at the expense of more qualitative objectives. For example, it might be much easier to agree on production goals than on goals that involve employee development, although both might be equally important. Also, excessive short-term orientation can be a problem with MBO. Finally, even if reasonable objectives are established, MBO can still be subverted if the performance review becomes an exercise in browbeating or punishing employees for failure to achieve objectives.[67]

FLEXIBLE WORK ARRANGEMENTS AS MOTIVATORS FOR A DIVERSE WORKFORCE

LO 6.6

Explain how flexible work work arrangements respect employee diversity.

Most Canadians work a five-day week of approximately 40 hours—the "nine-to-five grind." However, many organizations have modified these traditional working schedules. For example, employees at EllisDon can work flexible hours, telecommute, and participate in a reduced summer hours program. In fact, nearly half of Canadian workers say their workplaces offer some form of flexible work arrangement.

Flexible work arrangements are work options that permit flexibility in terms of "where" and/or "when" work is completed.[68] The purpose of these arrangements is not to motivate people to work harder and thus produce direct performance benefits. Rather, the purpose is to meet diverse workforce needs, promote job satisfaction, and help employees manage work and non-work responsibilities. In turn, this should facilitate recruiting and retaining the best talent and reduce costly absenteeism and turnover. Let's now take a closer look at some of the most common flexible work arrangements.

Flexible work arrangements. Work options that permit flexibility in terms of "where" and/or "when" work is completed.

Flex-Time

Flex-time. An alternative work schedule in which arrival and departure times are flexible.

One alternative to traditional working schedules is to provide flexibility in terms of when employees work, or **flex-time**. In its most simple and common form, management requires employees to report for work on each working day and work a given number of hours. However, the times at which they arrive and leave are flexible, as long as they are present during certain core times. For example, companies might permit employees to begin their day anytime after 7 a.m. and work until 6 p.m., as long as they put in eight hours and are present during the core times of 9:15 a.m. until noon and 2:00 p.m. until 4:15 p.m. (Exhibit 6.8). Other systems permit employees to tally hours on a weekly or monthly basis, although they are still usually required to be present during the core time of each working day.[69]

Flex-time is obviously well suited to meeting the needs of a diverse workforce, since it allows employees to tailor arrival and departure times to their own transportation and child care situations. It should reduce absenteeism, since employees can handle personal matters during conventional business hours.[70] Also, flexible working hours signal a degree of prestige and trust that is usually reserved for executives and professionals.

When jobs are highly interdependent, such as on an assembly line, flex-time becomes an unlikely strategy. To cite an even more extreme example, we simply cannot have members of a hospital operating room team showing up for work whenever it suits them! In addition, flex-time might lead to problems in achieving adequate supervisory coverage. For these reasons, not surprisingly, flex-time is most frequently implemented in office environments. For instance, in a bank, the core hours might be when the bank is open to the public.

Although flex-time has generally been limited to white-collar workers, it has been applied in a variety of organizations, including insurance companies (ING Insurance), financial institutions (RBC), and government offices (many Canadian and American public service positions). [71]

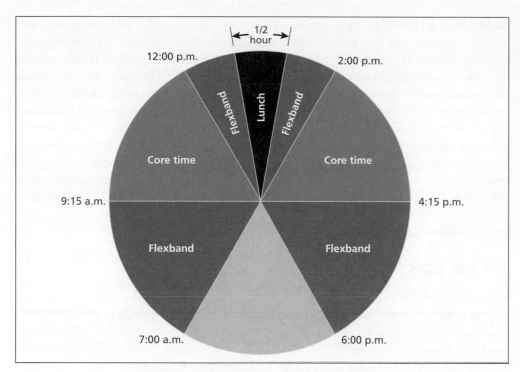

EXHIBIT 6.8
An example of a flex-time schedule.
Source: Ronen, S. (1981).
Flexible working hours: An innovation in the quality of work life.
New York, NY: McGraw-Hill, p.
42. Reprinted by permission of
the author.

RESEARCH EVIDENCE We can draw a number of conclusions from the research on flex-time.[72] First, employees who work under flex-time almost always prefer the system to fixed hours. In addition, work attitudes generally become more positive, and employers report minimal abuse of the arrangement. Absenteeism and tardiness have often shown decreases following the introduction of flex-time, and first-line supervisors and managers are usually positively inclined toward the system. Interestingly, slight productivity gains are often reported under flex-time, probably due to better use of scarce resources or equipment rather than to increased motivation. A review of research on flex-time concluded that it has a positive effect on productivity, job satisfaction, and satisfaction with work schedule, and that it lowers employee absenteeism.[73]

Compressed Workweek

A second alternative to traditional working schedules that provides flexibility in terms of when work is performed is the **compressed workweek**. This system compresses the hours worked each week into fewer days. The most common compressed workweek is the 4–40 system, in which employees work four 10-hour days each week rather than the traditional five 8-hour days. Thus, the organization or department might operate Monday through Thursday or Tuesday through Friday, although rotation schemes that keep the organization open five days a week are also employed.[74]

Like flex-time, the shorter workweek might be expected to reduce absenteeism because employees can pursue personal business or family matters in what had been working time. In addition, the 4–40 schedule reduces commuting costs and time by 20 percent and provides an extra day a week for leisure or family pursuits. Although the longer workday could pose a problem for single parents, a working couple with staggered off-days could actually provide their own child care on two of five "working" days.

Technical roadblocks to the implementation of the 4–40 workweek include the possibility of reduced customer service and the negative effects of fatigue that can accompany longer working days. The latter problem is likely to be especially acute when the work is strenuous.

Compressed workweek.
An alternative work schedule in which employees work fewer than the normal five days a week but still put in a normal number of hours per week.

RESEARCH EVIDENCE Although research on the effects of the four-day week is less extensive than that for flex-time, a couple of conclusions do stand out.[75] First, people who have experienced the four-day system seem to *like* it. Sometimes this liking is accompanied by increased job satisfaction, but the effect might be short-lived.[76] In many cases, the impact of the compressed workweek might be better for family life than for work life. Second, workers have often reported an increase in fatigue following the introduction of the compressed week. This might be responsible for the uneven impact of the system on absenteeism, sometimes decreasing it and sometimes not. Potential gains in attendance might be nullified as workers take an occasional day off to recuperate from fatigue.[77] Finally, the more sophisticated research studies do not report lasting changes in productivity due to the shortened workweek.[78] According to a review of research on the compressed workweek, there is a positive effect on job satisfaction and satisfaction with work schedule but no effect on absenteeism or productivity.[79]

Job and Work Sharing

Some flexible work arrangements involve sharing a job or work hours so that the amount of time at work is lower than the traditional 40 hours. **Job sharing** occurs when two part-time employees divide the work (and perhaps the benefits) of a full-time job.[80] The two can share all aspects of the job equally, or some kind of complementary arrangement can occur in which one party does some tasks and the co-holder does other tasks.

Job sharing. An alternative work schedule in which two part-time employees divide the work of a full-time job.

Job sharing is obviously attractive to people who want to spend more time with small children or sick elders than a conventional five-day-a-week routine permits. By the same token, it can enable organizations to attract or retain highly capable employees who might otherwise decide against full-time employment.

Work sharing. Reducing the number of hours employees work to avoid layoffs when there is a reduction in normal business activity.

Work sharing involves reducing the number of hours employees work, in order to avoid layoffs when there is a reduction in normal business activity. The Government of Canada has a work-sharing program that is designed to help employers and workers avoid temporary layoffs. For example, NORDX/CDT, a Montreal-based firm that makes cables used in fibre-optic networks, introduced a work-sharing program to cut costs while keeping workers employed. The program reduces the workweek by one to three days for some employees over a short-term period; 272 employees work one day less per week. Employees receive employment insurance benefits for the days they are not working, up to 55 percent of their salary.[81]

Many organizations in Canada have implemented work-sharing programs to save jobs and avoid layoffs during the recession. For example, Rogers Communications gave full-time staff the opportunity to reduce their workweek and accept a 20-percent pay cut to avoid layoffs to 20 percent of its staff. Buhler Industries Inc. of Winnipeg implemented a three-day workweek for its 200 employees instead of letting 90 workers go and shutting down its tractor-manufacturing plant for four months. In British Columbia, Photon Control Inc. saved 10 jobs by implementing a four-day workweek when its revenues declined, saving the company about $17 000 a month without having to downsize. Work sharing not only cuts costs, saves jobs, and avoids layoffs, but it allows organizations to retain highly skilled workers so they can quickly rebound when the economy and business improves.[82]

RESEARCH EVIDENCE There is virtually no hard research on job and work sharing. However, anecdotal reports suggest that the job sharers must make a concerted effort to communicate well with each other and with superiors, co-workers, and clients. Such communication is greatly facilitated by computer technology and voice mail. However, job sharing can result in coordination problems if communication is not adequate. Also, problems with performance appraisal can occur when two individuals share one job.

Telecommuting

In recent years, an increasing number of organizations have begun to offer employees flexibility in terms of where they perform their job, an arrangement known as telecommuting, telework, or teleworking. By **telecommuting**, employees are able to work at remote locations (e.g., home or satellite offices) but stay in touch with their offices through the use of information and communication technology, such as a computer network, voice mail, and electronic messages, to interact with others within and outside the workplace.[83] Like the other types of flexible work arrangements, telecommuting provides workers with greater flexibility in their work schedules.

Many companies first began implementing telecommuting in response to employee requests for more flexible work schedules.[84] With the growth in communication technologies, however, other factors have also influenced the spread of telecommuting. For example, telecommuting is changing the way that organizations recruit and hire people. When telecommuting is an option, companies can hire the best person for a job, regardless of where they live in the world, through *distant staffing*.[85] Distant staffing enables employees to work for a company without ever having to come into the office or even be in the same country!

Telecommuting has grown considerably over the past few years, and demand is expected to continue to grow in the coming years. It is estimated that approximately 11 million North Americans are telecommuting and that 51 percent of North American companies offer some form of telecommuting, including one in four Fortune 1000 companies. In Canada, it has been estimated that more than 1.5 million Canadians are telecommuting and about 23 percent of Canadian organizations offer it to their employees.[86]

An interesting trend in telecommuting is telework centres that provide workers all of the amenities of a home office in a location close to their home. Related to this is the emergence of *distributed work programs*, which involve a combination of remote work arrangements that allow employees to work at their business office, a satellite office, and a home office. At Bell Canada, all employees are eligible to participate in the company's distributed work program. Employees can choose to work from home all of the time, or they can work a few days a week at one of Bell's satellite offices. More than 2000 of its 42 000 workers in Canada telecommute, either from home or from one of 13 satellite offices.[87]

Telecommuting. A system by which employees are able to work at remote locations but stay in touch with their offices through the use of information and communication technology.

© David Anderson

RESEARCH EVIDENCE   Telecommuting has often been touted as having benefits to organizations and individuals. For example, organizations stand to benefit from lower costs as a result of a reduction in turnover and need for office space and equipment, and they can attract employees who see it as a desirable benefit. For individuals, it has been suggested that telecommuting can improve work–life balance and increase productivity.[88] But does telecommuting deliver on these benefits?

A review of research on telecommuting found that telecommuting has small but positive effects on perceived autonomy and lower work–family conflict. It also has a positive effect on job satisfaction and job performance, and results in lower stress and turnover intentions. Telecommuting was found to have no detrimental effect on the quality of workplace relationships or one's career prospects. In addition, a greater frequency of telecommuting (more than 2.5 days a week) was associated with a greater reduction in work–family conflict and stress. The authors found that the positive effects of telecommuting were mostly due to an increase in perceived autonomy. These findings were supported in a recent study in which telecommuting was positively related to job performance and citizenship behaviours in part because it increases employees' perceptions of autonomy.[89]

Negative aspects of telecommuting can result from damage to informal communication. These include decreased visibility when promotions are considered, problems in handling rush projects, and workload spillover for non-telecommuters. More frequent telecommuting also has a negative effect on relationships with co-workers.[90] Other potential problems include distractions in the home environment, feelings of isolation, and overwork. In addition, telecommuting may not be appropriate in organizations where customers are frequently at the office or where co-workers need to constantly collaborate on rush projects. Nor is telecommuting appropriate for all employees. As well, many companies are hesitant to implement telecommuting programs because of concerns about trust and worries that employees will not be as productive. In fact, in recent years several organizations, such as Yahoo, have banned employees from working at home.[91]

LO 6.7

Describe the factors that organizations should consider when choosing motivational practices.

MOTIVATIONAL PRACTICES IN PERSPECTIVE

As we have illustrated in this chapter, organizations have a lot of options when it comes to motivating their employees. Confused about what they should do?

As we indicated in Chapter 1, there are no simple formulas to improve employee attitudes and performance, nor is there a set of laws of organizational behaviour that can be used to solve organizational problems. Like all of organizational behaviour, when it comes to employee motivation, there is no "cookbook" to follow. Thus, while many of the best companies to work for in Canada use the motivational practices described in this chapter, this does not mean that these practices will always be effective or that other organizations should follow suit. Clearly, the motivational practices used by the best companies are effective because they *fit* in with and are part of a larger organizational culture and system of management practices. For example, the motivational practices of EllisDon described at the beginning of the chapter are part of an organizational culture that fosters entrepreneurship and employee ownership.

The choice of motivational practices requires a thorough diagnosis of the organization and the needs and desires of employees. The most effective approach will depend on a combination of contingency factors, including employee needs (e.g., money and challenging work), the nature of the job (e.g., individual or group work), characteristics of the organization (e.g., strategy and culture), and the outcome that an organization wants to achieve (e.g., job satisfaction, job performance). Ultimately, motivational systems that make use of a variety of motivators—such as performance-based pay and job enrichment—used in conjunction with one another are likely to be most effective.[92] Exhibit 6.9 summarizes the motivational practices described in this chapter and the contingency factors that should be considered when implementing them.

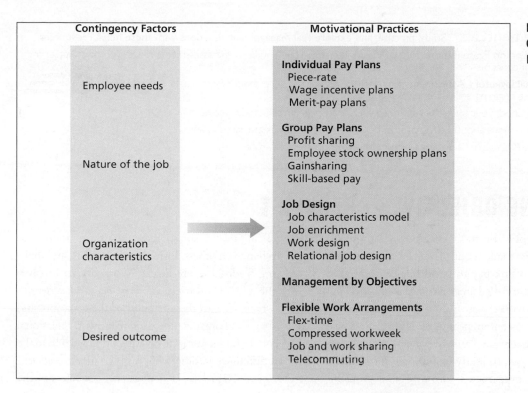

EXHIBIT 6.9
Contingency Factors and Motivational Practices.

THE MANAGER'S NOTEBOOK

Retention Bonuses at SNC-Lavalin

1. The purpose of a retention bonus is to keep managers and key employees in the organization during a critical period or during a crisis. They are often used when an organization is experiencing a change or some kind of transition and it needs to retain key people. They are also used when an organization is going through a difficult time and is worried that people are going to leave. A retention bonus can be effective if it helps to keep key people from leaving the organization and to complete projects that are in progress. On the other hand, if an organization is struggling, paying existing employees millions of dollars to stay might not solve its problems. Furthermore, employees who do not receive the bonus might be resentful, which can lower their motivation and/or increase their turnover. As a result, there must be clear and objective criteria used to decide who will receive a bonus. Finally, there is nothing to stop employees and managers from leaving SNC after they have received the bonuses. According to SNC, the bonuses were considered successful because no key employees have left since receiving the cash awards or RSU grants. Of course, this does not mean that they will not eventually leave, as there is no incentive in place to keep them.

2. An important consideration is the manner in which SNC provided the retention bonuses. In effect, they simply handed out the bonuses to managers and employees whom they decided were important to retain. In other words, those who received the bonus did not actually have to do anything to earn them. As a result, there was (and is) nothing keeping them from eventually leaving the organization. An alternative strategy would have been to provide the bonuses contingent on their remaining with the organization for a given period of time or following completion of a project. If they had done this, then the bonuses would have functioned as an incentive to motivate employees and managers to stay with the organization. Ideally, they could have provided various bonuses over a period of years or following completion of various projects, thereby requiring employees and managers to stay with the organization in order to receive the bonuses.

LEARNING OBJECTIVES CHECKLIST

6.1 Money should be most effective as a motivator when it is made contingent on performance. Schemes to link pay to performance on production jobs are called *wage incentive plans. Piece-rate*, in which workers are paid a certain amount of money for each item produced, is the prototype of all wage incentive plans. In general, wage incentives increase productivity, but their introduction can be accompanied by a number of problems, one of which is the restriction of production.

6.2 Attempts to link pay to performance on white-collar jobs are called *merit pay plans*. Evidence suggests that many merit pay plans are less effective than they could be, because merit pay is inadequate, performance ratings are mistrusted, or extreme secrecy about pay levels prevails.

6.3 Compensation plans to enhance teamwork include *profit sharing, employee stock ownership plans, gainsharing*, and *skill-based pay*. Each of these plans has a different motivational focus, so organizations must choose a plan that supports their strategic needs.

6.4 The traditional approach to the design of most non-managerial jobs was job simplification. Recent views advocate increasing the scope (breadth and depth) of jobs to capitalize on their inherent motivational properties, as opposed to the job simplification of the past. The *Job Characteristics Model*, developed by Hackman and Oldham, suggests that jobs have five core characteristics that affect their motivating potential: *skill variety, task identity, task significance, autonomy*, and *feedback*. When jobs are high in these characteristics, favourable motivational and attitudinal consequences should result. *Job enrichment* involves designing jobs to enhance intrinsic motivation, job involvement, and the quality of working life. Some specific enrichment techniques include combining tasks, establishing

client relationships, reducing supervision and reliance on others, forming work teams, and making feedback more direct. Work design involves the use of a variety of *work design characteristics* which refer to the attributes of the task, job, and social and organizational environment. Relational job design involves motivating employees to make a difference in other people's lives or *prosocial motivation*. The *relational architecture of jobs* refers to the structural properties of work that shape employees' opportunities to connect and interact with other people. The basic idea is that jobs can be designed to connect employees to those who benefit from their work, so that employees can see the impact of their actions on others.

6.5 *Management by Objectives (MBO)* is an elaborate goal-setting and evaluation process that organizations typically use for management jobs. Objectives for the organization as a whole are developed by top management and diffused down through the organization and translated into specific behavioural objectives for individual members.

6.6 Some organizations have adopted *flexible work arrangements* which permit flexibility in terms of where and when work is completed. Common examples include *flex-time, compressed workweeks, job and work sharing,* and *telecommuting*. These flexible work arrangements have the potential to meet diverse workforce needs and promote job satisfaction. They can also reduce absenteeism and turnover and enhance the quality of working life.

6.7 Organizations need to conduct a diagnostic evaluation to determine the motivational practices that will be most effective. This requires a consideration of employee needs, the nature of the job, organizational characteristics, and the outcome that is of most concern to the organization.

DISCUSSION QUESTIONS

1. Imagine two insurance companies that have merit pay plans for salaried, white-collar employees. In one organization, the plan truly rewards good performers, while in the other it does not. Both companies decide to make salaries completely public. What will be the consequences of such a change for each company? (Be specific, using concepts such as expectancy, instrumentality, job satisfaction, and turnover.)

2. Imagine an office setting in which a change to a four-day workweek, flex-time, or telecommuting would appear to be equally feasible to introduce. What would be the pros and cons of each system? How would factors such as the nature of the business, the age of the workforce, and the average commuting distance affect the choice of systems?

3. Refer to the work design characteristics in Exhibit 6.7. What work design characteristics are most important for you and why? If you

were to redesign the job you currently hold or a job you have previously held, what work design characteristics would you change? How would you change them?

4. Incentive compensation plans are believed to have a number of advantages for organizations. However, they can also have negative consequences for employees and organizations. Discuss how the design of compensation programs can lead to inappropriate and unethical behaviours. How should incentive compensation programs be designed to encourage positive behaviours and discourage negative ones?

5. What is the relational architecture of jobs, and why is this important for job design? Discuss your current or most recent job in terms of its relational architecture. How can the relational architecture of your job be improved, and what effect would this have on your motivation?

INTEGRATIVE DISCUSSION QUESTIONS

1. Merit pay plans often require managers to conduct performance evaluations of their employees to determine the amount of merit pay to be awarded. Discuss some of the perceptual problems and biases described in Chapter 3 that could create problems for a merit pay plan. What can be done to improve performance evaluations and the success of merit pay plans?

2. Using each of the motivation theories described in Chapter 5, explain how job design job enrichment, work design, and relational job design can be motivational. According to each theory, when are job design, job enrichment, work design, and relational job design most likely to be effective for motivating workers?

ON-THE-JOB CHALLENGE QUESTION

Your New Salary

Gravity Payments is a mobile credit-card payment processing company in Seattle, Washington that was started by its CEO Dan Price while he was still a freshman at Seattle Pacific University. Last year, Gravity Payments made $2.2 million in profits, and Price earned a salary of $1 million.

In April of 2015, Dan Price made a very surprising announcement to the company's 120 employees: "You might be making $35 000 a year right now but everyone in here will definitely be making $70 000 a year and I'm super excited about that." He told them that he would be cutting his $1 million salary and would use the company's profits so that all of the company's employees would earn a base salary of $70 000.

About 30 employees will have their salary double, while others will get raises to bring them up to $70 000, and about 50 employees are already paid above $70 000. Before the increase, the average salary at Gravity Payments was $48 000. The pay increases will cost about $1.7 million, most of the company's profits. In order to afford it, Price is taking a pay cut from $1 million to $70 000. Price said he did not think it was right that he should earn up to 100 times more than most of his employees.

Price says he got the idea from a Princeton University study that found that emotional well-being increases with income, but only to about $75 000. According to Price, if companies want to have happy, motivated employees, they should pay them enough to thrive, not survive. He says, "I think this is going to become a competitive imperative over time, and it will catch on."

What do you think of the new base salary at Gravity Payments? Do you think it will have a positive effect on employee motivation and performance? Should other companies consider paying their employees a base salary of $70 000? What are the pros and cons of this revolutionary approach to pay? Will it catch on?

Sources: Levinson King, R. (2015, April 17). Forget the minimum wage. Gravity Payments CEO Dan Price sets $70K "happiness" wage. *Toronto Star*, www.thestar.com/news/canada/2015/04/17/…; Ensor, J. (2015, April 16). How about a $70,000 minimum wage? That's what this CEO is offering his employees. *Financial Post*, www.business.financialpost.com/executive/….

EXPERIENTIAL EXERCISE

Task Characteristics Scale

How would you describe your job? The questions below are from the Work Design Questionnaire (WDQ). They provide you with the opportunity to evaluate the task characteristics of the job you currently hold or one you have held in the past. For each question, indicate the extent to which you agree or disagree. Alternatively, you can use this scale to assess your task characteristics preferences by replacing the beginning of each question with "I would like a job that allows me to…"

Use the following response scale when answering each question:

1–Strongly disagree

2–Disagree

3–Neither disagree nor agree

4–Agree

5–Strongly agree

____   1. The job allows me to make my own decisions about how to schedule my work.

____   2. The job allows me to decide on the order in which things are done on the job.

____   3. The job allows me to plan how I do my work.

____   4. The job gives me a chance to use my personal initiative or judgment in carrying out the work.

____   5. The job allows me to make a lot of decisions on my own.

____   6. The job provides me with significant autonomy in making decisions.

____   7. The job allows me to make decisions about what methods I use to complete my work.

____   8. The job gives me considerable opportunity for independence and freedom in how I do the work.

____   9. The job allows me to decide on my own how to go about doing my work.

____   10. The job involves a great deal of task variety.

____   11. The job involves doing a number of different things.

____   12. The job requires the performance of a wide range of tasks.

____   13. The job involves performing a variety of tasks.

____   14. The results of my work are likely to significantly affect the lives of other people.

____   15. The job itself is very significant and important in the broader scheme of things.

____   16. The job has a large impact on people outside the organization.

____   17. The work performed on the job has a significant impact on people outside the organization.

____   18. The job involves completing a piece of work that has an obvious beginning and end.

____   19. The job is arranged so that I can do an entire piece of work from beginning to end.

____   20. The job provides me the chance to completely finish the pieces of work I begin.

____   21. The job allows me to complete work I start.

____   22. The work activities themselves provide direct and clear information about the effectiveness (e.g., quality and quantity) of my job performance.

____   23. The job itself provides feedback on my performance.

____   24. The job itself provides me with information about my performance.

Scoring and Interpretation

You have just completed the task characteristics scales of the Work Design Questionnaire (WDQ). A study of a sample of 540 individuals who had at least 10 years of full-time work experience resulted in the following mean scores for each task characteristic (scores range from 1 to 5; note that there are three different scales for autonomy: work scheduling autonomy, decision making autonomy, and work methods autonomy):

Work-scheduling autonomy:	3.93
Decision-making autonomy:	4.12
Work-methods autonomy:	3.99
Task variety:	4.13
Task significance:	3.95
Task identity:	3.61
Feedback from the job:	3.91

To obtain your score on each task characteristic, calculate your scores as shown below. Note that your scores can range from 1 to 5, with higher scores indicating a greater amount of the task characteristic in your job (or in the case of preferences, a greater preference for the task characteristic).

Work scheduling autonomy: Add items 1, 2, and 3 and divide by three.

Decision making autonomy: Add items 4, 5, and 6 and divide by three.

Work methods autonomy: Add items 7, 8, and 9 and divide by three.

(Note that you can obtain an overall autonomy score by adding your score for questions 1 to 9 and dividing by nine).

Task variety: Add items 10, 11, 12, and 13 and divide by four.

Task significance: Add items 14, 15, 16, and 17 and divide by four.

Task identity: Add items 18, 19, 20, and 21 and divide by four.

Feedback from job: Add items 22, 23, and 24 and divide by three.

Source: Morgeson, F.P., & Humphrey, S.E. (2006). The work design questionnaire (WDQ): Developing and validating a comprehensive measure for assessing job design and the nature of work. *Journal of Applied Psychology*, *91*, 1321–1339. American Psychological Association.

To facilitate class discussion and your understanding of work design and task characteristics, form a small group with several other members of the class and consider the following questions:

1. Each group member should present his or her score on each task characteristic. What task characteristics do group members score high and low on? Is there any consistency among group members in terms of the highest and lowest task characteristics? (Note: If you answered the question in terms of task characteristics preferences, discuss your highest and lowest preferences).

2. Each group member should describe his or her job and provide specific examples of what contributes to their task characteristics scores. What is it about the job that contributes to a high or low score on each task characteristic? (Note: If you answered the question in terms of task characteristics preferences, discuss your ideal job based on your task characteristics scores. Be specific in terms of how you would like your job to be designed).

3. Consider your job attitudes (e.g., job satisfaction and organizational commitment) and behaviours (e.g., job performance, absenteeism, and intention to quit) in terms of your task characteristics scores. To what extent do the task characteristics contribute to your job attitudes and behaviours? (Note: If you answered the question in terms of task characteristics preferences, describe how the task characteristics might influence your job attitudes and behaviours. What task characteristics do you think would be most important for you and why?)

4. If you could redesign your job, what task characteristics would you focus on? What exactly would you do to redesign your job? Be specific in terms of how your job would change. What effect do you think these changes would have on your job attitudes and behaviours? (Note: If you answered the question in terms of task characteristics preferences, discuss how knowledge of your task characteristics scores can assist you in your job search, questions you will ask interviewers, and your job choice decision. How will knowledge of your task characteristics preferences assist in you in the future?)

5. What have you learned about job design and task characteristics? How can you use this information as a job seeker, an employee, and as a manager?

CASE INCIDENT

The Junior Accountant

After graduating from business school, Sabrita received a job offer from a large accounting firm to work as a junior accountant. She was ranked in the top 10 of her class and could not have been happier.

During the first six months, however, Sabrita began to reconsider her decision to join a large firm. This is how she described her job: Every day her supervisor brought several files for her to audit. He told her what order to do them in and how to plan her workday. At the end of the day, the supervisor would return to pick up the completed files. The supervisor collected the files from several other junior accountants and put them all together and completed the audit himself. The supervisor would then meet the client to review and discuss the audit. Sabrita did not ever meet the client, and her supervisor never talked about his meeting or the final report.

Sabrita felt very discouraged and wanted to quit. She was even beginning to reconsider her choice of accounting as a career.

1. Describe the job characteristics and critical psychological states of Sabrita's job. According to the Job Characteristics Model, how motivated

is Sabrita? What does the Job Characteristics Model predict about the way her job is designed and its affect on her job attitudes and behaviours?

2. Evaluate Sabrita's job on each of the work design characteristics described in Exhibit 6.7. What work design characteristics are particularly low? Based on your evaluation, what factors do you think are contributing to Sabrita's job attitudes and intention to quit?

3. How would you redesign Sabrita's job to increase her motivation? Be sure to describe changes you would make to the work design characteristics as well as job enrichment schemes that you would use to redesign her job.

CASE STUDY

Dr. Jack Perry, DDS

Source: Eleni Mitsis wrote this case under the supervision of Professor John Haywood-Farmer solely to provide material for class discussion. The authors do not intend to illustrate either effective or ineffective handling of a managerial situation. The authors might have disguised certain names and other identifying information to protect confidentiality.

Ivey Management Services prohibits any form of reproduction, storage or transmittal of this material without its written permission. Reproduction of this material is not covered under

authorization by any reproduction rights organization. To order copies or request permission to reproduce materials, contact Ivey Publishing, Ivey Management Services, c/o Richard Ivey School of Business, The University of Western Ontario, London, Ontario, Canada, N6A 3K7; phone (519) 661-3208; fax (519) 661-3882; e-mail cases@ivey.uwo.ca. Copyright © 2007, Ivey Management Services. Version: (A) 2007-03-12.

One time permission to reproduce granted by Richard Ivey School of Business Foundation on October 14, 2015.

"In dental school, they turned us into expert dentists, gave us our diplomas, and sent us out into the world with no sense of how to manage people. I wish they'd taught us how to manage a business," thought Dr. Jack Perry, a sole practitioner dentist in Cromwell, Ontario.

Perry had just returned from lunch one day in early 2006 with his newest team member, Sandi, a receptionist. Over lunch, she had expressed concern that during her four months working at Perry's office, she had concluded that morale was low and had noticed that staff members did not seem to be working as hard as they could to help increase billings. Sandi said that although all of the staff seemed to enjoy Perry's easygoing nature and pleasant demeanour, they did not seem motivated to grow the business, fill cancellations, follow up on collections, or cross-sell procedures. Perry was happy Sandi had raised the issue. Although he had observed the same behaviour himself, so far he had

ignored it, as he felt overwhelmed at how to deal with this people management issue.

THE CANADIAN DENTAL INDUSTRY

Canada had some 17 500 dentists[1]—professionals qualified to prevent, diagnose, evaluate and treat diseases and disorders of the human mouth, gums and teeth. Becoming a dentist in Canada was a rigorous process that included at least three years of study at the university undergraduate level, usually in natural sciences, followed by four more years at an accredited dental school. At the end of their studies, graduates had to pass a board examination before obtaining their doctor of dental surgery degree (DDS). Dentists choosing to specialize in particular areas, such as endodontics, oral

---

1 *Ontario Dental Association website, www.oda.com/stats, accessed January 15, 2006.*

surgery or prosthodontics, spent at least another two years in school to become specialists.[2]

Each province had its own governing professional body to monitor dentists' activities. To practise, dentists had to be members in good standing. In Ontario, the Royal College of Dental Surgeons of Ontario (RCDSO) represented about 7700 practising dentists.[3]

Dentists typically worked as small business owners operating dental offices. Most were sole practitioners. Only about three percent of dentists worked outside that environment in hospitals, research facilities, and public clinics.[4]

Within their practices, dentists typically employed dental hygienists, dental assistants, and receptionists. Hygienists were responsible for promoting proper oral hygiene, such as regular brushing and flossing. Hygienists held a professional licence that allowed them to scale human teeth to remove buildup such as plaque and tartar. They were not allowed to diagnose dental conditions, although they regularly alerted dentists to suspected problems. Hygienists were prohibited from drilling teeth. Assistants helped the dentist during treatments, handed the dentist materials and sterilized all instruments following procedures. Some assistants were trained by dentists and had no formal education, thus limiting the tasks they could perform. Depending on their level, assistants with formal certification from an accredited community college were allowed to assist the dentist in other ways, such as taking X-rays, taking impressions and placing rubber dams on a patient's tooth in preparation for a filling. The receptionist's tasks included answering the phone, booking patients, billing patients, and making daily deposits at the bank.

Some 63 percent of Canadians over 12 years of age visited their dentist once per year. Over half of these patients had dental insurance coverage. Full or partial dental insurance was a common employee benefit through individual or family plans, which covered spouses and children. Coverage, which depended on the plan, varied greatly from no coverage to full coverage. The other half of patients were uninsured; they paid for dental services out of their own pockets,

which affected demand for nonessential dental services, such as regular cleanings and cosmetic procedures. Many patients, because of financial limitations or fear of dental treatment, could be considered as "pain management" cases who sought treatment only when they experienced significant pain.

Each year, RCDSO issued a schedule of dental fees, which varied by procedure. Dentists were legally able to charge up to 20 percent more than the fee guide or a lower amount if they wanted. However, most dentists did not try to undercut each other on price and followed the RCDSO fee guide with little deviation.

PERRY'S DENTAL PRACTICE

Perry graduated at the top of his class from an Ontario university dental school in 2001 and purchased a dwindling practice from a nearly retired dentist in Cromwell, Ontario, a small town some 30 kilometres from Ottawa. Cromwell had a population of 3000 people and served an additional 7000 people in the surrounding area. Cromwell was a bedroom community; most of its employed citizens worked in Ottawa. In addition to Perry, Cromwell had three other dentists, two of whom worked few hours and were practically retired, and one dentist who was in his early 40s and had been practising in Cromwell about five years longer than Perry. Perry was very proud of the financial success of his practice, which had grown exceptionally and was now growing at 15 percent annually. Exhibit 1 shows a financial statement.

Perry employed two part-time receptionists, two full-time hygienists, one full-time assistant and one part-time assistant. All were women. Each member of the team had unique skills and specific duties in the practice. The hygienists were responsible for cleaning (or scaling) teeth, educating patients about their dental health during appointments, and bringing any potential dental problems to the attention of Perry for diagnosis and possibly treatment. The receptionists were in charge of booking patients, filling cancellations, collecting accounts receivable, and ensuring that patients had regular dental hygiene appointments, usually once every nine months. The assistants' primary task was to help Perry during procedures by passing him instruments, taking X-rays, taking impressions, setting up the operatory,[5] and sterilizing the equipment after each use. During their down time, assistants called patients

2 The American Dental Association recognizes nine dental specialties. Endodontists deal with tooth pulp or dentine; root canals are their most common procedure. Prosthodontists specialize in the restoration of oral function by creating prostheses or restorations. See: en.wikipedia.org/wiki, accessed March 10, 2006.

3 ODA website: www.oda.com, accessed January 22, 2006.
4 Royal College of Dental Surgeons of Ontario Newsletter, October 2005.

5 An operatory is the space in which the dentist performs dental procedures. It is equipped with a reclining dental chair for the patient, drills and handpieces for the dentist's work, cabinetry, and a mobile lamp.

Gross collections		
Dentist	$455 800	
Hygienist	303 900	
Total	$759 700	
Expenses		
Salaries and wages★	$299 700	
Supplies	50 800	
Depreciation	8000	
Marketing and promotion	10 600	
Rent	24 000	
Utilities and telephone	9200	
Insurance and licensing	15 300	
Equipment repairs	7200	
Professional development	19 000	
Interest and bank charges	5350	
Total	$449 150	
Net income	$310 550	

★ *This figure includes a salary for Perry of $72 000 per year. His personal income also included the practice's net income.*

EXHIBIT 1
2005 Income Statement for Dr. Jack Perry, Dentistry Professional Corporation

Source: Practice files.

on behalf of Perry to see how they were recovering following dental surgery procedures, such as extractions, implant therapy, and other intrusive treatments.

Like most Canadian dentists, Perry compensated his employees based on their position, credentials, and performance at the following hourly rates: hygienists, $31 per hour; receptionists, $18 per hour; full-time assistant (who was certified at Level 1), $19 per hour; part-time assistant, who had begun as a co-operative student from the local high school and who was hoping to be admitted into a formal dental assisting program, $11 per hour.

Perry met informally with staff on an individual basis annually to discuss their work and salary. According to an annual report from the Ontario Dental Association, Perry's compensation was competitive and his staff were near the top of the second quartile. Perry believed that this level was fair because smaller rural practices tended to pay lower hourly wages than those in large cities, where staff had to pay for parking and commuting costs. There was no shortage of qualified staff in the Cromwell area; Perry regularly received résumés from qualified professionals seeking work. Perry kept these résumés on file in case he had to replace a staff member.

Perry had virtually no staff turnover,[6] a situation he attributed to his easy-going manner, his competitive salary and the fairly pleasant atmosphere of the practice. Additionally, he knew that the women who worked at his office enjoyed working close to home. Moreover, Perry knew from local hygienists that the other active dentist in town experienced significant staff turnover and had a reputation as a difficult employer.

Perry's staff enjoyed three weeks of holiday per year, two weeks in the summer and one week at Christmas. In addition to this time off, Perry allowed staff to take further unpaid vacation time so long as they could arrange to have another staff member cover their shifts. The staff appreciated this flexibility, as it allowed them to spend time with their families during school breaks.

Every year, right before Christmas holidays, Perry held a staff party that included dinner and drinks and the exchanging of small gifts. The staff looked forward to this event and enjoyed planning it. In addition to the Christmas party, Perry gave each employee a

---

6 *Over the past five years, one of Perry's employees had left to join an upscale, downtown Ottawa dental office offering more money. He had dismissed two others, one for incompetence and one for unprofessional conduct.*

cash bonus for their hard work throughout the year. Although the amount was not rigorously calculated, the staff all seemed quite happy with an extra $400.

THE ISSUE

As Perry thought back to Sandi's comments, he wondered what he could do to motivate his staff to help the business grow. He thought that Sandi was probably right and that morale probably was low. Some of Perry's colleagues had warned him that the bigger his business grew, the less happy the staff would feel because they would begin to see themselves as slave labourers making little money relative to him. The receptionists and assistants were privy to the total billing amounts through daily and monthly reports outlining the practice's revenues. The staff would also know that every month, the business grew by adding more new patients. The hygienists were well aware that they generated about 40 percent of the practice's total billings. Unfortunately, staff members were unaware of the costs of the practice, such as lab materials, supplies, phone, salaries, advertising, continuing education, and insurance.

Perry knew that each of his employees played a role in the practice's financial health. For every cancellation the receptionists filled, Perry made money on what would otherwise have been lost billable time; Perry had to pay his staff regardless of whether or not the patient attended. His assistants played a role similar to nurses in a hospital setting in comforting patients and making sure they felt at ease. This action significantly affected patient retention and word-of-mouth referrals. The hygienists had a direct effect on revenue because their services were billable, and they had leverage in helping the dentist recommend further dental work if necessary.

As a result of their impact, Perry was not averse to sharing profits with his staff. He believed that such a move would cure the somewhat low morale and sluggish work and would make the staff understand the other side of the coin — the costs that he incurred each month while running his practice. However, Perry was unsure how to share profits.

Perry recalled a dental conference he had attended with some colleagues in Chicago in 2005, which featured a presentation by a business consultant on the topic of staff motivation and profit sharing. Perry had taken notes during the presentation, as he was intrigued by the concept of profit sharing for a dental office. The consultant, who was also acting as a salesman for his services, said that in 2005, over 30 percent of dental practices in the United States had profit-sharing programs compared to only five percent in 1998. The presentation showed statistically significant links between the introduction of a profit-sharing program and decreased staff turnover, higher morale, and increased productivity.[7] Unfortunately, the consultant did not provide a copy of his presentation to guests. The consultant outlined two popular ways to structure a profit-sharing program.

The first approach was to hire hygienists as separate contractors. This plan would fundamentally change the way in which more traditional offices, such as Perry's, compensated hygienists. Rather than paying hygienists by the hour, they would earn a percentage of their collections. The consultant had suggested that a commission rate of 40 percent was common in the marketplace. Because Perry's computer system identified the provider who performed each service, adopting this approach would require no changes in that sense. The consultant maintained that any office that introduced such a system would see hygienists' billings increase by seven percent to 13 percent in the first year.

Although Perry liked the idea of making the hygienists more responsible for their contribution to the practice, he wondered what effect such a structure would have on the hygienists' compensation if collections did not increase. Currently, the hygienists were paid approximately $52 000 per year before taxes and deductions. Would they be better off? If not, how could he sell the change without a massive revolt on their part? Perry also wondered whether adopting this system would encourage the hygienists to take more responsibility for reminding patients of their appointment the day ahead. Currently, this task belonged to the receptionists. Surely, missed appointments would begin to bother the hygienists, as they would now be affected financially. Currently, Perry did not charge for missed appointments, as no other dentist in the area did.

The consultant also noted that starting with the hygienists was critical because of their effect on practice billings. Once implemented, he stated that it was critical to look at the assistants and receptionists, who could have a lower base salary and commission linked to the overall performance of the practice, including the dentist's billings. This structure was less clear because the consultant said it varied significantly from practice to practice.

---

7 *Productivity is defined as the total collections of the dental practice divided by the total number of staff hours worked.*

The second structure identified by the consultant was to make everyone equally responsible for developing the practice through a form of profit sharing. Under such a scheme, the dentist would establish the percentage of total collections accounted for by the staff. The dentist would then guarantee that staff would receive that percentage of collections. In essence, if hourly wages and hours worked remained the same, but collections grew, the staff would share in the bonus, as their productivity had increased. The reward could be distributed in a number of ways: on the basis of seniority, by position, or by the percentage of hours worked by each staff member. The consultant suggested that this program would increase productivity by an extra 10 percent to 15 percent in the first year.

Perry wondered whether this option would provide enough additional payout to staff to motivate them to grow the practice. Currently, Perry's staff salaries accounted for about 30 percent of collections,[8] and his

8 *The figure of 30 percent is based on the total salary amount outlined in* **Exhibit 1**, *less the personal income Perry paid himself from the business.*

practice collections were naturally growing at an average rate of about 15 percent annually. He believed this performance was likely to continue for the next five years. Perry was concerned that this option did not reward the great performers differently from the mediocre ones. Also, he noted that it would give him less influence in changing specific behaviours than would the first option.

As Perry looked over his notes, he realized that he had listed only the structure types the consultant had outlined and not their benefits and drawbacks. Perry did not want to hire the consultant because he believed that the notes he had taken would allow him to perform his own analysis of what best suited his practice. He knew that his decision would be critical, as staff morale could be further ruined if he were to select the wrong structure. Perry wanted to understand the financial impact on his staff as well as on the practice if he were to introduce either incentive program. Furthermore, Perry wondered how he would implement a compensation structure change. He assembled his information on his desk and wondered which alternative, if either, would help address his staff issues.

QUESTIONS

1. Do you think Dr. Perry has a motivation problem in his office? If so, what is the evidence and nature of the problem, and why do you think it exists?

2. Compare and contrast the two pay plans. How are they similar and how are they different? What are the advantages and disadvantages of each plan?

3. What effect do you think each pay plan will have on Dr. Perry's employees? Be specific with respect to each group of employee (i.e., receptionists, hygienists, and assistants). What effect do you think each pay plan will have on office productivity?

4. What pay plan do you think Dr. Perry should implement and why? Explain how the plan should be implemented.

5. What factors might derail the successful implementation of a new pay plan? What will Dr. Perry have to do to make sure that a new pay plan is effective for motivating his employees and improving office productivity?

6. What other pay schemes should Dr. Perry consider besides the two alternatives described in the case? What do you recommend and why?

INTEGRATIVE CASE

IVEY | Publishing

Ken Private Limited: Digitization Project

At the end of Chapter 1, you were introduced to the Ken Private Limited: Digitization Project Integrative Case. The case questions focused on issues pertaining to the relevance and goals of organizational behaviour, managerial roles and activities, and contemporary management concerns. Now that you have completed

Part 2 of the text and the chapters on Individual Behaviour, you can return to the Integrative Case and focus on issues related to learning, perceptions, cross-cultural differences, and motivation by answering the following questions.

QUESTIONS

1. How important is learning for the success of the Genesis Digitization Project? Who needs to learn, and what do they need to learn?

2. What behaviours do you think need to be increased, decreased, and/or eliminated? Explain the implications of operant learning theory and social cognitive theory for employees working on the Genesis Digitization Project. Based on each theory, what would you do to facilitate learning and increase the probability of desirable behaviours?

3. What organizational learning practices would you recommend for employees working on the Genesis Digitization Project? Consider each of the organizational learning practices described in Chapter 2 and explain why you would or would not use them to change the behaviour of employees working on the Genesis Digitization Project.

4. Consider the perceptions held by employees on the Indian team and the Filipino team. How does each team perceive the other team and why?

5. Use social identity theory to explain the perceptions that employees on the Indian and Filipino team have of themselves and each other. How does social identity theory help us to understand their perceptions?

6. To what extent are person perception biases affecting the perceptions that each team has of the other? What are the implications of these perceptions for the success of the Genesis Digitization Project?

7. Consider the role of trust and perceived organizational support (POS) in the case. How important are they for the success of the Genesis

Digitization Project? To what extent do employees on each team have positive perceptions of trust, and what effect do these perceptions have on their attitudes and behaviours? What should Shekhar Sharma and Saiyumn Savarker do to create positive perceptions of trust and organizational support?

8. To what extent do you think national cultural differences contributed to the events in the case, as opposed to other factors? Before you answer, locate India and the Philippines in Exhibit 4.4, which cross-references power distance and individualism values.

9. Discuss the relevance of motivation for the successful completion of the Genesis Digitization Project, and describe the motivation of employees working on the project. How important is motivation? Describe what employees should be motivated to do and how to motivate them to do it.

10. Use each of the theories of work motivation to (a) describe the motivation of employees on the Indian and Filipino team, and (b) describe what to do to increase employee motivation. Based on your analysis, what do you think is most important for motivating employees on each team to successfully complete the project?

11. What motivational practices would you use to motivate employees working on the Genesis Digitization Project? Be sure to consider pay schemes, job design, Management by Objectives, and flexible work arrangements. What practice(s) would you recommend and why?

CHAPTER 7

GROUPS AND TEAMWORK

LEARNING OBJECTIVES

After reading Chapter 7, you should be able to:

7.1 Discuss group development.

7.2 Explain how group size and member diversity influence what occurs in groups.

7.3 Review how *norms*, *roles*, and *status* affect social interaction.

7.4 Discuss the causes and consequences of *group cohesiveness*.

7.5 Explain the dynamics of *social loafing*.

7.6 Discuss how to design and support *self-managed teams*.

7.7 Explain the logic behind *cross-functional teams,* and describe how they can operate effectively.

7.8 Understand *virtual teams* and what makes them effective.

IDEO

IDEO is considered to be one of the most innovative and influential global design and innovation consultancy firms in the world. IDEO has received numerous domestic and international awards for design excellence, including 38 Red Dot awards and 28 iF Hanover awards. Signature products have included the first Apple computer mouse, Nike sunglasses, and the Steelcase Node chair.

With offices in major cities in the U.S., Europe, and Asia, IDEO employs people working on projects for clients ranging from startups to premier organizations in food and beverage (Nestlé), retail (Target), philanthropy (Oxfam), telecommunications (Nokia), computing (Microsoft), medicine (Mayo Clinic), banking (Bank of America), and manufacturing (Ford Motor Company).

As a design firm, IDEO uses an approach that relies heavily on interdisciplinary project teams. For example, for a Kentucky-based project headed by The Community Builders, the largest nonprofit developer of public housing in the U.S., an IDEO team was assembled consisting of anthropologists, architects, psychologists, and industrial designers. To accomplish their mandate, team members interviewed builders, urban planners, municipal authorities, and service providers. The real insights, however, occurred when the team broke into groups to stay overnight with three families from Park DuValle, a mixed-income community in Louisville. By doing so, the team was able to uncover the latent needs of home dwellers whose income levels and life trajectories were vastly different from one another.

Since the challenges facing IDEO are complex, assembling the right teams is critical to ensuring its success. In his book *Change by Design*, CEO Tim Brown suggests that a popular saying throughout the company— "All of us are smarter than any of us"—is purportedly what drives the company's insistence on a collective ownership of ideas. Staffing a project with teammates from a multiplicity of disciplines takes patience, however. To become part of an IDEO team, an individual must possess not only depth in the skill required to make a tangible contribution but also a capacity for handling role ambiguity and a disposition for collaborating with others across fields. Several best practices are therefore instilled to provide the firm with guidance in designing effective teams.

First, since new teams are marshalled for every project, team members must be passionate about the project they are assigned to. Without passion, IDEO believes that the motivation needed to generate creative solutions will be absent.

Second, status differences between team members are eliminated because IDEO considers hierarchy as stifling to innovation. As such, formal position titles on business cards and segregated corner offices are rejected because they impose mental and physical barriers between teams

IDEO design team.

and individuals. Another element minimizing employee status differences and facilitating virtual communication is the company's intranet, known widely as "The Tube." Considered to be the centerpiece of how IDEO interacts as a global organization, The Tube encourages teams to collaborate and share their passions and expertise through social-networking tools such as blogs, wikis, and real-time screen sharing.

An innovation project with a dedicated beginning, middle, and end is more likely to keep the team motivated and focused on moving forward. Since clients may unnecessarily delay their engagement after the presentation of a consultant's report, IDEO encourages its clients to participate in all aspects of the team's research, analysis, and development process. Unlike many traditional design consulting firms, IDEO's teams help shorten the time between conception and sale, thereby reinforcing its competitive advantage.[1]

This vignette shows how critical groups or teams are in determining organizational success. In this chapter, we will define the term *group* and discuss the nature of formal groups and informal groups in organizations. After this, we will present the details of group development. Then, we will consider how groups differ from one another structurally and explore the consequences of these differences. We will also cover the problem of social loafing. Finally, we will examine how to design effective work teams.

WHAT IS A GROUP?

Group. Two or more people interacting interdependently to achieve a common goal.

We use the word "group" rather casually in everyday discourse—for example, special-interest group or ethnic group. However, for behavioural scientists, a **group** consists of two or more people interacting interdependently to achieve a common goal.

Interaction is the most basic aspect of a group—it suggests who is in the group and who is not. The interaction of group members need not be face to face, and it need not be verbal. For example, employees who telecommute can be part of their work group at the office even though they live kilometres away and communicate via email. Interdependence simply means that group members rely to some degree on each other to accomplish goals. All groups have one or more goals that their members seek to achieve. These goals can range from having fun to marketing a new product to achieving world peace.

Group memberships are very important for two reasons. First, groups exert a tremendous influence on us. They are the social mechanisms by which we acquire many beliefs, values, attitudes, and behaviours. Group membership is also important because groups provide a context in which *we* are able to exert influence on *others*.

Formal work groups. Groups that are established by organizations to facilitate the achievement of organizational goals.

Formal work groups are groups that organizations establish to facilitate the achievement of organizational goals. They are intentionally designed to channel individual effort in an appropriate direction. The most common formal group consists of a manager and the employees who report to that manager. In a manufacturing company, one such group might consist of a production manager and the six shift supervisors who report to him or her. In turn, the shift supervisors head work groups composed of themselves and their respective subordinates. Thus, the hierarchy of most organizations is a series of formal, interlocked work groups.

Other types of formal work groups include task forces, project teams, and committees. *Task forces* and *project teams* are temporary groups that meet to achieve particular goals or to solve particular problems, such as suggesting productivity improvements. At IDEO, the design of products and services is accomplished via formal but temporary interdisciplinary project teams. *Committees* are usually permanent groups that handle recurrent assignments outside the usual work group structures. For example, a firm might have a standing committee on work–family balance.

Informal groups. Groups that emerge naturally in response to the common interests of organizational members.

In addition to formal groups sanctioned by management to achieve organizational goals, informal grouping occurs in all organizations. **Informal groups** are groups that emerge naturally in response to the common interests of organizational members. They are seldom sanctioned by the organization, and their membership often cuts across formal groups. Informal groups can either help or hurt an organization, depending on their norms for behaviour. We will consider this in detail later.

LO 7.1

Discuss group development.

GROUP DEVELOPMENT

Even relatively simple groups are actually complex social devices that require a fair amount of negotiation and trial and error before individual members begin to function as a true group. While employees often know each other before new teams are formed, simple familiarity does not replace the necessity for team development.

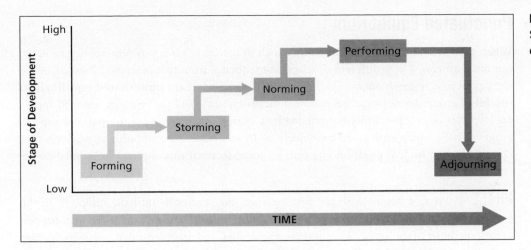

EXHIBIT 7.1
Stages of group development.

Typical Stages of Group Development

Leaders and trainers have observed that many groups develop through a series of stages over time.[2] Each stage presents the members with a series of challenges they must master to achieve the next stage. These stages (forming, storming, norming, performing, and adjourning) are presented in Exhibit 7.1.

FORMING At this early stage, group members try to orient themselves by "testing the waters." What are we doing here? What are the others like? What is our purpose? The situation is often ambiguous, and members are aware of their dependency on each other.

STORMING At this second stage, conflict often emerges. Confrontation and criticism occur as members determine whether they will go along with the way the group is developing. Sorting out roles and responsibilities is often at issue here. Problems are more likely to happen earlier, rather than later, in group development.

NORMING At this stage, members resolve the issues that provoked the storming, and they develop social consensus. Compromise is often necessary. Interdependence is recognized, norms are agreed to, and the group becomes more cohesive. (We will study these processes later.) Information and opinions flow freely.

PERFORMING With its social structure sorted out, the group devotes its energies toward task accomplishment. Achievement, creativity, and mutual assistance are prominent themes of this stage.

ADJOURNING Some groups, such as task forces and design project teams, have a definite lifespan and disperse after achieving their goals. Also, some groups disperse when corporate layoffs and downsizing occur. At this adjourning stage, rites and rituals that affirm the group's previous successful development are common (such as ceremonies and parties). Members often exhibit emotional support for each other.[3]

The stages model is a good tool for monitoring and troubleshooting how groups are developing. However, not all groups go through these stages of development. The process applies mainly to new groups that have never met before. Well-acquainted task forces and committees can short-circuit these stages when they have a new problem to work out.[4] Also, some organizational settings are so structured that storming and norming are unnecessary for even strangers to coalesce into a team. For example, most commercial airline cockpit crews perform effectively even though they can be made up of virtual strangers who meet just before takeoff.[5]

Punctuated Equilibrium

Punctuated equilibrium model. A model of group development that describes how groups with deadlines are affected by their first meetings and crucial midpoint transitions.

When groups have a specific deadline by which to complete some problem-solving task, we can often observe a very different development sequence from that described above. Connie Gersick, whose research uncovered this sequence, describes it as a **punctuated equilibrium model** of group development.[6] *Equilibrium* means stability, and the research revealed apparent stretches of group stability punctuated by a critical first meeting, a midpoint change in group activity, and a rush to task completion. In addition to many business work groups, Gersick studied student groups doing class projects, so see if this sequence of events sounds familiar to you.

PHASE 1   Phase 1 begins with the first meeting and continues until the midpoint in the group's existence. The very first meeting is critical in setting the agenda for what will happen in the remainder of this phase. Assumptions, approaches, and precedents that members develop in the first meeting end up dominating the first half of the group's life. Although it gathers information and holds meetings, the group makes little visible progress toward the goal.

MIDPOINT TRANSITION   The midpoint transition occurs at almost exactly the halfway point in time toward the group's deadline. For instance, if the group has a two-month deadline, the transition will occur at about one month. The transition marks a change in the group's approach, and how the group manages the change is critical for the group to show progress. The need to move forward is apparent, and the group may seek outside advice. This transition may consolidate previously acquired information or even mark a completely new approach, but it crystallizes the group's activities for Phase 2 just as the first meeting did for Phase 1.

PHASE 2   For better or for worse, decisions and approaches adopted at the midpoint get played out in Phase 2. It concludes with a final meeting that reveals a burst of activity and a concern for how outsiders will evaluate the product.

Exhibit 7.2 shows how the punctuated equilibrium model works for groups that successfully or unsuccessfully manage the midpoint transition.

What advice does the punctuated equilibrium model offer for managing product development teams, advertising groups, or class project groups?[7]

- Prepare carefully for the first meeting. What is decided here will strongly determine what happens in the rest of Phase 1. If you are the coach or adviser of the group, stress *motivation and excitement* about the project.

- As long as people are working, do not look for radical progress during Phase 1.

EXHIBIT 7.2
The punctuated equilibrium model of group development for two groups.

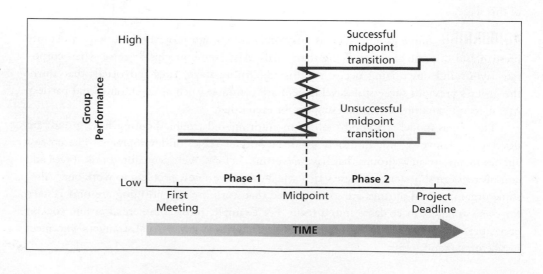

- Manage the midpoint transition carefully. Evaluate the strengths and weaknesses of the ideas that people generated in Phase 1. Clarify any questions with whoever is commissioning your work. Recognize that a fundamental change in approach must occur here for progress to occur. Essential issues are not likely to "work themselves out" during Phase 2. At this point, a group coach should focus on the *strategy* to be used in Phase 2.

- Be sure that adequate resources are available to actually execute the Phase 2 plan.

- Resist deadline changes. These could damage the midpoint transition.

As noted, the concept of punctuated equilibrium applies to groups with deadlines. Such groups might also exhibit some of the stages of development noted earlier, with a new cycle of storming and norming following the midpoint transition.

GROUP STRUCTURE AND ITS CONSEQUENCES

LO **7.2**

Explain how group size and member diversity influence what occurs in groups.

Group structure refers to the characteristics of the stable social organization of a group—the way a group is "put together." The most basic structural characteristics along which groups vary are size and member diversity. Other structural characteristics are the expectations that members have about each other's behaviour (norms), agreements about "who does what" in the group (roles), the rewards and prestige allocated to various group members (status), and how attractive the group is to its members (cohesiveness).

Group Size

Of one thing we can be certain—the smallest possible group consists of two people, such as a manager and a particular employee. It is possible to engage in much theoretical nitpicking about just what constitutes an upper limit on group size. However, given the definition of group that we presented earlier, it would seem that congressional or parliamentary size (300 to 400 members) is somewhere close to this limit. In practice, most work groups, including task forces and committees, usually have between 3 and 20 members.

SIZE AND SATISFACTION The more the merrier? In theory, yes. In fact, however, members of larger groups rather consistently report less satisfaction with group membership than those who find themselves in smaller groups.[8] What accounts for this apparent contradiction?

For one thing, as opportunities for friendship increase, the chance to work on and develop these opportunities might decrease owing to the sheer time and energy required. In addition, in incorporating more members with different viewpoints, larger groups might prompt conflict and dissension, which work against member satisfaction. As group size increases, the time available for verbal participation by each member decreases. Also, many people are inhibited about participating in larger groups.[9] Finally, in larger groups, individual members identify less easily with the success and accomplishments of the group. For example, a particular member of a 4-person cancer research team should be able to identify his or her personal contributions to a research breakthrough more easily than a member of a 20-person team can.

SIZE AND PERFORMANCE Satisfaction aside, do large groups perform tasks better than small groups? This question has great relevance to practical organizational decisions: How many people should a bank assign to evaluate loan applications? How many carpenters should a construction company assign to build a garage? If a school system decides to implement team teaching, how big should the teams be? The answers to these and similar questions depend on the exact task that the group needs to accomplish and on how we define good performance.[10]

Additive tasks. Tasks in which group performance is dependent on the sum of the performance of individual group members.

Disjunctive tasks. Tasks in which group performance is dependent on the performance of the best group member.

Process losses. Group performance difficulties stemming from the problems of motivating and coordinating larger groups.

Conjunctive tasks. Tasks in which group performance is limited by the performance of the poorest group member.

EXHIBIT 7.3
Relationships among group size, productivity, and process losses.
Source: Data from Steiner, I.D. (1972). *Group process and productivity.* New York: Academic Press, p. 96.

Some tasks are **additive tasks**. This means that we can predict potential performance by adding the performances of individual group members together. Building a house is an additive task, and we can estimate potential speed of construction by adding the efforts of individual carpenters. Thus, for additive tasks, the potential performance of the group increases with group size.

Some tasks are **disjunctive tasks**. This means that the potential performance of the group depends on the performance of its *best member*. For example, suppose that a research team is looking for a single error in a complicated computer program. In this case, the performance of the team might hinge on its containing at least one bright, attentive, logical-minded individual. Obviously, the potential performance of groups doing disjunctive tasks also increases with group size because the probability that the group includes a superior performer is greater.

We use the term "potential performance" consistently in the preceding two paragraphs for the following reason: As groups performing tasks get bigger, they tend to suffer from process losses.[11] **Process losses** are performance difficulties that stem from the problems of motivating and coordinating larger groups. Even with good intentions, problems of communication and decision making increase with size—imagine 50 carpenters trying to build a house. Thus, actual performance = potential performance − process losses.

These points are summarized in Exhibit 7.3. As you can see in part (a), both potential performance and process losses increase with group size for additive and disjunctive tasks. The net effect is shown in part (b), which demonstrates that actual performance increases with size up to a point and then falls off. Part (c) shows that the *average* performance of group members decreases as size gets bigger. Thus, up to a point, larger groups might perform better as groups, but their individual members tend to be less efficient.

We should note one other kind of task. **Conjunctive tasks** are those in which the performance of the group is limited by its *poorest performer*. For example, an assembly-line

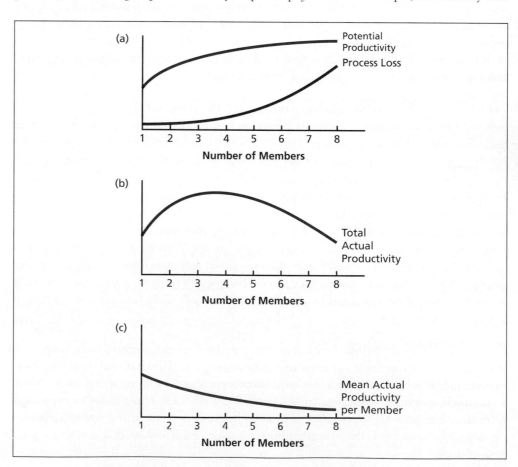

operation is limited by its weakest link. Also, if team teaching is the technique used to train employees how to perform a complicated, sequential job, one poor teacher in the sequence will severely damage the effectiveness of the team. Both the potential and actual performance of conjunctive tasks would decrease as group size increases, because the probability of including a weak link in the group goes up.

In summary, for additive and disjunctive tasks, larger groups might perform better up to a point but at increasing costs to the efficiency of individual members. By any standard, performance on purely conjunctive tasks should decrease as group size increases.

Diversity of Group Membership

Imagine an eight-member product development task force composed exclusively of 30-something white males of Western European heritage. Then imagine another task force with 50 percent men and 50 percent women from eight different ethnic or racial backgrounds and an age range from 25 to 55. The first group is obviously homogeneous in its membership, while the latter is heterogeneous or diverse. Which task force do you think would develop more quickly as a group? Which would be most creative?

Group diversity has a strong impact on interaction patterns—more diverse groups have a more difficult time communicating effectively and becoming cohesive (we will study cohesiveness in more detail shortly).[12] This means that diverse groups might tend to take longer to do their forming, storming, and norming.[13] Once they do develop, more and less diverse groups can be equally cohesive and productive.[14] However, diverse groups sometimes perform better on certain tasks. For example, diversity in educational background and functional specialty (e.g., marketing versus product design) enhances team creativity and innovation because a wider variety of ideas are considered.[15] In general, any negative effects of "surface diversity" in age, gender, or race are small or wear off over time. For instance, age diversity is unrelated to group performance, while racial and gender diversity have small negative effects.[16] However, "deep diversity" in attitudes toward work or how to accomplish a goal can badly damage cohesiveness.[17]

All this speaks well for the concepts of valuing and managing diversity, which we discussed in Chapter 3. When management values and manages diversity, it offsets some of the initial process loss costs of diversity and capitalizes on its benefits for group performance.

Group Norms

Social **norms** are collective expectations that members of social units have regarding the behaviour of each other. As such, they are codes of conduct that specify what individuals ought and ought not to do and standards against which we evaluate the appropriateness of behaviour.

Much normative influence is unconscious, and we are often aware of such influence only in special circumstances, such as when we see children struggling to master adult norms or international visitors sparring with the norms of our culture. We also become conscious of norms when we encounter ones that seem to conflict with each other ("Get ahead" but "Don't step on others") or when we enter new social situations. For instance, the first day on a new job, workers frequently search for cues about what is considered proper office etiquette: Should I call the boss "mister"? Can I personalize my workspace?

NORM DEVELOPMENT *Why* do norms develop? The most important function that norms serve is to provide regularity and predictability to behaviour. This consistency provides important psychological security and permits us to carry out our daily business with minimal disruption.

What do norms develop *about*? Norms develop to regulate behaviours that are considered at least marginally important to their supporters. For example, managers are more

Simulate

TEAMS

LO 7.3

Review how *norms*, *roles*, and *status* affect social interaction.

Norms. Collective expectations that members of social units have regarding the behaviour of each other.

likely to adopt norms regarding the performance and attendance of employees than norms concerning how employees personalize and decorate their offices. In general, less deviation is accepted from norms that concern more important behaviours.

How do norms develop? As we discussed in Chapter 4, individuals develop attitudes as a function of a related belief and value. In many cases, their attitudes affect their behaviour. When the members of a group *share* related beliefs and values, we can expect them to share consequent attitudes. These shared attitudes then form the basis for norms.[18] Notice that it really does not make sense to talk about "my personal norm." Norms are *collectively* held expectations, depending on two or more people for their existence.

Why do individuals tend to comply with norms? Much compliance occurs simply because the norm corresponds to privately held attitudes. In addition, even when norms support trivial social niceties (such as when to shake hands or when to look serious), they often save time and prevent social confusion. Most interesting, however, is the case in which individuals comply with norms that *go against* their privately held attitudes and opinions. For example, couples without religious convictions frequently get married in religious services, and people who hate neckties often wear them to work. In short, groups have an extraordinary range of rewards and punishments available to induce conformity to norms.

SOME TYPICAL NORMS
There are some classes of norms that seem to crop up in most organizations and affect the behaviour of members. They include the following:

- *Dress norms.* Social norms frequently dictate the kind of clothing people wear to work.[19] Military and quasi-military organizations tend to invoke formal norms that support polished buttons and razor-sharp creases. Even in organizations that have adopted casual dress policies, employees often express considerable concern about what they wear at work. Such is the power of social norms.

- *Reward allocation norms.* There are at least four norms that might dictate how rewards, such as pay, promotions, and informal favours could be allocated in organizations:

    a. Equity—reward according to inputs, such as effort, performance, or seniority.

    b. Equality—reward everyone equally.

    c. Reciprocity—reward people the way they reward you.

    d. Social responsibility—reward those who truly need the reward.[20]

    Most Western organizations tend to stress allocation according to some combination of equity and equality—give employees what they deserve, and no favouritism.

- *Performance norms.* The performance of organizational members might be as much a function of social expectations as it is of inherent ability, personal motivation, or technology.[21] Work groups provide their members with potent cues about what an appropriate level of performance is. New group members are alert for these cues: Is it all right to take a break now? Under what circumstances can I be absent from work without being punished? The official organizational norms that managers send to employees usually favour high performance. However, work groups often establish their own informal performance norms, such as those that restrict productivity under a piece-rate pay system. In accordance with the discussion in Chapter 5, groups that set specific, challenging goals will perform at a high level.[22]

Roles

Roles. Positions in a group that have a set of expected behaviours attached to them.

Roles are positions in a group that have a set of expected behaviours attached to them. Thus, roles represent "packages" of norms that apply to particular group members. As we implied in the previous section, many norms apply to all group members to be sure that they engage in *similar* behaviours (such as restricting productivity or dressing a certain way). However,

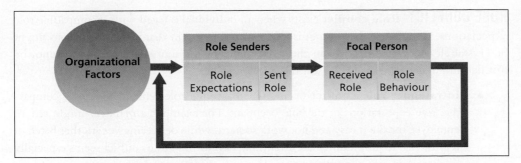

EXHIBIT 7.4
A model of the role assumption process.
Source: Adapted from Katz, D. et al. (1966, 1978). *The Social Psychology of Organizations*, 2nd edition, p. 196. © 1966, 1978 John Wiley & Sons Inc. New York. Reprinted by permission of John Wiley & Sons, Inc.

the development of roles is indicative of the fact that group members might also be required to act *differently* from one another.

In organizations, we find two basic kinds of roles. Designated or *assigned roles* are formally prescribed by an organization as a means of dividing labour and responsibility to facilitate task achievement. In general, assigned roles indicate "who does what" and "who can tell others what to do." In a software firm, labels that we might apply to formal roles include president, software engineer, analyst, programmer, and sales manager. In addition to assigned roles, we invariably see the development of *emergent roles*. These are roles that develop naturally to meet the social-emotional needs of group members or to assist in formal job accomplishment. The class clown and the office gossip fulfill emergent social-emotional roles, while an "old pro" might emerge to assist new group members learn their jobs. Other emergent roles might be assumed by informal leaders or by scapegoats who are the targets of group hostility.

ROLE AMBIGUITY **Role ambiguity** exists when the goals of one's job or the methods of performing it are unclear. Ambiguity might be characterized by confusion about how performance is evaluated, how good performance can be achieved, or what the limits of one's authority and responsibility are.

Exhibit 7.4 shows a model of the process that is involved in assuming an organizational role. As you can see, certain organizational factors lead role senders (such as managers) to develop role expectations and "send" roles to focal people (such as employees). The focal person "receives" the role and then tries to engage in behaviour to fulfill the role. This model reveals a variety of elements that can lead to ambiguity.

- *Organizational factors.* Some roles seem inherently ambiguous because of their function in the organization. For example, middle management roles might fail to provide the "big picture" that upper management roles do. Also, middle management roles do not require the attention to supervision necessary in lower management roles.

- *The role sender.* Role senders might have unclear expectations of a focal person. Even when the sender has specific role expectations, they might be ineffectively sent to the focal person. A weak orientation session, vague performance reviews, or inconsistent feedback and discipline may send ambiguous role messages to employees.

- *The focal person.* Even role expectations that are clearly developed and sent might not be fully digested by the focal person. This is especially true when he or she is new to the role. Ambiguity tends to decrease as length of time in the job role increases.[23]

What are the practical consequences of role ambiguity? The most frequent outcomes appear to be job stress, dissatisfaction, reduced organizational commitment, lowered performance, and intentions to quit.[24] Managers can do much to reduce unnecessary role ambiguity by providing clear performance expectations and performance feedback, especially for new employees and for those in more intrinsically ambiguous jobs.

Role ambiguity. Lack of clarity of job goals or methods.

Role conflict. A condition of being faced with incompatible role expectations.

Intrasender role conflict. A single role sender provides incompatible role expectations to a role occupant.

Intersender role conflict. Two or more role senders provide a role occupant with incompatible expectations.

Interrole conflict. Several roles held by a role occupant involve incompatible expectations.

Person–role conflict. Role demands call for behaviour that is incompatible with the personality or skills of a role occupant.

ROLE CONFLICT **Role conflict** exists when an individual is faced with incompatible role expectations. Conflict can be distinguished from ambiguity in that role expectations might be crystal clear but incompatible in the sense that they are mutually exclusive, cannot be fulfilled simultaneously, or do not suit the role occupant.

- **Intrasender role conflict** occurs when a single role sender provides incompatible role expectations to the role occupant. For example, a manager might tell an employee to take it easy and not work so hard, while delivering yet another batch of reports that require immediate attention. This form of role conflict seems especially likely to also provoke ambiguity.

- If two or more role senders differ in their expectations for a role occupant, **intersender role conflict** can develop. Employees who straddle the boundary between the organization and its clients or customers are especially likely to encounter this form of conflict. Intersender conflict can also stem exclusively from within the organization. The classic example here is the first-level manager, who serves as the interface between "management" and "the workers." From above, the manager might be pressured to get the work out and keep the troops in line. From below, he or she might be encouraged to behave in a considerate and friendly manner.

- Organizational members necessarily play several roles at one time, especially if we include roles external to the organization. Often, the expectations inherent in these several roles are incompatible, and **interrole conflict** results.[25] One person, for example, might fulfill the roles of a functional expert in marketing, head of the market research group, subordinate to the vice-president of marketing, and member of a product development task force. This is obviously a busy person, and competing demands for her time are a frequent symptom of interrole conflict.

- Even when role demands are clear and otherwise congruent, they might be incompatible with the personality or skills of the role occupant—thus, **person–role conflict** results.[26] Many examples of "whistle-blowing" are signals of person–role conflict. The organization has demanded some role behaviour that the occupant considers unethical.

As with role ambiguity, the most consistent consequences of role conflict are job dissatisfaction, stress reactions, lowered organizational commitment, and turnover intentions.[27] Managers can help prevent employee role conflict by avoiding self-contradictory messages, conferring with other role senders, being sensitive to multiple role demands, and fitting the right person to the right role.

Status

Status. The rank, social position, or prestige accorded to group members.

Status is the rank, social position, or prestige accorded to group members. Put another way, it represents the group's *evaluation* of a member. Just *what* is evaluated depends on the status system in question. However, when a status system works smoothly, the group will exhibit clear norms about who should be accorded higher or lower status.

FORMAL STATUS SYSTEMS All organizations have both formal and informal status systems. Since formal systems are most obvious to observers, let's begin there. The formal status system represents management's attempt to publicly identify those people who have higher status than others. It is so obvious because this identification is implemented by the application of *status symbols* that are tangible indicators of status. Status symbols might include titles, particular working relationships, pay packages, work schedules, and the physical working environment. Just what are the criteria for achieving formal organizational status? One criterion is often seniority in one's work group. Employees who have been with the group longer might acquire the privilege of choosing day shift work or a more favourable office location. Even more important than seniority, however, is one's assigned role in the organization—one's job. Because they perform different jobs, secretaries, labourers, managers, and executives acquire different statuses. Organizations often go to great pains to tie status symbols to assigned roles.

Why do organizations go to all this trouble to differentiate status? For one thing, status and the symbols connected to it serve as powerful magnets to induce members to aspire to higher organizational positions (recall Maslow's need for self-esteem). Second, status differentiation reinforces the authority hierarchy in work groups and in the organization as a whole, since people *pay attention* to high-status individuals.

INFORMAL STATUS SYSTEMS In addition to formal status systems, one can detect informal status systems in organizations. Such systems are not well advertised, and they might lack the conspicuous symbols and systematic support that people usually accord the formal system. Nevertheless, they can operate just as effectively. Sometimes, job performance is a basis for the acquisition of informal status. The "power hitters" on a baseball team or the "cool heads" in a hospital emergency unit might be highly evaluated by co-workers for their ability to assist in task accomplishment. Some managers who perform well early in their careers are identified as "fast trackers" and given special job assignments that correspond to their elevated status. Just as frequently, though, informal status is linked to factors other than job performance, such as gender or race. For example, the man who takes a day off work to care for a sick child may be praised as a model father. The woman who does the same may be questioned about her work commitment.

CONSEQUENCES OF STATUS DIFFERENCES Status differences have a paradoxical effect on communication patterns. Most people like to communicate with others at their own status or higher rather than with people who are below them.[28] The result should be a tendency for communication to move up the status hierarchy. However, if status differences are large, people can be inhibited from communicating upward. These opposing effects mean that much communication gets stalled.

People pay attention to and respect status.[29] Thus, status also affects the amount of various group members' communication and their influence in group affairs. As you might guess, higher status members do more talking and have more influence.[30] Some of the most convincing evidence comes from studies of jury deliberations, in which jurors with higher social status (such as managers and professionals) participate more and have more effect on the verdict.[31] Unfortunately, there is no guarantee that the highest-status person is the most knowledgeable about the problem at hand!

REDUCING STATUS BARRIERS Although status differences can be powerful motivators, their tendency to inhibit the free flow of communication has led many organizations to downplay status differentiation by doing away with questionable status symbols. The goal is to foster a culture of teamwork and cooperation across the ranks, as seen in the IDEO vignette that opened the chapter. The high-tech culture of Silicon Valley is egalitarian and lacking in conspicuous status symbols, but even old-line industries are getting on the bandwagon, doing away with reserved parking and fancy offices for executives.

Some organizations employ phoney or misguided methods to bridge the status barrier. Some examples of "casual Friday" policies (which permit the wearing of casual clothes on Fridays) only underline status differences the rest of the week if no other cultural changes are made.

Many observers note that email has levelled status barriers.[32] High-speed transmission, direct access, and the opportunity to avoid live confrontation often encourage lower-status parties to communicate directly with organizational VIPs. This has even been seen in the rank-conscious military.

LO 7.4

Discuss the causes and consequences of *group cohesiveness*.

Group cohesiveness. The degree to which a group is attractive to its members.

GROUP COHESIVENESS

Group cohesiveness is a critical property of groups. Cohesive groups are those that are especially attractive to their members. Because of this attractiveness, members are especially desirous of staying in the group and tend to describe the group in favourable terms.[33]

The arch-stereotype of a cohesive group is the major league baseball team that begins September looking like a good bet to win its division and make it to the World Series. On the field we see well-oiled, precision teamwork. In the clubhouse, all is sweetness and joviality, and interviewed players tell the world how fine it is to be playing with "a great bunch of guys."

Cohesiveness is a relative, rather than absolute, property of groups. While some groups are more cohesive than others, there is no objective line between cohesive and non-cohesive groups. Thus, we will use the adjective *cohesive* to refer to groups that are more attractive than average for their members.

Factors Influencing Cohesiveness

What makes some groups more cohesive than others? Important factors include threat and competition, success, member diversity, group size, and toughness of initiation.

THREAT AND COMPETITION   External threat to the survival of the group increases cohesiveness in a wide variety of situations.[34] As an example, consider the wrangling, uncoordinated corporate board of directors that quickly forms a united front in the face of a takeover bid. Honest competition with another group can also promote cohesiveness.[35] This is the case with the World Series contenders.

Why do groups often become more cohesive in response to threat or competition? They probably feel a need to improve communication and coordination so that they can better cope with the situation at hand. Members now perceive the group as more attractive because it is seen as capable of doing what has to be done to ward off threat or to win. However, under *extreme* threat or very *unbalanced* competition, increased cohesiveness will serve little purpose. For example, the partners in a firm faced with certain financial disaster would be unlikely to exhibit cohesiveness, because it would do nothing to combat the severe threat.

SUCCESS   It should come as no surprise that a group becomes more attractive to its members when it has successfully accomplished some important goal, such as defending itself against threat or winning a prize.[36] By the same token, cohesiveness will decrease after failure, although there may be "misery loves company" exceptions. The situation for competition is shown graphically in Exhibit 7.5. Fit-Rite Jeans owns two small clothing stores (A and B) in a large city. To boost sales, it holds a contest between the two stores, offering $150 worth of merchandise to each employee of the store that achieves the highest sales during the next business quarter. Before the competition begins, the staff of each store is equally cohesive. As we suggested above, when competition begins, both groups become more cohesive. The members become more cooperative with each other, and in each store there is much talk about "us" versus "them." At the end of the quarter, store A wins the prize and becomes yet more cohesive. The group is especially attractive to its members because it has succeeded in the attainment of a desired goal. On the other hand, cohesiveness plummets in the losing store B—the group has become less attractive to its members.

MEMBER DIVERSITY   Earlier, we pointed out that groups that are diverse in terms of gender, age, and race can have a harder time becoming cohesive than more homogeneous groups. However, if the group is in agreement about how to accomplish some particular task, its success in performing the task will often outweigh surface dissimilarity in determining cohesiveness.[37]

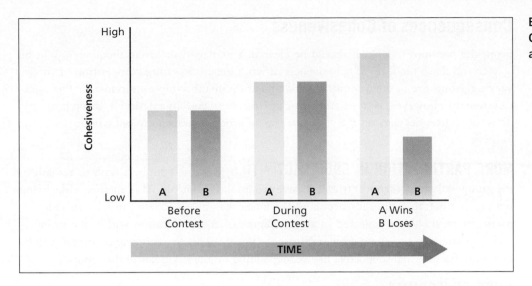

EXHIBIT 7.5
Competition, success, and cohesiveness.

GROUP SIZE Other things being equal, bigger groups should have a more difficult time becoming and staying cohesive. In general, such groups should have a more difficult time agreeing on goals and more problems communicating and coordinating efforts to achieve those goals. Large groups frequently divide into subgroups, and such subgrouping is contrary to the cohesiveness of the larger group.[38]

TOUGHNESS OF INITIATION Despite its rigorous admissions policies, the Harvard Business School does not lack applicants. Similarly, exclusive yacht and golf clubs might have waiting lists for membership extending several years into the future. All this suggests that groups that are tough to get into should be more attractive than those that are easy to join.[39] This is well known in the armed forces, where rigorous physical training and stressful "survival schools" precede entry into elite units such as the Canadian Special Operations Forces Command or the U.S. Army Rangers.

Cohesive groups lead to effective goal accomplishment.

Consequences of Cohesiveness

From the previous section, it should be clear that managers or group members might be able to influence the level of cohesiveness of work groups by using competition or threat, varying group size or composition, or manipulating membership requirements. The question remains, however, as to whether *more* or *less* cohesiveness is a desirable group property. This, of course, depends on the consequences of group cohesiveness and who is doing the judging.

MORE PARTICIPATION IN GROUP ACTIVITIES

Because members wish to remain in the group, voluntary turnover from cohesive groups should be low. Also, members like being with each other; therefore, absence should be lower than in less cohesive groups. In addition, participation should be reflected in a high degree of communication within the group as members strive to cooperate with and assist each other. This communication might well be of a more friendly and supportive nature, depending on the key goals of the group.[40]

MORE CONFORMITY

Because they are so attractive and coordinated, cohesive groups are well equipped to supply information, rewards, and punishment to individual members. These factors take on special significance when they are administered by those who hold a special interest for us. Thus, highly cohesive groups are in a superb position to induce conformity to group norms.

Members of cohesive groups are especially motivated to engage in activities that will *keep* the group cohesive. Chief among these activities is applying pressure to deviants to get them to comply with group norms. Cohesive groups react to deviants by increasing the amount of communication directed at these individuals.[41] Such communication contains information to help the deviant "see the light," as well as veiled threats about what might happen if he or she does not. Over time, if such communication is ineffective in inducing conformity, it tends to decrease. This is a signal that the group has isolated the deviant member to maintain cohesiveness among the majority.

MORE SUCCESS

Above, we pointed out that successful goal accomplishment contributes to group cohesiveness. However, it is also true that cohesiveness contributes to group success—in general, cohesive groups are good at achieving their goals. Research has found that group cohesiveness is related to performance.[42] Thus, there is a reciprocal relationship between success and cohesiveness.

Why are cohesive groups effective at goal accomplishment? Probably because of the other consequences of cohesiveness we discussed above. A high degree of participation and communication, coupled with active conformity to group norms and commitment, should ensure a high degree of agreement about the goals the group is pursuing and the methods it is using to achieve those goals. Thus, coordinated effort pays dividends to the group.

Since cohesiveness contributes to goal accomplishment, should managers attempt to increase the cohesiveness of work groups by juggling the factors that influence cohesiveness? To answer this question, we must emphasize that cohesive groups are especially effective at accomplishing *their own* goals. If these goals happen to correspond with those of the organization, increased cohesiveness should have substantial benefits for group performance. If not, organizational effectiveness might be threatened.[43] One large-scale study of work groups reached the following conclusions:

- In highly cohesive groups, the productivity of individual group members tends to be fairly similar to that of other members. In less cohesive groups there is more variation in productivity.

- Highly cohesive groups tend to be *more* or *less* productive than less cohesive groups, depending on a number of variables.[44]

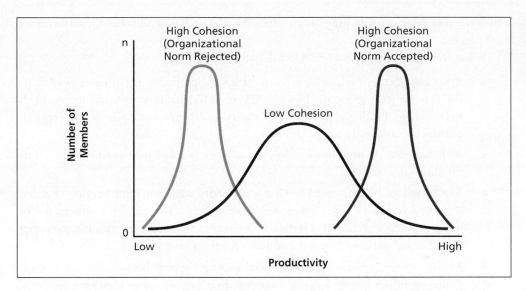

EXHIBIT 7.6
Hypothetical productivity curves for groups varying in cohesiveness.

These two facts are shown graphically in Exhibit 7.6. The lower variability of productivity in more cohesive groups stems from the power of such groups to induce conformity. To the extent that work groups have productivity norms, more cohesive groups should be better able to enforce them. Furthermore, if cohesive groups accept organizational norms regarding productivity, they should be highly productive. If cohesive groups reject such norms, they are especially effective in limiting productivity.

One other factor that influences the impact of cohesiveness on productivity is the extent to which the task really requires interdependence and cooperation among group members (e.g., a football team versus a golf team). Cohesiveness is more likely to pay off when the task requires more interdependence.[45]

In summary, cohesive groups tend to be successful in accomplishing what they wish to accomplish. In a good labour relations climate, group cohesiveness on interdependent tasks should contribute to high productivity. If the climate is marked by tension and disagreement, cohesive groups may pursue goals that result in low productivity.

SOCIAL LOAFING

Have you ever participated in a group project at work or school in which you did not contribute as much as you could have because other people were there to take up the slack? Or have you ever reduced your effort in a group project because you felt that others were not pulling their weight? If so, you have been guilty of social loafing. **Social loafing** is the tendency that people have to withhold physical or intellectual effort when they are performing a group task.[46] The implication is that they would work harder if they were alone rather than part of the group. Earlier we said that process losses in groups could be due to coordination problems or to motivation problems. Social loafing is a motivation problem.

People working in groups often feel trapped in a social dilemma, in that something that might benefit them individually—slacking off in the group—will result in poor group performance if everybody behaves the same way. Social loafers resolve the dilemma in a way that hurts organizational goal accomplishment. Notice that the tendency for social loafing is probably more pronounced in individualistic North America than in more collective and group-oriented cultures.

As the questions above suggest, social loafing has two different forms. In the *free rider effect*, people lower their effort to get a free ride at the expense of their fellow group members. In the *sucker effect*, people lower their effort because of the feeling that others are free riding, that is, they are trying to restore equity in the group. You can probably imagine a scenario in

LO **7.5**

Explain the dynamics of *social loafing*.

Social loafing. The tendency to withhold physical or intellectual effort when performing a group task.

which the free riders start slacking off and then the suckers follow suit. Group performance suffers badly.

What are some ways to counteract social loafing?[47]

- *Make individual performance more visible.* Where appropriate, the simplest way to do this is to keep the group small in size. Then, individual contributions are less likely to be hidden. Posting performance levels and making presentations of one's accomplishments can also facilitate visibility.

- *Make sure that the work is interesting.* If the work is involving, intrinsic motivation should counteract social loafing.

- *Increase feelings of indispensability.* Group members might slack off because they feel that their inputs are unnecessary for group success. This can be counteracted by using training and the status system to provide group members with unique inputs (e.g., having one person master computer graphics programs).

- *Increase performance feedback.* Some social loafing happens because groups or individual members simply are not aware of their performance. Increased feedback, as appropriate, from the boss, peers, and customers (internal or external) should encourage self-correction.

- *Reward group performance.* Members are more likely to monitor and maximize their own performance (and attend to that of their colleagues) when the *group* receives rewards for effectiveness.[48]

WHAT IS A TEAM?

Some have suggested that a team is something more than a group. They suggest that a group becomes a team when there exists a strong sense of shared commitment and when a synergy develops such that the group's efforts are greater than the sum of its parts.[49] While such differences might be evident in some instances, our definition of a group is sufficient to describe most teams that can be found in organizations. The term *team* is generally used to describe "groups" in organizational settings. Therefore, for our purposes in this chapter, we use the terms interchangeably. Teams have become a major building block of organizations and are now quite common in North America.[50] Research has shown improvements in organizational performance in terms of both efficiency and quality as a result of team-based work arrangements.[51]

Collective efficacy.
Shared beliefs that a team can successfully perform a given task.

You will recall that in Chapter 2 we defined self-efficacy as beliefs individuals have about their ability to successfully perform a task. When it comes to teams, collective efficacy is also important to ensure high performance.[52] **Collective efficacy** consists of *shared* beliefs that a team can successfully perform a given task. Notice that self-efficacy does not necessarily translate into collective efficacy—five skilled musicians do not necessarily result in a good band. In the following sections we cover the factors that contribute to collective efficacy in a team.

DESIGNING EFFECTIVE WORK TEAMS

The double-edged nature of group cohesiveness suggests that a delicate balance of factors dictates whether a work group is effective or ineffective. In turn, this suggests that organizations should pay considerable attention to how work groups are designed and managed.

A good model for thinking about the design of effective work groups is to consider a successful sports team. In most cases, such teams are small groups made up of highly skilled individuals who are able to meld these skills into a cohesive effort. The task they are performing is intrinsically motivating and provides very direct feedback. If there are status

PERSONAL INVENTORY ASSESSMENT
Learn About Yourself
Team Development Behaviours

differences on the team, the basis for these differences is contribution to the team, not some extraneous factor. The team shows an obsessive concern with obtaining the right personnel, relying on tryouts or player drafts, and the team is coached, not supervised. With this informal model in mind, let's examine the concept of group effectiveness more closely.

J. Richard Hackman (co-developer of the Job Characteristics Model, Chapter 6) has written extensively about work group effectiveness.[53] According to Hackman, a work group is effective when (1) its physical or intellectual output is acceptable to management and to the other parts of the organization that use this output, (2) group members' needs are satisfied rather than frustrated by the group, and (3) the group experience enables members to *continue* to work together.

What leads to group effectiveness? In colloquial language, "sweat, smarts, and style." Put more formally, as Hackman notes, group effectiveness occurs when high effort is directed toward the group's task, when great knowledge and skill are directed toward the task, and when the group adopts sensible strategies for accomplishing its goals. And just how does an organization achieve this? There is growing awareness in many organizations that the answer is self-managed work teams.

Self-Managed Work Teams

LO 7.6

Discuss how to design and support *self-managed teams*.

Self-managed work teams. Work groups that have the opportunity to do challenging work under reduced supervision.

Self-managed work teams generally provide their members with the opportunity to do challenging work under reduced supervision. Other labels that we often apply to such groups are autonomous, semi-autonomous, and self-directed. The general idea, which is more important than the label, is that the groups regulate much of their own members' behaviour. Much interest in such teams was spurred by the success of teams in Japanese industry. Critical to the success of self-managed teams are the nature of the task, the composition of the group, and the various support mechanisms in place.[54]

TASKS FOR SELF-MANAGED TEAMS Experts agree that tasks assigned to self-managed work teams should be complex and challenging, requiring high interdependence among team members for accomplishment. In general, these tasks should have the qualities of enriched jobs (Chapter 6). Thus, teams should see the task as significant, they should perform the task from beginning to end, and they should use a variety of skills. Self-managed teams have to have something useful to self-manage, and it is fairly complex tasks that capitalize on the diverse knowledge and skills of a group. Taking a number of olive stuffers on a food-processing assembly line, putting them in distinctive jumpsuits, calling them the Olive Squad, and telling them to self-manage will be unlikely to yield dividends in terms of effort expended or brainpower employed. The basic task will still be boring, a prime recipe for social loafing!

Outside the complexity requirement, the actual range of tasks for which organizations have used self-managed teams is wide, spanning both blue- and white-collar jobs. In the white-collar domain, complex service and design jobs seem especially conducive to self-management. In the blue-collar domain, General Mills and Chaparral Steel of Midlothian, Texas, make extensive use of self-managed work groups. In general, these groups are responsible for dividing labour among various subtasks as they see fit and making a variety of decisions about matters that impinge on the group. When a work site is formed from scratch and lacks an existing culture, the range of these activities can be very broad. Consider the self-managed teams formed in a new U.K. confectionery plant.

Production employees worked in groups of 8 to 12 people, all of whom were expected to carry out each of eight types of jobs involved in the production process. Group members were collectively responsible for allocating jobs among themselves, reaching production targets and meeting quality and hygiene standards, solving local production problems, recording production data for information systems, organizing breaks, ordering and collecting raw materials and delivering finished goods to stores, calling for engineering support, and training new recruits. They also participated in selecting new employees. Within each group, individuals had considerable control over the amount of variety they experienced by rotating their tasks, and each production group was responsible for one product line. Group members interacted informally throughout the working day but made the most important decisions—for example, regarding job allocation—at formal weekly group meetings where performance was also discussed.[55]

If a theme runs through this discussion of tasks for self-managed teams, it is the breakdown of traditional, conventional, specialized *roles* in the group. Group members adopt roles that will make the group effective, not ones that are simply related to a narrow specialty.

COMPOSITION OF SELF-MANAGED TEAMS

How should organizations assemble self-managed teams to ensure effectiveness? "Stable, small, and smart" might be a fast answer.[56]

- *Stability.* Self-managed teams require considerable interaction and high cohesiveness among their members. This, in turn, requires understanding and trust. To achieve this, group membership must be fairly stable. Rotating members into and out of the group will cause it to fail to develop a true group identity.[57]

- *Size.* In keeping with the demands of the task, self-managed teams should be as small as is feasible. The goal here is to keep coordination problems and social loafing to a minimum. These negative factors can be a problem for all groups, but they can be especially difficult for self-managed groups. This is because reduced supervision means that there is no boss to coordinate the group's activities and search out social loafers who do not do their share of the work.

- *Expertise.* Group members should have a high level of expertise about the task at hand. Everybody does not have to know everything, but the group as a *whole* should be very knowledgeable about the task. Again, reduced supervision discourages "running to the boss" when problems arise, but the group must have the resources to successfully solve these problems. One set of skills that all members should probably possess to some degree is social skills. Understanding how to talk things out, communicate effectively, and resolve conflict is especially important.

- *Diversity.* Put simply, a team should have members who are similar enough to work well together and diverse enough to bring a variety of perspectives and skills to the task at hand. A product-planning group consisting exclusively of new male MBAs might work well together but lack the different perspectives that are necessary for creativity.

One way of maintaining appropriate group composition might be to let the group choose its own members, as occurred at the confectionery plant we described above. A potential problem with this is that the group might use some irrelevant criterion (such as race or gender) to unfairly exclude others. Thus, human resources department oversight is necessary, as are very clear selection criteria (in terms of behaviours, skills, and credentials). The selection stage is critical, since some studies (including the one conducted in the confectionary plant) have shown elevated turnover in self-managed teams.[58] Such turnover can damage team effectiveness because it reduces the capacity for the team to learn and adapt.[59] Thus, "fit" is important, and it is well worth expending the extra effort to find the right people. At Britain's Pret A Manger sandwich and coffee shops, job seekers work in a shop for a day and then the staff votes on whether they can join the team.[60]

The theme running through this discussion of team composition favours *high cohesiveness* and the development of group *norms* that stress group effectiveness.

SUPPORTING SELF-MANAGED TEAMS

A number of support factors can assist self-managed teams in becoming and staying effective. Reports of problems with teams can usually be traced back to inadequate support.

- *Training.* In almost every conceivable instance, members of self-managed teams require extensive training. The kind of training depends on the exact job design and on the needs of the workforce. However, some common areas include:

  - *Technical training.* This might include math, computer use, or any tasks that a supervisor formerly handled. Cross-training in the specialties of other teammates is common.

  - *Social skills.* Assertiveness, problem solving, and routine dispute resolution are skills that help the team operate smoothly.

  - *Language skills.* This can be important for ethnically diverse teams. Good communication is critical on self-managed teams.

  - *Business training.* Some firms provide training in the basic elements of finance, accounting, and production so that employees can better grasp how their team's work fits into the larger picture.

- *Rewards.* The general rule here is to mostly tie rewards to team accomplishment rather than to individual accomplishment, while still providing team members with some individual performance feedback to counteract social loafing. Microsoft's European product support group went from individual rewards to team-based rewards when it found that the former discouraged engineers from taking on difficult cases.[61] Gain sharing, profit sharing, and skill-based pay (Chapter 6) are compatible reward systems for a team environment. Skill-based pay is especially attractive because it rewards the acquisition of multiple skills that can support the team.

- *Management.* Self-management will not receive the best support when managers feel threatened and see it as reducing their own power or promotion opportunities. Some schooled in the traditional role of manager may simply not adapt. Those who do can serve important functions by mediating relations *between* teams and by dealing with union concerns, since unions are often worried about the cross-functional job sharing in self-management. One study found that the most effective managers in a self-management environment encouraged groups to observe, evaluate, and reinforce their own task behaviour.[62] This suggests that coaching teams to be independent enhances their effectiveness.[63]

Exhibit 7.7 summarizes the factors that determine work group effectiveness. Michael Campion and colleagues studied these factors in teams of professional and non-professional workers.[64] Their results provide strong support for many of the relationships shown in the

PERSONAL INVENTORY ASSESSMENT

Learn About Yourself
Team Competencies

EXHIBIT 7.7
Factors influencing work group effectiveness.
Source: Based in part on Hackman, J.R. (1987). "The Design of Work Teams" in J.W. Lorsch (Ed.), *Handbook of organizational behaviour.* Englewood Cliffs, NJ: Pearson Education.

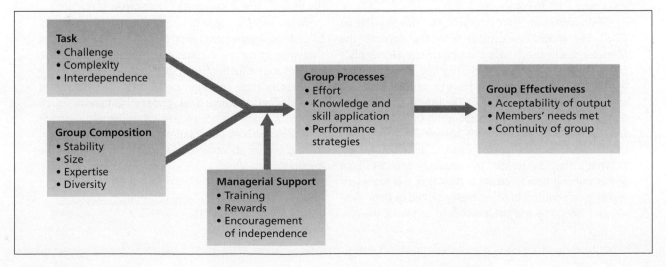

exhibit. Overall, research has shown improvements in team productivity, quality, customer satisfaction, and safety following the implementation of self-managed work teams.[65] For an example of a team with extraordinary need for good support, see Research Focus: *Supporting Teamwork on the Mission to Mars.*

RESEARCH FOCUS

SUPPORTING TEAMWORK ON THE MISSION TO MARS

Usually when co-workers irritate each other, they can let off steam by spending time with family or going for a jog. But in the cramped quarters of a space capsule, it's tough to find a place to decompress after a challenging workday. And over time, little disagreements can erode an astronaut's ability to function as part of a team, says Eduardo Salas, PhD, an industrial-organizational psychologist at the University of Central Florida (UCF). "It's not like someone can leave if they're not getting along," says Salas. "Team cohesion is paramount to success." In fact, a space mission can be disastrous without it. Errors indirectly caused by team members' conflicts can have dire consequences. "People can die," he says. To avert such human error, Salas and several other industrial-organizational psychologists are using NASA funding to conduct research that helps inform the team selection and training for the agency's mission to Mars, tentatively scheduled for 2030.

"No one has traveled that far out in space for that long, so it's not like we can take a look at research that's been done elsewhere," says Scott Tannenbaum, president of the consulting firm The Group for Organizational Effectiveness. "Probably the closest thing to the environment these astronauts will face is if you go back hundreds of years and look at the ships that crossed the ocean. So it's an interesting, exciting and important area of research to which I think psychologists have a lot to contribute."

"Astronauts at the International Space Station (ISS) live spaciously compared to the capsule the Mars team will use," says Michigan State University's Steve Kozlowski, PhD, who is using the NASA funding his team received to develop tools to monitor the Mars team's cohesiveness over time. The International Space Station's length and width is about the size of a football field. The Mars capsule, while not yet developed, will likely be closer to the size of a small kitchen.

That's the key reason Tannenbaum and his team are examining how to create a crew that will work well together in addition to being highly skilled at their individual tasks. "It's not just a matter of us taking the four or five most individually capable individuals and assuming that's going to make a good team for a three-year mission in that type of isolated, confined, and extreme environment," Tannenbaum says. "For example, can you imagine a team that's made up of all very strong challengers who tend to question a lot of things? Nothing would ever get done. But similarly, having a team that has none of them is a problem as well."

"A spat with one team member can lead to isolation or depression, and can affect not just the interactions with that team member but between all team members," Kozlowski says. How often will the team face such issues and how will they recover? Kozlowski and his colleagues are studying the dynamics of NASA teams living in environments such as Antarctica, which is similar to the extreme space environment the Mars team will face. They're also working with a group of engineers to develop a wireless "badge" that astronauts would wear to monitor team collaboration and cohesion while the Mars team is in transit. The badges would have motion detection built in and could monitor which astronaut approached the other, as well as the vocal intensity, heart rate, and face-time distance between other sensor-wearing team members. "From that, we might infer that there was an argument or altercation, and then we could monitor subsequent interactions more closely, provide the crew with feedback and alert the ground crew if necessary," Kozlowski says.

Salas and his team are using their NASA funding to develop, implement, and evaluate interventions to maximize space crew cohesion and mitigate negative psychosocial effects of long-duration missions, as well as measure crew cohesion over time. They're focused on identifying stressors among spaceflight crews—such as lack of space and privacy—and working to pinpoint strategies, such as team self-correction and regulation, to help astronauts cope with such stressors during the mission.

Source: Excerpted from Novotney, A. (2013, March). I/O psychology goes to Mars. *Monitor on Psychology*, 38–41.

Cross-Functional Teams

LO **7.7**

Let's look at another kind of team that contemporary organizations are using with increasing frequency. **Cross-functional teams** bring people with different functional specialties together to better invent, design, or deliver a product or service. For example, recall that the IDEO Kentucky public housing project brought together experts in architecture, design, anthropology, and psychology.

Explain the logic behind *cross-functional teams*, and describe how they can operate effectively.

A cross-functional team might be self-managed and permanent if it is doing a recurrent task that is not too complex. If the task is complex and unique (such as designing a car), cross-functional teams require formal leadership, and their lives will generally be limited to the life of the specific project. In both cases, the "cross-functional" label means that such diverse specialties are necessary that cross-training is not feasible. People have to be experts in their own area but able to cooperate with others.

Cross-functional teams. Work groups that bring people with different functional specialties together to better invent, design, or deliver a product or service.

Cross-functional teams, which have been used in service industries such as banking and hospitals, are probably best known for their successes in product development.[66] Thus, Rubbermaid uses teams to invent and design a remarkable variety of innovative household products. Pharmaceutical development teams at Novartis and Wyeth include toxicologists, biologists, clinicians, chemists, and marketers.

The general goals of using cross-functional teams include some combination of innovation, speed, and quality that comes from early coordination among the various specialties. We can see their value by looking at the traditional way auto manufacturers used to design cars in North America.[67] First, stylists determined what the car would look like and then passed their design on to engineering, which developed mechanical specifications and blueprints. In turn, manufacturing considered how to construct what the stylists and engineers designed. Somewhere down the line, marketing and accounting got their say. This process invariably leads to problems. One link in the chain might have a difficult time understanding what the previous link meant. Worse, one department might resist the ideas of another simply because they "were not invented here." The result of all this is slow, expensive development and early quality problems. In contrast, the cross-functional approach gets all the specialties working together from day one. A complex project, such as a car design, might have over 30 cross-functional teams working at the same time.

The speed factor can be dramatic. Manufacturers have reduced the development of a new car model by several years. Boeing used a cross-functional team to reduce certain design analyses from two weeks to only a few minutes.

PRINCIPLES FOR EFFECTIVENESS
A number of factors contribute to the effectiveness of cross-functional teams. We will illustrate several with examples from a past redesign of the Ford Mustang.[68]

- *Composition.* All relevant specialties are necessary, and effective teams are sure not to overlook anyone. Auto companies put labour representatives on car design teams to warn of assembly problems. On the Mustang project, outside suppliers were represented. At IDEO, clients are represented on design teams.

- *Superordinate goals.* **Superordinate goals** are attractive outcomes that can be achieved only by collaboration. They override detailed functional objectives that might be in conflict (e.g., finance versus design). On the Mustang project, the superordinate goal was to keep the legendary name alive in the face of corporate cost cutting.

Superordinate goals. Attractive outcomes that can be achieved only by collaboration.

- *Physical proximity.* Team members have to be located (sometimes relocated) close to each other to facilitate informal contact. Mustang used a former furniture warehouse in Allen Park, Michigan, to house its teams.

- *Autonomy.* Cross-functional teams need some autonomy from the larger organization, and functional specialists need some authority to commit their function to project decisions. This prevents meddling or "micromanaging" by upper-level or functional managers.

- *Rules and procedures.* Although petty rules and procedures are to be avoided, some basic decision procedures must be laid down to prevent anarchy. On the Mustang project, it was agreed that a single manufacturing person would have a veto over radical body changes.

- *Leadership.* Because of the potential for conflict, cross-functional team leaders need especially strong people skills in addition to task expertise. The "tough engineer" who headed the Mustang project succeeded in developing his people skills for that task.

Shared mental models.
Team members share identical information about how they should interact and what their task is.

Several of these principles ensure that team members share mental models. **Shared mental models** mean that team members share identical information about how they should interact and what their task is. Shared mental models enhance coordination and contribute greatly to effective team performance, at least when the shared knowledge reflects reality.[69] Although shared mental models are important for all teams, they are a particular challenge to instill in cross-functional teams due to the divergent backgrounds of the team members. Consider this product development team:

> *The team is given the mandate to make a "tough truck." The designer, thinking in terms of styling, conceptualizes "tough" as "powerful looking." The designer then sketches a vehicle with a large grille and large tires, creating a very powerful stance. When seeing this mock-up, an engineer, thinking in terms of functionality and conceptualizing tough as implying durability, is unhappy with the design because it compromises the vehicle's power. Maintaining hauling capacity with large tires implies the need for greater torque output from the engine, adding expense and difficulty to the engineer's part of the problem. When the engineer suggests 16- rather than 20-inch wheels, the designer balks, claiming it makes the vehicle look cartoonish rather than tough.*[70]

Clearly, the designer and the engineer don't share mental models of what "tough" means, and this problem can be greatly magnified with the participation of other functions and disciplines. It can also be magnified in virtual teams, a subject we will now turn to.

LO 7.8

Understand *virtual teams* and what makes them effective.

Virtual teams. Work groups that use technology to communicate and collaborate across time, space, and organizational boundaries.

PERSONAL INVENTORY ASSESSMENT

Learn About Yourself
Positive Practices Survey

Virtual Teams

With the increasing trends toward globalization and the rapid development of high-tech communication tools, a new type of team has emerged that will surely be critical to organizations' success for years to come: virtual teams. **Virtual teams** are work groups that use technology to communicate and collaborate across space, time, and organizational boundaries.[71] Along with their reliance on computer and electronic technology, the primary feature of these teams is the lack of face-to-face contact between team members due to geographic dispersion. This separation often entails linkages across countries and cultures. Furthermore, virtual teams are often cross-functional. Technologies used by virtual teams can be either asynchronous (email, fax, voice mail), allowing team members to reflect before responding, or synchronous (chat, groupware), allowing team members to communicate dynamically in real time. Although not so long ago they were only a dream, virtual teams are now spreading across the business landscape and are used by numerous companies, such as CAE, Sabre, IBM, and Texas Instruments. For an example of a virtual team in the nonprofit sector, see the Applied Focus: *Virtual Teams at Save the Children*.

ADVANTAGES OF VIRTUAL TEAMS   Why are these teams becoming so popular? Because linking minds through technology has some definite advantages:

- *Around-the-clock work.* Globally, a virtual team is a 24-hour team that never sleeps. In these "follow the sun" teams, a team member can begin a process in London and pass it on to another team member in New York for more input. From New York,

■ APPLIED FOCUS ■

VIRTUAL TEAMS AT SAVE THE CHILDREN

People at Save the Children are heavily reliant on virtual teams to get their work done. The London-based charity has offices in over 50 countries and is part of an international alliance of almost 30 Save the Children organisations that fight to protect and promote children's rights. A lot of co-ordination between the various entities is required. "All of our working practices are informed by our being acutely aware of the importance of the left hand knowing what the right hand is doing," says Jasmine Whitbread, the organisation's CEO. The charity's health team, for example, is made up of researchers and policy advisers in London, as well as project managers and in-country policy advisers in each of the countries in which the charity operates. The charity recently launched its biggest global campaign to date, EVERY ONE. Virtual teams around the globe ensured that branding, messaging, policy calls, information materials, fundraising and campaigning activities were synchronised and launched on time. Virtual teamwork has made Save the Children much more operationally efficient. For example, the speed and reach of new communications mean that

project designs, policy strategies or media reports that have worked in one country can easily be shared with another. However, Ms. Whitbread says that Save the Children works in very distinct and diverse countries, with individual cultures and languages, and these are sometimes glossed over in the "speed and universal application of new communication networks". "Working in virtual teams can lose the spontaneity of a face-to-face meeting in which you're required to use your full range of sensual perceptions," she says. "This is why I still make an effort, and encourage our managers, to travel out frequently to visit and hear what our programme offices have to say." There is also the more prosaic problem that ICT is not universally or equally diffuse. Many of the countries in which Save the Children operates, such as Côte d'Ivoire, Sudan and the Democratic Republic of the Congo, simply do not have high-speed Internet connections, or even a secure electricity supply.

Source: © Reproduced by permission of the The Economist Intelligence Unit.

---

the work can be forwarded to a colleague in San Francisco who, after more work, can send it along to Hong Kong for completion.[72] In today's non-stop economy, the benefits of such continuous workflows are huge.

- *Reduced travel time and cost.* Virtual teaming reduces travel costs associated with face-to-face meetings. In the past, important meetings, key negotiation sessions, and critical junctures in projects required team members to board planes and travel long distances. In the virtual environment, expensive and time-consuming travel can be mostly eliminated. Virtual teams can therefore lead to significant savings of time and money, and concerns over air travel also make virtual teams an attractive alternative.

- *Larger talent pool.* Virtual teams allow companies to expand their potential labour markets and to go after the best people, even if these people have no interest in relocating. The nature of virtual teams can also give employees added flexibility, allowing for a better work–life balance, which is an effective recruiting feature.[73]

CHALLENGES OF VIRTUAL TEAMS While the advantages highlighted above are appealing, virtual teams are not without disadvantages.[74] Managers must recognize that these teams present unique challenges and should not be treated as regular teams that just happen to use technology.

- *Trust.* Commentators have noted that trust is difficult to develop among virtual team members. People typically establish trust through physical contact and socialization, which are simply not available to virtual team members. For more on this challenge, see You Be the Manager: *Creating Trust in Virtual Teams at Orange.*

YOU BE THE MANAGER

Creating Trust in Virtual Teams at Orange

Multinational companies have a dual challenge of globalizing operations for purposes of efficiencies and localizing delivery of products and services to support national differences. At Orange, this challenge became all the more obvious when it expanded operations in the late 1990s to become a large, pan-European company. Orange is the mobile operator of France Telecom, providing services to 57 million customers across 17 countries. With presence in Europe, the Middle East, and Africa, Orange realized that to protect and strengthen the Orange brand, product development previously performed within host countries needed to become a global initiative. Although it is tempting to centralize a team that has a global mandate, Orange pursued virtual-team collaboration, which allows firms to increase diversity in their teams and potentially achieve greater productivity and creativity. At Orange, as in many high-tech, global corporations, virtual teams were becoming a way of life, but there were clearly challenges, rooted in the fact that there were fewer interpersonal similarities (e.g., common backgrounds and experience) among team members.

Within the product development organization at Orange, virtual teams were usually led by a product manager. Members of the team not only had primary responsibilities to the virtual team but also did work for local teams and various functions. Like other virtual teams, those at Orange were required to work across time zones, cultures, and reporting lines. Virtuality meant that team members were unable to interact informally, in face-to-face meetings. Communicating through electronic media (e.g., email, phone, and video conferencing) greatly reduced the ability to interact through non-verbal cues. The lack of informal communication was considered to be a large barrier in team productivity. As one team leader expressed, "Work really only starts after that first face-to-face meeting."

Cultural distance also affected the virtual teams at Orange. In one virtual team, conference calls between the U.K. and Paris offices became particularly strained. The British employees, in an effort to enhance meeting productivity, used humour to encourage participation, but this approach backfired. Without the benefit

Getstock.com

At Orange, the creation and leadership of virtual teams is based on the fundamental need to create trust quickly and embed this trust throughout the life of the team.

of seeing facial expressions, paired with the difficulty of relating to the jokes themselves, Parisian employees felt increasingly isolated from their British counterparts and, like other virtual teams at Orange, had low trust in their colleagues' ability to perform.

Because virtual teams at Orange were vital to the company's overall global strategy, management was keen to find ways to enhance team performance, productivity, and innovation. It was clear that work had to be done to overcome the trust barrier that existed between many of the virtual team members.

Questions

1. Why is trust important in virtual teams, and what influences the degree of trust among team members?

2. How can trust be developed and maintained in virtual teams?

To find out how Orange increased trust between virtual team members, see The Manager's Notebook at the end of this chapter.

Source: Adapted from Lawley, D. (2006). Creating trust in virtual teams at Orange. *Knowledge Management Review, 9* (2), 12–17.

● *Miscommunication.* The loss of face-to-face communication presents certain risks for virtual teams. Humans use many non-verbal cues to communicate meaning and feeling in a message. When they use technology, the richness of face-to-face communication is lost and miscommunication can result (see Chapter 10). These risks can be particularly high on global virtual teams, as attempts at humour or the use of unfamiliar terms can lead to messages being misconstrued. Some organizations, such as Chevron, encourage global team members to avoid humour or metaphors when communicating online.[75]

- *Isolation.* People have needs for companionship. In self-contained offices, co-workers can meet for lunch, share stories, talk about their kids, and socialize outside of work. Unfortunately, these more casual interactions are not usually possible for virtual teams, a lack that can lead to team members having feelings of isolation and detachment.

- *High costs.* Savings in areas such as travel must be weighed against the costs of cutting-edge technology. Initial set-up costs can be substantial. Budgets must also be devoted to maintenance since, in the virtual environment, the firm's technology must run flawlessly, 24 hours a day, 7 days a week.

- *Management issues.* For managers, virtual teams can create new challenges in terms of dealing with subordinates who are no longer in view. How can you assess individual performance, monitor diligence, and ensure fairness in treatment when your team is dispersed around the globe?

Jessica Mesmer-Magnus and colleagues conducted an informative review of the research on information sharing in virtual teams versus face-to-face teams.[76] They found that virtual teams engaged in a lower volume of information sharing but were in fact more likely to share unique information that was not known by other team members. They suggested that the uniqueness advantage arises because virtuality encourages more reflection compared to direct interaction. Paradoxically, however, the performance of virtual teams was especially dependent on them also having a high volume of open communication to complement the unique ideas. This is because openness facilitates the development of cooperation, cohesion, and trust, all of which are challenges for virtuality. The authors also found support for the idea that hybrid teams that combine face-to-face interaction with virtual interaction are especially likely to share information, a point reinforced in the following section.

LESSONS CONCERNING VIRTUAL TEAMS Overall, a number of lessons are beginning to emerge about what managers must do or watch out for when developing virtual teams.[77]

- *Recruitment.* Choose team members carefully in terms of attitude and personality, so that they are excited about these types of teams and can handle the independence and isolation that often define them. Find people with good interpersonal skills, not just technical expertise.

- *Training.* Invest in training for both technical and interpersonal skills. In many cases, virtual teams falter not due to weak technical skills but due to poor communication and cooperation.

- *Personalization.* Encourage team members to get to know one another, either by encouraging informal communication using technology or by arranging face-to-face meetings whenever possible. Reduce feelings of isolation by setting aside time for chit-chat, acknowledging birthdays, and so on.

- *Goals and ground rules.* On the management side, virtual team leaders should define goals clearly, set rules for communication standards and responses, and provide feedback to keep team members informed of progress and the big picture.

The key appears to be recognizing the ways in which these teams are different from those based in a single-office environment but not falling into the trap of focusing solely on technology. Many of the general recommendations that apply to any work team also apply to virtual teams. These teams are made up of individuals who have the same feelings and needs as workers in more traditional environments. Virtual teams must be real teams, if not by location, then in mind and spirit.

A WORD OF CAUTION: TEAMS AS A PANACEA

Teams can be a powerful resource for organizations, and this chapter has identified some of the important lessons leading to team success. However, switching from a traditional structure to a team-based configuration is not a cure-all for an organization's problems, even though some managers fall prey to the "romance of teams."[78] It is likely that the research to date on teams has focused almost exclusively on viable, ongoing teams, with little attention being paid to unsuccessful teams. Some observers suggest that the team approach puts unwanted pressure and responsibilities on workers. Others have noted that many organizations have rushed to deploy teams with little planning, often resulting in confusion and contradictory signals to employees. Good planning and continuing support are necessary for the effective use of teams.[79]

THE MANAGER'S NOTEBOOK

Creating Trust in Virtual Teams at Orange

1. Trust is an important ingredient in all teams, regardless of the proximity of members. Trust is considered to enhance overall team performance because it reduces the need for formal checks and balances and increases team members' ability to work through interpersonal challenges. When trust is low, teams require a higher degree of control and leadership, which reduces overall productivity and increases costs. In virtual teams, trust is harder to achieve due to the perceived distances (e.g., geographical and cultural) among team members. To overcome this challenge, members of virtual teams need to be aligned in their thoughts and actions about the work they have been assigned. In virtual teams, trust is built on the perceived ability of team members, benevolence among team members, positive feelings about each other, and the overall integrity of the group. At Orange, experience confirmed that three principles are necessary for building trust in teams: small team size, strong leadership, and a common working framework. At first, Orange attempted to run large, lengthy, cross-functional initiatives through the use of virtual teams. But the company found that the number of relationships and the complexity of the work created significant trust barriers. Over time, Orange moved to smaller virtual teams (under 10 members) to achieve more focused mandates over a shorter period. In addition, Orange recognized that more effective leaders were those who could recognize cultural differences and bridge those differences between members through the use of a common framework. For example, one way to ensure "equality" in a team is to have everyone join a conference call by phone, regardless of the fact that some members are located in the same place and could talk face to face.

2. At Orange, experience indicated that leaders of virtual teams are better off focusing on outputs rather than on team processes. Since it is impossible to know what each team member is doing at any particular time, measuring outputs allows each team member to work when and how he or she chooses, respecting local customs and norms. Orange and their consultants also realized that the start-up of a team is a crucial period when leaders need to develop clear team objectives. To encourage a culture of trust within the team, leaders must therefore be good communicators and coaches, be able to foster an atmosphere of trust, and be independent workers. From the start, the leader must demonstrate trust in team members and encourage trust among team members by identifying their track records and nature of expertise. This effort must be complemented by seeking trust from stakeholders of the project, which, in turn, will generate further trust within the team. At Orange, the creation and leadership of virtual teams is now based on the fundamental need to create trust quickly and to embed this trust throughout the life of the team. Trust has become a planned activity to be achieved through the building of knowledge (understanding objectives and the contribution of others) and team formation.

MyManagementLab Study, practise, and explore real management situations with these helpful resources:

- **Interactive Lesson Presentations:** Work through interactive presentations and assessments to test your knowledge of management concepts.
- **PIA (Personal Inventory Assessments):** Enhance your ability to connect with key concepts through these engaging, self-reflection assessments.
- **Study Plan:** Check your understanding of chapter concepts with self-study quizzes.
- **Videos:** Learn more about the management practices and strategies of real companies.
- **Simulations:** Practise decision-making in simulated management environments.

P I A PERSONAL INVENTORY ASSESSMENT

LEARNING OBJECTIVES CHECKLIST

7.1 A *group* consists of two or more people interacting interdependently to achieve a common goal. Some groups go through a series of developmental stages: forming, storming, norming, performing, and adjourning. However, the *punctuated equilibrium* model stresses a first meeting, a period of little apparent progress, a critical midpoint transition, and a phase of goal-directed activity.

7.2 As groups get bigger, they provide less opportunity for member satisfaction. When tasks are *additive* (performance depends on the addition of individual effort) or *disjunctive* (performance depends on that of the best member), larger groups should perform better than smaller groups if the group can avoid *process losses* due to poor communication and motivation. When tasks are *conjunctive* (performance is limited by the weakest member), performance decreases as the group gets bigger, because the chance of adding a weak member increases. Diverse groups generally develop at a slower pace and are less cohesive than homogeneous groups. While the effects of surface-level demographic diversity can wear off over time, deep diversity differences regarding attitudes are more difficult to overcome.

7.3 *Norms* are expectations that group members have about one another's behaviour. They provide consistency to behaviour and develop as a function of shared attitudes. In organizations, both formal and informal norms often develop to control dress, reward allocation, and performance. *Roles* are positions in a group that have a set of expected behaviours associated with them. *Role ambiguity* refers to a lack of clarity of job goals or methods. *Role conflict* exists when an individual is faced with incompatible role expectations, and it can take four forms: *intrasender, intersender, interrole,* and *person–role*. Both ambiguity and conflict

have been shown to provoke job dissatisfaction, stress, and lowered commitment. *Status* is the rank or prestige that a group accords its members. Formal status systems use status symbols to reinforce the authority hierarchy and reward progression. Informal status systems also operate in organizations. Although status differences are motivational, they also lead to communication barriers.

7.4 *Cohesive groups* are especially attractive to their members. Threat, competition, success, and small size contribute to cohesiveness, as does a tough initiation into the group. The consequences of cohesiveness include increased participation in group affairs, improved communication, and increased conformity. Cohesive groups are especially effective in accomplishing their own goals, which may or may not be those of the organization.

7.5 *Social loafing* occurs when people withhold effort when performing a group task. This is less likely when individual performance is visible, the task is interesting, there is good performance feedback, and the organization rewards group achievement.

7.6 Members of *self-managed work teams* do challenging work under reduced supervision. For greatest effectiveness, such teams should be stable, small, well trained, and moderately diverse in membership. Group-oriented rewards are most appropriate. Teams perform best when they have high *collective efficacy*, a shared belief that they can perform a given task. Sharing identical information (*shared mental models*) contributes to such efficacy.

7.7 *Cross-functional teams* bring people with different functional specialties together to better invent, design, or deliver a product or service. They should have diverse membership, a *superordinate* goal, some basic decision rules, and reasonable autonomy. Members should work in the same physical location, and team leaders require people skills as well as task skills.

7.8   *Virtual teams* use technology to communicate and collaborate across time, space, and organizational boundaries. These teams offer many advantages, such as reduced travel costs, greater potential talent, and continuous workflow, but present difficulties in terms of miscommunication, lack of trust, and feelings of isolation.

DISCUSSION QUESTIONS

1. Describe the kind of skills that you would look for in members of self-managed teams. Explain your choices. Do the same for virtual teams.

2. When would an organization create self-managed teams? When would it use cross-functional teams? When would it employ virtual teams?

3. Explain how a cross-functional team could contribute to product or service quality. Explain how a cross-functional team could contribute to speeding up product design.

4. Some organizations have made concerted efforts to do away with many of the status symbols associated with differences in organizational rank. All employees now park in the same lot, eat in the same dining room, and have similar offices and privileges. Discuss the pros and cons of such a strategy. How might such a change affect organizational communications?

5. You are an executive in a consumer products corporation. The president assigns you to form a task force to develop new marketing strategies for the organization. You are permitted to choose its members. What things would you do to make this group as cohesive as possible? What are the dangers of group cohesiveness for the group itself and for the organization of which the group is a part?

INTEGRATIVE DISCUSSION QUESTIONS

1. What role do perceptions play in group development? Refer to the discussion of perceptual process and biases in Chapter 3 and discuss the implications for each stage of group development. What are the implications for improving the development of groups?

2. How can groups be motivated? Consider the implications of each of the work motivation theories described in Chapter 5. What do the theories tell us about how to motivate groups?

ON-THE-JOB CHALLENGE QUESTION

Self-Managed Teams at ISE Communications

ISE Communications was one of the pioneers in using self-managed work teams. The teams were put in place to improve manufacturing flexibility and customer service, both factors being crucial in the highly competitive circuit board industry. Its conversion from an assembly-line style of circuit board manufacturing to teams who identified with "their own" products and customers was deemed a great success by industry observers. One interesting result was that the teams became extremely obsessed with monitoring the promptness and attendance of their members, more so than managers had been before the conversion to teams. They even posted attendance charts and created punishments for slack team members.

Use your understanding of both group dynamics and teams to explain why the employees became so concerned about attendance when they were organized into teams. What had changed?

Source: Adapted from Barker, J.R. (1993). Tightening the iron cage: Concertive control in self-managing teams. *Administrative Science Quarterly, 38*, 408–437.

EXPERIENTIAL EXERCISE

NASA

The purpose of this exercise is to compare individual and group problem solving and to explore the group dynamics that occur in a problem-solving session. It can also be used in conjunction with Chapter 11. The instructor will begin by forming groups of four to seven members.

The situation described in this problem is based on actual cases in which men and women lived or died, depending on the survival decisions they made. Your "life" or "death" will depend on how well your group can share its present knowledge of a relatively unfamiliar problem, so that the group can make decisions that will lead to your survival.

The Problem

You are a member of a space crew originally scheduled to rendezvous with a mother ship on the lighted surface of the moon. Due to mechanical difficulties, however, your ship was forced to land at a spot some 200 miles from the rendezvous point. During landing, much of the equipment aboard was damaged, and, because survival depends on reaching the mother ship, the most critical items available must be chosen for the 200-mile trip. On the next page are listed the 15 items left intact and undamaged after the landing. Your task is to rank them in terms of their importance to your crew in reaching the rendezvous point. In the first column (step 1) place the number 1 by the most important, and so on, through number 15, the least important. You have 15 minutes to complete this phase of the exercise.

After the individual rankings are complete, participants should be formed into groups having from four to seven members. Each group should then rank the 15 items as a team. This group ranking should be a general consensus after a discussion of the issues, not just the average of each individual ranking. While it is unlikely that everyone will agree exactly on the group ranking, an effort should be made to reach at least a decision that everyone can live with. It is important to treat differences of opinion as a means of gathering more information and clarifying issues and as an incentive to force the group to seek better alternatives.

The group ranking should be listed in the second column (step 2).

The third phase of the exercise consists of the instructor providing the expert's rankings, which should be entered in the third column (step 3). Each participant should compute the difference between the individual ranking (step 1) and the expert's ranking (step 3), and between the group ranking (step 2) and the expert's ranking (step 3). Then add the two "difference" columns—the smaller the score, the closer the ranking is to the view of the experts.

Source: Ritchie, *Organization and people*, 3rd ed. © 1984 South-Western, a part of Cenage Learning, Inc. Reproduced by permission. www.cengage.com/permissions.

Discussion

The instructor will summarize the results on the board for each group, including (a) the average individual accuracy score, (b) the group accuracy score, (c) the gain or loss between the average individual score and the group score, and (d) the lowest individual score (i.e., the best score) in each group.

The following questions will help guide the discussion:

1. As a group task, is the NASA exercise an additive, disjunctive, or conjunctive task?

2. What would be the impact of group size on performance in this task?

3. Did any norms develop in your group that guided how information was exchanged or how the decision was reached?

4. Did any special roles emerge in your group? These could include a leader, a secretary, an "expert," a critic, or a humourist. How did these roles contribute to or hinder group performance?

5. Consider the factors that contribute to effective self-managed teams. How do they pertain to a group's performance on this exercise?

6. How would group diversity help or hinder performance on the exercise?

NASA tally sheet

Items	Step 1 Your individual ranking	Step 2 The team's ranking	Step 3 Survival expert's ranking	Step 4 Difference between Step 1 & 3	Step 5 Difference between Step 2 & 3
Box of matches					
Food concentrate					
50 feet of nylon rope					
Parachute silk					
Portable heating unit					
Two .45 calibre pistols					
One case dehydrated milk					
Two 100-lb. tanks of oxygen					
Stellar map (of the moon's constellation)					
Life raft					
Magnetic compass					
5 gallons of water					
Signal flares					
First aid kit containing injection needles					
Solar-powered FM receiver-transmitter					
Total (The lower the score the better)				Your score	Team score

CASE INCIDENT

The Group Assignment

Janet, a student, never liked working on group assignments; however, this time she thought it would be different because she knew most of the people in her group. But it was not long before things started going badly. After the first meeting, the group could not agree when to meet again. When they finally did meet, nobody had done anything, and the assignment was due in two weeks. The group then agreed to meet again the next day to figure out what to do. However, two of the group members did not show up. The following week Janet tried in vain to arrange for another meeting, but the other group members said they were too busy and that it would be best to divide the assignment up and have each member work on a section.

The night before the assignment was due the group members met to give Janet their work. Finally, Janet thought, we are making progress. However, when she got home and read what the other members had written, she was shocked at how bad it was. Janet spent the rest of the night and early morning doing the whole assignment herself. Once the course ended, Janet never spoke to any of the group members again.

1. Refer to the typical stages of group development and explain the development of Janet's group.

2. To what extent was group cohesiveness a problem in Janet's work group? What might have made the group more cohesive?

CASE STUDY

Levi Strauss & Co.'s Flirtation with Teams

Levi Strauss & Co. is one of the largest makers of brand-name clothing in the world. It has had a long history of being profitable, good to its workers, and charitable to its factory towns. Compared with other companies in the apparel industry, Levi Strauss had been known for generous wages and good working conditions. When other American apparel firms moved their manufacturing offshore, Levi Strauss & Co. maintained a large American manufacturing base and was often ranked as one of the best companies to work for. In fact, in 1997 the company received an award from the United Nations for improving global workplace standards.

Up until 1992, Levi's employees worked on their own, operating machines on which they performed a single, specific, and repetitive task, such as sewing zippers or belt loops on jeans. Pay was based on a piece-rate system, in which workers were paid a set amount for each piece of work completed. A worker's productivity and pay were highly dependent on levels of skill, speed, and stamina.

By 1992, however, Levi Strauss & Company began to feel the pressure of overseas, low-cost competitors, and realized it needed to increase productivity and reduce costs to remain competitive and keep their North American plants open. The company decided that the best solution was teamwork. In a memo sent to workers, Levi's operations vice-president wrote, "This change will lead to a self-managed work environment that will reduce stress and help employees become more productive." Teamwork was felt to be a humane, safe, and profitable solution that would be consistent with the company's philosophy.

Under the new philosophy, gone was the old system of performing a single task all the time, and the piece-rate system that went with it. Now teams of 10 to 50 workers shared the tasks and would be paid for the total number of trousers that the group completed. The team system was expected to lower the monotony of piecework by enabling workers to do different tasks and to therefore lower repetitive-stress injuries.

Although employees were given brief seminars and training on team building and problem solving, it was not long before problems began to arise. Top performers complained about their less skilled and slower teammates who caused a decline in their wages. Meanwhile, the wages of lower-skilled workers increased.

Threats, insults, and group infighting became a regular part of daily work as faster workers tried to rid their group of slower workers. To make matters worse, top performers responded to their lower wages by reducing their productivity. Not surprisingly, employee morale began to deteriorate.

Another problem was that whenever a group member was absent or slow, the rest of the team had to make up for it. This exacerbated the infighting among team members and resulted in excessive peer pressure. In one instance, an enraged worker had to be restrained from throwing a chair at a team member who constantly harassed her about working too slowly, and in another incident, a worker threatened to kill a member of her team. An off-duty sheriff's deputy had to be placed at the plant's front entrance.

Because the groups had limited supervision, they had to resolve group problems on their own, and they also divided up the work of absent members themselves. In some plants, team members would chase each other out of the bathroom and nurse's station. Slower teammates were often criticized, needled, and resented by their group. Some could not take the resentment and simply quit. In one group, a member was voted off her team because she planned to have hand surgery. And although workers were now part of a team system, management was not given guidance on how to implement the system. As a result, each manager had his or her own idea of how the team system should work, including team size, structure, pay formulas, and shop-floor layouts. One former production manager described the situation as worse than chaos and more like hell!

To make matters worse, the team system did not improve the situation for Levi's. Labour and overhead costs increased by up to 25 percent during the first years of the team system. Efficiency, based on the quantity of pants produced per hour worked, dropped to 77 percent of pre-team levels. Although productivity began to improve, it is now only at 93 percent of the piecework level. Even in some of the company's best plants, production has fallen and remained at lower levels since the introduction of teams. And although one of the reasons for adopting the team system was to lower the high costs of injuries that resulted from workers pushing themselves to achieve piece-rate goals, these costs continued to rise in many plants even after the team approach was implemented.

Profit margins also began to decline as competitors began offering private-label jeans at two-thirds the price of Levi's, and Levi's market share of men's denim jeans in the United States fell from 48 percent in 1990 to 26 percent in 1997. As costs continued to increase, plant managers were warned that they would face an uncertain future unless they cut costs by 28 percent by the end of year.

Teams did, however, result in some improvements. For example, the average turnaround time of receiving an order and shipping it was reduced from nine to seven weeks. As well, because the teams were responsible for producing completed pairs of pants, there was less work-in-process at the end of each day compared with the piece-rate system, where each worker did only one part of the job. And teams allowed workers to manage themselves and to find better and safer ways of working.

Nonetheless, the team system did not help Levi's achieve its objectives. In February 1997, then-CEO Robert Haas announced that the company would cut its salaried workforce by 20 percent in the next 12 months. The following November, the company closed 11 factories in the United States and laid off 6395 workers. In an unusual response to being laid off, one worker described it as a "relief" from the burden and stress that had become part of her job.

Commenting on the team approach, a now-retired former manufacturing manager said, "We created a lot of anxiety and pain and suffering in our people, and for what?" According to a production manager who has taken early retirement, "It's just not the same company anymore. The perceived value of the individual and the concern for people just is not there." A veteran worker who had gone back to the old system of doing a single task and was now paid in part for what she produced said, "I hate teams. Levi's is not the place it used to be."

In February 1999, as sales of Levi's jeans continued to fall, the company let go another 5900 workers, or 30 percent of its workforce of 19 900 in the United States and Canada, and announced that it would close 11 of its remaining 22 plants in North America. According to company officials, plant closings might have been sooner and job losses greater if they had not adopted the team system. In 2003, due to substantial drops in net sales over the previous three years, the company implemented more measures to recoup some of its losses, including closing 37 of its factories worldwide and instead using independent contract manufacturers. The company closed its remaining North American manufacturing facilities; its San Antonio operations closed at the end of 2003, and its three Canadian operations closed in March 2004. The closures affected some 2000 employees. The Canadian plants were considered among the most efficient in the company. As such, Levi Strauss & Co. now manufactures 100 percent of its jeans for the North American market outside of North America, compared with 15 percent in 1991.

Sources: Gilbert, C. (1998, September). Did modules fail Levi's or did Levi's fail modules? *Apparel Industry Magazine*, 88–92; King, R.T., Jr. (1998, May 20). Levi's factory workers are assigned to teams and morale takes a hit. *Wall Street Journal*, A1, A6; Levi Strauss & Co. (2003, September 15). *Hoover's Company Capsules* (L), p. 40278. Retrieved September 30, 2003, from ProQuest database; McFarland, J. (1999, February 23). Levi Strauss slashes 5,900 jobs. *Globe and Mail*, B5; Paddon, D. (2003, September 26). Levi Strauss closing plants. *Montreal Gazette*, B2; Steinhart, D. (1999, February 23). Levi to shut plants in Cornwall, *U.S. Financial Post*, C1, C9.

QUESTIONS

1. Discuss the stages of group development and the implications of them for the development of the teams at Levi Strauss.
2. Discuss some of the norms that emerged in the teams. What was their function and how did they influence the behaviour of group members?

3. Discuss the role dynamics that emerged in the teams. Is there any evidence of role ambiguity or role conflict?

4. How cohesive were the teams at Levi Strauss? What factors contribute to the level of cohesiveness?

5. The teams were supposed to be self-managing teams. Critique this idea in terms of the principles for effectiveness for such teams given in the chapter.

6. Do you think it was a good idea for Levi Strauss & Co. to implement a team system? Was it the best solution to deal with increased global competition? Why wasn't the team approach at Levi Strauss & Co. more effective, and with your knowledge of groups, what might you have done differently if you had to implement a team system at Levi Strauss?

8 SOCIAL INFLUENCE, SOCIALIZATION, AND ORGANIZATIONAL CULTURE

LEARNING OBJECTIVES

After reading Chapter 8, you should be able to:

8.1 Understand the difference between *information dependence* and *effect dependence*, and differentiate *compliance*, *identification*, and *internalization* as motives for social conformity.

8.2 Describe the *socialization* process and the stages of organizational socialization.

8.3 Describe the implications of *unrealistic expectations* and the *psychological contract* for socialization.

8.4 Describe the main methods of socialization and how newcomers can be *proactive* in their socialization.

8.5 Define *organizational culture*, and discuss the assets and liabilities of *strong cultures*.

8.6 Discuss the contributors to an organization's culture.

8.7 Describe how to diagnose an organizational culture.

KICKING HORSE COFFEE

Kicking Horse Coffee was started in 1996 by Elana Rosenfeld and Leo Johnson when they began selling organic fair trade coffee out of their garage in Invermere, British Columbia. They were the first Fairtrade licensee in Western Canada.

Today, Kicking Horse Coffee is one of the largest and most notable business in Invermere. It is also the number one seller of organic fair trade coffee in Canada and can be found in major grocery stores across Canada, as well as in high-end chain stores in the United States.

The management style at Kicking Horse Coffee has been described as informal and accessible with regular communication with the company's 85 employees, and a relationship based on trust, employee autonomy, and a shared sense of mission. Employees receive perks such as incentive bonuses, free lunches, a cool staff lounge, regular days off, and no night shifts. There is a hostess in the lunch room, which is fitted out with easy chairs inside and Muskoka chairs outside, and employees receive a generous supply of coffee at work and home.

Active living, work–life balance, and a strong sense of fun and camaraderie permeate the company culture. The company is known for its playful spirit and cheeky irreverence. Employees receive information on how the company is performing as a whole during catered monthly meetings. They have two paid fun days each year where production shuts down and the whole team gets together for outdoor activities such as hiking, rafting, kayaking, mountain biking, and skiing. Employees also receive a wellness allowance to spend on things to get them active. RAVE awards (Recognizing Actions, Values, and Ethics) are given to employees whose behaviours demonstrate a strong work ethic and reflect the company's values, and CRACK awards (celebrating random acts of kindness) enable employees to recognize each other with gift cards. And when 20 centimetres or more of snow fall on Panorama Mountain, the Powder Day Rule comes into effect, which means that fresh tracks trump office time.

Kicking Horse Coffee has a strong organizational culture that emphasizes active living, work-life balance, fun and camaraderie.

Photo by Andreas Dyballa

"Our team kicks ass," says Rosenfeld, Kicking Horse Coffee, Co founder and Chief Executive Officer. "That means equal parts hard work and having fun. Our people are passionate about working together to wake people up with a delicious, mysterious, inspiring beverage. It's hard not to have fun at work." The fun culture can also be seen in some of the company's job titles such as Packaging Ninjas, Stage Horses, and Work Horses, as well as in the names of its coffees, such as Smart Ass®, Grizzly Claw®, Hoodoo Jo®, Cliff Hanger Espresso®, and—for one of its most potent coffee blends—Kick Ass®.

"Doing it from the heart is paying off for us. Our employees are highly motivated, very productive and usually stay with us a long time," says Rosenfeld. The company's attitude toward employees is part of a holistic approach to business. "Everything we do has to be high quality," Rosenfeld says. "And I don't just mean the product. We're passionate about contributing socially and environmentally. That commitment starts with our No. 1 asset, our people. Our priority is to make sure employees are looked after and can maintain healthy, fulfilling lives with their families." The company also participates in community events and contributes to conservation projects.

Rosenfeld describes her employees like this: "We have a very passionate, motivated team who really appreciate their jobs, appreciate that they can live here and have a great work environment and opportunities" and notes, "We've always believed that work should be fun. We always wanted to desire to come to work. That's why we're located in Invermere, in a Rocky Mountain playground. That's why our team smiles so much. We know that happy, healthy living translates to a happy healthy workplace."

In 2015, Kicking Horse Coffee was named the 15th Best Workplace in Canada by Great Place to Work®. "We're a small company and we're all committed to doing great work," Rosenfeld says. "Doing our best everyday requires depending on each other and when everyone you work with also wants to do a kick ass job; well, it makes things pretty fun. We're proud to be recognized for that."[1]

This description of Kicking Horse Coffee suggests that it has a strong organizational culture that is based on a shared set of values that influence employee attitudes and behaviours But what exactly is an organizational culture, and what effect does it have on employees? What does it mean to have a strong culture, and what are the assets and liabilities of strong cultures? How are cultures built and maintained, and how do new employees learn about an organization's culture? These are the kinds of questions that we will probe in this chapter.

First, we will examine the general issue of social influence in organizations—how members have an impact on each other's behaviour and attitudes. Social norms hold an organization together, and conformity to such norms is a product of the social influence process. Following this, we consider the elaborate process of organizational socialization: the learning of attitudes, knowledge, and behaviours that are necessary for a person to function in an organization. Socialization both contributes to and results from the organizational culture, the final topic that we will explore.

LO 8.1

Understand the difference between *information dependence* and *effect dependence*, and differentiate *compliance*, *identification*, and *internalization* as motives for social conformity.

SOCIAL INFLUENCE IN ORGANIZATIONS

In the previous chapter, we pointed out that groups exert influence over the attitudes and behaviour of their individual members. As a result of social influence, people often feel or act differently from how they would as independent operators. What accounts for such influence? In short, in many social settings, and especially in groups, people are highly *dependent* on others. This dependence sets the stage for influence to occur.

Information Dependence and Effect Dependence

Information dependence.
Reliance on others for information about how to think, feel, and act.

We are frequently dependent on others for information about the adequacy and appropriateness of our behaviour, thoughts, and feelings. How satisfying is this job of mine? How nice is our boss? How much work should I take home to do over the weekend? Should we protest the bad design at the meeting? Objective, concrete answers to such questions might be hard to come by. Thus, we must often rely on information that others provide.[2] In turn, this **information dependence** gives others the opportunity to influence our thoughts, feelings, and actions via the signals they send to us.[3]

Social information processing theory.
Information from others is used to interpret events and develop expectations about appropriate and acceptable attitudes and behaviours.

The process through which this occurs is explained by social information processing theory. According to **social information processing theory**, organizational members use information from others to interpret events and develop expectations about appropriate and acceptable attitudes and behaviours. Thus, organizational members look to others for information and cues about how they should behave.[4] Individuals are often motivated to compare their own thoughts, feelings, and actions with those of others as a means of acquiring information about their adequacy. The effects of social information can be very strong, often exerting as much or more influence over others as objective reality. As a result, individual behaviour is influenced and shaped by others.[5]

Effect dependence.
Reliance on others due to their capacity to provide rewards and punishment.

As if group members were not busy enough tuning in to information provided by the group, they must also be sensitive to the rewards and punishments the group has at its disposal. Thus, individuals are dependent on the *effects* of their behaviour as determined by the rewards and punishments provided by others. **Effect dependence** actually involves two complementary processes. First, the group frequently has a vested interest in how individual members think and act, because such matters can affect the goal attainment of the group. Second, the members frequently desire the approval of the group. In combination, these circumstances promote effect dependence.

In organizations, plenty of effects are available to keep individual members "under the influence." Managers typically have a fair array of rewards and punishments available, including promotions, raises, and the assignment of more or less favourable tasks. At the informal level, the variety of such effects available to co-workers is staggering. They might reward cooperative behaviour with praise, friendship, and a helping hand on the job. Lack of cooperation might result in nagging, harassment, name calling, or social isolation.

The Social Influence Process and Conformity

One of the most obvious consequences of information and effect dependence is the tendency for group members to conform to the social norms that have been established by the group. In the previous chapter, we discussed the development and function of such norms, but we have postponed until now the discussion of why norms are supported. Put simply, much of the information and many of the effects on which group members are dependent are oriented toward enforcing group norms. As described below, there are three different motives for social conformity.[6]

To understand the motives for social conformity, consider Mark, an idealistic graduate of a university social work program who acquires a job with a social services agency. Mark loves helping people but hates the bureaucratic red tape and reams of paperwork that are necessary to accomplish this goal. However, to acquire the approval of his boss and co-workers and to avoid trouble, he follows the rules to the letter of the law. This is pure compliance. **Compliance** is the simplest, most direct motive for conformity to group norms. It occurs because a member wishes to acquire rewards from the group and avoid punishment. As such, it primarily involves effect dependence. Although the complying individual adjusts his or her behaviour to the norm, he or she does not really subscribe to the beliefs, values, and attitudes that underlie the norm.

Over time, however, Mark begins to *identify* with his boss and more experienced co-workers because they are in the enviable position of controlling those very rewards and punishments that are so important to him. Obviously, if he is to *be* one of them, he must begin to think and feel like them. **Identification** as a motive for conformity is often revealed by an imitation process in which established members serve as models for the behaviour of others. Although there are elements of effect dependence here, information dependence is especially important — if someone is basically similar to you, then you will be motivated to rely on that person for information about how to think and act.

Finally, Mark is promoted to a supervisory position, partly because he is so cooperative. Breaking in a new social worker, Mark is heard to say, "Our rules and paperwork are very important. You don't understand now, but you will." The metamorphosis is complete— Mark has *internalized* the beliefs and values that support the bureaucratic norms of his agency. **Internalization** occurs when individuals have truly and wholly accepted the beliefs, values, and attitudes that underlie the norm. Conformity occurs because it is seen as *right*, not because it achieves rewards, avoids punishment, or pleases others. That is, conformity is due to internal, rather than external, forces.

Although this story is slightly dramatized, the point that it makes is accurate— simple compliance can set the stage for more complete identification and involvement with organizational norms and roles. The process through which this occurs in organizations is known as *organizational socialization*, and it is the focus of the next section.

ORGANIZATIONAL SOCIALIZATION

The story of Mark, the social worker, in the previous section describes how one individual was socialized into a particular organization. **Socialization** is the process by which people learn the attitudes, knowledge, and behaviours that are necessary for them to function in a group or organization. It is a learning process in which new members must acquire knowledge, change their attitudes, and perform new behaviours. Socialization is also the primary means by which organizations communicate their culture and values to new members.[7]

Exhibit 8.1 depicts the socialization process. In particular, it shows how different socialization methods (e.g., employee orientation programs) influence immediate or proximal

---

Compliance. Conformity to a social norm prompted by the desire to acquire rewards or avoid punishment.

Identification. Conformity to a social norm prompted by perceptions that those who promote the norm are attractive or similar to oneself.

Internalization. Conformity to a social norm prompted by true acceptance of the beliefs, values, and attitudes that underlie the norm.

Socialization. The process by which people learn the attitudes, knowledge, and behaviours that are necessary for a person to function in a group or organization.

LO 8.2

Describe the *socialization* process and the stages of organizational socialization.

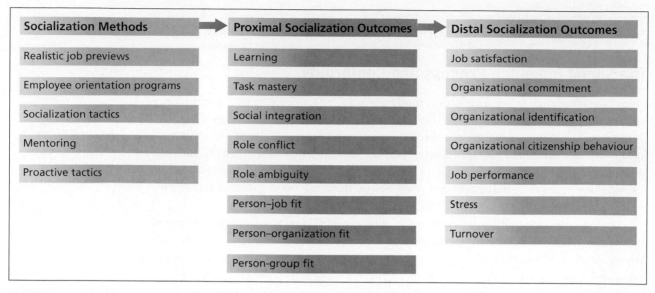

EXHIBIT 8.1
The socialization process.

socialization outcomes, such as learning, which lead to more distal or longer-term outcomes, such as attitudes (e.g., job satisfaction) and behaviours (e.g., turnover).

Learning during socialization has often been described in terms of content areas or domains of learning, such as the task, role, group, and organization domain. Newcomers need to acquire the knowledge and skills necessary to perform their job duties and *tasks*; they need to learn the appropriate behaviours and expectations of their *roles*; they need to learn the norms and values of their *work group*; and they need to learn about the *organization*, such as its history, traditions, language, politics, mission, and culture. As newcomers learn about each of these areas, they should begin to master their tasks and integrate with others in their work group and the organization. This should also help to reduce their role ambiguity and role conflict. In Chapter 7, we described how different factors can lead to role ambiguity and role conflict. One of the goals of socialization is to provide new hires with information and knowledge about their roles, in order to avoid problems of role conflict and role ambiguity.

An important objective of organizational socialization is for newcomers to achieve a good fit. There are generally three kinds of fit that are important for socialization. First, newcomers must acquire the knowledge and skills necessary to perform their work tasks and roles so they can develop a strong person–job fit, or PJ fit. **Person–job fit** refers to the match between an employee's knowledge, skills, and abilities and the requirements of a job. Second, newcomers must also learn the values and beliefs that are important to the organization so they can develop a strong person–organization, or PO fit. **Person–organization fit** refers to the match between an employee's personal values and the values of an organization. Third, newcomers must also learn the values and beliefs that are important to their work group so they can develop a strong person–group, or PG fit. **Person–group fit** refers to the match or compatibility between an employee's values and beliefs and the values and beliefs of his or her work group.[8] Research has found that PJ, PO, and PG fit are strongly influenced by the socialization process and are related to job attitudes and behaviours.[9]

One of the primary goals of organizational socialization is to ensure that new employees learn and understand the key beliefs, values, and assumptions of an organization's culture, and for individuals to define themselves in terms of the organization and what it is perceived to represent. This is known as **organizational identification**, and as shown in Exhibit 8.1, it is also a distal outcome of socialization. Organizational identification reflects an individual's learning and acceptance of an organization's culture.[10]

In summary, socialization is important because it has a direct effect on proximal socialization outcomes (e.g., learning, PJ fit, PO fit, and PG fit), which lead to distal outcomes (e.g., organizational identification). As we shall see, some of this process might occur before

Person–job fit. The match between an employee's knowledge, skills, and abilities and the requirements of a job.

Person–organization fit. The match between an employee's personal values and the values of an organization.

Person–group fit. The match between an employee's values and the values of his or her work group.

Organizational identification. The extent to which individuals define themselves in terms of the organization and what it is perceived to represent.

Cartoonresource/Shutterstock

"We only have a few rules around here, but we really enforce them."

organization membership formally begins, while some of it occurs once the new member enters the organization. Furthermore, socialization is an ongoing process by virtue of continuous interaction with others in the organization. However, socialization is most potent during certain periods of membership transition, such as when one is promoted or assigned to a new work group or department, and especially when one joins a new organization.[11]

Stages of Socialization

Since organizational socialization is an ongoing process, it is useful to divide this process into three stages.[12] One of these stages occurs before entry, another immediately follows entry, and the last occurs after one has been a member for some period of time. In a sense, the first two stages represent hurdles for achieving passage into the third stage (see Exhibit 8.2).

ANTICIPATORY SOCIALIZATION A considerable amount of socialization occurs even before a person becomes a member of a particular organization. This process is called anticipatory socialization. Some anticipatory socialization includes a formal process of skill and attitude acquisition, such as that which might occur by attending college or university. Other anticipatory socialization might be informal, such as that acquired through a series of summer jobs or even by watching the portrayal of organizational life in television shows and movies. Some organizations begin to socialize job candidates even before they are hired at recruitment events, where organizational representatives discuss the organization with potential hires. As we shall see shortly, organizations vary in the extent to which they encourage anticipatory socialization in advance of entry. As well, not all anticipatory socialization is accurate and useful for the new member.

ENCOUNTER In the encounter stage, the new recruit, armed with some expectations about organizational life, encounters the day-to-day reality of this life. Formal aspects of this stage

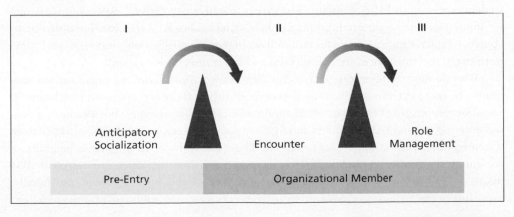

EXHIBIT 8.2
Stages of organizational socialization.
Source: Based on Feldman, D.C. (1976). A contingency theory of socialization. *Administrative Science Quarterly, 21,* 433–452; Feldman, D.C. (1981). The multiple socialization of organization members. *Academy of Management Review, 6,* 309–318.

might include orientation programs and rotation through various parts of the organization. Informal aspects include getting to know and understand the style and personality of one's boss and co-workers. At this stage, the organization and its experienced members are looking for an acceptable degree of conformity to organizational norms and the gradual acquisition of appropriate role behaviour. Recruits, on the other hand, are interested in having their personal needs and expectations fulfilled. If successful, the recruit will have complied with critical organizational norms and should begin to identify with experienced organizational members.

ROLE MANAGEMENT Having survived the encounter stage and acquired basic role behaviours, the new member's attention shifts to fine-tuning and actively managing his or her role in the organization. Following some conformity to group norms, the new recruit might now be in a position to modify the role to better serve the organization. This might require forming connections outside the immediate work group. The organizational member must also confront balancing the now-familiar organizational role with non-work roles and family demands. Each of these experiences provides additional socialization to the role occupant, who might begin to internalize the norms and values that are prominent in the organization.

Now that we have seen a basic sketch of how socialization proceeds, let's take a closer look at some of the key issues in the process.

LO 8.3

Describe the implications of *unrealistic expectations* and the *psychological contract* for socialization.

UNREALISTIC EXPECTATIONS AND THE PSYCHOLOGICAL CONTRACT

People seldom join organizations without expectations about what membership will be like and what they expect to receive in return for their efforts. In fact, it is just such expectations that lead them to choose one career, job, or organization over another. Management majors have some expectations about what they will be doing when they become management trainees at IBM. Similarly, even 18-year-old army recruits have notions about what military life will be like. Unfortunately, these expectations are often unrealistic, and agreements between new members and organizations are often breached. Let's now consider the implications of unrealistic expectations and the psychological contract.

Unrealistic Expectations

Research indicates that people entering organizations hold many expectations that are inaccurate and often unrealistically high. As a result, once they enter an organization they realize that their expectations are not being met and they experience what is known as "reality shock."[13] In one study of telephone operators, for example, researchers obtained people's expectations about the nature of the job *before* they started work. They also looked at these employees' perceptions of the actual job shortly *after* they started work. The results indicated that many perceptions were less favourable than expectations. A similar result occurred for students entering an MBA program. The extent to which newcomers' expectations are met (or unmet) has important implications for their socialization. Research has found that newcomers who have higher met expectations have higher job satisfaction, organizational commitment, job performance, and job survival and lower intentions to quit.[14]

Why do new members often have unrealistic expectations about the organizations they join?[15] To some extent, occupational stereotypes, such as those we discussed in Chapter 3, could be responsible. The media often communicate such stereotypes. For example, a person entering nursing training might have gained some expectations about hospital life from watching the television show *Grey's Anatomy*. Those of us who teach might also be guilty of communicating stereotypes. After four years of study, the new management trainee at IBM might be dismayed to find that the emphasis is on *trainee* rather than *management*! Finally, unrealistic expectations may also stem from overzealous recruiters who paint rosy pictures to attract job candidates to the organization. Taken together, these factors demonstrate the need for socialization and for helping recruits acquire more realistic expectations.

Psychological Contract

When people join organizations, they have beliefs and expectations about what they will receive from the organization in return for what they will give the organization. Such beliefs form what is known as the psychological contract. A **psychological contract** refers to beliefs held by employees regarding the reciprocal obligations and promises between them and their organization.[16] For example, an employee might expect to receive bonuses and promotions in return for hard work and loyalty.

Unfortunately, psychological contract breach appears to be a common occurrence. Perceptions of **psychological contract breach** occur when an employee perceives that his or her organization has failed to fulfill one or more of its promises or obligations in the psychological contract. One study found that 55 percent of MBA graduates reported that some aspect of their psychological contract had been broken by their employers.[17] This often results in feelings of anger and betrayal and can have a negative effect on employees' work attitudes and behaviour.

A review of research on the impact of psychological contract breach found that breach is related to affective reactions (higher feelings of contract violation and mistrust toward management), work attitudes (lower job satisfaction and organizational commitment, and higher turnover intentions), and work behaviours (lower organizational citizenship behaviour and job performance). These effects are due to the formation of negative emotions that stem from feelings of violation and mistrust toward management.[18] Employee perceptions of psychological contract breach have also been found to be associated with a decrease in innovation-related behaviours (e.g., coming up with new ideas) and lower customer satisfaction, both of which can have negative consequences for organizations.[19]

Why does psychological contract breach occur? As is the case with unrealistic expectations, recruiters are often tempted to promise more than their organization can provide to attract the best job applicants. In addition, newcomers often lack sufficient information to form accurate perceptions concerning their psychological contract. As a result, there will be some incongruence or differences in understanding between an employee and the organization about promised obligations. In addition, organizational changes, such as downsizing and restructuring, can cause organizations to knowingly break promises made to an employee whom they are either unable or unwilling to keep.[20]

It is therefore important that newcomers develop accurate perceptions in the formation of a psychological contract. Many of the terms of the psychological contract are established during anticipatory socialization. Therefore, organizations need to ensure that truthful and accurate information about promises and obligations is communicated to new members before and after they join an organization. Incongruence and psychological contract breach are less likely in organizations where socialization is intense.[21] Furthermore, there is some evidence that what organizations actually give employees is most important.[22] This further demonstrates the importance and need for organizational socialization. Let's now take a closer look at how organizations socialize new members.

METHODS OF ORGANIZATIONAL SOCIALIZATION

Organizations differ in the extent to which they socialize their new hires. This is in part owing to the fact that some organizations make use of other organizations to help socialize their members. For example, hospitals do not develop experienced cardiologists from scratch. Rather, they depend on medical schools to socialize potential doctors in the basic role requirements of being a physician. Similarly, business firms rely on business schools to send them recruits who think and act in a business-like manner. In this way, a fair degree

Psychological contract.
Beliefs held by employees regarding the reciprocal obligations and promises between them and their organization.

Psychological contract breach. Employee perceptions that his or her organization has failed to fulfill one or more of its promises or obligations in the psychological contract.

LO 8.4

Describe the main methods of socialization and how newcomers can be *proactive* in their socialization.

of anticipatory socialization may exist before a person joins an organization. On the other hand, organizations such as police forces, the military, and religious institutions are less likely to rely on external socialization. Police academies, boot camps, and seminaries are set up as extensions of these organizations to aid in socialization.

Organizations that handle their own socialization are especially interested in maintaining the continuity and stability of job behaviours over a period of time. Conversely, those that rely on external agencies to perform anticipatory socialization are oriented toward maintaining the potential for creative, innovative behaviour on the part of members—there is less "inbreeding." Of course, reliance on external agents might present problems. The engineer who is socialized in university courses to respect design elegance might find it difficult to accept cost restrictions when he or she is employed by an engineering firm. For this reason, organizations that rely heavily on external socialization always supplement it with formal training and orientation or informal on-the-job training.

The point is that organizations differ in terms of *who* does the socializing, *how* it is done, and *how much* is done. Most organizations, however, make use of a number of methods of socialization, including realistic job previews, employee orientation programs, socialization tactics, and mentoring. Let's now take a closer look at each of these methods of organizational socialization.

Realistic Job Previews

We noted earlier that new organizational members often have unrealistic, inflated expectations about what their jobs will be like. When the job actually begins and it fails to live up to these expectations, individuals experience "reality shock," and job dissatisfaction results. As a consequence, costly turnover is most likely to occur among newer employees who are unable to survive the discrepancy between expectations and reality. For the organization, this sequence of events represents a failure of socialization.

Obviously, organizations cannot control all sources of unrealistic job expectations, such as those provided by television shows and glorified occupational stereotypes. However, they *can* control those generated during the recruitment process by providing job applicants with realistic job previews. **Realistic job previews** provide a balanced, realistic picture of the positive and negative aspects of the job to applicants.[23] Thus, they provide "corrective action" to expectations at the anticipatory socialization stage. Exhibit 8.3 compares the realistic job

Realistic job previews. The provision of a balanced, realistic picture of the positive and negative aspects of a job to applicants.

EXHIBIT 8.3
Traditional and realistic job previews compared.
Source: Republished with permission of American Management Association, from Wanous, J.P. Tell it like it is at realistic job previews. Personnel, *52*(4), 50–60 © 1975; permission conveyed through Copyright Clearance Center, Inc.

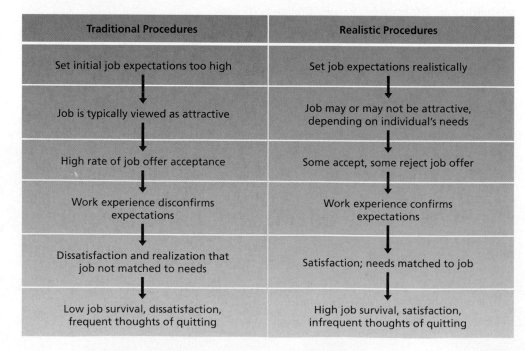

Traditional Procedures	Realistic Procedures
Set initial job expectations too high	Set job expectations realistically
Job is typically viewed as attractive	Job may or may not be attractive, depending on individual's needs
High rate of job offer acceptance	Some accept, some reject job offer
Work experience disconfirms expectations	Work experience confirms expectations
Dissatisfaction and realization that job not matched to needs	Satisfaction; needs matched to job
Low job survival, dissatisfaction, frequent thoughts of quitting	High job survival, satisfaction, infrequent thoughts of quitting

preview process with the traditional preview process that often sets expectations too high by ignoring the negative aspects of the job.

How do organizations design and conduct realistic job previews? Generally, they obtain the views of experienced employees and human resources staff about the positive and negative aspects of the job. Then, they incorporate these views into booklets or video presentations for applicants.[24] A video might involve interviews with job incumbents discussing the pros and cons of their jobs. Some companies have managers and employees communicate realistic information to job candidates in person. For example, Scotiabank has managers from various business lines explain the day-to-day job realities to prospective job candidates.[25] Realistic previews have been designed for jobs as diverse as telephone operators, life insurance salespeople, U.S. Marine Corps recruits, and supermarket workers.

Sometimes realistic previews use simulations to permit applicants to actually sample the work. For example, in an effort to recruit more women, the Ontario Provincial Police (OPP) have staged recruiting camps in which the women experience typical OPP policing activities, including shooting a handgun, completing 6 a.m. fitness drills, and responding to mock crimes.[26]

RESEARCH EVIDENCE Evidence shows that realistic job previews are effective in reducing inflated expectations and turnover, and in improving job performance.[27] What is less clear is exactly why turnover reduction occurs. Reduced expectations and increased job satisfaction are part of the answer. It also appears that realistic previews cause those not cut out for the job or who have low PJ and PO fit perceptions to withdraw from the application process, a process known as *self-selection*.[28] As a result, applicants who perceive a good PJ and PO fit are more likely to accept a job offer and remain on the job. There is also some evidence that organizations that provide realistic job previews are perceived by job applicants as more honest and trustworthy, and this encourages employees to remain with the organization once they are hired.[29] Although the turnover reductions generated by realistic previews are small, they can result in substantial financial savings for organizations.[30] Thus, providing realistic job previews is a low-investment strategy that can lower unrealistic expectations and reduce turnover. There is also some evidence that they can also help prevent perceptions of psychological contract breach.[31]

Employee Orientation Programs

Once newcomers enter an organization, socialization during the encounter stage usually begins with an orientation program. **Employee orientation programs** are designed to introduce new employees to their job, the people they will be working with, and the organization. The main content of most orientation programs consists of health and safety issues, terms and conditions of employment, and information about the organization, such as its history and traditions. Another purpose of employee orientation programs is to begin conveying and forming the psychological contract and to teach newcomers how to cope with stressful work situations.[32]

Orientation programs that are designed to help newcomers cope with stress are called **Realistic Orientation Program for Entry Stress (ROPES)**. Like a realistic job preview, ROPES provides newcomers with realistic information about work tasks and the organization; however, it also teaches newcomers how to use cognitive and behavioural coping techniques to manage workplace stressors.[33]

Most orientation programs take place during the first week of entry and last one day to one week. Some organizations realize the importance of orientation and invest a considerable amount of time and resources in it. For example, Capital Power, an independent power producer in Edmonton, designed and implemented an orientation program called "Strong

Employee orientation programs. Programs designed to introduce new employees to their job, the people they will be working with, and the organization.

Realistic Orientation Program for Entry Stress (ROPES). An orientation program that is designed to teach newcomers coping techniques to manage workplace stressors.

EXHIBIT 8.4
Socialization tactics.

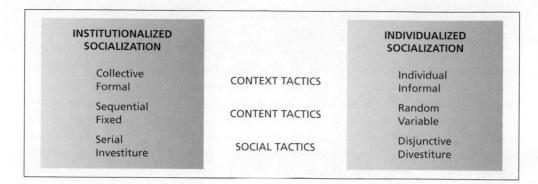

INSTITUTIONALIZED SOCIALIZATION		INDIVIDUALIZED SOCIALIZATION
Collective Formal	CONTEXT TACTICS	Individual Informal
Sequential Fixed	CONTENT TACTICS	Random Variable
Serial Investiture	SOCIAL TACTICS	Disjunctive Divestiture

Start." The program combines e-learning modules with classroom instruction that provides information about the organization (e.g., vision, values, and policies) and its business. The modules are interactive and include video clips, online coaching, an intranet scavenger hunt, and knowledge checks. After completing the e-learning modules, new hires participate in a day-and-a-half classroom session that includes a talk from the CEO or another senior executive. New hires are also required to create a 100-day initial development plan with their manager. Capital Power has seen a 30 percent increase in organizational knowledge among participants since the program was launched.[34]

RESEARCH EVIDENCE Orientation programs are an important method of socialization because they can have an immediate effect on learning and a lasting effect on the job attitudes and behaviours of new hires. One study found that newly hired employees who attended an orientation program were more socialized in terms of their knowledge and understanding of the organization's goals and values, history, and involvement with people, and also reported higher organizational commitment compared to employees who did not attend the orientation program.[35] A study conducted at Corning Inc. concluded that employees who completed a full orientation program were 69 percent more likely to remain employed with the company for at least three years. Other companies have also seen substantial decreases in their rate of turnover as a result of employee orientation programs.[36] Research on ROPES has found that it lowers participants' expectations and stress and improves newcomers' adjustment and retention.[37]

Socialization Tactics

Socialization tactics.
The manner in which organizations structure the early work experiences of newcomers and individuals who are in transition from one role to another.

John Van Maanen and Edgar Schein developed a theory of socialization that helps us understand and explain the socialization process. They suggested that there are six **socialization tactics** that organizations use to structure the early work experiences of new hires and individuals who are in transition from one role to another. As shown in Exhibit 8.4, each of the six tactics consists of a bipolar continuum that can be grouped into two separate patterns of socialization called institutionalized socialization and individualized socialization (see Exhibit 8.5 for descriptions of each of the tactics).[38]

Institutionalized socialization consists of collective, formal, sequential, fixed, serial, and investiture tactics. Individualized socialization consists of individual, informal, random, variable, disjunctive, and divestiture tactics. The main difference between these two approaches to socialization is that institutionalized socialization involves a more formalized and structured program of socialization that reduces uncertainty and encourages new hires to accept organizational norms and maintain the status quo. On the other hand, individualized socialization reflects a relative absence of structure that creates ambiguity and encourages new hires to question the status quo and develop their own approach to their role.

In addition, the tactics have also been distinguished in terms of the *context* in which information is presented to new hires, the *content* provided to new hires, and the *social* aspects of socialization.[39] As shown in Exhibit 8.4, the collective–individual and formal–informal

Collective versus Individual Tactics The collective tactic consists of a number of new members being socialized as a group, going through the same experiences and facing the same challenges. Army boot camps, fraternity pledge classes, and training classes for salespeople and flight attendants are common examples. In contrast, the individual tactic consists of socialization experiences that are tailor-made for each new member. Simple on-the-job training and apprenticeship to develop skilled craftspeople constitute individual socialization.

Formal versus Informal Tactics Formal tactics involve segregating newcomers from regular organizational members and providing them with formal learning experiences during the period of socialization. Informal tactics, however, do not distinguish a newcomer from more experienced members and rely more on informal and on-the-job learning.

Sequential versus Random Tactics The sequential tactic involves a fixed sequence of steps or stages leading to the assumption of the role, whereas with the random tactic, there is an ambiguous or changing sequence.

Fixed versus Variable Tactics The fixed tactic consists of a timetable for the newcomer's assumption of the role. If the tactic is variable, then there is no time frame to indicate when the socialization process ends and the newcomer assumes his or her new role.

Serial versus Disjunctive Tactics The serial tactic refers to a process in which newcomers are socialized by experienced members of the organization. The disjunctive tactic refers to a socialization process where role models and experienced organization members do not groom new members or "show them the ropes."

Investiture versus Divestiture Tactics Divestiture tactics (also known as debasement and hazing) involve putting new members through a series of experiences that are designed to humble them and strip away some of their initial self-confidence and change their attitudes and beliefs. Debasement is a way of testing the commitment of new members and correcting for faulty anticipatory socialization. Having been humbled and stripped of preconceptions, members are then ready to learn the norms of the organization. An extreme example is the rough treatment and shaved heads of U.S. Marine Corps recruits. The investiture socialization tactic affirms the incoming identity and attributes of new hires rather than denying them and stripping them away. Organizations that carefully select new members for certain attributes and characteristics would be more likely to use the investiture tactic.

EXHIBIT 8.5
Descriptions of the socialization tactics.
Source: Based on Van Maanen, J., & Schein, E.H. (1979). Toward a theory of organizational socialization. In B.M. Staw (Ed.), *Research in organizational behavior*, Vol. 1. Greenwich, CT: JAI Press, 209–264.

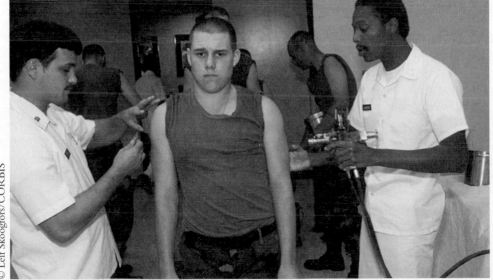

© Leif Skoogfors/CORBIS

Some socialization tactics, such as debasement and hazing, are designed to strip new members of their old beliefs, values, and attitudes and get them to internalize new ones.

tactics represent the context of socialization; the sequential–random and fixed–variable tactics represent the content of socialization; and the serial–disjunctive and investiture–divestiture tactics represent the social aspects of socialization.

Why would an organization choose institutionalized over individualized socialization? Institutionalized socialization tactics are effective in promoting organizational loyalty and uniformity of behaviour among those being socialized. This last characteristic is often very important. No matter where they are in the world, soldiers know whom to salute and how to do it. Similarly, air passengers need not expect any surprises from cabin crew, thanks to the flight attendants' institutionalized socialization.

When socialization is individualized, new members are more likely to take on the particular characteristics and style of those who are socializing them. Thus, two newly hired real estate agents who receive on-the-job training from their bosses might soon think and act more like their bosses than like each other. As you can see, uniformity is less likely under individualized socialization.

Institutionalized socialization is always followed up by some individualized socialization as the member joins his or her regular work unit. For example, rookie police officers are routinely partnered with more experienced officers. At this point, they will begin to develop some individuality in the style with which they perform their jobs.

RESEARCH EVIDENCE Research on socialization tactics supports the basic predictions regarding the effects of institutionalized and individualized socialization on newcomers' roles, attitudes, and behaviour. Institutionalized socialization tactics are related to proximal outcomes, such as lower role ambiguity and role conflict and more positive perceptions of PJ and PO fit, as well as distal outcomes, such as greater job satisfaction and organizational commitment and lower stress and turnover. In addition, institutionalized socialization tactics result in a custodial role orientation, in which new hires accept the status quo and the requirements of their tasks and roles. Individualized socialization tactics result in a more innovative role orientation, in which new recruits might change or modify the way they perform their tasks and roles.

It is also worth noting that among the different socialization tactics, the social tactics (serial–disjunctive and investiture–divestiture) have been found to be the most strongly related to socialization outcomes. This is consistent with research that has found that organizations that are more successful at socializing newcomers help them to establish a broad network of relationships with co-workers.[40] However, there is some evidence that social tactics can have negative consequences. To find out, see the Ethical Focus, *Socialization Tactics and Ethical Conflict*.

Mentoring

It should be apparent from our discussion of socialization tactics that supervisors and peers play an important role in the socialization process. While effective relationships between supervisors and their employees influence the socialization and career success of individuals within an organization, one particularly important relationship is between a newcomer or protégé and a mentor.

A **mentor** is an experienced or more senior person in the organization who provides a junior person with guidance and special attention, such as by giving advice and creating opportunities to assist him or her during the early stages of his or her career. While someone other than the junior person's boss can serve as a mentor, often the supervisor is in a unique position to provide mentoring.

Mentoring is a type of developmental relationship that produces benefits for a protégé's work and/or career.[41] However, for mentors to be effective they must perform two types of developmental functions: career and psychosocial functions.

CAREER FUNCTIONS OF MENTORING A mentor provides many career-enhancing benefits to newcomers.[42] These benefits are made possible by the senior person's experience,

Mentor. An experienced or more senior person in the organization who provides a junior person with guidance and special attention, such as giving advice and creating opportunities to assist him or her during the early stages of his or her career.

■ ETHICAL FOCUS

SOCIALIZATION TACTICS AND ETHICAL CONFLICT

Professionals in fields such as law, medicine, psychology, and teaching receive extensive training in ethics and resolving ethical conflicts that can arise in their fields. Thus, one might think that ethical misconduct would be rare among professionals. However, even trained professionals experience a significant amount of ethical conflict in their work, and these ethical conflicts can cause employees to feel frustrated and emotionally exhausted.

Ethical conflict is a subjective sense that expectations for one's behaviour are inconsistent with one's beliefs regarding what is right and wrong. Thus, ethical conflict arises when there is a perceived discrepancy between the ethical climate of the organization and the ethics of the individual and the individual must choose between two competing principles. This is especially problematic when the organization has lower ethical standards than the individual.

But what can cause an individual to experience ethical conflict at work and what are the consequences of it?

According to John D. Kammeyer-Mueller, Lauren S. Simon, and Bruce L. Rich, ethical conflicts can occur when an organization's socialization practices encourage new employees to behave counter to their own sense of right and wrong. In particular, they predicted that divestiture socialization tactics are most likely to result in ethical conflict because they discourage employees from using their own belief systems and replace them with the organization's attitudes and beliefs, whereas investiture socialization tactics encourage employees to rely on their own sense of what is right. The authors also predicted that divestiture tactics and ethical conflict will result in more emotional exhaustion and that ethical conflict will lead to lower career fulfillment.

To test these predictions, the authors conducted a study of 371 early-career lawyers. The lawyers completed a survey that asked them about their socialization, the extent to which they had experienced various conflicts during their first years on the job as practising lawyers (e.g., conflict between their personal values and the directives of their supervisors), and their experience of emotional exhaustion (e.g., feeling run down) and career fulfillment (e.g., pay level and promotion).

As predicted, divestiture socialization was positively related to ethical conflict and emotional exhaustion. In addition, ethical conflict was positively related to emotional exhaustion, and emotional exhaustion was negatively related to career fulfillment.

The results of this study indicate that early-career lawyers who experience higher levels of divestiture socialization experience more ethical conflict at work, which in turn results in more emotional exhaustion and lower career fulfillment.

These results do not mean that divestiture socialization should always be avoided. In fact, there are some occupations, such police, military, and emergency medical teams, where uniformity of behaviour is extremely important and divestiture socialization is required. The point that the authors are making is that divestiture socialization tactics should be designed to clarify and support newcomers' beliefs about ethical behaviour and teach them that following the organization's rules for behaviour is consistent with achieving their desired ethical ends.

Source: Based on Kammeyer-Mueller, J.D., Simon, L.S., & Rich, B.L. (2012). The psychic cost of doing wrong: Ethical conflict, divestiture socialization, and emotional exhaustion. *Journal of Management, 38*, 784–808.

status, knowledge of how the organization works, and influence with powerful people in the organization. The career functions of mentoring include

- *Sponsorship.* The mentor might nominate the newcomer for advantageous transfers and promotions.

- *Exposure and visibility.* The mentor might provide opportunities for the newcomer to work with key people and see other parts of the organization.

- *Coaching and feedback.* The mentor might suggest work strategies and identify strengths and weaknesses in the newcomer's performance.

- *Developmental assignments.* The mentor can provide challenging work assignments that will help the newcomer develop key skills and knowledge that are crucial to career progress.

PSYCHOSOCIAL FUNCTIONS OF MENTORING Besides helping directly with career progress, mentors can provide certain psychosocial functions that are helpful in developing the newcomer's self-confidence, sense of identity, and ability to cope with emotional traumas that can damage a person's effectiveness. These include

- *Role modelling.* This provides a set of attitudes, values, and behaviours for the newcomer to imitate.
- *Providing acceptance and confirmation.* This provides encouragement and support and helps the newcomer gain self-confidence.
- *Counselling.* This provides an opportunity to discuss personal concerns and anxieties concerning career prospects, work–family conflicts, and so on.

FORMAL MENTORING PROGRAMS Mentoring relationships have often been of an informal nature, in that the individuals involved chose to enter into a mentoring relationship with each other without the direct involvement of their organization. However, **formal mentoring programs**, in which seasoned employees are recruited as mentors and matched with newcomers as part of an organization sponsored program, have become increasingly popular in recent years and are now provided by many organizations.[43] For example, Telvent Canada Ltd., a Calgary-based company that develops information management systems, started a formal mentoring program a number of years ago. Although it was originally offered to new hires to help get them up to speed, it is now available to all of the company's employees. Bell Canada launched a company-wide online mentor program several years ago called Mentor Match, which is open to all of its employees. The program is available on the company's intranet, and employees must apply to be either a mentor or a protégé.[44]

DEVELOPMENTAL NETWORKS In recent years, it has become apparent that many newcomers have more than a single mentor and that mentoring support can come from several people inside and outside of the organization, or what is known as a developmental network. **Developmental networks** refer to groups of people who take an active interest in a protégé's career and take actions toward advancing it by providing developmental assistance. Thus, unlike in a traditional mentoring relationship, which involves one protégé and one mentor, in a developmental network a protégé can have multiple developers from inside

Formal mentoring programs. Organization sponsored programs in which seasoned employees are recruited as mentors and matched with protégés.

Developmental networks. Groups of people who take an active interest in a protégé's career and take actions toward advancing it by providing developmental assistance.

Many research efforts have documented the importance of having a mentor when starting one's career and how it can influence career success.

© Monkey Business/Fotolia

and outside (e.g., family and community) of the organization, and the network can include people from different hierarchical levels of the organization (e.g., peers, superiors, subordinates, and senior managers). With a developmental network, a newcomer is more likely to obtain different types of support (e.g., career and psychosocial) and to realize a broader range of career outcomes.[45]

WOMEN AND MENTORING One factor that inhibits women's career development compared with that of their male counterparts is the difficulty women have historically faced in establishing a mentor relationship with a senior person in the organization.[46] The lack of mentors and role models is a major barrier for the career advancement of many women.[47] The problem goes well beyond the traditional gender stereotyping we discussed in Chapter 3. It stems from the fact that the senior people who are in the best position to be mentors are frequently men, and men are more likely to serve as mentors than are women.[48] Further, a young woman attempting to establish a productive relationship with a senior male associate faces complexities that a male apprentice does not. Often, a woman's concerns are different from those her male mentor experienced at that stage in his career. As a result, the strategies that he models might have limited relevance for the female newcomer.

Because of these concerns, the prospective female newcomer faces more constraints than her male counterpart. Research has confirmed that cross-gender dyads are less likely to get involved in informal after-work social activities. These activities can help newcomers establish relationships with other influential people in a relaxed setting. Research also confirms that newcomers in a cross-gender dyad are less likely to see their mentor as a role model and, therefore, are less likely to realize the developmental benefits of an effective model.[49]

However, with many organizations now providing formal mentoring programs, the barriers facing women in finding a mentor have been removed. In fact, a review of gender differences in mentoring found that males and females are equally likely to have been protégés. And while male and female protégés report receiving equal amounts of career development mentoring, female protégés reported receiving more psychosocial support.[50] Similarly, a study on formal mentoring programs found that the negative effects associated with cross-gender dyads dissipates as the mentoring relationship develops over time. Thus, protégés in cross-gender dyads receive just as much career and psychosocial mentoring as those in same-gender relationships.[51]

The research evidence suggests that mentoring is even more critical to women's career success than it is to men's. Women who make it to executive positions have invariably had a mentor along the way. This is true for one-half to two-thirds of male executives.[52] Recent studies also indicate that a majority of women (61 percent) have had a mentor, and almost all (99 percent) say that their mentor has had an impact on the advancement of their career.[53] There is also some evidence that in male-dominated industries, female managers and professionals benefit the most from a senior male mentor.[54]

Thus, for women with career aspirations, finding a mentor appears to be a difficult but crucial task. The good news is that an increasing number of organizations are developing mentoring programs as well as women's internal networks to provide women with opportunities to network and find mentors. For example, Deloitte has a program called Developing Leaders, in which experienced partners mentor and coach male and female partners who demonstrate leadership potential. Mentors are carefully chosen, and their skills and experience are matched to the new partner's goals and aspirations. In addition, women at Deloitte have developed networking and mentoring opportunities for themselves through a program called Women's Business Development Groups. The group organizes networking events, meets with other women's business groups, and organizes an annual Spring Breakfast during which prominent women are invited to speak. ENMAX, a utility company in Calgary, has a women's internal network called EN-power that includes professional development, leadership, and soft skills training. Enbridge has a Women@Enbridge program, which is an employee resource group to support the career development of female employees.[55] These kinds of programs are extremely important, because research has found that exclusion from informal networks is one of the major roadblocks to the advancement of women.[56]

RACE, ETHNICITY, AND MENTORING   Limited racial and ethnic diversity at higher levels of organizations can also constrain the mentoring opportunities available to younger minority group employees. Research shows that mentors tend to select individuals to mentor who are similar to them in terms of race and nationality as well as gender.[57] While there are exceptions, research confirms that minority apprentices in cross-ethnic group mentoring

RESEARCH FOCUS

THE DISCRIMINATORY GAP IN UNIVERSITY MENTORING

If you are looking for a professor to mentor you at university, you might think that a university is one place where your gender and race would not matter. Unfortunately, the results of a recent study of prospective doctoral students seeking mentorship suggest that this is not the case.

Katherine Milkman, Modupe Akinola, and Dolly Chugh conducted a study in which they sent mock emails to more than 6,500 professors from 89 disciplines at 259 top universities in the United States. The messages were purported to be from prospective doctoral students with an interest in the professor's research and a request for a short meeting to discuss research opportunities before applying to a doctoral program. The emails were all the same, except that the name of the student varied and was meant to signal gender and race. The names were shown in previous research to be perceived as belonging to white, black, Hispanic, Indian, or Chinese students and included names such as Brad Anderson, Meredith Roberts, Lamar Washington, LaToya Brown, Juanita Martinez, Deepak Patel, Sonali Desai, Chang Wong, and Mei Chen. A total of 20 names were used, which made up 10 different race-gender categories (e.g., white male, Hispanic female). The main outcome of interest was whether the professors would respond to the request within one week.

The researchers sent the emails on a Monday morning and then waited to see which professors would respond. They expected that the treatment of any student on average should not differ from any other unless the professors were deciding which students they would help based on their race or gender. However, they also suggested that differential treatment on the basis of gender and race might be a factor in the under-representation of women and minority doctoral students and professors, especially in certain disciplines.

Most of the professors (67 percent) responded to the emails and 59 percent agreed to meet the student.

However, the professors were more responsive to white male students than to white females, black, Hispanic, Indian, or Chinese students. Although this was the case in every discipline and across all types of universities, it was especially the case in private schools and higher-paying disciplines. The greatest bias was in business, where 87 percent of white males received a response compared to 62 percent of all females and minorities combined. What's more, the results were the same for all professors, regardless of their gender and race, and it did not matter if the student was the same gender or race as the professor. Female and minority professors were just as likely to respond more often to white males, and they were not more likely to respond to requests from female or minority students. The results were no different in disciplines where there are more female and minority faculty.

The results of this study indicate that in almost every academic discipline, faculty exhibit a bias that favours white males and discriminates against female and minority group students seeking mentoring. The authors do not believe that the professors were intentionally discriminating against women and minorities, but rather that the bias was more likely unconscious and unintentional. Unfortunately, regardless of whether the bias was conscious or unconscious, it still contributes to discrimination, or what the authors refer to as a "discriminatory gap," that contributes to the under-representation of women and minorities in the ranks of both doctoral students and professors, and can have meaningful career consequences for individuals and society.

Sources: Milkman, K.L., Akinola, M., & Chugh, D. (2015). What happens before? A field experiment exploring how pay and representation differentially shape bias on the pathway into organizations. *Journal of Applied Psychology*; Waldman, K. (2014, April 27). The advantages of being white and male. *Toronto Star*, IN3; Matter, G. (2014, May 9). Professors are prejudiced, too. *The New York Times*, http://nyti.ms/1ghpQ8F.

relationships tend to report less assistance than those with same-race mentors.[58] There is also some evidence that women and minorities are less likely to find a mentor in academics. To learn more, see Research Focus: *The Discriminatory Gap in University Mentoring.*

Cross-race mentoring relationships seem to focus on instrumental or career functions of mentoring (e.g., sponsorship, coaching, and feedback) and provide fewer psychosocial support functions (e.g., role modelling and counselling) than is generally seen in same-race dyads.[59] Although the increasing diversity of organizations makes this tendency less problematic, it suggests that minority group members need to put extra efforts into developing a supportive network of peers who can provide emotional support and role modelling as well as the career functions. It also means that organizations must do more to provide mentoring opportunities for minority employees, just as some have done for women. Fortunately, many organizations now include mentoring and networking opportunities as part of their diversity strategy.[60]

RESEARCH EVIDENCE Many research studies have documented the importance of having a mentor when starting one's career and how it can influence career success.[61] A review of this research found that mentored individuals had higher objective career outcomes, such as compensation and number of promotions, and higher subjective outcomes, including greater satisfaction with their jobs and careers and greater career commitment. They were also more likely to believe that they would advance in their career. However, mentoring tends to be more strongly related to the subjective than to the objective career outcomes. Furthermore, in comparisons of the effects of the two mentoring functions, the psychosocial function is more strongly related to satisfaction with the mentoring relationship, while the career function is more strongly related to compensation and advancement. Both functions are just as important in generating positive attitudes toward one's job and career.[62]

Research on formal mentoring programs has found that they are just as beneficial as informal mentoring relationships and certainly more beneficial than no mentoring at all. In addition, formal mentoring programs have been found to be most effective when the mentor and protégé have input into the matching process and when they receive training prior to the mentoring relationship, especially training that is perceived to be of a high quality.[63]

Proactive Socialization

In Chapter 2 it was noted that individuals learn by observing and imitating the behaviour of others and that proactive behaviours involve taking initiative to improve current circumstances or create new ones. Thus, it should not surprise you that these forms of learning are also important for socialization. That is, newcomers can be proactive in their socialization and in the management of their careers through the use of proactive behaviours or what is known as proactive socialization.

Proactive socialization refers to the process in which newcomers play an active role in their socialization through the use of proactive behaviours. Exhibit 8.6 describes the major types of proactive socialization behaviours. Two of the most important are to request feedback about one's work and job performance (**feedback seeking**) and to seek information about one's work tasks, roles, work group, and organization (**information seeking**). Recall that organizational socialization is about learning the attitudes, knowledge, and behaviours that are necessary to function as an effective member of a group and organization. One way for newcomers to learn about their new job, role, and the organization is to seek information from others in the organization.[64]

Newcomers can acquire information by requesting it, by asking questions, and by observing the behaviour of others. In addition, there are different sources that can be used to acquire information, such as supervisors, co-workers, mentors, and written documents.

Proactive socialization.
The process through which newcomers play an active role in their own socialization through the use of a number of proactive socialization behaviours.

Feedback seeking.
Requesting information about how one is performing one's tasks and role.

Information seeking.
Requesting information about one's job, role, group, and organization.

EXHIBIT 8.6
Proactive socialization behaviours.
Source: Based on Ashford, S.J., & Black, J.S. (1996). Proactivity during organizational entry: The role of desire for control. *Journal of Applied Psychology, 81,* 199–214.

Feedback seeking Requesting information about how one is performing one's tasks and role.

Information seeking Requesting information about one's job, role, group, and organization.

General socializing Participating in social office events and attending social gatherings (e.g., parties, outings, clubs, and lunches).

Relationship building Initiating social interactions and building relationships with others in one's area or department.

Boss-relationship building Initiating social interactions to get to know and form a relationship with one's boss.

Networking Socializing with and getting to know members of the organization from various departments and functions.

Job change negotiation Attempts to change one's job duties or the manner and means by which one performs one's job in order to increase the fit between oneself and the job.

Research has found that newcomers rely primarily on observation, followed by interpersonal sources (i.e., supervisors and co-workers). Furthermore, they tend to seek out task-related information the most, especially during the early period of socialization, followed by role, group, and organization information.[65]

In addition to feedback seeking and information seeking, newcomers can also be proactive by participating in social events (general socializing), developing friendships and relationships with co-workers (relationship building), developing a friendship and relationship with their boss (boss-relationship building), getting to know people outside of their department or work area (networking), and attempting to change or modify their tasks to improve PJ fit (job change negotiation).[66]

RESEARCH EVIDENCE Research has found that newcomers who engage in proactive behaviours more frequently are more likely to obtain the corresponding proactive outcomes and to have more positive proximal socialization outcomes (e.g., fit perceptions) and distal socialization outcomes (e.g., job satisfaction). For example, newcomers who frequently seek feedback are more likely to obtain it and those who engage in relationship building are more likely to have developed friendships with co-workers. Thus newcomers who are more proactive obtain more feedback and information, and develop more friendships and relationships, all of which result in more positive proximal and distal socialization outcomes. Thus, it pays to be proactive![67]

LO **8.5**

Define *organizational culture*, and discuss the assets and liabilities of *strong cultures*.

PERSONAL INVENTORY ASSESSMENT

Learn About Yourself
Company Culture Assessment

ORGANIZATIONAL CULTURE

The previous several pages have been concerned with socialization into an organization. To a large degree, the course of that socialization both depends on and shapes the culture of the organization. As indicated in the chapter-opening vignette, Kicking Horse Coffee has a unique fun culture that emphasizes active living, wellness, work–life balance, and social and environmental issues. But what exactly is an organizational culture? Let's now examine culture, a concept that has gained the attention of both researchers and practising managers.

What Is Organizational Culture?

At the outset, we can say that organizational culture is not the easiest concept to define. But to get you thinking about what a culture is like, consider this example. The day before game seven of the 2011 Stanley Cup finals between the Vancouver Canucks and the Boston Bruins, Tracy Redies, former CEO of Coast Capital Savings Credit Union, received an email from a customer service representative asking her to consider closing branches with extended hours early so that employees would be able to watch game seven with their families. Many businesses would not have considered such a request. However, an important part of Coast Capital's culture is caring, and this was a great opportunity to show employees that the organization cared about them. So within a few hours, Redies sent out an email announcing that the branches would be closing early and customers would be directed to the call centre. Employees working at the call centre would get large screen TVs and pizza so they, too, could watch the game. Within 30 seconds of the announcement, Redies received hundreds of emails from thrilled employees, including many who did not even work at the extended-hour branches but were happy for their co-workers. One customer service representative sent her an email in bold that read: "I love you CEO."[68] Clearly, the CEO's actions were part and parcel of the company's culture.

Informally, culture might be thought of as an organization's style, atmosphere, or personality. This style, atmosphere, or personality is most obvious when we contrast what it must be like to work in various organizations, such as Suncor Energy Inc., the Royal Bank of Canada, WestJet, Google Canada, or Kicking Horse Coffee. Even from their mention in the popular press, we can imagine that these organizations provide very different work environments. Thus, culture provides uniqueness and social identity to organizations.

More formally, **organizational culture** consists of the shared beliefs, values, and assumptions that exist in an organization.[69] In turn, these shared beliefs, values, and assumptions determine the norms that develop and the patterns of behaviour that emerge from these norms. The term *shared* does not necessarily mean that members are in close agreement on these matters, although they may well be. Rather, it means that they have had uniform exposure to them and have some minimum common understanding of them. Several other characteristics of culture are important.

- Culture represents a true "way of life" for organizational members, who often take its influence for granted. Frequently, an organization's culture becomes obvious only when it is contrasted with that of other organizations or when it undergoes changes.

- Because culture involves basic assumptions, values, and beliefs, it tends to be fairly stable over time. In addition, once a culture is well established, it can persist despite turnover among organizational members, providing social continuity.

- The content of a culture can involve matters that are internal to the organization or external. Internally, a culture might support innovation, risk taking, or secrecy of information. Externally, a culture might support "putting the customer first" or behaving unethically toward competitors.

- Culture can have a strong impact on both organizational performance and member satisfaction.

Culture is truly a social variable, reflecting yet another aspect of the kind of social influence that we have been discussing in this chapter. Thus, culture is not simply an automatic consequence of an organization's technology, products, or size. For example, there is some tendency for organizations to become more bureaucratic as they get larger. However, the culture of a particular large organization might support an informal, non-bureaucratic atmosphere.

Can an organization have several cultures? The answer is yes. Often, unique **subcultures** develop that reflect departmental differences or differences in occupation or training.[70] A researcher who studied Silicon Valley computer companies found that technical and professional employees were divided into "hardware types" and "software types." In turn, hardware types subdivided into engineers and technicians, and software types subdivided

Organizational culture. The shared beliefs, values, and assumptions that exist in an organization.

Subcultures. Smaller cultures that develop within a larger organizational culture and are based on differences in training, occupation, or departmental goals.

into software engineers and computer scientists. Each group had its own values, beliefs, and assumptions about how to design computer systems.[71] Effective organizations will develop an overarching culture that manages such divisions. For instance, a widely shared norm might exist that in effect says, "We fight like hell until a final design is chosen, and then we all pull together."

The "Strong Culture" Concept

Strong culture. An organizational culture with intense and pervasive beliefs, values, and assumptions.

Kicking Horse Coffee is a good example of a company with a strong culture, and it highlights the fact that some cultures have more impact on the behaviour of organizational members than others. But what exactly is a strong culture? In a **strong culture**, the beliefs, values, and assumptions that make up the culture are both intense and pervasive across the organization.[72] In other words, they are strongly supported by the majority of members, even cutting across any subcultures that might exist. Thus, the strong culture provides great consensus concerning "what the organization is about" or what it stands for. In weak cultures, on the other hand, beliefs, values, and assumptions are less strongly ingrained or less widely shared across the organization. Weak cultures are thus fragmented and have less impact on organizational members. All organizations have a culture, although it may be hard to detect the details of weak cultures.

To firm up your understanding of strong cultures, let's consider thumbnail sketches of some organizations that are generally agreed to have strong cultures.

- *Hilti (Canada) Corp.* The construction-equipment manufacturer in Mississauga, Ontario, developed a can-do attitude, using "Gung Ho!" as its mantra and to promote a culture that emphasizes the importance of worthwhile work, being in control of achieving your goals, and celebrating others' successes. The company takes its culture so seriously that "Gung Ho!" was transformed into a program called "Our Culture Journey" to ensure that all employees know what Hilti stands for and expects. Most of the company's employees have gone through the mandatory two-day Culture Journey, which reintroduces them to the company's culture. In addition, all new recruits get two days of "culture training" before they begin four weeks of product and sales training, and that is after four weeks of pre-training! Hilti has been ranked as one of the best workplaces in Canada.[73]

- *Google Canada.* Google has more than 50 000 employees in offices around the world but has been able to maintain a small-company feel thanks to a culture of collaboration, a flat structure with very little hierarchy, small focused teams of employees, kitchens that serve healthy food and courage employees to eat together and socialize, and perks such as in-house massages. The culture also emphasizes innovation and entrepreneurship through its "20 percent time" program which enables employees to spend one day out of five on something other than their job that they are passionate about so that employees can work on new ideas and collaborate with each other. The company even has a chief culture officer to ensure that it maintains its core values and culture. [74]

- *Express Scripts Canada.* Express Scripts Canada, a provider of health benefits management services, has been named the World's Most Ethical Company thanks in part to its ethics-based culture and commitment to conduct business ethically. Employees at the company have a commitment to ethical behaviour, good governance, and top-notch service to clients and patients. The company has a set of values called "Express Way" that focuses on acting honestly and demonstrating integrity at all times. The company has a compliance program to prevent, detect, and address unlawful and unethical behaviour, and the compliance department hosts an annual Compliance Awareness Day to promote awareness of the program. Privacy protection

Google Canada has a strong corporate culture that emphasizes innovation, collaboration, and entrepreneurship.

is also embedded into the culture through mandatory annual training and a value of privacy vigilance that guides daily work and future planning.[75]

Three points are worth emphasizing about strong cultures. First, an organization need not be big to have a strong culture. If its members agree strongly about certain beliefs, values, and assumptions, a small business, school, or social service agency can have a strong culture. Second, strong cultures do not necessarily result in blind conformity. For example, a strong culture at 3M supports and rewards *non*-conformity in the form of innovation and creativity. Finally, Hilti, Google Canada, and Express Scripts are obviously successful organizations. Thus, strong cultures are associated with greater success and effectiveness. Let's now consider the assets and liabilities of strong cultures.

Assets of Strong Cultures

Organizations with strong cultures have several potential advantages over those lacking a strong culture.

COORDINATION In effective organizations, the right hand (e.g., finance) knows what the left hand (e.g., production) is doing. The overarching values and assumptions of strong cultures can facilitate such communication. In turn, different parts of the organization can learn from each other and can coordinate their efforts. This is especially important in decentralized, team-oriented organizations. At Google Canada, coordination and collaboration are facilitated by providing places for employees to communicate and socialize with each other, weekly TGIF meetings, and its "20 percent time" program, which enables employees to work together one day out of five on something other than their job that they are passionate about.[76]

CONFLICT RESOLUTION You might be tempted to think that a strong culture would produce strong conflicts within an organization—that is, you might expect the intensity associated with strongly held assumptions and values to lead to friction among organizational members. There may be some truth to this. Nevertheless, sharing core values can be a powerful mechanism that helps to ultimately resolve conflicts—a light in a storm, as it were. For example, in a firm with a core value of excellent customer service, it is still possible for managers to differ about how to handle a particular customer problem. However, the core value will often suggest an appropriate dispute resolution mechanism—"Let's have the person who is closest to the customer make the final decision."

FINANCIAL SUCCESS   Does a strong culture pay off in terms of dollars and cents—that is, do the assets we discussed above get translated into bottom-line financial success? The answer seems to be yes, as long as the liabilities discussed below can be avoided.

There is growing consensus that strong cultures contribute to financial success and other indicators of organizational effectiveness *when the culture supports the mission, strategy, and goals of the organization.*[77] A good example is WestJet Airlines. A key aspect of WestJet's corporate culture is a universal desire to maximize profits. The company has not only become one of the most profitable airlines in North America, but it is also the most successful low-cost carrier in Canadian history. According to former company CEO Clive Beddoe, WestJet's corporate culture is the primary reason for its extraordinary performance. "The entire environment is conducive to bringing out the best in people," he says. "It's the culture that creates the passion to succeed."[78]

Perhaps it is no wonder, then, that executives across Canada have consistently ranked WestJet as having one of the most admired corporate cultures in Canada. Most of the executive respondents also believe that there is a direct correlation between culture and an organization's health and financial performance and that corporate culture has a tangible impact on their long-term success and an organization's ability to recruit, manage, and retain the best people. In fact, the most admired corporate cultures have been found to have a three-year average revenue growth that has significantly outpaced the S&P/TSX compound annual growth rate (CAGR) by over 600 percent.[79]

Liabilities of Strong Cultures

On the other side of the coin, strong cultures can be a liability under some circumstances.

RESISTANCE TO CHANGE   The mission, strategy, or specific goals of an organization can change in response to external pressures, and a strong culture that was appropriate for past success might not support the new order. That is, the strong consensus about common values and appropriate behaviour that makes for a strong culture can prove to be very resistant to change. This means that a strong culture can damage a firm's ability to innovate.

An excellent example is the case of IBM. A strong culture dedicated to selling and providing excellent service for mainframe computers contributed to the firm's remarkable success. However, this strong culture also bred strong complacency that damaged the company's ability to compete effectively with smaller, more innovative firms. IBM's strong mainframe culture limited its competitiveness in desktop computing, software development, and systems compatibility.

Another good example is the sales culture of software giant Oracle Corporation, which has been described as hyperaggressive and tough as nails—the toughest ever seen in the industry. Oracle salespeople were accused of using brute-force tactics, heavy-handed sales pitches, and even routinely running roughshod over customers. Although the culture was once the envy of the industry and the major reason Oracle became the world's second-largest software company, when the industry changed, the culture was described as its own worst enemy. Former CEO Larry Ellison set out to change the company's aggressive sales culture, and one of the first things he did was eliminate a long-established incentive system that encouraged furious sales pushes, over-promising, and steep discounts.[80]

CULTURE CLASH   Strong cultures can mix as badly as oil and water when a merger or acquisition pushes two of them together under the same corporate banner.[81] Consider this: When HBC acquired 50 Towers department stores along with 3000 employees with plans to convert them to Zellers stores, almost every Towers store manager quit. Why? Because the culture of Towers was that management treated employees very positively, and believing that Zellers treated employees poorly, they feared that they would be forced to treat their employees badly.[82]

The merger of Hewlett-Packard and Compaq also raised concerns about a culture clash, given the different work habits, attitudes, and strategies of the two companies. For example, Hewlett-Packard was known for careful, methodical decision making, while Compaq had a reputation for moving fast and correcting mistakes later. Hewlett-Packard was engineering oriented and Compaq was sales oriented. The merger involved a vicious battle inside Hewlett-Packard that was described as a corporate civil war. When the companies merged, employees who were once rivals had to work together and learn new systems. They had to resolve culture clashes and overcome the fact that more often than not, high-tech mergers fail. This, however, was nothing new to Compaq. The company had already experienced a culture clash when it merged with Digital Equipment Corp. in 1998. Many of the promised benefits had not materialized, product decisions were not made quickly or were changed, and confused customers took their business elsewhere.[83]

PATHOLOGY Some strong cultures can threaten organizational effectiveness simply because the cultures are, in some sense, pathological.[84] Such cultures may be based on beliefs, values, and assumptions that support infighting, secrecy, and paranoia, pursuits that hardly leave time for doing business. The collapse of Enron has been blamed in part on a culture that valued lies and deception rather than honesty and truth, and the collapse of WorldCom has been attributed to a culture of secrecy and blind obedience in which executives were encouraged to hide information from directors and auditors and told to simply follow orders. The use of unethical and fraudulent accounting practices was part and parcel of both cultures. Similarly, when Garth Drabinsky and Myron Gottlieb, co-founders of the theatre company Livent Inc., were sentenced for fraud and forgery, Superior Court Justice Mary Lou Benotto stated that the two men presided over a corporation whose culture was one of dishonesty and what she called a "cheating culture."[85]

Another example of a pathological culture is NASA's culture of risk taking. Although the cause of the fatal crash of the *Columbia* space shuttle in February 2003 was a chunk of foam about the size of a briefcase, the root cause was NASA's culture, which downplayed space-flight risks and suppressed dissent. A report by the Columbia Accident Investigation Board concluded that "NASA's organizational culture had as much to do with this accident as foam did." The report indicated that the culture of NASA has sacrificed safety in the pursuit of budget efficiency and tight schedules. One of the board's recommendations was that the "self-deceptive" and "overconfident" culture be changed.[86]

The RCMP has also been singled out as having a pathological culture. Recent allegations and law suits of sexual harassment by former Mounties have been attributed to a culture of silence in which employees were afraid to speak up and sexual harassment was so pervasive that many victims felt that they had no choice but to tolerate it because their complaints went unanswered.[87]

Contributors to the Culture

How are cultures built and maintained? In this section, we consider two key factors that contribute to the foundation and continuation of organizational cultures: the founder's role and socialization.

THE FOUNDER'S ROLE It is certainly possible for cultures to emerge over time without the guidance of a key individual. However, it is remarkable how many cultures, especially strong cultures, reflect the values of an organization's founder.[88] One can clearly see the

LO **8.6**

Discuss the contributors to an organization's culture.

◄●► Simulate

ORGANIZATIONAL CULTURE

John Stanton, CEO of the Running Room, is a classic example of a founder whose values have shaped the organization's culture.

© CP PICTURE ARCHIVE/Jeff McIntosh

influence that the founders of Kicking Horse Coffee have had on the company's culture. Similarly, the imprint of Walt Disney on the Disney Company, Sam Walton on Walmart, Ray Kroc on McDonald's, Thomas Watson on IBM, John Stanton on the Running Room, Mary Kay Ash on Mary Kay Cosmetics, and Bill Gates on Microsoft is obvious. As we shall see shortly, such an imprint is often kept alive through a series of stories about the founder passed on to successive generations of new employees. This provides continuing reinforcement of the firm's core values.

In a similar vein, most experts agree that top management strongly shapes the organization's culture. The culture will usually begin to emulate what top management "pays attention to." For example, the culture of IBM today is much different than it was under the leadership of Thomas Watson, who created a culture that reflected his own personality. Louis Gerstner, Jr., who took over as CEO in 1993 until his retirement in 2002, made diversity a top priority. As a result, the culture of IBM became a more people-friendly one in which individuals are valued for their unique traits, skills, and contributions—a sharp contrast to the culture of conformity under the leadership of Thomas Watson. Today, IBM is regarded as a leader in workplace diversity.[89]

SOCIALIZATION The precise nature of the socialization process is a key to the culture that emerges in an organization, because socialization is one of the primary means by which individuals can learn the culture's beliefs, values, and assumptions. Weak or

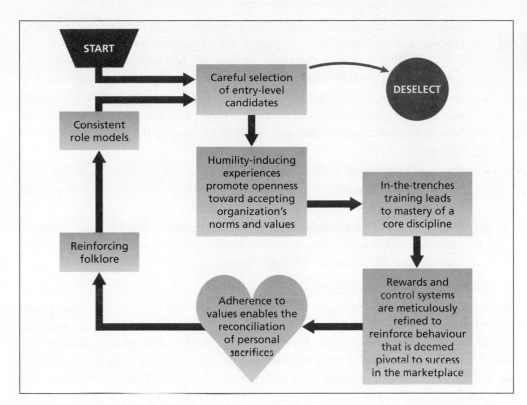

EXHIBIT 8.7
Socialization steps in strong cultures.
Source: The Regents of the University of California. (1985). Reprinted from the *California Management Review, 27*(2) by permission of The University of California Press.

fragmented cultures often feature haphazard selection and a nearly random series of job assignments that fail to present the new hire with a coherent set of experiences. On the other hand, Richard Pascale, of the University of Oxford, notes that organizations with strong cultures go to great pains to expose employees to a careful, step-by-step socialization process (Exhibit 8.7).[90]

- *Step 1—Selecting Employees.* New employees are carefully selected to obtain those who will be able to adapt to the existing culture, and realistic job previews are provided to allow candidates to deselect themselves (i.e., self-selection). As an example, Pascale cites Procter & Gamble's series of individual interviews, group interviews, and tests for brand management positions. Another good example is the interview process conducted by Google Canada, in which employees participate in the selection of new hires who fit the Google culture. At Kicking Horse Coffee, they look for employees who will be a good fit for the culture.[91] An increasing number of organizations now emphasize recruiting and selecting employees for their fit to the company's values and culture (PO fit).[92]

- *Step 2—Debasement and Hazing.* Debasement and hazing (divestiture socialization tactics) provoke humility in new hires so that they are open to the norms of the organization.

- *Step 3—Training "in the Trenches."* Training begins "in the trenches" so that employees begin to master one of the core areas of the organization. For example, even experienced MBAs will start at the bottom of the professional ladder to ensure that they understand how *this* organization works. At Lincoln Electric, an extremely successful producer of industrial products, new MBAs literally spend eight weeks on the welding line so that they truly come to understand and appreciate Lincoln's unique shop floor culture.

- *Step 4—Reward and Promotion.* The reward and promotion system is carefully used to reinforce those employees who perform well in areas that support the values and goals of the organization. For example, at Agrium Inc., a supplier of agricultural products and services, rewards and recognition programs are closely aligned with behaviours that exemplify the corporate values.[93] At Kicking Horse Coffee, the RAVE award is given to employees who exhibit the company's cultural values.

- *Step 5—Exposure to Core Culture.* Again and again, the culture's core beliefs, values, and assumptions are asserted to provide guidance for member behaviour. This is done to emphasize that the personal sacrifices required by the socialization process have a true purpose.

- *Step 6—Organizational Folklore.* Members are exposed to folklore about the organization, stories that reinforce the nature of the culture. We examine this in more detail below.

- *Step 7—Role Models.* Identifying people as "fast-trackers" provides new members with role models whose actions and views are consistent with the culture. These role models serve as tangible examples for new members to imitate.

Pascale is careful to note that it is the *consistency* among these steps and their mutually reinforcing properties that make for a strong culture. For example, it is remarkable how many of these tactics the Disney company uses. Selection is rigorous, and grooming standards serve as mild debasement. Everyone begins at the bottom of the hierarchy. Pay is low, but promotion is tied to performance. Folklore stresses core values ("Walt's in the park"). And better performers serve as role models at Disney University or in paired training.

At Four Seasons Hotels and Resorts, where the company wants new employees to buy in to the team philosophy and a "service mindset," all new hires—from hotel managers to dishwashers—go through four interviews during the selection process; once hired, they enter a three-month socialization program.[94]

Although we have been discussing how cultures are built and maintained, very often organizations have to change their culture, especially when there are changes in an organization's business strategy. We will have more to say about this in Chapter 15, but for now please consult You Be the Manager: *Changing the Culture at Kinaxis.*

LO 8.7

Describe how to diagnose an organizational culture.

Diagnosing a Culture

Earlier, we noted that culture represents a "way of life" for organizational members. Even when the culture is strong, this way of life might be difficult for uninitiated outsiders to read and understand. One way to grasp a culture is to examine the symbols, rituals, and stories that characterize the organization's way of life. For insiders, these symbols, rituals, and stories are mechanisms that teach, communicate, and reinforce the company's culture.

SYMBOLS At the innovative Chaparral Steel Company in Texas, employees have to walk through the human resources department to get to their lockers. Although this facilitates communication, it also serves as a powerful symbol of the importance that the company places on its human resources. For years, IBM's "respect for the individual" held strong symbolic value, which was somewhat shaken with its first-ever layoffs. Such symbolism is a strong indicator of corporate culture.[95]

Some executives are particularly skilled at consciously using symbols to reinforce cultural values. Retired chairman and CEO Carl Reichardt of Wells Fargo was known as a fanatical cost cutter. According to one story, Reichardt received managers requesting capital budget increases while sitting in a tatty chair. As managers made their cases, Reichardt picked at the chair's exposed stuffing, sending a strong symbolic message of fiscal austerity. This was in case they had missed the message conveyed by having to pay for their own coffee and their own office Christmas decorations![96]

YOU BE THE MANAGER

Changing the Culture at Kinaxis

Kinaxis is a provider of software for supply chain management (SCM) and sales and operations planning (S&OP). Founded in Ottawa in 1984, Kinaxis now has offices around the world.

After being in business for 20 years, Kinaxis underwent a major transformation. With the goal of growing faster and gaining more value, the software company completely changed what it sold, how it sold it, and who it sold it to.

According to company Chief Products Officer John Sicard, "We had to differentiate ourselves. We were competing with some pretty large competitors and we found ourselves competing under their terms, not our own."

While Kinaxis was seeing some surprising gains in its professional services, its software sales were sliding and software maintenance was growing only marginally—not a healthy trend, said Sicard. "We realized for us to actually win more and grow, we had to change our approach."

The company decided to make several business changes, including shifting the software to subscription from perpetual, to on-demand from on-premise, to and configured from custom. In 2008, Kinaxis attempted a similar change that was unsuccessful. After the executive team explained that the company was shifting to subscription software from perpetual, they went back on their word and approved a perpetual software sale for one employee, which quickly snowballed to many other employees.

Fundamentally changing the business—and implementing all the changes at the same time—required support from all employees because it affected every single department in the organization, said Sicard.

Kinaxis

Kinaxis made several business changes that required a change in the company's culture.

Since people are often uncomfortable with change, the executive team had to be prepared for resistance and figure out a way to gain employee support.

But what other changes are required to successfully transform the business? Does it require a change in culture? You be the manager.

Questions

1. Do you think that Kinaxis needs to change its culture? If so, how should they proceed? Explain your reasoning.

2. What can Kinaxis do to gain employee support, and how will the changes affect the selection of new employees?

To find out what Kinaxis did, see The Manager's Notebook at the end of the chapter.

Source: Based on material from Canadian HR Reporter (http://www.hrreporter.com/executiveseries/videodisplay/232hrsroleinabusinesstransformation).

RITUALS Observers have noted how rites, rituals, and ceremonies can convey the essence of a culture.[97] For example, at Coast Capital Savings Credit Union, Canada's second-largest credit union, the company's executives dress up in costumes during the employee recognition awards event. During the 2011 Stanley Cup playoffs, staff held noon-hour street hockey games in the parking lot to support the Vancouver Canucks. These events are indicative of a culture of fun and light-heartedness.[98] The Disney picnics, beach parties, and employee nights are indicative of a peer-oriented, youth-oriented culture. At Flight Centre, the monthly parties called "buzz nights," at which employees are recognized for their accomplishments, are indicative of a youthful, energetic, and fun culture. At Mary Kay Cosmetics, elaborate "seminars" with the flavour of a Hollywood premiere combined with a revival meeting are used to make the sales force feel good about themselves and the company. Pink Cadillacs and other extravagant sales awards reinforce the cultural imperative that any Mary Kay woman can be successful. Rituals need not be so exotic to send a cultural message. In some companies, the annual performance review is an act of feedback and development. In others, it might be viewed as an exercise in punishment and debasement.

STORIES Organizations often communicate their culture through the use of stories. For example, at the Rocky Mountain Soap Company in Canmore, Alberta, core value stories are presented at meetings, and posters at all locations feature a story for each of the company's five core values.[99] As we noted earlier, the folklore of organizations—stories about past organizational events—is a common aspect of culture. These stories, told repeatedly to successive generations of new employees, are evidently meant to communicate "how things work," whether they be true, false, or a bit of both. Anyone who has spent much time in a particular organization is familiar with such stories, and they often appear to reflect the uniqueness of organizational cultures.

However, research indicates that a few common themes underlie many organizational stories:

- Is the big boss human?
- Can the little person rise to the top?
- Will I get fired?
- Will the organization help me when I have to move?
- How will the boss react to mistakes?
- How will the organization deal with obstacles?[100]

Issues of equality, security, and control underlie the stories that pursue these themes. Also, such stories often have a "good" version, in which things turn out well, and a "bad" version, in which things go sour. For example, there is a story that Ray Kroc, McDonald's founder, cancelled a franchise after finding a single fly in the restaurant.[101] This is an example of a sour ending to a "How will the boss react to mistakes?" story. Whether the story is true, its retelling is indicative of one of the core values of the McDonald's culture—a fanatical dedication to clean premises.

Fun is an essential part of the culture of Flight Centre, where employees attend monthly parties called "buzz nights."

Daniel Alan/Stone/Getty

THE MANAGER'S NOTEBOOK

Changing the Culture at Kinaxis

The Kinaxis story is an excellent example of how changes in an organization's business strategy often require changes in the company's culture. In 2015, Kinaxis was named one of Canada's Top Employers for Young People, one of Canada's Top Small & Medium Employers for the second year in a row, and one of the National Capital Region's Top Employers, which recognizes Ottawa-area employers that offer an exceptional place to work.

1. The change in business strategy required a new culture that would support the business initiatives. To get employees behind the new plan, Kinaxis involved them in the new vision for the company. It created an online community shaped by four key pillars—learn, laugh, share, and connect—that became anchors to the new company culture. The website was also revamped to reflect the new culture, which included changing the title of a video from *Stuff Happens* to *Sh*t Happens*. "Everyone went, 'We can't have that on our website,' and we said, 'Yes, we can because that's what people think—it's edgy and it's OK,'" said Sicard. "We modernized the website, changed our voice. Rather than sounding like a big tech library, we really started to speak in a more conversational manner." Kinaxis also hired a community manager to help transform employees and get them used to being social. "That was a big part of our cultural shift. [We were] very enterprise-focused, closed doors, everything is very, very serious—and developers never came out," said Sicard. "But we had to change the way people thought about this."

2. To gain employee support, Kinaxis offered financial incentives for any employee who would contribute to the website. They were encouraged to be provocative, but respectful, bold, and edgy in their comments—because that's how you get people talking, said Sicard. In keeping with this new, edgy brand, Kinaxis developed its own TV show called the *Late Late Supply Chain Show*, starring Kinaxis employees, as well as a video comedy series called *New Kinexions*. Ongoing communication with employees was also a key aspect in how Kinaxis survived the transformation. The company's CEO "errs on telling everything"—through newsletters, one-on-one sessions, and town-hall meetings—so employees can really understand what's going on at the organization. The HR department was also affected by the change, and the biggest shift was in how it screened candidates and determined fit, said Sicard. "In the past, we might have been hyper-focused on a potential employee's fit from a technical know-how/skill side of the equation and, of course, we're still looking for 'Will they work well in a team?' but now [we look at] 'Will they thrive under this culture?'"

MyManagementLab   Study, practise, and explore real management situations with these helpful resources:

- **Interactive Lesson Presentations:** Work through interactive presentations and assessments to test your knowledge of management concepts.
- **PIA (Personal Inventory Assessments):** Enhance your ability to connect with key concepts through these engaging, self-reflection assessments.   **PIA** PERSONAL INVENTORY ASSESSMENT
- **Study Plan:** Check your understanding of chapter concepts with self-study quizzes.
- **Videos:** Learn more about the management practices and strategies of real companies.
- **Simulations:** Practise decision-making in simulated management environments.

LEARNING OBJECTIVES CHECKLIST

8.1 There are two basic forms of social dependence. *Information dependence* means that we rely on others for information about how we should think, feel, and act. *Effect dependence* means that we rely on rewards and punishments provided by others. Both contribute to conformity to norms. There are several motives for conformity to social norms. One is *compliance*, in which conformity occurs mainly to achieve rewards and avoid punishment. It is mostly indicative of effect dependence. Another motive for conformity is *identification* with other group members. Here, the person sees himself or herself as similar to other organizational members and relies on them for information. Finally, conformity may be motivated by the *internalization* of norms, and the person is no longer conforming simply because of social dependence.

8.2 *Socialization* is the process by which people learn the attitudes, knowledge, and behaviours that are necessary to function in a group or organization. It is a process that affects proximal socialization outcomes (e.g., learning about one's tasks, roles, group, and organization) as well as distal socialization outcomes (e.g., job satisfaction and turnover). Organizational members learn norm and role requirements through three stages of socialization: anticipatory, encounter, and role management.

8.3 People entering organizations tend to have expectations that are inaccurate and unrealistically high and that can cause them to experience reality shock. The *psychological contract* refers to beliefs held by employees regarding the reciprocal obligations and promises between them and their organization. *Psychological contract breach* is common and can have a negative effect on employees' work attitudes and behaviours. Socialization programs can help new hires form realistic expectations and accurate perceptions of the psychological contract.

8.4 *Realistic job previews* can help new members cope with initial unrealistic expectations. *Employee orientation programs* introduce new employees to

their job, the people they will be working with, and the organization. *Socialization tactics* refer to the manner in which organizations structure the early work experiences of newcomers and individuals who are in transition from one role to another. Institutionalized socialization reflects a formalized and structured program of socialization. Individualized socialization reflects a relative absence of structure. *Mentors* can assist new members during socialization and influence their career success by performing career and psychosocial functions. *Formal mentoring programs* are organizationally sponsored programs in which seasoned employees are recruited as mentors and matched with protégés. New members can play an active role in their socialization through the use of *proactive socialization* behaviours, such as feedback seeking and information seeking.

8.5 *Organizational culture* consists of the shared beliefs, values, and assumptions that exist in an organization. *Subcultures* can develop that reflect departmental or occupational differences. In *strong cultures*, beliefs, values, and assumptions are intense, pervasive, and supported by consensus. The assets of a strong culture include good coordination, appropriate conflict resolution, and financial success. Liabilities of a strong culture include inherent pathology, resistance to change, and culture clash when mergers or acquisitions occur.

8.6 Two key factors that contribute to the foundation and continuation of organizational cultures are the founder's role and a careful step-by-step socialization process.

8.7 Symbols, rituals, and stories are often useful for diagnosing a culture.

DISCUSSION QUESTIONS

1. Consider how you were socialized into the college or university where you are taking your organizational behaviour course. Did you have some unrealistic expectations? Where did your expectations come from? What outside experiences prepared you for college or university? Did you experience institutionalized or individualized socialization? What proactive socialization

behaviours did you employ to facilitate your socialization and which ones were most helpful?

2. Discuss the advantages and disadvantages of developing a strong organizational culture and some socialization practices that you would recommend for building a strong organizational culture.

3. Describe how you would design an orientation program. Be sure to indicate the content of your

program and what knowledge and information employees will acquire from attending the program. What are some of the outcomes that you would expect from your orientation program?

4. What does it mean to be proactive during the socialization process, and what are the different ways that newcomers can be proactive? To what extent have you used each of the proactive behaviours described in the chapter (see Exhibit 8.6) in a current or previous job, and what effect did it have on your socialization?

5. What are the main functions performed by mentors, and what effect do they have on protégés? Do you think organizations should implement formal mentoring programs, or should they remain informal? What are the advantages and disadvantages of each approach?

INTEGRATIVE DISCUSSION QUESTIONS

1. What are the implications of social cognitive theory for social influence and socialization? Discuss the practical implications of each component of social cognitive theory (i.e., observational learning, self-efficacy, and self-regulation) for the socialization of new organization members. Describe how you would design an orientation program for new employees based on social cognitive theory. Consider the implications of social cognitive theory for mentoring. What does social cognitive theory say about why mentoring is important and how to make it effective?

2. Refer to the work-related values that differ across cultures presented in Chapter 4 (i.e., work centrality, power distance, uncertainty avoidance, masculinity/femininity, individualism/collectivism, and long-term/short-term orientation) and consider how the culture of an organization in Canada might lead to conflicts in a country with different work-related values. Give some examples of the kind of organizational culture that might conflict with the various work-related values in other countries. What are the implications of this for Canadian companies that wish to expand abroad?

ON-THE-JOB CHALLENGE QUESTION

Culture or Biology?

A report by former Supreme Court justice Marie Deschamps on sexual misconduct and harassment in the Canadian Armed Forces found that women in the military endure a toxic work environment and are often the target of vulgar name calling, sexual innuendoes and jokes, harassment, and assault—behaviours that are condoned or ignored by senior military leaders. The report concludes that there is an "underlying sexualized culture" that is "hostile" to women as well as lesbian, gay, transgendered, bisexual, and queer members of the military.

After talking to hundreds of members of the forces across the country, Deschamps found that the armed forces are rife with discrimination and that abuse toward women starts from their first days in uniform. She found that the problems start in basic training, where inappropriate language by trainers goes unpunished, there are reports of "dubious" sexual encoun-

ters, and date rape is "prevalent." The use of language that belittles women is "commonplace." Women have been told to "stop being pussies" and "leave your purses at home," and graphic swear words and jokes about rape are tolerated. Women are often described as "ice princesses," "girls," "bitches," and "sluts" in what is perceived to be a "boys' club" culture. The report also noted that most men didn't see such language as harassment, with one saying, "Girls that come to the army know that to expect."

According to the report, "There is an undeniable problem of sexual harassment and sexual assault in the [Canadian Armed Forces], which requires direct and sustained action." However, military leaders are blind to the poisonous culture and excuse inappropriate conduct on the basis that the armed forces are simply a "reflection of society."

Most incidents of sexual harassment and assault were not reported because the victims feared their careers would be harmed, that they would not be believed, or that they would be branded as trouble-makers if they reported the incidents. Those who have reported incidents said that the experience was "atrocious."

Former Chief of Defence Staff General Tom Lawson promised that the armed forces will at long last acknowledge the seriousness of the issue and will develop a strategy to change the culture. However, shortly after the report's release, he told the CBC's Peter Mansbridge that he blamed biology for the problem of sexual harassment and misconduct in the military, stating that some male soldiers are "biologically wired in a certain way" that makes inappropriate behaviour seem acceptable to them.

What do you think about the report's findings and conclusions? What role does culture play in the sexual misconduct and abuse in the Canadian Forces? What advice would you give the armed forces about how culture affects people's attitudes and behaviour, and what they need to do to eliminate sexual misconduct and harassment?

Sources: Campion-Smith, B., & Boutilier, A. (2015, April 30). Canada's military suffers "sexualized culture," report says. *Toronto Star*, www.thestar.com/news/canada/2015/04/30/...; Editorial (2015, April 30). Canada's military needs an about-face on sexual misconduct: Editorial. *Toronto Star*, www.thestar.com/opinion/editorials/2015/04/30/...; Campion-Smith, B. (2015, June 17). General's sexual harassment remark denounced by Harper, Trudeau and Mulcair. *Toronto Star*, www.thestar.com/news/canada/2015/06/17/...

EXPERIENTIAL EXERCISE

Socialization Preferences and Experience

The purpose of this exercise is for you to learn about how you would like to be socialized when you join an organization and how you have been socialized in a current or previous organization. By comparing your preferences to your most recent socialization experience, you can better understand how socialization can influence your job attitudes and behaviour.

Part 1: Your Socialization Preferences

Indicate your preference for each of the socialization experiences listed below using the following response scale:

1–Dislike very much

2–Dislike

3–Neither like nor dislike

4–Like

5–Like very much

To what extent would you like or dislike

____ 1. To be (*I was*) extensively involved with other new hires in common, job-related training activities.

____ 2. To go (*I went*) through a set of training experiences that are specifically designed to give newcomers a thorough knowledge of job-related skills.

____ 3. The organization to change your (*changed my*) values and beliefs.

____ 4. To see a (*There was a*) clear pattern in the way one role leads to another or one job assignment leads to another.

____ 5. To have (*At my organization*) experienced organizational members see advising or training newcomers as one of their main job responsibilities.

____ 6. To be able to (*I was able to*) predict your (*my*) future career path in the organization by observing other people's experiences.

____ 7. To have other (*Other*) newcomers be (*were*) instrumental in helping you (*me*) to understand your (*my*) job requirements.

____ 8. To be (*I was*) physically apart from regular organizational members during your (*my*) training.

____ 9. To have (*I had*) to "pay your (*my*) dues" before you are (*I was*) fully accepted.

____ 10. For each stage (*Each stage*) of the training process to expand and build (*expanded and built*) upon the job knowledge gained during the preceding stages of the process.

____ 11. To gain (*I gained*) a clear understanding of your (*my*) role in the organization by observing your (*my*) senior colleagues.

____ 12. To have (*I had*) good knowledge of the time it will take you (*me*) to go through the various stages of the training process in the organization.

____ 13. For the organization to (*The organization*) put all newcomers through the same set of learning experiences.

____ 14. To avoid (*I avoided*) performing any of your (*my*) normal job responsibilities until you are (*I was*) thoroughly familiar with departmental procedures and work methods.

____ 15. To be (*I was*) transformed or changed into a different kind of person.

____ 16. For the movement (*The movement*) from role to role and function to function to build up (*built up*) experience and a track record to be (*was*) very apparent in the organization.

____ 17. To receive (*I received*) little guidance from experienced organizational members about how you should (*I should*) perform your (*my*) job.

____ 18. To have your (*I had my*) progress through the organization follow a fixed timetable of events.

____ 19. For most of your (*Most of my*) training to be (*was*) carried out apart from other newcomers.

____ 20. For much of your (*Much of my*) job knowledge to be (*was*) acquired informally on a trial and error basis.

____ 21. To be (*I was*) accepted by the organization for who you are (*I am*) as a person.

____ 22. For the organization to (*The organization*) put newcomers through an identifiable sequence of learning experiences.

____ 23. To have (*I had*) a lot of access to people who have previously performed your (*my*) role in the organization.

____ 24. To have (*I had*) a clear idea of when to expect a new job assignment or training exercise in the organization.

____ 25. To experience (*I experienced*) a sense of "being in the same boat" among newcomers in the organization.

____ 26. To be (*I was*) very aware that you are (*I was*) seen as "learning the ropes" in the organization.

____ 27. To feel (*I felt*) that experienced organizational members hold you (*me*) at a distance until you (*I*) conform to their expectations.

____ 28. To have (*I had*) the steps in the career ladder clearly specified in the organization.

____ 29. To generally be (*I was generally*) left alone to discover what your (*my*) role should be in the organization.

____ 30. For most of your (*Most of my*) knowledge of what may happen to you (*me*) in the future to come (*came*) informally, through the grapevine, rather than through regular organizational channels.

Part 2: Your Socialization Experience

Answer each of the questions above again, but this time in terms how you were socialized in your current organization if you are employed or the most recent organization where you were last employed. To answer the questions about your socialization experience, use the italicized words instead of the ones that precede them. For each statement, use the following scale to indicate how accurately it describes your socialization experiences when you joined the organization:

1 = Strongly disagree

2 = Disagree

3 = Neither agree nor disagree

4 = Agree

5 = Strong agree

Scoring and Interpretation

This scale measures the six socialization tactics discussed in the chapter (see Exhibit 8.5). To calculate your scores on each tactic, you first must subtract your response to questions 3, 9, 15, 17, 19, 20, 27, 29, and 39 from 6. For example, if you gave a response of 5 to question 3, give yourself a 1 (6 minus 5). Then calculate your score for each socialization tactic by adding up your answers as follows:

Collective versus individual tactic: Add your answers to questions 1, 7, 13, 19, and 25.

Formal versus informal tactic: Add your answers to questions 2, 8, 14, 20, and 26.

Investiture versus divestiture tactic: Add your answers to questions 3, 9, 15, 21, and 27.

Sequential versus random tactic: Add your answers to questions 4, 10, 16, 22, and 28.

Serial versus disjunctive tactic: Add your answers to questions 5, 11, 17, 23, and 29.

Fixed versus variable tactic: Add your answers to questions 6, 12, 18, 24, and 30.

For each scale, your total score should be somewhere between 5 and 25. Higher scores reflect the institutionalized end of the scale (collective, formal, investiture, sequential, serial, and fixed). You can calculate a total score for all tactics by adding your responses to all 30 questions. Your total scale should fall between 30 and 150. Higher scores reflect a preference for institutionalized socialization. To calculate your socialization experience scores, follow the same procedures but this time use your answers from Part 2.

To compare your socialization preferences to your socialization experience, calculate a socialization preference difference score by subtracting your socialization experience score from your socialization preference score for each tactic. For example, if your collective–individual socialization preference score was 25 and your socialization experience score was 10, the difference would be 15. A small difference indicates greater congruence between your socialization preference and experience. Large differences indicate a discrepancy between how you prefer to be socialized and the way you were socialized.

To facilitate class discussion and your understanding of socialization tactics, form a small group with several other members of the class and answer the following questions:

1. Each group member should present their preference score of each socialization tactic. What is the average of the group for each tactic? For each of the six tactics, do most group members prefer the institutionalized or individualized tactic?

Each group member should explain their preference for each tactic.

2. Each group member should present their experience score of each socialization tactic. What is the average of the group for each tactic? For each of the six tactics, did most group members experience institutionalized or individualized socialization? Each group member should explain how they were socialized and what effect it had on them.

3. Each group member should present their socialization preference–experience difference score for each tactic. What are largest and smallest differences and for which tactics? Do some members have larger differences than others? Compare and contrast the experiences and socialization of those who have large difference scores to those who have smaller difference scores. Be sure to consider the effect of your socialization and the preference–experience difference score on your learning, job attitudes, and behaviour.

4. How can an understanding of your socialization preferences assist in your future jobs? How can organizations improve their socialization process by understanding the socialization preferences of new hires?

5. What are the implications for organizations that do not consider the socialization preferences of new hires? What are the implications for new hires whose socialization experience is inconsistent with their preferences? What are the implications for organizations whose new hires have socialization experiences that are inconsistent with their preferences?

Source: The socialization preference and experience scale is based on Jones, G.R. (1986). Socialization tactics, self-efficacy, and newcomers' adjustments to organizations. *Academy of Management Journal, 29*, 262–279; Ashforth, B.E., Sluss, D.M., & Saks, A.M. (2007). Socialization tactics, proactive behavior, and newcomer learning: Integrating socialization models. *Journal of Vocational Behavior, 70*, 447–462.

CASE INCIDENT

The Reality Shock

Soon after starting his new job, Jason began to wonder about the challenging work he was supposed to be doing, the great co-workers he had been told about, and the ability to attend training and development programs. None of these things seemed to be happening as promised and as he had expected. To make matters worse, he had spent most of the first month working on his own and reading about the organization's mission, history, policies, and so on. Jason began to wonder whether he had chosen the right job and organization. He was very dissatisfied and seriously thinking about quitting.

1. Explain how Jason's anticipatory socialization might be contributing to his disappointment

and job attitudes. How might this situation have been prevented?

2. Explain how unrealistic expectations and the psychological contract can help us understand Jason's situation.

3. Comment on the use of socialization tactics in Jason's socialization. What tactics do you think were used and what effect did they have on Jason?

4. Given Jason's current situation, is there anything the organization can do to prevent him from quitting? What should Jason do? Is there anything the organization should do so that other new hires don't have the same experience as Jason?

CASE STUDY

THE WONDERFUL WORLD OF HUMAN RESOURCES AT DISNEY

You can design and create and build the most wonderful place in the world. But it takes people to make the dream a reality.
—Walt Disney[1]

1 "Walt Disney Quotes," JustDisney.com, http://www.justdisney.com/walt_disney/quotes/ (accessed May 28, 2013).

Five-year-old Oliver wanted to see the animals during his overnight stay at Disney's Animal Kingdom Lodge. It was early evening, too late to get in the park, so his grandmother took him to a scenic overlook at the back of the lobby. As Oliver walked around, there were no animals to be seen, only clusters of trees, some grasses, and dirt trails below the overlook. Oliver's grandmother could sense his disappointment. This was Oliver's first visit to a place that was supposed to enchant children so that parents or grandparents would bring them back. Expectations were sky-high.

ONCE UPON A TIME: DISNEY'S HERITAGE AND TRADITIONS

I only hope that we don't lose sight of one thing: that it was all started by a mouse.

—Walt Disney[2]

The mouse that started it all was a character idea born out of desperation. Walt's original character, Oswald the Rabbit, for which he had just signed a contract for an animated series, was stolen by the New York distributor, who then hired all of Walt's animators. On the train ride back home, Walt got the idea for a mouse. "A mouse had always appealed to me," he said. "While working in Kansas City, I caught several in wastebaskets around the studio. I kept them in a cage on my desk and enjoyed watching their antics."[3] The original name was to be Mortimer Mouse, but Walt's wife, Lilly, convinced him that the name Mortimer seemed too formal. Mickey Mouse, the character that people loved and the icon of an empire-to-be, was born.

The animated film company that Walt founded in 1923 with his brother Roy (who put up most of the money) got busy. Walt introduced the use of sound, then in its motion-picture infancy, in the first talking animated film, *Steamboat Willie*. The film debuted in New York City in 1928, and was a hit. Disney Brothers Studios was launched; a year later it was renamed "Walt Disney Productions."

To go along with the red-shorted, yellow-shoed mouse, Walt dreamed up some friends: Pluto in 1930, Goofy in 1932, and Donald Duck in 1934. The brothers licensed these Disney characters and began selling merchandise such as shirts, watches, and writing tablets with their images. By 1937, Mickey's image, on one distributed product or another, had found its way to 38 countries; to handle the volume, distribution offices for merchandise and films opened in Paris and London.

Mickey Mouse clubs started cropping up worldwide. Disney products had a global appeal and reach.

Walt Disney Productions struggled financially for a while, but with the help of Bank of America and some of their own money, the Disney brothers created a film in color called *Snow White and the Seven Dwarfs*. Premiering in 1937 and opening nationwide in 1938, it was a financial and artistic success, making millions of dollars. After that, Walt's imagination and Roy's business acumen were an unstoppable combination, and by 1940, the firm had issued its first stock. In 1954, they used another medium to share Walt's imagination with the world: the brothers created a television show called *Disneyland* (later called *The Wonderful World of Disney*). Now Disney movie fans turned on their television sets each Sunday evening and watched a variety of Disney characters and stories.

FROM FILM TO THEME PARK

As it turned out, filmmaking and television shows were not the only projects on the drawing board. The idea of expanding into theme parks came from the same guy who drew the famous mouse—Walt. Although Roy was against the concept at first, creating a theme park fit well with both Walt's urge to escape the real world and dream, and his goal to create happiness for those who visited.

To create his ideal world outside the film channel, Walt gathered a select group of animators, artists, directors, set designers, and writers from Walt Disney Productions—whom he called "Imagineers"—and told them about his park idea.[4] As with the sound stage of a film, setting was important. With the *Disneyland* TV show as both inspiration and source of funding, the Imagineers were asked to create a family-style amusement park in secret. Owned by Disneyland Inc., the park would be spotless and meticulously groomed (bushes cut into the shape of Disney characters, for example). "When I started on Disneyland," Walt said, "My wife used to say, 'but why do you want to build an amusement park? They're so dirty.' I told her that was just the point—mine wouldn't be."[5] In fact, imagineers studied human behaviour to discover the distance an

2 "Top 10 Walt Disney Quotes," MoveMeQuotes.com, http://www.movemequotes.com/top-10-walt-disney-quotes/ (accessed May 28, 2013).

3 James R. Stewart, *Disney War* (New York: Simon & Schuster, 2005), 23.

4 All designers, engineers, architects, and technicians that created and worked on park resorts were imagineers (imagination and engineer).

5 Richard Hoffer, "Disneyland Turns 50," *Via*, July/August 2005, http://www.viamagazine.com/attractions/disneyland-turns-50 (accessed August 21, 2012).

average person would walk holding an item before throwing it away (17 feet).

Disneyland Park was built on an 85-acre parcel of land in Anaheim, California and had attractions modeled after images from popular Disney films. The park, raised above ground like a *stage*, was to be "picture-perfect" in Walt's words.[6] Everything in the park was a *prop* that would allow a *make-believe show* to run flawlessly from opening to closing. Park visitors were *guests* and, during an average visit, would likely have as many as 60 encounters with employees, called *cast members*. The experience was to be magical, offering visitors the "happiest place on Earth," and appeal to young and old. After all, the Disney brothers were in show business, and Disneyland was a live show, every day, all day long. In 1955, one year after the debut of the *Disneyland* television show, Disneyland Park opened at a cost of $17 million.

When open, the park filled with pleasant, wholesome, *costume*-clad cast members who were *onstage* in the public areas of the park and eager to play a part in the *live show* while being helpful and friendly. Indeed, no matter what job a cast member was hired to perform, the standard was always "to exceed guests' expectations."[7] That point was so important to Walt that he would dress so no one could recognize him, tour the park, and go on attractions. One time he took the *Jungle Boat* ride and was unhappy that, instead of lasting seven minutes, it lasted only four. "How would you like to go to a movie and have the theater remove a reel in the middle of the picture?" he asked the ride supervisor. "Do you realize how much those hippos cost? I want people to see them, not be rushed through a ride by some guy who's bored with his work."[8]

Under the park, at ground level, was an area called *offstage,* where cast members changed into character, took breaks, and prepared for their parts. Connected through a maze of hallways or tunnels were well-appointed break areas, vending machines, hair designers, a notary, driver's-license renewal services, check cashing services, postage stamp machines, and, as cast members were provided fresh costumes daily, one of the largest wardrobe departments in the world.[9] An underground tram would transport cast members back and forth to quiet corners of the park where they would appear onstage discreetly through unmarked doors.

To Walt, every detail mattered. This was perhaps an extension of the painstaking nature of drawing animation, eventually referred to by animators as *bumping the lamp*.[10] Fostering a sense of pride was at the forefront of Walt's work and, he hoped, the work of every single person working for the company. To ensure that happened, Walt designed an elaborate employee hiring and training process that supported his management philosophy and, above all, allowed for a workplace where creativity could thrive. (See Exhibit 1 for the Disney creativity model.)

All hiring took place at the Walt Disney World Casting Center. Each cast member was trained to *perform* for the roles they would be playing while onstage. The only downtime allowed was when cast members were offstage, at which point they were allowed to be themselves. If by chance, a noncast member was in the offstage area, cast members were required to stay in character and were not allowed to speak or show the person underneath the costume.

Eager to open more, Walt secretly bought several acres of land on the opposite coast, just outside of Orlando, Florida. But before his plans to open another theme park could come to fruition, he died.

The years between 1939 and 1966, the year of Walt's passing, were considered the firm's golden years. Five years after his death, a second theme park, Walt Disney World Resort (Disney World) opened in Orlando, home to the Magic Kingdom and two hotels.

INSIDE THE MAGIC KINGDOMS

Disney World and Disneyland were both built and run on what had widely become known as "Disney magic." Disney values and beliefs, which for the most part were deliberately designed by Walt and Roy Disney, made up its corporate culture and became apparent with every visit to a park. The Disney brothers' strategy was to exceed customer expectations

---

6 Tom Peters as quoted in *In Search of Excellence*, Enterprise Media video, 1982.

7 Disney Institute and Theodore Kinni, *Be Our Guest: Perfecting the Art of Customer Service* (New York: Disney Editions, 2011), 14.

8 Disney Institute and Theodore Kinni, 130.

9 Peters.

10 The animators for *Who Framed Roger Rabbit* ended up adding more time and money to the film because when Roger Rabbit bumped into a swinging lamp they didn't see a shadow on the rabbit's face. They redid the animation to make sure it appeared despite the likelihood that most viewers never would have noticed.

EXHIBIT 1
The Wonderful World of Human Resources at Disney
WDC Inspiring Creativity Model
Data source: Adapted from Disney Institute and Theodore Kinni.

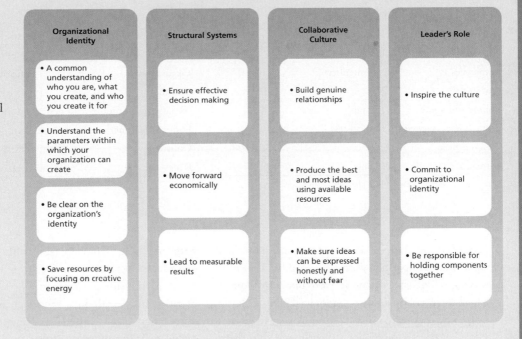

Organizational Identity	Structural Systems	Collaborative Culture	Leader's Role
• A common understanding of who you are, what you create, and who you create it for	• Ensure effective decision making	• Build genuine relationships	• Inspire the culture
• Understand the parameters within which your organization can create	• Move forward economically	• Produce the best and most ideas using available resources	• Commit to organizational identity
• Be clear on the organization's identity			
• Save resources by focusing on creative energy	• Lead to measurable results	• Make sure ideas can be expressed honestly and without fear	• Be responsible for holding components together

through strict attention to detail and policies and procedures designed to deliver quality. To do that, they believed that cast members must be enamored with being part of Disney and embrace the firm's purpose to bring entertainment to young and old—to make people happy. If that transpired, Walt believed a collaborative culture would emerge. And when that happened, he expected financial results would follow.

The goal was to captivate guests with everything Disney; the first step toward that goal was to treat potential employees well. Walt and Roy thought that if the company treated cast members as guests, they would treat guests and each other the same way. Whether one was a guest or a cast member, creating a supportive environment was all part of management's commitment to *keeping the magic going*

BECOMING PART OF THE WALT DISNEY COMPANY (WDC)[11]

As with most organizations, the first step to becoming a cast member at WDC was filling out an application onsite or remotely through a job line.[12] If there was interest in the applicant, he or she would be invited

to *audition* for a role, which included going through an interview process at the casting center. Opened in 1989, the center provided job seekers the first hint that Disney was about magic and make-believe. Like everything else Disney, Walt's presence could be felt throughout: diamond shapes in colors on the front of the casting building corresponded with a photo inside of him wearing his famed argyle socks with matching diamond shapes and colors. Awnings covering the entrance to the casting center building had a castle-like look, and once inside, the doorknobs were identical to the talking ones in Disney's famous film—*Alice in Wonderland*. The building's hallway walls, ceilings, and floors featured Disney characters and film scenes. "Let them wander," Robert A.M. Stern, the architect, once said. "Let them get a taste for Disney before they get here."[13] Once applicants reached the second-floor recruitment office, they would apply for *roles* and watch a film about Disney's heritage, regulations, and terms of employment. At that point, if still interested, applicants would be sent to an appropriate place to be interviewed for their chosen role.

The interviews were structured and purposeful. If an interviewee was auditioning for a position to accompany a character, they might be asked, "What would you do if you were paired with Donald Duck and someone kicked him?" If the interviewee laughed

11 In 1985, Walt Disney Productions became the Walt Disney Company.

12 With time, Disney used other channels for parts of its casting process such as job fairs, recruiting programs, and the Internet.

13 Disney Institute and Theodore Kinni, 63.

TABLE 1   Disney speak

Corporate World	Disney	Corporate World	Disney
Customers/clients	Guests	Job	Role
Employees	Cast members	On the job	Performance
Out front	Onstage	Working	Show
Behind the scene	Offstage	Negative customer experience	Bad show
Front-line employee	Host/hostess	Positive customer experience	Good show
Job interview	Audition	Courtesy	Performance tips
Human resources	Casting	Rides	Attractions

Data source: Disney Institute and Theodore Kinni.

or suggested they would "kick that person back," then being a character partner was not a good fit. If instead they said, "Tell the kicker it was time for Donald Duck's lunch, so we must get moving," then being a character partner made sense. The idea was that roles should play to cast members' strengths and that there was a place for every kind.

In addition to the interview questions, each person auditioning was once more informed of employment conditions. Perhaps the most talked-about condition was appearance—hair length, amount of facial hair, and quantity of jewelry. Following a successful audition, each new cast member, regardless of position in the firm, would be sent to Disney University.

Traditions I class

Walt established Disney University as a place for new cast members to rehearse for performances and practise all things Disney. Being selected to teach there was considered an honor, so each year hundreds of cast members applied to leave their roles and become Traditions assistants. Their job was to pass on Walt's legacy and help new cast members learn about Disney characters and films. Attendees engaged in Trivial Pursuit–like games by answering such questions as "What were the names of the Seven Dwarfs? What was Donald Duck's middle name?" meant to bolster their knowledge about the company's heritage, traditions, language, symbols, and shared values. The program was designed to instill a sense of excitement about working at Disney.

First-name-only tags were worn on the left side, as all new cast members discovered who Disney was as a firm (its vision), what Disney did (its mission), and for whom (guests). Throughout these lessons, cast members learned to act and speak courteously (welcome and thank every guest), became familiar

with the Disney language (see **Table 1** for examples), practised using an appropriate tone of voice, learned to focus on the positive and use humour instead of rules and regulations, and rehearsed appropriate body language.[14] At the same time, they were introduced to issues of safety (what to do in an event of an accident) and how to answer the numerous questions cast members were routinely asked. It turned out that the most frequently asked question at Disney theme parks was the location of the bathroom. (There were phones to a central answer service hidden in shrubbery around the parks.)[15] All cast members were trained to react and offer help if they saw a guest in need.

No cast member was allowed to complain about problems around guests; it was a cast member's job to ensure that all guests had a magical experience—regardless of how she or he was feeling. On the other hand, Disney recognized that working with the public was often difficult and that from time to time, despite the best planning, things would go wrong. How many times could a cast member answer the same questions, such as "What time does the 3:00 p.m. parade start?" For those moments, cast members were taught to *find your applause*. That meant discovering what their value to the organization was, something they did as a cast member that was meaningful to them, and focusing on it when they felt down or tired.

By the end of a day spent in the Traditions course, all new cast members would understand that at Disney all employees, no matter their job, were important to

---

14 Disney Institute and Theodore Kinni, 71–72.

15 Thomas J. Peters and Robert H. Waterman Jr., *In Search of Excellence: Lessons from America's Best-Run Companies* (New York: Harper & Row, 1982), 168.

EXHIBIT 2   The Wonderful World of Human Resources at Disney

The Walt Disney Company Human Resources[16]

We aspire to inspire together.

Diversity

Having a diverse work force is critical to our business. We welcome a variety of opinions, ideas, and perspectives to ensure we continue to top our own performance and represent our global marketplace. When our people reflect the communities we serve, it enhances the way we connect to our guests, audiences, and consumers. Together, we work toward an inclusive environment that fosters creativity, innovation, and camaraderie across all our companies.

Culture

Each of our companies has a unique ability to harness the imagination in a way that inspires others, improves lives across the world, and brings hope, laughter, and smiles to those who need it most. Together as one team, we embrace the values that make the Walt Disney Company an extraordinary place to work:

- Innovation
  - We are committed to a tradition of innovation and technology.
- Quality
  - We strive to set a high standard of excellence.
  - We maintain high-quality standards across all product categories.
- Community
  - We create positive and inclusive ideas about families.
  - We provide entertainment experiences for all generations to share.
- Storytelling
  - Timeless and engaging stories delight and inspire.
- Optimism
  - At the Walt Disney Company, entertainment is about hope, aspiration, and positive outcomes.
- Decency
  - We honor and respect the trust people place in us.
  - Our fun is about laughing at our experiences and ourselves.

These values live in everything we do. They create a unified mission that all our people believe in and work toward. And to recognize individual efforts, we have a variety of reward programs, including:

- Quality of Work
- Length of Service
- Community Volunteerism
- Employee of the Month Recognition

These are just some of the ways the Walt Disney Company commits to providing a rewarding, inclusive, and supportive work environment.

the company (see Exhibit 2 for values statement). To express this, cast members were asked to picture a bolt of polka dot fabric with each Disney cast member represented by one dot on yards and yards of material. If that was a cast member's position in the organization, what would happen to the fabric if a single dot was missing? At Disney, every dot counted.

Local traditions

After learning about the overall Disney culture on the first day, cast members were sent to the park, where

training at the local level was conducted in several steps according to job category. If, for example, a cast member was going to join the show as an operator of the *Jungle Boat* attraction, he or she would start with a safety course along with all the other new cast members training to be attraction operators. They would study how the equipment worked and what it took to be successful theme-park attraction operators.

Following that, the new operators would be sent for a local orientation. For the new *Jungle Boat* cast member, he or she would go to *Adventureland* to learn information about that show. Although aligned with Disney values, each theme area's performance culture had its own mission, vision, and values. The new cast member would shadow a seasoned cast member to learn

16 "Culture & Diversity," Disney Careers, http://disney-careers.com/en/working-here/culture-diversity/ (accessed May 28, 2013).

the special language, the script, and the planned and rehearsed steps to safely navigate the boat and guests through the make-believe, danger-infested river waters.

Once there was complete confidence that the new cast member could *perform*, he or she would be allowed to operate the attraction under the watchful eye of a mentor to ensure that the first few trips went smoothly, that the boat trip looked dramatic, that the new cast member had his or her lines down pat, and that the ride was the right length of time—never short of the seven full minutes!

While training at the local site, new cast members would meet their manager. In addition to making the workplace more comfortable, management worked to identify cast members doing a great job at the park. If, for example, a cast member learned that a guest was ill and arranged for a Mickey Mouse get-well card to be sent to their hotel room, the cast member would likely be given a *Guest Service Fanatic* card from his or her manager. Anyone receiving such a card would place it in a drop box from which five or six names were drawn each month and the chosen cast members rewarded with a prize. The drawing was a big deal, with either a senior executive or popular Disney character picking the names out of the box. Success was to be celebrated.

The attachment

Did Disney's distinctive culture really explain the company's popularity among children and adults? Based on its own research, Disney management thought that loyalty to its brand started through slightly different channels for children and adults. For children, exposure to the Disney brand usually began after watching a television show or movie. Each story generated a favorite or several favorite characters that often led children to pester their parents into taking them to a Disney theme park, where they could meet the characters, buy merchandise, and perhaps attend some stage shows. Those elements (movie, character, products, theme park rides) cross-fertilized each other's demand. For example, there was an attraction called the *Pirates of the Caribbean* in the theme park before the *Pirates of the Caribbean* movie came out. There had never been a Captain Jack in the attraction, but so many children asked where the movie character was (and cast members made a note each time they did) that Disney added him to the ride.

The Disney relationship with most adults generally started with their experiences as children. They would then encourage their children to watch Disney television and films, which most considered child-appropriate in content. In turn, adults were willing to spend money on Disney merchandise and trips to theme parks. All that ended up with the entire family sharing a *magical* experience (courtesy of Disney) and one that Disney hoped many families wanted to repeat. According to folks at the Disney Institute, "We may not remember what someone said to us, but we certainly remember how someone made us feel." Indeed, Disney World's repeat customer percentage was more than 70 percent, and hotel occupancy was usually more than 90 percent full, according to Bruce Jones, program director of the Disney Institute. Those kind of numbers suggested that, whether it was parents or their offspring, Disney park visitors liked to come back.

OUTSIDE THE MAGIC KINGDOMS

Following Walt and Roy Disney's deaths, their beloved company went through some rough times, frequently referred to as transition years (1971–1984). WDC had let its filmmaking business lag and had instead relied upon theme park revenue (in 1984, 80 percent of operating income was from theme parks and 1 percent from movies).[17] The greater part of revenue generation at parks and resorts was within the spring, summer, and last couple weeks of December, leaving several months unutilized. Neglect of its film business resulted in an exodus of creative talent to other studios, where they made hit films. As value for shareholders dropped, Saul Steinberg, a venture capitalist, tried to take over the company to sell piece by piece. A group of friendly investors (Bass Brothers Enterprises) helped the company out of the takeover crisis, and in 1984, Michael Eisner was appointed chairman and CEO, and Frank Wells was selected as president and COO.

The pair rejuvenated the company and built the foundation that Disney grew to a media empire by 2012. Disney's World Wide Parks and Resort were just one part of an integrated network, joined by studio entertainment companies (such as Disney Studios Motion Pictures, Disney Animation, Pixar, Touchstone, and Marvel), media networks (e.g., Disney Channel, ABC, ESPN), Disney Consumer Products

---

17 John Huey, Joe McGowan, and Therese Eiben, "Eisner Explains Everything," *Fortune,* April 17, 1995, http://money.cnn .com/magazines/fortune/fortune_archive/1995/04/17/202090/ index.htm (accessed Aug. 28, 2012).

(e.g., Disney Stores), and Disney Interactive (e.g., Disney Interactive Games).

Just as the company started with Walt the leader, WDC viewed leadership as the beginning of and support to a chain of excellence. When the story began just shy of a century ago, the longevity of Walt's leadership viewpoint was unclear. Yet in 1977, Disney documented the beginnings of a philosophy (see Exhibit 3) that had succeeded in maintaining a powerful connection between inspired leaders, motivated employees,

---

EXHIBIT 3 The Wonderful World of Human Resources at Disney

The Disney Way of Leadership (1977)[18]

A Disney Leader Gets Results Through People

Simplified, this means that a Disney Leader is a people specialist. He does not get results by doing his own thing; he works with other people and helps them put on a good show. It is a known fact that leadership is a science and can be learned like any other skill, but you have to work at it every day. There are some key skills important to the Disney Way of Leadership.

Human Relations Skills

Good Human Relations is a basic cornerstone of the Disney people philosophy. The success of our organization depends on the way we deal with people, and it begins with the way we deal with our employees. Our ability to work positively with people lies in continually putting to practice some key points.

- Set the example; it starts with you.
- Encourage a positive attitude.
- Get to know your employees, treat them as individuals.
- Be with your team; provide encouragement and attention.
- Use empathy; look at the other person's point of view.
- Have respect for others.
- Be objective; be firm, fair, and consistent.
- Give recognition for a job well done.
- Maintain your sense of humor.
- All problems are not the same; treat each individually.
- If an employee has a problem, help solve it.
- If a promise is made, keep it.
- See that your employees have good working conditions.

Communications Skills

One of the most valuable and important skills of the Disney Leader is his ability to effectively communicate. All the positive human relations techniques available today are virtually useless without effective communication.

Since communication means getting ideas across and finding out what other people have to say, we stress the following points in the Disney Way of Leadership:

- Communicate clearly; get your message across.
- Let your employees know how they're doing.
- Encourage upward and downward communications.
- Listen to what employees have to say.
- Keep an open door and an open mind.
- Tell employees how they fit in; explain the big picture.
- Let your employees feel like they belong.
- Communication should be direct, open, and honest.

(Continued)

---

18 *The Disney Management Style* (Walt Disney Productions, 1977), 32–34. Excerpt also used in Jeanne M. Liedtka, William E. Fulmer, and Robert M. Fulmer, "Walt Disney Productions (A): The Walt Years," UVA-BP-0332 (Charlottesville, VA: Darden Business Publishing, 1993): 21–23.

EXHIBIT 3   The Wonderful World of Human Resources at Disney (*Continued*)

Training Skills

Training is the method of developing the basic skills to create an efficient work group and is the responsibility of every Disney Leader.

An efficient operation can never come about as the result of a "happy accident." Each employee must have a clear-cut idea of what they are expected to accomplish and how to achieve it with the greatest proficiency.

Some key training points to remember:

- Be sure your employees receive the proper training, which they need for doing their job.
- Provide for your employees' future growth and development.
- Give employees a chance to learn and participate.
- Encourage new ideas and creative contributions.

Other Leadership Skills

In addition to the aforementioned skills, the Disney Leader also needs to be aware of and skillful in areas of planning, organizing, directing, and controlling his/her team's efforts.

Planning is really just looking ahead. Once objectives are understood, the means necessary to achieve them are presented in plans. Organizing is the process of putting all the resources together to carry out the plan. Directing involves the process of carrying out the plan using all the resources gathered. Controlling measures performance in relation to expected standards of performance.

The Disney Way of Leadership stresses arranging work into a logical and workable manner to insure its successful completion. Keep in mind these helpful points.

- A plan of action is the best control to make sure we get there.
- Don't over-structure a plan; stay flexible.
- Set clearly defined priorities and completion schedules.
- Be realistic with target dates but set them.
- Don't assume; follow-up on assignments and requests.
- Organize around jobs and people.
- Find the right person for the job.
- Issue effective and understandable instructions and directions.
- Establish effective controls to get things done in a timely manner and by priority.

In summary, the Disney Way of Leadership actually integrates all of these skills, applies them as appropriate at the point of action. It's only through daily application and practice that we "fine tune" the essential skills of effective leadership.

and satisfied customers who together drove financial results and brand loyalty.

Over the years, the human relations aspect of the leadership philosophy evolved from Walt's key points into a more holistic partnership between employees and company leaders that, in turn, benefited customers, whether the relationship was through sports or cinema. This partnership included encouraging employees to pursue healthy lifestyles, develop their careers, and take time off. To help with what the company described as "refueling," employees were given complimentary tickets to Disney's parks, discounts at company-operated shops, and an array of company-sponsored services such as computer assistance programs.[19]

As Disney leadership progressed, it continued to refer to the process as *storytelling*. Whether it was management supporting customized training programs, education reimbursement, or professional/career development for employees, "hope and positive outcomes" were part of the goal—and each employee's work experience was meant to be innovative and engaging, because Disney leadership continued to believe that the best ideas came from employees.[20] And championed employees ensured happy guests.

19 "Total Rewards: Support Beyond your Imagination," Disney Careers, http://disneycareers.com/en/working-here/total-rewards/ (accessed June 7, 2012).

20 "Learning & Development," Disney Careers, http://disneycareers.com/en/working-here/learning-development/ (accessed June 10, 2013).

WHAT LIVES ON?

Back at the Animal Kingdom Lodge overlook, with no animals in sight, a disappointed Oliver marched right up to a Disney cast member dressed as a park ranger and said, "Mr. Zookeeper, I want a tour to see the animals." As if on command, a zebra emerged from the distant trees and lay down. Without missing a beat, Mr. Zookeeper said, "See, the animals are starting to go to sleep, which is why you can't see them." Oliver beamed and asked a string of questions about animals sleeping: "Where are the rest of the animals? Where do they sleep? Do they have a house to go to?" All the way back to the room, he stopped at each overlook to see where other animals were going to sleep.

There were many different ways the interaction could have unfolded between this young guest and the cast member he encountered. What made this exchange a memorable experience for this young guest? Would Walt have been surprised?

Source: This case was prepared by Lynn A. Isabella, Gerry Yemen. Reprinted with permission. Copyright © 2015 by The University of Virginia Darden School Foundation. All rights reserved.

QUESTIONS

1. Describe the culture of the Walt Disney Company. What values, norms, and behaviours are associated with the culture? How does the culture influence the customer experience at its theme parks, and how has it contributed to its success?

2. Discuss the "strong culture" concept with respect to the culture of the Walt Disney Company. What are some examples that demonstrate it has a strong culture? What are its assets and liabilities?

3. What factors have contributed to the foundation and continuation of the culture of Walt Disney Company?

4. Discuss the process used to socialize new hires at Walt Disney Company. Refer to Exhibit 8.7 (Socialization steps in strong cultures) to answer this question and provide specific examples of how they perform each step. To what extent does the Walt Disney Company follow each of the steps? What is the effect of the socialization process on new employees?

5. Consider the role of fit at Walt Disney Company. What are the different types of fit and what types are especially important for Walt Disney Company? What does the company do to ensure that applicants are a good fit?

6. What are some of the ways that you can diagnose the culture of Walt Disney Company? Provide some specific examples and explain their purpose.

7. What can other organizations learn about socialization and culture from the Walt Disney Company?

CHAPTER **9** LEADERSHIP

LEARNING OBJECTIVES

After reading Chapter 9, you should be able to:

9.1 Define *leadership*, and discuss the role of *strategic* and formal leadership in organizations.

9.2 Explain and critically evaluate the *trait theory of leadership*.

9.3 Compare and contrast the following leadership behaviours and their consequences: *consideration, initiating structure, leader reward*, and *leader punishment*.

9.4 Describe and evaluate the situational theories of leadership: *contingency theory* and *path–goal theory*.

9.5 Discuss *participative leadership* and how and when to use participative leadership using the Vroom and Jago model.

9.6 Describe and evaluate *leader–member exchange (LMX) theory* and *transactional* and *transformational* leadership and their consequences.

9.7 Discuss the new and emerging theories of leadership including *empowering leadership, ethical leadership, authentic leadership*, and *servant leadership*.

9.8 Describe gender differences in leadership, and explain why women are underrepresented in leadership roles in organizations.

9.9 Discuss the GLOBE project, and explain the role that culture plays in leadership effectiveness.

9.10 Discuss *global leadership*, and describe the characteristics of global leaders.

SERGIO MARCHIONNE

"Chrysler's Man of Steel" was the headline of an article in the *Toronto Star* recognizing Sergio Marchionne as Wheels Newsmaker of the Year in 2012. The sub-headline read, "He brought a major automaker back from the brink, forged a contract with CAW and tore strips off a U.S. presidential hopeful. Fiat's tough CEO (and T.O. expat) gets it done ... and he's not finished yet."

So who is Sergio Marchionne? He is the CEO of Fiat Chrysler Automobiles (FCA), the seventh-largest automaker in the world. Marchionne was born in Italy and raised in Toronto, where his family moved when he was 14 years old. His father, a senior police officer in Chieti, Italy, wanted to ensure that his children received a good education. Marchionne attended the University of Toronto, University of Windsor, and York University's

Osgoode Hall and holds degrees in accounting, business, and law.

After university, he took on various financial management positions and was promoted all the way up to the board at Fiat, where the ailing company gambled in 2004 and made him CEO. Before he became CEO, Fiat had gone through four CEOs in three years and was a laughingstock. But Marchionne changed its entire top-down executive structure and turned the company around in 18 months, restoring it to profitability. He then did the same thing at Chrysler when he became CEO in 2009, where he has overseen a massive overhaul of a company that nearly went bankrupt during the recent auto industry crisis. Under his leadership, Chrysler went from bailout to profitability and paid off its $7.6 billion

Sergio Marchionne, CEO of Fiat Chrysler Automobiles, turned around Fiat and Chrysler and restored both to profitability.

in government loans in less than two years. In 2014, following Fiat's purchase of Chrysler, Marchionne became CEO of the newly merged company.

What sets Sergio Marchionne apart from other leaders? According to Joseph D'Cruz, professor emeritus of strategic management at the University of Toronto, it's charisma. "He's got a lot of charm and when he chooses he can turn it on, but underneath it all, there's steel." Ken Lewenza, president of the Canadian Auto Workers union, has said that Marchionne is a global CEO.

Marchionne is a hard-driving business executive who carries five cellphones with him at all times, and is a hard taskmaster who works all the time and expects his managers to do the same. He wakes at 3:30 in the morning and tries to go to bed at 10 at night, seven days a week. Ken Lewenza says, "Marchionne is absolutely hands-on, and when it comes to the decision-making process, he's got to have the final stamp. There's no doubt about that. He's very focused on product quality—which the union always was, though sometimes it fell on deaf ears; he's focused on design; he's focused on how you grow market share. Admittedly, what makes or breaks a company is product, and he spends a hell of a lot of time—I tell you, a hell of a lot of time—with his product development team."

He has developed a reputation for speaking his mind. According to automotive industry consultant Dennis DesRosiers, "He's a straight-up, shoot from the hip, go go guy." Marchionne is also considered to be one of the most interesting auto industry executives. He has a passion for vintage cars and classical music, and dresses differently from most business executives. At a recent auto show, he was seen among a sea of business suits in his trademark black crewneck wool sweater and black pants. He once told a group of reporters he kept his wardrobe simple so that he didn't have to waste time deciding what to wear in the morning. "I like simplicity almost to the point of being monastic" he said.

With his owlish glasses and hunched shoulders, he looks more like a university professor than a hard-driving business executive. But his looks are deceiving. "He's so smart, he can mesmerize a room" said Sean McAlinden, an analyst with the Center for Automotive Research. "He can pack three headlines into a single speech. The guppy in shark-infested seas. That's a classic Marchionneism." And indeed, at a recent auto show in Toronto, Marchionne warned, "Canada can't afford to be a guppy in shark-infested waters."

In an article in the *Harvard Business Review*, Marchionne commented on leadership at Fiat saying, "We've abandoned the Great Man model of leadership that long characterized Fiat and have created a culture where everyone is expected to lead. My job as CEO is not to make decisions about the business but to set stretch objectives and help our managers work out how to reach them." According to Ken Lewenza, "I think that what he's done is empower confidence in his top management team and they're producing results based on good leadership. I don't think one man in isolation can save a company, but he certainly deserves credit for playing the lead role in doing so."[1]

Sergio Marchionne is a case study in leadership. But what exactly is leadership, and what makes Sergio Marchioone a successful leader? Is it his charisma, his hands-on approach, empowerment, or does it perhaps have to do with strategic and global leadership? These are the kinds of issues and types of leadership that we will cover in this chapter.

First, we will define leadership and find out if we can identify special leadership traits associated with successful leaders. After this, we will examine the consequences of various leadership behaviours and examine theories contending that effective leadership depends on the nature of the work situation. Following this are discussions of participative leadership, leader–member exchange theory, and transactional and transformational leadership theory. Next, we discuss several new and emerging leadership theories, including empowering leadership, ethical leadership, authentic leadership, and servant leadership. We conclude the chapter with a discussion of gender differences and culture in leadership, and global leadership.

WHAT IS LEADERSHIP?

LO 9.1

Define *leadership*, and discuss the role of *strategic* and formal leadership in organizations.

Leadership. The influence that particular individuals exert on the goal achievement of others in an organizational context.

PERSONAL INVENTORY ASSESSMENT

Learn About Yourself
Leadership Style Inventory

Strategic leadership. Leadership that involves the ability to anticipate, envision, maintain flexibility, think strategically, and work with others to initiate changes that will create a viable future for the organization.

A recent survey found that the most pressing human capital challenge facing Canadian businesses today is leadership.[2] Perhaps it is not surprising that organizations in North America spend billions of dollars each year to develop their leaders to make them more effective. But what exactly is leadership and what makes a leader effective?

Leadership occurs when particular individuals exert influence on the goal achievement of others in an organizational context. Effective leadership exerts influence in a way that achieves organizational goals by enhancing the productivity, innovation, satisfaction, and commitment of the workforce. Leadership is about motivating people and gaining their commitment. Effective leaders can change the way people think, feel, and behave, and they can have a positive effect on individuals, groups, units, and even entire organizations.[3]

As demonstrated in the chapter-opening vignette, leadership has a strong effect on an organization's strategy, success, and very survival. Just consider Sergio Marchionne's role in transforming and saving Fiat and Chrysler and making them both profitable organizations. His role and actions demonstrate the important role that leaders play in changing the direction and strategy of an organization through what is known as strategic leadership.

Strategic leadership refers to a leader's "ability to anticipate, envision, maintain flexibility, think strategically, and work with others to initiate changes that will create a viable future for the organization." Strategic leaders can provide an organization with a sustainable competitive advantage by helping their organizations compete in turbulent and unpredictable environments and by exploiting growth opportunities. Strategic leaders are open and honest in their interactions with the organization's stakeholders, and they focus on the future.[4] Sergio Marchionne is an excellent example of strategic leadership.

In theory, *any* organizational member can exert influence on other members, thus engaging in leadership. In practice, though, some members are in a better position to be

" *Some men are born great, some achieve greatness, and
some are allowed to work for great men like me.* "

leaders than others. Individuals with titles such as *manager, executive, supervisor,* and *department
head* occupy formal or assigned leadership roles. As part of these roles they are *expected* to
influence others, and they are given specific authority to direct employees. Of course, the
presence of a formal leadership role is no guarantee that there is leadership. Some managers
and supervisors fail to exert any influence on others. These people will usually be judged to
be ineffective leaders. Thus, leadership involves going beyond formal role requirements to
influence others.

Individuals might also emerge to occupy informal leadership roles. Since informal leaders do not have formal authority, they must rely on being well liked or being perceived as
highly skilled to exert influence. In this chapter, we will concentrate on formal leadership.
In the next section, we discuss one of the earliest theories of leadership. Before continuing,
try to answer this question: *Are some people born leaders?*

ARE LEADERS BORN? THE TRAIT THEORY OF LEADERSHIP

Given Sergio Marchionne's track record as an effective leader, you might be tempted to conclude that he is a born leader. But then again, given his years of experience, you might just as
easily conclude that he has, in fact, learned how to become a good leader.

Throughout history, social observers have been fascinated by obvious examples of successful interpersonal influence, whether the consequences of this influence were good, bad,
or mixed. Individuals such as Henry Ford, Martin Luther King, Jr., Barbara Jordan, Ralph
Nader, and Jack Welch have been analyzed and reanalyzed to discover what made them leaders and what set them apart from less successful leaders. The implicit assumption here is that
those who become leaders and do a good job of it possess a special set of traits that distinguish
them from the masses of followers. This approach to leadership is known as the trait theory of
leadership. According to the **trait theory of leadership**, leadership depends on the personal
qualities or traits of the leader.[5] While philosophers and the popular media have advocated
such a position for centuries, trait theories of leadership did not receive serious scientific
attention until the 1900s. Let's take a closer look at the research on leadership traits.

LO 9.2

Explain and critically
evaluate the *trait theory
of leadership.*

Trait theory of leadership.
Leadership depends on the
personal qualities or traits of
the leader.

Research on Leadership Traits

During the First World War, the U.S. military recognized that it had a leadership problem. Never before had the country mounted such a massive war effort, and able officers were in short supply. Thus, the search for leadership traits that might be useful in identifying potential officers began. Following the war, and continuing through the Second World War, this interest expanded to include searching for leadership traits in populations as diverse as school children and business executives. Some studies tried to differentiate traits of leaders and followers, while others were a search for traits that predicted leader effectiveness or distinguished lower-level leaders from higher-level leaders.[6]

Just what is a trait, anyway? **Traits** are personal characteristics of individuals such as physical characteristics, intellectual ability, and personality. Research on leadership has mostly focused on traits associated with demographics (e.g., gender, age, and education), task competence (e.g., intelligence), and interpersonal attributes (e.g., extraversion).[7] Research has shown that many, many traits are not associated with whether people become leaders or how effective they are as leaders. Research also shows that some traits are associated with leadership. Exhibit 9.1 provides a list of the traits that have often been found to be related to leadership.[8] As you might expect, leaders (or more successful leaders) tend to be higher than average on these dimensions, although the connections are not very strong. Notice that the list portrays a high-energy person who really wants to have an impact on others but at the same time is smart and stable enough not to abuse his or her power. Interestingly, this is a very accurate summary description of Sergio Marchionne.

In recent years, there has been a renewed interest in the study of leadership traits, and a number of studies have shown that certain traits are more closely linked to leadership emergence and effectiveness. For example, all five of the Big Five dimensions of personality have been found to be related to leadership emergence and success, with extraversion and conscientiousness being the most consistent predictors of leadership effectiveness.[9] What's more, a recent study found that CEO and top management team conscientiousness were directly related to organizational performance.[10] A review of research on intelligence and leadership found that although there is a significant relationship between intelligence and leadership effectiveness, it is considerably lower than previously thought.[11] It is also worth noting that the relationship between traits and leadership effectiveness is stronger for affective and relational measures of effectiveness (e.g., satisfaction with the leader) than for performance-related measures. Perhaps not surprisingly, many contemporary organizations use a wide variety of trait-based assessments to measure leadership traits when making hiring and promotion decisions.[12] For another example of a trait that has often been associated with leadership, see the Research Focus: *Narcissism and Leadership*.

Traits. Individual characteristics such as physical attributes, intellectual ability, and personality.

EXHIBIT 9.1
Traits associated with leadership effectiveness.

Intelligence
Energy and drive
Self-confidence
Dominance
Motivation to lead
Emotional stability
Honesty and integrity
Need for achievement
Sociability

Limitations of the Trait Approach

Even though some traits appear to be related to leadership emergence and leadership effectiveness, there are several reasons why the trait approach is not the best means of understanding and improving leadership.

In many cases, it is difficult to determine whether traits make the leader or whether the opportunity for leadership produces the traits. For example, do dominant individuals tend to become leaders, or do employees become more dominant *after* they successfully occupy leadership roles? This distinction is important. If the former is true, we might wish to seek out dominant people and appoint them to leadership roles. If the latter is true, this strategy will not work.

Even if we know that dominance, intelligence, or tallness is associated with effective leadership, we have few clues about what dominant or intelligent or tall people *do* to influence others successfully. As a result, we have little information about how to train and develop leaders and no way to diagnose failures of leadership.

Furthermore, because the trait approach leads us to believe that a person is more likely to become a leader or to be a more effective leader simply because they possess certain traits,

■ RESEARCH FOCUS ■

NARCISSISM AND LEADERSHIP

Narcissism is a personality trait that describes people who have a grandiose sense of self-importance, require excessive admiration, have a sense of entitlement, lack empathy, and tend to be exploitive, manipulative, and arrogant. For years, it has been suggested that narcissism is an important factor for leadership success. In fact, a number of studies have reported positive relationships between narcissism and leadership. However, other studies have found negative relationships between narcissism and leadership. As a result, there is a lack of consensus on the impact of narcissism on leadership and whether narcissistic leaders hinder or benefit organizations.

There are a number of reasons for the inconsistency in research findings, such as whether or not one is predicting leadership emergence (whether one is viewed by others as a leader) or leadership effectiveness as well as the source of the leadership ratings (i.e., leader self-report or observer ratings).

In an attempt to assess the relationship between narcissism and leadership and to better understand the inconsistent findings, Emily Grijalva and colleagues reviewed past research on narcissism and leadership and conducted a meta-analytic review that combines the results of past studies. Their results provide a clearer picture of the role of narcissism in leadership.

First, they compared the results of studies that predicted leadership emergence versus leadership effectiveness. They expected narcissism to be positively related to leadership emergence but negatively related to leadership effectiveness. They found that while narcissism was positively related to leadership emergence, it was not significantly related to leadership effectiveness. Furthermore, the narcissism–leadership relationship was stronger for leadership emergence than for leadership effectiveness.

Second, they compared the source of the reports of the leadership effectiveness ratings (e.g., self-report by the leader versus observer). The results indicated that the relationship between narcissism and leadership effectiveness was stronger when the leader provided the ratings of his or her effectiveness rather than an observer (i.e., supervisor, peer, subordinate).

Third, the authors were also interested in whether the effect of narcissism on leadership emergence might be due to extraversion, which is a personality trait that overlaps with narcissism and is also associated with leadership. As expected, extraversion was positively related to leadership emergence. Furthermore, when narcissism and extraversion were both used to predict leadership emergence, narcissism was no longer a significant predictor. In other words, once extraversion is taken into account, narcissists are not more likely to emerge as leaders. Thus, narcissists emerge as leaders because they are more extraverted.

A fourth possible explanation for the inconsistent results for narcissism and leadership effectiveness is the possibility that the relationship is curvilinear rather than linear. Along these lines, the authors tested the possibility that only a moderate level of narcissism is related to leadership effectiveness, while too little or too much is associated with leadership dysfunction. The results did in fact support a curvilinear relationship between narcissism and leadership effectiveness such that the shape of the relationship is an inverted U. In other words, narcissism contributes to leadership effectiveness up to a point, beyond which it is detrimental to leadership effectiveness. Furthermore, unlike the linear relationship between narcissism and leadership emergence, this relationship was not explained by extraversion.

The results of this study help to clarify when, why, and by how much narcissism influences leadership. In particular, the results indicate that the effect of narcissism on leadership depends on the type of leadership (emergence versus effectiveness) and that narcissists are more likely to emerge as leaders, but only because they are more extraverted. Finally, leaders are more effective when they have moderate or average levels of narcissism rather than very high or very low levels. What this means is that while individuals high in narcissism are more likely to be selected into leadership roles, their high levels of narcissism will also hinder leadership effectiveness.

Source: Based on Grijalva, E., Harms, P.D., Newman, D.A., Gaddis, B.H., & Fraley, R.C. (2015). Narcissism and leadership: A meta-analytic review of linear and nonlinear relationships. *Personnel Psychology, 68*, 1–47.

it can lead to bias and discrimination when evaluating a leader's effectiveness and when making decisions about promoting people to leadership positions. According to **leadership categorization theory**, people are more likely to view somebody as a leader and to evaluate them as a more effective leader when they possess prototypical characteristics of leadership. For example, research has found that leaders, but not employees, were more often assumed to be white by white and non–white research participants, regardless of the percentage of white

Leadership categorization theory. People are more likely to view somebody as a leader and to evaluate them as a more effective leader when they possess prototypical characteristics of leadership.

individuals in an organization and in leadership positions. White and non-white participants also evaluated white leaders as more effective and as having more leadership potential than non-white leaders when the leader was credited with their organization's success.[13] Thus, it is not a good idea to focus exclusively on traits when making decisions and judgements about leadership potential and effectiveness.

Finally, the most crucial problem of the trait approach to leadership is its failure to take into account the *situation* in which leadership occurs. Intuitively, it seems reasonable that top executives and first-level supervisors might require different traits to be successful. Similarly, physical prowess might be useful in directing a logging crew but irrelevant to managing a team of scientists.

In summary, although there are some traits that are associated with leadership success, traits alone are not sufficient for successful leadership. Traits are only a precondition for certain actions that a leader must take to be successful. In other words, possessing the appropriate traits for leadership makes it possible—and even more likely—that certain actions will be taken and will be successful.[14] In fact, there is some evidence that one of the reasons that traits are related to leadership effectiveness is because of their association with leadership behaviours that are important for effective leadership. This research also indicates that leader behaviours have a greater impact on leadership effectiveness than leader traits and, unlike traits, behaviours can be learned and developed.[15]

THE BEHAVIOUR OF LEADERS

The trait approach is mainly concerned with what leaders *bring* to a group setting. The limitations of this approach gradually promoted an interest in what leaders *do* in group settings. Of particular interest were the behaviours of certain group members that caused them to *become* leaders and the behaviour of assigned or appointed leaders. What are the crucial

LO 9.3

Compare and contrast the following leadership behaviours and their consequences: *consideration, initiating structure, leader reward,* and *leader punishment.*

Co-operators president and CEO Kathy Bardswick is a good example of a leader who exhibits leader consideration behaviour.

Fred Lum/The Globe and Mail

behaviours such leaders engage in, and how do these behaviours influence employee performance and satisfaction? In other words, is there a particular *leadership style* that is more effective than other possible styles?

The most involved, systematic study of leadership took place at Ohio State University in the 1940s. The Ohio State researchers began by having employees describe their superiors along a number of behavioural dimensions. Statistical analyses of these descriptions revealed that they boiled down to two basic kinds of behaviour—consideration and initiating structure.

Consideration and Initiating Structure

Consideration is the extent to which a leader is approachable and shows personal concern and respect for employees. The considerate leader is seen as friendly and egalitarian, expresses appreciation and support, and is protective of group welfare. Co-operators Group president and CEO Kathy Bardswick is a good example of someone who exhibits leader consideration behaviour. After she became CEO in 2001, she participated in 90 town hall meetings across the country to learn about employee concerns and answer their questions. Upon learning that employees were stressed and feeling the heat of public outrage at the high cost of auto insurance, she introduced a number of initiatives to assist employees, including a wellness program, recognition programs, and flexible work hours. In 2004, for the first time, the Co-operators were named one of the 50 Best Employers in Canada and remains so today.[16]

Initiating structure is the degree to which a leader concentrates on group goal attainment. The structuring leader clearly defines and organizes his or her role and the roles of followers, stresses standard procedures, schedules the work to be done, and assigns employees to particular tasks.

It is important to note that consideration and initiating structure are not incompatible; a leader could be high, low, or average on one or both dimensions.

Consideration. The extent to which a leader is approachable and shows personal concern and respect for employees.

Initiating structure. The degree to which a leader concentrates on group goal attainment.

The Consequences of Consideration and Structure

The association between leader consideration, leader initiating structure, and employee responses has been the subject of hundreds of research studies. In general, this research shows that consideration and initiating structure both contribute positively to employees' motivation, job satisfaction, and leader effectiveness. However, consideration tends to be more strongly related to follower satisfaction (leader satisfaction and job satisfaction), motivation, and leader effectiveness, while initiating structure is slightly more strongly related to leader job performance and group performance.[17] In addition, there is some evidence that the relative importance of consideration and initiating structure varies according to the nature of the leadership situation. In particular, the effects of consideration and initiating structure often depend on the characteristics of the task, the employee, and the setting in which work is performed.[18] We will have more to say about this when we discuss the situational theories of leadership. But first, let's consider two more examples of leader behaviours.

Leader Reward and Punishment Behaviours

Two additional leader behaviours that have been the focus of research are leader reward behaviour and leader punishment behaviour. **Leader reward behaviour** provides employees with compliments, tangible benefits, and deserved special treatment. When such rewards are made *contingent on performance*, employees should perform at a high level and experience job satisfaction. Under such leadership, employees have a clear picture of what is expected of them, and they understand that positive outcomes will occur if they achieve these expectations.

Leader punishment behaviour involves the use of reprimands or unfavourable task assignments and the active withholding of raises, promotions, and other rewards. You will recall from Chapter 2 that punishment is extremely difficult to use effectively, and when it is

Leader reward behaviour. The leader's use of compliments, tangible benefits, and deserved special treatment.

Leader punishment behaviour. The leader's use of reprimands or unfavourable task assignments and the active withholding of rewards.

perceived as random and not contingent on employee behaviour, employees react negatively, with great dissatisfaction.

Research on leader reward and punishment behaviour has found them to be very effective. Contingent leader reward behaviour is positively related to employees' perceptions (e.g., trust in supervisor), attitudes (e.g., job satisfaction and organizational commitment), and behaviour (e.g., effort, performance, and organizational citizenship behaviour). And while contingent leader punishment behaviour is related to more favourable employee perceptions, attitudes, and behaviour, *non-contingent* punishment behaviour is related to unfavourable outcomes. Furthermore, the relationships are much stronger when rewards and punishment are made contingent on employee behaviour, which means that the manner in which leaders administer rewards and punishment is a critical determinant of their effectiveness. One of the reasons that leader reward and punishment behaviours are positively related to employee attitudes and behaviours is that they lead to more positive perceptions of justice and lower role ambiguity.[19]

LO **9.4**

Describe and evaluate the situational theories of leadership: *contingency theory* and *path–goal theory.*

Simulate

LEADERSHIP

SITUATIONAL THEORIES OF LEADERSHIP

We have referred to the potential impact of the situation on leadership effectiveness several times. Specifically, the *situation* refers to the *setting* in which influence attempts occur. The basic premise of situational theories of leadership is that the effectiveness of a leadership style is contingent on the setting. The setting includes the characteristics of the employees, the nature of the task they are performing, and characteristics of the organization.

The situational leadership theories described below are among the best known and most studied. They consider situational variables that seem especially likely to influence leadership effectiveness.

Fiedler's Contingency Theory

Contingency theory. Fred Fiedler's theory that states that the association between leadership orientation and group effectiveness is contingent on how favourable the situation is for exerting influence.

Least preferred co-worker. A current or past co-worker with whom a leader has had a difficult time accomplishing a task.

Fred Fiedler of the University of Washington spent decades developing and refining a situational theory of leadership called **contingency theory**.[20] This name stems from the notion that the association between *leadership orientation* and *group effectiveness* is contingent on (depends on) the extent to which the *situation is favourable* for the exertion of influence. In other words, some situations are more favourable for leadership than others, and these situations require different orientations on the part of the leader.

Leadership orientation is measured by having leaders describe their **least preferred co-worker** (LPC). This person may be a current or past co-worker. In either case, it is someone with whom the leader has had a difficult time getting the job done. The leader who describes the LPC relatively favourably (a high LPC score) can be considered *relationship* oriented— that is, despite the fact that the LPC is or was difficult to work with, the leader can still find positive qualities in him or her. On the other hand, the leader who describes the LPC unfavourably (a low LPC score) can be considered *task* oriented. This person allows the low task competence of the LPC to colour his or her views of the personal qualities of the LPC ("If he's no good at the job, then he's not good, period").

Fiedler has argued that the LPC score reveals a personality trait that reflects the leader's motivational structure. High–LPC leaders are motivated to maintain interpersonal relations, while low–LPC leaders are motivated to accomplish the task. Despite the apparent similarity, the LPC score is *not* a measure of consideration or initiating structure. These are observed *behaviours*, while the LPC score is an *attitude* of the leader toward work relationships.

Situational favourableness is the "contingency" part of contingency theory—that is, it specifies when a particular LPC orientation should contribute most to group effectiveness. A situation is considered to be most favourable when the relationship between the leader and the group members is good (leader–member relations), the task at hand is highly structured

© CP PHOTO/Kevin Frayer

Situational theories of leadership explain how leadership style must be tailored to the demands of the task and the qualities of employees.

(task structure), and when the leader has been granted formal authority by the organization to tell others what to do (position power). The situation is least favourable when leader–member relations are poor, the task is unstructured, and the leader has weak position power.

As shown in Exhibit 9.2, we can arrange the possible combinations of situational factors into eight octants that form a continuum of favourability. The model indicates that a task orientation (low LPC) is most effective when the leadership situation is very favourable (octants I, II, and III) *or* when it is very unfavourable (octant VIII). On the other hand, a relationship orientation (high LPC) is most effective in conditions of medium favourability (octants IV, V, VI, and VII). Why is this so? In essence, Fiedler argues that leaders can "get away" with a task orientation when the situation is favourable—employees are "ready" to be influenced. Conversely, when the situation is very unfavourable for leadership, task orientation is necessary to get anything accomplished. In conditions of medium favourability, the boss is faced with some combination of an unclear task or a poor relationship with employees. Here, a relationship orientation will help to make the best of a situation that is stress provoking but not impossibly bad.

RESEARCH EVIDENCE The conclusions about leadership effectiveness in Exhibit 9.2 are derived from many studies that Fiedler summarizes.[21] However, contingency theory has been the subject of as much debate as any theory in organizational behaviour.[22] Fiedler's explanation for the superior performance of high–LPC leaders in the middle octants is not especially convincing, and the exact meaning of the LPC score is one of the great mysteries

Favourableness	High							Low
Leader–Member Relations	Good				Poor			
Task Structure	Structured		Unstructured		Structured		Unstructured	
Position Power	Strong	Weak	Strong	Weak	Strong	Weak	Strong	Weak
	I	II	III	IV	V	VI	VII	VIII
Most Effective Leader Orientation	Task			Relationship				Task

EXHIBIT 9.2
Predictions of leader effectiveness from Fiedler's contingency theory of leadership.

of organizational behaviour. It does not seem to be correlated with other personality measures or predictive of specific leader behaviour. It now appears that a major source of the many inconsistent findings regarding contingency theory is the small sample sizes that researchers used in many of the studies. Advances in correcting for this problem statistically have led recent reviewers to conclude that there is reasonable support for the theory.[23] However, Fiedler's prescription for task leadership in octant II (good relations, structured task, weak position power) seems contradicted by the evidence, suggesting that his theory needs some refinement.

House's Path–Goal Theory

Path–goal theory. Robert House's theory concerned with the situations under which various leader behaviours (directive, supportive, participative, achievement oriented) are most effective.

Robert House, building on the work of Martin Evans, proposed a situational theory of leadership called path–goal theory.[24] Unlike Fiedler's contingency theory, which relies on the somewhat ambiguous LPC trait, **path–goal theory** is concerned with the situations under which various leader *behaviours* are most effective.

THE THEORY Why did House choose the name "path–goal" for his theory? According to House, the most important activities of leaders are those that clarify the paths to various goals of interest to employees. Such goals might include a promotion, a sense of accomplishment, or a pleasant work climate. In turn, the opportunity to achieve such goals should promote job satisfaction, leader acceptance, and high effort. Thus, *the effective leader forms a connection between employee goals and organizational goals.*

House argues that to provide *job satisfaction* and *leader acceptance*, leader behaviour must be perceived as immediately satisfying or as leading to future satisfaction. Leader behaviour that employees see as unnecessary or unhelpful will be resented. House contends that to promote employee *effort*, leaders must make rewards dependent on performance and ensure that employees have a clear picture of how they can achieve these rewards. To do this, the leader might have to provide support through direction, guidance, and coaching. For example, the bank teller who wishes to be promoted to supervisor should exhibit superior effort when his boss promises a recommendation contingent on good work and explains carefully how the teller can do better in his or her current job.

LEADER BEHAVIOUR Path–goal theory is concerned with the following four specific kinds of leader behaviour:

- *Directive behaviour.* Directive leaders schedule work, maintain performance standards, and let employees know what is expected of them. This behaviour is essentially identical to initiating structure.

- *Supportive behaviour.* Supportive leaders are friendly, approachable, and concerned with pleasant interpersonal relationships. This behaviour is essentially identical to consideration.

- *Participative behaviour.* Participative leaders consult with employees about work-related matters and consider their opinions.

- *Achievement-oriented behaviour.* Achievement-oriented leaders encourage employees to exert high effort and strive for a high level of goal accomplishment. They express confidence that employees can reach these goals.

According to path–goal theory, the effectiveness of each set of behaviours depends on the situation that the leader encounters.

SITUATIONAL FACTORS Path–goal theory concerns itself with two primary classes of situational factors—employee characteristics and environmental factors. Exhibit 9.3 illustrates

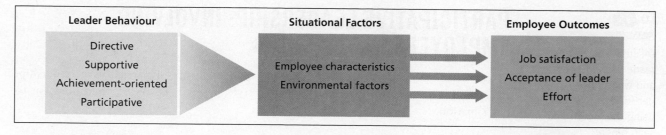

Leader Behaviour	Situational Factors	Employee Outcomes
Directive Supportive Achievement-oriented Participative	Employee characteristics Environmental factors	Job satisfaction Acceptance of leader Effort

the role of these situational factors in the theory. Put simply, the impact of leader behaviour on employee satisfaction, effort, and acceptance of the leader depends on the nature of the employees and the work environment. Let's consider these two situational factors in turn, along with some of the theory's predictions.

According to the theory, different types of employees need or prefer different forms of leadership. For example,

- Employees who are high need achievers (Chapter 5) should work well under achievement-oriented leadership.

- Employees who prefer being told what to do should respond best to a directive leadership style.

- When employees feel that they have rather low task abilities, they should appreciate directive leadership and coaching behaviour. When they feel quite capable of performing the task, they will view such behaviours as unnecessary and irritating.

As you can observe from these examples, leaders might have to tailor their behaviour to the needs, abilities, and personalities of individual employees.

Also, according to the theory, the effectiveness of leadership behaviour depends on the particular work environment. For example,

- When tasks are clear and routine, employees should perceive directive leadership as a redundant and unnecessary imposition. This should reduce satisfaction and acceptance of the leader. Similarly, participative leadership would not seem to be useful when tasks are clear, since there is little in which to participate. Obviously, such tasks are most common at lower organizational levels.

- When tasks are challenging but ambiguous, employees should appreciate both directive and participative leadership. Such styles should clarify the path to good performance and demonstrate that the leader is concerned with helping employees to do a good job. Obviously, such tasks are most common at higher organizational levels.

- Frustrating, dissatisfying jobs should increase employee appreciation of supportive behaviour. To some degree, such support should compensate for a disliked job, although it should probably do little to increase effort.

As you can see from these examples of environmental factors, effective leadership should *take advantage of* the motivating and satisfying aspects of jobs while *offsetting* or *compensating for* those job aspects that demotivate or dissatisfy.

RESEARCH EVIDENCE In general, there is some research support for most of the situational propositions discussed above. In particular, there is substantial evidence that supportive or considerate leader behaviour is most beneficial in supervising routine, frustrating, or dissatisfying jobs and some evidence that directive or structuring leader behaviour is most effective on ambiguous, less structured jobs.[25] The theory appears to work better in predicting employees' job satisfaction and acceptance of the leader than in predicting job performance.[26]

EXHIBIT 9.3
The path–goal theory of leadership.
Source: The path–goal theory of leadership. *Journal of Contemporary Business*, 3 (4), 89., Michael G. Foster School of Business.

Discuss *participative leadership* and how and when to use participative leadership using the Vroom and Jago model.

Participative leadership.
Involving employees in making work-related decisions.

PARTICIPATIVE LEADERSHIP: INVOLVING EMPLOYEES IN DECISIONS

In the discussion of path–goal theory, we raised the issue of participative leadership. Because this is such an important leadership style, we will devote further attention to participation.

What Is Participative Leadership?

At a very general level, **participative leadership** means involving employees in making work-related decisions. The term *involving* is intentionally broad. Participation is not a fixed or absolute property but a relative concept. This is illustrated in Exhibit 9.4. Here, we see that leaders can vary in the extent to which they involve employees in decision making. Minimally, participation involves obtaining employee opinions before making a decision. Maximally, it allows employees to make their own decisions within agreed-on limits. As the "area of freedom" on the part of employees increases, the leader is behaving in a more participative manner. There is, however, an upper limit to the area of employee freedom available under participation. Participative leadership should not be confused with the *abdication* of leadership, which is almost always ineffective.

Participation can involve individual employees or the entire group of employees that reports to the leader. For example, participation on an individual basis might work best when setting performance goals for particular employees, planning employee development, or dealing with problem employees. On the other hand, the leader might involve the entire work group in decision making when determining vacation schedules, arranging for telephone coverage during lunch hour, or deciding how to allocate scarce resources, such as travel money or secretarial help. As these examples suggest, the choice of an individual or group participation strategy should be tailored to specific situations.

Potential Advantages of Participative Leadership

Just why might participation be a useful leadership technique? What are its potential advantages?

MOTIVATION Participation can increase the motivation of employees.[27] In some cases, participation permits them to contribute to the establishment of work goals and to decide how they can accomplish these goals. It might also occur to you that participation can

EXHIBIT 9.4
Employee participation in decision making can vary.
Source: Tannenbaum, R., & Schmidt, W.H. (1958, March/April). "How to choose a leadership pattern." *Harvard Business Review.* Copyright © 1958 by the President and Fellows of Harvard College; all rights reserved. Reprinted by permission.

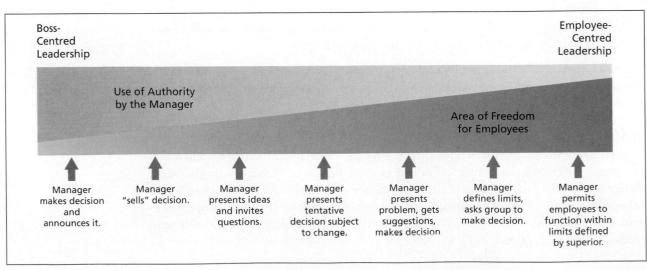

Boss-Centred Leadership

Employee-Centred Leadership

Use of Authority by the Manager

Area of Freedom for Employees

Manager makes decision and announces it.

Manager "sells" decision.

Manager presents ideas and invites questions.

Manager presents tentative decision subject to change.

Manager presents problem, gets suggestions, makes decision

Manager defines limits, asks group to make decision.

Manager permits employees to function within limits defined by superior.

increase intrinsic motivation by enriching employees' jobs. In Chapter 6, you learned that enriched jobs include high task variety and increased employee autonomy. Participation adds some variety to the job and promotes autonomy by increasing the "area of freedom" (see Exhibit 9.4).

QUALITY Participation can enhance quality in at least two ways. First, an old saying argues that "two heads are better than one." While this is not always true, there do seem to be many cases in which "two heads" (participation) lead to higher-quality decisions than the leader could make alone.[28] In particular, this is most likely when employees have special knowledge to contribute to the decision. In many research and engineering departments, it is common for the professional employees to have technical knowledge that is superior to that of their boss. This occurs either because the boss is not a professional or because the boss's knowledge has become outdated. Under these conditions, employee participation in technical matters should enhance the quality of decisions.

Participation can also enhance quality because high levels of participation often empower employees to take direct action to solve problems without checking every detail with the boss. Empowerment gives employees the authority, opportunity, and motivation to take initiative and solve problems. We will have more to say about empowering leadership later in the chapter.

ACCEPTANCE Even when participation does not promote motivation or increase the quality of decisions, it can increase the employees' acceptance of decisions. This is especially likely when issues of *fairness* are involved.[29] For example, consider the problems of scheduling vacations or telephone coverage during lunch hours. Here, the leader could probably make high-quality decisions without involving employees. However, the decisions might be totally unacceptable to the employees because they perceive them as unfair. Involving employees in decision making could result in solutions of equal quality that do not provoke dissatisfaction. Public commitment and ego involvement probably contribute to the acceptance of such decisions.

Potential Problems of Participative Leadership

You have no doubt learned that every issue in organizational behaviour has two sides. Consider the potential difficulties of participation.

TIME AND ENERGY Participation is not a state of mind. It involves specific behaviours on the part of the leader (soliciting ideas, calling meetings), and these behaviours use time and energy. When a quick decision is needed, participation is not an appropriate leadership strategy. The hospital emergency room is not the place to implement participation on a continuous basis!

LOSS OF POWER Some leaders feel that a participative style will reduce their power and influence. Sometimes they respond by asking employees to make trivial decisions of the "What colour shall we paint the lounge?" type. Clearly, the consequences of such decisions (for motivation, quality, and acceptance) are near zero. A lack of trust in employees and a fear that they will make mistakes is often the hallmark of an insecure manager. On the other hand, the contemporary call for flatter hierarchies and increased teamwork make such sharing of power inevitable.

LACK OF RECEPTIVITY OR KNOWLEDGE Employees might not be receptive to participation. When the leader is distrusted, or when a poor labour climate exists, they might resent "having to do management's work." Even when receptive, employees might lack the knowledge to contribute effectively to decisions. Usually, this occurs because they are unaware of *external constraints* on their decisions.

Vroom and Jago's Situational Model of Participation

How can leaders capitalize on the potential advantages of participation while avoiding its pitfalls? Victor Vroom and Arthur Jago developed a model that attempts to specify in a practical manner when leaders should use participation and to what extent they should use it. (The model was originally developed by Vroom and Philip Yetton).[30]

Vroom and Jago begin with the recognition that there are various degrees of participation that a leader can exhibit. For issues involving the entire work group, the following range of behaviours is plausible (A stands for autocratic, C for consultative, and G for group; I indicates an individual, and II indicates that a group is involved):

AI. You solve the problem or make the decision yourself, using information available to you at the time.

AII. You obtain the necessary information from your employees, then decide the solution to the problem yourself. You may or may not tell your employees what the problem is when getting the information from them. The role played by your employees in making the decision is clearly one of providing the necessary information to you, rather than generating or evaluating alternative solutions.

CI. You share the problem with the relevant employees individually, getting their ideas and suggestions without bringing them together as a group. Then you make the decision, which may or may not reflect your employees' influence.

CII. You share the problem with your employees as a group, obtaining their collective ideas and suggestions. Then you make the decision, which may or may not reflect your employees' influence.

GII. You share the problem with your employees as a group. Together you generate and evaluate alternatives and attempt to reach agreement (consensus) on a solution. Your role is much like that of chairperson. You do not try to influence the group to adopt "your" solution, and you are willing to accept and implement any solution that has the support of the entire group.[31]

Which of these strategies is most effective? According to Vroom and Jago, this depends on the situation or problem at hand. In general, the leader's goal should be to make high-quality decisions to which employees will be adequately committed without undue delay. To do this, he or she must consider the questions in Exhibit 9.5. The quality requirement (QR) for a problem might be low if it is very unlikely that a technically bad decision could be made or if all feasible alternatives are equal in quality. Otherwise, QR is probably high. The commitment requirement (CR) is likely to be high if employees are very concerned about which alternative will be chosen or if they will have to actually implement the decision. The problem is structured (ST) when the leader understands the current situation, the desired situation, and how to get from one to the other. Unfamiliarity, uncertainty, or novelty in any of these matters reduces problem structure. The other questions in Exhibit 9.5 are fairly self-explanatory. Notice, however, that all are oriented toward preserving either decision quality or commitment to the decision.

By tracing a problem through the decision tree, the leader encounters the prescribed degree of participation for that problem. In every case, the tree shows the fastest approach possible (i.e., the most autocratic) that still maintains decision quality and commitment. In many cases, if the leader is willing to sacrifice some speed, a more participative approach could stimulate employee development (as long as quality or commitment is not threatened).

RESEARCH EVIDENCE The original decision model developed by Vroom and Yetton, on which the Vroom and Jago model is based, has substantial research support.[32] Following

QR	Quality Requirement:	How important is the technical quality of this decision?
CR	Commitment Requirement:	How important is subordinate commitment to the decision?
LI	Leader's Information:	Do you have sufficient information to make a high-quality decision?
ST	Problem Structure:	Is the problem well structured?
CP	Commitment Probability:	If you were to make the decision by yourself, is it reasonably certain that your subordinate(s) would be commited to the decision?
GC	Goal Congruence:	Do subordinates share the organizational goals to be attained in solving the problem?
CO	Subordinate Conflict:	Is conflict among subordinates over preferred solutions likely?
SI	Subordinate Information:	Do subordinates have sufficient information to make a high-quality decision?

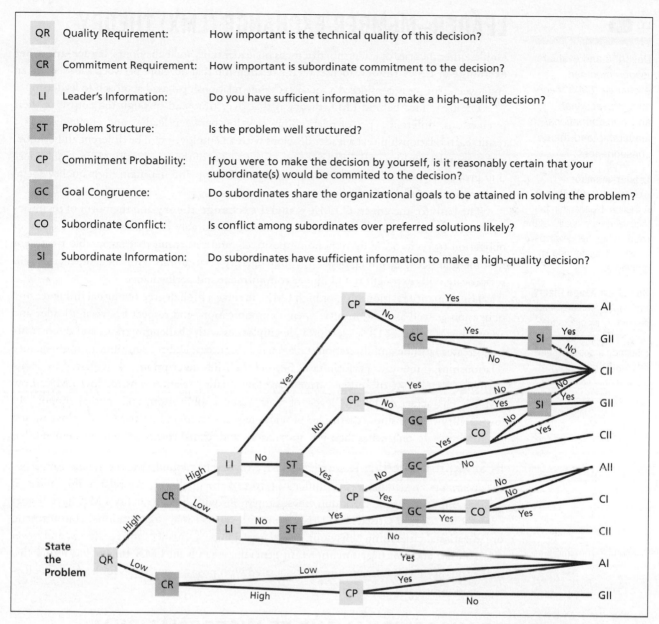

EXHIBIT 9.5

The Vroom and Jago decision tree for participative leadership.

Source: Vroom, V.H., & Jago, A.G. (1988). *The new leadership: Managing participation in organizations.* Reprinted by permission of Dr. Victor H. Vroom.

the model's prescriptions is more likely to lead to successful managerial decisions than unsuccessful decisions. The model has been used frequently in management development seminars.

But does participative leadership result in beneficial outcomes? There is substantial evidence that employees who have the opportunity to participate in work-related decisions report more job satisfaction and higher task performance and organizational citizenship behaviour toward the organization than those who do not. These results are due in part to a positive effect on employee empowerment and trust in one's supervisor. Thus, most workers seem to *prefer* a participative work environment. However, for participation to be translated into higher productivity, it would appear that certain facilitating conditions must exist. Specifically, participation should work best when employees feel favourably toward it, when they are intelligent and knowledgeable about the issue at hand, and when the task is complex enough to make participation useful.[33] In general, these conditions are incorporated into the Vroom and Jago model. Like any other leadership strategy, the usefulness of participation depends on the constraints of the situation.

LO 9.6

Describe and evaluate *leader–member exchange (LMX) theory* and *transactional* and *transformational* leadership and their consequences.

Leader–member exchange (LMX) theory.
A theory of leadership that focuses on the quality of the relationship that develops between a leader and an employee.

Social exchange theory.
Individuals who are treated favourably by others feel obliged to reciprocate by responding positively and returning that favourable treatment in some manner.

LEADER–MEMBER EXCHANGE (LMX) THEORY

Unlike other theories of leadership that focus on leader traits and behaviours, **leader–member exchange** or **LMX theory,** focuses on the relationship that develops between a leader and an employee. Thus, it is considered a social exchange relationship-based approach to leadership.

The basic idea behind LMX theory is that over time and through the course of their interactions, different types of relationships develop between leaders and employees. As a result, each relationship that a leader develops with an employee will be different and unique, and these relationships will differ in terms of the *quality* of the relationship. Effective leadership processes result when leaders and employees develop and maintain high-quality social exchange relationships.[34]

The basis for the effects of LMX is **social exchange theory** and the norm of reciprocity, which posits that individuals who are treated favourably by others will feel a sense of obligation to reciprocate by responding positively and returning that favourable treatment in some manner. Thus, employees in a high-quality relationship with their supervisor will reciprocate with extra effort and higher commitment and performance.[35]

High-quality relationships, or high LMX, involve a high degree of mutual influence and obligation as well as trust, loyalty, open communication, and respect between a leader and an employee. High LMX leaders provide employees with challenging tasks and opportunities, greater latitude and discretion, task-related resources, and recognition. In high-quality relationships, employees perform tasks beyond their job descriptions, as suggested by social exchange theory. At the other extreme are low-quality relationships, or low LMX. Low LMX is characterized by low levels of trust, respect, obligation, and mutual support. In low-quality relationships, the leader provides less attention and latitude to employees, and so employees do only what their job descriptions and formal role requirements demand.[36]

RESEARCH EVIDENCE Research on LMX theory has found that the relationships between leaders and employees do differ in terms of the quality of the relationship and that this has implications for work outcomes. Employees with higher quality LMX have higher self-efficacy, overall satisfaction, satisfaction with supervision, organizational commitment, organizational citizenship behaviour, role clarity, job performance, and creativity, and lower role conflict and turnover intentions. In general, research on LMX theory has found that higher quality LMX relationships are associated with positive outcomes for leaders, employees, work units, and organizations.[37]

TRANSACTIONAL AND TRANSFORMATIONAL LEADERSHIP THEORY

Transactional leadership.
Leadership that is based on a straightforward exchange relationship between the leader and the followers.

Thus far in the chapter, we have been describing traditional theories of leadership involving an approach to leadership that is known as transactional leadership. **Transactional leadership** is leadership that is based on a straightforward exchange relationship between the leader and the followers—leaders set goals and provide direction and support, employees perform well, and the leader rewards them; the leader uses a participatory style, and the employees come up with good ideas.

Management by exception. Leadership that involves the leader taking corrective action on the basis of the results of leader–follower transactions.

Transactional leadership behaviour involves *contingent reward behaviour*, as discussed earlier in the chapter, and management by exception. As in path–goal theory, the leader clarifies expectations and establishes the rewards for meeting them. **Management by exception** is the degree to which leaders take corrective action on the basis of results of leader–follower transactions. Thus, they monitor follower behaviour, anticipate problems, and take corrective actions before the behaviour creates serious problems.[38] Although it might be difficult to do well, such leadership is routine, in the sense that it is directed mainly toward bringing employee behaviour in line with organizational goals.

However, you might be aware of some more dramatic examples of leadership in which leaders have had a more profound effect on followers by giving them a new vision that instilled true commitment to a project, a department, or an organization. Such leadership is called **transformational leadership** because the leader decisively changes the beliefs and attitudes of followers to correspond to this new vision and motivates them to achieve performance beyond expectations.[39]

Popular examples of transformational leadership are easy to find—consider Herb Kelleher's founding of Southwest Airlines, former Disney CEO Michael Eisner's role in improving Disney's performance, the late Steven Jobs's vision in bringing the Apple Macintosh to fruition, or former Hewlett-Packard CEO Carly Fiorina's orchestration of the merger with Compaq Computer and her transformation of Hewlett-Packard's structure and culture. Each of these leaders went beyond playing a mere institutional figurehead role, and even beyond a transactional leadership role, to truly transform employees' thinking about the nature of their businesses. However, these prominent examples should not obscure the fact that transformational leadership can occur in less visible settings. For example, a new coach might revitalize a sorry peewee soccer team, or an energetic new director might turn around a moribund community association using the same types of skills.

But what *are* the behaviours of these transformational leaders who encourage considerable effort and dedication on the part of followers? The late Bernard Bass conducted extensive research on transformational leaders.[40] Bass notes that transformational leaders are usually good at the transactional aspects of clarifying paths to goals and rewarding good performance. But he also notes other qualities that set transformational leaders apart from their transactional colleagues. In particular, there are four key dimensions of transformational leader behaviour: intellectual stimulation, individualized consideration, inspirational motivation, and charisma.[41] Let's now take a closer look at each of these behaviours.

Intellectual Stimulation

Intellectual stimulation contributes, in part, to the "new vision" aspect of transformational leadership. People are stimulated to think about problems, issues, and strategies in new ways. The leader challenges assumptions, takes risks, and solicits followers' ideas. Often, creativity and novelty are at work here. For example, the late Steve Jobs was convinced that the Apple Macintosh had to be extremely user-friendly. As you might imagine, many of the technical types who wanted to sign on to the Mac project needed to be convinced of the importance of this quality, and Jobs was just the person to do it, raising their consciousness about what it felt like to be a new computer user.

Individualized Consideration

Individualized consideration involves treating employees as distinct individuals, indicating concern for their needs and personal development, and serving as a mentor or coach when appropriate. The emphasis is on one-on-one attempts to meet the concerns and needs of the individual in question in the context of the overall goal or mission. Bass implies that individualized consideration is particularly striking when military leaders exhibit it, because the military culture generally stresses impersonality and "equal" treatment. The late General "Stormin'" Norman Schwarzkopf, commander of American troops during the Gulf War, is a good example of this.

Inspirational Motivation

Inspirational motivation involves the communication of visions that are appealing and inspiring to followers. Leaders with inspirational motivation have a strong vision for the future based on values and ideals. They stimulate enthusiasm, challenge followers with high

Transformational leadership. Leadership that provides followers with a new vision that instills true commitment.

standards, communicate optimism about future goal attainment, and provide meaning for the task at hand. They inspire followers using symbolic actions and persuasion.[42]

Charisma

Charisma (also known as *idealized influence*) is the fourth and by far the most important aspect of transformational leadership. In fact, many authors simply talk about charismatic leadership, although a good case can be made that a person could have charisma without being a leader. As indicated in the chapter-opening vignette, Sergio Marchionne has been described as a charismatic leader. But what exactly does this mean?

Charisma. The ability to command strong loyalty and devotion from followers and thus have the potential for strong influence among them.

Charisma is a term stemming from a Greek word meaning *favoured* or *gifted*. Charismatic individuals have been portrayed throughout history as having personal qualities that give them the potential to have extraordinary influence over others. They tend to command strong loyalty and devotion, and this, in turn, inspires enthusiastic dedication and effort directed toward the leader's chosen mission. In terms of the concepts we developed in Chapter 8, followers come to trust and *identify* with charismatic leaders and to *internalize* the values and goals they hold. Charisma provides the *emotional* aspect of transformational leadership.

It appears that the emergence of charisma is a complex function of traits, behaviours, and being in the right place at the right time.[43] Prominent traits include self-confidence, dominance, and a strong conviction in one's beliefs. Charismatic leaders often act to create an impression of personal success and accomplishment. They hold high expectations for follower performance while at the same time expressing confidence in followers' capabilities. This enhances the self-esteem of the followers. The goals set by charismatic leaders often have a moral or ideological flavour to them. In addition, charismatic leaders often emerge to articulate the feelings of followers in times of stress or discord. If these feelings go against an existing power structure, the leader might be perceived as especially courageous.

RESEARCH EVIDENCE A review of all the studies on transformational leadership found that transformational leadership is strongly related to follower motivation and satisfaction (satisfaction with leader and job satisfaction), leader performance, leader effectiveness, and individual, group, and organizational performance.[44] In addition, charismatic leadership has been found to be strongly related to follower satisfaction and leadership effectiveness.[45]

The late Steve Jobs was a charismatic leader who commanded strong loylaty and devotion from his employees.

© dpa picture alliance archive / Alamy Stock Photo

Comparisons between transformational leadership and contingent reward behaviours indicate that transformational leadership is more strongly related to follower satisfaction with the leader and leader effectiveness, while contingent reward is more strongly related to follower's job satisfaction and leader job performance. However, compared to other forms of leader behaviour (initiating structure, consideration, contingent reward behaviour), transformational leadership has been found to be the most consistent predictor of effective leadership.[46] In addition, several studies have found that CEO transformational leadership is positively related to organizational performance, especially under conditions of environmental uncertainty and in small- to medium-sized organizations.[47] Transformational leadership seems to be especially effective during times of change and for obtaining employees' commitment to a change. Employees with transformational leaders have been found to be more committed to and less likely to resist a large-scale organizational change.[48] Overall, research indicates that the best leaders are both transformational and transactional.

NEW AND EMERGING THEORIES OF LEADERSHIP

LO 9.7

Over the past decade, leadership research has begun to focus on not only the leader but also the broader context of the leadership process. This has involved a greater focus on followers and it has led to the emergence of new forms of leadership behaviours and theories.[49] In this section we describe four new and emerging theories of leadership: empowering leadership, ethical leadership, authentic leadership, and servant leadership. Pay particular attention to how each of these new forms of leadership differs from the more traditional styles and theories of leadership described earlier in the chapter.

Discuss the new and emerging theories of leadership including *empowering leadership*, *ethical leadership*, *authentic leadership*, and *servant leadership*.

Empowering Leadership

Traditional theories of leadership focus on how leaders influence and motivate employees to work toward organizational goals largely through initiating structure and directive behaviours. These theories were developed at a time when organizations were more hierarchical and bureaucratic. Many organizations today, however, are flatter, more flexible, and less bureaucratic, and employees in these organizations have more autonomy and responsibility in how they perform their jobs. This calls for a style of leadership, known as empowering leadership, that enables employees to make decisions and take actions on their own without direct supervision.

Empowering leadership involves implementing conditions that enable power to be shared with employees. Empowering leaders highlight the significance of employees' work, provide participation and autonomy in decision making, express confidence in employees' capabilities, and remove bureaucratic constraints or hindrances to performance. As a result, employees experience a state of psychological empowerment that consists of a feeling that their work is personally important (meaning), a belief in their ability to successfully perform work tasks (competence), freedom to choose how to initiate and carry out their tasks (self-determination), and a belief that their behaviour is making a difference (impact). Thus, empowering leadership provides employees with a greater feeling of control over their work and a sense that they can make a difference in their organization's effectiveness.[50]

Empowering leadership. Implementing conditions that enable power to be shared with employees.

In one study, empowering leadership was found to be associated with higher self-efficacy and adaptability of salespeople in a pharmaceutical company, and this was related to higher job performance and customer-service satisfaction. Interestingly, employees with less product/industry knowledge and experience benefited the most from empowering leadership.[51] In another study, professional employees in a major information technology company in the People's Republic of China (PRC) who had empowering leaders experienced a greater degree of psychological empowerment, which was associated with more creativity-relevant behaviours.[52]

■ RESEARCH FOCUS

EMPOWERING LEADERSHIP AND NEWCOMER CREATIVITY

Organizations are increasingly concerned about the need for creativity (i.e., the production of novel and potentially useful ideas aimed at creating, improving, or altogether changing an organization's products, services, practices, and procedures) to ensure they are innovative, remain competitive, and can survive in the long term. Although it has often been assumed that newcomers bring something new to an organization, there are no guarantees that they will be creative. Therefore, two important issues are discovering how to bring out the creativity in newcomers and determining what leaders can do to facilitate it.

T. Brad Harris and colleagues suggested that empowering leadership might be important for newcomer creativity. They conducted two studies to investigate the relationship between empowering leadership and newcomer creativity. Empowering leadership focuses on power sharing and granting autonomy to employees, with the intent of activating intrinsic motivational reactions. Thus, they suggested that empowering leadership will activate newcomers' intrinsic motivations to autonomously learn about their new roles and engage creatively in ways to improve the organization.

The first study consisted of newcomers at two high-tech joint ventures operated in Shanghai, China, in a variety of jobs, such as IT engineering, computer programming, and new product development. The results indicated that empowering leadership was positively related to newcomers' creative performance, which was rated by newcomers' managers. In addition, leadership empowerment was most strongly related to creativity when newcomers' perceived a high level of organizational support for creativity (the organization encourages, rewards, and recognizes creative behaviour).

The second study consisted of newcomers in a shipbuilding company in Shanghai, China, working in a variety of jobs, as manufacturing engineers, technologists, production technicians, and designers. Once again, empowering leadership was positively related to newcomer creative performance as rated by managers and co-workers. The relationship between empowering leadership and creativity was stronger when trust in the leaders was high. In addition, the relationship between empowering leadership and newcomer creativity was explained by an increase in creative process engagement (an individual's involvement in identifying potential problems, searching for relevant information, and generating new or alternative approaches to problems). In other words, empowering leadership resulted in greater creative process engagement, and creative process engagement led to greater newcomer creativity. The authors also found that empowering leadership was positively related to socialization outcomes such as role clarity, organizational attachment, and task performance.

The results of this research indicate that empowering leadership plays a key role in predicting and facilitating newcomer creativity. What's more, the positive effects of empowering leadership on newcomer creativity are even greater when organizational support for creativity and newcomers' trust in their leader is high. This research also shows that empowering leadership has a positive effect on the socialization of newcomers. Thus, preparing and encouraging leaders to empower newcomers is beneficial to newcomers and organizations.

Source: Based on Harris, T.B., Li, N., Boswell, W.R., Zhang, X., & Xie, Z. (2014). Getting what's new from newcomers: Empowering leadership, creativity, and adjustment in the socialization context. *Personnel Psychology, 67*, 567-604.

A study on teams found that those with empowering leaders improved their performance over time to a greater extent than teams with directive leaders.[53] Empowering leadership has also been found to be important for facilitating the creativity and socialization of newcomers. To learn more, see Research Focus: *Empowering Leadership and Newcomer Creativity.*

Ethical Leadership

Most theories of leadership focus on how leaders can improve the performance and effectiveness of individuals and groups. This should not be surprising, as most organizations want competent leaders who can make their company profitable. However, given the profound impact that leaders can have on the lives of so many people inside and outside of an organization, it is now generally understood that ethical leadership is a critical component of effective leadership and long-term business success.

PERSONAL INVENTORY ASSESSMENT

Learn About Yourself
Ethical Leadership Assessment

Ethical leadership involves the demonstration of normatively appropriate conduct (e.g., openness, fairness, and honesty) through personal actions and interpersonal relationships, and the promotion of such conduct to followers through two-way communication, reinforcement, and decision making. Ethical leaders model what is considered to be normatively appropriate behaviour, such as honesty, trustworthiness, fairness, and care. They make ethics salient in the workplace and draw attention to it by engaging in explicit ethics-related communications and by setting ethical standards. They reward ethical behaviour, discipline those who do not follow ethical standards, and punish unethical behaviour. (Notice the use of contingent leader reward and punishment behaviour.) Ethical leaders also consider the ethical consequences of their decisions and make principled and fair decisions that can be observed and emulated by others. Ethical leaders care about people and the broader society and seek to do the right thing personally and professionally.[54]

> **Ethical leadership.** The demonstration of normatively appropriate conduct through personal actions and interpersonal relationships.

A recent review and analysis of research on ethical leadership found that ethical leadership is positively related to more favourable evaluations of leaders (e.g., satisfaction and trust in the leader), more positive job attitudes (e.g., job satisfaction, organizational commitment), and greater performance (e.g., job performance, organizational citizenship behaviour), and negatively related to job strains, turnover intentions, and counterproductive work behaviours. The relationship between ethical leadership and work outcomes was found to be due to trust in the leader. In other words, employees trust ethical leaders, and higher trust leads to more positive job attitudes and job performance. What's more, the relationships between ethical leadership and performance remained significant even when the effects of other types of leadership (e.g., transformational) were taken into account.[55]

Finally, it is also worth noting that the extent to which ethics is an important part of an organization's culture is influenced by the ethics and moral development of the leader. In other words, the ethical behaviour of leaders has a significant influence on the ethical culture of an organization. This is because ethical leaders set ethical standards, model ethical behaviours, and use rewards and punishment to ensure ethical behaviour on the part of employees. Furthermore, ethical leadership has been found to be related to less unethical behaviour in work units and less relationship conflict among employees.[56]

Although ethical leadership is important at all levels of an organization, ethical leadership on the part of the immediate supervisor is likely to have the greatest effect on employees.[57]

Authentic Leadership

Have you ever questioned the true feelings and beliefs of a leader? Have you ever wondered if a leader was hiding his or her real thoughts and beliefs? We like to believe that our leaders act in a manner that is consistent with their true personal values and beliefs and in the best interests of employees and the organization. However, some leaders are more authentic than others when it comes to what they say and what they do.

Authentic leadership is a positive form of leadership that involves being true to oneself. Authentic leaders know and act upon their true values, beliefs, and strengths, and they help others do the same. Their conduct and behaviour is guided by their internal values. In other words, there is a consistency between their true values, beliefs, and actions. As a result, authentic leaders earn the respect and trust of their followers. Authentic leaders are perceived by their followers as being high in moral perspective and as open and fair in decision making.[58]

> **Authentic leadership.** A positive form of leadership that involves being true to oneself.

A good example of an authentic leader is Maple Leafs Foods president and CEO Michael McCain. At the time of the listeriosis outbreak in 2008, he apologized and expressed sympathy for the victims, and accepted full responsibility and accountability. He said that he was doing what was right, and doing what was right came directly from the company's ingrained values. According to McCain, "The core principle here was to first do what's in the interest of public health, and second to be open and transparent in taking accountability. For the team, this was almost not a decision—it was obvious. It's just what we are."[59] McCain's words and actions are an excellent example of authentic leadership.

Authentic leadership involves four distinct but related behaviours:[60]

- *Self-awareness.* An accurate understanding of one's strengths and weaknesses and an awareness of one's impact on others. Authentic leaders gain insight into themselves through interactions with others and possess accurate self-knowledge.

- *Relational transparency.* The presenting of one's true or authentic self to others and the open sharing of information and expressions of one's true thoughts and feelings.

- *Balanced processing.* The objective analysis of all relevant information before making a decision and consideration of views that challenge one's own position.

- *Internalized moral perspective.* Internal moral standards and values that guide behaviour and decision making. Authentic leaders exhibit behaviour that is consistent with their internal values and standards, and they resist social pressures.

Over the past several years, an increasing number of studies have found that authentic leadership has positive effects on work-related outcomes. For example, followers of authentic leaders have been found to have higher organizational commitment, job satisfaction, and satisfaction with their supervisor and to exhibit higher organizational citizenship behaviour, work engagement, ethical, and pro-social behaviours.[61]

Authentic leadership has also been found to have a positive effect on work groups. For example, in a study on work groups in a large bank, authentic leadership was positively related to the psychological capital of the group (self-efficacy, hope, optimism, and resilience; see Chapter 1 for definitions) and trust among group members, which led to a higher level of group citizenship

Maple Leaf Foods CEO Michael McCain's words and actions in response to the listeriosis outbreak are an example of authentic leadership.

THE CANADIAN PRESS/Ryan Remiorz

behaviours and performance.[62] A study on military teams found that team leader authenticity was related to team members' authenticity. In other words, team members were more likely to be authentic when their leader was authentic. The study also found that team member authenticity was related to higher-quality teamwork behaviour and team productivity.[63]

Servant Leadership

Unlike other theories of leadership, the focus of servant leadership is a concern for the needs of followers and their well-being. **Servant leadership** is a form of leadership that involves going beyond one's own self-interests and having a genuine concern to serve others and a motivation to lead. Servant leadership emphasizes the needs of followers and their growth and development as well as the needs of communities within and outside of the organization.[64]

The phrase "servant leadership" was first coined by Robert Greenleaf, who described a servant leader as somebody who wants to serve first and lead second rather than somebody who wants to lead first. Thus, servant leaders have a need to serve combined with a motivation to lead. They place the needs of their followers before their own needs and focus on helping their followers grow to reach their maximum potential.[65] Servant leadership is believed to encourage followers to become the very best they can be and to lead to self-actualization, positive job attitudes, performance, and an organizational focus on sustainability and corporate social responsibility.

A review and synthesis of the research on servant leadership identified the following six key characteristics of servant leader behaviour:[66]

- *Empowering and developing people.* Providing others with a sense of personal power and encouraging their personal development. A belief in the intrinsic value of each individual and the realization of each person's abilities and what the person can still learn.

- *Humility.* Actively seeking the contributions of others and placing their interests first. Facilitating the performance of others and providing them with support.

- *Authenticity.* Similar to authentic leadership, this involves expressing one's true self in ways that are consistent with one's inner feelings and thoughts, and accurately representing internal states, intentions, and commitments.

- *Interpersonal acceptance.* The ability to understand and experience the feelings of others and to create an atmosphere of trust in which others will feel accepted.

- *Providing direction.* Ensuring that people know what is expected of them and considering followers' abilities, needs, and input when providing direction.

- *Stewardship.* Focusing on service rather than control and self-interest, and encouraging others to act in the common interest.

Research on servant leadership indicates that servant leadership is positively related to trust in management, perceptions of organizational justice, need satisfaction, job satisfaction, organizational commitment, and creative performance.[67] Servant leadership has also been found to be related to organizational citizenship behaviours, because it increases employees' self-efficacy, commitment to the supervisor, and perceptions of procedural justice. A study of departments in a chain of grocery stores found that employees in departments that had servant leaders had higher perceptions of being treated fairly and were more likely to exhibit helping behaviours.[68] Finally, a study of hairstylists in a Chinese chain of hair salons found that salon managers' servant leadership was positively related to stylists' service performance behaviours as rated by customers above and beyond the effects of transformational leadership.[69]

Now that you are familiar with the theories and styles of leadership, see You Be the Manager: *Leadership at the CBC.*

Servant leadership. A form of leadership that involves going beyond one's own self-interests and having a genuine concern to serve others and a motivation to lead.

YOU BE THE MANAGER

Leadership at the CBC

In October of 2014, the CBC fired its popular radio host Jian Ghomeshi of its flagship arts and culture radio program *Q*, amidst allegations of sexual assault. Ghomeshi was subsequently criminally charged and faces five counts of sexual assault and one of overcoming resistance by choking. His lawyer has stated that he plans to plead not guilty.

The CBC hired two employment lawyers to conduct an independent internal investigation into the CBC's response to Ghomeshi's inappropriate behaviour in the workplace and its dealings with him. The lawyers interviewed 99 former and current CBC employees and found that Ghomeshi's behaviour "consistently breached the behavioural standard" of the CBC's policies.

The report's findings indicated that Ghomeshi's behaviour had been abusive and harassing. He was chronically late and consistently disrespectful of colleagues' time; he was scheming, dismissive, moody, difficult, emotionally unpredictable, and harshly critical; he diminished the role and contribution of others; took credit for other people's work; was belittling and humiliating to others and made demeaning comments about co-workers' appearance; and he played pranks and cruel jokes on co-workers. Ghomeshi also gave unwanted back rubs and shoulder massages to female employees and shared intimate and graphic details about his sex life.

The report also found that those who directly managed Ghomeshi were aware of aspects of his behaviour but did nothing about it. The report identified three opportunities in which CBC executives were made aware of allegations of inappropriate behaviour on the part of Ghomeshi but failed to investigate and intervene: a "Red Sky Document" prepared in 2012 by members of the *Q* staff, outlining their concerns; an email from an inquiring journalist regarding inappropriate behaviour in 2014; and an email from a concerned employee. The information, however, became diluted as it moved up the organization, and in some cases managers failed to inquire about it or take adequate steps to stop the behaviour.

Regarding CBC leadership, the report stated, "We saw no compelling evidence that Mr. Ghomeshi was ever told his behaviour would have to improve or he would have to refrain from certain types of behaviour, or else face disciplinary action including termination." Employees who complained about Ghomeshi were told to "work around him" or solve problems themselves.

The report also indicated the following:

"Management knew or ought to have known of this behaviour and conduct and failed to take steps required of it in accordance with its own policies to ensure that the workplace was free from disrespectful and abusive conduct"

"We believe that management's failure to effectively deal with Mr. Ghomeshi's behaviour gave him license to continue."

© canada/Alamy Stock Photo

A report of the CBC's response to Jian Ghomeshi's workplace behaviour and its dealings with him concluded that CBC management was to blame.

"The evidence shows that while Mr. Ghomeshi's star was allowed to rise, his problematic behaviour was left unchecked."

"It is our conclusion that CBC management condoned this behaviour."

The report concluded that Ghomeshi's abusive and harassing behaviour created a stressful and dysfunctional environment and that CBC management was to blame. CBC management has accepted the "general conclusions" of the report and said it will take the necessary steps to implement the report's recommendations as quickly as possible.

Do you think leadership was to blame for Mr. Ghomeshi's behaviour? You be the manager.

Questions

1. Do you agree with the report that management was to blame for Mr. Ghomeshi's behaviour? Use the theories of leadership to support your answer.

2. What type of leadership would have been effective in preventing the abuse and harassment? What advice would you give the CBC about effective leadership?

To find out more about leadership at the CBC, see The Manager's Notebook: *Leadership at the CBC* at the end of the chapter.

Sources: Dobson, S. (2015, May 4). Ghomeshi report outlines troubled culture. *Canadian HR Reporter, 28*(8), 1, 12; Gallant, J. (2015, April 17). Ghomeshi scandal: CBC brass walloped. *Toronto Star*, A1, A10; Humphreys, A. (2015, April 16). 'Troubling and disappointing': CBC 'severing ties' with executives in Ghomeshi scandal. *National Post*, http://news.nationalpost.com/news/canada/cbc-severing-ties-with-executives-in-ghomeshi-scandal, Gunter, L. (2015, April 18). CBC failed us in Ghomeshi scandal. *Toronto Sun*, http://www.torontosun.com/2015/04/17/cbc-failed-us-in-ghomeshi-scandal.

LO **9.8**

Describe gender differences in leadership, and explain why women are under-represented in leadership roles in organizations.

GENDER AND LEADERSHIP

Do men and women adopt different leadership styles? A number of popular books have argued that women leaders tend to be more intuitive, less hierarchically oriented, and more collaborative than their male counterparts. Is this true? Notice that two opposing logics could be at work here. On the one hand, different socialization experiences could lead men and women to learn different ways of exerting influence on others. On the other hand, men and women should be equally capable of gravitating toward the style that is most appropriate in a given setting. This would result in no general difference in style.

However, a number of reviews have found that there are some differences in leadership style between men and women in organizational settings. For example, researchers Alice Eagly and Blair Johnson concluded that women have a tendency to be more participative or democratic than men, and as a result, they are changing the business world.[70] How is this so? One theory holds that women have better social skills, which enable them to successfully manage the give-and-take that participation requires. Another theory holds that women avoid more autocratic styles because they violate gender stereotypes and lead to negative reactions. This might explain why a study on gender and leadership found that women are perceived by themselves and their co-workers as performing significantly better as managers than do men.[71]

In a review of the leadership styles of men and women based on 45 studies, women leaders were found to be more transformational than men leaders, and they also engaged in more of the contingent reward behaviours associated with transactional leadership. Men leaders engaged in more of the other components of transactional leadership, such as management by exception and **laissez-faire leadership**, which is a passive form of leadership that involves the avoidance or absence of leadership and is negatively related to leader effectiveness.[72]

What is most interesting about these findings is that those aspects of leadership style in which women exceed men are all positively related to leadership effectiveness, while those leadership aspects in which men exceed women have weak, negative, or null relations to leadership effectiveness. The authors concluded that these findings attest to the ability of women to be highly effective leaders in contemporary organizations.[73]

So do men and women differ in leadership effectiveness? A recent review of 95 studies on gender differences in perceptions of leadership effectiveness over the last 49 years found that there are some differences but only in certain situations. For example, men are perceived as more effective in organizations that are masculine and male dominated (i.e., government) while women are perceived as more effective in feminine and female dominated organizations (e.g., social service organizations and education organizations). In addition, women are perceived as more effective leaders in middle management positions. Furthermore, when the ratings of effectiveness were made by the leaders themselves, men rated themselves as more effective than did women. However, when the ratings of effectiveness were made by others (e.g., peers, subordinates, bosses), women were perceived as more effective leaders than men. Once all these factors are taken into account, however, men and women do not differ in perceived leadership effectiveness.[74]

Unfortunately, while the evidence clearly indicates that women can be highly effective leaders, the reality is that women hold very few top leadership positions in Canadian organizations. Some exceptions are Bonnie Brooks, Vice Chairman of Hudson's Bay Company, and Elyse Allan, President and CEO of General Electric Canada, who has been recognized as one of the 25 Most Powerful People in Canada and one of Canada's Top Women of Influence.[75]

The most recent census of women corporate officers and top earners of the FP500 indicates that women hold only 18.1 percent of senior officer positions, and make up only 5.7 percent of CEOs. This is particularly low when you consider that women make up 47 percent of the total workforce and 37.2 percent of management positions. Women currently occupy 45 senior positions such as chief executive, chief financial officer, or vice-president of an organization,

Laissez-faire leadership. A style of leadership that involves the avoidance or absence of leadership.

Elyse Allan, President and CEO of General Electric Canada, and Bonnie Brooks, Vice Chairman of Hudson's Bay Company, are examples of women who hold senior leadership positions in Canada.

including eight CEOs. According to Statistics Canada, the proportion of women in senior management positions has not changed in the past two decades. Since 1987, men have been two to three times more likely to hold a senior management position and one-and-a-half times more likely to hold a middle management position. Women also hold a minority of senior leadership positions in the United States and Europe.[76] How can we explain this gender bias in leadership?

Glass ceiling. An invisible barrier that prevents women from advancing to senior leadership positions in organizations.

For decades the explanation has been the **glass ceiling** metaphor—the invisible barrier that prevents women from advancing to senior leadership positions in organizations. However, Alice Eagly and Linda Carli have suggested that a more accurate metaphor is a *labyrinth*, because of the many twists, turns, detours, and dead ends that women encounter along their way up the organizational hierarchy. In other words, the lack of women leaders is the sum of all of the barriers women face rather than one particular barrier (i.e., the glass ceiling) at the top of the organization.[77]

Role congruity theory. Prejudice against female leaders is the result of an incongruity between the perceived characteristics of women and the perceived requirements of leadership roles.

According to **role congruity theory** (RCT), prejudice against female leaders is the result of an incongruity between the perceived characteristics of women and the perceived requirements of leadership roles.[78] For example, leaders are perceived as similar to men and not very similar to women, as more "agentic" than communal, and as more masculine than feminine.[79] Men are perceived as having *agentic* traits, which convey assertion and control and are generally associated with effective leadership. Women are perceived as having *communal* traits, which convey a concern for the compassionate treatment of others. Agentic leadership traits tend to be associated with male leaders to a greater extent than with female leaders. In other words, males but not females are perceived as having traits that are associated with leadership.[80] Exhibit 9.6 shows some common agentic and communal leadership traits.

Given the many obstacles that women face, what can organizations do to increase the number of women in senior leadership positions? As shown in Exhibit 9.7, a combination of programs and interventions is required, such as reducing the subjectivity of performance evaluation, changing the norm of long work hours, and establishing family-friendly human resources practices.

Agentic Traits

Dedicated: Logs long hours to meet deadlines.

Charismatic: Motivates employees when speaking.

Intelligent: Displays talent and ability in all aspects of the job.

Determined: Does not give up easily when issues arise.

Aggressive: Fights to get necessary resources for one's team.

Communal Traits

Caring: Shows concern for the well being of one's team.

Sensitive: Sympathetic and responsive to the feelings of employees.

Honest: Does not take credit for employees' good ideas.

Understanding: Listens when subordinates are having a personal conflict.

Compassionate: Extends deadlines when employees have family commitments.

EXHIBIT 9.6
Agentic and communal leadership traits
Source: Republished with permission of Elsevier Science, Inc., from Organizational Behavior and Human Decision Processes 101 , Scott, K. A., & Brown, D. J. (2006). *Female first, leader second? Gender bias in the encoding of leadership behavior*, 230 -242; permission conveyed through Copyright Clearance Center, Inc.

According to Alice Eagly and Linda Carli, legislation that requires organizations to eliminate inequitable practices is not effective for the advancement of women when inequality in an organization is embedded in the organization's culture and structure. If organizations want to remove the barriers that prevent women from advancing to leadership roles, they should do the following:

- Increase people's awareness of the psychological drivers of prejudice toward female leaders, and work to dispel those perceptions.
- Change the long-hours norm.
- Reduce the subjectivity of performance evaluation.
- Use open-recruitment tools, such as advertising and employment agencies, rather than relying on informal social networks and referrals to fill positions.
- Ensure a critical mass of women in executive positions—not just one or two women—to head off the problems that come with tokenism.
- Avoid having a sole female member of any team.
- Help shore up social capital.
- Prepare women for line management with appropriately demanding assignments.
- Establish family-friendly human resources practices.
- Allow employees who have significant parental responsibility more time to prove themselves worthy of promotion.
- Welcome women back.
- Encourage male participation in family-friendly benefits.

EXHIBIT 9.7
The advancement of women in organizations
Source: A.H. Eagly and Carli, L.L. (2007). Exhibit from "Women and the Labyrinth of Leadership," 101. Reprinted by permission of the *Harvard Business Review*. Copyright © 2007 by the Harvard Business School Publishing Corporation; all rights reserved.

CULTURE AND LEADERSHIP

If you consider the cultural differences in values described in Chapter 4, you might be wondering if leadership styles are equally effective across cultures. This is a question that researchers have been asking for decades. Fortunately, we have learned a great deal over the past 25 years.

The Global Leadership and Organizational Behaviour Effectiveness (GLOBE) research project is the most extensive and ambitious study ever undertaken on culture and leadership. It involved 170 researchers who worked together for 10 years collecting and analyzing data on cultural values and practices and leadership attributes from over 17 000 managers in 62 societal cultures. The results provide a rich and detailed account of cultural attributes and global leadership dimensions around the world.[81]

The project team first identified nine cultural dimensions that distinguish one society from another. Some of these dimensions are similar to Hofstede's, which were described in Chapter 4, but many of them were developed by GLOBE. Exhibit 9.8 lists and defines the nine cultural dimensions. Using these nine dimensions, GLOBE identified 10 culture

LO 9.9

Discuss the GLOBE project, and explain the role that culture plays in leadership effectiveness.

EXHIBIT 9.8
**Cultural dimensions
from the GLOBE project**
Source: Republished with
permission of Academy of
Management, from Javidan,
M., Dorfman, P.W., de Luque,
M.S., & House, R.J. In the eye
of the beholder: Cross-cultural
lessons in leadership from
Project GLOBE. *Academy of
Management Perspectives,
20,* Table 4, p. 75; permission
conveyed through Copyright
Clearance Center, Inc.

The GLOBE project conceptualized and developed measures of nine cultural dimensions. These are aspects of a country's culture that distinguish one society from another and have important managerial implications. The nine cultural dimensions are as follows:

Performance Orientation: The degree to which a collective encourages and rewards (and should encourage and reward) its members for improvement and excellence in their performance.

Assertiveness: The degree to which individuals are (and should be) assertive, confrontational, and aggressive in their interactions with others.

Future Orientation: The extent to which individuals prepare (and should prepare) for the future, for example, by delaying gratification, planning ahead, and investing in the future.

Humane Orientation: The degree to which a collective encourages and rewards (and should encourage and reward) individuals for their fairness, altruism, generosity, caring, and kindness to others.

Institutional Collectivism: The degree to which the institutional practices of organizations and society encourage and reward (and should encourage and reward) collective distribution of resources and collective action.

In-Group Collectivism: The degree to which individuals express (and should express) pride, loyalty, and cohesiveness in their families or organizations.

Gender Egalitarianism: The degree to which a collective minimizes (and should minimize) gender inequality.

Power Distance: The degree to which members of a collective expect (and should expect) power to be distributed evenly.

Uncertainty Avoidance: The extent to which a society, organization, or group relies (and should rely) on social norms, rules, and procedures to lessen the unpredictability of future events.

clusters from the 62 culture samples. The culture clusters differ with respect to how they score on the nine culture dimensions.

GLOBE wanted to know whether the same attributes that lead to successful leadership in one country lead to success in other countries. What they found was that citizens in each nation have implicit assumptions regarding requisite leadership qualities, something known as implicit leadership theory. According to **implicit leadership theory**, individuals hold a set of beliefs about the kinds of attributes, personality characteristics, skills, and behaviours that contribute to or impede outstanding leadership. These belief systems are assumed to affect the extent to which an individual accepts and responds to others as leaders. GLOBE found that these belief systems are shared among individuals in common cultures, something they call *culturally endorsed implicit leadership theory (CLT).* Further, they identified 21 primary and 6 global leadership dimensions that are contributors to or inhibitors of outstanding leadership. The six global leadership dimensions are as follows:[82]

**Implicit leadership
theory.** A theory that states
that individuals hold a set
of beliefs about the kinds
of attributes, personality
characteristics, skills, and
behaviours that contribute
to or impede outstanding
leadership.

- *Charismatic/Value-Based.* A broadly defined leadership dimension that reflects the ability to inspire, to motivate, and to expect high performance outcomes from others on the basis of firmly held core beliefs.

- *Team-Oriented.* Emphasizes effective team building and implementation of a common purpose or goal among team members.

- *Participative.* The degree to which managers involve others in making and implementing decisions.

- *Humane-Oriented.* Reflects supportive and considerate leadership, but also includes compassion and generosity.

- *Autonomous.* Independent and individualistic leadership.
- *Self-Protective.* Focuses on ensuring the safety and security of the individual.

GLOBE then created leadership profiles for each national culture and cluster of cultures based on their scores on the six global leadership dimensions. They compared the ten culture clusters on the leadership profiles and found that cultures and clusters differ significantly on all six of the global leadership dimensions. For example, compared to other culture clusters, Canada and the United States score high on the charismatic/value-based, participative, and humane-oriented dimensions, low on the self-protective dimension, and medium on the team-oriented and the autonomous dimensions.

Finally, to determine what is considered important for leadership effectiveness across cultures, GLOBE examined a large number of leader attributes. They found that while the cultures do differ on many aspects of leadership effectiveness, they also have many similarities. In fact, they found many attributes, such as being honest, decisive, motivational, and dynamic, to be universally desirable; these are believed to facilitate outstanding leadership in all GLOBE countries. They also found leadership attributes such as being loners, irritable, egocentric, and ruthless to be deemed ineffective in all GLOBE countries. And as you might expect, they also found that some attributes are *culturally contingent*. In other words, some attributes are effective in some cultures but are either ineffective or even dysfunctional in others. Exhibit 9.9 provides some examples of universally desirable, universally undesirable, and culturally contingent leadership attributes.[83]

The results of the GLOBE project are important because they show that while there are similarities across cultures in terms of what are considered to be desirable and undesirable leadership attributes, there are also important differences. This means that managers need to understand the similarities and differences in what makes someone an effective leader across cultures if they are to be effective global leaders. Let's now consider what it means to be an effective global leader.

The following is a partial list of leadership attributes that are universal facilitators, universal inhibitors, or culturally contingent.

Universal Facilitators of Leadership Effectiveness

- Demonstrating trustworthiness, a sense of justice, and honesty
- Having foresight and planning ahead
- Encouraging, motivating, and building confidence; being positive and dynamic
- Being communicative, informed, a coordinator, and team integrator (team builder)

Universal Impediments to Leadership Effectiveness

- Being a loner and asocial
- Being irritable and uncooperative
- Imposing your views on others

Culturally Contingent Endorsement of Leader Attributes

- Being individualistic
- Being constantly conscious of status
- Taking risks

EXHIBIT 9.9
Cultural views of leadership effectiveness from the GLOBE project.

Source: Republished with permission of Academy of Management, from Javidan, M., Dorfman, P.W., de Luque, M.S., & House, R.J. In the eye of the beholder: Cross-cultural lessons in leadership from Project GLOBE. *Academy of Management Perspectives, 20,* 69–70; permission conveyed through Copyright Clearance Center, Inc.

LO 9.10

Discuss *global leadership*, and describe the characteristics of global leaders.

Global leadership. A set of leadership capabilities required to function effectively in different cultures and the ability to cross language, social, economic, and political borders.

GLOBAL LEADERSHIP

Given the cultural differences in leadership effectiveness described in the previous section, it should come as no surprise that it takes a special style of leadership to be an effective global leader. Therefore, to conclude this chapter we will discuss one final type of leadership: Global leadership.

Global leadership involves having leadership capabilities to function effectively in different cultures and being able to cross language, social, economic, and political borders.[84] The essence of global leadership is the ability to influence people who are not like the leader and come from different cultural backgrounds. This means that to succeed, global leaders need to have a global mindset, tolerate high levels of ambiguity, and exhibit cultural adaptability and flexibility.[85] For multinational organizations, global leadership is a critical success factor for the organization.

As indicated in the chapter-opening vignette, Sergio Marchionne is a good example of a global leader. Another example is Linda Hasenfratz, CEO of auto-parts manufacturer Linamar Corporation. Since becoming CEO in 2002, she has expanded into Europe and Asia and turned the company into a global business with 45 plants around the world. In 2014, Hasenfratz received the Ernst & Young Entrepreneur of the Year Award for Manufacturing and became the first woman ever to receive it.[86]

But what makes a leader a good global leader? According to Hal Gregersen, Allen Morrison, and Stewart Black, global leaders have the following four characteristics:[87]

- *Unbridled inquisitiveness.* Global leaders must be able to function effectively in different cultures in which they are required to cross language, social, economic, and political borders. A key characteristic of global leaders is that they relish the opportunity to see and experience new things.

- *Personal character.* Personal character consists of two components: an emotional connection to people from different cultures and an uncompromising integrity. The ability to connect with others involves a sincere interest and concern for them and a willingness to listen to and understand others' viewpoints. Global leaders also

Linda Hasenfratz, CEO of Linamar Corporation who has turned Linamar into a global business, is an example of a global business leader.

© Patti Gower/Canadian Press Images

demonstrate an uncompromising integrity by maintaining high ethical standards and loyalty to their organization's values. This demonstration of integrity results in a high level of trust throughout the organization.

- *Duality.* For global leaders, duality means that they must be able to manage uncertainty and balance global and local tensions. Global leaders are able to balance the tensions and dualities of global integration and local demands.

- *Savvy.* Because of the greater challenges and opportunities of global business, global leaders need to have business and organizational savvy. Global business savvy means that global leaders understand the conditions they face in different countries and are able to recognize new market opportunities for their organization's goods and services. Organizational savvy means that global leaders are well informed of their organization's capabilities and international ventures.

Individuals with the potential to become global leaders have experience working or living in different cultures, speak more than one language, and have an aptitude for global business. However, becoming an effective global leader requires extensive training that consists of travel to foreign countries, teamwork with members of diverse backgrounds, and formal training programs that provide instruction on topics such as international and global strategy, business and ethics, cross-cultural communication, and multicultural team leadership. The most powerful strategy for developing global leaders is work experience, transfers, and international assignments. Long-term international assignments are considered to be especially effective.[88] Many companies, such as GE, Citigroup, Shell, Siemens, and Nokia, use international assignments to develop global leaders.[89]

Developing global leaders is becoming increasingly important for organizations around the world. To be successful in the global economy, it is critical for an organization to identify and develop leaders who have the capability to become global leaders. For many organizations, however, this will not be easy, as many report that they do not have enough global leaders now or for the future, and they do not have a system in place for developing them.[90]

However, there is some evidence that certain countries produce more global leaders than others. Karl Moore and Henry Mintzberg of McGill University found that those countries that are considered to be the most global in terms of their involvement in world trade and investment, such as Canada, the Netherlands, Switzerland, Belgium, Ireland, Sweden, Denmark, Singapore, Australia, and Finland, tend to have more than their share of good global leaders, given their size. Why is this? They are all middle-economy countries that are dependent on foreign trade. As a result, they must be able to understand and empathize with persons in other cultures. For Canadians, this comes naturally. According to Moore and Mintzberg, it is a strength of Canadians that they learn from the cradle to take into account other perspectives, a key requirement of global managers working for global companies. Living in a multicultural environment like Canada is excellent preparation for being a global manager. As a result, Canadian companies like Bombardier are way ahead of most organizations in big countries like the United States when it comes to global leadership.[91]

WHAT STYLE OF LEADERSHIP IS BEST?

Now that you have learned about the many styles and theories of leadership, you might be asking yourself, *what style of leadership is best?* The answer of course, like so many things in organizational behaviour, is: *it depends.* First, it is important to recognize that an effective leader needs to be capable of employing various styles of leadership. For example, we noted earlier that consideration and initiating structure are not

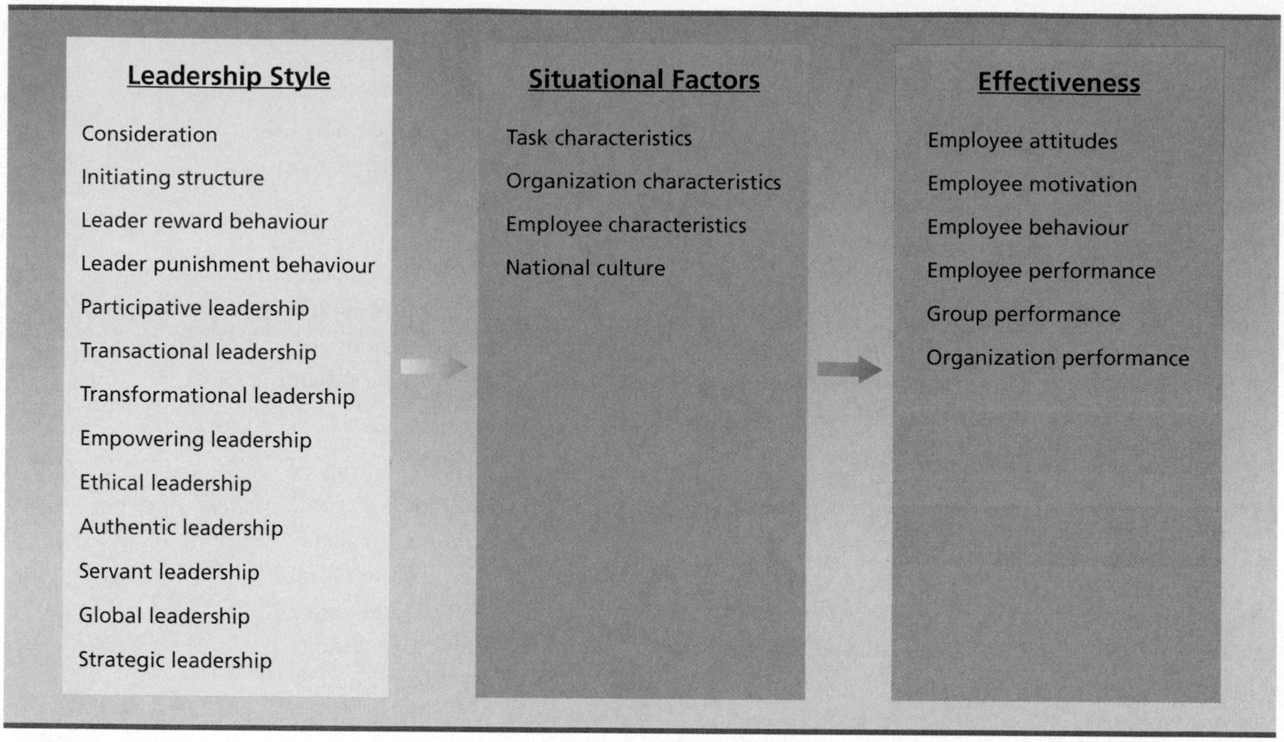

Leadership Style	Situational Factors	Effectiveness
Consideration	Task characteristics	Employee attitudes
Initiating structure	Organization characteristics	Employee motivation
Leader reward behaviour	Employee characteristics	Employee behaviour
Leader punishment behaviour	National culture	Employee performance
Participative leadership		Group performance
Transactional leadership		Organization performance
Transformational leadership		
Empowering leadership		
Ethical leadership		
Authentic leadership		
Servant leadership		
Global leadership		
Strategic leadership		

EXHIBIT 9.10
Leadership Styles, Situational Factors, and Effectiveness

incompatible and that a leader can be high, low, or average on one or both dimensions. It was also noted that the best leaders are both transformational and transactional. If you review the chapter-opening vignette on Sergio Marchionne, you will see that his leadership includes aspects of strategic leadership, empowering leadership, transformational leadership, global leadership, and servant leadership. Thus, a good leader must be able to use many different styles of leadership. So the issue is not what style of leadership is best, but rather what style of leadership is required in each situation that a leader encounters. This is where the situational theories of leadership come into play for we know that the most effective style of leadership depends on the situation. Based on what we have covered in this chapter, the situation consists of the nature of the task, employee characteristics, characteristics of the organization, and national culture. As shown in Exhibit 9.10, when the style of leadership is matched to the situation, a leader will be effective in terms of employee attitudes, behaviours, and performance, and organizational performance.

![] THE MANAGER'S NOTEBOOK

Leadership at the CBC

1. The report clearly places the blame on the CBC's leadership for turning a blind eye to Ghomeshi's behaviour, as they had numerous opportunities to investigate the concerns that were raised and to do something about them. The report states that senior management was aware of Ghomeshi's behaviour but failed to take steps to stop it. In fact, they failed to enforce CBC policies to ensure that the workplace was free from disrespectful and abusive conduct. What's more, this failure of leadership allowed the abusive behaviour to continue. As indicated in the report, "Had it taken proper steps, we believe that CBC management could have obtained a clearer picture of what was happening at *Q*. Moreover, Mr. Ghomeshi would have been presented with these allegations, had an opportunity to respond to them, and present his employer with his explanation and perspective." In terms of the leadership theories and behaviour, leader punishment behaviour in which the leader uses reprimands and the active withholding of raises, promotions, and other rewards should have been used. As indicated in the report, Mr. Ghomeshi was never told that he would face disciplinary action including termination if he did not improve his behaviour or if he did not refrain from certain types of behaviour. Thus, leadership punishment behaviour should have been used to reprimand, discipline, and/or punish Ghomeshi for his behaviour. In addition, the leadership was also lacking in consideration behaviour as management should have shown greater personal concern and respect towards employees who complained about Ghomeshi's behaviour and were subjected to his abuse. Instead, they were left on their own and told to "work around him" or solve problems themselves.

2. As indicated above, what was lacking in the Ghomeshi case was appropriate leadership punishment behaviour. Instead, CBC leadership continued to reward Ghomeshi with salary increases, more staff, more live shows in other cities, and higher-profile guests, despite his chronic and persistent inappropriate behaviour. Thus, leader punishment behaviour was needed to adequately discipline, sanction, and punish Ghomeshi for his abusive and inappropriate behavour, which violated the CBC's policies. In addition, leader reward behavour was ineffective, because Ghomeshi was rewarded regardless of his behaviour. If leader reward behaviour had been effective, then Ghomeshi would not have been rewarded and he would not only have had a clear picture of what was expected of him but he would also have realized that he would receive positive outcomes only if he changed and improved his behaviour. Finally, ethical leadership would have also been effective in preventing the abuse and harassment. If the leadership had been ethical, then there would have been ethical standards and expectations: ethical behaviour would be rewarded, and unethical behaviour would be disciplined and punished. Thus, with ethical leadership Ghomeshi's behaviour would not have been tolerated, and he would have been disciplined, punished, and perhaps terminated. Therefore, the best advice for the CBC regarding effective leadership is to establish better leader reward behaviour, leader punishment behaviour, and ethical leadership.

MyManagementLab Study, practise, and explore real management situations with these helpful resources:

- **Interactive Lesson Presentations:** Work through interactive presentations and assessments to test your knowledge of management concepts.
- **PIA (Personal Inventory Assessments):** Enhance your ability to connect with key concepts through these engaging, self-reflection assessments.
- **Study Plan:** Check your understanding of chapter concepts with self-study quizzes.
- **Videos:** Learn more about the management practices and strategies of real companies.
- **Simulations:** Practise decision-making in simulated management environments.

PIA PERSONAL INVENTORY ASSESSMENT

LEARNING OBJECTIVES CHECKLIST

9.1 *Leadership* occurs when an individual exerts influence on others' goal achievement in an organizational context. *Strategic leadership* refers to a leader's ability to anticipate, envision, maintain flexibility, think strategically, and work with others to initiate changes that will create a viable future for the organization. Individuals with titles such as manager, executive, supervisor, and department head occupy formal or assigned leadership roles. As part of these roles, they are expected to influence others, and they are given specific authority to direct employees. Individuals may also emerge to occupy informal leadership roles. Since informal leaders do not have formal authority, they must rely on being well liked or being perceived as highly skilled to exert influence.

9.2 The *trait theory of leadership* was concerned with identifying physical, psychological, and intellectual *traits* that might predict leader effectiveness. While some traits appear to be related to leadership capacity, there are no traits that guarantee leadership across various situations. However, of the Big Five dimensions of personality, extraversion and conscientiousness have been found to be the most consistent predictors of leadership effectiveness.

9.3 Studies of the behaviour of leaders have concentrated on *initiating structure* and *consideration* as well as *leader reward* and *punishment behaviours*. Both consideration and initiating structure contribute positively to employees' motivation, job satisfaction, and leader effectiveness. Consideration tends to be more strongly related to follower satisfaction, motivation, and leader effectiveness, while initiating structure is slightly more strongly related to leader job performance and group performance. Leader-contingent reward and punishment behaviour is positively related to employees' perceptions, attitudes, and behaviour.

9.4 *Fiedler's contingency theory* is a situational theory of leadership that suggests that different leadership orientations are necessary depending on the favourableness of the situation for the leader. Favourableness depends on the structure of the task, the position power of the leader, and the relationship between the leader and the group. Fiedler argues that *task-oriented* leaders perform best in situations that are either very favourable or very unfavourable. *Relationship-oriented* leaders are said to perform best in situations of medium favourability. *House's path–goal theory* is a situational theory of leadership that suggests that leaders will be most effective when they are able to clarify the paths to various subordinate goals that are also of interest to the organization. According to House, the effectiveness of directive, supportive, participative, and achievement-oriented behaviour depends on the nature of the subordinates and the characteristics of the work environment.

9.5 *Participative leadership* involves employees in making work-related decisions. Participation can increase employee motivation and lead to higher quality and more acceptable decisions. The *Vroom and Jago model* specifies how much participation is best for various kinds of decisions. Participation works best when employees are desirous of participation, when they are intelligent and knowledgeable, and when the task is reasonably complex.

9.6 *Leader–member exchange (LMX) theory* is concerned with the quality of the relationship that develops between a leader and an employee. High-quality relationships, or high LMX, involve a high degree of mutual influence and obligation as well as trust, loyalty, and respect between a leader and an employee. Higher-quality LMX relationships result in positive outcomes for leaders, employees, work units, and organizations. *Transactional leadership* is leadership that is based on a straightforward exchange relationship between the leader and followers and involves *contingent reward behaviour* and *management by exception*. *Transformational leadership* refers to leaders that provide followers with a new vision that instills true commitment. They provide intellectual stimulation, individualized consideration, and inspirational motivation. They also have *charisma*, the ability to command extraordinary loyalty, dedication, and effort from followers.

9.7 *Empowering leadership* involves implementing conditions that enable the sharing of power with employees. *Ethical leadership* involves the demonstration of normatively appropriate conduct through personal actions and interpersonal relationships and the promotion of such conduct to followers through two-way communication, reinforcement, and decision making. *Authentic leadership* is a positive form of leadership that involves being true to oneself. Authentic leaders know and act upon their true values, beliefs, and strengths and they help others do the same. *Servant leadership* is a form of leadership that involves going beyond one's own self-interests and having a genuine concern to serve others.

9.8 There are some differences in leadership style between men and women in organizational settings. Female leaders tend to be more transformational than male leaders, and they also engage in more contingent reward behaviours. Male leaders engage in more management by exception and laissez-faire leadership. In terms of effectiveness, there are no differences between men and women leaders except in a few certain situations. However, women remain under-represented in senior leadership positions as a result of many barriers and obstacles that have been described as a labyrinth of leadership.

9.9 The GLOBE project found that there are many leadership attributes that are universally desirable or universally undesirable in all cultures, as well as some attributes that are culturally contingent, that is, they will be effective in some cultures but ineffective or dysfunctional in others.

9.10 *Global leadership* involves having a set of leadership capabilities required to function effectively in different cultures and the ability to cross language, social, economic, and political borders. Global leaders are characterized by their inquisitiveness, personal character, global business and organizational savvy, and their ability to manage the dualities of global integration and local demands.

DISCUSSION QUESTIONS

1. Are leaders born or made? Consider each perspective (leaders born versus made) and the implications of each for organizations. What does each perspective suggest that organizations should do to ensure that they have effective leaders? Based on the information in this chapter, do you think that leaders can be developed?

2. Describe a situation that would be ideal for having employees participate in a work-related decision. Discuss the employees, the problem, and the setting. Describe a situation in which participative decision making would be an especially unwise leadership strategy. Why is this so?

3. What are transformational leaders skilled at doing that gives them extraordinary influence over others? Why do you think women are more likely to be transformational leaders than men?

Describe a leadership situation in which a transformational leader would probably not be the right person for the job.

4. What are the main findings from the GLOBE project, and what are the implications for leadership across cultures? If a leader from Canada takes on an assignment in another culture, will he or she be successful? What is most likely to improve the chances of success?

5. Discuss the four new and emerging theories of leadership (empowering, ethical, authentic, and servant). How is each type of leadership different from traditional theories of leadership? Do you think these theories extend our knowledge and understanding of effective leadership? Explain your answer.

INTEGRATIVE DISCUSSION QUESTIONS

1. Consider the relationship between leadership and organizational culture. Using the approaches to leadership discussed in this chapter (e.g., leadership traits, behaviours, situational theories, participative leadership, LMX theory, transformational leadership, and empowering, ethical, authentic, and servant leadership), describe how a leader can influence the culture of an organization. Based on your analysis, do you think that leaders have a strong influence on an organization's culture?

2. Refer to the material in Chapter 3 on perceptions and gender stereotypes and compare and contrast it with the material presented in this chapter on women and leadership. What does the material in Chapter 3 tell us about women and leadership? Why do you think women are more likely to be transformational leaders than men? Can women be more effective leaders than men? What have you learned about perceptions, stereotypes, and reality when it comes to women and leadership?

ON-THE-JOB CHALLENGE QUESTION

The RCMP's New Boss

In November of 2011, Bob Paulson was appointed as the new Commissioner of the Royal Canadian Mounted Police (RCMP), becoming the 23rd Commissioner. However, Paulson's appointment came at a critical time for the RCMP, amid a string of scandals, including numerous allegations of sexual harassment. Several former members of the RCMP stated that they had endured years of sexual harassment from senior officers. According to a staff relations representative, morale within the force had withered to an "all-time low."

During a press conference at the House of Commons, Paulson promised to reform the RCMP, stating, "First on my plate will be addressing the issue of harassment and sexual harassment" and "I will sort this out in a way that Canadians can have faith and trust in the RCMP." He said that "accountability and leadership" would be at the top of his long list of priorities.

Canadians had been questioning the RCMP's ability to safeguard the public, as complaints of botched investigations, excessive use of force, and institutional dysfunction had become routine.

The former Minister of Public Safety, Vic Toews, stated, "The RCMP has been pursuing an ambitious course of change over recent years, and navigating that change has been the challenge of successive commissioners over the years, and it will be no different for the new commissioner … [H]e recognizes that change is necessary."

Paulson replaced former Commissioner William Elliott, who stepped down after being accused by some senior members of the management team for having an abrasive leadership style.

Refer to the theories and styles to leadership discussed in the chapter and describe the kind of leader that Bob Paulson should be and the type of leadership that is required to change the RCMP. What do the theories of leadership suggest he needs to do to be an effective leader? What advice would you give him? What leadership style and behaviours do you recommend and why?

Sources: Freeze, C., LeBlanc, D., & Sher, J. (2011, November 16). New RCMP Commissioner sets out to rebuild trust. *The Globe and Mail*; Kennedy, M., & Quan, D. (2011, November 16). Bob Paulson to be named new RCMP commissioner. *National Post*; Kennedy, M. (2011, November 16). New RCMP boss named as sexual harassment claims are referred to police watchdog. *National Post*.

EXPERIENTIAL EXERCISE

Ethical Leadership Scale (ELS)

How ethical is your leader? To find out, answer as frankly and honestly as possible the 10 questions below about your current supervisor if you are employed or the most recent supervisor you had in your last job. Use the following response scale:

1–Strongly disagree

2–Disagree

3–Neither agree or disagree

4–Agree

5–Strongly agree

My supervisor …

____ 1. listens to what employees have to say.

____ 2. disciplines employees who violate ethical standards.

____ 3. conducts his/her personal life in an ethical manner.

____ 4. has the best interests of employees in mind.

____ 5. makes fair and balanced decisions.

____ 6. can be trusted.

____ 7. discusses business ethics or values with employees.

____ 8. sets an example of how to do things the right way in terms of ethics.

____ 9. defines success not just by results but also by the way that they are obtained.

____ 10. when making decisions, asks, "What is the right thing to do?"

Scoring and Interpretation

You have just completed the Ethical Leadership Scale (ELS) developed by Michael E. Brown, Linda K. Trevino, and David A. Harrison. To obtain your score, add up your responses to the 10 questions and divide by 10. Your total should be somewhere between 1 and 5. Higher scores indicate a more ethical leader. The average score of 87 MBA students in a large public university in the United States was 3.37. In a sample of 123 undergraduate seniors in business, the average ELS score was 3.46.

Source: Republished with permission of Elsevier Science, Inc., from Brown, M.E., Trevino, L.K. & Harrison, D.A. (2005). *Ethical leadership: A social learning perspective for construct development and testing Organizational Behavior and Human Decision Processes, 97*, 117–134; permission conveyed through Copyright Clearance Center, Inc.

To facilitate class discussion and your understanding of ethical leadership, form a small group with several members of the class and consider the following questions:

1. Each group member should present their ELS score. What is the range of scores (highest and lowest) and the average score in your group? Overall, how ethical are group members' supervisors?

2. Each group member should provide examples of what makes their supervisor an ethical or unethical leader. Be specific in describing supervisor behaviours that are ethical or unethical. Based on group members' answers, what are some of the main differences between ethical and unethical leaders?

3. Each group member should consider the impact that their supervisor has had on them, their co-workers, and the organization. Be specific in describing the effects that their ethical or unethical behaviour has had on people's attitudes and behaviours as well as on the organization (e.g., reputation, sales, or productivity).

4. What does your supervisor need to do differently to be a more ethical leader?

5. If you are now or have been in a leadership position in the past, how ethical have you been? Take the ELS again, but this time thinking about yourself in a current or previous leadership role. How ethical are you (or were you)? What do you have to do to become a more ethical leader?

EXPERIENTIAL EXERCISE

Leadership Empowerment Behaviour

Have you ever had a leader who was empowering? To find out, answer the 12 questions below as frankly and honestly as possible about your current supervisor if you are employed or the most recent supervisor you had in your last job. Use the following response scale:

1–Strongly disagree

2–Disagree

3–Neither agree or disagree

4–Agree

5–Strongly agree

My supervisor…

_____ 1. helps me understand how my objectives and goals relate to those of the company.

_____ 2. helps me understand the importance of my work to the overall effectiveness of the company.

_____ 3. helps me understand how my job fits into the bigger picture.

_____ 4. makes many decisions together with me.

_____ 5. often consults me on strategic decisions.

_____ 6. solicits my opinion on decisions that may affect me.

_____ 7. believes that I can handle demanding tasks.

_____ 8. believes in my ability to improve even when I make mistakes.

_____ 9. expresses confidence in my ability to perform at a high level.

_____ 10. allows me to do my job my way.

_____ 11. makes it more efficient for me to do my job by keeping the rules and regulations simple.

_____ 12. allows me to make important decisions quickly to satisfy customer needs.

Scoring and Interpretation

You have just completed the Leadership Empowerment Behaviour (LEB) scale developed by Michael Ahearne, John Mathieu, and Adam Rapp. The scale measures four dimensions of empowering leadership: (1) enhancing the meaningfulness of work (questions 1, 2, and 3); (2) fostering participation in decision making (questions 4, 5, and 6); (3) expressing confidence in high performance (questions 7, 8, and 9); and (4) providing autonomy from bureaucratic constraints (questions 10, 11, and 12). To obtain your overall score, add up your responses to the 12 questions and divide by 12. Your total should be somewhere between 1 and 5. Higher scores indicate a more empowering leader. The average score of 367 professional-level employees in a major information technology (IT) company in China was 3.67. You can also determine the score on each dimension by adding the three items for each dimension and then dividing by 3.

Sources: Zhang, X., & Bartol, K. (2010). Linking empowering leadership and employee creativity: The influence of psychological empowerment, intrinsic motivation, and creative process engagement. *Academy of Management Journal, 53*, 107–128; Ahearne, M., Mathieu, J., & Rapp, A. (2005). To empower or not to empower your sales force? An empirical examination of the influence of leadership empowerment behavior on customer satisfaction and performance. *Journal of Applied Psychology, 90*, 945–955.

To facilitate class discussion and your understanding of empowering leadership, form a small group with several members of the class and consider the following questions:

1. Each group member should present their LEB score. What is the range of scores (highest and low-

est) and the average score in your group? Overall, how empowering are group members' supervisors?

2. Each group member should provide examples of what makes their supervisor an empowering leader. Be specific in describing how your supervisor scored on each of the four dimensions. Based on group members' answers, what are some of the main reasons why a supervisor is or is not empowering?

3. Each group member should consider the impact that their supervisor has had on them, their co-workers, and the organization. Be specific in describing the effects that an empowering leader has had on people's attitudes, behaviours, performance, and creativity.

4. What does your supervisor need to do differently to be a more empowering leader?

5. Do you think that all leaders should be empowering leaders? Explain your answer. If you had a choice, would you want to have an empowering leader? Explain your answer.

EXPERIENTIAL EXERCISE

Servant Leadership Scale

Have you ever had a servant leader? To find out, answer the 28 questions below as frankly and honestly as possible about your current supervisor if you are employed or the most recent supervisor you had in your last job. Use the following response scale:

1–Strongly disagree

2–Disagree

3–Somewhat disagree

4–Neither agree nor disagree

5–Somewhat agree

6–Agree

7–Strongly agree

____ 1. I would seek help from my manager if I had a personal problem.

____ 2. My manager cares about my personal well-being.

____ 3. My manager takes time to talk to me on a personal level.

____ 4. My manager can recognize when I'm down without asking me.

____ 5. My manager emphasizes the importance of giving back to the community.

____ 6. My manager is always interested in helping people in our community.

____ 7. My manager is involved in community activities.

____ 8. I am encouraged by my manager to volunteer in the community.

____ 9. My manager can tell if something is going wrong.

____ 10. My manager is able to effectively think through complex problems.

____ 11. My manager has a thorough understanding of our organization and its goals.

____ 12. My manager can solve work problems with new or creative ideas.

____ 13. My manager gives me the responsibility to make important decisions about my job.

____ 14. My manager encourages me to handle important work decisions on my own.

____ 15. My manager gives me the freedom to handle difficult situations in the way that I feel is best.

____ 16. When I have to make an important decision at work, I do not have to consult my manager first.

____ 17. My manager makes my career development a priority.

____ 18. My manager is interested in making sure that I achieve my career goals.

____ 19. My manager provides me with work experiences that enable me to develop new skills.

____ 20. My manager wants to know about my career goals.

____ 21. My manager seems to care more about my success than his/her own.

____ 22. My manager puts my best interests ahead of his/her own.

____ 23. My manager sacrifices his/her own interests to meet my needs.

____ 24. My manager does what she/he can do to make my job easier.

____ 25. My manager holds high ethical standards.

____ 26. My manager is always honest.

____ 27. My manager would not compromise ethical principles in order to achieve success.

____ 28. My manager values honesty more than profits.

Scoring and Interpretation

You have just completed the Servant Leadership Scale developed by Robert Liden, Sandy Wayne, Hao Zhao, and David Henderson. The scale measures the following seven dimensions of servant leadership:

1. Emotional healing (the act of showing sensitivity to others' personal concerns): Questions 1, 2, 3 and 4.

2. Creating value for the community (a conscious, genuine concern for helping the community): Questions 5, 6, 7, and 8.

3. Conceptual skills (possessing the knowledge of the organization and tasks at hand so as to be in a position to effectively support and assist others, especially immediate followers): Questions 9, 10, 11, and 12.

4. Empowering (encouraging and facilitating others, especially immediate followers, in identifying and solving problems, as well as determining when and how to complete work tasks): Questions 13, 14, 15, and 16.

5. Helping subordinates grow and succeed (demonstrating genuine concern for others' career growth and development by providing support and mentoring): Questions 17, 18, 19, and 20.

6. Putting subordinates first (using actions and words to make it clear to others (especially immediate followers) that satisfying their work needs is a priority): Questions 21, 22, 23, and 24.

7. Behaving ethically (interacting openly, fairly, and honestly with others): Questions 25, 26, 27, and 28.

To obtain your overall score, add up your responses to the 28 questions and divide by 28. Your total should be somewhere between 1 and 7. Higher scores indicate a more servant leader. You can also determine the score for the seven dimensions by adding your responses to the four items for each dimension and dividing by 4. In a study of 183 employees of a production and distribution company, the average score for each dimension was as follows: emotional healing: 4.85; creating value for the community: 3.83; conceptual skills: 5.29; empowering: 5.13; helping subordinates grow and succeed: 4.68; putting subordinates first: 3.97; behaving ethically: 4.93. Servant leadership was found to be positively related to community citizenship behaviours, organizational commitment, and performance. Furthermore, servant leadership made a unique contribution to the prediction of these outcomes beyond transformational leadership and LMX.

Source: Republished with permission of Elsevier Science, Inc., from Liden, R. C., Wayne, S. J., Zhao, H., & Henderson, D. (2008). *Servant leadership: Development of a multidimensional measure and multi-level assessment. The Leadership Quarterly, 19*, 161-177; permission conveyed through Copyright Clearance Center, Inc.

To facilitate class discussion and your understanding of servant leadership, form a small group with several members of the class and consider the following questions:

1. Each group member should present their servant leadership score. What is the range of scores (highest and lowest) and the average score in your group? Overall, to what extent are group members' supervisors' servant leaders?

2. Each group member should provide examples of what makes their supervisor a servant leader. Be specific in describing servant behaviours in terms of your scores on the seven dimensions of the scale. Based on group members' answers, what are some of the main things that distinguish servant leaders from non-servant leaders?

3. Each group member should consider the impact that their supervisor has had on them, their co-workers, and the organization. Be specific in describing the effects that servant (or non-servant) leaders have had on people's attitudes and behaviours as well as on the organization (e.g., reputation, sales, or productivity).

4. What does your supervisor need to do differently to be a more servant leader? Be specific in terms of the scores on the seven dimensions.

5. If you are now or have been in a leadership position in the past, to what extent have you been a servant leader? Take the Servant Leadership Scale again, but this time thinking about yourself in a current or previous leadership role. To what extent are you (or were you) a servant leader? What do you have to do to become more of a servant leader?

CASE INCIDENT

Fran-Tech

A mid-level manager at Fran-Tech, a Seattle software company, received a CD-ROM set containing the source code for a competitor's software product. The competitor is the market leader in the software niche in which both companies compete; it is crushing Fran-Tech in the marketplace. An anonymous note accompanying the package stated that the package was sent by a disgruntled employee of the competitor and urged the recipient to use the data "as you see fit." The manager receiving the data was considered to be a "star" performer by her boss and her peers.

1. What do you think the manager is likely to do in this situation? What should she do and why?

2. Explain the relevance of ethical leadership in this situation. What will an ethical leader do and why? What will an unethical leader do?

3. Consider how the manager's response to this situation can impact the ethical behaviour of her employees in the organization. What are some of the potential implications of her actions for employees and the organization?

Source: Thomas, T., Schermerhorn, J.R., Jr., & Dienhart, J.W. (2004). Strategic leadership of ethical behavior in business. *Academy of Management Executive*, 18, 56–66.

CASE STUDY

Radio Station WEAA: Leading in a Challenging Situation

Corin Fiske, Director of News and Public Affairs at WEAA, a public radio station licensed and owned by Morgan State University (MSU) in Baltimore, Maryland, felt like she'd just had the wind knocked out of her. She'd just gotten off the phone with Micah Razan, host of the *Women Today* program, for the past 14 years. Razan was calling to let Fiske know that she was resigning from her volunteer on-air host position and that she would be taking the show's name and concept with her. As Fiske collected her thoughts, she realized that not only did she need to find a replacement host and new program concept quickly, but she also needed to deal with her staffing situation.

In August of 2006, Fiske had been recruited by the chair of the Communication Studies Department to be a change agent, to help the organization achieve its full potential. She planned and delivered 15 hours of world-class news and community affairs programming every week through a staff of 30 direct reports, 29 of whom were volunteers. In the two months Fiske had been at WEAA, she felt like some of her staff weren't fully supporting her or the organization's goals. As she reflected on the situation, she realized she needed to figure out what to do and quickly. She'd have to tell her new boss, Jabari Owens, the station general manager, about the resignation, the loss of the show concept, and the resistance from her staff. He would surely expect her to have a plan to deal with these urgent short- and long-term issues.

WEAA BACKGROUND

WEAA, a non-profit, National Public Radio (NPR) affiliated station,[1] served the Baltimore market. It was licensed and owned by Morgan State University. The station began operating on January 10, 1977 and operated at 12 600 watts, 24 hours a day, 365 days a year. WEAA, a community-oriented radio station, reached out to its multicultural audience with social, political, and multicultural programs and music. The station was committed to academic excellence and the professional development and training of students interested in careers in broadcasting. In 1999, *Gavin Magazine* named WEAA the Jazz Station of the Year. In 2000, 2002, and 2005 *Citypaper* newspaper[2] named WEAA the best radio station in Baltimore. The average WEAA listener was an affluent, educated, community-active, professional African American in the 25–54 age group (64 percent male, 36 percent female).[3]

According to the music director, Narius Coleman, the station started as a "refreshing, new African American perspective, playing jazz and R&B and having great talk shows. We were the voice of the community. Our call letters[4] stood for 'We educate African Americans.'" As the station evolved in the 1980s, he said, "they played less R&B and more jazz; talk shows remained an important part of the format." Coleman noted that in the 1990s the station became a "straight ahead" jazz station (i.e., focused on jazz without R&B) with talk shows. Now he says the station has evolved to be "a blend of contemporary and traditional jazz with

---

1 Unlike most NPR affiliated radio stations, WEAA did not run the full roster of NPR programming; most of WEAA's programming was original.

---

2 (2008). Best of Baltimore. 2008, from www.citypaper.com/bob/story.asp?id=12612.

3 (2007). WEAA. 2007, from http://www.weaa.org/index.html.

4 Letters assigned to broadcast stations by the Federal Communications Commission (FCC) by which stations identify themselves. In general, stations east of the Mississippi River have call letters beginning with W; those west of the Mississippi have call letters beginning with K.

TABLE 1   WEAA Profit and Loss Statement

	2004	2005	2006	2007 est.
Revenue				
Underwriting/membership (fund raising)	$234 000	$250 000	$113 000	$135 000
Studio rental				$5000
Grants	$200 000	$200 000	$200 000	$200 000
University Funds	$186 000	$300 000	$250 000	$200 000
Total	$620 000	$750 000	$563 000	$540 000
Expenses	$770 500	$770 500	$770 500	$770 500
Profit/Loss	−$150 500	−$20 500	−$207 500	−$230 500

Sources: 2004 Audited Financial Statement, General Manager estimates, 2007

some soul and R&B classics and talk shows, closer to its original format." According to Coleman, the definition of the call sign has been expanded to signify, "We educate African Americans and all who listen, whether they are Latino, Caucasian, or African … we speak to many different cultures."

The station competed in the Baltimore market, the 21st-largest radio market in the United States with a population of about 2.3 million people.[5] There were 24 other radio stations that competed in the market.[6] Three were public radio stations—WYPR, previously affiliated with Johns Hopkins University; WTMD, affiliated with Towson University; and WBJC, affiliated with Baltimore City Community College.[7] A number of for-profit radio stations also competed with news/talk, jazz, or mixed music formats in the market.

Fiske and Jabari Owens, the station general manager, admired WAMU, the leading public radio station for NPR news and information in the Washington D.C. area. They cited it as a role model for their station and what they hoped to achieve. WAMU was in the 9th-largest radio market in the country, with a population of 4.2 million people. On air since 1961, the station was member supported, professionally staffed, and licensed to American University. The station had about 580,000 unique listeners in 2006. In that same year, the station generated revenue of $11.4 million dollars, expenses of $10.3 million dollars, and a profit of about $1.1 million dollars.[8]

In comparison, WEAA had about 90 000 unique listeners in 2006. The station had annual revenue of $563 000, annual operating expenses of $770 500 and an annual loss of $207 500 in that same year. (See Table 1 for Profit and Loss Statements for WEAA.)

Like WAMU, their role model, and other public, non-profit radio stations (e.g., WTMD, WBJC), WEAA was licensed to and owned by a higher education institution. WEAA was part of Morgan State University's College of Liberal Arts, Communications Studies Department, telecommunications program.[9] The College of Liberal Arts, the largest academic division of the university, served over 30 percent of the university's 6 000 enrolled students. About 25 percent of the college's enrolled students majored in telecommunications, the most popular major. In the telecommunication program, students learned about telecommunications theory and practices, through on-campus media laboratory experiences, workshops, and internships. In 2006, a new, $21-million building was completed to house the Communications Studies Department, the Media Center, the journalism and writing programs of the College of Liberal Arts, and WEAA radio station. The station moved into their state-of-the art broadcasting facility, including modern offices and studios in the fall of 2006. According to Jabari Owens, the station "has a 'great stick.'"[10]

5 (2008). Arbitron radio stations. 2008, from www.arbitron.com/radio_stations/home.htm.

6 (2008). List of radio stations in Maryland. 2007, from http://en.wikipedia.org/wiki/List_of_radio_stations_in_Maryland.

7 (2008). On the radio dot.net. 2008, from http://www.onthcradio.nct/states/maryland.aspx.

8 (2007). WAMU. 2007, from http://wamu.org/.

9 (2007). Morgan State University. 2007, from www.morgan.edu.

10 A very powerful broadcast antenna for a public radio station.

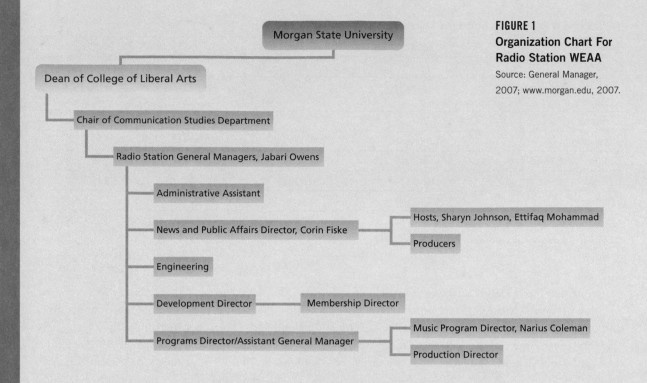

FIGURE 1
Organization Chart For Radio Station WEAA
Source: General Manager, 2007; www.morgan.edu, 2007.

The radio station was organized as outlined in Figure 1. Jabari Owens was the fourth general manager in four years. Volunteers typically have had little interaction with station management. Jabari Owens, the new general manager, noted that "turnover has hurt the organization, stalling growth and development." The membership director position, responsible for leading fund raising, had been open for over a year and consequently the station had not had a formal fund raising drive in at least two years. As he became familiar with the organization, Owens noticed that there were some unconventional aspects of the organization in terms of titles, reporting relationships, and business processes (e.g., directors reporting to directors, people reporting to whomever they wanted to, tasks allocated in inefficient ways). He also learned that volunteers typically have had little interaction with station management.

CORIN FISKE'S PERSPECTIVE

Fiske was attracted to the position at WEAA because she saw an opportunity to be part of building a radio station, transforming it from a small station to a larger, profitable, highly regarded station like WAMU. "I have an entrepreneurial spirit. Themes that have emerged over the course of my career are change and learning. I am a change agent. I also love to learn. So, I found the opportunity at WEAA very attractive. I think they

were looking for a leader to make things happen, to lead change. That's me."

Fiske had 10 years experience in the broadcasting industry. She started her career as a radio personality and entertainment reporter for radio station WAFL-FM in Dover, Delaware, the 75th-largest radio market in the United States. After two years, she became a TV reporter at the NBC affiliate KWES-TV in Midland, Texas (a market with a population of just under a 100 000 people) for a year. Next she jumped to Philadelphia, the fifth-largest city in the United States based on population, where she spent a year as a TV reporter and photographer for the number four ranked station, a 24-hour news station. Then she moved to Youngstown, Ohio (a market with a population of just under 100 000 people), where she was a TV reporter for CBS/Fox for two years. While at CBS/Fox she was recruited to be a reporter for a new station launch, a 24-hour news Time/Warner TV station in Houston, the fourth-largest market in the U.S. based on population. She spent two years there before she moved to Atlanta and helped build a broadcast school, the Connecticut School of Broadcasting (CSB). For two years she developed their TV curriculum, which was adopted at all their campuses. "Then I was wooed to Morgan to be part of building a radio station. I have industry experience. I am a teacher. I joined WEAA to develop curriculum, to leverage the radio station in the community, to develop and file content[11] locally and nationally, to grow," she explained.

The call from Micah Razan, resigning, was one of many incidents that contributed to Fiske's growing feeling that there were significant issues she needed to address, if she wanted to be successful in her new position. During the call, Razan said she had just gotten a promotion in her full-time job and would be moving. Razan told Fiske that she had come up with the original idea for the show and had been hosting the show for 14 years, and she planned to take the name and concept with her, so that she could use it when she relocated. Fiske said, "I know that the question of ownership of the intellectual property of the show is debatable." However, because of the turnover, turmoil, and the laissez-faire management approach at the station, any history or documentation about the intellectual property rights (e.g., evidence of a work for hire policy or contract) would be very difficult to find. She decided not to fight Razan; but to Fiske the situation illustrated the vulnerability of the station when policies and expectations were unclear. She viewed the lack of commitment to and agreement on operating policies and standards as a serious issue. She also thought some of her staff were resistant to change, disengaged, and lacking motivation.

She recalled, "Shortly after I started this job, I was in my office—we were in two buildings then, I still hadn't moved to the new building. A young woman came in to be a guest on a show. She'd come to the wrong building (the old building). I knew the show started at 6:00 PM, so I decided to speed-walk her to the other building where the show was being produced live. When we got there, just after 6:00, the show hadn't started yet. The theme song was playing; it played for ten minutes. Finally, the host ran in, saying, 'Oh !@%&, I know you're going to be upset,' then started the show."

"Later, I called him in for a meeting. I explained that the next time he was late, even if it was by one minute, we would air an encore presentation[12] ... Over the years we have had a history of this. Some volunteers who serve as hosts and are not working at a high effort undermine the quality of the programming." She explained that sometimes hosts do not have the skills, experience, or motivation to deliver high-quality, timely programming. For example, she noted that not all hosts called in if they were going to be late or miss the show. This resulted in shows not starting on time or having to substitute an encore presentation at the last minute instead of airing a live show as scheduled.

She recalled another situation during the fall of 2006. "This one was a nightmare. Ed Zeigler, a college professor from a local community college, hosted one of the shows, a political talk show. Zeigler and his producer couldn't understand the importance of balance in reporting on the show. A very strict balance is required to maintain credibility and have high journalistic integrity. As journalists we should investigate, report, and cover the story. We are not actors/actresses; we should not create the story. On one show, Zeigler talked about an individual, a prominent public figure, not doing his job. I explained that you are the host; you can't just present your opinion or even just one side of the story. Your job as host is to present both sides of the story, a balanced view. Zeigler said, 'Well, what about Rush Limbaugh, he presents his opinion. He doesn't present all sides of an issue.' I said 'Rush Limbaugh isn't on a public radio station.' I spent over an hour going back and forth with him about balance and our responsibility as a public radio station to offer listeners an opportunity to discover opposing views in a way that respects differences and our listeners. We should not be featuring shouting matches. If we want to criticize a public official for something, we need to invite him to explain his perspective or at least be able to say we asked the official for his response and he declined. It was a frustrating conversation."

As Fiske reviewed the situation, she noted, "Of the 20 volunteer talk show hosts that I'm responsible for, many have never been trained. Many do not understand public radio standards, and some are resisting and/or putting in a low effort. Some have never been oriented; some have never been evaluated. Most shows don't have a producer.[13] We have an issue of lack of consistency of programming standards across the board. And we don't have enough key personnel to facilitate the production of solid news."

Fiske experienced some resistance from her staff in terms of communicating and reporting. Volunteer staff members did not have offices (i.e., a room with

---

11 Radio programming content.

12 A repeat of a previously aired program.

13 A producer for a radio show is responsible for generating and researching ideas for show content, identifying and booking resources/guests, overseeing production, evaluating performance, and providing feedback and direction for performance improvement.

a phone and a computer) at the radio station. Most worked out of their homes or offices and came into the station only to work on their shows. When she was introduced to her staff at a meeting in September, she asked them to meet with her individually, on a regular basis, so they could get to know each other and work together on programming. Some staff members have never followed up on this request. Some did not return her phone calls or emails. Every quarter she needed to compile programming information for mandatory reporting to the FCC. It had been a struggle to get complete information from her staff on a timely basis. Recently, she tried a new approach. After explaining the importance of the information to her staff, she sent them, via email, a schedule of the due dates; she also sent them a reminder a few weeks before the deadline, and gave them a template document to fill in. This helped, Fiske explained; she got a great improvement in the response rate, receiving reports from half her staff.

"One of the challenges in my position has been the staffing philosophy of using mostly or all volunteer staff versus paid staff. I applaud volunteers working at a high effort level. I've been a volunteer; I was an executive on loan to the United Way for over a year. I was personally in charge of raising $8 million dollars. I exceeded the goal. I was very committed. All the volunteers were very committed. I knew they valued me. I knew they appreciated my skills. It was one of the best experiences of my life. They really worked hard to show their appreciation. They had a volunteer appreciation dinner. Every month they had one or two events honoring volunteers. So I know what it is to be a volunteer and to be committed. The United Way was an important part of my development, and I want to bring that emphasis on commitment and recognition to WEAA."

Fiske felt an urgent need to address the issues she faced; they could jeopardize her success and the success of WEAA. But, she had many other duties also, "I have been writing grants, developing curriculum, and recruiting, training, and managing volunteers. I am working long hours, 12- to 13-hour days. I return phone calls, respond to emails, and deal with operating priorities as they pop up. I have had to turn down opportunities to develop community relations, simply because I don't have time for it."

Fiske reviewed a list of priorities she had drafted when she first arrived (see Table 2). She wondered if they still made sense.

TABLE 2   Ideas For Change Within Department of News and Public Affairs

- Establish core values and standards
- Strengthen content
- Underwriting for all news and public affairs programming
- Discontinue and reposition all first Sunday and fifth week Tuesday, Wednesday and Thursday shows
- Diversify programming
- Develop volunteer curriculum and career development workshops
- Produce vignette, modules, and segment
- Purchase field reporting equipment for expansion
- Feature reporting
- Strengthen relationship with University
- Develop more versatile approach to programming (interactive via web, pod casting, etc., TV)
- Establish ownership of programs
- Explore syndication opportunities
- Establish relationship with NPR to file content nationally
- Develop volunteer appreciation awards ceremony

Source: Corin Fiske, 2007

To provide additional insight about the situation at WEAA, Fiske's boss, a peer, and two volunteer subordinates shared their perspectives.

JABARI OWENS' PERSPECTIVE

Jabari Owens, general manager of WEAA, since October of 2006, was a third-generation radio broadcaster and Fiske's boss. He had 10 years of experience in the radio business. He started in college radio at the University of Miami and had recently left a satellite radio firm to join WEAA. He was attracted to WEAA by the "turn around" opportunity and the chance to build a profitable, competitive public radio station from the ground up. His mission was to "run the station as a business … and to make the station financially self sufficient in five years so that it does not rely on the roughly $350 000 the university provides in yearly financial support."[14] He saw WAMU as a role model from which WEAA could learn.

Owens thought that the station's strong community connection was both a strength and a weakness. "Featuring members of the community on-air results in a high level of buy-in and ownership. However, over-reliance on volunteer community members has made the station vulnerable (sometimes unable to operate independently). One of my roles as the general

14 Dash, J. (2008). Whose public radio?, from http://baltimore. bizjournals.com/baltimore/stories/2008/03/10/focus1.html.

manager is to protect the station's license. The lack of direction, lack of structure, and lack of understanding can be dangerous."

He said, "Radio is an art and a science. We have the art down. But being opinionated and articulate is not enough. We need to get the science part of it down. Producing news, talk, and public affairs programming is the most difficult type of programming to create and we are doing it mostly with volunteers. We need qualified producers to manage the complete life cycle of every show. Some folks will welcome these changes and the opportunity to take it to the next level. Others will say 'I don't need any help, I want to do my own thing.' Some will think, 'This is just a way of trying to control me' versus trying to improve my show." Owens said that "as a management team we must set expectations, provide the tools and resources, and establish regular evaluations." He said Fiske will need to tackle the challenges of motivating a volunteer staff, reining in the types of programs on-air, and creating a culture of commitment.

Owens believed Fiske had a wealth of experience, and a desire to build, and that she would be instrumental in developing the station's mission and programming philosophy. "She instantly conveys an air of professionalism; she can and has established a higher level of professionalism. She has an ability to build relationships with students, with other departments, and within the university and the community. One opportunity for her to become even more effective is to develop a more fluid working relationship with the program director/assistant general manager." Owens said, "The only thing holding us back is us—the infrastructure is here. We have the art down. We have the passion, the stuff you can't teach. We need to teach the science."

NARIUS COLEMAN'S PERSPECTIVE

Narius Coleman, assistant program director, music director and *In the Groove* host had been in the radio business for 14 years and was a colleague/peer of Fiske's. He started working at WEAA as a student; after graduation, he left to work in commercial radio, and had now been back at the station for two years. Coleman saw the station "as a very small team (five full-time employees, a few part-time employees, and 30 plus volunteers). The advantage is that we are a small, close-knit group; the disadvantage is that the amount of work can be overwhelming at times. I'd love to see more full-time employees; unfortunately we just don't have the money. We have so many opportunities, if we

had free rein; but we have to abide by the rules and regulations of the communications department. There is a lot of red tape."

Coleman said, "You can only expect so much from volunteers. Sometimes they don't put their all into it. If talk show hosts can't make it, they just don't come in. Then we have to run an encore presentation. If they were paid, they'd be here, because time is money. One of our biggest challenges is to get folks to take ownership as if it was a paid job.

"Corin has a vision, she has the background. She's put together curriculum. She's trained students. She's making a difference. She is 'on point' on so many things. My only suggestion for her is to pick up her phone," he said with a smile. "She is so busy, she's hard to get on the phone."

SHARYN JOHNSON'S PERSPECTIVE

Sharyn Johnson, *Real Money* volunteer host for eight years, was a 20-year veteran of the financial services industry and one of Fiske's direct reports. When she had children, Johnson said, she "downshifted," (i.e., tried to work less and to achieve a better balance between work and family life), starting her own consulting business, Johnson's Media Group. Her firm specialized in consulting on how to sell financial services and the financial empowerment and education of consumers. Volunteering as a radio show host made a lot of sense to Johnson because she got a lot of return in terms of publicity and awareness for herself and ultimately her business.

Johnson noted that for many years WEAA had been considered a community service of the University, not a business. Johnson said, "Five years ago this was a little radio station; hosts said what they wanted to say; there was no rigour, most hosts were winging it." Johnson saw the station as a "diamond in the rough." She saw the value and potential of the station and believed that Fiske and the other managers needed to help the university administration see that potential also—"Get the leadership to see what's sitting in front of them." Johnson liked the fact that Fiske was introducing NPR standards and a higher level of expectations for the staff. She thought that Fiske should try to communicate more frequently with the staff. "People need to hear her voice, we need to hear praise when we're on track, and we need her to let us know when we're off track."

Johnson talked about the challenges of delivering quality programming with an all-volunteer staff.

"As soon as a volunteer intern is trained and ramped up, they're moving on. A show needs a producer to come up with story ideas, do research, book guests, 'feed the beast.' It is very difficult to produce quality programming with an all-volunteer staff. If people add value, you have to pay them. I think it would be much better to hire hosts versus have volunteers. Then we could set standards."

ETTIFAQ MOHAMMAD'S PERSPECTIVE

Ettifaq Mohammad, *Listen Up* volunteer host for three years and one of Fiske's direct reports, was the 27-year-old co-founder and president of New Light Leadership Coalition, Inc., a nonprofit organization devoted to leadership development among youth, by youth. Mohammad said, "I am very grateful to be part of WEAA. I feel like the organization has always been very supportive, giving me a platform to communicate with an audience of 100 000 at a young age with relatively little radio experience. If I could get paid it would be great, but I'm just so happy to be on air. I'm grateful for the opportunity."

Mohammad had seen a lot of changes and transitions at the station, and he thought they were generally positive; however, they hadn't really affected him. He noted that the station had different types of general managers, from Zack Johnson, who had been outgoing and emphasized getting Hollywood-style entertainment on air, to more introverted, "hands off" educators.

He noted that the culture had been one where most hosts did not have journalism or radio backgrounds. Mohammad believed the staff supported Fiske—she had good interpersonal skills. "It is comforting to know the news director and to know that she knows my name, she listens to my show and will give me feedback."

According to Mohammad, one of Fiske's biggest challenges was to get the support of the university administration. "Sometimes Morgan (MSU) suffers from administrative and management problems, so it can be a challenge to work through the red tape and politics. Fiske comes from a fast-paced TV environment; she may need to balance her passion and urgency with the level of passion and urgency of other people. She needs to work through the culture, helping to regain the trust and support of students and the administration that has been lost due to prior poor management."

Mohammad noted the challenges of a volunteer staff: "You can't put too many expectations on them.

I just lost a student intern producer; her grades were falling, so she just couldn't do the show." In closing, he said, "We all want to see WEAA thrive … we want to see WEAA get to the top of its game."

CONCLUSION

As Fiske reflected on her relatively short time at WEAA, she realized she faced some urgent issues, and she had concerns about the level of support and motivation among her staff for her and for the station's goals. She had a lot on her plate. The call from Razan, resigning, was still fresh on her mind. As was the frustrating conversation with Zeigler and his producer. She'd heard rumors that Zeigler was thinking of making their disagreements public (possibly talking to reporters). She was also concerned about hosts not showing up on time, missing meetings, not communicating, and not completing reports in a timely manner. She was still excited about the opportunities at WEAA. What could she do to ensure her success and the success of the organization? A serious strategy meeting with Owens, her boss, was urgently needed. She needed to share her ideas and concerns and get his ideas and advice about how to resolve these issues. Then she could develop a plan of action and focus on implementing it.

QUESTIONS

1. Discuss the issues, problems, and challenges facing Corin Fiske and WEAA. To what extent are these issues, problems, and challenges the result of the station's past and present leadership?

2. Evaluate Corin Fiske's success as a leader in terms of the meaning of leadership and what it means to be an effective leader. Do you think she has been an effective leader? Provide some specific examples to support your answer.

3. Consider Corin Fiske's leadership in terms of the different types of leadership behaviour (i.e., consideration, initiating structure, leader reward behaviour, and leader punishment behaviour). To what extent does she exhibit each of these behaviours, and how effective is she when she does? What leadership behaviours do you think are required to improve her effectiveness as a leader? Explain your answer.

4. Use the situational theories of leadership (contingency theory and path–goal theory) to explain the leadership style and behaviour that is most likely to be effective given Corin Fiske's situation. What is the difference between her current leadership style and behaviour and the style and behaviour suggested by each theory? What does she need to do according to each theory?

5. Discuss the merits of leader–member exchange (LMX) theory, transactional, and transformational leadership for the leadership situation facing Corin Fiske at WEAA. What type of leadership is necessary and why? What does each theory suggest that Corin Fiske should do to be a more effective leader?

6. Given the many challenges facing WEAA and Corin Fiske, what type of leadership is most important to improve the situation and the success of WEAA? Can Corin Fiske improve the situation by being a more effective leader, and if so, what type of leadership is required and why? Be sure to consider the merits of the different types and theories of leadership discussed in this chapter.

CHAPTER 10

COMMUNICATION

LEARNING OBJECTIVES

After reading Chapter 10, you should be able to:

10.1 Define *communication*, and explain why communication by the strict chain of command is often ineffective.

10.2 Explain the factors that contribute to *voice* versus *silence*.

10.3 Explain the organizational *grapevine*, and discuss its main features.

10.4 Review the role of verbal and *non-verbal communication* at work.

10.5 Discuss gender differences in communication, and identify how a failure to recognize these differences can cause communication problems.

10.6 Discuss challenges relating to *cross-cultural communication*, and identify useful strategies to deter miscommunication.

10.7 Define *computer-mediated communication*, and highlight its strengths and weaknesses.

10.8 Review personal strategies and organizational initiatives aimed at enhancing communication.

TORONTO'S SICK KIDS HOSPITAL BREAKS DOWN COMMUNICATION BARRIERS

In the stratified world of medical research, Roman Melnyk and Sheena Josselyn were at "opposite ends of the plant." He studies how the toxins in bacteria make people sick; she researches memory and neurological disease. But when Mr. Melnyk happened to hear a presentation by his colleague at the Hospital for Sick Children, it led to an intriguing collaboration: they're now trying to get those pushy toxins to deliver drugs to the brain and other hard-to-reach tissues. Their chance encounter happened at an annual hospital retreat. But Sick Kids is hoping the most distinctive feature of a gleaming new research building will encourage the same kind of cross-pollination between diverse scientists every day.

Each floor of the downtown Toronto structure is joined with another one or two to a light-filled, atrium-like common area, so researchers can mingle and trade ideas on breaks from the nearby laboratories. The labs themselves are unusually open-concept spaces where different research will take place within the same walls. In the heated debate about whether it's sufficient merely for workers to be connected virtually, the new $400-million tower is a forceful vote for bringing colleagues face to face.

"These sort of interactive spaces I think are going to be game changing," said Mr. Melnyk, a biochemist. "I think right now we're very siloed . . . [But] we're going to be all hanging out in the same space, and I think that's going to break down a lot of physical and virtual barriers to people talking to each other."

Scientists have traditionally toiled in small, self-contained labs, mixing mainly with those in the same narrow discipline and doing much of their communication via the Internet, said Janet Rossant, Sick Kids' chief of research. That fractured culture is not helped at the Toronto hospital, a major research centre as well as one of the country's foremost hospitals for children, by having scientists divided among six buildings.

At Sick Kids, the new hospital was designed to foster communication between research disciplines.

Andrew Francis Wallace/Toronto Star via Getty Images

All 2000 research staff will be moving into the new, 21-storey Peter Gilgan tower next month. To encourage more mingling, the building has been divided into "neighbourhoods" of two-to-three storeys each, such as one for genetics, another for neurosciences, and one for cell biology. The neighbourhood floors are linked by stairs to the common areas, which extend out from the building's façade behind striking, curved expanses of glass. Each lounge has a kitchen area and comfortable furniture. There are even plans for brown-bag lunches between neighbourhoods.

When Mr. Melnyk heard Ms. Josselyn's presentation, it occurred to him the toxins could be used to deliver medication across the "blood-brain barrier," the organ's natural defence against harmful substances that also makes it difficult to treat neurological diseases. Ms. Josselyn, a neurophysiologist, said she believes other workplaces can benefit from the human interaction that brought the two scientists together.

"I think it's always hugely important," she said. "If you encounter some problems or you just want to bounce an idea off somebody, it's so much easier if you already have a connection with them . . . I think non-work-related interacting with colleagues always promotes work."[1]

The Sick Kids Hospital story exemplifies the importance of good communication. In this chapter, we will define *communication* and present a model of the communication process. We will then investigate voice, silence, the "grapevine," the verbal and non-verbal language of work, gender differences, cross-cultural communication, and computer-mediated communication. Finally, we will discuss personal and organizational means of improving communication.

Define *communication*, and explain why communication by the strict chain of command is often ineffective.

Communication.
The process by which information is exchanged between a sender and a receiver.

PERSONAL INVENTORY ASSESSMENT

Learn About Yourself
Communication Styles

EXHIBIT 10.1
A model of the communication process and an example.
Source: Glueck, W.F. (1980). *Management,* 2nd ed. South-Western, a part of Cengage Learning, Inc. Reproduced by permission, www.cengage.com/permissions.

WHAT IS COMMUNICATION?

Communication is the process by which information is exchanged between a sender and a receiver. The kind of communication we are concerned with in this chapter is *interpersonal* communication—the exchange of information between people. The simplest prototype for interpersonal communication is a one-on-one exchange between two individuals. Exhibit 10.1 presents a model of the interpersonal communication process and an example of a communication episode between a purchasing manager and her assistant. As you can see, the sender must *encode* his or her thoughts into some form that can be *transmitted* to the receiver. In this case, the manager has chosen to encode her thoughts in writing and transmit them via email. Alternatively, the manager could have encoded her thoughts in speech and transmitted them via voice mail or face to face. The assistant, as a receiver, must *perceive* the message and accurately decode it to achieve accurate understanding. In this case, the assistant uses an online parts catalogue to decode the meaning of an "A-40." To provide *feedback*, the assistant might send the manager a copy of the order for the flange bolts. Such feedback involves yet another communication episode that tells the original sender that her assistant has received and understood the message.

This simple communication model is valuable because it points out the complexity of the communication process and demonstrates a number of points at which errors can occur. Such errors lead to a lack of correspondence between the sender's initial thoughts and the receiver's understanding of the intended message. A slip of the finger on the keyboard can lead to improper encoding. A poor email system can lead to ineffective transmission. An outdated parts catalogue can result in inaccurate decoding. Encoding and decoding may be prone to even more error when the message is inherently ambiguous or emotional. This is because the two parties may have very different perceptions of the "facts" at hand.

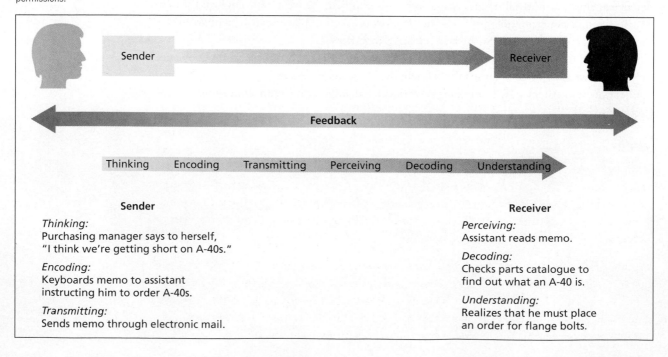

Effective communication occurs when the right people receive the right information in a timely manner. Violating any of these three conditions results in a communication episode that is ineffective.

Effective communication.
Communication whereby the right people receive the right information in a timely manner.

BASICS OF ORGANIZATIONAL COMMUNICATION

Let's consider a few basic issues about organizational communication.

Communication by Strict Chain of Command

The lines on an organizational chart represent lines of authority and reporting relationships. For example, a vice-president has authority over the plant manager, who has authority over the production supervisors. Conversely, production workers report to their supervisors, who report to the plant manager, and so on. In theory, organizational communication could stick to this strict **chain of command**. Under this system, three necessary forms of communication can be accomplished.

Downward communication flows from the top of the organization toward the bottom. For example, a vice-president of production might instruct a plant manager to gear up for manufacturing a new product. In turn, the plant manager would provide specifics to supervisors, who would instruct the production workers accordingly.

Upward communication flows from the bottom of the organization toward the top. For instance, a chemist might conceive a new plastic formula with unique properties. She might then pass this on to the research and development manager, who would then inform the relevant vice-president.

Horizontal communication occurs between departments or functional units, usually as a means of coordinating effort. Within a strict chain of command, such communication would flow up to and then down from a *common manager*. For example, suppose a salesperson gets an idea for a new product from a customer. To get this idea to the research staff, it would have to be transmitted up to and down from the vice-presidents of marketing and research, the common managers for these departments. At Sick Kids Hospital, the new research building is meant to improve horizontal communication between health science disciplines.

Clearly, a lot of organizational communication does follow the formal lines of authority shown on organizational charts. This is especially true for the examples of upward and downward communication given above—directives and instructions usually pass downward through the chain of command, and ideas and suggestions pass upward. However, the reality of organizational communication shows that the formal chain of command is an incomplete and sometimes ineffective path of communication.

Chain of command. Lines of authority and formal reporting relationships.

Downward communication. Information that flows from the top of the organization toward the bottom.

Upward communication. Information that flows from the bottom of the organization toward the top.

Horizontal communication. Information that flows between departments or functional units, usually as a means of coordinating effort.

Deficiencies in the Chain of Command

Managers recognize that sticking strictly to the chain of command is often ineffective.

INFORMAL COMMUNICATION The chain of command obviously fails to consider *informal* communication between members. In previous chapters, we discussed how informal interaction helps people accomplish their jobs more effectively. Of course, not all informal communication benefits the organization. An informal grapevine might spread unsavoury, inaccurate rumours across the organization.

FILTERING Getting the right information to the right people is often inhibited by filtering. **Filtering** is the tendency for a message to be watered down or stopped altogether at some point during transmission, and it is something of a double-edged sword. On the one hand, employees are *supposed* to filter information. For example, CEOs are not expected to communicate every detail of the management of the company right down to the shop floor.

Filtering. The tendency for a message to be watered down or stopped during transmission.

However, overzealous filtering will preclude the right people from getting the right information, and the organization will suffer accordingly. Upward filtering often occurs because employees are afraid that their boss will use the information against them. Downward filtering is often due to time pressures or simple lack of attention to detail, but more sinister motives may be at work. As the old saying goes, "Information is power," and some managers filter downward communications to maintain an edge on their subordinates. For example, a manager who feels that an up-and-coming employee could be promoted over him might filter crucial information to make the subordinate look bad at a staff meeting.

SLOWNESS Even when the chain of command transmits information faithfully, it can be painfully slow. The chain of command can be even slower for horizontal communication between departments, and it is not a good mechanism for reacting quickly to customer problems. Cross-functional teams and employee empowerment, concepts we introduced earlier in the text, have been used to improve communication in these areas by short-circuiting the chain of command.

In summary, informal communication and the recognition of filtering and time constraints guarantee that organizations will develop channels of communication beyond the strict chain of command.

LO 10.2

Explain the factors that contribute to *voice* versus *silence*.

Voice. The constructive expression of disagreement or concern about work unit or organizational practices.

VOICE, SILENCE, AND THE MUM EFFECT

Speaking generally, the free flow of information contributes to effective communication. One aspect of this free flow is employee **voice**, the constructive expression of disagreement or concern about work unit or organizational practices.[2] Voice refers to "speaking up" and can be contrasted with silence, which in this context means withholding relevant information. Voice might be directed horizontally, to teammates, or vertically, to the boss or to management in general. When it is not morally or legally required, voice can be considered a form of organizational citizenship behaviour (Chapter 4) that enables organizations to learn and change. Hence, it is in their interest to encourage voice. However, speaking up can be perceived as risky due to inherent power differentials in organizations.

Who is inclined to exercise voice, and when? Interestingly, more satisfied employees who identify more strongly with their work unit or organization are most likely to speak up, as are those who are conscientious and extraverted.[3] Also, direct supervisors and higher-level managers play an absolutely critical role in creating a climate in which constructive dissent can emerge.[4] Both direct support (or lack thereof) for dissent as well as symbolic stories about what has happened to those who exercise voice are strong determinants of such a climate. Meeting employees informally on their own turf and not unfairly punishing honest mistakes can foster a positive climate for voice. All of these factors can contribute to an atmosphere of **psychological safety**, a shared belief that it is safe to take social risks.[5] Indeed, high "voicers" report less work stress than those who remain silent.[6]

Psychological safety. A shared belief that it is safe to take social risks.

On the other hand, self-censorship will result in a climate of silence. One study found that the following implicit notions contributed to silence: I can't attack the boss's pet idea; I don't have solid data to speak up; I can't bypass the boss; I can't publicly embarrass the boss; I can't look like I'm not a team player.[7]

A more general factor that contributes to silence and works against voice is the **mum effect**, the tendency to avoid communicating unfavourable news to others.[8] Often, people would rather "keep mum" than convey bad news that might provoke negative reactions. The sender need not actually be responsible for the bad news for the mum effect to occur, but the tendency is even more likely when the sender *is* responsible for the bad news. For example, the nurse who mistakenly administers an incorrect drug dose might be very reluctant to inform the head nurse of his or her error. Employees with strong aspirations for upward mobility are especially likely to encounter communication difficulties with their bosses.[9]

Mum effect. The tendency to avoid communicating unfavourable news to others.

YOU BE THE MANAGER

Communicating Diversity and Inclusion at Ryder

Founded in 1933, Ryder System, Inc., a Fortune 500 company, provides commercial transportation, logistics, and supply chain support in North America, Asia, and Europe. Ryder's products and services include truck rental and leasing, fleet management, and turnkey supply chain and transportation solutions. Thus, Ryder can lease trucks to a customer, but it can also supply drivers, fuel, scheduling, and routing, spanning the chain from raw material acquisition to delivery of a final product. For many years, Ryder has shown a commitment to diversity and inclusion (D&I), seeing it as imperative to attracting and retaining the best workforce, generating diverse perspectives, and putting its best foot forward for its customers. Thus, it has a dedicated Office of D&I and a Council of D&I made up of 12 company leaders from a variety of functions. These two bodies chart strategy to enhance diversity and inclusion at Ryder. Part of that strategy has involved including effective D&I management among its required leadership competencies and tying success in fostering D&I to management compensation. However, the company wanted to involve *all* of its employees more fully in the D&I effort and really get them on board. Ryder realized that a multi-pronged communication strategy would be necessary to take its D&I efforts to the next level. But what exactly should they do? You be the manager.

Ryder realized the importance of communication in fostering diversity.

1. Employees are busy with their everyday jobs. How do you get their attention and focus them on the core importance of diversity and inclusion?

2. Having gotten employees' attention concerning D&I by communicating its importance, how can management reinforce this attention and galvanize employees into action?

To find out what Ryder did, see The Manager's Notebook at the end of the chapter.

Sources: Based on Amparo, B. (2010, November/December). Communicating diversity & inclusion at Ryder. *Profiles in Diversity Journal*, p. 70; Ryder System website.

This might be due, in part, to the mum effect—employees who desire to impress their bosses to achieve a promotion have strong motives to withhold bad news.[10]

The mum effect does not apply only to subordinates. A boss might be reluctant to transmit bad news downward. One of your authors found that employees who had good performance ratings were more likely to know those ratings than employees who had bad ratings. Managers evidently avoided communicating bad news for which they were partly responsible, since they themselves had done the ratings. Given this, it is not surprising that managers and their employees often differ in their perceptions of employee performance.[11]

Issues of voice and silence are especially relevant to power dynamics, organizational politics, and ethics, topics we will cover in Chapter 12. The subject of workforce diversity deserves less silence and more voice. Consider You Be the Manager: *Communicating Diversity and Inclusion at Ryder.*

THE GRAPEVINE

Just inside the gates of the steel mill where one of your authors used to work, there was a large sign that read "X days without a major accident." The sign was revised each day to impress on the workforce the importance of safe working practices. A zero posted on the sign caught one's attention immediately, since this meant that a serious accident or fatality had just occurred. Seeing a zero on entering the mill, workers seldom took more than five minutes to find someone who knew the details. While the victim's name might be unknown,

LO 10.3

Explain the organizational *grapevine*, and discuss its main features.

 Simulate

COMMUNICATION

the location and nature of the accident were always accurate, even though the mill was very large. How did this information get around so quickly? It travelled through the "grapevine."

Characteristics of the Grapevine

Grapevine. An organization's informal communication network.

The **grapevine** is the informal communication network that exists in any organization. As such, the grapevine often cuts across formal lines of communication that are recognized by management. Observation suggests several distinguishing features of grapevine systems:

- We generally think of the grapevine as communicating information by word of mouth. However, written notes, emails, and social media can contribute to the transmission of information.

- Organizations often have several grapevine systems, some of which may be loosely coordinated. For instance, a secretary who is part of the "office grapevine" might communicate information to a mail carrier, who passes it on to the "warehouse grapevine."

- The grapevine can transmit information relevant to the performance of the organization as well as personal gossip.[12] Many times, it is difficult to distinguish between the two: "You won't *believe* who just got fired!"

How accurate is the grapevine? One expert concludes that at least 75 percent of the non-controversial, organization-related information carried by the grapevine is correct.[13] Personal information and emotionally charged information are most likely to be distorted.

Who Participates in the Grapevine, and Why?

Who is likely to be a transmitter of grapevine information? Personality characteristics may play a role. For instance, extraverts might be more likely than introverts to pass on information. Similarly, those who lack self-esteem might pass on information that gives them a personal advantage. Also, the *physical* location of organizational members is related to their opportunity to receive and transmit news via the "vine." Occupants of work stations that receive a lot of traffic are good candidates to be transmitters. A warm control room in a cold plant or an air-conditioned computer room in a sweltering factory might provide their occupants with a steady stream of potential receivers for juicy information. On the other side of the coin, jobs that require movement throughout the organization also give their holders much opportunity to serve as grapevine transmitters. Mail carriers and IT troubleshooters are good examples.

What motivates people to gossip via the grapevine? For one thing, it can be a timely, inexpensive source of information that simply isn't available through other channels. In turn, this information can provide an alternative source of power and influence available to all, not just those with access to formal information channels. Much grapevine material involves

Patrick Hardin, www.CartoonStock.com

releasing pent-up emotions concerning bosses or customers that can't otherwise be comfortably expressed, and the exchange of delicate information thus builds a bond of trust between senders and receivers. Finally, some jobs are so boring that gossip provides one of the few available sources of social and intellectual stimulation.[14]

Pros and Cons of the Grapevine

Is the grapevine desirable from the organization's point of view? For one thing, it can keep employees informed about important organizational matters, such as job security. In some organizations, management is so notoriously lax at this that the grapevine is a regular substitute for formal communication. The grapevine can also provide a test of employee reactions to proposed changes without making formal commitments. Managers have been known to "leak" ideas to the grapevine to probe their potential acceptance. Anita Roddick, the late founder of The Body Shop, was known for planting ideas with the office gossips to tap in to the organization's informal networks.[15] Finally, when grapevine information extends outside the organization, it can serve as a potent informal recruiting source.[16]

The grapevine can become a real problem for the organization when it becomes a constant pipeline for rumours. A **rumour** is an unverified belief that is in general circulation.[17] The key word here is "unverified"—although it is possible for a rumour to be true, it is not likely to *remain* true as it runs through the grapevine. Because people cannot verify the information as accurate, rumours are susceptible to severe distortion as they are passed from person to person.

Rumour. An unverified belief that is in general circulation.

Rumours seem to spread fastest and farthest when the information is especially ambiguous, when the content of the rumour is important to those involved, when the rumour seems credible, and when the recipient is anxious.[18] Increasingly difficult global competition, staff reductions, and restructuring have placed a premium on rumour control. At the same time, organizations should avoid the tendency to be mum about giving bad news.

THE VERBAL LANGUAGE OF WORK

LO 10.4

Review the role of verbal and *non-verbal communication* at work.

A friend of one of your authors had just moved into a new neighbourhood. In casual conversation with a neighbour, he mentioned that he was "writing a book on OD." She replied with some enthusiasm, "Oh, that's great. My husband's in obstetrics too!" The author's friend, of course, is a management professor who was writing a book on organizational behaviour. The neighbour's husband was a physician who specialized in delivering babies.

Every student knows what it means to do a little "cramming in the caf" before an exam. Although this phrase might sound strange to the uninitiated listener, it reveals how circumstances shape our language and how we often take this shaping for granted. In many jobs, occupations, and organizations, we see the development of a specialized language, or **jargon**, that members use to communicate with one another. Thus, *OB* means *organizational behaviour* to management professors and *obstetrics* to physicians.

Jargon. Specialized language used by job holders or members of particular occupations or organizations.

Rosabeth Moss Kanter, in studying a large corporation, discovered its attempt to foster COMVOC, or "common vocabulary," among its managers.[19] Here, the goal was to facilitate communication among employees who were often geographically separated, unknown to each other, and "meeting" impersonally through memos. COMVOC provided a common basis for interaction among virtual strangers. In addition, managers developed their own informal supplements to COMVOC. Upward mobility, an especially important topic in the corporation, was reflected in multiple labels for the same concept:

Fast trackers	One performers
High fliers	Boy (girl) wonders
Superstars	Water walkers

While jargon is an efficient means of communicating with peers and provides a touch of status to those who have mastered it, it can also serve as a *barrier* to communicating with others. For example, local jargon might serve as a barrier to clear communication between departments such as sales and engineering. New organizational members often find the use of jargon especially intimidating and confusing. A second serious problem with the use of jargon is the communication barrier that it presents to those *outside* of the organization or profession. Consider the language of the corporate takeover, with its greenmail, poison pills, and white knights!

THE NON-VERBAL LANGUAGE OF WORK

Have you ever come away from a conversation having heard one thing yet believing the opposite of what was said? Professors frequently hear students say that they understand a concept but somehow know that they do not. Students often hear professors say, "Come up to my office any time" but somehow know that they do not mean it. How can we account for these messages that we receive in spite of the words we hear? The answer is often non-verbal communication.

Non-verbal communication. The transmission of messages by some medium other than speech or writing.

Non-verbal communication is the transmission of messages by some medium other than speech or writing. As indicated above, non-verbal messages can be very powerful in that they often convey "the real stuff," while words serve as a smokescreen. Raised eyebrows, an emphatic shrug, or an abrupt departure convey a lot of information with great economy. The minutes of dramatic meetings (or even verbatim transcripts) can make for extremely boring reading because they are stripped of non-verbal cues. These examples involve the transmission of information by body language. Body language and the manipulation of objects are major forms of non-verbal communication.

Body Language

Body language. Non-verbal communication by means of a sender's bodily motions, facial expressions, or physical location.

Body language is non-verbal communication that occurs by means of the sender's bodily motions and facial expressions or the sender's physical location in relation to the receiver.[20] Although we can communicate a variety of information via body language, two important messages are the extent to which the sender likes and is interested in the receiver, and the sender's views concerning the relative status of the sender and the receiver.

In general, senders communicate liking and interest in the receiver when they

- position themselves physically close to the receiver;
- touch the receiver during the interaction;
- maintain eye contact with the receiver;
- lean forward during the interaction; and
- direct their torso toward the receiver.[21]

Each of these behaviours demonstrates that the sender has genuine consideration for the receiver's point of view.

Senders who feel themselves to be of higher status than the receiver act more *relaxed* than those who perceive themselves to be of lower status. Relaxation is demonstrated by

- the casual, asymmetrical placement of arms and legs;
- a reclining, non-erect seating position; and
- a lack of fidgeting and nervous activity.[22]

In other words, the greater the difference in relaxation between two parties, the more they communicate a status differential to each other.

People often attempt to use non-verbal behaviour to communicate with others, just as they use verbal behaviour. This use could include showing our true feelings, "editing" our feelings, or trying to actively deceive others. It is difficult to regulate non-verbal behaviour when we are feeling very strong emotions. However, people are otherwise pretty good at non-verbal "posing," such as looking relaxed when they are not. On the other hand, observers also show some capacity to detect such posing.[23]

Employment interviewers are usually faced with applicants who are motivated to make a good verbal impression. Thus, in accordance with the idea that "the body doesn't lie," interviewers might turn their attention to non-verbal cues on the assumption that they are less likely to be censored than verbal cues. Non-verbal behaviours, such as smiling, gesturing, and maintaining eye contact, have a favourable impact on interviewers when they are not overdone.[24] However, it is unlikely that such body language can overcome bad credentials or poor verbal performance.[25] Rather, positive body language might give the edge to applicants who are otherwise equally well qualified. Remember, in an employment interview, it is not just what you say, but also what you do!

Props, Artifacts, and Costumes

In addition to the use of body language, non-verbal communication can also occur through the use of various objects such as props, artifacts, and costumes.

OFFICE DECOR AND ARRANGEMENT Consider the manner in which people decorate and arrange their offices. Does this tell visitors anything about the occupant? Does it communicate any useful information? The answer is yes. One study found that students would feel more welcome and comfortable in a professor's office when the office was (1) tidy, (2) decorated with posters and plants, and (3) the desk was against the wall instead of between the student and the professor.[26] A neat office evidently signalled that the professor was well organized and had time to talk to them. Perhaps personal decoration signalled "I'm human." When the desk was against the wall, there was no tangible barrier between the parties. Inferences of this type appear to have some validity. Another study found that strangers were able to accurately infer certain Big Five personality traits (Chapter 2) of the occupants of business offices. In particular, they could assess how conscientious and how open to experience the person was simply by seeing his or her office. Neatness was a typical cue for conscientiousness and distinctive decor for openness.[27]

Researcher Kimberly Elsbach found that middle managers working in the California information technology sector (mostly at Intel and Hewlett-Packard) used office decor to

The decor and arrangement of furniture in a person's office conveys non-verbal information to visitors.

Terry Vine/Getty Images

EXHIBIT 10.2
Inferences from office decor.

Source: Adapted from Elsbach, K.D. (2004). Interpreting workplace identities: The role of office décor. *Journal of Organizational Behavior*, *25*(1), 99–128. © 2004 John Wiley & Sons Limited. Reproduced with permission of John Wiley & Sons Ltd; permission conveyed through Copyright Clearance Center, Inc.

Office Decor	Distinctiveness Categorizations	Status Categorizations
Family photos	Family oriented, balanced, not work focused	Not a "player"
Hobby photos, calendar, poster, artifacts	Ambitious, outgoing, well-rounded	Unprofessional
Funny, unusual artifacts and conversation pieces	Fun person, joker, off-beat, approachable, lazy, needs attention	Not serious, unprofessional
Formal decor, artifacts	Professional, successful, vain, distant, snobbish	High status, authority figure
Informal, messy office	Easy-going, busy, true engineer, disorganized, unskilled	Unprofessional
Awards, diplomas	Show-off, hard-working, successful, pretentious, vain	Accomplished, intimidating
Professional products	Functional expert, "company person," geek	Accomplished
Ideological artifacts	Patriotic, says "I have a social conscience," extreme, radical	Insecure, unprofessional
Salient, flashy artifacts	Needs to get attention, flashy	Insecure
High conformity artifacts	Predictable, reliable, conservative, not innovative	Insecure

"profile" the identity and status of office occupants.[28] Exhibit 10.2 shows some of the inferences they made about their fellow employees, both flattering and unflattering.

DOES CLOTHING COMMUNICATE?
"Wardrobe engineer" John T. Molloy is convinced that the clothing organizational members wear sends clear signals about their competence, seriousness, and promotability—that is, receivers unconsciously attach certain stereotyped meanings to various clothing and then treat the wearer accordingly. For example, Molloy insists that a black raincoat is the kiss of death for an aspiring male executive. He claims that black raincoats signal "lower-middle class," while beige raincoats lead to "executive" treatment. For the same reason, Molloy strongly vetoes sweaters for women executives. Molloy stresses that proper clothing will not make up for a lack of ambition, intelligence, and savvy. Rather, he argues that the wrong clothing will prevent others from detecting these qualities. To this end, he prescribes detailed "business uniforms," the men's built around a conservative suit and the women's around a skirted suit and blouse.[29] For an exception to the business uniform rule, see Research Focus: *The Red Sneakers Effect: When Nonconformity Signals High Status.*

Clothing does indeed communicate.[30] Even at the ages of 10 to 12 years, children associate various brand names of jeans with different personality characteristics of the wearer! Such effects persist into adulthood. Research simulations have shown that more masculinely dressed and groomed women are more likely to be selected for executive jobs. However, there might be a point at which women's dress becomes "too masculine" and thus damages their prospects.[31] The non-profit organization Dress for Success provides disadvantaged women with professional apparel appropriate for job interviews in various industries and additional apparel when they are hired.[32]

Proper clothing may enhance self-esteem and self-confidence to a noticeable degree. One study contrived to have some student job applicants appear for an interview in street clothes, while others had time to dress in more appropriate formal interview gear. Those who wore more formal clothes felt that they had made a better impression. They also asked for a starting salary that was $4000 higher than job seekers who wore street clothes![33]

■ RESEARCH FOCUS ■

THE RED SNEAKERS EFFECT: WHEN NONCONFORMITY SIGNALS HIGH STATUS

Speaking generally, people who are conventionally well dressed communicate high status, competence, and authority to others. Hence, the well-tailored suit and shiny leather shoes have become something of a standard "business uniform," and both the 22-year-old business school graduate and the 50-year-old business magnate tend to conform to remarkably similar styles of dress to achieve and maintain social acceptance among their business peers. This strong degree of conformity is a reflection of the status and competence that such dress confers and the expected social costs of deviating from conventional standards of good dress.

But what about exceptions to the business uniform? What about Facebook CEO Mark Zukerberg's penchant for hoodies? And what about consultant Tom Searcy's observation that many of his super-rich Silicon Valley tech visionaries attend board meetings dressed like homeless people? Obviously, some successful people can "get away" with dressing how they want. But is it also possible that such nonconformity can actually *contribute to* perceptions of status and success? Researchers Silvia Bellezza, Francesca Gino, and Anat Keinan have studied the red sneakers effect, the occasional tendency for *non*conformity to signal status and competence. What they found is that such positive

signaling can occur under certain conditions. For one thing, the nonconformity has to be seen as intentional; accidentally dressing in a nonconforming way doesn't signal competence. Also, the nonconforming behavior has to occur in a prestigious context where there are general expectations that one might dress in a conventional manner; dressing down at the beach won't score any points, but doing so in the boardroom might work to one's advantage. How do red sneakers and other nonconforming dress communicate status and competence? The researchers found that the nonconformists were perceived as more autonomous, more in control, and these are valued qualities in our society.

Canadian clothier Larry Rosen insisted that the sloppy look is intended to make "some kind of counter-culture statement." Consultant Searcy said that the look is meant to communicate the notion that ideas are more important than appearances. In line with the Bellezza research, both men stressed that the look is intentionally cultivated.

Sources: Based on Bellezza, S., Gino, F., & Keinan, A. (2014). The red sneakers effect: inferring status and competence from signals of nonconformity. *Journal of Consumer Research, 41*, 35–54; Owram, K. (2014, September 11). Silicon valley's closet fashionistas. *Financial Post*, FP1, FP4.

GENDER DIFFERENCES IN COMMUNICATION

LO

According to Deborah Tannen, there are gender differences in communication styles, and these differences influence the way that men and women are perceived and treated in the workplace. Gender differences in communication have their origin in childhood. Girls see conversations as a way to develop networks of connection and intimacy. Boys view conversations as a way to achieve status and to maintain independence. These childhood differences persist in the workplace, where they influence who gets recognized and valued.[34]

A typical example of how these differences are played out is in a business meeting in which a woman comes up with a great idea and by the end of the meeting one of her male peers receives the credit for it.[35] What often happens is that a man picks up the idea of a female co-worker and spends more time talking about it. As a result, he gets the credit.[36]

Gender differences in communication revolve around what Tannen refers to as the "One Up, One Down" position. Men tend to be more sensitive to power dynamics and will use communication as a way to position themselves in a one-up situation. Women are more concerned with rapport building, and they communicate in ways that avoid putting others down. As a result, women often find themselves in a one-down position, which can have a negative effect on the rewards they receive and their careers.[37]

Discuss gender differences in communication, and identify how a failure to recognize these differences can cause communication problems.

On the basis of her research, Tannen has found that there are a number of key differences in male and female communication styles and rituals that often place women in a one-down position:

- *Getting credit.* Men are more likely than women to blow their own horn about something good they have done.

- *Confidence and boasting.* Compared with women, who downplay their certainty, men tend to be more boastful about themselves and their capabilities and to minimize their doubts. As a result, men tend to be perceived as more confident.

- *Asking questions.* Most people know that men do not like to ask for directions when they are lost. This is because they realize that asking questions can put them in a one-down position and reflect negatively on them. Therefore, men are less likely than women to ask questions.

- *Apologies.* Women will often say "I'm sorry" as a way of expressing concern, such as when a friend has had a bad day. For women, apologies are part of a ritual that is used to establish rapport. Men, however, see ritual apologies as weakness.

- *Feedback.* Women will often buffer criticism by beginning with praise as a way to save face for the person receiving the criticism and avoid putting them in a one-down position. Men, however, tend to be much more blunt and straightforward. These differences can lead to misunderstandings, as when a man interprets a woman's praise, rather than the criticism, as the main message.

- *Compliments.* If a friend of yours has just completed a class presentation and asks for your thoughts about it, what would you say? Women are more likely to provide a compliment such as "Great presentation" or "Good job." Men, however, are more likely to interpret the question literally and provide a critique.

- *Ritual opposition.* Men often use ritual opposition as a form of communication and to exchange ideas. This takes the form of attacking others' points of view, challenging them in public, and being argumentative. For women, ritual opposition is seen as a personal attack and something to be avoided.

- *Managing up and down.* Many women believe that, to be recognized and rewarded, what matters most is doing a good job. Unfortunately, this is not always the case. What also matters is who you communicate with and what you discuss. Men spend much more time communicating with their superiors and talking about their achievements. This type of communication influences who gets recognized and promoted.

- *Indirectness.* What would be your response if your supervisor asked you a relatively simple question such as "How would you feel about helping the human resources department hire a new person for our department?" Would you then think about how you "feel" about helping or would you interpret this as a request to actually do it? In North America, persons in positions of authority are expected to give direct orders when asking subordinates to do something. Women in positions of authority, however, tend to be indirect when giving orders. For instance, in the above example, what is really being said is, "Help the human resource department hire a person for our department." Such indirectness can lead to misunderstandings and be perceived as a lack of appropriate demeanour and confidence.[38]

The differences in communication styles between men and women almost always reflect negatively on women and place them in a one-down position. Does this mean that women should change the way they communicate? The communication styles that women are accustomed to are most appropriate when communicating with other women, and the same goes for men. The key, according to Deborah Tannen, is to recognize that people have different linguistic styles and to be flexible so that you can adjust your style when necessary. For example, men should learn to admit when they make a mistake and women should learn to be more direct when asking subordinates to do something.

CROSS-CULTURAL COMMUNICATION

LO **10.6**

Consider a commonplace exchange in the world of international business:

> A Japanese businessman wants to tell his Norwegian client that he is uninterested in a particular sale. To be polite, the Japanese says, "That will be very difficult." The Norwegian interprets the statement to mean that there are still unresolved problems, not that the deal is off. He responds by asking how his company can help solve the problems. The Japanese, believing he has sent the message that there will be no sale, is mystified by the response.[39]

Discuss challenges relating to *cross-cultural communication*, and identify useful strategies to deter miscommunication.

Obviously, ineffective communication has occurred between our international business people, since the Norwegian has not received the right information about the (non) sale. From the Norwegian's point of view, the Japanese has not encoded his message in a clear manner. The Japanese, on the other hand, might criticize the weak decoding skills of his Scandinavian client. Let's examine some important dimensions of cross-cultural communication.

Language Differences

Communication is generally better between individuals or groups who share similar cultural values. This is even more true when they share a common language. Thus, despite acknowledged differences in terminology ("lift" versus "elevator," "petrol" versus "gasoline"), language should not be a communication barrier for the North American executive who is posted to a British subsidiary. Despite this generality, the role of language in communication involves some subtle ironies. For example, a common language can sometimes cause visitors to misunderstand or be surprised by legitimate cultural differences, because they get lulled into complacency. Boarding a Qantas Airlines flight in Australia, one of your authors was attempting to pick up a magazine from a rack when he was admonished by a flight attendant with the sharp words "First class, mate." Grinning sheepishly, he headed back to his economy class seat without the magazine. Wise to the ways of Australia, he was not offended by this display of brash informality. However, a North American less familiar with local ways and assuming that "they speak English, they're just like us," might have been less forgiving, attributing the flight attendant's behaviour to a rude personality rather than national style. By the same token, the flight attendant would be surprised to learn that someone might be offended by his words.

As the Qantas example indicates, speaking the same language is no guarantee of perfect communication. In fact, the Norwegian and Japanese business people described above may have negotiated in a common language, such as English. Even then, the Norwegian did not get the message. Speaking generally, however, learning a second language should facilitate cross-cultural communication. This is especially true when the second-language facility provides extra insight into the communication style of the other culture. Thus, the Norwegian would profit from understanding that the Japanese have sixteen subtle ways to say no, even if he could not understand the language perfectly.[40]

To some extent, English has become the default language of global business. However, a recent study of over 800 foreign subsidiaries of multinational firms indicated that language differences between headquarters and subsidiaries pose substantial challenges.[41] Lack of a common language itself, distinct from cultural differences, fostered misunderstanding and conflict, resulting in the rise of parallel information networks and less face-to-face and telephone interaction. Hence, more personal forms of communication are replaced by less personal written communication via email. The study found that expatriate employees with skills in both relevant languages helped ease communication problems. One "solution" to language differences is the institution of English-only policies. Although commonly implemented (at, for instance, Nissan, Philips, Nokia, and Siemens), such policies have resulted in a host of problems.[42] Employees forced to speak English often feel reduced professional status and report extreme anxiety about having to communicate about important business matters in other than their native language.

Non-Verbal Communication across Cultures

From our earlier discussion of non-verbal communication, you might be tempted to assume that it would hold up better than verbal communication across cultures. While there are some similarities across cultures in non-verbal communication, there are also many differences. Here are a few examples.

- *Facial expressions.* People are very good at decoding basic, simple emotions in facial expressions, even across cultures. Americans, Japanese, and members of New Guinea tribes can accurately detect anger, surprise, fear, and sadness in the same set of facial photographs.[43] Thus, paying particular attention to the face in cross-cultural encounters will often yield communication dividends. However, this does not always work because some cultures (such as that of Japan) frown on the display of negative facial expressions, no doubt prompting the "inscrutable" label.

- *Gestures.* Except for literal mimicry ("I need food," "Sign here"), gestures do not translate well across cultures. This is because they involve symbolism that is not shared:

   In the United States, a raised thumb is used as a signal of approval or approbation, the thumbs-up signal, but in Greece, it is employed as an insult, often being associated with the expression katsa pano, or "sit on this." Another example is the ring sign, performed by bringing the tips of the thumb and finger together so that they form a circle. For most English-speaking people it means okay and is, in fact, known as the "okay gesture." But in some sections of France, the ring means zero or worthless. In English-speaking countries, disagreement is signalled by shaking the head, but in Greece and southern Italy the head-toss is employed to signify disagreement.[44]

- *Gaze.* There are cultural differences in the extent to which it is considered suitable to look others directly in the eye. Latin Americans and Arabs favour an extended gaze, while Europeans do not. In many parts of East Asia, avoiding eye contact is a means of showing respect. In North America, it often connotes disrespect.

- *Touch.* In some cultures, people tend to stand close to one another when meeting and often touch each other as an adjunct to conversation. This is common in Arab, Latin American, and Southern European countries. On the other hand, Northern Europeans and North Americans prefer to "keep their distance."[45]

In an interesting experiment, English people received training in social skills that were appropriate to the Arab world. These included standing or sitting close to others and looking into their eyes, coupled with extensive touching, smiling, and handshaking. Experimenters then introduced Arabs to a trained subject and to a control subject who had only been exposed to general information about the Middle East. When asked whom they liked better, the Arabs preferred the people who had received training in their own non-verbal communication style.[46] We can well imagine a business meeting between English and Saudi bankers, both true to their cultures. The Saudis, gazing and touching, finish the meeting wondering why the English are so inattentive and aloof. The English, avoiding eye contact and shrinking from touch, wonder why the Saudis are so aggressive and threatening!

■ GLOBAL FOCUS

SELF-PRESENTATION BIAS: WHO'S MOST AND LEAST MODEST IN JOB APPLICATIONS?

Cornelius König and colleagues studied an aspect of communication that is important to both job seekers and potential employers—self-presentation in the job application process. Self-presentation refers to a range of communication behaviours that might be subsumed under the label of faking. This could include exaggerating one's positive qualities and downplaying one's negative qualities as well as more blatant examples, such as fabricating experience that one does not really have. The overall goal of self-presentation is to create a favourable impression of the candidate in the eyes of HR personnel and managers. Using an elaborate technique designed to ensure anonymity and encourage honest responding, the researchers questioned Swiss and Icelandic respondents about what they had communicated during a recent job application. The goal was to compare the results with previous research done in the United States. Given that modesty is a particularly valued trait in both Iceland and Switzerland (e.g., tourist guidebooks often extol Swiss modesty), but less so in the United States, it was expected that the Icelanders and Swiss would report having employed less self-presentation in job applications. For the most part, the Europeans reported much less self-presentation bias than the Americans on a wide range of items. For example, while no Swiss or Icelandic respondents reported outright fabrication of information about themselves, 17% of U.S. respondents did so. Also, 5% of the Swiss, 17% of the Icelanders, and 56% of the Americans admitted to exaggerating their positive attributes, such as efficiency and industriousness. Such communication tendencies might favour U.S. applicants in international recruiting situations and lead to overlooking the positive qualities of more modest European applicants.

Source: Based on König, C.J., Hafsteinson, L.G., Jansen, A., & Stadelmann, E.H. (2011). Applicants' self-presentational behaviors across cultures: Less self-presentation in Switzerland and Iceland than in the United States. *International Journal of Selection and Assessment, 19,* 331–339.

Etiquette and Politeness across Cultures

Cultures differ considerably in how etiquette and politeness are expressed.[47] Very often, this involves saying things that one does not literally mean. The problem is that the exact form that this takes varies across cultures, and careful decoding is necessary to avoid confusion and embarrassment. Literal decoding will almost always lead to trouble. Consider the North American manager who says to an employee, "Would you like to calculate those figures for me?" This is really a mild order, not an opportunity to say no to the boss's "invitation." However, put yourself in the place of a foreign employee who has learned that Americans generally speak directly and expect directness in return. Should she say no to the boss?

In some cultures, politeness is expressed with modesty that seems excessive to North Americans. Consider, for example, the Chinese visitor's response to a Canadian who told him that his wife was very attractive. The Chinese modestly responded, "No, no, my wife is ugly." Needless to say, what was said was not what the Chinese visitor really meant. For an example of national variations in modesty, see the Global Focus: *Self-Presentation Bias: Who's Most and Least Modest in Job Applications?*

In social situations, the Japanese are particularly interested in maintaining feelings of interdependence and harmony. To do this, they use a large number of set phrases or "lubricant expressions" to express sympathy and understanding, soften rejection, say no indirectly, or facilitate apology.[48] When the Japanese told the Norwegian "that will be very difficult" rather than "no," he was using such an expression. To Northern Europeans and North Americans, who do not understand the purpose of these ritual expressions, they may seem at best to be small talk and at worst to be insincere.

Social Conventions across Cultures

Over and above the issue of politeness and etiquette, there are a number of social conventions that vary across cultures and can lead to communication problems.[49] We have already alluded to the issue of directness. Especially in business dealings, North Americans tend to favour "getting down to brass tacks" and being specific about the issue at hand. Thus, the uninitiated business person might be quite surprised at the rather long period of informal chat that will begin business meetings in the Arab world or the indirectness and vagueness of many Japanese negotiators.

Greetings and how people say hello also vary across cultures, and these differences can lead to misunderstandings. For example, in North America people often greet one another by asking, "How are you?" and yet seem uninterested in the response. While this is an acceptable way of saying hello to North Americans, visitors from other cultures find this to be hypocritical. In other cultures, people greet each other by asking, "Where are you going?" Such a question is considered intrusive to North Americans who do not realize that this, too, is just a way of greeting somebody.[50]

What individuals consider a proper degree of loudness for speech also varies across cultures, and people from "quieter" societies (such as the United Kingdom) might unfairly view those from "louder" societies (such as the Middle East) as pushy or intimidating.

What people consider proper punctuality also varies greatly around the world. In North America and Japan, punctuality at meetings is expected and esteemed. In the Arab world and Latin America, being late for a meeting is not viewed negatively. In fact, one study found that being on time for an appointment connoted success in the United States and being *late* connoted success in Brazil.[51] Notice how an American business person might decode a Brazilian's lateness as disrespect, while the Brazilian was just trying to make a proper impression. Exhibit 10.3 shows the results of a study of differences in the pace of life across cultures. It illustrates the accuracy of clocks, the time to walk 100 feet, and the time to get served in a post office. As you can see, Japan is the most time conscious, while Indonesia is quite leisurely.

Finally, what is considered proper professional behaviour varies across cultures. In North America, there is a social norm that professional people should not communicate too much

EXHIBIT 10.3
Pace of life in six countries.
Source: Levine, R., & Wolff, E. (1985, March). Social time: The heartbeat of culture. Psychology Today , 26–35. Reprinted with permission from Dr. Robert Levine.

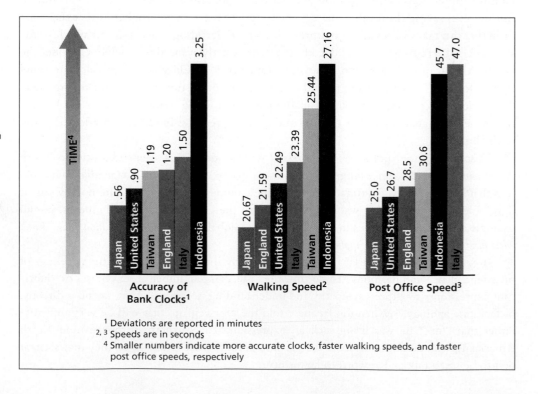

personal information in work settings. Thus, excessive personalization of one's office with non-work references (e.g., photos) concerning one's family, hobbies, or leisure travels is seen as less professional (Exhibit 10.2), as is trying to build rapport by discussing one's family life in a hiring interview or business negotiation. In other cultures, such as India, such non-work references may be seen as entirely appropriate.[52] This brings us to the subject of cultural context.

Cultural Context

In the previous sections, we provided many examples of communication differences across cultures. Is there some organizing principle underlying these differences, something that helps to summarize them? The concept of *cultural context* provides a partial answer. **Cultural context** is the cultural information that surrounds a communication episode. It is safe to say that context is always important in accurately decoding a message. Still, as Exhibit 10.4 shows, cultures tend to differ in the importance to which context influences the meaning to be put on communications.[53]

> **Cultural context.** The cultural information that surrounds a communication episode.

Some cultures, including many East Asian, Latin American, African, and Arab cultures, are high-context cultures. This means that the message contained in communication is strongly influenced by the context in which the message is sent. In high-context cultures, literal interpretations are often incorrect. Examples include those mentioned earlier—the Japanese really meant that the business deal was dead, and the Chinese did not really mean that his wife was unattractive.

Low-context cultures include North America, Australia, Northern Europe (excluding France), and Scandinavia. Here, messages can be interpreted more literally because more meaning resides in the message than in the context in which the communication occurs.

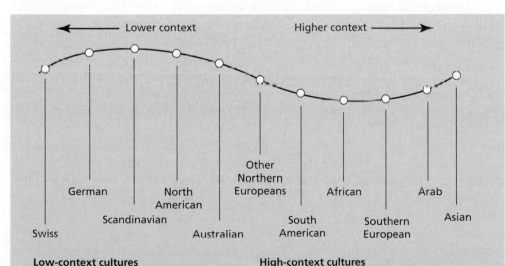

Low-context cultures
(Information must be provided explicitly, usually in words.)

- Less aware of non-verbal cues, environment and situation
- Lack well-developed networks
- Need detailed background information
- Tend to segment and compartmentalize information
- Control information on a "need to know" basis
- Prefer explicit and careful directions from someone who "knows"
- Knowledge is a commodity

High-context cultures
(Most information drawn from surroundings. Very little must be explicitly transferred.)

- Non-verbal important
- Information flows freely
- Physical context relied upon for information
- Environment, situation, gestures, mood all taken into account
- Maintain extensive information networks

EXHIBIT 10.4
High- versus low-context cultures.

Source: Klopf, D. W., & McCroskey, J., *Intercultural Communication Encounters*, Figure 10.1 "Where Different Cultures Fall on the Context Scale," p. 187, © 2007 Printed and Electronically reproduced by permission of Pearson Education, Inc., Upper Saddle River, New Jersey.

The "straight talk" that Americans favour is such an example. However, such straight talk is not any straighter in meaning than that heard in high-context cultures if one also learns to attend to the context when decoding messages.

Differences in the importance of context across cultures have some interesting implications for organizational communication, especially when we consider what might occur during business negotiations. Consider the following:[54]

- People from high-context cultures want to know about you and the company that you represent in great detail. This personal and organizational information provides a context for understanding your messages to them.

- Getting to the point quickly is not a style of communication that people in high-context cultures favour. Longer presentations and meetings allow people to get to know one another and to consider a proposal in a series of stages.

- When communicating with people from a high-context culture, give careful consideration to the age and rank of the communicator. Age and seniority tend to be valued in high-context cultures, and the status of the communicator is an important contextual factor that gives credibility to a message. Younger fast-trackers will do fine in low-context cultures where "it's the message that counts."

- Because they tend to devalue cultural context, people from low-context cultures tend to favour very detailed business contracts. For them, the meaning is in the message itself. High-context cultures place less emphasis on lengthy contracts because the context in which the deal is sealed is critical.

COMPUTER-MEDIATED COMMUNICATION

LO 10.7

Define *computer-mediated communication*, and highlight its strengths and weaknesses.

Information richness.
The potential information-carrying capacity of a communication medium.

Does communicating electronically differ from communicating face to face? This is clearly an important topic, given the pervasive use of routine email, "chat"-type decision-support software, teleconferencing, videoconferencing, and social media. A good way to begin thinking about this issue is to consider **information richness**, the potential information-carrying capacity of a communication medium.[55] Various media can be ranked in terms of their information richness. A face-to-face transmission of information is very high in richness because the sender is personally present, audio and visual channels are used, body language and verbal language are occurring, and feedback to the sender is immediate and ongoing. A phone conversation is also fairly rich, but it is limited to the audio channel, and it does not permit the observation of body language. At the other extreme, communicating via numeric computer output lacks richness because it is impersonal and uses only numeric language. Feedback on such communication might also be very slow. The chapter-opening vignette stresses the importance of rich face-to-face communication among researchers to create a synergy of ideas.

Exhibit 10.5 shows two important dimensions of information richness: the degree to which information is synchronous between senders and receivers, and the extent to which both parties can receive non-verbal and para-verbal cues. Highly synchronous communication, such as face-to-face speech, is two-way, in real time. On the low side of synchronization, memos, letters, and even emails are essentially a series of one-way messages, although email and especially texting have the clear potential for speedy response. Face-to-face interaction and videoconferencing are high in non-verbal (e.g., body language) and para-verbal (e.g., tone of voice) cues, while these are essentially absent in the text-based media. In general, the media in the upper right sector of Exhibit 10.5 (highly synchronous, high in non-verbal and para-verbal cues) exemplify the most information richness, and those in the lower left sector exhibit the least richness.

Computer-mediated communication (CMC).
Forms of communication that rely on computer technology to facilitate information exchange.

As shown in Exhibit 10.5, email, chat systems, teleconferencing, and videoconferencing are commonly classified as **computer-mediated communication (CMC)** in that

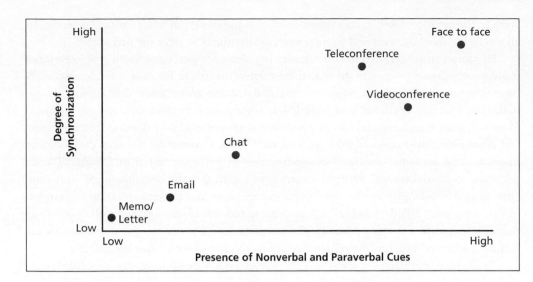

EXHIBIT 10.5
Communication media arranged according to synchronization and cue availability.

Source: Republished with permission of Elsevier Science, from Computer-mediated communication and group decision making: A meta-analysis, Boris B Baltes; Marcus W Dickson; Michael P Sherman; Cara C Bauer; Jacqueline S LaGanke, *Organizational Behavior and Human Decision Processes*, *87*, 156–179, 1985; permission conveyed through Copyright Clearance Center, Inc.

they rely on computer technology to facilitate information exchange. All of these media permit discussion and decision making without employees having to be in the same location, potentially saving time, money, and travel hassles. But does such potential efficiency result in effective communication as we defined it earlier?

Most research has focused on "chat"-type group-decision support systems that rely on text-based computer conferencing to generate ideas and make decisions. Such systems have been shown to enhance the sheer number of ideas generated when brainstorming a problem.[56] Several factors contribute to this. In electronic groups, computer memory means that people can "talk" at the same time. Also, some systems permit the anonymous generation of ideas. This means that those who are shy may be less inhibited in offering suggestions. Also, anonymity can erase perceived or actual status differences. In one study of executives, men

Computer-mediated communication includes videoconferencing.

John Fedele/Blend Images/Getty Images

were five times more likely than women to offer an initial idea in a face-to-face meeting. In an electronic meeting, men and women were equally likely to offer the first idea.[57]

By almost any criterion other than generating ideas, computer-mediated groups perform more poorly than face-to-face groups, at least when they meet for only a single session. A careful review concluded that computer-mediated decision groups generally take more time, make less effective decisions, and have less-satisfied members than face-to-face groups.[58] However, time is an issue, and computer-mediated groups gradually develop increased trust and cooperation over repeated meeting sessions.[59] What accounts for the slow development of trust using computer-mediated communication (a point we noted in Chapter 7 with reference to virtual teams)? Some observers have found that the detachment of electronic communication can give rise to rude, impulsive messages and to the expression of extreme views, sometimes called "flaming." Others have noted that electronic media elicit informal modes of expression that are prone to misinterpretation. The consequent use of emotional icons ("emoticons") such as the smiley face ☺ can go only so far as trust builders.[60]

In addition, the lack of non-verbal cues may make it difficult to recognize subtle trends toward consensus. Finally, although computer mediation can reduce status differences and promote equality, people can still detect some differences in text-based messages. For instance, people exhibit some degree of accuracy in deducing whether a message was sent by a man or a woman![61]

As suggested by Exhibit 10.5, email may be even more prone to miscommunication than chat formats. Jason Kruger and colleagues found that people strongly overestimated their skill in both communicating and interpreting sarcasm, humour, and emotions via email. They concluded that people tend to be egocentric and exaggerate the extent to which others share their own perspective.[62] Other research suggests that people may interpret some emails as more emotionally negative than they really are.[63] All of this would apply to social media as well.

As a form of computer-mediated communication, social media such as Facebook, Twitter, and YouTube have some special properties that deserve our attention. Although public social media sites are frequently used externally in support of marketing and public relations, the impact of such media on behaviour within organizations and at the interface between employees and their organizations has only recently received attention.

Observers have noted that social media pose both challenges and opportunities for organizations and their members. One challenge posed by social media is that they can be addictive to the extent that employees engage in "cyberloafing" while at work, updating their Facebook profiles rather than serving customers. A recent large-scale study found that cyberloafers tended to be younger, extraverted, better-educated males. People with demanding and challenging jobs and those working in organizations with policies prohibiting social media use at work reported less cyberloafing.[64] Furthermore, social media tend to blur the distinction between the work and non-work domains, and (unlike the communication episode shown in Exhibit 10.1) senders may not be aware of just who receives their messages. Thus, as recounted in the Experiential Exercise and the Case Study at the end of the chapter, employees have been fired for derogatory Facebook postings about their employers and judged to be faking illness or unfit for hiring because of leisure activities portrayed on Facebook. Many organizations have formal social media policies, and employees should be familiar with them.

On the other side of the coin, there is growing recognition that social media can play a positive role in organizational communication, aiding in problem solving and innovation. Some of the earliest applications were by interns and new university grads at firms such as Microsoft and IBM using public sites such as LinkedIn, Facebook, and Twitter to exchange information about work and co-workers. Various security concerns, such as losing information to competitors or blurring the distinction between work and personal life, has led many organizations to establish private **enterprise social media** platforms that are restricted to organizational members.[65] These platforms tend to mimic public sites such as Facebook in

Enterprise social media.
A private work-related social media platform that is accessible only by organizational members.

look and functionality, but they can also feature blogs, wikis, and document sharing. Their essential feature is the capacity to record, store, and share ideas such that they can be accessed by all organizational members. Ideally, this creates new social networks among employees and facilitates social learning and innovation. Your post a month ago may solve my problem today!

Telus, the telecommunications company based in Burnaby, British Columbia, employs an enterprise social media platform called TELUS Xchange. It is used to encourage a "media mindset and a culture of collaboration."[66] A typical scenario: an employee encounters an unfamiliar problem when doing a custom home installation. She videos the issue, narrates the problem, and uploads it to Xchange. In ten minutes, employees across the country advise her of potential solutions. The video is then tagged, archived, and available to others with an easy search. This is what is meant by social learning.

To conclude, a good rule to follow is that less routine communication requires richer communication media.[67] Memos, reports, emails, and web portals are fine for recurrent, non-controversial, impersonal communication in which information is merely being disseminated. Important decisions, intended changes, controversial messages, and emotional issues generally call for richer (i.e., face-to-face or video) media. The non-routine nature of scientific discovery prompted the Sick Kids Hospital to opt for an architectural design that would encourage rich face-to-face interaction.

PERSONAL APPROACHES TO IMPROVING COMMUNICATION

Review personal strategies and organizational initiatives aimed at enhancing communication.

More and more people are learning that developing their communication skills is just as sensible as developing their accounting skills, their computer skills, or anything else that will give them an edge in the job market. When you communicate well, people generally respond to you in a positive way, even if they are not totally happy with your message. Poor communication can provoke a negative response that leads to even *poorer* communication. This happens when the other party becomes resistant, defensive, deceptive, or hostile.

Basic Principles of Effective Communication

Let's consider some basic principles of effective face-to-face communication.[68]

Learn About Yourself
Communicating Supportively

TAKE THE TIME Good communication takes time. Managers in particular have to devote extra effort to developing good rapport with employees. Not taking adequate time often leads to the selection of the wrong communication medium. One of your authors has seen a "don't do this" memo sent to 130 employees because two of them committed some offence. Of course, the memo irritated 128 people, and the two offenders really did not grasp the problem. The boss should have taken the time to meet face to face with the two people in question.

BE ACCEPTING OF THE OTHER PERSON Try to be accepting of the other person as an individual who has the right to have feelings and perceptions that may differ from your own. You can accept the person even if you are unhappy with something that he or she has done. Having empathy with others (trying to put yourself in their place and see things from their perspective) will increase your acceptance of them. Acting superior or arrogant works against acceptance.

DO NOT CONFUSE THE PERSON WITH THE PROBLEM Although you should be accepting of others, it is generally useful to be problem oriented rather than person oriented. For example, suppose an employee does something that you think might have offended a client. It is probably better to focus on this view of the problem than to impute motives to the employee ("Don't you care about the client's needs?"). The focus should be on what the person did, not who the person is. Along these same lines, try to be more descriptive rather than evaluative. Again, focus on what exactly the employee did to the client, not how bad the consequences are.

SAY WHAT YOU FEEL   More specifically, be sure that your words, thoughts, feelings, and actions exhibit **congruence**—that they all contain the same message. A common problem is soft-pedalling bad news, such as saying that someone's job is probably secure when you feel that it probably is not. However, congruence can also be a problem with positive messages. Some managers find it notoriously difficult to praise excellent work or even to reinforce routine good performance. Congruence can be thought of as honesty or authenticity, but you should not confuse it with brutal frankness or cruelty. Also, remember that in some high-context cultures, "saying what you feel" is done very indirectly. Still, the words and feelings are congruent in their own context.

LISTEN ACTIVELY   Effective communication requires good listening. People who are preoccupied with themselves or who simply hear what they expect to hear are not good listeners. Good listening improves the accuracy of your reception, but it also shows acceptance of the speaker and encourages self-reflection on his or her part. Good listening is not a passive process. Rather, good communicators employ active listening to get the most out of an interaction. Techniques of **active listening** include the following:

- *Watch your body language.* Sit up, lean forward, and maintain eye contact with the speaker. This shows that you are paying attention and are interested in what the speaker is saying. (This is another aspect of congruence.)

- *Paraphrase what the speaker means.* Reflecting back what the speaker has said shows interest and ensures that you have received the correct message.

- *Show empathy.* When appropriate, show that you understand the feelings that the speaker is trying to convey. A phrase such as "Yes, that client has irritated me, too" might fill the bill.

- *Ask questions.* Have people repeat, clarify, or elaborate what they are saying. Avoid asking leading questions that are designed to pursue some agenda that *you* have.

- *Wait out pauses.* Do not feel pressured to talk when the speaker goes silent. This discourages him or her from elaborating.

GIVE TIMELY AND SPECIFIC FEEDBACK   When you initiate communication to provide others with feedback about their behaviour, do it soon and be explicit. Speed maximizes the reinforcement potential of the message, and explicitness maximizes its usefulness to the recipient. Say *what* was good about the person's presentation to the client, and say it soon.

When in Rome...

You are off to a pretty good start in cross-cultural communication if you can do a careful job of applying the basic communication principles we discussed above. However, people's basic skills sometimes actually *deteriorate* when they get nervous about a cross-cultural encounter. Let's cover a few more principles for those situations.

ASSUME DIFFERENCES UNTIL YOU KNOW OTHERWISE   The material we presented earlier on cross-cultural communication and that in Chapter 3 on workforce diversity should sensitize you to the general tendency for cross-cultural differences to exist. In a cross-cultural situation, caution dictates we should assume that such differences exist until we are proven wrong. Remember, we have a tendency to project our own feelings and beliefs onto ambiguous targets (Chapter 3), leading us to ignore differences. Be particularly alert when

Congruence. A condition in which a person's words, thoughts, feelings, and actions all contain the same message.

Active listening. A technique for improving the accuracy of information reception by paying close attention to the sender.

dealing with proficient English speakers from cultures that emphasize harmony and avoidance of conflict (e.g., Japan). Their good English will tempt you to think that they think like you do, and their good manners will inhibit them from telling you otherwise.

RECOGNIZE DIFFERENCES WITHIN CULTURES Appreciating differences between cultures can sometimes blind us to the differences among people within a culture. This, of course, is what stereotypes do (Chapter 3). Remember, your German employees will have as many different personalities, skills, and problems as your North American employees. Remember, too, that there are occupational and social class differences in other countries just like there are at home, although they can be harder to decipher. (This is why one of your authors once shook hands with the chef at a French business school, mistaking him for the dean!)

WATCH YOUR LANGUAGE (AND THEIRS) Unless the person with whom you are communicating is very fluent in English, speak particularly clearly, slowly, and simply. Avoid clichés, jargon, and slang. Consider how mystifying phrases such as "I'm all ears," "Let's get rolling," and "So long" must be.[69] By the same token, do not assume that those who can speak your language well are smarter, more skilled, or more honest than those who cannot.

ORGANIZATIONAL APPROACHES TO IMPROVING COMMUNICATION

Toronto's Sick Kids Hospital relied on innovative architecture to facilitate communication among medical researchers. In this section, we discuss some other organizational techniques that can improve communication. We consider other techniques in Chapter 13 (concerning conflict reduction) and Chapter 15 (with regard to organizational development).

Provision of Explanations

Organizations sometimes have to enact controversial policies that have the potential to spark much employee resistance. Examples might involve restructuring, layoffs, pay rollbacks, smoking bans, or affirmative action programs. Often, there are good reasons for the introduction of such policies. However, in line with the mum effect, many organizations simply announce such policies with little or no explanation, evidently fearing to dwell on negative news or provoke lawsuits. This is a bad idea, and there are communication approaches that can greatly improve the perceived fairness of controversial policies. Notions of procedural and interactional fairness (Chapter 4) underlie such effective communication.

Two factors are critical to the perceived fairness of controversial policies: the adequacy of the explanation and the style in which it is delivered.[70] Adequate explanations are specific and detailed, highlighting the reasons for the policy, how the decision was made, and the benefits that will accrue from it. Equally important, the message should be truthful, sincere, respectful, and sensitive. When appropriate, the communicator should express sincere remorse for having to implement the policy (e.g., a pay rollback) and acknowledge any suffering that the policy might cause. All of this requires the use of a rich communication medium, such as a personal appearance by the CEO or other high organizational representative. A research review concluded that an adequate explanation for a policy decision reduced employees' tendencies to retaliate by 43 percent, and that an inadequate explanation is seen as less fair than no explanation at all.[71]

360-Degree Feedback

Traditionally, employee performance appraisal has been viewed as an exercise in downward communication in which the boss tells the employee how he or she is doing. More recently, performance appraisal has become a two-way communication process in which employees are also able to have upward impact concerning their appraisal. Most recently, some firms have expanded the communication channels in performance appraisal to include not only superior and self-ratings but also ratings by subordinates, peers, and clients or customers. This is called *multisource* or **360-degree feedback**. Firms that use it include Air Canada and Bell Canada.

360-degree feedback. Performance appraisal that uses the input of supervisors, employees, peers, and clients or customers of the appraised individual.

The 360-degree system usually focuses on required behavioural competencies rather than bottom-line performance. It is usually used for employee development rather than salary determination. It is possible that the various sources of feedback could contradict each other, and ratees may need some assistance in putting all this input together. However, in a well-designed 360-degree system, the various information sources ideally should provide unique data about a person's performance. Research shows that 360-degree feedback leads to subsequent performance improvements.[72]

Employee Surveys and Survey Feedback

Surveys of the attitudes and opinions of current employees can provide a useful means of upward communication. Since surveys are usually conducted with questionnaires that provide for anonymous responses, employees should feel free to voice their genuine views. A good **employee survey** contains questions that reliably tap employee concerns and also provide information that is useful for practical purposes. Survey specialists must summarize (encode) results in a manner that is easily decoded by management. Surveys are especially useful when they are administered periodically. In this case, managers can detect changes in employee feelings that may deserve attention.

Employee survey. An anonymous questionnaire that enables employees to state their candid opinions and attitudes about an organization and its practices.

When survey results are fed back to employees, along with management responses and any plans for changes, this feedback should enhance downward communication. Survey feedback shows employees that management has heard and considered their comments. Plans for changes in response to survey concerns indicate a commitment to two-way communication.[73] In Chapter 15 you will learn more about employee surveys.

Suggestion Systems

Suggestion systems. Programs designed to enhance upward communication by soliciting ideas for improved work operations from employees.

Suggestion systems are designed to enhance upward communication by soliciting ideas for improved work operations from employees. They represent a formal attempt to encourage useful ideas and prevent their filtering through the chain of command. The simplest example of a suggestion system involves the use of a suggestion box into which employees put written ideas for improvements (usually anonymously). This simple system is usually not very effective, since there is no tangible incentive for making a submission and no clear mechanism to show that management has considered a submission.

Much better are programs that *reward* employees for suggestions that are actually adopted and provide feedback as to how management evaluated each suggestion. For simple suggestions, a flat fee is usually paid (perhaps $500). For complex suggestions of a technical nature that might result in substantial savings to the firm, a percentage of the anticipated savings is often awarded (perhaps several thousand dollars). An example of such a suggestion might be how to reduce paper use and promote environmental sustainability. When strong publicity follows the adopted suggestions (such as explaining them in the organization's employee newsletter), downward communication is also enhanced, since employees receive information about the kind of innovations desired.

Telephone Hotlines, Intranets, and Webcasts

Many organizations have adopted *telephone hotlines* to further communication. Some hotlines use a news format to present company information. News may be presented live at prearranged times or recorded for 24-hour availability. Such hotlines prove especially valuable at times of crisis, such as during storms or strikes.[74] Other hotlines serve as query systems, in that employees can call in for answers to their questions, either by using an automated attendant or by talking live to support personnel (e.g., Human Resources). In some instances, companies use hotlines for ethics reporting, so that employees can call in to report unethical behaviour they have either experienced or witnessed. These hotlines can support anonymous reporting. McMaster University uses such a system, which is operated by the firm EthicsPoint.[75]

Many companies use their corporate intranet portals and enterprise social media as a means of communicating important announcements or engaging employees in electronic discussions (e.g., corporate blogs). These provide an important information source on various topics of interest to employees and can also allow employees to communicate information to the organization, such as changes of address or benefits enrolment.[76]

One excellent technique for fostering communication is webcasting. Corporate webcasting constitutes a rich communication medium that allows for the broadcasting of both audio and video and can reach employees located anywhere in the world. Multipoint webcasting allows for a number of presenters who can be located in multiple cities. This medium is especially good for general information sessions, training, and new product introduction. The synchronous, interactive nature of webcasts supports audience engagement either through written questions, audio questions, or, where possible, video interaction. Employees who missed the original webcast or want to review what they learned can watch the webcast at their leisure.

Management Training

Managers face a fundamental challenge in balancing social-emotional and task demands in their communication with employees, and proper training can improve the communication skills of managers. Notice the specific use of the word "skills" here. Vague lectures about the importance of good communication simply do not tell managers how to communicate better. However, isolating specific communication skills and giving the boss an opportunity to practise these skills should have positive effects. The manager who has confidence in how to handle delicate matters should be better able to handle the balance between social-emotional and task demands.

Effective training programs often present videotaped models correctly handling a typical communication problem. Managers then role-play the problem and are reinforced by the trainers when they exhibit effective skills. At General Electric, for example, typical communication problems that this kind of training addresses have included discussing undesirable work habits, reviewing work performance, discussing salary changes, and dealing with employee-initiated discussions.[77] North Carolina's Center for Creative Leadership incorporates 360-degree feedback data from peers, superiors, and subordinates into its training.

THE MANAGER'S NOTEBOOK

Communicating Diversity and Inclusion at Ryder

1. Overall, Ryder used a variety of communication media to establish and reinforce the importance of D&I at the grassroots level. The key is to repeat the message through a series of mutually reinforcing channels. The firm took the unusual and old-school approach of mailing to every employee's home a letter from the CEO that explained Ryder's D&I vision and goals. The letter invited employees to view a more comprehensive video presentation by him on the organization's website, and it stressed the importance of employee involvement in the initiative. Communication from the CEO shows that D&I has top management support. Importantly, to foster two-way communication, the Office of Diversity also established an email address "Ask Diversity and Inclusion" to answer employee questions and take suggestions.

2. To reinforce the CEO's message, Ryder used branding techniques to establish D&I as a viable and important "brand" in the company. This included a distinct logo and a slogan ("Diversity and Inclusion: It Starts with You"). These were then featured in lapel pins and email stationery, and a special section of the corporate magazine *Ryder People* was dedicated to highlighting diversity and inclusion news. Importantly, a D&I toolkit was prepared to aid managers in introducing and discussing D&I with employees. Managers will vary in their comfort in dealing with D&I issues, and such a toolkit facilitates self-confidence in communicating about this vital subject.

MyManagementLab **Study, practise, and explore real management situations with these helpful resources:**

- **Interactive Lesson Presentations:** Work through interactive presentations and assessments to test your knowledge of management concepts.
- **PIA (Personal Inventory Assessments):** Enhance your ability to connect with key concepts through these engaging, self-reflection assessments.
- **Study Plan:** Check your understanding of chapter concepts with self-study quizzes.
- **Videos:** Learn more about the management practices and strategies of real companies.
- **Simulations:** Practise decision-making in simulated management environments.

P I A PERSONAL INVENTORY ASSESSMENT

LEARNING OBJECTIVES CHECKLIST

10.1 *Communication* is the process by which information is exchanged between a sender and a receiver. Effective communication involves getting the right information to the right people in a timely manner. Although much routine communication can occur via the chain of command, the chain tends to be slow and prone to filtering. It also ignores informal communication.

10.2 *Voice* is expressing constructive disagreement with organizational practices. It is most likely in an atmosphere of *psychological safety* that encourages social risk taking. The *mum effect* (the reluctance to transmit bad news) discourages voice.

10.3 The *grapevine* is an organization's informal communication network. Key physical locations or jobs that require movement around the organization encourage certain members to pass on information. The grapevine can be useful to the organization, and it often transmits information accurately. However, it becomes problematic when rumours (unverified beliefs) circulate.

10.4 Verbal language that is tailored to the needs of a particular occupation or organization is known as *jargon*. While jargon aids communication between experienced co-workers, it can often prove confusing for new organizational members and people outside the organization. *Non-verbal communication* is the transmission of messages by a medium other than speech or writing. One major form is *body language*, which involves body movement or the placement of the body in relation to the receiver. Much body language is subtle and automatic, communicating factors such as liking, interest, and status differences. Other forms of non-verbal communication involve office decoration, office arrangement, and the clothing worn at work.

10.5 Communication styles between men and women differ. Speaking generally, women are more inclined to ask questions, make apologies, and give compliments; men are more likely to take credit, act confident, and express opposition.

10.6 Communication across cultures can be difficult, owing to obvious language differences but also to less obvious differences in non-verbal style, social conventions, and matters of etiquette. In low-context cultures, individuals tend to interpret messages more literally than in high-context cultures, where issues surrounding a message are more critical to understanding it. When communicating cross-culturally, assume cultural differences until you know otherwise, recognize differences within cultures, and use simple language.

10.7 *Computer-mediated communication* is communication that relies on computer technology to facilitate information exchange. Examples include email, chat systems, teleconferencing, and social media. Computer-mediated communication is useful for disseminating routine messages and soliciting ideas, but richer (e.g., face-to-face) communication media are superior for non-routine decision tasks and messages.

10.8 Personal approaches to improving communication include taking time, being accepting of others, concentrating on the problem, saying what you feel, listening actively, and giving timely and specific feedback. Organizational approaches to improving communication include 360-degree feedback, employee surveys, suggestion systems, telephone hotlines, corporate intranets, webcasts, and management training.

DISCUSSION QUESTIONS

1. Why is computer-mediated communication attractive? What are its problems?

2. List six reasons why employees might respond with silence rather than voice to an organizational problem. Then, for each reason, explain how the organization could act to encourage voice.

3. Discuss the pros and cons of the existence of the grapevine in organizations. Suppose an organization wanted to "kill" the grapevine. How easy do you think this would be?

4. Under what conditions might body language or clothing have a strong communicative effect? When might the effect be weaker?

5. Debate: As more women move into management positions in organizations, the gender differences in communication between men and women will eventually disappear, and so will communication problems.

INTEGRATIVE DISCUSSION QUESTIONS

1. What role do perceptions play in gender differences in communication? Refer to the perceptual system in Chapter 3 and use its components—the perceiver, the target person, and the situation surrounding the communication—to explain how differences in communication styles between men and women can result in misunderstandings and inaccurate perceptions. What effect might these misunderstandings and inaccurate perceptions have on gender stereotypes?

2. How does a manager's leadership style affect manager–employee communication? Refer to the theories of leadership described in Chapter 9 (e.g., ethical and authentic leadership, leadership traits, behaviours, situational theories, participative leadership, and LMX theory) and explain their implications for effective manager–employee communication.

ON-THE-JOB CHALLENGE QUESTION

Carol Bartz and Yahoo!

Carol Bartz, Yahoo's hard-driving CEO, was fired "over the telephone" in a conversation with Chairman of the Board Roy Bostock. The firing came with more than a year left on her contract, as Yahoo continued to lose ground to Google and failed to recognize the competitive threat posed by Facebook. Bartz was well known for her abrasive, confrontational communication style, and she was especially known for her extreme use of profanity. A number of observers wondered whether Bartz's salty language was an issue because she is a woman.

Was it appropriate to fire Carol Bartz via a telephone call? Why or why not? Would a profane communication style be more likely to damage the reputation of a male or female CEO, and why? Do expectations play a role?

Sources: Grinberg, E. (2011, September 12). Carol Bartz, swearing and a —— in the workplace, www.CNN.com.; Efrati, A. & Lublin, J.S. (2011, September 7). Yahoo ousts Bartz as CEO, www.wsj.com.

EXPERIENTIAL EXERCISE

Communication Technology and Media Dilemmas

The advent of various forms of advanced communication technology and associated social media have benefited organizations and their employees in many ways, but they have also led to an assortment of problems and conflicts. Several themes are apparent in the scenarios presented below. For one thing, contemporary communication media have blurred the distinction between the work and non-work domains. Second, the scenarios suggest communication contradictions—Facebook postings could be grounds for firing, but the medium can also facilitate work-related communication. Third, much contemporary communication occurs in a context in which one is not sure just who the receiver might be.

The exercise can be conducted in several ways: Students can independently prepare their reflections on the scenarios for class discussion. Alternatively, learning teams can discuss one or more scenarios and report their reflections to the class. Finally, the instructor might organize a debate around each scenario. In any case, use your imagination when reflecting on the scenarios. How would you feel if you were an employee in the scenario? How would you feel if you were a manager?

1. The American Lifeguard Association has recorded a notable increase in complaints concerning lifeguards texting on the job, and some drowning tragedies have reportedly occurred at pools where such texting occurred. Many lifeguards are students who evidently feel the need to "stay connected" when at work, even though lifeguard training specifies vigilant 10-second scanning cycles of the water. Incidents of lifeguards concealing forbidden cellphones have been reported. Of course, it can be pretty boring sitting up there in a lifeguard's chair all day! What do you think about this issue?

2. A survey of Canadian companies found that 57 percent block access to online sites for shopping. Others reported keeping tabs on the frequency of use of such sites by their employees. On one hand, it seems reasonable to insist that workers do their personal shopping on their own time. On the other hand, many people are so overwhelmed by dual career juggling, child care logistics, and taking assignments home that a few spare minutes at work might be their only opportunity to shop. What's wrong with hitting e-Bay or Amazon during your break?

3. Would you hire BlazinWeedClown@mail.com? In a study of 15 000 online job applications for distribution centre positions, 3 percent of email addresses were judged antisocial (referencing insanity, sex, drugs, or meanness, e.g., insanekid33) and 22 percent were judged otherwise unprofessional (referencing hobbies, immaturity, popular culture, or nerdiness, e.g., cyborg22). The study also found that observers readily made attributions about the intelligence, professionalism, and conscientiousness of

these email applicants. Such judgments could, of course, affect an applicant's chances of being hired. But should they?

4. Two employees were fired by British Columbia's West Coast Mazda for making postings on their personal Facebook pages that were critical of the company and its management. Although the general public did not have access to the postings, nearly 500 Facebook friends, including former and current West Coast employees, did so. The comments, some lewd and others hinting at workplace violence, were deemed "offensive, insulting, and disrespectful" by an arbitration board, which upheld the dismissals as indicative of insubordination. Was this just natural, private grumbling about the workplace, or was it grounds to be fired?

5. PhoneDog, a web-based company that provides news, reviews, and advice concerning mobile phones and service providers, sued a former employee for taking his 17 000 Twitter followers with him when he changed jobs. The company contended that the followers comprised a customer database and that they had invested substantial resources to leverage social media to enhance awareness of their brand. Hence, the list was their "property." Is this list of followers some proprietary trade secret, or is it a list of people with too much time on their hands? And who "owns" it?

6. Atos, a European IT services firm with 74 000 employees in 42 countries, announced that it would put in place a "zero email policy" for internal communications, claiming that email contains too much (90 percent) time-wasting trivia. Instead, its CEO touted the advantages of communicating in person, by phone, by text, or via various real-time social media such as Facebook or business collaboration software. Supporters of the plan noted that younger people had already deserted email for more social media and texting. Critiques asserted that people will "waste" time communicating no matter what media or technology are used, as it's just human nature. What do you say? And is email passé for internal business communications?

7. Do U txt @ wrk? Some members of the police SWAT team in Ontario, California, did, and it got them into hot water. The officers were given department-issued pagers and were permitted to use them for personal texting if they reimbursed the department. Fed up with doing the account-

ing to get reimbursement, and surprised by the volume of personal texts (in a month, only 57 out of one officer's 456 texts were work related), the department accessed the texts via the mobile carrier. They contained a good bit of sexually explicit content. The department had a formal policy to monitor emails but had not explicitly mentioned pagers. The officers and a lower level court claimed that this was a violation of privacy rights. Under appeal, the U.S. Supreme Court was unanimous that the employer was within its rights to access the texts. Many employees are issued pagers, mobile phones, and so on for the convenience of the employer. Should employees expect some privacy if they use them occasionally for personal purposes?

8. A Quebec IBM employee on long-term disability leave for major depression was surprised when the company's insurance company terminated her benefits and declared her fit to work. It appeared that their decision was partly influenced by photos on her Facebook page showing her cavorting on a beach, enjoying a birthday celebration, and visiting a male strip bar. Is it fair game to use this social media source as evidence concerning a medical claim? Did the poster use good judgment?

9. Writer Bob Green puts it succinctly: In the days before cellphones, would an employer permit an employee to install a personal phone line in the office to make personal calls at will? Certainly not, but the advent of cellphones has effectively led to an analogous situation. Green recounts a series of complaints from store managers, restaurant proprietors, and factory bosses, some of whom have instituted no-cell policies. Especially worrisome are reports of extensive cell use by hospital staff, even in the operating room. Of course, as Green notes, some of these same employers see nothing unusual about texting or calling employees after work hours or on the weekend, expecting 24/7 responses. How big of an issue is this? Should personal cellphone use at work be prohibited or restricted in any way?

Sources: Exercise prepared by Gary Johns. (1) Tedeschi, B. (2010, September 10). Texts from lifeguard chair are raising concerns over safety. *The New York Times*, A21; (2) Simons, P. (2011, December 11). Personal browsing a workplace issue. *The Gazette* (Montreal), D20; (3) Blackhurst, E., Congemi, P., Meyer, J., & Sachau, D.

(2011). Should you hire BlazinWeedClown@Mail.Com? *The Industrial-Organizational Psychologist*, *49*(2), 27–37; (4) Ringseis, E. (2011). Careful what you write when you LOL. *The Canadian Industrial-Organizational Psychologist*, *27*(2), 6–7; (5) Booth, R. (2011, December 28). Company sues ex-worker for Twitter followers. *The Globe and Mail*, B10; (6) Staff. (2011, December 16). Work: Life without email. *THE WEEK*; (7) Groscup, J. (2010, May). RU

txting at wrk? *Monitor on Psychology*, 22; (8) Vicini, J. (2010, June 17). Court allows search of text messages on pager. Reuters, www.reuters.com; (9) Staff. (2009, November 21). Depressed woman loses benefits over Facebook photos. CBC News, www.cbc.ca/news; (10) Green, B. (2012, January 7). Is 2012 the year to hang up the phone? CNN opinion, www.CNN.com.

CASE INCIDENT

Email Madness

The email just said "Cancel it." Carol Graves couldn't believe her eyes. Carol was a marketing coordinator for Monkland Pharmaceuticals. One of her duties was to organize a professional development visiting speaker series for her marketing colleagues, mostly featuring prominent university professors or health care professionals. Given how busy people were, it was very hard to get a commitment from speakers and to schedule the talks at times that were suitable for all. Even getting a proper room for the speakers' presentations was difficult, due to competition for meeting space. The "cancel it" email had come from Carol's boss, Anastasia Bulos, when Carol had informed her (by email) that the monthly coordination meeting that Anastasia had just announced conflicted with one of Carol's hard-gotten scheduled speakers.

In response to the "cancel it" message, Carol had composed a heated message that accused Anastasia of undermining her, exhibiting professional disinterest, and ignoring the unit events calendar. Just before Carol was about to hit the send icon, a ping alerted her to another email from Anastasia. The sole message consisted of "☺". The "cancel it" message had been a joke! Shortly thereafter, Anastasia announced a new date for the monthly meeting that did not conflict with the planned speaker.

1. Communication problems can occur in any medium, but what particular problems with email are apparent in this incident?

2. What are some informal "rules" about using email that might avoid the problems illustrated in incidents of this nature?

CASE STUDY

Facebook (A)

Miranda Shaw was stymied. She had been on the verge of hiring a highly talented recent business school graduate, Rick Parsons, as a senior analyst for her project team. It had been a choice between Parsons and Deborah Jones, another very promising hire. Both Parsons and Jones had graduated from the same highly ranked business school that Shaw had attended, had the appropriate work backgrounds, and had performed well in their multiple rounds of interviews. From their conversations, Shaw believed either one would be a good choice for the company. While she had had a hard time deciding, she was leaning toward hiring Parsons because of his leadership skills and his reputation for tireless energy and great communication skills. Before making her final decision, Shaw—almost in desperation, because she needed to submit her recommendation to human

resources immediately—had "Googled" both of the candidates. What she had discovered about Parsons both on-line and at Facebook.com, while not necessarily a deal-breaker, was disturbing enough that she had to rethink her opinion.

Shaw was a manager at a leading consulting firm. She had worked her way up from intern after four years and was on the fast track to making partner. Her company was a special place and, as she had seen over the past few years, it took a special type of consultant to work there. She remembered plenty of cases where new hires had left the company in the first few months because they did not fit in with the high-energy and high-commitment work environment. She had seen several projects delayed or worse because of personnel issues. This high turnover was not good for the company, because it invested significant time, energy, and funds to train and mentor new hires. Shaw believed in the adage that "you are only as good as the people who work for you," and she knew that making the right hiring decisions was critical to her success at the firm. Shaw had to take these factors into consideration as she decided between two equally qualified candidates for the position.

In her web search, Shaw was initially impressed with Parsons. He was obviously very involved in non-profit work and had won a number of community service awards. But she then discovered his Facebook page and found herself quite dismayed. There were several pictures of Parsons with his fraternity brothers; in most, they were drinking, smoking cigarettes, and—in his own words—"smokin' blunts." This term, Shaw learned after a little research, meant smoking cigars hollowed out and stuffed with marijuana.

She then turned her Google efforts to Jones. She did not discover any personal information about Jones, nor did she find Jones on Facebook. There were only work-related sites that listed Jones as an effective project member.

Shaw sighed in dismay. She had been poised, only an hour earlier, to submit her recommendation to hire Parsons. Now she was not sure what to do.

QUESTIONS

1. Discuss how the web and new media such as Facebook have (a) aided and (b) complicated organizational communication. Be sure to consider the implications of sending a message when you do not know who the receiver might be.
2. Suppose that Miranda had just heard a rumour about Rick's activities as opposed to seeing them on Facebook. Would her reaction have been the same? Incorporate the concept of media richness in framing your answer.
3. Do the prominence of Rick on the web and the relative absence of Deborah reflect gender differences in communication?
4. What should Miranda do?

Facebook (B)

Based on her Google search and the Facebook.com photographs, Miranda Shaw concluded that Rick Parsons would not fit in with the professional work environment at the company and of the team in particular. She knew how much time and money could be wasted on hiring the wrong person. She concluded that she should offer the position to Deborah Jones.

While she was mostly proud of her resourcefulness, Shaw was a little uneasy about her decision. Although information on the internet was public and people controlled what they posted online, Shaw was not certain that it was fair to use web information in her hiring decision. After all, the candidate had not offered it willingly, and Shaw had not told Parsons or Jones that she would be researching them online. She did not, however, have either the time or resources to waste on hiring another bad fit. She was sure that most employers used Google and other internet sources in hiring, though few admitted it. Nonetheless, she was not comfortable with her research methods and wondered how long this discomfort would last.

QUESTIONS

5. Was it ethical for Miranda to avail herself of these indirect, web-based sources of communication to find out about the job applicants?
6. If Miranda hires Deborah, should she explain to Rick the issue that damaged his chances? Why or why not?
7. If Miranda does tell Rick, how should she do so? In answering, consider the chapter sections Basic Principles of Effective Communication and Provision of Explanations.

11

DECISION MAKING

LEARNING OBJECTIVES

After reading Chapter 11, you should be able to:

11.1 Define *decision making*, and differentiate well-structured and ill-structured problems.

11.2 Compare and contrast perfectly *rational decision making* with decision making *under bounded rationality*.

11.3 Discuss the impact of *framing* and *cognitive biases* on the decision process.

11.4 Explain the process of *escalation of commitment* to an apparently failing course of action.

11.5 Consider how emotions and mood affect decision making.

11.6 Summarize the pros and cons of using groups to make decisions, with attention to the *groupthink* phenomenon and risk assessment.

11.7 Discuss contemporary approaches to improving organizational decision making.

JPMORGAN CHASE LOSES $2 BILLION

In May of 2012, JPMorgan Chase CEO Jaime Dimon disclosed that the bank had incurred a $2-billion trading loss. As early as 2007, some of its top investment bankers and risk managers had questioned the bank's risk exposure as a result of the incredibly complex and arcane trading practices that were mainly centred in the London-based chief investment office, a unit that was originally and ironically designated to manage or hedge risk. These practices, involving derivative positions and credit-default swaps, were not well comprehended by senior management in New York. "There were many errors, sloppiness, and bad judgment," Dimon said as the company's stock fell in extended trading. "These were egregious mistakes; they were self-inflicted." Some observers, however, felt that Dimon himself had encouraged the riskier speculative trading, motivated by high initial investment profits accrued by the office, and it was he who had changed the mandate of the office from risk management to profit seeking, hiring a new breed of traders and offering incentives that encouraged risk. The doubter's concerns had been dismissed.

Dimon, known by some as the King of Wall Street, was credited with doing a good job of steering the bank through the 2008–2009 financial crisis, performance that was in line with its reputation for superior risk management. However, in London, a trader known as "the London whale" had amassed derivative positions of over $100 billion, and they had to be liquidated at fire-sale prices. Dimon had dismissed early media reports concerning this trader's massive credit-default gambles, in part due to reassurances from the head of the London office, Ina Drew. Some of the core problem stemmed from over-reliance on quantitative trading models that failed to take into account changes in the marketplace. In addition, the insularity of the London office and the complexity if the investment practices made oversight more difficult. Finally, Mr. Dimon at this point was extremely busy dealing with the losses stemming from the bad mortgages that had led to the earlier financial crisis and with the threat of new regulations designed to make the banking industry more accountable.

Bad decision making cost
JPMorgan Chase $2 billion.

© Brendan McDermid / Reuters Pictures

Erratic trading sessions featuring big gains and even bigger losses occurred in March and April in advance of Mr. Dimon's May announcement of the loss. The London traders increased their gambles rather than reducing them, trying to make up for prior losses. The market smelled blood, and the massively negative result sullied the reputation of the bank and its top management. Many intelligent observers wondered how America's biggest bank could have let this happen.[1]

At JPMorgan Chase, how could so many people misjudge the risks and make such a series of apparently bad decisions? We will find out in this chapter. First, we will define decision making and present a model of a rational decision-making process. As we work through this model, we will be especially concerned with the practical limitations of rationality. After this, we will investigate the use of groups to make decisions. Finally, the chapter closes with a description of some techniques to improve decision making.

WHAT IS DECISION MAKING?

Consider the following questions that might arise in a variety of organizational settings:

- How much inventory should our store carry?
- Where should we locate the proposed community mental health centre?
- Should I remain at this job or accept another?
- How many classes of Philosophy 200 should our department offer next semester?
- Should our diplomats attend the summit conference?

Common sense tells us that someone is going to have to do some decision making to answer such questions. **Decision making** is the process of developing a commitment to some course of action.[2] Three things are noteworthy about this definition. First, decision making involves making a *choice* among several action alternatives—the store can carry more or less inventory, and the mental health centre can be located at the north or south end of town. Second, decision making is a *process* that involves more than simply the final choice among alternatives—if you decide to accept the offer of a new job, we want to know *how* this decision was reached. Finally, the "commitment" mentioned in the definition usually involves some commitment of *resources*, such as time, money, or personnel—if the store carries a large inventory, it will tie up cash.

In addition to conceiving of decision making as the commitment of resources, we can describe it as a process of problem solving.[3] A **problem** exists when a gap is perceived between some existing state and some desired state. For example, the chairperson of the Philosophy department might observe that there is a projected increase in university enrolment for the upcoming year and that his course schedule is not completed (existing state). In addition, he might wish to adequately service the new students with Philosophy 200 classes and at the same time satisfy his dean with a timely, sensible schedule (desired state). In this case, the decision-making process involves the perception of the existing state, the conception of the desired state, and the steps that the chairperson takes to move from one state to the other.

Well-Structured Problems

For a **well-structured problem**, the existing state is clear, the desired state is clear, and how to get from one state to the other is fairly obvious. Intuitively, these problems are simple, and their solutions arouse little controversy. This is because such problems are repetitive and familiar.

- Assistant bank manager: Which of these 10 car loan applications should I approve?
- Welfare officer: How much assistance should this client receive?
- Courier: Which delivery route should I use?

Because decision making takes time and is prone to error, organizations (and individuals) attempt to program the decision making for well-structured problems. A **program** is simply a standardized way of solving a problem. As such, programs short-circuit the

decision-making process by enabling the decision maker to go directly from problem identification to solution.

Programs usually go under labels such as *rules, routines, standard operating procedures,* or *rules of thumb.* Some programs come from experience and exist only "in the head." Other programs are more formal. At UPS, drivers' routes are programmed to avoid left-hand turns so that they do not idle waiting for oncoming traffic to clear. In one year, this saved 3 million gallons of fuel and reduced emissions by 32 000 tonnes.[4] You are probably aware that routine loan applications are "scored" by banks according to a fixed formula that takes into account income, debt, previous credit, and so on.

Many of the problems encountered in organizations are well structured, and programmed decision making provides a useful means of solving these problems. However, programs are only as good as the decision-making process that led to the adoption of the program in the first place. In computer terminology, "garbage in" will result in "garbage out." For example, when the Canadian government revised the Temporary Foreign Worker Program to curb abuses in low-paying jobs such as fast-food work, it inadvertently affected the ability of universities to hire top-ranked foreign academics.[5]

Ill-Structured Problems

The extreme example of an **ill-structured problem** is one in which the existing and desired states are unclear and the method of getting to the desired state (even if clarified) is unknown. For example, a vice-president of marketing might have a vague feeling that the sales of a particular product are too low. However, she might lack precise information about the product's market share (existing state) and the market share of its most successful competitor (ideal state). In addition, she might be unaware of exactly how to increase the sales of this particular product.

Ill-structured problems are generally unique; that is, they are unusual and have not been encountered before. In addition, they tend to be complex and involve a high degree of uncertainty. As a result, they frequently arouse controversy and conflict among the people who are interested in the decision. For example, consider the following:

- Should we vaccinate the population against a new flu strain when the vaccination may have some bad side effects?
- Should we implement a risky attempt to rescue political hostages?
- In which part of the country should we build a new plant?

Ill-structured problems such as these cannot be solved with programmed decisions. Rather, the decision makers must resort to non-programmed decision making. This simply means that they are likely to try to gather more information and be more self-consciously analytical in their approach. Ill-structured problems can entail high risk and stimulate strong political considerations. There was some evidence of this in the JPMorgan Chase trading loss fiasco. We will concentrate on such ill-structured problems in this chapter.

Exhibit 11.1 presents a model of the decision process that a rational decision maker might use. When a problem is identified, a search for information is begun. This information clarifies the nature of the problem and suggests alternative solutions. These are carefully evaluated, and the best is chosen for implementation. The implemented solution is then monitored over time to ensure its immediate and continued effectiveness. If difficulties occur at any point in the process, repetition or recycling may be affected.

It might occur to you that we have not yet determined exactly what a "rational" decision maker is. Before we discuss the specific steps of the model in detail, let's contrast two forms of rationality.

Ill-structured problem.
A problem for which the existing and desired states are unclear and the method of getting to the desired state is unknown.

EXHIBIT 11.1
The rational decision-making process.

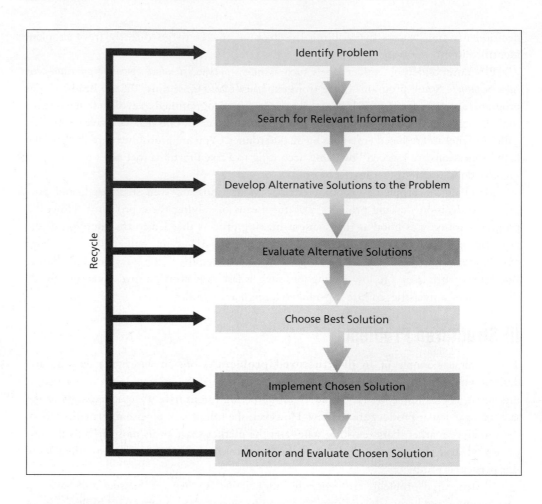

THE COMPLEAT DECISION MAKER
—A RATIONAL DECISION-MAKING MODEL

Perfect versus Bounded Rationality

Compare and contrast perfectly *rational decision making* with decision making *under bounded rationality.*

Perfect rationality. A decision strategy that is completely informed, perfectly logical, and oriented toward economic gain.

Bounded rationality. A decision strategy that relies on limited information and that reflects time constraints and political considerations.

Framing. Aspects of the presentation of information about a problem that are assumed by decision makers.

The prototype for **perfect rationality** is the familiar Economic Person (formerly Economic Man), whom we meet in the first chapter of most introductory textbooks in economics. Economic Person is the perfect, cool, calculating decision maker. More specifically, he or she

- can gather information about problems and solutions without cost and is thus completely informed;
- is perfectly logical: if solution A is preferred over solution B, and B is preferred over C, then A is necessarily preferable to C; and
- has only one criterion for decision making: economic gain.

While Economic Person is useful for theoretical purposes, the perfectly rational characteristics embodied in Economic Person do not exist in real decision makers. Nobel Prize winner Herbert Simon recognized this and suggested that managers use **bounded rationality** rather than perfect rationality.[6] That is, while they try to act rationally, they are limited in their capacity to acquire and process information. In addition, time constraints and political considerations (such as the need to please others in the organization) act as bounds to rationality.

Framing and cognitive biases both illustrate the operation of bounded rationality, as does the impact of emotions and mood on decisions. **Framing** refers to the (sometimes subtle) aspects of the presentation of information about a problem that are assumed by decision makers.[7] A frame could include assumptions about the boundaries of a problem, the possible outcomes of a decision, or the reference points used to determine if a decision is successful.[8] As we shall see, how problems and decision alternatives are framed can have a powerful impact on resulting decisions.

Cognitive biases are tendencies to acquire and process information in a particular way that is prone to error. These biases constitute assumptions and shortcuts that can improve decision-making efficiency, but they frequently lead to serious errors in judgment. We will see how they work in the following pages. For now, consider Applied Focus: *Decision Errors Lead to Target's Failure in Canada.*

Cognitive biases.
Tendencies to acquire and process information in an error-prone way.

APPLIED FOCUS

DECISION ERRORS LEAD TO TARGET'S FAILURE IN CANADA

Target's foray into Canada was seen as a natural expansion for the American retailer that for years had been a magnet for Canadians, attracting hordes of shoppers across the border. But nearly two years after its much hyped and heralded launch, Target threw in the towel, a victim, some analysts say, of bad management, poor planning, and misguided and overambitious expectations. Having lost nearly $1 billion in its first year in Canada, and facing more multimillion-dollar losses, Target announced it would discontinue its operations in Canada and close its 133 stores.

"I think it's a multifaceted failure," said Doug Stephens, retail analyst and author of *The Retail Revival: Re-Imagining Business for The New Age of Consumerism*. "The plan that they undertook was imperilled and overly ambitious from the beginning."

"When you open a retail store, the first three months are vital. You're trying to connect with your consumers, and they did not connect," said Brian Sozzi, CEO and chief equities strategist of Belus Capital Advisors. "And they've been trying to play catchup ever since. It's been downhill since they opened the first store."

"They overestimated the size of the potential market for them, for their business," said Antony Karabus, analyst and president of Hilco Retail Consulting. "They underestimated the fierceness of the competition and the loyalty to existing retailers," which included Walmart, Canadian Tire, and Home Depot. "You can only unseal an incumbent if you bring something better. That's the fundamental issue. They didn't bring something better."

Target also signed a costly "trainwreck" of a deal in which it inherited the leases and locations of Zellers stores across the country, said Sozzi. While Target would save money on building costs, most of its Canadian stores would not be based on their U.S. models, which had been so successful. As well, the Canadian stores were not in "Triple A locations," and many were not big enough, nor did they fit nicely with Target's brand, Stephens said. "In the U.S when you walk in the front door of a Target, you know exactly where to go. The floor plan is predictable, you know where to go for what you want," Karabus said. "So you're not getting the frustration of running around the store trying to find what you want. [In Canada], you didn't know where to go."

Then there was the issue of stock, or lack of it. "I recall going into one of their grand openings in Aurora, Ont., and seeing hundreds of linear feet of empty shelving. I was astonished," Stephens said. "It became a thing. People began to ask, 'Why is there so much empty space? Where are the products?'" Target admitted it had supply chain issues but promised to fix them. Instead, the problems persisted, even into the holiday season.

But Target also failed to acquire the sales history of the Zellers stores, meaning they were "essentially flying blind" upon their launch. "They had no idea what they would sell, what they should stock, how much of it. So Day 1, when they opened their stores, they had no clue," Stephens said. Meanwhile, the stock they did have failed to excite consumers. "I went to [Target] a number of times in Canada and I didn't see a lot worth buying whereas when I would go to Target in the U.S. . . . there's always a treasure hunt," Karabus said. "There's always something."

Pricing was another issue. Many consumers, used to the deals in the U.S., complained that Canadian prices were just too high. "They did not drive that right balance of great assortment and appropriate pricing," Sozzi said. "It wasn't until this holiday season where they tried to get much more aggressive on pricing, tried to be much more price competitive. But by then, the customer was already turned off by them."

Source: Excerpted from Gollom, M. (2015, January 16). Target's launch into Canada a multifaceted failure. *CBC News*, http://www.cbc.ca/news/business/target-s-launch-into-canada-a-multifaceted-failure-1.2901789.

After we work through the rational decision-making model, we will consider how emotions and mood affect decisions.

LO **11.3**

Discuss the impact of *framing* and *cognitive biases* on the decision process.

Problem Identification and Framing

You will recall that a problem exists when a gap occurs between existing and desired conditions. Such gaps might be signalled by dissatisfied customers or vigilant employees. Similarly, the press might contain articles about legislation or ads for competing products that signal difficulties for the organization. The perfectly rational decision maker, infinitely sensitive and completely informed, should be a great problem identifier. Bounded rationality, however, can lead to the following difficulties in problem identification:[9]

- *Perceptual defence.* In Chapter 3, we pointed out that the perceptual system may act to defend the perceiver against unpleasant perceptions. For example, at JPMorgan Chase, executives might have been unconsciously motivated not to "see" signals of the trading problem.

- *Problem defined in terms of functional specialty.* Selective perception can cause decision makers to view a problem as being in the domain of their own specialty even when some other perspective might be warranted. For example, employees with a marketing background might fixate on a marketing solution to poor sales even though the problem resides in bad design.

- *Problem defined in terms of solution.* This form of jumping to conclusions effectively short-circuits the rational decision-making process. When Coca-Cola changed its time-honoured formula in 1985 to produce a "new" Coke, it appears that it prematurely defined its market share problem in terms of a particular solution—we need to change our existing product.

- *Problem diagnosed in terms of symptoms.* "What we have here is a morale problem." While this might be true, a concentration on surface symptoms will provide the decision maker with few clues about an adequate solution. The real problem here involves the cause of the morale problem. Low morale due to poor pay suggests different solutions than does low morale due to boring work.

When a problem is identified, it is necessarily framed in some way. Consider how different it is to frame a $10 000 expenditure as a cost (something to be avoided) versus an investment (something to be pursued). Or, consider how different it is to frame a new product introduction as a military campaign against competitors versus a crusade to help customers. In each case, the facts of the matter might be the same, but the different decision frames might lead to very different decisions.

Rational decision makers should try to be very self-conscious about how they have framed problems ("We have assumed that this is a product innovation problem"). Also, they should try out alternative frames ("Let's imagine that we don't need a new product here"). Finally, decision makers should avoid overarching, universal frames (corporate culture gone wild). While it is a good idea to "put customers first," we do not want to frame every problem as a customer service problem.[10]

Information Search

As you can see in Exhibit 11.1, once a problem is identified, a search for information is instigated. This information search may clarify the nature or extent of the problem and begin to suggest alternative solutions. Again, our perfectly rational Economic Person is in good shape at this second stage of the decision-making process. He or she has free and instantaneous access to all information necessary to clarify the problem and develop alternative solutions.

Bounded rationality, however, presents a different picture. The information search might be slow and costly.

TOO LITTLE INFORMATION Sometimes decision makers do not acquire enough information to make a good decision. Several cognitive biases contribute to this. For one thing, people tend to be mentally lazy and use whatever information is most readily available to them. Often, this resides in the memory, and we tend to remember *vivid recent* events.[11] Although such events might prove irrelevant in the context of the current problem, we curtail our information search and rely on familiar experience. The manager who remembers that "the last time we went to an outside supplier for parts, we got burned" may be ignoring the wisdom of contracting out a current order.

Another cognitive bias that contributes to an incomplete information search is the well-documented tendency for people to be overconfident in their decision making.[12] This difficulty is exacerbated by **confirmation bias**, the tendency to seek out information that conforms to one's own definition of or solution to a problem. According to one expert, this ceremonial information search leads to "decision-based evidence making" rather than evidence-based decision making![13]

Critics of the U.S. invasion of Iraq cited both overconfidence and confirmation bias. Similarly, in the fatal 1986 *Challenger* space launch, only a limited range of data about the impact of temperature on mechanical failure were examined, leading to a disastrous cold-weather launch choice. Another sort of inadequate information was apparent in the JPMorgan Chase loss of $2 billion. Many of the bank's derivative financial products were so mathematically complicated that executives simply did not understand how risky they were.

TOO MUCH INFORMATION While the bounds of rationality often force us to make decisions with incomplete or imperfect information, *too much* information can also damage the quality of decisions. **Information overload** is the reception of more information than is necessary to make effective decisions. As you might guess, information overload can lead to errors, omissions, delays, and cutting corners.[14] In addition, decision makers facing overload often attempt to use all the information at hand, then get confused and permit low-quality information or irrelevant information to influence their decisions.[15] Perhaps you have experienced this when writing a term paper—trying to incorporate too many references and too

Confirmation bias. The tendency to seek out information that conforms to one's own definition of or solution to a problem.

Information overload. The reception of more information than is necessary to make effective decisions.

Information overload can lead to errors, omissions, delays, and stress.

Blend Images - Jade/Brand X Pictures/Getty Images

many viewpoints into a short paper can lead to a confusing, low-quality end product. More is not necessarily better. The chapter-opening vignette suggests that information overload might have distracted chief executive Jaime Dimon at JPMorgan Chase from attending to the evolving trading irregularities. This would not be unusual, as star employees are prone to overload due to their many social connections.[16]

However, decision makers seem to *think* that more is better. Why is this so? For one thing, even if decisions do not improve with additional information, confidence in the decisions will increase.[17] Second, decision makers may fear being "kept in the dark" and associate the possession of information with power. One research review concludes that managers

- gather much information that has little decision relevance;
- use information that they collected and gathered after a decision to justify that decision;
- request information that they do not use;
- request more information, regardless of what is already available; and
- complain that there is not enough information to make a decision even though they ignore available information.[18]

Finally, information search often involves seeking advice from various parties, including trade associations, government agencies, and consultants. Research reveals that people have a cognitive bias to value advice for which they have paid over free advice of equal quality. No wonder there are so many consulting firms![19]

Alternative Development, Evaluation, and Choice

Perfectly informed or not, the decision maker can now list alternative solutions to the problem, examine the solutions, and choose the best one. For the perfectly rational, totally informed, ideal decision maker, this is easy. He or she conceives of all alternatives, knows the ultimate value of each alternative, and knows the probability that each alternative will work. In this case, the decision maker can exhibit **maximization**—that is, he or she can choose the alternative with the greatest expected value. Consider a simple example:

Maximization. The choice of the decision alternative with the greatest expected value.

	Ultimate Value	Probability	Expected Value
Alternative 1	$100 000 Profit	.4	$40 000 Profit
Alternative 2	$ 60 000 Profit	.8	$48 000 Profit

Here, the expected value of each alternative is calculated by multiplying its ultimate value by its probability. In this case, the perfectly rational decision maker would choose to implement the second alternative.

Unfortunately, things do not go so smoothly for the decision maker working under bounded rationality. He may not know all alternative solutions, and he may be ignorant of the ultimate values and probabilities of success of those solutions that he knows. Again, cognitive biases come into play. In particular, people are especially weak intuitive statisticians, and they frequently violate standard statistical principles. For example,[20]

- People avoid incorporating known existing data about the likelihood of events ("base rates") into their decisions. For instance, firms continue to launch novelty food products (e.g., foods squeezed from tubes or foods developed by celebrities) even though they have a very high failure rate in the market.
- Large samples warrant more confidence than small samples. Despite this, data from a couple of (vivid) focus groups might be given more weight than data from a large (but anonymous) national survey.
- Decision makers often overestimate the odds of complex chains of events occurring— the scenario sounds sensible despite being less likely with every added link in the

chain. During the 2008–2009 economic meltdown, it was implicitly assumed that the economy would remain healthy *and* real estate prices would continue to rise *and* people would find a way to pay their escalating mortgages.

- People are poor at revising estimates of probabilities and values as they acquire additional information. A good example is the **anchoring effect**, which illustrates that decision makers do not adjust their estimates enough from some initial estimate that serves as an anchor. For example, in one study, real estate agents allowed the *asking price* of a house to unduly influence their *professional evaluation* of the house.[21]

Anchoring effect. The inadequate adjustment of subsequent estimates from an initial estimate that serves as an anchor.

It is possible to reduce some of these basic cognitive biases by making people more accountable for their decisions. This might include requiring reasoned reports, formal presentations of how the decision was reached, and so on. However, it is critical that this accountability be in place *before* a decision is reached. After-the-fact accountability often increases the probability of biases, as people try to protect their identity as good decision makers.[22] It is now clear that deregulation of the banking industry reduced accountability and contributed to the 2008–2009 economic meltdown.

The perfectly rational decision maker can evaluate alternative solutions against a single criterion: economic gain. The decision maker who is bounded by reality might have to factor in other criteria as well, such as the political acceptability of the solution to other organizational members: Will the boss like it? Since these additional criteria have their own values and probabilities, the decision-making task increases in complexity.

The bottom line here is that the decision maker working under bounded rationality frequently "satisfices" rather than maximizes.[23] **Satisficing** means that the decision maker establishes an adequate level of acceptability for a solution and then screens solutions until he or she finds one that exceeds this level. When this occurs, evaluation of alternatives ceases, and the solution is chosen for implementation. For instance, the human resources manager who feels that absenteeism has become too high might choose a somewhat arbitrary acceptable level (e.g., the rate one year earlier), and then accept the first solution that seems likely to achieve this level. Few organizations seek to *maximize* attendance.

Satisficing. Establishing an adequate level of acceptability for a solution to a problem and then screening solutions until one that exceeds this level is found.

Decision expert Paul Nutt found that the search for alternatives is often very limited in strategic decision making and that firms invest very little money in exploring alternatives.[24] What this leads to is a kind of tunnel vision in which some hastily chosen option is viewed much too favourably.[25] Thus, the provision of information concerning alternatives is crucial to good decision making.[26] Successful consulting firms often fulfill this role.

Many students want to start their own companies, so you should be aware that entrepreneurs are especially prone to overconfidence, too much optimism, and other cognitive biases that cloud decision making.[27] These biases can threaten the survival of new firms.

Risky Business

Choosing between decision alternatives often involves an element of risk, and the research evidence on how people handle such risks is fascinating. Consider this scenario that decision researcher Max Bazerman developed. Which alternative would you choose?

Robert Davis, head of the legal staff of a Fortune 500 company, has delayed making one of the most critical recommendations in the organization's history. The company is faced with a class action suit from a hostile group of consumers. While the organization believes that it is innocent, it realizes that a court may not have the same perspective. The organization is expected to lose $50 million if the suit is lost in court. Davis predicts a 50 percent chance of losing the case. The organization has the option of settling out of court by paying $25 million to the "injured" parties. Davis's senior staff has been collecting information and organizing the case for over six months. It is time for action. What should Davis recommend?

> Alternative A   Settle out of court and accept a sure *loss* of $25 million,
>
> or
>
> Alternative B   Go to court expecting a 50 percent probability of a $50 million loss.[28]

Notice that these two solutions are functionally equivalent in terms of dollars and cents (50 percent of $50 million = $25 million). Nonetheless, you probably tended to choose alternative B—about 80 percent of students do. Notice also that alternative B is the riskier of the two alternatives in that it exposes the firm to a *potential* for greater loss.

Now, consider two further descriptions of the alternatives. Which solution would you choose?

> Alternative C   Settle out of court and *save* $25 million that could be lost in court,
>
> or
>
> Alternative D   Go to court expecting a 50 percent probability of *saving* $50 million.

Again, these two solutions are functionally equivalent in monetary terms (and equivalent to options A and B). Yet, you probably chose solution C—80 percent of students do. Notice that this is the *less* risky alternative, in that the firm is not exposed to a potential $50 million loss.

This is a graphic example of the power of framing. Alternatives A and B frame the problem as a choice between losses, while C and D frame it as a choice between gains or savings. Research by Daniel Kahneman and Amos Tversky shows that when people view a problem as a choice between losses, they tend to make risky decisions, rolling the dice in the face of a sure loss. When people frame the alternatives as a choice between gains they tend to make conservative decisions, protecting the sure win.[29] It is very important to be aware of what reference point you are using when you frame decision alternatives. It is not necessarily wrong to frame a problem as a choice between losses, but this can contribute to a foolish level of risk taking.

Solution Implementation

When a decision is made to choose a particular solution to a problem, the solution must be implemented. The perfectly rational decision maker will have factored any possible implementation problems into his or her choice of solutions. Of course, the bounded decision maker will attempt to do the same when estimating probabilities of success. However, in organizations, decision makers are often dependent on others to implement their decisions, and it might be difficult to anticipate their ability or motivation to do so.

An example of implementation problems occurs when products are designed, engineered, and produced in a lengthy series of stages. For example, engineering might have to implement decisions made by designers, and production planning might have to implement decisions made by engineering. As we noted in Chapter 7, this sequential process frequently leads to confusion, conflict, and delay unless cross-functional teams are used during the decision-making process. When they work well, such teams are sensitive to implementation problems.

LO 11.4

Explain the process of *escalation of commitment* to an apparently failing course of action.

Solution Evaluation

When the time comes to evaluate the implemented solution, the decision maker is effectively examining the possibility that a new problem has occurred: Does the (new) existing state match the desired state? Has the decision been effective? For all the reasons we stated previously, the perfectly rational decision maker should be able to evaluate the effectiveness of the decision with calm, objective detachment. Again, however, the bounded decision maker might encounter problems at this stage of the process.

JUSTIFICATION
As we said earlier, people tend to be overconfident about the adequacy of their decisions. Thus, substantial dissonance can be aroused when a decision turns out to be faulty. One way to prevent such dissonance is to avoid careful tests of the adequacy of the decision. As a result, many organizations are notoriously lax when it comes to evaluating the effectiveness of expensive training programs or advertising campaigns. If the bad news cannot be avoided, the erring decision maker may devote his or her energy to trying to justify the faulty decision.

The justification of faulty decisions is best seen in the irrational treatment of sunk costs. **Sunk costs** are permanent losses of resources incurred as the result of a decision.[30] The key word here is *permanent*. Since these resources have been lost (sunk) due to a past decision, they should not enter into future decisions. Psychologist Barry Staw has studied how, despite this, people often "throw good resources after bad," acting as if they could recoup sunk costs. This process is **escalation of commitment** to an apparently failing course of action, in which the escalation involves devoting more and more resources to actions implied by the decision.[31] For example, suppose an executive authorizes the purchase of several new machines to improve plant productivity. The machines turn out to be very unreliable, and they are frequently out of commission for repairs. Perfect rationality suggests admitting to a mistake here. However, the executive might authorize an order for more machines from the same manufacturer to "prove" that he was right all along, hoping to recoup sunk costs with improved productivity from an even greater number of machines. As indicated in the final paragraph of the chapter-opening vignette, escalation seems to have contributed to the JPMorgan Chase trading loss.

Dissonance reduction is not the only reason that escalation of commitment to a faulty decision may occur. A social norm that favours *consistent* behaviour by managers may also be at work.[32] Changing one's mind and reversing previous decisions might be perceived as a sign of weakness, a fate to be avoided at all costs.

Escalation of commitment sometimes happens even when the current decision maker is not responsible for previous sunk costs. For example, politicians might continue an expensive, unnecessary public works project that was begun by a previous political administration. Here, dissonance reduction and the appearance of consistency are irrelevant, suggesting some other causes of escalation. For one thing, decision makers might be motivated to not appear wasteful.[33] ("Even though the airport construction is way over budget and flight traffic doesn't justify a new airport, let's finish the thing. Otherwise, the taxpayers will think we've squandered their money.") Also, escalation of commitment might be due to the way in which decision makers frame the problem once some resources have been sunk. Rather than seeing the savings involved in reversing the decision, they may frame the problem as a decision between a sure loss of x dollars (which have been sunk) and an uncertain loss of $x + y$ dollars (maybe the additional investment will succeed). As we noted earlier, when problems are framed this way, people tend to avoid the certain loss and go with the riskier choice, which in this case is escalation.[34] In addition to these situational causes, personality, moods, and emotions can affect escalation. For instance, people high on neuroticism and negative affectivity (Chapter 2) are *less* likely to escalate since they try to avoid stressful predicaments.[35]

Escalation can occur in both competitive and non-competitive situations. A non-competitive example can be seen in the overvaluation of stocks by Wall Street analysts in advance of a market crash. Competitive, auction-like situations seem especially likely to prompt escalation, because they often involve time pressure, rivalry, interested audiences, and the desire to be the first mover. These factors contribute to emotional arousal (see below) and stimulate escalation.[36] The Vietnam and Iraq wars have been cited as prime examples of competitive escalation.

Sunk costs. Permanent losses of resources incurred as the result of a decision.

Escalation of commitment. The tendency to invest additional resources in an apparently failing course of action.

Are there any ways to prevent the tendency to escalate commitment to a failing course of action? Logic and research suggest the following:[37]

- Encourage continuous experimentation with reframing the problem to avoid the decision trap of feeling that more resources *have* to be invested. Shift the frame to saving rather than spending.

- Set specific goals for the project in advance that must be met if more resources are to be invested. This prevents escalation when early results are "unclear."

- Place more emphasis when evaluating managers on *how* they made decisions and less on decision outcomes. This kind of accountability is the sensible way to teach managers not to fear or hide failure.

- Separate initial and subsequent decision making so that individuals who make the initial decision to embark on a course of action are assisted or replaced by others who decide if a course of action should be continued. Banks often do this when trying to decide what to do about problem loans. However, at JPMorgan Chase, risk managers failed to flag problematic trading.

It may be tempting to think that using groups to make decisions will reduce the tendency toward escalation. However, groups are *more* prone than individuals to escalate commitment.[38]

Hindsight. The tendency to review the decision-making process to find what was done right or wrong.

HINDSIGHT   The careful evaluation of decisions is also inhibited by faulty hindsight. **Hindsight** refers to the tendency to review the decision-making process that was used to find out what was done right (in the case of success) or wrong (in the case of failure). While hindsight can prove useful, it often reflects a cognitive bias.

The classic example of hindsight involves the armchair quarterback who "knew" that a chancy intercepted pass in the first quarter was unnecessary because the team won the game anyway! The armchair critic is exhibiting the knew-it-all-along effect. This is the tendency to assume, after the fact, that we knew all along what the outcome of a decision would be. In effect, our faulty memory adjusts the probabilities that we estimated before making the decision to correspond to what actually happened.[39] This can prove quite dangerous. The money manager who consciously makes a very risky investment that turns out to be successful might revise her memory to assume that the decision was a sure thing. The next time, the now-confident investor might not be so lucky!

Another form of faulty hindsight is the tendency to take personal responsibility for successful decision outcomes while denying responsibility for unsuccessful outcomes.[40] Thus, when things work out well, it is because *we* made a careful, logical decision. When things go poorly, some unexpected *external* factor messed up our sensible decision!

LO 11.5

Consider how emotions and mood affect decision making.

How Emotions and Mood Affect Decision Making

Thus far we have discussed decision making from a mainly cognitive perspective, focusing on the rational decision-making model and illustrating the limits to rationality. However, our coverage of decision justification and hindsight suggests a considerable emotional component to many organizational decisions—people do not like to be wrong, and they often become emotionally attached to the failing course of action that signals escalation of commitment.

At the outset, it should be emphasized that emotionless decision making would be poor decision making, and the rational model is not meant to suggest otherwise. Some of the most graphic evidence for this comes from unfortunate cases in which people suffer brain injuries that blunt their emotions while leaving their intellectual functions intact. Such individuals often proceed to make a series of poor life decisions, because they are unable to properly evaluate the impact of these decisions on themselves and others; they have no feeling.[41]

rawpixel.com/Shutterstock

Decision makers in a good mood can overestimate the likelihood of good events and use shortcut decision strategies.

During the 2005 NASA *Discovery* space mission, it was suggested that some of the caution-focused decisions, such as a delay in landing and a decision to set down in California, were made by mission control personnel still suffering emotional effects of the 2003 *Columbia* tragedy. Strong emotions frequently figure in the decision-making process that corrects ethical errors (Chapter 12), and so-called whistle-blowers often report that they were motivated by emotion to protest decision errors. Strong (positive) emotion has also been implicated in creative decision making and the proper use of intuition to solve problems. Such intuition (Chapter 1) can lead to the successful short-circuiting of the steps in the rational model when speed is of the essence.

Despite these examples of how emotion can help decision making, there are many cases in which strong emotions are a hindrance. The folk saying "blinded by emotion" has some truth to it, as people experiencing strong emotions are often self focused and distracted from the actual demands of the problem at hand. Most of our information about the impact of emotions on decisions is anecdotal, because people are often reluctant to participate in field research about emotional issues and because it is not ethical to invoke strong emotions in lab research. One clever field study did document how excessive pride led highly paid CEOs to pay too much for firms they were acquiring.[42] Other business–press evidence implicates angry CEOs losing their heads in competitive bidding for acquisitions (escalation of commitment). A common theme over the years has been how excessive emotional conflict between business partners or family business members provokes questionable business decisions.

In contrast to the case for strong emotions, there is much research on the impact of mood on decision making. You will recall from Chapter 4 that moods are relatively mild, unfocused states of positive or negative feeling. The research on mood and decision making reveals some very interesting paradoxes. For one thing, mood is a pretty low-key state, and you might be inclined to think it would not have much impact on decisions. In fact, there is plenty of evidence that mood affects *what* and *how* people think when making decisions. Also, you might imagine that the impact of mood would be restricted to mundane, structured decision problems. In fact, mood has its greatest impact on uncertain, ambiguous decisions of the type that are especially crucial for organizations. Here is what the research reveals:[43]

- People in a positive mood tend to remember positive information. Those in a negative mood remember negative information.

- People in a positive mood tend to evaluate objects, people, and events more positively. Those in a negative mood provide more negative evaluations.

YOU BE THE MANAGER

Preventing Surgical Decision Errors at Toronto General Hospital

Every year, between 9000 and 23 000 people die in Canadian hospitals due to surgical errors. Although many preventable deaths occur during operations, some of them also stem from pre-op or post-op errors. Surgical operations are done by some of the most highly trained professionals, yet still mistakes are made in this emotion-laden environment.

Toronto General Hospital and its two sister hospitals, Toronto Western and Princess Margaret, form the University Health Network (UHN). These hospitals, like all other hospitals in the country, sometimes fall victim to human error. Considering that the complication rate in higher-income area hospitals is approximately 10.3 percent, more than 2000 of the UHN's 23 000 annual surgical patients may suffer from preventable complications.

"[Surgery] is one of the areas where we have tremendous skills and resources," says Dr. Ross Baker, a health policy professor at the University of Toronto. "And then we go in and somebody forgets to do something they should do as a matter of course, and the outcome is an infection or complication of some sort."

For years, medical researchers have sought ways to reduce errors that occur in the operating room, not only to save lives but also to save money. Prevention requires an understanding of possible negative events and their associated causes. Once the scenarios have been identified, a set of procedures can be created to help prevent them from occurring. Also at issue is establishing means to manage any negative events that do occur to avoid adverse complications. Both approaches come with challenges. First, it may be difficult to predict potential problems, because hospital staff and procedures are constantly changing. Second, errors may not always be identified in real time.

One might wonder why a highly professional team of doctors and nurses would fail to identify or respond to a potentially deadly error, especially when they have the collective technical knowledge to identify such errors. The problem, it seems, is not so much related to knowledge; rather, it often stems from the complex professional relationships that exist between doctors and nurses, and between the surgical leader and the rest of the team. Like a pilot in command of a plane, the lead surgeon carries significant responsibility and authority. Team members often feel threatened about

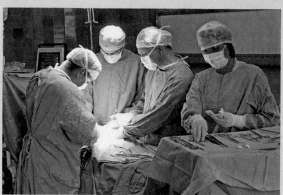

In surgical teams, members often find it difficult to speak up, even if they believe that a problem exists.

speaking up, even if they believe that a problem exists. Eliminating preventable complications, therefore, requires both systemic and behavioural changes.

Dr. Bryce Taylor, UHN's surgeon-in-chief, takes the problem very seriously: "With approximately 234 million surgeries performed each year worldwide, we owe it to our patients to look at every opportunity to prevent complications during and after surgery."

Questions

1. Is there a programmed decision-making process that would support the prevention and correction of surgical errors?

2. What role may emotions play in the decision behaviour of operating room personnel?

To find out what happened at Toronto General, see The Manager's Notebook at the end of the chapter.

Sources: Blackwell, T. (2009, January 15). Checklists cut surgical mistakes by a third. *National Post*, A1, A5 (Baker quote); Blatt, R., Christianson, M.K., & Sutcliffe, K.M. (2006). A sensemaking lens on reliability. *Journal of Organizational Behavior, 27,* 491–515; Haynes, A.B., Weiser, T.G., Berry, W.R., Lipsitz, S.R., Breizat, A-H.S., Dellinger, et al. (2009). A surgical safety checklist to reduce morbidity and mortality in a global population. *New England Journal of Medicine, 360,* 491–499; Nembhardi, I.M., & Edmondson, A.C. (2006). Making it safe: The effects of leader inclusiveness and professional status on psychological safety and improvement efforts in health care teams. *Journal of Organizational Behavior, 27,* 941–966; Priest, L. (2009, January 15). Simple checklist saves lives in the operating room, study finds. *Globe and Mail*, A4; Anonymous (2009, January 14). Results show surgical safety checklist drops deaths and complications by more than one third. University Health Network, www.uhn.ca (Taylor quote).

- People in a good mood tend to overestimate the likelihood that good events will occur and underestimate the occurrence of bad events. People in a bad mood do the opposite.

- People in a good mood adopt simplified, shortcut decision-making strategies, more likely violating the rational model. People in a negative mood are prone to approach decisions in a more deliberate, systematic, detailed way.

- Positive mood promotes more creative, intuitive decision making.

As you can see, it makes perfect sense to hope for your job interview to be conducted by a person in a good mood or to try to create a good mood on the part of your clients! Notice that the impact of mood on decision making is not necessarily dysfunctional. If the excesses of optimism can be controlled, those in a good mood can make creative decisions. If the excesses of pessimism can be controlled, those in a negative mood can actually process information more carefully and effectively. In a simulation, it was found that foreign currency traders in a good mood performed more poorly (by losing money) than those in bad or neutral moods. Those in a bad mood performed better, but were rather conservative. Traders in a neutral mood did best, tolerating risk but not being overconfident.[44] Thus, the investment practitioners' advice to remain calm during turbulent markets has some validity.

A fine example of how mood and emotion can lead to faulty decision making can be seen in the "dot.com meltdown" that began in the late 1990s. In this era, hundreds of firms were formed to exploit the potential wealth of ecommerce. An economic boom, ready capital, advancing technology, and the model of a few overnight "internet millionaires" created a positive mood that led to overly intuitive decisions, false creativity, and exaggerated optimism. Mood is contagious, and many start-up firms, fearing to be left behind, were founded with vague goals and even vaguer business plans. Many consisted of little more than a website, and "hits" were confused with cash flow. The ensuing crash left those firms founded on careful business decision-making principles to enjoy the spoils of the technology revolution. It was exactly this kind of giddy emotion, fuelled by big bonuses, that led Wall Street executives to ignore the subprime mortgage meltdown that occurred in 2008–2009.

Before continuing, check out You Be the Manager: *Preventing Surgical Decision Errors at Toronto General Hospital.*

Rational Decision Making—A Summary

The rational decision-making model in Exhibit 11.1 provides a good guide for how many decisions *should* be made but offers only a partially accurate view of how they *are* made. For complex, unfamiliar decisions, such as choosing an occupation, the rational model provides a pretty good picture of how people actually make decisions.[45] Also, organizational decision makers often follow the rational model when they agree about the goals they are pursuing.[46] On the other hand, there is plenty of case study evidence of short-circuiting the rational model in organizational decisions, in part because of the biases we discussed above.[47] A study of 356 decisions in medium to large organizations found that half of them failed. These failures were found to be primarily due to the use of poor tactics on the part of managers who impose solutions, limit the search for alternatives, and use power to implement their plans.[48] However, true experts in a field will often short-circuit the rational model, using their intuitive knowledge base stored in memory to skip steps logically.[49] Exhibit 11.2 summarizes the operation of perfect and bounded rationality at each stage of the decision process. Exhibit 11.3 summarizes the various cognitive biases that we have covered.

EXHIBIT 11.2
Perfectly rational decision making contrasted with bounded rationality.

Stage	Perfect Rationality	Bounded Rationality
Problem Identification	Easy, accurate perception of gaps that constitute problems	Perceptual defence; jump to solutions; attention to symptoms rather than problems; mood affects memory
Information Search	Free; fast; right amount obtained	Slow; costly; reliance on flawed memory; obtain too little or too much
Development of Alternative Solutions	Can conceive of all	Not all known
Evaluation of Alternative Solutions	Ultimate value of each known; probability of each known; only criterion is economic gain	Potential ignorance of or miscalculation of values and probabilities; criteria include political factors; affected by mood
Solution Choice	Maximizes	Satisfies
Solution Implementation	Considered in evaluation of alternatives	May be difficult owing to reliance on others
Solution Evaluation	Objective, according to previous steps	May involve justification, escalation to recover sunk costs, faulty hindsight

EXHIBIT 11.3
Summary of cognitive biases in decision making.

- Decision makers tend to be overconfident about the decisions that they make.
- Decision makers tend to seek out information that confirms their own problem definitions and solutions. (Confirmation bias)
- Decision makers tend to remember and incorporate vivid, recent events into their decisions.
- Decision makers fail to incorporate known existing data about the likelihood of events into their decisions.
- Decision makers ignore sample sizes when evaluating samples of information.
- Decision makers overestimate the odds of complex chains of events occurring.
- Decision makers do not adjust estimates enough from some initial estimate that serves as an anchor as they acquire more information. (Anchoring effect)
- Decision makers have difficulty ignoring sunk costs when making subsequent decisions.
- Decision makers overestimate their ability to have predicted events after-the-fact, take responsibility for successful decision outcomes, and deny responsibility for unsuccessful outcomes. (Hindsight)

LO 11.6

Summarize the pros and cons of using groups to make decisions, with attention to the *groupthink* phenomenon and risk assessment.

GROUP DECISION MAKING

Many, many organizational decisions are made by groups rather than individuals, especially when problems are ill structured. In this section, we consider the advantages and problems of group decision making.

Why Use Groups?

There are a number of reasons for employing groups to make organizational decisions.

DECISION QUALITY Experts often argue that groups or teams can make higher-quality decisions than individuals. This argument is based on the following three assumptions:

- Groups are *more vigilant* than individuals are—more people are scanning the environment.

- Groups can *generate more ideas* than individuals can.
- Groups can *evaluate ideas better* than individuals can.

At the problem identification and information search stages, vigilance is especially advantageous. For example, a member of the board of directors might notice a short article in an obscure business publication that has great relevance for the firm. In searching for information to clarify the problem suggested in the article, other members of the board might possess unique information that proves useful.

When it comes to developing alternative solutions, more people should literally have more ideas, if only because someone remembers something that others have forgotten. In addition, members with different backgrounds and experiences may bring different perspectives to the problem. This is why undergraduate students, graduate students, faculty, and administrators are often included on university task forces to improve the library or course evaluation system.

When it comes to evaluating solutions and choosing the best one, groups have the advantage of checks and balances—that is, an extreme position or incorrect notion held by one member should be offset by the pooled judgments of the rest of the group.

These characteristics suggest that groups *should* make higher-quality decisions than individuals can. Shortly, we will find out whether they actually do.

DECISION ACCEPTANCE AND COMMITMENT As we pointed out in our discussion of participative leadership in Chapter 9, groups are often used to make decisions on the premise that a decision made in this way will be more acceptable to those involved. Again, there are several assumptions underlying this premise:

- People wish to be involved in decisions that will affect them.
- People will better understand a decision in which they participated.
- People will be more committed to a decision in which they invested personal time and energy.

The acceptability of group decisions is especially useful in dealing with a problem described earlier: getting the decision implemented. If decision makers truly understand the decision and feel committed to it, they should be willing to follow through and see that it is carried out.

DIFFUSION OF RESPONSIBILITY High quality and acceptance are sensible reasons for using groups to make decisions. A less admirable reason to employ groups is to allow for **diffusion of responsibility** across the members in case the decision turns out poorly. In this case, each member of the group will share part of the burden of the negative consequences, and no one person will be singled out for punishment. Of course, when this happens, individual group members often "abandon ship" and exhibit biased hindsight—"I knew all along that the bid was too high to be accepted, but they made me go along with them."

Diffusion of responsibility. The ability of group members to share the burden of the negative consequences of a poor decision.

Do Groups Actually Make Higher-Quality Decisions than Individuals?

Is the frequent use of groups to make decisions warranted by evidence? The answer is yes. One review concludes that "groups usually produce more and better solutions to problems than do individuals working alone."[50] Another concludes that group performance is superior to that of the average individual in the group.[51] More specifically, groups should perform better than individuals when

- the group members differ in relevant skills and abilities, as long as they do not differ so much that conflict occurs;

- some division of labour can occur;

- memory for facts is an important issue; and

- individual judgments can be combined by weighting them to reflect the expertise of the various members.[52]

Equal weighting of opinions and averaging are inappropriate when some group members have more expertise concerning a particular problem, and it is critical for decision success that such expertise be recognized by the group. However, if several group members share the same view about a problem, this shared view can prevail in spite of the knowledge held by a single expert.[53] Extensive discussion of the problem is one way that accurate but minority viewpoints can positively influence decisions.[54]

Disadvantages of Group Decision Making

Although groups have the ability to develop high-quality, acceptable decisions, there are a number of potential disadvantages to group decision making.

TIME   Groups seldom work quickly or efficiently compared with individuals. This is because of the process losses (Chapter 7) involved in discussion, debate, and coordination. The time problem increases with group size. When the speed of arriving at a solution to a problem is a prime factor, organizations should avoid using groups.

CONFLICT   Participants in group decisions may have their own personal axes to grind or their own resources to protect. When this occurs, decision quality may take a back seat to political wrangling and infighting. In general, groups will make better decisions when their members feel psychologically safe.

DOMINATION   The advantages of group decision making will seldom be realized if meetings are dominated by a single individual or a small coalition. Even if a dominant person has good information, this style is not likely to lead to group acceptance and commitment. If the dominant person is particularly misinformed, the group decision is very likely to be ineffective.

GROUPTHINK   Have you ever been involved in a group decision that you knew was a "loser" but that you felt unable to protest? Perhaps you thought you were the only one who had doubts about the chosen course of action. Perhaps you tried to speak up, but others criticized you for not being on the team. Maybe you found yourself searching for information to confirm that the decision was correct and ignoring evidence that the decision was bad. What was happening? Were you suffering from some strange form of possession? Mind control?

In Chapter 8, we discussed the process of conformity, which can have a strong influence on the decisions that groups make. The most extreme influence is seen when **groupthink** occurs. This happens when group pressures lead to reduced mental efficiency, poor testing of reality, and lax moral judgment.[55] In effect, unanimous acceptance of decisions is stressed over quality of decisions.

Psychologist Irving Janis, who developed the groupthink concept, felt that high group cohesiveness was at its root. It now appears that other factors are more important.[56] These include strong identification with the group, concern for their approval, and the isolation of the group from other sources of information. However, the promotion of a particular decision by the group leader appears to be the strongest cause.[57] Janis provides a detailed list of groupthink symptoms:

Groupthink. The capacity for group pressure to damage the mental efficiency, reality testing, and moral judgment of decision-making groups.

- *Illusion of invulnerability.* Members are overconfident and willing to assume great risks. They ignore obvious danger signals.

- *Rationalization.* Problems and counter-arguments that members cannot ignore are "rationalized away." That is, seemingly logical but improbable excuses are given.

- *Illusion of morality.* The decisions the group adopts are not only perceived as sensible, they are also perceived as *morally* correct.

- *Stereotypes of outsiders.* The group constructs unfavourable stereotypes of those outside the group who are the targets of their decisions.

- *Pressure for conformity.* Members pressure each other to fall in line and conform with the group's views.

- *Self-censorship.* Members convince themselves to avoid voicing opinions contrary to the group.

- *Illusion of unanimity.* Members perceive that unanimous support exists for their chosen course of action.

- *Mindguards.* Some group members may adopt the role of "protecting" the group from information that goes against its decisions.[58]

We can see groupthink in the decision-making process concerning NASA's Hubble Space Telescope in the 1990s, where an aberration in the telescope's primary mirror was the source of astronomical repair costs.[59] To begin with, a dominant leader in charge of the internal mirror tests appears to have isolated the mirror project team from outside sources of information. Symptoms of groupthink followed: at least three sets of danger signals that the mirror was flawed were ignored or explained away (illusion of invulnerability and rationalization); an outside firm, Kodak, was dismissed as too incompetent to test the mirror (stereotype of outsiders); the consultant who suggested that Kodak test the mirror received bitter criticism but still felt he did not protest enough in the end (mindguarding and self censorship); and the defence of the isolated working methods was viewed as more "theological" than technical (illusion of morality).

What can prevent groupthink? Leaders must be careful to avoid exerting undue pressure for a particular decision outcome and concentrate on good decision processes. Also, leaders should establish norms that encourage and even reward responsible dissent, and outside experts should be brought in from time to time to challenge the group's views.[60] Some of the decision-making techniques we discuss later in the chapter should help prevent the tendency as well.

Stimulating and Managing Controversy

Full-blown conflict among organizational members is hardly conducive to good decision making. Individuals will withhold information, and personal or group goals will take precedence over developing a decision that solves organizational problems. On the other hand, a complete lack of controversy can be equally damaging, since alternative points of view that may be very relevant to the issue at hand will never surface. Such a lack of controversy is partially responsible for the groupthink effect, and it also contributes to many cases of escalation of commitment.

One interesting method of controversy stimulation is the appointment of a **devil's advocate** to challenge existing plans and strategies. The advocate's role is to challenge the weaknesses of the plan or strategy and state why it should not be adopted. For example, a bank might be considering offering an innovative kind of account. Details to be decided include interest rate, required minimum balance, and so on. A committee might be assigned to develop a position paper. Before a decision is made, someone would be assigned to read the paper and "tear it apart," noting potential weaknesses. Thus, a decision is made in full recognition of the pros and cons of the plan. The controversy promoted by the devil's

Devil's advocate. A person appointed to identify and challenge the weaknesses of a proposed plan or strategy.

advocate improves decision quality.[61] However, to be effective, the advocate must present his or her views in an objective, unemotional manner.

How Do Groups Handle Risk?

Almost by definition, problems that are suitable for group decision making involve some degree of risk and uncertainty. This raises a very important question: Do groups make decisions that are more or less risky than those of individuals? Or will the degree of risk assumed by the group simply equal the average risk preferred by its individual members? Consider the following scenario:

> *An accident has just occurred at a nuclear power plant. Several corrections exist, ranging from expensive and safe to low-cost but risky. On the way to an emergency meeting, each nuclear engineer formulates an opinion about what should be done. But what will the group decide?*

Conventional wisdom provides few clear predictions about what the group of engineers will decide to do. It is sometimes argued that groups will make riskier decisions than individuals because there is security in numbers—that is, diffusion of responsibility for a bad decision encourages the group to take greater chances. On the other hand, it is often argued that groups are cautious, with the members checking and balancing each other so much that a conservative outcome is sure to occur. Just contrast the committee-laden civil service with the swashbuckling style of independent operators such as Richard Branson and Donald Trump!

Given this contradiction of common sense, the history of research into group decision making and risk is instructive. A Massachusetts Institute of Technology student, J.A.F. Stoner, reported in a master's thesis that he had discovered clear evidence of a **risky shift** in decision making.[62] Participants in the research reviewed hypothetical cases involving risk, such as those involving career choices or investment decisions. As individuals, they recommended a course of action. Then they were formed into groups, and the groups discussed each case and came to a joint decision. In general, the groups tended to advise riskier courses of action than the average risk initially advocated by their members. This is the risky shift. As studies were conducted by others to explore the reasons for its causes, things got more complicated. For some groups and some decisions, **conservative shifts** were observed. In other words, groups came to decisions that were *less* risky than those of the individual members before interaction.

It is now clear that both risky and conservative shifts are possible, and that they occur in a wide variety of real settings, including investment and purchasing decisions. But what determines which kind of shift occurs? A key factor appears to be the initial positions of the group members before they discuss the problem. This is illustrated in Exhibit 11.4. As you can see, when group members are somewhat conservative before interaction (the Xs), they tend to exhibit a conservative shift when they discuss the problem. When group members are somewhat risky initially (the dots), they exhibit a risky shift after discussion. In other words, *group discussion seems to polarize or exaggerate the initial position of the group.*[63] Returning to the nuclear accident, if the engineers initially prefer a somewhat conservative solution, they will likely adopt an even more conservative strategy during the meeting.

Why do risky and conservative shifts occur when groups make decisions? Evidence indicates two main factors:[64]

Risky shift. The tendency for groups to make riskier decisions than the average risk initially advocated by their individual members.

Conservative shift. The tendency for groups to make less risky decisions than the average risk initially advocated by their individual members.

- Group discussion generates ideas and arguments that individual members have not considered before. This information naturally favours the members' initial tendency toward risk or toward conservatism. Since discussion provides "more" and "better" reasons for the initial tendency, the tendency ends up being exaggerated.

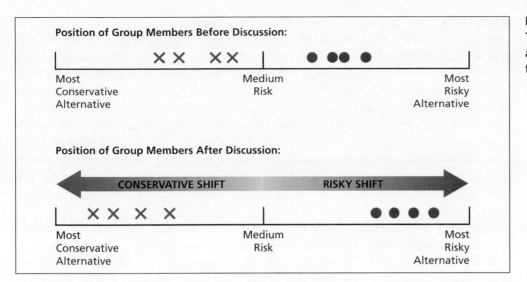

EXHIBIT 11.4
The dynamics of risky and conservative shifts for two groups.

- Group members try to present themselves as basically similar to other members but "even better." Thus, they try to one-up others in discussion by adopting a slightly more extreme version of the group's initial stance.

In summary, managers should be aware of the tendency for group interaction to polarize initial risk levels. If this polarization results from the sensible exchange of information, it might actually improve the group's decision. However, if it results from one-upmanship, it might lead to low-quality decisions.

CONTEMPORARY APPROACHES TO IMPROVING DECISION MAKING

LO 11.7

Discuss contemporary approaches to improving organizational decision making.

Good decisions are vital for organizational success, and decisions can be improved if decision makers are encouraged to adhere to the rational model shown in Exhibit 11.1. This should help preclude the various biases and errors that we have alluded to earlier. Each of the contemporary approaches discussed in this section has this goal, and several themes are apparent in what follows. In particular, managers have to be more mindful of the quality of the *evidence* they are using to make decisions. Also, managers have to be open to new and improved *sources* of evidence. Finally, they may have involve an array of *new people* in the decision-making process.

Evidence-Based Management

At its core, **evidence-based management** is "making decisions through the conscientious, explicit, and judicious use of the best available evidence from multiple sources."[65] Wishful thinking and intuition are no substitute for high-quality evidence. The practice has its roots in evidence-based medicine, a movement that summarizes the results of thousands of medical studies to provide solid evidence for good clinical practice.[66] Unfortunately, much of what passes for decision making in organizations consists of guessing what the boss favours, indiscriminately copying competitors (defended as "benchmarking"), or buying canned consulting packages, none of which passes the test for the best available evidence.

What is good evidence?[67] If available for a particular problem, scientifically conducted peer-reviewed research is the gold standard. This is especially true when multiple

Evidence-based management. Making decisions through the conscientious, explicit, and judicious use of the best available evidence from multiple sources.

independent research studies are summarized in a systematic review using a technique called meta-analysis. If you look at the References section at the back of this book, you will see that we rely on many meta-analyses to support our writing. Much social science research is underappreciated by managers, but it can be a source of competitive advantage in decisions concerning human resources, strategy, and marketing. Data generated by or for a specific organization can also constitute reasonable evidence. Traditional customer and employee surveys (if professionally constructed), financial data, and human resources data can all be valuable sources of information. In addition, as discussed below, new sources of data are coming into vogue, including seeking the views of the masses (crowdsourcing) and mining the massive wealth of archived internet traffic. Finally, the views of experts and professionals with profound experience in a particular domain can constitute evidence.

Speaking very generally, harder sources of evidence (scientific research and company data) are most useful at the information search and solution evaluation stages of the decision cycle shown in Exhibit 11.1. Expert and professional judgment tend to be most valuable in identifying the problem and mid-process, when developing, choosing, and implementing solutions. Even the highest-quality evidence does not speak for itself, and context is important in applying evidence in a particular setting.

As a student of organizational behaviour, you should develop an evidence-based mindset. Always ask yourself: What is the precise evidence being brought to bear concerning this decision? How high is the quality of this evidence? Can we obtain higher quality evidence?

Crowdsourcing

Crowdsourcing.

Outsourcing aspects of a decision process to a large collection of people.

Crowdsourcing involves "outsourcing" aspects of a decision process to a large collection of people.[68] In essence, it is meant to capitalize on the merits of group decision making that were discussed earlier, but on a large scale. In terms of the rational decision model (Exhibit 11.1), crowdsourcing can be used to develop alternative solutions to a problem, to choose the best solution, or both. Usually, the crowd in question is outside of the organization in which a decision is being made, although a very large organization might open a decision process up to all of its employees, using a kind of internal crowdsourcing. Crowdsourcing is not the same as contracting with outside experts, such as in a consulting relationship. Rather it is a much more open and organic process in which expertise is sought among the masses, which might range from everyday people to experts in their fields. One familiar application of crowdsourcing is employed by Wikipedia, the online encyclopedia. As you may know, Wikipedia entries are created, edited, and reviewed by volunteers who have an interest (and, one hopes, expertise) in a particular domain. As indicated in Applied Focus: Some *Applications of Crowdsourcing*, the practice has been applied to problems as diverse as discovering gold, curing illness, and choosing what fashions to produce.

Two basic ideas underpin the effective use of crowdsourcing for decision making. One is that the information required to make a particular decision is not available to those charged with making that decision. That is, in evidence-based management terms, evidence is needed, but it is not available in house. For example, a team of 50-year-old male apparel executives is unlikely to have much insight into what colour preferences preteen girls will have next summer. The other is that a large collection of diverse individuals is likely to contain either a single superior solution to a problem or, on average, the collection will be correct. Single superior solutions usually involve technical problems such as finding gold or designing an app. Averages of a large number of opinions usually work best for problems dealing with style or taste. Thus, the fashion business relies heavily on crowdsourcing to guide its choice of designs for production.

APPLIED FOCUS

SOME APPLICATIONS OF CROWDSOURCING

Goldcorp, a Vancouver-based gold mining company, had spent millions of dollars using its own geologists trying to find gold on its northern Ontario holdings, without great success. In what is normally an extremely secretive business, the CEO decided to make all of its geological data and related software publicly available on the firm's website and established the Goldcorp Challenge, offering $575 000 in prize money for successful solutions. Over 1000 people from 50 nations participated, bringing to bear disciplines such as geology, math, physics, computer graphics, and intelligent systems. New sources rich in gold were identified, transforming Goldcorp into a major player in precious metals mining.

Harvard Medical School used crowdsourcing to find new treatments and potential cures for Type 1 diabetes. The winning proposals contained innovative ideas well beyond the domain of conventional diabetes research, coming from a retired dentist, an undergrad chemistry student, a geophysicist, and a famous genetics researcher.

Netflix funded a $1-million contest to develop a new algorithm to be used to recommend movies to its clients. Much information sharing occurred among competitors, and the winning team was made up of competing teams that merged late in the contest.

Threadless, a Chicago design company and artists' community, provides design tools, such as guidelines and templates for T-shirts, backpacks, and laptop cases, to encourage a wide range of solutions from a wide range of designers. Then, it goes a step further and has its online community give feedback and vote on which designs they like. Threadless executives then use this information to make final production decisions.

Sources: Goldcorp from Tapscott, D., & Williams, A.D. (2008). *Wikinomics: How mass collaboration changes everything* (Expanded ed.). New York, NY: Portfolio; other examples from King, A., & Lakhani, K.R. (2013, Fall). Using open innovation to identify the best ideas. *MIT Sloan Management Review*, 41–48.

Low-cost information technology and the rise of social media have contributed to the growth of crowdsourcing as a decision aid. It is best employed when in-house expertise is lacking, the nature of the problem can be clearly stated, and a large, diverse crowd is both knowledgeable and motivated to participate. Concerning motivation, much crowdsourcing has relied on enthusiastic volunteers. However, as illustrated in the Applied Focus, contests involving considerable prizes have been used for certain high-payoff problems. In this case, organizations must cultivate trust that good ideas will not be unfairly taken without compensation. Many companies have used InnoCentive, a reputable innovation contest platform, to serve as an intermediary in such circumstances.[69]

Analytics and Big Data

Like crowdsourcing, analytics and big data are other facets of evidence-based management. **Analytics** concerns finding meaningful patterns in large datasets using conventional statistics, mathematical modeling, and various techniques to represent data visually. In some cases, the revealed patterns show that problems are more well structured than was thought. An interesting example of analytics can be found in the bestselling book *Moneyball* by Michael Lewis, the basis for a movie starring Brad Pitt. Lewis recounts how the general manager of the Oakland Athletics major league baseball team used an array of new performance statistics to evaluate players and implement tactics during games. The interesting thing about these analytic applications is that they showed that many intuitive and time-honoured decision rules used by managers (e.g., telling players to steal a base) were statistically incorrect. Using analytics enabled the Athletics to field highly competitive teams while paying comparatively modest salaries.[70]

Analytics. Finding meaningful patterns in large datasets.

Much of the sports establishment has remained hostile toward analytics, revering intuition and folklore over data-based decision making. Less so in business, where Netflix uses analytics to recommend movies and StyleSeek uses analytics to recommend fashion choices to online shoppers. One company strongly identified with the use of analytics is General Electric. Despite being a giant conglomerate, it has instilled a data-driven analytics culture into its various divisions.[71]

Big data. Copious amounts of information that are often collected in real time and can come from a wide variety of sources, particularly digital.

The term **big data** is not exactly a technical term. Rather, it refers loosely to copious amounts of information that are often collected in real time and can come from a wide variety of sources, particularly digital.[72] These sources include messages and images from social media, blog postings, cellphone data (including GPS), online shopping records, news articles, and data captured by sensors in cars and machinery. Such data tend to be unstructured and not easily incorporated into standard databases.

THE MANAGER'S NOTEBOOK

Preventing Surgical Decision Errors at Toronto General Hospital

1. To help cut surgical errors, medical researchers drew upon the experience of airline pilots, who use a safety checklist before takeoff. In 2008, the World Health Organization issued a set of guidelines for safe surgery. Harvard professor Dr. Atul Gawande and a team of physicians from eight city hospitals worldwide (including Toronto General) transformed the WHO guidelines into a 19-item Surgical Safety Checklist. Such checklists are especially effective for preventing procedural errors. The checklist is applied at three critical stages of the surgical process: before anaesthesia, before skin incision, and before the patient leaves the operating room. As part of their research, Dr. Gawande and his team, including UHN Chief Surgeon Dr. Bryce Taylor, tested the checklist in each of the eight hospitals, with impressive results. Although there was a greater decrease in preventable deaths in lower-income versus higher-income hospitals, all eight institutions experienced significant drops in complication rates. Dr. Taylor was so impressed with the results that the checklist is now being used by all three UHN hospitals under his watch. Should the checklist be fully implemented across Canada, it is possible that more than 60 000 complications could be avoided each year. Dr. Gawande's own experience convinced him that the checklist should be used worldwide; he argues that its use could prevent millions of complications and deaths each year and save billions of dollars in health-care costs.

2. Studies have indicated that nurses do not always speak up in the operating room, out of fear of reprisal. Although both nurses and doctors ultimately serve the needs of the patient, their respective training serves different purposes. Physicians have in-depth knowledge on surgical procedures, positioning them as leaders in the operating room. Consequently, because nurses are on the lower end of the status hierarchy, they may refrain from challenging physicians out of fear of being punished. The traditional operating-room command structure, in which the lead surgeon is considered to be the ultimate boss, may also intimidate residents and anaesthesiologists. So when problems do arise, they may be overlooked by a submissive surgical team. The essential problem is one in which the emotions of discomfort or outright fear lead to decisions being made with inadequate information. Thus, the person on the team who is most knowledgeable about a problem may not offer decision input. Toronto General Hospital understood that changing the surgical team culture from one of command-and-control to one of collaborative learning could encourage effective group decision making through the elimination of fear. The introduction of the Surgical Safety Checklist encouraged all team members to speak up either prior to, during, or after the operation. The researchers from Toronto General Hospital were so convinced that the procedures borrowed from aviation could save lives that they even invited a senior Air Canada training pilot to talk with the surgical teams.

Google and Facebook are two companies that have profited greatly from applying sophisticated analytics to big data to facilitate decisions about targeted advertising. Amazon knows what books online customers considered, what reviews they examined, and what they bought, enabling them to make recommendations for further reading. Acceptance or rejection of these suggestions allows them to refine future suggestions, all in real time. Health researchers have used aggregated Google search data concerning the flu to predict hospital visits in advance of flu alerts from the Centers for Disease Control.[73]

Privacy concerns have certainly been raised concerning the rise of big data, but it is clear that such data will continue to fascinate organizational decision makers.

MyManagementLab   Study, practise, and explore real management situations with these helpful resources:

- **Interactive Lesson Presentations:** Work through interactive presentations and assessments to test your knowledge of management concepts.
- **PIA (Personal Inventory Assessments):** Enhance your ability to connect with key concepts through these engaging, self-reflection assessments.   **P I A** PERSONAL INVENTORY ASSESSMENT
- **Study Plan:** Check your understanding of chapter concepts with self-study quizzes.
- **Videos:** Learn more about the management practices and strategies of real companies.
- **Simulations:** Practise decision-making in simulated management environments.

LEARNING OBJECTIVES CHECKLIST

11.1 *Decision making* is the process of developing a commitment to some course of action. Alternatively, it is a problem-solving process. A problem exists when a gap is perceived between some existing state and some desired state. Some problems are well structured. This means that existing and desired states are clear, as is the means of getting from one state to the other. Well-structured problems are often solved with programs that simply standardize solutions. Programmed decision making is effective as long as the program is developed rationally and as long as conditions do not change. Ill-structured problems contain some combination of an unclear existing state, an unclear desired state, or unclear methods of getting from one state to the other. They tend to be unique and non-recurrent, and they require non-programmed decision making, in which the rational model comes into play.

11.2 *Rational decision making* includes (1) problem identification, (2) information search, (3) development of alternative solutions, (4) evaluation of alternatives, (5) choice of the best alternative, (6) implementation, and (7) ongoing evaluation of the implemented alternative. The imaginary, perfectly rational decision maker has free and easy access to all relevant information, can process it accurately, and has a single ultimate goal: economic maximization. Real decision makers must suffer from *bounded rationality*. They do not have free and easy access to information, and the human mind has limited information processing capacity and is susceptible to a variety of cognitive biases. In addition, time constraints and political considerations can outweigh anticipated economic gain. As a result, bounded decision makers usually *satisfice* (choose a solution that is "good enough") rather than maximize.

11.3 *Framing* refers to the aspects of the presentation of information about a problem that are assumed by decision makers. A frame could include assumptions about the boundaries of a problem, the possible outcomes of a decision, or the reference points used to decide if a decision is successful. Problems that are framed as an investment versus a cost, or as a potential gain versus a potential loss, can affect decision-making processes. *Cognitive biases* are tendencies to acquire and process information in a particular way that is prone to error. These biases constitute assumptions and shortcuts that can improve decision-making efficiency, but they frequently lead to serious errors in judgment. Examples include overemphasizing recent information, overconfidence based on past success, perceptual defence, and faulty hindsight.

11.4 *Escalation of commitment* is the tendency to invest additional resources in an apparently failing course of action. This tendency emerges from people's desires to justify past decisions and attempts to recoup sunk costs incurred as the result of a past decision.

11.5 Although emotions can enhance the decision-making process in relation to correcting ethical errors or when dealing with creative problems, they can also distract and unsettle decision makers and lead to poor choices. Research has shown that mood can also have an important impact on the decision-making process, especially for uncertain or ambiguous problems. Mood can affect information recall, evaluation, creativity, time reference, and projected outcomes.

11.6 Groups can often make higher-quality decisions than individuals because of their vigilance and their potential capacity to generate and evaluate more ideas. Also, group members might accept more readily a decision that they have been involved in making. Given the appropriate problem, groups will frequently make higher-quality decisions than individuals. However, using groups takes a lot of time and may provoke conflict. In addition, groups may fall prey to *groupthink*, in which social pressures to conform to a particular decision outweigh rationality. Groups may also make decisions that are more risky or conservative than those of individuals.

11.7 Contemporary approaches to improving organizational decision making include evidence-based management, crowdsourcing, analytics, and the use of big data.

DISCUSSION QUESTIONS

1. The director of an urban hospital feels that there is a turnover problem among the hospital's nurses. About 25 percent of the staff resigns each year, leading to high replacement costs and disruption of services. Use the decision model in Exhibit 11.1 to explore how the director might proceed to solve this problem. Discuss probable bounds to the rationality of the director's decision.

2. Describe a decision-making episode (in school, at work, or in your personal life) in which you experienced information overload. How did you respond to this overload? Did it affect the quality of your decision?

3. A very cohesive planning group for a major oil company is about to develop a long-range strategic plan. The head of the unit is aware of the groupthink problem and wishes to prevent it. What steps should she take?

4. Discuss the implications of diffusion of responsibility, risky shift, and conservative shift for the members of a parole board. Also, consider the role of emotion and mood.

5. Discuss how the concepts of groupthink and escalation of commitment might be related to some cases of unethical decision making (and its cover-up) in business.

INTEGRATIVE DISCUSSION QUESTIONS

1. Consider the role of communication in decision making. Explain how various communication problems can affect decision making in organizations. How can personal and organizational approaches for improving communication improve decision making?

2. Does group structure influence group decision making? Explain how each of the following structural characteristics might influence group decision quality, acceptance and commitment, and diffusion of responsibility: group size, diversity, norms, roles, status, and cohesiveness.

ON-THE-JOB CHALLENGE QUESTION

Toronto Ritz-Carlton Nixes Poppies

It happens every year: A prominent organization bans a practice the public holds dear; an uproar ensues; the organization backs down in the face of bad publicity. So it happened at Toronto's posh new Ritz-Carlton hotel. The hotel had issued a memo to employees forbidding the wearing of poppies as a reminder of Remembrance Day, November 11, which marks the end of the First World War and serves to honour all military veterans. In general, Ritz policy forbids the wearing of any ribbons, pins, or badges that make a statement or support a cause. After complaints and media attention, the poppy ban was withdrawn. About the same time, the international soccer association FIFA initially banned the English team from wearing poppies in a match against Spain and then backed down after a public uproar and an intervention by Prince William.

Imagine the decision process that underpins the Ritz-Carlton policy against wearing ribbons, pins, or badges on one's uniform. What are some pros and some cons of such a policy? What does this story say about the role of rationality versus emotion in decision making? How do you account for the regularity with which managers reverse themselves on decisions like this?

Sources: Staff. (2011, November 10). Hotel rescinds poppy ban. *National Post*, A5; Burtt, J. (November 9, 2011). FIFA backs down and allows England players to wear poppies on black armband against Spain. *The Telegraph*.

EXPERIENTIAL EXERCISE

The New Truck Dilemma
Preparation for Role-Playing

The instructor will

1. Read the general instructions to the class as a whole.

2. Place data regarding name, length of service, and make and age of truck on the board for ready reference by all.

3. Divide the class into groups of six. Ask any remaining members to join one of the groups and serve as observers.

4. Assign roles to each person by handing out slips with the names Chris Marshall, Terry, Sal, Jan, Sam, and Charlie. Ask each person to read his or her own role only. Instructions should not be consulted once role-playing has begun.

5. Ask the Chris Marshalls to stand up when they have completed reading their instructions.

6. When all Chris Marshalls are standing, ask that each crew member display conspicuously the slip of paper with his or her role name so that Chris Marshalls can tell who is who.

The Role-Playing Process

1. The instructor will start the role-playing with a statement such as the following: "Chris Marshall has asked the crew to wait in the office. Apparently Chris wants to discuss something with the crew. When Chris sits down that will mean he or she has returned. What you say to each other is entirely up to you. Are you ready? All Chris Marshalls please sit down."

2. Role-playing proceeds for 25 to 30 minutes. Most groups reach agreement during this interval.

Collection of Results

1. Each supervisor in turn reports his or her crew's solution. The instructor summarizes these on the board by listing the initials of each repair person and indicating with arrows which truck goes to whom.

2. A tabulation should be made of the number of people getting a different truck, the crew members considering the solution unfair, and the supervisor's evaluation of the solution.

Discussion of Results

1. A comparison of solutions will reveal differences in the number of people getting a different truck, who gets the new one, the number dissatisfied, and so on. Discuss why the same facts yield different outcomes.

2. The quality of the solution can be measured by the trucks retained. Highest quality would require the poorest truck to be discarded. Evaluate the quality of the solutions achieved.

3. Acceptance is indicated by the low number of dissatisfied repair people. Evaluate solutions achieved on this dimension.

4. List problems that are similar to the new truck problem. See how widely the group will generalize.

General Instructions

This is a role-playing exercise. Do not read the roles given below until assigned to do so by your instructor!

Assume that you are a repair person for a large utility company. Each day you drive to various locations in the city to do repair work. Each repair person drives a small truck, and you take pride in keeping yours looking good. You have a possessive feeling about your truck and like to keep it in good running order. Naturally, you would like to have a new truck too, because a new truck gives you a feeling of pride.

Here are some facts about the trucks and the crew that reports to Chris Marshall, the supervisor of repairs:

> Terry—17 years with the company, has a 2-year-old Ford
>
> Sal—11 years with the company, has a 5-year-old Dodge
>
> Jan—10 years with the company, has a 4-year-old Ford
>
> Sam—5 years with the company, has a 3-year-old Ford
>
> Charlie—3 years with the company, has a 5-year-old Chevrolet

Most of you do all your driving in the city, but Jan and Sam cover the jobs in the suburbs.

You will be one of the people mentioned above and will be given some further individual instructions. In acting your part in role-playing, accept the facts as well as assume the attitude supplied in your specific role. From this point on, let your feelings develop in accordance with the events that transpire in the role-playing process. When facts or events arise that are not covered by the roles, make up things that are consistent with the way it might be in a real-life situation.

When the role-playing begins, assume that Chris Marshall called the crew into the repair office.

Role for Chris Marshall, Supervisor. You are the supervisor of a repair crew, each of whom drives a small service truck to and from various jobs. Every so often you get a new truck to exchange for an old one, and you have the problem of deciding which one of your crew gets the new truck. Often there are hard feelings because each person seems to feel entitled to the new truck, so you have a tough time being fair. As a matter of fact, it usually turns out that whatever you decide, most of the crew consider it wrong. You now have to face the issue again because a new truck has just been allocated to you for assignment. The new truck is a Chevrolet.

To handle this problem, you have decided to put the decision up to the crew themselves. You will tell them about the new truck and will put the problem in terms of what would be the fairest way to assign the truck. Do not take a position yourself because you want to do what the crew thinks is most fair. However, be sure that the group reaches a decision.

Role for Terry. When a new Chevrolet truck becomes available, you think you should get it because you have most seniority and do not like your present truck. Your own car is a Chevrolet, and you prefer a Chevrolet truck such as you drove before you got the Ford.

Role for Sal. You feel you deserve a new truck. Your present truck is old, and since the more senior crew member has a fairly new truck, you should get the next one. You have taken excellent care of your present Dodge and have kept it looking like new. People deserve to be rewarded if they treat a company truck like their own.

Role for Jan. You have to do more driving than most of the other crew because you work in the suburbs. You have a fairly old truck and feel you should have a new one because you do so much driving.

Role for Sam. The heater in your present truck is inadequate. Since Charlie backed into the door of your truck, it has never been repaired to fit right. The door lets in too much cold air, and you attribute your frequent colds to this. You want a warm truck since you have a good deal of driving to do. As long as it has good tires, brakes, and is comfortable, you do not care about its make.

Role for Charlie. You have the poorest truck in the crew. It is five years old, and before you got it, it had been in a bad wreck. It has never been good, and you have put up with it for three years. It is about time you got a good truck to drive, and you feel the next one should be yours. You have a good accident record. The only accident you had was when you sprung the door of Sam's truck when he opened it as you were backing out of the garage. You hope the new truck is a Ford, since you prefer to drive one.

Source: Maier, N.R.F., & Verser, G.C. (1982). *Psychology in industrial organizations* (5th ed.). Copyright 1982 Wadsworth, a part of Cengage Learning, Inc. Adapted by permission, www.cengage.com/permissions.

CASE INCIDENT

The Restaurant Review

After emigrating from New Orleans to his adopted city of Vancouver, Christophe Touché had worked as head chef at a neighbourhood pub for five years while saving money and planning to open his own restaurant. At the pub, he perfected several Cajun specialties that would form the core of the menu of his new restaurant, Cajun Sensation. After his restaurant had been open for two months, Christophe was delighted to receive a phone call from the local newspaper food critic who had dined anonymously at the restaurant the previous evening and was calling to verify some of the ingredients and techniques he used in his cooking. Two days later, delight turned to dismay as Christophe read the restaurant review. Although the critic praised the inventiveness of some dishes, others were described as "heavy handed." The staff was described as "charming but amateurish." And the wine list was described as "well chosen but overpriced." The review concluded, "In sum, this very new restaurant has both problems and promise." It was local custom to post restaurant reviews prominently at the restaurant entrance to capture walk-by trade. At a staff meeting, opinions varied about what to do. One member suggested posting the review, as it noted that the new establishment had been open only two months. Another suggested posting only favourable excerpts from the review. A third offered to write an angry letter to the paper's editor. Christophe wasn't sure what to do.

1. What are some of the factors that might lead Christophe to make a poor decision about the review?

2. What would you do in this situation, and why?

CASE STUDY

The Admissions Dilemma

Having just returned from a lengthy meeting with the dean of Birdwood Business School and the director of its development office, Janel Lehman sat down at her desk to gather her thoughts. As Birdwood's director of admissions, Lehman knew her recommendation to admit the daughter of a trustee and prominent businessman would not only have an immediate impact on the future of two applicants, but also might affect the capital campaign Birdwood had recently initiated. Additionally, Lehman realized that her decision would set a precedent upon which future admissions criteria could be based.

BIRDWOOD BUSINESS SCHOOL

Birdwood Business School had long been regarded as one of the premier business schools in the country. Like other top programs, the school relied heavily on the generous financial contributions of its alumni and other wealthy patrons to help finance the program and its continued development. To maintain its strong academic reputation and its elite status among business school programs, Birdwood attracted top faculty and provided cutting-edge resources and classes to its students. These efforts came at a hefty price, but they set Birdwood apart and allowed it to attract the best applicants and a long list of corporate recruiters year after year. To build and maintain a top program was expensive, and tuition alone did not cover a substantial part of the overall program cost.

To effectively cultivate the necessary contributions to finance a top-tier program, Birdwood maintained a development office that staffed four full-time and four part-time employees. The office kept a database of both personal and professional information on all graduates dating back to the first graduating class in 1957. This information was used to develop relationships with current and potential donors. For the wealthiest alumni, the office kept personal files, the contents of which reflected years of fundraising efforts. Birdwood believed this detailed and long-term commitment to fundraising resulted in the largest donations. During the previous capital campaign, the department's efforts brought in several $10 million commitments, which helped build a new library and computer centre and funded several full scholarships for outstanding applicants. Coincidentally, several recipients of this scholarship would graduate from Birdwood in the spring.

A year earlier, Birdwood had initiated a highly publicized multiyear capital campaign. One of the most-talked-about alumni within the development office was Joseph Lipscomb, class of 1970. After graduating from Birdwood, Joseph had started LipCo, one of the largest oil services companies in the world. At the company's stock price of $70, Joseph had a net worth estimated to be $800 million. Birdwood's development office had been courting him for the past year and had made significant strides toward securing a potentially sizable donation. He had been invited to join the board of trustees two years earlier and had taken an active role on the policy committee. In a private conversation that followed one of these meetings, Birdwood's dean had learned Joseph wanted his daughter Caroline to follow in his footsteps and attend Birdwood. Caroline had been working at LipCo since her graduation from Yale three years prior, and Joseph hoped that one day she would have the interest and skill set to take over control of the company.

THE DEAN'S "WATCH LIST"

At the request of the dean and the director of development, Lehman pulled Caroline Lipscomb's application from the pile of packets that made up the "Dean's Watch List" and began reading through it once again. Similar to its peer institutions, Birdwood maintained a list of candidates who were personally sponsored by

distinguished alumni, faculty members, and influential outside patrons. This list, known within the office as the "Dean's Watch List," was handled with extreme sensitivity. While some of the candidates on this list met the school's academic standards for admission, many did not. This latter group of candidates posed a dilemma for the office each year. For various reasons, Birdwood had historically admitted several candidates from this list, often applicants who would not have been accepted based upon their academic merit. If an applicant from this list was denied admission, the dean would make a personal phone call to the applicant's sponsor about the decision and the reasoning behind it. From Birdwood's perspective, greater communication with the sponsor might mitigate any damage to the school's relationship with that person.

Birdwood's application process was highly competitive. The school received roughly 3000 applications annually for just 300 spots. So far, this year's applicants had been extremely competitive on all fronts. Historically, those admitted to Birdwood averaged a 3.5 GPA, a 690 GMAT score, and four years of work experience and were quite active in their communities. There were subsets of candidates within the applicant pool, which helped add context to the evaluation process. This process was typical for most business schools. The basis for these subsets could include gender, ethnicity, cultural background, and previous work experience. The disparity between the average grades and test scores of the different groups could often be significant, so the school made an effort to recruit the top candidates from each subset. While the admissions office might find it easy to fill a class with "white male bankers" or "Indian engineers," the goal was to deliver a class of candidates that would best contribute to the program's rich diversity and academic excellence. Falling short in either area would undermine the school's effort to provide its students with a rich and well-rounded experience.

3.0 GPA/580 GMAT

Caroline Lipscomb's 3.0 GPA at Yale University and her 580 GMAT score were below both the school average and that of the admitted females in the class. On the positive side, Caroline had played field hockey at Yale and served as vice president of her sorority for two years. Caroline was also active in her community and, according to her references, had outperformed her peers during her three years at LipCo. Clearly, Caroline was intelligent and driven, two essential qualities in all Birdwood students. Yet while Caroline's application was good, given the strong current class of applicants, she fell short of being admitted based upon her own merit.

As Lehman sipped her coffee, she thought about Birdwood's relationship with LipCo and how it had weakened over the past few years after the company had stopped recruiting at Birdwood in favour of other top programs. Lehman could not avoid thinking about the $10 million donation Joseph Lipscomb had made to Yale when Caroline graduated in 2002, a gift that funded the Yale Center for Investment Management.

Lehman was well aware of the importance of large donors in any capital campaign and had seen Birdwood's capital campaign goals. These goals were based upon widely used fundraising statistics that showed that during a typical capital campaign, roughly 2.4% of a school's graduates provided 78% of the funding. (See Exhibit 1.)

Taking her thoughts one step further, Lehman wondered if she could consider admitting Caroline through the perspective of diversity. The "subset" of legacy applicants with wealthy families and a higher

(and in some cases known) propensity to donate large sums of money was quite small. Clearly, the school relied upon a small group of alumni to provide a disproportionate amount of the school's funding. If her office were to maintain a unique set of standards by which females, African-Americans, Europeans, and even bankers were to be evaluated, should applicants similar to Caroline also be evaluated separately? The decision would not be easy, but it had to be made soon. The school was sending out its admittance letters the next day.

This case was prepared by Jonathan England (MBA '06) under the supervision of Andrew C. Wicks, Associate Professor of Business Administration, and Jenny Mead, Senior Researcher. It was written as a basis for class discussion rather than to illustrate effective or ineffective handling of an administrative situation. Copyright © 2010 by the University of Virginia Darden School Foundation, Charlottesville, VA. All rights reserved. *To order copies, send an e-mail to sales@dardenbusinesspublishing.com. No part of this publication may be reproduced, stored in a retrieval system, used in a spreadsheet, or transmitted in any form of by any means—electronic, mechanical, photocopying, recording, or otherwise—without the permission of the Darden School Foundation.*

EXHIBIT 1   The Admissions Dilemma

Alumni Contribution Data and Forecast

(a) Percentage of Alumni Who Contribute and Percentage of Goal They Provide

Percentage of Alumni	Percentage of Goal
0.08%	40.0%
0.11%	56.7%
0.79%	66.0%
2.39%	78.0%
5.32%	83.3%

(b) Expected Breakout of Capital Campaign

■ 97.6% of alumni

■ 2.4% of alumni

Source: Created by case writer.

QUESTIONS

1. Is selecting applicants for business school a well-structured or an ill-structured problem? Explain your reasoning.

2. Is it possible to program the decision to select applicants for admission for business school? Is it advisable? Explain your answers.

3. Does Janel Lehman have enough information to make an appropriate decision? Does she have too much?

4. Explain how mood and emotion might affect decision making in this case.

5. Give an example of how hindsight might apply to the forthcoming decision.

6. Is this a decision that is appropriate for a group to make?

7. What are the ethical issues raised by this case?

12 POWER, POLITICS, AND ETHICS

LEARNING OBJECTIVES

After reading Chapter 12, you should be able to:

12.1 Define *power*, and review the bases of individual power.

12.2 Explain how people obtain power in organizations.

12.3 Discuss the concept of *empowerment*.

12.4 Provide a profile of power seekers.

12.5 Explain *strategic contingencies*, and discuss how subunits obtain power.

12.6 Define *organizational politics*, and discuss its various forms.

12.7 Define *ethics*, and review the ethical dilemmas that managers and employees face.

12.8 Define *sexual harassment*, and discuss what organizations can do to prevent it and how they should respond to allegations.

SEXUAL HARASSMENT AT THE ROYAL CANADIAN MOUNTED POLICE

The Royal Canadian Mounted Police (RCMP) recruited its first female officers in May 1974, some 101 years after its founding. Occasionally making headlines, sexual harassment has been an issue in the force for years. In 2004, the RCMP reached a settlement on a lawsuit filed by four female officers claiming they had been sexually harassed. More recently, in 2011, Corporal Catherine Galliford, the spokesperson for the RCMP on several high-profile investigations, made public her allegations of sexual harassment against several superior officers and colleagues. Galliford, in a 115-page complaint, described how for almost two decades she was the target of harassment and bullying due to her gender. Galliford's courage emboldened several other female officers to come forward with similar stories of abuse. The allegations spanned years and snowballed into one of the biggest scandals to hit the force since its creation. By 2015, more than 350 victims had started organizing for a possible class action lawsuit against the RCMP. Their allegations include indecent exposure, sexual remarks and advances, coerced sexual activities, double standards, and threats to benefits. Harassment has had serious effects on the victims. Most who went public have taken sick leave after being diagnosed with post-traumatic stress disorder, depression, anxiety, and insomnia, and some have even attempted suicide. Some substance abuse has occurred, but the more common story is one of failed careers, damaged family relations, and low quality of life.

As allegations have been brought to light, it becomes clear that power, politics, and a strict hierarchal organizational structure play a role in fuelling the unethical behaviour. On one hand, the RCMP provides not-so-easily replaceable service in many of the provinces, which causes provincial and federal authorities to be more forgiving about some of the transgressions that have been attributed to the force. On the other hand, the RCMP has all the ingredients needed for a perfect storm when it comes to harassment issues. Similar to other paramilitary organizations, it has a rigid male-dominated hierarchy with strict power differentials under which Mounties are expected to follow commands or risk being punished. Within such organizations, criticizing and whistle-blowing are often not tolerated and can have serious consequences for complainants. Female officers have reported observing or experiencing how voicing one's opinions about such issues have led to poor performance evaluations, transfer to less desirable assignments, being labelled as a whiner, and eventually being "stressed" out of the force. Even those who dare to object have had their complaints fall onto deaf ears. Constable Janet Merlo, at

The RCMP has been plagued by repeated charges of sexual harassment and power abuse.

CP PHOTO/Chuck Stoody

the centre of the possible class action lawsuit, wrote to former RCMP commissioner William Elliott concerning an unfair transfer, only to get a standard reply more than two years later. Former commissioner Elliott was himself on the receiving end of intimidation accusations by his deputies. A senior officer charged with fixing the harassment mess was accused of brokering a deal that got a staff sergeant accused of harassing two female Mounties off the hook with a deduction of a day's pay and an order to get counselling after pleading guilty to charges well below what the two women were accusing him of. The same transgressor was soon after promoted.

Yet another problem is inadequate policies and procedures to investigate and manage such incidents. The Division Staff Relations Representative Program, the body responsible for handling formal complaints within the RCMP, rarely acted when it came to harassment issues. Victims can go on indefinite paid sick leave, which basically avoids anyone having to fix the problem. A 2007 task force on RCMP governance and culture heavily criticized its management structure and suggested that complaints against Mounties be handled by a civilian body rather than an internal division. The suggestion has yet to be implemented.

Following Catherine Galliford's public accusations and the storm that followed, steps have been taken to initiate change. The RCMP Public Complaints Commission was assigned to inspect whether regulations were impartially respected when investigating complaints of harassment and whether existing RCMP guidelines in that respect needed updating. An informal review based on focus group meetings with some 400 female Mounties found that there is a general distrust of the current reporting system. As such, recommendations were made for a new, more confidential system for reporting incidents and better harassment awareness programs. Building on these findings, a gender-based, nation-wide audit is being conducted by the RCMP to tackle those subjects in addition to areas such as women's engagement and advancement in the workplace. The supervision of harassment complaints has been centralized in Ottawa, and British Columbia has trained 100 RCMP officers in harassment investigation.[1]

This vignette illustrates the main themes of this chapter—power, politics, and ethics. First, we will define power and discuss the bases of individual power. Then, we will examine how people get and use power and who seeks it. After this, we will explore how organizational subunits, such as particular departments, obtain power, define organizational politics, and explore the relationship of politics to power. Finally, we will look at ethics in organizations and sexual harassment.

WHAT IS POWER?

LO 12.1

Define *power*, and review the bases of individual power.

Power. The capacity to influence others who are in a state of dependence.

PERSONAL INVENTORY ASSESSMENT

Learn About Yourself
Personal Empowerment Assessment

Power is the capacity to influence others who are in a state of dependence.[2] First, notice that power is the *capacity* to influence the behaviour of others. Power is not always perceived or exercised.[3] For example, most professors hold a great degree of potential power over students in terms of grades, assignment load, and the ability to embarrass students in class. Under normal circumstances, professors use only a small amount of this power.

Second, the fact that the target of power is dependent on the power holder does not imply that a poor relationship exists between the two. For instance, your best friend has power to influence your behaviour and attitudes because you are dependent on him or her for friendly reactions and social support. Presumably, you can exert reciprocal influence for similar reasons.

Third, power can flow in any direction in an organization. Often members at higher organizational levels have more power than those at lower levels. However, in specific cases, reversals can occur. For example, the janitor who finds the president in a compromising position with a subordinate might find himself in a powerful position if the president wishes to maintain his reputation in the organization!

Finally, power is a broad concept that applies to both individuals and groups. On the one hand, an individual marketing manager might exert considerable influence over the staff who report to her. On the other hand, the marketing department at XYZ Foods might be the most powerful department in the company, able to get its way more often than other departments. But from where do the marketing manager and the marketing department obtain their power? We explore this issue in the following sections.

THE BASES OF INDIVIDUAL POWER

If you wanted to marshal some power to influence others in your organization, where would you get it? As psychologists John French and Bertram Raven have explained, power can be found in the *position* that you occupy in the organization or the *resources* that you are able to command.[4] The first base of power—legitimate power—is dependent on one's position or job. The other bases (reward, coercive, referent, and expert power) involve the control of important resources.

Legitimate Power

Legitimate power. Power derived from a person's position or job in an organization.

Legitimate power derives from a person's position or job in the organization. It constitutes the organization's judgment about who is formally permitted to influence whom, and it is often called "authority." As we move up the organization's hierarchy, we find that members possess more and more legitimate power. In theory, organizational equals (e.g., all vice-presidents) have equal legitimate power. Of course, some people are more likely than others to *invoke* their legitimate power—"Look, *I'm* the boss around here." In the RCMP, one's legitimate power corresponds to one's rank in the organization's hierarchy.

Organizations differ greatly in the extent to which they emphasize and reinforce legitimate power. At one extreme is the military, which has many levels of command, differentiating uniforms, and rituals (e.g., salutes), all designed to emphasize legitimate power. On the other hand, the academic hierarchy of universities tends to downplay differences in the legitimate power of lecturers, professors, chairpeople, and deans.

When legitimate power works, it often does so because people have been socialized to accept its influence. Experiences with parents, teachers, and law enforcement officials cause members to enter organizations with a degree of readiness to submit to (and exercise) legitimate power. In fact, employees consistently cite legitimate power as a major reason for following their boss's directives, even across various cultures.[5] This is one reason why juries often fail to believe that top executives are "out of the loop" in ethical scandals.

Reward Power

Reward power means that the power holder can exert influence by providing positive outcomes and preventing negative outcomes. In general, it corresponds to the concept of positive reinforcement discussed in Chapter 2. Reward power often backs up legitimate power. That is, managers are given the chance to recommend raises, do performance evaluations, and assign preferred tasks to employees. Of course, *any* organizational member can attempt to exert influence over others with praise, compliments, and flattery, which also constitute rewards.

Reward power. Power derived from the ability to provide positive outcomes and prevent negative outcomes.

Coercive Power

Coercive power is available when the power holder can exert influence using punishment and threat. Like reward power, it is often a support for legitimate power. Managers might be permitted to dock pay, assign unfavourable tasks, or block promotions. Despite a strong civil service system, even US government agencies provide their executives with plenty of coercive power. In the RCMP, some more senior male officers have abused their legitimate power and engaged in sexual coercion.

Of course, coercive power is not perfectly correlated with legitimate power. Lower-level organizational members can also apply their share of coercion. For example, consider work-to-rule campaigns that slow productivity by strictly adhering to organizational procedures. Cohesive work groups are especially skilful at enforcing such campaigns.

In Chapter 2, we pointed out that the use of punishment to control behaviour is very problematic because of emotional side effects. Thus, it is not surprising that when managers use coercive power, it is generally ineffective and can provoke considerable employee resistance.[6]

Coercive power. Power derived from the use of punishment and threat.

Referent Power

Referent power exists when the power holder is *well liked* by others. It is not surprising that people we like readily influence us. We are prone to consider their points of view, ignore their failures, seek their approval, and use them as role models. In fact, it is often highly dissonant to hold a point of view that is discrepant from that held by someone we like.[7]

Referent power is especially potent for two reasons. First, it stems from *identification* with the power holder. Thus, it represents a truer or deeper base of power than reward or coercion, which may stimulate mere compliance to achieve rewards or avoid punishment. In this sense, charismatic leaders (Chapter 9) have referent power. Second, *anyone* in the organization may be well liked, irrespective of his or her other bases of power. Thus, referent power is available to everyone from the janitor to the president.

Friendly interpersonal relations often permit influence to extend across the organization, outside the usual channels of legitimate authority, reward, and coercion. For example, a production manager who becomes friendly with the design engineer through participation in a task force might later use this contact to ask for a favour in solving a production problem.

Referent power. Power derived from being well liked by others.

EXHIBIT 12.1
Employee responses to bases of power.
Source: Steers, Richard M. Introduction Organizational Behaviour, 4th ed. ©1991. Printed and Electronically reproduced by permission of Pearson Education, Inc., Upper Saddle River, New Jersey.

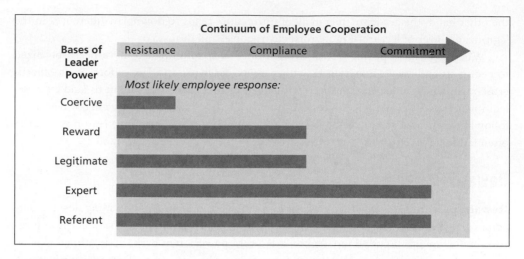

Expert Power

Expert power. Power derived from having special information or expertise that is valued by an organization.

A person has **expert power** when he or she has special information or expertise that the organization values. In any circumstance, we tend to be influenced by experts or by those who perform their jobs well. However, the more crucial and unusual this expertise, the greater the expert power available. Thus, expert power corresponds to difficulty of replacement. Consider the business school that has one highly published professor who is an internationally known scholar and past federal cabinet minister. Such a person would obviously be difficult to replace and should have much greater expert power than an unpublished lecturer.

One of the most fascinating aspects of expert power occurs when lower-level organizational members accrue it. Many secretaries have acquired expert power through long experience in dealing with clients, keeping records, or sparring with the bureaucracy. Frequently they have been around longer than those they serve. In this case, it is not unusual for bosses to create special titles and develop new job classifications to reward their expertise and prevent their resignation.

Of all the bases of managerial power, expertise is most consistently associated with employee effectiveness.[8] Also, research shows that employees perceive women managers as more likely than male managers to be high in expert power.[9] Women often lack easy access to more organizationally based forms of power, and expertise is free for self-development. Thus, being "better" than their male counterparts is one strategy that women managers have used to gain influence.

Exhibit 12.1 summarizes likely employee responses to various bases of managerial power. As you can see, coercion is likely to produce resistance and lack of cooperation. Legitimate power and reward power are likely to produce compliance with the boss's wishes. Referent and expert power are most likely to generate true commitment and enthusiasm for the manager's agenda.

LO 12.2

Explain how people obtain power in organizations.

Learn About Yourself
Gaining Power and Influence

HOW DO PEOPLE OBTAIN POWER?

Now that we have discussed the individual bases of power, we can turn to the issue of how people *get* power. Rosabeth Moss Kanter has provided a succinct recipe: Do the right things, and cultivate the right people.[10]

Doing the Right Things

According to Kanter, some activities are "righter" than others for obtaining power. She argues that activities lead to power when they are extraordinary, highly visible, and especially relevant to the solution of organizational problems.

EXTRAORDINARY ACTIVITIES Excellent performance of a routine job might not be enough to obtain power. What one needs is excellent performance in *unusual* or *non-routine* activities. In the large company that Kanter studied, these activities included occupying new positions, managing substantial changes, and taking great risks. For example, consider the manager who establishes and directs a new customer service program. This is a risky, major change that involves the occupancy of a new position. If successful, the manager should acquire substantial power.

VISIBLE ACTIVITIES Extraordinary activities will fail to generate power if no one knows about them. People who have an interest in power are especially good at identifying visible activities and publicizing them. The successful marketing executive whose philosophy is profiled in *Fortune* will reap the benefits of power. Similarly, the innovative surgeon whose techniques are reported in the *New England Journal of Medicine* will enhance his influence in the hospital.

RELEVANT ACTIVITIES Extraordinary, visible work may fail to generate power if no one cares. If nobody sees the work as relevant to the solution of important organizational problems, it will not add to one's influence. The English professor who wins two Pulitzer Prizes will probably not accrue much power if his small college is financially strapped and hurting for students. He would not be seen as contributing to the solution of pressing organizational problems. In another college, these extraordinary, visible activities might generate considerable influence.

Cultivating the Right People

An old saying advises, "It's not what you know, it's *who* you know." In reference to power in organizations, there is probably more than a grain of truth to the latter part of this statement. Kanter explains that developing informal relationships with the right people can prove a useful means of acquiring power.

OUTSIDERS Establishing good relationships with key people outside one's organization can lead to increased power within the organization. Sometimes this power is merely a reflection of the status of the outsider, but, all the same, it may add to one's internal influence. The assistant director of a hospital who is friendly with the president of the American Medical Association might find herself holding power by association. Cultivating outsiders may also contribute to more tangible sources of power. Organizational members who are on the boards of directors of other companies might acquire critical information about business conditions that they can use in their own firms.

SUBORDINATES At first blush, it might seem unlikely that power can be enhanced by cultivating relationships with subordinates. However, as Kanter notes, an individual can gain influence if she is closely identified with certain up-and-coming subordinates—"I taught her everything she knows." In academics, some professors are better known for the brilliant PhD students they have supervised than for their own published work. Of course, there is also the possibility that an outstanding subordinate will one day become one's boss! Having cultivated the relationship earlier, one might then be rewarded with special influence.

Cultivating subordinate interests can also provide power when a manager can demonstrate that he or she is backed by a cohesive team. The research director who can oppose a policy change by honestly insisting that "My people won't stand for this" knows that there is strength in numbers.

PEERS Cultivating good relationships with peers is mainly a means of ensuring that nothing gets in the way of one's *future* acquisition of power. As one moves up through the ranks, favours can be asked of former associates, and fears of being "stabbed in the back" for a past misdeed are precluded. Organizations often reward good "team players" with promotions on the assumption that they have demonstrated good interpersonal skills. On the other side of the coin, people often avoid contact with peers whose reputation is seen as questionable.

SUPERIORS Liaisons with key superiors probably represent the best way of obtaining power through cultivating others. As we discussed in Chapter 8, such superiors are often called *mentors* or *sponsors* because of the special interest they show in a promising subordinate. Mentors can provide power in several ways. Obviously, it is useful to be identified as a protégé of someone higher in the organization. More concretely, mentors can provide special information and useful introductions to other "right people."

Although cultivating others can add to one's power base, associates of people who have power sometimes develop an exaggerated and illusory sense of their own power, status, and influence. This phenomenon seems much more prevalent among men than women.[11] Celebrity hangers-on and political staff personnel (e.g., aides to prime ministers and senators) can be classic examples of this illusory power by association.

LO 12.3

Discuss the concept of *empowerment*.

Empowerment. Giving people the authority, opportunity, and motivation to take initiative and solve organizational problems.

PERSONAL INVENTORY ASSESSMENT

Learn About Yourself
Effective Empowerment and Enagagement

EMPOWERMENT—PUTTING POWER WHERE IT IS NEEDED

Early organizational scholars treated power as something of a fixed quantity: an organization had so much, the people on the top had a lot, and lower-level employees had a little. Our earlier analysis of the more informal sources of power (such as being liked and being an expert) hints at the weakness of this idea. Thus, contemporary views of power treat it less as a fixed-sum phenomenon. This is best seen in the concept of **empowerment**, which means giving people the authority, opportunity, and motivation to take initiative to solve organizational problems.[12]

In practice, having the authority to solve an organizational problem means having legitimate power. This might be included in a job description, or a boss might delegate it to a subordinate.

Having opportunity usually means freedom from bureaucratic barriers and other system problems that block initiative. In a service encounter, if you have ever heard "Sorry, the computer won't let me do that" or "That's not my job," you have been the victim of limited opportunity. Opportunity also includes any relevant training and information about the impact of one's actions on other parts of the organization.

The motivation part of the empowerment equation suggests hiring people who will be intrinsically motivated by power and opportunity and aligning extrinsic rewards with successful performance. Also, leaders who express confidence in subordinates' abilities and foster conditions that facilitate the sharing of power (see transformational and empowering leadership, Chapter 9) can contribute to empowerment.[13] A good example occurred when a nay-saying union shop steward, doubting General Electric's commitment to changing its corporate culture, explained a recurrent problem with a supplier's component. His manager, sensing he was correct, chartered a plane, and the subordinate left that same night to visit the supplier and solve the problem.[14] It goes without saying that managers have to be tolerant of occasional mistakes from empowered employees.

People who are empowered have a strong sense of self-efficacy (Chapter 2), the feeling that they are capable of doing their jobs well and "making things happen." Empowering

Delta Hotels focuses on empowerment.

David Cooper/Getty Images

lower-level employees can be critical in service organizations, where providing customers with a good initial encounter or correcting any problems that develop can be essential for repeat business. The Nordstrom chain of stores is one firm that is known for empowering sales personnel to make on-the-spot adjustments or search out merchandise at other stores. Customers have even had enthusiastic store personnel change flat tires.

Under its Power to Please program, staff at Canada's Delta Hotels have the authority to handle special guest requests without seeking manager approval, deal with customer complaints on the spot, and have input on how they fulfill their tasks. For example, staff can handle requests for extra towels or more coffee directly, housekeepers have input on the type of cleaning products the hotel uses, and front desk staffers can take it upon themselves to send up a platter from room service following a guest complaint.[15]

There is growing evidence that empowerment fosters job satisfaction, organizational commitment, organizational citizenship behaviours, and high performance.[16] However, empowerment does not mean providing employees with a maximum amount of unfettered power. Rather, used properly, empowerment puts power where it is *needed* to make the organization effective. This depends on organizational strategy and customer expectations. The average Taco Bell customer does not expect highly empowered counter personnel who offer to make adjustments to the posted menu—a friendly, fast, efficient encounter will do. On the other hand, the unempowered waiter in a fancy restaurant who is fearful of accommodating reasonable adjustments and substitutions can really irritate customers. Speaking generally, service encounters predicated on high volume and low cost need careful engineering. Those predicated on customized, personalized service need more empowered personnel.[17]

You might wonder whether organizational members could have *too much* power. Exhibit 12.2 nicely illustrates the answer. People are empowered, and should exhibit effective performance, when they have sufficient power to carry out their jobs. Above, we mainly contrasted empowerment with situations in which people had inadequate power for effective performance. However, as the exhibit shows, excessive power can lead to abuse and ineffective performance. One is reminded of the recurrent and inappropriate use

EXHIBIT 12.2
Relationship between power and performance.
Source: Whetten, David A. Developing Management Skills, 3rd ed. ©1995. Printed and Electronically reproduced by permission of Pearson Education, Inc., Upper Saddle River, New Jersey.

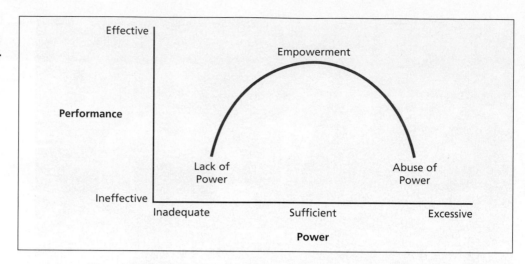

of government aircraft by political bigwigs as an example. As we will see in the following sections, the fact that people can have too much power does not always inhibit them from seeking it anyway!

INFLUENCE TACTICS—PUTTING POWER TO WORK

Influence tactics. Tactics that are used to convert power into actual influence over others.

As we discussed earlier, power is the potential to influence others. But exactly how does power result in influence? Research has shown that various **influence tactics** convert power into actual influence. These are specific behaviours that people use to affect others and manage other's impressions of themselves.[18] These tactics include the following:

- *Assertiveness:* ordering, nagging, setting deadlines, and verbally confronting others
- *Ingratiation:* using flattery and acting friendly, polite, or humble
- *Rationality:* using logic, reason, planning, and compromise
- *Exchange:* doing favours or offering to trade favours
- *Upward appeal:* making formal or informal appeals to organizational superiors for intervention
- *Coalition formation:* seeking united support from other organizational members

PERSONAL INVENTORY ASSESSMENT

Learn About Yourself
Using Influencing Strategies

What determines which influence tactics you might use? For one thing, your bases of power.[19] Other things being equal, someone with coercive power might gravitate toward assertiveness, someone with referent power might gravitate toward ingratiation, and someone with expert power might try rationality. Of course, rationality or its appearance is a highly prized quality in organizations, and its use is viewed positively by others. Thus, surveys show that people report trying to use rationality very frequently.

As you can guess, the use of influence tactics is also dependent on just whom you are trying to influence—subordinates, peers, or superiors. Subordinates are more likely to be the recipients of assertiveness than peers or superiors. Despite the general popularity of rationality, it is most likely to be directed toward superiors. Exchange, ingratiation, and upward appeal are favoured tactics for influencing both peers and subordinates.[20]

Which influence tactics are most effective? Some of the most interesting research has concerned upward influence attempts directed toward superiors. It shows that, at least for men, using rationality as an influence tactic was associated with receiving better performance evaluations, earning more money, and experiencing less work stress. A particularly ineffective influence style is a "shotgun" style that is high on all tactics with particular emphasis on assertiveness and exchange. In this series of studies, women who used ingratiation as an influence tactic received the highest performance evaluations (from male managers).[21] Another study showed that top managers who used ingratiation with their CEOs were inclined to receive appointments to corporate boards with whom the CEO was connected.[22] Thus, flattery and opinion conformity work even at the very top of organizations!

WHO WANTS POWER?

LO 12.4

Provide a profile of power seekers.

Who wants power? At first glance, the answer would seem to be everybody. After all, it is both convenient and rewarding to be able to exert influence over others. Power whisks celebrities to the front of movie lines, gets rock stars the best restaurant tables, and enables executives to shape organizations in their own image. Actually, there are considerable individual differences in the extent to which individuals pursue and enjoy power. On television talk shows, we occasionally see celebrities recount considerable embarrassment over the unwarranted power that public recognition brings.

Earlier we indicated that some people consider power a manifestation of evil. This is due, in no small part, to the historic image of power seekers that some psychologists and political scientists have portrayed. This is that power seekers are neurotics who are covering up feelings of inferiority, striving to compensate for childhood deprivation, or substituting power for lack of affection.[23]

There can be little doubt that these characteristics do apply to some power seekers. Underlying this negative image of power seeking is the idea that some power seekers feel weak and resort primarily to coercive power to cover up, compensate for, or substitute for this weakness. Power is sought for its own sake and is used irresponsibly to hurt others. Adolf Hitler comes to mind as an extreme example.

But can one use power responsibly to influence others? Psychologist David McClelland says yes. In Chapter 5, we discussed McClelland's research on need for power (n Pow). You will recall that n Pow is the need to have strong influence over others. This need is a reliable personality characteristic—some people have more n Pow than others.[24] Also, just as many women have high n Pow as men.[25] People who are high in n Pow in its "pure" form conform to the negative stereotype depicted above—they are rude, sexually exploitative, abuse alcohol, and show a great concern with status symbols. However, when n Pow is responsible and controlled, these negative properties are not observed. Specifically, McClelland argues that the most effective managers

- have high n Pow;
- use their power to achieve organizational goals;
- adopt a participative or "coaching" leadership style; and
- are relatively unconcerned with how much others like them.

McClelland calls such managers *institutional managers* because they use their power for the good of the institution rather than for self-aggrandizement. They refrain from coercive leadership and do not play favourites, since they are not worried about being well liked. His research reveals that institutional managers are more effective than *personal power managers* (who use their power for personal gain) and *affiliative managers* (who are more concerned with being liked than with exercising power). Exhibit 12.3 shows that institutional managers are generally superior in giving subordinates a sense of responsibility, clarifying organizational priorities, and instilling team spirit.[26] We can conclude that the need for power can be a useful asset, as long as it is not a neurotic expression of perceived weakness.

Research has shown that CEOs who are very powerful relative to their top management team tend to pursue extreme strategies, with big successes or failures. However, a powerful board of directors can temper these extremes and promote successful strategic outcomes.[27]

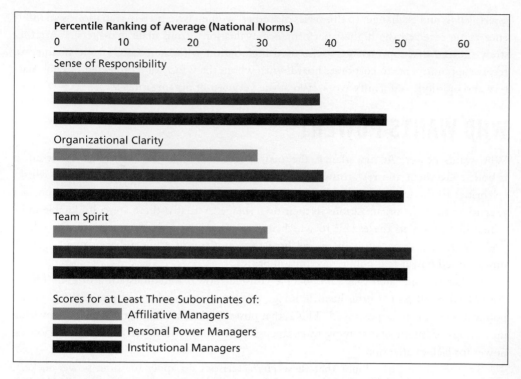

LO 12.5

Explain *strategic contingencies*, and discuss how subunits obtain power.

Subunit power. The degree of power held by various organizational subunits, such as departments.

Strategic contingencies. Critical factors affecting organizational effectiveness that are controlled by a key subunit.

CONTROLLING STRATEGIC CONTINGENCIES —HOW SUBUNITS OBTAIN POWER

Thus far, we have been concerned with the bases of *individual* power and how individual organizational members obtain influence. In this section, we shift our concern to **subunit power**. Most straightforwardly, the term *subunit* applies to organizational departments. In some cases, subunits could also refer to particular jobs, such as those held by software engineers or environmental lawyers.

How do organizational subunits acquire power—that is, how do they achieve influence that enables them to grow in size, get a bigger share of the budget, obtain better facilities, and have greater impact on decisions? In short, they control **strategic contingencies**, which are critical factors affecting organizational effectiveness. This means that the work *other* subunits perform is contingent on the activities and performance of a key subunit. Again, we see the critical role of *dependence* in power relationships. If some subunits are dependent on others for smooth operations (or their very existence), they are susceptible to influence. We turn now to the conditions under which subunits can control strategic contingencies.

Scarcity

Differences in subunit power are likely to be magnified when resources become scarce.[28] When there is plenty of budget money or office space or support staff for all subunits, they will seldom waste their energies jockeying for power. If cutbacks occur, however, differences in power will become apparent. For example, well-funded quality-of-work-life programs or organizational development efforts might disappear when economic setbacks occur, because the subunits that control them are not essential to the firm's existence.

Subunits tend to acquire power when they are able to *secure* scarce resources that are important to the organization as a whole. One study of a large American state university found that the power of academic departments was associated with their ability to obtain funds through consulting contracts and research grants. This mastery over economic resources was more crucial to their power than was the number of undergraduates taught by the department.[29]

Uncertainty

Organizations detest the unknown. Unanticipated events wreak havoc with financial commitments, long-range plans, and tomorrow's operations. The basic sources of uncertainty exist mainly in the organization's environment: government policies might change, sources of supply and demand might dry up, or the economy might take an unanticipated turn. It stands to reason that the subunits that are most capable of coping with uncertainty will tend to acquire power.[30] In a sense, these subunits are able to protect the others from serious problems. By the same token, uncertainty promotes confusion, which permits *changes* in power priorities as the organizational environment changes. Those functions that can provide the organization with greater control over what it finds problematic and can create more certainty will acquire more power.[31]

Changes in the sources of uncertainty frequently lead to shifts in subunit power. Thus, HR departments gained power when government legislation regarding employment opportunity was first passed, and departments concerned with environmental impact have gained power with the current interest in "green" organizations. Units dealing with business ethics or environmental concerns gain or lose power in response to the latest scandal or the newest piece of legislation involving clean air or water.

Centrality

Other things being equal, subunits whose activities are most central to the mission or work flow of the organization should acquire more power than those whose activities are more peripheral.[32] A subunit's activities can be central in at least three senses. First, it may influence the work of most other subunits. The finance or accounting department is a good example here—its authority to approve expenses and make payments affects every other department in the firm.

Centrality also exists when a subunit has an especially crucial impact on the quantity or quality of the organization's key product or service. This is one reason for the former low power of human resources departments—their activities were then seen as fairly remote from the primary goals of the organization.

Finally, a subunit's activities are more central when their impact is more immediate. As an example, consider a large city government with a fire department, a police department, and a public works department. The impact of a lapse in fire or police services will be felt more immediately than a lapse in street repairs. This gives the former departments more potential for power acquisition.

One of the reasons that organizations such as the RCMP have trouble instituting effective anti-harassment units is that the role of such units is not seen as central to the organization's primary mission of crime fighting.

Substitutability

A subunit will have relatively little power if others inside or outside the organization can perform its activities. If the subunit's staff is non-substitutable, however, it can acquire substantial power.[33] One crucial factor here is the labour market for the specialty performed by the subunit. A change in the labour market can result in a change in the subunit's influence. For example, the market for scientists and engineers is notoriously cyclical. When jobs are plentiful, these professionals command high salaries and high influence in organizations. When jobs are scarce, this power wanes. In the 1990s, there was a shortage of engineers and scientists, with a consequent increase in their bargaining power. Precisely in line with the strategic contingencies idea, this shortage provided real opportunities for properly trained women and members of minorities to move into positions of power from which they were excluded when there were plenty of white male engineers and scientists to go around.[34]

If work can be contracted out, the power of the subunit that usually performs these activities is reduced. Typical examples include temporary office help, off-premises data entry, and contracted maintenance, laboratory, and security services. The subunits that control these activities often lack power because the threat of "going outside" can counter their influence attempts.

LO 12.6

Define *organizational politics*, and discuss its various forms.

ORGANIZATIONAL POLITICS —USING AND ABUSING POWER

In the previous pages, we have avoided using the terms "politics" or "political" in describing the acquisition and use of power. This is because not all uses of power constitute politics.

The Basics of Organizational Politics

Organizational politics.
The pursuit of self-interest in an organization, whether or not this self-interest corresponds to organizational goals.

Organizational politics is the pursuit of self-interest within an organization, whether or not this self-interest corresponds to organizational goals.[35] Frequently, politics involves using means of influence that the organization does not sanction or pursuing ends or goals that it does not sanction.[36]

Political activity is self-conscious and intentional. This separates politics from ignorance or lack of experience with approved means and ends. Also, we can conceive of politics as either individual activity or subunit activity. Either a person or a whole department could act politically. Finally, it is possible for political activity to have beneficial outcomes for the organization, even though these outcomes are achieved by questionable tactics.

We can explore organizational politics using the means/ends matrix in Exhibit 12.4. It is the association between influence means and influence ends that determines whether activities are political and whether these activities benefit the organization.

- *I. Sanctioned means/sanctioned ends.* Here, power is used routinely to pursue agreed-on goals. Familiar, accepted means of influence are employed to achieve sanctioned outcomes. For example, a manager agrees to recommend a raise for an employee if she increases her net sales by 30 percent in the next six months. There is nothing political about this.

- *II. Sanctioned means/not-sanctioned ends.* In this case, acceptable means of influence are abused to pursue goals that the organization does not approve of. For instance, a head nurse agrees to assign a subordinate nurse to a more favourable job if the nurse agrees not to report the superior for stealing medical supplies. While job assignment is often a sanctioned means of influence, covering up theft is not a sanctioned end. This is dysfunctional political behaviour.

- *III. Not-sanctioned means/sanctioned ends.* Here, ends that are useful for the organization are pursued through questionable means. For example, although Qatar officials were pursuing a sanctioned end—the 2022 World Cup of soccer—the alleged use of bribery and vote-buying as a means of influence were not sanctioned tactics.

EXHIBIT 12.4
The dimensions of organizational politics.
Source: Mayes, B.T., & Allen, R.T. (1977). Toward a definition of organizational politics, *Academy of Management Review, 2,* 672–678.

Influence Means	Influence Ends	
	Organizationally Sanctioned	Not Sanctioned by Organization
Organizationally Sanctioned	Nonpolitical job behaviour **I**	**II** Organizationally dysfunctional political behaviour
Not Sanctioned by Organization	Political behaviour potentially functional to the organization **III**	**IV** Organizationally dysfunctional political behaviour

- *IV. Not-sanctioned means/not-sanctioned ends.* This quadrant may exemplify the most flagrant abuse of power, since disapproved tactics are used to pursue disapproved outcomes. For example, to increase his personal power, the head of an already over-staffed legal department wishes to increase its size. He intends to hire several of his friends in the process. To do this, he falsifies workload documents and promises special service to the accounting department in exchange for the support of its manager.

We have all seen cases in which politics have been played out publicly to "teach someone a lesson." More frequently, though, politicians conceal their activities with a "cover story" or "smokescreen" to make them appear legitimate.[37] Such a tactic will increase the odds of success and avoid punishment from superiors. A common strategy is to cover non–sanctioned means and ends with a cloak of rationality. For an example, see the Ethical Focus: *Knowledge Hiding in Organizations*.

Do political activities occur under particular conditions or in particular locations in organizations? Research suggests the following:[38]

- Managers report that most political manoeuvring occurs at middle and upper management levels rather than at lower levels.

- Some subunits are more prone to politicking than others. Clear goals and routine tasks (e.g., production) might provoke less political activity than vague goals and complex tasks (e.g., research and development).

- Some issues are more likely than others to stimulate political activity. Budget allocation, reorganization, and personnel changes are likely to be the subjects of politicking. Setting performance standards and purchasing equipment are not.

- In general, scarce resources, uncertainty, and important issues provoke political behaviour.

Highly political climates result in lowered job satisfaction, commitment, and organizational citizenship, and increased stress and turnover intentions.[39] When it comes to performance, politics take a toll on older workers but not on younger workers, perhaps due to stress factors.[40]

ETHICAL FOCUS

KNOWLEDGE HIDING IN ORGANIZATIONS

Canadian researchers Catherine Connelly, David Zweig, Jane Webster, and John Trougakos studied knowledge hiding in organizations. Knowledge hiding is a form of political behaviour that entails intentionally concealing or withholding information that has been requested by or is relevant to another organizational member. Although the sharing of knowledge is essential for organizational success and has been extensively studied, little is known about the active hiding of organization-relevant knowledge from co-workers. A preliminary study determined that about 10 percent of knowledge transfer events consisted of knowledge hiding rather than sharing, and that people were quite open about the process: "There are always ways to answer questions without answering questions.... " A second study established three forms of hiding: *Playing dumb* (pretending to be ignorant about requested knowledge); *evasive hiding* (providing misinformation or falsely promising knowledge in the future); *rationalized hiding* (justifying the failure to share by claiming extenuating circumstances or blaming others). What factors promote knowledge hiding? Interpersonal mistrust of the other party is a critical motivator of all three types of hiding. In addition, evasive hiding is more likely when knowledge is complex and more task related. The researchers also expect that knowledge hiding is elevated when there is great competition among employees for individual recognition.

Source: Based on Connelly, C., Zweig, D., Webster, J. & Trougakos, J. (2012). Knowledge hiding in organizations. *Journal of Organizational Behavior, 33*, 64–88.

The Facets of Political Skill

It is one thing to engage in organizational politics, but it is another thing to do it skilfully, because pursuing self-interest can encounter resistance. Gerald Ferris and colleagues define **political skill** as "the ability to understand others at work and to use that knowledge to influence others to act in ways that enhance one's personal or organizational objectives."[41] Notice that this definition includes two aspects—comprehending others and translating this comprehension into influence. Research by Ferris and colleagues indicates that there are four facets to political skill:

Political skill. The ability to understand others at work and to use that knowledge to influence others to act in ways that enhance one's personal or organizational objectives.

- *Social astuteness.* Good politicians are careful observers who are tuned in to others' needs and motives. They can "read" people and thus possess emotional intelligence, as discussed in Chapter 5. They are active self-monitors (Chapter 2) who know how to present themselves to others.

- *Interpersonal influence.* The politically skilled have a convincing and persuasive interpersonal style but employ it flexibly to meet the needs of the situation. They put others at ease.

- *Apparent sincerity.* Influence attempts will be seen as manipulative unless they are accompanied by sincerity. A good politician comes across as genuine and exhibits high integrity.

Networking. Establishing good relations with key organizational members and outsiders to accomplish one's goals.

- *Networking ability.* **Networking** involves establishing good relations with key organizational members or outsiders to accomplish one's goals. Networks provide a channel for favours to be asked for and given. An effective network enhances one's organizational reputation, thus aiding influence attempts.

Political skill, as measured by these four facets, is positively related to job performance, job satisfaction, and career success.[42] If you would like to assess your own political skill, complete the Experiential Exercise *Political Skill Inventory* at the end of the chapter.

Because networking is such a critical aspect of power acquisition and political success, let's examine it in more detail. In essence, networking involves developing informal social contacts to enlist the cooperation of others when their support is necessary. Upper-level managers often establish very large political networks both inside and outside the organization (Exhibit 12.5). Lower-level organizational members might have a more restricted network, but the principle remains the same. One study of general managers found that they used face-to-face encounters and informal small talk to bolster their political networks. They also did favours for others and stressed the obligations of others to them. Personnel were hired, fired, and transferred to bolster a workable network, and the managers forged connections among network members to create a climate conducive to goal accomplishment.[43]

Monica Forret and Thomas Dougherty determined that there are several aspects to networking:[44]

- *Maintaining contacts:* giving out business cards, sending gifts and thank you notes
- *Socializing:* playing golf, participating in company sports leagues, having drinks after work
- *Engaging in professional activities:* giving a workshop, accepting a speaking engagement, teaching, publishing, appearing in the media
- *Participating in community activities:* being active in civic groups, clubs, church events
- *Increasing internal visibility:* accepting high-profile work projects, sitting on important committees and task forces

The authors found that those high in self-esteem and extraversion (Chapter 2) were more likely to engage in networking behaviours. They also found that engaging in professional activities and increasing internal visibility were most associated with career success

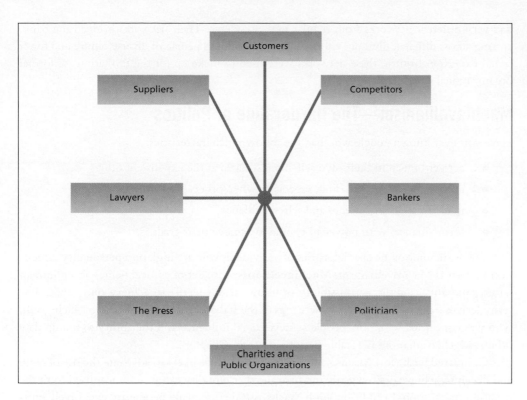

EXHIBIT 12.5
A typical upper-level manager's external network.

(i.e., compensation, promotions, and perceived success).[45] However, this applied only to men, despite the fact that men and women engaged in networking equally, except for socializing, where men perhaps had the edge. Forret and Dougherty make the important point that networking has increased in importance as people become more self-reliant and less reliant on organizations to plot their career futures. This is why many MBA and executive MBA programs foster social media such as LinkedIn, Facebook, and Twitter to maintain trusted networks among their alumni.

Being central in a large network provides power because you have access to considerable resources, such as knowledge. This is especially true if the network is diverse (the people you know do not know each other) and consists of those who themselves hold power.[46] One study in a leading bank revealed that those who were promoted most quickly to senior vice-president

Mark Leibowitz/Masterfile

Networking is an effective way to develop informal social contacts.

had very different networks from regular vice-presidents. Their networks bridged the bank, cutting across different divisions and regions and including people of diverse tenure and functional expertise. In turn, these networks were used to make up for the limitations of formal organizational structure.[47]

Machiavellianism—The Harder Side of Politics

Have you ever known people who had the following characteristics?

- act very much in their own self-interest, even at the expense of others
- appear cool and calculating, especially when others get emotional
- manifest high self-esteem and self-confidence
- form alliances with powerful people to achieve their goals

Machiavellianism. A set of cynical beliefs about human nature, morality, and the permissibility of using various tactics to achieve one's ends.

These are some of the characteristics of individuals who are high on a personality dimension known as Machiavellianism. **Machiavellianism** is a set of cynical beliefs about human nature, morality, and the permissibility of using various tactics to achieve one's ends. The term derives from the 16th-century writings of the Italian civil servant Niccolo Machiavelli, who was concerned with how people achieve social influence and the ability to manipulate others. Machiavellianism is a stable personality trait (Chapter 2).

Compared with "low Machs," "high Machs" are more likely to advocate the use of lying and deceit to achieve desired goals and to argue that morality can be compromised to fit the situation in question. In addition, high Machs assume that many people are excessively gullible and do not know what is best for themselves. Thus, in interpersonal situations, the high Mach acts in an exceedingly practical manner, assuming that the ends justify the means. Not surprisingly, high Machs tend to be convincing liars and good at "psyching out" competitors by creating diversions. Furthermore, they are quite willing to form coalitions with others to outmanoeuvre or defeat people who get in their way.[48] In summary, high Machs are likely to be enthusiastic organizational politicians.

Do high Machs feel guilty about the social tactics they utilize? The answer would appear to be no. Since they are cool and calculating rather than emotional, high Machs seem to be able to insulate themselves from the negative social consequences of their tactics. You might wonder how successful high Machs are at manipulating others and why others would tolerate such manipulation. After all, the characteristics we detail above are hardly likely to win a popularity contest, and you might assume that targets of a high Mach's tactics would vigorously resist manipulation by such a person. Again, the high Mach's rationality seems to provide an answer. Put simply, it appears that high Machs are able to accurately identify situations in which their favoured tactics will work. Such situations have the following characteristics:

- the high Mach can deal face to face with those he or she is trying to influence;
- the interaction occurs under fairly emotional circumstances; and
- the situation is fairly unstructured, with few guidelines for appropriate forms of interaction.[49]

In combination, these characteristics reveal a situation in which the high Mach can use his or her tactics because emotion distracts others. High Machs, by remaining calm and rational, can create a social structure that facilitates their personal goals at the expense of others. Thus, high Machs are especially skilled at getting their way when power vacuums or novel situations confront a group, department, or organization. For example, imagine a small family business whose president dies suddenly without any plans for succession. In this power vacuum, a high Mach vice-president would have an excellent chance of manipulating the choice of a new president. The situation is novel, emotion provoking, and unstructured, since no guidelines for succession exist. In addition, the decision-making body would be small enough for face-to-face influence and coalition formation.

Despite sometimes being able to get their own way, research shows that high Machs are unlikely to be high performers. In fact, they are inclined toward counterproductive behaviours such as sabotage and theft.[50]

Defensiveness—Reactive Politics

So far, our discussion of politics has focused mainly on the proactive pursuit of self-interest. Another form of political behaviour, however, is more reactive in that it concerns the defence or protection of self-interest. The goal here is to reduce threats to one's own power by avoiding actions that do not suit one's own political agenda or avoiding blame for events that might threaten one's political capital. Blake Ashforth and Ray Lee describe some tactics for doing both.[51]

Astute organizational politicians are aware that sometimes the best action to take is no action at all. A number of defensive behaviours can accomplish this mission:

- *Stalling.* Moving slowly when someone asks for your cooperation is the most obvious way of avoiding taking action without actually saying no. With time, the demand for cooperation may disappear. The civil service bureaucracy is infamous for stalling on demands from acting governments.

- *Overconforming.* Sticking to the strict letter of your job description or to organizational regulations is a common way to avoid action. Of course, the overconformer may be happy to circumvent his job description or organizational regulations when it suits his political agenda.

- *Buck passing.* Having someone else take action is an effective way to avoid doing it yourself. Buck passing is especially dysfunctional politics when the politician is best equipped to do the job but worries that it might not turn out successfully ("Let's let the design department get stuck with this turkey").

Another set of defensive behaviours is oriented around the motto "If you can't avoid action, avoid blame for its consequences." These behaviours include

- *Buffing.* Buffing is the tactic of carefully documenting information showing that an appropriate course of action was followed. Getting "sign-offs," authorizations, and so on are examples. Buffing can be sensible behaviour, but it takes on political overtones when doing the documenting becomes more important than making a good decision. It is clearly dysfunctional politics if it takes the form of fabricating documentation.

- *Scapegoating.* Blaming others when things go wrong is classic political behaviour. Scapegoating works best when you have some power behind you. One study found that when organizations performed poorly, more powerful CEOs stayed in office and the scapegoated managers below them were replaced. Less powerful CEOs were dismissed.[52]

The point of discussing these defensive political tactics is not to teach you how to do them. Rather, it is to ensure that you recognize them as political behaviour. Many of the tactics are quite mundane. However, viewing them in context again illustrates the sometimes subtle ways that individuals pursue political self-interest in organizations.

ETHICS IN ORGANIZATIONS

LO 12.7

Define *ethics*, and review the ethical dilemmas that managers and employees face.

Linda Keen, the president of the Canadian Nuclear Safety Commission, was dismissed from her post by the Conservative government, citing her "lack of leadership." The commission headed by Keen had ordered a shutdown of the 50-year-old Chalk River nuclear reactor because of safety concerns. The reactor, which generates 40 to 60 percent of the world's vital medical isotopes used in nuclear medicine, was restarted following an emergency measure in the House of Commons. Prime Minster Stephen Harper had called Keen a partisan because she was appointed by the Liberal government. In the following months, heavy water leaks occurred, which eventually forced the shutdown of the reactor.[53] What are the ethics of this story?

Ethics. Systematic thinking about the moral consequences of decisions.

Stakeholders. People inside or outside of an organization who have the potential to be affected by organizational decisions.

For our purposes, **ethics** can be defined as systematic thinking about the moral consequences of decisions. Moral consequences can be framed in terms of the potential for harm to any stakeholders in the decision. **Stakeholders** are simply people inside or outside the organization who have the potential to be affected by the decision. This could range from the decision makers themselves to "innocent bystanders."[54]

Researchers have conducted a number of surveys to determine managers' views about the ethics of decision making in business.[55] Some striking similarities across studies provide an interesting picture of the popular psychology of business ethics. First, far from being shy about the subject, a large majority agree that unethical practices occur in business. Furthermore, a substantial proportion (between 40 and 90 percent, according to the particular study) report that they have been pressured to compromise their own ethical standards when making decisions. In line with the concept of self-serving attributions, managers invariably tend to see themselves as having higher ethical standards than their peers and sometimes their superiors.[56] The unpleasant picture here is one in which unethical behaviour tempts managers, who sometimes succumb but feel that they still do better than others on moral grounds. This situation is not helped by the fact that top managers tend to see their organizations as being more ethical than do those lower in the hierarchy.[57] This is not a recipe for ethical vigilance, and it contributes to the majority of ethical violations made by managers.[58]

Among business students, undergraduates have been found to be more ethical than MBA students.[59] In fact, in a large survey, 56 percent of MBA students admitted to cheating during the past year, compared with 47 percent of non-business grad students.[60] Research indicates that women are marginally more ethical than men and that older people are marginally more ethical than the young. However, these associations are very small compared to those for personality (discussed below).[61]

The Nature of Ethical Misconduct

What kinds of ethical misconduct occur in organizations? Exhibit 12.6 shows the percentage of employees who reported having observed ethical misconduct in response to the *National Business Ethics Survey of the US Workforce*. As you can see, abusive behavior, lying to employees, and conflicts of interest topped the list, perhaps given the fact that they are mostly internal to the organization and thus more observable. Bribery, manipulating financial data, and falsifying expenses are reported less commonly, perhaps in part because they are easier to hide.

Ethical issues are often occupationally specific. As an example, let's consider the ethical dilemmas faced by the various subspecialties of marketing.[62] Among market researchers, telling research participants the true sponsor of the research has been an ongoing topic of debate. Among purchasing managers, where to draw the line in accepting favours (e.g., sports tickets) from vendors poses ethical problems. Among product managers, issues of planned obsolescence, unnecessary packaging, and differential pricing (e.g., charging more in the inner city) raise ethical concerns. When it comes to salespeople, how far to go in enticing customers and how to be fair in expense account use have been prominent ethical themes. Finally, in advertising, the range of ethical issues can (and does) fill books. Consider, for example, the decision to use sexual allure to sell a product.

In contrast to these occupationally specific ethical dilemmas, what are the common themes that run through ethical issues that managers face? An in-depth interview study of an

EXHIBIT 12.6
Issues covered in
corporate codes of
ethics.

*Percentages refer to the
percent of survey respondents
who observed the ethical
misconduct.
Source: Adapted from Ethics
Resource Center (2014).
*National business ethics
survey of the US workforce.*
Arlington, VA: Author. Used by
permission.

Observed Ethical Misconduct

OVERALL	41%*
Abusive behaviour or behaviour that creates a hostile work environment	18%
Lying to employees	17%
A conflict of interest – that is, behaviour that places an employee's interests over the company's interests	12%
Violating company policies related to internet use	12%
Discriminating against employees	12%
Violations of health or safety regulations	10%
Lying to customers, vendors, or the public	10%
Retaliation against someone who has reported misconduct	10%
Falsifying time reports or hours worked	10%
Stealing or theft	9%
Violating employee wage, overtime, or benefit rules	9%
Delivery of substandard goods or services	9%
Abusing substances, such as drugs or alcohol, at work	9%
Breaching employee privacy	8%
Improper hiring practices	7%
Sexual harassment	7%
Breaching customer or consumer privacy	5%
Violation of environmental regulations	4%
Misuse of company's confidential information	4%
Violating contract terms with customers or suppliers	4%
Falsifying invoices, books, and/or records	4%
Accepting inappropriate gifts or kickbacks from suppliers or vendors	4%
Offering anything of value (e.g., cash, gifts, entertainment) to influence a potential/existing client or customer	4%
Falsifying expense reports	4%
Falsifying and/or manipulating financial reporting information	3%
Improper use of competitor's proprietary information	3%
Offering anything of value (e.g., cash, gifts, entertainment) to influence a public official	2%
Making improper political contributions to officials or organizations	2%

occupationally diverse group of managers discovered seven themes that defined their moral standards for decision making.[63] Here are those themes and some typical examples of associated ethical behaviour:

- *Honest communication.* Evaluate subordinates candidly; advertise and label honestly; do not slant proposals to senior management.

- *Fair treatment.* Pay equitably; respect the sealed bid process; do not give preference to suppliers with political connections; do not use lower-level people as scapegoats.

- *Special consideration.* The "fair treatment" standard can be modified for special cases, such as helping out a long-time employee, giving preference to hiring the disabled, or giving business to a loyal but troubled supplier.

- *Fair competition.* Avoid bribes and kickbacks to obtain business; do not fix prices with competitors.

- *Responsibility to organization.* Act for the good of the organization as a whole, not for self-interest; avoid waste and inefficiency.

- *Corporate social responsibility.* Do not pollute; think about the community impact of plant closures; show concern for employee health and safety.

- *Respect for law.* Legally avoid taxes, do not evade them; do not bribe government inspectors; follow the letter and spirit of labour laws.

Before continuing, have a look at the You Be the Manager: *Yahoo's Resume Scandal* feature.

Causes of Unethical Behaviour

Knowing the causes of unethical behaviour can aid in its prevention. Because the topic is sensitive, you should appreciate that this is not the easiest area to research. The major evidence comes from surveys of executive opinion, case studies of prominent ethical failures, business game simulations, and responses to written scenarios involving ethical dilemmas.

GAIN Although the point might seem mundane, it is critical to recognize the role of temptation in unethical activity. The anticipation of healthy reinforcement for following an unethical course of action, especially if no punishment is expected, should promote unethical decisions.[64] Consider Dennis Levine, an investment banker who was convicted of insider trading in one of Wall Street's biggest scandals.

> *It was just so easy. In seven years I built $39 750 into $11.5 million, and all it took was a 20-second phone call to my offshore bank a couple of times a month—maybe 200 calls total. My account was growing at 125% a year, compounded. Believe me, I felt a rush when I would check the price of one of my stocks on the office Quotron and learn I'd just made several hundred thousand dollars. I was confident that the elaborate veils of secrecy I had created—plus overseas bank-privacy laws—would protect me.[65]*

A slightly more subtle example of the role of gain can be seen in compensation systems designed around very high bonuses. Such systems have often been implicated in ethically questionable behaviour, as ethics are sacrificed to boost income. On the opposite side of the coin, people who are unfairly underpaid are also more inclined to act unethically to offset this underpayment, especially when they have knowledge of others who are more fairly paid.[66]

EXTREME PERFORMANCE PRESSURE Although challenging goals lead to higher performance (Chapter 5), there is a point at which goal challenge can be so extreme as to induce unethical behavior. This is especially true when a consecutive series of high or increasing performance goals results in extreme performance pressure. In this situation, people's ethical focus is depleted.[67] Also, at the organizational level, pressure from analysts and investors for better and better financial performance has been implicated in ethical lapses among prominent and successful firms.[68]

ROLE CONFLICT Many ethical dilemmas are actually forms of role conflict (Chapter 7) that get resolved in an unethical way. For example, consider the ethical theme of corporate social responsibility we listed above. Here, an executive's role as custodian of the environment (do not pollute) might be at odds with his or her role as a community employer (do not close the plant that pollutes).

■ YOU BE THE MANAGER ■

Yahoo's Resume Scandal

"And computer science" were three words that Yahoo CEO Scott Thompson would come to regret. Thompson, the former president of PayPal, had been at Yahoo for only four months when Third Point, an activist shareholder group seeking representation on the board, claimed that he had misrepresented his academic credentials in the Yahoo annual report filed with the U.S. Securities and Exchange Commission. The report, which CEOs must certify as true, stated that "Mr. Thompson holds a B.S. in accounting and computer science from Stonehill College." In fact, Thompson held an accounting degree, but not one in computer science. The press quickly ascertained that Thompson's degree had in the past also been inaccurately stated on the PayPal website but that it was accurately described in formal SEC filings by PayPal parent eBay and another firm where Thompson was a board member.

The degree scandal occurred against a backdrop of turmoil at Yahoo, which had been losing ground to web-based companies Google, Facebook, and YouTube. The previous CEO had been fired within a year, and there had been recent staff layoffs. Third Point was the largest shareholder in Yahoo and had launched a proxy war to place its founder Daniel Loeb and other Third Point nominees on the board to assert and protect its interests. Discrediting Scott Thompson was a step in this direction.

Was this scenario a serious ethical violation by Scott Thompson or just a manifestation of power and politics?

Questions

1. How serious of an ethical violation was Scott Thompson's misstatement of academic qualifica-

Yahoo CEO Scott Thompson was challenged concerning resume irregularities.

Noah Berger/Polaris/Newscom

tions in the Yahoo annual report? Who are the relevant stakeholders here? What might have motivated this misrepresentation?

2. What should Thompson have done to resolve this? What should the board of directors have done?

To find out what happened, see The Manager's Notebook at the end of the chapter.

Sources: Pepitone, J. (2012, May 13). Yahoo CEO out after resume scandal—reports. *CNNMoney*, http://money.cnn.com/2012/05/13/technology/yahoo-ceo-out-rumor/index.htm; Saginor, J. (2012, May 13). Yahoo! CEO Scott Thompson resigns amid resume scandal. *Digital Trends*, www.digitaltrends.com/web/yahoo-ceo-scott-thompson-resigns-amid-resume-scandal/; Saginor, J. (2012, April 6). Yahoo versus the hedge fund millionaire: A Silicon Valley soap opera. *Digital Trends*, 2012, www.digital trends.com/web/yahoo-versus-the-hedge-fund-billionaire-a-silicon-valley-soap-opera/.

A very common form of role conflict that provokes unethical behaviour occurs when our "bureaucratic" role as an organizational employee is at odds with our role as the member of a profession.[69] For example, engineers who in their professional role opposed the fatal launch of the space shuttle *Challenger* due to cold weather were pressured to put on their bureaucratic "manager's hats" and agree to the launch. Both the insurance and brokerage businesses have been rocked by similar ethics problems. Agents and brokers report being pressured as employees to push products that are not in the best interests of their clients. Frequently, reward systems (i.e., the commission structure) heighten the conflict, which then becomes a conflict of interest between self and client.

STRONG ORGANIZATIONAL IDENTIFICATION Some employees identify very strongly with their organizations, seeing their membership as an integral part of their identity. This can sometimes lead them to engage in unethical activities to "help" the organization. Many instances of covering up previous ethical violations have this motivation. Strong identifiers seem most likely to do this when they expect their "loyalty" will be reciprocated with favours.[70]

COMPETITION Stiff competition for scarce resources can stimulate unethical behaviour. This has been observed in both business game simulations and industry studies of illegal acts, in which trade offences, such as price fixing and monopoly violations, have been shown to increase with industry decline.[71] For example, observers cite a crowded and mature market as one factor prompting price-fixing violations in the folding-carton packaging industry.[72] We should note one exception to the "competition stresses ethics" thesis. In cases in which essentially *no* competition exists, there is also a strong temptation to make unethical decisions. This is because the opportunity to make large gains is not offset by market checks and balances. Prominent examples have occurred in the defence industry, in which monopoly contracts to produce military hardware have been accompanied by some remarkable examples of overcharging taxpayers. The understandable monopolies that police forces such as the RCMP have in law enforcement have sometimes been linked to ethical breaches.

PERSONALITY Are certain types of personalities more prone to unethical decisions? In fact, the cynical and those with external locus of control (Chapter 2) are less tuned in to ethical matters. Also, people with a high need for personal power (especially Machiavellians) may be prone to make unethical decisions, using this power to further self-interest rather than for the good of the organization.[73] Finally, people with strong economic values (Chapter 4) are more likely to behave unethically.[74]

More broadly, there are marked individual differences in the degree of sophistication that people use in thinking about moral issues.[75] Some people are morally disengaged, rejecting responsibility for their actions and using euphemistic labelling to obscure moral issues.[76] For example, a broken political promise might be described as a "non-core promise" to deflect censure. Other people are morally attentive, spotting moral issues and thinking about moral matters.[77] Research shows that less disengagement and more attentiveness is associated with more ethical behaviour.[78]

Remember that we have a tendency to exaggerate the role of dispositional factors, such as personality, in explaining the behaviour of others (Chapter 3). Thus, when we see unethical behaviour, we should look at situational factors, such as competition and the organization's culture, as well as the personality of the actor.

ORGANIZATIONAL AND INDUSTRY CULTURE Bart Victor and John Cullen found that there were considerable differences in ethical values across the organizations they studied.[79] These differences involved factors such as consideration for employees, respect for the law, and respect for organizational rules. In addition, there were differences across groups within these organizations. This indicates that aspects of an organization's culture (and its subcultures) can influence ethics.[80] This corresponds to the repeated finding in executive surveys that the conduct of peers and superiors is viewed as strongly influencing ethical behaviour, for good or for bad. The presence of role models helps to shape the culture (Chapter 8). If these models are actually rewarded for unethical behaviour, rather than punished, the development of an unethical culture is likely. In fact, firms convicted of illegal acts often tend to be repeat offenders.[81] Remember, no one thing creates a "culture of corruption" in organizations. Rather, it is often a combination of factors, such as evaluating managers solely "by the numbers," denying responsibility, denying injury to others, and teaching (low-power) newcomers corrupt practices that lead to unethical corporate cultures.[82]

Observers of the folding-carton price-fixing scandal we mentioned above noted how top managers frequently seemed out of touch with the difficulty of selling boxes in a mature, crowded market. They put in place goal setting and reward systems (e.g., commission forming 60 percent of income), systems that are much more appropriate for products on a growth cycle, that almost guaranteed unethical decisions.[83] In fact, research shows that upper-level managers generally tend to be naïve about the extent of ethical lapses in those below them. This can easily contribute to a success-at-any-cost culture.[84]

Finally, a consideration of culture suggests the conditions under which corporate codes of ethics might actually have an impact on decision making. If such codes are specific, tied to the actual business being done, correspond to the reward system, and are rigorously enforced, they should bolster an ethical culture. If vague codes that do not correspond to other cultural elements exist, the negative symbolism might actually damage the ethical culture. To see how time of day affects ethical decisions see Research Focus: *Are You More Ethical in the Morning?*

Whistle-Blowing

In spite of the catalogue of causes of unethical behaviour discussed above, individuals occasionally step forward and "blow the whistle" on unethical actions. For instance, former tobacco executive Dr. Jeffrey Wigand (portrayed in the movie *The Insider*) leaked evidence to *60 Minutes* that consumers had been misled about the addictiveness of nicotine for many years. Similarly, Catherine Galliford blew the whistle on sexual harassment at the RCMP.

Whistle-blowing occurs when a current or former organizational member discloses illegitimate practices to some person or organization that may be able to take action to correct these practices.[85] Thus, the whistle may be blown either inside or outside of the offending organization, depending on the circumstances. The courage of insiders to call attention to organizational misdoing is especially important in large contemporary organizations,

Whistle-blowing.
Disclosure of illegitimate practices by a current or former organizational member to some person or organization that may be able to take action to correct these practices.

▉ RESEARCH FOCUS ▉

ARE YOU MORE MORAL IN THE MORNING?

Are you more moral in the morning? Or are ethical lapses equal opportunity when it comes to time of day? Researchers Maryam Kouchaki and Isaac Smith set out to examine this issue in a series of four studies that assigned computer-mediated tasks to people in such way that they were able to cheat or lie in order to obtain extra compensation for their work. In all four studies there was more cheating and lying when the task was completed in the afternoon rather than in the morning. What causes the "morning morality effect"? The authors argue that the gradual fatigue associated with mundane activities throughout the day slowly depletes people's resources and causes them to be less alert to moral and ethical decision points, resulting in less ethical behavior. Ironically, people who are generally morally engaged and alert to moral issues are most susceptible to losing their moral compass in the afternoon. People who are morally disengaged and insensitive to moral issues are less ethical no matter the time of day.

The authors conclude "our findings suggest that mere time of day can lead to a systematic failure of good people to act morally." The findings also suggest that individuals and organizations should, if possible, exercise care in scheduling meetings in which difficult decisions with ethical ramifications are to be made. Morning meetings seem preferable, and in general, such decisions should be avoided when people are fatigued, overloaded, or distracted.

Source: Based on Kouchaki, M., & Smith, I.H. (2014). The morning morality effect: The influence of time of day on unethical behavior. *Psychological Science, 25*, 95-102.

because their very complexity often allows for such misdoing to be disguised from outsiders. Also, given pervasive conflicts of interest, there is no guarantee that external watchdogs (such as accounting firms that perform audits) will do the job.[86] Most organizations seem to rely on vague open-door policies rather than having specific channels and procedures for whistle-blowers to follow. This is not the best way to encourage principled dissent.

Not everyone at the failed energy-trading giant Enron stood idly by while massive fraud unfolded around them. Sherron Watkins, a vice-president with a master's degree in accounting, courageously spoke out against fraudulent accounting practices and notified the CEO. Watkins' testimony at the hearings into the scandal also provided crucial information as to the breadth and depth of the problems at Enron. At telecommunications giant WorldCom, Cynthia Cooper, an internal auditor, discovered fraudulent bookkeeping entries. Cooper discussed her findings with the company's controller and with the CFO, but was told not to worry about it and to stop her review. Instead, she immediately went over her boss's head and called the board chair's audit committee. Two weeks later, WorldCom disclosed its misstatements, leading to the largest bankruptcy in American history.[87]

Despite these success stories, whistle-blowers are often the victims of considerable retaliation for their efforts because they have challenged the status quo and embarrassed those in power. For instance, three Health Canada scientists were fired for insubordination (one finally being reinstated) for making public that they had been pressured to declare various hormones and antibiotics as safe for consumption without proper testing.[88] The *National Business Ethics Survey* indicated that about one in five US employees faces retaliation when reporting unethical activity.[89]

<table>
<tr><td>LO **12.8**</td></tr>
</table>

Define *sexual harassment*, and discuss what organizations can do to prevent it and how they should respond to allegations.

Sexual Harassment—When Power and Ethics Collide

In recent years, a number of high-profile sexual harassment cases have made news headlines and brought increased attention to this problem. In addition to numerous cases reported in the American and Canadian military, many organizations, including Mitsubishi, Astra, Sears, and Del Laboratories, have found themselves involved in costly litigation cases.[90] The failure of these organizations to effectively respond to charges of sexual harassment has cost them millions of dollars in settlements as well as lower productivity, increased absenteeism, and turnover. As well, the effects on employees can include decreased job satisfaction and organizational commitment as well as reduced psychological and physical well-being.[91]

The following is a fairly comprehensive definition of sexual harassment:

> *The EEOC [Equal Employment Opportunity Commission] regulatory guidelines state that unwelcome sexual advances, requests for sexual favours, and other verbal or physical conduct of a sexual nature constitute sexual harassment when submission to requests for sexual favours is made explicitly or implicitly a term or condition of employment; submission to or rejection of such requests is used as a basis for employment decisions; or such conduct unreasonably interferes with work performance or creates an intimidating, hostile, or offensive work environment. On the basis of these guidelines, current legal frameworks generally support two causes of action that claimants may state: coercion of sexual cooperation by threat of job-related consequences (quid pro quo harassment) and unwanted and offensive sex-related verbal or physical conduct, even absent any job-related threat (hostile work environment).[92]*

Sexual harassment is a form of unethical behaviour that stems, in part, from the abuse of power and the perpetuation of a gender power imbalance. Managers who use their position, reward, or coercive power to request sexual favours or demonstrate verbal or physical conduct of a sexual nature as a basis for employment decisions toward those in less powerful positions are abusing their power and acting unethically. While the most severe forms of sexual harassment are committed by supervisors, the most frequent perpetrators are actually co-workers. Although co-workers do not necessarily have the same formal power bases as supervisors, power differences often exist among co-workers and can also play a role in sexual harassment. Whether the harasser is a supervisor or a co-worker, he or she is likely to be more powerful than the person being harassed,[93] and the most vulnerable victims are those who cannot afford to lose their jobs.[94]

Sexual harassment is also prevalent in hostile work environments that perpetuate the societal power imbalance between men and women. For example, the higher incidence of harassment reported in the military is believed to be partly a function of its rigid hierarchy and power differentials.[95] Incidents of harassment and organizational inaction to complaints of harassment are also more likely in male-dominated industries in which men attempt to maintain their dominance relative to women.[96]

Clients and customers can also engage in harassment. Many service jobs are performed by women, who are required to spend virtually their entire workday with customers. Other jobs (e.g., sales rep) require the development of strong client relationships. In a web-based survey of professional women, 86 percent reported having experienced sexist hostility; 40 percent reported unwanted sexual attention; and 8 percent reported sexual coercion. Harassment increased when the proportion of men in the client base increased and when the clients were perceived as holding a lot of power (e.g., were very important to company business). Also, minority women were more likely to be harassed.[97] Jennifer Berdahl found that harassment was more likely to be experienced by women who exhibited traditionally masculine personality traits (such as independence and assertiveness). Thus, the motive was punishment for gender role "deviance" rather than sexual desire.[98]

Like the RCMP, many organizations are slow to react to complaints of sexual harassment. This has been labelled the "deaf ear syndrome," which refers to the "inaction or complacency of organizations in the face of charges of sexual harassment."[99] The deaf ear syndrome doubtless contributes immensely to the marked tendency for harassment to go unreported. An Angus Reid poll found that nearly a third of Canadians reported sexual harassment at work, but 78 percent of these respondents did not report the behaviour.[100] Management at CBC Radio was accused by some of turning a deaf ear to harassment complaints about fired radio host Jian Ghomeshi because he was such a successful "talent" fronting the well-regarded progressive pop culture program Q.[101]

Organizations can effectively deal with allegations of sexual harassment and increase their responsiveness by taking a number of important measures.

- *Examine the characteristics of deaf ear organizations.* Managers should examine their own organizations to determine if they have any of the characteristics that would make them susceptible to the deaf ear syndrome.

- *Foster management support and education.* Sexual harassment training programs are necessary to educate managers on how to respond to complaints in a sensitive and respectful manner.

- *Stay vigilant.* Managers must monitor the work environment and remove displays of a sexual nature and factors that can contribute to a hostile work environment.

- *Take immediate action.* Failure to act is likely to result in negative consequences for the organization and the victims of sexual harassment. Organizations considered to be the best places for women to work are known for their swift action and severe handling of harassers.

- *Create a state-of-the-art policy.* Sexual harassment policies and procedures need to clearly define what constitutes harassment and the sanctions that will be brought to bear on those found guilty of it.

- *Establish clear reporting procedures.* User-friendly policies need to be designed so that there are clear procedures for filing complaints and mechanisms in place for the impartial investigation of complaints. The privacy of those involved must also be protected.[102]

Organizations that are responsive to complaints of sexual harassment have top management commitment, provide comprehensive education programs, continuously monitor the work environment, respond to complaints in a thorough and timely manner, and have clear policies and procedures.[103] An example is DuPont, which has developed a sexual harassment awareness program called A Matter of Respect. It includes interactive training programs, peer-level facilitators who are trained to meet with victims or potential victims, and a 24-hour hotline.[104]

Employing Ethical Guidelines

A few simple guidelines, regularly used, should help in the ethical screening of decisions. The point is not to paralyze your decision making but to get you to think seriously about the moral implications of your decisions before you make them.[105]

- Identify the stakeholders that will be affected by any decision.
- Identify the costs and benefits of various decision alternatives to these stakeholders.
- Consider the relevant moral expectations that surround a particular decision. These might stem from professional norms, laws, organizational ethics codes, and principles such as honest communication and fair treatment.
- Be familiar with the common ethical dilemmas that decision makers face in your specific organizational role or profession.
- Discuss ethical matters with decision stakeholders and others. Do not think ethics without talking about ethics.
- Convert your ethical judgments into appropriate action.

THE MANAGER'S NOTEBOOK

Yahoo's Resume Scandal

1. Opinions will vary about the seriousness of Scott Thompson's misstatement of his academic qualifications in the Yahoo annual report. Perhaps it was an honest mistake. Alternatively, some might see it as somewhat of a victimless crime, as it is hard pinpoint exactly whose interests were damaged by the event. On the other hand, consider some stakeholders: Yahoo as a company clearly did not need such bad publicity, especially given its recent turmoil. And the board member who headed the search committee that recruited Thompson felt compelled to announce she would step down. Investors might take unwarranted comfort in seeing that the head of a web-embedded company held a computer science degree. Finally, actions such as this by high-profile business leaders may convince some people that "everybody does it," serving as a negative role model for many future leaders. As news stories reported at the time, this was not the first case of a business leader being derailed by bogus academic qualifications. However, the technology and web sectors may be especially prone to this, as some will feel a need to signal their technical legitimacy in web-related matters.

2. Scott Thompson resigned from Yahoo, citing personal reasons, including a diagnosis of thyroid cancer. There is reason to believe that the move was motivated in part by a subcommittee of outside directors who had been appointed to examine the matter, because Daniel Loeb and two Third Point nominees were immediately appointed to the board. All in all, the three words "and computer science" provided a rational excuse for the board to jettison Thompson and resolve a contentious proxy war with Third Point, Yahoo!'s biggest shareholder.

What this advice does is enable you to recognize ethical issues, make ethical judgments, and then convert these judgments into behaviour.[106]

Training and education in ethics have become very popular in North American organizations. Evidence indicates that formal education in ethics does have a positive impact on ethical attitudes.[107]

MyManagementLab Study, practise, and explore real management situations with these helpful resources:

- **Interactive Lesson Presentations:** Work through interactive presentations and assessments to test your knowledge of management concepts.
- **PIA (Personal Inventory Assessments):** Enhance your ability to connect with key concepts through these engaging, self-reflection assessments.   **P I A** PERSONAL INVENTORY ASSESSMENT
- **Study Plan:** Check your understanding of chapter concepts with self-study quizzes.
- **Videos:** Learn more about the management practices and strategies of real companies.
- **Simulations:** Practise decision-making in simulated management environments.

LEARNING OBJECTIVES CHECKLIST

12.1 *Power* is the capacity to influence others who are in a state of dependence. People have power by virtue of their position in the organization (legitimate power) or by virtue of the resources that they command (reward, coercion, friendship, or expertise).

12.2 People can obtain power by doing the right things and cultivating the right people. Activities that lead to power acquisition need to be extraordinary, visible, and relevant to the needs of the organization. People to cultivate include outsiders, subordinates, peers, and superiors.

12.3 *Empowerment* means giving people the authority, opportunity, and motivation to solve organizational problems. Power is thus located where it is needed to give employees the feeling that they are capable of doing their jobs well.

12.4 Effective managers often have a high need for power. While individuals with high *n* Pow can, in some circumstances, behave in an abusive or dominating fashion, they can also use their power responsibly. Managers with high *n* Pow are effective when they use this power to achieve organizational goals.

12.5 Organizational subunits obtain power by controlling *strategic contingencies*. This means that they are able to affect events that are critical to other subunits. Thus, departments that can obtain resources for the organization will acquire power. Similarly, subunits gain power when they are able to reduce uncertainty, when their function is central to the organizational mission or workflow, and when other subunits or outside contractors cannot perform their tasks.

12.6 *Organizational politics* occur when non-sanctioned ends are pursued or when influence in the form of non-sanctioned means is used. The pursuit of non-sanctioned ends is always dysfunctional, but the organization may benefit when non-sanctioned means are used to achieve approved goals. Several political tactics were discussed: *Networking* is establishing good relations with key people to accomplish goals. It contributes to political skill along with political astuteness, interpersonal influence, and apparent sincerity. *Machiavellianism* is a set of cynical beliefs about human nature, morality, and the permissibility of using various means to achieve one's ends. Situational morality, lying, and "psyching out" others are common tactics. *Defensiveness* means avoiding taking actions that do not suit one's political agenda and avoiding blame for negative events.

12.7 *Ethics* is systematic thinking about the moral consequences of decisions. Of particular interest is the impact on stakeholders, people who have the potential to be affected by a decision. Ethical dilemmas that managers face involve honest communication, fair treatment, special consideration, fair competition, responsibility to the organization, social responsibility, and respect for law. Causes of unethical behaviour include the potential for gain, extreme performance pressure, role conflict, strong organizational identification, the extremes of business competition (great or none), organizational and industry culture, and certain personality characteristics.

12.8 *Sexual harassment* is a form of unethical behaviour that stems from the abuse of power and the perpetuation of a gender imbalance in the workplace. Steps that can be taken to prevent and deal with harassment include training and education, clear and formal policies, vigilance, detection of the "deaf ear" syndrome, and rapid response.

DISCUSSION QUESTIONS

1. Are the bases of individual power easily substitutable for each other? Are they equally effective? For example, can coercive power substitute for expert power?

2. Suppose that you are an entrepreneur who has started a new chain of consumer electronics stores. Your competitive edge is to offer excellent customer service. What would you do to empower your employees to help achieve this goal?

3. Imagine that you are on a committee at work or in a group working on a project at school that includes a "high Mach" member. What could you do to neutralize the high Mach's attempts to manipulate the group?

4. Discuss the conditions under which the following subunits of an organization might gain or lose power: legal department; research and development unit; public relations department. Use the concepts of scarcity, uncertainty, centrality, and substitutability in your answers.

5. Is sexual harassment more likely to be a problem in some occupations and types of organizations? Describe those occupations and organizational cultures where sexual harassment is most likely to be a problem. What can be done to prevent sexual harassment in these occupations and organizations?

INTEGRATIVE DISCUSSION QUESTIONS

1. Consider the role of politics and ethics in decision making. How can organizational politics be a source of effective or ineffective decision making in organizations? In what way can the causes of unethical behaviour influence decision making?

2. How can an organization create an ethical workplace where ethical behaviour is the norm? Refer to the organizational learning practices in Chapter 2, attitudes in Chapter 4, ethical leadership in Chapter 9, and the contributors to organizational culture in Chapter 8 to answer this question.

ON-THE-JOB CHALLENGE QUESTION

CBC's Steven Smart

Canadian Broadcasting Corporation (CBC) journalist Stephen Smart didn't anticipate that getting married would get him in hot water with his employer. However, Smart, a reporter in the British Columbia provincial legislature, had married Rebecca Scott, the premier's deputy press secretary. Shortly thereafter, the marriage came to the attention of the CBC ombudsperson, who declared that Smart was in a conflict of interest position, and that it was not possible for him to be fair and impartial in his reporting concerning the premier, given his wife's close connection to her. Mr. Smart's regional director, noting that no evidence of partiality had been presented, explained that ground rules had been established with him regarding his reporting and that no other action would be taken.

Who are the stakeholders in this ethical scenario? What kinds of role conflicts are operating here? Should Smart continue on the provincial legislature beat, or is this ethically unacceptable?

Source: Based on Woo, A. (2012, January 23). Marriage violates CBC standards: Ombudsman. *National Post*, p. A3.

EXPERIENTIAL EXERCISE

Political Skill Inventory

Early in the chapter we discussed political skill. This exercise will allow you to assess your political skill set.

Instructions: Using the following 7-point scale, place the number on the blank before each item that best describes how much you agree with each statement about yourself.

1–Strongly disagree

2–Disagree

3–Slightly disagree

4–Neutral

5–Slightly agree

6 Agree

7–Strongly agree

1. ____ I spend a lot of time and effort at work networking with others.

2. ____ I am able to make most people feel comfortable and at ease around me.

3. ____ I am able to communicate easily and effectively with others.

4. ____ It is easy for me to develop good rapport with most people.

5. ____ I understand people very well.

6. ____ I am good at building relationships with influential people at work.

7. ____ I am particularly good at sensing the motivations and hidden agendas of others.

8. ____ When communicating with others, I try to be genuine in what I say and do.

9. ____ I have developed a large network of colleagues and associates at work whom I can call on for support when I really need to get things done.

10. ____ At work, I know a lot of important people and am well connected.

11. ____ I spend a lot of time at work developing connections with others.

12. ____ I am good at getting people to like me.

13. ____ It is important that people believe I am sincere in what I say and do.

14. ____ I try to show a genuine interest in other people.

15. ____ I am good at using my connections and network to make things happen at work.

16. ____ I have good intuition or savvy about how to present myself to others.

17. ____ I always seem to instinctively know the right things to say or do to influence others.

18. ____ I pay close attention to people's facial expressions.

Scoring and Interpretation

To compute your overall political skill, add up your scores and divide the total by 18. Scores below 2.3 indicate low political skill and scores over 4.6 signal high political skill. You can also compute your scores for the various dimensions of political skill. To determine your social astuteness, sum answers 5, 7, 16, 17, and 18 and divide by 5. To determine your interpersonal influence, sum answers 2, 3, 4, and 12 and divide by 4. To assess your networking ability, sum answers 1, 6, 9, 10, 11, and 15 and divide by 6. Finally, to compute your apparent sincerity, sum answers 8, 13, and 14 and divide by 3. It is also useful to see how others rate your political skill. Have someone who knows you well use the scale to rate you and compare his or her rating with yours.

Source: Ferris, G.R., Treadway, D.C., Kolodinsky, R.W., Hochwarter, W.A., Kacmar, C.J., Douglas, C., & Frink, D.D. (2005). Development and validation of the Political Skill Inventory. *Journal of Management*, *31*, 126–152, Sage Publications (US) Inc.

CASE INCIDENT

Doubling Up

The business school at Canadian Anonymous University prided itself on its international programs, which spanned Eastern Europe, North Africa, and South America. Many of the faculty enjoyed teaching in these programs, as it offered them a chance for free travel and the opportunity to sometimes avoid the harsh extremes of the Canadian climate. In addition, the teaching was well paid, offering a more reliable source of additional income than consulting. The university's auditor recently determined that several faculty members had been teaching in the international programs at the same time that they were scheduled to be teaching undergraduate classes at CAU. This was possibly due to the loose connection between the international programs office and the academic departments. After

some investigation, it was determined that these faculty members had been subcontracting their CAU teaching to graduate students (at rather low rates) to enable themselves to teach internationally. One faculty member defended the practice as "gaining global exposure." Another claimed that developing countries "deserved experienced professors." A third claimed to be underpaid without the international teaching.

1. What kind of organizational politics are at work here?

2. What influence tactics might the profs have used to get the grad students to fill in for them?

3. Discuss the ethics of the professors "doubling up" on their teaching.

CASE STUDY

To Tell the Truth

It's natural to want to correct a mistake when you find one. But Kyle Singer was discovering life isn't always so simple. The production manager for Vancouver-based food contract manufacturer Devonshire Milton, which had just delivered 30 000 packages of candy to AG Distributing of Carol Stream, Ill., happened to be in the customer's warehouse delivering a batch of samples when he discovered that the incorrect expiry date had been printed on 10 of the 75 packages he had inspected. It was Sept. 1, 2011, and earlier that day Singer had been walking to a meeting with Cyrus Nell, AG's operations manager, to talk about an unrelated issue. He didn't mention the mistake to anyone at AG at the time, but was now wondering what to do. "Short of going through the warehouse and checking each package, we won't be able to isolate the misprinted product," Singer told a friend he was meeting for drinks.

Devonshire produced private-label candy for regional grocery stores, and one of its subcontractors, FulthrenFood, packaged it into foil bags and usually printed the expiry dates. But because of special Halloween packaging, the location of the expiry date had to be moved and the packages could be printed only at

AG's warehouse. Adrian Borscoe, FulthrenFood's customer service contact, provided the batch and expiry dates to AG's production manager. Borscoe confirmed that to Singer in a meeting, telling him that the expiry date code "01122011" was provided, referring to Dec. 1, 2011.

Singer had now discovered the date coding machines in AG Distributing's warehouse were different, and that number combination had resulted in "January 12th, 2011" being printed on some packages. AG Distributing relied on part-time, transient labour to receive and prepare inventory for delivery to stores. A large percentage of this labour force had minimal education and did not speak English as a first language. Singer suspected the date code had been entered—as it was given—and printed, but a correction must have been made because the majority of the batch seemed to be correctly labelled. However, it seemed the incorrectly labelled packages were not isolated from the rest of the order. After discovering the error, Singer had called Borscoe, who told him the right date code sequence, 12012011, was given and "there was no confusion."

Now, over drinks, Singer was replaying the day's events with his friend. "I'm not sure who is at fault, but FulthrenFood is our subcontractor, and this is our order," he continued. "There is a big chance that the mistake lies with the customer's warehouse staff."

Singer did not want to take the blame for the misprints if it meant he would risk affecting the AG candy contract, which represented 12 percent of Devonshire's revenues. Devonshire was one of three contract manufacturers delivering the same product to AG Distributing. Although it sounded a little selfish, he rued the fact that he had even checked the date codes. There was no way for Singer to recall the product for reprinting without raising concerns on the customer's side. But when the product reached store shelves, there was a significant chance returns, typically 2 percent of sales, would dramatically rise, perhaps to 10 percent. If the customer started to ask questions, the issue would have to be delicately handled.

Singer's bias was to immediately inform the client and tell them exactly what he believed had happened. But he wondered whether his customer's assertion—made at the start of their working relationship—that

they wanted their suppliers to be "transparent" and to "collaboratively work on difficult issues" was real or just surface deep. "I would like to take them at their word," he observed, "but I know they will not appreciate that a mistake has been made—either by them or by us."

Source: Material republished with the express permission of: *Financial Post*, a division of Postmedia Network Inc.

QUESTIONS

1. Using your own judgment and the material in the section *The Nature of Ethical Misconduct*, describe the ethical dilemma facing Kyle Singer.
2. Who are the relevant stakeholders in this case?
3. What are some factors that might lead Kyle Singer to act unethically in this situation?
4. Could political skill be of use to Kyle in dealing with this problem?
5. What should Kyle do now? What is your reasoning?

13 CONFLICT AND STRESS

CHAPTER

LEARNING OBJECTIVES

After reading Chapter 13, you should be able to:

13.1 Define *interpersonal conflict*, and review its causes in organizations.

13.2 Explain the *types of conflict* and the process by which conflict occurs.

13.3 Discuss the various *modes of managing conflict*.

13.4 Review a range of *negotiation techniques*.

13.5 Distinguish among *stressors*, *stress*, and *stress reactions*.

13.6 Discuss the role that personality plays in stress.

13.7 Review the sources of stress encountered by various organizational role occupants.

13.8 Describe *behavioural*, *psychological*, and *physiological reactions* to stress, and discuss techniques for managing stress.

ORANGE FRANCE INVESTIGATES SECOND WAVE OF STAFF SUICIDES

The French telecom company Orange is on "serious alert" after reports of a fresh spate of work-related suicides. Since the beginning of the year, 10 of its employees have killed themselves—most for reasons "explicitly related" to their jobs, according to the company's own stress and mental health watchdog.

Orange was formerly the state-owned France Telecom, which reported a similar wave of deaths between 2008 and 2009. The number of suicides so far this year is almost as high as for the whole of last year, when 11 workers took their own lives. Of the 10 deaths this year—three women and seven men, the youngest aged 25—eight have been directly linked to work, according to the observatory for stress and forced mobility, which is responsible for monitoring work conditions at the company. The observatory was set up after the earlier wave of suicides caused widespread concern about working conditions and practices at the firm.

The French health minister, Marisol Touraine, called the new deaths worrying. "The company has to take the necessary measures. I know that the company and the unions are alert to this ... we cannot leave the situation as it is," she told French radio.

The company's former boss Didier Lombard resigned after 35 employees killed themselves between 2008 and 2009. He was lambasted and forced to apologize after suggesting suicide was a "fashion" at the company. In 2012, Lombard was put under formal police investigation accused of installing "brutal management methods" that amounted to "moral harassment." *Le Parisien* published an internal company document from 2006 in which Lombard allegedly told directors he was determined to cut 22 000 jobs, adding "I'll do it in one way or the other, by the window or by the door." Lombard denied that his methods were the cause of the deaths. He remains under investigation.

An official report by the works inspectorate in 2010 blamed a climate of "management harassment" that it said had "psychologically weakened staff and attacked their physical and mental health." Since then, Patrick Ackermann, delegate for the SUD union and member of the observatory, said the situation had eased, but last month the group issued a warning to management of a "dramatic worsening" of morale within the company to 2007 levels. "For the last two years, the pressure from management has started again and working conditions have once more

Work stress at Orange France prompted protests.

GERARD JULIEN/AFP/Getty Images

deteriorated," it said. Factors driving workers to depression included a reduced workforce being asked to produce better results, staff being obliged to relocate, the threat of site closures and job losses, and an atmosphere of increased competition between workers.

"Also, what we are seeing among mid-level directors is a return to old and brutal methods of management," the observatory said in a statement.

France Telecom was privatized in 2004, sparking a major restructuring and the loss of scores of jobs. The company, known since last year as Orange to match the name of its mobile phone operation, currently employs around 100,000 but has pledged further cuts to the workforce.

In a statement, Orange admitted there had been "several suicides" this year, adding, "Each of these acts is by its nature singular and stem from different contexts. But these situations remind us to be vigilant and for the need to repeatedly question the efficiency of the numerous preventative measures put in place several for the past few years."[1]

In this chapter, we will define *interpersonal conflict*, discuss its causes, and examine various ways of handling conflict, including negotiation. Then we will explore *work stress*, noting its causes and the consequences that it can have for both individuals and organizations. Various strategies for managing stress will be considered.

LO **13.1**

Define *interpersonal conflict*, and review its causes in organizations.

Interpersonal conflict. The process that occurs when one person, group, or organizational subunit frustrates the goal attainment of another.

WHAT IS CONFLICT?

Interpersonal conflict is a process that occurs when one person, group, or organizational subunit frustrates the goal attainment of another. Thus, the curator of a museum might be in conflict with the director over the purchase of a particular work of art. Likewise, the entire curatorial staff might be in conflict with the financial staff over cutbacks in acquisition funds.

In its classic form, conflict often involves antagonistic attitudes and behaviours, as seen in the drama at Orange France. As for attitudes, the conflicting parties might develop a dislike for each other, see each other as unreasonable, and develop negative stereotypes of their opposites ("Those scientists should get out of the laboratory once in a while"). Antagonistic behaviours might include name calling, sabotage, or even physical aggression. In some organizations, the conflict process is managed in a collaborative way that keeps antagonism at a minimum. In others, conflict is hidden or suppressed and not nearly so obvious (e.g., some gender conflict).[2]

CAUSES OF ORGANIZATIONAL CONFLICT

It is possible to isolate a number of factors that contribute to organizational conflict.[3]

Group Identification and Intergroup Bias

An especially fascinating line of research has shown how identification with a particular group or class of people can set the stage for organizational conflict. In this work, researchers have typically assigned people to groups randomly or on the basis of some trivial characteristic, such as eye colour. Even without interaction or cohesion, people have a tendency to develop a more positive view of their own "in-group" and a less positive view of the "out-group," of which they are not a member.[4] The ease with which this unwarranted intergroup bias develops is disturbing.

Why does intergroup bias occur? Self-esteem is probably a critical factor. Identifying with the successes of one's own group and disassociating oneself from out-group failures boosts self-esteem and provides comforting feelings of social solidarity. Research by one of your authors, for example, found that people felt that their work group's attendance record was superior to that of their occupation in general (and, by extension, other work groups).[5] Attributing positive behaviour to your own work group should contribute to your self-esteem.

In organizations, there are a number of groups or classes with which people might identify. These might be based on personal characteristics (e.g., race or gender), job function (e.g., sales or production), or job level (e.g., manager or non-manager). Furthermore, far from being random or trivial, differences between groups might be accentuated by real differences in power, opportunity, clients serviced, and so on. The best prognosis is that people who identify with some groups will tend to be leery of out-group members. The likelihood of conflict increases as the factors we cover below enter into the relationship between groups.

The increased emphasis on teams in organizations generally places a high premium on getting employees to identify strongly with their team. The prevalence of intergroup bias suggests that organizations will have to pay special attention to managing relationships *between* these teams.

Interdependence

When individuals or subunits are mutually dependent on each other to accomplish *their own* goals, the potential for conflict exists. For example, the sales staff is dependent on the production department for the timely delivery of high-quality products. This is the only way sales can maintain the goodwill of its customers. On the other hand, production depends on the sales staff to provide routine orders with adequate lead times. Custom-tailored emergency orders will wreak havoc with production schedules and make the production department look bad. In contrast, the sales staff and the office maintenance staff are not highly interdependent. Salespeople are on the road a lot and should not make great demands on maintenance. Conversely, a dirty office probably will not lose a sale.

Interdependence can set the stage for conflict for two reasons. First, it necessitates interaction between the parties so that they can coordinate their interests. Conflict will not develop if the parties can "go it alone." Second, as we noted in the previous chapter, interdependence implies that each party has some *power* over the other. It is relatively easy for one side or the other to abuse its power and create antagonism.

Interdependence does not *always* lead to conflict. In fact, it often provides a good basis for collaboration through mutual assistance. Whether interdependence prompts conflict depends on the presence of other conditions, which we will now consider.

Differences in Power, Status, and Culture

Conflict can erupt when parties differ significantly in power, status, or culture.

POWER If dependence is not mutual but one way, the potential for conflict increases. If party A needs the collaboration of party B to accomplish its goals but B does not need A's assistance, antagonism may develop. B has power over A, and A has nothing with which to bargain. A good example is the quality control system in many factories. Production workers might be highly dependent on inspectors to approve their work, but this dependence is not reciprocated. The inspectors might have a separate boss, their own office, and their own circle of friends (other inspectors). In this case, production workers might begin to treat inspectors with hostility, one of the symptoms of conflict.

STATUS Status differences provide little impetus for conflict when people of lower status are dependent on those of higher status. This is the way organizations often work, and most members are socialized to expect it. However, because of the design of the work, there are occasions when employees who technically have lower status find themselves giving orders to, or controlling the tasks of, higher-status people. The restaurant business provides a good example. In many restaurants, lower-status servers give orders and initiate queries to higher status chefs. The latter might come to resent this reversal of usual lines of influence.[6] In some organizations, junior staff are more adept with information technology than senior staff. Some executives are defensive about this reversal of roles.

CULTURE When two or more very different cultures develop in an organization, the clash in beliefs and values can result in overt conflict. Hospital administrators who develop a strong culture centred on efficiency and cost-effectiveness might find themselves in conflict with physicians who share a strong culture based on providing excellent patient care at any cost. At Orange France, the culture change that accompanied privatization stimulated considerable conflict. A telling case of cultural conflict occurred when Apple expanded and hired professionals away from several companies with their own strong cultures.

During the first couple of years Apple recruited heavily from Hewlett-Packard, National Semiconductor, and Intel, and the habits and differences in style among these companies were reflected in Cupertino. There was a general friction between the rough and tough ways of the semiconductor men (there were few women) and the people who made computers, calculators, and instruments at Hewlett-Packard. . . . Some of the Hewlett-Packard men began to see themselves as civilizing influences and were horrified at the uncouth rough-and-tumble practices of the brutes from the semiconductor industry. . . . Many of the men from National Semiconductor and other stern backgrounds harboured a similar contempt for the Hewlett-Packard recruits. They came to look on them as prissy fusspots.[7]

Ambiguity

Ambiguous goals, jurisdictions, or performance criteria can lead to conflict. Under such ambiguity, the formal and informal rules that govern interaction break down. In addition, it might be difficult to accurately assign praise for good outcomes or blame for bad outcomes when it is hard to see who was responsible for what. For example, if sales drop following the introduction of a "new and improved" product, the design group might blame the marketing department for a poor advertising campaign. In response, the marketers might claim that the "improved" product is actually inferior to the old product.

Ambiguous performance criteria are a frequent cause of conflict between managers and employees. The basic scientist who is charged by a chemical company to "discover new knowledge" might react negatively when her boss informs her that her work is inadequate. This rather open-ended assignment is susceptible to a variety of interpretations. Conflict is not uncommon in the film and entertainment industry, in part because a great deal of ambiguity surrounds just what is needed to produce a hit movie or show.

Scarce Resources

In the previous chapter we pointed out that differences in power are magnified when resources become scarce. This does not occur without a battle, however, and conflict often surfaces in the process of power jockeying. Limited budget money, secretarial support, or lab space can contribute to conflict. Scarcity has a way of turning latent or disguised conflict into overt conflict. Two scientists who do not get along very well may be able to put up a peaceful front until a reduction in lab space provokes each to protect his or her domain. At Orange France, job cutbacks increased competition among employees.

LO 13.2

Explain the *types of conflict* and the process by which conflict occurs.

Relationship conflict.
Interpersonal tensions among individuals that have to do with their relationship per se, not the task at hand.

Task conflict.
Disagreements about the nature of the work to be done.

Process conflict.
Disagreements about how work should be organized and accomplished.

TYPES OF CONFLICT

Is all conflict the same? The answer is no. It is useful to distinguish among relationship, task, and process conflict.[8] **Relationship conflict** concerns interpersonal tensions among individuals that have to do with their relationship per se, not the task at hand. So-called personality clashes are examples of relationship conflicts. **Task conflict** concerns disagreements about the nature of the work to be done. Differences of opinion about goals or technical matters are examples of task conflict. Finally, **process conflict** involves disagreements about how work should be organized and accomplished. Disagreements about responsibility, authority, resource allocation, and who should do what all constitute process conflict.

In the context of work groups and teams, relationship and process conflict tend to be detrimental to member satisfaction and team performance. In essence, such conflict prevents the development of cohesiveness (Chapter 7). Occasionally, some degree of task conflict is actually beneficial for team performance, especially when the task is non-routine and requires a variety of perspectives to be considered and when it does not degenerate into relationship conflict.[9] Thus, not all conflict is detrimental, and we shall return to some potential benefits of conflict later in the chapter.

CONFLICT DYNAMICS

A number of events occur when one or more of the causes of conflict we noted above take effect. We will assume here that the conflict in question occurs between groups, such as organizational departments. However, much of this is also relevant to conflict within teams or between individuals. Specifically, when conflict begins, we often see the following events transpire:

- "Winning" the conflict becomes more important than developing a good solution to the problem at hand.

- The parties begin to conceal information from each other or to pass on distorted information.

- Each side becomes more cohesive. Deviants who speak of conciliation are punished, and strict conformity is expected.

- Contact with the opposite party is discouraged except under formalized, restricted conditions.

- While the opposite party is negatively stereotyped, the image of one's own position is boosted.

- On each side, more aggressive people who are skilled at engaging in conflict may emerge as leaders.[10]

You can certainly see the difficulty here. What begins as a problem of identity, interdependence, ambiguity, or scarcity quickly escalates to the point that the conflict process *itself* becomes an additional problem. The elements of this process then work against the achievement of a peaceful solution. The conflict continues to cycle "on its own steam."

MODES OF MANAGING CONFLICT

How do you tend to react to conflict situations? Are you aggressive? Do you tend to hide your head in the sand? As conflict expert Kenneth Thomas notes, there are several basic reactions that can be thought of as styles, strategies, or intentions for dealing with conflict. As shown in Exhibit 13.1, these approaches to managing conflict are a function of both how *assertive* you are in trying to satisfy your own or your group's concerns and how *cooperative* you are in trying to satisfy those of the other party or group.[11] It should be emphasized that none of

LO 13.3

Discuss the various *modes of managing conflict.*

PERSONAL INVENTORY ASSESSMENT
Learn About Yourself
Strategies for Handling Conflict

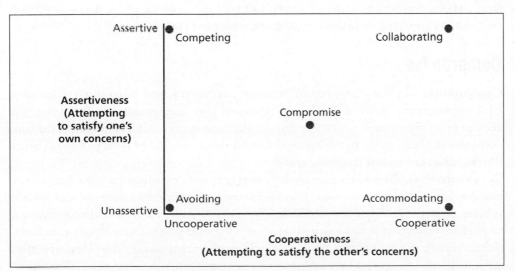

EXHIBIT 13.1
Approaches to managing organizational conflict.
Source: Thomas, K.W. (1992). Conflict and negotiations in organizations," in M.D. Dunnette, & L.M. Hough, (Eds.) *Handbook of industrial and organizational psychology* (2nd ed., Vol. 3). Palo Alto, CA: Consulting Psychologists Press. Used by permission of the author.

the five styles for dealing with conflict in Exhibit 13.1 is inherently superior. As we will see, each style might have its place given the situation in which the conflict episode occurs. To diagnose how you manage conflict, try the Experiential Exercise at the end of the chapter.

Avoiding

Avoiding. A conflict management style characterized by low assertiveness of one's own interests and low cooperation with the other party.

The **avoiding** style is characterized by low assertiveness of one's own interests and low cooperation with the other party. This is the "hiding one's head in the sand" response. Although avoidance can provide some short-term stress reduction from the rigours of conflict, it does not really change the situation. Thus, its effectiveness is often limited.

Of course, avoidance does have its place. If the issue is trivial, information is lacking, people need to cool down, or the opponent is very powerful and very hostile, avoidance might be a sensible response.

Accommodating

Accommodating. A conflict management style in which one cooperates with the other party while not asserting one's own interests.

Cooperating with the other party's wishes while not asserting one's own interests is the hallmark of **accommodating**. If people see accommodation as a sign of weakness, it does not bode well for future interactions. However, it can be an effective reaction when you are wrong, the issue is more important to the other party, or you want to build good will.

Competing

Competing. A conflict management style that maximizes assertiveness and minimizes cooperation.

A **competing** style tends to maximize assertiveness for your own position and minimize cooperative responses. In competing, you tend to frame the conflict in strict win–lose terms. Full priority is given to your own goals, facts, or procedures. Microsoft founder Bill Gates tends to pursue the competing style:

> *Gates is famously confrontational. If he strongly disagrees with what you're saying, he is in the habit of blurting out, "That's the stupidest … thing I've ever heard!" People tell stories of Gates spraying saliva into the face of some hapless employee as he yells, "This stuff isn't hard! I could do this stuff in a weekend!" What you're supposed to do in a situation like this, as in encounters with grizzly bears, is stand your ground: if you flee, the bear will think you're game and will pursue you, and you can't outrun a bear.[12]*

The competing style holds promise when you have a lot of power, you are sure of your facts, the situation is truly win–lose, or you will not have to interact with the other party in the future. This style is illustrated in the chapter-opening vignette.

Compromise

Compromise. A conflict management style that combines intermediate levels of assertiveness and cooperation.

Compromise combines intermediate levels of assertiveness and cooperation. Thus, it is itself a compromise between pure competition and pure accommodation. In a sense, you attempt to satisfice (Chapter 11) rather than maximize your outcomes and hope that the same occurs for the other party. In the law, a plea bargain is an example of a compromise between the defending lawyer and the prosecutor.

Compromise places a premium on determining rules of exchange between the two parties. As such, it always contains the seeds for procedural conflict in addition to whatever else is being negotiated. Also, compromise does not always result in the most creative response to conflict. Compromise is not so useful for resolving conflicts that stem from power asymmetry, because the weaker party may have little to offer the stronger party. However, it is a sensible reaction to conflict stemming from scarce resources. Also, it is a good fallback position if other strategies fail.

Integrative negotiation can result in win—win solutions.

Collaborating

In the **collaborating** mode, both assertiveness and cooperation are maximized in the hope that an integrative agreement occurs that fully satisfies the interests of both parties. Emphasis is put on a win—win resolution, in which there is no assumption that someone must lose something. Rather, it is assumed that the solution to the conflict can leave both parties in a better condition. Ideally, collaboration occurs as a problem-solving exercise (Chapter 11). It probably works best when the conflict is not intense and when each party has information that is useful to the other. Although effective collaboration can take time and practice to develop, it frequently enhances productivity and achievement.[13]

Some of the most remarkable examples of collaboration in contemporary organizations are those between companies and their suppliers. Traditionally, adversarial competition in which buyers try to squeeze the very lowest price out of suppliers, who are frequently played off against each other, has dominated these relationships. This obviously does not provide much incentive for the perpetually insecure suppliers to invest in improvements dedicated toward a particular buyer. Gradually, things have changed, and now it is common for organizations to supply extensive engineering support and technical advice to their suppliers. In a related example, after the 2011 Japanese earthquake and tsunami the country's car manufacturers, usually fierce competitors, collaborated to get the nation's parts suppliers back on line.[14]

Collaborating. A conflict management style that maximizes both assertiveness and cooperation.

MANAGING CONFLICT WITH NEGOTIATION

The stereotype we have of negotiation is that it is a formal process of bargaining between labour and management or buyer and seller. However, job applicants negotiate for starting salaries, employees negotiate for better job assignments, and people with sick kids negotiate to leave work early. To encompass all these situations, we might define **negotiation** as "a decision-making process among interdependent parties who do not share identical preferences."[15] Negotiation constitutes conflict management, in that it is an attempt to either prevent conflict or resolve existing conflict.

Negotiation is an attempt to reach a satisfactory exchange among or between the parties. Sometimes, negotiation is very explicit, as in the case of the labour negotiation or the

LO 13.4

Review a range of *negotiation techniques*.

Negotiation. A decision-making process among interdependent parties who do not share identical preferences.

buyer–seller interaction. However, negotiation can also proceed in a very implicit or tacit way.[16] For instance, when an employee is trying to get a more interesting job assignment or to take off from work early, the terms of the exchange are not likely to be spelled out very clearly. Still, this is negotiation.

It has become common to distinguish between distributive and integrative negotiation tactics.[17] **Distributive negotiation** assumes a zero-sum, win–lose situation in which a fixed pie is divided up between the parties. If you re-examine Exhibit 13.1, you can imagine that distributive negotiation occurs on the axis between competition and accommodation. In theory, the parties will more or less tend toward some compromise. On the other hand, **integrative negotiation** assumes that mutual problem solving can result in a win–win situation in which the pie is actually enlarged before distribution. Integrative negotiation occurs on the axis between avoiding and collaborating, ideally tending toward the latter.

Distributive and integrative negotiations can take place simultaneously. We will discuss them separately for pedagogical purposes.

Distributive Negotiation Tactics

Distributive negotiation is essentially single-issue negotiation. Many potential conflict situations fit this scenario. For example, suppose you find a used car that you really like. Now things boil down to price. You want to buy the car for the minimum reasonable price, while the seller wants to get the maximum reasonable price.

The essence of the problem is shown in Exhibit 13.2. Party is a consulting firm who would like to win a contract to do an attitude survey in Other's firm. Party would like to make $90 000 for the job (Party's target) but would settle for $70 000, a figure that provides for minimal acceptable profit (Party's resistance point). Other thinks that the survey could be done for as little as $60 000 (Other's target) but would be willing to spend up to $80 000 for a good job (Other's resistance point). Theoretically, an offer in the settlement range between $70 000 and $80 000 should clinch the deal, if the negotiators can get into this range. Notice that every dollar that Party earns is a dollar's worth of cost for Other. How will they reach a settlement?[18]

> **Distributive negotiation.**
> Win–lose negotiation in which a fixed amount of assets is divided between parties.
>
> **Integrative negotiation.**
> Win–win negotiation that assumes that mutual problem solving can enlarge the assets to be divided between parties.

EXHIBIT 13.2
A model of distributive negotiation.

Source: Thomas, K.W. (1992). Conflict and negotiations in organizations in M.D. Dunnette, & L.M. Hough (Eds.) *Handbook of industrial and organizational psychology* (2nd ed., Vol. 3). Palo Alto, CA: Consulting Psychologists Press. Used by permission of the author.

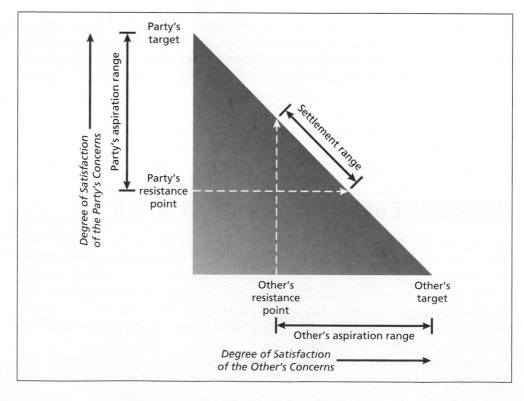

THREATS AND PROMISES *Threat* consists of implying that you will punish the other party if he or she does not concede to your position. For example, the Other firm might imply that it will terminate its other business with the consulting company if Party does not lower its price on the attitude survey job. *Promises* are pledges that concessions will lead to rewards in the future. For example, Other might promise future consulting contracts if Party agrees to do the survey at a lower price. Of course, the difference between a threat and a promise can be subtle, as when the promise implies a threat should no concession be made.

Threat has some merit as a bargaining tactic if one party has power over the other that corresponds to the nature of the threat, especially if no future negotiations are expected or if the threat can be posed in a civil and subtle way.[19] If power is more balanced and the threat is crude, a counter-threat could scuttle the negotiations, despite the fact that both parties could be satisfied in the settlement range. Promises have merit when your side lacks power and anticipates future negotiations with the other side. Both threats and promises work best when they send interpretable signals to the other side about your true position, what really matters to you. Careful timing is critical.

FIRMNESS VERSUS CONCESSIONS How about intransigence—sticking to your target position, offering few concessions, and waiting for the other party to give in? Research shows that such a tactic yields superior economic results, especially in face-to-face negotiations.[20] When some concessions are thought to be appropriate, good negotiators often use face-saving techniques to explain them. For example, the consulting firm might claim that it could reduce the cost of the survey by making it web-based rather than based on paper questionnaires.

PERSUASION Verbal persuasion or debate is common in negotiations. Often, it takes a two-pronged attack. One prong asserts the technical merits of the party's position. For example, the consulting firm might justify its target price by saying "We have the most qualified staff. We do the most reliable surveys." The other prong asserts the fairness of the target position. Here, the negotiator might make a speech about the expenses the company would incur in doing the survey.

Verbal persuasion is an attempt to change the attitudes of the other party toward your target position. Persuaders are most effective when they are perceived as expert, likable, and unbiased. The obvious problem in distributive negotiations is bias—each party knows the other is self-interested. One way to deal with this is to introduce some unbiased parties. For example, the consulting firm might produce testimony from satisfied survey clients. Also, disputants often bring third parties into negotiations on the assumption that they will process argumentation in an unbiased manner.

Salary negotiation is a traditional example of distributive bargaining. A review of studies on gender differences in negotiation outcomes found that although men negotiated significantly better outcomes than women, the overall difference between men and women was small. However, even small differences in salary negotiations would be perpetuated through subsequent salary increases based on percentage of pay. Thus, training programs that enable women to negotiate better starting salaries comparable with men can have short- and long-term benefits.[21] Negotiation is worth doing, as a study showed that new hires who negotiated received a $5000 salary premium. Collaborating and competing strategies were superior to compromising and accommodating.[22]

Integrative Negotiation Tactics

As we noted earlier, integrative negotiation rejects a fixed-pie assumption and strives for collaborative problem solving that advances the interests of both parties. This requires trust between the parties, but this trust is often rewarded with superior negotiation outcomes.[23]

At the outset, it is useful but sobering to realize that people have a decided bias for fixed-pie thinking. Integrative negotiation requires a degree of creativity. Many people are not especially creative, and the stress of typical negotiation does not provide the best climate for creativity in any event. This means that many of the role models that negotiators have (e.g., following labour negotiations on TV) are more likely to use distributive than integrative tactics. To complicate matters, if you are negotiating for constituents, they are also more likely to be exposed to distributive tactics and likely to pressure you to use them. Nevertheless, attempts at integrative negotiation can be well worth the effort.[24]

COPIOUS INFORMATION EXCHANGE Most of the information exchanged in distributive bargaining is concerned with attacking the other party's position and trying to persuade them of the correctness of yours. Otherwise, mum's the word. A freer flow of information is critical to finding an integrative settlement. The problem, of course, is that we all tend to be a bit paranoid about information being used against us in bargaining situations. This means that trust must be built slowly. One way to proceed is to give away some non-critical information to the other party to get the ball rolling. As we noted earlier, much negotiation behaviour tends to be reciprocated. Also, ask the other party a lot of questions, and *listen* to their responses. This is at odds with the tell-and-sell approach used in most distributive negotiations. If all goes well, both parties will begin to reveal their true interests, not just their current positions.

FRAMING DIFFERENCES AS OPPORTUNITIES Parties in a negotiation often differ in their preferences, for everything from the timing of a deal to the degree of risk that each party wants to assume. Traditionally, such differences are framed as barriers to negotiations. However, such differences can often serve as a basis for integrative agreements because, again, they contain information that can telegraph each party's real interests. For instance, imagine that two co-workers are negotiating for the finishing date of a project that they have to complete by a certain deadline. Due to competing demands, one wants to finish it early, and the other wants to just make the deadline. In the course of the discussion, they realize that they can divide the labour such that one begins the project while the other finishes it, satisfying both parties fully (notice that this is not a compromise).

CUTTING COSTS If you can somehow cut the costs that the other party associates with an agreement, the chance of an integrative settlement increases. For example, suppose that you are negotiating with your boss for a new, more interesting job assignment, but she does not like the idea because she relies on your excellent skills on your current assignment. By asking good questions (see above), you find out that she is ultimately worried about the job being done properly, not about your leaving it. You take the opportunity to inform her that you have groomed a subordinate to do your current job. This reduces the costs of her letting you assume the new assignment. Integrative solutions are especially attractive when they reduce costs for *all* parties in a dispute.

INCREASING RESOURCES Increasing available resources is a very literal way of getting around the fixed-pie syndrome. This is not as unlikely as it sounds when you realize that two parties, working together, might have access to twice as many resources as one party. One of your authors once saw two academic departments squabbling to get the approval to recruit one new faculty member for whom there was a budget line. Seeing this as a fixed pie leads to one department winning all or to the impossible compromise of half a recruit for each department. The chairs of the two departments used their *combined* political clout to get the dean to promise that they could also have exclusive access to one budget line the following year. The chairs then flipped a coin to see who would recruit immediately and who would wait a year. This minor compromise on time was less critical than the firm guarantee of a budget line.

INTRODUCING SUPERORDINATE GOALS As discussed in Chapter 7, **superordinate goals** are attractive outcomes that can be achieved only by collaboration.[25] Neither party can attain the goal on its own. Superordinate goals probably represent the best example of creativity in integrative negotiation, because they change the entire landscape of the negotiation episode. Over the years various terrorist attacks have created superordinate goals that prompt collaboration among nations that otherwise might have been mired in conflict over more trivial matters.

Superordinate goals. Attractive outcomes that can be achieved only by collaboration.

Third-Party Involvement

Sometimes, third parties come into play to intervene between negotiating parties.[26] Often, this happens when the parties reach an impasse. For example, a manager might have to step in to a conflict between two employees or even between two departments. In other cases, third-party involvement exists right from the start of the negotiation. For example, real estate agents serve as an interface between home sellers and buyers.

MEDIATION The process of mediation occurs when a neutral third party helps to facilitate a negotiated agreement. Formal mediation has a long history in labour disputes, international relations, and marital counselling. However, by definition, almost any manager might occasionally be required to play an informal mediating role.

What do mediators do?[27] First, almost anything that aids the *process* or *atmosphere* of negotiation can be helpful. Of course, this depends on the exact situation at hand. If there is tension, the mediator might serve as a lightning rod for anger or try to introduce humour. The mediator might try to help the parties clarify their underlying interests, both to themselves and to each other. Occasionally, imposing a deadline or helping the parties deal with their own constituents might be useful. Introducing a problem-solving orientation to move toward more integrative bargaining might also be appropriate.

The mediator might also intervene in the *content* of the negotiation, highlighting points of agreement, pointing out new options, or encouraging concessions.

Research shows that mediation has a fairly successful track record in dispute resolution. However, mediators cannot turn water into wine, and the process seems to work best when the conflict is not too intense and the parties are resolved to use negotiation to deal with their conflict. If the mediator is not seen as neutral, or if there is dissension in the ranks of each negotiating party, mediation does not work so well.[28]

ARBITRATION The process of arbitration occurs when a third party is given the authority to dictate the terms of settlement of a conflict (there is also non-binding arbitration, which we will not consider here). Although disputing parties sometimes agree to arbitration, it can also be mandated formally by law or informally by upper management or parents. The key point is that negotiation has broken down, and the arbitrator has to make a final distributive allocation. This is not the way to integrative solutions.

In *conventional arbitration*, the arbitrator can choose any outcome, such as splitting the difference between the two parties. In *final offer arbitration*, each party makes a final offer, and the arbitrator chooses one of them. This latter invention was devised to motivate the two parties to make sensible offers that have a chance of being upheld. Also, fear of the all-or-nothing aspect of final arbitration seems to motivate more negotiated agreement.[29]

One of the most commonly arbitrated disputes between employers and employees is dismissal for excessive absenteeism. One study found that the arbitrators sided with the company in over half of such cases, especially when the company could show evidence of a fair and consistently applied absentee policy.[30]

IS ALL CONFLICT BAD?

In everyday life, there has traditionally been an emphasis on the negative, dysfunctional aspects of conflict. However, as suggested in our previous distinction among task, process, and relationship conflict, there is growing awareness of some potential benefits of organizational conflict.[31] The argument that conflict can be functional rests mainly on the idea that it can improve decision making and promote necessary organizational change. For example, consider the museum that relies heavily on government funding and consistently mounts exhibits that are appreciated only by "true connoisseurs" of art. Under a severe funding cutback, the museum can survive only if it begins to mount exhibits with more popular appeal. Such a change might occur only after much conflict within the board of directors.

Constructive conflict is most likely to promote good decisions and positive organizational change. Such conflict means that the parties to the conflict agree that its benefits outweigh its costs.[32] This is most likely when the tendency to avoid conflict is suppressed and the parties engage in open-minded discussion of their differences, being open to evidence that is counter to their current positions.

If conflict can be constructive, then there are times when managers might use a strategy of **conflict stimulation** to foster change. But how does a manager know when some conflict might be a good thing? One signal is the existence of a "friendly rut," in which peaceful relationships take precedence over organizational goals. Another signal is seen when parties that should be interacting closely have chosen to withdraw from each other to avoid overt conflict. A third signal occurs when conflict is suppressed or downplayed by denying differences, ignoring controversy, and exaggerating points of agreement.[33]

The causes of conflict, discussed earlier, such as scarcity and ambiguity, can be manipulated by managers to achieve change.[34] For example, when he was appointed vice-chairman of product development at General Motors, Robert Lutz sent out a memo entitled "Strongly-Held Beliefs." In it, the product czar said that GM undervalued exciting design, and he panned corporate sacred cows, such as the extensive use of consumer focus groups and product planning committees. Lutz stimulated conflict by signalling a shift of resources from marketing to design.[35]

Conflict in organizations, warranted or not, often causes considerable stress. Let's now turn to this topic.

A MODEL OF STRESS IN ORGANIZATIONS

During the past two decades, stress has become a serious concern for individuals and organizations. In fact, in an American Psychological Association survey, work was reported to be a potent source of stress, edging out health and relationships.[36] Stress has been estimated to cost U.S. businesses $300 billion annually and Canadian businesses $16 billion.[37] The model of a stress episode in Exhibit 13.3 can guide our introduction to this topic.[38]

Stressors

Stressors are environmental events or conditions that have the potential to induce stress. There are some conditions that would prove stressful for just about everyone. These include such things as extreme heat, extreme cold, isolation, or hostile people. More interesting is the fact that the individual personality often determines the extent to which a potential stressor becomes a real stressor and actually induces stress.

Stress

Stress is a psychological reaction to the demands inherent in a stressor that has the potential to make a person feel tense or anxious because the person does not feel capable of coping

---

Constructive conflict.
Conflict for which the benefits outweigh the costs.

Conflict stimulation.
A strategy of increasing conflict to motivate change.

LO **13.5**

Distinguish among *stressors, stress,* and *stress reactions.*

PERSONAL INVENTORY ASSESSMENT

Learn About Yourself
Stress Management Assessment

Stressors. Environmental events or conditions that have the potential to induce stress.

Stress. A psychological reaction to the demands inherent in a stressor that has the potential to make a person feel tense or anxious.

with these demands.[39] Stress is not intrinsically bad. All people require a certain level of stimulation from their environment, and moderate levels of stress can serve this function. In fact, one would wonder about the perceptual accuracy of a person who *never* experienced tension. On the other hand, stress does become a problem when it leads to especially high levels of anxiety and tension. Obviously, the restructuring at Orange France described in the chapter-opening vignette provoked much stress.

Stress Reactions

Stress reactions are the behavioural, psychological, and physiological consequences of stress. Some of these reactions are essentially passive responses over which the individual has little direct control, such as elevated blood pressure or a reduced immune function. Other reactions are active attempts to *cope* with some previous aspect of the stress episode. Exhibit 13.3 indicates that stress reactions that involve coping attempts might be directed toward dealing directly with the stressor or simply reducing the anxiety generated by stress. In general, the former strategy has more potential for effectiveness than the latter because the chances of the stress episode being *terminated* are increased.[40]

Often, reactions that are useful for the individual in dealing with a stress episode may be very costly to the organization. The individual who is conveniently absent from work on the day of a difficult inventory check might prevent personal stress but leave the organization short-handed (provoking stress in others). Thus, organizations should be concerned about the stress that individual employees experience.

Throughout the book, we have been careful to note cross-cultural differences in OB. However, the stress model presented here appears to generalize across cultures. That is, similar factors provoke stress and lead to similar stress reactions around the globe.[41]

Stress reactions. The behavioural, psychological, and physiological consequences of stress.

Personality and Stress

Personality (Chapter 2) can have an important influence on the stress experience. As shown in Exhibit 13.3, it can affect both the extent to which potential stressors are perceived as stressful and the types of stress reactions that occur. Let's look at three key personality traits.

LOCUS OF CONTROL You will recall from Chapter 2 that **locus of control** concerns people's beliefs about the factors that control their behaviour. Internals believe that they control their own behaviour, while externals believe that their behaviour is controlled by luck, fate, or powerful people. Compared with internals, externals are more likely to feel anxious in the face of potential stressors.[42] Most people like to feel in control of what happens to them, and externals feel less in control. Internals are more likely to confront stressors directly because they assume that this response will make a difference. Externals, on the other hand, are anxious but do not feel that they are masters of their own fate. Thus, they are more prone to simple anxiety-reduction strategies that work only in the short run.

LO 13.6

Discuss the role that personality plays in stress.

Locus of control. A set of beliefs about whether one's behaviour is controlled mainly by internal or external forces.

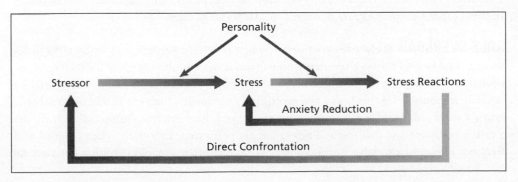

EXHIBIT 13.3
Model of a stress episode.

Type A behaviour pattern.
A personality pattern that includes aggressiveness, ambitiousness, competitiveness, hostility, impatience, and a sense of time urgency.

TYPE A BEHAVIOUR PATTERN Interest in the **Type A behaviour pattern** began when physicians noticed that many sufferers of coronary heart disease, especially those who developed the disease relatively young, exhibited a distinctive pattern of behaviours and emotions.[43] Individuals who exhibit the Type A behaviour pattern tend to be aggressive and ambitious. Their hostility is easily aroused, and they feel a great sense of time urgency. They are impatient, competitive, and preoccupied with their work. The Type A individual can be contrasted with the Type B, who does not exhibit these extreme characteristics. Compared with Type B individuals, Type A people report heavier workloads, longer work hours, and more conflicting work demands.[44] We will see later that such factors turn out to be potent stressors. Thus, either Type A people encounter more stressful situations than Type B people do, or they perceive themselves as doing so. In turn, Type A individuals are likely to exhibit adverse physiological reactions in response to stress. These include elevated blood pressure, elevated heart rate, and modified blood chemistry. Frustrating, difficult, or competitive events are especially likely to prompt these adverse reactions. Type A individuals seem to have a strong need to control their work environment, a full-time task that stimulates their feelings of time urgency and leads them to overextend themselves physically.[45]

The major component of Type A behaviour that contributes to adverse physiological reactions is hostility and repressed anger. This may also be accompanied by exaggerated cynicism and distrust of others. When these factors are prominent in a Type A individual's personality, stress is most likely to take its toll.[46]

Negative affectivity.
Propensity to view the world, including oneself and other people, in a negative light.

NEGATIVE AFFECTIVITY **Negative affectivity** is the propensity to view the world, including oneself and other people, in a negative light. It is a stable personality trait that is a major component of the Big Five personality dimension neuroticism (Chapter 2). People high in negative affectivity tend to be pessimistic and downbeat. As a consequence, they tend to report more stressors in the work environment and to feel more subjective stress. They are particularly likely to feel stressed in response to the demands of a heavy workload.[47]

Several factors might be responsible for the susceptibility to stress of those who are high in negative affectivity. These include (a) a predisposition to *perceive* stressors in the workplace, (b) hypersensitivity to existing stressors, (c) a tendency to gravitate to stressful jobs, (d) a tendency to *provoke* stress through their negativity, or (e) the use of passive, indirect coping styles that avoid the real sources of stress.[48]

STRESSORS IN ORGANIZATIONAL LIFE

LO 13.7

Review the sources of stress encountered by various organizational role occupants.

In this section, we will examine potential stressors in detail. Some stressors can affect almost everyone in any organization, while others are likely to affect people who perform particular roles.

Executive and Managerial Stressors

Executives and managers make key organizational decisions and direct the work of others. In these capacities, they experience some special forms of stress.

Role overload. The requirement for too many tasks to be performed in too short a time period or to work too many hours.

ROLE OVERLOAD **Role overload** occurs when one must perform too many tasks in too short a time period or work too many hours, and it is a common stressor for managers, especially in today's downsized organizations. The open-ended nature of the managerial job is partly responsible for this heavy and protracted workload, which might add up to 60 or 70 hours a week. Management is an ongoing *process*, and there are few signposts to signify that a task is complete and that rest and relaxation are permitted. Especially when coupled with frequent moves or excessive travel, a heavy workload often provokes conflict between the

© Randy Glasbergen

"You've been working awfully hard lately.
If you need a little fresh air and sunshine,
you can go to www.fresh-air-and-sunshine.com"

manager's role as an organizational member and his or her role as a spouse or parent. Thus, role overload may provoke stress, at the same time preventing the manager from enjoying the pleasures of life that can reduce stress.

HEAVY RESPONSIBILITY Not only is the workload of the executive heavy, but it can have extremely important consequences for the organization and its members. A vice-president of labour relations might be in charge of a negotiation strategy that could result in either labour peace or a protracted and bitter strike. To complicate matters, the personal consequences of an incorrect decision can be staggering. For example, the courts have fined and even jailed executives who have engaged in illegal activities on behalf of their organizations. Finally, executives are responsible for people as well as things, and this influence over the future of others has the potential to induce stress. The executive who must terminate the operation of an unprofitable division, putting many out of work, or the manager who must lay off an employee, putting one out of work, may experience guilt and tension.[49]

Operative-Level Stressors

Operatives are individuals who occupy non-professional and non-managerial positions in organizations. In a manufacturing organization, operatives perform the work on the shop floor and range from skilled craftspeople to unskilled labourers. As is the case with other organizational roles, the occupants of operative positions are sometimes exposed to a special set of stressors.

POOR PHYSICAL WORKING CONDITIONS Operative-level employees are more likely than managers and professionals to be exposed to physically unpleasant and even dangerous working conditions. Although social sensibility and union activity have improved working conditions over the years, many employees must still face excessive heat, cold, noise, pollution, and the chance of accidents.

POOR JOB DESIGN Although bad job design can provoke stress at any organizational level (executive role overload is an example), the designs of lower-level blue- and white-collar jobs are particular culprits. It might seem paradoxical that jobs that are too simple or not challenging enough can act as stressors. However, monotony and boredom can prove extremely frustrating to people who feel capable of handling more complex tasks. Thus, research has found that job scope can be a stressor at levels that are either too low or too high.[50]

Boundary Role Stressors, Burnout, and Emotional Labour

Boundary roles. Positions in which organizational members are required to interact with members of other organizations or with the public.

Boundary roles are positions in which organizational members are required to interact with members of other organizations or with the public. For example, a vice-president of public relations is responsible for representing his or her company to the public. At other levels, receptionists, sale reps, and installers often interact with customers or suppliers.

People are especially likely to experience stress as they straddle the imaginary boundary between the organization and its environment. This is yet another form of role conflict in which one's role as an organizational member might be incompatible with the demands made by the public or other organizations. A classic case of boundary role stress involves sales reps. In extreme cases, customers desire fast delivery of a custom-tailored product, such as a new software application. The sales rep might be tempted to "offer the moon" but at the same time is aware that such an order could place a severe strain on his or her organization's software development team. Thus, the sales rep is faced with the dilemma of doing his or her primary job (selling), while protecting another function (software development) from unreasonable demands that could result in a broken delivery contract.

Burnout. A syndrome of emotional exhaustion, cynicism, and reduced self-efficacy.

A particular form of stress (and accompanying stress reactions) experienced by some boundary role occupants is burnout. **Burnout**, as Christina Maslach, Michael Leiter, and Wilmar Schaufeli define it, is a syndrome made up of emotional exhaustion, cynicism, and low self-efficacy (Chapter 2).[51] Burnout was originally studied among those working in some capacity with people. Frequently, these people are organizational clients who require special attention or who are experiencing severe problems. Thus, teachers, nurses, paramedics, social workers, and police are especially likely candidates for burnout. However, burnout can occur even among non–boundary spanners.

Burnout follows a process that begins with emotional exhaustion (left side of Exhibit 13.4). The person feels fatigued in the morning, drained by the work, and frustrated by the day's events. One way to deal with this extreme exhaustion is to become cynical and distance oneself from one's clients, the "cause" of the exhaustion. In the extreme, this might involve depersonalizing them, treating them like objects, and lacking concern for what happens to them. The clients might also be seen as blaming the employee for their problems. Finally, the burned-out individual develops feelings of low self-efficacy and low personal accomplishment—"I can't deal with these people; I'm not helping them; I don't understand them." In fact, because of the exhaustion and depersonalization, there might be more than a grain of truth to these feelings. Although the exact details of this progression are open to some question, these three symptoms paint a reliable picture of burnout.[52]

Burnout seems to be most common among people who entered their jobs with especially high ideals. Their expectations of being able to "change the world" are badly frustrated when they encounter the reality shock of troubled clients (who are often perceived as

EXHIBIT 13.4
The burnout–engagement continuum.

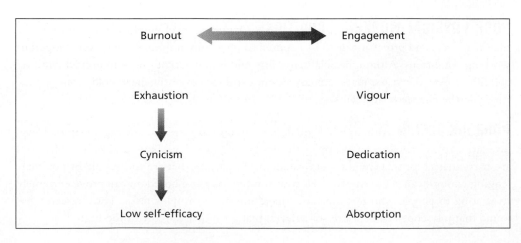

Many service jobs require emotional labour, suppressing negative emotions and exaggerating positive ones.

unappreciative) and the inability of the organization to help them. Teachers get fed up with being disciplinarians; nurses get upset when patients die; and police officers get depressed when they must constantly deal with the "losers" of society. Gender and personality are also related to burnout. Women are more likely to report emotional exhaustion and men are more likely to report depersonalization. In general, those with high self-esteem, high conscientiousness, and internal control report less burnout.[53]

What are the consequences of burnout? Some individuals bravely pursue a new occupation, often experiencing guilt about not having been able to cope in the old one. Others stay in the same occupation but seek a new job. For instance, the burned-out nurse may go into nursing education to avoid contact with sick patients. Some people pursue administrative careers in their profession, attempting to "climb above" the source of their difficulties. These people often set cynical examples for idealistic subordinates. Finally, some people stay in their jobs and become part of the legion of "deadwood," collecting their paycheques but doing little to contribute to the mission of the organization. Many "good bureaucrats" choose this route.[54]

Much boundary role stress stems from the frequent need for such employees to engage in "emotional labour." You will recall from Chapter 4 that emotional labour involves regulating oneself to suppress negative emotions or to exaggerate positive ones. Thus, police officers are not supposed to express anger at unsafe motorists or drunks, and salon employees are supposed to act friendly and sympathetic to boorish clients. Such suppression and acting takes a toll on cognitive and emotional resources over time.[55]

The Job Demands–Resources Model and Work Engagement

It is obvious that organizations should strive to avoid causing burnout and the extreme detachment from the job that it causes. In fact, organizations should strive to foster exactly the *opposite* of burnout—extreme engagement and enthusiasm for the job. In recent years, the subject of engagement has captured the attention of both researchers and managers. In part, this is due to rather low self-reported levels of engagement. Surveys indicate that only 17 percent of Canadians are highly engaged in their work, 66 percent are moderately engaged, and 17 percent are disengaged.[56] **Work engagement** can be defined as "a positive

Work engagement. A positive work-related state of mind that is characterized by vigour, dedication, and absorption.

Compassionate Eye Foundation/Justin Pumfrey/Getty Images

work-related state of mind that is characterized by vigor, dedication, and absorption."[57] (See the right side of Exhibit 13.4.) Vigour involves high levels of energy and mental resilience at work; dedication means being strongly involved in your work and experiencing a sense of significance, enthusiasm, and challenge; absorption refers to being fully concentrated on and engrossed in your work. In particular, the first two dimensions—vigour and dedication— position engagement as the opposite of burnout.[58]

What determines whether employees tend toward engagement versus burnout? According to the **job demands–resources model** the work environment can be described in terms of demands and resources.[59] Job demands are physical, psychological, social, or organizational features of a job that require sustained physical or psychological effort that in turn can result in physiological or psychological costs. Common demands include work overload, time pressure, role ambiguity, and role conflict. Job resources refer to features of a job that are functional in that they help achieve work goals, reduce job demands, and stimulate personal growth, learning, and development. Job resources can come from the organization (e.g., pay, career opportunities, and job security), interpersonal and social relations (e.g., supervisor and co-worker support, team climate), the organization of work (e.g., role clarity, participation in decision making), and the task itself (e.g., task significance, autonomy, and performance feedback). A central assumption of the model is that high job resources foster work engagement, while high job demands exhaust employees physically and mentally and lead to burnout. Indeed, research has found that job demands are related to burnout, disengagement, and health problems, while job resources lead to work engagement, organizational citizenship behaviour, and organizational commitment. Also, it shows that resources can buffer the negative impact of job demands on well-being.[60]

Exhibit 13.5 shows the results of a survey of 11 000 U.K. workers in 26 occupations. The occupations are ranked in terms of several outcomes of stress. The low-ranked jobs are "worse," and those in italics are worse than average. These are the jobs that make high demands while supplying limited resources. Later in the chapter we will suggest some ways to reduce stress or improve the ability to cope that involve reducing demands and/or increasing resources.

Some General Stressors

To conclude our discussion of stressors that people encounter in organizational life, we will consider some that are probably experienced equally by occupants of all roles.

INTERPERSONAL CONFLICT Interpersonal conflict can be a potent stressor, especially for those with strong avoidance tendencies. The entire range of conflict, from personality clashes to intergroup strife, is especially likely to cause stress when it leads to real or perceived attacks on our self-esteem or integrity. Although conflict can lead to stress in many settings outside of work, we often have the option of terminating the relationship, of "choosing our friends," as it were. This option is often not available at work.

A particular manifestation of interpersonal conflict is workplace bullying. **Bullying** is repeated negative behaviour that is directed toward one or more individuals of lower power or status and creates a hostile work environment.[61] Research has clearly demonstrated that it is a potent source of stress and negative well-being.[62]

A number of factors distinguish bullying as a stress-inducing form of conflict.[63] Although bullying can involve physical aggression, it is most commonly a more subtle form of psychological aggression and intimidation. This can take many forms, such as incessant teasing, demeaning criticism, social isolation, or sabotaging others' tools and equipment. An essential feature of bullying is its persistence, and a single harsh incident would not constitute such behaviour. Rather, it is the *repeated* teasing, criticism, or undermining that signals bullying. Another key feature of the bullying process is some degree of power or status imbalance between the bully and the victim. Power imbalance can be subtle, and some people might

Job demands–resources model. A model that specifies how job demands cause burnout and job resources cause engagement.

PERSONAL INVENTORY ASSESSMENT
Learn About Yourself
Managing Interpersonal Conflict

Bullying. Repeated negative behaviour that is directed toward one or more individuals of lower power or status and creates a hostile work environment.

Rank	Physical Health	Psychological Well–being	Job Satisfaction
1	*Ambulance*	*Social services providing care*	*Prison officer*
2	*Teachers*	*Teachers*	*Ambulance*
3	*Social services providing care*	*Fire brigade*	*Police*
4	*Customer services–call centre*	*Ambulance*	*Customer services–call centre*
5	*Bar staff*	*Vets*	*Social services providing care*
6	*Prison officer*	*Lecturers*	*Teachers*
7	*Mgmt (private sector)*	*Clerical and admin*	*Nursing*
8	*Clerical and admin*	*Mgmt (private sector)*	*Medical/dental*
9	*Police*	*Prison officer*	*Allied health professionals*
10	Teaching assistant	*Research–academic*	Bar staff
11	Head teachers	*Police*	Mgmt (private sector)
12	Secretarial/business support	*Customer services–call centre*	Fire brigade
13	Research–academic	Director (public sector)	Vets
14	Lecturers	Allied health professionals	Clerical and admin
15	Senior police	Bar staff	Mgmt (public sector)
16	Nursing	Nursing	Lecturers
17	Mgmt (public sector)	Medical/dental	Head teachers
18	Allied health professionals	Senior police	Teaching assistant
19	Medical/dental	Secretaria/business support	Secretarial/business support
20	Accountant	Head teachers	Director (public sector)
21	Fire brigade	Mgmt (public sector)	Research–academic
22	Vets	Accountant	Senior police
23	Director (public sector)	Teaching assistant	School lunchtime supervisors
24	Analyst	Analyst	Accountant
25	School lunchtime supervisors	School lunchtime supervisors	Analyst
26	Director/MD (private sector)	Director/MD (private sector)	Director/MD (private sector)

EXHIBIT 13.5
Occupations ranked on physical health, psychological well-being, and job satisfaction.
Note: The most stressful jobs have the lowest ranks. Jobs worse than average are indicated in italics.
Source: Johnson S. (2009). Organizational screening: The ASSET model. In S. Cartwright & C.L. Cooper (Eds.), *The Oxford handbook of organizational well-being.* Oxford: Oxford University Press, p. 145.

lack power due to their gender, race, physical stature, low job security, or educational credentials. Also, there is power in numbers, in that subordinates might team up to harass their boss. This is an example of a phenomenon closely associated to bullying called *mobbing*. Mobbing occurs when a number of individuals, usually direct co-workers, "gang up" on a particular employee.[64] Mobbing can be especially intimidating and stressful because it restricts the availability of social support that might be present when there is only a single bully. Even smart people can be bullied, as illustrated in Research Focus: *Get Smarty Pants*.

The role of differential power is most apparent when managers engage in the bullying of subordinates, a condition called **abusive supervision**. Abusive supervision is especially damaging to employee well-being, because managers control considerable resources of interest to employees (e.g., access to promotions) and are a natural place to turn to for support when experiencing abuse. This is impossible when it is the manager who is the abuser. Research has shown that the negative behaviour can "trickle down" from managers to supervisors to workers, creating a climate of abuse.[65] A profile of abusive managers shows that they often come from abusive families, are themselves experiencing stress at work, and feel they have been treated unfairly.[66] Given this, organizations should obviously pay careful attention to who is assigned to leadership positions.

Although bullying has occurred as long as people have worked, **cyberbullying** is a fairly new form of bullying in which the abuse occurs electronically via email, texting, social network platforms, or blogs. In some cases, the cyberbullying is direct in that it consists of

Abusive supervision. The bullying of subordinates by managers.

Cyberbullying. Bulling via email, texting, social network platforms, or blogs.

RESEARCH FOCUS

GET SMARTY PANTS

Organizations generally try to hire smart people and reward good performance. However, co-workers of smart, well-performing employees may not always be so generous. In a series of studies Eugene Kim and Theresa Glomb explored the possibility that star performers can often be the victims of bullying. In one study, they found that smart employees (as determined by a cognitive test) were more likely to report having been bullied. This was especially likely when the smart people were dominant and assertive types rather than agreeable and social. In other studies, they found that high performers were more likely to be bullied, and that this bullying might have been caused by co-workers' envy of their high performance. Again, however, the extent of bullying depended on other aspects of the potential victim. Good performers who identified more strongly with their work group were less likely to be victimized than those who were more detached from the group. The research sites spanned health care, university support staff, government work, and small advertising agencies. It would be interesting to see if the results hold in competitive high-tech environments. However, the urge to "get smarty pants" occurred in both the individualistic United States and in collectivist South Korea.

Source: Based on Kim, E., & Glomb, T.M. (2014). Victimization of high performers: The roles of envy and work group identification. *Journal of Applied Psychology, 99,* 619-634.

harassing messages (e.g., emails or texts) sent explicitly to the target of abuse. In other cases, it is indirect in that messages are posted publicly on Facebook, Twitter, YouTube, blogs, and web pages.[67] The content of some cyberbullying constitutes sexual harassment (see below). Cyberbullying can be especially destructive because the perpetrator might be anonymous, the audience for the abuse can be large, and the abuse extends into the non-work domain, so people feel they cannot get away from it.[68]

Victims of bullying, mobbing, or abusive supervision experience stress because they feel powerless to deal with the perpetrator(s). Norway, Sweden, France, and several Canadian provinces have enacted laws that pertain to bullying in the workplace. Various organizations have also done their part. The U.S. Department of Veterans Affairs and IBM both have active anti-bullying programs. To drive home its seriousness about its policy, IBM fired several factory workers who mobbed their new supervisor.[69]

Before continuing, consider You Be the Manager: *Bullying at Veterans Affairs.*

WORK–FAMILY CONFLICT Work–family conflict occurs when either work duties interfere with family life or family life interferes with work responsibilities.[70] A national Canadian survey determined that it results in decreased work performance and increased absenteeism.[71]

Two facts of life in contemporary society have increased the stress stemming from the interrole conflict between being a member of one's family and the member of an organization. First, the increase in the number of households in which both parents work and the increase in the number of single-parent families has led to a number of stressors centred around child care. Finding adequate daycare and disputes between partners about sharing child-care responsibilities can prove to be serious stressors. Second, increased life spans have meant that many people in the prime of their careers find themselves providing support for elderly parents, some of whom may be seriously ill. This inherently stressful eldercare situation is often compounded by feelings of guilt about the need to tend to matters at work.[72]

Women are particularly victimized by stress due to work–family conflict, although it is a rapidly growing problem for men as well. Women who take time off work to deal with pressing family matters are more likely than men to be labelled disloyal or undedicated to

YOU BE THE MANAGER

Bullying at Veterans Affairs

Jobs in the social service sector regularly entail emotional labour, with workers confronted on a daily basis with high demands from clients concerning social, emotional, and medical problems. While such client–service provider interactions can be emotionally draining, such a work environment can also be a breeding ground for workplace aggression and bullying.

With this in mind, the United States Department of Veterans Affairs (VA), in collaboration with university researchers, launched the Workplace Stress and Aggression Project. The VA provides patient care and federal benefits to veterans and their dependents through central offices, benefits offices, and medical facilities. In the post–September 11 era, the VA had seen an increase in activity with the conflicts in Afghanistan and Iraq. The goal of the project was to assess the prevalence of workplace aggression and bullying within the VA; to understand their impact on employee satisfaction, VA performance, and veteran satisfaction; and to develop intervention strategies.

The research team used archival data, questionnaires, interviews, and discussion groups. Results of the initial surveys clearly indicated that workplace aggression and bullying were issues within the VA. Overall, 36 percent of employees surveyed reported being bullied at work. Bullying was defined as persistent patterns of aggression that workers experienced at least once a week. Of the 36 percent, 29 percent indicated they experienced aggression in the workplace one to five times a week, while 7 percent reported experiencing six or more aggression episodes a week. Another 58 percent of employees reported that they experienced workplace aggression, albeit not on a weekly basis, while only 6 percent of employees indicated that they suffered no workplace aggression. Aggression could be physical or verbal, active (e.g., in a confrontation) or passive (e.g., through exclusion), or direct (e.g., personally targeted) or indirect (e.g., defacing property or spreading rumours). Most incidents were of the verbal, passive, and indirect variety.

Employees indicated that 44 percent of the aggression they experienced emanated from co-workers, 35 percent came from supervisors, and 12 percent came from veterans. In terms of impact on personal well-being, they suffered more stress and lower job satisfaction when a supervisor was the source of the aggression than when co-workers or clients were the source. The

Chip Somodevilla/Getty Images

High levels of bullying at
various Veterans Affairs
facilities worried executives.

research team also found that bullying was linked to lower employee and organizational performance and increases in stress, absenteeism, lateness, turnover, and worker compensation claims. With these data in hand, the project team's focus turned to understanding why aggression occurred and what could be done to reduce it.

Questions

1. What do you think some of the primary causes of workplace aggression and bullying within the VA might be? Do you think the causes would be different across the various VA facilities?

2. Suggest an intervention strategy to reduce the incidence of aggression and bullying in the VA workplace. Who should be involved?

To find out how the VA responded, see The Manager's Notebook at the end of the chapter.

Sources: Scaringi, J., et al. (n.d.). *The VA workplace stress and aggression project—Final report*; Neuman, J.H., and Keashly, L. (2005, August). Reducing aggression and bullying: An intervention project in the U.S. Department of Veterans Affairs. In J. Raver (Chair), *Workplace bullying: International perspectives on moving from research to practice*. Symposium presented at the annual meeting of the Academy of Management, Honolulu, HI; Neuman, J.H. (2004). Injustice, stress, and aggression in organizations. In R.W. Griffin and A.M. O'Leary-Kelly (Eds.), *The dark side of organizational behavior*. San Francisco, CA: Jossey-Bass.

their work. Also, many managers seem to be insensitive to the demands that these basic demographic shifts are making on their employees, again compounding the potential for stress and burnout.[73]

Occupations that require a high degree of teamwork or responsibilities for others tend to provoke the most work–family conflict (e.g., police detectives, firefighters, and family doctors). At the other extreme, tellers, insurance adjusters, and taxi drivers report much lower levels.[74] Also, people who are highly engaged in their work have been shown to have elevated work-to-family conflict, but more conscientious employees seem to handle this tension between work and family better.[75]

JOB INSECURITY AND CHANGE Secure employment is an important goal for almost everyone, and stress may be encountered when it is threatened, as illustrated in the Orange France vignette that began the chapter. During the past decade, organizations have undergone substantial changes that have left many workers unemployed and threatened the security of those who have been fortunate enough to remain in their jobs. The trend toward mergers and acquisitions, along with reengineering, restructuring, and downsizing, has led to increasingly high levels of stress among employees who either have lost their jobs or must live with the threat of more layoffs, the loss of friends and co-workers, and an increased workload.[76]

At the operative level, unionization has provided a degree of employment security for some, but the vagaries of the economy and the threat of technology and other organizational changes hang heavily over many workers. Among professionals, the very specialization that enables them to obtain satisfactory jobs becomes a millstone whenever social or economic forces change. For example, aerospace scientists and engineers have long been prey to the boom-and-bust nature of their industry. When layoffs occur, these people are often perceived as overqualified or too specialized to easily obtain jobs in related industries. Finally, the executive suite does not escape job insecurity. Recent pressures for corporate performance have made cost-cutting a top priority, and one of the surest ways to cut costs in the short run is to reduce executive positions and thus reduce the total management payroll. Many corporations have greatly thinned their executive ranks in recent years.

ROLE AMBIGUITY We have already noted how role conflict—having to deal with incompatible role expectations—can provoke stress. There is also substantial evidence that role ambiguity can provoke stress.[77] From Chapter 7, you will recall that role ambiguity exists when the goals of one's job or the methods of performing the job are unclear. Such a lack of direction can prove stressful, especially for people who are low in their tolerance for such ambiguity. For example, the president of a firm might be instructed by the board of directors to increase profits and cut costs. While this goal seems clear enough, the means by which it can be achieved might be unclear. This ambiguity can be devastating, especially when the organization is doing poorly and no strategy seems to improve things.

SEXUAL HARASSMENT In Chapter 12, we discussed sexual harassment in terms of the abuse of power and a form of unethical behaviour. Sexual harassment is a major workplace stressor, with serious consequences for employees and organizations that are similar to or more negative than those of other types of job stressors.[78] Sexual harassment in the workplace is now considered to be widespread in both the public and private sectors, and most harassment victims are subjected to ongoing harassment and stress.[79] The negative effects of sexual harassment include decreased morale, job satisfaction, organizational commitment, and job performance and increased absenteeism, turnover, and job loss. Sexual harassment has also been found to have serious effects on the psychological and physical well-being of harassment victims.[80] Victims of sexual harassment experience depression, frustration, nervousness, fatigue, nausea, hypertension, and symptoms of post-traumatic stress disorder.[81] Organizations in which sexual harassment is most likely to be a problem are those that have

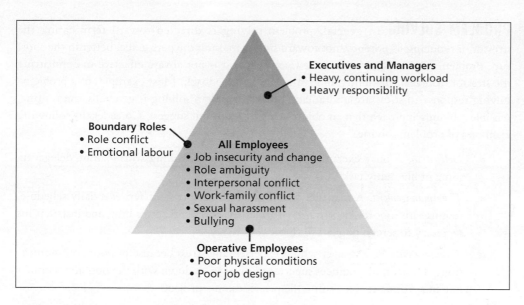

EXHIBIT 13.6
Sources of stress at various points in the organization.

a climate that is tolerant of sexual harassment and where women are working in traditionally male-dominated jobs and in a male-dominated workplace.[82]

Exhibit 13.6 summarizes the sources of stress at various points in the organization.

REACTIONS TO ORGANIZATIONAL STRESS

In this section, we examine the reactions that people who experience organizational stress might exhibit. These reactions can be divided into behavioural, psychological, and physiological responses. In general, reactions that result in an addition to one's resources can be seen as good coping with stress. Reactions that increase demands constitute bad coping. Exhibit 13.7 shows how a sample of more than 31 000 Canadian employees reported coping with stress.

Behavioural Reactions to Stress

Behavioural reactions to stress are overt activities that the stressed individual uses in an attempt to cope with the stress. They include problem solving, seeking social support, modified performance, withdrawal, presenteeism, and the use of addictive substances.

LO 13.8

Describe *behavioural*, *psychological*, and *physiological reactions* to stress, and discuss techniques for managing stress.

Coping Strategies	% of Sample Who Use		
	Rarely	Weekly	Daily
Prioritize	9%	21%	69%
Schedule, organize, and plan my time more carefully	22%	32%	47%
Talk with family or friends	26%	29%	45%
Just work harder (I try to do it all)	31%	26%	43%
Find some other activity to take my mind off it	36%	32%	32%
Talk with colleagues at work	40%	27%	32%
Delegate work to others	49%	24%	27%
Search for help from family or friends	51%	25%	23%
Just try and forget about it	60%	20%	19%
Search for help from colleagues at work	65%	19%	16%
Have an alcoholic drink	65%	23%	12%
Use prescription, over-the-counter, or other drugs	86%	4%	11%
Reduce the quality of the things I do	72%	18%	10%

EXHIBIT 13.7
How Canadian employees cope with stress.
Source: Higgins, C., Duxbury, L., & Lyons, S. (2006). *Reducing work-life conflict: What works? What doesn't?* Ottawa: Health Canada, p. 131. Reproduced with the permission of the Minister of Public Works and Government Services Canada, 2009.

PROBLEM SOLVING In general, problem solving is directed toward terminating the stressor or reducing its potency, not toward simply making the person feel better in the short run. Problem solving is reality oriented, and while it is not always effective in combatting the stressor, it reveals flexibility and realistic use of feedback. Most examples of a problem-solving response to stress are undramatic because problem solving is generally the routine, sensible, obvious approach that an objective observer might suggest. Consider the following examples of problem solving:

- *Delegation.* A busy executive reduces her stress-provoking workload by delegating some of her many tasks to a capable assistant.

- *Time management.* A manager who finds the day too short writes a daily schedule, requires his subordinates to make formal appointments to see him, and instructs his secretary to screen phone calls more selectively.

- *Talking it out.* An engineer who is experiencing stress because of poor communication with her non-engineer superior resolves to sit down with the boss and hammer out an agreement concerning the priorities on a project.

- *Asking for help.* A salesperson who is anxious about his company's ability to fill a difficult order asks the production manager to provide a realistic estimate of the probable delivery date.

- *Searching for alternatives.* A machine operator who finds her monotonous job stress provoking applies for a transfer to a more interesting position for which the pay is identical.

SEEKING SOCIAL SUPPORT Speaking generally, social support simply refers to having close ties with other people. In turn, these close ties can affect stress by bolstering self-esteem, providing useful information, offering comfort and humour, or even providing material resources (such as a loan). Research evidence shows that the benefits of social support are double-barrelled. First, people with stronger social networks exhibit better psychological and physical well-being. Second, when people encounter stressful events, those with good social networks are likely to cope more positively. Thus, the social network acts as a buffer against stress.[83]

Off the job, individuals might find social support in a spouse, family, or friends. On the job, social support might be available from one's superior or co-workers. Research evidence suggests that the buffering aspects of social support are most potent when they are directly connected to the source of stress. This means that co-workers and superiors may be the best sources of support for dealing with work-related stress. But most managers need better training to recognize employee stress symptoms, clarify role requirements, and so on. Unfortunately, some organizational cultures, especially those that are very competitive, do not encourage members to seek support in a direct fashion. In this kind of setting, relationships that people develop in professional associations can sometimes serve as an informed source of social support.

PERFORMANCE CHANGES Stress or stressors frequently cause reduced job performance.[84] However, this statement needs to be qualified slightly. Some stressors are "hindrance" stressors in that they directly damage goal attainment. These include things like role ambiguity and interpersonal conflict. Such stressors damage performance. On the other hand, some stressors are challenging. These include factors such as heavy workload and responsibility. Such stressors may damage performance, but they sometimes stimulate it via added motivation.[85] Because they are discretionary, organizational citizenship behaviours (Chapter 4) are especially likely to decrease under stressful conditions.[86]

WITHDRAWAL AND PRESENTEEISM Withdrawal from the stressor is one of the most basic reactions to stress. In organizations, this withdrawal takes the form of absence and turnover. Compared with problem-solving reactions to stress, absenteeism fails to attack the stressor directly. Rather, the absent individual is simply attempting short-term reduction of the anxiety prompted by the stressor. When the person returns to the job, the stress is still there. From this point of view, absence is a dysfunctional reaction to stress for both the individual and the organization. The same can be said about turnover if a person resigns from a stressful job on the spur of the moment merely to escape stress. However, a good case can be made for a well-planned resignation in which the intent is to assume another job that should be less stressful. This is actually a problem-solving reaction that should benefit both the individual and the organization in the long run. Absence, turnover, and turnover intentions have often been linked with stress and its causes.[87]

Perhaps ironically, stress can also prompt the opposite of withdrawal, to the extent that people go to work ill. This is known as **presenteeism**. Presentees are at work, but they are not working at full capacity. What would cause people to go to work even though they are suffering from asthma, migraines, or respiratory problems? Many factors are stress-related. Thus, some stressors can cause both absenteeism and presenteeism. High job demands and time pressure have been associated with presenteeism; people feel under pressure to get work done and sense the work piling up if they are absent. This is especially likely if there is understaffing, an increasing possibility in today's downsized organizations. Also, bullying and harassment are related to presenteeism, causing stress but often occurring to those with little power and few options to take time off. Depression, frequently associated with stress, is a common health problem connected to presenteeism. This may be because people do not view it as a legitimate reason to be absent or fear disclosing it as the reason for their absence.[88]

> **Presenteeism.** Attending work when ill.

USE OF ADDICTIVE SUBSTANCES Smoking, drinking, and drug use represent the least satisfactory behavioural responses to stress for both the individual and the organization. These activities fail to terminate stress episodes, and they leave employees less physically and mentally prepared to perform their jobs. We have all heard of hard-drinking newspaper reporters and advertising executives, and it is tempting to infer that the stress of their boundary role positions is responsible for their drinking. Indeed, cigarette and alcohol use are associated with work-related stress.[89]

Psychological Reactions to Stress

Psychological reactions to stress primarily involve emotions and thought processes rather than overt behaviour, although these reactions are frequently revealed in the individual's speech and actions. The most common psychological reaction to stress is the use of defence mechanisms.[90]

Defence mechanisms are psychological attempts to reduce the anxiety associated with stress. Notice that, by definition, defence mechanisms concentrate on *anxiety reduction* rather than on actually confronting or dealing with the stressor. Some common defence mechanisms include the following:

- *Rationalization* is attributing socially acceptable reasons or motives to one's actions so that they will appear reasonable and sensible, at least to oneself. For example, a male nurse who becomes very angry and abusive when learning that he will not be promoted to supervisor might justify his anger by claiming that the female head nurse discriminates against men.

- *Projection* is attributing one's own undesirable ideas and motives to others so that they seem less negative. For example, a sales executive who is undergoing conflict about offering a bribe to an official of a foreign government might reason that the official is corrupt.

PERSONAL INVENTORY ASSESSMENT

Learn About Yourself
Psychological Flourishing Assessment

> **Defence mechanisms.** Psychological attempts to reduce the anxiety associated with stress.

- *Displacement* is directing feelings of anger at a "safe" target rather than expressing them where they may be punished. For example, a construction worker who is severely criticized by the boss for sloppy workmanship might take out his frustrations in an evening hockey league.

- *Reaction formation* is expressing oneself in a manner that is directly opposite to the way one truly feels, rather than risking negative reactions to one's true position. For example, a low-status member of a committee might vote with the majority on a crucial issue rather than stating his true position and opening himself up to attack.

- *Compensation* is applying one's skills in a particular area to make up for failure in another area. For example, a professor who is unable to get his or her research published might resolve to become a superb teacher.

Is the use of defence mechanisms a good or bad reaction to stress? Used occasionally to temporarily reduce anxiety, they appear to be a useful reaction. For example, the construction worker who displaces aggression in an evening hockey league rather than attacking a frustrating boss might calm down, return to work the next day, and "talk it out" with the boss. Thus, the occasional use of defence mechanisms as short-term anxiety reducers probably benefits both the individual and the organization. In fact, people with "weak defences" can be incapacitated by anxiety and resort to dysfunctional withdrawal or addiction.

When the use of defence mechanisms becomes a chronic reaction to stress, however, the picture changes radically. The problem stems from the very character of defence mechanisms—they simply do not change the objective character of the stressor, and the basic conflict or frustration remains in operation. After some short-term relief from anxiety, the basic problem remains unresolved. In fact, the stress might *increase* with the knowledge that the defence has been essentially ineffective.

Physiological Reactions to Stress

Can work-related stress kill you? This is clearly an important question for organizations, and it is even more important for individuals who experience excessive stress at work. Many studies of physiological reactions to stress have concentrated on the cardiovascular system, specifically on the various risk factors that might prompt heart attacks. For example, work stress is associated with electrocardiogram irregularities and elevated levels of blood pressure, cholesterol, and pulse.[91] Stress has also been associated with the onset of diseases such as respiratory and bacterial infections due to its ill effects on the immune system.[92] The accumulation of stress into burnout has been particularly implicated in cardiovascular problems.[93]

ORGANIZATIONAL STRATEGIES FOR MANAGING STRESS

This chapter would be incomplete without a discussion of personal and organizational strategies to manage stress. In general, these strategies either reduce demands on employees or enhance their resources.

Job Redesign

Organizations can redesign jobs to reduce their stressful characteristics. In theory, it is possible to redesign jobs anywhere in the organization to this end. Thus, an overloaded executive might be given an assistant to reduce the number of tasks he or she must perform. In practice, most formal job redesign efforts have involved enriching operative-level jobs to make them more stimulating and challenging.

Especially for service jobs, there is growing evidence that providing more autonomy in how service is delivered can alleviate stress and burnout.[94] Call-centre workers, fast-food employees, some salespeople, and some hospitality workers are highly "scripted" by employers, with the idea that uniformity will be appreciated by customers. This idea is debatable, but what is not debatable is that this lack of personal control goes against the research-supported prescriptions of job enrichment (Chapter 6) and empowerment (Chapter 12), and the job demands–resources model of stress. Boundary role service jobs require a high degree of emotional regulation in any event, and some autonomy allows employees to cope with emotional labour by adjusting their responses to the needs of the moment in line with their own personalities. Guidelines about desired service outcomes can replace rigid scripts, especially for routine (non-emergency) encounters. Also, excessive electronic monitoring should be avoided in call centres.[95]

A special word should be said about the stressful job designs that often emerge from heavy-handed downsizings, restructurings, and mergers. Common symptoms of such jobs are extreme role overload, increased responsibility without corresponding authority to act, and the assignment of tasks for which no training is provided. Executives overseeing such change efforts should obtain professional assistance to ensure proper job designs.

"Family-Friendly" Human Resource Policies

To reduce stress associated with dual careers, child care, and eldercare, many organizations are beginning to institute "family-friendly" human resource policies to improve work–life balance.[96] These policies generally include some combination of formalized social support, material support, and increased flexibility to adapt to employee needs. In the domain of social support, some firms distribute newsletters, such as *Work & Family Life*, that deal with work–family issues. Others have developed company support groups for employees dealing with eldercare problems. Some companies have contracted specialized consultants to provide seminars on eldercare issues.

A welcome form of material support consists of corporate daycare centres. Flexibility (which provides more *control* over family issues) is also important, and includes flextime, telecommuting, and job sharing (Chapter 6), as well as family leave policies that allow time off for caring for infants, sick children, and aged dependents. Although many firms boast of having such flexible policies, a common problem is encouraging managers to *use* them in an era of downsizing and lean staffing. According to a Mediacorp study, some of Canada's most family-friendly employers include Mountain Equipment Co-op, University of Toronto, and Desjardins.[97] There is growing evidence that such policies contribute to improved health, lower turnover, and higher organizational performance.[98] In general, perceptions of flexibility, a reasonable workload, supportive supervision, and a supportive culture are associated with less work–family conflict and higher job satisfaction and organizational commitment.[99] For an example of a family-friendly organization, see Applied Focus: *Vancity Offers Family-Friendly Policies*.

The province of Quebec has established a voluntary certification program for work–life balance. Firms can apply for up to four levels of certification, depending on the exact features they offer to employees and the extent of commitment to balance. Frima Studio, a Quebec City video game developer, was the first organization to be certified. The commitment needed for certification was seen as a way to attract and retain the best talent in a competitive industry.[100]

Stress Management Programs

Some organizations have experimented with programs designed to help employees "manage" work-related stress. Such programs are also available from independent off-work sources.

■ APPLIED FOCUS

VANCITY OFFERS FAMILY-FRIENDLY POLICIES

Vancouver City Savings Credit Union, popularly known as Vancity, is a cooperative credit union that offers financial products and services to its members across British Columbia. It is Canada's largest community-based credit union, providing loans, mortgages, investments, credit cards, and insurance. Vancity is among Canada's Top 100 Employers and Canada's Top Family-Friendly Employers, as determined by Mediacorp. At the core of its many family-friendly policies, Vancity is Canada's largest Living Wage Employer, subscribing to a program that ensures that wages and salaries are set to provide a genuine living wage. This means that the lowest-paid Vancity employees make about twice the provincial minimum wage, enabling adequate provision for child care and avoiding the need to hold multiple jobs. Vancity also offers generous maternity and parental benefits, ranging up to 85% of salary for 35 weeks. Various family-friendly options that allow people to tailor their work schedules to their family lives include flextime, telecommuting, a compressed workweek (fewer days at more hours per day), shortened work weeks (fewer hours for less pay), job sharing with coworkers, and up to 24 months of unpaid leave, and a free week's summer camp retreat for teens.

In addition to its family-friendly policies, Vancity offers a number of other benefits that combat daily hassles and help deal with stress. Smaller perks are free parking, a public transit subsidy, secure bike parking, and fitness classes. More substantial ones include solid health and pension plans and a beginning minimum of three weeks of vacation per year.

Source: Based on Yerema, R. & Leung, K. (2014, November 3). Vancouver City Savings Credit Union. Mediacorp Canada Inc. website http://www.canadastop100.com/national/, accessed November 25, 2014.

Some of these programs help physically and mentally healthy employees prevent problems due to stress. Others are therapeutic in nature, aimed at individuals who are already experiencing stress problems. Although the exact content of the programs varies, most involve one or more of the following techniques: meditation, training in muscle-relaxation exercises, biofeedback training to control physiological processes, training in time management, and training to think more positively and realistically about sources of job stress.[101] Evidence suggests that these applications are useful in reducing physiological arousal, sleep disturbances, and self-reported tension and anxiety.[102]

Corporate fitness centres can combat work stress.

Alexander Zemlianichenko Jr./Bloomberg via Getty Images

Work–Life Balance, Fitness, and Wellness Programs

Many people have argued that a balanced lifestyle that includes a variety of leisure activities combined with a healthy diet and physical exercise can reduce stress and counteract some of the adverse physiological effects of stress. For some organizations, work–life balance programs and quality-of-life benefits have become a strategic retention tool. Employees are increasingly demanding work–life balance benefits, and employers are realizing that by providing them they can increase commitment and reduce turnover.

At Husky Injection Molding Systems, the cafeteria serves only healthy food. The company's head office in Bolton, Ontario, has a naturopath, a chiropractor, a medical doctor, a nurse, and a massage therapist on staff, and employees are encouraged to use the company's large fitness centre.[103] The DundeeWealth investment firm features weight-loss contests, fitness classes, and consultation on home training programs.[104]

Studies show that fitness training is associated with improved mood, a better self-concept, reduced absenteeism, enhanced job satisfaction, and reports of better performance.[105] Work–life programs are also believed to result in lower health-care costs. Some of these improvements probably stem from stress reduction.

■ THE MANAGER'S NOTEBOOK

Bullying at Veterans Affairs

1. Many of the well-known sources of conflict in the workplace can lead to aggression and bullying. Power and status differences between individuals, rivalries between groups, uncertainty and competition, and a noxious organizational culture can all facilitate bullying and aggression. The VA project team found many of these conditions at the various sites. However, they generally found a distinctive pattern of causes of bullying at each facility. At some sites, a lack of cooperation, respect, and fairness were drivers of aggression and bullying. At other sites, diversity management was the primary issue. Sites that had recently made significant new hires often had clashes between newcomers and old-timers. Sites with poor leadership and a lack of goal alignment were also problems. The results were often communication breakdowns, misinformation, and the growth of rumours. Overall, the project team identified issues in the work climate—although these varied in content from site to site—as the key factor in workplace aggression and bullying.

2. The VA project team realized that, unlike many organizational development prescriptions advocating the establishment of best practices to resolve problems, interventions to quell workplace aggression and bullying would need to be customized at each site to deal with each specific work climate. However, the general process they developed to do this was common to all. In the 11 sites that participated in the more comprehensive version of the project, the research team created action teams of organizational members to guide the project and develop needed interventions. The exercise of bringing people together to learn and discuss issues surrounding bullying and aggression in itself transformed the work climate in a positive way. Interventions often focused on some form of what are known as High Involvement Work Systems, involving information sharing and empowerment. In a follow-up two years after the original data-gathering exercise, the research team found that, compared with the 15 sites that did not participate in the intervention, the 11 focal sites reported fewer incidents of aggressive behaviour and fewer injury stress–related behaviours. Work attitudes and performance indicators also improved at the 11 intervention sites compared with the 15 other sites.

MyManagementLab Study, practise, and explore real management situations with these helpful resources:

- **Interactive Lesson Presentations:** Work through interactive presentations and assessments to test your knowledge of management concepts.
- **PIA (Personal Inventory Assessments):** Enhance your ability to connect with key concepts through these engaging, self-reflection assessments.
- **Study Plan:** Check your understanding of chapter concepts with self-study quizzes.
- **Videos:** Learn more about the management practices and strategies of real companies.
- **Simulations:** Practise decision-making in simulated management environments.

P I A PERSONAL INVENTORY ASSESSMENT

LEARNING OBJECTIVES CHECKLIST

13.1 *Interpersonal conflict* is a process that occurs when one person, group, or organizational unit frustrates the goal attainment of another. Such conflict can revolve around facts, procedures, or the goals themselves. Causes of conflict include intergroup bias, high interdependence, ambiguous jurisdictions, and scarce resources. Differences in power, status, and culture are also a factor.

13.2 *Types of conflict* include *relationship*, *task*, and *process* conflict. Conflict dynamics include the need to win the dispute, withholding information, increased cohesiveness, negative stereotyping of the other party, reduced contact, and emergence of aggressive leaders.

13.3 Modes of managing conflict include *avoiding*, *accommodating*, *competing*, *compromise*, and *collaborating*.

13.4 *Negotiation* is a decision-making process among parties that do not have the same preferences. *Distributive negotiation* attempts to divide up a fixed amount of outcomes. Frequent tactics include threats, promises, firmness, concession making, and persuasion. *Integrative negotiation* attempts to enlarge the number of available outcomes via collaboration or problem solving. Tactics include exchanging copious information, framing differences as opportunities, cutting costs, increasing resources, and introducing *superordinate goals*.

13.5 *Stressors* are environmental conditions that have the potential to induce stress. *Stress* is a psychological reaction that can prompt tension or anxiety because an individual feels incapable of coping with the demands made by a stressor. *Stress reactions* are the behavioural,

psychological, and physiological consequences of stress.

13.6 Personality characteristics can cause some individuals to perceive more stressors than others, experience more stress, and react more negatively to this stress. In particular, people with *external locus of control*, high *negative affectivity*, and *Type A behaviour pattern* are prone to such reactions.

13.7 At the managerial or executive level, common stressors include *role overload* and high responsibility. At the *operative level*, poor physical working conditions and underutilization of potential owing to poor job design are common stressors. *Boundary role occupants* often experience stress in the form of conflict between demands from inside the employing organization and demands from outside. Emotional labour may also provoke stress. *Burnout* may occur when a job produces emotional exhaustion, cynicism, and low self-efficacy. Job insecurity and change, role ambiguity, sexual harassment, interpersonal conflict, and work–family conflicts have the potential to induce stress in all organizational members.

Work engagement is a positive state of mind about work involving dedication, absorption, and vigour. The job demands–resources model explains how demands lead to burnout and resources lead to engagement.

13.8 *Behavioural reactions* to stress include problem solving, modified performance, withdrawal, presenteeism, and the use of addictive substances. *Problem solving* is the most effective reaction because it confronts the stressor directly and thus has the potential to terminate the stress episode. The most common psychological reaction to stress is the use of *defence mechanisms* to temporarily reduce anxiety. The majority of studies on physiological reactions to stress implicate cardiovascular risk factors. Strategies that can reduce organizational stress include job redesign, family-friendly human resource policies, stress-management programs, and work–life balance programs.

DISCUSSION QUESTIONS

1. The manager of a fast-food restaurant sees that conflict among the staff is damaging service. How might she implement a superordinate goal to reduce this conflict?

2. A company hires two finance majors right out of college. Being in a new and unfamiliar environment, they begin their relationship cooperatively. However, over time, they develop a case of deep interpersonal conflict. What factors could account for this?

3. Two social workers just out of college join the same social welfare agency. Both find their caseloads very heavy and their roles very ambiguous. One exhibits negative stress reactions, including absence and elevated alcohol use. The other seems to cope very well. Use the stress episode model to explain why this might occur.

4. Imagine that a person who greatly dislikes bureaucracy assumes her first job as an investigator in a very bureaucratic government tax office. Describe the stressors that she might encounter in this situation. Give an example of a problem-solving reaction to this stress. Give an example of a defensive reaction to it.

5. What factors might explain why bullying persists? How do workplace bullies get away with it?

INTEGRATIVE DISCUSSION QUESTIONS

1. Does personality influence the way individuals manage conflict? Consider the relationship among each of the following personality characteristics and the five approaches to managing conflict described in this chapter: the Big Five dimensions of personality, locus of control, self-monitoring, self-esteem, need for power, and Machiavellianism.

2. Can leadership be a source of stress in organizations? Refer to the leadership theories described in Chapter 9 (e.g., leadership traits, behaviours, situational theories, participative leadership, strategic leadership, and LMX theory) and explain how leadership can be a source of stress. According to each theory, what can leaders do to reduce stress and help employees cope with it?

ON-THE-JOB CHALLENGE QUESTION

Why Don't People Take Their Vacations?

A Harris/Decima poll determined that almost 25 percent of Canadians fail to use all the vacation days they are entitled to during the year. The unused days ranged from 1.39 in the province of Quebec to 2.81 in Alberta. Although these numbers seem small, they project nationally to 34 million unused days a year. Despite this, 42 percent of those polled reported being tired, stressed, and in need of a vacation. A similar Harris Interactive U.S. poll found that 57 percent of Americans reported unused vacation days.

What do you think explains the willingness of so many people to forgo deserved vacation time? If you were or are a manager, how would you react to staff who don't use all their vacation days? What are the long-term implications of this behaviour?

Sources: Based on Covert, K. (2009, July 9). Vacation phobia spreads. *National Post*, FP11; Censky, A. (2012, May 18). Vacation? No thanks, boss. *CNNMoney*.

EXPERIENTIAL EXERCISE

Strategies for Managing Conflict

Indicate how often you use each of the following by writing the appropriate number in the blank. Choose a number from a scale of 1 to 5, with 1 being "rarely," 3 being "sometimes," and 5 being "always." After you have completed the survey, use the scoring key to tabulate your results.

____ 1. I argue my position tenaciously.

____ 2. I put the needs of others above my own.

____ 3. I arrive at a compromise both parties can accept.

____ 4. I don't get involved in conflicts.

____ 5. I investigate issues thoroughly and jointly.

____ 6. I find fault in other persons' positions.

____ 7. I foster harmony.

____ 8. I negotiate to get a portion of what I propose.

____ 9. I avoid open discussions of controversial subjects.

____ 10. I openly share information with others in resolving disagreements.

____ 11. I enjoy winning an argument.

____ 12. I go along with the suggestions of others.

____ 13. I look for a middle ground to resolve disagreements.

____ 14. I keep my true feelings to myself to avoid hard feelings.

____ 15. I encourage the open sharing of concerns and issues.

____ 16. I am reluctant to admit I am wrong.

____ 17. I try to help others avoid "losing face" in a disagreement.

____ 18. I stress the advantages of "give and take."

____ 19. I encourage others to take the lead in resolving controversy.

____ 20. I state my position as only one point of view.

Scoring Key

Managing Strategy

Total your responses to these questions

Competing 1, 6, 11, 16 ____

Accommodating 2, 7, 12, 17 ____

Compromising 3, 8, 13, 18 ____

Avoiding 4, 9, 14, 19 ____

Collaborating 5, 10, 15, 20 ____

Primary conflict management strategy (highest score): ____

Secondary conflict management strategy (next-highest score): ____

Source: Whetten, D.A., & Cameron, K.S. *Developing management skills* (7th ed.) © 2007, p.379. Reprinted and Electronically reproduced by permission of Pearson Education, Inc., New York, NY.

CASE INCIDENT

Bringing Baby to Work

Ted Swanson liked to think of himself as a progressive, family-friendly kind of guy. Consequently, he couldn't quite believe the words coming out of his mouth, directed at Bryan Papis, his boss and owner of the creative media company ZeusAd. "Bryan, that baby is driving me crazy! The cooing, laughing, and crying are one thing, but some of the creative team and support staff make such a fuss over him that it drives me to distraction. I had a client in here yesterday who didn't know what to make of the whole thing. This just isn't professional."

The four-month-old baby to which Ted was referring belonged to Glenda Fox, one of the more clever creative types in the company. Although she was eligible for extended maternity leave, she had chosen not to take it. She said she didn't want to "get out of the loop" or let her current project team down. These motives, and Glenda's espoused beliefs in "attachment parenting" had led her to bring her new baby to work on a fairly regular basis, except when her husband could occasionally provide care.

Bryan Papis also prided himself on being a family-friendly employer, but he wondered if ZeusAd needed a formal policy concerning babies at work.

Source: Based on Boesveld, S. (2012, March 8). When every day is take your kids to work day. *National Post*, A1, A2.

1. A number of news stories have appeared suggesting that babies in the workplace are a source of considerable interpersonal conflict. What are some likely reasons for this?

2. Is bringing a baby to work the ultimate example of work–family integration? Or does it go too far in blurring the distinction between work and family?

3. What considerations should underpin a formal policy concerning babies at work?

CASE STUDY

Tough Guy

A mere half-block away from the office on a pleasing fall day—the kind that caught the attention of most New Yorkers—Jeremy Frazer, an associate at the investment bank Hudson Smith Gordon ("Hudson") thought about Chip Mazey, one of the vice presidents he was working with on a negotiation. Frazer and three other members working on the deal, Jean Fenster, Rich Patten, and Payton Edwards, had finally confided in each other about what it was like to work for the VP.

They found themselves in a difficult situation, one that most of them thought they had no power to change. After all, doing something about Mazey's behavior was tricky business. First was the fear of confronting Mazey. Another concern was the likelihood that Mazey would probably deny his behavior or wouldn't think that a problem existed. Then there was the unease about escalating the discussion to include a conversation with Mazey's boss. Going upstairs might cause a tense situation to become even worse. Not really knowing what to do irked Frazer, though he couldn't exactly say why. He thought about the stories his co-workers had shared.

BULGE, MIDDLE, OR BOUTIQUE?

The lure of high risk and high reward made investment banking an attractive career for many in the world of finance. Organizations employed investment banks to help work out financial problems. Offering a mix of business activities, investment banks issued securities, helped investors to purchase securities, managed financials assets, traded securities, and provided financial advice. Investment banks came in several sizes. The largest were called "bulge bracket" firms; the "middle market" companies tended to be regionally based; and "boutique" banks were smaller and more specialized. As a "middle market" firm, Hudson was oriented toward financial analysis and program trading.

To support their security sales and trading activities, investment banks hired and maintained large staffs of research analysts. As Frazer described,

> *In investment banking, you make deals for companies to raise capital—debt or equity. Research supports that effort. By becoming expert in a particular field, you generate more business. My firm is considered the leading expert on wireless carriers. This reputation translates into wireless communication companies' wanting Hudson to do research on them.*

MAKING THE DEAL WITH A FAST-TRACKER

Chip Mazey had been with Hudson 10 years and followed the "kiss up, kick down" mantra. His verbal lashings were sharp, unrelenting, and unprovoked. He had developed a nasty reputation among analysts and associates, which was passed to the firm's top management only through their 360-degree review system. Mazey was very careful not to show his true colours when senior management was within earshot, but as result of the negative comments from below, his initial promotion to vice president was postponed. The decision came as a shock to him, because he believed he had always been submissive to upper management. Despite his poor people skills, Mazey was a solid banker, and he received the promotion as scheduled one year later.

As a vice president, Mazey's swagger and bravado increased exponentially. Mazey always had trouble interacting with his peers, but after his promotion, he was more ruthless to his subordinates than his peers. He often referred to subordinates as "you" or "analyst" and he reminded others of his new title by telling them, "I am superior to you." It was common for him to yell at a subordinate in a rage, only to discover that he had made an error and there was no problem. In such a situation, Mazey would abruptly hang up the phone when he realized his error without a goodbye or apology. The targets of his verbal abuse disliked working with him and tried to spend time working on projects with other bankers.

The first time Frazer worked with Mazey was on a project Mazey was heading up. "I was assigned to this kick-ass multibillion dollar deal," Frazer said. "Even better than that was the fact that the deal team included the vice president, so I was extremely excited about the opportunity." The vice president was in charge of leading the deal and had a reputation of being "dynamic" and on the "fast track." Frazer's enthusiasm faded somewhat when he stepped into Mazey's office. During their initial meeting, Mazey ordered Frazer to stand "right here" and pointed to a spot on the floor in front of his desk. The associate felt uneasy about being spoken to in this manner, but because it was the first time he had worked with Mazey, he decided not to mention anything—it was best to let things go. After all, investment banks had a reputation for being infested with Type A personalities. Some "I-bankers" had told Frazer that the biggest challenge in an investment banking career was to manage upward.

Over the next several weeks, Frazer witnessed Mazey's insulting and derogatory behavior toward other associates and analysts. Tension was part of being around him. "Fortunately, I worked on multiple assignments, reporting to various other managers at the same time," Frazer said. "The dynamics on other assignment were in stark contrast to this particular one. So I realized how much I like the job and how well I fit in—despite being so heavily reprimanded on a continual basis with that VP."

ON A NEED-TO-KNOW BASIS

That Mazey was difficult to deal with was hardly news to most at Hudson. What was worthy of a headline was that Frazer seemed more willing than most to talk about his supervisor's questionable behavior. Others who had been in the organization much longer than Frazer just learned to work around Mazey's behavior—he was a control freak who made a lot of money for the company and that translated into wielding a lot of power. "I became more comfortable with some of my peers and started confiding in a few of them," Frazer said. "I realized my situation was hardly unique since everyone who had at one time worked with that VP had the same story." Things became so ugly, Frazer learned, that some full-time associates within the group bluntly refused to work with him. Jean Fenster,

an analyst who also worked with Mazey on a few deals, described her experience:

> When I first started, Chip asked me to complete an assignment which would typically take a novice at least three days to finish. I was handed the assignment at 8 p.m. and instructed to have it finished and on his desk to look at first thing the following morning. I sat through the night cracking on the assignment and finally completed what I thought was a pretty comprehensive product. To my good fortune, there were a few experienced staff members at the office during the night who offered to vet my product. They seemed pretty happy with my work. Slightly before dawn, I laid the finalized assignment on Chip's desk. I thought it would be a great idea to go home, catch up on a couple hours of sleep, and clean up. I arrived back at the office at least 15 minutes before Chip—ready to answer any questions.

As expected Fenster was called over to Mazey's desk the next morning. What followed, however, was unexpected. He questioned every assumption she had made, countered every explanation she offered in a derogatory manner, and nitpicked her work for an entire hour. He then asked her to redo the work based on information he forwarded via e-mail. When Fenster sat down at her desk to rework the material, she was shocked to learn that the VP was privy to that additional information *before he handed her the assignment*, information that would have made it easier to complete the work. She just couldn't fathom why this information was not forwarded to her earlier. Even more discouraging was that although she was asked to complete the work within 24 hours, the e-mail indicated they had two weeks before it was even due. That assignment was a nightmare, and every effort Fenster made toward working on it contributed to the bad dream. "Each session I had with Chip included a series of derogatory and demeaning remarks directed toward me," she said. "From my communication skills, my accent, to the way I dressed, this VP was critical."

Fenster's story sounded eerily familiar to Rich Patten, who described a couple of his experiences with the vice president. During a conference call with a client, Patten was unable to answer a question the client posted. Mazey became enraged and began screaming at both him and the other analyst in the room. Patten said he could have helped Mazey answer the client's questions but Mazey's ranting prevented him from even speaking. "The outburst resembled that of a two-year-old, and both of us were speechless," Patten said. "Then, still in a rage, Chip grabbed a calculator from his desktop and shattered it against the wall, just above my head!"

Later that day, Mazey apologized for his outburst, and Patter believed his apology was sincere. "I had considered going to speak with the vice president who hired me about the incident," Patten said, "but after the apology I changed my mind." Mazey asked the associate to focus on the task at hand. It was 7 p.m. and there were still at least nine hours of work that had to be completed by an 8 a.m. conference call the next morning. Mazey instructed Patten to come in to work an hour early to prepare for the call.

"I spent the entire night working, arrived home at 4:30 a.m., slept for an hour and a half, and then returned to the office at 7 a.m.," Patten recalled. "Gulping down my coffee, I went to Chip's office only to find it empty." The 8 a.m. showtime came and went without any word from Mazey, who eventually rolled into the office at 10 a.m. without a word. Patten asked him about the meeting, and Mazey simply said that the meeting was changed. Patten asked another associate who was staffed on the deal about the meeting, and found out that no such meeting was ever planned!

GET TO WORK—EVERYONE!

Payton Edwards had another Mazey characteristic to share. "He's very bright and certainly very capable, but he demands complete perfection and treats subordinates as if they were subservient to him and only him," Edwards said. "Occasionally, this man would compliment me for a 'job well done.'" Yet within five minutes, Mazey would come back with some reason why it wasn't "quite right" and force him to redo his work. He was also known for forcing people to do useless, menial tasks. For example, he frequently had his administrative assistant, as well as two analysts, complete the *exact* same task. Mazey said he just want to make absolutely sure that when all was said and done, the task was completed perfectly. Eventually, the analysts and administrative assistant found out that they were all assigned the same task and they were peeved. They felt like he didn't trust them—and he didn't. Edwards said,

Even when it was apparent that Chip had made a mistake, he never openly acknowledged it. One time, he denied that that there were multiple buyers on a particular deal and created a hostile deal environment for many of the concerned parties. He also did not like initiative-taking, much less even consider rewarding it.

When I went to him with ideas on topics to research relevant ongoing deals, he shot down my ideas and told me to work on what he wanted me to get done. When it turned out later that my ideas were good, he never gave me credit and pretended that he had thought of them himself. In fact, he went out of his way to discredit me. For example, when I was still a very novice drinker, Chip would get a kick out of having me order the wine at closing dinners. He wanted to embarrass me in public because of my lack of knowledge about wine.

Chip also made fun of the secretary who came from a poorer part of the city and where everyone seemed to have the same last name. At Christmas parties, the support staff was not allowed to bring spouses, while analysts and associates were invited to bring their spouses. Chip told me that he did not feel that it was necessary to "pay to feed the secretary's husband."

ANY MORE QUESTIONS?

Life for support staff working for Mazey was a challenge as well. He had an incessant need to know what every person was working on at all times. This was even more pronounced the lower an employee was within the organizational hierarchy. His administrative assistant, Gabriela Salaberrios, found it surprising that the VP needed to know what a secretary was typing at a given moment. Yet Mazey had to know where all employees were at all times. He provided Salaberrios with a cell phone so that he could contact her in the middle of the night to work on last-minute deal items. He was never polite, and refused to take no for an answer. More than a few times, Mazey called in the middle of the night and demanded her presence at the office. Many times he had already sent a car to get Salaberrios before she had said yes. One time, she was vacationing in Tunisia, and he called to demand her immediate return—it seemed that his idea on how a deal should go from beginning to end was to be followed by all.

SO WHAT?

Proud of his accomplishment in his career so far, Frazer had sashayed into New York with a youthful certainty that attitude would carry him. He held a job he had thought about for some time in a firm he was convinced would offer even more opportunities. Not once had he expected to get sidetracked over some middle-aged, disgruntled vice president. Yet that same VP possessed many of the characteristics Frazer had expected and indeed admired on Wall Street. Gathering all this information on Mazey had been almost cathartic. Now what, if anything, should he do with it?

QUESTIONS

1. Earlier in the chapter *conflict* was defined as a process that occurs when one person, group, or organizational subunit frustrates the goal attainment of another. Speculate about how Chip Mazey has frustrated the goal attainment of personnel at Hudson Smith Gordon.

2. Is the conflict observed in the case relationship, task, or process conflict? Please explain your reasoning.

3. The chapter outlined a number of causes of conflict. Which seem to be prevalent in this case? Feel free to cite some other contributors as well.

4. The chapter discusses five modes of managing conflict: avoiding, accommodating, competing, compromise, and collaborating. What mode does Chip Mazey employ? What mode does his staff employ?

5. Chip Mazey's subordinates seem to be suffering from stress, but what is its exact causes? That is, how does his behaviour translate into stress for others?

6. Is Chip a bully? Defend your answer.

7. Despite his obvious reputation, how has Chip managed to retain a position of power?

8. What should Jeremy Frazer do now? What should his goals be?

INTEGRATIVE CASE

IVEY | Publishing

Ken Private Limited: Digitization Project

At the end of Part 2 of the text, on Individual Behaviour, you answered a number of questions about the Ken Private Limited: Digitization Project Integrative Case that dealt with issues related to learning, perceptions, cross-cultural differences, and motivation. Now that you have completed Part 3 of the text and the chapters on Social Behaviour and Organizational Processes, you can return to the Integrative Case and enhance your understanding of some of the main issues associated with social behaviour and organizational processes by answering the following questions that deal with groups, subcultures, leadership, communication, decision making, and conflict.

QUESTIONS

1. Although the "teams" at Ken Private Limited are actually large organizational units, many of the principles of group dynamics and teamwork still apply. How do the concepts of group development, norms, diversity, and cohesiveness apply to the case?

2. What are the advantages and challenges of virtual teamwork displayed in the case? What caused the challenges? How could these challenges have been avoided?

3. Consider the existence of any subcultures at Ken Private Limited. What is the nature of these subcultures, and how and why do they differ?

4. How important and effective is leadership at Ken Private Limited with respect to the Genesis Digitization Project? Be sure to provide examples of effective and ineffective leadership.

5. Discuss Shekhar Sharma's leadership behaviours with respect to consideration, initiating structure, leader reward behaviour, and leader punishment

behaviour. What behaviours does he exhibit, and what behaviours are absent? What behaviours does he need to exhibit and why?

6. Use the situational theories of leadership to determine the type of leadership that Shekhar Sharma should be exhibiting. Is his leadership consistent with the situational theories of leadership?

7. What does Shekhar Sharma need to do to be a more effective leader? To answer this question, refer to the following theories of leadership: leader–member exchange (LMX), transactional and transformational leadership, empowering leadership, ethical leadership, authentic leadership, and servant leadership.

8. Is culture an issue with respect to Shekhar Sharma's approach to leadership? In other words, is the effectiveness of his approach to leadership dependent on culture, and is this a factor in the case with regard to the Indian and Filipino teams? Refer to Exhibit 9.8 to answer this question. What universal facilitators of leadership effectiveness (see Exhibit 9.9) should Shekhar Sharma be exhibiting to a greater extent?

9. Is there evidence of ineffective communication in the case? If so, please give specific examples, including any that pertain to cross-cultural factors.

10. Both too little information and too much information can result in low-quality decisions. Which is the problem here: too much or too little? Give examples to support your choice.

11. What is the main evidence of conflict in the case, and what are its causes? What might contribute to its resolution?

CHAPTER 14
ENVIRONMENT, STRATEGY, AND STRUCTURE

LEARNING OBJECTIVES

After reading Chapter 14, you should be able to:

14.1 Discuss the *open systems* concept of an organization and the components of an organization's *external environment*, and explain how *environmental uncertainty* and *resource dependence* affect what happens in organizations.

14.2 Define *strategy*, and describe how organizational structure can serve as a strategic response to environmental demands.

14.3 Define *organizational structure*, and explain how it corresponds to division of labour.

14.4 Discuss the relative merits of various forms of *departmentation*.

14.5 Review the more basic and more elaborate means of achieving organizational *coordination*.

14.6 Discuss the nature and consequences of *traditional structural characteristics*, and explain the distinction between *organic* and *mechanistic* structures.

14.7 Discuss the emergence of *ambidextrous*, *network*, *virtual*, and *modular* organizations.

14.8 Explain how vertical *integration, mergers and acquisitions, strategic alliances*, and the establishment of *legitimacy* reflect strategic responses.

MCDONALD'S

McDonald's is the largest food-service company in the world, with more than 36 000 restaurants worldwide. In Canada, McDonald's and its franchisees own and operate over 1400 restaurants and employ more than 80 000 workers. McDonald's has been named one of Canada's Best Workplaces and Best Employers.

In recent years, McDonald's has been struggling amid slumping sales due to increasing competition and changes in consumer tastes. On March 1, 2015, Steve Easterbrook became the company's new president and chief executive officer following one of its most dismal years on record.

In May of 2015, Easterbrook announced McDonald's long-awaited turnaround strategy. While many were expecting changes to address concerns over the company's menu, slow service, and the perception of low-quality food, the focus of the turnaround is a corporate restructuring that will strip away bureaucracy and enable McDonald's to keep up with consumer tastes.

The plan includes reorganizing domestic and international operating units, selling more restaurants to franchisees, and cutting costs. Easterbrook said, "Today we are announcing the initial steps to reset and turn around our business.... I will not shy away from the urgent need to reset this business.... The reality is our recent performance has been poor. The numbers don't lie."

On the turnaround strategy, Easterbrook said, "The immediate priority for our business is restoring growth under a new organizational structure and ownership mix designed to provide greater focus on the customer, improve our operating fundamentals, and drive a recommitment to running great restaurants. As we turn around our business, we will look to create more excitement around the brand and ensure that we build on our rich heritage of positively impacting the communities we serve."

The focus of the strategy is a change in McDonald's organizational structure. "The first critical step of our operational growth-led plan is to strengthen our effectiveness and efficiency to drive faster and more customer-led decisions" Easterbrook said. "We will restructure our

When Steve Easterbrook became McDonald's president and chief executive officer, one of the first things he did was change McDonald's organizational structure as part of the company's turnaround strategy.

business into four new segments that combine markets with similar needs, challenges, and opportunities for growth."

Easterbrook described McDonald's current structure, which is segmented by geography (e.g., United States, Europe, Asia/Pacific, the Middle East, Africa), as "cumbersome." The new organizational structure will be based on the maturity of its presence in the market and will consist of four segments of similar markets. One segment will focus on the United States, which is the company's largest segment and accounts for more than 40 percent of its operating income. A second segment will focus on international lead markets, which are established markets with similar economic and competitive dynamics and include countries such as Canada, Australia, France, Germany, and the United Kingdom. The third segment consists of high-growth markets, which have higher restaurant expansion and franchising potential and include China, Italy, Russia, South Korea, Spain, Switzerland, and the Netherlands. The fourth segment, which will focus on foundational markets, includes all of the remaining countries where McDonalds operates.

In commenting on the new structure, Easterbrook said, "Our new structure will be supported by streamlined teams with fewer layers and less bureaucracy, and our markets will be better organized around their growth drivers, resource needs and contributions to the Company's overall profitability. McDonald's new structure will more closely align similar markets so they can better leverage their collective insights, energy and expertise to deliver a stronger menu, service, and overall experience for our customers." Easterbrook also announced the leaders of each segment and stated that under the new structure the "leadership of McDonald's new segments will be able to more effectively address the common needs of their markets and customers."

McDonald's chief administrative officer, Pete Bensen, said that the new organizational structure "will unleash more entrepreneurial spirit and more innovation across our system while bolstering what makes McDonald's a formidable leader in the industry: our incredible network of dedicated franchisees."

The new structure, along with plans to franchise more restaurants, is expected to improve performance. In addition, Easterbrook says that it will cut $300 million (U.S.) in general and administrative costs by the end of 2017. The changes are intended to shape McDonald's future as a "modern, progressive burger company." In the words of Easterbrook, "We are taking decisive and necessary action to drive foundational improvements in our business and position the Company for long-term growth."[1]

The story of McDonald's turnaround strategy and change in organizational structure illustrates some of the major questions that we will consider in this chapter. How does the external environment influence organizations? How can an organization develop a strategy to cope with the environment? What forms of strategic response do organizations employ to cope with environmental uncertainty? And how does organizational structure affect employees and the overall effectiveness of organizations? These are the kinds of questions that we shall attempt to answer in this chapter.

First, we will discuss the external environment of organizations and how organizations respond to uncertainty and resource dependence. Then, we will define organizational structure and discuss the methods for dividing labour and forming departments. We will then consider some methods for coordinating labour as well as traditional structural characteristics and some contemporary organizational structures. Finally, we will review several other strategic responses to uncertainty and resource dependence.

THE EXTERNAL ENVIRONMENT OF ORGANIZATIONS

In previous chapters, we have been concerned primarily with the internal environments of organizations—those events and conditions inside the organization—that affect the attitudes and behaviours of members. In this section, we turn our interest to the impact of the **external environment**—those events and conditions surrounding the organization that influence its activities.

External environment.
Events and conditions surrounding an organization that influence its activities.

There is ample evidence in everyday life that the external environment has tremendous influence on organizations. For example, consider the SARS (Severe Acute Respiratory Syndrome) outbreak of 2003. When SARS hit Toronto, bus, hotel, restaurant, theatre, and travel companies were deluged with cancellations and experienced a sharp decline in business. SARS forced Toronto-based Cullingford Coaches to idle many of its 17 coaches and face the prospect of having part of its fleet repossessed.[2] It has been estimated that the overall effect of SARS on the economy from lost tourism and airport revenues was about $570 million in Toronto and another $380 million in the rest of Canada. The losses were even greater in some Asian countries, which experienced SARS outbreaks that were much worse than Canada's.[3] But many companies noticed that they could operate just as well with less business travel than they had undertaken before SARS. Some realized large savings in time and money by using technology like videoconferencing.[4]

A more recent example of the influence of the external environment is the economic crisis and global recession several years ago, in which manufacturing production plunged and thousands of employees lost their jobs. Particularly hard hit was the global auto industry. Companies such as General Motors and Chrysler had to shut down their North American operations and close plants and dealerships in the face of major declines in sales. The rise in gasoline prices triggered the collapse of the market for trucks and SUVs and resulted in the closure of GM's award-winning truck assembly plant in Oshawa, Ontario, after 44 years of operation. As a result, for the first time since 1918, GM stopped manufacturing trucks in Oshawa. GM filed for bankruptcy protection and had to scale back its business by selling off its Hummer and Saab brands and discontinuing the manufacture of Pontiacs. GM and Chrysler made major reductions in their workforce and negotiated new contracts with the Canadian Auto Workers and United Auto Workers unions to cut costs and change work rules. They also received $40 billion in government loans from the U.S. and Canadian governments to restructure. When the federal and Ontario governments announced a combined $10.6 billion in loans to help GM restructure, the headline on the front page of the *Toronto Star* read "Government Motors." The restructuring plan was expected to result in leaner, greener companies that manufacture smaller and more fuel-efficient vehicles.[5] As always, the external environment profoundly shaped organizational behaviour.

The final truck rolls off the assembly line, marking the close of GM's award-winning truck assembly plant in Oshawa, Ontario.

Joe Sarnovsky, CAW Local 222

Organizations as Open Systems

Organizations can be described as open systems. **Open systems** are systems that take inputs from the external environment, transform some of these inputs, and send them back into the external environment as outputs (Exhibit 14.1).[6] Inputs include capital, energy, materials, information, technology, and people; outputs include various products and services. Some inputs are transformed (e.g., raw materials), while other inputs (e.g., skilled craftspeople) assist in the transformation process. Transformation processes may be physical (e.g., manufacturing or surgery), intellectual (e.g., teaching or programming), or even emotional (e.g., psychotherapy). For example, an insurance company imports actuarial experts, information about accidents and mortality, and capital in the form of insurance premiums. Through the application of financial knowledge, it transforms the capital into insurance coverage and investments in areas like real estate. Universities and colleges import seasoned scholars and aspiring students from the environment. Through the teaching process, they return educated individuals to the community as outputs.

The value of the open systems concept is that it sensitizes us to the need for organizations to cope with the demands of the environment on both the input side and the output side. As we will see, some of this coping involves adaptation to environmental demands. On the other hand, some coping may be oriented toward changing the environment.

First, let's examine the external environment in greater detail.

Components of the External Environment

The external environment of any given organization is obviously a "big" concept. Technically, it involves any person, group, event, or condition outside the direct domain of the organization. For this reason, it is useful to divide the environment into a manageable number of components.[7]

THE GENERAL ECONOMY Organizations that survive through selling products or services often suffer from an economic downturn and profit from an upturn. When a downturn occurs, competition for remaining customers increases, and organizations might postpone needed capital improvements. Of course, some organizations thrive under a poor economy,

LO 14.1

Discuss the *open systems* concept of an organization and the components of an organization's *external environment*, and explain how *environmental uncertainty* and *resource dependence* affect what happens in organizations.

Open systems. Systems that take inputs from the external environment, transform some of them, and send them back into the environment as outputs.

EXHIBIT 14.1
The organization as an open system.

including welfare offices and law firms that deal heavily in bankruptcies. In addition, if a poor economy is accompanied by high unemployment, some organizations might find it opportune to upgrade the quality of their staff, since they will have an ample selection of candidates. This is exactly what Blackberry Limited and other tech firms did during the last recession. They hired thousands of employees, including tech gurus laid off by other firms, in hopes of gaining an edge on their competitors. Of course, when Blackberry Limited faced slumping sales of its BlackBerry smartphones a few years later, it too had to lay off thousands of workers.[8]

CUSTOMERS All organizations have potential customers for their products and services. Piano makers have musicians, and consumer activist associations have disgruntled consumers. The customers of universities include not only their students but also the firms that employ their graduates and seek their research assistance. Organizations must be sensitive to changes in customer demands. For example, the small liberal arts college that resists developing a business school might be faced with declining enrolment.

Successful firms are generally highly sensitive to customer reactions. Automobile manufacturers are now making smaller and more energy-efficient vehicles including hybrids and fully electric cars. Ford's flexible Michigan Assembly Plant was a response to the increasing customer demand for fuel-efficient and green vehicles, and the Ford Focus and the Focus Electric are examples of this.

SUPPLIERS Organizations are dependent on the environment for supplies, which include labour, raw materials, equipment, and component parts. Shortages can cause severe difficulties. For instance, the lack of a local technical school might prove troublesome for an electronics firm that requires skilled labour. Similarly, a strike by a company that supplies component parts might cause the purchaser to shut down its assembly line.

COMPETITORS Environmental competitors vie for resources that include both customers and suppliers.[9] Thus, private schools compete for students, and consulting firms compete for clients. Similarly, utility companies compete for coal, and professional baseball teams compete for free-agent ballplayers. Successful organizations devote considerable energy to monitoring the activities of competitors.

SOCIAL/POLITICAL FACTORS Organizations cannot ignore the social and political events that occur around them. Changes in public attitudes toward ethnic diversity, the proper age for retirement, the environment, corporate social responsibility, or the proper role of big business will soon affect them. Frequently, these attitudes find expression in law through the political process. Thus, organizations must cope with a series of legal regulations that prescribe fair employment practices, proper competitive activities, product safety, clients' rights, and environmental protectionism.

TECHNOLOGY The environment contains a variety of technologies that are useful for achieving organizational goals. Technology refers to ways of doing things, not simply to some form of machinery. The ability to adopt the proper technology should enhance an organization's effectiveness. For a business firm, this might involve the choice of an appropriate computer system or production technique. For a mental health clinic, it might involve implementing a particular form of psychotherapy that is effective for its clients. For an automotive firm, it might involve flexible manufacturing and smart robots.

Now that we have outlined the basic components of organizational environments, a few more detailed comments are in order. First, this brief list does not provide a perfect picture of the large number of actual interest groups that can exist in an organization's environment. **Interest groups** are parties or organizations other than direct competitors that have some vested interest in how an organization is managed. For example, Exhibit 14.2 shows the interest groups that surround a university. As you can see, our list of six environmental components actually involves quite an array of individuals and agencies with which the university must contend. To

Interest groups. Parties or organizations other than direct competitors that have some vested interest in how an organization is managed.

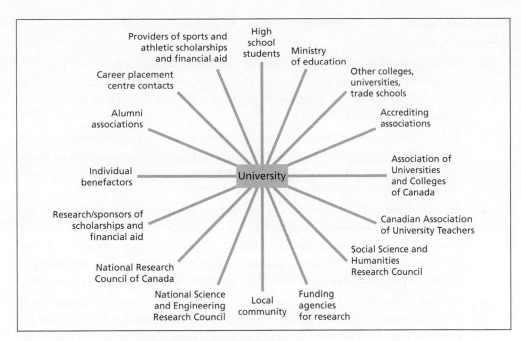

EXHIBIT 14.2
Interest groups in the external environment of a university.
Source: Based on Brown, W.B., & Moberg, D.J. (1980). *Organization theory and management*, p. 45. Copyright © 1980 by John Wiley & Sons, Inc.

complicate matters, some of these individuals and agencies might make competing or conflicting demands on the university. For instance, sponsors of athletic and sports scholarships might press the university to allocate more funds to field a winning hockey team, while research scholarship sponsors might insist that the university match their donations for academic purposes. Such competition for attention from different segments of the environment is not unusual. Obviously, different interest groups evaluate organizational effectiveness according to different criteria.[10]

Different parts of the organization are often concerned with different environmental components. For instance, we can expect a marketing department to be tuned in to customer demands and a legal department to be interested in regulations stemming from the social/political component. The coordination of this natural division of interests is a crucial concern for all organizations. Also, as environmental demands change, it is important that power shifts occur to allow the appropriate functional units to cope with these demands.

Finally, events in various components of the environment provide both constraints and opportunities for organizations. Although environments with many constraints (e.g., high interest rates, strong competition, and so on) appear pretty hostile, an opportunity in one environmental sector might offset a constraint in another. For example, the firm that is faced with a dwindling customer base might find its salvation by exploiting new technologies that give it an edge in costs or new product development.

Environmental Uncertainty

In our earlier discussion of environmental components we implied that environments have considerable potential for causing confusion among managers. Customers may come and go, suppliers may turn from good to bad, and competitors may make surprising decisions. The resulting uncertainty can be both challenging and frustrating. **Environmental uncertainty** exists when an environment is vague, difficult to diagnose, and unpredictable. We all know that some environments are less certain than others. Your hometown provides you with a fairly certain environment. There, you are familiar with the transportation system, the language, and necessary social conventions. Thrust into the midst of a foreign culture, you encounter a much less certain environment. How to greet a stranger, order a meal, and get around town become significant issues. There is nothing intrinsically bad about this uncertainty. It simply requires you to marshal a particular set of skills to be an effective visitor.

Like individuals, organizations can find themselves in more or less certain environments. But just exactly what makes an organizational environment uncertain? Put simply,

PERSONAL INVENTORY ASSESSMENT

Learn About Yourself
Tolerance of Ambiguity Scale

Environmental uncertainty. A condition that exists when the external environment is vague, difficult to diagnose, and unpredictable.

uncertainty depends on the environment's *complexity* (simple versus complex) and its *rate of change* (static versus dynamic).[11]

- *Simple environment.* A simple environment involves relatively few factors, and these factors are fairly similar to each other. For example, consider the pottery manufacturer that obtains its raw materials from two small firms and sells its entire output to three small pottery outlets.

- *Complex environment.* A complex environment contains a large number of dissimilar factors that affect the organization. For example, the university in Exhibit 14.2 has a more complex environment than the pottery manufacturer. In turn, McDonald's has a more complex environment than the university.

- *Static environment.* The components of this environment remain fairly stable over time. The small-town radio station that plays the same music format, relies on the same advertisers, and works under the same CRTC (Canadian Radio-television and Telecommunications Commission) regulations year after year has a stable environment. (Of course, no environment is *completely* static; we are speaking in relative terms here.)

- *Dynamic environment.* The components of a highly dynamic environment are in a constant state of change, which is unpredictable and irregular, not cyclical. For example, consider the firm that designs and manufactures microchips for electronics applications. New scientific and technological advances occur rapidly and unpredictably in this field. In addition, customer demands are highly dynamic as firms devise new uses for microchips. A similar dynamic environment faces auto manufacturers, owing in part to the vagaries of the energy situation and cost of fuel and in part to the fact that marketing automobiles has become an international rather than a national business. For example, fluctuations in the relative value of international currencies can radically alter the cost of competing imported cars quite independently of anything management does.

As we see in Exhibit 14.3, it is possible to arrange rate of change and complexity in a matrix. A simple/static environment (Cell 1) should provoke the least uncertainty, while a dynamic/complex environment (Cell 4) should provoke the most. Some research suggests that change has more influence than complexity on uncertainty.[12] Thus, we might expect a static/complex environment (Cell 2) to be somewhat more certain than a dynamic/simple environment (Cell 3).

Earlier, we stated that different parts of the organization are often interested in different components of the environment. And we have just shown that some aspects of the environment are less certain than others. Thus, some subunits might be faced with more uncertainty than others. For example, the research and development department of a microchip company would seem to face a more uncertain environment than the human resources department.

Increasing uncertainty has several predictable effects on organizations and their decision makers.[13] For one thing, as uncertainty increases, cause-and-effect relationships become less clear. If we are certain that a key competitor will not match our increased advertising budget, we may be confident that our escalated ad campaign will increase our market share. Uncertainty about the competitor's response reduces confidence in this causal inference. Second, environmental uncertainty tends to make priorities harder to agree on, and it often stimulates a fair degree of political jockeying within the organization. To continue the example, if the consequences of increased advertising are unclear, other functional units might see the increased budget allocation as being "up for grabs." Finally, as environmental uncertainty increases, more information must be processed by the organization to make adequate decisions. Environmental scanning, boundary spanning, planning, and formal management information systems will become more prominent.[14] This illustrates that organizations will act to cope with or reduce uncertainty, because uncertainty increases the difficulty of decision making and thus threatens organizational effectiveness. Shortly, we will examine in

	Complexity	
	Simple	Complex
Static	**Cell 1** *Low perceived uncertainty* 1. Small number of factors and components in the environment 2. Factors and components are somewhat similar to one another 3. Factors and components remain basically the same and are not changing	**Cell 2** *Moderately low perceived uncertainty* 1. Large number of factors and components in the environment 2. Factors and components are not similar to one another 3. Factors and components remain basically the same
Dynamic	**Cell 3** *Moderately high perceived uncertainty* 1. Small number of factors and components in the environment 2. Factors and components are somewhat similar to one another 3. Factors and components of the environment are in continual process of change	**Cell 4** *High perceived uncertainty* 1. Large number of factors and components in the environment 2. Factors and components are not similar to one another 3. Factors and components of environment are in a continual process of change

(Rate of Change: Static / Dynamic)

EXHIBIT 14.3
Environmental uncertainty as a function of complexity and rate of change.
Source: Duncan, R.B. (1972). Characteristics of organizational environments and perceived environment uncertainty. *Administrative Science Quarterly*, *17*(3), 313–327, p. 320. Used by permission of Cornell University Johnson School.

greater detail the means of managing uncertainty. First, we explore resource dependence, another aspect of the impact of the environment on organizations.

Resource Dependence

Earlier we noted that organizations are open systems that receive inputs from the external environment and transfer outputs into this environment. Many inputs from various components of the environment are valuable resources that are necessary for organizational survival. These include such things as capital, raw materials, and human resources. By the same token, other components of the environment (such as customers) represent valuable resources on the output end of the equation. All this suggests that organizations are in a state of **resource dependence** with regard to their environments.[15] Carefully managing and coping with this resource dependence is a key to survival and success.

Although all organizations are dependent on their environments for resources, some organizations are more dependent than others. This is because some environments have a larger amount of readily accessible resources.[16] A classic case of a highly resource-dependent organization is a newly formed small business. Cautious bank managers, credit-wary suppliers, and a dearth of customers all teach the aspiring owner the meaning of dependence. Also, many organizations in traditional manufacturing industries encounter a much less munificent environment. Investors are wary, customers are disappearing, and skilled human resources are attracted to situations with better career prospects. Historically, the computer and software industries were located in munificent environments. Capital was readily available, human resources were trained in relevant fields, and new uses for computers were continually being developed. Although this is still the case to some extent, we have already alluded to the shakeout in the market for basic software. The days are gone when business amateurs can develop a new word-processing package and become multi-millionaires, like the founders of WordPerfect. The big firms have consolidated the market.

Resource dependence. The dependency of organizations on environmental inputs, such as capital, raw materials, and human resources as well as outputs such as customers.

Resource dependence can be fairly independent of environmental uncertainty, and dealing with one issue will not necessarily have an effect on the other. For example, although the computer industry generally faces a fairly munificent environment, this environment is uncertain, especially with regard to rate of change. On the other hand, many mature small businesses exist in a fairly certain environment but remain highly resource dependent.

Competitors, regulatory agencies, and various interest groups can have a considerable stake in how an organization obtains and transforms its resources.[17] In effect, the organization might be indirectly resource dependent on these bodies and thus susceptible to a fair degree of social control.

The concept of resource dependence does not mean that organizations are totally at the mercy of their environments. Rather, it means that they must develop strategies for managing both resource dependence and environmental uncertainty.[18] Let's now consider strategic responses to uncertainty and resource dependence.

LO 14.2

Define *strategy*, and describe how organizational structure can serve as a strategic response to environmental demands.

Strategy. The process by which top executives seek to cope with the constraints and opportunities that an organization's environment poses.

STRATEGIC RESPONSES TO UNCERTAINTY AND RESOURCE DEPENDENCE

Organizations devote considerable effort to developing and implementing strategies to cope with environmental uncertainty and resource dependence. **Strategy** can be defined as the process by which top executives seek to cope with the constraints and opportunities posed by an organization's environment.

Exhibit 14.4 outlines the nature of the relationship between environment and strategy. At the top, the objective organizational environment is portrayed in terms of uncertainty

EXHIBIT 14.4
Environment, strategy, and organizational effectiveness.

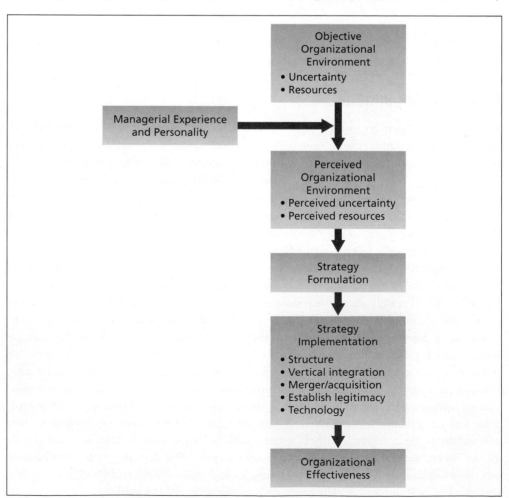

and available resources, as we discussed above. However, much of the impact that the environment has on organizations is indirect rather than direct, filtered through the perceptual system of managers and other organizational members.[19] By means of the perceptual process we discussed in Chapter 3, personality characteristics and experience may colour managers' perceptions of the environment. For example, the environment might seem much more complex and unstable for a manager who is new to his job than for one who has years of experience. Similarly, the optimistic manager might perceive more resources than the pessimistic manager.[20] It is the perceived environment that comprises the basis for strategy formulation. For a good example of this, see the Research Focus: *CEO Narcissism and Firm Strategy*.

Strategy formulation itself involves determining the mission, goals, and objectives of the organization. At the most basic level, for a business firm, this would even involve consideration of just what business the organization should pursue. Then the organization's orientation toward the perceived environment must be determined. This might range from being defensive and protective of current interests (such as holding market share) to prospecting vigorously for new interests to exploit (such as developing totally new products).[21] There is no single correct strategy along this continuum. Rather, the chosen strategy must correspond to the constraints and opportunities of the environment. Finally, the strategy must be implemented by selecting appropriate managers for the task and employing appropriate techniques, as shown in Exhibit 14.4. One of the most common strategic responses

◼ RESEARCH FOCUS ◼

CEO NARCISSISM AND FIRM STRATEGY

Research has found that top executives inject a great deal of themselves into their decisions and that the characteristics of top management teams affect strategic behaviour and performance. However, little attention has been given to one of the most vivid qualities of some CEOs: high levels of narcissism.

Narcissism is a recognized personality dimension that is defined as the degree to which an individual has an inflated sense of self and is preoccupied with having that self-view continually reinforced. The main manifestations of narcissism include feelings of superiority, entitlement, and a constant need for attention and admiration.

Highly narcissistic CEOs are defined as those who have very inflated self-views and who are preoccupied with having those self-views continuously reinforced. Narcissists seek out and pursue actions that are bold, distinctive, risky, and dramatic. As a result, they engage in behaviours and make decisions that have major consequences not only for individuals who interact directly with them but also for broader sets of stakeholders.

But can CEO narcissism influence an organization's strategy? To find out, Arijit Chatterjee and Donald C. Hambrick conducted a study of 111 CEOs in 105 firms in the computer software and hardware industries in the period 1992–2004. They argued that narcissism may impel CEOs to take actions that defy convention as a way to garner attention and applause and that these actions will affect their companies' strategy and performance. They hypothesized that narcissistic CEOs will favour strategic dynamism (the degree of change in an organization's strategy) and grandiosity rather than incrementalism and stability, which will result in extreme performance (big wins or big losses) and wide fluctuations in firm performance. They also predicted that narcissistic CEOs would be involved in more and larger acquisitions because they are among the most visible initiatives a CEO can take. To measure CEO narcissism, the researchers used unobtrusive indicators such as the prominence of the CEO's photograph in the company's annual report.

The results indicated that CEO narcissism is significantly positively related to strategic dynamism, number and size of acquisitions made, extreme performance, and fluctuating performance. Narcissistic CEOs change their organization's strategy more often and engage in bold actions that attract attention (e.g., acquisitions) and result in big wins or big losses and extreme and irregular firm performance.

Source: Chatterjee, A., & Hambrick, D.C. (2007). CEO Narcissism and Firm Strategy. *Administrative Science Quarterly, 52,* 351–386.

employed by organizations is a change in organizational structure. As described in the chapter-opening vignette, this is exactly what McDonald's did. Let's now take a closer look at organizational structure.

WHAT IS ORGANIZATIONAL STRUCTURE?

To achieve its goals, an organization has to do two very basic things: *divide* labour among its members and then *coordinate* what has been divided. For example, consider how a university divides its labour: some members teach, some run the graduate programs, some take care of accounts, and some handle registration. It is simply unlikely that anyone could do *all* these things well. Furthermore, within each of these subunits, labour would be further divided. For example, the registrar's office would include a director, secretaries, clerks, and so on. With all this division, some coordination is obviously necessary. We can conclude that **organizational structure** is the manner in which an organization divides its labour into specific tasks and achieves coordination among these tasks.[22]

Labour must be divided because individuals have physical and intellectual limitations. *Everyone* cannot do *everything*—even if this were possible, tremendous confusion and inefficiency would result. There are two basic dimensions to the division of labour: a vertical dimension and a horizontal dimension. Once labour is divided, it must be coordinated to achieve organizational effectiveness.

Vertical Division of Labour

The vertical division of labour is concerned primarily with apportioning authority for planning and decision making—who gets to tell whom what to do? As we can see in Exhibit 14.5, in a manufacturing firm, the vertical division of labour is usually signified by titles such as *president*, *manager*, and *supervisor*. In a university, it might be denoted by titles such as *president*, *dean*, and *chairperson*. Organizations differ greatly in the extent to which labour is divided vertically. For example, the Canadian Army has 19 levels of command, ranging from full generals to privates. Walmart U.S. has six levels. On the other hand, an automobile dealership might have only two or three levels, and a university would usually fall between the extremes. Separate departments, units, or functions *within* an organization will also often vary in the extent to which they vertically divide labour. A production unit might have several levels of management, ranging from supervisor to general manager. A research unit in the same company might have only two levels of management. A couple of key themes underlie the vertical division of labour.

AUTONOMY AND CONTROL Holding other factors constant, the domain of decision making and authority is reduced as the number of levels in the hierarchy increases. Put

EXHIBIT 14.5
The dimensions of division of labour in a manufacturing firm.

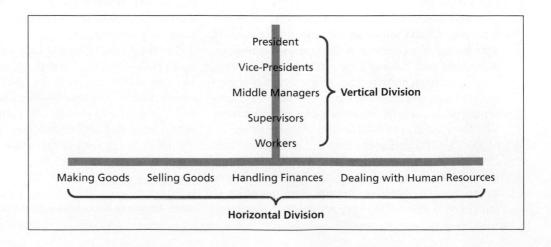

another way, managers have less authority over fewer matters. On the other hand, a flatter hierarchy pushes authority lower and involves people further down the hierarchy in more decisions.

COMMUNICATION A second theme underlying the vertical division of labour is communication or coordination between levels. As labour is progressively divided vertically, timely communication and coordination can become harder to achieve. Recall our discussion in Chapter 10 on information filtering as a barrier to communication. As the number of levels in the hierarchy increases, filtering is more likely to occur.

These two themes illustrate that labour must be divided vertically enough to ensure proper control but not so much as to make vertical communication and coordination impossible. The proper degree of such division will vary across organizations and across their functional units.

Horizontal Division of Labour

The horizontal division of labour groups the basic tasks that must be performed into jobs and then into departments so that the organization can achieve its goals. Required workflow is the main basis for this division. The firm schematized in Exhibit 14.5 must produce and sell goods, keep its finances straight, and keep its employees happy. A hospital must admit patients, subject them to lab tests, fix what ails them, and keep them comfortable, all the while staying within its budget. Just as organizations differ in the extent to which they divide labour vertically, they also differ in the extent of horizontal division of labour. In a small business, the owner might be a "jack of all trades," making estimates, delivering the product or service, and keeping the books. As the organization grows, horizontal division of labour is likely, with different groups of employees assigned to perform each of these tasks. Thus, the horizontal division of labour suggests some specialization on the part of the workforce. Up to a point, this increased specialization can promote efficiency. A couple of key themes underlie the horizontal division of labour.

JOB DESIGN The horizontal division of labour is closely tied to our earlier consideration of job design (Chapter 6). An example will clarify this. Suppose that an organization offers a product or service that consists of A work, B work, and C work (e.g., fabrication, inspection, and packaging). There are at least three basic ways in which it might structure these tasks:

- Form an ABC Department in which all workers do ABC work.
- Form an ABC Department in which workers specialize in A work, B work, or C work.
- Form a separate A Department, B Department, and C Department.

There is nothing inherently superior about any of these three designs. Notice, however, that each has implications for the jobs involved and how these jobs are coordinated. The first design provides for enriched jobs in which each worker can coordinate his or her own A work, B work, and C work. It also reduces the need for supervision and allows for self-managed teams. However, this design might require highly trained workers, and it might be impossible if A work, B work, and C work are complex specialties that require (for example) engineering, accounting, and legal skills. The second design involves increased horizontal division of labour in which employees specialize in tasks and in which the coordination of A work, B work, and C work becomes more critical. However, much of this coordination could be handled by properly designing the head of the department's job. Finally, the third design offers the greatest horizontal division of labour in that A work, B work, and C work are actually performed in separate departments. This design provides for great control and accountability for the separate tasks, but it also suggests that someone above the department heads will have to get involved in coordination.

Differentiation. The tendency for managers in separate units, functions, or departments to differ in terms of goals, time spans, and interpersonal styles.

DIFFERENTIATION As organizations engage in increased horizontal division of labour, they usually become more and more differentiated. **Differentiation** is the tendency for managers in separate units, functions, or departments to differ in terms of goals, time spans, and interpersonal styles.[23] In tending to their own domains and problems, managers often develop distinctly different psychological orientations toward the organization and its products or services. Under high differentiation, various organizational units tend to operate more autonomously.

A classic case of differentiation is that which often occurs between marketing managers and those in research and development. The goals of the marketing managers might be external to the organization and oriented toward servicing the marketplace. Those of R&D managers might be oriented more toward excellence in design and state-of-the-art use of materials. While marketing managers want products to sell *now*, R&D managers might feel that "good designs take time." Finally, marketing managers might believe that they can handle dispute resolution with R&D through interpersonal tactics learned when they were on the sales force ("Let's discuss this over lunch"). R&D managers might feel that "the design speaks for itself" when a conflict occurs. The essential problem here is that the marketing department and the R&D department *need* each other to do their jobs properly![24] Shortly, we will review some tactics to help achieve necessary coordination.

Differentiation is a natural consequence of the horizontal division of labour, but it again points to the need for coordination, a topic that we will consider in more detail below. For now, let's examine more closely how organizations can allocate work to departments.

LO 14.4

Discuss the relative merits of various forms of *departmentation*.

Departmentation

As we suggested above, once basic tasks have been combined into jobs, a question still remains as to how to group these jobs so that they can be managed effectively. The assignment of jobs to departments is called departmentation, and it represents one of the core aspects of the horizontal division of labour.

Functional departmentation. Employees with closely related skills and responsibilities are assigned to the same department.

FUNCTIONAL DEPARTMENTATION This form of organization is basic and familiar. Under **functional departmentation**, employees with closely related skills and responsibilities (functions) are located in the same department (Exhibit 14.6). Thus, those with skills in sales and advertising are assigned to the marketing department, and those with skills in accounting and credit are assigned to the finance department. Under this kind of design, employees are grouped according to the kind of resources they contribute to achieving the overall goals of the organization.[25]

The most cited advantage of functional departmentation is efficiency. When all the engineers are located in an engineering department, rather than scattered throughout the organization, it is easier to be sure that they are neither overloaded nor underloaded with work. Also, support factors, such as reference books, specialized software, and laboratory space can be allocated more efficiently with less duplication. Some other advantages of functional departmentation include the following:

- Communication within departments should be enhanced, since everyone "speaks the same language."

EXHIBIT 14.6 Functional departmentation.

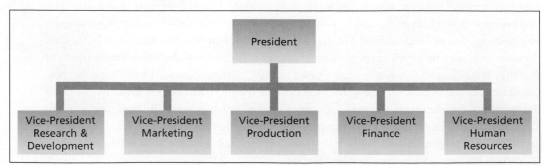

- Career ladders and training opportunities within the function are enhanced because all parties will share the same view of career progression.

- The performance of functional specialists should be easier to measure and evaluate when they are all located in the same department.

What are the disadvantages of functional departmentation? Most of them stem from the specialization within departments that occurs in the functional arrangement. As a result, a high degree of differentiation can occur between functional departments. At best, this can lead to poor coordination and slow response to organizational problems. At worst, it can lead to open conflict between departments, in which the needs of clients and customers are ignored. Departmental empires might be built at the expense of pursuing organizational goals. There is consensus that functional departmentation works best in small- to medium-sized firms that offer relatively few product lines or services. It can also be an effective means of organizing the smaller divisions of large corporations. When the scale gets bigger and the output of the organization gets more complex, most firms gravitate toward product departmentation or its variations.

PRODUCT DEPARTMENTATION Under **product departmentation**, departments are formed on the basis of a particular product, product line, or service. Each of these departments can operate fairly autonomously because it has its own set of functional specialists dedicated to the output of that department. For example, a personal care firm might have a shampoo division and a cosmetics division, each with its own staff of production people, marketers, and research and development personnel (Exhibit 14.7).

One key advantage of product departmentation is better coordination among the functional specialists who work on a particular product line. Since their attentions are focused on one product and they have fewer functional peers, fewer barriers to communication should develop. Other advantages include flexibility, since product lines can be added or deleted without great implications for the rest of the organization. Also, product-focused departments can be evaluated as profit centres, since they have independent control over costs and revenues. This is not feasible for most functional departments (e.g., the research and development department does not have revenues). Finally, product departmentation often serves the customer or client better, since the client can see more easily who produced the product (the software group, not Ajax Consulting). All in all, product structures have more potential than functional structures for responding to customers in a timely way. This is one reason why Hewlett-Packard recently adopted a functional design, consolidating its printer and PC operations in one unit and its enterprise software services in another.[26]

Product departmentation.
Departments are formed on the basis of a particular product, product line, or service.

EXHIBIT 14.7
Product departmentation.

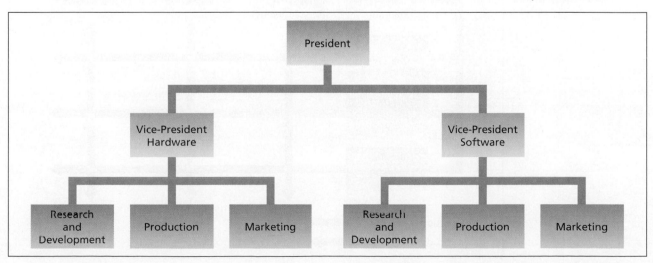

Are there any disadvantages to product departmentation? Professional development might suffer without a critical mass of professionals working in the same place at the same time. Also, economies of scale might be threatened and inefficiency might occur if relatively autonomous product-oriented departments are not coordinated. R&D personnel in an industrial products division and a consumer products division might work on a similar problem for months without being aware of each other's efforts. Worse, product-oriented departments might actually work at cross purposes.

Canadian Tire moved from a product-oriented structure (e.g., automotive, housewares, and hardware) to a more functional one. This redesign, meant to reduce "silo" thinking and cut costs, centralized such functions as human resources, finance, and information technology.[27]

Matrix departmentation.
Employees remain members of a functional department while also reporting to a product or project manager.

MATRIX DEPARTMENTATION The system of **matrix departmentation** is an attempt to capitalize simultaneously on the strengths of both functional and product departmentation.[28] In its most literal form, employees remain tied to a functional department such as marketing or production, but they also report to a product manager who draws on their services (Exhibit 14.8). For example, in a firm in the chemical industry, a marketing expert might matrix with the household cleaning products group. Familiar firms that have matrix designs include Procter & Gamble, IBM, Boeing, and BMW.

There are many variations on matrix design. Most of them boil down to what exactly gets crossed with functional areas to form the matrix and the degree of stability of the matrix relationships. For example, besides products, a matrix could be based on geographical regions or projects. For instance, a mechanical engineer in a global engineering company could report to both the mechanical engineering department at world headquarters and the regional manager for Middle East operations. This would probably be a fairly stable arrangement. Cisco Technical Services, which supplies equipment and 24/7 help desk support worldwide, converted from a regular functional design to a matrix based on geographic regions in order to better provide integrated services.[29] In fact, integrating business in multiple geographic regions is a common stimulus for the matrix design.[30]

EXHIBIT 14.8
Matrix departmentation.

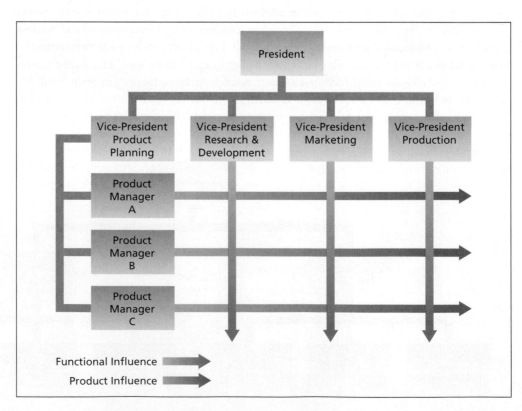

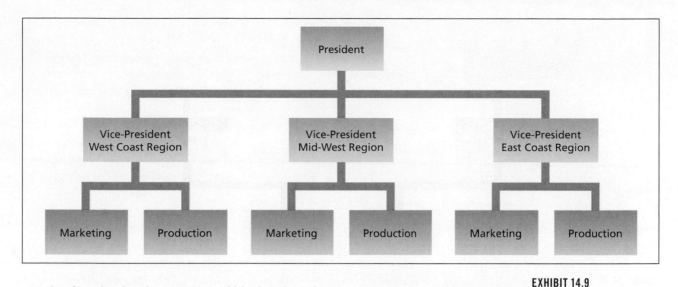

EXHIBIT 14.9
Geographic departmentation.

On the other hand, a matrix could be based on shorter term projects. NASA uses this system, as do many consulting firms and research labs. The cross-functional teams that design cars (Chapter 7) draw members from various functions (e.g., styling, marketing, and engineering). When the design is completed, members go on to other assignments.

The matrix system is quite elegant when it works well. Ideally, it provides a degree of *balance* between the abstract demands of the product or project and the people who actually do the work, resulting in a better outcome. Also, it is very flexible. People can be moved around as project flow dictates, and projects, products, or new regions can be added without total restructuring. Being focused on a particular product or project can also lead to better communication among the representatives from the various functional areas.

Two interrelated problems threaten the matrix structure. First, there is no guarantee that product or project managers will see eye to eye with various functional managers. This can create conflict that reduces the advantages of the matrix. Also, employees assigned to a product or project team in essence report to two managers, their functional manager and their product or project manager. This violation of a classical management principle (every employee should have only one boss) can result in role conflict and stress, especially at performance review time. The upshot of this is that managers need to be well trained under matrix structures.

OTHER FORMS OF DEPARTMENTATION Several other forms of departmentation also exist.[31] Two of these are simply variations on product departmentation. One is geographic departmentation, which is how McDonald's was previously structured. Under **geographic departmentation**, relatively self-contained units deliver the organization's products or services in specific geographic territories (Exhibit 14.9). This form of departmentation shortens communication channels, allows the organization to cater to regional tastes, and gives some appearance of local control to clients and customers. National retailers, insurance companies, and oil companies generally exhibit geographic departmentation.

Another form of departmentation closely related to product departmentation is **customer departmentation**. Under customer departmentation, relatively self-contained units deliver the organization's products or services to specific customer groups (Exhibit 14.10). The obvious goal is to provide better service to each customer group through specialization. For example, many banks have commercial lending divisions that are separate from the consumer loan operations. An engineering firm might have separate divisions to cater to civilian and military customers. In general, the advantages and disadvantages of geographic and customer departmentation parallel those for product departmentation. McDonald's new organizational structure is customer focused in that it is based on the firm's maturity in various markets and customer familiarity with the brand, cutting across geographical divides.

Geographic departmentation.
Relatively self-contained units deliver an organization's products or services in a specific geographic territory.

Customer departmentation.
Relatively self-contained units deliver an organization's products or services to specific customer groups.

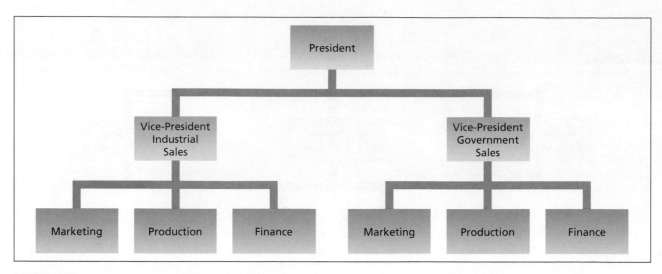

EXHIBIT 14.10
Customer
departmentation.

Hybrid departmentation.
A structure based on some
mixture of functional,
product, geographic, or
customer departmentation.

Finally, we should recognize that few organizations represent "pure" examples of functional, product, geographic, or customer departmentation. It is not unusual to see **hybrid departmentation**, which involves some combination of these structures.[32] For example, a manufacturing firm might retain human resources, finance, and legal services in a functional form at headquarters but use product departmentation to organize separate production and sales staffs for each product. Similarly, Walmart centralizes many activities at their headquarters but also has geographic divisions that cater to regional tastes and promote efficient distribution. The hybrids attempt to capitalize on the strengths of various structures, while avoiding the weaknesses of others.

Basic Methods of Coordinating Divided Labour

LO **14.5**

Review the more basic
and more elaborate
means of achieving
organizational
coordination.

Coordination. A process
of facilitating timing,
communication, and
feedback among work
tasks.

When the tasks that will help the organization achieve its goals have been divided among individuals and departments, they must be coordinated so that goal accomplishment is actually realized. We can identify five basic methods of **coordination**, which is a process of facilitating timing, communication, and feedback.[33]

DIRECT SUPERVISION This is a very traditional form of coordination. Working through the chain of command, designated supervisors or managers coordinate the work of their subordinates. For instance, a production supervisor coordinates the work of his or her subordinates. In turn, the production superintendent coordinates the activities of all the supervisors.

STANDARDIZATION OF WORK PROCESSES Some jobs are so routine that the technology itself provides a means of coordination. Little direct supervision is necessary for these jobs to be coordinated. The automobile assembly line provides a good example. When a car comes by, worker X bolts on the left door, and worker Y bolts on the right door. These workers do not have to interact, and they require minimal supervision. Work processes can also be standardized by rules and regulations. McDonald's stringent routine for constructing a burger is an example of such standardization.

STANDARDIZATION OF OUTPUTS Even when direct supervision is minimal and work processes are not standardized, coordination can be achieved through the standardization of work outputs. Concern shifts from how the work is done to ensuring that the work meets certain physical or economic standards. For instance, employees in a machine shop might be required to construct complex valves that require a mixture of drilling, lathe work, and finishing. The physical specifications of the valves will dictate how this work is to be coordinated. Standardization of outputs is often used to coordinate the work of separate product or geographic divisions. Frequently, top management assigns each division a profit target. These standards ensure that each division "pulls its weight." Thus, budgets are a form of standardizing outputs.

STANDARDIZATION OF SKILLS Even when work processes and output cannot be standardized and direct supervision is unfeasible, coordination can be achieved through standardization of skills. This is seen very commonly in the case of technicians and professionals. For example, a large surgery team can often coordinate its work with minimal verbal communication because of its high degree of interlocked training—surgeons, anaesthesiologists, and nurses all know what to expect from each other because of their standard training. MBA programs provide some standardized skills (e.g., the ability to read a balance sheet) to people with different functional specialties.

MUTUAL ADJUSTMENT Mutual adjustment relies on informal communication to coordinate tasks. Paradoxically, it is useful for coordinating the most simple and the most complicated divisions of labour. For example, imagine a small florist shop that consists of the owner-operator, a shop assistant, and a delivery person. It is very likely that these individuals will coordinate their work through informal processes, mutually adjusting to each other's needs. At the other extreme, consider the top executive team of virtually any corporation. Such teams are generally composed of people with a variety of skills and backgrounds (e.g., finance, marketing) and tend to be preoccupied with very non-routine problems. Again, mutual adjustment would be necessary to coordinate their efforts because standardization would be impossible.

The coordination methods we have discussed can be crudely ordered in terms of the degree of *discretion* they permit in terms of task performance. Applied strictly, direct supervision permits little discretion. Standardization of processes and outputs permits successively more discretion. Finally, standardization of skills and mutual adjustment put even more control into the hands of those who are actually doing the work.

Just as division of labour affects the design of jobs, so does the method of coordination employed. As we move from direct supervision toward mutual adjustment, there is greater potential for jobs to be designed in an enriched manner. By the same token, improper coordination can destroy intrinsic motivation. Traditionally, much work performed by professionals (e.g., scientists and engineers) is coordinated by their own skill standardization. If the manager of a research lab decides to coordinate work with a high degree of direct supervision, the motivating potential of the scientists' jobs might be damaged.

The use of the various methods of coordination tends to vary across different parts of the organization. As we noted, upper management relies heavily on mutual adjustment for coordination. Where tasks are more routine, such as in the lower part of the production subunit, we tend to see coordination via direct supervision or standardization of work processes or outputs.[34] Advisory subunits staffed by professionals, such as a legal department or a marketing research group, often rely on a combination of skill standardization and mutual adjustment.

Other Methods of Coordination

The forms of coordination we discussed above are very basic, in that almost every organization uses them. Sometimes, however, coordination problems are such that more customized, elaborate mechanisms are necessary to achieve coordination. This is especially true when we are speaking of lateral coordination across highly differentiated departments. Recall that the managers of such departments might vary greatly in goals, time spans, and interpersonal orientation. Figuratively at least, they often "speak different languages." The process of attaining coordination across differentiated departments usually goes by the name of **integration**.[35] Good integration achieves coordination without reducing the differences

Integration. The process of attaining coordination across differentiated departments.

that enable each department to do its own job well.[36] For example, in a high-technology firm, we do not *want* production and engineering to be so cozy that innovative tension is lost.[37] Ideally, integration specifies who is accountable for what, enables one department to predict the activities of another, and creates a shared understanding of overarching goals.[38]

In ascending order of elaboration, three methods of achieving integration include the use of liaison roles, task forces, and full-time integrators.[39]

LIAISON ROLES   A **liaison role** is occupied by a person in one department who is assigned, as part of his or her job, to achieve coordination with another department. In other words, one person serves as a part-time link between two departments. Sometimes the second department might reciprocate by nominating its own liaison person. For example, in a university library, reference librarians might be required to serve as liaison people for certain academic departments or schools. In turn, an academic department might assign a faculty member to "touch base" with its liaison in the library. Sometimes, liaison people might actually be located physically in the corresponding department.

TASK FORCES AND TEAMS   When coordination problems arise that involve several departments simultaneously, liaison roles are not very effective. **Task forces** are temporary groups set up to solve coordination problems across several departments. Representatives from each department are included on a full-time or part-time basis, but when adequate integration is achieved, the task force is disbanded.

Self-managed and cross-functional teams (Chapter 7) are also an effective means of achieving coordination. Such teams require interaction among employees who might otherwise operate in an independent vacuum. Cross-functional teams are especially useful in achieving coordination for new-product development and introduction.

INTEGRATORS   **Integrators** are organizational members who are permanently installed between two departments that are in clear need of coordination. Integrators are especially useful for dealing with conflict between departments that (1) are highly interdependent, (2) have very diverse goals, and (3) operate in a very ambiguous environment. Such a situation occurs in many high-tech companies.[40] For example, a biotech firm might introduce new products almost every month. This is a real strain on the production department, which might need the assistance of the lab to implement a production run. The lab scientists, on the other hand, rely on production to implement last-minute changes because of the rapidly changing technology. This situation badly requires coordination.

Integrators usually report directly to the executive to whom the heads of the two departments report. Ideally, they are rewarded according to the success of both units. A special kind of person is required for this job, since he or she has great responsibility but no direct authority in either department. The integrator must be unbiased, "speak the language" of both departments, and rely heavily on expert power.[41] He or she should also identify strongly with the overall organization and its goals.[42] An engineer with excellent interpersonal skills might be an effective integrator for the biotech firm.

TRADITIONAL STRUCTURAL CHARACTERISTICS

Every organization is unique in the exact way that it divides and coordinates labour. However, management scholars and practising managers have agreed on a number of characteristics that summarize the structure of organizations.[43]

Span of Control

The **span of control** is the number of subordinates supervised by a manager. The larger the span, the less *potential* there is for coordination by direct supervision. As the span increases,

---

Liaison role. Role occupied by a person who is assigned to help achieve coordination between his or her department and another department.

Task forces. Temporary groups set up to solve coordination problems across several departments.

Integrators. Organizational members permanently assigned to facilitate coordination between departments.

LO 14.6

Discuss the nature and consequences of *traditional structural characteristics*, and explain the distinction between *organic* and *mechanistic* structures.

Span of control. The number of subordinates supervised by a manager.

the attention that a supervisor can devote to each subordinate decreases. When work tasks are routine, coordination of labour through standardization of work processes or output often substitutes for direct supervision. Thus, at lower levels in production units, it is not unusual to see spans of control ranging to more than 20. In the managerial ranks, tasks are less routine and adequate time is necessary for informal mutual adjustment. As a result, spans at the upper levels tend to be smaller. Also, at lower organizational levels, workers with only one or a few specialties report to a supervisor. For instance, an office supervisor might supervise only clerks. As we climb the hierarchy, workers with radically different specialties might report to the boss. For example, the president might have to deal with vice-presidents of human resources, finance, production, and marketing. Again, the complexity of this task dictates smaller spans.[44]

Flat versus Tall

Holding size constant, a **flat organization** has relatively few levels in its hierarchy of authority, while a **tall organization** has many levels. Thus, flatness versus tallness is an index of the vertical division of labour. Again, holding size constant, it should be obvious that flatness and tallness are associated with the average span of control. This is shown in Exhibit 14.11. Both schematized organizations have 31 members. However, the taller one has five hierarchical levels and an average span of two, while the flatter one has three levels and an average span of five. Flatter structures tend to push decision-making powers downward in the organization because a given number of decisions are apportioned among fewer levels. Also, flatter structures generally enhance vertical communication and coordination. The Danish toy company Lego flattened its manufacturing division from four levels of management to three levels composed of teams. In the process, the number of managers was reduced by 40 percent.[45]

Formalization

Formalization is the extent to which work roles are highly defined by the organization.[46] A very formalized organization tolerates little variability in the way members perform their

◄●─ **Simulate**

ORGANIZATIONAL STRUCTURE

Flat organization. An organization with relatively few levels in its hierarchy of authority.

Tall organization. An organization with relatively many levels in its hierarchy of authority.

Formalization. The extent to which work roles are highly defined by an organization.

EXHIBIT 14.11
The relationship between span of control and organizational flatness and tallness.

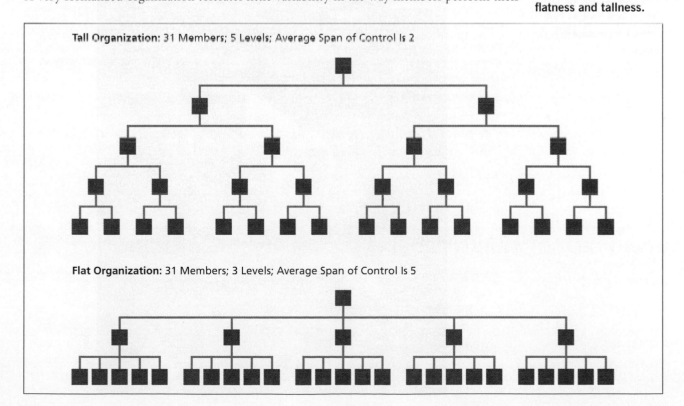

Tall Organization: 31 Members; 5 Levels; Average Span of Control Is 2

Flat Organization: 31 Members; 3 Levels; Average Span of Control Is 5

tasks. Some formalization stems from the nature of the jobs themselves; the work requirements of the assembly line provide a good example of this. More interesting, however, is
formalization that stems from rules, regulations, and procedures that the firm or institution
chooses to implement. Detailed, written job descriptions, thick procedure manuals, and
the requirement to "put everything in writing" are evidence of such formalization. At
McDonald's, strict standards dictate how customers are greeted, how burgers are cooked, and
how employees are dressed and groomed.

Very complex tasks dictate high formalization. In designing its 777 aircraft, Boeing
used information technology to manage the development and modification of thousands of
drawings and documents, thus coordinating the work of 5000 individuals at more than 20
locations.[47]

Sometimes, formalization seems excessive. Perhaps this is why so many fast-food
employees ignore the hairnet rule. A U.S. Department of Energy document detailing how to
change a light bulb in a radioactive area is 317 pages long and specifies duties for 43 people.[48]

Centralization

**Centralization. The
extent to which decision-
making power is localized
in a particular part of an
organization.**

Centralization is the extent to which decision-making power is localized in a particular
part of the organization. In the most centralized organization, the power for all key decisions
would rest in a single individual, such as the president. In a more decentralized organization,
decision-making power would be dispersed down through the hierarchy and across departments. Limitations to individual brainpower often prompt decentralization:

> *How can the Baghdad salesperson explain the nature of his clients to the Birmingham manager?
> Sometimes the information can be transmitted to one centre, but a lack of cognitive capacity
> (brainpower) precludes it from being comprehended there. How can the president of the conglom-
> erate corporation possibly learn about, say, 100 different product lines? Even if a report could be
> written on each, he would lack the time to study them all.*[49]

At Food Lion, buying is centralized, but local managers have
autonomy to stay close to
customers.

©Will McIntyre / Getty Images

Of course, the information-processing capacity of executives is not the only factor that dictates the degree of centralization. Some organizations consciously pursue a more participative climate through decentralization. In others, top management might wish to maintain greater control and opt for stronger centralization. One of founder Ray Kroc's innovations was not to permit *regional* franchises that could grow powerful and challenge the basic business principles of McDonald's.[50] The successful North Carolina–based supermarket chain Food Lion has generally decentralized with growth, giving local managers more autonomy to stay close to customers and cater to regional differences. However, the buying function and store design and construction have remained centralized to maintain efficiency and contain costs. Also, the lighting in all of its more than 1200 stores spanning 11 states is centralized via a computer system.[51]

Walmart and its French retail competitor Carrefour have pursued different degrees of centralization in their efforts to penetrate the Chinese market. Walmart has mostly replicated its extremely centralized U.S. structure. On the other hand, Carrefour has not centralized logistics and distribution, and it has granted much more autonomy to local store managers. The latter structure seems more appropriate for dealing with China's geographically fragmented and rapidly changing consumer demands.[52]

The proper degree of centralization should put decision-making power where the best *knowledge* is located. Often, this means decentralizing functions with direct customer contact, while centralizing functions that have a more internal orientation (e.g., information technology group). For an example of the pros and cons of centralization, see the Applied Focus: *Did BP's Organizational Structure Contribute to the Gulf Oil Spill?*

Complexity

Complexity is the extent to which organizations divide labour vertically, horizontally, and geographically.[53] A fairly simple organization will have few management levels (vertical division) and not many separate job titles (horizontal division). In addition, jobs will be grouped into a small number of departments, and work will be performed in only one physical location (geographic division). At the other extreme, a very complex organization will be tall, will have a large number of job titles and departments, and might be spread around the world. The essential characteristic of complexity is *variety*—as the organization becomes more complex, it has more kinds of people performing more kinds of tasks in more places, whether these places be departments or geographic territories.

Complexity. The extent to which an organization divides labour vertically, horizontally, and geographically.

Size and Structure[54]

In general, large organizations (measured by number of employees) are more complex than small organizations.[55] For example, a small organization is unlikely to have its own legal department or market research group, and these tasks will probably be contracted out. Economies of scale enable large organizations to perform these functions themselves, but with a consequent increase in the number of departments and job titles. In turn, this horizontal specialization often stimulates the need for additional complexity in the form of appointing integrators or creating planning departments. As horizontal specialization increases, management levels must be added (making the organization taller) so that spans of control do not get out of hand.[56]

Complexity means coordination problems, in spite of integrators, planning departments, and the like. This is where other structural characteristics come into play. In general, bigger organizations are less centralized than smaller organizations.[57] In a small company, the president might be involved in all but the least critical decisions. In a large company, the president would be overloaded with such decisions, and they could not be made in a timely manner. In addition, since the large organization will also be taller, top management is often too far removed from the action to make many operating decisions. How is control retained with decentralization? The answer is formalization—large organizations tend to be more

■ APPLIED FOCUS

DID BP'S ORGANIZATIONAL STRUCTURE CONTRIBUTE TO THE GULF OIL SPILL?

An organization that decentralized with some apparent success was the energy giant British Petroleum (BP). Over the years, the firm became so tall and bureaucratic that both its exploration and production functions suffered from slow, ponderous decision making and a lack of the kind of entrepreneurial spirit that the smaller energy companies had. BP was thus redesigned to allocate these functions into about 20 "assets," smaller business units, such as a single oil field. The managers of these assets were accorded much freedom as long as they met performance targets. Since some centralized forces for information sharing and integration were removed with this design, these managers formed small peer groups to share ideas and help each other solve problems.

Although decentralization can facilitate speed and flexibility, it can also damage coordination and remove important oversight. And this can contribute to disaster. In 2010, an explosion on the BP oil rig Deepwater Horizon killed 11 workers and led to the largest oil spill in history. For three months, unprecedented volumes of crude oil gushed into the waters of the Gulf of Mexico, devastating sea life and severely damaging the fishing and tourism industries. Jeffrey Stamps and Jessica Lipnack argued that this ecological disaster occurred in part due to a flat, decentralized organizational structure that was inappropriate for managing the complexity of safely finding and extracting oil from the depths of the seabed. They pointed to conflict and confusion about staunching the oil blowout, getting the cleanup underway, and facilitating claims for damages

as evidence of a lack of coordinated oversight. In similar fashion, a U.S. Department of the Interior report concluded that local business units were responsible for implementing their own operating systems and that this led to localized, idiosyncratic, and inadequate risk management procedures.

Did BP's decentralized design contribute to the Gulf oil disaster?

Sources: Fairtlough, G., & Beckham, R. (2009). Organizational design. In S.R. Clegg & C.L. Cooper (Eds.), *The Sage handbook of organizational behavior* (Vol. 2). London: Sage; Roberts, J. (2004). *The modern firm: Organizational design for growth and performance*. Oxford: Oxford University Press; Stamps, J., & Lipnack, J. (2010, June 23). Why BP crashed and killed the Gulf. *HBR Blog Network*, http://blogs.hbr.org/cs/2010/06/why_bp_crashed_and_killed_the.html; U.S. Department of the Interior. (2011, September 14). *Report regarding the causes of the April 20, 2010 Macondo well blowout.*

formal than small organizations. Rules, regulations, and standard procedures help to ensure that decentralized decisions fall within accepted boundaries.

You will recall that product departmentation is often preferable to functional departmentation as the organization increases in size. Logically, then, organizations with product departmentation should exhibit more complexity and more decentralization than those with functional departmentation. A careful comparison of Exhibits 14.6 and 14.7 will confirm this logic. In the firm structured by product, research, production, and marketing are duplicated, increasing complexity. In addition, since each product line is essentially self-contained, decisions can be made at a lower organizational level.

SUMMARIZING STRUCTURE —ORGANIC VERSUS MECHANISTIC

Do the various structural characteristics that we have been reviewing have any natural relationship to one another? Is there any way to summarize how they tend to go together?

In general, the classical organizational theorists tended to favour **mechanistic structures**.[58] As Exhibit 14.12 demonstrates, these structures tend toward tallness, narrow spans of control, specialization, high centralization, and high formalization. The other structural and human resources aspects in the exhibit complement these basic structural prescriptions. By analogy, the organization is structured as a mechanical device, each part serving a separate function, each part closely coordinated with the others. Speaking generally, functional structures tend to be rather mechanistic.

We can contrast mechanistic structures with organic structures. As shown in Exhibit 14.6, **organic structures** tend to favour wider spans of control, fewer authority levels, less specialization, less formalization, and decentralization. Flexibility and informal communication are favoured over rigidity and the strict chain of command. Thus, organic structures are more in line with the dictates of the human relations movement. Speaking generally, the matrix form is organic.

The labels *mechanistic* and *organic* represent theoretical extremes, and structures can and do fall between these extremes. But is one of these structures superior to the other? To answer this, pause for a moment and consider the structures of a fast-food restaurant chain like McDonald's and the structure of W.L. Gore & Associates, Inc. At the restaurant level, McDonald's is structured very mechanistically. This structure makes perfect sense for the rather routine task of delivering basic convenience food to thousands of people every day and doing it with uniform quality and speed. Of course, McDonald's headquarters, which deals with less routine tasks (e.g., product development, strategic planning), would be more organically structured. W.L. Gore & Associates, Inc. develops and manufactures products that are highly dependent on fast-changing high technology. Although its GORE-TEX brand breathable waterproof fabric is likely most familiar to you, the company also produces a wide range of medical and environmental products. Gore limits its plants to 200 people and retains a very flat structure to stimulate communication and innovation. New ideas spin off new business units. Its founder also despised bureaucracy.[59] An organic structure suits Gore perfectly.

There is no "one best way" to organize. In general, more mechanistic structures are called for when an organization's external environment is more stable and its technology is more routine. Organic structures work better when the environment is uncertain, the technology is less routine, and innovation is important.[60] Many organizations do not have only a single structure, and structure can and should change over time. Innovation (which we will study in detail in Chapter 15) is one factor that often dictates multiple structures, as we will see in the following section.

Mechanistic structures.
Organizational structures characterized by tallness, specialization, centralization, and formalization.

Organic structures.
Organizational structures characterized by flatness, low specialization, low formalization, and decentralization.

EXHIBIT 14.12
Mechanistic and organic structures.
Source: From Seiler, J.A. (1967). *Systems analysis in organizational behavior.* Homewood, IL: Irvin, p. 168. This exhibit is an adaptation of one prepared by Paul T. Lawrence and Jay W. Lorsch in an unpublished "Working Paper on Scientific Transfer and Organizational Structure," 1963. The latter, in turn, draws heavily on criteria suggested by W. Evans (1963). "Indices of hierarchical structure of industrial organizations." *Management Science, 9,* 468–477, Burns and Stalker, op cit., and Woodward, op cit., as well as those suggested by R.H. Hall (1962). "Intraorganizational structure variables." *Administrative Science Quarterly, 9,* 295–308.

Organizational Characteristics	Types of Organization Structure	
Index	**Organic**	**Mechanistic**
Span of control	Wide	Narrow
Number of levels of authority	Few	Many
Ratio of administrative to production personnel	High	Low
Range of time span over which an employee can commit resources	Long	Short
Degree of centralization in decision making	Low	High
Proportion of persons in one unit having opportunity to interact with persons in other units	High	Low
Quantity of formal rules	Low	High
Specificity of job goals	Low	High
Specificity of required activities	Low	High
Content of communications	Advice and information	Instructions and decisions
Range of compensation	Narrow	Wide
Range of skill levels	Narrow	Wide
Knowledge-based authority	High	Low
Position-based authority	Low	High

LO

Discuss the emergence of *ambidextrous*, *network*, *virtual*, and *modular* organizations.

CONTEMPORARY ORGANIC STRUCTURES

Recent years have seen the advent of new, more organic organizational structures.[61] Global competition and deregulation, as well as advances in technology and communications, have motivated the creation of these structures. Typically, the removal of unnecessary bureaucracy and the decentralization of decision making result in a more adaptable organization. In this section, we will examine some contemporary organic organizational structures. But first, consider You Be the Manager: *Zappos New Organizational Structure*.

The Ambidextrous Organization

Ambidextrous organization. An organization that can simultaneously exploit current competencies and explore emerging opportunities.

An **ambidextrous organization** is one that can simultaneously exploit current competencies and explore emerging opportunities.[62] The word *ambidextrous* means equally capable of using both hands, and the ideal ambidextrous organization is *partly* organic in form. On the other hand, it also exhibits more mechanistic characteristics. The need for ambidexterity stems from an age-old dilemma: how to pursue the core business while engaging in radical innovation. There is an essential tension between getting the most out of existing technology and the bread-and-butter products or services being offered (the firm's current competencies) and at the same time searching for new opportunities and innovating. This distinction is sometimes described as *exploiting* versus *exploring*. The tension between these two strategies stems from the fact that both require organizational resources, most of which are being generated by exploitation. It also stems from the fact that exploiting is a more certain activity, but one with diminishing returns, while exploring is a highly uncertain activity but has the potential to unlock fabulous opportunities for renewal. The question then becomes how to manage this essential tension, and it is generally conceded that proper structuring is part of the solution. This solution is important, because ambidexterity is hard to accomplish and thus rare and difficult to imitate, providing a distinct source of competitive advantage.[63] Indeed, ambidexterity has been associated with superior innovation, better financial performance, and longer survival, because it provides a dynamic capability for change.[64]

Two firms noted for their ambidexterity are Apple and Singapore Airlines.[65] Apple consistently manages to excel in innovation and design while achieving extreme efficiency and low costs. Singapore Airlines is also a cost leader among airlines, while offering service innovations and personalized customer interactions.

There is general agreement among experts that exploration and its quest for innovation require a more organic structure, while exploitation—extracting value from existing competencies—requires a more mechanistic approach. This means that ambidexterity provides great pressure for differentiation, clearly separating the creation of new ideas from the fine-tuning of established ideas. We have seen that differentiation in turn requires special attention to integration. This is particularly true in the case of ambidexterity because of the need to have *synergy* between exploitation and exploration while protecting the exploratory unit from creeping bureaucracy.

Charles O'Reilly and Michael Tushman studied how well-established organizations were structured to support radical innovation, the ultimate test of ambidexterity.[66] Some firms tried to innovate using regular functional structures. Others set up completely separate innovation units, the ultimate in differentiation. Some used cross-functional teams within an existing structure. However, the most successful structure for achieving ambidexterity was one in which an innovative unit maintained its own culture, structure, and processes but was integrated with the core of the firm by existing senior management. This structure provided resources and protection for the innovative unit and allowed established units to perfect their own business. This suggests that, with proper structure, exploitation and exploration are complementary rather than contradictory.[67]

O'Reilly and Tushman cite *USA Today* as an example of an organization that made a successful transition to ambidexterity, integrating traditional printed news with the burgeoning but uncertain internet news business. A false start positioned USAToday.com as a completely

YOU BE THE MANAGER

Zappos New Organizational Structure

Zappos is an online shoe retailer that was founded in by Nick Swinmurn in 1999. His plan was to create a website to offer the best selection of shoes and the best customer service. By 2003, gross merchandise sales had grown to $70 million up from $1.6 in 2000 and reached $1 billion in 2008.

In 2009, Zappos was purchased by Amazon.com for about $1.2 billion. It operates as an autonomous subsidiary and has become one of the largest online shoe retailers in the world. Zappos has grown so much that in 2010 it was restructured into ten separate companies and now sells a wide assortment of clothing, housewares, cosmetics, and other items in addition to shoes.

In 2014, Zappos made another change to its organizational structure following a six-month pilot project. Gone is the traditional hierarchical organizational structure. The new structure will not have any managers or job titles, and instead employees will decide how to perform their jobs. They will work in circles and will often have multiple roles and responsibilities, which will give them more autonomy.

Zappos CEO Tony Hsieh said that the change was critical to ensure that bureaucracy does not stifle growth. In a four-hour meeting about the change he told employees, "Darwin said that it's not the fastest or strongest that survive. It's the ones most adaptive to change."

Zappos's new organizational structure is known as Holacracy which comes from the word *holarchy*. Holarchy refers to organizing units that combine to form a larger organization. There are about 300 organizations that have adopted a Holacracy structure, and Zappos is the largest and most well-known.

The Holacracy structure was developed by Brian Robertson, who says, "It's not about throwing out managers. Managers provide important functions such as alignment, accountability, results. It's about replacing that with a more effective way of getting those functions met.... We're changing how power works and how people influence each other."

The basic idea behind a Holacracy is that people are accountable for their work and everyone should feel comfortable enough to speak up. Work teams are replaced by circles that employees can start or join based on the type of work they want to do. Each circle has a "lead link" which is like a project manager but has limited authority. The members of a circle decide on their tasks, roles, and responsibilities in "governance meetings" and they track their progress in "tactical" meetings. Employees have an opportunity to speak up and say what is on their minds at these meetings.

Zappos which has a ball pit at its headquarters in Las Vegas, recently adopted a new organizational structure that is known as a Holacracy.

To date, there are more than 300 circles at Zappos in areas such as customer service, social media, and Holacracy implementation. The plan is to have all of its 1500 employees in 400 circles by the end of the year.

Changes in organizational structure are often made when an organization is struggling and attempting a turnaround, such as the change made by McDonald's described in the chapter-opening vignette. This, however, is not the case with Zappos, which has been thriving. So why make such a change? And what effect will it have on employees and the organization? You be the manager.

Questions

1. What do you think of Zappos's new organizational structure? What effect do you think it will have on employees and the organization?

2. Do you think other organizations should adopt a Holacracy? Why or why not? Explain your answer.

To find out more, consult The Manager's Notebook at the end of the chapter.

Sources: Lu, V. (2014, January 21). Zappos to toss out manager roles, *Toronto Star*, B1, B7; Sherman, L. (2015, April 14). Inside the Zappos Holacracy, *The Business of Fashion*, http://www.businessoffashion.com/articles/intelligence/inside-the-zappos-holacracy; Hsieh, T. (2010, July-August). Zappo's CEO on going to extremes for customers. *Harvard Business Review, 88(7/8)*, 41-45; Silverman, R. E. (2015, May 21). At Zappos, banishing the bosses brings confusion, *Wall Street Journal (Online)*, http://www.wsj.com/articles/at-zappos-banishing-the-bosses-brings-confusion-1432175402; Helmore, E. (2015, May 30). Bring back the boss class, say employees fed up with self-ruling 'holacracy.' *The Guardian*, http://www.theguardian.com/business/2015/may/30/bring-back-boss-class-holacracy-zappos; Greenfield, R. (2015, April 3). Holawhat? Meet the alt-management system invented by a programmer and used by Zappos. *Fastcompany*, http://www.fastcompany.com/3044352/the-secrets-of-holacracy; *About Zappos, The Zappos family story: In the beginning – Let there be shoes*, www.zappos.com/d/about zappos.

independent operation from the print unit, so isolated that it could not capitalize on the newspaper's resources. Then the publisher reframed *USA Today* as a news *network* that would span paper, web, and TV coverage. This meant that a valuable resource, news content, would be shared, not hoarded (providing integration) but that each part of the news empire could use the content in its own way (maintaining differentiation).

As the *USA Today* story illustrates, innovations often require difficult decisions about existing structures and how to incorporate the innovation. A particular dilemma is the following: innovations entail a good deal of uncertainty, and more organic structures are best for dealing with uncertainty because of their capacity for adjustment. However, existing organizations are often structured more mechanistically to capitalize on the efficiencies of such a structure. Also, innovations have life cycles and organizational structures have to correspond to these cycles. Autonomy and differentiation are helpful for introducing innovations, but more integration leads to efficiency as the innovation becomes familiar.[68]

In theory, it makes sense for established firms to pursue ambidexterity by acquiring more innovative exploratory firms. However, research suggests that acquisitions are often assimilated for exploitation unless they are technologically unique and thus incompatible with the existing order.[69]

Network and Virtual Organizations

Network organization.
Liaisons between specialist organizations that rely strongly on market mechanisms for coordination.

In a **network organization**, various functions are coordinated as much by market mechanisms as by managers and formal lines of authority.[70] That is, emphasis is placed on who can do what most effectively and economically rather than on fixed ties dictated by an organizational chart. All the assets necessary to produce a finished product or service are present in the network as a whole, not held in house by one firm. Ideally, the network members cooperate, share information, and customize their services to meet the needs of the network. Indeed, diffusion of information and innovation are two important outcomes of network forms, especially when the partner firms are technologically diverse.[71] However, via resource synergies, networks can also facilitate exploitation of established assets.[72]

In stable networks, core firms that are departmentalized by function, product, or some other factor contract out some functions to favoured partners, so that they can concentrate on the things that they do best (see the left side of Exhibit 14.13). Chrysler, for instance, has its car seats supplied by an upstream firm that also does all the research associated with seating.

EXHIBIT 14.13
Types of network organizations.

Source: Copyright © 1992, by The Regents of the University of California. Reprinted from the *California Management Review*, Vol. *34*, No. 4. By permission of The University of California Press.

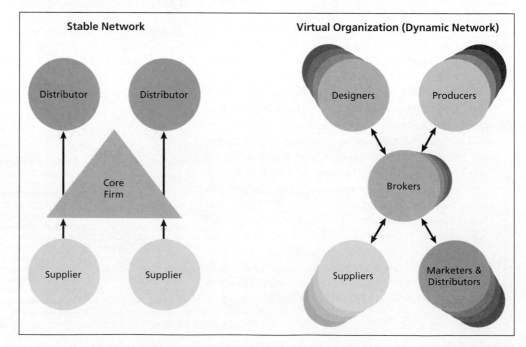

Particularly interesting networks are dynamic or virtual organizations, such as that illustrated on the right side of Exhibit 14.13. In a **virtual organization**, an alliance of independent companies shares skills, costs, and access to one another's markets. Thus, they consist of a network of continually evolving independent companies.[73] A "broker" firm with a good idea invents a network in which a large amount of the work is done by other network partners, who might change over time or projects. Each partner in a virtual organization contributes only in its area of core competencies. Contemporary book publishers are good examples. These firms do not employ authors, print books, or distribute books. Rather, they specialize in contracting authors for a particular project, providing developmental assistance, and marketing the final product. Printing, distribution, and some editorial and design work are handled by others in the network. Such networks are not new, as they have been used for years in the fashion and film industries. However, many firms in other industries, such as computers and biotechnology, now adopt network forms.

A familiar organization that is essentially virtual is Visa, which is at the centre of a network of thousands of financial institutions and many more retailers. Another organization with virtual properties is Google, which licenses its Android operating system at no charge to mobile phone companies and gives applications developers free access to related software. In turn, Google takes a cut of the revenues generated by thousands of applications.[74]

As indicated, a key advantage of the network form is its flexibility and adaptability. Networks also allow organizations to specialize in what they do best. In its network, Chrysler has intentionally positioned itself as a car manufacturer, not a car seat manufacturer. In turn, its supplier has a strong incentive to specialize in its product because Chrysler is a good customer.

The joint operation of specialization and flexibility can be seen in the video game industry.[75] Although there are some exceptions, the development of video games (e.g., *Minecraft*) and the design and sale of video game consoles (e.g., Xbox, PlayStation, and Wii) are done by separate, specialist organizations. In fact, there are hundreds of game developers (e.g., Ubisoft) and just a few console producers. Game developers make choices about which consoles their games can run on, thus establishing a network tie. Factors such as the age and market dominance of the console affect this choice. On their part, console designers such as Sony and Nintendo have to synchronize the timing of new products so as to cater to the needs of game designers and thus maintain and enlarge their networks.[76] Wireless gaming has led to even more complex networks, involving game developers, wireless carriers (e.g., Bell), handset makers (e.g., Samsung), platform providers (e.g., Oracle), and game publishers (e.g., Sega).[77]

Networking often breeds networking. Ubisoft, a French company, has a large and well-established game development studio in Montreal. Many of its veterans have started their own ventures, which then do business with Ubisoft. Such concentrations of talent, often supported by local universities and government subsidies, foster the advent of network organizations.[78]

Network and virtual organizations face some special problems.[79] Stable networks can deteriorate when the companies dealing with the core firm devote so much of their effort to this firm that they are isolated from normal market demands. This can make them "lazy," resulting in a loss of their technological edge. Virtual organizations lose their organic advantage when they become legalistic, secretive, and too binding of the other partners. On the other side of the coin, virtual partners sometimes exploit their loose structure to profit at the expense of the core firm. The computer industry has experienced both problems with its network arrangements. For instance, the main beneficiaries of the advent of the PC were Microsoft (the operating system supplier) and Intel (the microprocessor supplier), not IBM.[80]

The Modular Organization

Many organizations are realizing that there are advantages to not becoming a large and vertically integrated bureaucracy. Instead, they focus on a few core activities that they do best, such as designing and marketing computers, and let other companies perform all

Virtual organization.
A network of continually evolving independent organizations that share skills, costs, and access to one another's markets.

AP/John Froschauer

The video game industry uses networks extensively to develop and design games and gaming consoles.

Modular organization.
A network organization
that performs a few core
functions and outsources
other activities to specialists
and suppliers.

the other activities. A **modular organization** is a network organization that performs a few core functions and outsources other activities to specialists and suppliers. These core functions tend to focus on intellectual property, such as patents, brands, advertising, and distribution channels.[81] Services that are often outsourced include the manufacturing of parts, trucking, catering, data processing, and accounting. Thus, modular organizations are like hubs that are surrounded by networks of suppliers that can be added or removed as needed. And unlike a virtual organization, in which the participating firms give up part of their control and are interdependent, the modular organization maintains complete strategic control.[82]

By outsourcing non-core activities, modular organizations are able to keep unit costs low and develop new products more rapidly. It also allows them to use their capital in areas where they have a competitive advantage, such as design and marketing. This has enabled companies such as Dell Computer and Nike to experience large and rapid growth in a relatively short period of time, as they have not had to invest heavily in fixed assets. Nike and Reebok concentrate on designing and marketing high-tech fashionable sports and fitness footwear. Both organizations contract out production to suppliers in countries with low-cost labour.[83]

Modular organizations in the electronics industry buy their products already built, or they buy the parts from suppliers and then assemble them. Dell Computer, for example, assembles computers from outsourced parts, and this allows it to focus on marketing and service. Given this leanness, Dell can afford to invest in areas such as training salespeople and service technicians, although even most of its technicians are outsourced.[84] The automotive industry in North America is heavily involved in outsourcing and is thus increasingly modular. An increasing number of automakers are now outsourcing major parts of their vehicles (e.g., seats, doors) to parts suppliers like Magna in an effort to improve efficiency and quality. The practice is also apparent in Europe and Japan. For example, Toyota has achieved great success by relying on a network of suppliers.[85]

One familiar firm with modular network properties is Sweden's IKEA, the biggest furniture retailer in the world. IKEA restricts its own activities to inventing, distributing, and retailing its products. However, the company has 1300 suppliers who manufacture these products, 10 000 sub-suppliers (e.g., wood, coatings), and 500 logistical transportation partners. A key strength of IKEA is its skill in working with its suppliers to *develop* its products and to sustain efficiency in its operations.[86]

Although there are many advantages to the modular organization, there are also some disadvantages. Modular organizations work best when they focus on the right specialty and have good suppliers. Because they are dependent on so many outsiders, it is critical that they find suppliers who are reliable and loyal and can be trusted with trade secrets. Modular organizations also must be careful not to outsource critical technologies, which could diminish future competitive advantages.[87]

In summary, the modular organization is a streamlined structure with great flexibility, making it particularly well suited to rapidly changing environments. And although modular structures have been most popular in the trendy, fast-paced apparel and electronics industries, other industries, such as automotive, chemicals, and photographic equipment, are also becoming more modular.[88]

LO 14.8

Explain how *vertical integration, mergers* and *acquisitions, strategic alliances,* and the establishment of *legitimacy* reflect strategic responses.

Other Forms of Strategic Response

Changes in organizational structure are not the only strategic response that organizations can make. Structural variations often accompany other responses that are oriented toward coping with environmental uncertainty or resource dependence. Some forms of strategy implementation appear extremely routine, yet they might have a strong effect on the performance of the organization. For example, economic forecasting might be used to predict the demand for goods and services. In turn, formal planning might be employed to synchronize the organization's actions with the forecasts. All this is done to reduce uncertainty and to predict trends in resource availability. Lobbying and public relations are also common strategic responses. Simple negotiating and contracting are other forms of implementing strategy.

Some more elaborate forms of strategic response are worth a more detailed look and are discussed below. Notice how many of these concern relationships *between* organizations. The global automotive crisis resulted in dramatic changes and a restructuring of the industry, with a number of examples of strategic responses that involved relationships between organizations, such as mergers, acquisitions, and joint ventures.

VERTICAL INTEGRATION

Many managers live in fear of disruption on the input or output end of their organizations. A lack of raw materials to process or a snag in marketing products or services can threaten the very existence of the organization. One basic way to buffer the organization against such uncertainty over resource control is to use an inventory policy of stockpiling both inputs and outputs. For example, an automaker might stockpile needed parts in advance of an anticipated strike at a supplier. At the same time, it might have a 30-day supply of new cars in its distribution system at all times. Both inventories serve as environmental "shock absorbers." A natural extension of this logic is **vertical integration**, the strategy of formally taking control of sources of supply and distribution.[89] Major oil companies, for instance, are highly vertically integrated, handling their own exploration, drilling, transport, refining, retail sales, and credit. Starbucks, the Seattle-based chain of espresso bars, imports, roasts, and packages its own coffee and, in order to maintain high quality, refuses to franchise its bars.

Vertical integration. The strategy of formally taking control of sources of organizational supply and distribution.

MERGERS AND ACQUISITIONS

In the past decade, a number of very big Canadian mergers and acquisitions have taken place, such as the merger between Tim Hortons and Burger King. The new combined company became the third-largest fast-food company in the world.

Mergers of two firms and the **acquisition** of one firm by another have become increasingly common strategic responses in recent years. Some mergers and acquisitions are stimulated simply by economies of scale. For example, a motel chain with 100 motels might have the same advertising costs as one with 50 motels. Other mergers and acquisitions are pursued for purposes of vertical integration. For instance, a paper manufacturer might purchase a timber company. Similarly, Oracle Corp., the world's largest business software company, acquired Sun Microsystems Inc., which sells high-end servers and key software technologies. The acquisition allows Oracle to offer one-stop shopping for all the hardware and software required for complex corporate networks, thereby joining the ranks of IBM, Hewlett-Packard, Dell, and Cisco.[90]

Merger. The joining together of two organizations.

Acquisition. The purchase of one organization by another.

When mergers and acquisitions occur within the *same* industry such as the one between Tim Hortons and Burger King, they are being effected partly to reduce the uncertainty prompted by competition. When they occur across *different* industries (a diversification strategy), the goal is often to reduce resource dependence on a particular segment of the environment. A portfolio is created so that if resources become threatened in one part of the environment, the organization can still prosper.[91] This was one motive for Philip Morris to take over food companies such as Kraft; anti-smoking sentiments and legislation have provided much uncertainty for the firm's core cigarette business.

STRATEGIC ALLIANCES

We have all heard about bad blood following a merger or acquisition, especially after a hostile takeover. This failure of cultures to integrate smoothly (Chapter 8) is only one reason that mergers that look good from a financial point of view often end up as operational disasters. Is there any way to have the benefits of matrimony

© David Anderson

Strategic alliances.
Actively cooperative
relationships between legally
separate organizations.

without the attendant risks? Increasingly, the answer seems to be **strategic alliances**—that is, actively cooperative relationships between legally separate organizations. The organizations in question retain their own cultures, but true cooperation replaces distrust, competition, or conflict for the project at hand. Properly designed, such alliances reduce risk and uncertainty for all parties and recognize resource *interdependence*. The network organization we discussed earlier in the chapter is one form of strategic alliance.

Organizations can engage in strategic alliances with competitors, suppliers, customers, and unions.[92] Among competitors, one common alliance is a research and development consortium in which companies band together to support basic research that is relevant for their products. For example, several Canadian producers of audio speakers formed a consortium under the National Research Council to perfect the technology for "smart speakers" that adjust automatically to room configuration. Another common alliance between competitors is the joint venture, in which organizations combine complementary advantages for economic gain or new experience. In a **joint venture**, two or more organizations form an alliance in the creation of a new organizational entity. Organizations form joint ventures to create new products and services and, in the case of an international joint venture (IJV), to enter new and foreign markets.

Joint venture. Two or
more organizations form an
alliance in the creation of a
new organizational entity.

ESTABLISHING LEGITIMACY

It is something of a paradox that environmental uncertainty seems to increase the need to make correct organizational responses, but at the same time makes it harder to know which response is correct! One strategic response to this dilemma is to do things that make the organization appear *legitimate* to various constituents.[93] **Establishing legitimacy** involves taking actions that conform to prevailing norms and expectations. This will often be strategically correct, but equally important, it will have the *appearance* of being strategically correct. In turn, management will appear to be rational, and providers of resources will feel comfortable with the organization's actions.

Establishing legitimacy.
Taking actions that conform
to prevailing norms and
expectations.

How can legitimacy be achieved? One way is by associating with higher-status individuals or organizations. For example, an organization without much established status might put a high-status outsider on its board or form a strategic alliance with a more prestigious partner. Consider how WestJet first established its legitimacy:

In its formative year, the Calgary-based company had no direct experience in running an airline and it expected to be treated with skepticism by potential investors. To pre-empt this, it approached David Neeleman, former president of Morris Air, which had just been acquired by Dallas-based Southwest Airlines. Mr. Neeleman became one of WestJet's initial investors and joined its board of directors. In this way, WestJet was able to demonstrate that it had not just a business plan that copied Southwest's successful style but also an experienced entrepreneur on side, committed to the idea. WestJet took off. WestJet continues to pay attention to public legitimacy, or what its [former] CEO, Clive Beddoe, describes as "winning the hearts and minds of customers and employees."[94]

THE MANAGER'S NOTEBOOK

Zappos New Organizational Structure

1. In a Holacracy, there are no managers who oversee workers, and workers can decide for themselves what to do and speak their minds. This provides employees with a great deal of autonomy and empowers them to make decisions about their work. For some workers, the increased autonomy and lack of a manager is a welcome change. Still others prefer a more traditional organizational structure. At Zappos, 14 percent or 210 of its 1500 employees decided the change was not for them and quit. It was also reported that employees found the new structure confusing and time consuming, and it required long meetings to organize circles and learn about a Holacracy. Employees have also expressed concerns about how they will receive pay increases and advance in their careers if there are no managerial roles. Zappos CEO Tony Hsieh has said that Holacracy "takes time and a lot of trial and error" and that it can take three to five years to fully implement holacratic values. He believes that it empowers employees "to act more like entrepreneurs" and stokes faster "idea flow," collaboration and innovation. While this could help Zappos sell more merchandise, the company declines to comment on the financial impact it has had and does not disclose revenue or profits. Several reports have indicated that the transition at Zappos has not been smooth and that people are not happy about giving up their managerial titles. In a memo from Hsieh to Zappos employees, he confirmed Zappos's commitment to Holacracy and offered employees three months of severance if they preferred to quit.

2. Although some 300 hundred companies have adopted a Holacracy, its effectiveness will depend on a number of factors. For example, an organization's culture is very important. At Zappos, Hsieh has said that he is more interested in the Zappos culture than footwear. Zappos has ten core values that they live by such as, "Deliver WOW through service" and "Embrace and Drive Change." The core values of an organization's culture must support a Holacracy if it is to succeed. A Holacracy is consistent with Zappos's values, such as providing WOW service and driving change. A Holacracy is more likely to succeed in organizations whose cultures value employee autonomy and empowerment. At Zappos, employee independence has always been valued. In addition, a Holacracy might not be as effective for certain types of jobs and organizations where accountability and standardized working procedures are required (e.g., financial institutions). Some organizations have tried to implement a Holacracy but abandoned it, claiming it had led to too many meetings and vague decision-making authority. At Zappos, Hsieh has stated that it could take two to five years to complete the transition, and he isn't discouraged that 14 percent of employees have quit. He has also stated, "Like all the bold steps we've made in the past, it feels a little scary, but it also feels like exactly the type of thing that only a company such as Zappos would dare to attempt at this scale."

Another way to achieve legitimacy is to be seen as doing good deeds in the community. Thus, many companies engage in corporate philanthropy and various charity activities. A third way is to make very visible responses to social trends and legal legislation; many firms have appointed task forces and directors of workforce diversity or established official units to deal with employment equity guidelines. For example, the Bank of Montreal has an executive committee that oversees equity and diversity issues. Although such highly visible responses are not the only way to proceed with these matters, they do send obvious signals to external constituents that the organization is meeting social expectations. Probably the most common way of achieving legitimacy is to imitate management practices that other firms have institutionalized.

MyManagementLab Study, practise, and explore real management situations with these helpful resources:

- **Interactive Lesson Presentations:** Work through interactive presentations and assessments to test your knowledge of management concepts.
- **PIA (Personal Inventory Assessments):** Enhance your ability to connect with key concepts through these engaging, self-reflection assessments.
- **Study Plan:** Check your understanding of chapter concepts with self-study quizzes.
- **Videos:** Learn more about the management practices and strategies of real companies.
- **Simulations:** Practise decision-making in simulated management environments.

 PERSONAL INVENTORY ASSESSMENT

LEARNING OBJECTIVES CHECKLIST

14.1 Organizations are *open systems* that take inputs from the external environment, transform some of these inputs, and send them back into the environment as outputs. The *external environment* includes all the events and conditions surrounding the organization that influence this process. Major components of the environment include the economy, customers, suppliers, competitors, social/political factors, and existing technologies. *Environmental uncertainty* exists when an environment is vague, difficult to diagnose, and unpredictable. Uncertainty is a function of complexity and rate of change. *Resource dependence* refers to the dependency of organizations on environmental inputs, such as capital, raw materials, and human resources, and outputs such as customers. Organizations must develop strategies for managing environmental uncertainty and resource dependence for their survival and success.

14.2 *Strategy* is the process that executives use to cope with the constraints and opportunities posed

by the organization's environment, including uncertainty and scarce resources. One critical strategic response involves tailoring the organization's structure to suit the environment.

14.3 *Organizational structure* is the manner in which an organization divides its labour into specific tasks and achieves coordination among these tasks. Labour is divided vertically and horizontally. *Vertical division of labour* concerns the apportioning of authority. *Horizontal division of labour* involves designing jobs and grouping them into departments.

14.4 While *functional departmentation* locates employees with similar skills in the same department, other forms of departmentation locate employees in accordance with *product*, *geography*, or *customer requirements*.

14.5 Basic methods of coordinating divided labour include direct supervision, standardization of work processes, standardization of outputs, standardization of skills, and mutual adjustment. Workers are permitted more discretion as coordination moves from direct supervision through mutual adjustment. More elaborate methods of coordination are aimed specifically at achieving integration across departments. These include liaison roles, task forces, teams, and integrators.

14.6 *Traditional structural characteristics* include span of control, flatness versus tallness, formalization, centralization, and complexity. Larger organizations tend to be more complex, more formal, and less centralized than smaller organizations. The classical organizational theorists tended to favour *mechanistic organizational structures* (small spans, tall, formalized, and fairly centralized). More recent trends tend to favour *organic structures* (larger spans, flat, less formalized, and less centralized). However, there is no one best way to organize, and both mechanistic and organic structures have their places.

14.7 Traditional organizational structures are being replaced with more flexible structures that break down external and internal boundaries and facilitate innovation. *Ambidextrous organiza-*

tions simultaneously exploit current competencies and explore emerging opportunities. In a *network organization*, emphasis is placed on who can do what most effectively and economically rather than on fixed ties dictated by an organizational chart. In a *virtual organization*, an alliance of independent companies shares skills, costs, and access to one another's markets. In a *modular organization*, a network organization performs a few core functions and outsources other activities to specialists and suppliers.

14.8 Some of the more elaborate strategic responses include vertical integration, mergers and acquisitions, strategic alliances, and establishing legitimacy. Many of these involve relationships between organizations. *Vertical integration* involves taking control of sources of organizational supply and distribution; *mergers* and *acquisitions* involve two firms joining together or one taking over another; *strategic alliances* involve cooperative relationships between legally separate organizations; and *establishing legitimacy* involves taking actions that conform to prevailing norms and expectations.

DISCUSSION QUESTIONS

1. Construct a diagram of the various interest groups in the external environment of CBC Television. Discuss how some of these interest groups might make competing or contradictory demands on the CBC. Now do the same for your organization or the most recent organization you worked in.

2. Which basic method(s) of coordination is (are) most likely to be found in a pure research laboratory? On a football team? In a supermarket?

3. What are the relative merits of mechanistic versus organic structures?

4. As Spinelli Construction Company grew in size, its founder and president, Joe Spinelli, found that he was overloaded with decisions. What two basic structural changes should Spinelli make to rectify this situation without losing control of the company?

5. Explain why organizations operating in more uncertain environments require more organic structures.

INTEGRATIVE DISCUSSION QUESTIONS

1. Consider the effect of environmental uncertainty and resource dependence on power and politics in organizations. To what extent is subunit power and organizational politics a function of environmental uncertainty and resource dependence? Do environmental uncertainty and resource dependence predict and explain the dis-

tribution and use of power and politics in organizations?

2. How do the structural characteristics of organizations influence leadership, communication, decision making, and power in organizations? Discuss the implications of each of the structural characteristics (i.e., span of control, organization

levels, formalization, centralization, and complexity) for leadership behaviour, communication and decision-making processes, and the distribution and use of power in organizations.

3. Discuss the implications of mergers and acquisitions for organizational culture. In particular,

consider mergers and acquisitions in light of the assets and liabilities of strong cultures. How will culture influence the success or failure of mergers and acquisitions, and what can organizations do to increase the chances of success?

ON-THE-JOB CHALLENGE QUESTION

Span of Control at Google

Google, the internet innovator par excellence, relies less on top-down strategies and more on grassroots ideas for new products and services. These ideas are often developed in small project teams that have little supervision. In a typical organization, the span of control of a manager might range between 5 and 30 subordinates. However, according to consultant Gary Hamel, a single manager at Google professed to have 160 employees reporting to him!

What does this structural feature tell you about how work is organized at Google? How does a large span of control promote grassroots innovation?

Source: Based on Hamel, G. (2006, February). The why, what, and how of management innovation. *Harvard Business Review*, 72–84.

EXPERIENTIAL EXERCISE

Organizational Structure Preference Scale

In most organizations, there are differences of opinion and preferences as to how the organization should be structured and how people should conduct themselves. Following are a number of statements concerning these matters. The purpose of this survey is for you to learn about your own preferences regarding the structure of organizations. Please use the response scale below to indicate the extent to which you agree with each statement.

1–Disagree strongly

2–Disagree

3–Neither agree nor disagree

4–Agree

5–Agree strongly

_____ 1. I get most of my motivation to work from the job itself rather than from the rewards the company gives me for doing it.

_____ 2. I respect my supervisors for what they know rather than for the fact that the company has put them in charge.

_____ 3. I work best when things are exciting and filled with energy. I can feel the adrenalin rushing through me and I like it.

_____ 4. I like it best if we can play things by ear. Going by the book means you do not have any imagination.

_____ 5. People who seek security at work are boring. I don't go to work to plan my retirement.

_____ 6. I believe that planning should focus on the short term. Long-term planning is unrealistic. I want to see the results of my plan.

_____ 7. Don't give me a detailed job description. Just point me in the general direction and I will figure out what needs to be done.

_____ 8. I don't expect to be introduced to new people. If I like their looks, I'll introduce myself.

_____ 9. Goals should be set by everyone in the organization. I prefer to achieve my own goals rather than those of someone else.

_____ 10. One of the things I prefer most about a job is that it be full of surprises.

_____ 11. I like a job that is full of challenges.

_____ 12. Organization charts are only needed by people who are already lost.

_____ 13. Technology is constantly changing.

_____ 14. Supervision and control should be face to face.

_____ 15. If organizations focus on problem solving, the bottom line will take care of itself.

____ 16. I would never take a job that involved repetitive activities.

____ 17. Organizations are constantly in a state of change. I don't worry about how the players line up.

____ 18. Every decision I make is a new one. I don't look for precedents.

____ 19. When people talk about efficiency, I think they really don't want to do a good job.

____ 20. The people who know the most about the work should be put in charge.

Scoring and Interpretation

To calculate your organizational structure preference score, simply add up your responses to each of the 20 questions. Scores can range from 20 to 100. Your score on this survey indicates your preference for a mechanistic or organic organizational structure. A score of less than 50 indicates a preference for a mechanistic or formal organizational structure. Mechanistic structures tend to favour tallness, narrow spans of control, specialization, centralization, and formalization. Scores above 50 indicate a preference for a more organic or informal organizational structure. Organic structures tend to favour wider spans of control, fewer authority levels, less specialization, less formalization, and decentralization. Flexibility and informal communication are favoured over rigidity and the strict chain of command.

Source: Hoffman, R., & Ruemper, F. (1997). "Exercise 20: Mechanistic or Organic Organizational Design." In *Organizational behaviour: Canadian cases and exercises*, 3rd ed. Toronto: Captus Press Inc.), 298–299. Reprinted with permission of Captus Press Inc. www.captus.com.

CASE INCIDENT

Conway Manufacturing

Conway Manufacturing is a large organization that manufactures machine tools used by workers in various industries. In recent years, sales of the company's products have begun to fall as a result of increasing competition. Customers have also begun to complain about the quality of Conway's products. In response, Conway decided to design some new, high-quality products.

The research and development department was asked to develop some new designs for several of Conway's best-selling products. When the engineering department looked at the designs, they rejected them outright, saying that they were not very good. Engineering then revised the designs and sent them to the production department. However, the production department responded by sending them back to the engineering department, insisting that they would be impossible to produce. In the meantime, the marketing department had begun a campaign based on the material they had received from the research and development department. One year later, Conway was still no closer to producing new products. In the meantime, more customers were complaining and threatening to find new suppliers, and the competition continued to take more and more of Conway's business.

1. Describe the structure of Conway Manufacturing. What are some of the problems that Conway is having? Is organizational structure a factor?

2. What would be the most effective structure to design new, high-quality products in a short period of time? What are some methods for improving coordination?

CASE STUDY

Chris Peterson at DSS Consulting

Late Thursday afternoon, Chris Peterson was reflecting on the meeting she would have tomorrow with her boss, Meg Cooke. The purpose of the meeting was to give Meg an update on the status of the integrated budget and planning system her team had been working on over the past six months and plans for the team to begin marketing this system and other new DSS consulting services to clients.

Overall, Chris was quite pleased with the work her team had done. The team had been formed as part of a strategic change, including a somewhat controversial re-organization at DSS. The changes and new structure had created dissatisfaction and a fair amount of anxiety among many of DSS's consultants, but Chris felt her team had overcome their concerns to become a very effective group. They had worked together well, avoided the conflicts that often plague these kinds of teams, and generally maintained a high level of motivation and satisfaction. Most of all, Chris was proud of the work her team had done. They had created a budget and planning system that the team believed would be embraced by DSS's clients. The team had not gotten much support from other groups at DSS in developing the system, so team members had done much of the technical work on their own that would have normally been done by support people in the company. Despite this, Chris was very pleased with the system and looked forward to sharing her team's accomplishments with Meg.

DSS CONSULTING

DSS Consulting was formed in 1997 to provide administrative support to small school districts primarily in the mid-west and mountain west. The company was founded by three retired school district administrators to help small school districts that had limited staff deal with difficult and somewhat specialized administrative problems, such as negotiating labor agreements or setting up procurement systems.

During the late 1990s, DSS grew rapidly as small school districts faced more complex challenges and pressures to cut costs, particularly in administration. In response to this growth, DSS organized itself into four practice departments—Procurement and Systems, Information Technology, Contract Negotiation, and Facilities Planning—to deal with different types of engagements. Business came primarily through contacts the five founders had developed. Once DSS was engaged, the project would be referred to the head of the appropriate practice group who would assign consultants to the project.

By 2005, a number of changes had begun to affect DSS. First, the founders were cutting back their involvement in the company. As a result, management decisions were being passed on to new leaders, including people hired from other consulting companies. In addition, since much of DSS's business was generated through contacts established by the founders, their reduced involvement was creating a need for new marketing strategies. Second, the types of problems for which districts were looking for help were becoming more diverse and often didn't fit clearly into a specific practice area. The increasing complexities districts were facing were both reducing the need for the relatively straightforward projects DSS had been working on and creating demands for new types of services. Finally, state standards for school districts were diverging from one another, so that certain issues were more important in one region than in another. All of these changes led to stagnation in revenue growth for DSS.

Because of these changes, the founders decided that a shift in strategy would be necessary for DSS to continue to grow and be successful. As a first step, they promoted Meg Cooke to the position of Chief Operating Officer. Meg had joined DSS in the Contract Negotiation group about four years earlier after spending time with a larger east coast firm. Two years after joining DSS, she had been promoted to head the Contract Negotiation group. The founders and Meg had concluded that if DSS was to continue to be successful, it would need to expand beyond its traditional customer base of small districts and offer services to larger districts much more than it had in the past. They felt that accomplishing this would require developing new services and reorganizing into a more cross-functional, customer-focused organization. A major part of the strategic change involved reorganizing DSS from a purely practice-oriented functional structure to a hybrid structure. Most of the consultants would now be assigned to new cross-functional teams that would be responsible for marketing and delivering services to districts within a particular geographic region. The practice groups were maintained to provide specialized expertise to support the cross-functional teams in their work but with many fewer staff members than in the past.

The new cross-functional teams were given two responsibilities. Over the long run, the teams were to build relationships with the school districts in their regions and provide a full range of DSS consulting services to those districts. The teams were also to develop new consulting offerings in response to district needs. The expectations were that the cross-functional teams would eliminate the functional "silos" that constrained the services DSS could provide and help DSS develop services that could be sold to larger districts. Both these were seen as crucial steps in the plan to grow DSS.

CHRIS PETERSON AND THE SOUTHWEST REGION TEAM

Chris Peterson joined DSS in 2001. She had started her career as a high school teacher in a small school district in Iowa. When the district began to deploy personal computers, she was asked to head up the implementation in her school. The process went so smoothly that she was asked to give up classroom teaching and work full-time for the district in rolling out technology across all the schools. After five years in that job she joined DSS as a consultant in the Information Technology group. She rose to the position of project manager in the group and had been very successful in leading consulting projects. When the decision was made to reorganize into cross-functional teams, Chris was seen as a "natural" to lead one of the teams and was assigned to head the Southwest Region team.

Chris looked on her new assignment with a mixture of excitement and apprehension. Much of the excitement came from the opportunity to lead a permanent team rather than coordinate individuals for short consulting projects. Her apprehension came in large part because of some uncertainties about how the new strategy would unfold. Chris was aware that many people were ambivalent about the new strategy and uncertain about the necessity of the change and whether or not it was likely to be successful. The result of this was that there was a great deal of anxiety among many consultants about the future of DSS and their roles in the new structure. Chris also suspected that the strategy was still evolving and might change as management got a sense of how well the new organization was working.

One of the decisions that Meg had made about the new teams was that the team leaders ought to have a great deal of flexibility in inviting people to join their teams. Chris welcomed this opportunity. In thinking about who she wanted for the team, she considered two factors. First, she wanted people who had good skills and were experienced in the DSS consulting process. Second, she felt she needed people who would be able to work together well. She believed this would be important because of both the nature of the work to be done and her fear that the anxiety created by the change would boil over into dissatisfaction if people had trouble working together.

Chris gave a great deal of thought about who to ask to join the Southwest Region team. She decided that one thing that would help the group work together smoothly would be to select people who already had some experience in working with one another. Overall, Chris was quite happy with the team she was able to put together. She ended up asking two consultants each from Contract Negotiations, Procurement and Systems, and Information Technology, and one consultant from the Facilities group to join the team, all of whom accepted. Even though the consultants had not worked on specific projects with each other in the past, they knew one another and had a great deal in common. Nearly all of them had worked on DSS's annual Habitat for Humanity project, and all had started at DSS at about the same time. Many members of the group socialized with one another outside of work. At the first group meeting Chris realized that her strategy had worked well. Two of the consultants marveled about how nice it would be to work with people who were both very competent and friends as well. Another consultant mentioned that he didn't know many people at DSS other than the members of his new team and he was really looking forward to the project. Like most DSS consultants, members of Chris's new team had some questions about the new strategy and leadership; however, all believed that their new team had tremendous potential.

BEGINNING THE WORK

As DSS was making the transition to the new structure, consultants continued to finish existing projects even as they began working with their new teams. Chris believed it was very important that her team members be located together as soon as possible even though the team would not be working together full-time right away. She believed that co-locating the team would allow the group to get a quick start on the major deliverable of developing new products for DSS and prevent the group from getting distracted by some of the uncertainties created by the new structure. Chris was able to identify some space and a plan that could bring the full team together. Since none of the other new team managers felt as strongly about the co-location of their teams as Chris did, Meg allowed Chris's team to move together before the other teams did.

Once the team got settled into its new location, they quickly got to work. Chris believed that the first issue for the team would be to share their experiences and use their collective knowledge to identify one or more potential new products, and that her initial job would be to help the group pull together their experiences. The group had a number of meetings over the next month, discussing their perspectives. Chris was very pleased with what happened in the meetings. The team members seemed comfortable sharing information with one another. If a disagreement emerged, the team dealt with it without creating animosity or substantial delay. Chris was particularly pleased when two of the team members told her that this was one of the best groups they had ever been a part of.

Even though they were from different functional areas, the team members found that they had very similar experiences in dealing with districts. All of them had at least one story about how they had been delayed in a project because the people they were working with in the district were not able to get accurate data about budgets or long term plans. What emerged from the discussions was that small districts seemed to lack any integrated system for linking plans and budgets over time. The superintendent of the district seemed to be the only person who knew everything that was going on, and if he or she was not available it was difficult to get timely information. The team concluded that what small districts needed was an integrated system for planning and budgeting. Although most large districts had the systems or the human resources to do this, the costs were prohibitive for a small district. The team determined, therefore, that a scaled down system could provide the level of planning small districts needed at a price they could afford. Further, this project both excited the team and was something they felt they could do well.

PLANNING THE NEW PRODUCT

As members of the team began finishing the consulting projects they had been working on, they were able to devote more time to developing specifications for the new system. The majority of the team were now spending nearly all their time working with one another and saw less and less of the other consultants who were not on the team. Occasionally people would bring up what other consultants had said their teams were doing, but this seldom generated much interest and was sometimes seen as almost a distraction to the group. At this point in time, Chris had two primary goals for the team. First, she wanted to keep the group focused on the jobs of defining the new system and determining exactly how DSS consultants would use it. Second, she wanted to help the group avoid distractions and continue to build cohesion.

In addition to working with the team, Chris tried to deal with people outside the group. She had developed friendships with two superintendents in small districts, and when she saw them, she took the opportunity to describe the system her team was developing. Generally, the feedback she received was positive, and she relayed this to her team. Chris also met occasionally with Meg to update her on the project; however, these meetings were generally short. Chris observed that some of the other team leaders spent more time meeting with Meg than she did, but she didn't see that there was much need for her to do so, given the progress her team was making.

DEVELOPING THE PLANNING AND BUDGETING SYSTEM

Once the specific design of the proposed budget and planning system was complete, Chris felt it was time to share the work of the team with others. She took a detailed description of the program out to a number of districts she had worked with in the past and asked for comments. She also emailed the program description to Meg and some of the DSS functional specialists who would have to provide some technical support in developing the consulting protocols and specifying parts of the code for managing the data base.

The conversations with people in the districts were informative and more or less positive. While generally expressing support for the new system, people in the districts raised some specific questions. Many of the comments or questions were about how the system would deal with issues that were unique to a district. A few questions emerged about the price of the product and how it would differ from other products already on the market. When Chris took these comments back to the group they tried to modify the initial design and specifications of the program to meet the concerns that were raised. This worked well in the short run, but as more comments came in, the group began to flounder as the team tried to adapt the design to meet many of the questions from outsiders.

The reactions from others inside DSS were different from those in the districts. Most of the functional specialists who received descriptions of the project simply acknowledged receiving them but did not offer any real comments. Meg responded by asking a couple of questions and saying that she and Chris would talk more about it later. Overall, the group was pleased with these responses; no one had raised any objections to the program design or identified any difficulties that would slow the project down.

As the group worked to change the project specifications in response to the comments coming in from the districts, Chris felt that the effective process the group had developed was beginning to break down. There were disagreements about how important various comments actually were and progress in finalizing the specifications seemed to slow. Team members began to voice more concerns than they had in the past about the direction DSS was going and question whether the team would be able to accomplish its task. Chris decided that something needed to be done to get the group back on track. She cancelled work on the next Friday and had the whole team meet at a nearby nature preserve. After a hike, the group returned to Chris's house for a barbeque lunch. Following lunch, the members spent the rest of the afternoon discussing how they were performing and what they needed to do to finish designing the project. Overall, this seemed to work quite well. When the team got back to work on Monday, they quickly finalized the specifications and identified the steps that would be necessary to actually develop the product and consulting protocols.

The team turned its attention to completing the project. The project had four components: a database program provided by a third-party vendor, a program for putting information into the database program written by an outside consulting firm, a set of forms districts would use to organize information about schedules and budgets, and a set of instructions for consultants to use in helping districts use the program and its results. The team split into sub-groups to work on pieces of the final project.

Putting together the forms and developing instructions for consultants were the most challenging parts of the project. Both of these tasks required detailed knowledge about the different types of projects districts might undertake. Although members of the team had the knowledge and experience to complete most of this work, they often found that they needed to draw on the specialized knowledge of the DSS specialists in the practice groups. When a specific question came up that the team could not answer, one member of the Southwest team would either email a question or have a face-to-face meeting with the specialist. This worked well for simple issues but not for more complex problems. When team members tried to get functional specialists to spend time working on these more complex problems, they were often not given much help and were occasionally rebuffed. Chris found that she often had to go directly to the manager

of the practice area to try to get support. Even this didn't always work. One event typified the problem Chris was experiencing. She met with the head of Contract Negotiation to identify the specific information about a district's employees that would need to be entered into the program. He told Chris that he would ask one of his specialists to work on it with the team. When one member of Chris's team contacted the specialist, he was told that this project had not been built into her schedule and that she would not be able to help him until other things got done.

When Chris learned of this she scheduled a meeting with Meg to discuss the difficulty her team was having in getting support. From Chris's perspective, the meeting with Meg did not go particularly well. Meg seemed sympathetic to the difficulty Chris was having getting support and suggested that she could keep working with the practice group managers to get the final elements of the project completed. Chris had hoped that Meg would take more direct action. When Chris reported back to the team, the overall reaction by team members was negative. There were a number of comments about how decisions at DSS seemed to be more "political" under the new organization and how the "new Meg" seemed to be playing favorites.

FINISHING THE PROJECT

Despite the difficulty in getting support from others in the organization, Chris knew that the project was close to completion and could still be a success in the market. Chris conveyed this to her team. She reminded them that even if they were not getting the type of support they would like, they had the experience necessary to finish the program on their own. Chris's optimism was contagious. The team increased their efforts and did independent research to fill in their own knowledge gaps. The project came together quickly and within 10 days the team had a full product ready for beta testing. A few weeks earlier, Chris had recruited a district that would be willing to serve as a test site, and a date was scheduled for the team to go into the district to demonstrate the product.

THE MEETING WITH MEG COOKE

As Chris came into work on Friday morning, she thought back over the past few months and was quite pleased. The group had done a terrific job of specifying and developing a new product that was ready for a beta test. Initially her team members had had doubts about the new strategy and their new roles, but they had overcome those, and some real obstacles, to finish the assignment. Chris was looking forward to sharing this with Meg.

From Chris's perspective, the Friday morning meeting with Meg started off very well. Chris outlined the progress her team had made on the integrated budget and planning system. She spoke about how she was managing the beta test for the program and of the positive comments she was getting from the district. She also talked about how effective her team was. They worked together very well, were cohesive, and made decisions easily and quickly. Chris also mentioned that a number of the team members had not supported the reorganization at first but despite that had invested a great deal of effort in making the team and project work and were now committed to the new direction for DSS. In particular, Chris complimented the team members on their initiative in finishing the project even when they didn't have a great deal of help from the specialists in the practice groups.

Meg thanked Chris for all the hard work on the project and mentioned that she had heard very positive things about Chris's leadership from members of the Southwest Region team. Meg then shifted the conversation and asked Chris for a report about the types of services districts in her region might be looking for DSS to provide in the future and whether some of the other projects the DSS regional teams were working on would be of interest to the districts. Chris responded that she had a general idea of what the other teams had been working on but did not feel she had sufficient information to present them to districts at this time. She went on to say that her team had focused on their project and that the plan was for them to go out and meet with all districts in the region after the project was in a beta test so that they would have something specific to discuss. She reassured Meg that although she did not have a clear answer to the question right now, she would in the near future. Meg then asked Chris how she saw the integrated budget and planning system being marketed to large school districts, given that most of them already seemed to have either systems or personnel to do this. Chris responded that she understood the concern and that, at this point in time, large districts might not be interested in the system in its current form. She went to say that as the system was modified and expanded it would very likely be of interest to larger districts. After this, Chris and Meg exchanged a few pleasantries and the meeting ended.

THE MONDAY MORNING MEETING

When Chris arrived for work on Monday morning she found that she had a message from Meg asking if they could meet for coffee at 10:30. Chris was curious about the meeting but quickly responded that she would be available, and the two agreed to meet at a nearby coffee shop. After getting coffee and talking a bit about the weekend, Meg told Chris that after reviewing her team's project and its potential, she had decided that DSS would not go forward with the scheduling and budgeting project. When Chris asked for the reasons for this decision, Meg replied that the number of new products DSS could support was limited and that teams in the other regions had not reported any interest on the part of the districts they had worked with for this type of product. Meg also said that she was concerned that the project would not be of interest to the large districts. Chris responded that she certainly understood the issue about large districts but did not agree with Meg's observation. She went on to say that she did not understand how other regional teams could say that there would not be a demand for the product when they did not even know what the planning and scheduling system could do. Meg said that she appreciated Chris's concerns but that the decision to cancel the project was final.

An awkward silence followed this last exchange. After a moment or two, Meg said that there was one more thing left to discuss. She said that the Southwest Region Team would focus exclusively on marketing DSS products and not be involved in product development work in the future and that there would be some change to the composition of the team. Meg ended by asking Chris if she was prepared to lead the group in a new direction or if she would be more comfortable and successful returning to the IT practice group as a functional specialist.

Case titled "Chris Peterson at DSS Consulting" by Deborah Ancona and David Caldwell. Retrieved from https://mitsloan.mit.edu/LearningEdge/Leadership/DSSConsulting/Pages/default.aspx. Used by permission from MIT Sloan Management Review.

QUESTIONS

1. Describe the organizational structure of DSS Consulting in the late 1990s. What method of departmentation did they use, and why did they choose it?

2. Discuss the changes that began to affect DSS in 2005. Use the material in the chapter on the components of the external environment, interest groups, environmental uncertainty, and

resource dependence to explain how the environment was affecting DSS.

3. How did DSS Consulting respond to the changes in the environment? Use Exhibit 14.4 to explain their response. Do you think this was an appropriate response to the changes in the environment?

4. Discuss the new organizational structure in terms of the division and coordination of labour and departmentation. What are the pros and cons of the new organizational structure? What effect did the new organizational structure have on the Southwest Region team and its ability to successfully complete its project?

5. What effect do you think the new organizational structure had on the decision to cancel the Southwest Region's project? Explain your answer.

6. Do you think the outcome of the Southwest Region's project would have been more positive if a different organizational structure had been adopted? Is there anything else that might have prevented the cancellation of the project? Consider the potential effects of the different methods of coordinating divided labour. What might have saved the project?

15

ORGANIZATIONAL CHANGE, DEVELOPMENT, AND INNOVATION

LEARNING OBJECTIVES

After reading Chapter 15, you should be able to:

15.1 Explain the environmental forces that motivate organizational change, and describe the factors that organizations can change.

15.2 Explain how organizations learn and what makes an organization a *learning organization*.

15.3 Describe the basic *change process* and the issues that require attention at various stages of change.

15.4 Explain how organizations can deal with *resistance to change*.

15.5 Define *organizational development,* and discuss its general philosophy.

15.6 Discuss *team building, survey feedback, total quality management*, and *reengineering* as organizational development efforts.

15.7 Define *innovation*, and discuss the factors that contribute to successful organizational innovation.

15.8 Understand the factors that help and hurt the diffusion of innovations.

MICROSOFT'S STRUGGLE

In early 2015 what some thought was unthinkable happened—Apple's market capitalization, at $683 billion, more than doubled that of its competitor Microsoft. Although Microsoft had posted solid financial performance over the years, many industry observers attributed the disparity in performance between the two firms to Microsoft's inability to truly master the lucrative electronic consumer products market. The company that challenged IBM's mainframe dominance by putting a PC on every desk wasn't able to keep up with Apple's strategy of putting a smartphone in everyone's pocket. Although Microsoft consumer products such as the Xbox have been successful, its Windows Phone, Windows 8, and the early Surface tablets were less than well received. A *Vanity Fair* article by award-winning writer Kurt Eichenwald described then-CEO Steve Ballmer's reign as "Microsoft's lost decade." Reportedly, Ballmer had dismissed the best-selling Apple iPhone and iPad as inconsequential when they were introduced.

At the core of Microsoft's struggle has been the company's inability to identify important consumer trends and tolerate, let alone nurture, disruptive innovation. While Apple was happy to allow its iPhone to cannibalize the sales of its iPod, Microsoft exhibited a near-obsessive desire to retain the centrality of its Windows operating system and Office software suite, despite the need at hand, and it was slow to identify the core importance of mobile, touchscreen, and web-based technologies. In a telling example, the company's pioneering effort in ebooks was abandoned, reportedly because the user interface didn't have a Windows-like look. Although many insiders boast of the company's engineering-focused culture, this often clashes with consumer culture. Consumers want intuitive and easy-to-use products, while much Microsoft thinking is dominated by small business owners and IT specialists who are impressed by complex features and arcane technical performance data.

Despite its success, Microsoft needs more innovation.

© Agencja Fotograficzna Caro/Alamy Stock Photo

In addition to a rather insular engineering culture, Microsoft was known for meetings, red tape, and bureaucracy, all of which work against innovation. Furthermore, its brutal "stack ranking" performance review, held every six months, required managers to give negative reviews to those lowest ranked, even if they were actually good performers. This reportedly led to a severe lack of teamwork and to short-term political activity, rather than motivating attention to the longer-term big picture that can foster real innovation.

Following the publication of the *Vanity Fair* article, Microsoft abandoned the "stack-ranking review system, and Satya Nadella was named CEO in early 2014. Recent events suggest that Microsoft might be on an improved path. Both Windows 10 and its recent Surface tablets have been well received by the public. Time will tell if the company can make solid breakthroughs in mobile phone and computing technology and truly innovate for the future.[1]

This story reflects some key themes of our chapter. Although Microsoft has been a solid financial performer, it has been less successful in innovating and changing its culture to embrace the needs of the consumer market place. In this chapter we will discuss the concept of organizational change, including the whys and whats of change. Then we will consider the process by which change occurs and examine problems involved in managing change. Following this we will define organizational development and explore several development strategies as well as innovation, a special class of organizational change.

THE CONCEPT OF ORGANIZATIONAL CHANGE

LO 15.1

Explain the environmental forces that motivate organizational change, and describe the factors that organizations can change.

Common experience indicates that organizations are far from static. Our favourite small restaurant experiences success and expands. We return for a visit to our alma mater and observe a variety of new programs and new buildings. Toyota starts building trucks in Texas. As consumers, we are aware that such changes may have a profound impact on our satisfaction with the product or service offered. By extension, we can also imagine that these changes have a strong impact on the people who work at the organizations in question. In and of themselves, such changes are neither good nor bad. Rather, it is the way in which the changes are *implemented* and *managed* that is crucial to both customers and members. This is the focus of the present chapter.

Why Organizations Must Change

All organizations face two basic sources of pressure to change—external sources and internal sources.

In Chapter 14, we pointed out that organizations are open systems that take inputs from the environment, transform some of these inputs, and send them back into the environment as outputs. Organizations work hard to stabilize their inputs and outputs. For example, a manufacturing firm might use a variety of suppliers to avoid a shortage of raw materials and attempt to turn out quality products to ensure demand. However, there are limits on the extent to which such control over the environment can occur. In this case, environmental changes must be matched by organizational changes if the organization is to remain effective. For example, consider the successful producer of record turntables in 1970. In only a few years, the turntable market virtually disappeared with the advent of reasonably priced cassette and CD players. Now, downloaded music is commonplace.

Probably the best recent example of the impact of the external environment in stimulating organizational change is the increased competitiveness of business. Brought on, in part, by a more global economy, deregulation, and advanced technology, this competitiveness has forced businesses to become, as the cliché goes, leaner and meaner. Many firms have laid off thousands of employees and done away with layers of middle managers, developing flatter structures that are more responsive to competitive demands. Mergers, acquisitions, and joint ventures with foreign firms have become commonplace, as have less adversarial relationships with unions and suppliers.

Change can also be provoked by forces in the internal environment of the organization. Low productivity, conflict, strikes, sabotage, and high absenteeism and turnover are some of the factors that signal that change is necessary. Employee opinion can also be a force for change. For example, a number of Microsoft employees publish online blogs, some of which are critical of the firm's business strategy.[2] Very often, internal forces for change occur in response to organizational changes that are designed to deal with the external environment. Thus, many mergers and acquisitions that were to bolster the competitiveness of an organization have been followed by cultural conflict between the merged parties.

A word should be said about the perception of threat and change. Sometimes, when threat is perceived, organizations "unfreeze" (see below), scan the environment for solutions,

PERSONAL INVENTORY ASSESSMENT

Learn About Yourself
Comfort with Change Scale

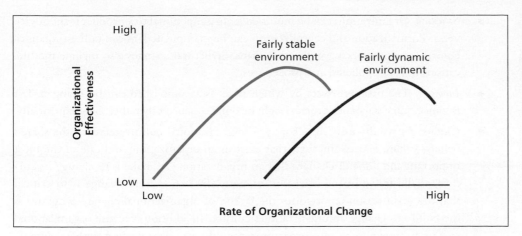

EXHIBIT 15.1
Relationships among environmental change, organizational change, and organizational effectiveness.

and use the threat as a motivator for change. Other times, though, organizations seem paralyzed by threat, behave rigidly, and exhibit extreme inertia. Change almost always entails some investment of resources, be it money or management time. Also, it almost always requires some modification of routines and processes.[3] If either of these prerequisites is missing, inertia will occur. For example, one of your authors observed a university program threatened by low enrolment. The involved faculty spent many hours ostensibly revising the curriculum. However, the revised curriculum looked much like the old curriculum. Here, resources were invested, but the routines of teaching were not modified to counter the threat.

In spite of trends toward change, the internal and external environments of various organizations will be more or less dynamic. In responding to this, organizations should differ in the amount of change they display. Exhibit 15.1 shows that organizations in a dynamic environment must generally show more change to be effective than those operating in a more stable environment. Also, change is in and of itself not a good thing, and organizations can exhibit too much change as well as too little. The company that is in constant flux fails to establish the regular patterns of organizational behaviour that are necessary for effectiveness, and employees become cynical.

Despite the importance of change, an IBM study, *Making Change Work*, found that most CEOs saw their organizations as being poor at executing change. Project leaders responsible for changes reported only a 41 percent success rate. The majority reported budget, quality, or time problems, and 15 percent of projects were complete failures.[4]

What Organizations Can Change

Since *change* is a broad concept, it is useful to identify several specific domains in which modifications can occur. Of course, the choice of what to change depends on a well-informed analysis of the internal and external forces signalling that change is necessary.[5] Factors that can be changed include

- *Goals and strategies.* Organizations frequently change their goals and the strategies they use to reach these goals. Expansion, the introduction of new products, and the pursuit of new markets represent such changes. Electronics giant Samsung changed its strategy from producing low-cost, imitative products to pursuing quality, collaboration, and innovation. Over the years, Microsoft's strategy has been reinvented several times to cope with changes in its external environment.

- *Technology.* Technological changes can vary from minor to major. The introduction of online portal access for employees is a fairly minor change. Moving from a rigid assembly line to flexible manufacturing is a major change.

- *Job design.* Companies can redesign individual groups of jobs to offer more or less variety, autonomy, identity, significance, and feedback, as we discussed in Chapter 6.

- *Structure.* Organizations can be modified from a functional to a product form or vice versa. Formalization and centralization can be manipulated, as can tallness, spans of control, and networking with other firms. Structural changes also include modifications in rules, policies, and procedures.

- *Processes.* The basic processes by which work is accomplished can be changed. For instance, some stages of a project might be done concurrently rather than sequentially.

- *Culture.* As we discussed in Chapter 8, organizational culture refers to the shared beliefs, values, and assumptions that exist in an organization, and one of the most important and difficult changes that an organization can make is to change its culture, as illustrated in the Microsoft vignette. In fact, culture change is so critical that the main reason reported for the failure of organizational change programs is the failure to change an organization's culture. In addition, because organizational culture is known to be a major factor in providing an organization with a competitive advantage and long-term effectiveness, changing an organization's culture is considered to be a fundamental aspect of organizational change.[6]

- *People.* The membership of an organization can be changed in two senses. First, the actual *content* of the membership can be changed through a revised hiring process. This is often done to introduce "new blood" or to take advantage of the opportunities that a more diverse labour pool offers. Second, the existing membership can be changed in terms of skills and attitudes by various training and development methods.

Two important points should be made about the various areas in which organizations can introduce change. First, a change in one area very often calls for changes in others. Failure to recognize this systemic nature of change can lead to severe problems. For example, consider the functionally organized East Coast chemical firm that decides to expand its operations to the West Coast. To be effective, this goal and strategy change might require some major structural changes, including a more geographic form and decentralization of decision-making power.

Second, changes in goals, strategies, technology, structure, process, job design, and culture almost always require that organizations give serious attention to people changes. As much as possible, necessary skills and favourable attitudes should be fostered *before* these changes are introduced. For example, although providing bank employees with a revised IT system is a fairly minor technological change, it might provoke anxiety on the part of those whose jobs are affected. Adequate technical training and clear, open communication about the change can do much to alleviate this anxiety.

The Change Process

By definition, change involves a sequence of events or a psychological process that occurs over time. The distinguished psychologist Kurt Lewin suggested that this sequence or process involves three basic stages—unfreezing, changing, and refreezing.[7]

Unfreezing. The recognition that some current state of affairs is unsatisfactory.

UNFREEZING **Unfreezing** occurs when it is recognized that some current state of affairs is unsatisfactory. This might involve the realization that the present structure, task design, or technology is ineffective, or that member skills or attitudes are inappropriate. Crises are especially likely to stimulate unfreezing. A dramatic drop in sales, a big lawsuit, or an unexpected strike are examples of such crises. Samsung's former chairperson, dismayed by product quality, burned 150 000 phones and fax machines in a giant bonfire, a dramatic unfreezing ploy meant to signal crisis. The leaked video "What if Microsoft made the iPod?" was meant to have a similar effect. Of course, unfreezing can also occur without crisis. Employee attitude surveys, customer surveys, and accounting data are often used to anticipate problems and to initiate change before crises are reached.

CHANGE Change occurs when some program or plan is implemented to move the organization or its members to a more satisfactory state. Change efforts can range from minor to major. A simple skills training program and a revised hiring procedure constitute fairly minor changes, in which few organizational members are involved. Conversely, major changes that involve many members might include extensive job enrichment, radical restructuring, or serious attempts at empowering the workforce.

In order for change to occur, people must have the capability *and* the opportunity *and* the motivation to change. In other words, some degree of all three factors must be present for successful change.[8] For example, suppose top management envisions a cultural change to make a traditional firm more innovative and entrepreneurial. This might suggest creativity training to enhance the capability of key employees. Also, opportunities for innovation must be presented to employees. For example, idea fairs and design competitions might be instituted to signal openness to new ideas. Finally, for motivation, incentive systems should be aligned to reward innovative ideas and avoid punishment for the inevitable failures that accompany innovation.

REFREEZING When changes occur, the newly developed behaviours, attitudes, or structures must be subjected to **refreezing**—that is, they must become an enduring part of the organization. At this point, the effectiveness of the change can be examined, and the desirability of extending the change further can be considered. It should be emphasized that refreezing is a relative and temporary state of affairs, as future changes may surely be required.

In recent years, there has been much debate about whether Lewin's simple model of change, especially the refreezing component, applies to firms in so-called hyperturbulent environments, where constant, unpredictable, non-linear change is the norm.[9] Although this turbulence clearly applies to the software, nanotechnology, and biotechnology industries, it can also be seen in a less extreme form in consumer electronics, as the Microsoft story illustrates. While the model probably applies, there is little doubt that organizations in hyperturbulent environments face special challenges that require them to be constantly acquiring, assimilating, and disseminating information so that they are ready for rapid change. Ideally, this permits something that looks like seamless "morphing" rather than the step-like process described by Lewin.[10] To achieve this seamless change, they have to have the qualities of a learning organization, a subject we will now explore.

Change. The implementation of a program or plan to move the organization or its members to a more satisfactory state.

Refreezing. The condition that exists when newly developed behaviours, attitudes, or structures become an enduring part of the organization.

LO **15.2**

Explain how organizations learn and what makes an organization a *learning organization*.

Organizational learning.
The process through which an organization acquires, develops, and transfers knowledge throughout the organization.

Learning organization.
An organization that has systems and processes for creating, acquiring, and transferring knowledge to modify and change its behaviour to reflect new knowledge and insights.

The Learning Organization

Organizational learning refers to the process through which organizations acquire, develop, and transfer knowledge throughout the organization. There are two primary methods of organizational learning. First, organizations learn through *knowledge acquisition*. This involves the acquisition, distribution, and interpretation of knowledge that already exists but which is external to the organization. Second, organizations also learn through *knowledge development*. This involves the development of new knowledge that occurs in an organization primarily through dialogue and experience. Organizational learning occurs when organizational members interact and share experiences and knowledge, and through the distribution of new knowledge and information throughout the organization.[11] Nokia and Samsung are prominent learning organizations.

Some organizations are better at learning than others, because they have processes and systems in place to facilitate learning and the transfer of knowledge throughout the organization. These kinds of organizations are known as learning organizations. A **learning organization** is an organization that has systems and processes for creating, acquiring, and transferring knowledge to modify and change its behaviour to reflect new knowledge and insights.[12] As a result, organizational change is much more likely to occur in a learning organization. In fact, it has even been suggested that a learning organization is "an organization that is adaptive in its capacity for change."[13]

There are four key dimensions that are critical for a learning organization:[14]

- *Vision/support.* Leaders must communicate a clear vision of the organization's strategy and goals, in which learning is a critical part and key to organizational success.

- *Culture.* A learning organization has a culture that supports learning. Knowledge and information sharing, risk taking, and experimentation are supported, and continuous learning is considered to be a regular part of organizational life and the responsibility of everybody in the organization.

- *Learning systems/dynamics.* Employees are challenged to think, solve problems, make decisions, and act according to a systems approach by considering patterns of interdependencies and by "learning by doing." Managers must be active in coaching, mentoring, and facilitating learning.

BMO Financial Group's Institute for Learning serves as the organization's strategic learning base and is a tangible symbol of the company's commitment to lifelong learning.

- *Knowledge management/infrastructure.* Learning organizations have established systems and structures to acquire, code, store, and distribute important information and knowledge so that it is available to those who need it, when they need it. This requires the integration of people, processes, and technology.

Conference Board of Canada research has shown that learning organizations are almost 50 percent more likely to have higher overall levels of profitability than those organizations not rated as learning organizations, and they are also better able to retain essential employees.[15]

Some companies, like BMO Financial Group, have realized the strategic importance of learning and the link between learning and achieving business objectives. Thus, the bank invested in the construction of the Institute for Learning, which serves as the organization's strategic learning base and a tangible symbol of BMO's commitment to lifelong learning. The institute serves as an agent of strategic and cultural alignment by providing individuals and teams with opportunities to acquire corporate knowledge and perspective through the learning process.[16]

One organization that excels at learning is Singapore Airlines. The company has created a culture that values extracting copious information from customers and using the information in a systematic way to improve customer service. In addition to using formal surveys and analyses of complaints, the airline has a system in place to note and codify verbal complaints and suggestions made to aircrew personnel. The level of detail achieved has led to many very specific innovations in customer service, such as in-flight email.[17]

Learning organizations are better able to change and transform themselves because of their greater capacity for acquiring and transferring knowledge. Thus, learning is an important prerequisite for organizational change and transformation. Next, we consider some issues in the change process. But first, consider the Research Focus: *Do Organizations Learn More from Success or Failure?*

■ RESEARCH FOCUS ■

DO ORGANIZATIONS LEARN MORE FROM SUCCESS OR FAILURE?

As long as organizations survive, they typically improve their performance with increasing experience, and this is generally attributed to organizational learning. But experience includes both successes and failures. Thus, is the experience effect mostly due to the fact that organizations learn from failures, learn from successes, or learn from a combination of the two outcomes? Peter Madsen and Vinit Desai studied the global orbital launch vehicle industry to find out. More precisely, they examined 4220 successful orbital rocket launches and 443 failed launches, beginning with Sputnik's success in 1957. Essentially, they were interested in the impact of launch success versus failure on future launch success, which would be indicative of organizational learning. The authors hypothesized that failure would lead to more learning than success because failure stimulates far greater information search and acquisition. They confirmed their hypothesis that failure is a more potent determinant of organizational learning than success. Although there was some evidence that organizations learned from the failure of other launch organizations, direct experience with failure was a more impactful experience in terms of learning. Also, although major failures (e.g., rocket blew up) contributed to learning, lesser failures (e.g., improper orbit) did not. This is unfortunate, because it precludes learning from "near misses." The authors note the paradox that while organizations learn the most from failure, failure is frequently stigmatized, and thus ignored, hidden, or redefined as success. Thus, taking a less punitive, more supportive stance toward failures might garner great benefits. Madsen and Desai discuss evidence that less exotic failures, such as airplane and railroad accidents and automotive safety recalls, may also be stimuli for organizational learning and improved organizational performance.

Source: Based on Madsen, P.M., & Desai, V. (2010). Failing to learn? The effects of failure and success on organizational learning in the global orbital launch vehicle industry. *Academy of Management Journal, 53,* 451-476.

LO 15.3

Describe the basic *change process* and the issues that require attention at various stages of change.

ISSUES IN THE CHANGE PROCESS

The simple sketch of the change process presented earlier neglects several important issues that organizations must confront during the process. These issues represent problems that must be overcome if the process is to be effective. Exhibit 15.2 illustrates the relationship between the stages of change and these problems, which include diagnosis, resistance, evaluation, and institutionalization.

Diagnosis

Diagnosis. The systematic collection of information relevant to impending organizational change.

Diagnosis is the systematic collection of information relevant to impending organizational change. Initial diagnosis can provide information that contributes to unfreezing by showing that a problem exists. Once unfreezing occurs, further diagnosis can clarify the problem and suggest just what changes should be implemented. It is one thing to feel that "hospital morale has fallen drastically," but quite another to be sure that this is true and to decide what to do about it.

Change agents. Experts in the application of behavioural science knowledge to organizational diagnosis and change.

For complex, non-routine problems, there is considerable merit in seeking out the diagnostic skills of a change agent. **Change agents** are experts in the application of behavioural science knowledge to organizational diagnosis and change. Some large firms have in-house change agents who are available for consultation. In other companies, outside consultants might be brought in. In any event, the change agent brings an independent, objective perspective to the diagnosis.

It is possible to obtain diagnostic information through a combination of observations, interviews, questionnaires, and the scrutiny of records. Attention to the views of customers or clients is critical. As the next section will show, there is usually considerable merit in using surveys to involve the intended targets of change in the diagnostic process.

The importance of careful diagnosis cannot be overemphasized. Proper diagnosis clarifies the problem and suggests what should be changed and the appropriate *strategy* for implementing change without resistance.[18] Unfortunately, many firms imitate the change programs of their competitors or other visible firms without doing a careful diagnosis of their own specific needs. A symptom of this is buying some pre-packaged intervention from a consulting firm. Similarly, managers sometimes confuse symptoms with underlying problems. This usually leads to trouble.

Resistance

CHANGE

As the saying goes, people are creatures of habit, and change is frequently resisted by those at whom it is targeted.[19] More precisely, people may resist both unfreezing and change. At the unfreezing stage, defence mechanisms (Chapter 13) might be activated to deny or rationalize the signals that change is needed.[20] Even if there is agreement that change is necessary, any specific plan for change might be resisted.

EXHIBIT 15.2
The change process and change problems.

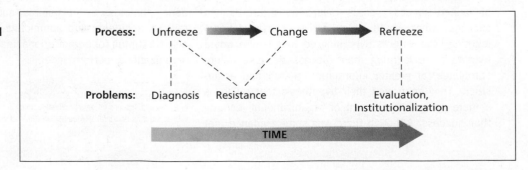

CAUSES OF RESISTANCE

Resistance to change occurs when people either overtly or covertly fail to support the change effort. Why does such failure of support occur, leading to a lack of readiness for change? Several common reasons include the following:[21]

Resistance. Overt or covert failure by organizational members to support a change effort.

- *Politics and self-interest.* People might feel that they personally will lose status, power, or even their jobs with the advent of the change. For example, individual departments will lose power and autonomy when a flat and decentralized structure is centralized and made more hierarchical.

- *Low individual tolerance for change.* Predispositions in personality make some people uncomfortable with changes in established routines. People who seek routine, are cognitively rigid, and have a short-term focus are inclined to resist change.[22] Those who feel self-efficacy to change tend to be committed to proposed changes.[23]

- *Lack of trust.* People might clearly understand the arguments being made for change but not trust the motives of those proposing the change.

- *Different assessments of the situation.* The targets of change might sincerely feel that the situation does not warrant the proposed change and that the advocates of change have misread the situation. For example, at UPS, managers saw the introduction of scanning bar-coded packages as a way to help customers trace goods. Employees saw it as a way to track them and spy on them.[24]

- *Strong emotions.* Change has the capacity to induce strong emotions in people trying to make sense of the change, emotions that often make people feel helpless and resistant.[25]

- *A resistant organizational culture.* Some organizational cultures have especially stressed and rewarded stability and tradition. Advocates of change in such cultures are viewed as misguided deviants or aberrant outsiders. Microsoft has a culture that is somewhat resistant to the realities of consumer electronics.

Underlying these various reasons for resistance are two major themes: (1) change is unnecessary because there is only a small gap between the organization's current identity and its ideal identity; and (2) change is unobtainable (and threatening) because the gap between the current and ideal identities is too large. Exhibit 15.3 shows that a moderate identity gap is probably most conducive to increased acceptance of change because it unfreezes people while not provoking maximum resistance.[26]

Exhibit 15.4 highlights the challenges to change reported by IBM's Making Change Work survey respondents. Notice that "soft," OB-type factors top the list rather than harder, technical factors.

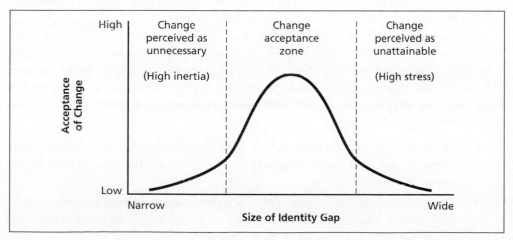

EXHIBIT 15.3
Probability of acceptance of change.
Source: From Reger, R.K., Gustafson, L.T., DeMarie, S.M., & Mullane, J.V. (1994). Reframing the organization: Why implementing total quality is easier said than done. *Academy of Management Review, 19,* 565–584.

EXHIBIT 15.4
Major change challenges.

Source: Courtesy of International Business Machines Corporation, © (2008) International Business Machines Corporation.

The most significant challenges when implementing change projects are people-oriented – topping the list are *changing mindsets* and *corporate culture*.

■ *Soft Factors*   ■ *Hard Factors*

Changing mindsets and attitudes	58%
Corporate culture	49%
Complexity is underestimated	35%
Shortage of resources	33%
Lack of commitment of higher management	32%
Lack of change know how	20%
Lack of transparency because of missing or wrong information	18%
Lack of motivation of involved employees	16%
Change of process	15%
Change of IT systems	12%
Technology barriers	8%

LO 15.4

Explain how organizations can deal with *resistance to change*.

PERSONAL INVENTORY ASSESSMENT

Learn About Yourself
Leading Positive Change

DEALING WITH RESISTANCE Low tolerance for change is mainly an individual matter, and it can often be overcome with supportive, patient supervision.

If politics and self-interest are at the root of resistance, it might be possible to co-opt the reluctant by giving them a special, desirable role in the change process or by negotiating special incentives for change. For example, consider office computing. Initially, many IT directors resisted the proliferation of personal computers, feeling that this change would reduce their power as departments moved away from dependence on the mainframe. Most organizations countered this resistance by giving IT control over the purchase, maintenance, and networking of personal computers, providing an incentive for change.

If misunderstanding, lack of trust, or different assessments are provoking resistance, good communication can pay off. Contemporary organizations are learning that obsessive secrecy about strategy and competition can have more internal costs than external benefits. It is particularly critical that lower-level managers understand the diagnosis underlying intended change and the details of the change so that they can convey this information to employees accurately. Springing "secret" changes on employees, especially when these changes involve matters such as workforce reduction, is sure to provoke resistance. Managers who are generally perceived as fair have a real advantage here because this can lead to the anticipation that change efforts will unfold fairly.[27]

Involving the people who are the targets of change in the change process often reduces their resistance.[28] This is especially appropriate when there is adequate time for participation, when true commitment ("ownership") to the change is critical, and when the people who will be affected by the change have unique knowledge to offer.

Finally, transformational leaders (Chapter 9) are particularly adept at overcoming resistance to change.[29] One way they accomplish this is by "striking while the iron is hot"—that is, by being especially sensitive to when followers are ready for change. The other way is to unfreeze current thinking by installing practices that constantly examine and question the status quo. One research study of CEOs who were transformational leaders noted the following unfreezing practices:[30]

● An atmosphere is established in which dissent is not only tolerated but encouraged. Proposals and ideas are given tough objective reviews, and disagreement is not viewed as disloyalty.

● The environment is scanned for objective information about the organization's true performance. This might involve putting lots of outsiders on the board of directors or sending technical types out to meet customers.

- Organizational members are sent to other organizations and even other countries to see how things are done elsewhere.

- The organization compares itself along a wide range of criteria *against the competition*, rather than simply comparing its performance against last year's. This avoids complacency.

Transformational leaders are skilled at using the new ideas that stem from these practices to create a revised vision for followers about what the organization can do or be. Often, a radically reshaped culture is the result. In the process, transformational leaders are good at inspiring trust and encouraging followers to subordinate their individual self-interests for the good of the organization. They are also adept at countering employee cynicism so that the proposed change is not seen as the new "flavour of the month."[31] This combination of tactics keeps followers within the zone of acceptance shown in Exhibit 15.3. By the way, that "flavour of the month" feeling is a bad thing because it suggests poor planning, and perceptions of poor planning provide stressful uncertainty.[32]

Evaluation and Institutionalization

It seems only reasonable to evaluate changes to determine whether they have accomplished what they were supposed to and whether that accomplishment is now considered adequate. Obviously, objective goals, such as return on investment or market share, might be easiest and most likely to be evaluated. Of course, organizational politics can intrude to cloud even the most objective evaluation.

Organizations are notorious for doing a weak job of evaluating "soft" change programs that involve skills, attitudes, and values. However, it is possible to do a thorough evaluation by considering a range of variables:

- *Reactions.* Did participants like the change program?

- *Learning.* What knowledge was acquired in the program?

- *Behaviour.* What changes in job behaviour occurred?

- *Outcomes.* What changes in productivity, absence, and so on occurred?[33]

To some extent, reactions measure resistance, learning reflects change, and behaviour reflects successful refreezing. Outcomes indicate whether refreezing is useful for the organization. Unfortunately, many evaluations of change efforts never go beyond the measurement of reactions. Again, part of the reason for this may be political. The people who propose the change effort fear reprisal if failure occurs.

If the outcome of change is evaluated favourably, the organization will wish to institutionalize that change. This means that the change becomes a permanent part of the organizational system, a social fact that persists over time, despite possible turnover by the members who originally experienced the change.[34]

It should be fairly easy to institutionalize a change that has been deemed successful. However, we noted that many change efforts are only weakly evaluated, and without hard proof of success it is very easy for institutionalization to be rejected by disaffected parties. This is a special problem for extensive, broad-based change programs that call for a large amount of commitment from a variety of parties (e.g., extensive participation, job enrichment, or work restructuring). It is one thing to institutionalize a simple training program, but quite another to do the same for complex interventions that can be judged from a variety of perspectives.

Studies of more complex change efforts indicate that a number of factors can inhibit institutionalization. For example, promised extrinsic rewards (such as pay bonuses) might not be developed to accompany changes. Similarly, initial changes might provide intrinsic rewards that create higher expectations that cannot be fulfilled. Institutionalization might also be damaged if new hires are not carefully socialized to understand the unique

■ YOU BE THE MANAGER ■

Transforming a Legacy Culture at 3M

3M, founded in 1902 as Minnesota Mining and Manufacturing Company, is one of the world's most admired companies. From its beginnings making sandpaper, the company has leveraged technology and innovation to become a multinational conglomerate employing over 80 000 people in more than 60 countries. In addition to the familiar Scotch Tape and Post-It Notes, its over 55 000 other products span applications from dentistry to biometrics to nanotechnology. The traditional hallmark of 3M's culture has been a fanatical dedication to radical innovation, bolstered by the practice of allowing its scientists to devote 15 percent of their working time to pet "blue sky" projects that might result in radical breakthroughs. However, several years ago some of its innovative spirit had been sapped by the negative spillover into the R&D environment of systems designed to enhance production efficiency. The result was a focus on easy-to-measure incremental product improvements rather than the risky but hard-to-predict breakthroughs that 3M was noted for. At the same time, the firm was facing increasing global competition and a proliferation of private-label brands. Although the company had low turnover, some felt that an entitlement mindset made employees too complacent. Although 3M was performing well, new CEO George Buckley wondered how the culture could be realigned to make the firm even more innovative and competitive.

© 3M Company

3M is dedicated to innovation.

Questions

1. How can 3M rekindle its innovative spirit and at the same time maintain efficient operations in the face of global competition?

2. What kinds of tools are required to effect the desired change at 3M?

To see what 3M did, consult The Manager's Notebook at the end of the chapter.

Source: Based on Paul, K.B., & Fenlason, K.J. (2014). Transforming a legacy culture at 3M: Teaching an elephant how to dance. In B. Schneider & K.M. Barbera (Eds.). *The Oxford handbook of organizational climate and culture.* Oxford: Oxford University Press.

environment of the changed organization. As turnover occurs naturally, the change effort might backslide. In a similar vein, key management supporters of the change effort might resign or be transferred. Finally, environmental pressures, such as decreased sales or profits, can cause management to regress to more familiar behaviours and abandon change.[35]

Let's now examine organizational development, a means of effecting planned change. But first, please consult You Be the Manager: *Transforming a Legacy Culture at 3M.*

LO **15.5**

Define *organizational development*, and discuss its general philosophy.

Organizational development (OD). A planned, ongoing effort to change organizations to be more effective and more human.

ORGANIZATIONAL DEVELOPMENT: PLANNED ORGANIZATIONAL CHANGE

Organizational development (OD) is a planned, ongoing effort to change organizations to be more effective and more human. It uses the knowledge of behavioural science to foster a culture of organizational self-examination and readiness for change. A strong emphasis is placed on interpersonal and group processes.[36]

The fact that OD is *planned* distinguishes it from the haphazard, accidental, or routine changes that occur in all organizations. OD efforts tend to be *ongoing* in at least two senses. First, many OD programs extend over a long period of time, involving several distinct phases of activities. Second, if OD becomes institutionalized, continual re-examination and readiness for further change become permanent parts of the culture. In trying to make organizations more *effective* and more *human*, OD gives recognition to the critical link between personal processes, such as leadership, decision making, and communication, and organizational outcomes, such as productivity and efficiency. The fact that OD uses *behavioural science knowledge* distinguishes it from other change strategies that rely solely on principles of accounting, finance, or engineering. However, an OD intervention may also incorporate these principles. OD seeks to modify *cultural norms and roles* so that the organization remains self-conscious and prepared for adaptation. Finally, a focus on *interpersonal* and *group* processes recognizes that all organizational change affects members and that their cooperation is necessary to implement change.

Traditionally, the values and assumptions of OD change agents were decidedly humanistic and democratic. Thus, self-actualization, trust, cooperation, and the open expression of feelings among all organizational members have been viewed as desirable.[37] In recent years, OD practitioners have shown a more active concern with organizational effectiveness and with using development practices to further the strategy of the organization. This joint concern with both people and performance has thus become the credo of many contemporary OD change agents. The focus has shifted from humanistic advocacy to generating data or alternatives that allow organizational members to make informed choices.[38]

SOME SPECIFIC ORGANIZATIONAL DEVELOPMENT STRATEGIES

The organization that seeks to "develop itself" has recourse to a wide variety of specific techniques. We discussed some of these techniques earlier in the book. For example, job enrichment and management by objectives (Chapter 6) are usually classed as OD efforts, as are diversity training (Chapter 3), self-managed and cross-functional teams (Chapter 7), and empowerment (Chapter 12). In this section, we will discuss four additional OD strategies that illustrate the diversity of the practice. Team building and survey feedback are limited in scope and are often a part of other change efforts. Total quality management and reengineering are broader in scope and lead to more sweeping organizational change.

Team Building

Team building attempts to increase the effectiveness of work teams by improving interpersonal processes, goal clarification, and role clarification.[39] (What is our team trying to accomplish, and who is responsible for what?) As such, it can facilitate communication and coordination. The term *team* can refer to intact work groups, special task forces, new work units, or people from various parts of an organization who must work together to achieve a common goal.

Team building usually begins with a diagnostic session, often held away from the workplace, in which the team explores its current level of functioning. The team might use several sources of data to accomplish its diagnosis. Some data might be generated through sensitivity training, outdoor "survival" exercises, or open-ended discussion sessions. In addition, "hard" data, such as attitude survey results and production figures, might be used. The goal at this stage is to paint a picture of the current strengths and weaknesses of the team. The ideal outcome of the diagnostic session is a list of needed changes to improve team functioning. Subsequent team-building sessions usually have a decidedly task-oriented slant—how can we actually implement the changes indicated by the diagnosis? Problem solving by subgroups might be used at this stage. Between the diagnostic and follow-up sessions, the change agent might hold confidential interviews with team members to anticipate implementation problems. Throughout, the change agent acts as a catalyst and resource person.

When team building is used to develop new work teams, the preliminary diagnostic session might involve attempts to clarify expected role relationships, and additional training

LO 15.6

Discuss *team building*, *survey feedback*, *total quality management*, and *reengineering* as organizational development efforts.

Team building. An effort to increase the effectiveness of work teams by improving interpersonal processes, goal clarification, and role clarification.

PERSONAL INVENTORY ASSESSMENT

Learn About Yourself
Diagnosing the Need for Team Building

Outdoor training programs are a popular method of team building in which team members participate in structured outdoor activities to improve their communication and coordination skills and learn how to work together as a team.

© Corbis

to build trust among team members. In subsequent sessions, the expected task environment might be simulated with role-playing exercises.

One company used this integrated approach to develop the management team of a new plant.[40] In the simulation portion of the development, typical problems encountered in opening a new plant were presented to team members via hypothetical in-basket memos and telephone calls. In role-playing the solutions to these problems, they reached agreement about how they would have to work together on the job and gained a clear understanding of each other's competencies. Plant start-ups were always problem laden, but this was the smoothest in the history of the company.

Survey Feedback

Survey feedback. The collection of data from organizational members and the provision of feedback about the results.

In bare-bones form, **survey feedback** involves collecting data from organizational members and feeding these data back to them in a series of meetings in which members explore and discuss the data.[41] The purpose of the meetings is to suggest or formulate changes that emerge from the data.

As its name implies, survey feedback's basic data generally consist of questionnaires completed by organizational members. Before data are collected, a number of critical decisions must be made by the change agent and organizational management. First, who should participate in the survey? Sometimes, especially in large organizations, the survey could be restricted to particular departments, jobs, or organizational levels where problems exist. However, most survey feedback efforts attempt to cover the entire organization. This approach recognizes the systemic nature of organizations and permits a comparison of survey results across various subunits. It is generally conceded that all members of a target group should be surveyed. This procedure builds trust and confidence in survey results.

Second, what questions should the survey ask? Two approaches are available. Some change agents use pre-packaged, standardized surveys covering areas such as communication and decision-making practices, and employee satisfaction. Such questionnaires are usually carefully constructed and permit comparisons with other organizations in which the survey has been conducted. However, there is some danger that pre-packaged surveys might neglect critical areas for specific consideration, and so many change agents choose to devise their own custom-tailored surveys or seek help from consulting firms. Some firms, such as

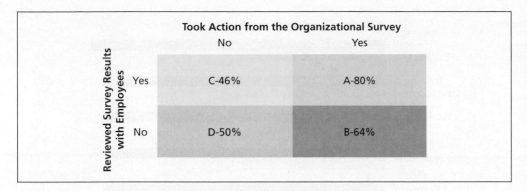

EXHIBIT 15.5 Percentage of favourable responses to a survey in terms of perceptions that results were reviewed with employees and action was taken.

Source: Reprinted with permission from Emerald Group Publishing Limited, originally published in *Research in organizational change and development* Vol. 20, 223–264 © Emerald Group Publishing Limited (2012).

the Hay Group, have large databases that enable organizations to compare their employees' responses with those of other organizations on core questions.

Feedback seems to be most effective when it is presented to natural working units in face-to-face meetings. This method rules out presenting only written feedback or feedback that covers only the organization as a whole. In a software firm, a natural working unit might consist of a department, such as development or marketing. In a school district, such units might consist of individual schools. Many change agents prefer that the manager of the working unit conduct the feedback meeting. This demonstrates management commitment and acceptance of the data. The change agent attends such meetings and helps facilitate discussion of the data and plans for change.

It bears emphasis that surveys have the most beneficial effects when the results are indeed reviewed with employees and when action is taken in response to the survey. Exhibit 15.5 shows the percentage of favourable survey responses in a multinational consumer products company. The survey is delivered in 40 languages in 200 nations. As you can see, the most favourable responses (80 percent) occur in quadrant A, where survey results were shared and action occurred as a result of the survey. Sharing results but not acting (C), or doing neither (D), were both associated with much less favourable responses. The motto is clear: Share and act.

IBM was one of the pioneers in employee surveys, beginning back in 1957. Given its business sector, it was also one of the first firms to use computerized surveying with integrated data collection and data processing, allowing for fast feedback. The company uses quarterly surveys of random samples of employees in 70 countries using 13 languages.[42] There are core questions and others tailored to local concerns. The company has validated the links from employee job satisfaction to client satisfaction to business performance.

Ford Motor Company also has a comprehensive, yearly, worldwide employee attitude survey called Ford Pulse.[43] Fifty-five core questions that are linked to strategic issues are always completed by salaried employees. Supplemental questions are custom-developed to cover local issues. On average, around 80 000 employees in 50 countries respond online in 23 languages. Ford validated the importance of the Pulse results at 147 Ford Credit branches in Canada and the United States.[44] The results showed that branches with higher Pulse scores had higher customer satisfaction, market share, and business volume and lower loan delinquency and employee turnover. The top part of Exhibit 15.6 shows the association between several Pulse dimensions and customer satisfaction with the branch. The lower part shows the association between Pulse scores and market share. These kinds of bottom-line results go a long way toward enhancing the credibility of the survey to managers and underlining the importance of accountability for "people issues."

Ford is a member of a consortium of over 40 large premier companies known as the Mayflower Group. Other participants include Microsoft, Boeing, 3M, and Target. Participating firms agree to include a number of core items in their employee surveys and share the responses with the consortium at least once every two years. This has provided a normative benchmarking database of over 3 million employees that enables member companies to compare where they stand on matters such as employee job satisfaction, work engagement, and diversity.[45]

EXHIBIT 15.6
Relationship between Ford Pulse survey scores and customer satisfaction and market share at Ford Credit branches.
Source: From Johnson, R.H., Ryan, A.M., & Schmit, M. (1994). *Employee Attitudes and Branch Performance at Ford Motor Credit.* Presentation at the annual conference of the Society for Industrial and Organizational Psychology, Nashville, TN. © 1994 Raymond Johnson. Used with permission.

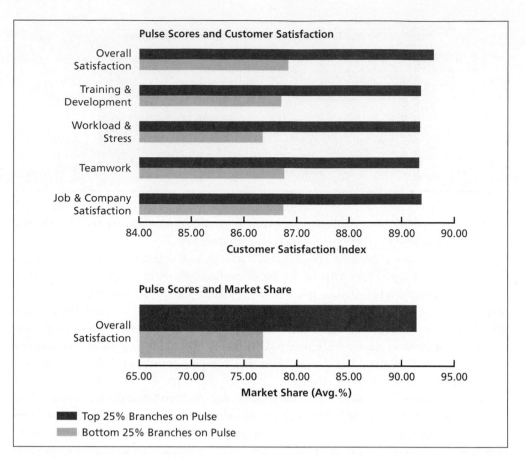

Total Quality Management

Total quality management (TQM). A systematic attempt to achieve continuous improvement in the quality of an organization's products or services.

Total quality management (TQM) is a systematic attempt to achieve continuous improvement in the quality of an organization's products or services. Typical characteristics of TQM programs include an obsession with customer satisfaction; a concern for good relations with suppliers; continuous improvement of work processes; the prevention of quality errors; frequent measurement and assessment; extensive training; and high employee involvement and teamwork.[46]

Prominent names associated with the quality movement include W. Edwards Deming, Joseph Juran, and Philip Crosby.[47] Although each of these "quality gurus" advocates somewhat different paths to quality, all three are concerned with using teamwork to achieve continuous improvement to please customers. Exhibit 15.7 highlights the key principles underlying customer focus, continuous improvement, and teamwork. In turn, each of these principles is associated with certain practices and specific techniques that typify TQM.

The concept of continuous improvement sometimes confuses students of TQM—how can something be more than 100 percent good? To clarify this, it is helpful to view improvement as a continuum ranging from responding to product or service problems (a reactive strategy) to creating new products or services that please customers (a proactive strategy).[48]

For example, suppose that you check in to a hotel and find no towels in your room. Obviously, a fast and friendly correction of this error is better than a slow and surly response, and cutting response time from 15 minutes to 5 minutes would be a great improvement. Better yet, management will try to prevent missing-towel episodes altogether, perhaps using training to move from 96 percent toward 100 percent error-free towel stocking. Although such error *prevention* is a hallmark of TQM, it is also possible to upgrade the service episode. For example, the hotel might work closely with suppliers to provide fluffier towels at the same price or encourage guests to not use too many towels, thus reducing laundry and room

	Customer Focus	**Continuous Improvement**	**Teamwork**
Principles	Paramount importance of providing products and services that fulfill customer needs; requires organizationwide focus on customers	Consistent customer satisfaction can be attained only through relentless improvement of processes that create products and services	Customer focus and continuous improvement are best achieved by collaboration throughout an organization as well as with customers and suppliers
Practices	Direct customer contact Collecting information about customer needs Using information to design and deliver products and services	Process analysis Reengineering Problem solving Plan/do/check/act	Search for arrangements that benefit all units involved in a process Formation of various types of teams Group skills training
Techniques	Customer surveys and focus groups Quality function deployment (translates customer information into product specifications)	Flowcharts Pareto analysis Statistical process control Fishbone diagrams	Organizational development methods such as the nominal group technique Team-building methods (e.g., role clarification and group feedback)

EXHIBIT 15.7
Principles, practices, and techniques of total quality management.
Source: From Dean, J.W., Jr., & Bowen, D.E. (1994). Management theory and total quality: Improving research and practice through theory development. *Academy of Management Review, 19,* 392–418.

costs. Finally, a new service opportunity might be identified and acted on. For example, the Chicago Marriott hotel discovered (after 15 years) that 66 percent of all guests' calls to the housekeeping department were requests for irons or ironing boards. The manager took funds earmarked to replace black-and-white bathroom TVs with colour sets and instead equipped each room with an iron and ironing board. No one had ever complained about black-and-white TVs in the bathroom.[49]

This series of hotel examples illustrates several features of the continuous improvement concept and TQM in general.[50] First, continuous improvement can come from small gains over time (e.g., gradually approaching 100 percent error-free room servicing) or from more radical innovation (e.g., offering a new service). In both cases, the goal is long-term improvement, not a short-term "fix." Next, improvement requires knowing where we are in the first place. Thus, TQM is very concerned with measurement and data collection; in our examples, we alluded to speed of service, percent of error-free performance, and frequency of customer requests as examples. Next, TQM stresses teamwork among employees and (in the examples given here) with suppliers and customers. Finally, TQM relies heavily on training to achieve continuous improvement.

Although simple job training can contribute to continuous improvement (as in the towel-stocking example), TQM is particularly known for using specialized training in tools that empower employees to diagnose and solve quality problems on an ongoing basis. Some tools, noted in the bottom row of Exhibit 15.7, include

- *Flowcharts of work processes.* Flowcharts illustrate graphically the operations and steps in accomplishing some task, noting who does what, and when. For instance, what happens when hotel housekeeping receives a guest request for towels?

- *Pareto analysis.* Pareto analysis collects frequency data on the causes of errors and problems, showing where attention should be directed for maximum improvement. For instance, the Marriott data on reasons for calls to housekeeping corresponds to Pareto data.

- *Fishbone diagrams.* Fishbone (cause-and-effect) diagrams illustrate graphically the factors that could contribute to a particular quality problem. Very specific causes ("small bones") are divided into logical classes or groups ("large bones"). In the hotel example, classes of causes might include people, equipment, methods, and materials.

● *Statistical process control.* Statistical process control gives employees hard data about the quality of their own output that enables them to correct any deviations from standard performance. TQM places particular emphasis on reducing variation in performance over time.

These tools to improve the diagnosis and correction of quality problems will not have the desired impact if they fail to improve quality in the eyes of the customer. An essential problem here is that quality has many different and potentially incompatible definitions. For example, *ultimate excellence, value for the money, conformance to specifications,* or *meeting or exceeding customer expectations* are all potential definitions of quality.[51] Although this last definition would seem to be closest to the TQM principle of customer focus, it is not without its weaknesses. For example, customers might have contradictory expectations. Also, they are more likely to have clear expectations about familiar products and services than about new or creative products or services. Nevertheless, organizations with a real commitment to TQM make heavy use of customer surveys, focus groups, mystery shoppers, and customer clinics to stay close to their customers. Harley-Davidson holds customer clinics and sponsors bike rallies to learn from its customers. Also, survey feedback programs allow organizations to obtain information about internal customers (such as how the adjacent department views your department's performance).

TQM programs have succeeded in firms such as L.L. Bean, Motorola, and Ritz-Carlton Hotels. However, they have also had their share of problems, which ultimately get expressed as resistance. Despite allowing for radical innovation, TQM is mainly about achieving small gains over a long period of time. This long-term focus can be hard to maintain, especially if managers or employees expect extreme improvements in the short term.

Reengineering

Reengineering. The radical redesign of organizational processes to achieve major improvements in such factors as time, cost, quality, or service.

Organizational processes. Activities or work that have to be accomplished to create outputs that internal or external customers value.

Reengineering is the radical redesign of organizational processes to achieve major improvements in such factors as time, cost, quality, or service.[52] Reengineering does not fine-tune existing jobs, structures, technology, or human resources policies. Rather, it uses a "clean slate" approach that asks basic questions, such as, *What business are we really in?* and *If we were creating this organization today, what would it look like?* Then, jobs, structure, technology, and policy are redesigned around the answers to these questions.

A key word in our definition of reengineering is *processes*. **Organizational processes** are *activities* or *work* that the organization must accomplish to create outputs that customers (internal or external) value.[53] For example, designing a new product is a process that might involve people holding a variety of jobs in several different departments (R&D, marketing, production, and finance). In theory, the gains from reengineering will be greatest when the process is complex and cuts across a number of jobs and departments. In contrast to TQM, which usually seeks incremental improvements in existing processes, reengineering involves radical revisions of processes. However, a TQM effort could certainly be part of a reengineering project.

What factors prompt interest in reengineering? One factor is "creeping bureaucracy," which is especially common in large, established firms. With growth, rather than rethinking basic work processes, many firms have simply tacked on more bureaucratic controls to maintain order. This leads to overcomplicated processes and an internal focus on satisfying bureaucratic procedures rather than tending to the customer. Many corporate downsizings have been unsuccessful because they failed to confront bureaucratic controls and basic work processes.

New information technology has also stimulated reengineering. Many firms were disappointed that initial investments in information technology did not result in anticipated reductions in costs or improved productivity. This is because existing processes were simply automated rather than reengineered to correspond to the capabilities of the new technology.

Now it is commonly recognized that advanced technology allows organizations to radically modify (and usually radically simplify) important organizational processes. In other words, work is modified to fit technological capabilities rather than simply fitting the technology to existing jobs. At Ford Motor Company, for example, a look at the entire process for procuring supplies revealed great inefficiencies.[54] Ford employed a large accounts payable staff to issue payments to suppliers when it received invoices. Now employees at the receiving dock can approve payment when the *goods* are received. Information technology enables them to tap a database to verify that the goods were ordered and issue a payment to the supplier.

How does reengineering actually proceed? In essence, much reengineering is oriented toward one or both of the following goals:[55]

- The number of mediating steps in a process is reduced, making the process more efficient.

- Collaboration among the people involved in the process is enhanced.

Removing the number of mediating steps in a process, if done properly, reduces labour requirements, removes redundancies, decreases chances for errors, and speeds up the production of the final output. All of this happened with Ford's revision of its procurement process. Enhanced collaboration often permits simultaneous, rather than sequential, work on a process and reduces the chances for misunderstanding and conflict.

Some of the nitty gritty aspects of reengineering include the following practices. You will notice that we have covered many of them in other contexts earlier in the book.[56]

- *Jobs are redesigned and usually enriched.* Frequently, several jobs are combined into one to reduce mediating steps and provide greater employee control.

- *A strong emphasis is placed on teamwork.* Teamwork (especially cross-functional) is a potent method of enhancing collaboration.

- *Work is performed by the people most logically suited to the task.* Some firms train customers to do minor maintenance and repairs themselves or turn over the management of some inventory to their suppliers.

- *Unnecessary checks and balances are removed.* When processes are simplified and employees are more collaborative, expensive and redundant controls can sometimes be removed.

- *Advanced technology is exploited.* Computerized technology not only permits combining of jobs, it also enhances collaboration via email, groupware, and so on.

It is easiest to get a feel for the success of reengineering by considering some of the reductions in mediating steps and improvements in speed that have resulted. Using software that allows clients to file electronic claims, Blue Cross of Washington and Alaska handled 17 percent more volume with a 12 percent smaller workforce and halved the time to handle a claim. Using cross-functional teams and advanced technology, Chrysler cut the design time of its successful Jeep Cherokee by 40 percent.[57] Such "concurrent engineering" is now the norm. At popular clothing stores, fashions move from design to store in days rather than the former two *seasons.* Thus, a firm is much more responsive to fickle swings in trends and taste.

Because reengineering has the goal of radical change, it requires strong CEO support and transformational leadership. Also, before reengineering begins, it is essential that the organization clarify its overall strategy. What business should we really be in? (Do we want to produce hardware, software, or both?) Given this, who are our customers, and what core processes create value for them? If such strategic clarification is lacking, processes that do not matter to the customer will be reengineered. Strong CEO support and a clear strategy are important for overcoming resistance that simply dismisses people who advocate reengineering as "more efficiency experts." Resistance due to self-interest and organizational politics is likely when radical change may lead to layoffs or major changes in work responsibilities.

Reengineering must be both broad and deep to have long-lasting, bottom-line results—that is, it should span a large number of activities that cut costs or add customer value, and it should affect a number of elements, including skills, values, roles, incentives, structure, and technology.[58] Half-hearted attempts do not pay off.

DOES ORGANIZATIONAL DEVELOPMENT WORK?

Does it work? That is, do the benefits of OD outweigh the heavy investment of time, effort, and money? At the outset, we should reemphasize that most OD efforts are *not* carefully evaluated. Political factors and budget limitations might be prime culprits, but the situation is not helped by some OD practitioners who argue that certain OD goals (e.g., making the organization more human) are incompatible with impersonal, scientifically rigorous evaluation. Two large-scale reviews of a wide variety of OD techniques (including some we discussed in this chapter as well as job redesign, MBO, and goal setting from Chapters 5 and 6) reached the following conclusions:[59]

- Most OD techniques have a positive impact on productivity, job satisfaction, or other work attitudes.

- OD seems to work better for supervisors or managers than for blue-collar workers.

- Changes that use more than one technique seem to have more impact.

- There are great differences across sites in the success of OD interventions.

Exhibit 15.8 summarizes the results of a large number of research studies on the impact of OD efforts on changes in a variety of outcomes such as performance and turnover. Organizational arrangements included changes in formal structure and some quality interventions. Social factors included the use of team building and survey feedback. Technology changes mainly involved job redesign. Finally, physical-setting interventions (which were rare) included things such as changes to open-plan offices.

As you can see, a healthy percentage of studies reported positive changes following an OD effort. However, many studies also reported no change. This underlines the difficulty of introducing change, and it also suggests that variations in how organizations actually implement change may greatly determine its success. The relative lack of negative change is encouraging, but it is also possible that there is a bias against reporting bad outcomes.[60]

EXHIBIT 15.8
Organizational change due to organizational development efforts.

Source: Modified and reproduced by special permission of the Publisher, Davies-Black Publishing, an imprint of CCP Inc., Palo Alto, CA 94303 from Dunnette, M.D., & Hough, L.M. (Eds.). (1992). *Handbook of industrial and organizational psychology*, 2nd ed. (Vol. 3). Copyright by Davies-Black Publishing, an imprint of CPP, Inc. All rights reserved. Further reproduction is prohibited without the publisher's written consent.

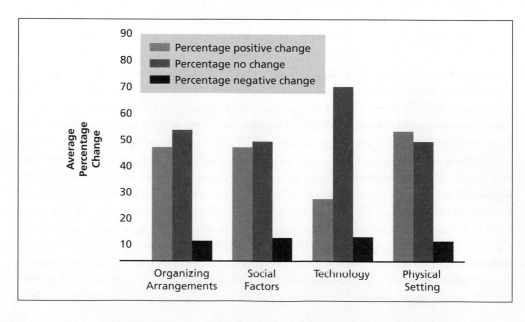

Weak methodology has sometimes plagued research evaluations of the success of OD interventions, although the quality of research seems to be improving over time.[61] Some specific problems include the following:[62]

- OD efforts involve a complex series of changes. There is little evidence of exactly which of these changes produce changes in processes or outcomes.

- Novelty effects or the fact that participants receive special treatment might produce short-term gains that really do not persist over time.

- Self-reports of changes after OD might involve unconscious attempts to please the change agent.

- Organizations may be reluctant to publicize failures.

Let's hope that promise will overcome problems as organizations try to respond effectively to their increasingly complex and dynamic environments. Speaking of such responses, let's turn now to innovation.

THE INNOVATION PROCESS

LO 15.7

Do you recognize the name Arthur Fry? Probably not. But Arthur Fry is famous in his own way as the inventor of the ubiquitous, sticky-backed Post-It Notes, a top seller among paper office supplies. Fry, a researcher at the innovative 3M Company, developed the product that became Post-Its in response to a personal problem: how to keep his place marker from falling out of his church choir hymnal.

What accounts for the ability of individuals like Arthur Fry and organizations like 3M to think up and exploit such innovative ideas? This is the focus of this section of the chapter.[63]

Define *innovation*, and discuss the factors that contribute to successful organizational innovation.

What Is Innovation?

Innovation is the process of developing and implementing new ideas in an organization. The term *developing* is intentionally broad. It covers everything from the genuine invention of a new idea to recognizing an idea in the environment, importing it to the organization, and giving it a unique application.[64] The essential point is a degree of creativity. Arthur Fry did not invent glue, and he did not invent paper, but he did develop a creative way to use them together. Then, 3M was creative enough to figure out how to market what might have appeared to less probing minds to be a pretty mundane product.

We can roughly classify innovations as product (including service) innovations, process innovations, or managerial innovations.[65] *Product innovations* have a direct impact on the cost, quality, style, or availability of a product or service. Thus, they should be very obvious to clients or customers. It is easiest to identify with innovations that result in tangible products, especially everyday consumer products. Thus, we can surely recognize that the iPhone, the iPod, and Post-It Notes have been innovative products. Perhaps coming less readily to mind are service innovations, such as purchasing via eBay, researching via Google, and downloading music via the iTunes Store.

Process innovations are new ways of designing products, making products, or delivering services. In many cases, process changes are invisible to customers or clients, although they help the organization to perform more effectively or efficiently. Thus, new technology is a process innovation, whether it be new manufacturing technology or a new management information system.

Managerial innovations are new forms of strategy, structure, human resource systems, and managerial practices that facilitate organizational change and adaptation. Examples might include job enrichment, participation, reengineering, and quality programs.[66] Visa, GE, DuPont, and Procter & Gamble are particularly noted for managerial innovations.[67]

Innovation. The process of developing and implementing new ideas in an organization.

PERSONAL INVENTORY ASSESSMENT

Learn About Yourself
Innovative Attitude Scale

Innovation is often conceived of as a stage-like process that begins with idea generation and proceeds to idea implementation. For some kinds of innovations, it is also hoped that the implemented innovation will diffuse to other sites or locations. This applies especially to process innovations that have begun as pilot or demonstration projects:

IDEA GENERATION → IDEA IMPLEMENTATION → IDEA DIFFUSION

In advance of discussing these stages, let us note several interesting themes that underlie the process of innovation. First, much idea generation is due to serendipity. Thus, IKEA's signature flat-packed "take it home yourself" furniture actually stemmed from a temporary labour shortage, not some grand plan to lower costs and save warehouse space.[68] Second, the beginning of innovation can be pretty haphazard and chaotic, and the conditions necessary to create new ideas might be very different from the conditions necessary to get these ideas implemented. In a related vein, although organizations have to innovate to survive, such innovation might be resisted just like any other organizational change. The result of these tensions is that innovation is frequently a highly political process (Chapter 12).[69] This important point is sometimes overlooked because innovation often involves science and technology, domains that have a connotation of rationality about them. However, both the champions of innovation and the resisters might behave politically to secure or hold on to critical organizational resources. Finally, the generation of good ideas is no guarantee that they will be implemented and diffused.[70]

Generating and Implementing Innovative Ideas

Innovation requires creative ideas, someone to fight for these ideas, good communication, and the proper application of resources and rewards.

INDIVIDUAL CREATIVITY Creative thinking by individuals or small groups is at the core of the innovation process. **Creativity** is usually defined as the production of novel but potentially useful ideas. Thus, creativity is a key aspect of the "developing new ideas" part of our earlier definition of innovation. However, innovation is a broader concept, in that it also involves an attempt to implement new ideas. Not every creative idea gets implemented.

Creativity. The production of novel but potentially useful ideas.

When we see a company like Corning, which is known for its innovations, or we see an innovative project completed successfully, we sometimes forget about the role that individual creativity plays in such innovations. However, organizations that have a consistent reputation for innovation have a talent for selecting, cultivating, and motivating creative individuals. Such creativity can come into play at many "locations" during the process of innovation. Thus, the salesperson who discovers a new market for a product might be just as creative as the scientist who developed the product.

What makes a person creative?[71] For one thing, you can pretty much discount the romantic notion of the naïve creative genius. Research shows that creative people tend to have an excellent technical understanding of their domain—that is, they understand its basic practices, procedures, and techniques. Thus, creative chemists will emerge from those who are well trained and up-to-date in their field. Similarly, creative money managers will be among those who have a truly excellent grasp of finance and economics. Notice, however, that the fact that creative people have good skills in their area of specialty does not mean that they are extraordinarily intelligent. Once we get beyond subnormal intelligence, there is no correlation between level of intelligence and creativity.

Most people with good basic skills in their area are still not creative. What sets the creative people apart are additional *creativity-relevant* skills. These include the ability to tolerate ambiguity, withhold early judgment, see things in new ways, and be open to new and diverse experiences. Some of these skills reflect certain personality characteristics, such as curiosity and persistence. Interestingly, creative people tend to be socially skilled but lower than average

PERSONAL INVENTORY ASSESSMENT

Learn About Yourself
Creativity Scale

PERSONAL INVENTORY ASSESSMENT

Learn About Yourself
Problem Solving, Creativity, and Innovation

in need for social approval. They can often interact well with others to learn and discuss new ideas, but they do not see the need to conform just to get others to like them.

Many creativity-related skills can actually be improved by training people to think in divergent ways and to withhold early evaluation of ideas.[72] Frito-Lay and DuPont are two companies that engage in extensive creativity training.

Finally, people can be experts in their field and have creativity skills, but still not be creative if they lack intrinsic motivation for generating new ideas. Such motivation is most likely to occur when there is genuine interest in and fascination with the task at hand. This is not to say that extrinsic motivation is not important in innovation, as we shall see shortly. Rather, it means that creativity itself is not very susceptible to extrinsic rewards.

Having a lot of potentially creative individuals is no guarantee in itself that an organization will innovate. Let's now turn to some other factors that influence innovation.

IDEA CHAMPIONS Again and again, case studies of successful innovations reveal the presence of one or more **idea champions**, people who see the kernel of an innovative idea and help guide it through to implementation.[73] This role of idea champion is often an informal emergent role, and "guiding" the idea might involve talking it up to peers, selling it to management, garnering resources for its development, or protecting it from political attack by guardians of the status quo. Champions often have a real sense of mission about the innovation. Idea champions have frequently been given other labels, some of which depend on the exact context or content of the innovation. For example, in larger organizations, such champions might be labelled *intrapreneurs* or *corporate entrepreneurs*. In R&D settings, one often hears the term *project champion*; *product champion* is another familiar moniker. The exact label is less important than the function, which is one of sponsorship and support.

For a modest innovation whose merits are extremely clear, it is possible for the creative person who thinks up the idea to serve as its sole champion and to push the idea into practice. In the case of more complex and radical innovations, especially those that demand heavy resource commitment, it is common to see more than one idea champion emerge during the innovation process. For example, a laser scientist might invent a new twist to laser technology and champion the technical idea within her R&D lab. In turn, a product division line manager might hear of the technical innovation and offer to provide sponsorship to develop it into an actual commercial product. This joint emergence of a technical champion and a management champion is typical. Additional idea champions might also emerge. For example, a sales manager in the medical division might lobby to import the innovation from the optics division.

An interesting program of research headed by Jane Howell examined champions who spearheaded the introduction of technology or product innovations in their firms (e.g., new management information systems).[74] This research compared "project champions" with non-champions who had also worked on the same project. The champions had very broad interests and saw their roles as being broad. They were very active in scouting for new ideas, using a wide variety of media for stimulation. They were skilled at presenting the innovation in question as an opportunity rather than framing it as countering a threat (e.g., "This will give us a whole new line of business" versus "This will keep us from getting sued"). Also, they exhibited clear signs of transformational leadership (Chapter 9), using charisma, inspiration, and intellectual stimulation to get people to see the potential of the innovation. They used a wide variety of influence tactics to gain support for the new system. In short, the champions made people truly want the innovation despite its disruption of the status quo.

Some idea champions feel compelled to engage in **creative deviance**, which means they defy orders by management to stop work on a creative idea. This sometimes involves "bootlegging" funds from other (approved) projects or camouflaging one's creative work from management scrutiny. Creative successes as diverse as the production of *The Godfather* to the advent of LED lighting have been attributed to creative deviance.[75]

Idea champions. People who recognize an innovative idea and guide it through to implementation.

Creative deviance. Defying orders by management to stop working on a creative idea.

EXTERNAL COMMUNICATION
Effective communication with the external environment and effective communication within the organization are vital for successful innovation.

The most innovative firms seem to be those that are best at recognizing the relevance of new, external information, importing and assimilating this information, and then applying it.[76] You might recall from earlier in the chapter that such processes are consistent with organizational learning. Experience shows that recognition and assimilation are a lot more chaotic and informal than one might imagine. Rather than relying on a formal network of journal articles, technical reports, and internal memoranda, technical personnel are more likely to be exposed to new ideas via informal oral communication networks. In these networks, key personnel function as **gatekeepers** who span the boundary between the organization and the environment, importing new information, translating it for local use, and disseminating it to project members. These people have well-developed communication networks with other professionals outside the organization and with the professionals on their own team or project. Thus, they are in key positions to both receive and transmit new technical or scientific information.[77] "Well developed" does not necessarily mean large. Strong ties with a sparse but diverse network seem to be key.[78] Also, they are perceived as highly competent and as a good source of new ideas. Furthermore, they have an innovative orientation, they read extensively, and they can tolerate ambiguity.[79] Gatekeeping is essentially an informal, emergent role, since many gatekeepers are not in supervisory positions.

Organizations can do several things to enhance the external contact of actual or potential gatekeepers. Generous allowances for subscriptions, telephone use, and database access might be helpful. The same applies to travel allowances for seminars, short courses, and professional meetings.

Technical gatekeepers are not the only means of extracting information from the environment. Many successful innovative firms excel at going directly to users, clients, or customers to obtain ideas for product or service innovation. This works against the development of technically sound ideas that nobody wants, and it also provides some real focus for getting ideas implemented quickly. For example, Nike uses internet-based engagement platforms designed around global customer experiences, such as enthusiasm for soccer or running. These "communities" of customers possess creativity that can find its way into new Nike designs.[80] Willie G. Davidson, retired chief styling officer and grandson of one of the founders of Harley-Davidson, got ideas from customers at Harley-Davidson bike rallies, where he often walked around with a notebook in hand and had one-on-one sessions with customers.[81] Notice that we are speaking here about truly getting "close to the customer," not simply doing abstract market research on large samples of people. Such market research does not have a great track record in prompting innovation; talking directly to users does. The chapter-beginning vignette suggests that Microsoft should spend more time consulting the users of consumer electronics. For a related example see Applied Focus: *Guests Help Hotels Innovate*.

Information can also be extracted from the environment by hiring employees with multicultural experience or providing opportunities for such experience, which has been shown to enhance creativity.[82] Also, research shows that firms that put their R&D activities in several geographic locations exhibit higher levels of imitative innovation, because they can access a broader set of knowledge.[83] For instance, appliance giant Whirlpool has design centres in Shanghai, Milan, New Delhi, São Paulo, Monterrey, Mexico, and Benton Harbor, Michigan.[84]

Finally, innovative ideas can be extracted from the external environment by holding design competitions and/or using crowdsourcing (Chapter 11) to broadcast design problems to a large audience of potential innovators. Such strategies are often termed *open innovation* in that they eschew the secrecy frequently associated with the process and invite input from a wide variety of external sources.[85] For example, the App Store facilitates access to external software developers in order to come up with innovative new applications.

INTERNAL COMMUNICATION
Now that we have covered the importation of information into the organization, let's focus on the requirements of *internal* communication for innovation.

Gatekeepers. People who span organizational boundaries to import new information, translate it for local use, and disseminate it.

APPLIED FOCUS

GUESTS HELP HOTELS INNOVATE

There's a "war room" in the basement of Marriott International's headquarters, and it's not one where its executives plot against Hilton. No, this war room is part of Marriott's new 10 000-square-foot Innovation Lab, a place where employees and hotel owners brainstorm, design, and refine their ideas for what the hotel of the future will look like. But they're not doing it all on their own. They're taking their cues from the people they want to please the most—their guests—as part of a new effort to "co-create" with their frequent travelers. "It's really consumer-driven," says Michael Dail, vice president of Global Brand Marketing for Marriott Hotels. "Rather than someone at the company coming up with the idea and letting consumers validate it, with co-creation the idea starts with the consumer."

Hotels have always turned to focus groups to provide input on ideas and initiatives. But social media have empowered guests to let hotels know what they like and don't like in real time. Hotel companies are now responding to this more demanding traveler by including them in their design and development process in a much more collaborative way. "For the longest time, hotel brands have followed the 'closed' model of innovation by creating amenities in-house and force feeding them to guests," says Chekitan Dev, an associate professor at Cornell University's School of Hotel Administration. "With an increasingly dynamic marketplace, and the emergence of a younger and more sophisticated travel consumer, this model no longer works."

Co-creation, or "crowdsourcing" opinions from the public, is another play for lucrative Millennial travelers, whose purchasing power is rapidly rising. Millennials, those born in the 1980s to the early 2000s, have unique habits that are influencing hotel design. They like to stay constantly connected through social media, they like to work and play in coffeehouse-like spaces, they pay attention to design, and they want instant gratification.

"When it comes to the preferences of the newest emerging market—the Millennial—firms have realized that to respond to the guest mantra of 'I want what I want and I want it now,' a smart way is to open the innovation process to the collective wisdom of its guests," Dev says.

In addition to inviting frequent guests to its Innovation Lab, Marriott Hotels and Resorts launched a "Travel Brilliantly" campaign this year aimed at Millennials. The company solicited ideas from travelers on everything from design to technology to food and beverage on its website, travelbrilliantly.com.

Last month, Hyatt Hotels partnered with innovation consultancy gravitytank at Chicago Ideas Week to solicit ideas from travelers on how they would reimagine the hotel experience. In September, Hyatt also hosted what it called "The World's Largest Focus Group," during which Hyatt employees around the world led discussions about travel via Twitter and Facebook. The focus group was the second phase in Hyatt's 18-month listening exercise, which includes more than 40 group discussions around the world. The company says the talks have led to new amenities such as Hyatt Has It, a service providing forgotten items like deodorant and curling irons, and healthier menu items.

Consumer input was key in the redesign of InterContinental Hotels Group's Holiday Inn lobbies. IHG reached out to about 5 000 consumers for direction on the kind of food, design, and amenities they wanted to see in the lobby. They took the best ideas and created a full-size mock-up of the "Active Lobby Concept" in a warehouse in Boston. Eventually, the concept, which turned separate public areas into one cohesive space for work and play, was tested out at the Holiday Inn Gwinnett Center in Atlanta.

Excerpted from Trejos, N. (2013, November 15). Guests help design the hotel of the future. *USA TODAY*.

At least during the idea-generation and early design phase, the more the better. Thus, it is generally true that organic structures (Chapter 14) facilitate innovation more easily than mechanistic structures.[86] Decentralization, informality, and a lack of bureaucracy all foster the exchange of information that innovation requires. To this mixture, add small project teams or business units and a diversity of member backgrounds to stimulate cross–fertilization of ideas and creative synthesis.[87] One study of more than 211 000 patents found that the exchange of knowledge among the divisions of diversified firms resulted in the most cited patents.[88] Interdivision communication is a driver of innovation.

In general, internal communication can be stimulated with in-house training, cross-functional transfers, and varied job assignments.[89] One study even found that the actual physical location of gatekeepers was important to their ability to convey new information to co-workers.[90] This suggests the clustering of offices and the use of common lounge areas as a means of facilitating communication. Organizations could give equal thought to the design of electronic communication media.

One especially interesting line of research suggests just how important communication is to the performance of research and development project groups.[91] This research found that groups with members who had worked together a short time or a long time engaged in less communication (within the group, within the organization, and externally) than groups that had medium longevity. In turn, performance mirrored communication, the high-communicating, medium-longevity groups being the best performers (Exhibit 15.9). Evidently, when groups are new, it takes time for members to decide what information they require and to forge the appropriate communication networks. When groups get "old," they sometimes get comfortable and isolate themselves from critical sources of feedback. Understand that the age of the group is at issue here, not the age of the employees or their tenure in the organization.

Although organic structures seem best in the idea-generation and design phases of innovation, more mechanistic structures are often better for actually implementing innovations.[92] Thinking up new computer programs is an organic task. Marketing them and distributing them online requires more bureaucratic procedures. This transition is important. Although audio and video recording innovations were pioneered in the United States, it was the Japanese who successfully implemented recording products in the marketplace. In part, this stemmed from a recognition of the different organizational requirements for idea generation versus idea implementation.

RESOURCES AND REWARDS Despite the romance surrounding the development of innovations on a shoestring, using unauthorized, "bootlegged" funds, abundant resources greatly enhance the chances of successful innovation. Not only do these resources provide funds in the obvious sense, they also serve as a strong cultural symbol that the organization

EXHIBIT 15.9
Group longevity, communication, and performance of research and development groups.

Source: From Katz, R. (1992). Group longevity, communication, and performance of research and development groups, the effects of group longevity on project communication and performance, Figure 3: Standardized Performance and Communication Means as a Function of Group Longevity. *Administrative Science Quarterly,* *27*(1), p. 96. Administrative Science Quarterly.

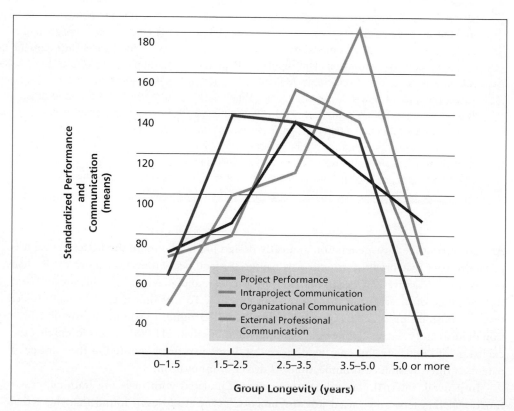

Martin Cooper, the inventor of the cellphone.

© AP Photo/Charles Sykes/Canadian Press Images

truly supports innovation.[93] Martin Cooper, the recognized inventor of the cellphone, noted that his employer, Motorola, invested $100 million over 10 years before any revenues were earned![94]

Funds for innovation should be seen as an *investment*, not a *cost*. Several observers have noted that such a culture is most likely when the availability of funding is anarchic and multisourced—that is, because innovative ideas often encounter resistance from the status quo under the best of circumstances, innovators should have the opportunity to seek support from more than one source. At 3M, for instance, intrapreneurs can seek support from their own division, from another division, from corporate R&D, or from a new ventures group.[95] (Notice how other idea champions might be cultivated during this process.)

Money is not the only resource that spurs innovation. *Time* can be an even more crucial factor for some innovations. At Google, employees can devote up to 20 percent of work time to any personal project that will help advertisers or users.[96]

Reward systems must match the culture that is seeded by the resource system. Coming up with new ideas is no easy job, so organizations should avoid punishing failure. Many false starts with dead ends will be encountered, and innovators need support and constructive criticism, not punishment. In fact, Hallmark puts its executives through a simulation in which they must design a line of greeting cards, so that they can better appreciate the frustrations felt by the creative staff.

A survey of research scientists found that freedom and autonomy were the *most*-cited organizational factors leading to creativity.[97] Since intrinsic motivation is necessary for creativity, these results support rewarding good past performance with enhanced freedom to pursue personal ideas. In a related vein, many organizations have wised up about extrinsic rewards and innovation. In the past, it was common for creative scientists and engineers to have to move into management ranks to obtain raises and promotions. Many firms now offer dual career ladders that enable these people to be extrinsically rewarded while still doing actual science or engineering. When Hewlett-Packard implemented an incentive program to pay researchers for each patent they filed, the number of filings doubled.[98] This corresponds to extensive research evidence that extrinsic rewards that are clearly tied to creativity do indeed increase creative behaviour, especially when accompanied by autonomy and feedback.[99]

We have been concerned here mainly with rewarding the people who actually generate innovative ideas. But how about those other champions who sponsor such ideas and push them into the implementation stage? At 3M, bonuses for division managers are contingent on 25 percent of their revenues coming from products that are less than five years old.[100] This stimulates them to pay attention when someone drops by with a new idea.

To summarize this section, we can conclude that innovation depends on individual factors (creativity), social factors (a dedicated champion and good communication), and organizational factors (resources and rewards).

LO 15.8

Understand the factors that help and hurt the diffusion of innovations.

Diffusion. The process by which innovations move through an organization.

Diffusing Innovative Ideas

Many innovations, especially process innovations, begin as limited experiments in one section or division of an organization. This is a cautious and reasonable approach. For example, a company might introduce new automated technology for evaluation in one plant of its multi-plant organization. Similarly, an insurance company might begin a limited exploration of job enrichment by concentrating only on clerical jobs at the head office. If such efforts are judged successful, it seems logical to extend them to other parts of the organization. **Diffusion** is the process by which innovations move through an organization. However, this is not always as easy as it might seem!

Richard Walton of Harvard University studied the diffusion of eight major process innovations in firms such as Volvo, Alcan, General Foods, Corning, and Shell UK. Each effort was rigorous and broad based, generally including changes in job design, compensation, and supervision.[101] All the pilot projects were initially judged successful, and each received substantial publicity, a factor that often contributes to increased commitment to further change. Despite this, substantial diffusion occurred in only one of the observed firms—Volvo. What accounted for this poor record of diffusion?

- Lack of support and commitment from top management.
- Significant differences between the technology or setting of the pilot project and those of other units in the organization, raising arguments that "it won't work here."
- Attempts to diffuse particular *techniques* rather than *goals* that could be tailored to other situations.
- Management reward systems that concentrate on traditional performance measures while ignoring success at implementing innovation.
- Union resistance to extending the negotiated "exceptions" in the pilot project.
- Fears that pilot projects begun in non-unionized locations could not be implemented in unionized portions of the firm.
- Conflict between the pilot project and the bureaucratic structures in the rest of the firm (e.g., pay policies and staffing requirements).

Because of these problems, Walton raises the depressing spectre of a "diffuse or die" principle. That is, if diffusion does not occur, the pilot project and its leaders become more and more isolated from the mainstream of the organization and less and less able to proceed alone. As we noted earlier, innovation can be a highly politicized process. Several of the barriers to diffusion that Walton cites were implicated in limiting the influence that the innovative Saturn project had on General Motors, including top management changes, union resistance, and competition for resources from old-line GM divisions.

Some research suggests that innovations are especially difficult to diffuse in organizations dominated by professionals, who tend to focus on their own "silos." Thus, in hospitals, doctors, nurses, and physiotherapists can have trouble working as multi-disciplinary teams to introduce new practices.[102]

One classic review suggests that the following factors are critical determinants of the rate of diffusion of a wide variety of innovations:[103]

- *Relative advantage.* Diffusion is more likely when the new idea is perceived as truly better than the one it replaces.
- *Compatibility.* Diffusion is easier when the innovation is compatible with the values, beliefs, needs, and current practices of potential new adopters.
- *Complexity.* Complex innovations that are fairly difficult to comprehend and use are less likely to diffuse.
- *Trialability.* If an innovation can be given a limited trial run, its chances of diffusion will be improved.
- *Observability.* When the consequences of an innovation are more visible, diffusion will be more likely to occur.

To this list we might add *adaptability*, since innovations often have to be custom-tailored to diffuse effectively.[104] In combination, these determinants suggest that there is considerable advantage to thinking about how innovations are "packaged" and "sold," so as to increase their chances of more widespread adoption. Also, they suggest the value of finding strong champions to sponsor the innovation at the new site.

A FOOTNOTE: THE KNOWING–DOING GAP

Despite the need for organizations to change, develop, and innovate, they often exhibit considerable inertia. This is particularly ironic, given that managers are better educated than ever, and there are well-developed bodies of research (many documented in your text) showing that some management practices are better than others. In addition, short courses, consulting firms, and popular books by management gurus frequently describe in detail the "best practices" of successful firms in various industries. Thus, it seems that many managers know what to do, but have considerable trouble *implementing* this knowledge in the form of action. In a very insightful book, Jeffrey Pfeffer and Robert Sutton describe this situation as the *knowing–doing gap*.[105] To take just one of their examples, they note that the much-admired and highly efficient Toyota Production System (TPS) has been featured in many books and articles. Toyota readily gives plant tours to illustrate its features. Despite this, firms have had considerable trouble in trying to imitate Toyota.

Why does the knowing–doing gap happen? Pfeffer and Sutton cite a number of reasons. One is the tendency for some organizational cultures to reward short-term talk rather than longer-term action. Meetings, presentations, documentation, and mission statements thus take precedence over action and experimentation. This is only reinforced when mistrust permeates a firm and employees fear reprisals for mistakes. Also, many changes require cooperation among organizational units, but many organizations foster internal competition that is not conducive to such cooperation. Finally, Pfeffer and Sutton note that when managers do manage to make changes, these changes sometimes fail because techniques are adopted without an understanding of their underlying philosophy. For instance, the TPS is based in part on TQM principles described earlier in this chapter, but some observers just see visible manifestations such as the cords that workers can pull to stop the assembly line. Similarly, one of the authors once heard a consultant say that one of his clients was all in favour of teamwork but did not want to actually implement any teams!

We hope that our book and your professor have provided you with the knowing. Now it's your turn to do the doing!

THE MANAGER'S NOTEBOOK

Transforming a Legacy Culture at 3M

1. 3M employees were generally satisfied with their jobs and committed to the organization. The new CEO reasoned that increasing employee *engagement* (Chapter 13) would be the correct path to align employee interests with those of the organization, because the factors associated with engagement (vigour, dedication, absorption) are the same as those that lead to innovation. Engaged employees would be willing to take risks through individual initiative while at the same time being mindful of the business necessity for disciplined creativity. Engagement was meant to counter a mentality of entitlement that had built up over time.

2. One of the first things 3M did was to add a measure of engagement to its traditional employee survey, which had focused on job satisfaction. This enabled the firm to track engagement over time, and it also allowed it to benchmark against other major corporations that used the same measure. Managers were trained to probe which aspects of work R&D personnel found most engaging and to communicate the firm's tolerance for failure. Employees must feel protected to "think big" and take risks in an atmosphere of trust. At the same time, the pay and benefits packages were modified to link compensation more directly to individual performance and focus people on external competition. Also, in addition to hiring new graduates, as was company tradition, 3M also acquired experienced people from outside the firm to infuse new ideas. Both the revised pay system and revised hiring strategy were meant to counter the entitlement mentality, reinforcing the need for continuous innovation. Engagement scores increased steadily during the change effort, and an increased percentage of revenues are coming from newly introduced products.

MyManagementLab   **Study, practise, and explore real management situations with these helpful resources:**

- **Interactive Lesson Presentations:** Work through interactive presentations and assessments to test your knowledge of management concepts.
- **PIA (Personal Inventory Assessments):** Enhance your ability to connect with key concepts through these engaging, self-reflection assessments.
- **Study Plan:** Check your understanding of chapter concepts with self-study quizzes.
- **Videos:** Learn more about the management practices and strategies of real companies.
- **Simulations:** Practise decision-making in simulated management environments.

P I A PERSONAL INVENTORY ASSESSMENT

LEARNING OBJECTIVES CHECKLIST

15.1 All organizations must change because of forces in the external and internal environments. Although more environmental change usually requires more organizational change, organizations can exhibit too much change as well as too little. Organizations can change goals and strategies, technology, job design, structure, processes, culture, and people. People changes should almost always accompany changes in other factors.

15.2 Organizations learn through the acquisition, distribution, and interpretation of knowledge that already exists but is external to the organization, and through the development of new knowledge that occurs in an organization primarily through dialogue and experience. *Learning organizations* have systems and processes for creating, acquiring, and transferring knowledge throughout the organization to modify and change behaviour.

15.3 The general *change process* involves unfreezing current attitudes and behaviours, changing them, and then refreezing the newly acquired attitudes and behaviours. Several key issues or problems must be dealt with during the general change process. One is accurate diagnosis of the current situation. Another is the resistance that might be provoked by unfreezing and change. A third issue is performing an adequate evaluation of the success of the change effort. Many such evaluations are weak or non-existent.

15.4 Organizations can deal with *resistance to change* by being supportive, providing clear and upfront communication about the details of the intended change, involving those who are targets of the change in the change process, and by co-opting reluctant individuals by giving them a special or desirable role in the change process or by negotiating special incentives for change. Transformational leaders are particularly adept at overcoming resistance to change.

15.5 *Organizational development (OD)* is a planned, ongoing effort to change organizations to be more effective and more human. It uses the knowledge of behavioural science to foster a culture of organizational self-examination and readiness for change. A strong emphasis is placed on interpersonal and group processes.

15.6 Four popular OD techniques are team building, survey feedback, total quality management, and reengineering. *Team building* attempts to increase the effectiveness of work teams by concentrating on interpersonal processes, goal clarification, and role clarification. *Survey feedback* requires that organizational members generate data that are fed back to them as a basis for inducing change. *Total quality management (TQM)* is an attempt to achieve continuous improvement in the quality of products or services. *Reengineering* is the radical redesign of organizational processes to achieve major improvements in time, cost, quality, or service.

15.7 *Innovation* is the process of developing and implementing new ideas in an organization. It can include new products, new processes, and new management practices. Innovation requires individual creativity and adequate resources and rewards to stimulate and channel that creativity. Also, *idea champions* who recognize and sponsor creative ideas are critical. Finally, internal and external communication is important for innovation. The role of gatekeepers who import and disseminate technical information is especially noteworthy.

15.8 Innovations will diffuse most easily when they are not too complex, can be given a trial run, are compatible with existing practices, and offer a visible advantage over current practices. Factors that can hurt diffusion include a lack of support and commitment from top management, reward systems that focus on traditional performance and ignore success at implementing innovation, union resistance, and conflict between pilot projects and the bureaucratic structures in the rest of the organization.

DISCUSSION QUESTIONS

1. You have been charged with staffing and organizing an R&D group in a new high-tech firm. What will you do to ensure that the group is innovative?

2. What qualities would the ideal gatekeeper possess to facilitate the communication of technical information in his or her firm?

3. Suppose a job enrichment effort in one plant of a manufacturing firm is judged to be very successful. You are the corporate change agent responsible for the project, and you wish to diffuse it to other plants that have a similar technology. How would you sell the project to other plant managers? What kinds of resistance might you encounter?

4. Discuss: The best organizational structure to generate innovative ideas might not be the best structure to implement those ideas.

5. Debate: Survey feedback can be a problematic OD technique, because it permits people who are affected by organizational policies to generate data that speak against those policies.

INTEGRATIVE DISCUSSION QUESTIONS

1. Do leadership, organizational culture, and communication influence the effectiveness of organizational change programs? Discuss the effect that leadership behaviour, strong cultures, and personal and organizational approaches to communication have on the change process and change problems. What should organizations do in terms of leadership, culture, and communication to overcome problems and ensure that the change process is effective?

2. How can organizational learning practices, pay, and socialization influence organizational learning and innovation in organizations? Design a program to improve an organization's ability to learn or generate and implement innovative ideas; the program should combine organizational learning practices (Chapter 2), pay systems (Chapter 6), and socialization methods (Chapter 8). What effect does organizational culture have on an organization's ability to learn and innovate?

3. Review the chapter-opening vignette on Microsoft and identify some of the most relevant issues that have been covered in previous chapters. In particular, consider the vignette in terms of some of the following topics: learning (Chapter 2), perceptions (Chapter 3), groups and teamwork (Chapter 7), culture (Chapter 8), leadership (Chapter 9), communication (Chapter 10), organizational structure (Chapter 14), and strategy (Chapter 14).

ON-THE-JOB CHALLENGE QUESTION

The Hacker Way at Facebook

Facebook's campus in Menlo Park, California, includes a large sign reading *The Hacker Company* and a giant HACK configured into the surface of one of its many pedestrian plazas. Founder Mark Zuckerberg is fond of extolling the virtues of the Hacker Way, an obsessive-compulsive need to change, fix, and improve systems, rejecting the status quo even in the face of outright resistance or claims that some innovation is impossible to accomplish. The company often sponsors Hackathons in which teams of employees work together to design a new concept in a short spurt of creativity. In fact,

the Facebook Timeline service was conceived in a Hackathon.

Given that Facebook itself is the frequent target of malicious hacking, Zuckerberg's use of the term and glorification of the spirit of hacking is ironic. Why does he extol the Hacker Way? How is it connected to the concept of organizational learning? What does it signal to organizational insiders and outsiders about change and innovation?

Source: Based on Hartley, M. (2012, March 19). Facebook makes room for everyone. *National Post*, FP3.

EXPERIENTIAL EXERCISE

Measuring Tolerance for Ambiguity

Please read each of the following statements carefully. Then use the following scale to rate each of them in terms of the extent to which you either agree or disagree with the statement.

Completely disagree		Neither agree nor disagree			Completely agree	
1	2	3	4	5	6	7

Place the number that best describes your degree of agreement or disagreement in the blank to the left of each statement.

____ 1. An expert who does not come up with a definite answer probably does not know too much.

____ 2. I would like to live in a foreign country for a while.

____ 3. The sooner we all acquire similar values and ideals, the better.

____ 4. A good teacher is one who makes you wonder about your way of looking at things.

____ 5. I like parties where I know most of the people more than ones where all or most of the people are complete strangers.

____ 6. Teachers or supervisors who hand out vague assignments give a chance for one to show initiative and originality.

____ 7. A person who leads an even, regular life in which few surprises or unexpected happenings arise really has a lot to be grateful for.

____ 8. Many of our most important decisions are based on insufficient information.

____ 9. There is really no such thing as a problem that cannot be solved.

____ 10. People who fit their lives to a schedule probably miss most of the joy of living.

____ 11. A good job is one in which what is to be done and how it is to be done are always clear.

12. It is more fun to tackle a complicated problem than to solve a simple one.

____ 13. In the long run, it is possible to get more done by tackling small, simple problems than large and complicated ones.

____ 14. Often the most interesting and stimulating people are those who do not mind being different and original.

____ 15. What we are used to is always preferable to what is unfamiliar.

____ 16. People who insist on a yes or no answer just do not know how complicated things really are.

Scoring and Interpretation

You have just completed the Tolerance for Ambiguity Scale. It was adapted by Paul Nutt from original work by S. Budner. The survey asks about personal and work-oriented situations that involve various degrees of ambiguity. To score your own survey, add 8 to each of your responses to the odd-numbered items. Then, add up the renumbered *odd* items. From this total, subtract your score from the sum of the *even* numbered items. Your score should fall between 16 and 112. People with lower scores are tolerant of and even enjoy ambiguous situations. People with high scores are intolerant of ambiguity and prefer more structured situations. In Paul Nutt's research, people typically scored between 20 and 80, with a mean around 45. People with a high tolerance for ambiguity respond better to change. They also tend to be more creative and innovative than those with low tolerance for ambiguity.

Source: From Nutt, P. (1989). *Making tough decisions.* John Wiley & Sons. Reprinted with permission of John Wiley & Sons, Inc.

CASE INCIDENT

Dandy Toys

Company president George Reed had built a successful toy company called Dandy Toys, which specialized in manufacturing inexpensive imitations of more expensive products. However, with increasing domestic and global competition, he became concerned that his cheap imitations would not be enough to maintain the company's current success. George decided to call a meeting with all the company's managers to express his concerns. He told them that Dandy Toys must change and become more innovative in its products. He told the managers that rather than just knock off other companies' toys, they must come up with creative and innovative ideas for new and more upscale toys. "By the end of this year," George told the managers, "Dandy Toys must begin making its own in-house–designed quality toys." When the managers left the meeting, they were surprised, and some were even shocked, about this new direction for Dandy Toys.

Although a few of the managers suggested some ideas for new toys during the next couple of months, nobody really seemed interested. In fact, business pretty much continued as always at Dandy Toys, and by the end of the year not a single new in-house toy had been made.

1. Comment on the change process at Dandy Toys. What advice would you give the president about how to improve the change process? What are some of the things that might be changed at Dandy Toys as part of the change process?

2. Why wasn't the innovation process more successful at Dandy Toys, and what can be done to improve it?

3. Consider the relevance of organizational learning for change and innovation at Dandy Toys.

What should the company do to improve learning? Will this help to create change and improve innovation?

CASE STUDY

IVEY | Publishing

Ions Consulting: The MP^2 Training Program

It was 7:00 p.m. on April 25, 2007 and Clark Loon only had three days left to show the executive board of Ions Consulting Services (ICS) that his newly developed Mentoring Management Project for Professionals (MP^2) training program was indeed worth the cost, the time and the resources to implement it across the company. Loon, the newly hired human resources director for ICS, was in charge of developing and implementing a training program that would meet the company's needs of transferring knowledge from older, more experienced project consultants to the junior, inexperienced associates. Loon envisioned that the MP^2 program would reshape the company's training practices and retain employees over the long term. However, implementing the program proved to be much more difficult than he ever imagined.

Clark turned on his computer and started to replay in his mind the meetings he had during the day. He wondered how to assess the success of the program, how to convince the board that it would work, and whether there was anything that he should be doing differently.

CLARK LOON

Clark Loon had worked in the consulting industry for over 20 years, with experience at six different consulting firms in various cities across North America. At the outset of his career, he never intended to move quickly from one firm to the next, but he longed to

experience living in different parts of the continent. Prior to joining ICS as the human resources director, Loon worked as a project management consultant for three years at a small advisory services firm in Detroit, Michigan. He attracted several blue-chip clients to the company's portfolio, considerably enhancing the firm's profile and reputation. However, as time went on, he became less happy being based in Detroit, which prompted him to look for another opportunity.

Ultimately, he returned to ICS in his hometown of Vancouver. Loon was familiar with ICS because he had worked there 14 years previously as an associate consultant, when the firm was just beginning its operation. Although he had decided to leave ICS after six years of service—for reasons of geographic relocation—he continued to maintain close ties with the president of the company. Ultimately, his close relationship with the president is what helped him land his current position as human resources director. However, at no time in the eight months that he had been there did Loon feel at ease. Loon felt that the company had changed for the worse in the 14 years of his absence and was facing severe human resource challenges.

IONS CONSULTING SERVICES (ICS)

ICS started in 1989 in downtown Vancouver with the concept of offering superior solutions that enabled client organizations to improve project execution with regards to budget, schedule and efficiency. Over the years, ICS had achieved success by developing its client portfolio primarily with health care and telecom companies, assisting them in various IT-related projects. ICS's core competence lay in IT project solutions, including system integration, network management, custom application development and e-commerce development.

Founded by three experienced aspiring individuals, ICS grew quickly. In 2003, three years prior to Loon rejoining the company, ICS had added offices in two different Canadian cities (Winnipeg and Toronto) in addition to their Vancouver office. At the same time, the firm grew to just over 60 employees. A recent downturn in the IT market had forced ICS to lay off some of its employees in an effort to reduce costs. By the time Loon rejoined the company in 2006, the total number of employees across the three offices had been reduced to approximately 40 employees. As a result, employee morale was low, and the employee turnover rate was the highest it had ever been.

The recent downsizing not only had detrimental effects on the low-performing employees that were let go, but also on some of the high-performing employees, who no longer wanted to remain with the firm because of perceived job insecurity. Among the layoff survivors, employees began to look for jobs elsewhere. Soon enough, the turnover rate soared and the firm was beginning to lose its edge on delivering quality solutions to its customers, as their top performing professional consultants bolted for jobs with competitors. When Loon rejoined ICS in 2006, nearly 60 percent of the employees in the company had fewer than five years of consulting experience. This was a stark contrast to 2001, when the company make-up was a 70 to 30 ratio in favor of employees with five or more years of experience.

ICS's competitive advantage came from having a large pool of experienced consultants. High-profile clients often stated that their satisfaction with ICS resulted from the experienced consultants who produced dynamic results. Unfortunately, ICS had recently been hiring based on availability rather than on consulting experience (that is, they needed "bodies"). This often meant hiring lower paid and less experienced consultants to fill the void, reducing the quality of work provided to the customers. ICS's former director of human resources was blamed for these results, and was asked to resign. Clark Loon joined the firm to replace her.

LOON'S MP^2 TRAINING PROGRAM

Drawing on his past experience, Loon believed that the best way to improve the quality of consultants would be to create a dynamic training program that would assist not only the inexperienced newcomers, but also the experienced professionals in the organization. Loon wanted to create a program that would facilitate teamwork among the employees, provide skill upgrades, and improve the quality of client service. Furthermore, Loon hoped that his new initiative would increase job satisfaction and commitment in order to combat the low morale and rising turnover rates of the company.

Loon's MP^2 program was designed to pair experienced consultants with inexperienced associates to work on complex and expensive projects for ICS clients. The benefits of this mentoring training program would be two-fold, as inexperienced associates would gain the opportunity to learn from experienced consultants in a structured, supported environment; and the experienced consultants would now have more resources and assistance to complete major projects as required.

The MP^2 program provided an opportunity for allowing associates to obtain valuable training in the presence of experienced consultants, in a mentoring relationship. The inexperienced associates would receive a small-scale project (within a major project) and work under the guidance and leadership of a mentor. Each time associates completed a task, they would be awarded a certain number of credits based on their contributions and the complexity of the task. This program was designed in such a way that each newcomer with fewer than three years of experience had to earn 30 credits before having the opportunity to lead a project on their own. Loon expected that the average time for an incoming associate to complete 30 credits would be approximately two to three years. Furthermore, the mentor was required to provide regular feedback and evaluations to his or her junior associates in order to further guide their development as a consultant.

LOON'S MP^2 PROPOSAL

Before the program was launched, Loon shared his MP^2 plan with some of the members of the firm to generate feedback. However, to Loon's surprise, the MP^2 proposal was met with great resistance from both the executive board and from the employees:

Senior VP of Operations Dale Ellis: "We can't afford to have 80 percent of our employees tied up in projects. If we go with this plan, we are really going to reduce our client portfolio and drive ourselves to the ground! We need to let even the less experienced lead projects on their own."

Managing Director of Client Services, Ray Rones: "What's wrong with our current training program? Our problem isn't training; it's about hiring and retaining the right people."

Senior Consultant Bob Dowry: "I am already overworked with my own projects. I don't have time to hand-hold and look over the work of the new recruits. Some of this stuff is complicated, and I just don't have the time to teach them everything. I want to help, but it's not realistic."

Senior Consultant Jane Platt: "What's the point of helping them when they are going to leave anyway after they have built up their contacts and padded their resumes? But on the other hand, I guess I can use some help in some areas."

Senior Consultant Larry Lay: "I don't need help. They're just going to slow me down. And what if I don't want to be a mentor … what are you going to do? Fire me? After working here for 10 years, I wouldn't be surprised if you do!"

Third-year Associate Consultant Sue Kay: "How is this program going to benefit me? I don't want to do someone else's dirty work. Let me get out there and work. I can do it. I can prove to you that I am capable of managing big projects. I really don't want to put in the unnecessary time."

Incoming Associate Jin Chang: "Three years is a long time before I actually get to do something."

MP^2 DEPLOYMENT

Despite facing great resistance from some of the board members and the employees, Loon remained persistent in deploying the MP^2 program. Eventually, the board collectively agreed on a pilot launch of the MP^2 program. The board decided on having a few mentors work with several inexperienced associates and they would observe the results. They decided that the company-wide deployment of the MP^2 would ultimately be based on the success of this initial pilot study. After a four-month trial period, Loon's program received mixed reviews:

Senior Vice-president Operations Dale Ellis: "Despite my initial reservations … having more members working on a single project has improved the efficiency and the speed of service. But I still believe we are tying up too many employees on single projects and missing out on new potential projects as a result of this program."

Managing Director of Client Services Ray Rones: "I haven't heard anything different from our clients. Have you?"

Senior Consultant Bob Dowry: "Having to look over three members is way too tough. I feel extremely overworked and burnt out. I'm having trouble looking over the work of the new recruits, let alone focusing on my own work, which I think is more important!"

Senior Consultant Jane Platt: "The associates have been very pleasant to work with. I was extremely impressed with how well they responded to the tasks that were given to them. I really felt like we were a team working together to help our clients reach their goal. I certainly want to work with them again! And I will certainly recommend this program to my colleagues."

Senior Consultant Larry Lay: "They can't do it. They just can't do the work. These young recruits are useless!"

Third year Associate Consultant Sue Kay: "What a waste of my time. My son, who is in high school, could do the type of work that I'm being asked to do. Also, my mentor doesn't seem to listen to anything that I say … well … not that we ever talk much … and just between you and me, I think he is utterly incompetent. By the way, after all this is over, how about giving me some 'real' work?"

Incoming Associate Jin Chang: "Wow, I was initially worried that I wasn't going to be involved or actually get to do anything. But my mentor really challenged me to get certain things done. I am just beginning to realize that I have lots more to learn before I can get really comfortable leading a project on my own."

MAKING CHANGES?

Once the four-month trial period was over, Loon had only three days left to revise the program, if necessary, and suggest a format that would guarantee the success of the MP^2 training program. The fiscal year end was approaching, and the executive board would have to approve adding this project into next year's budget. However, after having reviewed the feedback (most of which echoed the comments shown above), Loon couldn't really tell whether the program was working or failing. Loon also didn't know if this program had the potential to resolve the recent turnover issues of the firm. He had to decide what revisions, if any, he should make in his project proposal. Assuming the board gave him the go-ahead, he still had to take steps to ensure employee acceptance of the program. If this program faced employee rejection, it would never work. Thinking about employee acceptance led Loon to muse over the benefits of the MP^2 program, and he wondered what benefits he should focus on when telling senior and junior employees about it. A final issue of concern for Loon was just how to measure the success of a program like MP^2. Indeed, it was going to be a long night.

QUESTIONS

1. How does the MP^2 program relate to the concept of organizational learning, and why is organizational learning a particular issue for consulting firms?

2. Some specific examples of resistance to change are given in the case. How would you summarize these? That is, what are the core factors that provoke resistance to the new program?

3. The MP^2 program is a combination of a process innovation with a managerial innovation. Should Clark Loon have proceeded differently to institutionalize and diffuse the innovation? If so, how?

4. What should Clark do now? Be sure to consider the issues raised in the last paragraph of the case.

INTEGRATIVE CASE

IVEY | Publishing

Ken Private Limited: Digitization Project

At the end of Part 3 of the text, on Social Behaviour and Organizational Processes, you answered a number of questions about the Ken Private Limited: Digitization Project Integrative Case that dealt with issues related to groups, subcultures, leadership, communication, decision making, and conflict. Now that you have completed Part 4 of the text and the chapters on The Total Organization, you can return to the Integrative Case and enhance your understanding of some of the main issues associated with the total organization by answering the following questions that deal with organizational structure, change, and innovation.

QUESTIONS

1. What kind of organizational structure does Ken Private Limited employ in terms of departmentation, and how does this have consequences for differentiation and the need for integration?

2. The case recounts the need for change and innovation in the production department located in the Philippines. Why is it being resisted? What errors did Shekhar Sharma make, and what could have been done differently?

3. What should Saiyumm Savarker do to salvage the Genesis Digitization Project?

REFERENCES

Chapter 1

1. Dobson, S. (2013, April 22). Spirit, results, community. *Canadian HR Reporter, 26*(8), 1, 8; Scott, G. F. (2014, June 12). The smart way to sell a movement, *Profitguide.com,* www.profitguide .com...; Profit 500 – 2013 BDO Business Value Award – Vega (2013). www .bdo.ca.en/about.Sponsorships/pages/ PROFIT-500-2013-BBVA-Vega.aspx; Ayub, T. (2012). As I see it. Charles Chang, President Vega. www.pwc.com/ ca/private; O'Grady, M. (2014, May 29). Making millions selling vegan shakes, *The Globe and Mail,* www .theglobeandmail.com/...; Vega named one of Canada's Best Managed Companies. (2015, March 10). http://myvega.com/vega-life/vega-blog/.

2. Pfeffer, J. (2010). Business and the spirit: Management practices that sustain values. In R. A., Giacalone & C. L. Jurkiewicz (Eds.), *Handbook of workplace spirituality and organizational performance* (27–43). Armonk, NY: M. E. Sharpe.

3. Katz, D. (1964). The motivational basis of organizational behavior. *Behavioral Science, 9,* 131–146.

4. Peters, T. (1990, Fall). Get innovative or get dead. *California Management Review, 33,* 9–26.

5. Lu, V. (2011, July 26). RIM layoffs blamed on failure to innovate. *Toronto Star,* A1, A18; Silliker (2013, February 25). 9 in 10 execs say innovation top priority: Survey. *Canadian HR Reporter, 26*(4), 10.

6. Pfeffer, J. (1994). *Competitive advantage through people: Unleashing the power of the work force.* Boston: Harvard Business School Press.

7. Crook, T. R., Todd, S. Y., Combs, J. G., Woehr, D. J., & Ketchen, D. J., Jr. (2011). Does human capital matter? A meta-analysis of the relationship between human capital and firm performance. *Journal of Applied Psychology, 96,* 443–456.

8. Fulmer, I. S., Gerhart, B., & Scott, K. S. (2003). Are the 100 best better? An empirical investigation of the relationship between being a "great place to work" and firm performance. *Personnel Psychology, 56,* 965–993; Romero, E. J. (2004). Are the great places to work also great performers? *Academy of Management Executive, 18,* 150–152.

9. Wren, D. (1987). *The evolution of management thought* (3rd ed.). New York, NY: Wiley.

10. Rousseau, D. M. (2006). Is there such a thing as "evidence-based management"? *Academy of Management Review, 31,* 256–269; Pfeffer, J., & Sutton, R. I. (2006, January). Evidence-based management. *Harvard Business Review,* 62–74.

11. For a summary of their work and relevant references, see Wren, 1987.

12. Taylor, F. W. (1967). *The principles of scientific management.* New York, NY: Norton.

13. Weber, M. (1974). *The theory of social and economic organization.* A. M. Henderson & T. Parsons (Trans.). New York, NY: Free Press.

14. See Wren, 1987.

15. Roethlisberger, F. J., & Dickson, W. J. (1939). *Management and the worker.* Cambridge, MA: Harvard University Press; Wrege, C. D., & Greenwood, R. G. (1986). The Hawthorne studies. In D. A. Wren & J. A. Pearce II (Eds.) (1986), *Papers dedicated to the development of modern management.* Briarcliff Manor, NY: Academy of Management.

16. Argyris, C. (1957). *Personality and organization.* New York, NY: Harper.

17. Likert, R. (1961). *New patterns of management.* New York, NY: McGraw-Hill.

18. Gouldner, A.W. (1954). *Patterns of industrial bureaucracy.* New York, NY: Free Press.

19. Selznick, P. (1949). *TVA and the grass roots: A study in the sociology of formal organizations.* Berkeley: University of California Press.

20. Abrahamson, E. (1991). Managerial fads and fashions: The diffusion and rejection of innovations. *Academy of Management Review, 16,* 586–612; Johns, G. (1993). Constraints on the adoption of psychology-based personnel practices: Lessons from organizational innovation. *Personnel Psychology, 46,* 569–592.

21. Mintzberg, H. (1973). *The nature of managerial work.* New York, NY: Harper & Row. See also Mintzberg, H. (1994, Fall). Rounding out the manager's job. *Sloan Management Review,* 11–26.

22. Gibbs, B. (1994). The effects of environment and technology on managerial roles. *Journal of Management, 20,* 581–604; Kraut, A. I., Pedigo, P. R., McKenna, D. D., & Dunnette, M. D. (1989, November). The role of the manager: What's really important in different management jobs. *Academy of Management Executive,* 286–293.

23. Luthans, F., Hodgetts, R. M., & Rosenkrantz, S. A. (1988). *Real managers.* Cambridge, MA: Ballinger.

24. Kotter, J. P. (1982). *The general managers.* New York, NY: Free Press.

25. Simon, H. A. (1987, February). Making management decisions: The role of intuition and emotion. *Academy of Management Executive,* 57–64; Isenberg, D. J. (1984, November–December). How senior managers think. *Harvard Business Review,* 80–90. See also Sims, H. P., Jr., & Gioia, D. A. (Eds.) (1986). *The thinking organization: Dynamics of organizational social cognition.* San Francisco, CA: Jossey-Bass.

26. Hofstede, G. (1993, February). Cultural constraints in management theories. *Academy of Management Executive,* 81–94.

27. Crawford, M. (1993, May). The new office etiquette. *Canadian Business,* 22–31.

28. Kanungo, R. N. (1998). Leadership in organizations: Looking ahead to the 21st century. *Canadian Psychology, 39*(1–2), 71–82.

29. Mahoney, J. (2005, March 23). Visible majority by 2017. *The Globe and Mail,* A1, A7.

30. Galt, V. (2006, March 15). 65 means freedom to start a whole new career. *The Globe and Mail,* C1, C2.

31. Galt, V. (2005, September 20). Few firms adopt plans to retain aging staff. *The Globe and Mail,* B7.

32. Javidan, M., Dorfman, P. W., de Luque, M. S., & House, R. J. (2006). In the eye of the beholder: Cross cultural lessons in leadership from Project GLOBE. *Academy of Management Perspectives, 20,* 67–90; Absent workers cost Canadian economy $16.6-billion last year. (2013, September 23). *The Canadian Press,* www.theglobeandmail.com.

33. Attersley, J. (2005, November 7). Absence makes the bottom line wander. *Canadian HR Reporter,* R2; Galt, V. (2003, June 4). Workers rack up increased sick time. *The Globe and Mail,* C1, C3; Bernier, L. (2015, April 6). High stress, high stakes. *Canadian HR Reporter, 28*(6), 3, 10; Bernier, L. (2015, March 23). Work-life balance a struggle

for both men and women. *Canadian HR Reporter, 28*(5), 1, 7.

34. Duxbury, L., & Higgins, C. (2003). *Work–life conflict in Canada in the new millennium: A status report.* Ottawa, ON: Health Canada.

35. Gordon, A. (2013, January 17). National standards unveiled. *Toronto Star*, B4.

36. Saks, A. M. (2011). Workplace Spirituality and Employee Engagement. *Journal of Management, Spirituality & Religion, 8*, 317–340.

37. Myers, J. (2009, November 13). Nurturing spirituality in the workplace. *The Globe and Mail (Breaking News), GMBN.*

38. Luthans, F. (2002). The need for and meaning of positive organizational behavior. *Journal of Organizational Behavior, 23*, 695–706; Luthans, F. & Youssef, C. M. (2007). Emerging positive organizational behavior. *Journal of Management, 33*, 321–349.

39. Avey, J. B., Reichard, R. J., Luthans, F., & Mhatre, K. H. (2011). Meta-analysis of the impact of positive psychological capital on employee attitudes, behaviors, and performance. *Human Resource Development Quarterly, 22*, 127–152.

40. Avey, J. B., Luthans, F., & Youssef, C. M. (2010). The additive value of positive psychological capital in predicting work attitudes and behaviors. *Journal of Management, 36*, 430–452.

41. Avey et al., 2010, 2011; Culbertson, S. S., Fullagar, C. J., & Mills, M. J. (2010). Feeling good and doing great: The relationship between psychological capital and well-being. *Journal of Occupational Health Psychology, 15*, 421–433; Avey, J. B., Luthans, F., Smith, R. M., & Palmer, N. F. (2010). Impact of positive psychological capital on employee well-being over time. *Journal of Occupational Health Psychology, 15*, 17–28; Peterson, S. J., Luthans, F., Avolio, B. J., Walumbwa, F. O., & Zhang, Z. (2011). Psychological capital and employee performance: A latent growth modeling approach. *Personnel Psychology, 64*, 427–450.

42. Luthans, F., Avey, J. B., Avolio, B. J., & Peterson, S. J. (2010). The development and resulting performance impact of positive psychological capital. *Human Resource Development Quarterly, 21*, 41–67.

43. Ray, R. L. (2011, October). CEO challenge reflections: Talent matters. Report Nr. A-364-11-EA. *The Conference Board.*

44. Lockwood, N. R. (2006). Talent management: Driver for organizational success. *2006 SHRM Research Quarterly.* Alexandria, VA: Society for Human Resource Management.

45. McLaren, C. (2002, February 8). Ways to win top talent. *The Globe and Mail*, C1.

46. Bakker, A. B., & Demerouti, E. (2008). Towards a model of work engagement. *Career Development International, 13*, 209–223.

47. Ray, 2011; Saks, A. M. (2006). Antecedents and consequences of employee engagement. *Journal of Managerial Psychology, 21*, 600–619; Christian, M. S., Garza, A. S., & Slaughter, J. E. (2011). Work engagement: A quantitative review and test of its relations with task and contextual performance. *Personnel Psychology, 64*, 89–136; Rich, B. L., Lepine, J. A., & Crawford, E. R. (2010). Job engagement: antecedents and effects of job performance. *Academy of Management Journal, 53*, 617–635; Macey, W. H., Schneider, B., Barbera, K. M., & Young, S. A. (2009). *Employee engagement: Tools for analysis, practice, and competitive advantage.* Malden, WA: Wiley-Blackwell; Ross, P. (2015, April 6). Does HR need tech training? *Canadian HR Reporter, 28*(6), 15.

48. Lawler, E. E. (2008). *Talent: Making people your competitive advantage.* San Francisco, CA: John Wiley & Sons.

49. McKay, S. (2001, February). The 35 best companies to work for in Canada. *Report on Business Magazine*, 53–62; Toda, B. H. (2000, February). The rewards: Being a good employer draws talent and unlocks success. *Report on Business Magazine*, 33.

50. Bansal, P., Maurer, C., & Slawinski, N. (2008, January/February). Beyond good intentions: Strategies for managing your CSR performance. *Ivey Business Journal, 72*(1), 1–8; Morgeson, F. P., Aguinis, H., Waldman, D. A., & Siegel, D. S. (2013). Extending corporate social responsibility research to the human resource management and organizational behavior domains: A look into the future. *Personnel Psychology, 66*, 805–824.

51. Bansal, P., Maurer, C., & Slawinski, N. (2008, January/February).

52. Birenbaum, R., Lang, H., Linley, D., MacMahon, S., Mann, B., Sabour, A., Sosa, I., Stein, G., & White, A. (2009, June 22). 50 most socially responsible corporations. *Maclean's, 122*(23), 42–49.

53. McLaren, D. (2008, December 10). Doing their part—with goals in mind. *The Globe and Mail*, B7.

54. Johne, M. (2007, October 10). Show us the green, workers say. *The Globe and Mail*, C1, C6.

55. Aguinis, H., & Glavas, A. (2012). What we know and don't know about corporate social responsibility: A review and research agenda. *Journal of Management, 38*, 932–968.

56. Johne, M. (2007, October 10).

57. Gully, S. M., Phillips, J. M., Castellano, W. G., Han, K., & Kim, A. (2013). A mediated moderation model of recruiting socially and environmentally responsible job applicants. *Personnel Psychology, 66*, 935–973.

Chapter 2

1. Wingrove, J. (2010, October 19). Calgary's Naheed Nenshi becomes Canada's first Muslim mayor. *The Globe and Mail*, http://www.theglobeandmail.com/news/politics/calgarys-naheed-nenshi-becomes-canadas-first-muslim-mayor/article1215182/?page=all; Gerson, J. (2013, October 22). Nenshi won a landslide, but not without showing the cracks in his armour. *National Post*, http://news.nationalpost.com/full-comment/nenshi-won-a-landslide-but-not-without-showing-the-cracks-in-his-armour; Boushy, D. (2015, February 2). Naheed Nenshi awarded the 2014 World Mayor Prize, *Global News*, http://globalnews.ca/news/1807107/naheed-nenshi-awarded-the-2014-world-mayor-prize/; Gerson, J. (2015, January 28). Nenshi may be popular, but is his acerbic leadership style making work at Calgary City Hall impossible? *National Post*, http://www.springfreetrampoline.ca/summer-promotions-gta?utm_source=display&utm_medium=adwords&utm_content=gta&utm_campaign=CASUMMER15&gclid=CNaL8dOL_MYCFQ2OaQodlHsLhA; Taylor, S. (2015, March 12). "All about connectedness:" Calgary mayor inspires hundreds in Halifax to reimagine city. *Metro News*, http://metronews.ca/news/halifax/1311365/its-all-about-connectedness-calgary-mayor-inspires-hundreds-in-halifax-to-re-imagine-city/; Hopper, T. (2014, November 14). "Post-partisan purple": The rise of Canada's newest (and most fabulous) political colour. *National Post*, http://news.nationalpost.com/news/canada/canadian-politics/post-partisan-purple-the-rise-of-canadas-newest-and-most-fabulous-political-colour; Prest, S. (2014, April 4). Alberta's political scene needs a shakeup. Nenshi is the man for the job. *National Post*, http://news.nationalpost.com/full-comment/stewart-prest-albertas-political-scene-needs-a-shakeup-nenshi-is-the-man-for-the-job; Geddes, L. (2014, June 15). Nenshi on the 2013 flood: 5 memorable quotes. *Global News*, http://globalnews.ca/news/1374259/nenshi-on-the-2013-flood-five-memorable-quotes/; Bennett, D. (2013, June 28). "The voice of all Calgarians": Flood leaves Mayor Naheed Nenshi with Superman status. *National Post*, http://news.nationalpost.com/news/canada/the-voice-of-all-calgarians-flood-leaves-mayor-naheed-nenshi-with-superman-status; Rieti, J. (2013,

June 25). Alberta floods: Keeping up with Calgary Mayor Nenshi. *CBC News*, http://www.cbc.ca/news/canada/alberta-floods-keeping-up-with-calgary-mayor-nenshi-1.1303739; Editorial (2013, June 26). Calgary Mayor Naheed Nenshi deserves praise for his leadership during the flood crisis. *Calgary Sun*, http://www.calgarysun.com/2013/06/26/calgary-mayor-naheed-nenshi-deserves-praise-for-his-leadership-during-the-flood-crisis; Gandia, R. (2010, October 19). Calgary, meet your new mayor. *Calgary Sun*, http://www.torontosun.com/news/calgaryvotes/2010/10/19/15740951.html; vom Hove, T., Baker, B., & Schorr, J. (2015, February 3). Naheed Nenshi, Mayor of Calgary, Canada, awarded the 2014 World Mayor Prize. *World Mayor.com*, http://www.worldmayor.com/contest_2014/world-mayor-2014-winners.html.

2. Dobson, S. (2012, February 13). Revving up interest. *Canadian HR Reporter*, *25*(3), 13, 18; Silliker, A. (2013, July 15). HR by the numbers (Personality traits outrank credentials for grads). *Canadian HR Reporter*, *26*(13), 4; Bernier, L. (2014, February 24). Out of this world recruitment. *Canadian HR Reporter*, *27*(4), 1, 9.

3. George, J. M. (1992). The role of personality in organizational life: Issues and evidence. *Journal of Management*, *18*, 185–213; Mount, M. K., & Barrick, M. R. (1995). The big five personality dimensions: Implications for research and practice in human resources management. In K. M. Rowland & G. Ferris (Eds.), *Research in personnel and human resources management* (Vol. 13, 153–200). Greenwich, CT: JAI Press.

4. George, 1992; Weiss, H. M., & Adler, S. (1984). Personality and organizational behavior. In B. M. Staw & L. L. Cummings (Eds.), *Research in organizational behavior* (Vol. 6, 1–50). Greenwich, CT: JAI Press.

5. Adler, S., & Weiss, H. M. (1988). Recent developments in the study of personality and organizational behavior. In C. L. Cooper & I. Robertson (Eds.), *International review of industrial and organizational psychology*. New York, NY: Wiley.

6. Tett, R. P., & Burnett, D. D. (2003). A personality trait–based interactionist model of job performance. *Journal of Applied Psychology*, *88*, 500–517.

7. Moses, S. (1991, November). Personality tests come back in I/O. *APA Monitor*, 9.

8. Mount & Barrick, 1995.

9. Digman, J. M. (1990). Personality structure: Emergence of the five-factor model. *Annual Review of Psychology*, *41*, 417–440; Hogan, R. T. (1991).

Personality and personality measurement. In M. D. Dunette & L. M. Hough (Eds.), *Handbook of industrial and organizational psychology* (2nd ed., Vol. 2). Palo Alto, CA: Consulting Psychologists Press; Barrick, M. R., & Mount, M. K. (1991). The big five personality dimensions and job performance: A meta-analysis. *Personnel Psychology*, *44*, 1–26; Barrick, M. R., Mount, M. K., & Judge, T. A. (2001). Personality and performance at the beginning of the new millennium: What do we know and where do we go next? *International Journal of Selection and Assessment*, *9*, 9–30; Barrick, M. R., Mount, M. K., & Gupta, R. (2003). Meta-analysis of the relationship between the five-factor model of personality and Holland's occupational types. *Personnel Psychology*, *56*, 45–74; Ng, T. W. H., Eby, L. T., Sorensen, K. L., & Feldman, D. C. (2005). Predictors of objective and subjective career success: A meta-analysis. *Personnel Psychology*, *58*, 367–408.

10. Judge, T. A., Higgins, C. A., Thorensen, C. J., & Barrick, M. R. (1999). The Big Five personality traits, general mental ability, and career success across the life span. *Personnel Psychology*, *52*, 621–652.

11. Chiaburu, D. S., Oh, I., Berry, C. M., Li, N., & Gardner, R. G. (2011). The five-factor model of personality traits and organizational citizenship behaviors: A meta-analysis. *Journal of Applied Psychology*, *96*, 1140–1166; Hough, L. M., Eaton, N. K., Dunnette, M. D., Kamp, J. D., & McCloy, R. A. (1990). Criterion-related validities of personality constructs and the effect of response distortion on those validities. *Journal of Applied Psychology*, *75*, 581–595; Tett, R. P., Jackson, D. N., & Rothstein, M. (1991). Personality measures as predictors of job performance: A meta-analytic review. *Personnel Psychology*, *44*, 703–742.

12. Barrick & Mount, 1991; Ones, D. S., Dilchert, S., Viswesvaran, C., & Judge, T. A. (2007). In support of personality assessment in organizational settings. *Personnel Psychology*, *60*, 995–1027; Barrick, Mount, & Judge, 2001.

13. Ones, D. S., Viswesvaran, C., & Schmidt, F. L. (1993). Comprehensive meta-analysis of integrity test validities: Findings and implications for personnel selection and theories of job performance. *Journal of Applied Psychology*, *78*, 679–703.

14. Judge, Higgins, Thorensen, & Barrick, 1999; Beus, J. M., Dhanani, L. Y., & McCord, A. (2015). A meta-analysis of personality and workplace safety: Addressing unanswered questions. *Journal of Applied Psychology*, *100*, 481–498; Kluemper, D. H., McLarty, B. D., &

Bing, M. N. (2014). Acquaintance ratings of the big five personality traits: Incremental validity beyond and interactive effects with self-reports in the prediction of workplace deviance. *Journal of Applied Psychology*, *100*, 237–248.

15. Judge, T. A., & Ilies, R. (2002). Relationship of personality to performance motivation: A meta-analytic review. *Journal of Applied Psychology*, *87*, 797–807.

16. Judge, T. A., Heller, D., & Mount, M. K. (2002). Five-factor model of personality and job satisfaction: A meta-analysis. *Journal of Applied Psychology*, *87*, 530–541; Morgeson, F. P., Reider, M. H., & Campion, M. A. (2005). Selecting individuals in team settings: The importance of social skills, personality characteristics, and team work knowledge. *Personnel Psychology*, *58*, 583–611.

17. Judge, Higgins, Thorensen, & Barrick, 1999.

18. Rotter, J. B. (1966). Generalized expectancies for internal versus external controls of reinforcement. *Psychological Monographs*, *80* (1, Whole No. 609).

19. Szilagyi, A. D., & Sims, H. P., Jr. (1975). Locus of control and expectancies across multiple organizational levels. *Journal of Applied Psychology*, *60*, 638–640.

20. Szilagyi, A. D., Sims, H. P., Jr., & Keller, R. T. (1976). Role dynamics, locus of control, and employee attitudes and behavior. *Academy of Management Journal*, *19*, 259–276.

21. Andrisani, P. J., & Nestel, G. (1976). Internal-external control as contributor to and outcome of work experience. *Journal of Applied Psychology*, *61*, 156–165.

22. Wang, Q., Bowling, N. A., & Eschleman, K. J. (2010). A meta-analytic examination of work and general locus of control. *Journal of Applied Psychology*, *95*, 761–768. For evidence on stress and locus of control, see Anderson, C. R. (1977). Locus of control, coping behaviors, and performance in a stress setting: A longitudinal study. *Journal of Applied Psychology*, *62*, 446–451. For evidence on career planning, see Thornton, G. C., III. (1978). Differential effects of career planning on internals and externals. *Personnel Psychology*, *31*, 471–476.

23. Snyder, M. (1987). *Public appearances/private realities: The psychology of self-monitoring*. New York, NY: W. H. Freeman; Gangestad, S. W., & Snyder, M. (2000). Self-monitoring: Appraisal and reappraisal. *Psychological Bulletin*, *126*(4), 530–555.

24. Snyder, 1987; Gangestad & Snyder, 2000.

25. Day, D. V., Schleicher, D. J., Unckless, A. L., & Hiller, N. J. (2002). Self-monitoring

personality at work: A meta-analytic investigation of construct validity. *Journal of Applied Psychology, 87,* 390–401.

26. Brockner, J. (1988). *Self-esteem at work: Research, theory, and practice.* Lexington, MA: Lexington.

27. Brockner, 1988.

28. Brockner, 1988.

29. Pierce, J. L., Gardner, D. G., Cummings, L. L., & Dunham, R. B. (1989). Organization-based self-esteem: Construct definition, measurement, and validation. *Academy of Management Journal, 32,* 622–648; Tharenou, P. (1979). Employee self-esteem: A review of the literature. *Journal of Vocational Behavior, 15,* 1–29.

30. Pierce, J. L., Gardner, D. G., Dunham, R. B., & Cummings, L. L. (1993). Moderation by organization-based self-esteem of role condition—employee response relationships. *Academy of Management Journal, 36,* 271–288.

31. George, J. M. (1996). Trait and state affect. In K. R. Murphy (Ed.), *Individual differences and behavior in organizations.* San Francisco, CA: Jossey-Bass.

32. Johnson, R. E., Tolentino, A. L., Rodopman, O. B., & Cho, E. (2010). We (sometimes) know not how we feel: Predicting job performance with an implicit measure of trait affectivity. *Personnel Psychology, 63,* 197–219.

33. Johnson et al., 2010; George, 1996; Thoresen, C. J., Kaplan, S. A., Barsky, A. P., Warren, C. R., & de Chermont, K. (2003). The affective underpinnings of job perceptions and attitudes: A meta-analytic review and integration. *Psychological Bulletin, 129,* 914–945; Lyubomirsky, S., King, L., & Diener, E. (2005). The benefits of frequent positive affect: Does happiness lead to success? *Psychological Bulletin, 131,* 803–855; Kaplan, S., Bradley, J. C., Luchman, J. N., & Haynes, D. (2009). On the role of positive and negative affectivity in job performance: A meta-analytic investigation. *Journal of Applied Psychology, 94,* 162–176.

34. Crant, M. J. (2000). Proactive behaviour in organizations. *Journal of Management, 26,* 435–462; Seibert, S. E., Kraimer, M. L., & Crant, J. M. (2001). What do proactive people do? A longitudinal model linking proactive personality and career success. *Personnel Psychology, 54,* 845–874.

35. Bateman, T. S., & Crant, J. M. (1993). The proactive component of organizational behavior: A measure and correlates. *Journal of Organizational Behavior, 14,* 103–118.

36. Li, N., Liang, J., & Crant, J. M. (2010). The role of proactive personality in job

satisfaction and organizational citizenship behavior: A relational perspective. *Journal of Applied Psychology, 95,* 395–404; Seibert, Kraimer, & Crant, 2001; Thompson, J. A. (2005). Proactive personality and job performance: A social capital perspective. *Journal of Applied Psychology, 90,* 1011–1017; Brown, D. J., Cober, R. T., Kane, K., Levy, P. E., & Shalhoop, J. (2006). Proactive personality and the successful job search: A field investigation with college graduates. *Journal of Applied Psychology, 91,* 717–726.

37. Chen, G., Gully, S. M., & Eden, D. (2001). Validation of a new general self-efficacy scale. *Organizational Research Methods, 4,* 62–83.

38. Chen, Gully, & Eden, 2001.

39. Judge, T. A., Erez, A., Bono, J. E., & Thoresen, C. J. (2003). The core self-evaluation scale: Development of a measure. *Personnel Psychology, 56,* 303–331.

40. Chang, C., Ferris, D. L., Johnson, R. E., Rosen, C. C., & Tan, J. A. (2012). Core self-evaluations: A review and evaluation of the literature. *Journal of Management, 38,* 81–128; Judge, T. A., & Bono, J. E. (2001). Relationship of core self-evaluations traits—self-esteem, generalized self-efficacy, locus of control, and emotional stability—with job satisfaction and job performance: A meta-analysis. *Journal of Applied Psychology, 86,* 80–92; Judge, T. A., Bono, J. E., & Locke, E. A. (2000). Personality and job satisfaction: The mediating role of job characteristics. *Journal of Applied Psychology, 85,* 237–249; Judge, Erez, Bono, & Thoresen, 2003; Judge, T. A., Locke, E. A., & Durham, C. C. (1997). The dispositional causes of job satisfaction: A core evaluations approach. In B. M. Staw & L. L. Cummings (Eds.), *Research in organizational behavior* (Vol. 19, 151–188). Greenwich, CT: JAI Press; Judge, T. A., Bono, J. E., Erez, A., & Locke, E. A. (2005). Core self-evaluations and job and life satisfaction: The role of self-concordance and goal attainment. *Journal of Applied Psychology, 90,* 257–268; Kammeyer-Mueller, J. D., Judge, T. A., & Scott, B. A. (2009). The role of core self-evaluations in the coping process. *Journal of Applied Psychology, 94,* 177–195; Judge, T. A. (2009). Core self-evaluations and work success. *Current Directions in Psychological Science, 18,* 58–62; Johnson, R. E., Rosen, C. C., & Levy, P. E. (2008). Getting to the core of core self-evaluation: A review and recommendations. *Journal of Organizational Behavior, 29,* 391–413.

41. Day, N. (1998, June). Informal learning gets results. *Workforce,* 31–35.

42. Pfeffer, J. (1994). *Competitive advantage through people: Unleashing the power of the work force.* Boston, MA: Harvard Business School Press.

43. Immen, W. (2012, June 20). Companies boosting incentive programs. *The Globe and Mail,* B17; HR by the numbers (Generational differences in rewards). (2013, May 20). *Canadian HR Reporter, 26*(10), 4.

44. Peterson, S. J., & Luthans, F. (2006). The impact of financial and nonfinancial incentives on business-unit outcomes over time. *Journal of Applied Psychology, 91,* 156–165.

45. Peterson & Luthans, 2006.

46. Luthans, F., & Kreitner, R. (1975). *Organizational behavior modification.* Glenview, IL: Scott, Foresman.

47. However, more research is necessary to establish the extent of this in organizations. See Arvey, R. D., & Ivancevich, J. M. (1980). Punishment in organizations: A review, propositions, and research suggestions. *Academy of Management Review, 5,* 123–132.

48. Punishment in front of others can be effective under restricted conditions. See Trevino, L. K. (1992). The social effects of punishment in organizations: A justice perspective. *Academy of Management Review, 17,* 647–676.

49. Orsgan, D. W., & Hamner, W. C. (1982). *Organizational behavior: An applied psychological approach* (Rev. ed.). Plano, TX: Business Publications.

50. See Parmerlee, M. A., Near, J. P., & Jensen, T. C. (1982). Correlates of whistle-blowers' perceptions of organizational retaliation. *Administrative Science Quarterly, 27,* 17–34.

51. Bandura, A. (1991). Social cognitive theory of self-regulation. *Organizational Behavior and Human Decision Processes, 50,* 248–287.

52. Bandura, A. (1989). Human agency in social cognitive theory. *American Psychologist, 44,* 1175–1184. For a presentation of operant learning theory, see Honig, W. K., & Staddon, J. E. R. (Eds.). (1977). *Handbook of operant behavior.* Englewood Cliffs, NJ: Prentice-Hall. For a presentation of social learning theory, see Bandura, A. (1986). *Social foundations of thought and action.* Englewood Cliffs, NJ: Prentice-Hall.

53. Bandura, 1986.

54. Luthans, F., & Kreitner, R. (1985). *Organizational behavior modification and beyond: An operant and social learning approach.* Glenview, IL: Scott, Foresman; Manz, C. C., & Sims, H. P., Jr. (1981). Vicarious learning: The influence of modeling on organizational behavior. *Academy of Management Review, 6,* 105–113.

55. Bandura, 1986; Goldstein, A. P., & Sorcher, M. (1974). *Changing supervisor behavior.* New York, NY: Pergamon.

56. Robinson, S. L., & O'Leary-Kelly, A. M. (1998). Monkey see, monkey do: The influence of work groups on the antisocial behavior of employees. *Academy of Management Journal, 41,* 658–672; Goulet, L. R. (1997). Modeling aggression in the workplace: The role of role models. *Academy of Management Executive, 11,* 84–85.

57. Bandura, A. (1997). *Self-efficacy: The exercise of control.* New York, NY: W. H. Freeman.

58. Bandura, 1997; Stajkovic, A. D., & Luthans, F. (1998). Self-efficacy and work-related performance: A meta-analysis. *Psychological Bulletin, 124,* 240–261.

59. Bandura, 1991; Manz, C. C., & Sims, H. P., Jr. (1980). Self-management as a substitute for leadership: A social learning theory perspective. *Academy of Management Review, 5,* 361–367; Hackman, J. R. (1986). The psychology of self-management in organizations. In M. S. Pollack & R. Perloff (Eds.), *Psychology and work.* Washington, DC: American Psychological Association.

60. Bandura, 1986, 1989, 1991; Kanfer, F. H. (1980). Self-management methods. In F. H. Kanfer & A. P. Goldstein (Eds.), *Helping people change: A textbook of methods* (2nd ed.). New York, NY: Pergamon.

61. Luthans & Kreitner, 1985; Manz & Sims, 1980.

62. Frayne, C., & Latham, G. (1987). Application of social learning theory to employee self-management of attendance. *Journal of Applied Psychology, 72,* 387–392.

63. Frayne, C. A., & Geringer, J. M. (2000). Self-management training for improving job performance: A field experiment involving salespeople. *Journal of Applied Psychology, 85,* 361–372.

64. Gist, M. E., Stevens, C. K., & Bavetta, A. G. (1991). Effects of self-efficacy and post-training intervention on the acquisition and maintenance of complex interpersonal skills. *Personnel Psychology, 44,* 837–861; Stevens, C. K., Bavetta, A. G., & Gist, M. E. (1993). Gender differences in the acquisition of salary negotiation skills: The role of goals, self-efficacy, and perceived control. *Journal of Applied Psychology, 78,* 723–735.

65. Komaki, J., Barwick, K. D., & Scott, L. R. (1978). A behavioral approach to occupational safety: Pinpointing and reinforcing safe performance in a food manufacturing plant. *Journal of Applied Psychology, 63,* 434–445. For a similar study, see Haynes, R. S., Pine, R. C., & Fitch, H. G. (1982). Reducing accident rates with organizational behavior modification. *Academy of Management Journal, 25,* 407–416.

66. Stajkovic, A. D., & Lutans, F. (1997). A meta-analysis of the effects of organizational behavior modification on task performance, 1975–95. *Academy of Management Journal, 40,* 1122–1149; Stajkovic, A. D., & Luthans, F. (2003). Behavioral management and task performance in organizations: Conceptual background, meta-analysis, and test of alternative models. *Personnel Psychology, 56,* 155–194; Stajkovic, A. D., & Luthans, F. (2001). Differential effects of incentive motivators on work performance. *Academy of Management Journal, 44,* 580–590.

67. Markham, S. E., Scott, K. D., & McKee, G. H. (2002). Recognizing good attendance: A longitudinal, quasi-experimental field study. *Personnel Psychology, 55,* 639–660.

68. The power of peer recognition. A special report for the Great Place to Work® Institute Canada. (2008, April 28). *The Globe and Mail,* GPTW5; Marron, K. (2006, February 15). High praise from colleagues counts. *The Globe and Mail,* C1, C6; Dobson, S. (2013, October 7). Spontaneity makes recognition stand out. *Canadian HR Reporter, 26*(17), 25, 26; Silliker, A. (2013, April 22). Staff instructors offer training at CBC. *Canadian HR Reporter, 26*(8), 10; Byam, M. (2015, April 20). Peer-to-peer recognition. *Canadian HR Reporter, 28*(7), 15.

69. Bursch, J., & Van Strander, A. Well-structured employee reward/recognition programs yield positive results. (1999, November). *HRFocus, 1,* 14, 15.

70. Markham, Scott, & McKee, 2002.

71. Klie, S. (2006, August 14). Recognition equals profits. *Canadian HR Reporter, 19*(14), 18.

72. Saks, A. M., & Haccoun, R. R. (2010). *Managing performance through training and development* (5th ed.). Toronto, ON: Nelson.

73. Taylor, P. J., Russ-Eft, D. F., & Chan, D. W. L. (2005). A meta-analytic review of behavior modeling training. *Journal of Applied Psychology, 90,* 692–709.

74. Taylor, Russ-Eft, & Chan, 2005.

Chapter 3

1. Bernier, L. (2015, January 26). Pursuing their fullest potential. *Canadian HR Reporter, 28*(1), 3, www.rbc.com/careers/who-we-are.html; RBC holds strong market positions in its five business segments, www.rbc.com/aboutus/index/html; RBC is recognized as one of Canada's Best Diversity Employers for 2014, www.rbc.com.aboutus/2014-02-10-best-diversity-employers.html; Leung, K., & Yerema, R. (2015). RBC: Chosen as one of Canada's best diversity employers for 2015. *Canada's Best Diversity Employers,* http://www.canadastop100.com/diversity/. Reprinted by permission of *Canadian HR Reporter.* © Copyright Thomson Reuters Canada Ltd., Jan 26, 2015; 28, 1, Toronto, Ontario, 1-800-387-5164. Web: www.hrreporter.com.

2. Cox, T., Jr. (1993). *Cultural diversity in organizations: Theory, research, & practice.* San Francisco, CA: Berrett-Koehler.

3. Ashforth, B. E. (2001). *Role transitions in organizational life: An identity-based persepctive.* Mahwah, NJ: Lawrence Erlbaum Associates, Inc.; Ashforth, B. E., & Mael, F. (1989). Social identity theory and the organization. *Academy of Management Review, 14,* 20–39.

4. Ashforth, 2001; Ashforth & Mael, 1989.

5. Bruner, J. S. (1957). On perceptual readiness. *Psychological Review, 64,* 123–152.

6. Eagly, A. H., Ashmore, R. D., Makhijani, M. G., & Longo, L. C. (1991). What is beautiful is good, but…: A meta-analytic review of research on the physical attractiveness stereotype. *Psychological Bulletin, 110,* 109–128; Hosoda, M., Stone-Romero, E. F., & Coats, G. (2003). The effects of physical attractiveness on job-related outcomes: A meta-analysis of experimental studies. *Personnel Psychology, 56,* 431–462.

7. Stone, E. F., Stone, D. L., & Dipboye, R. L. (1992). Stigmas in organizations: Race, handicaps, and physical unattractiveness. In K. Kelley (Ed.), *Issues, theory and research in industrial/organizational psychology.* New York, NY: Elsevier; Hosoda, Stone-Romero, & Coats, 2003.

8. Judge, T. A., & Cable, D. M. (2004). The effect of physical height on workplace success and income: Preliminary test of a theoretical model. *Journal of Applied Psychology, 89,* 428–441.

9. Rudolph, C.W., Wells, C.L., Weller, M.D., & Baltes, B. B. (2009). A meta-analysis of empirical studies of weight-based bias in the workplace. *Journal of Vocational Behavior, 74,* 1–10.

10. See Krzystofiak, F., Cardy, R., & Newman, J. E. (1988). Implicit personality and performance appraisal: The influence of trait inferences on evaluations of behavior. *Journal of Applied Psychology, 73,* 515–521.

11. Fiske, S. T. (1993). Social cognition and social perception. *Annual Review of Psychology, 44,* 155–194.

12. Secord, P. F., Backman, C. W., & Slavitt, D. R. (1976). *Understanding social life: An*

introduction to social psychology. New York, NY: McGraw-Hill. For elaboration, see Wilder, D. A. (1986). Social categorization: Implications for creation and reduction of intergroup bias. *Advances in Experimental Social Psychology, 19,* 291–349.

13. Dion, K. L., & Schuller, R. A. (1991). The Ms. stereotype: Its generality and its relation to managerial and marital status stereotypes. *Canadian Journal of Behavioural Science, 23,* 25–40.

14. For a more complete treatment see Falkenberg, L. (1990). Improving the accuracy of stereotypes within the workplace. *Journal of Management, 16,* 107–118.

15. Kelley, H. H. (1972). Attribution in social interaction. In E. E. Jones, D. E. Kanhouse, H. H. Kelley, R. E. Nisbett, S. Valins, & B. Weiner (Eds.), *Attribution: Perceiving the causes of behavior.* Morristown, NJ: General Learning Press. For an integrative attribution model, see Medcof, J. W. (1990). PEAT: An integrative model of attribution processes. *Advances in Experimental Social Psychology, 23,* 111–209.

16. This discussion of attribution biases draws upon Fiske, S. T., & Taylor, S. E. (1984). *Social cognition.* Reading, MA: Addison-Wesley.

17. Jones, E. E. (1979). The rocky road from acts to dispositions. *American Psychologist, 34,* 107–117; Ross, L. (1977). The intuitive psychologist and his shortcomings: Distortions in the attribution process. *Advances in Experimental Social Psychology, 10,* 173–220.

18. Mitchell, T. R., & Kalb, L. S. (1982). Effects of job experience on supervisor attributions for a subordinate's poor performance. *Journal of Applied Psychology, 67,* 181–188.

19. Watson, D. (1982). The actor and the observer: How are their perceptions of causality divergent? *Psychological Bulletin, 92,* 682–700.

20. Sonnenfeld, J. (1981). Executive apologies for price fixing: Role biased perceptions of causality. *Academy of Management Journal, 24,* 192–198; Waters, J. A. (1978). Catch 20.5. Corporate morality as an organizational phenomenon. *Organizational Dynamics, 6*(4), 2–19.

21. Malle, B. F. (2006). The actor-observer asymmetry in attribution: A (surprising) meta-analysis. *Psychological Bulletin, 132,* 895–919.

22. Greenwald, A. G. (1980). The totalitarian ego: Fabrication and revision of personal history. *American Psychologist, 35,* 603–618; Tetlock, P. E. (1985). Accountability: The neglected social context of judgment and choice. *Research in Organizational Behavior, 7,* 297–332.

23. Pyszczynski, T., & Greenberg, J. (1987). Toward an integration of cognitive and motivational perspectives on social inference: A biased hypothesis-testing model. *Advances in Experimental Social Psychology, 20,* 197–340.

24. This section relies on Jackson, S. E., & Alvarez, E. B. (1992). Working through diversity as a strategic imperative. In S. E. Jackson (Ed.), *Diversity in the workplace: Human resources initiatives.* New York, NY: Guilford Press; Mahoney, J. (2005, March 23). Visible majority by 2017. *The Globe and Mail,* A1, A7.

25. Mahoney, 2005, March 23.

26. Mingail, H. (2004, September 29). Wise ways for retraining older workers. *The Globe and Mail,* C8; Dobson, S. (2010, April 5). HR by the numbers. *Canadian HR Reporter, 23*(7), 4.

27. Crawford, T. (2006, April 1). A better mix. *Toronto Star,* L1, L2; Galt, V. (2005, March 2). Diversity efforts paying off: Shell CFO. *The Globe and Mail,* B1, B20; Vu, U. (2004, November 8). FedEx holds managers accountable for diversity. *Canadian HR Reporter, 17*(19), 3; Shaw, A. (2006, May 22). Hiring immigrants makes good business sense. *Canadian HR Reporter, 19*(10), 21; Keung, N. (2006, March 18). Wanted: Minorities. *Toronto Star,* B1, B3; Dobson, S. (2013, March 25). Awards, "inclusion lens" among supports at top diversity employers. *Canadian HR Reporter, 26*(6), 2.

28. Cox, 1993, Cox, T., Jr. (1991). The multicultural organization. *Academy of Management Executive, 5,* 34–47.

29. Crone, G. (1999, February 18). Companies embracing workplace diversity. *Financial Post,* C11; Galt, V. (2004, January 27). Firms excel with women in senior ranks: Study. *The Globe and Mail,* B5; McKay, P. F., Avery D. R., & Morris, M. A. (2009). A tale of two climates: Diversity climate from subordinates' and managers' perspectives and their role in store unit sales performance. *Personnel Psychology, 62,* 767–791; Avery, D. R., McKay, P. F., Tonidandel, S., Volpone, S. D., & Morris, M. A. (2012). Is there method to the madness? Examining how racioethnic matching influences retail store productivity. *Personnel Psychology, 65,* 167–199.

30. Nguyen, H.-H. D., & Ryan, A. M. (2008). Does stereotype threat affect test performance of minorities and women? A meta-analysis of experimental evidence. *Journal of Applied Psychology, 93,* 1314–1334.

31. Bernier, L. (2014, October 20). The undercover employee. *Canadian HR Reporter, 27*(18), 1, 6.

32. Hartley, E. L. (1946). *Problems in prejudice.* New York, NY: King's Crown Press.

33. Sharpe, R. (1993, September 14). Losing ground. *Wall Street Journal,* A1, 12, 13.

34. King, E. B., & Ahmad, A. S. (2010). An experimental field study of interpersonal discrimination toward Muslim job applicants. *Personnel Psychology, 63,* 881–906.

35. Immen, W. (2007, June 29). Minorities still see barriers in way to the top. *The Globe and Mail,* C1.

36. Discrimination reported as a continuing issue in U.S. (2007, June 29). *The Globe and Mail,* C1.

37. Greenhaus, J. H., & Parasuraman, S. (1993). Job performance attributions and career advancement prospects: An examination of gender and race effects. *Organizational Behavior and Human Decision Processes, 55,* 273–297.

38. Powell, G. N. (1992). The good manager: Business students' stereotypes of Japanese managers versus stereotypes of American managers. *Group & Organizational Management, 17,* 44–56.

39. Galt, V. (2005, May 4). Glass ceiling still tough to crack. *The Globe and Mail,* C1, C2; Flavelle, D. (2005, April 28). Women advance up ranks slowly. *Toronto Star,* D1, D12; Perry, A. (2009, March 6). Women climbing corporate ranks: Study. *Toronto Star,* B3.

40. Brenner, O. C., Tomkiewicz, J., & Schein, V. E. (1989). The relationship between sex role stereotypes and requisite management characteristics revisited. *Academy of Management Journal, 32,* 662–669; Heilman, M. E., Block, C. J., Martell, R. F., & Simon, M. C. (1989). Has anything changed? Current characterizations of men, women, and managers. *Journal of Applied Psychology, 74,* 935–942; Schein, V. E. (1975). Relationships between sex role stereotypes and requisite management characteristics among female managers. *Journal of Applied Psychology, 60,* 340–344.

41. Brenner et al., 1989; Powell, G. N., Butterfield, D. A., & Parent, J. D. (2002). Gender and managerial stereotypes: Have the times changed? *Journal of Management, 28*(2), 177–193; Koenig, A. M., Eagly, A. H., Mitchell, A. A., & Ristikari, T. (2011). Are leader stereotypes masculine? A meta-analysis of three research paradigms. *Psychological Bulletin, 137,* 616–642; Koch, A. J., D'Mello, S. D., & Sackett, P. R. (2015). A meta-analysis of gender stereotypes and bias in experimental simulations of employment decision making. *Journal of Applied Psychology, 100,* 128–161.

42. Rosen, B., & Jerdee, T. H. (1974). Influence of sex role stereotypes on personnel decisions. *Journal of Applied Psychology, 59,* 9–14.

43. Cohen, S. L., & Bunker, K. A. (1975). Subtle effects of sex role stereotypes on

recruiters' hiring decisions. *Journal of Applied Psychology, 60,* 566–572. See also Rose, G. L., & Andiappan, P. (1978). Sex effects on managerial hiring decisions. *Academy of Management Journal, 21,* 104–112.

44. Heilman, M. E., Wallen, A. S., Fuchs, D., & Tamkins, M. M. (2004). Penalties for success: Reactions to women who succeed at male gender-typed tasks. *Journal of Applied Psychology, 89,* 416–427.

45. Parasuraman, S., & Greenhaus, J. H. (1993). Personal portrait: The lifestyle of the woman manager. In E. A. Fagenson (Ed.), *Women in management: Trends, issues, and challenges in managerial diversity.* Newbury Park, CA: Sage; Cleveland, J. N., Vescio, T. K., & Barnes-Farrell, J. L. (2005). Gender discrimination in organizations. In R. L. Dipboye & A. Colella (Eds.), *Discrimination at work: The psychological and organizational bases.* Mahwah, NJ: Lawrence Erlbaum Associates; Dobson, S. (2014, January 27). Female MBAs seeing less pay, lower job levels and fewer key career opportunities: Survey. *Canadian HR Reporter, 27*(2), 3, 9.

46. Tosi, H. L., & Einbender, S. W. (1985). The effects of the type and amount of information in sex discrimination research: A meta-analysis. *Academy of Management Journal, 28,* 712–723; Koch, A. J., D'Mello, S. D., & Sackett, P. R. (2015).

47. For a review, see Latham, G. P., Skarlicki, D., Irvine, D., & Siegel, J. P. (1993). The increasing importance of performance appraisals to employee effectiveness in organizational settings in North America. In C. L. Cooper & I. Robertson (Eds.), *International review of industrial and organizational psychology.* New York, NY: Wiley. For a representative study, see Pulakos, E. D., White, L. A., Oppler, S. A., & Borman, W. C. (1989). Examination of race and sex effects on performance ratings. *Journal of Applied Psychology, 74,* 770–780; Cleveland, Vescio, & Barnes-Farrell, 2005.

48. Roth, P. L., Purvis, K. L., & Bobko, P. (2012). A meta-analysis of gender group differences for measures of job performance in field studies. *Journal of Management, 38,* 719–739.

49. Bernier, L. (2014, October 6). Performance review or personal attack? *Canadian HR Reporter, 27*(17), 1, 8.

50. Galt, 2005, March 2.

51. Galt, 2005, May 4; McFarland, J. (2014, December 4). Canada third in ranking of female executives in financial services. *The Globe and Mail,* http://www.theglobeandmail.com/report-on-

business/canada-third-in-ranking-of-women-executives-in-financial-services/article21952110/.

52. Rosen, B., & Jerdee, T. H. (1976). The nature of job-related age stereotypes. *Journal of Applied Psychology, 61,* 180–183. See also Gibson, K. J., Zerbe, W. J., & Franken, R. E. (1992). Job search strategies for older job hunters: Addressing employers' perceptions. *Canadian Journal of Counselling, 26,* 166–176.

53. Gibson et al., 1992.

54. Ng, T. W. H., & Feldman, D. C. (2008). The relationship of age to ten dimensions of job performance. *Journal of Applied Psychology, 93,* 392–423; McEvoy, G. M., & Cascio, W. F. (1989). Cumulative evidence of the relationship between employee age and job performance. *Journal of Applied Psychology, 74,* 11–17. For a broader review on age, see Rhodes, S. R. (1983). Age-related differences in work attitudes and behavior. *Psychological Bulletin, 93,* 328–367.

55. Rosen, B., & Jerdee, T. H. (1976). The influence of age stereotypes on managerial decisions. *Journal of Applied Psychology, 61,* 428–432. Also see Dietrick, E. J., & Dobbins, G. J. (1991). The influence of subordinate age on managerial actions: An attributional analysis. *Journal of Organizational Behavior, 12,* 367–377.

56. Galt, V. (2002, October 16). What am I, chopped liver? *The Globe and Mail,* C1, C6.

57. Dobson, S. (2011, March 14). 50-plus awards celebrate older workers. *Canadian HR Reporter, 24*(5), 1, 6; Smolkin, S. (2013, February 25). Older workers finding success in second careers. *Toronto Star,* B1, B2; Silliker, A. (2013, January 14). 7 in 10 firms not hiring older workers. *Canadian HR Reporter, 26*(1), 1, 10; Bernier, L. (2013, October 7). Mature workers alienated by workplace policies. *Canadian HR Reporter, 26*(17), 3, 8.

58. Chamberlain, B. (2012, July 16). LGBT-friendly workplaces make business sense. *Canadian HR Reporter, 25*(13), 15; Silliker, A. (2011, December 19). LGBT staff still face bias. *Canadian HR Reporter, 24*(22), 1, 9; Shannon, K. (2009, July 13). LGBT employees still face barriers. *Canadian HR Reporter, 22*(13), 8; Bernier, L. (2015, June 15). LGBT community still facing misperceptions. *Canadian HR Reporter, 28*(11), 1, 17; Dobson, S. (2014, December 1). Out and proud at work. *Canadian HR Reporter, 27*(21), 1, 2.

59. Falkenberg, 1990; Fiske, S. T., Beroff, D. N., Borgida, E., Deaux, K., & Heilman, M. E. (1991). Use of sex stereotyping research in Price Waterhouse v. Hopkins. *American Psychologist, 46,* 1049–1060.

60. Bernier, L. (2015, January 26).

61. Dobson, S. (2014, April 21). TD recognized for focus on diversity. *Canadian HR Reporter, 27*(8), 8, 9.

62. Caudron, S. (1993, April). Training can damage diversity efforts. *Personnel Journal,* 51–62.

63. Scott, K. A., Heathcote, J. M., & Gruman, J. A. (2011). The diverse organization: Finding gold at the end of the rainbow. *Human Resource Management, 50,* 735–755; Bernier, L. (2014, March 10). Diversity not just about compliance. *Canadian HR Reporter, 27*(5), 1, 6.

64. Mayer, R. C., & Davis, J. H. (1999). The effect of the performance appraisal system on trust for management: A field quasi-experiment. *Journal of Applied Psychology, 84,* 123–136.

65. Lee, C. (1997, January). Trust. *Training, 34*(1), 28–37.

66. Anonymous (2014, May 19). HR by the numbers (Trust issues). *Canadian HR Reporter, 27*(10), 4; Silliker, A. (2012, November 19). 6 in 10 employees don't trust what leaders saying: Survey. *Canadian HR Reporter, 25*(20), 3, 5.

67. Mayer & Davis, 1999; Davis, J. H., Mayer, R. C., & Schoorman, F. D. (1995, October). The trusted general manager and firm performance: Empirical evidence of a strategic advantage. Paper presented at the 15th annual meeting of the Strategic Management Society, Mexico City, Mexico. Cited in Mayer & Davis, 1999.

68. Davis, Mayer, & Schoorman, 1995; Mayer, R. C., Davis, J. H., & Schoorman, F. D. (1995). An integrative model of organizational trust. *Academy of Management Review, 20,* 709–734; Rousseau, D. M., Sitkin, S. B., Burt, R. S., & Camerer, C. (1998). Not so different after all: A cross-discipline view of trust. *Academy of Management Review, 23,* 393–404.

69. Mayer, Davis, & Schoorman, 1995.

70. Mayer & Davis, 1999; Mayer, Davis, & Schoorman, 1995.

71. Colquitt, J. A., & Rodell, J. B. (2011). Justice, trust, and trustworthiness: A longitudinal analysis integrating three theoretical perspectives. *Academy of Management Journal, 54,* 1183–1206.

72. Dirks, K. T., & Ferrin, D. L. (2002). Trust in leadership: Meta-analytic findings and implications for research and practice. *Journal of Applied Psychology, 87,* 611–628.

73. Colquitt, J. A., Lepine, J. A., Zapata, C. P., & Wild, R. E. (2011). Trust in typical and high-reliability contexts: Building and reacting to trust among firefighters. *Academy of Management Journal, 54,* 999–1015.

74. Neto, J. T. (2009, April 6). About this survey. *A Special National Report for the*

Great Place to Work Institute Canada. The Globe and Mail, GPTW2.

75. Rhoades, L., & Eisenberger, R. (2002). Perceived organizational support: A review of the literature. *Journal of Applied Psychology, 87,* 698–714.

76. Rhoades & Eisenberger, 2002.

77. Shanock, L. R., & Eisenberger, R. (2006). When supervisors feel supported: Relationships with subordinates' perceived supervisor support, perceived organizational support, and performance. *Journal of Applied Psychology, 91,* 689–695.

78. Allen, D. G., Shore, L. M., & Griffeth, R. W. (2003). The role of perceived organizational support and supportive human resource practices in the turnover process. *Journal of Management, 29*(1), 99–118.

79. Rynes, S. L., Bretz, R., & Gerhart, B. (1991). The importance of recruitment in job choice: A different way of looking. *Personnel Psychology, 44,* 487–521.

80. Hausknecht, J. P., Day, D. V., & Thomas, S. C. (2004). Applicant reactions to selection procedures: An updated model and meta-analysis. *Personnel Psychology, 57,* 639–683.

81. Campion, M. A., Palmer, D. K., and Campion, J. E. (1997). A review of structure in the selection interview. *Personnel Psychology, 50,* 655–702; McDaniel, M. A., Whetzel, D. L., Schmidt, F. L., & Maurer, S. D. (1994). The validity of employment interviews: A comprehensive review and meta-analysis. *Journal of Applied Psychology, 79,* 599–616; Wiesner, W. H., & Cronshaw, S, F. (1988). A meta-analytic investigation of the impact of interview format and degree of structure on the validity of the employment interview. *Journal of Occupational Psychology, 61,* 275–290.

82. Hakel, M.D. (1982). Employment interviewing. In K. M. Rowland & G. R. Ferris (Eds.), *Personnel management.* Boston, MA: Allyn and Bacon.

83. Hakel, 1982; Dipboye, R. L. (1989). Threats to the incremental validity of interviewer judgments. In R. W. Eder & G. R. Ferris (Eds.), *The employment interview: Theory, research, and practice.* Newbury Park, CA: Sage.

84. Hollmann, T. D. (1972). Employment interviewers' errors in processing positive and negative information. *Journal of Applied Psychology, 56,* 130–134.

85. Rowe, P. M. (1989). Unfavorable information in interview decisions. In R. W. Eder & G. R. Ferris (Eds.), *The employment interview: Theory, research, and practice.* Newbury Park, CA: Sage.

86. Maurer, T. J., & Alexander, R. A. (1991). Contrast effects in behavioral measurement: An investigation of alternative process explanations. *Journal of Applied Psychology, 76,* 3–10; Maurer, T. J., Palmer, J. K., & Ashe, D. K. (1993). Diaries, checklists, evaluations, and contrast effects in measurement of behavior. *Journal of Applied Psychology, 78,* 226–231; Schmitt, N. (1976). Social and situational determinants of interview decisions: Implications for the employment interview. *Personnel Psychology, 29,* 70–101.

87. Chapman, D. S., & Zweig, D. I. (2005). Developing a nomological network for interview structure: Antecedents and consequences of the structured selection interview. *Personnel Psychology, 58,* 673–702.

88. For other reasons and a review of the interview literature, see Harris, M. M. (1989). Reconsidering the employment interview: A review of recent literature and suggestions for future research. *Personnel Psychology, 42,* 691–726.

89. Yam, K. C., Fehr, R., & Barnes, C. M. (2014). Morning employees are perceived as better employees: Employees' start times influence supervisor performance ratings. *Journal of Applied Psychology, 6,* 1288–1299.

90. Balzer, W. K., & Sulsky, L. M. (1992). Halo and performance appraisal research: A critical examination. *Journal of Applied Psychology, 77,* 975–985; Cooper, W. H. (1981). Ubiquitous halo. *Psychological Bulletin, 90,* 218–244; Murphy, K. R., Jako, R. A., & Anhalt, R. L. (1993). Nature and consequences of halo error: A critical analysis. *Journal of Applied Psychology, 78,* 218–225.

91. Kingstrom, P. D., & Bass, A. R. (1981). A critical analysis of studies comparing behaviorally anchored rating scales (BARS) and other rating formats. *Personnel Psychology, 34,* 263–289; Landy, F. J., & Farr, J. L. (1983). *The measurement of work performance.* New York, NY: Academic Press.

92. Roch, S. G., Woehr, D. J., Mishra, V., & Kieszczynska, U. (2012). Rater training revisited: An updated meta-analytic review of frame-of-reference training. *Journal of Occupational and Organizational Psychology, 85,* 370–395.

Chapter 4

1. Excerpted from Albergotti, R. (2014, December 26). At Facebook, boss is a dirty word. *The Wall Street Journal.* B1, B2. Reprinted with permission of *The Wall Street Journal,* Copyright © 2014 Dow Jones & Company, Inc. All Rights Reserved Worldwide.

2. Hofstede, G. (1980). *Culture's consequences: International differences in work-related values.* Beverly Hills, CA: Sage (p. 19); see also Rokeach, M. (1973). *The nature of human values.* New York: Free Press.

3. Meglino, B. M., & Ravlin, E. C. (1998). Individual values in organizations: Concepts, controversies, and research. *Journal of Management, 24,* 351–389.

4. Schwartz, S. H. (1992). Universals in the content and structure of values: Theoretical advances and empirical tests in 20 countries. *Advances in Experimental Social Psychology, 25,* 1–65.

5. See for example Hammill, G. (2005, Winter/Spring). Mixing and managing four generations of employees. *FDU Magazine*(online), http://view.fdu.edu/default.aspx?id=1144.

6. Lyons, S., & Kuron, L. (2014). Generational differences in the workplace: A review of the evidence and directions for future research. *Journal of Organizational Behavior, 35,* S139–S157.

7. Costanza, D. P., Badger, J. M., Fraser, R. L., Severt, J. B., & Gade, P. A. (2012). Generational differences in work-related attitudes: A meta-analysis. *Journal of Business and Psychology, 27,* 375–394; Cennamo, L., & Gardner, D. (2008). Generational differences in work values, outcomes and person–organisation fit. *Journal of Managerial Psychology, 23,* 891–906; Hess, N., & Jepsen, D. M. (2009). Career stage and generational differences in psychological contracts. *Career Development International, 14,* 261–283; Wong, M., Gardiner, E., Lang, W., & Coulon, L. (2008). General differences in personality and motivation: Do they exist and what are the implications for the workplace? *Journal of Managerial Psychology, 23,* 878–890; Deal, J. J. (2007). *Retiring the generation gap: How employees young and old can find common ground.* San Francisco: Jossey-Bass.

8. Westerman, J. W., & Yamamura, J. H. (2007). Generational preferences for work environment fit: Effects on employee outcomes. *Career Development International, 12,* 150–161; Cennamo & Gardner, 2008; Wong et al., 2008.

9. Twenge, J. M. (2010). A review of the empirical evidence on generational differences in work attitudes. *Journal of Business and Psychology, 25,* 201–210; Lyons & Kuron, 2014.

10. Twenge, 2010; Twenge, J. M., Campbell, S. M., Hoffman, B. J., & Lance, C. E. (2010). Generational differences in work values: Leisure and extrinsic values increasing, social and intrinsic values decreasing. *Journal of Management, 36,* 1117–1142; Lyons & Kuron, 2014.

11. Deal, 2007.

12. Meglino & Ravlin, 1998; Kristof, A. L. (1996). Person-organization fit: An integrative review of its conceptualizations,

measurement, and implications. *Personnel Psychology, 49,* 1–49.

13. Black, J. S., & Mendenhall, M. (1990). Cross-cultural training effectiveness: A review and theoretical framework for future research. *Academy of Management Review, 15,* 113–136.

14. MOW International Research Team. (1987). *The meaning of working.* London: Academic Press.

15. Hofstede, G., Hofstede, G. J., Minkov, M. (2010). *Cultures and organizations: Software of the mind* (3rd ed.). New York: McGraw-Hill.

16. Hofstede, G. (1991). *Cultures and organizations: Software of the mind.* London: McGraw-Hill; Hofstede, G., & Bond, M. H. (1988). The Confucius connection: From cultural roots to economic growth. *Organizational Dynamics, 16*(4), 4–21.

17. House, R. J., Hanges, P. J., Javidan, M., Dorfman, P. W., & Gupta, V. (Eds.) (2004). *Culture, leadership, and organizations: The GLOBE study of 62 societies.* Thousand Oaks, CA: Sage.

18. Daniels, M. A., & Greguras, G. J. (2014). Exploring the nature of power distance: Implications for micro- and macro-level theories, processes, and outcomes. *Journal of Management, 40,* 1202–1229.

19. For a meta-analysis of the correlates of Hofstede's cultural dimensions, see Taras, V., Kirkman, B. L., & Steel, P. (2010). Examining the impact of *Culture's Consequences*: A three-decade, multilevel, meta-analytic review of Hofstede's cultural value dimensions. *Journal of Applied Psychology, 95,* 405–439.

20. Beugelsdijk, S., Maseland, R., Onrust, O., van Hoorn, A., & Slangen, A. (2015). Cultural distance in international business and management: From mean-based to variance-based measures. *International Journal of Human Resource Management, 26,* 165–191.

21. Dragoni, L., Oh, I.-S., Tesluk, P. E., Moore, O. A., VanKatwyk, P., & Hazucha, J. (2014). Developing leaders' strategic thinking through global work experience: The moderating role of cultural distance. *Journal of Applied Psychology, 99,* 867–882.

22. Hofstede, G. (1984). The cultural relativity of the quality of life concept. *Academy of Management Review, 9,* 389–398; Hofstede, G. (1993, February). Cultural constraints in management theories. *Academy of Management Executive,* 81–94.

23. Young, S. M. (1992). A framework for successful adoption and performance of Japanese manufacturing practices in the United States. *Academy of Management Review, 17,* 677–700; Basadur, M. (1992, May). Managing creativity: A Japanese

model. *Academy of Management Executive,* 29–42.

24. Leung, K., Ang, S., & Tan, M. L. (2014). Intercultural competence. *Annual Review of Organizational Psychology and Organizational Behavior, 1,* 489–519.

25. Glasman, L. R., & Albarracín, D. (2006). Forming attitudes that predict future behavior: A meta-analysis of the attitude-behavior relation. *Psychological Bulletin, 132,* 778–821.

26. The following syllogistic construction of attitudes can be found in Jones, E. E., & Gerard, H. B. (1967). *Foundations of social psychology.* New York: Wiley.

27. Harrison, D. A., Newman, D. A., & Roth, P. L. (2006). How important are job attitudes? Meta-analytic comparisons of integrative behavioral outcomes and time sequences. *Academy of Management Journal, 49,* 305–325.

28. Locke, E. A. (1976). The nature and causes of job satisfaction. In M. D. Dunnette (Ed.), *Handbook of industrial and organizational psychology.* Chicago: Rand McNally. See also Rice, R. W., Gentile, D. A., & McFarlin, D. B. (1991). Facet importance and job satisfaction. *Journal of Applied Psychology, 76,* 31–39.

29. Smith, P. C. (1992). In pursuit of happiness: Why study general job satisfaction? In C. J. Cranny, P. C. Smith, & E. F. Stone (Eds.), *Job satisfaction.* New York: Lexington.

30. Smith, P. C., Kendall, L. M., & Hulin, C. L. (1969). *The measurement of satisfaction in work and retirement.* Chicago: Rand McNally; Bowling Green State University (2009). *The job descriptive index.* Bowling Green, OH: Department of Psychology, Bowling Green State University.

31. Weiss, D. J., Dawis, R. V., England, G. W., & Lofquist, L. H. (1967). *Manual for the Minnesota satisfaction questionnaire: Minnesota studies in vocational rehabilitation.* Minneapolis: Vocational Psychology Research, University of Minnesota.

32. Locke, E. A. (1969). What is job satisfaction? *Organizational Behavior and Human Performance, 4,* 309–336; Rice, R. W., McFarlin, D. B., & Bennett, D. E. (1989). Standards of comparison and job satisfaction. *Journal of Applied Psychology, 74,* 591–598.

33. Williams, M. L., McDaniel, M. A., & Nguyen, N. T. (2006). A meta-analysis of the antecedents and consequences of pay level satisfaction. *Journal of Applied Psychology, 91,* 392–413.

34. For a good overview of fairness research, see Greenberg, J., & Colquitt, J. A. (2005). *Handbook of organizational justice.* Mahwah, NJ: Lawrence Erlbaum Associates. For a recent empirical review, see Colquitt, J. A., Scott, B. A., Rodell,

J. B., Long, D. M., Zapata, C. P., & Conlon, D. E. (2013). Justice at the millennium, a decade later: A meta-analytic test of social exchange and affect-based perspectives. *Journal of Applied Psychology, 98,* 199–236.

35. Adams, J. S. (1963). Toward an understanding of inequity. *Journal of Abnormal and Social Psychology, 67,* 422–436.

36. See Kulik, C. T., & Ambrose, M. L. (1992). Personal and situational determinants of referent choice. *Academy of Management Review, 17,* 212–237.

37. Sharp, I. (2009, April 15). A few bumps in the road. *The Globe and Mail,* B3.

38. Greenberg, J. (1987). A taxonomy of organizational justice theories. *Academy of Management Review, 12,* 9–22.

39. Brockner, J., & Wiesenfeld, B. M. (1996). An integrative framework for explaining reactions to decisions: Interactive effects of outcomes and procedures. *Psychological Bulletin, 120,* 189–208; Brockner, J., & Wiesenfeld, B. (2005). How, when, and why does outcome favorability interact with procedural fairness? In Greenberg & Colquitt, 2005.

40. Cropanzano, R., & Folger, R. (1989). Referent cognitions and task decision autonomy: Beyond equity theory. *Journal of Applied Psychology, 74,* 293. See also Folger, R. (1987). Reformulating the preconditions of resentment: A referent cognitions model. In J. C. Masters & W. P. Smith (Eds.), *Social comparison, justice, and relative deprivation: Theoretical, empirical, and policy perspectives.* Hillsdale, NJ: Erlbaum.

41. Colquitt, J. A., Greenberg, J., & Zapata-Phelan, C. P. (2005). What is organizational justice? A historical overview. In Greenberg & Colquitt, 2005; Bies, R. J. (2005). Are procedural justice and interactional justice conceptually distinct? In Greenberg & Colquitt, 2005.

42. Judge, T. A. (1992). The dispositional perspective in human resources research. *Research in Personnel and Human Resources Management, 10,* 31–72. See also Staw, B. M., & Cohen-Charash, Y. (2005). The dispositional approach to job satisfaction: More than a mirage, but not yet an oasis. *Journal of Organizational Behavior, 26,* 59–78; Bowling, N. A., Beehr, T. A., Wagner, S. H., & Libkuman, T. M. (2005). Adaptation-level theory, opponent process theory, and dispositions: An integrated approach to the stability of job satisfaction. *Journal of Applied Psychology, 90,* 1044–1053.

43. Song, Z., Li, W., & Arvey, R. D. (2011). Associations between dopamine and serotonin genes and job satisfaction: Preliminary evidence from the Add Health Study. *Journal of Applied Psychology, 96,* 1223–1233.

44. Judge, T. A., Heller, D., & Mount, M. K. (2002). Five-factor model of personality and job satisfaction: A meta-analysis. *Journal of Applied Psychology, 87,* 530–541.

45. Judge, T. A., Bono, J. E., & Locke, E. A. (2000). Personality and job satisfaction: The mediating role of job characteristics. *Journal of Applied Psychology, 85,* 237–249.

46. Weiss, H. M., & Cropanzano, R. (1996). Affective events theory: A theoretical discussion of the structure, causes and consequences of affective experiences at work. *Research in Organizational Behavior, 18,* 1–74.

47. Colquitt et al., 2013; Barsky, A., Kaplan, S. A., & Beal, D. J. (2011). Just feelings? The role of affect in the formation of organizational fairness judgments. *Journal of Management, 37,* 248–279.

48. Elfenbein, H. A. (2014). The many faces of emotional contagion: An affective process theory of affective linkage. *Organizational Psychology Review, 4,* 326–362.

49. Barsade, S. G. (2002). The ripple effect: Emotional contagion and its influence on group behavior. *Administrative Science Quarterly, 47,* 644–675; see also Vijayalakshmi, V., & Bhattacharyya, S. (2012). Emotional contagion and its relevance to individual behavior and organizational processes: A position paper. *Journal of Business and Psychology,* 1–12.

50. Grandey, A. A., Dickter, D. N., & Sin, H. P. (2004). The customer is *not* always right: Customer aggression and emotion regulation of service employees. *Journal of Organizational Behavior, 25,* 397–418.

51. Kammeyer-Mueller, J. D., Rubenstein, A. L., Long, D. M., Odio, M. A., Buckman, B. R., Zhang, Y., & Halvorsen-Ganepola, M. D. K. (2013). A meta-analytic structural model of dispositional affectivity and emotional labor. *Personnel Psychology, 66,* 47–90; Hülsheger, U. R., & Schewe, A. F. (2011). On the costs and benefits of emotional labor: A meta-analysis of three decades of research. *Journal of Occupational Health Psychology, 16,* 361–389.

52. Kim, E., & Yoon, D. J. (2012). Why does service with a smile make employees happy? A social interaction model. *Journal of Applied Psychology, 97,* 1059–1067.

53. Glomb, T. M., Kammeyer-Mueller, J. D., & Rotundo, M. (2004). Emotional labor demands and compensating wage differentials. *Journal of Applied Psychology, 89,* 700–714.

54. This material draws upon Locke, 1976.

55. Hackett, R. D. (1989). Work attitudes and employee absenteeism: A synthesis of the literature. *Journal of Occupational Psychology, 62,* 235–248; Hackett, R. D., & Guion, R. M. (1985). A reevaluation of the absenteeism-job satisfaction relationship. *Organizational Behavior and Human Decision Processes, 35,* 340–381.

56. Johns, G. (2008). Absenteeism and presenteeism: Not at work or not working well. In C. L. Cooper & J. Barling (Eds.), *The Sage handbook of organizational behavior* (Vol. 1). London: Sage; Nicholson, N., & Johns, G. (1985). The absence culture and the psychological contract—Who's in control of absence? *Academy of Management Review, 10,* 397–407.

57. Li, Y., & Jones, C. B. (2013). A literature review of nursing turnover costs. *Journal of Nursing Management, 21,* 405–418.

58. Farris, G. F. (1971). A predictive study of turnover. *Personnel Psychology, 24,* 311–328. However, the more general relationship between performance and voluntary turnover is negative, as shown by Bycio, P., Hackett, R. D., & Alvares, K. M. (1990). Job performance and turnover: A review and meta-analysis. *Applied Psychology: An International Review, 39,* 47–76; Williams, C. R., & Livingstone, L. P. (1994). Another look at the relationship between performance and voluntary turnover. *Academy of Management Journal, 37,* 269–298.

59. Park, T.-Y., & Shaw, J. D. (2013). Turnover rates and organizational performance: A meta-analysis. *Journal of Applied Psychology, 98,* 268–309.

60. Griffeth, R. W., Hom, P. W., & Gaertner, S. (2000). A meta-analysis of antecedents and correlates of employee turnover: Update, moderator tests, and research implications for the next millennium. *Journal of Management, 26,* 463–488.

61. This model is based on Hom & Griffeth, 1995; Lee, T. W., & Mitchell, T. R. (1994). An alternative approach: The unfolding model of voluntary employee turnover. *Academy of Management Review, 19,* 51–89; Mitchell, T. R., Holtom, B. C., Lee, T. W., Sablynski, C. J., & Erez, M. (2001). Why people stay: Using job embeddedness to predict voluntary turnover. *Academy of Management Journal, 44,* 1102–1121.

62. Griffeth et al., 2000.

63. For further development of this see Hom, P. W., Mitchell, T. R., Lee, T. W., & Griffeth, R. W. (2012). Reviewing employee turnover: Focusing on proximal withdrawal states and an expanded criterion. *Psychological Bulletin, 138,* 831–858.

64. Carsten, J. M., & Spector, P. E. (1987). Unemployment, job satisfaction, and employee turnover: A meta-analytic test of the Muchinsky model. *Journal of Applied Psychology, 72,* 374–381.

65. Boswell, W. R., Boudreau, J. W., & Tichy, J. (2005). The relationship between employee job change and job satisfaction: The honeymoon-hangover effect. *Journal of Applied Psychology, 90,* 882–892; see also Boswell, W. R., Shipp, A. J., Payne, S. C., & Culbertson, S. S. (2009). Changes in newcomer satisfaction over time: Examining the pattern of honeymoons and hangovers. *Journal of Applied Psychology, 94,* 844–858.

66. Judge, T. A., Thoresen, C. J., Bono, J. E., & Patton, G. K. (2001). The job satisfaction-job performance relationship: A qualitative and quantitative review. *Psychological Bulletin, 127,* 376–407.

67. Iaffaldano, M. T., & Muchinsky, P. M. (1985). Job satisfaction and job performance: A meta-analysis. *Psychological Bulletin, 97,* 251–273.

68. Lawler, E. E., III (1973). *Motivation in organizations.* Monterey, CA: Brooks/Cole.

69. Riketta, M. (2008). The causal relationship between job attitudes and performance: A meta-analysis of panel studies. *Journal of Applied Psychology, 93,* 472–481.

70. Organ, D. W. (1988). *Organizational citizenship behavior: The good soldier syndrome.* Lexington, MA: Lexington; Podsakoff, P. M., MacKenzie, S. B., Paine, J. B., & Bachrach, D. G. (2000). Organizational citizenship behaviors: A critical review of the theoretical and empirical literature and suggestions for future research. *Journal of Management, 26,* 513–563.

71. Lepine, J. A., Erez, A., & Johnson, D.E. (2002). The nature and dimensionality of organizational citizenship behavior: A critical review and meta-analysis. *Journal of Applied Psychology, 87,* 52–65; Organ, D. W., & Ryan, K. (1995). A meta-analytic review of attitudinal and dispositional predictors of organizational citizenship behavior. *Personnel Psychology, 48,* 775–802; Hoffman, B. J., Blair, C. A., Meriac, J. P., & Woehr, D. J. (2007). Expanding the criterion domain? A quantitative review of the OCB literature. *Journal of Applied Psychology, 92,* 555–566.

72. Organ, 1988.

73. Lepine et al., 2002; Fassina, N. E., Jones, D. A., & Uggerslev, K. L. (2008). Meta-analytic tests of relationships between organizational justice and citizenship behavior: Testing agent-system and shared-variance models. *Journal of Organizational Behavior, 29,* 805–828.

74. George, J. M. (1991). State or trait: Effects of positive mood on prosocial

behaviors at work. *Journal of Applied Psychology, 76,* 299–307.

75. Podsakoff, N. P., Podsakoff, P. M., Mackenzie, S. B., Maynes, T. D., & Spoelma, T. M. (2014). Consequences of unit-level organizational citizenship behaviors: A review and recommendations for future research. *Journal of Organizational Behavior, 35,* S87–S119; Podsakoff, N. P., Whiting, S. W., Podsakoff, P. M., & Blume, B. D. (2009). Individual- and organizational-level consequences of organizational citizenship behaviors: A meta-analysis. *Journal of Applied Psychology, 94,* 122–141.

76. Berry, C. M., Lelchook, A. M., & Clark, M. A. (2011). A meta-analysis of the interrelationships between employee lateness, absenteeism, and turnover: Implications for models of withdrawal behavior. *Journal of Organizational Behavior, 33,* 678–699; Harrison et al., 2006.

77. Harter, J. K, Schmidt, F. L., & Hayes, T. L. (2002). Business-unit-level relationship between employee satisfaction, employee engagement, and business outcomes: A meta-analysis. *Journal of Applied Psychology, 87,* 268–279.

78. Edmans, A. (2012, November). The link between job satisfaction and firm value, with implications for corporate social responsibility. *Academy of Management Perspectives, 26*(4), 1–19.

79. Meyer, J. P., & Allen, N. J. (1997). *Commitment in the workplace.* Thousand Oaks, CA: Sage; for a recent critique and revised conception of commitment, see Klein, H. J., Molloy, J. C., & Brinsfield, C. T. (2012). Reconceptualizing workplace commitment to redress a stretched construct: Revisiting assumptions and removing confounds. *Academy of Management Review, 37,* 130–151.

80. Meyer, J. P., Allen, N. J., & Topolnytsky, L. (1998). Commitment in a changing world of work. *Canadian Psychology, 39,* 83–93; see also Meyer, J. P., Jackson, T. A., & Maltin, E. R. (2008). Commitment in the workplace: Past, present, and future. In J. Barling & C. L. Cooper (Eds.), *The Sage handbook of organizational behavior* (Vol. 1). London: Sage.

81. Meyer, J. P, Stanley, D. J., Herscovitch, L., & Topolnytsky, L. (2002). Affective, continuance, and normative commitment to the organization: A meta-analysis of antecedents, correlates, and consequences. *Journal of Vocational Behavior, 61,* 20–52.

82. Meyer et al., 2002.

83. Meyer et al., 2002; for a careful study, see Jaros, S. J., Jermier, J. M., Koehler, J. W., & Sincich, T. (1993). Effects of continuance, affective, and moral commitment on the withdrawal process: An evaluation of eight structural equation models. *Academy of Management Journal, 36,* 951–995.

84. Meyer, J. P., Becker, T. E., & Vandenberghe, C. (2004). Employee commitment and motivation: A conceptual analysis and integrative model. *Journal of Applied Psychology, 89,* 991–1007.

85. Meyer, J. P., Paunonen, S. V., Gellatly, I. R., Goffin, R. D., & Jackson, D. N. (1989). Organizational commitment and job performance: It's the nature of the commitment that counts. *Journal of Applied Psychology, 74,* 152–156.

86. Randall, D. M. (1987). Commitment and the organization: The organization man revisited. *Academy of Management Review, 12,* 460–471.

87. Meyer, Allen, & Topolnytsky, 1998; see also Meyer et al., 2008.

Chapter 5

1. Quan, K. (2014, November 10). Canada's best employers 2015: How DevFacto keeps its culture strong. *Canadian Business,* http://www.canadianbusiness.com/lists-and-rankings/best-jobs/2015-best-employers-devfacto-technologies/; Best Workplaces 2011: Best workplace for millenials (Devfacto Technologies Inc). *Alberta Venture* (2011, May 1), http://albertaventure.com/2011/05/best-workplaces-2011-best-workplace-for-perks-and-incentives-2/; Best workplaces 2012: Best workplaces under 100 employees (Devfacto). *Best Workplaces 2012* (2012, May 1), http://albertaventure.com/2012/05/best-workplaces-2012-best-workplace-under-100-employees; Chris Izquierdo and David Cronin (DevFacto Technologies Inc.). *Ernst & Young Entrepreneur of the Year 2012* (2012), http://business.queensu.ca/centres/business-venturing/bsme/pdf/entrepreneuroftheyearaward.pdf. Used by permission from David Cronin, CTO and Co-founder at DevFacto Technologies Inc.

2. Campbell, J. P., Dunnette, M. D., Lawler, E. E., III, & Weick, K. E., Jr. (1970). *Managerial behavior, performance, and effectiveness.* New York, NY: McGraw-Hill. Also see Blau, G. (1993). Operationalizing direction and level of effort and testing their relationship to job performance. *Organizational Behavior and Human Decision Processes, 55,* 152–170.

3. Dyer, L., & Parker, D. F. (1975). Classifying outcomes in work motivation research: An examination of the intrinsic-extrinsic dichotomy. *Journal of Applied Psychology, 60,* 455–458; Kanungo, R. N., & Hartwick, J. (1987). An alternative to the intrinsic-extrinsic dichotomy of work rewards. *Journal of Management, 13,* 751–766. Also see Brief, A. P., & Aldag, R. J. (1977). The intrinsic-extrinsic dichotomy: Toward conceptual clarity. *Academy of Management Review, 2,* 496–500.

4. Vallerand, R. J. (1997). Toward a hierarchical model of intrinsic and extrinsic motivation. *Advances in Experimental Social Psychology, 29,* 271–360.

5. Deci, E. L., & Ryan, R. M. (1985). *Intrinsic motivation and self-determination in human behavior.* New York, NY: Plenum.

6. Deci & Ryan, 1985.

7. Eisenberger, R., & Cameron, J. (1996). Detrimental effects of reward: Reality or myth? *American Psychologist, 51,* 1153–1166.

8. Guzzo, R. A. (1979). Types of rewards, cognitions, and work motivation. *Academy of Management Review, 4,* 75–86; Wiersma, U. J. (1992). The effects of extrinsic rewards in intrinsic motivation: A meta-analysis. *Journal of Occupational and Organizational Psychology, 65,* 101–114.

9. Based on Campbell, J. P., & Pritchard, R. D. (1976). Motivation theory in industrial and organizational psychology. In M. D. Dunnette (Ed.), *Handbook of industrial and organizational psychology.* Chicago, IL: Rand McNally.

10. O'Reilly, C. A. III, & Chatman, J. A. (1994). Working smarter and harder: A longitudinal study of managerial success. *Administrative Science Quarterly, 39,* 603–627.

11. Lang, J. W. B., Kersting, M., Hulsheger, U. R., & Lang, J. (2010). General mental ability, narrower cognitive abilities, and job performance: The perspective of the nested-factors model of cognitive abilities. *Personnel Psychology, 63,* 595–640; Hunter, J. E. (1986). Cognitive ability, cognitive aptitudes, job knowledge, and job performance. *Journal of Vocational Behavior, 29,* 340–362; Schmidt, F. L., & Hunter, J. E. (1998). The validity and utility of selection methods in personnel psychology: Practical and theoretical implications of 85 years of research findings. *Psychological Bulletin, 124,* 262–274; Judge, T. A., Klinger, R. L., & Simon, L. S. (2010). Time is on my side: Time, general mental ability, human capital, and extrinsic career success. *Journal of Applied Psychology, 95,* 92–107.

12. Mayer, J. D., Caruso, D. R., & Salovey, P. (2000). Emotional intelligence meets traditional standards for an intelligence. *Intelligence, 27,* 267–298; Salovey, P., & Mayer, J. D. (1990). Emotional

intelligence. *Imagination, Cognition and Personality, 9,* 185–211.

13. Mayer, Caruso, & Salovey, 2000.

14. George, J. M. (2000). Emotions and leadership: The role of emotional intelligence. *Human Relations, 53,* 1027–1055.

15. George, 2000.

16. George, 2000.

17. Van Rooy, D. L., & Viswesvaran, C. (2004). Emotional intelligence: A meta-analytic investigation of predictive validity and nomological net. *Journal of Vocational Behavior, 65,* 71–95.

18. O'Boyle, E. H., Jr., Humphrey, R. H., Pollack, J. M., Hawver, T. H., & Story, P. A. (2011). The relation between emotional intelligence and job performance: A meta-analysis. *Journal of Organizational Behavior, 32,* 788–818.

19. Schutte, N. S., Malouff, J. M., Hall, L. E., Haggerty, D. J., Cooper, J. T., Golden, C. J., & Dornheim, L. (1998). Development and validation of a measure of emotional intelligence. *Personality and Individual Differences, 25,* 167–177; Wong, C., & Law, K. S. (2002). The effects of leader and follower emotional intelligence on performance and attitude: An exploratory study. *The Leadership Quarterly, 13,* 243–274; Daus, C. S., & Ashkanasy, N. M. (2005). The case for the ability-based model of emotional intelligence in organizational behaviour. *Journal of Organizational Behavior, 26,* 453–466; Joseph, D. L., & Newman, D. A. (2010). Emotional intelligence: An integrative meta-analysis and cascading model. *Journal of Applied Psychology, 95,* 54–78.

20. Côté, S., & Miners, C. T. H. (2006). Emotional intelligence, cognitive intelligence, and job performance. *Administrative Science Quarterly, 51,* 1–28.

21. See Henkoff, R. (1993, March 22). Companies that train best. *Fortune,* 62–75.

22. The distinction between need (content) and process theories was first made by Campbell et al., 1970.

23. Maslow, A. H. (1970). *Motivation and personality* (2nd ed.). New York, NY: Harper & Row.

24. Alderfer, C. P. (1969). An empirical test of a new theory of human needs. *Organizational Behavior and Human Performance, 4,* 142–175. Also see Alderfer, C. P. (1972). *Existence, relatedness, and growth: Human needs in organizational settings.* New York, NY: The Free Press.

25. McClelland, D. C. (1985). *Human motivation.* Glenview, IL: Scott, Foresman.

26. McClelland, D. C., & Winter, D. G. (1969). *Motivating economic achievement.* New York, NY: The Free Press, 50–52.

27. McClelland, D. C., & Boyatzis, R. E. (1982). Leadership motive pattern and long-term success in management. *Journal of Applied Psychology, 67,* 737–743; McClelland, D. C., & Burnham, D. (1976, March–April). Power is the great motivator. *Harvard Business Review,* 159–166. However, need for power might not be the best motive pattern for managers of technical and professional people. See Cornelius, E. T., III, & Lane, F. B. (1984). The power motive and managerial success in a professionally oriented service industry organization. *Journal of Applied Psychology, 69,* 32–39.

28. Wahba, M. A., & Bridwell, L. G. (1976). Maslow reconsidered: A review of research on the need hierarchy theory. *Organizational Behavior and Human Performance, 15,* 212–240.

29. Schneider, B., & Alderfer, C. P. (1973). Three studies of measures of need satisfaction in organizations. *Administrative Science Quarterly, 18,* 498–505. Also see Alderfer, C. P., Kaplan, R. E., & Smith, K. K. (1974). The effect of relatedness need satisfaction on relatedness desires. *Administrative Science Quarterly, 19,* 507–532. For a disconfirming test, see Rauschenberger, J., Schmitt, N., & Hunter, J. E. (1980). A test of the need hierarchy concept by a Markov model of change in need strength. *Administrative Science Quarterly, 25,* 654–670.

30. McClelland, 1985; Spangler, W. D. (1992). Validity of questionnaire and TAT measures of need for achievement: Two meta-analyses. *Psychological Bulletin, 112,* 140–154.

31. Herzberg, F. (1966). *Work and the nature of man.* Cleveland, OH: World Publishing.

32. Lawler, E.E., III. (1973). *Motivation in work organizations.* Monterey, CA: Brooks/Cole.

33. Gagné, M., & Deci, E. L. (2005). Self-determination theory and work motivation. *Journal of Organizational Behavior, 26,* 331–362.

34. Gagné, M., & Deci, E. L. (2005).

35. Gillet, N., Gagné, M., Sauvagere, S., & Fouquereau, E. (2013). The role of supervisor autonomy support, organizational support, and autonomous and controlled motivation in predicting employees' satisfaction and turnover intentions. *European Journal of Work and Organizational Psychology, 22,* 450–460; Gagne, M. et al. (2015). The multidimensional work motivation scale: Validation evidence in seven languages and nine countries. *European Journal of Work and Organizational Psychology, 24,* 178–196; Gagne, M., Forest, J., Gilbert, M. H., Aube, C., Morin, E., & Malorni,

A. (2010). The motivation at work scale: Validation evidence in two languages. *Educational and Psychological Measurement, 70,* 628–646; Gagne, M. (2003). The role of autonomy support and autonomy orientation in prosocial behavior engagement. *Motivation and Emotion, 27,* 199–223.

36. Gagné, M., & Deci, E. L. (2005).

37. Vroom, V. H. (1964). *Work and motivation.* New York, NY: Wiley.

38. Mitchell, T. R. (1974). Expectancy models of job satisfaction, occupational preference, and effort: A theoretical, methodological, and empirical appraisal. *Psychological Bulletin, 81,* 1053–1077. Also see Pinder, C. C. (1984). *Work motivation: Theory, issues, and applications.* Glenview, IL: Scott, Foresman; Kanfer, R. (1990). Motivation theory in industrial and organizational psychology. In M. D. Dunnette & L. M. Hough (Eds.), *Handbook of industrial and organizational psychology* (2nd ed., Vol. 1). Palo Alto, CA: Consulting Psychologists Press.

39. A good discussion of how managers can strengthen expectancy and instrumentality relationships is presented by Strauss, G. (1977). Managerial practices. In J. R. Hackman & J. L. Suttle (Eds.), *Improving life at work: Behavioral science approaches to organizational change.* Glenview, IL: Scott, Foresman.

40. Adams, J. S. (1965). Injustice in social exchange. *Advances in Experimental Social Psychology, 2,* 267–299.

41. Kulik, C. T., & Ambrose, M. L. (1992). Personal and situational determinants of referent choice. *Academy of Management Review, 17,* 212–237.

42. Carrell, M. R., & Dittrich, J. E. (1978). Equity theory: The recent literature, methodological considerations, and new directions. *Academy of Management Review, 3,* 202–210; Mowday, R. T. (1991). Equity theory predictions of behavior in organizations. In R. M. Steers & L. W. Porter (Eds.), *Motivation and work behavior,* 111–131. New York, NY: McGraw-Hill.

43. Mowday, 1991; Carrell & Dittrich, 1978.

44. See Kulik & Ambrose, 1992.

45. Locke, E. A., & Latham, G. P. (2002). Building a practically useful theory of goal setting and task motivation. *American Psychologist, 57,* 705–717.

46. The best-developed theoretical position is that of Locke, E. A., & Latham, G. P. (1990). *A theory of goal setting and task performance.* Englewood Cliffs, NJ: Prentice-Hall.

47. Locke & Latham, 2002.

48. Locke & Latham, 2002.

49. Locke, E. A., Latham, G. P., & Erez, M. (1988). The determinants

of goal commitment. *Academy of Management Review, 13*, 23–39.

50. See Erez, M., Earley, P. C., & Hulin, C. L. (1985). The impact of participation on goal acceptance and performance: A two-step model. *Academy of Management Journal, 28*, 50–66.

51. Latham, G. P., Erez, M., & Locke, E. A. (1988). Resolving scientific disputes by the joint design of crucial experiments by the antagonists: Application to the Erez-Latham dispute regarding participation in goal setting. *Journal of Applied Psychology, 73*, 753–772.

52. Latham, G. P., Mitchell, T. R., & Dosset, D. L. (1978). The importance of participative goal setting and anticipated rewards on goal difficulty and job performance. *Journal of Applied Psychology, 63*, 163–171; Saari, L. M., & Latham, G. P. (1979). The effects of holding goal difficulty constant on assigned and participatively set goals. *Academy of Management Journal, 22*, 163–168.

53. For a discussion of this issue, see Saari & Latham, 1979.

54. Payne, S. C., Youngcourt, S. S., & Beaubien, J. M. (2007). A meta-analytic examination of the goal orientation nomological net. *Journal of Applied Psychology, 92*,128–150; Zweig, D., & Webster, J. (2004). Validation of a multidimensional measure of goal orientation. *Canadian Journal of Behavioural Science, 36*(3), 232–243.

55. Seijts, G. H., Latham, G. P., Tasa, K., & Latham, B. W. (2004). Goal setting and goal orientation: An integration of two different yet related literatures. *Academy of Management Journal, 47*, 227–239; Button, S. B., Mathieu, J. E., & Zajac, D. M. (1996). Goal orientation in organizational research: A conceptual and empirical foundation. *Organizational Behavior and Human Decision Processes, 67*, 26–48; VandeWalle, D., Brown, S. P., Cron, W. L., & Slocum, J.W., Jr. (1999). The influence of goal orientation and self-regulation tactics on sales performance: A longitudinal field test. *Journal of Applied Psychology, 84*, 249–259; VandeWalle, D., Cron, W.L., & Slocum, J. W., Jr. (2001). The role of goal orientation following performance feedback. *Journal of Applied Psychology, 86*, 629–640; Kozlowski, S. W. J., Gully, S. M., Brown, K. G., Salas, E., Smith, E. M., & Nason, E. R. (2001). Effects of training goals and goal orientation traits on multidimensional training outcomes and performance adaptability. *Organizational Behavior and Human Decision Processes, 85*, 1–31.

56. Latham, G. P., & Seijts, G. H. (1999). The effects of proximal and distal goals on performance on a moderately complex task. *Journal of Organizational Behavior, 20*, 421–429; Seijts, G. H., & Latham, G. P. (2001). The effect of distal learning, outcome, and proximal goals on a moderately complex task. *Journal of Organizational Behavior, 22*, 291–307.

57. Latham & Seijts, 1999; Seijts & Latham, 2001.

58. O'Leary-Kelly, A. M., Martocchio, J. J., & Frink, D. D. (1994). A review of the influence of group goals on group performance. *Academy of Management Journal, 37*, 1285–1301; Kleingeld, A., van Mierlo, H., & Arends, L. (2011). The effect of goal setting on group performance: A meta-analysis. *Journal of Applied Psychology, 96*, 1289–1304.

59. Locke, E. A., & Latham, G. P. (1984). *Goal setting: A motivational technique that works.* Englewood Cliffs, NJ: Prentice-Hall.

60. Latham, G. P., & Baldes, J. J. (1975). The "practical significance" of Locke's theory of goal setting. *Journal of Applied Psychology, 60*, 122–124; Latham, G. P., & Locke, E. (1979). Goal setting: a motivational technique that works. *Organizational Dynamics, 8*(2), 68–80.

61. Payne et al., 2007; Seijts, Latham, Tasa, & Latham, 2004; Seijts, G., & Latham, G. P. (2005). Learning versus performance goals: When should each be used? *Academy of Management Executive, 19*, 124–131.

62. Shantz, A., & Latham, G. P. (2009). An exploratory field experiment of the effect of subconscious and conscious goals on employee performance. *Organizational Behavior and Human Decision Processes, 109*, 9–17; Stajkovic, A. D., Locke, E. A., & Blair, E. S. (2006). A first examination of the relationships between primed subconscious goals, assigned conscious goals, and task performance. *Journal of Applied Psychology, 91*, 1172–1180.

63. Seijts, Latham, Tasa, & Latham, 2004; Seijts & Latham, 2005; Latham & Seijts, 1999; Seijts & Latham, 2001.

64. Kagitcibasi, C., & Berry, J. W. (1989). Cross-cultural psychology: Current research and trends. *Annual Review of Psychology, 40*, 493–531.

65. Hofstede, G. (1980). *Culture's consequences: International differences in work-related values.* Beverly Hills, CA: Sage.

66. Gagne, M. et al. (2015).

67. For a review, see Kagitcibasi & Berry, 1989.

68. Adler, N. J. (1992). *International dimensions of organizational behavior* (2nd ed.). Belmont, CA: Wadsworth.

69. Locke & Latham, 2002.

70. Kirkman, B. L., & Shapiro, D. L. (1997). The impact of cultural values on employee resistance to teams: Toward a model of globalized self-managing work team effectiveness. *Academy of Management Review, 22*, 730–757.

71. Adler, 1992, 159.

Chapter 6

1. Gerstel, J. (2011, November 24). Best GTA employers: Building on a solid foundation, *Toronto Star*, X4, X5; Chosen as one of Canada's top 100 employers, top employers for Canadians over 40 and greater Toronto's top employers for 2012, www.eluta.ca/top-employer-ellisdon; Brent, P. (2008, April 29). Who's on top?: EllisDon, www.workopolis.com; www.ellisdon.com/careers/culture; Pitts, G. (2013, April 7). EllisDon CEO Geoff Smith: Building a different construction company. *The Globe and Mail*, http://www.theglobeandmail.com/report-on-business/careers/careers-leadership/ellisdon-ceo-geoff-smith-building-a-different-construction-company/article10835783/; Moneo, S. (2014, October 14). EllisDon triumphs with UBC laboratory project. *Journal of Commerce*, http://journalofcommerce.com/Associations/News/2014/10/EllisDon-triumphs-with-UBC-laboratory-project-1002651W/; EllisDon CEO Geoffrey Smith named Canada's Entrepreneur of the Year, *Financial Post* (2013, November 28), http://business.financialpost.com/entrepreneur/fp-startups/ellis-don-entrepreneur-year-2013; Yerema, R., & Leung, K. (2014, November 3). EllisDon Corporation, Canada's top 100 employers 2015, http://www.eluta.ca/jobs-at-ellisdon#winner:winner-more; Spence, R. (2014, September 28). Can you grow your business by putting employees first? *Financial Post*, http://business.financialpost.com/entrepreneur/can-you-grow-your-business-by-putting-employees-first; Canada's 10 most admired corporate cultures: Reaching the top. *National Post* (2014, February 3), JV1, JV2.

2. Rynes, S. L., Gerhart, B., & Minette, K. A. (2004). The importance of pay in employee motivation: Discrepancies between what people say and what they do. *Human Resource Management, 43*, 381–394.

3. Immen, W. (2012, June 20). Companies boosting incentive programs. *The Globe and Mail*, B17; Jenkins, G. D., Jr., Mitra, A., Gupta, N., & Shaw, J. D. (1998). Are financial incentives related to performance? A meta-analytic review of empirical research. *Journal of Applied Psychology, 83*, 777–787; Sturman, M. C., Trevor, C. O., Boudreau, J. W., &

Gerhart, B. (2003). Is it worth it to win the talent war? Evaluating the utility of performance-based pay. *Personnel Psychology, 56*, 997–1035; Rynes, Gerhart, & Minette, 2004.

4. For reviews, see Chung, K. H. (1977). *Motivational theories and practices.* Columbus, OH: Grid; Lawler, E. E., III. (1971). *Pay and organizational effectiveness: A psychological view.* New York, NY: McGraw-Hill. For a careful study, see Wagner, J. A., III, Rubin, P. A., & Callahan, T. J. (1988). Incentive payment and nonmanagerial productivity: An interrupted time series analysis of magnitude and trend. *Organizational Behavior and Human Decision Processes, 42*(1), 47–74.

5. Locke, E. A., Feren, D. B., McCaleb, V. M., Shaw, K. N., & Denny, A. T. (1980). The relative effectiveness of four methods of motivating employee performance. In K. D. Duncan, M. M. Gruneberg, & D. Wallis (Eds.), *Changes in working life.* London: Wiley.

6. Fein, M. (1973, September). Work measurement and wage incentives. *Industrial Engineering*, 49–51.

7. Perry, N. J. (1988, December 19). Here come richer, riskier pay plans. *Fortune*, 50–58; Sharplin, A. D. (1990). Lincoln Electric Company, 1989. In A. A. Thompson, Jr., & A. J. Strickland, III. (Eds.), *Strategic management: Concepts and cases.* Homewood, IL: BPI/Irwin.

8. For a general treatment of why firms fail to adopt state-of-the-art personnel practices, see Johns, G. (1993). Constraints on the adoption of psychology-based personnel practices: Lessons from organizational innovation. *Personnel Psychology, 46*, 569–592.

9. Posner, B. G. (1989, May). If at first you don't succeed. *Inc.*, 132–134.

10. Lawler, 1971.

11. Lawler, 1971; Nash, A., & Carrol, S. (1975). *The management of compensation.* Monterey, CA: Brooks/Cole.

12. Bertin, O. (2003, January 31). Is there any merit in giving merit pay? *The Globe and Mail*, C1, C7.

13. Sethi, C. (2006, September 5). Calgary wages rising at record pace. *The Globe and Mail*, B1, B2.

14. Young, G. J., Beckman, H., & Baker, E. (2012). Financial incentives, professional values and performance: A study of pay-for-performance in a professional organization. *Journal of Organizational Behavior*, doi: 10.1002/job.1770

15. Chu, K. (2004, June 15). Firms report lackluster results from pay-for-performance plans. *Wall Street Journal*, D2.

16. Heneman, R.L. (1990). Merit pay research. *Research in Personnel and Human Resources Management, 8*, 203–263; Tosi,

H. L., & Gomez-Mejia, L. R. (1989). The decoupling of CEO pay and performance: An agency theory perspective. *Administrative Science Quarterly, 34*, 169–189; Ungson, G. R., & Steers, R. M. (1984). Motivation and politics in executive compensation. *Academy of Management Review, 9*, 313–323.

17. Haire, M., Ghiselli, E. E., & Gordon, M. E. (1967). A psychological study of pay. *Journal of Applied Psychology Monograph, 51*, (Whole No. 636).

18. Meyer, H. H. (1991, February). A solution to the performance appraisal feedback enigma. *Academy of Management Executive*, 68–76.

19. See Zenga, T. R. (1992). Why do employers only reward extreme performance? Examining the relationships among pay, performance, and turnover. *Administrative Science Quarterly, 37*, 198–219.

20. Benzie, R. (2011, June 25). OLG reports record $6.7B revenues, $11.6M in bonuses. *Toronto Star*, B1, B2.

21. Lawler, E. E., III. (1972). Secrecy and the need to know. In H. L. Tosi, R. J. House, & M. D. Dunnette (Eds.), *Managerial motivation and compensation.* East Lansing: Michigan State University Press.

22. Futrell, C. M., & Jenkins, O. C. (1978). Pay secrecy versus pay disclosure for salesmen: A longitudinal study. *Journal of Marketing Research, 15*, 214–219, 215.

23. Dobson, S. (2014, April 7). "You make how much?" *Canadian HR Reporter, 27*(7), 1, 10.

24. For a study of the prevalence of these plans, see Lawler, E. E. III, Mohrman, S. A., & Ledford, G. E. (1992). *Employee involvement and total quality management: Practices and results in Fortune 1000 companies.* San Francisco, CA: Jossey-Bass.

25. Vermond, K. (2008, October 11). Bonus planning in a bear market. *The Globe and Mail*, B16; Gooderham, M. (2007, November 20). A piece of the pie as motivational tool. *The Globe and Mail*, B8.

26. (2003, October). The goals of stock option programs. www.workforce.com.

27. Gordon, A. (February 2000). 35 best companies to work for. *Report on Business Magazine*, 24–32.

28. Brearton, S., & Daly, J. (2003, January). The 50 best companies to work for in Canada. *Report on Business*, 53–65.

29. Hays, S. (1990). "Ownership cultures" create unity. *Workforce, 78*(2), 60–64.

30. Vermond, K. (2008, March 29). Worker as shareholder: Is it worth it? *The Globe and Mail*, B21.

31. Graham-Moore, B., & Ross, T. L. (1990). *Gainsharing: Plans for improving performance.* Washington, DC: Bureau of National Affairs; Markham, S. E., Scott,

K. D., & Little, B. L. (1992, January–February). National gainsharing study: The importance of industry differences. *Compensation & Benefits Review*, 34–45; Miller, C. S., & Shuster, M. H. (1987, Summer). Gainsharing plans: A comparative analysis. *Organizational Dynamics*, 44–67.

32. Davis, V. (1989, April). Eyes on the prize. *Canadian Business*, 93–106.

33. Graham-Moore & Ross, 1990; Moore, B. E., & Ross, T. L. (1978). *The Scanlon way to improved productivity: A practical guide.* New York, NY: Wiley.

34. Perry, N. J., 1988; Lawler, E. E. (1984). Whatever happened to incentive pay? *New Management, 1*(4), 37–41.

35. Arthur, J. B., & Huntley, C. L. (2005). Ramping up the organizational learning curve: Assessing the impact of deliberate learning on organizational performance under gainsharing. *Academy of Management Journal, 48*, 1159–1170.

36. Hammer, T. H. (1988). New developments in profit sharing, gainsharing, and employee ownership. In J. P. Campbell & R. J. Campbell (Eds.), *Productivity in organizations.* San Francisco, CA: Jossey-Bass.

37. Cooper, C. L., Dyck, B., & Frohlich, N. (1992). Improving the effectiveness of gainsharing: The role of fairness and participation. *Administrative Science Quarterly, 37*, 471–490.

38. Lawler, E. E., III, & Jenkins, G. D., Jr. (1992). Strategic reward systems. In M. D. Dunette & L. M. Hough (Eds.), *Handbook of industrial and organizational psychology* (2nd ed., Vol. 3). Palo Alto, CA: Consulting Psychologists Press.

39. Murray, B., & Gerhart, B. (1998). An empirical analysis of a skill–based pay program and plant performance outcomes. *Academy of Management Journal, 41*, 68–78.

40. Peterson, S., & Luthans, F. (2006). The impact of financial and nonfinancial incentives on business-unit outcomes over time. *Journal of Applied Psychology, 91*, 156–165.

41. Erez, M. (2010). Culture and job design. *Journal of Organizational Behavior, 31*, 389–400.

42. Immen, W. (2009, February 27). Meaning means more than money at work: Poll. *The Globe and Mail*, B14; Immen, W. (2008, January 23). Forget pay: Challenging work counts for top talent. *The Globe and Mail*, C2.

43. Taylor, F. W. (1967). *The principles of scientific management.* New York, NY: Norton.

44. This discussion draws upon Gibson, J. L., Ivancevich, J. M., & Donnelly, J. H., Jr. (1991). *Organizations* (7th ed.). Homewood, IL: Irwin.

45. Ray, R. (2006, April 19). New assignments a stretch but not a yawn. *The Globe and Mail*, C1, C6.

46. Immen, W. (2007, October 17). Starting rotation adds bench strength. *The Globe and Mail*, C1, C2.

47. Hackman, J. R., & Oldham, G. R. (1980). *Work redesign*. Reading, MA: Addison-Wesley.

48. Oldham, G. R., Hackman, J. R., & Stepina, L. P. (1979). Norms for the job diagnostic survey. *JSAS Catalog of Selected Documents in Psychology, 9*, 14. (Ms. No. 1819).

49. See, for example, Johns, G., Xie, J. L., & Fang, Y. (1992). Mediating and moderating effects in job design. *Journal of Management, 18*, 657–676.

50. Humphrey, S. E., Nahrgang, J. D., & Morgeson, F. P. (2007). Integrating motivational, social, and contextual work design features: A meta-analytic summary and theoretical extension of the work design literature. *Journal of Applied Psychology, 92*(5), 1332–1356.

51. Johns et al., 1992; Tiegs, R. B., Tetrick, L. E., & Fried, Y. (1992). Growth need strength and context satisfactions as moderators of the relations of the job characteristics model. *Journal of Management, 18*, 575–593.

52. Brown, S. P. (1996). A meta-analysis and review of organizational research on job involvement. *Psychological Bulletin, 120*, 235–255.

53. This section draws in part on Hackman & Oldham, 1980.

54. Dumaine, B. (1989, November 6). P&G rewrites the marketing rules. *Fortune*, 34–48, 46.

55. Campion, M. A., Mumford, T. V., Morgeson, F. P., & Nahrgang, J. D. (2005). Work redesign: Eight obstacles and opportunities. *Human Resource Management, 44*, 367–390.

56. Stonewalling plant democracy. *Business Week*. (1977, March 28).

57. Morgeson, F. P., & Humphrey, S. E. (2006). The work design questionnaire (WDQ): Developing and validating a comprehensive measure for assessing job design and the nature of work. *Journal of Applied Psychology, 91*, 1321–1339; Humphrey et al., 2007.

58. Grant, A. M. (2008). Does intrinsic motivation fuel the prosocial fire? Motivational synergy in predicting persistence, performance, and productivity. *Journal of Applied Psychology, 93*, 48–58.

59. Grant, A. M. (2007). Relational job design and the motivation to make a prosocial difference. *Academy of Management Review, 32*, 393–417.

60. Grant, 2008; Grant, A. M. (2008). The significance of task significance: Job performance effects, relational mechanisms, and boundary conditions. *Journal of Applied Psychology, 93*, 108–124; Grant, A. M., Campbell, E. M., Chen, G., Cottone, K., Lapedis, D., & Lee, K. (2007). Impact and the art of motivation maintenance: The effects of contact with beneficiaries on persistence behavior. *Organizational Behavior and Human Decision Processes, 103*, 53–67; Grant, A. M., & Parker, S. K. (2009). Redesigning work design theories. *The Academy of Management Annals, 3*, 317–375.

61. Good descriptions of MBO programs can be found in Mali, P. (1986). *MBO updated: A handbook of practices and techniques for managing by objectives*. New York, NY: Wiley; Odiorne, G. S. (1965). *Management by objectives*. New York, NY: Pitman; Raia, A. P. (1974). *Managing by objectives*. Glenview, IL: Scott, Foresman.

62. Beer, M., & Cannon, D. (2004). Promise and peril in implementing pay-for-performance. *Human Resource Management, 43*, 3–48.

63. Brearton, S., & Daly, J. (2003, January). The 50 best companies to work for in Canada. *Report on Business*, 53–66.

64. Brearton & Daly, 2003; Rodgers, R., & Hunter, J. E. (1991). Impact of management by objectives on organization productivity. *Journal of Applied Psychology, 76*, 322–336.

65. Rodgers & Hunter, 1991.

66. See Rodgers, R., Hunter, J. E., & Rogers, D. L. (1993). Influence of top management commitment on management program success. *Journal of Applied Psychology, 78*, 151–155.

67. For discussions of these and other problems with MBO, see Levinson, H. (1979, July–August). Management by whose objectives. *Harvard Business Review*, 125–134; McConkey, D. D. (1972, October). 20 ways to kill management by objectives. *Management Review*, 4–13; Pringle, C. D., & Longenecker, J. G. (1982). The ethics of MBO. *Academy of Management Review, 7*, 305–312.

68. Myers, J. (2010, June 26). The flex factor. *The Globe and Mail*, B15; Allen, T. D., Johnson, R. C., Kiburz, K. M., & Shockley, K. M. (2013). Work-family conflict and flexible work arrangements: Deconstructing flexibility. *Personnel Psychology, 66*, 345–376.

69. See Nollen, S. D. (1982). *New work schedules in practice: Managing time in a changing society*. New York, NY: Van Nostrand Reinhold; Ronen, S. (1981). *Flexible working hours: An innovation in the quality of work life*. New York, NY: McGraw-Hill; Ronen, S. (1984). *Alternative work schedules: Selecting, implementing, and evaluating*. Homewood, IL: Dow Jones-Irwin.

70. For a good study showing absence reduction, see Dalton, D. R., & Mesch, D. J. (1990). The impact of flexible scheduling on employee attendance and turnover. *Administrative Science Quarterly, 35*, 370–387.

71. Baltes, B., Briggs, T. E., Huff, J. W., Wright, J. A., & Neuman, G. A. (1999). Flexible and compressed workweek schedules: A meta-analysis of their effects on work-related criteria. *Journal of Applied Psychology, 84*, 496–513.

72. Golembiewski, R. T., & Proehl, C. W. (1978). A survey of the empirical literature on flexible workhours: Character and consequences of a major innovation. *Academy of Management Review, 3*, 837–853; Pierce, J. L., Newstrom, J. W., Dunham, R. B., & Barber, A. E. (1989). *Alternative work schedules*. Boston, MA: Allyn and Bacon; Ronen, 1981 and 1984.

73. Baltes et al., 1999.

74. Ronen, 1984; Nollen, 1982.

75. Pierce et al., 1989; Ronen, 1984; Ronen, S., & Primps, S. B. (1981). The compressed workweek as organizational change: Behavioral and attitudinal outcomes. *Academy of Management Review, 6*, 61–74.

76. Pierce et al., 1989; Ivancevich, J. M., & Lyon, H. L. (1977). The shortened workweek: A field experiment. *Journal of Applied Psychology, 62*, 34–37.

77. Johns, G. (1987). Understanding and managing absence from work. In S. L. Dolan & R. S. Schuler (Eds.), *Canadian readings in personnel and human resource management*. St. Paul, MN: West.

78. Ivancevich & Lyon, 1977; Calvasina, E. J., & Boxx, W. R. (1975). Efficiency of workers on the four-day workweek. *Academy of Management Journal, 18*, 604–610; Goodale, J. G., & Aagaard, A. K. (1975). Factors relating to varying reactions to the 4-day workweek. *Journal of Applied Psychology, 60*, 33–38.

79. Baltes et al., 1999.

80. This section relies on Pierce et al., 1989.

81. MacGregor, A. (2001, December 29). Sharing jobs gets trendy. *The Gazette*, Montreal, C1.

82. Popplewell, B. (2009, March 10). Staying at home so others don't have to. *Toronto Star*, B1, B4; Grant, T. (2009, June 23). Buying jobs and buying time. *The Globe and Mail*, B4.

83. DeFrank, R. S., & Ivancevich, J. M. (1998). Stress on the job: An executive update. *Academy of Management Executive, 12*, 55–66; Gajendran, R. S., Harrison, D. A., & Delaney-Klinger, K. (2015). Are telecommuters remotely good citizens? Unpacking telecommuting's effects on performance via I-deals and job resources. *Personnel Psychology, 68*, 353–393.

84. Grensing-Pophal, L. (1997, March). Employing the best people—from afar. *Workforce, 76*(3), 30–38; Piskurich, G. M. (1998). *An organizational guide to*

telecommuting: Setting up and running a successful telecommuter program. Alexandria, VA: American Society for Training and Development.

85. Grensing-Pophal, 1997.

86. DeFrank & Ivancevich, 1998; Goldsborough, R. (1999, May 14). Make telecommuting work for you. *Computer Dealer News,* 19–20; Fortier, B. (2005, June 6). Ergonomics for teleworkers often overlooked. *Canadian HR Reporter, 18*(11), 18, 21; Karstens-Smith, G. (2014, May 29). Remote work an escape when trapped by gridlock. *Toronto Star,* B1, B6.

87. Galt, V. (2003, September 24). Drive is on for telework. *The Globe and Mail,* C7; Vu, U. (2006, August 14). A variety of options gives boost to remote work. *Canadian HR Reporter, 19*(14), 15, 21; Myers, R. C. (2008, March 8). The back and forth of working from home. *The Globe and Mail,* B16.

88. DeFrank & Ivancevich, 1998; Grensing-Pophal, 1997.

89. Gajendran, R. S., & Harrison, D. A. (2007). The good, the bad, and the unknown about telecommuting: Meta-analysis of psychological mediators and individual consequences. *Journal of Applied Psychology, 92,* 1524–1541; Gajendran, R. S., Harrison, D. A., & Delaney-Klinger, K. (2015).

90. Bailey, D. S., & Foley, J. (1990, August). Pacific Bell works long distance. *HRMagazine,* 50–52.

91. Myers, 2008; Klie, S. (2008, June 2). Mistrust "number one barrier" to telework. *Canadian HR Reporter, 21*(11), 13, 19; Grensing-Pophal, 1997; Kane, L. (2015, March 2). Does working from home make sense? *Toronto Star,* B7.

92. Rynes et al., 2004.

Chapter 7

1. Borden, M. Most innovative companies 2010: 35_IDEO, http://www.fastcompany.com/3017932/most-innovative-companies-2010/35ideo; IDEO. (n.d.). Fact sheet, www.ideo.com/images/uploads/home/IDEO_Fact_Sheet.pdf; Brown, T. (2009). *Change by design: How design thinking transforms organizations and inspires innovation.* New York, NY: HarperCollins; Recruiting Q&A: IDEO. (2001, January 10). www.businessweek.com/careers/content/jan2001/ca20010111_923.htm; http://pages.towson.edu/aclardy/Working%20Papers/IDEO.pdf; The Tube for IDEO: The centerpiece of how IDEO interacts as a global organization, www.ideo.com/work/the-tube/; http://charleslawportfolio.com/charleslaw_assets/charleslaw_creativeessay.pdf; www.ideo

.com/images/uploads/hcd_toolkit/IDEO_HCD_ToolKit.pdf.

2. Tuckman, B. W. (1965). Developmental sequence in small groups. *Psychological Bulletin, 63,* 384–399; Tuckman, B. W., & Jensen, M. A. C. (1977). Stages of small-group development revisited. *Group & Organization Studies, 2,* 419–427.

3. Harris, S. G., & Sutton, R. I. (1986). Functions of parting ceremonies in dying organizations. *Academy of Management Journal, 29,* 5–30.

4. Seger, J. A. (1983). No innate phases in group problem solving. *Academy of Management Review, 8,* 683–689. For a study comparing phases with punctuated equilibrium, see Chang, A., Bordia, P., & Duck, J. (2003). Punctuated equilibrium and linear progression: Toward a new understanding of group development. *Academy of Management Journal, 46,* 106–117.

5. Ginnett, R. C. (1990). Airline cockpit crew. In J. R. Hackman (Ed.), *Groups that work (and those that don't).* San Francisco, CA: Jossey-Bass.

6. Gersick, C. J. G. (1989). Marking time: Predictable transitions in task groups. *Academy of Management Journal, 32,* 274–309; Gersick, C. J. G. (1988). Time and transition in work teams: Toward a new model of group development. *Academy of Management Journal, 31,* 9–41.

7. Gersick, 1989, 1988; Hackman, J. R., & Wageman, R. (2005). A theory of team coaching. *Academy of Management Review, 30,* 269–287.

8. Hare, A. P. (1976). *A handbook of small group research.* New York, NY: The Free Press; Shaw, M. E. (1981). *Group dynamics: The psychology of small group behavior* (3rd ed.). New York, NY: McGraw-Hill; Jones, E. E., & Gerard, H. B. (1967). *Foundations of social psychology.* New York, NY: Wiley.

9. Hare, 1976; Shaw, 1981.

10. The following discussion relies upon Steiner, I. D. (1972). *Group process and productivity.* New York, NY: Academic Press.

11. Steiner, 1972; Hill, G. W. (1982). Group versus individual performance: Are n+1 heads better than one? *Psychological Bulletin, 91,* 517–539.

12. Williams, K. Y., & O'Reilly, C. A. III. (1998). Demography and diversity in organizations: A review of 40 years of research. *Research in Organizational Behavior, 20,* 77–140; Jackson, S. E., Stone, V. K., & Alvarez, E. B. (1993). Socialization amidst diversity: The impact of demographics on work team oldtimers and newcomers. *Research in Organizational Behavior, 15,* 45–109.

13. Watson, W. E., Kumar, K., & Michaelson, L. K. (1993). Cultural

diversity's impact on interaction process and performance: Comparing homogeneous and diverse task groups. *Academy of Management Journal, 36,* 590–602.

14. van Dijk, H., van Engen, M. L., & van Knippenberg, D. (2012). Defying conventional wisdom: A meta-analytical examination of the differences between demographic and job-related diversity relationships with performance. *Organizational Behavior and Human Decision Processes, 119,* 38–53; Webber, S. S., & Donahue, L. M. (2001). Impact of highly and less job-related diversity on work group cohesion and performance: A meta-analysis. *Journal of Management, 27,* 141–162.

15. Bell, S. T., Villado, A. J., Lukasik, M. A., Belau, L., & Briggs, A. L. (2011). Getting specific about demographic diversity variable and team performance relationships: A meta-analysis. *Journal of Management, 37,* 709–743; see also Joshi, A., & Roh, H. (2009). The role of context in work team diversity research: A meta-analytic review. *Academy of Management Journal, 52,* 599–627.

16. Bell et al., 2011; Joshi & Roh, 2009.

17. Harrison, D. A., Price, K. H., & Bell, M. P. (1998). Beyond relational demography: Time and effects of surface- and deep-level diversity on work group cohesion. *Academy of Management Journal, 41,* 96–107; see also Bell, S. T. (2007). Deep-level composition variables as predictors of team performance: A meta-analysis. *Journal of Applied Psychology, 92,* 595–615.

18. For an example of the social process by which this sharing may be negotiated in a new group, see Bettenhausen, K., & Murnighan, J. K. (1991). The development of an intragroup norm and the effects of interpersonal and structural challenges. *Administrative Science Quarterly, 36,* 20–35.

19. Kanter, R. M. (1977). *Men and women of the corporation.* New York, NY: Basic Books, 37.

20. Leventhal, G. S. (1976). The distribution of rewards and resources in groups and organizations. In L. Berkowitz & E. Walster (Eds.), *Advances in experimental social psychology* (Vol. 9). New York, NY: Academic Press.

21. See Mitchell, T. R., Rothman, M., & Liden, R. C. (1985). Effects of normative information on task performance. *Journal of Applied Psychology, 70,* 48–55.

22. Kleingeld, A., van Mierlo, H., & Arends, L. (2011). The effect of goal setting on group performance: A meta-analysis. *Journal of Applied Psychology, 96,* 1289–1304.

23. Jackson, S. E., & Schuler, R. S. (1985). A meta-analysis and conceptual critique

of research on role ambiguity and role conflict in work settings. *Organizational Behavior and Human Decision Processes, 36,* 16–78. For a methodological critique of this domain, see King, L. A., & King, D. W. (1990). Role conflict and role ambiguity: A critical assessment of construct validity. *Psychological Bulletin, 107,* 48–64.

24. Jackson & Schuler, 1985; Tubre, T. C., & Collins, J. M. (2000). Jackson and Shuler (1985) revisited: A meta-analysis of the relationship between role ambiguity, role conflict, and job performance. *Journal of Management, 26,* 155–169.

25. O'Driscoll, M. P., Ilgen, D. R., & Hildreth, K. (1992). Time devoted to job and off-job activities, interrole conflict, and affective experiences. *Journal of Applied Psychology, 77,* 272–279.

26. See Latack, J. C. (1981). Person/role conflict: Holland's model extended to role-stress research, stress management, and career development. *Academy of Management Review, 6,* 89–103.

27. Jackson & Schuler, 1985.

28. Shaw, 1981.

29. Fiske, S. T. (2010). Interpersonal stratification: Status, power, and subordination. In S. T. Fiske, D. T. Gilbert, & G. Lindzey (Eds.), *Handbook of social psychology* (5th ed., Vol. 2). Hoboken, NJ: Wiley.

30. Kiesler, S., & Sproull, L. (1992). Group decision making and communication technology. *Organizational Behavior and Human Decision Processes, 52,* 96–123; Fiske, 2010.

31. Strodbeck, F. L., James, R. M., & Hawkins, C. (1957). Social status in jury deliberations. *American Sociological Review, 22,* 713–719.

32. Kiesler & Sproull, 1992.

33. For other definitions and a discussion of their differences, see Mudrack, P. E. (1989). Defining group cohesiveness: A legacy of confusion? *Small Group Behavior, 20,* 37–49.

34. Stein, A. (1976). Conflict and cohesion: A review of the literature. *Journal of Conflict Resolution, 20,* 143–172. For an interesting example, see Haslam, S. A., & Reicher, S. (2006). Stressing the group: Social identity and the unfolding dynamics of responses to stress. *Journal of Applied Psychology, 91,* 1037–1052.

35. Cartwright, D. (1968). The nature of group cohesiveness. In D. Cartwright & A. Zander (Eds.), *Group dynamics: Research and theory* (3rd ed., pp. 91–109). New York, NY: Harper & Row.

36. Lott, A., & Lott, B. (1965). Group cohesiveness as interpersonal attraction: A review of relationships with antecedent and consequent variables. *Psychological Bulletin, 64,* 259–309.

37. Anderson, A. B. (1975). Combined effects of interpersonal attraction and goal-path clarity on the cohesiveness of task-oriented groups. *Journal of Personality and Social Psychology, 31,* 68–75; see also Cartwright, 1968.

38. See Carton, A. M., & Cummings, J. N. (2012). A theory of subgroups in work teams. *Academy of Management Review, 37,* 441–470.

39. Aronson, E., & Mills, J. (1959). The effects of severity of initiation on liking for a group. *Journal of Abnormal and Social Psychology, 59,* 177–181.

40. Cartwright, 1968; Shaw, 1981.

41. Schacter, S. (1951). Deviation, rejection, and communication. *Journal of Abnormal and Social Psychology, 46,* 190–207; see also Barker, J. R. (1993). Tightening the iron cage: Concertive control in self-managing teams. *Administrative Science Quarterly, 38,* 408–437.

42. Beal, D. J., Cohen, R. R., Burke, M. J., & McLendon, C. L. (2003). Cohesion and performance in groups: A meta-analytic clarification of construct relations. *Journal of Applied Psychology, 88,* 989–1004; Mullen, B., & Copper, C. (1994). The relation between group cohesiveness and performance: An integration. *Psychological Bulletin, 115,* 210–227.

43. Podsakoff, P. M., MacKenzie, S. B., & Ahearne, M. (1997). Moderating effects of goal acceptance on the relationship between group cohesiveness and productivity. *Journal of Applied Psychology, 82,* 974–983.

44. Seashore, S. (1954). *Group cohesiveness in the industrial workgroup.* Ann Arbor, MI: Institute for Social Research; see also Stogdill, R. M. (1972). Group productivity, drive, and cohesiveness. *Organizational Behavior and Human Performance, 8,* 26–43. For a critique, see Mudrack, P. E. (1989). Group cohesiveness and productivity: A closer look. *Human Relations, 42,* 771–785.

45. Gulley, S. M., Devine, D. J., & Whitney, D. J. (1995). A meta-analysis of cohesion and performance: Effects of level of analysis and task interdependence. *Small Group Research, 26,* 497–520.

46. Shepperd, J. A. (1993). Productivity loss in small groups: A motivation analysis. *Psychological Bulletin, 113,* 67–81; Kidwell, R. E., III, & Bennett, N. (1993). Employee propensity to withhold effort: A conceptual model to intersect three avenues of research. *Academy of Management Review, 18,* 429–456.

47. Shepperd, 1993; Kidwell & Bennett, 1993; George, J. M. (1992). Extrinsic and intrinsic origins of perceived social loafing in organizations. *Academy of Management Journal, 35,* 191–202.

48. Barnes, C. M., Hollenbeck, J. R., Jundt, D. K., DeRue, D. S., & Harmon, S. J. (2011). Mixing individual incentives and group incentives: Best of both worlds or social dilemma? *Journal of Management, 37,* 1611–1635.

49. Guzzo, R. A., & Dickson, M. W. (1996). Teams in organizations: Recent research on performance and effectiveness. *Annual Review of Psychology, 47,* 307–338.

50. Kirkman, B. L., & Shapiro, D. L. (1997). The impact of cultural values on employee resistance to teams: Toward a model of globalized self-managing work team effectiveness. *Academy of Management Review, 22,* 730–757.

51. Guzzo & Dickson, 1996; Kirkman & Shapiro, 1997; Banker, R. D., Field, J. M., Schroeder, R. G., & Sinha, K. K. (1996). Impact of work teams on manufacturing performance: A longitudinal field study. *Academy of Management Journal, 39,* 867–890.

52. Tasa, K., Taggar, S., & Seijts, G. H. (2007). The development of collective efficacy in teams: A multi-level and longitudinal perspective. *Journal of Applied Psychology, 92,* 17–27; Gibson, C. B., & Earley, P. C. (2007). Collective cognition in action: Accumulation, interaction, examination, and accommodation in the development and operation of efficacy beliefs in the workplace. *Academy of Management Review, 32,* 438–458; Tasa, K., Sears, G. J., & Schat, A. C. H. (2011). Personality and teamwork behavior in context: The cross-level moderating role of collective efficacy. *Journal of Organizational Behavior, 32,* 65–85; Stajkovic, A. D., Lee, D., & Nyberg, A. J. (2009). Collective efficacy, group potency, and group performance: Meta-analyses of their relationships, and test of a mediation model. *Journal of Applied Psychology, 94,* 814–828.

53. Hackman, J. R. (1987). The design of work teams. In J. W. Lorsch (Ed.), *Handbook of organizational behavior.* Englewood Cliffs, NJ: Prentice-Hall; see also Hackman, J. R. (2002). *Leading teams: Setting the stage for great performances.* Boston, MA: Harvard Business School Press.

54. Campion, M. A., Medsker, G. J., & Higgs, A. C. (1993). Relations between work group characteristics and effectiveness: Implications for designing effective work groups. *Personnel Psychology, 46,* 823–850.

55. Wall, T. D., Kemp, N. J., Jackson, P. R., & Clegg, C. W. (1986). Outcomes of autonomous workgroups: A field experiment. *Academy of Management Journal, 29,* 280–304.

56. Parts of this section rely on Hackman, 1987.

57. See Ashforth, B. E., & Mael, F. (1989). Social identity theory and the organization. *Academy of Management Review, 14,* 20–39.

58. Wall et al., 1986; Cordery, J. L., Mueller, W. S., & Smith, L. M. (1991). Attitudinal and behavioral effects of autonomous group working: A longitudinal field study. *Academy of Management Journal, 34,* 264–276.

59. van der Vegt, G. S., Bunderson, S., & Kuipers, B. (2010). Why turnover matters in self-managing work teams: Learning, social integration, and task flexibility. *Journal of Management, 36,* 1168–1191.

60. Bainbridge, J. (2009). Inspire and innovate: Personal services. www.guardian .co.uk.

61. Hayward, D. (2003, May 20). Management through measurement. *Financial Post,* BE5.

62. Manz, C. C., & Sims, H. P., Jr. (1987). Leading workers to lead themselves: The external leadership of self-managing work teams. *Administrative Science Quarterly, 32,* 106–128.

63. For reviews of research on self-managed teams, see Chapter 3 of Cummings, T. G., & Molloy, E. S. (1977). *Improving productivity and the quality of working life.* New York, NY: Praeger; Goodman, P. S., Devadas, R., & Hughes, T. L. G. (1988). Groups and productivity: Analyzing the effectiveness of self managing teams. In J. P. Campbell & R. J. Campbell (Eds.), *Productivity in organizations.* San Francisco, CA: Jossey Bass; Pearce, J. A., III, & Ravlin, E. C. (1987). The design and activation of self-regulating work groups. *Human Relations, 40,* 751–782.

64. Campion, M. A., Papper, E. M., & Medsker, G. J. (1996). Relations between work team characteristics and effectiveness: A replication and extension. *Personnel Psychology, 19,* 429–452; Campion, Medsker, & Higgs, 1993.

65. Kirkman & Shapiro, 1997; Banker et al., 1996.

66. Farnham, A. (1994, February 7). America's most admired company. *Fortune,* 50–54; Dumaine, B. (1993, December 13). Payoff from the new management. *Fortune,* 103–110.

67. Waterman, R. H., Jr. (1987). *The renewal factor.* New York, NY: Bantam Books; McElroy, J. (1985, April). Ford's new way to build cars. *Road & Track,* 156–158.

68. Pinto, M. B., Pinto, J. K., & Prescott, J. E. (1993). Antecedents and consequences of project team cross-functional cooperation. *Management Science, 39,* 1281–1297; Henke, J. W., Krachenberg, A. R., & Lyons, T. F. (1993). Cross-functional teams: Good concept, poor implementation! *Journal of Product Innovation Management, 10,* 216–229. Mustang examples from White, J. B., & Suris, O. (1993, September 21). How a "skunk works" kept the Mustang alive—on a tight budget. *Wall Street Journal,* A1, A12.

69. Mathieu, J., Maynard, M. T., Rapp, T., & Gilson, L. (2008). Team effectiveness 1997–2007: A review of recent advancements and a glimpse into the future. *Journal of Management, 34,* 410–476; Mesmer-Magnus, J. R., & DeChurch, L. A. (2009). Information sharing and team performance. *Journal of Applied Psychology, 94,* 535–546; Mohammed, S., Ferzandi, L., & Hamilton, K. (2010). Metaphor no more: A 15-year review of the team mental model construct. *Journal of Management, 36,* 876–910; DeChurch, L. A., & Mesmer-Magnus, J. R. (2010). The cognitive underpinnings of effective teamwork: A meta-analysis. *Journal of Applied Psychology, 95,* 32–53.

70. Cronin, M. A., & Weingart, L. R. (2007). Representational gaps, information processing, and conflict in functionally diverse teams. *Academy of Management Review, 32,* 761–773, p. 761.

71. Lipnack, J., & Stamps, J. (2000). *Virtual teams: People working across boundaries with technology.* (2nd ed.). New York, NY: Wiley; Axtell, C. M., Fleck, S. J., & Turner, N. (2004). Virtual Teams: Collaborating across distance. *International Review of Industrial and Organizational Psychology, 19,* 205–248; Successfully transitioning to a virtual organization: Challenges, impact and technology. (2010, 1st quarter). *SHRM Research Quarterly.* Alexandria, VA: Society for Human Resource Management.

72. Willmore, J. (2000, February). Managing virtual teams. *Training Journal,* 18–21.

73. Joinson, C. (2002, June). Managing virtual teams. *HR Magazine,* 68–73.

74. Cascio, W. F. (2000, August). Managing a virtual workplace. *Academy of Management Executive,* 81–90; see also Malhotra, A., Majchrzak, A., & Rosen, B. (2007). Leading virtual teams. *Academy of Management Perspectives,* 60–70; and Gibson, C. B., & Gibbs, J. L. (2006). Unpacking the concept of virtuality: The effects of geographic dispersion, electronic dependence, dynamic structure, and national diversity on team innovation. *Administrative Science Quarterly, 51,* 451–495.

75. Willmore, 2000.

76. Mesmer-Magnus, J. R., DeChurch, L. A., Jimenez-Rodriguez, M., Wildman, J., & Shuffler, M. (2011). A meta-analytic investigation of virtuality and information sharing in teams. *Organizational Behavior and Human Decision Processes, 115,* 214–225.

77. Cascio, 2000; Joinson, 2002; Kirkman, B. L., Rosen, B., Gibson, C. B., Tesluk, P. E., & McPherson, S. O. (2002, August). Five challenges to virtual team success: Lessons from Sabre, Inc. *Academy of Management Executive, 16,* 67–79.

78. Allen, N. J., & Hecht, T. D. (2004). The "romance of teams": Toward an understanding of its psychological underpinnings and implications. *Journal of Occupational and Organizational Psychology, 77,* 439–461.

79. Vallas, S. P. (2003). Why teamwork fails: Obstacles to workplace change in four manufacturing plants. *American Sociological Review, 68,* 223–250; Tudor, T. R., Trumble, R. R., & Diaz, J. J. (1996, Autumn). Work-teams: Why do they often fail? *S.A.M. Advanced Management Journal,* 31–39.

Chapter 8

1. Andrews, R. (2011, Winter). A shared sense of mission. *Profits (Business Development Bank of Canada), 31*(1), 6–8, MacGregor, R. (2014, September 19). Small-town success Kicking Horse Coffee brews bold move to the U.S. *The Globe and Mail,* http://www.theglobeandmail .com/report-on-business/small-business/ sb-growth/small-town-success-kicking-horse-coffee-brews-bold-move-to-the-us/article20707819/; Massey, B. (2015, April 17). Kick ass crew love what they do. *The Columbia Valley Pioneer, 12*(16), 5, 31; Lee, J. (2012, November 28). B. C. entrepreneur celebrates the sweet smell of (Kicking Horse Coffee) success. *The Vancouver Sun,* http:// www.vancouversun.com/business/ smallbusiness/Vancouver+entrepreneur +celebrates+sweet+smell/7617938/ story.html; Whoa! Kicking Horse Coffee named one of Canada's best places to work. (2015, April 10). Press Release, https://www.kickinghorsecoffee.com/ files/2015_04_10%20KHC%20Press%20 Release.pdf; Brown, L. (2012, November 16). Healthy employees, healthy business, says this SME owner. *Smallbizadvisor,* http://www.smallbizadvisor .ca/group-benefits/healthy-employees-healthy-business-says-this-sme-owner-1700; McTavish, V. (2013, December 2). Engaging workplaces: Case Study: Kicking Horse Coffee Co. Ltd., *BC Business,* https://www.kickinghorsecoffee .com/files/2013_12_02_BCBusiness_ Engaging%20Workplaces.pdf; Kerr, M. (2014, September 15). A kickass

approach to building a great culture. *Humor at Work*, http://www.mikekerr.com/humour-at-work-blog/a-kickass-approach-to-building-a-great-culture/.

2. See Morrison, E. W. (1993). Newcomer information seeking: Exploring types, modes, sources, and outcomes. *Academy of Management Journal, 36*, 557–589.

3. The terms *information dependence* and *effect dependence* are used by Jones, E. E., & Gerard, H. B. (1967). *Foundations of social psychology*. New York, NY: Wiley.

4. Salancik, G. R., & Pfeffer, J. (1978). A social information processing approach to job attitudes and task design. *Administrative Science Quarterly, 23*, 224–253.

5. Festinger, L. (1954). A theory of social comparison processes. *Human Relations, 7*, 117–140; Thomas, J., & Griffin, R. (1983). The social information processing model of task design: A review of the literature. *Academy of Management Review, 8*, 672–682.

6. Kelman, H. C. (1961). Processes of opinion change. *Public Opinion Quarterly, 25*, 57–78.

7. Bauer, T. N., Morrison, E. W., & Callister, R. R. (1998). Organizational socialization: A review and directions for future research. In G. R. Ferris & K. M. Rowland (Eds.), *Research in Personnel and Human Resources Management*, (Vol. 16, pp. 149–214). Greenwich, CT: JAI Press; Saks, A. M., & Ashforth, B. E. (1997a). Organizational socialization: Making sense of the past and present as a prologue for the future. *Journal of Vocational Behavior, 51*, 234–279.

8. Saks, A. M., & Ashforth, B. E. (1997b). A longitudinal investigation of the relationships between job information sources, applicant perceptions of fit, and work outcomes. *Personnel Psychology, 50*, 395–426; DeRue, D. S., & Morgeson, F. P. (2007). Stability and change in person-team and person-role fit over time: The effects of growth satisfaction, performance, and general self-efficacy. *Journal of Applied Psychology, 92*, 1242–1253.

9. Kristof-Brown, A. L., Zimmerman, R. D., & Johnson, E. C. (2005). Consequences of individuals' fit at work: A meta-analysis of person-job, person-organization, person-group, and person-supervisor fit. *Personnel Psychology, 58*, 281–342; Kristof, A. L. (1996). Person-organization fit: An integrative review of its conceptualizations, measurement, and implications. *Personnel Psychology, 49*, 1–49; Saks & Ashforth, 1997b; Saks, A. M., & Ashforth, B. E. (2002). Is job search related to employment quality? It all depends on the fit. *Journal of Applied Psychology, 87*, 646–654; Oh, I., Guay,

R. P., Kim, K., Harold, C. M., Lee, J., Heo, C., & Shin, K. (2014). Fit happens globally: A meta-analytic comparison of the relationships of person-environment fit dimensions with work attitudes and performance across East Asia, Europe, and North America. *Personnel Psychology, 67*, 99–152.

10. Ashforth, B. E., & Saks, A. M. (1996). Socialization tactics: Longitudinal effects on newcomer adjustment. *Academy of Management Journal, 39*, 149–178; Riketta, M. (2005). Organizational identification: A meta-analysis. *Journal of Vocational Behavior, 66*, 358–384.

11. Van Maanen, J., & Schein, E. H. (1979). Toward a theory of organizational socialization. *Research in Organizational Behavior, 1*, 209–264.

12. Feldman, D. C. (1976). A contingency theory of socialization. *Administrative Science Quarterly, 21*, 433–452.

13. Wanous, J. P. (1992). *Organizational entry: Recruitment, selection, orientation, and socialization of newcomers*. (2nd ed.). Reading, MA: Addison-Wesley.

14. Wanous, J. P. (1976). Organizational entry: From naive expectations to realistic beliefs. *Journal of Applied Psychology, 61*, 22–29; Wanous, J. P., Poland, T. D., Premack, S. L., & Davis, K. S. (1992). The effects of met expectations on newcomer attitudes and behaviors: A review and meta-analysis. *Journal of Applied Psychology, 77*, 288–297.

15. See Breaugh, J. A. (1992). *Recruitment: Science and practice*. Boston, MA: PWS-Kent.

16. Morrison, E. W., & Robinson, S. L. (1997). When employees feel betrayed: A model of how psychological contract violation develops. *Academy of Management Review, 22*, 226–256.

17. Robinson, S. L., & Rousseau, D. M. (1994). Violating the psychological contract: Not the exception but the norm. *Journal of Organizational Behavior, 15*, 245–259.

18. Zhao, H., Wayne, S. J., Glibkowski, B. C., & Bravo, J. (2007). The impact of psychological contract breach on work-related outcomes: A meta-analysis. *Personnel Psychology, 60*, 647–680.

19. Bordia, P., Restubog, S. L. D., Bordia, S., & Tang, R. L. (2010). Breach begets breach: Trickle-down effects of psychological contract breach on customer service. *Journal of Management, 36*, 1578–1607; Ng, T. W. H., Feldman, D. C., & Lam, S. S. K. (2010). Psychological contract breaches, organizational commitment, and innovation-related behaviors: A latent growth modeling approach. *Journal of Applied Psychology, 95*, 744–751.

20. Morrison & Robinson, 1997.

21. Morrison & Robinson, 1997.

22. Montes, S. D., & Zweig, D. (2009). Do promises matter? An exploration of the role of promises in psychological contract breach. *Journal of Applied Psychology, 94*, 1243–1260.

23. Wanous, 1992; Breaugh, 1992.

24. Wanous, 1992; Breaugh, 1992.

25. Galt, V. (2005, March 9). Kid-glove approach woos new grads. *The Globe and Mail*, C1, C3.

26. Harding, K. (2003, July 16). Police aim to hire officers. *The Globe and Mail*, C1.

27. Phillips, J. M. (1998). Effects of realistic job previews on multiple organizational outcomes: A meta-analysis. *Academy of Management Journal, 41*, 673–690.

28. Premack, S. L., & Wanous, J. P. (1985). A meta-analysis of realistic job preview experiments. *Journal of Applied Psychology, 70*, 706–719. See also Wanous, J. P., Poland, T. D., Premack, S. L., & Davis, K. S. (1992). The effects of met expectations on newcomer attitudes and behaviors: A review and meta-analysis. *Journal of Applied Psychology, 77*, 288–297.

29. Earnest, D. R., Allen, D. G., & Landix, R. S. (2011). Mechanisms linking realistic job previews with turnover: A meta-analytic path analysis. *Personnel Psychology, 64*, 865–897.

30. Premack & Wanous, 1985; McEvoy, G. M., & Cascio, W. F. (1985). Strategies for reducing employee turnover: A meta-analysis. *Journal of Applied Psychology, 70*, 342–353.

31. Morrison & Robinson, 1997.

32. Wanous, J. P., & Reichers, A. E. (2000). New employee orientation programs. *Human Resource Management Review, 10*, 435–451.

33. Fan, J., & Wanous, J. P. (2008). Organizational and cultural entry: A new type of orientation program for multiple boundary crossings. *Journal of Applied Psychology, 93*, 1390–1400.

34. Mitchell, B. (2012, January 30). Power to the people. *Canadian HR Reporter, 25*(2), 23, 25.

35. Klein, H. J., & Weaver, N. A. (2000). The effectiveness of an organizational-level orientation training program in the socialization of new hires. *Personnel Psychology, 53*, 47–66.

36. Schettler, J. (2002, August). Welcome to ACME Inc. *Training, 39*(8), 36–43.

37. Fan, J., & Wanous, J. P. (2008).

38. Van Maanen, J., & Schein, E. H. (1979). Toward a theory of organizational socialization. In B. M. Staw (Ed.), *Research in organizational behavior*, Vol. 1. Greenwich, CT: JAI Press, 209–264.

39. Ashforth & Saks, 1996; Jones, G. R. (1986). Socialization tactics, self-efficacy,

and newcomers' adjustments to organizations. *Academy of Management Journal, 29,* 262–279.

40. Ashforth & Saks, 1996; Jones, 1986; Cable, D. M., & Parsons, C. K. (2001). Socialization tactics and person-organization fit. *Personnel Psychology, 54,* 1–23; Rollag, K., Parise, S., & Cross, R. (2005). Getting new hires up to speed quickly. *MIT Sloan Management Review,* 35–41.

41. Haggard, D. L., Dougherty, T. W., Turban, D. B., & Wilbanks, J. E. (2011). Who is a mentor? A review of evolving definitions and implications for research. *Journal of Management, 37,* 280–304.

42. Kram, K. (1985). *Mentoring.* Glenview, IL: Scott, Foresman.

43. Weinberg, F. J., & Lankau, M. J. (2011). Formal mentoring programs: A mentor-centric and longitudinal analysis. *Journal of Management, 37,* 1527–1557; Allen, T. D., Eby, L. T., & Lentz, E. (2006a). Mentorship behaviours and mentorship quality associated with formal mentoring programs: Closing the gap between research and practice. *Journal of Applied Psychology, 91,* 567–578; Murray, M. (1991). *Beyond the myths and magic of mentoring: How to facilitate an effective mentoring program.* San Francisco, CA: Jossey-Bass; Lawrie, J. (1987). How to establish a mentoring program. *Training & Development Journal, 41*(3), 25–27.

44. Harding, K. (2003, March 12). Your new best friend. *The Globe and Mail,* C1, C10.

45. Dobrow, S. R., Chandler, D. E., Murphy, W. M., & Kram, K. E. (2012). A review of developmental networks: Incorporating a mutuality perspective. *Journal of Management, 38,* 210–242.

46. Cox, T., Jr. (1993). *Cultural diversity in organizations: Theory, research, & practice.* San Francisco, CA: Berrett-Koehler; Noe, R. A. (1988). Women and mentoring: A review and research agenda. *Academy of Management Review, 13,* 65–78; Ragins, B. R. (1989). Barriers to mentoring: The female manager's dilemma. *Human Relations, 42,* 1–22.

47. Dreyfus, J., Lee, M. J., & Totta, J. M. (1995, December). Mentoring at the Bank of Montreal: A case study of an intervention that exceeded expectations. *Human Resource Planning, 18*(4), 45–49.

48. O'Brien, K. E., Biga, A., Kessler, S. R., & Allen, T. D. (2010). A meta-analytic investigation of gender differences in mentoring. *Journal of Management, 36,* 537–554.

49. Ragins, B., & McFarlin, D. (1990). Perceptions of mentor roles in cross-gender mentoring relationships. *Journal of Vocational Behavior, 37,* 321–339.

50. O'Brien et al., 2010.

51. Weinberg & Lankau, 2011.

52. Burke, R., & McKeen, C. (1990). Mentoring in organizations: Implications for women. *Journal of Business Ethics, 9,* 317–322; Dennett, D. (1985, November). Risks, mentoring helps women to the top. *APA Monitor, 26;* Morrison, A., White, R., & Van Velsor, E. (1987). *Breaking the glass ceiling: Can women reach the top of America's largest corporations?* Reading, MA: Addison-Wesley.

53. Purden, C. (2001, June). Rising to the challenge. *Report on Business Magazine, 17*(12), 31.

54. Ramaswami, A., Dreher, G. F., Bretz, R., & Wiethoff, C. (2010). Gender, mentoring, and career success: The importance of organizational context. *Personnel Psychology, 63,* 385–405.

55. Purden, 2001; Dobson, S. (2015, May 4). Women's internal networks connecting to bottom line: Study. *Canadian HR Reporter, 28*(8), 6.

56. Church, E. (2001, March 8). Mentors guide women through career roadblocks. *The Globe and Mail,* B12.

57. Cox, 1993; Ibarra, H. (1993). Personal networks of women and minorities in management. *Academy of Management Review, 18,* 56–87.

58. Nkomo, S., & Cox, T. (1989). Gender differences in the upward mobility of black managers: Double whammy or double advantage? *Sex Roles, 21,* 825–839.

59. Thomas, D. (1989). Mentoring and irrationality: The role of racial taboos. *Human Resource Management, 28,* 279–290; Thomas, D. (1990). The impact of race on managers' experiences of developmental relationships: An intraorganizational study. *Journal of Organizational Behavior, 11,* 479–492.

60. Bernier, L. (2014, March 10). Diversity not just about compliance. *Canadian HR Reporter, 27*(5), 1, 6.

61. Dalton, G. W., Thompson, P. H., & Price, R. (1977, Summer). The four stages of professional careers: A new look at performance by professionals. *Organizational Dynamics,* 19–42; Fagenson, E. (1988). The power of a mentor: Protégés and nonprotégés' perceptions of their own power in organizations. *Group and Organization Studies, 13,* 182–192; Fagenson, E. (1989). The mentor advantage: Perceived career/job experiences of protégés versus non-protégés. *Journal of Organizational Behavior, 10,* 309–320; Scandura, T. (1992). Mentorship and career mobility: An empirical investigation. *Journal of Organizational Behavior, 13,* 169–174; Dreher, G., & Ash, R. (1990). A comparative study of mentoring among men and women in managerial, professional and technical positions. *Journal of Applied Psychology, 75,* 539–546; Whitely, W., Dougherty, T., & Dreher, G. (1991). Relationship of career mentoring and socioeconomic origin to managers' and professionals' early career progress. *Academy of Management Journal, 34,* 331–351.

62. Allen, T.D., Eby, L.T., Poteet, M.L., Lentz, E., & Lima, L. (2004). Career benefits associated with mentoring for protégés: A meta-analysis. *Journal of Applied Psychology, 89,* 127–136.

63. Chao, G., Walz, P., & Gardner, P. (1992). Formal and informal mentorships: A comparison on mentoring functions and contrast with nonmentored counterparts. *Personnel Psychology, 45,* 619–636; Noe, R. (1988). An investigation of the determinants of successful assigned mentoring relationships. *Personnel Psychology, 41,* 457–479; Allen, Eby, & Lentz, 2006a; Allen, T. D., Eby, L. T., & Lentz, E. (2006b). The relationship between formal mentoring program characteristics and perceived program effectiveness. *Personnel Psychology, 59,* 125–153.

64. Ostroff, C., & Kozlowski, S. W. J. (1992). Organizational socialization as a learning process: The role of information acquisition. *Personnel Psychology, 45,* 849–874; Saks, A. M., & Ashforth, B. E. (1996). Proactive socialization and behavioral self-management. *Journal of Vocational Behavior, 48,* 301–323.

65. Morrison, E. W. (1993). Newcomer information seeking: Exploring types, modes, sources, and outcomes. *Academy of Management Journal, 36,* 557–589; Morrison, E. W. (1993). Longitudinal study of the effects of information seeking on newcomer socialization. *Journal of Applied Psychology, 78,* 173–183.

66. Ashford, S. J., & Black, J. S. (1996). Proactivity during organizational entry: The role of desire for control. *Journal of Applied Psychology, 81,* 199–214; Griffin, A. E. C., Colella, A., & Goparaju, S. (2000). Newcomer and organizational socialization tactics: An interactionist perspective. *Human Resource Management Review, 10,* 453–474; Wanberg, C. R., & Kammeyer-Mueller, J. D. (2000). Predictors and outcomes of proactivity in the socialization process. *Journal of Applied Psychology, 85,* 373–385; Whitely, W. T., Peiró, J. M., Feij, J. A., & Taris, T. W. (1995). Conceptual, epistemological, methodological, and outcome issues in work-role development: A reply. *Journal of Vocational Behavior, 46,* 283–291.

67. Ostroff & Kozlowski, 1992; Ashforth, B. E., Sluss, D. M., & Saks, A. M. (2007). Socialization tactics, proactive behavior, and newcomer learning: Integrating socialization models. *Journal of Vocational Behavior, 70,* 447–462; Saks, A. M., Gruman, J. A., & Cooper-Thomas, H. (2011). The neglected role of proactive behavior and outcomes in newcomer socialization. *Journal of Vocational Behavior, 79,* 36–46.

68. Deveau, D. (2012, February 3). Canada's 10 most admired corporate cultures ("People here really believe in our purpose"). *National Post,* JV6.

69. For a more complete discussion of various definitions, theories, and concepts of culture, see Allaire, Y., & Firsirotu, M. E. (1984). Theories of organizational culture. *Organization Studies, 5,* 193–226; Hatch, M. J. (1993). The dynamics of organizational culture. *Academy of Management Review, 18,* 657–693; Schein, E. H. (1992). *Organizational culture and leadership,* 2nd ed. San Francisco, CA: Jossey-Bass; Smircich, L. (1983). Concepts of culture and organizational analysis. *Administrative Science Quarterly, 28,* 339–358.

70. Sackmann, S. A. (1992). Culture and subculture: An analysis of organizational knowledge. *Administrative Science Quarterly, 37,* 140–161.

71. Gregory, K. L. (1983). Native-view paradigms: Multiple cultures and culture conflicts in organizations. *Administrative Science Quarterly, 28,* 359–376.

72. Deal, T. E., & Kennedy, A. A. (1982). *Corporate cultures: The rites and rituals of corporate life.* Reading, MA: Addison-Wesley; Kilmann, R., Saxton, M. J., & Serpa, R. (1986, Winter). Issues in understanding and changing culture. *California Management Review,* 87–94. For a critique, see Saffold, G. S., III. (1988). Culture traits, strength, and organizational performance: Moving beyond "strong" culture. *Academy of Management Review, 13,* 546–558.

73. Holloway, A. (2006, April 10–23). Hilti (Canada) Corp. *Canadian Business, 79*(8), 78.

74. Anonymous (2012, April 19). Canada's best workplaces: Google Canada tops list of large employers. *A Special National Report for the Great Place to Work Institute, The Globe and Mail,* GPTW1, GPTW6; Anonymous (2009, April 6). Canada's best workplaces: Google Canada, World's top search engine also ranked Canada's best place to work. *A Special National Report for the Great Place to Work Institute, The Globe and Mail,* GPTW1, GPTW3; Abel, K. (2008, November 24). Google Canada's new eco-friendly home enjoys playful work philosophy: Part One and Part Two [Web log message]. www .krisable.ctv.ca/blog; Mills, E. (2007, April 27). Newsmaker: Meet Google's culture czar. *CNET News,* www.news.cnet.com; Google corporate information, The Google culture, www.google.ca.

75. Biskey, M. (2015, February 23). Raising the bar on ethical culture. *Canadian HR Reporter, 28(3),* 16.

76. Canada's best workplaces: Google Canada tops list of large employers. (2012, April 19). *A Special National Report for the Great Place to Work Institute, The Globe and Mail,* GPTW1, GPTW6; Canada's best workplaces: Google Canada, World's top search engine also ranked Canada's best place to work. (2009, April 6). *A Special National Report for the Great Place to Work Institute, The Globe and Mail,* GPTW1, GPTW3; Abel, K. (2008, November 24). Google Canada's new eco-friendly home enjoys playful work philosophy: Part One and Part Two [Web log message]. www .krisable.ctv.ca/blog; Mills, E. (2007, April 27). Newsmaker: Meet Google's culture czar. *CNET News,* www.news. cnet.com; Google corporate information, The Google culture, www.google.ca.

77. Lorsch, J.W. (1986, Winter). Managing culture: The invisible barrier to strategic change. *California Management Review,* 95–109.

78. Verburg, P. (2000, December 25).

79. Waterstone Human Capital: Announcing Canada's 10 Most Admired Corporate Cultures of 2014. (2014, November 20). *Waterstone News and Events,* http://www .waterstonehc.com/news-events/news/ announcing-canadas-10-most-admired-corporate-cultures-2014.

80. Mount, I. (2002, August). Out of control. *Business 2.0, 3*(8), 38–44.

81. Cartwright, S., & Cooper, C.L. (1993, May). The role of culture compatibility in successful organizational marriage. *Academy of Management Executive,* 57–70.

82. Dobson, S. (2013, March 11). Retention, culture critical to M&As: Surveys. *Canadian HR Reporter, 26(5),* 5, 8.

83. Fordahl, M. (2002, March 28). HP, Compaq face ghosts of mega-mergers past. *The Globe and Mail,* B17.

84. Kets de Vries, M. F. R., & Miller, D. (1984). *The neurotic organization: Diagnosing and changing counterproductive styles of management.* San Francisco, CA: Jossey-Bass.

85. Lardner, J. (2002, March). Why should anyone believe you? *Business 2.0, 3*(3), 40–48; Waldie, P., & Howlett, K. (2003, June 11). Reports reveal tight grip of Ebbers on WorldCom. *The Globe and Mail,* B1, B7; Wells, J. (2009, August 6). Now playing: Garth Drabinsky stars in the 7-year stretch. *Toronto Star,* A1, A12; Blackwell, R., & MacMillan, J. (2009, August 6). They built a theatre empire that crumbled, bilking investors and cleaning out creditors. Now Garth Drabinsky and his partner are going to jail for their "deception" and "dishonest dealing." *The Globe and Mail,* A1, A7.

86. McKenna, B. (2003, August 27). Shuttle probe blasts NASA's dysfunctional atmosphere. *The Globe and Mail,* A9; Schwartz, J., & Wald, M. L. (2003, August 27). Shuttle probe faults NASA. *Toronto Star* (online), www.thestar.ca (orig. pub. *The New York Times*).

87. Maccharles, T. (2011, November 17). Sexual harassment tops RCMP agenda. *Toronto Star,* A4; Keller, J. (2012, May 10). RCMP corporal files sexual harassment suit. *The Canadian Press,* www .metronews.ca/news.

88. See Schein, 1992.

89. Papmehl, A. (2002, October 7). Diversity in workplace paying off, IBM finds. *Toronto Star.* http://www-2 .rotman.utoronto.ca/~verma/Media%20 Publications%20featuring%20Anil%20 Verma/Diversity%20in%20workforce%20 paying%20off,%20IBM%20finds.htm.

90. Pascale, R. (1985, Winter). The paradox of "corporate culture": Reconciling ourselves to socialization. *California Management Review,* 26–41. For some research support, see Caldwell, D. F., Chatman, J. A., & O'Reilly, C. A. (1990). Building organizational commitment: A multifirm study. *Journal of Occupational Psychology, 63,* 245–261.

91. Kerr, M. (2014, September 15).

92. Deveau, D. (2012, February 3). Canada's 10 most admired corporate cultures (Culture aids recruiting process). *National Post,* JV1.

93. Deveau, D. (2012, February 3). Canada's 10 most admired corporate cultures (No cultural divides for Agrium employees). *National Post,* JV4.

94. Gordon, A. (2000, February). 35 best companies to work for. *Report on Business Magazine,* 24–32.

95. Hatch, 1993; Ornstein, S. (1986). Organizational symbols: A study of their meanings and influences on perceived organizational climate. *Organizational Behavior and Human Decision Processes, 38,* 207–229.

96. Nulty, P. (1989, February 27). America's toughest bosses. *Fortune,* 40–54.

97. Trice, H.M., and Beyer, J.M. (1984). Studying organizational cultures through rites and ceremonials. *Academy of Management Review, 9,* 653–669.

98. Deveau, D. (2012, February 3). Canada's 10 most admired corporate cultures ('People here really believe in our purpose'). *National Post*, JV6.

99. Dobson, S. (2013, January 28). Award-winning corporate cultures about values, feedback, communication. *Canadian HR Reporter*, 26(2), 8, 26.

100. Martin, J., Feldman, M. S., Hatch, M. J., & Sitkin, S. B. (1983). The uniqueness paradox in organizational stories. *Administrative Science Quarterly*, 28, 438–453.

101. Peters, T., & Austin, N. (1985). *A passion for excellence: The leadership difference.* New York, NY: Random House.

Chapter 9

1. Richardson, M. (2012, December 29). Chrysler's man of steel. *Toronto Star*, W1, W4; Flavelle, D. (2014, March 8). CEO aims to steer Chrysler back on track. *Toronto Star*, B1, B7; Marchionne, S. (2008, December). Fiat's extreme makeover. *Harvard Business Review*, 86(12), 45–48; Ebhardt, T. (2014, January 13). Fiat CEO Marchionne to stay minimum three years. *Financial Post*, http://business.financialpost.com/news/transportation/fiat-ceo-marchionne-to-stay-minimum-three-years; Associated Press (2014, October 13). Fiat Chrysler shares bounce around in first day of trading. *Toronto Star*, http://www.thestar.com/business/2014/10/13/fiat_chrysler_shares_bounce_around_in_first_day_of_trading.html. Reprinted with permission - Torstar Syndication Services.

2. Dobson, S. (2015, May 18). Leadership is most pressing human capital challenge: Survey. *Canadian HR Reporter*, 28(9), 3, 9.

3. Hiller, N. J., DeChurch, L. A., Murase, T., & Doty, D. (2011). Searching for outcomes of leadership: A 25-year review. *Journal of Management*, 37, 1137–1177.

4. Ireland, R. D., & Hitt, M. A. (1999). Achieving and maintaining strategic competitiveness in the 21st century: The role of strategic leadership. *Academy of Management Executive*, 13, 43–57.

5. Judge, T. A., Bono, J. E., Ilies, R., & Gerhardt, M. W. (2002). Personality and leadership: A qualitative and quantitative review. *Journal of Applied Psychology*, 87, 765–780.

6. Bass, B. M. (1990). *Bass & Stogdill's handbook of leadership: A survey of research* (3rd ed.). New York, NY: Free Press.

7. Derue, D. S., Nahrgang, J. D., Wellman, N., & Humphrey, S. E. (2011). Trait and behavioral theories of leadership: An integration and meta-analytic test of their relative validity. *Personnel Psychology*, 64, 7–52.

8. This list is derived from Bass, 1990; House, R. J., & Baetz, M. L. (1979). Leadership: Some empirical generalizations and new research directions. *Research in Organizational Behavior*, 1, 341–423; Locke, E. A. & Associates (1992). *The essence of leadership: The four keys to leading effectively.* New York, NY: Free Press; Lord, R. G., DeVader, C. L., & Alliger, G. M. (1986). A meta-analysis of the relationship between personality traits and leadership perceptions: An application of validity generalization procedures. *Journal of Applied Psychology*, 71, 402–410.

9. Derue et al., 2011; Judge et al., 2002; Grant, A. M., Gino, F., & Hofmann, D. A. (2011). Reversing the extraverted leadership advantage: The role of employee proactivity. *Academy of Management Journal*, 54, 528–550; Van Iddekinge, C. H., Ferris, G. R., & Heffner, T. S. (2009). Test of a multistage model of distal and proximal antecedents of leader performance. *Personnel Psychology*, 62, 463–495.

10. Colbert, A. E., Barrick, M. R., & Bradley, B. H. (2014). Personality and leadership composition in top management teams: Implications for organizational effectiveness. *Personnel Psychology*, 67, 351–387.

11. Judge, T. A., & Bono, J. E. (2000). Five-factor model of personality and transformational leadership. *Journal of Applied Psychology*, 85, 751–765; Judge, T. A., Colbert, A. E., & Ilies, R. (2004). Intelligence and leadership: A quantitative review and test of theoretical propositions. *Journal of Applied Psychology*, 89, 542–552.

12. Derue et al., 2011.

13. Rosette, A. S., Leonardelli, G. J., & Phillips, K. W. (2008). The White standard: Racial bias in leader categorization. *Journal of Applied Psychology*, 93, 758–777.

14. Kirkpatrick, S. A., & Locke, E. A. (1991). Leadership: Do traits matter? *Academy of Management Executive*, 5, 48–60.

15. Derue et al., 2011.

16. Hannon, G. (2004, January). The great transformation. *Report on Business Magazine*, 20(7), 43–46.

17. Judge, T. A., Piccolo, R. F., & Ilies, R. (2004). The forgotten ones? The validity of consideration and initiating structure in leadership research. *Journal of Applied Psychology*, 89, 36–51.

18. Kerr, S., Schriesheim, C. A., Murphy, C. J., & Stogdill, R. M. (1974). Toward a contingency theory of leadership based upon the consideration and initiating structure literature. *Organizational Behavior and Human Performance*, 12, 62–82.

19. Podsakoff, P. M., Bommer, W. H., Podsakoff, N. P., & MacKenzie, S. B. (2006). Relationships between leader reward and punishment behaviour and subordinate attitudes, perceptions, and behaviors: A meta-analytic review of existing and new research. *Organizational Behavior and Human Decision Processes*, 99, 113–142.

20. Fiedler, F. E. (1967). *A theory of leadership effectiveness.* New York, NY: McGraw-Hill; Fiedler, F. E. (1978). The contingency model and the dynamics of the leadership process. In L. Berkowitz (Ed.), *Advances in experimental social psychology* (Vol. 11). New York, NY: Academic Press; Fiedler, F. E., & Chemers, M. M. (1974). *Leadership and effective management.* Glenview, IL: Scott, Foresman.

21. For a summary, see Fiedler, 1978.

22. See Ashour, A.S. (1973). The contingency model of leader effectiveness: An evaluation. *Organizational Behavior and Human Performance*, 9, 339–355; Graen, G. B., Alvares, D., Orris, J. B., & Martella, J. A. (1970). The contingency model of leadership effectiveness: Antecedent and evidential results. *Psychological Bulletin*, 74, 285–296.

23. Peters, L. H., Hartke, D. D., & Pohlmann, J. T. (1985). Fiedler's contingency theory of leadership: An application of the meta-analysis procedures of Schmidt and Hunter. *Psychological Bulletin*, 97, 274–285; Schriesheim, C. A., Tepper, B. J., & Tetreault, L. A. (1994). Least preferred co-worker score, situational control, and leadership effectiveness: A meta-analysis of contingency and performance predictions. *Journal of Applied Psychology*, 79, 561–573; Strube, M. J., & Garcia, J. E. (1981). A meta-analytic investigation of Fiedler's contingency model of leadership effectiveness. *Psychological Bulletin*, 90, 307–321.

24. House, R. J., & Dessler, G. (1974). The path-goal theory of leadership: Some post hoc and a priori tests. In J.G. Hunt & L.L. Larson (Eds.), *Contingency approaches to leadership.* Carbondale, IL: Southern Illinois University Press; House, R. J., & Mitchell, T. R. (1974, Autumn). Path-goal theory of leadership. *Journal of Contemporary Business*, 81–97. See also Evans, M. G. (1970). The effects of supervisory behavior on the path-goal relationship. *Organizational Behavior and Human Performance*, 5, 277–298.

25. Filley, A. C., House, R. J., & Kerr, S. (1976). *Managerial process and organizational behavior* (2nd ed.). Glenview, IL:

Scott, Foresman; House & Dessler, 1974; House & Mitchell, 1974; Wofford, J. C., & Liska, L. Z. (1993). Path-goal theories of leadership: A meta-analysis. *Journal of Management, 19,* 857–876.

26. See, for example, Greene, C. N. (1979). Questions of causation in the path-goal theory of leadership. *Academy of Management Journal, 22,* 22–41; Griffin, R. W. (1980). Relationships among individual, task design, and leader behavior variables. *Academy of Management Journal, 23,* 665–683.

27. Mitchell, T. R. (1973). Motivation and participation: An integration. *Academy of Management Journal, 16,* 160–179.

28. Maier, N. R. F. (1970). *Problem solving and creativity in individuals and groups.* Belmont, CA: Brooks/Cole; Maier, N. R. F. (1973). *Psychology in industrial organizations* (4th ed.). Boston, MA: Houghton Mifflin.

29. Maier, 1970, 1973.

30. Vroom, V. H., & Jago, A. G. (1988). *The new leadership: Managing participation in organizations.* Englewood Cliffs, NJ: Prentice-Hall; Vroom, V. H., & Yetton, P. W. (1973). *Leadership and decision-making.* Pittsburgh, PA: University of Pittsburgh Press.

31. Vroom & Yetton, 1973, 13.

32. See Vroom & Jago, 1988, for a review. See also Field, R. H. G., Wedley, W. C., & Hayward, M. W. J. (1989). Criteria used in selecting Vroom-Yetton decision styles. *Canadian Journal of Administrative Sciences, 6*(2), 18–24.

33. Reviews on participation reveal a complicated pattern of results. See Miller, K. I., & Monge, P. R. (1986). Participation, satisfaction, and productivity: A meta-analytic review. *Academy of Management Journal, 29,* 727–753; Wagner, J. A., III, & Gooding, R. Z. (1987a). Shared influence and organizational behavior: A meta-analysis of situational variables expected to moderate participation–outcome relationships. *Academy of Management Journal, 30,* 524–541; Wagner, J. A., III, & Gooding, R. Z. (1987b). Effects of societal trends on participation research. *Administrative Science Quarterly, 32,* 241–262; Huang, X., Iun, J., Liu, A., & Gong, Y. (2010). Does participative leadership enhance work performance by inducing empowerment or trust? The differential effects on managerial and non-managerial subordinates. *Journal of Organizational Behavior, 31,* 122–143.

34. Graen, G. B., & Uhl-Bien, M. (1995). Relationship-based approach to leadership: Development of leader–member exchange (LMX) theory of leadership over 25 years: Applying a multi-level,

multi-domain perspective. *Leadership Quarterly, 6*(2), 219–247.

35. Walumbwa, F. O., Mayer, D. M., Wang, P., Wang, H., Workman K., & Christensen, A. L. (2011). Linking ethical leadership to employee performance: The roles of leader-member exchange, self-efficacy, and organizational identification. *Organizational Behavior and Human Decision Processes, 115,* 204–213; Walumbwa, F. O., Cropanzano, R., & Goldman, B. M. (2011). How leader–member exchange influences effective work behaviors: Social exchange and internal-external efficacy perspectives. *Personnel Psychology, 64,* 739–770.

36. Gerstner, C. R., & Day, D. V. (1997). Meta-analytic review of leader-member exchange theory: Correlates and construct issues. *Journal of Applied Psychology, 82,* 827–844; Graen & Uhl-Bien, 1995; Schriesheim, C. A., Castro, S. L., & Cogliser, C. C. (1999). Leader–member exchange (LMX) research: A comprehensive review of theory, measurement, and data-analytic practices. *Leadership Quarterly, 10*(1), 63–113; House, R. J., & Aditya, R. N. (1997). The social scientific study of leadership: Quo vadis? *Journal of Management, 23,* 409–473; Tierney, P., Farmer, S. M., & Graen, G. B. (1999). An examination of leadership and employee creativity: The relevance of traits and relationships. *Personnel Psychology, 52,* 591–620.

37. Gerstner & Day, 1997; Graen & Uhl-Bien, 1995; Ilies, R., Nahrgang, J. D., & Morgeson, F. P. (2007). Leader-member exchange and citizenship behaviors: A meta-analysis. *Journal of Applied Psychology, 92,* 269–277; Liao, H., Liu, D., & Loi, R. (2010). Looking at both sides of the social exchange coin: A social cognitive perspective on the joint effects of relationship quality and differentiation on creativity. *Academy of Management Journal, 53,* 1090–1109.

38. Judge, T. A., & Piccolo, R. F. (2004). Transformational and transactional leadership: A meta-analytic test of their relative validity. *Journal of Applied Psychology, 89,* 755–768.

39. The transformational/transactional distinction is credited to Burns, J. M. (1978). *Leadership.* New York, NY: Harper & Row.

40. Bass, B.M. (1985). *Leadership and performance beyond expectations.* New York, NY: Free Press; Bass, B. M. (1990, Winter). From transactional to transformational leadership: Learning to share the vision. *Organizational Dynamics,* 19–31.

41. Judge & Piccolo, 2004.

42. Judge & Piccolo, 2004; Bono, J. E., & Judge, T. A. (2004). Personality and

transformational and transactional leadership: A meta-analysis. *Journal of Applied Psychology, 89,* 901–910.

43. House, R. J. (1977). A 1976 theory of charismatic leadership. In J. G. Hunt & L. L. Larson (Eds.), *Leadership: The cutting edge.* Carbondale, IL: Southern Illinois University Press.

44. Judge & Piccolo, 2004.

45. DeGroot, T., Kilker, D. S., & Cross, T. C. (2000). A meta-analysis to review organizational outcomes related to charismatic leadership. *Canadian Journal of Administrative Sciences, 17,* 356–371; Fuller, J. B., Patterson, C. E. P., Hester, K., & Stringer, D. Y. (1996). A quantitative review of research on charismatic leadership. *Psychological Reports, 78,* 271–287; Agle, B. R., Nagarajan, N. J., Sonnenfeld, J. A., & Srinivasan, D. (2006). Does CEO charisma matter? An empirical analysis of the relationships among organizational performance, environmental uncertainty, and top management team perceptions of CEO charisma. *Academy of Management Journal, 49,* 161–174; Waldman, D. A., Ramirez, G. G., House, R. J., & Puranam, P. (2001). Does leadership matter? CEO leadership attributes and profitability under conditions of perceived environmental uncertainty. *Academy of Management Journal, 44,* 134–143.

46. Derue et al., 2011.

47. Colbert, A. E., Kristof-Brown, A. L., Bradley, B. H., & Barrick, M. R. (2008). CEO transformational leadership: The role of goal importance congruence in top management teams. *Academy of Management Journal, 51,* 81–96; Ling, Y., Simsek, Z., Lubatkin, M. H., & Veiga, J. F. (2008). The impact of transformational CEOs on the performance of small- to medium-sized firms: Does organizational context matter? *Journal of Applied Psychology, 93,* 923–934; Colbert, Barrick, & Bradley, 2014.

48. Seo, M., Taylor, M. S., Hill, N. S., Zhang, X., Tesluk, P. E., & Lorinkova, N. M. (2012). The role of affect and leadership during organizational change. *Personnel Psychology, 65,* 121–165; Oreg, S., & Berson, Y. (2011). Leadership and employees' reactions to change: The role of leaders' personal attributes and transformational leadership style. *Personnel Psychology, 64,* 627–659; Herold, D. M., Fedor, D. B., Caldwell, S., & Liu, Y. (2008). The effects of transformational and change leadership on employees' commitment to a change: A multilevel study. *Journal of Applied Psychology, 93,* 346–357.

49. Avolio, B. J., Walumbwa, F. O., & Weber, T. J. (2009). Leadership: Current

theories, research, and future directions. *Annual Review of Psychology, 60*, 421–449.

50. Zhang, X., & Bartol, K. M. (2010). Linking empowering leadership and employee creativity: The influence of psychological empowerment, intrinsic motivation, and creative process engagement. *Academy of Management Journal, 53*, 107–128.

51. Ahearne, M., Mathieu, J., & Rapp, A. (2005). To empower or not to empower your sales force? An empirical examination of the influence of leadership empowerment behavior on customer satisfaction and performance. *Journal of Applied Psychology, 90*, 945–955.

52. Zhang & Bartol, 2010.

53. Lorinkova, N. M., Pearsall, M. J., & Sims, Jr., H. P. (2013). Examining the differential longitudinal performance of directive versus empowering leadership in teams. *Academy of Management Journal, 56*, 573–596.

54. Brown, M. E., Trevino, L. K., & Harrison, D. A. (2005). Ethical leadership: A social learning perspective for construct development and testing. *Organizational Behavior and Human Decision Processes, 97*, 117–134; Brown, M. E., & Trevino, L. K. (2006). Ethical leadership: A review and future directions. *The Leadership Quarterly, 17*, 595–616.

55. Ng, T. W. H., & Feldman, D. C. (2015). Ethical leadership: Meta-analytic evidence of criterion-related and incremental validity. *Journal of Applied Psychology, 100*, 948–965.

56. Mayer, D. M., Aquino, K., Greenbaum, R. L., & Kuenzi, M. (2012). Who displays ethical leadership, and why does it matter? An examination of antecedents and consequences of ethical leadership. *Academy of Management Journal, 55*, 151–171; Kacmar, K. M., Bachrach, D. G., & Harris, K. J. (2011). Fostering good citizenship through ethical leadership: Exploring the moderating role of gender and organizational politics. *Journal of Applied Psychology, 96*, 633–642; Schminke, M., Ambrose, M. L., & Neubaum, D. O. (2005). The effects of leader moral development on ethical climate and employee attitudes. *Organizational Behavior and Human Decision Processes, 97*, 135–151.

57. Brown, Trevino, & Harrison, 2005; Mayer, D. M., Kuenzi, M., Greenbaum, R., Bardes, M., & Salvador, R. (2009). How low does ethical leadership flow? Test of a trickle-down model. *Organizational Behavior and Human Decision Processes, 108*, 1–13.

58. Hannah, S. T., Avolio, B. J., & Walumbwa, F. O. (2011). Relationships between authentic leadership, moral courage, and ethical and pro-social behaviors. *Business Ethics Quarterly, 21*, 555–578; Gardner, W. L., Avolio, B. J., Luthans, F., May, D. R., & Walumbwa, F. (2005). "Can you see the real me?" A self-based model of authentic leader and follower development. *The Leadership Quarterly, 16*, 343–372; Ilies, R., Morgenson, F. P., & Nahrgang, J. D. (2005). Authentic leadership and eudaemonic well-being: Understanding leader-follower outcomes. *The Leadership Quarterly, 16*, 373–394.

59. Pitts, G. (2008, December). The testing of Michael McCain. *Report on Business*, 60–66; Pitts, G. (2008, August 30). Man under fire. *The Globe and Mail*, B1, B6.

60. Walumbwa, F. O., Avolio, B. J., Gardner, W. L., Wernsing, T. S., & Peterson, S. J. (2008). Authentic leadership: Development and validation of a theory-based measure. *Journal of Management, 34*, 89–126.

61. Walumbwa et al., 2008; Hannah et al., 2011; Walumbwa, F. O., Wang, P., Wang, H., Schaubroeck, J., & Avolio, B. J. (2010). Psychological processes linking authentic leadership to follower behaviors. *The Leadership Quarterly, 21*, 901–914.

62. Walumbwa, F. O., Luthans, F., Avey, J. B., & Oke, A. (2011). Authentically leading groups: The mediating role of collective psychological capital and trust. *Journal of Organizational Behavior, 32*, 4–24.

63. Hannah, S. T., Walumbwa, F. O., & Fry, L. W. (2011). Leadership in action teams: Team leader and members' authenticity, authenticity strength, and team outcomes. *Personnel Psychology, 64*, 771–802.

64. Liden, R. C., Wayne, S. J., Zhao, H., & Henderson, D. (2008). Servant leadership: Development of a multidimensional measure and multi-level assessment. *The Leadership Quarterly, 19*, 161–177.

65. Van Dierendonck, D. (2011). Servant leadership: A review and synthesis. *Journal of Management, 37*, 1228–1261; Liden et al., 2008.

66. Van Dierendonck, 2011.

67. Van Dierendonck, 2011; Mayer, D. M., Bardes, M., & Piccolo, R. F. (2008). Do servant-leaders help satisfy follower needs? An organizational justice perspective. *European Journal of Work and Organizational Psychology, 17*, 180–197; Neubert, M. J., Kacmar, K. M., Carlson, D. S., Chonko, L. B., & Roberts, J. A. (2008). Regulatory focus as a mediator of the influence of initiating structure and servant leadership on employee behavior. *Journal of Applied Psychology, 93*, 1220–1233.

68. Walumbwa, F. O., Hartnell, C. A., & Oke, A. (2010). Servant leadership, procedural justice climate, service climate, employee attitudes, and organizational citizenship behavior: A cross-level investigation. *Journal of Applied Psychology, 95*, 517–529; Ehrhart, M. G. (2004). Leadership and procedural justice climate as antecedents of unit-level organizational citizenship behavior. *Personnel Psychology, 57*, 61–94.

69. Chen, Z., Zhu, J., & Zhou, M. (2015). How does a servant leader fuel the service fire? A multilevel model of servant leadership, individual self identity, group competition climate, and customer service performance. *Journal of Applied Psychology, 100*, 511–521.

70. Eagley, A. H., & Johnson, B. T. (1990). Gender and leadership style: A meta-analysis. *Psychological Bulletin, 108*, 233–256.

71. Kass, S. (September 1999). Employees perceive women as better managers than men, finds five-year study. *ADA Monitor, 30*(8), 6.

72. Derue et al., 2011.

73. Eagly, A.H., Johannesen-Schmidt, M.C., & van Engen, M.L. (2003). Transformational, transactional, and laissez-faire leadership styles: A meta-analysis comparing women and men. *Psychological Bulletin, 120*, 569–591.

74. Paustian-Underdahl, S. C., Walker, L. S., & Woehr, D. J. (2014). Gender and perceptions of leadership effectiveness: A meta-analysis of contextual moderators. *Journal of Applied Psychology, 99*, 1129–1145.

75. Financial Post Staff (2011, December 11). Canada's most powerful women: Top 100, *Financial Post*, www.financialpost.com; www.ge.com.ca/en/company/leadership,bios/elyse_allan.html.

76. Wohlbold, E., & Chenier, L. (2011). Women in senior management: Where are they? *The Conference Board of Canada*. Ottawa; Kopun, F. (2011, August 31). Women's workplace mobility 'flatlined.' *Toronto Star*, B4; McFarland, J., & McNish, J. (2010, October 15). Firms creating diversity programs to break down systemic barriers. *The Globe and Mail*, A14; Klie, S. (2009, April 6). Women make small gains. *Canadian HR Reporter, 22*(7), 1, 2; Morra, M. (2008, June–July). The broad perspective. *HR Professional*, 22–28; Anonymous (2015, March 19). Women now hold 8.5% of Canada's top jobs, *CBC News*, http://www.cbc.ca/news/business/women-now-hold-8-5-of-canada-s-top-jobs-1.3001744; Silliker, A. (2013, April 22). MPI tops list of FP500 companies with most women at the top: Report. *Canadian HR Reporter, 26*(8), 2, 6.

77. Eagly, A.H., & Carli, L.L. (2007, September). Women and the labyrinth of leadership. *Harvard Business Review, 85*, 63–71.

78. Eagly, A. H., & Karau, S. J. (2002). Role congruity theory of prejudice toward female leaders. *Psychological Review, 109*, 573–598.

79. Koenig, A.M., Eagly, A.H., Mitchell, A.A., & Ristikari, T. (2011). Are leader stereotypes masculine? A meta-analysis of three research paradigms. *Psychological Bulletin, 137*, 616–642.

80. Eagly & Carli, 2007.

81. Javidan et al., 2006.

82. Javidan et al., 2006.

83. Javidan et al., 2006.

84. Gregersen, H.B., Morrison, A.J., & Black, J.S. (1998, Fall). Developing leaders for the global frontier. *Sloan Management Review*, 21–32.

85. Javidan, M., Dorfman, P.W., de Luque, M.S., & House, R.J. (2006). In the eye of the beholder: Cross-cultural lessons in leadership from Project GLOBE. *Academy of Management Perspectives, 20*, 67–90.

86. Bitti, M. T. (2014, December 15). Linamar chief Linda Hasenfratz continues to prove she belongs at the top. *Financial Post*, http://business .financialpost.com/entrepreneur/linamar-chief-linda-hasenfratz-continues-to-prove-she-belongs-at-the-top.

87. Gregersen, Morrison, & Black, 1998.

88. Gregersen, Morrison, & Black, 1998; Javidan et al., 2006.

89. Javidan et al., 2006.

90. Gregersen, Morrison, & Black, 1998; Church, E. (1999, January 7). Born to be a global business leader. *The Globe and Mail*, B8.

91. Moore, K. (2002, August 21). Multicultural Canada breeds managers with global outlook. *The Globe and Mail*, B9.

Chapter 10

1. Excerpted from Blackwell, T. (2013, August 27). Building chemistry. *National Post*, A9.

2. Morrison, E. W. (2014). Employee voice and silence. *Annual Review of Organizational Psychology and Organizational Behavior, 1*, 173–197; Morrison, E. W. (2011). Employee voice behavior: Integration and directions for future research. *Academy of Management Annals, 5*, 373–412.

3. Morrison, E. W., Wheeler-Smith, S. L., & Kamdar, D. (2011). Speaking up in groups: A cross-level study of group voice climate and voice. *Journal of Applied Psychology, 96*, 183–191; Ng, T. W. H., & Feldman, D. C. (2012). Employee voice behavior: A meta-analytic test of the conservation of resources framework. *Journal of Organizational Behavior, 33*, 216–234; LePine & Van Dyne, 2001.

4. Detert, J. R., & Treviño, L. K. (2010). Speaking up to higher-ups: How supervisors and skip-level leaders influence employee voice. *Organization Science, 21*, 249–270.

5. Edmondson, A. C., & Lei, Z. (2014). Psychological safety: The history, renaissance, and future of an interpersonal construct. *Annual Review of Organizational Psychology and Organizational Behavior, 1*, 23–43.

6. Ng & Feldman, 2012.

7. Detert, J. R., & Edmondson, A. C. (2011). Implicit voice theories: Taken-for-granted rules of self-censorship at work. *Academy of Management Journal, 54*, 461–488.

8. Tesser, A., & Rosen, S. (1975). The reluctance to transmit bad news. In L. Berkowitz (Ed.), *Advances in experimental social psychology* (Vol. 8). New York, NY: Academic Press.

9. Read, W. (1962). Upward communication in industrial hierarchies. *Human Relations, 15*, 3–16; for related studies, see Jablin, F. M. (1979). Superior–subordinate communication: The state of the art. *Psychological Bulletin, 86*, 1201–1222.

10. Evidence that subordinates suppress communicating negative news to the boss can be found in O'Reilly, C. A., & Roberts, K. H. (1974). Information filtration in organizations: Three experiments. *Organizational Behavior and Human Performance, 11*, 253–265. For evidence that this is probably self-presentational, see Bond, C. F., Jr., & Anderson, E. L. (1987). The reluctance to transmit bad news: Private discomfort or public display? *Journal of Experimental Social Psychology, 23*, 176–187.

11. Ashford, S.J. (1989). Self-assessments in organizations: A literature review and integrated model. *Research in Organizational Behavior, 11*, 133–174; Heidemeier, H., & Moser, K. (2009). Self-other agreement in job performance ratings: A meta-analytic test and a process model. *Journal of Applied Psychology, 94*, 353–370.

12. Grosser, T. J., Lopez-Kidwell, V., Labianca, G., & Ellwardt, L. (2012). Hearing it through the grapevine: Positive and negative workplace gossip. *Organizational Dynamics, 41*, 52–61.

13. Davis, K. (1977). *Human behavior at work* (5th ed.). New York, NY: McGraw-Hill.

14. Grosser et al., 2012.

15. Bartlett, C. A., & Ghosal, S. (1995, May–June). Changing the role of top management: Beyond systems to people. *Harvard Business Review*, 132–142; for more on gossip, see the June 2004 special issue of the *Review of General Psychology*.

16. Van Hoye, G., & Lievens, F. (2009). Tapping the grapevine: A closer look at word-of-mouth as a recruitment source. *Journal of Applied Psychology, 94*, 341–352.

17. Rosnow, R. L. (1980). Psychology of rumor reconsidered. *Psychological Bulletin, 87*, 578–591.

18. Rosnow, R. L. (1991). Inside rumor: A personal journey. *American Psychologist, 46*, 484–496; see also DiFronzo, N. & Bordia, P. (2007). *Rumor psychology: Social and organizational approaches*. Washington, DC: American Psychological Association.

19. Kanter, R. M. (1977). *Men and women of the corporation*. New York, NY: Basic Books.

20. For reviews, see Heslin, R., & Patterson, M. L. (1982). *Nonverbal behavior and social psychology*. New York, NY: Plenum; Harper, R.G., Wiens, A. N., & Matarazzo, J. D. (1978). *Nonverbal communication: The state of the art*. New York, NY: Wiley; for a popular treatment, see Goman, C. K. (2008). *The nonverbal advantage: Secrets and science of body language at work*. San Francisco, CA: Berrett-Koehler.

21. Mehrabian, A. (1972). *Nonverbal communication*. Chicago, IL: Aldine-Atherton.

22. Mehrabian, 1972; see also Hall, J. A., Coats, E. J., & Smith LeBeau, L. (2005). Nonverbal behavior and the vertical dimension of social relations: A meta-analysis. *Psychological Bulletin, 131*, 898–924.

23. DePaulo, B. M. (1992). Nonverbal behavior and self-presentation. *Psychological Bulletin, 111*, 203–243.

24. Edinger, J. A., & Patterson, M. L. (1983). Nonverbal involvement and social control. *Psychological Bulletin, 93*, 30–56.

25. Rasmussen, K. G., Jr. (1984). Nonverbal behavior, verbal behavior, resume credentials, and selection interview outcomes. *Journal of Applied Psychology, 69*, 551–556.

26. Campbell, D. E. (1979). Interior office design and visitor response. *Journal of Applied Psychology, 64*, 648–653. For a replication, see Morrow, P. C., & McElroy, J. C. (1981). Interior office design and visitor response: A constructive replication. *Journal of Applied Psychology, 66*, 646–650.

27. Gosling, S. D., Ko, S. J., Mannarelli, T., & Morris, M. E. (2002). A room with a cue: Personality judgments based on offices and bedrooms. *Journal of Personality and Social Psychology, 82*, 379–398.

28. Elsbach, K. D. (2004). Interpreting workplace identities: The role of office decor. *Journal of Organizational Behavior, 25,* 99–128.

29. Molloy, J. T. (1993). *John T. Molloy's new dress for success.* New York, NY: Warner; Molloy, J. T. (1987). *The woman's dress for success book.* New York, NY: Warner.

30. Rafaeli, A., & Pratt, M. G. (1993). Tailored meanings: On the meaning and impact of organizational dress. *Academy of Management Review, 18,* 32–55; Solomon, M. R. (Ed.). (1985). *The psychology of fashion.* New York, NY: Lexington; Solomon, M.R. (1986, April). Dress for effect. *Psychology Today,* 20–28.

31. Forsythe, S., Drake, M. F., & Cox, C. E. (1985). Influence of applicant's dress on interviewer's selection decisions. *Journal of Applied Psychology, 70,* 374–378.

32. Dress for Success Worldwide, www .dressforsuccess.org.

33. Solomon, 1986.

34. Tannen, D. (1994). *Talking from 9 to 5.* New York, NY: William Morrow.

35. Koonce, R. (1997, September). Language, sex, and power: Women and men in the workplace. *Training & Development,* 34–39.

36. Tannen, D. (1995, September–October). The power of talk: Who gets heard and why. *Harvard Business Review,* 138–148.

37. Koonce, 1997.

38. Tannen, 1994.

39. Adler, N. J. (1992). *International dimensions of organizational behavior* (2nd ed.). Belmont, CA: Wadsworth, 66.

40. Ramsey, S., & Birk, J. (1983). Preparation of North Americans for interaction with Japanese: Considerations of language and communication style. In D. Landis & R. W. Brislin (Eds.), *Handbook of intercultural training* (Vol. 3). New York, NY: Pergamon.

41. Harzing, A.-W., & Pudelko, M. (2014). Hablas vielleicht un peu la mia language? A comprehensive overview of the role of language differences in headquarters-subsidiary communication. *International Journal of Human Resource Management, 25,* 696–717.

42. Neeley, T. B., Hinds, P. J., & Cramton, C. D. (2012). The (un)hidden turmoil of language in global collaboration. *Organizational Dynamics, 41,* 236–244.

43. Ekman, P., & Rosenberg, E. (1997). *What the face reveals.* New York, NY: Oxford University Press.

44. Furnham, A., & Bochner, S. (1986). *Culture shock: Psychological reactions to unfamiliar environments.* London, UK: Methuen, 207–208; for a more general perspective on how gestures relate to verbal communication, see Hostetter,

A. B. (2011). When do gestures communicate? A meta-analysis. *Psychological Bulletin, 137,* 297–315.

45. Examples on gaze and touch draw on Argyle, M. (1982). Inter-cultural communication. In S. Bochner (Ed.), *Cultures in contact: Studies in cross-cultural interaction.* Oxford, UK: Pergamon; Furnham & Bochner, 1986.

46. Collett, P. (1971). Training Englishmen in the non-verbal behaviour of Arabs: An experiment on intercultural communication. *International Journal of Psychology, 6,* 209–215.

47. Furnham & Bochner, 1986; Argyle, 1982.

48. Ramsey & Birk, 1983.

49. Furnham & Bochner, 1986; Argyle, 1982.

50. Tannen, 1995.

51. Levine, R., West, L. J., & Reis, H. T. (1980). Perceptions of time and punctuality in the United States and Brazil. *Journal of Personality and Social Psychology, 38,* 541–550.

52. Uhlmann, E. L., Heaphy, E., Ashford, S. J., Zhu, L., & Sanchez-Burks, J. (2013). Acting professional: An exploration of culturally bounded norms against nonwork role referencing. *Journal of Organizational Behavior, 34,* 866–886.

53. Hall, E. T., & Hall, M. R. (1990). *Understanding cultural differences.* Yarmouth, ME: Intercultural Press.

54. Dulek, R. E., Fielden, J. S., & Hill, J. S. (1991, January–February). International communication: An executive primer. *Business Horizons,* 20–25.

55. Daft, R. L., & Lengel, R. H. (1984). Information richness: A new approach to managerial behavior and organizational design. *Research in Organizational Behavior, 6,* 191–233.

56. Dennis, A. R., & Wixom, B. H. (2001). Investigating the moderators of the group support systems use with meta-analysis. *Journal of Management Information Systems, 18,* 235–257.

57. McGuire, T., Kiesler, S., & Siegel, J. (1987). Group and computer-mediated discussion effects in risk decision making. *Journal of Personality and Social Psychology, 52,* 917–930.

58. Baltes, B. B., Dickson, M. W., Sherman, M. P., Bauer, C. C., & LaGanke, J. S. (2002). Computer-mediated communication and group decision making: A meta-analysis. *Organizational Behavior and Human Decision Processes, 87,* 156–179.

59. Wilson, J. M., Straus, S. G., & McEvily, B. (2006). All in due time: The development of trust in computer-mediated and face-to-face teams. *Organizational Behavior and Human Decision Processes, 99,* 16–33.

60. Skovholt, K., Grønning, A., & Kankaanranta, A. (2014). The communicative functions of emoticons in workplace e-mails: :-). *Journal of Computer-Mediated Communication, 19,* 780–797.

61. O'Mahony, S., & Barley, S. R. (1999). Do digital telecommunications affect work organization? The state of our knowledge. *Research in Organizational Behavior, 21,* 125–161; Thomson, R., & Murachver, T. (2001). Predicting gender from electronic discourse. *British Journal of Social Psychology, 40,* 193–208.

62. Kruger, J., Epley, N., Parker, J., & Ng, Z. W. (2005). Egocentrism over e-mail: Can we communicate as well as we think? *Journal of Personality and Social Psychology, 89,* 925–936; see also Byron, K. (2008). Carrying too heavy a load? The communication and miscommunication of emotion by email. *Academy of Management Review, 33,* 309–327.

63. Byron, 2008.

64. Andreassen, C. S., Torsheim, T., & Pallesen, S. (2014). Predictors of use of social networking sites at work – a specific type of cyber loafing. *Journal of Computer-Mediated Communication, 19,* 906–921.

65. Leonardi, P. M., Huysman, M., & Steinfield, C. (2013). Enterprise social media: Definition, history, and prospects for the study of social technologies in organizations. *Journal of Computer-Mediated Communication, 19,* 1–19.

66. Bingham, T., & Conner, M. (2010). *The new social learning: A guide to transforming organizations through social media.* San Francisco, CA: Berret-Koehler, p. 58.

67. Lengel, R. H., & Daft, R. L. (1988, August). The selection of communication media as an executive skill. *Academy of Management Executive,* 225–232.

68. The following relies in part on Athos, A. G., & Gabarro, J. J. (1978). *Interpersonal behavior.* Englewood Cliffs, NJ: Prentice-Hall; DeVito, J. A. (1992). *The interpersonal communication book* (6th ed.). New York, NY: HarperCollins; Whetten, D. A., & Cameron, K. S. (2007). *Developing management skills* (7th ed.). Upper Saddle River, NJ: Prentice Hall.

69. Dulek et al., 1991.

70. Bobocel, D. R., & Zdaniuk, A. (2005). How can explanations be used to foster organizational justice? In J. Greenberg & J. A. Colquitt (Eds.), *Handbook of organizational justice* (pp. 469–498). Mahwah, NJ: Lawrence Erlbaum; Bies, R. J. (2013). The delivery of bad news in organizations: A framework for analysis. *Journal of Management, 39,* 136–162.

71. Shaw, J. C., Wild, E., & Colquitt, J. A. (2003). To justify or excuse? A meta-analytic review of the effects of

explanations. *Journal of Applied Psychology, 88,* 444–458.

72. Smither, J. W., London, M., & Reilly, R. R. (2005). Does performance improve following multisource feedback? A theoretical model, meta-analysis, and review of empirical findings. *Personnel Psychology, 58,* 33–66.

73. For a good description of how to develop and use organizational surveys, see Kraut, A. I. (Ed.). (1996) *Organizational surveys.* San Francisco, CA: Jossey-Bass; Edwards, J. E., Thomas, M. D., Rosenfeld, P., & Booth-Kewley, S. (1996). *How to conduct organizational surveys: A step-by-step guide.* Thousand Oaks, CA: Sage.

74. Taft, W. F. (1985). Bulletin boards, exhibits, hotlines. In C. Reuss & D. Silvis (Eds.), *Inside organizational communication* (2nd ed.). New York, NY: Longman.

75. Tamburri, R. (2011, January). Making it safe to report wrongdoing. *University Affairs,* 12–16.

76. Chamine, S. (1998, December). Making your intranet an effective HR tool. *HR Focus,* 11–12.

77. Burnaska, R. (1976). The effects of behavior modeling training upon managers' behaviors and employees' perceptions. *Personnel Psychology, 29,* 329–335.

Chapter 11

1. Silver-Greenberg, J., & Schwartz, N. D. (2012, May 15). Warnings said to go unheeded by Chase bosses. *The New York Times,* A1, B5; Kopecki, D., Moore, M. J., & Harper, C. (2012, May 11). JPMorgan loses $2 Billion on unit's "egregious mistakes." *BloombergBusiness,* http://www.bloomberg.com/news/articles/2012-05-11/jpmorgan-loses-2-billion-as-mistakes-trounce-hedges (Dimon quote); Fitzpatrick, D., Zuckerman, G., & Rappaport, L. (2012, May 11). J.P. Morgan's $2 billion blunder. *Wall Street Journal,* http://www.wsj.com/articles/SB10001424052702304070304577396511420792008; Seligson, S. (2012, July 24). How does a bank lose $5.8 billion? *BU Today,* http://www.bu.edu/today/2012/how-does-a-bank-lose-billions/. (Online material accessed September 16, 2015).

2. Mintzberg, H. (1979). *The structuring of organizations.* Englewood Cliffs, NJ: Prentice-Hall.

3. MacCrimmon, K. R., & Taylor, R. N. (1976). Decision making and problem solving. In M. D. Dunnette (Ed.), *Handbook of industrial and organizational psychology.* Chicago, IL: Rand McNally.

4. No left turn. (2008, November). *Road & Track,* 40.

5. Tamburri, R. (2014, November 10). Universities caught up in overhaul of foreign workers program. Universityaffaires.ca.

6. Simon, H. A. (1957). *Administrative behavior* (2nd ed.). New York, NY: Free Press. See also: Kahneman, D. (2003). A perspective in judgment and choice: Mapping bounded rationality. *American Psychologist, 56,* 697–720.

7. Cornelissen, J. P., & Werner, M. D. (2014). Putting framing in perspective: A review of framing and frame analysis across the management and organizational literature. *Academy of Management Annals, 8,* 181–235; Bazerman, M. (2006). *Judgment in managerial decision making* (6th ed.). Hoboken, NJ: Wiley; Kahneman, 2003.

8. Russo, J. E., & Schoemaker, P. J. H. (1989). *Decision traps.* New York,NY: Doubleday; Whyte, G. (1991, August). Decision failures: Why they occur and how to prevent them. *Academy of Management Executive,* 23–31.

9. The latter two difficulties are discussed by Huber, G. P. (1980). *Managerial decision making.* Glenview, IL: Scott, Foresman. For further discussion of problem identification, see Cowan, D. A. (1986). Developing a process model of problem recognition. *Academy of Management Review, 11,* 763–776; Kiesler, S., & Sproull, L. (1982). Managerial response to changing environments: Perspectives on problem sensing from social cognition. *Administrative Science Quarterly, 27,* 548–570.

10. Whyte, 1991; Russo & Schoemaker, 1989.

11. Tversky, A., & Kahneman, D. (1973). Availability: A heuristic for judging frequency and probability. *Cognitive Psychology, 5,* 207–232. Also see Taylor, S. E., & Fiske, S. T. (1978). Salience, attention, and attribution: Top of the head phenomena. In L. Berkowitz (Ed.), *Advances in experimental social psychology* (Vol. 11). New York, NY: Academic Press.

12. Lichtenstein, S., Fischhoff, B., & Phillips, L. D. (1982). Calibration of probabilities: The state of the art in 1980. In D. Kahneman, P. Slovic, & A. Tversky (Eds.), *Judgment under uncertainty: Heuristics and biases.* Cambridge, MA: Cambridge University Press.

13. Tingling, P. (2009, April 21). Fact or fantasy. *National Post,* FP12.

14. Miller, J. G. (1960). Information input, overload, and psychopathology. *American Journal of Psychiatry, 116,* 695–704.

15. Manis, M., Fichman, M., & Platt, M. (1978). Cognitive integration and referential communication: Effects of information quality and quantity in message decoding. *Organizational Behavior and Human Performance, 22,* 417–430; Troutman, C. M., & Shanteau, J. (1977). Inferences based on nondiagnostic information. *Organizational Behavior and Human Performance, 19,* 43–55; Wiltermuth, S. S., & Neale, M. A. (2011). Too much information: The perils of nondiagnostic information in negotiation. *Journal of Applied Psychology, 96,* 192–201.

16. Oldroyd, J. B., & Morris, S. S. (2012). Catching falling stars: A human resource response to social capital's detrimental effect of information overload on star employees. *Academy of Management Review, 37,* 396–418.

17. Tsai, C. I., Klayman, J., & Hastie, R. (2008). Effects of amount of information on judgment accuracy and confidence. *Organizational Behavior and Human Decision Processes, 107,* 97–105.

18. Feldman, M. S., & March, J. G. (1981). Information in organizations as signal and symbol. *Administrative Science Quarterly, 26,* 171–186.

19. Gino, F. (2008). Do we listen to advice just because we paid for it? The impact of advice cost on its use. *Organizational Behavior and Human Decision Processes, 107,* 234–245. For a review of advice taking, see Bonaccio, S., & Dalal, R.S. (2006). Advice taking and decision-making: An integrative literature review and implications for the organizational sciences. *Organizational Behavior and Human Decision Processes, 101,* 127–151.

20. Kahneman et al., 1982; Tversky, A., & Kahneman, D. (1976). Judgment under uncertainty: Heuristics and biases. *Science, 185,* 1124–1131.

21. Northcraft, G. B., & Neale, M. A. (1987). Experts, amateurs, and real estate: An anchoring-and-adjustment perspective on property pricing decisions. *Organizational Behavior and Human Decision Processes, 39,* 84–97.

22. Johns, G. (1999). A multi-level theory of self-serving behavior in and by organizations. *Research in Organizational Behavior, 21,* 1–38; Tetlock, P. E. (1999). Accountability theory: Mixing properties of human agents with properties of social systems. In L. L. Thompson, J. M. Levine, & D. M. Messick (Eds.), *Shared cognition in organizations: The management of knowledge.* Mahwah, NJ.: Lawrence Erlbaum.

23. Simon, H. A. (1957). *Models of man.* New York, NY: Wiley; Cyert, R. M., & March, J. G. (1963). *A behavioral theory of the firm.* Englewood Cliffs, NJ: Prentice-Hall. For an example, see Bower, J., & Zi-Lei, Q. (1992). Satisficing when

buying information. *Organizational Behavior and Human Decision Processes, 51,* 471–481.

24. Nutt, P. C. (2004, November). Expanding the search for alternatives during strategic decision-making. *Academy of Management Executive,* 13–28.

25. Posavac, S. S., Kardes, F. R., & Brakus, J. J. (2010). Focus induced tunnel vision in managerial judgment and decision making: The peril and the antidote. *Organizational Behavior and Human Decision Processes, 113,* 102–111.

26. Dalal, R. S., & Bonaccio, S. (2010). What types of advice do decision-makers prefer? *Organizational Behavior and Human Decision Processes, 112,* 11–23.

27. Shepherd, D. A., Williams, T. A., & Patzelt, H. (2015). Thinking about entrepreneurial decision making: Review and research agenda. *Journal of Management, 41,* 11–46; Gudmundsson, S. V., & Lechner, C. (2013). Cognitive biases, organization, and entrepreneurial firm survival. *European Management Journal, 31,* 278–294.

28. Bazerman, M. (1990). *Judgment in managerial decision making* (2nd ed.). New York, NY: Wiley.

29. Kahneman, D., & Tversky, A. (1979). Prospect theory: An analysis of decision under risk. *Econometrica, 47,* 263–291; see also Holmes, M. R. Jr., Bromiley, P., Devers, C. E., Holcomb, T. R., & McGuire, J. B. (2011). Management theory applications of prospect theory: Accomplishments, challenges, and opportunities. *Journal of Management, 37,* 1069–1107.

30. For a detailed treatment and other perspectives, see Northcraft, G. B., & Wolf, G. (1984). Dollars, sense, and sunk costs: A life cycle model of resource allocation decisions. *Academy of Management Review, 9,* 225–234.

31. Brockner, J. (1992). The escalation of commitment to a failing course of action: Toward theoretical progress. *Academy of Management Review, 17,* 39–61; Staw, B. M. (1997). Escalation of commitment: An update and appraisal. In Z. Shapira (Ed.), *Organizational decision making.* Cambridge, MA: Cambridge University Press; for a meta-analysis, see Sleesman, D. J., Conlon, D. E., McNamara, G., & Miles, J. E. (2012). Cleaning up the big muddy: A meta-analytic review of the determinants of escalation of commitment. *Academy of Management Journal, 55,* 541–562.

32. Staw, B. M. (1981). The escalation of commitment to a course of action. *Academy of Management Review, 6,* 577–587. For the limitations of this view, see Knight, P. A. (1984). Heroism versus competence: Competing explanations for the effects of experimenting and consistent management. *Organizational Behavior and Human Performance, 33,* 307–322.

33. Arkes, H. R., & Blumer, C. (1985). The psychology of sunk cost. *Organizational Behavior and Human Decision Processes, 35,* 124–140.

34. Whyte, G. (1986). Escalating commitment to a course of action: A reinterpretation. *Academy of Management Review, 11,* 311–321.

35. Wong, K. F. E., Yik, M., & Kwong, J. Y. Y. (2006). Understanding the emotional aspects of escalation of commitment: The role of negative affect. *Journal of Applied Psychology, 91,* 282–297.

36. Ku, G., Malhotra, D., & Murnighan, J. K. (2005). Towards a competitive arousal model of decision-making: A study of auction fever in live and internet auctions. *Organizational Behavior and Human Decision Processes, 96,* 89–103.

37. Simonson, I., & Nye, P. (1992). The effect of accountability on susceptibility to decision errors. *Organizational Behavior and Human Decision Processes, 51,* 416–446; Simonson, I., & Staw, B. M. (1992). Deescalation strategies: A comparison of techniques for reducing commitment to losing courses of action. *Journal of Applied Psychology, 77,* 419–426; Whyte, 1991.

38. Whyte, G. (1993). Escalating commitment in individual and group decision making: A prospect theory approach. *Organizational Behavior and Human Decision Processes, 54,* 430–455.

39. Hawkins, S. A., & Hastie, R. (1990). Hindsight: Biased judgments of past events after outcomes are known. *Psychological Bulletin, 107,* 311–327; for a recent refinement, see Fessel, F., Epstude, K., & Roese, N. J. (2009). Hindsight bias redefined: It's about time. *Organizational Behavior and Human Decision Processes, 110,* 56–64.

40. Greenwald, A. G. (1980). The totalitarian ego: Fabrication and revision of personal history. *American Psychologist, 35,* 603–618.

41. Forgas, J. P., & George, J. M. (2001). Affective influences on judgments and behavior in organizations: An information processing perspective. *Organizational Behavior and Human Decision Processes, 86,* 3–34.

42. Hayward, M. L. A., & Hambrick, D. C. (1997). Explaining the premiums paid for large acquisitions: Evidence of CEO hubris. *Administrative Science Quarterly, 42,* 103–127.

43. Forgas & George, 2001; Weiss, H. M. (2002). Conceptual and empirical foundations for the study of affect at work. In R. G. Lord, R. J. Klimoski, & R. Kanfer (Eds.), *Emotions in the workplace: Understanding the structure and role of emotions in organizational behavior.* San Francisco, CA: Jossey-Bass; Davis, M. A. (2009). Understanding the relationship between mood and creativity: A meta-analysis. *Organizational Behavior and Human Decision Processes, 108,* 25–38; Baas, M., De Dreu, C. K. W., & Nijstad, B. A. (2008). A meta-analysis of 25 years of mood-creativity research: Hedonic tone, activation, or regulatory focus? *Psychological Bulletin, 134,* 779–806.

44. Au, K., Chan, F., Wang, D., & Vertinsky, I. (2003). Mood in foreign exchange trading: Cognitive processes and performance. *Organizational Behavior and Human Decision Processes, 91,* 322–338; see also Fenton-O'Creevy, M., Soane, E., Nicholson, N., & Willman, P. (2011). Thinking, feeling and deciding: The influence of emotions on the decision making and performance of traders. *Journal of Organizational Behavior, 32,* 1044–1061.

45. Mitchell, T. R., & Beach, L. R. (1977). Expectancy theory, decision theory, and occupational preference and choice. In M. F. Kaplan & S. Schwartz (Eds.), *Human judgment and decision processes in applied settings.* New York, NY: Academic Press.

46. Pinfield, L. T. (1986). A field evaluation of perspectives on organizational decision making. *Administrative Science Quarterly, 31,* 365–388.

47. Nutt, P.C. (1989). *Making tough decisions.* San Francisco, CA: Jossey-Bass.

48. Nutt, P.C. (1999, November). Surprising but true: Half the decisions in organizations fail. *Academy of Management Executive,* 75–90.

49. Salas, E., Rosen, M. A., & DiazGranados, D. (2010). Expertise-based intuition and decision making in organizations. *Journal of Management, 36,* 941–973; Kahneman, D., & Klein, G. (2009). Conditions for intuitive expertise: A failure to disagree. *American Psychologist, 64,* 515–526; Gigerenzer, G., & Gaissmaier, W. (2011). Heuristic decision making. *Annual Review of Psychology, 62,* 451–482.

50. Shaw, M. E. (1981). *Group dynamics* (3rd ed.). New York, NY: McGraw-Hill, 78.

51. Hill, G. W. (1982). Group versus individual performance: Are n+1 heads better than one? *Psychological Bulletin, 91,* 517–539.

52. Shaw, 1981; Davis, J. H. (1969). *Group performance.* Reading, MA: Addison-Wesley; Libby, R., Trotman, K. T., & Zimmer, I. (1987). Member variation, recognition of expertise, and group performance. *Journal of Applied Psychology, 72,* 81–87.

53. Van Ginkel, W. P., & van Knippenberg, D. (2009). Knowledge about the distribution of information and group decision making: When and why does it work? *Organizational Behavior and Human Decision Processes, 108*, 218–229; Brodbeck, F. C., Kerschreiter, R., Mojzisch, A., & Schulz-Hardt, S. (2007). Group decision making under conditions of distributed knowledge: The information asymmetries model. *Academy of Management Review, 32*, 459–479.

54. Park, G., & DeShon, R.P. (2010). A multilevel model of minority opinion expression and team decision-making effectiveness. *Journal of Applied Psychology, 95*, 824–833.

55. Janis, I. L. (1972). *Victims of groupthink.* Boston, MA: Houghton Mifflin.

56. Esser, J. K. (1998). Alive and well after 25 years: A review of groupthink research. *Organizational Behavior and Human Decision Processes, 73*, 116–141.

57. Aldag, R. J., & Fuller, S. R. (1993) Beyond fiasco: A reappraisal of the groupthink phenomenon and a new model of group decision processes. *Psychological Bulletin, 113*, 533–552; McCauley, C. (1989). The nature of social influence in groupthink: Compliance and internalization. *Journal of Personality and Social Psychology, 57*, 250–260; Baron, R. S. (2005). So right it's wrong: Groupthink and the ubiquitous nature of polarized group decision making. *Advances in Experimental Social Psychology, 37*, 219–253.

58. Janis, 1972.

59. This is our analysis. The data cited are from Capers, R. S., & Lipton, E. (1993, November). Hubble error: Time, money, and millionths of an inch. *Academy of Management Executive*, 41–57 (originally published in *Hartford Courant*).

60. Hart, P. (1998). Preventing groupthink revisited: Evaluating and reforming groups in government. *Organizational Behavior and Human Decision Processes, 73*, 306–326.

61. Schwenk, C. R. (1984). Devil's advocacy in managerial decision-making. *Journal of Management Studies, 21*, 153–168; for a study, see Schwenk, C., & Valacich, J.S. (1994). Effects of devil's advocacy and dialectical inquiry on individuals versus groups. *Organizational Behavior and Human Decision Processes, 59*, 210–222.

62. Stoner, J. A. F. (1961). *A comparison of individual and group decisions involving risk.* Unpublished master's thesis. School of Industrial Management, Massachusetts Institute of Technology.

63. Lamm, H., & Myers, D. G. (1978). Group-induced polarization of attitudes and behavior. In L. Berkowitz (Ed.), *Advances in experimental social psychology* (Vol. 11, pp. 145–195). New York, NY: Academic Press.

64. Isenberg, D. J. (1986). Group polarization: A critical review and meta-analysis. *Journal of Personality and Social Psychology, 50*, 1141–1151.

65. Barends, E., Rousseau, D. M., & Briner, R. B. (2014). *Evidence-based management: The basic principles.* Amsterdam, NL: Center for Evidence-Based Management.

66. For a good review of the history of evidence-based management see Baba, V. V, & HakemZadeh, F. (2012). Toward a theory of evidence based decision making. *Management Decision, 50*, 832–867.

67. Barends et al., 2014; Rousseau, D. M. (2012). Envisioning evidence-based management. In D. M. Rousseau (Ed.), *The Oxford handbook of evidence-based management.* New York, NY: Oxford University Press.

68. Afuah, A., & Tucci, C. L. (2012). Crowdsourcing as a solution to distant search. *Academy of Management Review, 37*, 355–375.

69. Afuah & Tucci, 2012; King, A., & Lakhani, K. R. (2013, Fall). Using open innovation to identify the best ideas. *MIT Sloan Management Review*, 41–48.

70. Wolfe, R., Wright, P. M., & Smart, D. L. (2006). Radical HRM innovation and competitive advantage: The *Moneyball* story. *Human Resource Management, 45*, 111–145.

71. Ferguson, R. B. (2014, Spring). GE and the culture of analytics. *MIT Sloan Management Review*, 1–4.

72. McAfee, A., & Brynjolfsson, E. (2012, October). Big data: The management revolution. *Harvard Business Review*, 60–68.

73. McAfee & Brynjolfsson (2012); see also Lohr, S. (2012, February 11). The age of big data. *The New York Times.* NYTimes.com.

Chapter 12

1. Root out sexual harassment from the RCMP. (2011, November 16). *The Globe and Mail*, www.theglobeandmail.com/news/opinions/editorials/root-out-sexual-harassment-from-the-rcmp/article2238700/; Expand RCMP sexual harassment hearings, Liberals urge. (2012, April 23). CBCnews, www.cbc.ca/news/canada/story/2012/04/23/rcmp-sexual-harassment-hearings-paulson.html; Bailey, I. (2011, December 20). Lawyers preparing possible class-action suit against RCMP. *The Globe and Mail*, www.theglobeandmail.com/news/politics/lawyers-preparing-possible-class-action-suit-against-rcmp/article2278817/; Burgmann, T. (2012, April 16). RCMP to train B.C. officers to investigate sex harassment within force. *The Globe and Mail*, www.theglobeandmail.com/news/national/rcmp-to-train-bc-officers-to-investigate-sex-harassment-within-force/article2403389/; Clancy, N. (2011, November 7). B.C. Mountie alleges years of sexual harassment. CBCnews British Columbia: www.cbc.ca/news/canada/british-columbia/story/2011/11/07/bc-rcmp-harassment-galiford.html; Gillis, C., & MacQueen, K. (2011, November 28). The RCMP: A Royal Canadian disgrace. Macleans.ca, http://www2.macleans.ca/2011/11/18/a-royal-canadian-disgrace/; Keller, J. (2012, January 6). Another sexual harassment suit filed against RCMP. *The Globe and Mail*, www.theglobeandmail.com/news/national/british-columbia/another-sexual-harassment-suit-filed-against-rcmp/article2294125/; Mason, G. (2011, December 3). Former Mountie paints picture of near daily harassment. *The Globe and Mail*, www.theglobeandmail.com/news/national/former-mountie-paints-picture-of-near-daily-harassment/article2259072/; Mason, G. (2011, December 12). Inaction in RCMP harassment scandal should bother us all. *The Globe and Mail*, www.theglobeandmail.com/news/national/british-columbia/gary_mason/inaction-in-rcmp-harassment-scandal-should-bother-us-all/article2268808/; Mason, G. (2011, December 5). RCMP took two years to respond to officer's sexual harassment complaint. *The Globe and Mail*, www.theglobeandmail.com/news/national/british-columbia/gary_mason/rcmp-took-two-years-to-respond-to-officers-sexual-harassment-complaint/article2261049/; Theodore, T. (2012, March 27). Ex-Mountie's lawsuit accuses RCMP of bullying, sexual discrimination. *The Globe and Mail*, www.theglobeandmail.com/news/national/british-columbia/ex-mounties-lawsuit-accuses-rcmp-of-bullying-sexual-discrimination/article2383538/.

2. For recent reviews of power, see Sturm, R. E., & Antonakis, J. (2015). Interpersonal power: A review, critique, and research agenda. *Journal of Management, 41*, 136–163; Anderson, C., & Brion, S. (2014). Perspectives on power in organizations. *Annual Review of Organizational Psychology and Organizational Behavior, 1*, 67–97.

3. Brass, D. J., & Burkhardt, M. E. (1993). Potential power and power use: An

investigation of structure and behavior. *Academy of Management Journal, 36,* 441–470; see also Kim, P. H., Pinkley, R. L., & Fragale, A. R. (2005). Power dynamics in negotiation. *Academy of Management Review, 30,* 799–822.

4. These descriptions of bases of power were developed by French, J. R. P., Jr., & Raven, B. (1959). In D. Cartwright (Ed.), *Studies in social power.* Ann Arbor, MI: Institute for Social Research; see also Elias, S. (2008). Fifty years of influence in the workplace: The evolution of the French and Raven power taxonomy. *Journal of Management History, 14,* 267–283.

5. Rahim, M. A. (1989). Relationships of leader power to compliance and satisfaction with supervision: Evidence from a national sample of managers. *Journal of Management, 15,* 545–556; Tannenbaum, A. S. (1974). *Hierarchy in organizations.* San Francisco, CA: Jossey-Bass.

6. Podsakoff, P. M., & Schriesheim, C. A. (1985). Field studies of French and Raven's bases of power: Critique, reanalysis, and suggestions for future research. *Psychological Bulletin, 97,* 387–411.

7. Heider, F. (1958). *The psychology of interpersonal relations.* New York, NY: Wiley.

8. Podsakoff & Schriesheim, 1985.

9. Ragins, B. R., & Sundstrom, E. (1990). Gender and perceived power in manager-subordinate dyads. *Journal of Occupational Psychology, 63,* 273–287.

10. The following is based upon Kanter, R. M. (1977). *Men and women of the corporation.* New York, NY: Basic Books. For additional treatment, see Pfeffer, J. (2010). *Power: Why some people have it – and others don't.* New York, NY: HarperCollins.

11. Goldstein, N. J., & Hays, N. A. (2011). Illusory power transference: The vicarious experience of power. *Administrative Science Quarterly, 56,* 593–621.

12. See Thomas, K. W., & Velthouse, B. A. (1990). Cognitive elements of empowerment: An "interpretative" model of intrinsic task motivation. *Academy of Management Review, 15,* 668–681; Conger, J. A., & Kanungo, R. N. (1988). The empowerment process: Integrating theory and practice. *Academy of Management Review, 13,* 471–482. For a good review of this area, see Spreitzer, G. (2008). Taking stock: A review of more than twenty years of research on empowerment at work. In J. Barling and C. L. Cooper (Eds.), *The Sage handbook of organizational behavior* (Vol. 1). London, UK: Sage.

13. Dust, S. B., Resick, C. J., & Mawritz, M. B. (2014). Transformational leadership, psychological empowerment, and the moderating role of mechanistic-organic contexts. *Journal of Organizational Behavior, 35,* 413–433; Chen, G., Kirkman, B. L., Kanter, R., Allen, D., & Rosen, B. (2007). A multilevel study of leadership, empowerment, and performance in teams. *Journal of Applied Psychology, 92,* 331–346; Srivastava, A., Bartol, K. M., & Locke, E. A. (2006). Empowering leadership in management teams: Effects on knowledge sharing, efficacy, and performance. *Academy of Management Journal, 49,* 1239–1251.

14. Tichy, N. M., & Sherman, S. (1993, June). Walking the talk at GE. *Training and Development,* 26–35.

15. Lowe, E. (2005, October). Response-ability and the Power to Please: Delta Hotels. *Social Innovations,* 7–8; Vanier Institute of the Family. www.vifamily.ca/library/social/delta.html.

16. Seibert, S. E., Wang, G., & Courtright, S. H. (2011). Antecedents and consequences of psychological and team empowerment in organizations: A meta-analytic review. *Journal of Applied Psychology, 96,* 981–1003; Maynard, M. T., Gilson, L. L., & Mathieu, J. E. (2012). Empowerment–fad or fab? A multilevel review of the past two decades of research. *Journal of Management, 38,* 1231–1281; Wall, T. D., Wood, S. J., & Leach, D. J. (2004). Empowerment and performance. *International Review of Industrial and Organizational Psychology, 19,* 1–46.

17. Bowen, D. E., & Lawler, E. E., III. (1992, Spring). The empowerment of service workers: What, why, how, and when. *Sloan Management Review,* 31–39.

18. Kipnis, D., Schmidt, S. M., & Wilkinson, I. (1980). Intra-organizational influence tactics: Explorations in getting one's way. *Journal of Applied Psychology, 65,* 440–452; Kipnis, D., & Schmidt, S. M. (1988). Upward-influence styles: Relationship with performance evaluation, salary, and stress. *Administrative Science Quarterly, 33,* 528–542; Bolino, M. C., Kacmar, K.M., Turnley, W. H., & Gilstrap, J. B. (2008). A multilevel review of impression management motives and behaviors. *Journal of Management, 34,* 1080–1109.

19. See Brass & Burkhardt, 1993.

20. Kipnis et al., 1980. See also Keys, B., & Case, T. (1990, November). How to become an influential manager. *Academy of Management Executive,* 38–51.

21. Kipnis & Schmidt, 1988.

22. Westphal, J. D., & Stern, I. (2006). The other pathway to the boardroom: Interpersonal influencing behavior as a substitute for elite credentials and majority status in obtaining board appointments. *Administrative Science Quarterly, 51,* 169–204.

23. Kipnis, D. (1976). *The powerholders.* Chicago, IL: University of Chicago Press.

24. McClelland, D.C. (1975). *Power: The inner experience.* New York: Irvington.

25. Winter, D. G. (1988). The power motive in women—and men. *Journal of Personality and Social Psychology, 54,* 510–519.

26. McClelland, D. C., & Burnham, D. H. (1976, March–April). Power is the great motivator. *Harvard Business Review,* 100–110.

27. Tang, J., Crossan, M., & Glenn Rowe, W. (2011). Dominant CEO, deviant strategy, and extreme performance: The moderating role of a powerful board. *Journal of Management Studies, 48,* 1479–1503.

28. Salancik, G. R., & Pfeffer, J. (1977, Winter). Who gets power—and how they hold on to it: A strategic contingency model of power. *Organizational Dynamics,* 3–21.

29. Salancik, G. R., & Pfeffer, J. (1974). The bases and use of power in organizational decision making: The case of a university. *Administrative Science Quarterly, 19,* 453–473. Also see Pfeffer, J., & Moore, W. L. (1980). Power in university budgeting: A replication and extension. *Administrative Science Quarterly, 25,* 637–653. For conditions under which the power thesis breaks down, see Schick, A. G., Birch, J. B., & Tripp, R. E. (1986). Authority and power in university decision making: The case of a university personnel budget. *Canadian Journal of Administrative Sciences, 3,* 41–64.

30. Hickson, D. J., Hinings, C. R., Lee, C. A., Schneck, R. E., & Pennings, J. M. (1971). A strategic contingency theory of intraorganizational power. *Administrative Science Quarterly, 16,* 216–229; for support of this theory, see Hinings, C. R., Hickson, D. J., Pennings, J. M., & Schneck, R. E. (1974). Structural conditions of intraorganizational power. *Administrative Science Quarterly, 19,* 22–44; Saunders, C. S., & Scamell, R. (1982). Intraorganizational distributions of power: Replication research. *Academy of Management Journal, 25,* 192–200; Hambrick, D. C. (1981). Environment, strategy, and power within top management teams. *Administrative Science Quarterly, 26,* 253–276.

31. Kanter, 1977, 170–171.

32. Hickson et al., 1971; Hinings et al., 1974.

33. Hickson et al., 1971; Hinings et al., 1974; Saunders & Scamell, 1982.

34. Nulty, P. (1989, July 31). The hot demand for new scientists. *Fortune,* 155–163.

35. Nord, W. R., & Tucker, S. (1987). *Implementing routine and radical innovations.* Lexington, MA: Lexington Books.

36. Mayes, B. T., & Allen, R. W. (1977). Toward a definition of organizational politics. *Academy of Management Review, 2,* 672–678.

37. Porter, L. W., Allen, R. W., & Angle, H. L. (1981). The politics of upward influence in organizations. *Research in Organizational Behavior, 3,* 109–149.

38. Porter et al., 1981; Madison, D. L., Allen, R. W., Porter, L. W., Renwick, P. A., & Mayes, B. T. (1980). Organizational politics: An exploration of managers' perceptions. *Human Relations, 33,* 79–100.

39. Chang, C.- H., Rosen, C. C., & Levy, P. E. (2009). The relationship between perceptions of organizational politics and employee attitudes, strain, and behavior: A meta-analytic examination. *Academy of Management Journal, 52,* 779–801.

40. Treadway, D. C., Ferris, G. R., Hochwarter, W., Perrewé, P., Witt, L. A., & Goodman, J. M. (2005). The role of age in the perceptions of politics-job performance relationship: A three-study constructive replication. *Journal of Applied Psychology, 90,* 872–881.

41. Ferris, G. D., Davidson, S. L., & Perrewé, P. L. (2005). *Political skill at work: Impact on effectiveness.* Mountain View, CA: Davies-Black, 7; see also Ferris, G. R., Treadway, D. C., Kolodinsky, R. W., Hochwarter, W. A., Kacmar, C. J., Douglas, C., & Frink, D. D. (2005). Development and validation of the Political Skill Inventory. *Journal of Management, 31,* 126–152.

42. Munyon, T. P., Summers, J. K., Thompson, K. M., & Ferris, G. R. (2015). Political skill and work outcomes: A theoretical extension, meta-analytic investigation, and agenda for the future. *Personnel Psychology,* in press; Kimura, T. (2015). A review of political skill: Current research trend and directions for future research. *International Journal of Management Reviews,* in press.

43. Kotter, J.P. (1982). *The general managers.* New York, NY: Free Press.

44. Forret, M. L., & Dougherty, T. W. (2004). Networking behaviors and career outcomes: Differences for men and women. *Journal of Organizational Behavior, 25,* 419–437; Forret, M. L., & Dougherty, T. W. (2001). Correlates of networking behavior for managerial and professional employees. *Group & Organization Management, 26,* 283–311.

45. See also Wolff, H.- G., & Maser, K. (2009). Effects of networking on career success: A longitudinal study. *Journal of Applied Psychology, 94,* 196–206.

46. Brass, D. J., Galaskiewicz, J., Greve, H. R., & Tsai, W. (2004). Taking stock of networks and organizations: A multi-level perspective. *Academy of Management Journal, 47,* 795–817.

47. Cross, R., Cowen, A., Vertucci, L., & Thomas, R. J. (2009). How effective leaders drive results through networks. *Organizational Dynamics, 38,* 93–105.

48. Geis, F., & Christie, R. (1970). Overview of experimental research. In R. Christie & F. Geis (Eds.), *Studies in Machiavellianism.* New York, NY: Academic Press; Wilson, D. S., Near, D., & Miller, R. W. (1996). Machiavellianism: A synthesis of the evolutionary and psychological literatures. *Psychological Bulletin, 119,* 285–299.

49. Geis & Christie, 1970; Wilson et al., 1996.

50. O'Boyle, E. H., Jr., Forsyth, D. R., Banks, G. C., & McDaniel, M. A. (2012). A meta-analysis of the Dark Triad and work behavior: A social exchange perspective. *Journal of Applied Psychology, 97,* 557–579.

51. What follows relies on Ashforth, B. E., & Lee, R. T. (1990). Defensive behavior in organizations: A preliminary model. *Human Relations, 43,* 621–648.

52. Boeker, W. (1992). Power and managerial dismissal: Scapegoating at the top. *Administrative Science Quarterly, 37,* 400–421.

53. Galloway, G. (2009, May 21). Watchdog predicted reactor's demise. *The Globe and Mail,* A5; (2008, January 16). Nuclear safety watchdog head fired for "lack of leadership": Minister. www.cbc.ca/news.

54. This draws loosely on Glenn, J. R., Jr. (1986). *Ethics in decision making.* New York, NY: Wiley.

55. For reviews, see Treviño, L. K. (1986). Ethical decision making in organizations: A person-situation interactionist model. *Academy of Management Review, 11,* 601–617; Tsalikis, J., & Fritzsche, D. J. (1989). Business ethics: A literature review with a focus on marketing ethics. *Journal of Business Ethics, 8,* 695–743.

56. Tyson, T. (1992). Does believing that everyone else is less ethical have an impact on work behavior? *Journal of Business Ethics, 11,* 707–717.

57. Treviño, L. K., Weaver, G. R., & Brown, M. E. (2008). It's lovely at the top: Hierarchical levels, identities, and perceptions of organizational ethics. *Business Ethics Quarterly, 18,* 233–252.

58. Ethics Resource Center (2014). *National business ethics survey of the US workforce.* Arlington, VA: Ethics Resource Center.

59. Kaynama, S. A., King, A., & Smith, L. W. (1996). The impact of a shift in organizational role on ethical perceptions: A comparative study. *Journal of Business Ethics, 15,* 581–590.

60. McCabe, D. L., Butterfield, K. D., & Treviño, L. K. (2006). Academic dishonesty in graduate business programs: Prevalence, causes, and proposed action. *Academy of Management Learning & Education, 5,* 294–305.

61. Kish-Gephart, J. J., Harrison, D. A., & Treviño, L. K. (2010). Bad apples, bad cases, and bad barrels: Meta-analytic evidence about sources of unethical decisions at work. *Journal of Applied Psychology, 95,* 1–31; see also Pan, Y., & Sparks, J. R. (2012). Predictors, consequence, and measurement of ethical judgments: Review and meta-analysis. *Journal of Business Research, 65,* 84–91.

62. Tsalikis & Fritzsche, 1989.

63. Bird, F., & Waters, J. A. (1987). The nature of managerial moral standards. *Journal of Business Ethics, 6,* 1–13.

64. Hegarty, W. H., & Sims, H. P., Jr. (1978). Some determinants of unethical behavior: An experiment. *Journal of Applied Psychology, 63,* 451–457; Treviño, L. K., Sutton, C. D., & Woodman, R. W. (1985). *Effects of reinforcement contingencies and cognitive moral development on ethical decision-making behavior: An experiment.* Paper presented at the annual meeting of the Academy of Management, San Diego, CA.

65. Levine, D. B. (1990, May 21). The inside story of an inside trader. *Fortune,* 80–89, 82.

66. John, L. K., Lowenstein, G., & Rick, S. I. (2014). Cheating more for less: Upward social comparisons motivate the poorly compensated to cheat. *Organizational Behavior and Human Decision Processes, 123,* 101–109.

67. Welsh, D. T., & Ordóñez, L. D. (2014). The dark side of consecutive high performance goals: Linking goal setting, depletion, and unethical behavior. *Organizational Behavior and Human Decision Processes, 123,* 79–89.

68. Mishina, Y., Dykes, B. J., Block, E. S., & Pollock, T. G. (2010). Why "good" firms do bad things: The effects of high aspirations, high expectations, and prominence on the incidence of corporate illegality. *Academy Management Journal, 53,* 701–722.

69. Grover, S. L. (1993). Why professionals lie: The impact of professional role conflict on reporting accuracy. *Organizational Behavior and Human Decision Processes, 55,* 251–272.

70. Umphress, E. E., & Bingham, J. B. (2011). When employees do bad things for good reasons: Examining unethical pro-organizational behaviors. *Organization Science, 22,* 621–640;

Umphress, E. E., Bingham, J. B., & Mitchell, M. S. (2010). Unethical behavior in the name of the company: The moderating effect of organizational identification and positive reciprocity beliefs on unethical pro-organizational behavior. *Journal of Applied Psychology, 95,* 769–780.

71. Staw, B. M., & Szwajkowski, E. W. (1975). The scarcity-munificence component of organizational environments and the commission of illegal acts. *Administrative Science Quarterly, 20,* 345–354.

72. Sonnenfeld, J., & Lawrence, P. R. (1989). Why do companies succumb to price fixing? In K. R. Andrew (Ed.), *Ethics in practice: Managing the moral corporation.* Boston, MA: Harvard Business School Press.

73. Hegarty & Sims, 1978; Hegarty, W. H., & Sims, H. P., Jr. (1979). Organizational philosophy, policies, and objectives related to unethical decision behavior: A laboratory experiment. *Journal of Applied Psychology, 64,* 331–338.

74. Kish-Gephart et al., 2010; Detert, J. R., Treviño, L. K., & Sweitzer, V. L. (2008). Moral disengagement in ethical decision making: A study of antecedents and outcomes. *Journal of Applied Psychology, 93,* 374–391.

75. Colby, A., & Kohlberg, L. (1987). *The measurement of moral judgment. Volume 1: Theoretical foundations and research validation.* Cambridge, MA: Cambridge University Press; see also Treviño, 1986; Grover, 1993.

76. Detert et al., 2008.

77. Reynolds, S. J., (2008). Moral attentiveness: Who pays attention to the moral aspects of life? *Journal of Applied Psychology, 93,* 1027–1041.

78. Kish-Gephart et al., 2010.

79. Victor, B., & Cullen, J. B. (1988). The organizational bases of ethical work climates. *Administrative Science Quarterly, 33,* 101–125; for a review, see Simha, A., & Cullen, J. B. (2012, November). Ethical climates and their effects on organizational outcomes: Implications from the past and prophecies for the future. *Academy of Management Perspectives,* 20–34.

80. Kish-Gephart et al., 2010; Tenbrunsel, A. E., & Smith-Crowe, K. (2008). Ethical decision making: Where we've been and where we're going. *Academy of Management Annals, 2,* 545–607; Mayer, D. M. (2014). A review of the literature on ethical climate and culture. In B. Schneider & K. M. Barbera (Eds). *The Oxford handbook of organizational climate and culture.* Oxford, UK: Oxford University Press.

81. Baucus, M. S., & Near, J. P. (1991). Can illegal corporate behavior be predicted? An event history analysis. *Academy of Management Journal, 34,* 9–16.

82. Anand, V., Ashforth, B. E., & Joshi, M. (2004, May). Business as usual: The acceptance and perpetuation of corruption in organizations. *Academy of Management Executive,* 39–53.

83. Sonnenfeld & Lawrence, 1989; see also Hosmer, L. T. (1987). The institutionalization of unethical behavior. *Journal of Business Ethics, 6,* 439–447.

84. Morgan, R. B. (1993). Self- and co-worker perceptions of ethics and their relationships to leadership and salary. *Academy of Management Journal, 36,* 200–214.

85. This definition and other material in this paragraph are from Miceli, M. P., & Near, J. P. (2005). Standing up or standing by: What predicts blowing the whistle on organizational wrongdoing? *Research in Personnel and Human Resources Management, 24,* 95–136.

86. Moore, D. A, Tetlock, P. H., Tanlu, L., & Bazerman, M. H. (2006). Conflicts of interest and the case of auditor independence: Moral seduction and strategic issue cycling. *Academy of Management Review, 31,* 10–29.

87. Ripley, A. (2002, December 30/2003, January 6). The night detective. *Time,* 45; Morse, J., & Bower, A. (2002, December 30/2003, January 6). The party crasher. *Time,* 53.

88. Hutton, D. (2011, August 13). Effectively silencing Canada's whistleblowers. *Toronto Star.* http://www.thestar.com/opinion/editorialopinion/2011/08/13/effectively_silencing_canadas_whistleblowers.html

89. Ethics Resource Center, 2014.

90. Peirce, E., Smolinski, C. A., & Rosen, B. (1998, August). Why sexual harassment complaints fall on deaf ears. *Academy of Management Executive,* 41–54.

91. O'Leary-Kelly, A. M., Bowes-Sperry, L., Bates, C. A., & Lean, E. R. (2009). Sexual harassment at work: A decade (plus) of progress. *Journal of Management, 35,* 503–536; Willness, C. R., Steel, P., & Lee, K. (2007). A meta-analysis of the antecedents and consequences of workplace sexual harassment. *Personnel Psychology, 60,* 127–162.

92. Schneider, K. T., Swan, S., & Fitzgerald, L. F. (1997). Job-related and psychological effects of sexual harassment in the workplace: Empirical evidence from two organizations. *Journal of Applied Psychology, 82,* 401–415.

93. O'Leary-Kelly et al., 2009.

94. Seppa, N. (1997, May). Sexual harassment in the military lingers on. *APA Monitor,* 40–41.

95. Seppa, 1997.

96. Peirce et al., 1998; Seppa, 1997.

97. Gettman, H. J., & Gelfand, M. J. (2007). When the customer shouldn't be king: Antecedents and consequences of sexual harassment by clients and customers. *Journal of Applied Psychology, 92,* 757–770.

98. Berdahl, J. L. (2007). The sexual harassment of uppity women. *Journal of Applied Psychology, 92,* 425–437.

99. Peirce et al., 1998.

100. Brean, J. (2014, December 5). Most harassment in workplaces goes unreported: Poll. *Montreal Gazette,* A13.

101. Kingston, A. (2014, November 6). Gian Ghomeshi: How he got away with it. *Maclean's.* http://www.macleans.ca/news/canada/jian-ghomeshi-how-he-got-away-with-it/.

102. Peirce et al., 1998.

103. Flynn, G. (1997, February). Respect is key to stopping harassment. *Workforce,* 56.

104. Peirce et al., 1998.

105. This draws on Waters, J. A., & Bird, F. (1988). *A note on what a well-educated manager should be able to do with respect to moral issues in management.* Unpublished manuscript.

106. See Jones, T. M. (1991). Ethical decision making by individuals in organizations: An issue-contingent model. *Academy of Management Journal, 16,* 366–395.

107. Weber, J. (1990). Measuring the impact of teaching ethics to future managers: A review, assessment, and recommendations. *Journal of Business Ethics, 9,* 183–190.

Chapter 13

1. Excerpted with minor editing from Willsher, K. (2014, March 19). Orange France investigates second wave of suicides among staff. Theguardian.com.

2. Kolb, D. M., & Bartunek, J. M. (Eds.) (1992). *Hidden conflict in organizations: Uncovering behind-the-scenes disputes.* Newbury Park, CA: Sage.

3. This section relies partly on Walton, R. E., & Dutton, J. M. (1969). The management of interdepartmental conflict: A model and review. *Administrative Science Quarterly, 14,* 73–84; see also De Dreu, C. K. W., & Gelfand, M. J. (2008). Conflict in the workplace: Sources, functions, and dynamics across multiple levels of analysis. In C. K. W. De Dreu & M. J. Gelfand (Eds.), *The psychology of conflict and conflict management in organizations.* New York, NY: Lawrence Erlbaum.

4. Balliet, D., Wu, J., & De Dreu, C. K. W. (2014). Ingroup favoritism in cooperation: A meta-analysis. *Psychological*

Bulletin, 140, 1556–1581; Greenwald, A. G., & Pettigrew T. F. (2014). With malice toward none and charity for some: Ingroup favoritism enables discrimination. *American Psychologist, 69,* 669–684; Ashforth, B. E., & Mael, F. (1989). Social identity theory and the organization. *Academy of Management Review, 14,* 20–39.

5. Johns, G. (1994). Absenteeism estimates by employees and managers: Divergent perspectives and self-serving perceptions. *Journal of Applied Psychology, 79,* 229–239.

6. See Whyte, W. F. (1948). *Human relations in the restaurant industry.* New York, NY: McGraw-Hill.

7. Moritz, M. (1984). *The little kingdom: The private story of Apple Computer.* New York, NY: William Morrow, 246–247.

8. Jehn, K. A., & Mannix, E. A. (2001). The dynamic nature of conflict: A longitudinal study of intragroup conflict and group performance. *Academy of Management Journal, 44,* 238–251.

9. De Dreu, C. K. W., & Weingart, L. R. (2003). Task versus relationship conflict, team performance, and team member satisfaction: A meta-analysis. *Journal of Applied Psychology, 88,* 741–749; de Wit, F. R. C., Greer, L. L., & Jehn, K. A. (2012). The paradox of intragroup conflict: A meta-analysis. *Journal of Applied Psychology, 97,* 360–390; de Wit, F. R. C., Jehn, K. A., & Scheepers, D. (2013). Task conflict, information processing, and decision-making: The damaging effect of relationship conflict. *Organizational Behavior and Human Decision Processes, 122,* 177–189.

10. See Blake, R. R., Shepard, M. A., & Mouton, J. S. (1964). *Managing intergroup conflict in industry.* Houston: Gulf; Sherif, M. (1966). *In common predicament: Social psychology of intergroup conflict and cooperation.* Boston, MA: Houghton Mifflin; Wilder, D. A. (1986). Social categorization: Implications for creation and reduction of intergroup bias. *Advances in Experimental Social Psychology, 19,* 291–349; Pruitt, D. G. (2008). Conflict escalation in organizations. In De Dreu & Gelfand, 2008.

11. Thomas, K. W. (1992). Conflict and negotiation in organizations. In M. D. Dunnette & L. M. Hough (Eds.), *Handbook of industrial and organizational psychology* (2nd ed., Vol. 3). Palo Alto, CA: Consulting Psychologists Press.

12. Seabrook, J. (1994, January 10). E-mail from Bill. *The New Yorker,* 48–61, 52.

13. Johnson, D. W., Maruyama, G., Johnson, R., Nelson, D., & Skon, L. (1981). Effects of cooperative and individualistic goal structures on achievement: A meta-analysis. *Psychological Bulletin, 89,* 47–62; see also Tjosvold, D. (1991). *The conflict-positive organization.* Reading, MA: Addison-Wesley.

14. Keenan, G. (2011, December 28). Earthquake. Tsunami. Floods. How Japan's car makers are rebuilding after a year of disasters. *The Globe and Mail,* B1, B4, B5.

15. Neale, M. A., & Bazerman, M. H. (1992, August). Negotiating rationally: The power and impact of the negotiator's frame. *Academy of Management Executive,* 42–51, p. 42; for a recent review, see Thompson, L. L., Wang, J., & Gunia, B. C. (2010). Negotiation. *Annual Review of Psychology, 61,* 491–515.

16. Wall, J. A., Jr. (1985). *Negotiation: Theory and practice.* Glenview, IL: Scott, Foresman.

17. Walton, R. E., & McKersie, R. B. (1991). *A behavioral theory of labor negotiations* (2nd ed.). Ithaca, NY: ILR Press.

18. What follows draws on Pruitt, D. G. (1981). *Negotiation behavior.* New York, NY: Academic Press.

19. Wall, J. A., Jr., & Blum, M. (1991). Negotiations. *Journal of Management, 17,* 273–303.

20. Hüffmeier, J., Freund, P. A., Zerres, A., Backhaus, K., & Hertel, G. (2014). Being tough or being nice? A meta-analysis on the impact of hard- and soft-line strategies in distributive negotiations. *Journal of Management, 40,* 866–892.

21. Stuhlmacher, A. F., and Walters, A. E. (1999). Gender differences in negotiation outcome: A meta-analysis. *Personnel Psychology, 52,* 653–677; see also Kulik, C. T., & Olekalns, M. (2012). Negotiating the gender divide: Lessons from the negotiation and organizational behavior literatures. *Journal of Management, 38,* 1387–1415.

22. Marks, M., & Harold, C. (2011). Who asks and who receives in salary negotiation. *Journal of Organizational Behavior, 32,* 371–394.

23. Kong, D. T., Dirks, K. T., & Ferrin, D. L. (2014). Interpersonal trust within negotiations: Meta-analytic evidence, critical contingencies, and directions for future research. *Academy of Management Journal, 57,* 1235–1255.

24. The following draws on Bazerman, M. H., & Neale, M. A. (1992). *Negotiating rationally.* New York, NY: The Free Press; see also Bazerman, M. H. (2006). *Judgment in managerial decision making* (6th ed.). Hoboken, NJ: Wiley.

25. Sherif, 1966; Hunger, J. D., & Stern, L. W. (1976). An assessment of the functionality of the superordinate goal in reducing conflict. *Academy of Management Journal, 19,* 591–605.

26. Goldman, B. M., Cropanzano, R., Stein, J., & Benson, L. III. (2008). The role of third parties/mediation in managing conflict in organizations. In De Dreu & Gelfand, 2008.

27. Pruitt, 1981; Kressel, K., & Pruitt, D. G. (1989). *Mediation research.* San Francisco: Jossey-Bass.

28. Kressel & Pruitt, 1989.

29. Pruitt, 1981; Wall & Blum, 1991.

30. Moore, M. L., Nichol, V. W., & McHugh, P. P. (1992). Review of no-fault absenteeism cases taken to arbitration, 1980–1989: A rights and responsibilities analysis. *Employee Rights and Responsibilities Journal, 5,* 29–48; Scott, K. D., & Taylor, G. S. (1983, September). An analysis of absenteeism cases taken to arbitration: 1975–1981. *The Arbitration Journal, 61*–70.

31. For a spirited debate on this, see De Dreu, C. K. W. (2008). The virtue and vice of workplace conflict: Food for (pessimistic) thought. *Journal of Organizational Behavior, 29,* 5–18, and Tjosvold, D. (2008). The conflict-positive organization: It depends on us. *Journal of Organizational Behavior, 29,* 19–28.

32. Tjosvold, D., Wong, A. S. H., & Chen, N. Y. F. (2014). Constructively managing conflicts in organizations. *Annual Review of Organizational Psychology and Organizational Behavior, 1,* 545–568; see also Coleman, P. T., & Ferguson, R. (2014). *Making conflict work: Harnessing the power of disagreement.* Boston, MA: Houghton Mifflin Harcourt.

33. Brown, L. D. (1983). *Managing conflict at organizational interfaces.* Reading, MA: Addison-Wesley.

34. Robbins, S. P. (1974). *Managing organizational conflict: A nontraditional approach.* Englewood, Cliffs, NJ: Prentice-Hall, 20; see also Brown, 1983.

35. Raynal, W., & Wilson, K. A. (2001, October 15). What about Bob? *Autoweek,* 5.

36. American Psychological Association (2014). *Stress in America.* Washington, DC: APA.

37. Tangri, R. (2007, September). Putting a price on stress. *Canadian Healthcare Manager, 14,* 24–25.

38. This model has much in common with many contemporary models of work stress. For a comprehensive summary, see Kahn, R. L., & Byosiere, P. (1992). Stress in organizations. In M. D. Dunnette & L. M. Hough (Eds.), *Handbook of industrial and organizational psychology* (2nd ed., Vol. 3). Palo Alto, CA: Consulting Psychologists Press.

39. McGrath, J. E. (1970). A conceptual formulation for research on stress. In J.

E. McGrath (Ed.), *Social and psychological factors in stress*. New York, NY: Holt, Rinehart, Winston.

40. Roth, S., & Cohen, L. J. (1986). Approach, avoidance, and coping with stress. *American Psychologist, 41*, 813–819.

41. Glazer, S., & Beehr, T. A. (2005). Consistency of implications of three role stressors across four countries. *Journal of Organizational Behavior, 26*, 467–487.

42. Ng, T. W. H., Sorensen, K. L., & Eby, L. T. (2006). Locus of control at work: A meta-analysis. *Journal of Organizational Behavior, 27*, 1057–1087.

43. Friedman, M., & Rosenman, R. (1974). *Type A behavior and your heart*. New York, NY: Knopf.

44. Chesney, M. A., & Rosenman, R. (1980). Type A behavior in the work setting. In C. L. Cooper and R. Payne (Eds.), *Current concerns in occupational stress*. Chichester, UK: Wiley. For a typical study, see Jamal, M., & Baba, V. V. (1991). Type A behavior, its prevalence and consequences among women nurses: An empirical examination. *Human Relations, 44*, 1213–1228.

45. Fine, S., & Stinson, M. (2000, February 3). Stress is overwhelming people, study shows. *The Globe and Mail*, A1, A7; Matthews, K.A. (1982). Psychological perspectives on the Type A behavior pattern. *Psychological Bulletin, 91*, 293–323.

46. Booth-Kewley, S., & Friedman, H. S. (1987). Psychological predictors of heart disease: A quantitative review. *Psychological Bulletin, 101*, 343–362; Smith, D. (2003, March). Angry thoughts, at-risk hearts. *Monitor on Psychology*, 46–48; Ganster, D. C., Schaubroeck, J., Sime, W. E., & Mayes, B. T. (1991). The nomological validity of the Type A personality among employed adults. *Journal of Applied Psychology, 76*, 143–168.

47. Houkes, I., Janssen, P. P. M., de Jonge, J., & Bakker, A. B. (2003). Personality, work characteristics, and employee well-being: A longitudinal analysis of additive and moderating effects. *Journal of Occupational Health Psychology, 8*, 20–38; Grant, S., & Langan-Fox, J. (2007). Personality and the stressor-strain relationship: The role of the Big Five. *Journal of Occupational Health Psychology, 12*, 20–33; Kammeyer-Mueller, J. D., Judge, T. A., & Scott, B. A. (2009). The role of core self-evaluations in the coping process. *Journal of Applied Psychology, 94*, 177–195.

48. Spector, P. E., Zapf, D., Chen, P. Y., & Frese, M. (2000). Why negative affectivity should not be controlled in stress research: Don't throw out the baby with the bath water. *Journal of Organizational*

Behavior, 21, 79–95. For a relevant study, see Barsky, A., Thoresen, C. J., Warren, C. R., & Kaplan, S. A. (2004). Modeling negative affectivity and job stress: A contingency-based approach. *Journal of Organizational Behavior, 25*, 915–936.

49. An excellent review of managerial stressors can be found in Marshall, J., & Cooper, C. L. (1979). *Executives under pressure*. New York, NY: Praeger.

50. Xie, J. L., & Johns, G. (1995). Job scope and stress: Can job scope be too high? *Academy of Management Journal, 38*, 1288–1309.

51. Maslach, C., Leiter, M. P., & Schaufeli, W. (2009). Measuring burnout. In S. Cartwright & C. L. Cooper (Eds.), *The Oxford handbook of organizational well-being*. Oxford, UK: Oxford University Press; Maslach, C., & Leiter, M. P. (2008). Early predictors of burnout and engagement. *Journal of Applied Psychology, 93*, 498–512.

52. Maslach, C., Schaufeli, W. B., & Leiter, M. P. (2001). Job burnout. *Annual Review of Psychology, 52*, 397–422; Cordes, C. L., & Dougherty, T. W. (1993). A review and integration of research on job burnout. *Academy of Management Review, 18*, 621–656. For a comprehensive study, see Lee, R. T., & Ashforth, B. E. (1993). A longitudinal study of burnout among supervisors and managers: Comparisons of the Leiter and Maslach (1988) and Golembiewski et al. (1986) models. *Organizational Behavior and Human Decision Processes, 54*, 369–398.

53. Purvanova, R. K., & Muros, J. P. (2010). Gender differences in burnout: A meta-analysis. *Journal of Vocational Behavior, 77*, 168–185; Alarcon, G., Eschleman, K. J., & Bowling, N. A. (2009). Relationships between personality variables and burnout: A meta-analysis. *Work & Stress, 23*, 244–263.

54. See Pines, A. M., & Aronson, E. (1981). *Burnout: From tedium to personal growth*. New York, NY: The Free Press.

55. Hülsheger, U. R., & Schewe, A. F. (2011). On the costs and benefits of emotional labor: A meta-analysis of three decades of research. *Journal of Occupational Health Psychology, 16*, 361–389; see also Mesmer-Magnus, J. R., DeChurch, L. A., & Wax, A. (2012). Moving emotional labor beyond surface and deep acting: A discordance–congruence perspective. *Organizational Psychology Review, 2*, 6–53.

56. Galt, V. (2005, November 15). Fewer workers willing to put in 110%. *The Globe and Mail*, B8; Carniol, N. (2005, November 15). Fewer workers willing to give 100 percent. *Toronto Star*, D1, D11;

Galt, V. (2005, January 26). This just in: Half your employees ready to jump ship. *The Globe and Mail*, B1, B9.

57. Schaufeli, W. B., Bakker, A. B., & Van Rhenen, W. (2009). How changes in job demands and resources predict burnout, work engagement, and sickness absenteeism. *Journal of Organizational Behavior, 30*, 893–917; see also Bakker, A. B., & Demerouti, E. (2008). Towards a model of work engagement. *Career Development International, 13*, 209–223.

58. Cole, M. S., Walter, F., Bedeian, A. G., & O'Boyle, E. H. (2012). Job burnout and employee engagement: A meta-analytic examination of construct proliferation. *Journal of Management, 38*, 1550–1581.

59. Bakker, A. B., Demerouti, E., & Sanz-Vergel, A. I. (2014). Burnout and work engagement: The JD-R approach. *Annual Review of Organizational Psychology and Organizational Behavior, 1*, 389–411; Schaufeli, W., & Taris, T. (2014). A critical review of job demands resources model. Implications for improving work and health. In G. Bauer & O. Hämmig (Eds.), *Bridging occupational, organizational and public health*. Dordrecht, NL: Springer.

60. Bakker et al., 2014; Schaufeli et al., 2009.

61. Salin, D. (2003). Ways of explaining workplace bullying: A review of enabling, motivating and precipitating structures in the work environment. *Human Relations, 56*, 1213–1232.

62. Nielsen, M. B., & Einarsen, S. (2012). Outcomes of exposure to workplace bullying: A meta-analytic review. *Work & Stress, 26*, 309–332; Bowling, N. A., & Beehr, T. A. (2006). Workplace harassment from the victim's perspective: A theoretical model and meta-analysis. *Journal of Applied Psychology, 91*, 998–1012.

63. Salin, 2003; Rayner, C., & Keashly, L. (2005). Bullying at work: A perspective from Britain and North America. In S. Fox & P. E. Spector (Eds.), *Counterproductive work behavior: Investigations of actors and targets*. Washington, DC: American Psychological Association.

64. This is one interpretation of the distinction between bullying and mobbing. See Zapf, D., & Einarsen, S. (2005). Mobbing at work: Escalated conflicts in organizations. In Fox & Spector, 2005.

65. Mawritz, M. B., Mayer, D. M., Hoobler, J. M., Wayne, S. J., & Marinova, S. V. (2012). A trickle-down model of abusive supervision. *Personnel Psychology, 65*, 325–357; Priesemuth, M., Schminke, M., Ambrose, M. L., & Folger, R.

(2014). Abusive supervision climate: A multiple-mediation model of its impact on group outcomes. *Academy of Management Journal, 57,* 1513–1534.

66. Martinko, M. J., Harvey, P., Brees, J. R., & Mackey, J. (2013). A review of abusive supervision research. *Journal of Organizational behavior, 34,* S120–S137.

67. Langos, C. (2012). Cyberbullying: The challenge to define. *Cyberpsychology, Behavior, and Social Networking, 15,* 285-289.

68. Dobson, S. (2012, December 3). Cyberbullying can be harsher than other forms of workplace bullying: Study. *Canadian HR Reporter, 9,* 19.

69. Dingfelder, S.F. (2006, July–August). Banishing bullying. *Monitor on Psychology,* 76–78.

70. See Ford, M. T., Heinen, B. A., & Langkamer, K. L. (2008). Work and family satisfaction and conflict: A meta-analysis of cross-domain relations. *Journal of Applied Psychology, 92,* 57–80.

71. Duxbury, L., & Higgins, C. (undated). *Revisiting Work-Life Issues in Canada: The 2012 National Study on Balancing Work and Caregiving in Canada.*

72. For a review of the antecedents of work–family conflict, see Michel, J. S., Kotrba, L. M., Mitchelson, J. K., Clark, M. A., & Baltes, B. B. (2011). Antecedents of work-family conflict: A meta-analytic review. *Journal of Organizational Behavior, 32,* 689–725.

73. Bellavia, G. M., & Frone, M. R. (2005). Work–family conflict. In J. Barling, E. K. Kelloway, & M. R. Frone (Eds.), *Handbook of work stress.* Thousand Oaks, CA: Sage; Reichl, C., Leiter, M. P., & Spinath, F. M. (2014). Work-nonwork conflict and burnout: A meta-analysis. *Human Relations, 67,* 979–1005.

74. Dierdorff, E. C., & Ellington, J. K. (2008). It's the nature of the work: Examining behavior-based sources of work–family conflict across occupations. *Journal of Applied Psychology, 93,* 883–892.

75. Halbesleben, J. R. B., Harvey, J., & Bolino, M. C. (2009). Too engaged? A conservation of resources view of the relationship between work engagement and work interference with family. *Journal of Applied Psychology, 94,* 1452–1465.

76. For job loss in particular, see McKee-Ryan, F. M., Song, Z., Wanberg, C. R., & Kinicki, A. J. (2005). Psychological and physical well-being during unemployment: A meta-analytic study. *Journal of Applied Psychology, 90,* 53–76; for mergers and acquisitions, see Cartwright, S. (2005). Mergers and acquisitions: An update and appraisal. *International Review of Industrial and Organizational Psychology, 20,* 1–38.

77. Jackson, S. E., & Schuler, R. S. (1985). Meta-analysis and conceptual critique of research on role ambiguity and conflict in work settings. *Organizational Behavior and Human Decision Processes, 36,* 16–78. For a critique of some of this research, see Fineman, S., & Payne, R. (1981). Role stress: A methodological trap? *Journal of Occupational Behaviour, 2,* 51–64.

78. Fitzgerald, L. F., Drasgow, F., Hulin, C. L., Gelfand, M. J., & Magley, V. J. (1997). Antecedents and consequences of sexual harassment in organizations: A test of an integrated model. *Journal of Applied Psychology, 82,* 578–589; Schneider, K. T., Swan, S., & Fitzgerald, L. F. (1997). Job-related and psychological effects of sexual harassment in the workplace: Empirical evidence from two organizations. *Journal of Applied Psychology, 82,* 401–415.

79. Fitzgerald et al., 1997; Schneider et al., 1997.

80. O'Leary-Kelly, A. M., Bowes-Sperry, L., Bates, C. A., & Lean, E. R. (2009). Sexual harassment at work: A decade (plus) of progress. *Journal of Management, 35,* 503–536; Willness, C. R., Steel, P., & Lee, K. (2007). A meta-analysis of the antecedents and consequences of workplace sexual harassment. *Personnel Psychology, 60,* 127–162.

81. Peirce, E., Smolinski, C. A., & Rosen, B. (1998, August). Why sexual harassment complaints fall on deaf ears. *Academy of Management Executive,* 41–54; Schneider et al., 1997.

82. Fitzgerald et al., 1997; Glomb, T. M., Munson, L. J., Hulin, C. L., Bergman, M. E., & Drasgow, F. (1999). Structural equation models of sexual harassment: Longitudinal explorations and cross-sectional generalizations. *Journal of Applied Psychology, 84,* 14–28.

83. Cohen, S., & Wills, T. A. (1985). Stress, social support, and the buffering hypothesis. *Psychological Bulletin, 98,* 310–357; Kahn & Byosiere, 1992. For recent treatments of social support and relational views of work, see Grant, A. M., & Parker, S. K. (2009). Redesigning work design theories: The rise of relational and proactive perspectives. *Academy of Management Annals, 3,* 317–375, and Baran, B. E., Shanock, L. R., & Miller, L. R. (2012). Advancing organizational support theory into the twenty-first century world of work. *Journal of Business and Psychology, 27,* 123–147.

84. Gilboa, S., Shirom, A., Fried, Y., & Cooper, C. (2008). A meta-analysis of work demand stressors and job performance: Examining main and moderating effects. *Personnel Psychology, 61,* 227–271. For a classic study, see Jamal, M. (1984). Job stress and job performance controversy: An empirical assessment. *Organizational Behavior and Human Performance, 33,* 1–21.

85. LePine, J. A., Podsakoff, N. P., & LePine, M. A. (2005). A meta-analytic test of the challenge stressor-hindrance stressor framework: An explanation for inconsistent relationships among stressors and performance. *Academy of Management Journal, 48,* 764–775.

86. Eatough, E. M., Chang, C.-H., Miloslavic, S. A., & Johnson, R. E. (2011). Relationships of role stressors with organizational citizenship behavior: A meta-analysis. *Journal of Applied Pscyhology, 96,* 619–632.

87. Darr, W., & Johns, G. (2008). Work strain, health, and absenteeism from work: A meta-analysis. *Journal of Occupational Health Psychology, 13,* 293–318; Podsakoff, N. P., LePine, J. A., & LePine, M. A. (2007). Differential challenge stressor-hindrance stressor relationships with job attitudes, turnover intentions, turnover, and withdrawal behavior: A meta-analysis. *Journal of Applied Psychology, 92,* 438–454.

88. Miraglia, M., & Johns, G. (2016). Going to work ill: A meta-analysis of the correlates of presenteeism and a dual-path model. *Journal of Occupational Health Psychology,* in press; Johns, G. (2010). Presenteeism in the workplace: A review and research agenda. *Journal of Organizational Behavior, 31,* 519–532.

89. Kahn & Byosiere, 1992; Frone, M. R. (2008). Employee alcohol and illicit drug use: Scope, causes, and organizational consequences. In J. Barling & C. L. Cooper (Eds.), *Sage handbook of organizational behavior* (Vol. 1). London, UK: Sage.

90. For reviews, see Cramer, P. (2000). Defense mechanisms in psychology today: Further processes for adaptation. *American Psychologist, 55,* 637–646; Baumeister, R. F., Dale, K., & Sommer, K. L. (1998). Freudian defense mechanisms and empirical findings in modern social psychology: Reaction formation, projection, displacement, undoing, isolation, sublimation, and denial. *Journal of Personality, 66,* 1081–1124.

91. Ganster, D. C., & Rosen, C. C. (2013). Work stress and employee health: A multidisciplinary review. *Journal of Management, 39,* 1085–1122.

92. Cohen, S., & Herbert, T. B. (1996). Health psychology: Psychological and physical disease from the perspective of human psychoneuroimmunology. *Annual*

Review of Psychology, 47, 113–142; Cohen, S., & Williamson, G. M. (1991). Stress and infectious disease in humans. *Psychological Bulletin*, 109, 5–24.

93. Melamed, S., Shirom, A., Toker, S., Berliner, S., & Shapira, I. (2006). Burnout and risk of cardiovascular disease: Evidence, possible causal paths, and promising research directions. *Psychological Bulletin*, 132, 327–353; Kivimaki, M., Virtanen, M., Elovainio, M., Kouvonen, A., Vaananen, A., & Vahtera, J. (2006). Work stress in the etiology of coronary heart disease: A meta-analysis. *Scandinavian Journal of Work, Environment and Health*, 32, 431–442; see also the special issue Stress and the Heart, *Stress and Health*, August 2008.

94. Grandey, A. A., Fisk, G. M., & Steiner, D. D. (2005). Must "service with a smile" be stressful? The moderating role of personal control for American and French employees. *Journal of Applied Psychology*, 90, 893–904; Grandey, A. A., Dickter, D. N., & Sin, H. P. (2004). The customer is not always right: Customer aggression and emotion regulation of service employees. *Journal of Organizational Behavior*, 25, 397–418.

95. See Spriggs, C. A., & Jackson, P. R. (2006). Call centers as lean service environments: Job related strain and the mediating role of work design. *Journal of Occupational Health Psychology*, 11, 197–212.

96. This section relies on a *Wall Street Journal* special section on Work & Family (1993, June 21) and Shellenbarger, S. (1993, June 29). Work & family. *Wall Street Journal*, B1.

97. Canadastop100.com/family/, retrieved November 19, 2014.

98. Ngo, H.-Y., Foley, S., & Loi, R. (2009). Family friendly work practices, organizational climate, and firm performance: A study of multinational corporations in Hong Kong. *Journal of Organizational Behavior*, 30, 665–680; Van Steenbergen, E. F., & Ellemers, N. (2009). Is managing the work–family interface worthwhile? Benefits for employee health and performance. *Journal of Organizational Behavior*, 30, 617–642.

99. Butts, M. M., Casper, W. J., & Yang, T. S. (2013). How important are work-family support policies? A meta-analytic investigation of their effects on employee outcomes. *Journal of Applied Psychology*, 98, 1–25; Kelly, E. L., Kossek, E. E., Hammer, L. B., Durhman, M., Bray, J., Chermack, K., Murphy, L. A., & Kaskubar, D. (2008). Getting there from here: Research on the effects of work-family initiatives on work-family conflict and business outcomes. *Academy of Management Annals*, 2, 305–309.

100. Dobson, S. (2011, May 23). Quebec certifies work-life balance. *Canadian HR Reporter*, 1, 19; Dobson, S. (2012, May 7). Quebec certification hits 1-year mark. *Canadian HR Reporter*, 7, 10.

101. Richardson, K. M., & Rothstein, H. R. (2008). Effects of occupational stress management intervention programs: A meta-analysis. *Journal of Occupational Health Psychology*, 13, 69–93; Ivancevich, J. M., Matteson, M. T., Freedman, S. M., & Phillips, J. S. (1990). Worksite stress management interventions. *American Psychologist*, 45, 252–261; Cartwright, S., & Cooper, C. (2005). Individually targeted interventions. In Barling et al., 2005.

102. Richardson & Rothstein, 2008; Ivancevich et al., 1990.

103. Lush, T. (1998, October 3). Company with a conscience. *The Gazette* (Montreal), C3.

104. Immen, W., & Brown-Bowers, A. (2008, April 16). Employers get the fitness bug. *The Globe and Mail*, C1, C2.

105. Parks, K. M., & Steelman, L. A. (2008). Organizational wellness programs: A meta-analysis. *Journal of Occupational Health Psychology*, 13, 58–63; DeGroot, T., & Kiker, D. S. (2003). A meta analysis of the non-monetary effects of employee health management programs. *Human Resource Management*, 42, 53–69; Jex, S. M. (1991). The psychological benefits of exercise in work settings: A review, critique, and dispositional model. *Work & Stress*, 5, 133–147.

Chapter 14

1. Wright, L. (2015, May 5). McDonald's plan leaves investors hungry. *Toronto Star*, B1, B2; (Anonymous, Retrieved May 16, 2015). McDonald's announces initial steps in turnaround plan including worldwide business restructuring and financial updates. *McDonald's Official Global Corporate Website*, http://news .mcdonalds.com; Choi, C. (2015, May 4). McDonald's to simplify corporate structure, focus on customers, *Daily News*, www.dailynews.com/busines/20150504/...;Choi, C. (2015, May 3). McDonald's maps out revival plan: Simplified structure, more choices. *The Associated Press*, www.montreal-gazette.com/business/McDonald's...; Baertlein, L. (2015, May 4). McDonald's CEO Steve Easterbrook says he will do whatever it takes to "reset" struggling restaurant chain. *National Post*, http://business.financialpost.com/investing/mcdonalds-ceo-easterbrook...;

2. McNish, J. (2003, June 11). Skittish travelers shifting bus tour firm into reverse. *The Globe and Mail*, B1, B4.

3. Little, B. (2003, June 11). Second SARS outbreak barely noticed. *The Globe and Mail*, B4.

4. Neuman, S. (2003, June 4). SARS travel slump could last. *The Globe and Mail*, B6.

5. Scoffield, H. (2009, May 16). Manufacturing production sinks 2.7%. *The Globe and Mail*, B6; Ferguson, R., & Van Alphen, T. (2009, June 2). Government Motors. *Toronto Star*, A1, A12; Keenan, G., Howlett, K., & McCarthy, S. (2009, June 2). High stakes, high costs and high hopes. *The Globe and Mail*, A1, A14; Van Alphen, T. (2009, May 15). Truck stop. *Toronto Star*, B1, B4; Van Alphen, T. (2009, May 15). Oshawa reels as truck plant closes. *Toronto Star*, B4.

6. Katz, D., & Kahn, R.L. (1978). *The social psychology of organizations* (2nd ed.). New York, NY: Wiley.

7. This list relies on Duncan, R. (1972). Characteristics of organization environments and perceived environmental uncertainty. *Administrative Science Quarterly*, 17, 313–327.

8. Friend, D. (2009, March 13). RIM stays ahead of the curve with hiring frenzy. *The Globe and Mail*, B14; Rubin, J. (2012, May 26). RIM expected to announce major layoffs this week. *Toronto Star*, http://www.thestar.com/business/2012/05/26/rim_expected_to_announce_major_layoffs_this_week.html.

9. See Khandwalla, P. (1981). Properties of competing organizations. In P. C. Nystrom & W. H. Starbuck (Eds.), *Handbook of organization design* (Vol. 1). Oxford, UK: Oxford University Press.

10. Connolly, T., Conlon, E. J., & Deutsch, S. J. (1980). Organizational effectiveness: A multiple-constituency approach. *Academy of Management Review*, 5, 211–217.

11. Duncan, 1972. Just how to measure uncertainty has provoked controversy; see Downey, H. K., & Ireland, R. D. (1979). Quantitative versus qualitative: Environmental assessment in organizational studies. *Administrative Science Quarterly*, 24, 630–637; Milliken, F. J. (1987). Three types of perceived uncertainty about the environment: State, effect, and response uncertainty. *Academy of Management Review*, 12, 133–143.

12. Duncan, 1972; Tung, R. L. (1979). Dimensions of organizational environments: An exploratory study of their impact on organization structure. *Academy of Management Journal*, 22, 672–693. For contrary evidence, see Downey, H., Hellriegel, D., & Slocum, J. (1975). Environmental uncertainty: The construct and its application. *Administrative Science Quarterly*, 20, 613–629.

13. See Leblebici, H., & Salancik, G. R. (1981). Effects of environmental uncertainty on information and decision processes in banks. *Administrative Science Quarterly, 26,* 578–596.

14. See At-Twaijri, M.I.A., & Montanari, J.R. (1987). The impact of context and choice on the boundary-spanning process: An empirical extension. *Human Relations, 40,* 783–798.

15. Pfeffer, J., & Salancik, G. R. (1978). *The external control of organizations: A resource dependence perspective.* New York, NY: Harper & Row; Yasai-Ardekani, M. (1989). Effects of environmental scarcity and munificence on the relationship of context to organizational structure. *Academy of Management Journal, 32,* 131–156.

16. Castrogiovanni, G. J., (1991). Environmental munificence: A theoretical assessment. *Academy of Management Review, 16,* 542–565.

17. Pfeffer & Salancik, 1978.

18. Hillman, A. J., Withers, M. C., & Collins, B. J. (2009). Resource dependence theory: A review. *Journal of Management, 35,* 1404–1427.

19. Boyd, B. K., Dess, G. G., & Rasheed, A. M. A. (1993). Divergence between archival and perceptual measures of the environment: Causes and consequences. *Academy of Management Review, 18,* 204–226.

20. For an analogue, see Miller, D., Dröge, C., & Toulouse, J. M. (1988). Strategic process and content as mediators between organizational context and structure. *Academy of Management Journal, 31,* 544–569.

21. Miles, R. C., & Snow, C. C. (1978). *Organizational strategy, structure, and process.* New York, NY: McGraw-Hill.

22. Mintzberg, H. (1979). *The structuring of organizations.* Englewood Cliffs, NJ: Prentice-Hall. For a more recent review of some of the issues involved in structuring organizations, see Dunbar, R. L., & Starbuck, W. H. (2006). Learning to design organizations and learning from designing them. *Organization Science, 17,* 171–178.

23. Lawrence, P. R., & Lorsch, J. W. (1969). *Organization and environment: Managing differentiation and integration.* Homewood, IL: Irwin.

24. For an extended treatment of the role of interdependence between departments, see McCann, J., & Galbraith, J. R. (1981). Interdepartmental relations. In P. C. Nystrom & W. H. Starbuck (Eds.), *Handbook of organizational design* (Vol. 2). Oxford, UK: Oxford University Press.

25. For a comparison of functional and product departmentation, see McCann & Galbraith, 1981; Walker, A. H., & Lorsch, J. W. (1968, November–December). Organizational choice: Product vs. function. *Harvard Business Review,* 129–138.

26. Wallace, G., & Isidore, C. (2014, October 6). HP to split into two companies. *CNNMoney.*

27. Flynn, A., & Freeman, S. (2010, September 16). Canadian Tire tweaks managers' roles. *The Globe and Mail,* B10.

28. Galbraith, J. R. (2009). *Designing matrix organizations that actually work.* San Francisco, CA: Jossey-Bass; see also Davis, S. M., & Lawrence, P. M. (1977). *Matrix.* Reading, MA: Addison-Wesley.

29. Novak, B. (2008, July–August). Cisco connects the dots: Aligning leaders with a new organizational structure. *Global Business and Organizational Excellence,* 22–32.

30. Qiu, J. X. J., & Donaldson, L. (2011). Stopford and Wells were right! MNC matrix structures do fit a "high-high" strategy. *Management International Review,* 1–19.

31. Treatment of these forms of departmentation can be found in Daft, R. L. (2009). *Organization theory and design* (10th ed.). Mason, OH: Thompson South-Western; Robey, D. (1991). *Designing organizations* (3rd ed.). Homewood, IL: Irwin.

32. Battilana, J., & Lee, M. (2014). Advancing research on hybrid organizing – Insights from the study of social enterprises. *Academy of Management Annals, 8,* 397–441.

33. Mintzberg, 1979.

34. See Hall, R. H. (1962). Intraorganizational structural variation: Application of the bureaucratic model. *Administrative Science Quarterly, 7,* 295–308.

35. Lawrence & Lorsch, 1969.

36. Galbraith, J. R. (1977). *Organization design.* Reading, MA: Addison-Wesley.

37. See Birnbaum, P. H. (1981). Integration and specialization in academic research. *Academy of Management Journal, 24,* 487–503.

38. Okhuysen, G. A., & Bechky, B. A. (2009). Coordination in organizations: An integrative perspective. *Academy of Management Annals, 3,* 463–502.

39. This discussion relies on Galbraith, 1977.

40. Lawrence & Lorsch, 1969.

41. Galbraith, 1977.

42. Richter, A. W., West, M. A., Van Dick, R., & Dawson, J. F. (2006). Boundary spanners' identification, intergroup contact, and effective intergroup relations. *Academy of Management Journal, 49,* 1252–1269.

43. These definitions of structural variables are common. However, there is considerable disagreement about how some should be measured. See Walton, E. J. (1981). The comparison of measures of organizational structure. *Academy of Management Review, 6,* 155–160.

44. Research on these hypotheses is sparse and not always in agreement. See Dewar, R. D., & Simet, D. P. (1981). A level specific prediction of spans of control examining effects of size, technology, and specialization. *Academy of Management Journal, 24,* 5–24; Van Fleet, D. D. (1983). Span of management research and issues. *Academy of Management Journal, 26,* 546–552.

45. Lüscher, L. S., & Lewis, M. W. (2008). Organizational change and managerial sensemaking: Working through paradox. *Academy of Management Journal, 51,* 221–240.

46. For a study, see Hetherington, R. W. (1991). The effects of formalization on departments of a multi-hospital system. *Journal of Management Studies, 28,* 103–141.

47. Groth, L. (1999). *Future organizational design: The scope for the IT-based enterprise.* Chichester, UK: Wiley.

48. *60 Minutes,* October 17, 1993.

49. Mintzberg, 1979, 182.

50. Ritzer, G., (2013). *The McDonaldization of society* (7th ed.). Thousand Oaks, CA: Sage.

51. Personal communication from Food Lion's Jeff Lowrance, August 7, 2006.

52. Chuang, M. -L., Donegan, J. J., Ganon, M. W., & Wei, K. (2011). Walmart and Carrefour experiences in China: Resolving the structural paradox. *Cross Cultural Management, 18,* 443–463.

53. Daft, 2009.

54. For a good general review of size research, see Bluedorn, A. C. (1993). Pilgrim's progress: Trends and convergence in research on organizational size and environments. *Journal of Management, 19,* 163–191.

55. Much of this research was stimulated by Blau, P.M. (1970). A theory of differentiation in organizations. *American Sociological Review, 35,* 201–218. For a review and test, see Cullen, J. B., Anderson, K. S., & Baker, D. D. (1986). Blau's theory of structural differentiation revisited: A theory of structural change or scale? *Academy of Management Journal, 29,* 203–229.

56. Dewar, R., & Hage, J. (1978). Size, technology, complexity, and structural differentiation: Toward a theoretical synthesis. *Administrative Science Quarterly, 23,* 111–136; Marsh, R. M., & Mannari, H. (1981). Technology and size as determinants of the organizational structure of Japanese factories. *Administrative Science Quarterly, 26,* 33–57.

57. Hage, J., & Aiken, M. (1967). Relationship of centralization to other structural properties. *Administrative Science Quarterly, 12*, 79–91; Mansfield, R. (1973). Bureaucracy and centralization: An examination of organizational structure. *Administrative Science Quarterly, 18*, 77–88.

58. The terms *mechanistic* and *organic* (to follow) were first used by Burns, T., & Stalker, G. M. (1961). *The management of innovation.* London, UK: Tavistock Publications. For a relevant study, see Courtright, J. A., Fairhurst, G. T., & Rogers, L. E. (1989). Interaction patterns in organic and mechanistic systems. *Academy of Management Journal, 32,* 773–802.

59. Anfuso, D. (1999, March). Core values shape W. L. Gore's innovative culture. *Workforce,* 48–53; Deutschman, A. (2004, December). The fabric of creativity. *Fast Company,* 54–62; Weinreb, M. (2003, April). Power to the people. *Sales and Marketing Management,* 30–35.

60. Lawrence, P. R., & Lorsch, J. W. (1967). *Organization and environment: Managing differentiation and integration.* Homewood, IL: Irwin. For a follow-up study, see Lorsch, J. W., & Morse, J. J. (1974). *Organizations and their members: A contingency approach.* New York, NY: Harper & Row. For a review of the somewhat mixed evidence on this, see Miner, J. B. (1982). *Theories of organizational structure and process.* Chicago, IL: Dryden.

61. Puranam, P., Alexy, O., & Reitzig, M. (2014). What's "new" about new forms of organizing? *Academy of Management Review, 39,* 162–180.

62. Raisch, S., Birkinshaw, J., Probst, G., & Tushman, M. L. (2009). Organizational ambidexterity: Balancing exploitation and exploration for sustained performance. *Organization Science, 20,* 685–695; Simsek, Z., Heavey, C., Viega, J. F., & Souder, D. (2009). A typology for aligning ambidexterity's conceptualizations, antecedents, and outcomes. *Journal of Management Studies, 46,* 864–894.

63. Jansen, J. J. P., Tempelaar, M. P., van den Bosch, F. A. J., & Volberda, H. W. (2009). Structural differentiation and ambidexterity: The mediating role of integration mechanisms. *Organization Science, 20,* 797–811.

64. Junni, P., Sarala, R. M., Taras, V., & Tarba, S. Y. (2013). Organizational ambidexterity and performance: A meta-analysis. *Academy of Management Perspectives, 27,* 299–312; O'Reilly, C.A. III, & Tushman, M. L. (2008). Ambidexterity as a dynamic capability: Resolving the innovator's dilemma. *Research in Organizational Behavior, 28,* 185–206.

65. Heracleous, L. (2013). Quantum strategy at Apple Inc. *Organizational Dynamics, 42,* 92–99; Heracleous, L., & Wirtz, J. (2014). Singapore Airlines: Achieving sustainable advantage through mastering paradox. *Journal of Applied Behavioral Science, 50,* 150–170.

66. O'Reilly, C. A. III, & Tushman, M. L. (2004, April). The ambidextrous organization. *Harvard Business Review,* 74–82; see also Jansen et al., 2009, and O'Reilly, C. A. III, Tushman, M. L. (2011, Summer). Organizational ambidexterity in action: How managers explore and exploit. *California Management Review, 53,* 5–22.

67. Farjoun, M. (2010). Beyond dualism: Stability and change as a duality. *Academy of Management Review, 35,* 202–225.

68. Westerman, G., McFarlan, F. W., & Iansiti, M. (2006). Organization design and effectiveness over the innovation life cycle. *Organization Science, 17,* 230–238; Puranam, P., Singh, H., & Zollo, M. (2006). Organizing for innovation: Managing the coordination autonomy dilemma in technology acquisitions. *Academy of Management Journal, 49,* 263–280.

69. Phene, A., Tallman, S., & Almeida, P. (2012). When do acquisitions facilitate technological exploration and exploitation? *Journal of Management, 38,* 753–783.

70. Miles, R. E., & Snow, C. C. (1992, Summer). Causes of failure in network organizations. *California Management Review,* 53–72; Snow, C. C., Miles, R. F., & Coleman, H. J., Jr. (1992, Winter). Managing 21st century network organizations. *Organizational Dynamics, 20,* 5–20.

71. Brass, D. J., Galaskiewicz, J., Greve, H. R., & Tsai, W. (2004). Taking stock of networks and organizations: A multi-level perspective. *Academy of Management Journal, 47,* 795–817; Phelps, C. C. (2010). A longitudinal study of the influence of alliance network structure and composition on firm exploratory innovation. *Academy of Management Journal, 53,* 890–913.

72. Parmigiani, A., & Rivera-Santos, M. (2011). Clearing a path through the forest: A meta-review of interorganizational relationships. *Journal of Management, 37,* 1108–1136.

73. Dess, G. G., Rasheed, A. M. A., McLaughlin, K. J., & Priem, R. L. (1995, August). The new corporate architecture. *Academy of Management Executive, 9,* 7–20.

74. Magder, J. (2011, February 12). Risky business of Google. *The Gazette* (Montreal). B1, B4.

75. This example is from Venkatraman, N., & Lee, C. H. (2004). Preferential linkage and network evolution: A conceptual model and empirical test in the U.S. video game sector. *Academy of Management Journal, 47,* 876–892.

76. Davis, J. P. (2013, Summer). Capturing the value of synchronized innovation. *MIT Sloan Management Review,* 55–62.

77. Ozcan, P., & Eisenhardt, K. M. (2009). Origin of alliance portfolios: Entrepreneurs, network strategies, and firm performance. *Academy of Management Journal, 52,* 246–279.

78. Hartley, M. (2012, May). Doubling down. *Financial Post Magazine,* 24–28.

79. Miles & Snow, 1992.

80. Chesbrough, H. W., & Teece, D. J. (2002, August). Organizing for innovation: When is virtual virtuous? *The Innovative Enterprise,* 127–134.

81. Davis, G. F. (2009, August). The rise and fall of finance and the end of the society of organizations. *Academy of Management Perspectives,* 27–44.

82. Dess et al., 1995; Tully, S. (1993, February 8). The modular corporation. *Fortune,* 106–114.

83. Tully, 1993; Dess et al., 1995.

84. Magretta, J. (1998, March–April). The power of virtual integration: An interview with Dell Computer's Michael Dell. *Harvard Business Review,* 72–84; Tully, 1993.

85. Dess et al., 1995.

86. Baraldi, E. (2008, Summer). Strategy in industrial networks: Experiences from IKEA. *California Management Review,* 99–126.

87. Dess et al., 1995; Tully, 1993.

88. Tully, 1993.

89. Romme, A. G. L. (1990). Vertical integration as organizational strategy formation. *Organization Studies, 11,* 239–260.

90. Hartley, M. (2009, April 21). Oracle deal for Sun creates one-stop shop. *The Globe and Mail,* B13.

91. Lubatkin, M., & O'Neill, H. M. (1987). Merger strategies and capital market risk. *Academy of Management Journal, 30,* 665–684; Pfeffer & Salancik, 1978; Hill, C. W. L., & Hoskisson, R. E. (1987). Strategy and structure in the multiproduct firm. *Academy of Management Review, 12,* 331–341.

92. Kanter, R. M. (1989, August). Becoming PALS: Pooling, allying, and linking across companies. *Academy of Management Executive,* 183–193.

93. See Davis, G. F., & Powell, W. W. (1992). Organization-environment relations. In M. D. Dunnette & L. M. Hough (Eds.), *Handbook of industrial and organizational psychology* (2nd ed., Vol. 3). Palo Alto, CA: Consulting Psychologists Press; Oliver, C. (1991). Strategic responses to institutional processes.

Academy of Management Review, 16, 145–179.

94. Greenwood, R., & Deephouse, D. (2001, December 26). Legitimacy seen as key. *The Globe and Mail*, B7.

Chapter 15

1. Stewart, J. B. (2015, January 29). How, and why, Apple overtook Microsoft. *The New York Times* online; Bilton, N. (2013, July 29). Microsoft's struggle to make things simple. *The New York Times*, B4; Eichenwald, K. (2012, August). Microsoft's lost decade. *Vanity Fair*; Farnham, A. (2013, November 16). Microsoft: "Stack-ranking" gets heave ho. *ABC News*.

2. Kirby, J. (2006, June 19). Awakening Microsoft. *National Post*, FP1, FP4.

3. Gilbert, C. G. (2005). Unbundling the structure of inertia: Resource versus routine rigidity. *Academy of Management Journal, 48,* 741–763; see also Vincente-Lorente, J. D., & Zúñiga-Vincente, J. A. (2006). Testing the time-variancy of explanatory factors of strategic change. *British Journal of Management, 17,* 93–114.

4. Jørgensen, H. H., Owen, L., & Neus, L. (2009). Stop improvising change management! *Strategy & Leadership, 37,* 38–44.

5. This list relies mostly on Leavitt, H. (1965). Applied organizational changes in industry: Structural, technological, and humanistic approaches. In J. G. March (Ed.), *Handbook of organizations*. Chicago, IL: Rand McNally.

6. Cameron, K. S., & Quinn, R. E. (1999). *Diagnosing and changing organizational culture*. Reading, MA: Addison-Wesley.

7. Lewin, K. (1951). *Field theory in social science*. New York, NY: Harper & Row; see also Burnes, B. (2004). Kurt Lewin and the planned approach to change: A re-appraisal. *Journal of Management Studies, 41,* 977–1002.

8. Michie, S., van Stralen, M. M., & West, R. (2011). The behaviour change wheel: A new method for characterising and designing behaviour change interventions. *Implementation Science, 6,* 42.

9. Rafferty, A. E., & Griffin, M. A. (2008). Organizational change. In J. Barling & C. L. Cooper (Eds.), *The Sage handbook of organizational behavior* (Vol. 1). London, UK: Sage.

10. Marshak, R.J. (2004). Morphing: The leading edge of organizational change in the twenty-first century. *Organization Development Journal, 22,* 8–21.

11. Tetrick, L. E., & Da Silva, N. (2003). Assessing the culture and climate for organizational learning. In S. E. Jackson, M. A. Hitt, and A. S. Denisi (Eds.), *Managing knowledge for sustained competitive advantage*. San Francisco, CA: Jossey-Bass.

12. Garvin, D. A. (1993, July–August). Building a learning organization. *Harvard Business Review*, 78–91.

13. Corley, K. G., & Gioia, D. A. (2003). Semantic learning as change enabler: Relating organizational identity and organizational learning. In M. Easterby-Smith and M. A. Lyles (Eds.), *Handbook of organizational learning and knowledge management*. Oxford: Blackwell.

14. Harris-Lalonde, S. (2001). *Training and development outlook 2001*. Ottawa, ON: The Conference Board of Canada.

15. Harris-Lalonde, 2001; see also Ellinger, A. D., Ellinger, A. E., Baiyin, Y., & Howton, S. W. (2002). The relationship between the learning organization concept and firms' financial performance: An empirical assessment. *Human Resource Development Quarterly, 13,* 5–21.

16. Flynn, G. (1997, December). Bank of Montreal invests in its workers. *Workforce*, 30–38.

17. Wirtz, J., Heracleous, L., & Menkhoff, T. (2007). Value creation through strategic knowledge management: The case of Singapore Airlines. *Journal of Asian Business, 23,* 249–263.

18. See Levinson, H. (2002). *Organizational assessment: A step-by-step guide to effective consulting*. Washington, DC: American Psychological Association; Howard, A. (Ed.) (1994). *Diagnosis for organizational change: Methods and models*. New York, NY: Guilford.

19. Ford, J. D., & Ford, L. W. (2009). Resistance to change: A reexamination and extension. *Research in Organizational Change and Development, 17,* 211–239.

20. Sonenshein, S. (2010). We're changing—or are we? Untangling the role of progressive, regressive, and stability narratives during strategic change implementation. *Academy of Management Journal, 53,* 477–512.

21. The first five reasons are from Kotter, J. P., & Schlesinger, L. A. (1979, March–April). Choosing strategies for change. *Harvard Business Review*, 106–114.

22. Oreg, S., Bayazit, M., Vakola, M., Arciniega, L., Armenakis, A., Barkauskiene, R., Bozionelos, N., et al. (2008). Dispositional resistance to change: Measurement equivalence and the link to personal values across 17 nations. *Journal of Applied Psychology, 93,* 935–944.

23. Herold, D. M., Fedor, D. B., & Caldwell, S. D. (2007). Beyond change management: A multilevel investigation of contextual and personal influences on employees' commitment to change. *Journal of Applied Psychology, 92,* 942–951; see also Shin, J., Taylor, M. S., & Seo, M.-G. (2012). Resources for

change: The relationships of organizational inducements and psychological resilience to employees' attitudes and behaviors toward organizational change. *Academy of Management Journal, 55,* 727–748.

24. Frank, R. (1994, May 23). As UPS tries to deliver more to its customers, labor problems grow. *Wall Street Journal*, A1, A8.

25. George, J. M., & Jones, G. R. (2001). Towards a process model of individual change in organizations. *Human Relations, 54,* 419–444. Unfortunately, research has often ignored the emotional component of change; see Rafferty, A. E., Jimmieson, N. L., & Armenakis, A. A. (2013). Change readiness: A multilevel review. *Journal of Management, 39,* 110–135.

26. The following relies partly on Kotter & Schlesinger, 1979.

27. Rodell, J. B., & Colquitt, J. A. (2009). Looking ahead in times of uncertainty: The role of anticipatory justice in an organizational change context. *Journal of Applied Psychology, 94,* 989–1002.

28. For reviews, see Macy, B. A., Peterson, M. F., & Norton, L. W. (1989). A test of participation theory in a work redesign field setting: Degree of participation and comparison site contrasts. *Human Relations, 42,* 1095–1165; Filley, A. C., House, R. J., & Kerr, S. (1976). *Managerial process and organizational behavior* (2nd ed.). Glenview, IL: Scott, Foresman.

29. See, for example, Seo, M.-G., Taylor, M. S., Hill, N. S., Zhang, X., Tesluk, P. E., & Lorinkova, N. M. (2012). The role of affect and leadership during organizational change. *Personnel Psychology, 65,* 121–165.

30. Tichy, N. M., & Devanna, M. A. (1986). *The transformational leader*. New York, NY: Wiley.

31. Bommer, W. H., Rich, G. A., & Rubin, R. S. (2005). Changing attitudes about change: Longitudinal effects of transformational leader behavior on employee cynicism about organizational change. *Journal of Organizational Behavior, 26,* 733–753; Herold, D. M., Fedor, D. B., Caldwell, S., & Liu, Y. (2008). The effects of transformational and change leadership on employees' commitment to change: A multilevel study. *Journal of Applied Psychology, 93,* 346–357.

32. Rafferty, A. E., & Griffin, M. A. (2006). Perceptions of organizational change: A stress and coping perspective. *Journal of Applied Psychology, 91,* 1154–1162.

33. Catalanello, R. F., & Kirkpatrick, D. L. (1968). Evaluating training programs: The state of the art. *Training and Development Journal, 22,* 2–9.

34. Goodman, P.S., Bazerman, M., & Conlon, E. (1980). Institutionalization of planned organizational change. *Research in Organizational Behavior, 2,* 215–246.

35. Goodman et al., 1980.

36. For a review of various definitions, see Porras, J. I., & Robertson, P. J. (1992). Organizational development: Theory, practice, and research. In M. D. Dunnette & L. M. Hough (Eds.), *Handbook of industrial and organizational psychology,* (2nd ed., Vol. 3). Palo Alto, CA: Consulting Psychologists Press; for a good history, see Burnes, B., & Cooke, B. (2012). The past, present and future of organization development: Taking the long view. *Human Relations, 65,* 1395–1429.

37. French, W. L., & Bell, C. H., Jr. (1973). *Organization development.* Englewood Cliffs, NJ: Prentice-Hall.

38. Burnes & Cooke, 2012; Beer, M., & Walton, E. (1990). Developing the competitive organization: Interventions and strategies. *American Psychologist, 45,* 154–161.

39. Beer, M. (1976). The technology of organizational development. In M. D. Dunnette (Ed.) *Handbook of industrial and organizational psychology.* Chicago, IL: Rand McNally. See also Dyer, W. (1987). *Team building: Issues and alternatives* (2nd ed.). Reading, MA: Addison-Wesley.

40. Wakeley, J. H., & Shaw, M. E. (1965). Management training: An integrated approach. *Training Directors Journal, 19,* 2–13.

41. This description relies upon Beer, M. (1980). *Organization change and development: A systems view.* Glenview, IL: Scott, Foresman; Huse, E. F., & Cummings, T. G. (1985). Organization development and change (3rd ed.). St. Paul, MN: West; Nadler, D. A. (1977). *Feedback and organization development: Using data-based methods.* Reading, MA: Addison-Wesley.

42. Weiner, S. P. (2006). *Driving change with IBM's bimonthly global pulse survey.* Paper presented at the annual conference of the Society for Industrial and Organizational Psychology, Dallas, TX.

43. Smith, R. L., Rauschenberger, J. M., Bastos, M. W., Jayne, M. A. E., Mills, N. E., & Tripp, R. E. (2006). *Ford Motor Company Pulse trend analysis—Making and breaking trends.* Paper presented at the annual conference of the Society for Industrial and Organizational Psychology, Dallas, TX; see also Pulse Survey Offers Employees a Voice, Measures Satisfaction. (2011, August 26) www.at.ford.com/news/cn/Pages/Pulse%20Survey%20Offers%20Employees%20a%20Voice%20Measures%20Satisfaction.aspx.

44. Johnson, R. H., Ryan, A. M., & Schmit, M. (1994). Employee attitudes and branch performance at Ford Motor Credit. Presentation at the annual conference of the Society for Industrial and Organizational Psychology, Nashville, TN.

45. Mayflower Group, www.mayflower-group.org.

46. For an eclectic view of TQM concerns, see the Total Quality Special Issue of the July 1994 *Academy of Management Review.*

47. Crosby, P. B. (1979). *Quality is free.* New York, NY: McGraw-Hill; Deming, W. E. (1986). *Out of the crisis.* Cambridge, MA: Massachusetts Institute of Technology Center for Advanced Engineering Study; Juran J. M. (1992). *Juran on quality by design.* New York, NY: Free Press.

48. Kinlaw, D. C. (1992). *Continuous improvement and measurement for total quality: A team-based approach.* San Diego, CA: Pfeiffer.

49. Berry, L. L., Parasuraman, A., & Zeithaml, V. A. (1994, May). Improving service quality in America: Lessons learned. *Academy of Management Executive, 8,* 32–45.

50. Kinlaw, 1992; Bounds, G., Yorks, L., Adams, M., & Ranney, G. (1994). *Beyond total quality management: Toward the emerging paradigm.* New York, NY: McGraw-Hill.

51. Reeves, C. A., & Bednar, D. A. (1994). Defining quality: Alternatives and implications. *Academy of Management Review, 19,* 419–445.

52. Greengard, S. (1993, December). Reengineering: Out of the rubble. *Personnel Journal,* 48B–48O; Hammer, M., & Champy, J. (1993). *Reengineering the corporation: A manifesto for business revolution.* New York, NY: HarperBusiness; Stewart, T. A. (1993, August 23). Reengineering: The hot new management tool. *Fortune,* 41–48.

53. Hammer & Champy, 1993.

54. Hammer & Champy, 1993.

55. Teng, J. T. C., Grover, V., & Fiedler, K. D. (1994, Spring). Business process reengineering: Charting a strategic path for the information age. *California Management Review, 36,* 9–31.

56. Hammer & Champy, 1993; Teng et al., 1994.

57. Examples from Greengard, 1993; Teng et al., 1994.

58. Hall, G., Rosenthal, J., & Wade, J. (1993, November–December). How to make reengineering really work. *Harvard Business Review,* 119–131.

59. Guzzo, R. A., Jette, R. D., & Katzell, R. A. (1985). The effects of psychologically based intervention programs on worker productivity: A meta-analysis.

Personnel Psychology, 38, 275–291; Neuman, G. A., Edwards, J. E., & Raju, N. S. (1989). Organizational development interventions: A meta-analysis of their effects on satisfaction and other attitudes. *Personnel Psychology, 42,* 461–489.

60. For a meta-analytic summary, see Robertson, P. J., Roberts, D. R., & Porras, J. I. (1993). Dynamics of planned organizational change: Assessing support for a theoretical model. *Academy of Management Journal, 36,* 619–634. See also Macy, B. A., & Izumi, H. (1993). Organizational change, design, and work innovation: A meta-analysis of 131 North American field studies—1961–1991. *Research in Organizational Change and Development, 7,* 235–313.

61. Porras & Robertson, 1992; Nicholas, J. M., & Katz, M. (1985). Research methods and reporting practices in organization development: A review and some guidelines. *Academy of Management Review, 10,* 737–749.

62. White, S. E., & Mitchell, T. R. (1976). Organization development: A review of research content and research design. *Academy of Management Review, 1,* 57–73.

63. For reviews of creativity and innovation research, see Anderson, N., Potočnik, K., & Zhou, J. (2014). Innovation and creativity in organizations: A state-of-the-science review, prospective commentary, and guiding framework. *Journal of Management, 40,* 1297–1333; Zhou, J., & Hoever, I. J. (2014). Research on workplace creativity: A review and redirection. *Annual Review of Organizational Psychology and Organizational Behavior, 1,* 333–359; George, J. M. (2007) Creativity in organizations. *Academy of Management Annals, 1,* 439–477; Hennessey, B. A., & Amabile, T.M. (2010). Creativity. *Annual Review of Psychology, 61,* 569–598.

64. For an attempt to provide some order to this subject, see Wolfe, R. A. (1994). Organizational innovation: Review, critique and suggested research directions. *Journal of Management Studies, 31,* 405–431.

65. Tushman, M., & Nadler, D. (1986, Spring). Organizing for innovation. *California Management Review, 28,* 74–92; Damanpour, F., & Aravind, D. (2012). Managerial innovation: Conceptions, processes, and antecedents. *Management and Organization Review, 8,* 423–454.

66. Damanpour & Aravind, 2012.

67. Hamel, G. (2006, February). The why, what, and how of management innovation. *Harvard Business Review,* 72–84.

68. Birkinshaw, J., Hamel, G., & Mol, M. J. (2008). Management innovation.

Academy of Management Review, 33, 825–845.

69. Frost, P. J., & Egri, C. P. (1991). The political process of innovation. *Research in Organizational Behavior, 13,* 229–295.

70. Baer, M. (2012). Putting creativity to work: The implementation of creative ideas in organizations. *Academy of Management Journal, 55,* 1102–1119.

71. This three-part view of creativity is from Amabile, T. M. (1988). A model of creativity and innovation in organizations. *Research in Organizational Behavior, 10,* 123–167; see also Woodman, R. W., Sawyer, J. E., & Griffin, R. W. (1993). Toward a theory of organizational creativity. *Academy of Management Review, 18,* 293–321.

72. Basadur, M. (1994). Managing the creative process in organizations. In M. A. Runco (Ed.), *Problem finding, problem solving, and creativity.* Norwood, NJ: Ablex; Kabanoff, B., & Rossiter, J. R. (1994). Recent developments in applied creativity. *International Review of Industrial and Organizational Psychology, 9,* 283–324.

73. Galbraith, J. R. (1982, Winter). Designing the innovating organization. *Organizational Dynamics,* 4–25.

74. Howell, J. M. (2005, May). The right stuff: Identifying and developing effective champions of innovation. *Academy of Management Executive,* 108–119; Howell, J.M., & Higgins, C.A. (1990). Champions of technological innovation. *Administrative Science Quarterly, 35,* 317–341.

75. Definition and examples from Mainemelis, C. (2010). Stealing fire: Creative deviance in the evolution of new ideas. *Academy of Management Review, 35,* 558–578.

76. Cohen, W. M., & Levinthal, D.A. (1990). Absorptive capacity: A new perspective on learning and innovation. *Administrative Science Quarterly, 35,* 128–152; for an update see Lane, P.J., Koka, B.R., & Pathak, S. (2006). The reification of absorptive capacity: A critical review and rejuvenation of the construct. *Academy of Management Review, 31,* 833–863.

77. Tushman, M. L., & Scanlan, T. J. (1981a). Characteristics and external orientations of boundary spanning individuals. *Academy of Management Journal, 24,* 83–98; Tushman, M. L., & Scanlan, T. J.

(1981b). Boundary spanning individuals: Their role in information transfer and their antecedents. *Academy of Management Journal, 24,* 289–305.

78. McFadyen, A. M., Semadeni, M., & Cannella, A. A., Jr. (2009). Value of strong ties to disconnected others: Examining knowledge creation in biomedicine. *Organizational Science, 20,* 552–564.

79. Keller, R. T., & Holland, W. E. (1983). Communicators and innovators in research and development organizations. *Academy of Management Journal, 26,* 742–749.

80. Ramaswamy, V. (2008). Co-creating value through customers' experiences: The Nike case. *Strategy & Leadership, 36,* 9–14.

81. Bertin, O. (2003, July 14). Harley-Davidson's great ride to the top. *The Globe and Mail,* B1, B4.

82. Leung, A.K.-Y., Maddux, W. W., Galinsky, A. D., & Chiu, C.-Y. (2008). Multicultural experience enhances creativity: The when and how. *American Psychologist, 63,* 169–181.

83. Leiponen, A., & Helfat, C. E. (2011). Location, decentralization, and knowledge sources for innovation. *Organization Science, 22,* 641–658.

84. Wilson, K. A. (2011, February 7). From the inside, out. *Autoweek,* 22–23.

85. Lampel, J., Jha, P. P., & Bhalla, A. (2012, May). Test-driving the future: How design competitions are changing innovation. *Academy of Management Perspectives,* 71–85.

86. Kanter, R. M. (1988). When a thousand flowers bloom: Structural, collective, and social conditions for innovation in organization. *Research in Organizational Behavior, 10,* 169–211; Nord, W. R., & Tucker, S. (1987). *Implementing routine and radical innovations.* Lexington, MA: Lexington Books; Damanpour, F. (1991). Organizational innovation: A meta-analysis of effects of determinants and moderators. *Academy of Management Journal, 34,* 555–590.

87. Harvey, S. (2014). Creative synthesis: Exploring the process of extraordinary group creativity. *Academy of Management Review, 39,* 324–343.

88. Miller, D. J., Fern, M. J., & Cardinal, L. B. (2007). The use of knowledge for technological innovation within diverse

firms. *Academy of Management Journal, 50,* 308–326.

89. Tushman & Scanlan, 1981b.

90. Keller & Holland, 1983.

91. Katz, R. (1982). The effects of group longevity on project communication and performance. *Administrative Science Quarterly, 27,* 81–104.

92. For a review, see Nord & Tucker, 1987. However, this prescription is controversial. For other views, see Kanter, 1988; Marcus A. A. (1988). Implementing externally induced innovations: A comparison of rule-bound and autonomous approaches. *Academy of Management Journal, 31,* 235–256.

93. Damanpour, 1991; Kanter, 1988.

94. Ulanoff, L. (2011, April 15). Inventor of cell phone says no to AT&T Mobile, yes to apps, and more. pcmag.com

95. Galbraith, 1982.

96. Hamel, 2006.

97. Amabile, 1988.

98. Damsell, K. (2003, October 29). CEO Fiorina touts HP's ability to adapt. *The Globe and Mail,* B3.

99. Byron, K., & Khazanchi, S. (2012). Rewards and creative performance: A meta-analytic test of theoretically derived hypotheses. *Psychological Bulletin, 138,* 809–830.

100. Galbraith, 1982.

101. Walton, R. E. (1975, Winter). The diffusion of new work structures: Explaining why success didn't take. *Organizational Dynamics, 3,* 3–22.

102. Ferlie, E., Fitzgerald, L., Wood, M., & Hawkins, C. (2005). The nonspread of innovations: The mediating role of professionals. *Academy of Management Journal, 48,* 117–134.

103. Rogers, E. M. (2003). *Diffusion of innovations* (5th ed.). New York, NY: Free Press.

104. Ansari, S. M., Fiss, P. C., & Zajac, E. J. (2010). Made to fit: How practices vary as they diffuse. *Academy of Management Review, 35,* 67–92.

105. Pfeffer, J., & Sutton, R. I. (2000). *The knowing-doing gap: How smart companies turn knowledge into action.* Boston, MA: Harvard Business School Press; see also Johns, G. (1993). Constraints on the adoption of psychology-based personnel practices: Lessons from organization innovation. *Personnel Psychology, 46,* 569–592.

INDEX

A

Aboriginal peoples, 19, 84
absenteeism, 6, 20, 49, 53, 482, 486, 491
   as consequence of job satisfaction, 145–146
   patterns of, 145
abusive management, 64
abusive supervision, 481
accommodating style (of conflict management), 468
Ackermann, Patrick, 462
acquisitions, 529, 544
active listening, 388
actor-observer effect, 94
Adams, J. Stacey, 174
adaptive performance, 49
   relationship to personality, 51
additive tasks, 246, 247
Adler, Nancy, 185
affective (organizational) commitment, 150
affective personality traits, 54
affiliative managers, 439
age diversity, 19
agenda implementation, 16–17
agenda setting, 16
age stereotyping, 101–103
   effect on human resource decisions, 102
   inaccuracy of, 101
agreeableness dimension of personality, 49
Akinola, Modupe, 290
Alderfer, Clayton, 166, 167, 169, 202
Allan, Elyse, 343
Allen, Natalie, 150, 151
ambidextrous organization, 524–525
ambiguity, organizational conflict and, 466
American Express Canada, 106, 114
American Medical Association, 435
American Psychological Association, 474
analytics, 421–422, 423
anchoring effect, 407
anticipatory socialization, 279
Apple Inc., 103, 126, 524, 542
arbitration, 473
Argyris, Chris, 13
Ash, Mary Kay, 298
Ashforth, Blake, 447
attitudes,
   behaviours and, 136
   compared to values, 136
   definition of, 136
   development of, 136

   evaluative aspect of, 136
   job satisfaction, 136–137
attributions, 22, 91
   actor-observer bias effect in, 94
   biases in, 93–94
   consensus cues, 92
   consistency cues, 91–92
   dispositional, 91
   distinctiveness cues, 92
   examples of, 92–93
   fundamental error as bias in, 93
   importance in job performance interpretation, 98
   self-serving bias in, 94
   situational, 91
authentic leadership, 339–341
   balanced processing behaviour in, 340
   internalized moral perspective behaviour in, 341
   relational transparent behaviour in, 340
   self-awareness behaviour in, 340
   work groups and, 341
   work-related outcomes and, 341
autonomous motivation, 170
autonomy, 217
autonomy support, 170–171
avoiding style (of conflict management), 468

B

Baby Boomers (born 1946–1964), 128
backstabbing, 436
Ballmer, Steve, 542
Baloun, Karel, 126
Bandura, Albert, 62
Barrick, Murray R., 25
Bartol, Kathryn, 207
Bass, Bernard, 335
Bazerman, Max, 407
Beddoe, Clive, 296, 631
behaviourally anchored rating scale (BARS), 113
behavioural plasticity theory, 52–53
behavioural science knowledge, 555
behaviour modelling training (BMT), 70
Bell Canada, 215, 227, 288, 390
Bellezza, Silvia, 377
Belus Capital Advisors, 403
Bensen, Pete, 501
Berdahl, Jennifer, 455
big data, 421, 422
Big Five personality traits. *See* personality, Five Factor Model
   (FFM) of

Black, Stewart, 348
Blackberry Limited, 504
BMO Financial Group, 549
body language, 374–375
Bond, Michael, 131
boundary role stress, 478–479
    emotional labour and, 479
bounded rationality, 402
    cognitive biases and, 414
    problem identification difficulties and, 404
Branson, Richard, 418
breadth (of job), 214
British Petroleum (BP), 522
broad tendency, 128
Brooks, Bonnie, 343
Brown, Tim, 240
Bruner, Jerome, 87, 88
Bruner's perception model, 87–88
    perceptual consistency characteristic of perception
        process, 88
    perceptual constancy characteristic of perception
        process, 88
    selective characteristic of perception process, 88
Buckley, George, 554
buck passing, 447
buffing, 447
Buhler Industries Inc., 226
bullying, 480
    cyberbullying, 481–482
    forms of, 480
    in social service sector, 483, 491
    star performers as victims of, 481
bureaucracy, 12
    critique of, 12, 13
    human relations movement and, 12–13
    qualities of, 12
burnout, 478–479
    consequences of, 479
    gender and personality and, 479
    job demands-resources model and, 480
    work engagement as opposite of, 479–480
business communication,
    common vocabulary (COMVOC), 373
    jargon, 373–374
    non-verbal, 374–377
    verbal, 373–374

C

Cadsby, C. Bram, 208
Calgary Airport Authority, 69
Calgary International Airport, 69, 70
Calgary Sun, 45
Cameo Corp, 24
Campion, Michael, 259
Canadian Auto Workers (CAW) union, 319, 502
Canadian Broadcasting Corporation (CBC), 342, 351, 455
Canadian HR Reporter, 114

Canadian Nuclear Safety Commission, 447
Canadian Radio-television and Telecommunications
    Commission (CRTC), 506
Capital Power, 283, 284
Cappelli, Peter, 127
career development, 3
    coaching and feedback mentoring functions in, 287
    developmental assignments mentoring function in, 287
    exposure and visibility mentoring functions in, 287
    networking and, 444–445
    personality dimensions links to, 50
    sponsorship mentoring function in, 287
Carli, Linda, 344, 345
Carlsberg Group, 134, 152
casual Friday policies, 251
Catalyst Canada, 98
CBS Radio, 126
Center for Automobile Research, 319
Center for Creative Leadership, 129
Centers for Disease Control, 423
centralization, 12, 520–521
    factors dictating degree of, 520–521
central tendency (rater error in performance appraisal), 111
central traits, 89
chain of command, 12
    communication, 369
    filtering deficiencies in, 369–370
    informal communication deficiencies in, 369
    slowness deficiency in, 370
Challenger space launch (1986), 405, 451
Chang, Charles, 2, 3
change agents, 550
Change by Design, 240
change in organization, 547
Chapman, Derek, 110
charisma (idealized influence), 320, 336, 565
Chatterjee, Arijit, 509
Chugh, Molly, 290
classical viewpoint, 10, 12
    advocates of, 12
    compared to human relations approach, 13–14
    qualities of, 12
Coast Capital Savings Credit Union, 293, 301
coercive power, 433
cognitive biases, 402, 403
    after-the-fact accountability and, 407
    bounded rationality and, 406
    confirmation bias and, 405
    for paid information over free advice, 406
collaborating style (of conflict management), 469
collective efficacy, 256
collective organizational engagement, 25
collectivist societies, 131
Columbia space shuttle crash (2003), 297, 411
common vocabulary (COMVOC), 373
communication,
    see also organizational communication

business, 373–376
chain of command, 369
computer-mediated, 384–386
cross-cultural, 379–380
cultural context for, 383–384
definition of, 368
downward, 369
effective, 369
electronic, 384–385
etiquette differences across cultures, 381
gender differences in styles of, 377–378
grapevine, 371–373
horizontal, 369
informal, 369
information richness, 384
interpersonal, 368
language differences and, 379–380
non-verbal, 374–375
politeness differences across cultures, 381
process, 368
self-presentation bias, 381
social conventions across cultures, 382–383
upward, 369
companies,
American Express Canada, 106, 114
Apple Inc., 103, 126, 524, 542
Bell Canada, 215, 227, 288, 390
Blackberry Limited, 504
BMO Financial Group, 549
British Petroleum (BP), 522
Buhler Industries Inc., 226
Cameo Corp., 24
Capital Power, 283, 284
Carlsberg Group, 134, 152
Delta Hotels, 437
DevFacto Technologies Inc., 158–159, 160, 170
Disney Corp., 134
eBay, 451
Eli Lilly Canada, 68
EllisDon Corporation, 200–201, 202, 211, 219, 224, 228
Express Scripts Canada, 294–295
Facebook Inc., 44, 126–127, 377, 423, 451, 567
Fairmont Hotels and Resorts, 26
Federal Express Canada Ltd., 95
Fiat Chrysler Automobiles (FCA), 318
Ford Motor Company, 557, 561
General Electric Corp., 63
Goldcorp, 421
Google Canada, 294, 295, 299
Google Inc., 126, 423, 451
Hilti (Canada) Corp., 294, 295
Home Depot, 102
HP Advance Solutions, 102
Hudson's Bay Company (HBC), 26, 211, 297, 343
Husky Injection Molding Systems Ltd., 26, 211, 491
IBM, 103, 130, 298, 542, 545, 551, 557
IDEO, 240–241, 242, 251, 261
IT/NET Ottawa Inc., 68
Javelin Technologies Inc., 215
JPMorgan Chase, 398, 400, 401, 405, 409
Kicking Horse Coffee, 274–275, 276, 294, 298, 299, 300
Kinaxis, 301, 303
Kirmac Collection Services, 46
Lincoln Electric Company, 203
Marriott International, 567
McDonald's Corp., 500–501, 502, 521, 523
McKinney & Company, 44
Microsoft Corp., 63, 542–543, 544, 546
Minnesota Mining and Manufacturing Company (3M), 554, 563, 569, 570, 572
Netflix, 421, 422
NORDX/CDT, 226
Oracle Corporation, 296
Orange (prev. France Telecom), 264, 266, 462–463, 464, 475, 482
Orkin/PCO Services Corp., 19
PayPal, 451
PCL Constructors, 211
Photon Control Inc., 226
Rocky Mountain Soap Company, 301
Rogers Communications, 226
Royal Bank of Canada (RBC), 68, 82–83, 95, 211
Ryder System Inc., 371, 392
Samsung Corp., 134
Scotiabank, 103
Shell Canada Ltd., 95, 101
SNC-Lavalin Group Inc., 210, 229
Solar Press, 204
Target Inc., 403
Telus Corp., 21, 215
Telvent Canada Ltd., 288
Threadless, 421
Unilever Canada, 26
Vancouver City Savings Credit Union (*a.k.a.* Vancity), 490
Vega, 2–3
W. L. Gore & Associates Inc., 523
Walmart Canada, 102, 403
Western Electric, 12
WestJet Airlines, 296, 531
Weyerhaeuser Company, 180–181
Yahoo Inc., 126, 451, 456
Zappos, 525, 531
compensation, 6
competing style (of conflict management), 468
Competitive Advantage Through People, 7
complexity, 521
compliance, 277
compressed work week, 224, 225
research evidence for, 226
compromise style (of conflict management), 468
computer-mediated communication (CMC), 384–386
see also social media
compared to face-to-face groups, 386
Conference Board of Canada, 549

confirmation bias, 405
conflict stimulation, 474
congruence, 388
conjunctive tasks, 246–247
Connelly, Catherine, 443
conscientiousness dimension of personality, 49
    leadership and, 322
    relation to work behaviours, 49
consensus cues, 92
conservative shifts, 418
consideration, 325
    association between employees and leadership, 325
    consequences for leadership, 325
consistency cues, 91–92
constructive conflict, 474
contingency management approach, 13–14
    definition of, 14
contingency theory of leadership, 326–328
    measurement of LPC for orientation, 326
    situational favourableness in, 326–327
contingent reward leadership, 207
    compared to transformational leadership, 337
continuance (organizational) commitment, 150
continuous improvement concept, 558–559
contrast effects, 110
controlled motivation, 170
Cook, Tim, 103
Cooper, Cecily, 179
Cooper, Martin, 569
coordination of divided labour, 516–517
    direct supervision method, 516
    integration method, 517–518
    mutual adjustment method, 517
    output standardization method, 516–517
    skill standardization method, 517
    work process standardization method, 516
core-self-evaluations, 54–55
    four traits that make up, 54–55
    job performance and, 162
Cornell University, 567
corporate social responsibility (CSR), 24, 26
    report, 26
Courtright, Stephen H., 25
Crawford, Neil, 200
creative deviance, 565–566
creativity, individual, 564–565
creativity-related skills, 564–565
Cronin, David, 158, 159
Cropanzano, Russell, 140
Crosby, Philip, 558
cross-cultural communication, 379–381
cross-functional teams, 261
    autonomy factor in effectiveness of, 261–262
    composition factor in effectiveness of, 261
    leadership factor in effectiveness of, 262
    physical proximity factor in effectiveness of, 261
    rules and procedures factors in effectiveness of, 262

shared mental models and, 262
    superordinate goals factor in effectiveness of, 261
Crossley, Craig, 179
crowdsourcing, 420–421
    low-cost information technology and, 421
    social media and, 421
Cullen, John, 452
cultural context, 383–384
    high-context vs. low-context cultures, 383–384
    organizational communication and, 384
    organizational conflict and, 465
cultural distance, 132
cultural diversity, 19
    appreciation of global, 134–135
    in collectivist societies, 131, 132
    equity theory and, 184
    expectancy theory and, 184
    fairness and, 140
    gender roles, 131
    globalization and, 129
    implications of, 132–133
    importing of organizational theories to North America, 133–134
    in individualistic societies, 131, 132
    long-term orientation, 131
    personality and, 49
    power distance, 131
    self-determination theory (SDT) and, 184
    short-term orientation, 131
    translation of organizational theories to other cultures, 132–133
    uncertainty avoidance, 131
    work motivation theories and, 181, 183–184
    in work values, 129–130
cultural intelligence (CI), 135
    in Canada, 135
cultural maps, 132
culture, 292–293
    organizational, 292–294
    as social variable, 293
    strong as concept of, 294–295
culture clash, 296–297
customer departmentation, 515
cyberbullying, 481–482
cyberloafing, 386

D

Davidson, Willie G., 566
D'Cruz, Joseph, 319
deaf ear syndrome, 455
decentralization, 522
Dechief, Diane, 99
decisional roles of management, 14, 15
decision making,
    see also group decision making
    anchoring effect in, 407
    characteristics of top management and, 509

cognitive biases in, 404, 405, 406, 407

crowdsourcing as approach to improving, 420–421

definition of, 400

emotions involved in, 410–411

evidence-based management as approach to improve, 419–420

group, 414–415

group *vs.* individual, 415–416

information search for, 404–406

justification for faulty decisions, 409

maximization of alternative solutions, 406–407

moods involved in, 411, 413

problem identification, 403

problems and, 400–401

rational, 401–402

rational model of, 402–404

risk handling in, 407–408

satisficing in, 407

solution evaluation in, 408–409

solution implementation in, 408

vertical division of labour and, 510–511

well-structured problem and, 400–401

defence mechanisms, 487–488

  compensation, 488

  displacement, 488

  projection, 487

  rationalization, 487

  reaction formation, 488

defensive behaviours (in self-interest), 447

  buck passing, 447

  buffing, 447

  overconforming, 447

  scapegoating, 447

  stalling, 447

Delta Hotels, 437

Deming, W. Edwards, 558

demographics. *See* workplace demographics

departmentation, 512

  customer, 515

  functional, 512–513, 522

  geographic, 515

  hybrid, 516

  matrix, 514–515

  product, 513–514, 522

depth (of job), 214

Desai, Vinit, 549

DesRosiers, Dennis, 319

Dev, Chekitan, 567

developmental networks, 288–289

DevFacto Technologies Inc., 158–159, 160, 170

devil's advocate, 417

diagnosis, 550

Dickson, William J., 13

differentiation, 512

diffusion of innovative ideas, 570–571

  critical determinants in rate of, 571

  diffuse or die principle, 570

  factors in poor record of, 570

diffusion of responsibility, 415

Dimon, Jaime, 398, 399, 406

Discovery space mission (2005), 411

discrepancy reduction, 65

discrepancy theory of job satisfaction, 138

discrimination, 98

  age, 102

  ethnic-sounding names and, 99

  gender, 101

  LGBT, 103

disjunctive tasks, 246, 247

Disney Corp., 134

disposition, 140–141

  job satisfaction and, 140–141

dispositional approach, 47

dispositional attributions, 91

dissonance (from faulty decision), 409

distal goal, 180

distinctiveness cues, 92

distributed work programs, 227

distributive fairness (justice), 138–139

distributive negotiation, 470–471

  firmness *vs.* concessions in, 471

  persuasion as tactic in, 471

  promises as tactic in, 471

  salary negotiation as example of, 471

  tactics, 470–471

  threats as tactic in, 471

diversity. *See* workforce diversity

diversity training programs, 104–105

divestiture socialization, 284–285, 287

Dougherty, Thomas, 444, 445

Dow, Douglas, 82, 83

downward communication, 369

Drabinski, Garth, 297

Drew, Ina, 398

Drucker, Peter, 223

Duhaime, Pierre, 210

Durham, Cathy, 54

E

Eagly, Alice, 343, 344, 345

Easterbrook, Steve, 500, 501

eBay, 451

effect dependence, 276

  active listening principle of, 388

  social norms effects from, 277

effective communication, 369

  acceptance of other person principle of, 387

  difference assumption principle of, 388–389

  employee voice in, 370

  exhibit congruence principle of, 388

  non-confusion of person with problem principle of, 387–388

  recognition of cultural differences principle of, 389

  take the time principle for, 387

  timely and specific feedback principle of, 388

  watch your language principle of, 389

Eichenwald, Kurt, 542
Eisner, Michael, 335
Eli Lilly Canada, 68
Elliott, William, 431
EllisDon Corporation, 200–201, 202, 211, 219, 224, 228
Ellison, Larry, 296
Elsbach, Kimberly, 375
emotional contagion, 141
emotional intelligence (EI), 135, 162–164
    research, 164
emotional intelligence (EI) model, 163–164
    four sets of interrelated skills in, 163–164
emotional labour, 142
    boundary role stress and, 479
emotional regulation, 141–142
    consequences of requirement for, 142
emotional stability/neuroticism dimension of personality, 49
emotions, 141
employee orientation programs, 283–284
    Realistic Orientation Program for Entry Stress (ROPES), 283
    research evidence for, 284
employee recognition programs, 67–69
    effectiveness of, 67
    peer recognition programs, 68–69
employee stock ownership plans (ESOPs), 211
employee surveys, 6, 390
employee turnover, 20
Employment and Immigration Canada, 19
Employment Equity Act, 19
Employment Standards Act, 183
empowering leadership, 337
    high self-efficacy and, 337
    newcomer creativity and, 338
empowerment, 2, 3, 4, 6, 331
    definition of, 436
    high performance and, 437
    job satisfaction and, 437
    motivation part of, 436
    opportunity part of, 436
    organizational citizenship behaviours and, 437
    organizational commitment and, 437–438
    self-efficacy part of, 436–437
encounter stage (of organizational socialization), 279–280
enterprise social media, 386–387
entrepreneurship, 2, 4, 6
    corporate, 565
environmental, social, and governance (ESG) issues, 24, 26, 505
environmental uncertainty, 505–507
    complexity and rate of change in, 506
    effects of an increase in, 506–507
    resource dependence and, 507–508
Equal Employment Opportunity Commission (EEOC), 454
equity theory, 138, 174–175

cultural diversity and, 184
gender and equity, 175
inputs, 138
managerial implications of, 175–176
outcomes, 138
research support for, 175
work motivation and, 174–175
ERG (existence, relatedness, and growth) theory, 166–167
    compared to Maslow's hierarchy of needs, 166–167
    existence needs, 166
    growth needs, 166
    high- and low-scope jobs and, 215
    motivational premises of, 167
    relatedness needs, 166
    simplicity and flexibility of, 168–169
escalation of commitment, 409
    prevention of, 410
establishing legitimacy, 530, 532
ethical conflict, 287
ethical dilemmas, 450
ethical guidelines, 456–457
ethical leadership, 338–339
ethical misconduct, 448–449
    extreme performance pressure as cause of, 450
    gain as cause of, 450
    organizational and industry culture as causes of, 452–453
    personality as cause of, 452
    role conflict as cause of, 450–451
    sexual harassment, 454–455
    strong competition as cause of, 452
    strong organizational identification as cause of, 451–452
    time of day and, 453
ethics, 447–449
    definition of, 448
ethnic stereotyping, 98
Evans, Martin, 328
evidence-based management, 10
    analytics in, 421–422, 423
    as approach to improve decision making, 419–420
    big data in, 421, 422
    crowdsourcing in, 420–421
expectancy (component of expectancy theory), 172
expectancy theory of motivation, 171–173
    basis of, 173
    contingencies reward as managerial implication of, 174
    cultural diversity and, 184
    diverse needs appreciation as managerial implication of, 174
    expectancies boost as managerial implication of, 173–174
    expectancy component, 172
    force component, 172–173
    instrumentality component, 171
    mechanics of, 173
    outcomes component, 171
    relationship between performance and pay, 202
    research support for, 173
    valence component, 171–172

expert power, 434
explicit bias, 97
Express Scripts Canada, 294–295
external environment (of organizations), 502
   competitors as component of, 504
   complex, 506
   customers as component of, 504
   dynamic, 506
   environmental components of, 505
   environmental uncertainty in, 505–506
   general economy component of, 503–504
   interest groups as components of, 504–505
   simple, 506
   social and political factors as components of, 504
   static, 506
   suppliers as component of, 504
   technology as component of, 504
extinction strategy, 60
extraversion dimension of personality, 48–49
   leadership and, 322
   links to work behaviours, 49
   narcissism and, 323
   networking and, 444
extrinsic motivation, 161–162

F

Facebook Inc., 44, 126–127, 128, 377, 386, 423, 451, 482, 567
Fair and Impartial Policing (FIP), 97
Fairmont Hotels and Resorts, 26
fairness, 138–139, 331
   cultural differences in, 140
   distributive, 138–139
   procedural, 139–140
Faul, Don, 126
Fayol, Henri, 12
Federal Express Canada Ltd., 95
feedback, 217
feedback seeking, 291–292
Ferris, Gerald, 444
Fiat Chrysler Automobiles (FCA), 318
Fiedler, Fred, 326
filtering of information, 369–370
Fiorina, Carly, 335
First World War, 322
five-factor model (FFM) of personality, 48–49
   agreeableness dimension, 49
   conscientiousness, 49
   emotional stability/neuroticism dimension, 49
   extraversion dimension, 48–49
   links to job satisfaction, 50
   links to organizational behaviour, 49–50
   links to work motivation, 50
   openness to experience dimension, 49
flat organization, 519
flexibility, 5
flexible work arrangements, 224–225

compressed work week, 225
   distributed work programs, 227
   flex-time, 224
   job sharing, 224, 226
   telecommuting, 224, 227
   work sharing, 224, 226
flex-time, 224
   research evidence for, 225
Follett, Mary Parker, 12
force (component of expectancy theory), 172–173
Ford, Henry, 321
Ford Motor Company, 557, 561
formalization, 519–520
formal mentoring programs, 288
formal status systems, 250–251
formal work groups, 242
Forret, Monica, 444, 445
frame-of-reference (FOR) training, 113
framing, 402–403
   problem identification and, 404
French, John, 432
Fridell, Dr. Lorie, 97
Fry, Arthur, 563
functional departmentation, 512–513, 522
   career ladders advantage of, 513
   communication advantage of, 512
   disadvantages of, 513
   efficiency advantage of, 512
   measurement of specialists advantage of, 513
   training opportunities advantage of, 513
functional foremanship, 12
fundamental attribution error, 93

G

gainsharing, 212
   Scanlon Plan, 212
Galliford, Catherine, 430, 431, 453
gatekeepers, 566
Gates, Bill, 63, 298
Gawande, Dr. Atul, 422
gender stereotyping, 98–101, 343
   biased human resources decisions from, 100
   cultural differences in, 131
   nature of, 99–100
   performance evaluations and, 100–101
   training to reduce, 100
general cognitive ability, 162–163
General Electric Corp., 63
general self-efficacy (GSE), 54
Generation X (born 1965-1980), 128
geographic departmentation, 515
Gersick, Connie, 244
Gerstner, Louis, Jr., 298
Ghomeshi, Jian, 342, 351, 455
Giambrone, Adam, 11
Gino, Francesca, 377
glass ceiling, 344

globalization, 95
    appreciation of cross-cultural differences and, 134–135
    cultural differences and, 129
    cultural intelligence (CI) in, 135
    English as business language, 379–380
    racial and ethnic stereotypes in, 98
global leadership, 348–349
    dimensions in, 346–347
    duality characteristic in, 349
    personal character characteristic in, 348–349
    savvy characteristic in, 349
    unbridled inquisitiveness characteristic in, 348
Global Leadership and Organizational Behaviour Effectiveness
    (GLOBE) research project, 345
    cultural dimensions that distinguish societies, 345–346
    culturally endorsed implicit leadership theory, 346
    national leader profiles and attributes, 247
global leadership dimensions, 346–347
global recession, 502
GLOBE project, 131
Glomb, Theresa, 142, 482
goal accomplishment, 5, 22
goal orientation, 178
    learning, 178
    performance-avoid, 178
    performance-prove, 178
    research, 178
goal(s), 176
    see also Management by Objectives (MBO)
    distal, 180
    do-your-best (DYB), 181
    high-learning, 181
    high-performance, 181, 182
    low-performance, 182
    motivational, 176–177
    proximal, 180
    subconscious, 181
    superordinate, 261
goal(s), definition of, 176
goal setting, 22
    ethical behaviour in, 182
    goal orientation development in, 178
    management proactivity in, 179
    managerial trust in, 179
    negative effects of, 182
    proximal vs. distal goals, 180
    as self-regulation technique, 66
goal setting theory, 175–177
    factors in effects on performance, 181
    goal challenge characteristic of, 177
    goal commitment characteristic of, 177
    goal feedback characteristic of, 177
    goal specificity characteristic of, 176–177
    management support as effect in, 178
    managerial implications of, 181
    participation as an effect in, 177–178
    research support for, 180–181

rewards as effects in, 178
Goldcorp, 421
Google Canada, 294, 295, 299
Google Inc., 126, 423, 451
Gottlieb, Myron, 297
Gouldner, Alvin, 13
Graham, Molly, 127
Grant, Adam, 222
grapevine, 371–373
    characteristics, 372
    participants in, 372–373
    pros and cons, 373
    rumour and, 373
Great Place to Work Institute Canada, 107
Greenleaf, Robert, 341
Greenpeace, 7
Gregersen, Hal, 348
Grey's Anatomy (television show), 280
Grijalva, Emily, 323
group cohesiveness, 252–253
    group size factor influencing, 253
    increase in conformity consequence of, 254
    increase in effectiveness consequence of, 254–255
    increase in group activity participation consequence
        of, 254
    member diversity factor influencing, 252
    success factor influencing, 252
    threat and competition factors influencing, 252
    toughness of initiation factor influencing, 253
group decision making,
    acceptability of, 415
    commitment to, 415
    conflict disadvantage of, 415
    conservative shifts in, 418
    decision quality in, 414–415
    devil's advocate in, 417
    diffusion of responsibility in, 415
    domination disadvantage of, 416
    dynamics of shifts within, 418–419
    groupthink disadvantage of, 416–417
    managing controversy in, 417–418
    risk handling in, 418
    risky shifts in, 418
    stimulating controversy in, 417–418
    time disadvantage of, 415
group development, 242–243
    adjourning stage of, 243
    forming stage of, 243
    norming stage of, 243
    norms and, 247–249
    performing stage of, 243
    potential performance and, 245–246
    punctuated equilibrium model of, 244
    roles and, 248–250
    stability in, 244
    status and, 250–251
    storming stage of, 243

group effectiveness, 257
  in cross-functional teams, 260–261
  factors influencing work, 258–259
  in self-managed work teams, 259–260
  in virtual teams, 262–263
  work team composition and, 257–258
group identification,
  bases for, 464
  as factor in organizational conflict, 464–465
group membership, 242
  diversity in, 247
group norms, 258
group(s),
  definition of, 242
  formal work, 242
  informal work, 242
  interaction aspect of, 242
  project teams, 242
  task forces, 242
group structures, 245
  additive tasks and performance, 246, 247
  conjunctive tasks and performance, 246–247
  disjunctive tasks and performance, 246, 247
  group size characteristic, 245
  performance and size, 245
  satisfaction and size, 245
  size and process losses, 246
groupthink, 414, 416–417
  conformity pressure symptom of, 417
  illusion of invulnerability symptom of, 416
  illusion of morality symptom of, 417
  lack of controversy in, 418
  mindguards symptom of, 417
  outsider stereotypes symptom of, 417
  rationalization symptom of, 417
  self-censorship symptom of, 417
  symptoms of, 417
  unanimity illusion symptom of, 417
growth need strength, 218

H

Hackman, J. Richard, 215, 217, 218, 257
halo effect (in performance appraisal), 112
Hambrick, Donald C., 509
Han, Joo Hun, 207
hangover effect, 147
Harper, Stephen, 448
Harris, T. Brad, 338
harshness (rater error in performance appraisal), 111
Harvard Business Review, 320
Harvard Medical School, 421
Harvard University, 13, 44, 570
Hasenfrantz, Linda, 348
Hawthorne studies, 12–13
health and wellness, 4
Health Canada, 454
hierarchical organization, 430

Hilco Retail Consulting, 403
Hilti (Canada) Corp., 294, 295
hindsight, 410
Hodgetts, Richard, 15
Hofstede, Geert, 18, 130
Hofstede's study of value dimensions, 130–131,
  132, 345
holacracy organizational structure, 525, 531
Home Depot, 102
homophobia, 103
honeymoon effect, 147
horizontal communication, 369
horizontal division of labour,
  differentiation theme in, 512
  job design theme in, 511
Hospital for Sick Children, Toronto, 366, 368, 369, 389
House, Robert, 131, 328
Howell, Jane, 565
HP Advance Solutions, 102
Hsieh, Tony, 525
Hubble Space Telescope, 417
Hudson's Bay Company (HBC), 26, 211, 297, 343
human capital, 7
human relations movement,
  bureaucracy and, 12–13
  compared to classical viewpoint, 10, 12, 13–14
  definition of, 13
human resource management (HRM), 6, 25, 207
  compensation, 6
  definition of, 5–6
  effective, 6
  organizational behaviour and, 6
  recruitment, 6
  training, 6
Humphrey, Stephen, 221
Husky Injection Molding Systems Ltd., 26, 211, 491
Hutchinson, Angela, 2, 3
hybrid departmentation, 516

I

IBM, 103, 130, 298, 542, 545, 551, 557
idea champions, 565–566
  creative deviance and, 565
  intrapreneurs (corporate entrepreneurs), 565
  product champion, 565
identification, 277
IDEO, 240–241, 242, 251, 261
ill-structured problem, 401
immigration,
  workforce diversity and, 106
implicit bias, 97
implicit leadership theory, 346
implicit personality theories, 89
individualistic societies, 131
individualized socialization, 284–286
  compared to organizational socialization, 284–286
Industrial Revolution, 214

influence tactics, 438–439
  effectiveness of, 438
informal communication, 369
  grapevine, 372
informal status systems, 250, 251
  job performance and, 251
informal (work) groups, 242
informational roles of management, 14, 15
information dependence, 276
  social norm effects from, 277
information overload, 405
information richness, 384
  dimensions of, 384
  ranking media in terms of, 384
information search (after problem identification), 404
  cognitive biases in, 405
  more information is better, 406
information seeking, 291–292
initiating structure, 325
  association between employees and leadership, 325
  consequences for leadership, 325
innovation(s), 5
  creative deviance in, 565
  creativity-related skills in, 564–565
  definition of, 563
  design competitions for, 566
  effective communication with external
    environment and, 566
  effective communication within organization and, 566–568
  gatekeepers and, 566
  idea champions and, 565–566
  implementation of, 568
  individual creativity in, 564–565
  managerial, 563
  organizational factors in, 569
  as political process, 564
  process, 563
  product, 563
  resources for, 568–569
  rewards, 569–570
  serendipity of, 564
  time factor in, 569
Insider, The, (movie), 453
institutional managers, 439
instrumentality (component of expectation theory), 171
integration, 517–518
  integrator method of achieving, 518
  liaison role method of achieving, 518
  task force method of achieving, 518
integrative negotiation, 470, 471–472
  copious information exchange tactic in, 472
  cost cutting as tactic in, 472
  framing differences as opportunities tactic in, 472
  increasing resources tactic in, 472–473
  superordinate goals introduction as tactic in, 473
  tactics in, 471–472
integrators, 518

intelligence quotient (IQ), 135
  emotional intelligence (EI) and, 162–163
  general cognitive ability and, 162–163
  leadership and, 322
  role in performance of, 162–163
interactional fairness, 140
interactionist approach, 47–48
  trait activation theory and, 48
interest groups, 504–505
intergroup bias,
  emphasis on teams and, 464
  as factor in organizational conflict, 464–465
  self-esteem as factor in, 464
internalization, 277
international joint venture (IJV), 530
international management, 18
International Space Station (ISS), 260
interpersonal communication, 368
interpersonal conflict, 464
  abusive supervision, 481
  cyberbullying, 481–482
  definition of, 464
  job insecurity, 484
  role ambiguity, 484
  sexual harassment, 484–485
  work-family conflict, 482
  workplace bullying, 480
interpersonal roles of management, 14, 15
interrole conflict, 250
intersender role conflict, 250
interviews (for employment), 109–110
  contrast effects in, 110
  evaluation standardization structure of, 110
  perceptual tendencies in, 110
  question consistency structure of, 110
  question sophistication structure of, 110
  signalling theory and, 109
  structured, 110
  support building structure of, 110
intranets, 391
intrasender role conflict, 250
intrinsic motivation, 161–162
Isenberg, Daniel, 17
IT/NET Ottawa Inc., 68
Izquierdo, Chris, 158

J

Jago, Arthur, 332
Janis, Irving, 416
Japanese management techniques, 133–134
jargon, 373–374
Javelin Technologies Inc., 215
job characteristics model, 215–217
  autonomy, 217
  core job characteristics, 216–217
  critical psychological states, 218
  feedback, 217

growth need strength, 218
moderators, 218
outcomes, 218
research evidence, 218–219
skill variety, 217
task identity, 217
task significance, 217
job demands–resources model of work environment, 480
Job Descriptive Index (JDI), 137
job design, 213–214
historical views of, 214
Job Diagnostics Survey (JDS), 217–218
job enlargement, 220
job enrichment, 219–220
external client relationship establishment procedures in, 219
internal client relationship establishment procedures in, 219
lack of desire or skill problems with, 220
more direct feedback procedures in, 220
poor diagnosis problems with, 220
reward demand problems with, 220
supervision reduction procedures in, 219
supervisory resistance to, 221
task combination procedures in, 219
union resistance to, 220–221
work team formation procedures in, 219–220
job involvement, 219
job rotation, 215
Jobs, Steven, 335
job satisfaction, 49, 491
absenteeism as consequence of, 145–146
adequate compensation as contributor to, 144
affect as determinant of, 141–142
career opportunities as contributor to, 144
colleagues and superiors as contributors to, 144
context as contributor to, 144
core self-evaluations and, 55
customer satisfaction and, 149
desire differences in, 138
determinants of, 142–143, 145
discrepancy theory of, 137–138
disposition and, 140–141
distributive fairness and, 138–139
emotional contagion influence on, 141
emotional regulation influence on, 141–142
emotions affect in, 141
empowerment and, 437
facet aspect of, 136
interactional fairness and, 140
measurement of, 137
mental challenges as contributor to, 143
moods affect in, 141
organizational citizenship behaviour (OCB) and, 148
organizational profitability and, 149
overall aspect of, 137
perception differences in, 137–138
performance and, 147–148
personality and, 140–141
personality dimensions links to, 50, 53
proactive personality and, 54
procedural fairness and, 139–140
turnover as consequence of, 145–147
job scope, 214–215
breadth, 214
depth, 214
high function, 214–215
job rotation to increase, 215
low function, 214–215
motivational theories and, 215
motivation and, 214–215
stretch assignments and, 215
job sharing, 226
research evidence for, 226
Johnson, Blair, 343
Johnson, Leo, 274
joint venture, 530, 544
Jordan, Barbara, 321
Josselyn, Sheena, 366, 367
JPMorgan Chase, 398, 400, 401, 406, 409
Judge, Timothy, 54
Juran, Joseph, 558

K
Kahneman, Daniel, 408
Kammeyer-Mueller, John D., 142, 287
Kanter, Rosabeth Moss, 373, 434, 435
Karabus, Antony, 403
Keen, Linda, 447, 448
Keinan, Anat, 377
Kelleher, Herb, 335
Kicking Horse Coffee, 274–275, 276, 294, 298, 299, 300
Kim, Eugene, 482
Kim, Seongsu, 207
Kinaxis, 301, 303
King, Martin Luther, Jr., 321
Kirmac Collection Services, 46
knowing-doing gap, 571
reasons for, 571
knowledge hiding, 443
König, Cornelius, 381
Kotter, John, 16, 17
Kouchaki, Maryam, 453
Kozlowski, Steve, 260
Kroc, Ray, 298, 301, 521
Kruger, Jason, 386

L
labour pool, 95
laissez-faire leadership, 343
latchkey kids, 129
Lawson, Andrea, 22
leader-member exchange (LMX) theory, 334
research evidence for, 334
leader punishment behaviour, 325–326
leader reward behaviour, 325–326

leadership, 9
  association between orientation and group effectiveness, 326
  authentic, 339–341
  categorization theory of, 323–324
  charismatic, 336
  consideration behaviour in group setting, 325
  culture and, 345–346
  definition of, 320
  effectiveness and research evidence, 327–328
  effectiveness and traits, 322
  empowering, 337–338
  ethical, 338–339
  Five Factor Model (FFM) of personality and, 322
  formal, 321
  gender and, 343–344
  gender traits, 344–345
  global, 348–349
  global dimensions in, 346–347
  group setting behaviours of, 324–325
  informal, 321
  intelligence and, 322
  laissez-faire, 343
  leader-member exchange (LMX) theory of, 334
  least preferred co-worker (LPC) to measure orientation, 326
  narcissism and, 323
  participative, 330
  reward and punishment behaviours, 325–326
  servant, 341
  situational theories of, 326–327
  strategic, 320–321
  structure initiation behaviour in group setting, 325
  study of traits, 322
  styles, situational factors and effectiveness of, 349–350
  trait theory of, 321
  transactional, 334–335
  transformational, 335–337
leadership categorization theory, 323–324
leadership orientation, 326
  measurement of, 326
learning, 55
  cultural awareness category of, 55
  interpersonal skills category of, 55
  intrapersonal skills category of, 55
  operant learning theory, 56
  practical skills category of, 55
  reinforcement process and, 56–60
  self-regulation and, 66
  social cognitive theory (SCT) of, 62–63
  during socialization, 278
learning goal orientation, 178
learning organization, 548–549
  critical dimensions for, 548–549
  success *vs.* failure outcomes for, 549
least preferred co-worker (LPC), 326
  high *vs.* low LPC, 326–328
Lee, Ray, 447
legitimate power, 432–433

Leiter, Michael, 478
leniency (rater error in performance appraisal), 111
lesbian, gay, bisexual, and transgender (LGBT), 19, 84, 97
Levine, Dennis, 450
Lewenza, Ken, 319, 320
Lewin, Kurt, 546
Lewis, Michael, 421
LGBT, 19, 84, 97
LGBT-inclusive workplace, 103
LGBT stereotyping, 103
Li, Andrew, 140
liaison role, 518
Likert, Rensis, 13
Lincoln Electric Company, 203
line-of-sight and performance-reward expectancy, 207
Lipnack, Jessica, 522
Locke, Edwin, 54
locus of control personality dimension, 50–51, 475–476
Loeb, Daniel, 451
Lombard, Didier, 462
LPC. *See* least preferred co-worker (LPC)
lump sum bonus, 206
Luthans, Fred, 15, 16
Lutz, Robert, 474

M

Machiavelli, Niccolo, 446
Machiavellianism, 446–447
  characteristics of situations favoured by, 446
  high *vs.* low, 446
Maclean's, 24, 44
Madsen, Peter, 549
Making Change Work, 545
management, 4
  abusive, 64
  classical viewpoint of, 10, 12
  complexity of roles of, 15
  contemporary concerns of, 18–19
  contingency approach to, 13–14
  decisional roles, 14, 15
  definition of, 10
  disseminator role of, 15
  disturbance handler role of, 15
  entrepreneur role of, 15
  evidence-based, 10
  figurehead role of, 15
  human relations movement, 10, 12
  human resource management activities of, 15
  informational roles, 14, 15
  international, 18
  interpersonal roles, 14, 15
  leadership role of, 15
  liaison role, 15
  monitor role of, 15
  negotiator role of, 15
  networking activities of, 15
  practices and organizational behaviour, 8

resource allocation role of, 15
roles, 14–15
routine communication activities of, 15
spokesperson role of, 15
talent, 23
traditional management activities of, 15
management by exception, 334
Management by Objectives (MBO), 223–224
management-individual workers interactions, 223
research evidence for, 223–224
management incentive program (MIP), 219
management style, 274
managerial activities, 15–16
agenda implementation, 16–17
agenda setting, 16
intuition, 17
networking, 16
managerial intuition, 17
Manitoba Hydro, 95
Marchionne, Sergio, 318, 319, 320, 322, 336, 348, 350
Marriott International, 567
Maslach, Christine, 478
Maslow, Abraham, 165, 166, 167, 202, 251
Maslow's hierarchy of needs, 165–166
belongingness needs, 165
compared to ERG theory, 166–167
esteem needs, 165
high- and low scope jobs and, 215
hypotheses of, 168–169
physiological needs, 165
relationship between pay and performance and, 202
safety needs, 165
self-actualization needs, 165–166
Massachusetts Institute of Technology (MIT), 14, 418
master of business administration (MBA), 50
matrix departmentation, 514–515
variations of, 514–515
Mawritz, Mary Bardes, 64
maximization (of alternative solutions), 406–407
Mayer, John, 163
Mayflower Group, 557
Mayo, Elton, 13
McAlinden, Sam, 319
McCain, Michael, 339, 340
McClelland, David, 167, 438
McClelland's theory of needs, 167–168
need for achievement (n Ach), 167–168
need for affiliation (n Aff), 168
need for power (n Pow), 168
predictions based on, 169
McDonald's Corp., 500–501, 502, 510, 521, 523
McGill University, 349
McKinney & Company, 44
McKinnon, Mike, 158
mechanistic structures, 523
mediation, 473
Melnyk, Roman, 366, 367

mental ability, 162
mental health, 22
mental illness, 20–21
mentor(ing), 286–287
career developmental function of, 286–288
cross-race programs, 291
formal mentoring programs, 288
psychological developmental function of, 286, 288
race and ethnicity in, 290–291
research evidence for, 291
university, 290
women and, 289–290
mergers, 529, 544
merit pay plans, 205
compared to wage incentive plans, 205–206
low discrimination problem with, 206
lump sum bonus, 206
pay secrecy problem with, 206–207, 208–209
small increases problem with, 206
Merlo, Janet, 430
Mesmer-Magnus, Jessica, 265
Metro Vancouver Transit Police, 97
Meyer, John, 150, 151
Michigan State University, 260
Microsoft Corp., 63, 542–543, 544, 546
Milkman, Katherine, 290
Millennials (born 1981–2000), 126, 128, 567
Minnesota Mining and Manufacturing Company (3M), 554, 563, 569, 570, 572
Minnesota Satisfaction Questionnaire (MSQ), 137
Mintzberg, Henry, 14, 15, 349
modular organization, 527–528
Molly, John T., 376
Moneyball (movie), 421
moods, 141
Mooney, James D., 12
Moore, Karl, 349
Morgeson, Frederick, 221
Morrison, Allen, 348
motivating work design, 25
motivation. *See* work motivation
motivational personality traits, 54
motivational work practices, 228
summary of, 229
Mount Royal University, 44
multinationals, 19, 264
mum effect, 370–371

N

Nadella, Satya, 543
Nader, Ralph, 321
narcissism, 322
chief executive officer (CEO), 509
National Aeronautics and Space Administration (NASA), 260, 411, 417
pathological culture at, 297
National Business Ethics Survey of the US Workforce, 448, 454

National Research Council, 530

need for achievement (n Ach), 167–168

need for affiliation (n Aff), 168

need for power (n Pow), 168

need theories (of work motivation), 164–165
diversity appreciation and, 169
ERG theory, 166–167
ERG theory compared to Maslow's hierarchy of needs, 166–167
intrinsic motivation appreciation and, 169
Maslow's hierarchy of needs, 165–166
McClelland's theory of needs, 167–168
relationship between performance and pay and, 202
research support for, 168–169

Neeleman, David, 531

negative affectivity (NA), 53
emotional tendencies and, 53
stress and, 476

negative reinforcement, 56–57

negotiation, 469–470
arbitration and, 473
in conflict management, 469–470
distributive, 470–471
integrative, 470, 471–472
mediation and, 473
stereotype of, 469
third-party involvement in, 473

Nenshi, Naheed, 44, 45, 46, 50

Netflix, 421, 422

networking, 16
as aspect of political skill, 444–446
aspects of, 444
diverse, 445–446
extraversion and, 444
high self-esteem and, 444
increase in importance of, 445

network organization, 526
flexibility and adaptability advantages of, 527

non-verbal communication, 374–377
body language, 374–375
clothing and, 376–377
cultural differences in, 380
employment interviewers and, 375
nonconformists and, 377
office decor and arrangement, 375–376

NORDX/CDT, 226

normative (organizational) commitment, 150

norms, 247
see also social norms
dress, 248
equality, 248
equity, 248
group, 258
official organizational, 248
performance, 248
reciprocity, 248
reward allocation, 248
social responsibility, 248

Nutt, Paul, 407

O

observational learning, 63
as component of social cognitive theory (SCT), 62–63
as a process, 63
self-reinforcement in, 63

occupational injury, 53

Office, The (television program), 69

Ohio State University, 325

Oldham, Greg, 215, 217, 218

Ontario Human Rights Commission, 102

Ontario Lottery and Gaming Corporation (OLG), 206

Ontario Provincial Police (OPP), 283

open-door policy, 3, 4

openness to experience dimension of personality, 49

open systems concept of an organization, 503

operant learning theory, 56
compared to social cognitive theory (SCT), 62

Oracle Corporation, 296

Orange (prev. France Telecom), 264, 266, 462–463, 464, 475, 482

O'Reilly, Charles, 524

Oreopoulos, Philip, 99

organic structures, 523
ambidextrous organization, 524–525
modular organization, 527–528
network and virtual organizations, 526–527
strategic response, forms of, 528–531

organizational behaviour, 4
attitude formation and, 128–130
attitudes as interest of, 5
company effectiveness from, 7–8
compensation aspects of, 4
corporate social responsibility (CSR) and, 24, 26
cultural aspects of, 4
definition of, 4, 5–6
dispositional approach to, 47
diversity and, 19
empowerment aspect of, 3, 4, 6
engagement aspect of, 4
entrepreneurship aspect of, 2, 4, 6
explanation goal of, 9–10
fields in, 6
health and wellness aspect of, 4
human resource management and, 6
importance of, 7
interactionist approach to, 47–48
issues involved in, 6
links to five-factor model (FFM) of personality, 49–50
locus of control personality dimension and, 49–50
management goal of, 10
motivational aspects of, 4
national cultures and, 18
personality and, 47–48
predictions goal of, 9
reasons for studying, 6–7
reward aspect of, 4
self-monitoring and, 52
situational approach to, 47

to survive and adapt, 5
value aspect of, 4
valuing diversity, 95–96
variances in, 7
work-life conflict and, 19–20, 20–21
organizational behaviour modification (O.B. Mod), 66–67
organizational change, 544–546
   see also organizational development (OD)
   change agents in, 550
   change stage in process of, 547
   culture as factor in, 546
   diagnosis stage in process of, 550
   evaluation stage in process of, 553
   goals and strategies as factors in, 545
   impact of external environment on, 544–545
   impact of internal environment on, 544–545
   institutionalization stage in process of, 553–554
   job design as factor in, 545–546
   knowing-doing gap in, 571
   people as factor in, 546
   processes as factors in, 546
   reengineering, 560–561
   refreezing stage in process of, 547
   resistance stage in process of, 550–551
   structure as factor in, 546
   technology as factor in, 545
   unfreezing stage in process of, 546
organizational citizenship behaviour (OCB), 148–149
   forms of, 148
   job satisfaction and, 148
organizational commitment,
   affective type of, 150
   changes in employee's commitment, 151
   changes in focus of employee's commitment, 151
   consequences of, 150–151
   continuance type of, 150
   definition of, 150
   key contributors to, 150
   multiplicity of employer-employee relationship, 151
   normative type of, 150
organizational communication, 369–371
   see also communication
   cultural context and, 384
   effective management training to improve, 391
   employee surveys to improve, 390
   explanation provision to improve, 389
   intranets to improve, 391
   suggestion systems to improve, 390
   telephone hotlines to improve, 390
   360-degree feedback to improve, 389–390
   webcasts to improve, 391
organizational conflict, 464–466
   accommodating style of managing, 468
   ambiguity and, 466
   avoiding style of managing, 468
   collaborating style of managing, 469
   competing style of managing, 468
   compromise style of managing, 468

conflict stimulation and, 474
constructive, 474
culture and, 465
dynamics of, 467
group identification as factor in, 464–465
heavy executive responsibility as stressor in, 477
interdependence as stage for, 465
intergroup bias as factor in, 464–465
negotiating style of managing, 469–470
power and, 465
process conflict type of, 466
relationship type of, 466
role overload as stressor in, 476–477
scare resources and, 466
status and, 465
strategies for managing, 467–468
stress model of, 474–475
task conflict type of, 466
workplace bullying, 480
organizational culture, 6
   characteristics of, 293
   definition of, 292 293
   founder's role in, 297 298
   learning of, 55
   rituals, 300, 301–302
   socialization as key to, 298–299
   socialization steps in creating a strong, 299–300
   stories, 300, 302
   strong as concept of, 294–295
   subcultures, 293–294
   symbols, 300
organizational development (OD), 554–556
   see also organizational change
   change agents in, 555
   definition of, 554–555
   research into, 562–563
   reviews of, 562–563
   survey feedback strategy of, 556–557
   team building strategy in, 555–556
   total quality management (TQM) and, 558–559
   use of behavioural science knowledge, 555
   weak methodology in reviews of, 563
organizational ethics, 447–449
   definition of, 448
   ethical misconduct, 448–450
   stakeholders and, 448
organizational identification, 278
organizational justice theory, 109
organizational learning, 548
   knowledge acquisition process of, 548
   knowledge development process of, 548
organizational learning practices, 66–70
   behaviour modelling training (BMT), 70
   employee recognition programs, 67–69
   organizational behaviour modification
       (O.B. Mod), 66–67
   training and development programs, 69–70
organizational membership, 202

organizational politics, 442–443
  defensive behaviours, 447
  definition of, 442
  ethical guidelines, 456–457
  Machiavellianism, 446–447
  means/end matrix for, 442
  particular conditions and locations for, 443
  political skill in, 444–445
organizational processes, 560
  reengineering as, 560–561
organizational socialization, 277–279
  anticipatory stage of, 279
  compared to individualized socialization, 284–286
  culture as key to, 298–299
  developmental networks, 288–289
  employee orientation programs, 283–284
  encounter stage of, 279–280
  ethical conflict and, 287
  methods, 281–282
  organizational identification objective
    of, 278–279
  person-group fit objective of, 278
  person-job fit objective of, 278
  person-organization fit objective of, 278
  process, 277–278
  role management stage of, 280
  socialization tactics, 284–286
  steps in creating strong culture, 299–300
  unrealistic expectations in, 280–281
organizational strategy, 508–510
organizational structure,
  centralization characteristic of, 520–521
  complexity of, 521
  decentralized, 522
  definition of, 510
  departmentation, 512–513
  flat organization characteristic of, 519
  formalization characteristic of, 519–520
  holacracy, 525
  horizontal division of labour, 511–512
  mechanistic, 523
  mechanistic vs. organic, 523
  modular organization, 527–528
  network organization, 526
  organic, 523
  size of, 521–522
  span of control characteristic of, 518–519
  tall organization characteristic of, 519
  vertical division of labour, 510–511
  virtual organization, 526–527
organizational support theory, 107–108
organizations,
  definition of, 4
  effective teamwork characteristic of, 5
  factors that make successful, 6
  goal accomplishment component of, 5
  group effort component of, 5
  innovation as strategic priority, 5

  as social inventions, 4
  socialization process of, 6
Orkin/PCO Services Corp., 19
outcomes (component of expectancy theory), 171
outsourcing, 528
overconforming, 447

P

Parisien, La, 462
Parsons, Lee, 200
participative leadership, 330
  acceptance as potential advantage of, 331
  beneficial outcomes from, 333
  decision tree for, 332–333
  lack of knowledge as potential problem of, 331
  lack of receptivity as potential problem of, 331
  loss of power as potential problem of, 331
  motivation as potential advantage of, 330–331
  quality as potential advantage of, 331
  situational model of participation, 332
  time and energy as potential problems of, 331
Pascale, Richard, 299
path-goal theory, 328, 334
  achievement-oriented leader behaviour, 328
  directive leader behaviour, 328
  employee characteristics as situational factors in, 328–329
  employee types need different leadership forms, 329
  environmental factors as situational factors in, 328, 329
  participative leader behaviour, 328, 330
  research evidence for, 329
  supportive leader behaviour, 328
pay-for-performance programs, 202–207
PayPal, 451
pay (wages), 202–203
  see also teamwork pay plans
  expectancy theory and, 202
  hierarchy terminology and, 202
  lump sum bonus, 206
  to motivate teamwork, 210–211
  need theories and, 202
  piece rate, 202
  relationship to performance, 202–206
  wage incentive plans, 202–205
PCL Constructors, 211
peer recognition programs, 68
perceived organizational support (POS), 107–108
  factors that contribute to employees', 108
  job performance and, 108
  perceived supervisor support as contribution to, 108
perceived supervisor support, 108
perceiver, 84, 85
  perceptual defence phenomenon, 85
perceptions, 84–86
  attributions and, 91
  basic biases in, 88–89
  definition of, 84
  in employment interview, 109–110
  in human resources, 108–110

perceiver component of, 84–85
perceiver target component of, 84, 85–86
perception context component of, 84
perceptual defence phenomenon in, 85
in performance appraisal, 111–112
primacy effect of, 88
process of, 87–88
projection of thoughts and feelings on, 89
recency effect of, 88
reliance on central traits for, 89
signalling theory and, 109
stereotyping and, 90–91
perceptual consistency, 88
perceptual constancy, 88
perceptual defence, 85
perfect rationality, 402
  cognitive biases and, 414
  justification of faulty decisions and, 409–410
performance, 162
  emotional intelligence (EI) as predictor of, 163–164
  general cognitive ability as predictor of, 163
  intelligence role in, 162–163
  motivational components of, 164–165
  over-reporting of, 208
  production jobs and pay linkage to, 205–206
  relationship to pay, 202–206
  relationship with motivation, 164–165
  white collar jobs and pay linkage to, 205–206
performance appraisal, 111–112
  behaviourally anchored rating scale (BARS), 113
  frame-of-reference (FOR) training, 113
  objective measures in, 111
  rater errors in, 111–112
  subjective measures in, 111
performance-avoid goal orientation, 178
performance bonuses, 3, 4
performance feedback, 58
performance-prove goal orientation, 178
performance-reward expectancy, 207
personal identity, 86
personality, 46–47
  agreeableness dimension of, 49
  burnout and, 479
  as cause of ethical misconduct, 452
  characteristics of, 47–48
  conscientiousness dimension of, 49
  constituents of, 46
  cultural differences and, 49
  definition of, 46
  emotional stability/neuroticism dimension of, 49
  extraversion dimension of, 48–49
  five factor model (FFM) (*a.k.a.* Big Five traits) of, 48–49,
    141, 162, 322, 375
  implicit theories of, 89
  links to career success, 50
  links to job satisfaction, 50
  links to motivation, 50
  locus of control dimension of, 50–51

motivational compared to affective traits of, 54
  narcissism as trait, 323
  negative affectivity (NA) trait of, 53
  openness to experience dimension of, 49
  organizational behaviour and, 47–48
  positive affectivity (PA) trait of, 53
  proactive, 54
  relationship to adaptive performance, 51
  self-esteem dimension of, 52–53
  self-monitoring dimension of, 51–52
  stress and, 475–476
personality tests, 47
personal power managers, 439
person-group (PG) fit, 278
person-job (PJ) fit, 278, 286, 292
person-organization (PO) fit, 278, 286
person-role conflict, 250
person-situation debate, 47
Peters, Tom, 5
Pfeffer, Jeffrey, 7, 571
Photon Control Inc., 226
piece rate, 202
Pitt, Brad, 421
political skill,
  apparent sincerity facet of, 444
  interpersonal influence facet of, 444
  networking ability facet of, 444–446
  social astuteness facet of, 444
positive affectivity (PA), 53
  emotional tendencies and, 53
positive organizational behaviour (POB), 22–23
  psychological capital (PsyCap) and, 22–23
positive reinforcement, 56
power,
  coercive, 433
  cultivating the right people in obtaining, 435
  definitions of, 432
  dependence in relationships of, 440
  doing the right things in obtaining, 434–435
  expert, 434
  extraordinary activities in obtaining, 435
  influence tactics in, 438–439
  legitimate, 432–433
  need for, 439
  organizational conflict and, 465
  outsiders cultivation in obtaining, 435
  peer cultivation in obtaining, 436
  referent, 433
  relevant activities in obtaining, 435
  responsible use of, 439
  reward, 433
  seekers of, 439
  subordinate cultivation in obtaining, 435
  subunit, 440
  superior cultivation in obtaining, 436
  visible activities in obtaining, 435
power distance, 131
presenteeism, 486–487

primacy effect, 88
Princess Margaret Hospital, Toronto, 412
proactive behaviour, 54
  in goal setting, 179
proactive personality, 54
  relationship to work outcomes, 54
proactive socialization, 291–292
  boss-relationship-building behaviour, 292
  feedback-seeking behaviour, 291–292
  general socializing behaviour, 292
  information-seeking behaviour, 291–292
  job-change-negotiation behaviour, 292
  networking behaviour, 292
  relationship-building behaviour, 292
  research evidence for, 292
problem, 400
  alternative solutions to, 406
  cognitive biases and, 403
  framing, 402–403
  ill-structured, 401
  program as standardized way of solving, 400–401
  solution evaluation, 408–409
  solution implementation, 408
  well-structured, 400–401
problem identification,
  framing and, 404
  functional specialty definition difficulties with, 404
  perceptual defence difficulties with, 404
  problem solution definition difficulties with, 404
  problem symptom diagnosis difficulties with, 404
problem solving, 486
procedural fairness (justice), 139–140
process conflict, 466
process losses, 246
process theories (of work motivation), 165, 171–174
product departmentation, 513–514, 522
  advantages of, 513
  disadvantages of, 514
profit sharing, 3, 4, 6, 207
  as group-oriented incentive system, 211
program, 400–401
projection of thoughts and feelings, 89
prosocial motivation, 222–223
proximal goal, 180
proximal socialization outcomes, 278–279
Prue, Michael, 183
PsyCap interventions (PCI), 23
psychological capital (PsyCap), 22–23
  components of, 22–23
psychological characteristics, 46
psychological contract, 281
psychological contract breach, 281
psychological safety, 370
punctuated equilibrium model (of group development),
  244–245
  advice from, 244–245
  midpoint transition in, 244

  phase 1 of, 244
  phase 2 of, 244
punishment strategy, 59, 60
  characteristics of punishment and, 60–61
  to control behaviour, 433
  difficulties with, 61
  effectiveness of, 60–62
  principles to increase effectiveness of, 61–62

Q
Q (radio program), 342, 351, 455
Quinton, Leslie, 210

R
racial stereotyping, 98, 99
rater errors (in performance appraisal), 111–112
  central tendency, 111
  halo effect, 112
  harshness, 111
  leniency, 111
  similar-to-me effect, 112
rational decision-making model, 402–404
Raven, Bertram, 432
realistic job previews, 282–283
  compared to traditional job previews, 282–283
  research evidence into, 283
Realistic Orientation Program for Entry Stress (ROPES), 283
recency effect, 88
recruitment, 6
Redies, Tracy, 293
reengineering, 560–561
  creeping bureaucracy factor in, 560
  definition of, 560
  goals of, 561
  new information technology as stimulant for, 560–561
  organizational processes in, 560
  practices, 561
  radical change goal of, 560, 561
referent power, 433
refreezing, 547
registered retirement savings plan (RRSP), 159
Reichardt, Carl, 300
reinforcement process, 56
  diversity-neglecting organizational error in, 57–58
  extinction strategy in, 60
  learning of values through, 128
  negative, 57, 59, 61
  performance feedback and, 58
  positive, 56, 59, 61
  punishment strategy in, 59, 60
  reward confusion organizational error in, 57
  social recognition and, 58
  strategies, 58–59
relational architecture of jobs, 222–223
relationship conflict, 466
religious stereotyping, 98
resistance (to organizational change), 550–551

different assessments of situation cause of, 551, 552
lack of trust cause of, 551, 552
low individual tolerance cause of, 551, 552
methods for overcoming, 552–553
politics and self-interest causes of, 551, 552
resistant organized culture cause of, 551, 552
strong emotions cause of, 551, 552
unnecessary theme as challenge to, 551
unobtainable theme as challenge to, 551
resource dependence, 507–508
strategic responses to, 508–509
restricted stock-unit (RSU) grants, 210
restriction of productivity, 204
restructuring, 500–501
Retail Survival, The: Re-Imagining Business for The New Age of Consumerism, 403
retention bonuses, 210
return on assets (ROA), 23
reward power, 433
Rich, Bruce L., 287
Richardson, Michele, 22
risky shift, 418
Robertson, Brian, 525
Rocky Mountain Soap Company, 301
Roddick Anita, 373
Roethlisberger, Fritz, 13
Rogers Communications, 226
role ambiguity, 249–250
see also role assumption process
interpersonal conflict and, 484
practical consequences of, 149
role assumption process, 249–250
see also role ambiguity
focal person factor in ambiguity in, 249
organizational factors and ambiguity in, 249
role sender factor and ambiguity in, 249
role conflict, 250
interrole, 250
intrasender, 250
intresender, 250
person-role, 250
practical consequences of, 250
role congruity theory, 344
role management, 280
role overload, 476–477
role(s), 248–250
designated (assigned), 249
emergent, 249
Rosen, Larry, 377
Rosenfeld, Elana, 274, 275
Rosenkrantz, Stuart, 15
Rotundo, Maria, 142
Royal Bank of Canada (RBC), 68, 82–83, 95, 211
Royal Canadian Mounted Police (RCMP), 210, 297, 430–431, 432, 433, 452, 455
rumour, 373
Ryder System Inc., 370, 392

S

Salas, Eduardo, 260
Salovey, Peter, 163
Samsung Corp., 134
satisficing, 407
Save the Children, 263
Scanlon, Joe, 212
Scanlon (gainsharing) Plan, 212
scapegoating, 447
Schaufeli, Wilmar, 478
Schein, Edgar, 284
Schwarzkopf, "Stormin" Norman, 335
scientific management, 12
qualities of, 12
Scotiabank, 103
Searcy, Tom, 377
Second World War, 13, 47, 322
self-determination theory (SDT) of motivation, 169–170
autonomy support, 170–171
cultural diversity and, 184
importance of basic psychological needs, 170
needs as universal necessities for psychological health, 170
self-efficacy, 22, 256
behavioural plasticity theory of, 52–53
burnout and low, 478
empowering leadership and high, 337
empowerment and, 436–437
self-efficacy beliefs, 64–65
as component of social cognitive theory (SCT), 62, 64–65
determinants of, 65
importance of, 65
self-esteem, 46
comparison of high and low, 52–53
as factor in intergroup bias, 464
networking and, 111
self-evaluation, 65
self-interest,
buck-passing defensive behaviours for, 447
buffing defensive behaviour for, 447
overconforming defensive behaviour for, 447
protection of, 447
scapegoating defensive behaviour for, 447
stalling defensive behaviour for, 447
self-managed work teams, 257–258
business training support for, 259
diversity of membership in effectiveness of, 258
expertise of membership in effectiveness of, 258
language skills support for, 259
management support for, 259
reward support for, 259
size of membership in effectiveness of, 258
social skills support for, 259
stability of membership in effectiveness of, 258
tasks for, 257–258
technical training support for, 259
training support for, 259

self-monitoring, 51–52
　organizational behaviour and, 52
self-observation, 65, 66
self-perception, 86
self-presentation bias, 381
self-regulation, 65–66
　as component of social cognitive theory (SCT), 62, 65–66
　discrepancy reduction in, 65
　goal-setting technique of, 66
　high-performance goals and, 182
　learning and, 66
　model observation technique of, 66
　rehearsal technique of, 66
　self-observation data collection technique of, 66
　self-reinforcement technique of, 66
self-reinforcement, 63, 65
　as self-regulation technique, 66
self-selection application process, 283
self-serving bias, 94
servant leadership, 341
　authenticity characteristic of, 341
　empowering and developing people characteristic of, 341
　humility characteristic of, 341
　interpersonal acceptance characteristic of, 341
　providing direction characteristic of, 341
　stewardship characteristic of, 341
severe acute respiratory syndrome (SARS), 502
sexual harassment, 430–431
　deaf ear syndrome and, 455
　definition of, 454
　as form of unethical behaviour, 454–455
　interpersonal conflict and, 484
　minority women and, 455
　organizational measures to deal with, 455
　prevalence of, 455
shared mental models, 262
Sheldon, Courtney, 82
Shell Canada Ltd., 95, 101
Sicard, John, 301
Sierra Club, 7
signalling theory, 109
similar-to-me effect (in performance appraisal), 112
Simon, Herbert, 17, 402
Simon, Lauren S., 287
situational approach, 47
situational attributions, 91
situational model of participation, 332
　effective strategies in, 332
　research evidence for, 332–333
situational theories of leadership, 326–327
　contingency theory, 326–328
　path-goal theory, 328–329
situation (component of perception), 84, 86
60 Minutes (television program), 453
skill-based pay, 212–213
skill variety, 217
Skinner, B. F., 56

Smith, Geoff, 200
Smith, Isaac, 453
Smith, Troy A., 25
SNC-Lavalin Group Inc., 210, 229
social categorizations, 86
social cognitive theory (SCT), 62–63
　compared to operant learning theory, 62
　observational learning component of, 62–63
　self-efficacy beliefs component of, 62, 64–65
　self-regulation component of, 62, 65–66
　triadic reciprocal causation in, 62
social conformity, 277
　compliance motive for, 277
　identification motive for, 277
　internalization motive for, 277
social dilemma, 255
social exchange theory, 334
social identity theory, 86–87
　in perception formation, 87
social influence, 276–277
social information processing theory, 276
　compliance, 277
　identification, 277
　internalization, 277
socialization,
　see also organizational socialization
　of Baby Boomers, 128–129
　definition of, 277–278
　divestiture, 284–285, 287
　of Generation X, 129
　of Generation Y, 129
　importance of, 278–279
　as key to culture of organization, 298–299
　during learning, 278
　mentoring as process in, 286–287
　proactive, 291–292
　process, 277–278
　steps in creating strong culture in, 299–300
　of Traditionalists, 128
socialization tactics, 284–286
　collective vs. individual tactics, 284–285, 286
　ethical conflict and, 287
　fixed vs. variable tactics, 284–285
　formal vs. informal tactics, 284–285
　investiture vs. divestiture tactics, 284–285
　research evidence into, 286
　sequential vs. random tactics, 284–285
　serial vs. variable tactics, 284–285
social loafing, 255–256, 258
　counteractions, 256
　effect of on group performance, 256
　free rider effect, 255
　sucker effect, 255–256
social media, 44, 386, 567
　see also computer-mediated
　　communication (CMC),
　crowdsourcing and, 421

enterprise, 386–387
    to improve organizational communication, 391
    organizational challenges of, 386
    organizational opportunities for, 386–387
social norms, 55
    see also norms
    compliance, 248
    definition of, 247
    development of, 247–248
    information and effect dependency effects on, 277
social recognition, 58
Solar Press, 204
Song, Fei, 208
Sozzi, Brian, 403
span of control, 518–519
specialization, 12
stage model of group development, 243
stakeholders, 448
stalling, 447
Stamps, Jeffrey, 522
standardization, 12
Stanford University, 88
Stanton, John, 298
Statistics Canada, 20, 344
status, 250–251
    consequences of differences in, 251
    formal status systems, 250–251
    informal status systems, 250, 251
    organizational conflict and, 465
    reduction of barriers to, 251
status symbols, 250
Staw, Barry, 409
Steele, Nancy, 106, 114
Stephens, Doug, 403
stereotype threat, 96–97
stereotyping, 90–91, 169
    accuracy and inaccuracy of, 90–91
    age, 101–103
    aspects of, 90
    as barrier to valuing diversity, 95–96
    ethnic, 98, 99
    gender, 98–101
    of generations, 129
    LGBT, 103
    negative effects of, 97
    racial, 98
    religious, 98
    unrealistic expectations from, 280–281, 282
Steven M. Ross School of Business, University
    of Michigan, 127
Stoner, J. A. F., 418
strategic alliances, 529–530
strategic contingencies, 440
strategic leadership, 320–321
strategy,
    chief executive officer (CEO) narcissism and, 509
    definition of, 508

formulation, 509–510
    relationship to environmental uncertainty, 508–509
stress, 474–475
    addictive substances and, 487
    burnout as type of, 478–479
    defence mechanisms to reduce, 487–488
    family-friendly human resource organizational
        strategy for, 489
    fitness programs for, 491
    job insecurity and, 484
    job redesign organizational strategy for, 488–489
    negative affectivity (NA) and, 476
    performance changes behavioural reaction to, 486
    personality and, 475–476
    presenteeism behavioural reaction to, 486–487
    problem solving behavioural reaction to, 486
    psychological reactions to, 487
    social support behavioural reaction to, 486
    Type A behaviour pattern and, 476
    wellness programs for, 491
    work-family conflict and, 482
    work-life balance programs for, 491
stress management programs, 489–491
stress model of organizational conflict, 474–476
    stress, 474–475
    stressors, 474
    stress reactions, 475
stressors, 474
    boundary role, 478–479
    executive and managerial, 476–477
    heavy responsibility as, 477
    interpersonal conflict, 481
    operative-level, 477
    poor job design as operative-level, 477
    poor working conditions as operative-level, 477
    role ambiguity as, 484
    role overload as, 476–477
    sexual harassment as, 484–485
    withdrawal from, 487
stress reactions, 475
stretch assignments, 215
strong culture, 294–295
    conflict resolution advantage in, 295–296
    coordination advantage in, 295
    culture clash liability of, 296–297
    financial success advantage of, 296
    pathology liability of, 297
    resistance to change liability of, 296
    steps in socialization process for, 299–300
subunit power, 440
    centrality and, 441
    scarcity of resources and, 440
    substitutability and, 441–442
    uncertainty and, 441
suggestion systems, 390
suicides, 462, 463
sunk costs, 409

superordinate goals, 261
  as tactic in integrative negotiation, 473
survey feedback, 556–557
  effectiveness of, 557
  questionnaires, 556
  questions, 556–557
  results review of, 557
Sutton, Robert, 571
Swinmurn, Nick, 525
Szczepanowski, Janine, 200

T

talent management, 23
tall organization, 519
Tannen, Deborah, 377, 378
Tannenbaum, Scott, 260
Tapon, Francis, 208
target-based incentive systems, 208
  unethical behaviour and, 208
target (component of perception), 84, 85–86
Target Inc., 403
task conflict, 466
task forces, 518
task identity, 217
task significance, 217
Taylor, Dr. Bryce, 412, 422
Taylor, Frederick Winslow, 12, 214
team building, 555–556
team players, 436
team(s), 256
  compared to a group, 256
  cross-functional, 261
  model for an effective work, 256–257
  as panacea, 266
  self-managed work, 259–260
  virtual, 262–263
teamwork, 5
teamwork pay plans,
  employee stock ownership plans (ESOPs), 211, 213
  gainsharing, 212, 213
  profit sharing, 211, 213
  skill-based pay, 212–213
telecommuting, 224, 227
  negative aspects of, 228
  positive aspects of, 228
  research evidence for, 228
telephone hotlines, 390–391
Telus Corp., 21, 215
Telvent Canada Ltd., 288
Third Point, 451
Thomas, Kenneth, 467
Thompson, Scott, 451, 456
Threadless, 421
360-degree feedback, 389–390
Thurgood, Gary R., 25
Tombari, Norman, 82
Topolnytsky, Laryssa, 151
Toronto General Hospital, 412, 422

Toronto Police Service, 97
Toronto Region Immigrant Employment Council (TRIEC), 114
Toronto Star, 11, 183, 318, 502
Toronto Stock Exchange (TSE), 211
Toronto Transit Commission (TTC), 10, 11, 27
Toronto Western Hospital, 412
total quality management (TQM), 558–559
  characteristics of, 558–559
  continuous improvement concept in, 558–559
  customer satisfaction characteristic of, 558, 559
  definition of, 558
  error prevention hallmark of, 558–559
  knowing-doing gap and, 571
  specialized training tools for, 559–560
  supplier relationship characteristic of, 558
Touraine, Marisol, 462
Toyota Production System (TPS), 571
Traditionalists (born 1922-1945), 128
traditional job previews, 282–283
training, 6
training and development, 69–70
trait activation theory, 48
traits, 322
  limitations in the approach to leadership, 322–324
  Machiavellianism as personality, 446
trait theory of leadership, 321
  limitations of, 322–324
transactional leadership theory, 334–335
  contingent reward behaviour in, 334
  management by exception in, 334
transformational leadership, 25
  compared to contingent reward leadership, 337
  innovation and, 565
  as method for overcoming resistance to change, 552
  unfreezing tactics of, 552–553
transformational leadership theory, 335
  individualized consideration behaviours, 335
  inspirational motivation behaviours, 335–336
  intellectual stimulation behaviours, 335
  research evidence for, 336–337
Tremblay, Cynthia, 69
triadic reciprocal causation, 62
Trougakos, John, 443
Trump, Donald, 418
trust perceptions, 105–107
  ability influence on, 105
  benevolence influence on, 105
  camaraderie as, 107
  credibility as, 107
  fairness as, 106
  in goal setting, 179
  importance of, 106
  integrity influence on, 105
  model of, 107
  pride as, 107
  respect as, 107
turnaround strategy, 500–501, 502

turnover, 145–147
  costs of, 145–146
  hangover effect and, 147
  honeymoon effect and, 147
  model, 146
  predictors of, 146
  reasons for satisfied employees quitting, 146–147
  relationship to job satisfaction, 146
Tushman, Michael, 524
Twitter, 44, 386, 482, 567
Type A behaviour pattern, 476

U

uncertainty avoidance, 131
Underwood, Paddy, 127
unfreezing, 546
  transformational leaders and tactics of, 552
Unilever Canada, 26
United Auto Workers union, 502
United States Department of Veteran Affairs (VA), 483, 491
University Health Network (UHN), 412, 422
University of British Columbia, 200
University of Calgary, 44, 110
University of Central Florida (UCF), 260
University of Oxford, 299
University of Saskatchewan, 26
University of Toronto, 99, 110, 319
University of Washington, 326
unrealistic expectations, 280–281
  realistic job previews and, 282–283
  reality shock from, 282
  stereotyping and, 280–281, 282
upward communication, 369
Urwick, Lyndall, 12
USA Today, 524, 525, 526
US Securities and Exchange Commission, 451

V

valence (component of expectation theory), 171–172
values,
  compared to attitudes, 136
  cultural differences in, 129–130, 132
  definition of, 128
  generational differences in, 128–129
  learned through reinforcement process, 128
  motivational aspect of, 128
  preference aspect of, 128
valuing diversity, 95–96
Vancouver City Savings Credit Union (*a.k.a.* Vancity), 490
Vanity Fair, 542, 543
Van Maanen, John, 284
Vega, 2–3, 4, 6, 7, 21, 24
vertical division of labour, 510–511
  autonomy and control themes of, 510–511
  communication theme in, 511
vertical integration, 529
Victor, Bart, 452

virtual organization, 526–527
virtual teams, 262–263
  around-the-clock work advantage of, 262–263
  compared to face-to-face teams, 265
  goals and ground rules lessons from, 265
  high costs challenge of, 265
  isolation challenge of, 265
  larger talent pool advantage of, 263
  management issues challenge of, 265
  miscommunication challenges of, 264–265
  personalization lessons from, 265
  recruitment lessons from, 265
  reduce travel costs and time advantage of, 263
  training lessons from, 265
  trust challenge of, 263
visible minorities, 19, 84, 96
voice (employee), 370
  mum effect and, 370–371
  psychological safety for, 370
Vroom, Victor, 171, 172, 332

W

W. L. Gore & Associates Inc., 523
wage incentive plans, 202–203
  compared to hourly pay, 203
  compared to merit pay plans, 205–206
  differential opportunity problems with, 203–204
  incompatible job design problems with, 204
  lowered quality problems with, 203
  reduced cooperation problems with, 204
  restriction of productivity problems with, 204–205
Walmart Canada, 102, 403
Walton, Richard, 570
Walton, Sam, 298
Watkins, Sherron, 454
Watson, Thomas, 298
webcasts, 391
Weber, Max, 12
Webster, Gary, 11
Webster, Jane, 443
Welch, Jack, 63, 321
Wernsing, Tara, 179
Western Electric, 12
WestJet Airlines, 296, 531
Weyerhaeuser Company, 180–181
Wharton School, University of Pennsylvania, 127
whistleblowing, 453–454
Whitbread, Jasmine, 263
Wigand, Dr. Jeffrey, 453
Wikipedia, 420
Winning Behaviours campaign (Carlsberg Group), 134
work design characteristics, 221–222
  knowledge characteristics, 221–222
  social characteristics, 221–222
  task characteristics, 221–222
  work context characteristics, 221–222
Work Design Questionnaire (WDQ), 221

work engagement, 23–24
  job demands-resources model and, 480
  as opposite of burnout, 479
work environment, 3
  job demands-resources model of, 480
work-family conflict, 482
workforce diversity, 94–95
  advantages to valuing, 96
  group cohesiveness and, 252
  group development and, 247
  immigrant strategy for, 106
  interaction patterns within groups and, 247
  management of, 104–105
  mentoring and, 290–291
  stereotypes and, 96
  stereotype threat to, 96–97
  training programs for, 104–105
  trust model for, 107
  valuing, 95–96
work-life conflict, 19–20
  workplace spirituality and, 21
work motivation, 6, 10, 159
  autonomous (self-determined) type of, 169–170
  controlled (not self-determined) type of, 170
  cultural diversity and theories of, 181, 183–184
  definition of, 160
  effort characteristic of, 160
  equity theory of, 174–175
  expectancy theory of, 171–173
  extrinsic, 161–162
  flexible work arrangements in, 224–225
  goal characteristic of, 161
  goal setting theory of, 176–177
  integrating theories of, 185–187
  intrinsic, 161–162

  job design and, 213–214
  job scope and, 214–215
  need theories of, 164–165
  pay and, 202
  performance and, 162
  persistence characteristic of, 160–161
  personality dimensions links to, 50
  process theories of, 165, 171–174
  prosocial, 222–223
  relationship between extrinsic and intrinsic, 161–162
  relationship with performance, 164–165
  self-determination theory (SDT) of, 169–170
  summary of organizational practices, 228–229
workplace aggression, 483
workplace demographics, 126–127, 128–129
workplace spirituality, 21–22
work sharing, 226
  research evidence for, 226
work teams, 256–257
  compared to a work group, 256
  effectiveness of, 257
  self-managed, 257–258
World Health Organization (WHO), 422

Y

Yahoo Inc., 126, 451, 456
Yewell, Peter, 126
Young Men's Christian Association (YMCA), 95
YouTube, 44, 386, 451, 482
Yversky, Amos, 408

Z

Zappos, 525, 531
Zuckerberg, Mark, 377
Zweig, David, 110, 443